# Lecture Notes in Computer Science 16480

Founding Editors

Gerhard Goos
Juris Hartmanis

Editorial Board Members

Elisa Bertino, *Purdue University, West Lafayette, IN, USA*
Wen Gao, *Peking University, Beijing, China*
Bernhard Steffen, *TU Dortmund University, Dortmund, Germany*
Moti Yung, *Columbia University, New York, NY, USA*

The series Lecture Notes in Computer Science (LNCS), including its subseries Lecture Notes in Artificial Intelligence (LNAI) and Lecture Notes in Bioinformatics (LNBI), has established itself as a medium for the publication of new developments in computer science and information technology research, teaching, and education.

LNCS enjoys close cooperation with the computer science R & D community, the series counts many renowned academics among its volume editors and paper authors, and collaborates with prestigious societies. Its mission is to serve this international community by providing an invaluable service, mainly focused on the publication of conference and workshop proceedings and postproceedings. LNCS commenced publication in 1973.

Jan Mendling · Sander Leemans ·
Boudewijn F. van Dongen · Hajo Reijers

Editors

# Mining a Scientist's Process

Essays Dedicated to Wil van der Aalst on the
Occasion of His 60th Birthday

 Springer

*Editors*
Jan Mendling
HU Berlin
Berlin, Germany

Boudewijn F. van Dongen
TU Eindhoven
Eindhoven, The Netherlands

Sander Leemans
RWTH Aachen
Aachen, Germany

Hajo Reijers
Utrecht University
Utrecht, The Netherlands

ISSN 0302-9743　　　　　　　　ISSN 1611-3349　(electronic)
Lecture Notes in Computer Science
ISBN 978-3-032-17617-2　　　ISBN 978-3-032-17618-9　(eBook)
https://doi.org/10.1007/978-3-032-17618-9

Wil van der Aalst

# Preface

Wil van der Aalst came of (academic) age as he pursed his M.Sc. and Ph.D. degrees at Eindhoven University of Technology during the 1980s. The "Eindhoven School" of computer science at the time, with Edsger Dijkstra as one of the most notable members, was known for their embrace of formal methods, their pursuit of radical innovation, and their general dislike of the industrial approach to relevant problems. These have all become trademarks of the work of Wil van der Aalst, one of the foremost computer scientists of our age.

In over 35 years as a researcher in computer science, Wil has managed to keep his work firmly embedded in the formal foundations of computer science, while at the same time he has never lost sight of the applications of his work. He founded the scientific disciplines of Business Process Management and Process Mining – both are thriving communities, as can be seen from the scientific conferences organized by these disciplines and the breadth and depth of their publications. Wil is renowned for his relentless efforts to publish theory and support the development of open-source tools implementing that theory, while also providing open access to the datasets used to demonstrate the benefits of both theory and tools.

## Early Career

Wil started his scientific career in the early 1990s by studying the practical problem of logistics, a discipline that is important to The Netherlands and to which it owes much of its wealth. In search of an adequate formalism to capture and analyze logistical processes, he discovered the elegance and expressiveness of Petri nets, first proposed by Carl Adam Petri in his 1962 dissertation [7]. Petri nets provide a subtle balance between modeling power and analyzability, which allowed Wil to realistically capture complex logistical processes and, surprisingly, prove important properties of such processes without the need to inject domain knowledge into the models. This was the first link in a lifelong chain of creating radically new insights by using mathematical rigor to solve industrially relevant problems.

## The Start: Process Modeling

Wil picked up on the topic of process modeling, a stream of work that became popular in the 1990s, partly due to the attention paid to it in an article by Bill Curtis et al. in the Communications of the ACM [2]. Wil noticed the plethora of commercial languages being proposed by many different vendors of process management software. He soon realized that almost none of these languages were properly grounded in formal methods. Many systems had internal inconsistencies in their languages or had hacks built into their execution engines. Wil, therefore, found inspiration from his previous work on Petri nets and he defined how one can (and should) model processes using Petri nets. Moreover, he defined a formal notion of soundness, a notion that specifies when a process model is correct.

Never losing sight of the application of his work, he analyzed many commercial systems and showed how their modeling concepts could be translated into a formal, Petri-net-based language, and to demonstrate that systems based on such a language could be implemented he developed the open-source framework YAWL during his visiting professorship at the Queensland University of Technology in Brisbane. The idea of YAWL was that it implemented all patterns of process modeling found in real life, i.e., it provided the union of all commercial tools.

His research on the soundness of process models sparked a range of related work. Today, there are dozens of soundness notions, all serving different purposes, all founded on the notions of soundness introduced by Wil, it's his strict notion of soundness of process models that is used to teach computer science students when they first learn about process modeling.

It is hard to overestimate the industrial importance of this line of work on soundness. In Europe, one of the leading languages for modeling processes is EPCs [5], originally developed at August-Wilhelm Scheer's Institut für Wirtschaftsinformatik at Saarland University, part of the ARIS platform for process modeling. Many European companies use SAP, which in turn has provided a collection of reference models in the form of such EPCs. When developing the patterns catalogue implemented in YAWL and the soundness notions, one of the subjects of study was this SAP reference model, and Wil and colleagues showed that a substantial percentage of models in this collection was actually unsound [6], i.e., if anybody built their company's processes around these models, their processes would have built-in inconsistencies and other problems. Needless to say, this work was not well received by SAP at the time, which only emphasizes the seriousness of the problems Wil unveiled.

## Process Models in Practice: Workflow Management Systems

Wil took his insights to the area of workflow management systems, a central subject at the time within the ACM's community studying computer-supported cooperative work (CSCW). His interest in the correctness of process models turned out to be a good foundation for studying the adaptability of these systems. In 1995, the late Clarence "Skip" Ellis at the University of Colorado at Boulder had formulated the "dynamic change bug", which refers to errors being introduced by migrating a case (i.e., a process instance) from its old process definition to a new one. During his stay in 2001 at the Large-Scale Distributed Information Systems Laboratory at the University of Georgia, Wil developed the notion of change regions for which he proved that process instances could be safely transferred between these [10].

This became one of the many different solutions that Wil developed to make workflow technology more adaptable. Other notable contributions relate to his work on case management technology, an altogether new paradigm for CSCW, and the use of inheritance-preserving transformation rules for workflow processes, which drew inspiration from object-oriented design. One of his most influential works to this day is the publication of a set of workflow patterns to comprehensively capture the functionality of workflow management systems, in particular with respect to their dynamic capabilities [11]. This work, inspired by the pattern-oriented approach of Martin Fowler, is used to this day as the backbone by thousands of academics and software engineers to analyze, design, and evaluate process-aware information systems.

## Data-Driven Modeling: Process Mining

While both research on and industrial applications of process modelling and workflow technology were at their peak in the late 1990s and early 2000s, there was an emerging discipline that caught Wil's attention, namely that of machine learning and its potential to discover workflow models [4, 1, 3]. Wil asked himself and his colleagues the question: Why should we model processes at all if we can use machine learning techniques to discover processes from data? This question sparked a completely new research field, called workflow mining at the time, but today commonly known as process mining.

And again, as he did earlier, Wil resorted to formal methods. In his early process mining work, he formally showed that the problem of discovering process models from event data was actually feasible. He was the first to show that even without complete information of a system, the models for such a system could be discovered [9]. The alpha-algorithm was the first-ever process discovery algorithm that did not require complete input data and provided formal guarantees. It relied on a very elegant concept: direct succession of tasks in a process hints at causality between these tasks.

His work on workflow mining came at the exact right time in history. With the growing availability of data since the year 2000, there also was a need for the structured analysis of processes using this data. The ever-growing sizes of available data also presented a challenge for the field as it became increasingly important that technical contributions were accompanied by open-source implementations able to handle larger and larger quantities of data.

For this reason, Wil initiated the development of an open-source platform for process mining called ProM: a Java-based framework, hosted by the Eindhoven University of Technology, open to researchers worldwide providing a standardized way for people to interact with event data, for researchers to contribute new algorithms as well as to plug them into a tooling pipeline, and for students to learn the fundamentals of real-life examples.

While the discovery of process models from data is an important challenge, Wil also identified the need to determine how well a model describes the data and the process that generated this data [8]. This led to a sub-stream of process mining research called conformance checking. Interestingly, together with his Ph.D. student Arya Adriansyah, Wil resorted to the shortest path techniques of Dijkstra to solve the fundamental question of how and where a process model differs from an event log. Conformance checking is also making a huge impact on practice, since the techniques can be used by finance and IT auditors to perform automated checks on whether organizational statements conform with actual data.

The size of datasets gradually became bigger and open-source implementation initiatives supported by Wil struggled to deal with the ever-increasing volume. Therefore, when Wil was already at RWTH Aachen and got the chance to join Celonis in 2021 as chief scientist, he jumped at the opportunity. He saw the potential of working with a large company and a team of skilled software engineers to build industry-strength implementations of his ideas able to deal with the ever-larger datasets.

Over time, event data continued to evolve. Where event logs were historically seen as datasets representing the execution of individual cases, each an instance of a process, real-life applications showed that events in data often refer to many processes at once, touching many objects at once. For example, a package that is delivered to a customer relates to the ordering process of the customer, to the invoicing process of the seller, to the delivery process of the postman, etc. This realization led to Wil's most recent work, where he focuses on graph-structured data, where each event is a node in a complex knowledge graph. And yet again, he invokes fundamental computer science subjects such as graph databases and graph queries to work with such data sets. The impact of this work is already showing in recent publications on process mining, where the first discovery and conformance checking technology is being developed on graph-based event data. There are early signs that industrial parties are keen to embrace the concept as well.

## Education

While the scientific and industrial impact have always been great drivers for Wil's research, he often states that the true impact of an academic is through education. A very notable achievement in this area is the development of several Massive Open Online Courses (MOOCs), taken by tens of thousands of people annually. Both his textbooks and these MOOCs are available in multiple languages providing a truly global community broad access to the fruits of his research.

## Conclusion

At the time of writing, Wil had a H-index of 182 (Google Scholar) and a D-index of 178, which firmly places him in the top-10 computer scientists worldwide. He has almost 1500 publications, including almost 300 journal articles, 35 books (as author or editor), 675 refereed conference/workshop papers, and 85 book chapters. He holds honorary degrees from the Moscow Higher School of Economics, Tsinghua University, and Hasselt University. He is an ACM Fellow, IFIP Fellow, and IEEE Fellow, and an elected member of the Royal Netherlands Academy of Arts and Sciences (Koninklijke Nederlandse Akademie van Wetenschappen), the Royal Holland Society of Sciences and Humanities (Koninklijke Hollandsche Maatschappij der Wetenschappen), Academia Europaea, the North Rhine-Westphalian Academy of Sciences, Humanities and the Arts (Nordrhein-Westfälische Akademie der Wissenschaften und der Künste), and the German Academy of Science and Engineering (Deutsche Akademie der Technikwissenschaften). In 2018 he was awarded an Alexander-von-Humboldt Professorship, Germany's most prestigious research award (5 million euros).

In this volume, many scientists and practitioners from across the world share their experiences of working with Wil and their views on his contribution to their fields, both academic, professional and in education.

November 2025

Jan Mendling
Sander Leemans
Hajo Reijers
Boudewijn F. van Dongen

# References


1. Jonathan E. Cook, Alexander L. Wolf. Automating process discovery through event-data analysis. Proc. 17th Intl. Conf. on Software Engineering, pp. 73–82, ACM, 1995
2. Bill Curtis, Marc I. Kellner, Jim Over. Process modeling. Commun. ACM **35**(9):75–90, September 1992
3. Anindya Datta. Automating the discovery of as-is business process models: Probabilistic and algorithmic approaches. Information Systems Research **9**(3): 275–301, 1998
4. Joachim Herbst, Dimitris Karagiannis. Integrating machine learning and workflow management to support acquisition and adaptation of workflow models. Intl. J. of Intelligent Systems in Accounting, Finance and Management **9**(2): 67–92, 2000
5. Gerhard Keller, Markus Nüttgens, August-Wilhelm Scheer. Semantische Prozessmodellierung auf der Grundlage Ereignisgesteuerter Prozessketten (EPK). Technical Report 89, Institut für Wirtschaftsinformatik, Saarbrücken, 1992
6. Jan Mendling, H.M.W. Verbeek, Boudewijn F. van Dongen, Wil M.P. van der Aalst, Gustaf Neumann. Detection and prediction of errors in EPCs of the SAP reference model. Data & Knowledge Engineering **64**(1): 312–329, 2008
7. Carl Adam Petri. Kommunikation mit Automaten. PhD thesis, Universität Bonn, 1962
8. Anne Rozinat, Wil M.P. Van der Aalst. Conformance testing: Measuring the fit and appropriateness of event logs and process models. Proc. Intl. Conf. on Business Process Management, pp. 163–176. Springer, 2005
9. Wil M.P. van der Aalst, Ton Weijters, Laura Maruster. Workflow mining: Discovering process models from event logs. IEEE Trans. on Knowledge and Data Engineering **16**(9):1128–1142, 2004
10. [10] Wil M.P. van der Aalst. Exterminating the dynamic change bug: A concrete approach to support workflow change. Information Systems Frontiers **3**(3):297–317, 2001
11. Wil M.P. van Der Aalst, Arthur H.M. ter Hofstede, Bartek Kiepuszewski, Alistair P. Barros. Workflow patterns. Distributed and Parallel Databases **14**(1):5–51, 2003

# Organization

## Program Committee

| | |
|---|---|
| Rafael Accorsi | Accenture, Switzerland |
| Arya Adriansyah | ABN AMRO, Netherlands |
| Elisabetta Benevento | University of Pisa, Italy |
| Alessandro Berti | RWTH Aachen University, Germany |
| Harry Beyel | RWTH Aachen University, Germany |
| Christian Brecher | RWTH Aachen University, Germany |
| Tobias Brockhoff | RWTH Aachen University, Germany |
| Edyta Brzychczy | AGH University of Science and Technology, Poland |
| Andrea Burattin | Technical University of Denmark, Denmark |
| Jochen De Weerdt | KU Leuven, Belgium |
| Adela del Río Ortega | University of Seville, Spain |
| Benoît Depaire | Hasselt University, Belgium |
| Jörg Desel | FernUniversität in Hagen, Germany |
| Claudio Di Ciccio | Utrecht University, Netherlands |
| Marlon Dumas | University of Tartu, Estonia |
| Dirk Fahland | Eindhoven University of Technology, Netherlands |
| Sandro Franzoi | Universität Münster, Germany |
| Hector Geffner | RWTH Aachen University, Germany |
| Sandra Geisler | RWTH Aachen University, Germany |
| Laura Genga | Eindhoven University of Technology, Netherlands |
| Chiara Ghidini | Free University of Bozen-Bolzano, Italy |
| Eduardo González López de Murillas | Eindhoven University of Technology, Netherlands |
| Florian Gottschalk | Thyssenkrupp Uhde, Germany |
| Eduardo Goulart Rocha | Celonis Labs, Germany |
| Marwan Hassani | Eindhoven University of Technology, Netherlands |
| Andreas V. Hense | Hochschule Bonn-Rhein-Sieg, Germany |
| Martin Henze | RWTH Aachen University and Fraunhofer FKIE, Germany |
| Anna Kalenkova | University of Adelaide, Australia |
| István Koren | RWTH Aachen University, Germany |
| Humam Kourani | Fraunhofer FIT, Germany |
| Maciej Koutny | Newcastle University, UK |
| Akhil Kumar | Pennsylvania State University, USA |

| | |
|---|---|
| Aaron Küsters | RWTH Aachen University, Germany |
| Marcello La Rosa | University of Melbourne, Australia |
| Gerhard Lakemeyer | RWTH Aachen University, Germany |
| Sander J.J. Leemans | RWTH Aachen University, Germany |
| Peter Letmathe | RWTH Aachen University, Germany |
| Lukas Liss | RWTH Aachen University, Germany |
| Cong Liu | Nova Information Management School, Portugal |
| Xixi Lu | Utrecht University, Netherlands |
| Lisa Luise Mannel | RWTH Aachen University, Germany |
| Felix Mannhardt | Eindhoven University of Technology, Netherlands |
| Laura Maruster | University of Groningen, Netherlands |
| Renata Medeiros de Carvalho | Eindhoven University of Technology, Netherlands |
| Jan Mendling | Humboldt-Universität zu Berlin, Germany |
| Marco Montali | Free University of Bozen-Bolzano, Italy |
| Jorge Munoz-Gama | Pontificia Universidad Católica de Chile, Chile |
| Joyce Nabende Nakatumba | Makerere University, Uganda |
| Verena Nitsch | RWTH Aachen University, Germany |
| Thomas Noll | RWTH Aachen University, Germany |
| Ali Norouzifar | RWTH Aachen University, Germany |
| Alex Norta | Tallinn University of Technology, Estonia |
| Wied Pakusa | Federal University of Applied Administrative Sciences, Germany |
| Gyunam Park | RWTH Aachen University, Germany |
| Viki Peeva | RWTH Aachen University, Germany |
| Marco Pegoraro | RWTH Aachen University, Germany |
| Jan Pennekamp | RWTH Aachen University, Germany |
| Artem Polyvyanyy | University of Melbourne, Australia |
| Mahsa Pourbafrani | RWTH Aachen University, Germany |
| Luise Pufahl | Technical University of Munich, Germany |
| Jagadeesh Chandra Bose | Skan, USA |
| Majid Rafiei | SAP SE, Germany |
| Jan Recker | University of Hamburg, Germany |
| Hajo Reijers | Utrecht University, Netherlands |
| Lars Reinkemeyer | Celonis, Germany |
| Wolfgang Reisig | Humboldt-Universität zu Berlin, Germany |
| Kate Revoredo | Humboldt-Universität zu Berlin, Germany |
| Stefanie Rinderle-Ma | Technical University of Munich, Germany |
| Rainer Röhrig | RWTH Aachen University, Germany |
| Thomas Rose | Fraunhofer FIT, Germany |
| Michael Rosemann | Queensland University of Technology, Australia |
| Wolfgang Rumpe | RWTH Aachen University, Germany |
| Shazia Sadiq | University of Queensland, Australia |

# Wil van der Aalst: A Scientific Guide Through Complexity

Alexander Rinke, Bastian Nominacher, Martin Klenk
Celonis SE

When we look back at the beginnings of Celonis, the story doesn't start with software or algorithms. It starts with spreadsheets, reports, interviews, and PowerPoint templates: the traditional consulting toolkit. We were spending hours preparing slides that we knew could never capture the complexity and truth of how things really worked. It was as if we were trying to map a living, breathing system with nothing but pen-and-paper sketches. But pen and paper reduced a living system to a sketch. As we worked through that student project that would later become Celonis, we realized we needed a way to understand the entire system.

That was the moment of serendipity. Around the same time, Wil and his colleagues published the *Process Mining Manifesto*. We stumbled upon it while searching for new ideas. Here was a method that seemed designed exactly for the problem we were facing: extracting the story from the data, seeing processes as they actually happened rather than how people imagined them to be. Looking back, it feels like destiny that the manifesto appeared almost at the same time that our student project took place. Celonis was in a sense born into Process Mining through Wil's intellectual spark.

## 1 From Advisor to Chief Scientist

As Celonis grew from a student project into a startup, and then from a startup into a global software company, Wil's role in the story also evolved. At first, he was the intellectual lighthouse we looked toward from afar. Even in those early days Wil and his students' findings around the Fuzzy, Alpha, Heuristic and Inductive Miner guided us in setting the foundations of the Celonis software and its process discovery algorithms. And it wasn't until 2015 that we started our first pilgrimage to Eindhoven to finally meet the godfather of Process Mining, to whom we had looked in awesome admiration, in person over a burger.

Later, he became an advisor, guiding us with both patience and challenge. Wil himself became intrigued by the idea of working directly with the data and real-world insight that we at Celonis could provide. Finally, he formally joined Celonis as Chief Scientist. It is difficult to overstate our gratitude for this. His new role symbolized the fusion of academia and industry in our field that had never been there before. Wil brought to Celonis the same intellectual rigor that had defined his career: a demand for clear, precise, and formally correct concepts. He reminded us that scientific discipline and conceptual clarity are not constraints, but the very compass that ensures meaningful innovation.Without Wil's pioneering research, there would be no Celonis, indeed, no field of Process Mining as it exists today. The very foundations of what the company built trace back to his early frameworks, algorithms, and ideas.

Long before the industry realized it could be transformative, Wil had legitimized and popularized Process Mining in academia. For this, thousands of practitioners worldwide owe him a debt of thanks.

## 2 Wil's Impact on an Industry

A central feature of Wil's work has been its transition from academic theory into practical application. Concepts that first appeared in his papers and lectures have steadily moved into the way organizations understand and manage their processes. The Inductive Miner and Object-Centric Process Mining (OCPM) are clear examples: developed as research ideas, they have since become practical approaches that organizations now rely on to analyze and improve their operations.

This trajectory reflects more than the strength of the ideas themselves. It also highlights Wil's role in shaping a research community that bridges theory and practice. Many of his former students now lead their own groups, expanding the reach of Process Mining research around the world. At the same time, Wil has remained closely connected to industry, working with Celonis customers and partners, supervising PhD projects in collaboration with companies, and supporting joint developments that bring academic insight into applied settings. From customer PhD projects to co-developed marketplace apps created by his students and ecosystem partners, he is constantly weaving the fabric between academia and industry. The active exchange between academia and industry also underscores one of Wil's enduring contributions: showing that formalism and practical application must go hand in hand. Formal methods such as Petri nets, for example, provide a strong conceptual foundation, yet their complexity can make them difficult to interpret in day-to-day business environments. Wil reminds us that formalism and real-world applicability are not opposites but essential complements.

Wil has spent decades shaping both the scientific foundations of the field and its practical adoption. Few scientists manage to build such a global movement in their lifetime. But Wil established a global movement and succeeded in sustaining an active dialogue between both communities over decades.

## 3 A Steady Compass for Future Horizons

From the beginning, there has been a strong resonance between Wil's academic mission and the path taken by Celonis. Wil has always challenged us to respect the core of our software: Process Mining, while also daring to expand its horizons. Wil's research uncovers the true behavior of processes unfolding in data, while Celonis set out to translate such insights into software that organizations could use in practice. He continues to remind us to stay true to our process identity, even as we now venture into new spaces such as Process Intelligence and AI. In doing so, he helps ensure that these new directions remain grounded in the same principle that defined the field from the start: making reality understandable. Wil has urged the company to preserve the methodological core of Process Mining, even as the technology expands into new applications and industries. His perspective has been a valuable counterbalance to the pressures of economic development and commercialization, ensuring that the discipline continues to be anchored in its scientific foundations.

Object-Centric Process Mining is a perfect example. We are far from finished in exploring and understanding process complexity. Traditional Process Mining approaches often impose linear structures on reality, but OCPM shows that processes rarely exist in isolation. Instead, they intersect, overlap, and evolve. OCPM allows us to capture complexity without reducing it to overly simple representations. It reminds us that every step forward in this field must begin with an honest view of reality. This insight is especially relevant as Celonis ventures into the intersection of processes and AI. The promise of AI lies in prediction, automation, and guidance, but these capabilities only create value if they are built on a truthful understanding of how processes actually work. OCPM provides that foundation. It shows us that even as technology advances, the scientific grounding of Process Mining remains essential. Wil's research continues to remind us that the journey is ongoing. There will always be new layers of complexity to uncover, and it is by embracing this complexity that meaningful innovation can emerge. For Celonis this is a central commitment: to embrace complexity instead of ignoring it.

## 4 At the Core of It All

It is rare in the software world to witness a category spring directly from academic research. It is rarer still to see it succeed on a global scale. Wil's research lit the spark for Process Mining, and today it stands alongside the most impactful software innovations, most recently making it into the *Fortune Future 50* list at rank 3. Throughout this journey, Process Mining has consistently stood out as one of the few innovations to spearhead software development in Germany. From *Gartner* defining a dedicated category, to receiving the *German President's Award*, to recognition in the *Forbes Cloud 100*, we have seen the field emerge together from two perspectives that once were separate yet by now have become deeply interwoven: academia and industry. On a personal level, we admire the way one person's research can ignite not only a company, not only an industry, but a global community. Wil's influence lives not only in algorithms and citations, but in the daily decisions of companies, the careers of students, and the shared mission of thousands of Celonauts and Process Mining practitioners worldwide.

As we look ahead, we are committed to continuing to bridge academia and industry. The field will keep evolving, new paradigms will emerge, but Wil's contributions will remain foundational. So let us close with a simple truth: without you, none of this would exist. Thank you for being more than a godfather. Thank you for being the pioneer, the guide, the Chief Scientist, and the friend that you are.

With admiration and gratitude,
Alex, Basti and Martin

# Contents

**Petri Nets and Formalisms**

**Process Mining Foundations**

## Process Applications

# Reflections About Wil's Career

# Are You a Process Guy or a Data Guy?

Mathias Weske[✉]

Hasso Plattner Institute, University of Potsdam, Potsdam, Germany
**mathias.weske@hpi.de**

**Abstract.** Remembering a conversation with Wil van der Aalst many years ago, this paper explores the relationships between business processes and data. It argues that the role of data in business processes has become more and more prominent over the years. In the early days of business process management, data was not prominent at all. Over the years, data became increasingly important in process modeling and analysis, process verification, and, most prominently, in process mining. At a BPM keynote in 2010, the keynote speaker indicated that data and processes are two sides of the same coin. Wil van der Aalst laid out what this really means: object-centric business process management.

**Keywords:** Processes · Data

## 1   Introduction

Strolling through Paviljoen at TU Eindhoven with Wil van der Aalst on a sunny day in the early summer of 2000, Wil asked me 'Are you a process guy or a data guy?'. Having worked on distributed databases during my PhD and having switched to workflow management after that, I replied, 'both'. I am not sure that Wil was happy with the reply from his new group member.

In this paper, I review the relationships between processes and data and how they have evolved over the years. Given the breadth of the topic, this discussion is rather personal than exhaustive. I will discuss the early days of business process management, when it was still called workflow management, and when data did not play any role at all. Yes, we needed data to implement workflow management systems, such as parameters for function calls, but we did not consider it conceptually interesting or worthy of scientific investigation.

The focus on activities and their execution ordering was still prominent when process mining entered the scene. Even though process mining is supposedly based on process execution data, data did not play an important role in early process mining research; it was only about the activities and their ordering, i.e., control flow.

The business process management community has always a strong application focus, which, over the years, led to the insight that data is actually key to understanding how processes operate and how processes can be improved and automated. This was eloquently stated in a keynote speech at BPM 2010 by Clay Richardson, who rendered data and processes as two sides of the same coin.


J. Mendling et al. (Eds.): Wil van der Aalst Festschrift, LNCS 16480, pp. 3–14, 2026.
https://doi.org/10.1007/978-3-032-17618-9_1

The role of data in process modeling and analysis became more important when BPMN entered the scene. Still, data modeling was relatively poor, since only data objects and their read and write relationships to process activities were discussed, while data structures and object behavior were not.

With the increasing adoption of process mining, data has entered the center stage. Also, in process modeling and analysis, the role of data was investigated in more detail. It turned out that attributes of data objects and associations between data objects are important aspects of business processes and might even influence process execution semantics. Several approaches to represent data objects and processes have been developed. However, the approaches have been scattered. This was the situation when Wil van der Aalst defined a focal point by coining the term object-centric process mining. With data objects and processes being two sides of the same coin, key concepts in business process management that have been stable for many years, e.g., the notion of process instances or cases, have to be revisited.

This paper will also shed light on a pattern of Wil's research work that proved instrumental in shaping our field. He comes up with an original idea that is then taken up and used by fellow researchers as a starting point of their investigations. On the shoulders of giants. Wil's work has inspired generations of young researchers and, ultimately, contributed to the formation of the BPM community that we know today.

The remainder of this paper is organized as follows. In Sect. 2, new a variant of the well-known business process lifecycle is introduced, which differentiates between different types of process models. Section 3 sketches the business process landscape before the advent of data. Data in process models is discussed in Sect. 4, while Sect. 5 focuses on object-centric business processes. The paper closes with a personal concluding remark.

## 2   Broadening the BPM Lifecycle

To set the scene for the investigations in this paper, we introduce a new variant of the business process management lifecycle, a framework that relates the main phases in business process management. This version differentiates between two types of process models that were not differentiated in traditional BPM lifecycles [19]. These types of process models have different goals, are designed quite differently, and use different representation languages. This lifecycle allows us to investigate the role of data in business process management in an adequate manner.

- *Blueprint process models* are designed as blueprints for process execution, i.e., they define how the process should be executed.
- *Discovered process models* represent the process as it was actually executed. They are discovered from event logs, based on process execution data.

Business Process Model and Notation or BPMN is the industry standard to define blueprint process models [15]. If we aim at a formal analysis of process

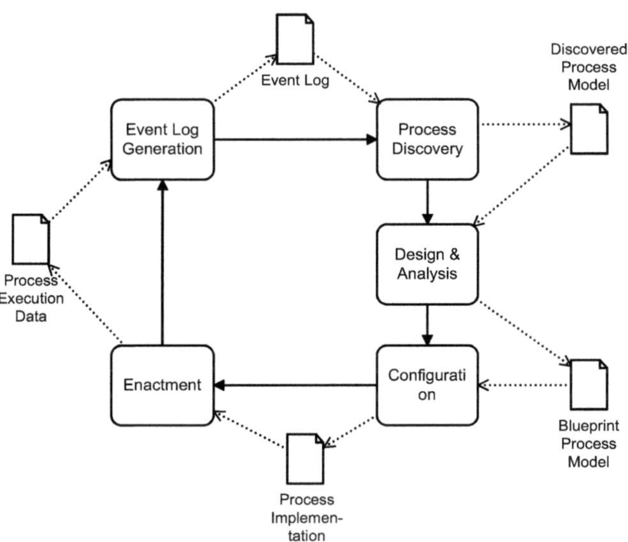


**Fig. 1.** BPM lifecycle that distinguishes two types of business process models: a blueprint model that is used to implement business processes and a discovered process model that is derived from event logs generated from process execution data.

models, we translate BPMN process diagrams to Petri nets, which can then be formally analyzed. Petri net are not only useful to represent blueprint process models, but also discovered ones. In particular, the alpha algorithm [5] and its variants, and a wide variety of other process discovery algorithms use Petri nets as representation.

Figure 1 distinguishes between those types of process models. This lifecycle covers not only the engineering perspective in business process management, but also the process mining perspective. After process identification and scoping (outside the scope of this lifecycle), the process design and analysis phase is entered. It results in a process model that serves as a blueprint for the implementation of the process. This process model is the basis for process configuration, where information systems are configured in a way that the process is implemented. In addition to the technical part, the configuration phase involves organizational aspects as well, such as training colleagues involved in the process. The outcome of this phase is a process implementation.

During process enactment, a myriad of data is created. This data comes in a wide variety of data formats, such as, for example, text files, database entries, and spreadsheet documents. An important first step in any process mining project is the generation of event logs, based on process execution data. These can be case-centric or object-centric. Event logs are input to process discovery algorithms, which discover process models that exhibit the same behavior as observed in the event logs. Discovered process models are input to the process design phase, starting the next iteration of the lifecycle.

To keep the lifecycle concise, I abstracted from other essential tasks in process mining, including conformance checking. We could add conformance checking as an additional phase and link it to event logs and blueprint process models. We could also link it to discovered process models, if we intend to check the conformance of an event log with a process model that was discovered, e.g., to investigate properties of a specific process discovery algorithm.

It is worth noting that the lifecycle does not rely on the presence of a blueprint process model. The process might just be defined by text or by informal process representations. In any case, there is a process implementation and in any case data is produced during process execution. Hence, we can derive an event log and we can discover a process model that provides us with insights on the process. The people involved might decide to use the discovered process model, to refine and enhance it and use it as blueprint process model in the continuous effort to improve the process.

## 3 Processes Only

When we were having our conversation at TU Eindhoven, workflow management had just emerged as a research topic, from two directions. On one hand, we find colleagues with a mathematical background who are interested in the formal analysis of workflows, typically using Petri nets. The second camp comes from database management, where a more pragmatic approach was followed, typically engineering process-oriented information systems based on database technologies. Wil comes from the former, and I from the latter camp.

While we shared – and still share – a deep adoration for business processes, we had complementary views on the subject. For Wil, the execution of an activity is the firing of a transition. For me, it is the invocation of a service, which typically has data parameters. Still, my data perspective was purely on a technical implementation level and not on a conceptual level; data was required to implement workflow systems, but it was not a subject of scientific investigation.

### 3.1 Blueprint Process Models

A typical blueprint process model, defined as a workflow net, is shown in Fig. 2. Workflow nets have been introduced by Wil van der Aalst as early as 1997 [1]. Workflow nets are a specific type of Petri nets that can be used for process verification, for example, using the soundness property [1]. Based on Wil's soundness property, fellow researchers have worked on various kinds of soundness, such as, for instance, relaxed soundness [7], interaction soundness [16], and decision soundness [6]. This showcases an early example of how Wil opens new research fields to be further explored by researchers and his active role in the initial forming the BPM community.

While workflow nets abstract from many aspects of the process, including data, they define in which order the activities of a workflow should be executed. In particular, the workflow net in Fig. 2 shows how the activities in a simplified

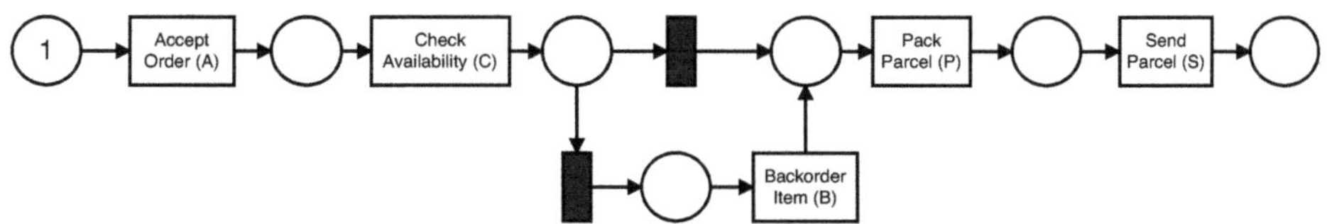


**Fig. 2.** Order handling process defined as a workflow net

ordering process should be executed. Hence, the workflow net can serve as a blueprint for an order handling process.

After the process has started and an order is accepted, the availability of the ordered item is checked. If the item is available, it can be packed and sent; otherwise, it has to be back-ordered first. Notice that activities are represented as transitions, and that the execution of an activity is abstracted to the timeless firing of a transition. No data is involved; just the labels of the transitions provide us with hints on the data involved. The process seems to deal with orders, items, and parcels.

## 3.2  Discovered Process Models

In the early 2000s, process mining entered the scene. What we find very intuitive these days was nothing more than a paradigm shift in those days. At that time, it was generally accepted that processes are executed just as they were defined in process models. After all, this is what process management is all about. Process engines were the software components that made it happen. In this spirit, the Workflow Management Coalition proposed an architecture that organized process engines, invoked applications, and several other software components, such as work item lists [11].

Wil van der Aalst challenged the assumption. Rather than assuming the process is executed as defined, he assumed the contrary: The process is not executed as defined. And we need to find out how the process was actually executed, and why. This question keeps us busy still today.

In real-world applications, the typical situation is that processes are not executed as defined in the blueprint process model, but there are deviations. The notion of event logs has been developed, which represent the activities that happened during process execution. Again, Wil was instrumental in this development. The alpha algorithm and its variants take an event log and discover a workflow net, which exposes the same behavior as we see in the event log [5].

A typical example of a discovered workflow net is shown in Fig. 3; the underlying event log can be found in the caption. It has been the assumption that each event represents an activity that has occurred during process execution. At that time, it was not investigated how the event log was generated, and we did not care about the data that might have led to events in the event log.

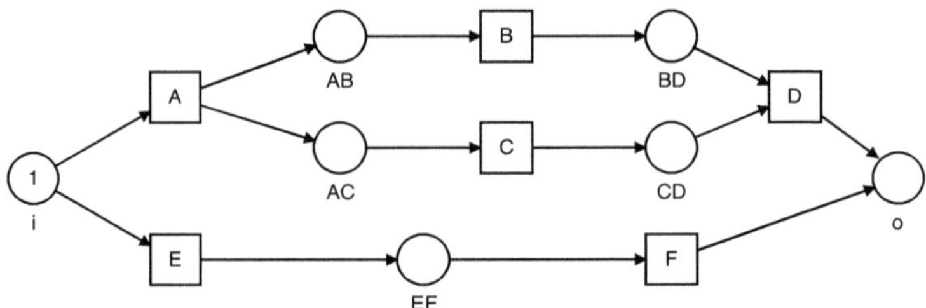

**Fig. 3.** Workflow net, resulting from applying the alpha algorithm to the event log {ABCD, ACBD, EF }. Data did not play any role in the early days of process mining; it was just activities, typically A's and B's.


To summarize, in the early days of business process management, data did not play any significant role, neither in process design and verification, nor in process mining.

## 4    Data in Process Models

Data in process modeling entered the scene with BPMN. In BPMN process diagrams, we can define data objects and how those are read and written by process activities during process executions. While data objects can be represented in process models, the support for data was relatively weak indeed. Data objects did not have any types, nor was there any relationship to a data model. In an extension to BPMN process diagrams, recently introduced in [19], data objects are typed and related to UML class diagrams, and variables are used to refer to different data objects of a given type. This extension helps us to represent data objects more precisely than in the BPMN standard.

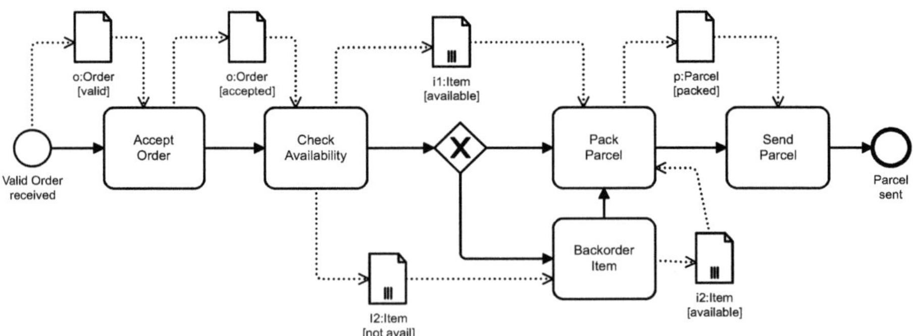

**Fig. 4.** Order handling process that involves variables, types, and states of data objects


An example is shown in Fig. 4, where a variant of the order management process discussed above is sketched. Each data object is represented by a variable, a type, and a state. For instance, after a valid order has been received, a data object $o$ of type *Order* is created in a state *valid*. Links to a class diagram make sure that not only the structure of data objects is defined, but also the associations to other data objects, as will be discussed below. As an extension to the initial example, each order consists of a list of items.

Data objects in process models can have states. The traditional assumption is that each data object is in a single state at every point in time. This is in line with object-oriented design and analysis, where objects have identity, structure and behavior. The behavior of objects can be represented by object lifecycles, which are state transition diagrams where the nodes represent states of objects and the arcs represent state transitions. The link between object behavior and process behavior is defined by process activities triggering state transitions.

In the example shown in Fig. 4, the order data object $o$ is in state *valid* when it is received. The process activity *Accept Order* triggers a transition to the state *accepted*. Recently, states have been investigated in more detail, so that states of data objects can take into account not only attribute values, but also associations between objects, and a given data object might in several states at a time, to cater for different perspectives on a given data object [12].

Once an order is accepted, the list of items that relate to this order is checked for availability. In this simplified example, we assume that either all items in the order are available or none is available, so that all items need to be back-ordered before the parcel can be packed and shipped. List data objects represent multiple items, represented by the respective data object marker in Fig. 4.

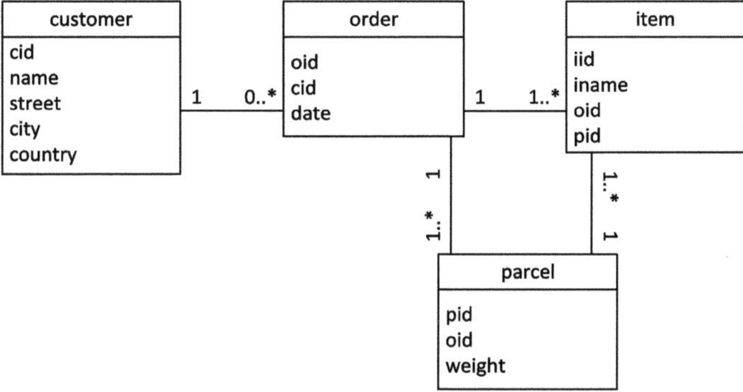

**Fig. 5.** UML class diagram shows the relationship between customers, orders, items, and parcels. Data objects in the ordering process need to satisfy the associations between the respective classes in the class diagram. Notice that there might be classes that do not have any data objects in a particular process model, like the class customer in the ordering process example.

Data objects in business process models show which data is read and written during process execution. It does not represent the structure of data objects nor the relationships between data objects of different classes. As defined by the multiplicities in the UML class diagram shown in Fig. 5, each item belongs to exactly one order, and each parcel is related to one or more items. Data objects as well as data models are important ingredients to define processes and their relationships in the blueprint process model. They are also instrumental in process mining, as will be investigated in the next section.

## 5   Object-Centric Business Process Management

Based on early works in process mining, the field has developed amazingly in the last decade. This development was fueled by the significant interest of the industry. Influenced by joint research projects, the focus in process mining turned from formal analysis of workflows to data-driven insights of operational business processes. As a result, a large variety of data in the information systems of organizations became the basis of process mining endeavors.

By studying the impact of data objects on business processes, it became clear that data objects are typically accessed and modified by several business processes, and not only by a single process instance specified by a single blueprint process model. It turns out that more relevant business insights can be generated when we can analyze business processes from different perspectives, driven by different objects involved in business process executions. These observations caused Wil van der Aalst to postulate a paradigm shift from activities and processes to data objects and their relationships with activities. Data objects were no longer a marginal aspect in process mining, but became the center. Wil called this paradigm object-centric process mining [2].

This novel perspective has massive implications on how we look at business processes today, both from a process engineering perspective and from a process mining perspective. Since the early phases of our discipline in the 1990s, the focus has always been on a single process model, as a blueprint for many process instances that are executed according to that model. Putting data objects in the center of attention and organizing activities and processes around them, the traditional view of one process model and many process instances was challenged. Processes share objects, and activities are executed on objects. This new perspective opens a large field of research.

To formally represent object-centric business processes on the level of Petri nets, Wil van der Aalst proposes object-centric Petri nets [4], based on earlier work on object-centric behavioral constraints [3]. These were developed in process mining to replay object-centric event logs, but they can also be used to design business processes that manipulate data objects.

Based on the traditional mapping of process diagrams to Petri nets introduced in [8], an object-centric Petri net can be derived from a process diagram as follows. Each activity in the process is mapped to a transition; a dedicated transition represents each decision that an activity can take. In addition to those traditional mapping rules, for each data object and each state the data object can assume, a place is defined. In addition, each object has specific source and sink states, represented by a play icon and a stop icon, respectively.

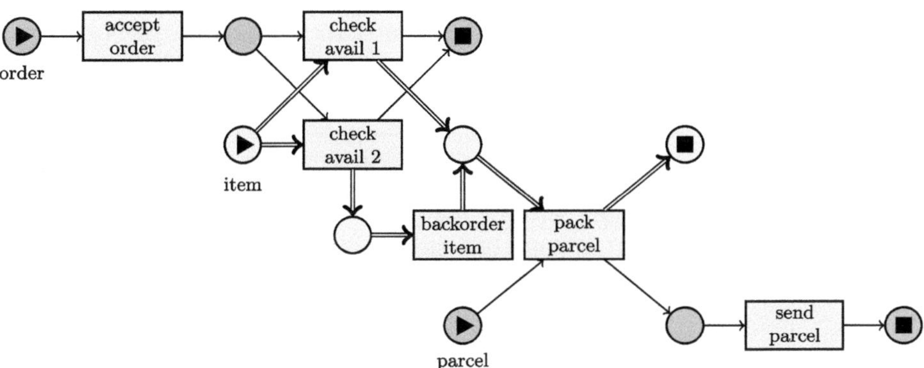


**Fig. 6.** Object-centric Petri net of the ordering process that allows us to represent data objects and their states explicitly. For each data object, a dedicated place represents the source of the object and its sink, marked by play and stop symbols, respectively.

Figure 6 shows an object-centric Petri net of the ordering process that was introduced above as a BPMN process diagram. The net covers data objects of three data object types: orders, items, and parcels. The respective places are colored to indicate their specific data object types. Tokens represent data objects, such that a token representing data object $o$ can only reside on a place with a matching data object type. In the example, tokens representing order data objects can only reside on pink places, items on yellow places, and parcels on violet places.

It is a good practice and improves the understanding of those nets to align places that belong to a given object type. For instance, all places that relate to an order are horizontally aligned. It is an assumption that all tokens pertaining to orders, items, and parcels are known and present in the source places of the respective object types. We now investigate the execution semantics, defined by the object-centric Petri net. In the initial state, only the *accept order* transition can fire. Once it has fired, the availability of the ordered items can be checked, i.e., the transitions *check avail 1* and *check avail 2* are enabled.

A double arc to a transition indicates that more than one token can be consumed (produced, analogously). We assume that all items need to be back-ordered, so that all tokens in the source item place are consumed, and *check avail 2* fires.[1] At this point, the items can be back-ordered, so that the items are available and can be packed, and the parcel can be sent.

Object-centric Petri nets allow us to investigate the process from different perspectives. In fact, we can use any data object as a separate perspective, for instance, the *order* data object. Each order is accepted before one of the check availability transitions can fire. The object-centricity allows us to precisely identify that two activities are executed on any given *order* data object, resulting in traces *<accept order, check avail 1>* and *<accept order, check avail 2>*, respectively. Along these lines, we can investigate the activities that are executed on items and on parcels as well. Related to items, first, the availability of the items is checked before the items are packed. In case the items are not available, they need to be back-ordered before packing.

**Fig. 7.** Wil van der Aalst demoing OCPQ, Object-Centric Process Querying & Constraints, to members of the business process technology group at BPM 2025 in Seville.

Object-centric Petri nets are another example of how Wil van der Aalst opens up new research directions. After their introduction, OCPN were discussed and critically evaluated. Researchers argued that links between data objects were not explicitly represented, so that those links could not be used during event log

---

[1] To be more precise, a transition with a double incoming arc can consume any non-empty subset of tokens, and OCPNs are accepting Petri nets, so that incomplete consumptions do not lead to accepting runs. Readers interested in the details of OCPN are referred to [4].

replay. Based on OCPN and Petri nets with identifiers [18], object-centric Petri nets with identifiers or OPID were introduced in [9]. Object identities can be used to establish links between related objects, avoiding the issues mentioned above. In the example, each item belongs to exactly one order.

To explicitly represent data on the Petri net level, DB-Nets have been proposed [14]. Combined with OPID, we arrive at data-aware object-centric Petri nets with identifiers, or DOPID, introduced in [10]. Using identifiers, we can explicitly represent those links between objects, so that, in our example, items do not move from one order to another. These types of binding relationships were recently investigated in [17]. This is another example where Wil opened a new research area that is then further developed by fellow researchers.

## 6    Closing

I close this paper with a photograph that I took during the Demo and Resources Session at BPM 2025 in Seville, shown in Fig. 7. Wil gave a demo on OCPQ, a tool that allows us to extract insights from process execution data based on object-centric event logs [13]. As is evident from that picture, members of the business process technology group were quite impressed by Wil's presentation. He showed how queries can be defined in a graphical editor and how those queries can be evaluated on object-centric event data. This picture nicely shows how Wil interacts with the next generation of researchers in BPM, contributing to the continuous development of the BPM community.

If I were to return the question that Wil asked me 25 years ago, 'Wil, are you a process guy or a data guy?', he would probably answer, 'both'.

## References


1. Aalst, W.M.P.: Verification of workflow nets. In: Azéma, P., Balbo, G. (eds.) ICATPN 1997. LNCS, vol. 1248, pp. 407–426. Springer, Heidelberg (1997). https://doi.org/10.1007/3-540-63139-9_48
2. Aalst, W.M.P.: Object-Centric Process Mining: Dealing with Divergence and Convergence in Event Data. In: Ölveczky, P.C., Salaün, G. (eds.) SEFM 2019. LNCS, vol. 11724, pp. 3–25. Springer, Cham (2019). https://doi.org/10.1007/978-3-030-30446-1_1
3. van der Aalst, W.M.P., Artale, A., Montali, M., Tritini, S.: Object-centric behavioral constraints: Integrating data and declarative process modelling. In: Artale, A., Glimm, B., Kontchakov, R. (eds.) Proceedings of the 30th International Workshop on Description Logics. CEUR Workshop Proceedings, vol. 1879. CEUR-WS.org (2017). https://ceur-ws.org/Vol-1879/paper51.pdf
4. van der Aalst, W.M.P., Berti, A.: Discovering object-centric petri nets. CoRR (2020) **abs/2010.02047**, https://arxiv.org/abs/2010.02047
5. van der Aalst, W.M.P., Weijters, T., Maruster, L.: Workflow mining: discovering process models from event logs. IEEE Trans. Knowl. Data Eng. **16**(9), 1128–1142 (2004). https://doi.org/10.1109/TKDE.2004.47

6. Batoulis, K., Weske, M.: Soundness of Decision-Aware Business Processes. In: Carmona, J., Engels, G., Kumar, A. (eds.) BPM 2017. LNBIP, vol. 297, pp. 106–124. Springer, Cham (2017). https://doi.org/10.1007/978-3-319-65015-9_7
7. Dehnert, J., Rittgen, P.: Relaxed Soundness of Business Processes. In: Dittrich, K.R., Geppert, A., Norrie, M.C. (eds.) CAiSE 2001. LNCS, vol. 2068, pp. 157–170. Springer, Heidelberg (2001). https://doi.org/10.1007/3-540-45341-5_11
8. Dijkman, R.M., Dumas, M., Ouyang, C.: Semantics and analysis of business process models in BPMN. Inf. Softw. Technol. **50**(12), 1281–1294 (2008). https://doi.org/10.1016/J.INFSOF.2008.02.006
9. Gianola, A., Montali, M., Winkler, S.: Object-Centric Conformance Alignments with Synchronization (extended version) (2024). https://arxiv.org/abs/2312.08537
10. Gianola, A., Montali, M., Winkler, S.: Object-centric processes with structured data and exact synchronization - formal modelling and conformance checking. In: Krogstie, J., Rinderle-Ma, S., Kappel, G., Proper, H.A. (eds.) Advanced Information Systems Engineering - 37th International Conference, CAiSE 2025. Lecture Notes in Computer Science, vol. 15702, pp. 185–202. Springer (2025). https://doi.org/10.1007/978-3-031-94571-7_11
11. Hollingsworth, D.: The Workflow Reference Model. Tech. Rep. Document Number TC00-1003, Workflow Management Coalition (1995)
12. König, M., Gießler, R., Brandt, W., Seidel, A., Weske, M.: A unified view on data object states. In: Krogstie, J., Rinderle-Ma, S., Kappel, G., Proper, H.A. (eds.) Advanced Information Systems Engineering - 37th International Conference, CAiSE 2025. Lecture Notes in Computer Science, vol. 15702, pp. 259–276. Springer (2025).https://doi.org/10.1007/978-3-031-94571-7_15
13. Küsters, A., van der Aalst, W.M.P.: OCPQ: object-centric process querying and constraints. In: Grabis, J., Vos, T.E.J., Escalona, M.J., Pastor, O. (eds.) Research Challenges in Information Science - 19th International Conference, RCIS 2025. LNBIP, vol. 547, pp. 383–400. Springer (2025)
14. Montali, M., Rivkin, A.: DB-Nets: On the Marriage of Colored Petri Nets and Relational Databases. In: Koutny, M., Kleijn, J., Penczek, W. (eds.) Transactions on Petri Nets and Other Models of Concurrency XII. LNCS, vol. 10470, pp. 91–118. Springer, Heidelberg (2017). https://doi.org/10.1007/978-3-662-55862-1_5
15. Object Management Group: Business Process Model and Notation (BPMN) Version 2.0, formal/2011-01-03 edn. (2011)
16. Puhlmann, F., Weske, M.: Interaction Soundness for Service Orchestrations. In: Dan, A., Lamersdorf, W. (eds.) ICSOC 2006. LNCS, vol. 4294, pp. 302–313. Springer, Heidelberg (2006). https://doi.org/10.1007/11948148_25
17. Seidel, A., Winkler, S., Gianola, A., Montali, M., Weske, M.: To bind or not to bind? discovering stable relationships in object-centric processes. In: Bork, D., Lukyanenko, R., Sadiq, S., Bellatreche, L., Pastor, O. (eds.) Conceptual Modeling - 44th International Conference, ER 2025. Lecture Notes in Computer Science, vol. 16189, pp. 223–241. Springer (2025). https://doi.org/10.1007/978-3-032-08623-5_12
18. van der Werf, J.M.E.M., Rivkin, A., Montali, M., Polyvyanyy, A.: Correctness notions for petri nets with identifiers. Fundam. Informaticae **190**(2–4), 159–207 (2024). https://doi.org/10.3233/FI-242169
19. Weske, M.: Business Process Management - Concepts, Languages, Architectures. Springer, fourth edn. (2024). https://doi.org/10.1007/978-3-662-69518-0

# A Brief History and Overview of the Chair of Process and Data Science (PADS)


Bianka Bakullari[3] , Alessandro Berti[1] , Harry H. Beyel[1] ,
Tobias Brockhoff[1] , Eduardo Goulart Rocha[1,3](✉) , Nina Graves[1] ,
Hannes Häfke[5] , Tsung-Hao Huang[1] , Benedikt Knopp[1] , István Koren[1] ,
Humam Kourani[1,2] , Aaron Küsters[1] , Chiao-Yun Li[1] , Lukas Liss[1] ,
Lisa Luise Mannel[1] , Jan Niklas Adams[1] , Ali Norouzifar[1] ,
Gyunam Park[2] , Viki Peeva[1] , Marco Pegoraro[1] , Cameron Pitsch[1] ,
Mahsa Pourbafrani[1] , Majid Rafiei[1] , Christian Rennert[1] ,
Daniel Schuster[4] , Christopher T. Schwanen[1] ,
Leah Tacke genannt Unterberg[1] , Merih Seran Uysal[1] , Miriam Wagner[1] ,
and Sebastiaan J. van Zelst[3]

[1] Chair of Process and Data Science (PADS), RWTH Aachen University,
Aachen, Germany
[2] Fraunhofer FIT, Birlinghoven Castle, Sankt Augustin, Germany
[3] Celonis Labs GmbH, Munich, Germany
e.goulartrocha@celonis.com
[4] Process Intelligence Solutions GmbH, Aachen, Germany
[5] GWQ ServicePlus AG, Düsseldorf, Germany



**Abstract.** This paper documents the foundation and subsequent growth of the Chair of Process and Data Science (PADS) at RWTH Aachen University, reflecting on the milestones that shaped its trajectory between 2018 and 2025 from the perspectives of its current and former members. We describe the conditions that enabled the establishment of the research group, the strategy used to assemble and manage a diverse team, and how the chair pursued its mission of research and knowledge transfer through numerous initiatives. The paper is written as a small case study that celebrates the chair's achievements while also reflecting on the lessons learned during these eight years.

**Keywords:** Academic Leadership · Research Group Formation · Industry–Academia Collaboration · Technology Transfer


## 1 Introduction

In 2018, Wil took the step of leaving a well-established, world-leading research group at Eindhoven University of Technology (TU/e) to establish the new Chair of Process and Data Science (PADS) at RWTH Aachen University. Founding a new research group is as much of an organizational challenge as it is a scientific


© The Author(s), under exclusive license to Springer Nature Switzerland AG 2026
J. Mendling et al. (Eds.): Wil van der Aalst Festschrift, LNCS 16480, pp. 15–29, 2026.
https://doi.org/10.1007/978-3-032-17618-9_2

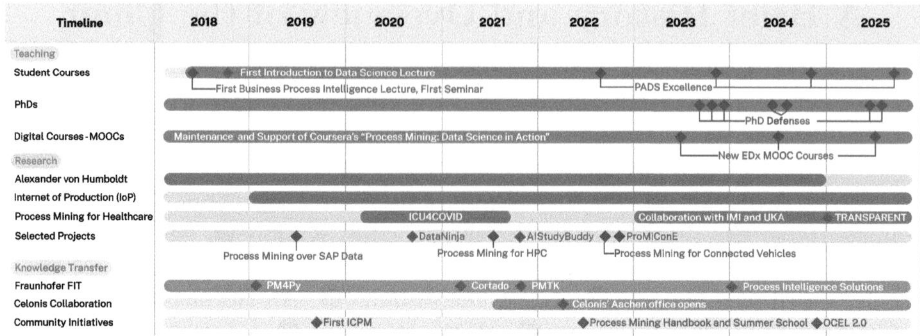

**Fig. 1.** A summary of the history of the PADS research group at RWTH Aachen University.

one. It requires designing a research agenda, fostering industrial partnerships, provisioning infrastructure, and establishing processes to manage a diverse team, that has to be assembled from scratch.

This paper documents the journey of the PADS Chair from its founding in 2018 to the present day (2025), describing the chair's key developments and accomplishments along the way. The goal is not to formally evaluate the group's success, but rather to provide a record of what was done, why it was done, and how these efforts fit together in pursuing the chair's core mission of research and knowledge transfer. The account is written to the best of our knowledge as current and former members of PADS. But it is inevitably incomplete, as Wil's perspective is missing. Nevertheless, we hope this serves as a useful resource for others looking to learn more on the inner workings of a research chair.

Figure 1 provides an overview of the chair's evolution from 2018 to 2025, organized around our three core responsibilities: teaching, research, and knowledge transfer. The upper "Teaching" lane records the first offerings of the *Introduction to Data Science* and *Business Process Intelligence* lectures and the later expansion to MOOCs, as well as the timeline of PhD projects at PADS. The "Research" lane highlights major research initiatives (e.g., the Alexander-von-Humboldt (AvH) professorship and the Internet of Production project) as well as selected research projects. The "Knowledge Transfer" lane captures milestones such as the establishment of Fraunhofer FIT, the start of the RWTH-Celonis cooperation, and our participation in broader community initiatives. We use this timeline as a roadmap for what follows: Sect. 2 covers organization and people, Sect. 3 details our research program, and Sect. 4 reviews our knowledge transfer initiatives.

## 2   The Chair

The PADS chair was established at RWTH Aachen University on *January 1st, 2018*, following the award of the *Alexander-von-Humboldt Professorship* to Wil in *2017*. As one of Germany's most prestigious research awards, the professorship provided the visibility and resources necessary to recruit talent, establish infrastructure, and launch both intra- and inter-university collaboration initiatives.

The chair's mission was framed as *"process science meets data science"*, aiming to solve organizational challenges through the development of rigorous methods. This guiding principle led to the formation of four research lines: *Foundations of Process Mining*, *Big & Uncertain Event Data*, *Automated Operational Process Improvement*, and *Responsible Process Mining*. With its initial research program defined, the next priority was to assemble a team capable of realizing this vision.

**Hiring the Team.** From the beginning, PADS was built as an international, gender-inclusive team. Over the years *2018–2025*, **43** researchers and staff were employed at the chair, with gender parity ($\approx 49\,\%$ women)—a figure that stood out in the context of a computer science discipline where such balance remains rare. Team members came from at least **17** different national backgrounds, and more than half held a non-German nationality ($\approx 58\,\%$). Recruitment and supervision was open to talent, irrespective of their background. The diversity shaped the daily work at the chair: the mix of perspectives and cultures made research discussions, meetings, and everyday interactions feel like those of a global team—united by a shared interest in process mining.

## 2.1   Organizing Work

Managing a research group in academia comes with unique organizational challenges. Unlike in industry, where teams often work on a shared product or deliverable, academic researchers typically pursue individual research agendas while also juggling teaching and project duties. High turnover—especially due to the limited-term nature of PhD contracts—adds further complexity to continuity and collaboration on shared operational tasks.

At PADS, these realities led to a structure that emphasized distributed responsibility and focused coordination. Internal working groups were created to ensure that critical operational tasks were not overlooked. The presently 17 teams took ownership of a specific area such as Administration and Finance, Organization of Teaching, Hardware and Software Support, Celonis Working Group, Social Media, or Social Activities. This setup ensures accountability by assigning a clear owner to each topic.

**Internal Processes.** As in any organization, PADS also structures its work through processes. While many internal processes, such as submitting a paper or requesting a reimbursement, are only informally described in our internal knowledge base, our thesis supervision process was so complex and critical that it required a more structured approach.

The supervision of Bachelor's and Master's theses is governed by strict university regulations and deadlines, making adherence to all formal requirements

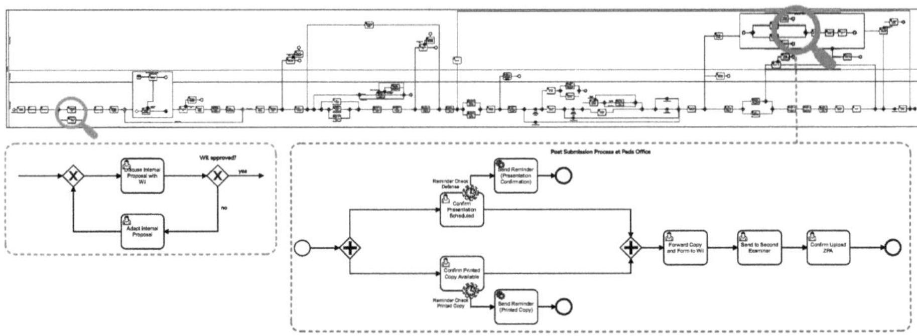

**Fig. 2.** Operational support for the thesis process at PADS using a workflow management system (top). Particularities of the PADS chair in the topic definition process (bottom left) and secretaries' involvement (bottom right) complete the picture.

critically important. With over 50 theses supervised annually, managing this process required a significant effort and was a clear source of friction. To handle these projects effectively and provide a consistent experience for all students, we have implemented the process as an executable workflow in the Camunda[1] system. As shown in Fig. 2, the BPMN model defines a standard process from topic selection to final submission. It automates administrative steps, clarifies the responsibilities of students, supervisors, and staff, and introduces structure to what is often an informal process. A small event log even allows us to analyze how well the process is running, detecting overloaded supervisors, and long-running theses.

## 3    Research

Alongside teaching, conducting research is a core responsibility of a university chair. At PADS, the first four lines of research were established upon receiving the Alexander-von-Humboldt grant. Below we detail each of them:

- **Foundations of Process Mining** This line of research extends foundational methods (process discovery, conformance checking, and performance analysis) to cope with complex, noisy event data while maintaining formal guarantees, ensuring that theory keeps pace with the growing scale and heterogeneity of logs in practice [39].
- **Big & Uncertain Event Data** This line of research addresses the challenges of applying process mining to large-scale, distributed, and streaming data by developing scalable techniques to handle uncertain data found in real-world infrastructures [35].
- **Automated Operational Process Improvement** This line of research develops techniques that combine continuous monitoring and iterative

---

[1] https://camunda.com.

redesign into "closed-loop" support for automated operational process improvement, anticipating execution-oriented mining where recommendations and changes are derived directly from event data [32].
- **Responsible Process Mining** This line of research investigates fairness, accuracy, privacy (confidentiality), and transparency in the analysis and deployment of process-analytic systems, embedding ethical safeguards alongside algorithmic innovation to prevent making unfair conclusions or revealing sensitive information [37].

Complementing the research lines established by the Alexander-von-Humboldt grant, Wil recognized the need to lift the initial single-case assumption from traditional process mining to capture many-to-many relations between objects and events, resulting in the emergence of **Object-Centric Process Mining (OCPM)**. Its shift in perspective can lead to new insights and allow previously impossible types of analysis [2].

Furthermore, PADS derived new research directions from a diverse project portfolio built over the years. These projects, which span fields like manufacturing, healthcare, education, and connected vehicles, reflecting Wil's belief in cross-fertilization. They serve to explore applications of process mining beyond conventional business processes. In the following sections, we provide an overview of these projects.

## 3.1 Internet of Production: Process Mining Analytics for Manufacturing

With the launch of the DFG Cluster of Excellence "Internet of Production" (IoP) at RWTH Aachen University in 2019, Wil took over a key position as deputy CEO, playing a central role in defining and steering the cluster's computer science involvements. Under his guidance, PADS, in collaboration with multiple industrial partners, applied process-centric analysis to the inherently complex field of manufacturing, navigating challenges such as large volumes and missing semantics [14]. For instance, the integration of *multi-level bills of materials* enabled a structured, top-down performance analysis of complex assembly processes, directly addressing the lack of explicit process information [15]. To overcome operational friction, such as rework and delays, process mining was further positioned to analyze variants, predictive simulation, and last but not least, handling interacting objects, by building accurate *digital shadows* that enable organizations to visualize, predict, and optimize their processes [4]. The research advanced data-driven simulation approaches for digital twin environments, establishing event logs as a foundation for predictive analysis and decision support [21,36]. The cluster's *models-in-the-middle* approach, informed by a large-scale study [23] and substantially inspired by the emerging OCEL 2.0 standard, introduced a number of data models with the prospect of streamlining data pipelines. Later, the cluster's move towards sustainability aspects enabled a new generation of process mining research on environmental analysis [18], e.g., with the *OCEAn* tool that enriches event data with emission factors to allocate carbon footprints per activity and object [17].

## 3.2   Process Mining for Healthcare

Process mining in healthcare has been a significant research area since at least 2004, representing a key application outside of traditional business and logistics. At RWTH Aachen University, the university hospital (UKA) provides a rich source of medical event data, which has been instrumental for developing and applying descriptive, predictive, and prescriptive analytics. Early contributions from PADS in this field include the ICU4COVID project (2020–2021), which focused on improving telemedicine in intensive care using robotics, cybernetics, data science, and medical expertise. This work led to some of the earliest publications on process mining using COVID-19 data, providing a normative care model and analyzing the challenges of quickly implementing new treatment guidelines in intensive care [5,34].

In Germany, the adoption of process mining in healthcare is hampered by strict data protection laws and a lack of standardized data formats. To address these issues, a collaboration with the Institute of Medical Informatics (IMI) began in 2023. This partnership aims to generalize the use of process mining for healthcare data across Germany, using the UKA as a model. Initial projects are focused on identifying commonalities between different datasets and creating intermediate models (models in the middle) that bridge the gap between healthcare data formats and those required for process mining [20].

The strong collaboration between PADS and the UKA is still ongoing. The TRANSPARENT project, started in *January 2025*, focuses on analyzing processes in emergency medicine within the Aachen region. This is the first project of its kind in Germany, bringing together data from the UKA, insurance companies, emergency services, and other providers. The primary goal is to link these diverse data sources in a way that respects patient privacy. By transforming this combined data into event logs, researchers can analyze patient journeys across different scopes, providing unprecedented insights into the previously opaque pathways of emergency medical care.

## 3.3   Selected Initiatives and Case Studies

In this subsection, we list further projects and case studies conducted by PADS that highlight the breadth of topics covered by the chair.

**Process Mining for Education: Analyzing Student Cohorts and Finding Recommendations.** Even before PADS, Wil's previous chair, the process analytics group at TU/e, laid the foundations for the research in process mining for education. With this background—and with the PADS chair being co-located in one institute with the Learning Technologies (LT) chair—the "AIStudyBuddy" research project emerged. The collaboration took place between 2021 and 2025 and also included further chairs from RWTH Aachen University, the University of Wuppertal, and Ruhr-University Bochum. The project allowed PADS to advertise process mining across universities and to showcase its capabilities by developing process mining algorithms for recommendations, discovery, and conformance checking on students' course-taking behavior [33].

**Analyzing Driver Behavior in Connected Vehicles.** This project, conducted from 2022 to 2024 in collaboration with an industrial partner, analyzed operational data (collected with the user's consent) from connected vehicles equipped with a hands-free driving mode. The research focused on *modeling* the system's underlying processes, *checking the conformance* of recorded data against this model, evaluating if the system follows its intended behavior, and identifying reasons why drivers disabled the hands-free driving mode. Research results [11–13] were not only published in academic venues, but also much appreciated in roundtable discussions with the industrial partner.

**DataNinja (ML4ProM).** The ML4ProM project was a collaborative effort within the DataNinja research training group, a program established by the Ministry of Culture and Education of North Rhine-Westphalia (Germany). Wil initiated the project together with Barbara Hammer from the CITEC group at Bielefeld University with the objective of combining process mining and machine learning expertise to develop novel, multidisciplinary approaches that advance both fields. Among its main outcomes are innovative methods for process discovery supporting desirable event logs while avoiding undesirable event logs [29], rule-guided process discovery [30], and LLM-assisted process discovery [31]. While the project is officially concluded, many of its research lines are still under active development, ensuring long-term collaborations between the institutions.

**Process Mining Applied to High Performance Computing Workloads.** Starting in *2021*, PADS joined Germany's National High Performance Computing Alliance (NHR) through the project NHR4CES, together with the Technical University of Darmstadt. The goal is to optimize and provide insights into the process of using computing clusters, from both the perspective of machine activity and user behavior. Participating PADS members set out to collect event data from HPC clusters, to conduct process mining case studies [38], and provide process-aware tooling and analysis support to HPC administrators [28]. Among the main challenges identified in this project, we list missing data associated with some commands, the difficulty of assigning a case ID notion to each event, and the confidentiality constraints related to accessing HPC logs. Currently, ongoing efforts focus on extracting object-centric event data to holistically analyze different perspectives.

**Process Mining Connector for ERP Systems (ProMiConE).** The ProMiConE project is a collaboration with RWTH's *Research Institute for Industrial Management (FIR)* to enable process mining for small and medium-sized enterprises by developing methods to assess the potential of process mining, particularly in the manufacturing domain (e.g., supported by the *Process Mining Use Case Canvas* [19]), and developing representative transactional reference process and data models that serve as a basis for an event data extraction prototype. The resulting extractor[2] leverages the user's domain knowledge of the process and data structure and, in return, relieves them of the usually required expertise to create an object-centric event log. Exporting an OCEL allows companies to import the extracted data to various proprietary or academic process mining tools for targeted analyses. Once configured, the extraction can be repeated for recurring evaluations.

**Process Mining over SAP Data.** This project focused specifically on enabling object-centric process mining using data from SAP systems. The extraction, transformation, and loading (ETL) of event logs from information systems represent the initial—and often most resource-intensive phase of process mining. Extracting event data from widely used ERP systems like SAP is particularly challenging due to the complexity and volume of the underlying data. The main objective of this project was to extract object-centric event data from SAP ERP systems and subsequently discover and analyze both known and previously undocumented processes. The project also involved several collaborations [6,9], with ECE Group Services as the main industry partner.

## 4   Knowledge Transfer

Research is not an end in itself. Therefore, a university chair is expected to foster the transfer of knowledge into application and ultimately generate societal value. In PADS, this is pursued via a wide variety of initiatives, such as industry collaborations, contributions to the process mining community and to open source initiatives, and open educational initiatives. In this section, we detail each of these initiatives.

### 4.1   Industry Collaborations

In Germany, research groups are expected to partake in broader cross-disciplinary initiatives and to foster the exchange of knowledge between academia and industry. Such partnerships are also beneficial for researchers, as they feed them with novel, relevant real-world problems. At PADS, these collaborations are structured across two pillars.

**An Applied Counterpart: Fraunhofer FIT.** The Process Mining group at Fraunhofer FIT was established in *2018*, taking shape alongside Wil's move to Aachen. The group was built under Wil's scientific guidance to translate the

---

[2] https://promicone.fir.de.

principle of "process science meets data science" into industry-focused research. Embracing the typical Fraunhofer mission of blending publicly funded research and industry projects, the unit became PADS' applied counterpart, focused on transforming methods and standards into tools, pilot projects, and partnerships.

On the research side, the group built a broad portfolio addressing a wide spectrum of challenges from foundational projects like Automated Operational Process Improvement to cutting-edge explorations into how generative AI and large language models can enable more intuitive and intelligent ways of working with business processes [24,25]. On the industry collaboration side, the group boasts a series of industry engagements that brought process mining into real-world applications across various sectors. Collaborations include the long-term project to integrate process mining functionalities into the KNIME Platform [26], a project with GWQ ServicePlus to analyze health insurance data, and numerous partnerships supporting companies from startups to large corporations in adopting process mining.

On the software development side, the group has created some of the most widely used tools in the field such as PM4Py [10], the leading open-source Python library for process mining; the Process Mining Toolkit (PMTK) [8] for comprehensive process analysis; and Cortado [40], an interactive process discovery environment. The success of the group's tools, especially PM4Py, has led to the spin-off Process Intelligence Solutions, ensuring sustainable enterprise-grade support while preserving open-source accessibility.

**Fostering Technology Transfer: The Celonis–RWTH Aachen University Cooperation.** In *August 2021*, Celonis and RWTH entered a formal cooperation to accelerate the transfer of knowledge from academia to industry and to give researchers access to real-world problems. This collaboration resulted in multiple initiatives, including a fully funded industrial PhD position, sponsored Master theses to be supervised in cooperation with Celonis (many of which make an impact in Celonis' product), new lab courses and guest lectures at RWTH, and the collaboration with PADS researchers, who (in cooperation with Celonis' customers) can test their solutions in real-world settings. In *May 2022*, the collaboration was further strengthened with the opening of Celonis' engineering hub in Aachen, where many of PADS' former students find full-time positions after graduating, establishing Aachen as a hub for the process mining industry.

## 4.2   Participating in Community-Defining Initiatives

Besides nurturing the community, contributing to such initiatives helps "put the group on the map" and establish it as a well-known actor in the field.

**Launching the ICPM Conference: A Flagship Venue (2019).** The idea of a dedicated, vendor-neutral conference for process mining matured in late *2017* and culminated in the inaugural International Conference on Process Mining (ICPM) in Aachen on *June 24–26, 2019*. Hosted by the PADS chair at

RWTH Aachen University and held under the auspices of the IEEE Task Force on Process Mining, ICPM 2019 was co-located with the Petri Nets and ACSD conferences to underline the field's formal roots while creating a forum squarely focused on process mining. The program combined a peer-reviewed research track with an industry program and community competitions, turning Aachen into the first neutral meeting ground for researchers, vendors, and end-users.

From the first edition, ICPM achieved critical mass: more than 420 participants gathered in Aachen, producing the "unique atmosphere" the community had long sought and immediately setting the template for an annual series. The blend of academic talks, invited industry case studies, and contests such as the BPI Challenge and the Process Discovery Contest established ICPM as the flagship venue of a fast-maturing discipline, with subsequent editions rotating internationally while preserving the spirit of the first edition.

**The Process Mining Summer School and Handbook (2022).** To meet increased demand for structured training, the first Process Mining Summer School took place in Aachen on *July 4–8, 2022*. Jointly organized by the IEEE Task Force on Process Mining and hosted by the PADS chair, the school admitted roughly 130 participants from doctoral students to practitioners, offered lectures by about 20 experts, and balanced foundational sessions with hands-on labs on both open-source and industrial tools, all hosted in RWTH's SuperC building and complemented by community events for networking. Its legacy was captured in the open-access *Process Mining Handbook*, edited by Wil and Josep Carmona and released in *mid-2022* [3]. The volume compiles 17 chapters arranged across eight sections, going from process discovery and conformance checking to data preparation, monitoring, and industrial perspectives, and has since become a widely consulted reference, with strong download and citation figures by the current year. The school and handbook together provided a snapshot of the state of the art while setting a road map for young researchers in process mining.

**The Push for OCPM and the OCEL 2.0 Initiative.** OCPM emerged from the recognition that real processes involve multiple interacting objects that cannot be flattened into a single case. The formative steps are clear: the Object-Centric Behavioral Constraints (OCBC) model laid conceptual foundations in *2017*; a keynote paper in *2019* formalized divergence and convergence in object-centric event data [1]; and OCEL 1.0 (*2020–2021*) provided a logging standard to capture events linked to many object types [16]. These strands laid the foundation for research in object-centric process analysis.

Through the subsequent years, PADS released a series of object-centric research tools and libraries, including the *OC-PM* tool for object-centric process discovery, the *OC-π* tool for object-centric performance analysis, and the *ocpa* library, collecting a variety of methods for object-centric process analysis. Later on, these tools were consolidated within the broader OCEL 2.0 initiative, which introduced the OCEL 2.0 standard [7], a complete tool set[3] for extracting, con-

---

[3] Available at https://www.ocel-standard.org/.

verting, storing, and managing the new format, as well as example datasets to help practitioners get started [22].

## 4.3   Contributing to Open-Source Software

Since its foundation, PADS has been committed to creating and maintaining open-source software. Some of the tools developed and maintained by PADS were already presented in previous sections. Here, we detail other tools that were not directly connected to other initiatives:

- *OCPQ* is an object-centric process querying tool written in Rust for interactive filtering and constraint checking on object-centric data [28].
- *Rust4PM* is a high-performance Rust library that parses XES/OCEL logs and implements core discovery and analysis routines with strong memory-safety guarantees and bindings for other languages [27].
- *Ocelot* is a web-based OCEL 2.0 inspector linked with Zenodo for fast online event log exploration[4].

## 4.4   Education and Outreach

Finally, PADS pursues educational initiatives that go beyond classrooms.

**Open Education (MOOCs).** The PADS chair maintains several online courses aimed at disseminating process mining knowledge worldwide, reaching both academic audiences and practitioners in organizations. The *Process Mining: Data Science in Action* MOOC[5], first launched on Coursera in 2015, has remained active and has been maintained and supported by the PADS team since 2018. In 2023, a new EdX MOOC titled *A Hands-On Introduction to Process Mining*[6] was launched in collaboration with Celonis. This course provides an accessible introduction to the fundamental concepts of process mining through hands-on tutorials and assignments. It was followed by two successive MOOCs: *Basics of Data Science* (2024)[7], providing a broad introduction to data science concepts and techniques, enabling a wide audience to acquire essential skills at the same quality level as taught at RWTH Aachen University, featuring lectures by Wil, and *Object-Centric Process Mining* (2025)[8], introducing learners to the most recent advances in the field, focusing on the object-centric paradigm that is reshaping how businesses analyze their processes in realistic, real-world settings.

---

[4]  https://ocelot.pm.

[5]  https://www.coursera.org/learn/process-mining.

[6]  https://www.edx.org/learn/computer-programming/rwth-aachen-university-process-mining.

[7]  https://www.edx.org/learn/data-science/rwth-aachen-university-basics-of-data-science.

[8]  https://www.edx.org/learn/computer-science/rwth-aachen-university-bai-process-mining.

**PADS Excellence.** In 2022, PADS established its alumni network *PADS Excellence* to honor its outstanding students and graduates and to form an alliance that extends beyond their studies. The annual PADS Excellence Symposium is the central networking event which brings the whole network of currently over 200 students, graduates, and professionals together. With scientific and industry keynotes, research exhibitions, and a networking reception, this event offers unique opportunities for members from different stages of their careers to connect and cooperate.

## 5    Conclusion and Lessons Learned

The previous sections have detailed the initiatives that established PADS as a new research hub in process mining. While the catalytic funding from the Alexander-von-Humboldt Professorship was instrumental in the group's rapid expansion, this initial support did not by itself guarantee success. Sustained growth required independent initiatives, including securing new research projects, fostering industry collaborations, and participating in community-defining events.

Reflecting on this journey, we attribute the group's success largely to Wil's distinctive approach to science. His philosophy can be distilled into the set of principles below, which, though not always explicitly stated, are consistently instilled by his leadership and implicitly guide our daily work.

1. **Pioneering Novel Research Topics:** Wil encourages researchers to move away from incremental work on well-established problems to explore unique, emerging areas where they can make a distinct and impactful contribution.
2. **Fostering Interdisciplinary Collaboration:** Wil views cross-fertilization between fields as an essential driver of research. This principle is reflected in our heterogeneous project portfolio, spanning a wide range of areas.
3. **Championing Open-Source Software and Education:** The success of our research group is intrinsically linked to the growth of process mining as a field. Since his early days at TU/e, Wil has championed open-source tools and free learning materials to accelerate the field's development. This principle was also imported into PADS.
4. **Materializing Research:** This is connected to the point above and is best synthesized in Wil's *"No paper without a tool"* motto, which ensures your work gets visibility and can be adopted and built upon by other researchers.
5. **Participating in Key Community Initiatives:** Wil actively contributes to pivotal initiatives that shape our community, such as the first International Conference on Process Mining, the Process Mining Summer School, and the OCEL 2.0 standard. This not only advances the field but also helps position the group within the research community, enhancing our visibility and impact.

Over the last eight years, the authors—as current and former members of PADS—have had the opportunity to learn from Wil how to conduct impactful research. We feel privileged to have (at least partially) experienced the process of founding a new research group and wish to take this opportunity to thank him for his invaluable mentorship.

# References


1. van der Aalst, W.M.P.: Object-Centric Process Mining: Dealing with Divergence and Convergence in Event Data. In: In: Ölveczky, P., Salaün, G. (eds.) SEFM. Lecture Notes in Computer Science, vol. 11724, pp. 3–25. Springer, Cham (2019). https://doi.org/10.1007/978-3-030-30446-1_1
2. van der Aalst, W.M.P., Berti, A.: Discovering object-centric petri nets. Fundam. Informaticae **175**(1–4), 1–40 (2020)
3. van der Aalst, W.M.P., Carmona, J. (eds.): Process Mining Handbook, Lecture Notes in Business Information Processing, vol. 448. Springer, Cham (2022). https://doi.org/10.1007/978-3-031-08848-3
4. van der Aalst, W.M.P., Brockhoff, T., Ghahfarokhi, A.F., Pourbafrani, M., Uysal, M.S., van Zelst, S.J.: Removing Operational Friction Using Process Mining: Challenges Provided by the Internet of Production (IoP). In: Hammoudi, S., Quix, C., Bernardino, J. (eds.) Data Management Technologies and Applications, vol. 1446, pp. 1–31. Springer, Cham (2021)
5. Benevento, E., et al.: Process Modeling and Conformance Checking in Healthcare: A COVID-19 Case Study. In: Montali, M., Senderovich, A., Weidlich, M. (eds.) ICPM Workshops. Lecture Notes in Business Information Processing, vol. 468, pp. 315–327. Springer, Cham (2022). https://doi.org/10.1007/978-3-031-27815-0_23
6. Berti, A., Jessen, U., Park, G., Rafiei, M., van der Aalst, W.M.P.: Analyzing interconnected processes: using object-centric process mining to analyze procurement processes. Int. J. Data Sci. Anal. **20**(2), 475–497 (2025)
7. Berti, A., et al.: OCEL (object-centric event log) 2.0 specification. CoRR **abs/2403.01975** (2024)
8. Berti, A., Li, C.Y., Schuster, D., van Zelst, S.J.: The process mining toolkit (PMTK): Enabling advanced process mining in an integrated fashion. In: Proceedings of the ICPM demo track. CEUR Workshop Proceedings, vol. 3098, pp. 43–44 (2021)
9. Berti, A., Park, G., Rafiei, M., van der Aalst, W.M.P.: A generic approach to extract object-centric event data from databases supporting SAP ERP. J. Intell. Inf. Syst. **61**(3), 835–857 (2023)
10. Berti, A., van Zelst, S.J., Schuster, D.: Pm4py: a process mining library for python. Softw. Impacts **17**, 100556 (2023)
11. Beyel, H.H., Makke, O., Gusikhin, O., van der Aalst, W.M.P.: Analyzing behavior in cyber-physical systems in connected vehicles: a case study. In: De Weerdt, J., Pufahl, L. (eds.) BPM Workshops. pp. 92–104. Springer, Cham (2023). https://doi.org/10.1007/978-3-031-50974-2_8
12. Beyel, H.H., Makke, O., Pourbafrani, M., Gusikhin, O., van der Aalst, W.M.P.: Analyzing data streams from cyber-physical-systems: a case study. SN Comput. Sci. **5**(6), 706 (2024)
13. Beyel, H.H., Makke, O., Yuan, F., Gusikhin, O., van der Aalst, W.M.P.: Analyzing Cyber-Physical Systems in Cars: A Case Study. In: DATA. pp. 195–204. SCITEPRESS (2023)
14. Brauner, P., et al.: A computer science perspective on digital transformation in production. ACM Trans. Internet Things. **3**(2), 1–32 (2022)
15. Brockhoff, T., Uysal, M.S., Terrier, I., Göhner, H., van der Aalst, W.M.P.: Analyzing multi-level BOM-structured event data. In: Munoz-Gama, J., Lu, X. (eds.) Process Mining Workshops, vol. 433, pp. 47–59. Springer, Cham (2022)

16. Ghahfarokhi, A.F., Park, G., Berti, A., van der Aalst, W.M.P.: OCEL: A Standard for Object-Centric Event Logs. In: Bellatreche, L., et al. (eds.) New Trends in Database and Information Systems. ADBIS (Short Papers). Communications in Computer and Information Science, vol. 1450, pp. 169–175. Springer (2021). https://doi.org/10.1007/978-3-030-85082-1_16
17. Graves, N., Fritsch, A., Hensen, R., Koren, I., Aalst, W.M.P.: Object-centric process mining for semi-automated and multi-perspective sustainability analyses (2025)
18. Graves, N., Koren, I., van der Aalst, W.M.P.: ReThink Your Processes! A Review of Process Mining for Sustainability. In: ICT4S. pp. 164–175. IEEE (2023)
19. Hardjosuwito, D., Braucks, F.L., Schröer, T., Schwanen, C.T., van der Aalst, W.M.P.: The process mining use case canvas: a framework for developing and specifying use cases. In: Conference on Production Systems and Logistics (CPSL) (2023)
20. Heidemeyer, H., et al.: A pipeline for the usage of the core data set of the medical informatics initiative for process mining - A technical case report. In: GMDS. Studies in Health Technology and Informatics, vol. 317, pp. 30–39. IOS Press (2024)
21. Knopp, B., Pourbafrani, M., van der Aalst, W.M.P.: Root cause analysis using rule mining on object-centric event logs. Delgado, A., Slaats, T. (eds.) ICPM Workshops. Lecture Notes in Business Information Processing, vol. 533, pp. 57–69. Springer, Cham (2024). https://doi.org/10.1007/978-3-031-82225-4_5
22. Koren, I., Adams, J.N., Berti, A., van der Aalst, W.M.P.: OCEL 2.0 Resources - www.ocel-standard.org In: ICPM Doctoral Consortium / Demo. CEUR Workshop Proceedings, vol. 3648 (2023)
23. Koren, I., Jarke, M., Michael, J., Heithoff, M.F., Tacke Genannt Unterberg, L., Stachon, M.P., Rumpe, B., van der Aalst, W.M.P.: Navigating the Data Model Divide in Smart Manufacturing: An Empirical Investigation for Enhanced AI Integration. In: van der Aa, H., Bork, D., Schmidt, R., Sturm, A. (eds.) Enterprise, Business-Process and Information Systems Modeling: 25th International Conference, BPMDS 2024. LNBIP, vol. 511, pp. 275–290. Springer, Cham, Switzerland (2024). https://doi.org/10.1007/978-3-031-61007-3_21
24. Kourani, H., et al.: Leveraging large language models for enhanced process model comprehension. Decis. Support Syst. **200**, 114563 (2026)
25. Kourani, H., Berti, A., Schuster, D., van der Aalst, W.M.P.: Process modeling with large language models. In: van der Aa, H., Bork, D., Schmidt, R., Sturm, A. (eds.) BPMDS/EMMSAD@CAiSE. Lecture Notes in Business Information Processing, vol. 511, pp. 229–244. Springer (2024). https://doi.org/10.1007/978-3-031-61007-3_18
26. Kourani, H., van Zelst, S.J., Lehmann, B., Einsdorf, G., Helfrich, S., Liße, F.: PM4KNIME: Process Mining Meets the KNIME Analytics Platform (Extended Abstract). In: ICPM Doctoral Consortium / Demo. CEUR Workshop Proceedings, vol. 3299, pp. 65–69 (2022)
27. Küsters, A., van der Aalst, W.M.P.: Rust4PM: a Versatile Process Mining Library for When Performance Matters. In: BPM (Demos / Resources Forum). CEUR Workshop Proceedings, vol. 3758, pp. 91–95 (2024)
28. Küsters, A., van der Aalst, W.M.P.: OCPQ: Object-Centric Process Querying and Constraints. In: In: Grabis, J., Vos, T.E.J., Escalona, M.J., Pastor, O. (eds.) RCIS (1). Lecture Notes in Business Information Processing, vol. 547, pp. 383–400. Springer (2025). https://doi.org/10.1007/978-3-031-92474-3_23

29. Norouzifar, A., van der Aalst, W.M.P.: Discovering Process Models that Support Desired Behavior and Avoid Undesired Behavior. In: SAC. pp. 365–368. ACM (2023)
30. Norouzifar, A., Dees, M., van der Aalst, W.M.P.: Rule-guided process discovery. Data & Knowl. Eng. **161**, 102508 (2026)
31. Norouzifar, A., Kourani, H., Dees, M., van der Aalst, W.M.P.: Bridging domain knowledge and process discovery using large language models. In: Gdowska, K., Gémez-Lépez, M.T., Rehse, Jr. (eds) Business Process Management Workshops. LNBIP, vol. 534, pp. 44–56. Springer, Cham (2024). https://doi.org/10.1007/978-3-031-78666-2_4
32. Park, G., van der Aalst, W.M.P.: Realizing a digital twin of an organization using action-oriented process mining. In: ICPM. pp. 104–111. IEEE (2021)
33. Park, G., Liss, L., van der Aalst, W.M.P.: Learning recommendations from educational event data in higher education. J. Intell. Inf. Sys. pp. 1–20 (2024)
34. Pegoraro, M., Narayana, M.B.S., Benevento, E., van der Aalst, W.M.P., Martin, L., Marx, G.: Analyzing Medical Data with Process Mining: A COVID-19 Case Study. In: Abramowicz, W., Auer, S., Stróżyna, M. (eds.) BIS (Workshops). Lecture Notes in Business Information Processing, vol. 444, pp. 39–44. Springer (2021). https://doi.org/10.1007/978-3-031-04216-4_4
35. Pegoraro, M., Uysal, M.S., van der Aalst, W.M.P.: Efficient time and space representation of uncertain event data. Algorithms **13**(11), 285 (2020)
36. Pourbafrani, M., van der Aalst, W.M.P.: Discovering system dynamics simulation models using process mining. IEEE Access **10**, 78527–78547 (2022)
37. Rafiei, M., van der Aalst, W.M.P.: Group-based privacy preservation techniques for process mining. Data Knowl. Eng. **134**, 101908 (2021)
38. Sadeghibogar, Z., Berti, A., Pegoraro, M., van der Aalst, W.M.P.: SLURMminer: a tool for slurm system analysis with process mining. In: BPM (Demos / Resources Forum). CEUR Workshop Proceedings, vol. 3469, pp. 97–101 (2023)
39. Sani, M.F., van Zelst, S.J., van der Aalst, W.M.P.: Improving Process Discovery Results by Filtering Outliers Using Conditional Behavioural Probabilities. In: Teniente, E., Weidlich, M. (eds.) Business Process Management Workshops. Lecture Notes in Business Information Processing, vol. 308, pp. 216–229. Springer (2017). https://doi.org/10.1007/978-3-319-74030-0_16
40. Schuster, D., van Zelst, S.J., van der Aalst, W.M.P.: Cortado - an interactive tool for data-driven process discovery and modeling. In: Buchs, D., Carmona, J. (eds.) Petri Nets. Lecture Notes in Computer Science, vol. 12734, pp. 465–475. Springer (2021). https://doi.org/10.1007/978-3-030-76983-3_23

# From Eindhoven to Everywhere: An Academic Spark that Lit Up Classrooms Around the World

Angela-Sophia Gebert[(✉)]

Celonis Deutschland GmbH, Munich, Germany
`as.gebert@celonis.com`

**Abstract.** This tribute, written by the Celonis Academic Alliance, celebrates the academic legacy of Professor Wil van der Aalst with a particular focus on his foundational role in shaping education within the field of Process Mining and Process Intelligence. His groundbreaking research in Eindhoven started a global movement that continues to shape how we teach, learn, and apply Process Intelligence today. From lecture halls to online classrooms, Wil's gospel and continued support is deeply embedded in the teaching materials and mission of our Academic Alliance. With over 1,500 academic partners the Celonis Academic Alliance exists because of the academic rigour and vision Wil brought to the field. This tribute honours the spark and continuous effort that lit thousands of classrooms worldwide, shaping the Process Intelligence Workforce of tomorrow.

It's a late evening in Eindhoven, the Netherlands. A single office light is still on inside the university's industrial engineering department, where Wil collaborated with Ton Weijters—a partnership that gave rise to the first paper explicitly describing Process Mining [1]. Professor Wil van der Aalst leans over a stack of event logs. Thousands of data points. Each one a breadcrumb of how real processes actually unfold. He doesn't see random noise. He sees patterns. Connections. A living map of how work really flows through organisations. That moment, more than two decades ago, sparked what would become one of the most important academic discoveries in modern business transformation: Process Mining. And from that spark, an entire field has grown.

## 1 Academia at the Core of Process Intelligence

At Celonis, we often say that **academia is in our DNA**. That's not a slogan. It's a fact. The algorithms and methods that underpin the Celonis platform trace back to university lecture halls and research labs. From Alpha Miner to conformance checking to object-centric modelling [2–5], the discipline of Process Mining was born from Wil's work and from the rigour of academic curiosity. In those early years, process models were still drawn on whiteboards or tucked away in manuals. They rarely matched the messy, complex reality of business life. While everyone was busy studying Workflow Management, Wil asked a different question:

*What if processes could be discovered from data rather than described on paper?*
That academic question changed everything.


J. Mendling et al. (Eds.): Wil van der Aalst Festschrift, LNCS 16480, pp. 30–32, 2026.
https://doi.org/10.1007/978-3-032-17618-9_3

Process Mining has since evolved into the broader field of Process Intelligence, combining data-driven discovery with operational excellence, predictive analytics, and increasingly object-centric representations. The academic heritage remains visible in every component of the discipline's evolution.

## 2  From Research to a Global Movement

Great ideas do not always make it out of academia. But this one did. The Celonis founders recognised the power of Process Mining early on. And they built a company anchored in the principles of academic rigour. This industry–academic bridge is part of the field's identity: research prototypes became algorithms, which became platforms, which in turn generated new research questions.

That DNA gave rise to the Celonis Academic Alliance: today one of the world's largest educational networks in enterprise technology. More than 1,500 professors and 600,000 students trained across 900 + institutions are now part of the programme. Academic curiosity and vivid exchange between academia and industry stands at the heart of the programme.

## 3  Wil's Lasting Contributions

Wil never stopped inspiring the field and advocating for academic excellence. As advisor to the Celonis Academic Alliance, he continues to build the bridge between theory and practice. At RWTH Aachen, his PADS group remains a global hub for cutting-edge Process Mining research and holds the title of Celonis Academic Center of Excellence. His group works closely with the Celonis product team based in Aachen shaping the product and developing IP on a daily basis. The presence of many of his former PhD students within Celonis is a testament to the strength of this continuous exchange. And his contributions to learning extend far beyond traditional academia:

- The world-famous Coursera MOOC is still seen as the bible for Process Mining education.
- Two MOOCs on EdX have brought Process Mining to tens of thousands of learners worldwide.
- The Celonis Academy course "From Theory to Execution" translates research into practical application for practitioners everywhere.
- And his guest appearance on the Trust the Process podcast is a must-listen.

Process Mining is not only a research discipline but an accessible, global learning movement. And Wil embodies what makes Process Intelligence unique: a living exchange between universities and companies, between students and consultants, between research and real-world challenges.

## 4  A Community that Trusts the Process

The beauty of Process Mining is that it has never been confined to the ivory tower. Students bring fresh questions. Professors bring thoroughness. Practitioners bring urgency. And in that cycle of exchange, the field keeps evolving from Object-Centric Process Mining, to predictive models to compliance by design. Wil often reminds us that *theories inspire tools, and tools create new questions for research. It's a cycle.*

That cycle is alive and thriving today thanks to Wil's vision. Process Intelligence grows not only through innovation, but through the classroom environments where future researchers and practitioners first encounter these ideas. Today, this cycle is more vibrant than ever. Student projects, research papers, and real-world applications feed back into the loop, reinforcing the very educational ecosystem Wil has championed for decades. The field expands not only through discoveries, but through the students and teachers who carry these discoveries forward.

## 5  Honouring the Spark

From Eindhoven to classrooms in Costa Rica, Bangalore, and Stockholm, Wil's spark has traveled the world. Today, students everywhere learn about Wil's theory in the classroom. We as Academic Alliance have supported over 5,000 classrooms alone. Tomorrow, they'll be the consultants, analysts, and leaders driving Process Intelligence forward. That is Wil's true legacy: A discovery that became a discipline and a movement that continues to grow rooted in academia, trusted by practice, and carried forward by a global learning community.

On behalf of the Celonis Academic Alliance, I want to honour Professor Wil van der Aalst as a tireless advocate for the vital role of academia in shaping the future of Process Intelligence. Because without academia, there would be no Process Mining.

Without Wil, there would be no spark. And without that spark, we wouldn't be here trusting the process together.

## References


1. Weijters, A.J.M.M., van der Aalst, W.M.P.: Process mining: discovering workflow models from event-based data. In: Kröse, B., de Rijke, M., Schreiber, G., van Someren, M. (eds.) Proceedings of the 13th Belgium–Dutch Conference on Artificial Intelligence (BNAIC 2001), pp. 283–290. Amsterdam (2001)
2. van der Aalst, W.M.P., Weijters, A.J.M.M., Maruster, L.: Workflow mining: discovering process models from event logs. IEEE Trans. Knowl. Data Eng. **16**(9), 1128–1142 (2004)
3. van der Aalst, W.M.P.: Process Mining: Discovery, Conformance and Enhancement of Business Processes. Springer, Berlin (2011). https://doi.org/10.1007/978-3-662-49851-4
4. van der Aalst, W.M.P., Adriansyah, A., van Dongen, B.F.: Replaying historic events on process models. Computing **94**(4), 299–330 (2012)
5. van der Aalst, W.M.P.:Object-centric process mining: dealing with divergence and convergence in event data. In: Giorgini, P., Weber, B. (eds.) CAiSE 2019. LNCS, vol. 11483, pp. 3–21. Springer, Cham (2019). https://doi.org/10.1007/978-3-030-30446-1_1

# From Theory to Practice: How Fraunhofer FIT and Its Ecosystem Brought Wil van der Aalst's Process Mining Vision to Market


Humam Kourani[1], Wolfgang Kratsch[1,3], Christoph Lange-Bever[1], Maximilian Röglinger[1,4], Daniel Schuster[5], Sebastiaan J. van Zelst[6], and Gyunam Park[1,2(✉)]

[1] Fraunhofer Institute for Applied Information Technology FIT,
Sankt Augustin, Germany
`gyunam.park@fit.fraunhofer.de, g.park@tue.nl`
[2] Eindhoven University of Technology, Eindhoven, The Netherlands
[3] Technical University of Applied Sciences Augsburg, Augsburg, Germany
[4] University of Bayreuth, Bayreuth, Germany
[5] Process Intelligence Solutions GmbH, Aachen, Germany
[6] Celonis SE, Munich, Germany



**Abstract.** This article chronicles the journey of translating Wil van der Aalst's foundational process mining concepts into practical, market-ready applications through the collaborative efforts of Fraunhofer FIT's Process Mining research group, the Center for Process Intelligence (CPI), and the Process Intelligence Solutions (PIS) spin-off. Since 2018, this three-dimensional ecosystem has generated over 2.5 million software downloads, many industry projects, and 100+ peer-reviewed publications while successfully bridging academic excellence with commercial impact. We demonstrate how van der Aalst's theoretical contributions enabled not just scientific advancement but sustainable institution building, creating a self-reinforcing cycle of research, consulting, and commercialization that continues to advance the field of process mining.

**Keywords:** Process Mining · Technology Transfer · Industry Applications · Open Source Software · Academic-Industry Collaboration


## 1 Introduction

When Wil van der Aalst pioneered the field of process mining, he envisioned a discipline that would bridge the gap between theoretical computer science and practical business applications [4]. His foundational contributions, from the $\alpha$-algorithm [3] to conformance checking [17], from performance analysis [2] to process monitoring [15], provided not just academic insights but a roadmap for transforming how organizations understand and optimize their processes.



J. Mendling et al. (Eds.): Wil van der Aalst Festschrift, LNCS 16480, pp. 33–45, 2026.
https://doi.org/10.1007/978-3-032-17618-9_4

Fraunhofer FIT, with its unique mission of conducting applied information technology research in the context of real-world problems, proved to be the ideal environment for realizing van der Aalst's vision. The institute's philosophy of bridging academic research with industrial applications aligned perfectly with process mining's inherent dual nature: rigorous in its theoretical foundations, yet practical in its applications.

This chapter documents how, since 2018, Fraunhofer FIT has successfully translated van der Aalst's theoretical contributions into a thriving ecosystem encompassing academic research, vendor-independent consulting, and commercial solutions. Through a three-pronged approach involving the Process Mining research group, the Center for Process Intelligence (CPI), and the Process Intelligence Solutions (PIS) spin-off, we have demonstrated that foundational research can indeed generate sustained practical impact while maintaining scientific excellence (Fig. 1).

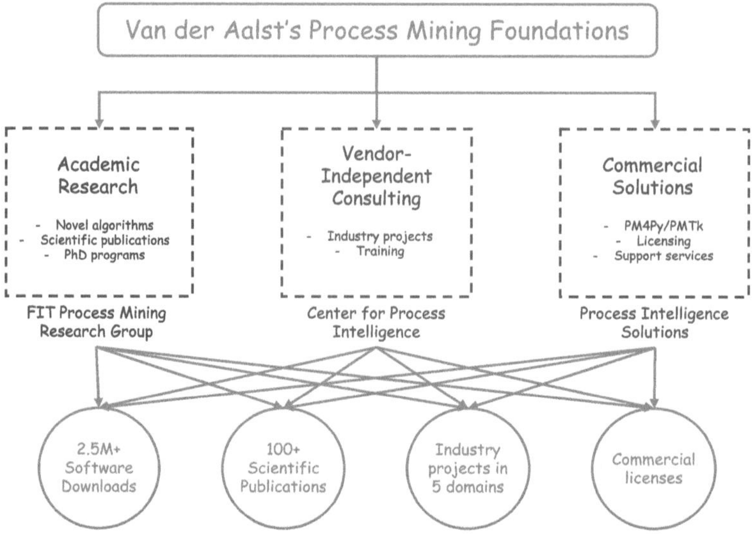


**Fig. 1.** The three-pronged approach: academic research (FIT PM research group), vendor-independent consulting (CPI), and commercial solutions (PIS)

The results obtained by the Fraunhofer process mining group are impressive: over 2.5 million downloads of our PM4Py library, making it the world's largest open-source process mining solution; 100+ peer-reviewed publications building directly on van der Aalst's foundations; industry projects across insurance, manufacturing, energy, and transportation sectors; and several successful commercial licensing agreements. More importantly, this ecosystem has become self-sustaining, generating the resources and market validation needed to continue advancing the field.

## 2    The Academic Foundation: Fraunhofer FIT Process Mining Research Group

### 2.1    The AOPI Project: Building on Van der Aalst's Framework

The foundation for Fraunhofer FIT's process mining success was laid through "Automated Operational Process Improvement Using Process Mining" (AOPI), a project in Fraunhofer's internal Impuls programme that began in 2018 coinciding with van der Aalst's appointment as Alexander von Humboldt Professor at RWTH Aachen University. The project's ambitious goal was to establish a self-sustaining process mining research group that could maintain close connections to both academic excellence and industrial relevance.

Under van der Aalst's invaluable guidance and mentorship, the research group systematically addressed five key work packages:

- **Guided Process Discovery** aimed to develop novel process discovery techniques using domain knowledge and event data together—addressing the fundamental limitation that event logs are often incomplete and at inappropriate granularity levels. This work recognized van der Aalst's insight that pure algorithmic approaches, while theoretically sound, often require human expertise to produce practically useful models.
- **Comparative Process Mining** focused on identifying and highlighting commonalities and differences among process variants, different episodes, and different case groups. This extended van der Aalst's foundational work on conformance checking into the realm of process evolution and organizational learning, recognizing that processes naturally drift and vary over time and context.
- **Operational Process Support** developed techniques for providing actionable real-time information, including remaining processing time predictions and resource recommendations. This work addressed van der Aalst's vision of process mining as not just retrospective analysis but forward-looking process intelligence.
- **Process Constraint Elicitation** tackled the challenge of understanding what aspects of a process can be changed during improvement efforts. This work recognized that van der Aalst's process improvement framework required explicit modeling of organizational constraints and degrees of freedom.
- **Automated Process Improvement** represented the project's most ambitious goal: automatically generating improved process models using constraint information, organizational goals, and raw event data. This work aimed to operationalize van der Aalst's vision of data-driven process optimization at scale.

### 2.2    Breakthrough Research Contributions

The research group's contributions consistently built upon van der Aalst's foundational work while addressing real-world constraints and requirements.

***Interactive Process Discovery.*** Process discovery is a foundational research area within the broader field of process mining. Over the years, a wide range of algorithms have been proposed to automatically derive process models from event data. One of the earliest and most influential among them is the Alpha Miner [1], introduced by Wil van der Aalst. Traditionally, process discovery techniques have been fully automated, relying solely on event logs to generate process models without any human input. However, the emerging field of interactive process discovery, to which the Fraunhofer research group has made significant contributions, aims to enrich this paradigm by integrating domain knowledge from process participants alongside event data. This shift has given rise to research on incremental process discovery [18], which enables users to iteratively construct process models. In this approach, users are actively involved in guiding and refining the discovery process, contributing contextual insights that go beyond what is available in the event logs. By incorporating human expertise, the resulting process models tend to be more accurate, interpretable, and representative of actual operational processes. To demonstrate the practical relevance of this vision, particularly in bridging the gap between academic research and industrial application, the Fraunhofer group has developed an advanced open-source software demonstrator, Cortado [19], which implements various interactive and incremental process discovery methods.

***Partially Ordered Workflow Language.*** One of the main research contributions of the group was the introduction of the Partially Ordered Workflow Language (POWL), first presented in [10] and later extended in [9] to increase its expressiveness. POWL provides essential quality guarantees for automated process model generation, while being more expressive than traditional hierarchical languages. Conceived as an intermediate representation, it captures both complex decisions and concurrent relations in a structured way, making it a bridge between event data, textual descriptions, and established notations such as Petri nets or BPMN. POWL was initially applied in discovery algorithms for event logs [11] and later proved useful in pipelines where Large Language Models (LLMs) generate formal process models from textual descriptions [8].

***Event Abstraction.*** The group made significant contributions to event abstraction, addressing the challenge that raw event data are often too fine-grained for human interpretation. Chiao-Yun Li and colleagues developed groundbreaking approaches, including an event abstraction framework based on partial order patterns [13] and a fully unsupervised framework for automated abstraction class detection [12]. These techniques enable lifting system-level event data to higher abstraction levels while preserving partial order relationships, making process mining outcomes more interpretable for business analysts. The unsupervised approach eliminates the need for manual specification of abstraction rules, allowing for arbitrary levels of abstraction and more precise process model discovery.

***Object-Centric Process Mining.*** Van der Aalst recognized that traditional process mining approaches, which assume a single case notion, fail to capture the complexity of real-world processes where multiple interrelated objects interact throughout execution. His pioneering work on object-centric process mining established a new research agenda that fundamentally challenges the single-case assumption underlying much of process mining. The Fraunhofer research group has made contributions to advancing this agenda. The group developed novel approaches for operational process monitoring in object-centric business processes [16], directly addressing van der Aalst's vision of accurately assessing operational problems that span multiple object types rather than being confined to a single object perspective. Further advancing this research direction, the group introduced GOProQ [14], a graphical query language for object-centric service processes. By operationalizing Object-Centric Event Logs (OCELs) as graphs of interconnected events and objects, GOProQ provides analysts with tools to navigate and query the complex, multi-object nature of service-oriented architectures that traditional approaches cannot adequately address.

***Business Process Simulation.*** The research group advanced van der Aalst's vision of predictive process analytics through innovative simulation techniques. Two major contributions emerged: a streaming process simulation discovery technique that integrates Incremental Process Discovery with Online Machine Learning methods [22], and white-box predictors based on probabilistic decision trees for business process simulation [21]. The streaming approach addresses the limitation of existing simulation techniques in dynamic environments, prioritizing recent data while preserving historical knowledge to handle concept drift effectively. The white-box predictor approach provides intelligible simulation models that service architects can understand and modify, overcoming the "black-box" limitation of traditional simulation approaches while capturing uncertainty through probabilistic modeling. The developments are supported by ProSiT [20], a tool for interactive and transparent process simulations.

***Generative AI for Process Mining.*** In recent years, Fraunhofer FIT has embraced the opportunities of generative AI to explore new forms of humanâĂŞtechnology interaction, and the process mining group at Fraunhofer FIT has been at the forefront of translating this vision into concrete research contributions. Building on the institute's tradition of combining methodological rigor with practical innovation, the group has advanced several complementary directions: designing process mining artifacts that can be consumed by LLMs and integrating natural-language querying support into PM4Py [6]; developing methods for deriving formal business process models directly from textual descriptions [8]; investigating the role of LLMs in enhancing process comprehension and making analytical results more interpretable [7]; and establishing benchmarks to evaluate LLM capabilities in process mining systematically [5]. Together, these contributions illustrate how Fraunhofer FIT is extending van der Aalst's vision into the era of generative AI, ensuring that process mining remains both scientifically rigorous and accessible to a broad range of stakeholders.

## 2.3   Scientific Impact and Recognition

The academic impact of the Fraunhofer FIT process mining group reflects both quantity and quality of contributions. Since 2018, the group has published 29 journal papers and 69 conference/workshop papers among other publications, with several appearing in top-tier venues including A-ranked conferences and journals.

The group's commitment to open science has been exemplified by the development of PM4Py, which has become the de facto standard for process mining research and education and also commercially successful (cf. Sect. 4.2). The library's success with over 2.5 million downloads demonstrates how process mining algorithms from the research community, when implemented accessibly in a comprehensive open-source framework, can achieve global adoption and impact.

A crucial milestone in making process mining accessible to a broad community was the collaboration between Fraunhofer FIT and KNIME AG[1]. The KNIME Analytics Platform provided the perfect environment to embed process mining capabilities into the daily toolkit of data scientists and business analysts who may not be specialists in the field. The resulting Process Mining Extension of KNIME offers seamless integration of core algorithms such as process discovery, conformance checking, and event data exploration within the KNIME ecosystem. By lowering technical barriers, the extension enables organizations to experiment with process mining using familiar data science workflows, bridging the gap between research-grade methods and real-world adoption.

# 3   Bridging Research and Practice: The Center for Process Intelligence (CPI)

## 3.1   Strategic Vision

The Center for Process Intelligence (CPI), established in January 2021, represents a unique institutional innovation that directly addresses van der Aalst's vision of process mining as both academically rigorous and practically transformative. CPI emerged from the recognition that successful technology transfer requires more than just good algorithms. It demands deep understanding of organizational contexts, business constraints, and implementation challenges.

The center's founding reflected a strategic collaboration between Fraunhofer FIT's Process Mining research group and the branch Business & Information Systems Engineering. This partnership combined expertise in value-based process management of the Digital Business and Information Systems Engineering departments with the technical process mining capabilities of the Process Mining research group. The result was an institution capable of supporting companies from their first process mining experiments through enterprise-wide scaling.

CPI's strategic positioning as vendor-independent reflects a deliberate choice to prioritize customer needs over product promotion. By using PM4Py as its primary technological foundation, CPI can focus entirely on delivering value rather

---

[1] https://www.knime.com/blog/process-mining-meets-knime.

than promoting particular commercial solutions. This approach has proven crucial for building trust with organizations considering process mining adoption.

## 3.2 Three-Dimensional Service Approach

CPI's success stems from its systematic approach to addressing different organizational needs through three complementary service dimensions:

- **Business Process Consulting** provides insights and advice regarding business processes through systematic analysis of organizational event data. This service dimension directly operationalizes van der Aalst's vision of process mining as organizational learning, helping companies understand how their processes actually execute rather than how they are supposed to execute.
- **Process Mining Software Development** focuses on creating and maintaining tools that make advanced process mining techniques accessible to practitioners. This dimension recognizes that van der Aalst's theoretical contributions require sophisticated tooling to achieve practical impact.
- **Joint Industrial Research** leverages cutting-edge academic knowledge to solve specific industrial challenges. This dimension ensures that van der Aalst's ongoing theoretical contributions continue to inform practical problem-solving while ensuring that real-world challenges drive continued academic innovation.

## 3.3 Industry Partnerships and Market Validation

Long-standing industry partnerships are a hallmark of Fraunhofer FIT's Business Information & Systems Engineering branch. Brought together with the deep technical foundations of FIT's Process Mining research group under the umbrella of the Center for Process Intelligence (CPI), this collaboration has created a unique opportunity to validate the latest research in longitudinal studies. In addition to advancing technical methods, these industry cooperations have also addressed critical organizational questions, such as how to establish centers of excellence and governance structures, ensuring the sustainable success of process mining in practice.

# 4 Commercialization and Market Impact: The PIS Success Story

## 4.1 From Academic Research to Commercial Reality

The founding of Process Intelligence Solutions (PIS) as a spin-off from the Process Mining research group at Fraunhofer FIT represents a major success in the commercialization of academic research. This achievement exemplifies Fraunhofer's core mission to foster effective technology transfer from academia to industry.

PIS's emergence closely aligns with Wil van der Aalst's vision of process mining as a broadly accessible capability, i.e., one that requires both free access to foundational tools and sustainable business models to support advanced, enterprise-grade applications. The spin-off illustrates how this vision can be realized by bridging rigorous applied research with practical industrial solutions.

This success story highlights the value of sustained investment in applied research as a driver of both technological innovation and commercial impact. By establishing PIS, the Process Mining group at Fraunhofer FIT has created a lasting pathway for transforming scientific advances into tangible benefits, empowering organizations worldwide while reinforcing the role of research in driving industry progress.

### 4.2    PM4Py: Open Source as Market Foundation

PM4Py (Process Mining for Python) is a comprehensive open-source software library that provides a wide range of process mining algorithms. Originally developed at the Fraunhofer Institute, PM4Py is now maintained and further developed by its spin-off, Process Intelligence Solutions (PIS). The library has achieved broad adoption, serving both researchers worldwide and numerous industrial partners. Its trajectory exemplifies the Fraunhofer philosophy of technology transfer, demonstrating how academic results can be effectively translated into impactful industrial solutions.

PM4Py's dual licensing model, i.e., free for open-source use, with dedicated licenses for closed-source commercial applications, represents an established and sustainable business strategy. This model enables the continued evolution of the library while aligning academic openness with commercial relevance. The success of PM4Py illustrates that advanced research outputs, when implemented in an accessible and adaptable way, can lower barriers to entry, foster global collaboration, and drive progress across both academic and industrial domains.

### 4.3    PMTk: From Research to Enterprise Solutions

The Process Mining Toolkit (PMTk) marks a significant advancement in the evolution of process mining, exemplifying the transition from academic research to enterprise-ready solutions. Uniquely, PMTk builds upon PM4Py, a sophisticated open-source process mining library, making it one of the few commercial tools grounded in a transparent and extensible academic core.

This integration of advanced algorithms with a user-friendly interface reflects a deep understanding of the practical challenges organizations face in adopting process mining technologies. PMTk's success across diverse domains, from insurance to manufacturing, demonstrates both the generality of process mining techniques and their ability to generate actionable, context-specific insights.

Widely used in R&D projects and governed by numerous commercial licenses, PMTk has achieved clear product-market fit. It also serves as the primary platform in many of CPI's consulting engagements, enabling rapid and tailored deployments. As such, PMTk stands as a strong example of the Fraunhofer philosophy of fostering technology transfer, showing how open-source academic innovation can be transformed into impactful, commercially viable solutions.

## 5  Fraunhofer FIT's Strategic Vision: Multi-dimensional Market Approach

### 5.1  The Strategic Framework

Fraunhofer FIT's success in translating van der Aalst's process mining vision into market reality reflects a sophisticated understanding that sustainable technology transfer requires multiple, mutually reinforcing approaches. The institute therefore acts simultaneously as an **R&D Partner**, developing advanced solutions for both technology users and vendors so that van der Aalst's theoretical ideas continue to inform practical problem-solving. In its **Analytics Partner** role, FIT embeds consulting expertise within event-data analysis projects, turning process insights into organizational learning and measurable performance improvements. Finally, as an **Organizational Partner**, the institute helps companies design governance structures, centers of excellence, and capability-building programs, ensuring that process mining adoption becomes embedded rather than project-based.

### 5.2  Sector-Specific Innovation and Learning

The institute's experience across diverse industry sectors demonstrates the generalizability of van der Aalst's theoretical foundations while revealing sector-specific adaptation requirements. Work with multi-national insurers such as Talanx AG/HDI Mexico showed how process mining can offer cross-organizational transparency while remaining sensitive to regulatory heterogeneity and cultural norms. In manufacturing, the Infineon collaboration emphasized integration of operational, financial, and quality metrics so that process mining augments existing systems rather than displacing them. Transportation and logistics engagements, including Munich Airport, highlighted the need for near real-time monitoring and predictive capabilities that tolerate high operational volatility. Partnerships with financial institutions like KfW underscored the importance of privacy-preserving conformance checking to satisfy supervisory expectations. In the energy sector, the Uniper assessment compressed diagnostic work into two weeks, illustrating that process mining can deliver rapid, high-stakes insights even in heavily regulated infrastructures.

Operating across these domains surfaced challenges that rarely appear in celebratory narratives. Balancing academic rigor with commercial timelines required explicit decision frameworks for allocating researcher time between exploratory topics and contract deliverables, while cross-subsidization mechanisms ensured that open-source commitments such as PM4Py remained funded. Governance structures had to mediate tensions between vendor independence and client-specific customization, leading to steering boards that include representatives from research, consulting, and commercial units. These lessons highlight that sustainable technology transfer depends as much on managing constraints, such as funding cycles, IP policies, talent retention, as on inventing algorithms, and they offer a transparent blueprint for institutions facing similar academia-industry junctions.

# 6    Lessons Learned and Future Vision

## 6.1    Critical Success Factors

Five critical success factors emerge from Fraunhofer FIT's experience translating van der Aalst's process mining vision into market reality. A **multi-dimensional strategic approach** that intertwined academic research, vendor-independent consulting, and commercial development proved essential for sustaining momentum; none of these elements would have had comparable reach on its own. **Open source as strategic foundation** ensured that PM4Py simultaneously nurtured a global research community and underpinned commercial offerings, demonstrating that transparency and sustainability need not be at odds. An **industry-first research orientation** kept scientific work grounded in real problems, which in turn sharpened theoretical contributions instead of diluting them. Finally, **strong academic leadership** provided a stable compass while allowing day-to-day autonomy for teams executing research, consulting, and commercialization mandates.

## 6.2    Technological Integration

The success of Fraunhofer FIT's process mining ecosystem provides a foundation for addressing next-generation challenges that build upon van der Aalst's theoretical contributions. **Advanced AI integration** is making discovery methods conversational and explainable, expanding access for non-experts while raising expectations for robustness. **Industry 4.0 applications** couple IoT sensor streams with classical event logs, forcing extensions of process models into cyber-physical settings without sacrificing analytic rigor. Meanwhile, **Sustainability and ESG analysis** elevates process mining from efficiency improvements to broader societal accountability, inviting new metrics and governance concerns.

These trajectories prompt reflective questions that reconnect directly to van der Aalst's original vision. How can object-centric process mining and generative AI co-evolve to provide faithful yet interpretable models for multi-object services? What governance mechanisms ensure that dual-licensing and open ecosystems remain viable once charismatic leaders move on? Which evaluation frameworks can quantify environmental or social outcomes of process optimization alongside throughput and compliance? Addressing such questions will determine whether the next decade of process mining remains as transformative as the last.

# 7   Conclusion

The success of Fraunhofer FIT's process mining ecosystem, spanning academic excellence, consulting impact, and commercial viability, provides compelling evidence for the transformative potential of van der Aalst's theoretical contributions. This success story demonstrates that fundamental research, when conducted with vision and persistence, can indeed generate sustained practical impact while advancing scientific knowledge.

The quantitative evidence speaks clearly: 2.5 million software downloads, industry projects in five different domains, 100+ peer-reviewed publications, and multiple successful commercial partnerships represent substantial impact across multiple dimensions. More importantly, this ecosystem has achieved self-sustainability, generating the resources and market validation needed to continue advancing the field.

The continuing evolution of this ecosystem, from the AOPI project's 2018 launch through 2023's thriving multi-dimensional platform, demonstrates that academic research and market success can be mutually reinforcing rather than competing objectives. Van der Aalst's vision of process mining as both scientifically rigorous and practically transformative has proven remarkably prescient.

As we look toward the future, the foundation van der Aalst established continues to enable new innovations, new applications, and new success stories. The process mining field he created has become sufficiently robust to support diverse approaches while maintaining coherent theoretical foundations.

Our gratitude to Wil van der Aalst extends beyond appreciation for specific theoretical contributions to recognition of his unique ability to envision practical applications for fundamental research while maintaining uncompromising scientific standards. The success of Fraunhofer FIT's process mining ecosystem stands as testimony to the enduring value of his vision and the continuing relevance of his contributions to both academic knowledge and practical organizational improvement.

Looking ahead, sustaining this trajectory will require the same balance of rigor and pragmatism that defined van der Aalst's career: institutionalizing mentorship pipelines, codifying decision frameworks that reconcile open science with commercial viability, and investing in evaluation methods that capture societal impact. By confronting these open issues explicitly, the ecosystem not only honors his legacy but also equips the broader community with a reproducible pathway from foundational insight to enduring market relevance.

**Acknowledgments.** We thank all the former/current colleagues in Fraunhofer FIT who worked on process mining research/industry projects, contributing to the development of process mining.

# References


1. van der Aalst, W., Weijters, T., Maruster, L.: Workflow mining: discovering process models from event logs. IEEE Trans. Knowl. Data Eng. **16**(9), 1128–1142 (2004). https://doi.org/10.1109/TKDE.2004.47
2. van der Aalst, W.M.P.: Process mining: Overview and opportunities. ACM Trans. Manag. Inf. Syst. **3**(2), 7:1–7:17 (2012). https://doi.org/10.1145/2229156.2229157
3. van der Aalst, W.M.P., van Dongen, B.F.: Discovering workflow performance models from timed logs. In: EDCIS 2002. LNCS, vol. 2480, pp. 45–63. Springer Heidelberg (2002). https://doi.org/10.1007/3-540-45785-2_4
4. van der Aalst, W.M.P., Weijters, T., Maruster, L.: Workflow mining: Discovering process models from event logs. IEEE Trans. Knowl. Data Eng. **16**(9), 1128–1142 (2004). https://doi.org/10.1109/TKDE.2004.47
5. Berti, A., Kourani, H., van der Aalst, W.M.P.: PM-LLM-Benchmark: Evaluating large language models on process mining tasks. In: Delgado, A., Slaats, T. (eds.) ICPM 2024 Workshops. LNBIP, vol. 533, pp. 610–623. Springer, Cham (2024). https://doi.org/10.1007/978-3-031-82225-4_45
6. Berti, A., Schuster, D., van der Aalst, W.M.P.: Abstractions, scenarios, and prompt definitions for process mining with LLMs: A case study. In: De Weerdt, J., Pufahl, L. (eds.) BPM 2023 Workshops. LNBIP, vol. 492, pp. 427–439. Springer, Cham (2023). https://doi.org/10.1007/978-3-031-50974-2_32
7. et al.: Leveraging large language models for enhanced process model comprehension. CoRR **abs/2408.08892** (2024). https://doi.org/10.48550/ARXIV.2408.08892
8. Kourani, H., Berti, A., Schuster, D., van der Aalst, W.M.P.: Process modeling with large language models. In: van der Aa, H., Bork, D., Schmidt, R., Sturm, A. (eds.) Enterprise, Business-Process and Information Systems Modeling 2024. LNBIP, vol. 511, pp. 229–244. Springer, Cham (2024). https://doi.org/10.1007/978-3-031-61007-3_18
9. Kourani, H., Park, G., van der Aalst, W.M.P.: Unlocking non-block-structured decisions: Inductive mining with choice graphs. In: Senderovich, A., Cabanillas, C., Vanderfeesten, I., A. Reijers, H. (eds.) BPM 2025. LNCS, vol. 16044, pp. 144–161. Springer, Cham (2025). https://doi.org/10.1007/978-3-032-02867-9_10
10. Kourani, H., van Zelst, S.J.: POWL: partially ordered workflow language. In: BPM 2023. LNCS, vol. 14159, pp. 92–108. Springer, CHam (2023). https://doi.org/10.1007/978-3-031-41620-0_6
11. Kourani, H., van Zelst, S.J., Schuster, D., van der Aalst, W.M.P.: Discovering partially ordered workflow models. Inf. Syst. **128**, 102493 (2025). https://doi.org/10.1016/J.IS.2024.102493
12. Li, C., van Zelst, S.J., van der Aalst, W.M.P.: A framework for automated abstraction class detection for event abstraction. In: Abraham, A., Pllana, S., Casalino, G., Ma, K., Bajaj, A. (eds.) ISDA 2022. LNNS, vol. 715, pp. 126–136. Springer, Cham (2022). https://doi.org/10.1007/978-3-031-35507-3_13
13. Li, C., van Zelst, S.J., van der Aalst, W.M.P.: Event abstraction for partial order patterns. In: Di Francescomarino, C., Burattin, A., Janiesch, C., Sadiq, S. (eds.) BPM 2023. LNCS, vol. 14159, pp. 38–54. Springer,Cham (2023). https://doi.org/10.1007/978-3-031-41620-0_3
14. Park, G., Adams, N., Schuster, D.: Goproq: A graphical query language for object-centric process analysis. In: Aiello, M., Deng, S., Murillo, JM., Georgievski, I., Benatallah, B., Wang, Z. (eds.) Service-Oriented Computing - 23rd International

Conference, ICSOC, Proceedings, Part I. Lecture Notes in Computer Science, Springer, Cham (2025). https://doi.org/10.1007/978-981-95-5015-9_21

15. Park, G., Song, M.: Predicting performances in business processes using deep neural networks. Decis. Support Syst. **129** (2020)

16. Park, G., van der Aalst, W.M.: Operational process monitoring: An object-centric approach. Comput. Ind. **164**, 104170 (2025)

17. Rozinat, A., van der Aalst, W.M.P.: Conformance checking of processes based on monitoring real behavior. Inf. Syst. **33**(1), 64–95 (2008). https://doi.org/10.1016/J.IS.2007.07.001

18. Schuster, D.: Incremental process discovery. (2025). https://doi.org/10.1007/978-3-031-80565-3

19. Schuster, D., van Zelst, S.J., van der Aalst, W.M.: Cortado: a dedicated process mining tool for interactive process discovery. SoftwareX **22**, 101373 (2023). https://doi.org/10.1016/j.softx.2023.101373

20. Vinci, F., Park, G., van der Aalst, W., de Leoni, M.: Prosit: A tool for interactive and transparent process simulations. In: Proceedings of the 23rd International Conference on Service-Oriented Computing (ICSOC 2025), Demo Track. Lecture Notes in Computer Science, Springer,Cham (2025)

21. Vinci, F., Park, G., van der Aalst, W., de Leoni, M.: Reliable and configurable process simulations via probabilistic white-box models. In: Aiello, M., Dong, S., Murillo, J.M., Georgievski, I., Benatallah, B., Wang, Z. (eds.) Service-Oriented Computing - 23rd International Conference, ICSOC, Proceedings, Part I. Lecture Notes in Computer Science, Springer, Cham (2025). https://doi.org/10.1007/978-981-95-5015-9_24

22. Vinci, F., Park, G., van der Aalst, W.M.P., de Leoni, M.: Online discovery of simulation models for evolving business processes. In: Senderovich, A., Cabanillas, C., Vanderfeesten, I., A. Reijers, H. (eds) BPM 2025. LNCS, vol. 16044, pp. 451–468. Springer, Cham (2025). https://doi.org/10.1007/978-3-032-02867-9_27

# Business Process Management Concepts

# From Vision to Community: The Origins and Evolution of the BPM Conference

Adela del-Río-Ortega[1]([✉])[ID] and Mathias Weske[2][ID]

[1] SCORE Lab, I3US, Universidad de Sevilla, Seville, Spain
adeladelrio@us.es
[2] HPI, University of Potsdam, Potsdam, Germany
mathias.weske@hpi.de

**Abstract.** This paper reflects on the origins and evolution of the BPM Conference, which has grown over the past decades into one of the premier information systems conferences and the flagship event in Business Process Management. Initiated by Wil van der Aalst, the conference was conceived to provide a dedicated forum for advancing research, fostering collaboration, and bridging academia with industry. We document its history, including the development of its program structure, international reach, and community culture. Among the many research lines that have been nurtured within the BPM community, we briefly note the emergence of process mining, which found some of its earliest publications at the conference before maturing into a thriving subfield with its own dedicated venue and industrial applications. We highlight Wil's vision and leadership, not only in establishing the conference and fostering its early growth, but also in shaping the trajectory of the BPM field as a whole. The paper provides both a historical account and a tribute, illustrating how individual contribution can have a lasting impact on the advancement of science and the building of research communities.

**Keywords:** Business Process Management (BPM) · BPM Conference · Research community building · Conference history

## 1 Introduction

It is exciting to witness the forming of a new research discipline. One of the most important ingredients in this process is a flagship conference that brings together people. People who share the enthusiasm for the new research area and who, through their work, begin forming a community.

This paper looks at the International Conference on Business Process Management and the role of Wil van der Aalst in forming what we today know as the BPM Community. Why do hundreds of researchers from all parts of the world meet annually at the BPM conference? How come they speak the same language, follow established and devising novel research methods and directions in our field?

We describe the origins of the BPM conference in Sect. 2. Next, in Sect. 3, we analyse how the conference has evolved over the years, navigating through its 23 editions. Section 4 highlights the scientific contributions associated with the conference, beginning with a review of topic evolution (Sect. 4.2) and then focusing on the specific contributions of Wil van der Aalst (Sect. 4.3). Section 5 reflects on Wil's personal role in shaping the conference, enriched with testimonies from esteemed members of our community. Finally, We present our concluding remarks in Sect. 6, offered both as a synthesis of the conference's journey and as a tribute to Wil's enduring legacy.

## 2   Origins of the BPM Conference

To understand the role of the BPM Conference in the forming of our community, we have to look back to its first edition in 2003 and beyond. The early establishment of the field can be traced back to two research streams, the first of which started in the 1980s. With the increasing availability of workstation computers in business organizations and in public administrations, researchers started looking at office automation [8] and computer supported cooperative work [30].

Together with the seminal work *Re-Engineering the Corporation* by Hammer and Champy in 1993 [11], this has led to a increasing interest in business processes, at that time called workflows. The Workflow Management Coalition formed as a body to strengthen industrial update in the field. This body is well known for WfMC reference architecture [14]. The process trend was taken up by several academic database research groups, who focused on the challenges in engineering workflow management systems. Those included the groups led by Peter Dadam in Ulm and Gottfried Vossen in Münster. At that time, Manfred Reichert was a doctoral student in Ulm and the second author a postdoctoral researcher in Münster.

The second stream of research address workflows from a formal, mathematical perspective. The goal back then was to formally describe workflows and to verify their properties. As we all know, Petri nets are an excellent formalisms to do so. Wil van der Aalst was instrumental in this research stream; workflow nets were and are still the cornerstone in formal process verification. Colleagues like Jörg Desel and Andreas Oberweis in Karlsruhe also followed this stream of research.

The Dagstuhl seminar "Petri Nets and Business Process Management" in 1998 was organized by Jörg Desel and Andreas Oberweis, and Wolfgang Reisig and Grzegorz Rozenberg were involved as experienced colleagues with many contacts. Wil was a participant at that seminar. With his clear ideas, formulations, and structuring in this new area, he has made a significant contribution to the success of the seminar. Consequently, Jörg Desel and Andreas Oberweis invited him to be co-editor of the LNCS volume "Business Process Management" that appeared early 2000 [4].

This was the situation when in 2003 the 24th International Conference Applications and Theory of Petri nets (ATPN) [3] was organized at the Technical University in Eindhoven, with Wil van der Aalst serving as "PC Co-chair, applications". Wil had this wonderful idea to organize a new event, co-located to

ATPN in Eindhoven: the First International Conference on Business Process Management, BPM 2003. He approached Arthur ter Hofstede and the second author and together with Wil we formed the team of PC Chairs at the first BPM conference. According to Wil, the 1998 Dagstuhl Seminar together with the LNCS volume from two years later can be viewed the embryo of the BPM conference.

We had a wonderful first BPM conference in the summer of 2003, with exciting paper presentations on a broad range of topics, including dynamic change, web service composition, process mining, exception handling, and supporting collaborative work in organizations.

On the evening the conference closed on June 27, 2003, there was a meeting in a ridiculously small room at TU/e to review the conference. The PC Chairs Wil van der Aalst, Arthur ter Hofstede, the second author, and the organizing chair Hajo Reijers hardly fitted in that room. BPM 2003 was a big success, we were very happy with the quality of the presentations, and participation numbers of BPM matched those of ATPN, which was in its 24th iteration already. So we agreed that, yes, we should organize BPM 2004. We looked at each other and I, the second author of this paper, agreed to organize BPM 2004 in Potsdam.

A few years later, at BPM 2005 in Nancy, a Steering Committee of the BPM conference series was established . Founding members were the PC Chairs of the first three editions of the conference: Wil van der Aalst, Mathias Weske, Arthur ter Hofstede, Barbara Pernici, Fabio Casati, and Boualem Benatallah. Wil was the chairperson of the Steering Committee until 2017, when Mathias took office. In his openings, Wil used to say that every conference has a strong man (woman, resp.), who drives the conference. Wil, you did not only establish the BPM conference series, but you drove it for many years with responsibility and care. Today, BPM is a well-managed conference series and, as such, an important pillar in the establishment of the BPM community as we know it today.


## 3    Evolution over Time

Over the course of more than two decades, the BPM Conference has grown into a truly global series. After its inaugural edition in Eindhoven (2003), the conference quickly established a tradition of rotating venues across different countries and continents. From Potsdam, Nancy, and Vienna in its early European editions, the conference expanded to Australia (2007, 2018), North America (2010), Asia (2013), and South America (2016). By regularly revisiting Europe while also reaching out to other regions, BPM developed into an inclusive international community with strong local engagement wherever it was hosted. The series has also demonstrated resilience in the face of unexpected challenges, such as the last-minute relocation of the 2014 edition from Haifa to Eindhoven and the transformation of the 2020 edition, planned for Seville, into a fully online conference due to the COVID-19 pandemic. Figure 1 provides a map of the host cities, illustrating both the geographic spread and the deliberate effort to strengthen

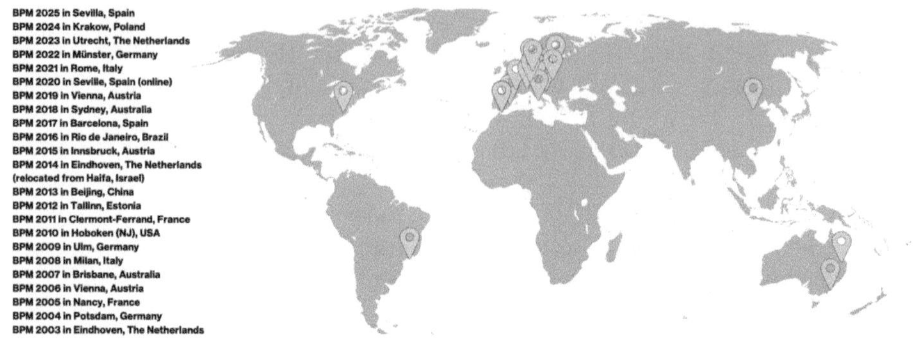


**Fig. 1.** BPM Conference Editions (2003–2025).

ties across continents. And we are looking forward to including Toronto (2026) and many more interesting locations to come!

The success of this internationalization is also evident in the evolution of submissions. As Fig. 2a shows, the conference consistently attracts between 120 and 170 submissions per year, reflecting its role as the flagship venue of the BPM community. Despite fluctuations, the overall trend demonstrates the maturity and sustainability of the field.

Figure 2b illustrates how acceptance rates have remained within the 14–19% range for much of the conference's history, underscoring its status as a highly selective and prestigious venue. In recent years, however, the community has made a conscious effort to broaden participation. This has included recognizing new forms of contributions and supporting diverse voices. The culmination of this trend occurred in 2025, when, for the first time, the acceptance rate surpassed 20%. This should not be read as a decline in rigor but rather as a reflection of inclusiveness, interdisciplinarity, and the community's willingness to adapt.

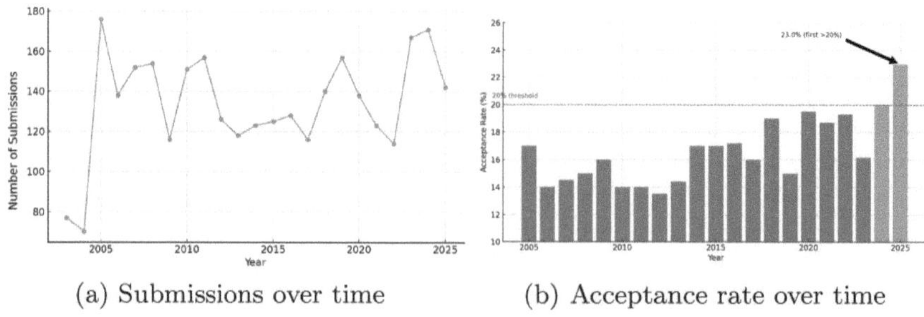

(a) Submissions over time          (b) Acceptance rate over time

**Fig. 2.** BPM Conference Submissions and Acceptance Rate over time.

Another sign of the conference's vitality and eagerness to improve and grow lies in the steady expansion of its program. Over time, new tracks and formats were introduced, reflecting both the maturation of the BPM discipline and broader developments in computer science and other neighbouring disciplines. Colocated workshops were already organized in 2005. The demo track was officially launched in 2006, followed shortly after by tutorials and panels (2007–2008). The Doctoral Consortium was first organized in 2012, strengthening support for junior researchers. Also in 2012, the program was extended with a dedicated track for education papers, covering another important aspect of academic life. In 2016 the BPM Forum was launched as a new sub-track with the aim to host innovative yet not mature research with high potential of stimulating discussions at the conference. To accommodate for the diversity of the BPM field, in 2018 and for the first time since its foundation, the conference run a multi-track system, with tracks for foundations, engineering, and management [33]. More recently, specialized forums have been introduced, such as those on Blockchain, RPA, Responsible BPM or Process Technology, along with initiatives to strengthen transparency, reproducibility and open science. These innovations highlight the conference's adaptability and its responsiveness to the changing needs of academia, industry and society in general.

In addition to programmatic innovations, the BPM Conference has increasingly emphasized diversity, equity, and inclusion (DEI), culminating in the creation of a DEI Committee in 2023. The 2025 DEI report showed submissions from 28 countries across six continents, up from 25 the year before, with several new countries represented for the first time. This broader international distribution underscores the community's commitment to global reach and inclusiveness.

Gender diversity has also received growing attention. For BPM 2025, women were first authors in 32.5% of all submissions (19% in the main track), and in some countries they even outnumbered male counterparts. That same year marked an important milestone: for the first time, keynote speakers were majority female. Moreover, across several events, including the Workshops, Demos & Resources, Education Forum, and Doctoral Consortium, the number of female chairs exceeded that of male chairs. Gender parity was also achieved among program committee and session chairs for the main tracks and the BPM Forum. Equally important has been the conference's firm commitment to rejuvenating its leadership by regularly renewing the Steering Committee and inviting younger scholars into it, such as Matthias Weidlich and the first author of this paper, and by systematically involving junior researchers in chairing roles across workshops, tracks, and forums. This renewal has gone hand in hand with continuity provided by the successive SC chairs: first Wil van der Aalst (2003–2017), then the second author of this paper (2017–2022), and today Jan Mendling (since 2022). Together, this deliberate rotation of responsibilities has kept the conference open to fresh perspectives while ensuring long-term stability.

These achievements reflect an active effort to create a more inclusive and representative community, not only in terms of geographical diversity and gender balance, but also by ensuring generational renewal.

This interest in improving and broadening the community remains very much alive. A clear example was the panel "Quo Vadis, BPM Conference?" held at the 2025 edition, conceived as a town-hall meeting to collectively reflect on the future of the series, with Irene Vanderfeesten, Hajo Reijers, Jan Mendling and the first author of this paper as invited panelists. The discussion covered key challenges such as managing scientific output and quality in the face of growing submission volumes, attracting and integrating researchers from related disciplines, and strengthening the conference's connection to real-world problems. Participants also debated how career incentives and the publishing ecosystem affect engagement with BPM, particularly for early-career researchers. The session underscored that the BPM community is both self-critical and forward-looking, willing to adapt its structures and formats to ensure continued relevance, rigor, and inclusiveness.

Together, these developments reveal a story of growth, inclusiveness, and community building: the BPM Conference has combined academic excellence with diversity and global reach, while continuing to reflect on its future to remain relevant for both research and practice.

## 4   Scientific Contributions Linked to the BPM Conference

Over the years, the BPM Conference has offered a fascinating journey through research contributions that have shaped the BPM field. In this section, we reflect on this journey (4.1), analyze the evolution of research topics (4.2), and take a special look at the specific contributions of Wil van der Aalst (4.3).

### 4.1   A Scientific Journey Through the BPM Conference

The BPM conference was born in 2003, but its roots extend further back, to the workflow management and formal methods communities. Early collections such as [4] framed the agenda: rigorous modeling languages, formal verification (often Petri-net–based), flexibility, and interoperability. These themes carried directly into the first BPM proceedings in Eindhoven. The 2003 survey in [5] already argued for more scientific foundations and a unified view of "Business Process Management" beyond fragmented terms like WfM (Workflow Management), BAM (Business Activity Monitoring), or BPA (Business Process Analysis). This positioning gave BPM a clear intellectual identity and justified the launch of a dedicated conference.

Wil van der Aalst's retrospective on the first decade [2] identified six core concerns that shaped the conference: (1) process modeling languages, (2) enactment infrastructures, (3) process model analysis, (4) process mining, (5) flexibility, and (6) reuse. He also noted 20 use cases illustrating how BPM research should connect to practice. Yet, he emphasized a central tension: while research matured, adoption by vendors and organizations lagged. In this way, he positioned the BPM Conference not just as a research venue, but as a community anchor tasked with bridging academia and practice, and with setting clear challenges for the next decade.

Mid-2010s analyses reinforced this need for reflection. Recker and Mendling [24] examined the proceedings from 2003 to 2014 and highlighted maturity, methodological quality, and impact as areas for growth. Around the same time, a community survey [25] confirmed that participants valued BPM's reputation, networking, and journal fast-tracks most, while tutorials and alternative formats mattered less. Recommendations included expanding the scope to interdisciplinary areas, stimulating industry involvement, and offering support for first-time submitters. These suggestions soon materialized: BPM broadened its call for papers, diversified its PC, and introduced new feedback mechanisms. The most significant shift came in 2018, when the conference adopted a three-track system (Foundations, Engineering, Management), with separate program committees and criteria, to ensure fairer evaluation and attract a wider set of contributions, especially those that fell in the managerial and organizational areas.

## 4.2  Topic Evolution Across Two Decades

The BPM Conference has always reflected the shifting boundaries of its discipline. A review of the proceedings over the past 23 editions shows how certain topics have persisted as pillars of the field, while others have emerged in response to technological advances and organizational needs.

**Foundational Continuity.** From the outset, the conference included papers on modeling languages, formal verification, semantics, and simulation. These themes, deeply rooted in computer science and information systems, remain constant across editions. For example, Rinderle-Ma's work on correctness [18, 27] illustrate how rigorous formalism became a backbone of the conference.

**Process Mining: from Fringe to Flagship.** A defining development has been the rise of process mining. First introduced in early BPM editions through exploratory work on workflow logs (e.g., [10, 29]), process mining soon established itself as a recurring theme. By the late 2000s, dedicated sessions on discovery and conformance checking had become standard [9]. Over the following decade, process mining grew to dominate proceedings, with contributions spanning predictive and prescriptive analytics [15, 31], streaming discovery [16], and, most recently, object-centric process mining (OCPM) [6]. The field's growth at BPM, as well as Wil's initiator role, were instrumental in the creation of a dedicated venue in 2019, ICPM (International Conference on Process Mining), while BPM itself continues to serve as a home for its latest advances.

**Managerial and Organizational Aspects.** While BPM has long been associated with technical advances, managerial and organizational contributions have also been present, although less prominently. Early editions included sporadic papers on maturity models, governance, and cultural factors (e.g. Neiger & Churilov's Structuring Business Objectives [22] and Reijers et al.'s work on business process redesign [19]), but these were often overshadowed by technical tracks. The introduction of a dedicated Management track in 2018 provided structural recognition to this line of research. Since then, contributions have broadened to address digital process innovation, the adoption of BPM techniques in practice and human-centric and ethical dimensions in BPM (like Rosemann's work on Benevolent BPM [7] and Zerbato et al.'s work on process mining practices [35]). Although smaller in volume, these works are vital in reminding the community that BPM is as much about people and organizations as it is about models and algorithms.

**Other Emerging Topics.** Over the years, new areas have regularly entered the program. IoT [17], blockchain [32], RPA [20], and AI for BPM [1] have each found their way into the main track. Recent editions highlight the growing emphasis on process intelligence, combining mining with machine learning, generative AI and decision support [26], while initiatives such as the Responsible BPM Forum underscore the community's responsiveness to societal expectations.

Taken together, these trajectories reveal the dual character of the BPM Conference: on the one hand, continuity through core topics that ensure intellectual stability; on the other, adaptability in embracing new technologies, practices, and organizational perspectives. Few conferences can claim to have spawned an entirely new discipline, as BPM did with process mining, while also opening itself to practice-driven innovations such as RPA and the broader managerial agenda. This dynamic balance has been central to the conference's longevity and prestige.

### 4.3 Wil van der Aalst's Research Contributions in the BPM Conference

Wil van der Aalst's research trajectory is inseparable from the history of the BPM Conference. With 178 publications across its 23 editions, he is by far the most prolific contributor, and his work reflects the evolving identity of the conference itself. His papers chart the community's shift from formal workflow verification to process mining, and more recently toward data-driven process intelligence and AI integration (see Fig. 3).

In the early years (2003–2007), Wil's contributions concentrated on workflow models, Petri nets, and formal verification. These works, such as [34] on the suitability of BPMN to model processes based on the workflow patterns, provided the methodological rigor that distinguished BPM from purely managerial or system-building traditions, establishing a scientific foundation for process modeling and analysis.

From the mid-2000s to the mid-2010s, his focus moved toward the development and maturation of process mining. During this period, the BPM Conference became the premier venue for presenting mining algorithms, conformance-checking techniques, and quality metrics such as fitness and precision. Wil was central to this transformation: he and his co-authors not only introduced the algorithms but also demonstrated their applicability through the ProM framework, which soon became a community-wide reference platform[1]. These contributions helped establish process mining as the defining research line of the conference.

---

[1] https://promtools.org/.

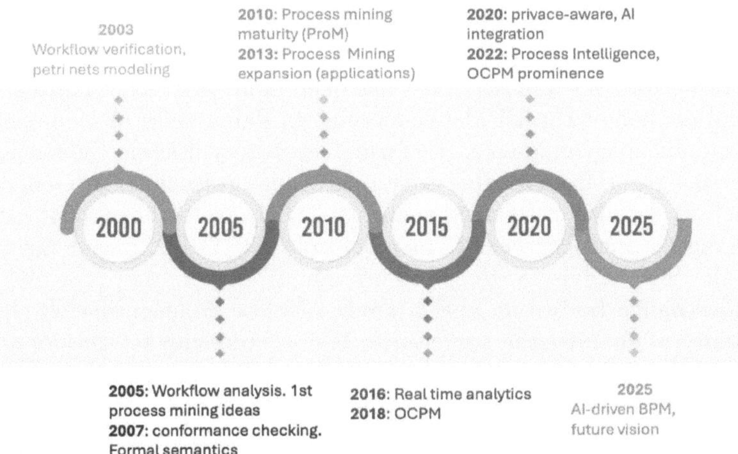


**Fig. 3.** Wil's contributions at the BPM Conference.

In the most recent decade (2016–2025), Wil's BPM papers expanded into new frontiers: privacy-preserving analysis [23], blockchain [13] and above all, object-centric process mining [6]. His work increasingly bridges BPM with machine learning and AI, advancing predictive and prescriptive process analytics. Recent proceedings show how these themes, object-centricity, data-awareness, and AI for process intelligence, now occupy a prominent position in the research program, underscoring Wil's role as both pioneer and guide. Equally important is the breadth of his contributions. While process mining dominates, Wil's BPM publications also touch on workflow verification, declarative modeling, performance analysis, and even early discussions of RPA and digital transformation. This breadth reflects his enduring commitment to keeping BPM rigorous, comprehensive, and relevant to both academia and practice. The alignment between Wil's work and the evolution of the conference proceedings' topics is striking. Topics that first appeared in his papers, such as conformance checking, performance analysis, and OCPM, later grew into recurring themes across sessions and workshops. Conversely, his sustained involvement in established areas (verification, semantics, formal modeling) provided continuity and stability. This dual role, anticipating new directions while consolidating existing ones, explains why colleagues often describe him as the intellectual anchor of the BPM community.

All in all, Wil's BPM publications illustrate more than scholarly productivity. They embody a research vision that is both consistent and forward-looking: rigorous formalism complemented by empirical validation, data-driven analysis tied to organizational relevance, and technical innovation aimed at real-world transformation. His contributions did not merely mirror the evolution of the BPM Conference—they actively shaped it.

## 5    Personal Role of Wil van der Aalst

From its inception, Wil van der Aalst has been more than an organizer; he is the intellectual anchor of the BPM Conference, bridging roles of leadership, mentorship, and visionary guidance. His formal trajectory mirrors the maturation of the conference itself: from leading most operational roles in 2003 (General Chair, PC Chair), to decades of steering committee (SC) leadership (2004–2017), then transitioning to a supportive SC member role (2017–2022), and now advising through the SC's Advisory Board. Throughout this journey, the SC was not only a governance body but also a circle of close colleagues who shared the responsibility of shaping the conference. Wil's leadership set the tone, and the SC provided the collective support and continuity that allowed the series to grow into a stable, inclusive, and internationally recognized community anchor.

Wil's leadership was not only organizational but also strategic. As Hajo Reijers recalls about the first BPM conference:

> As a young assistant professor, I was involved as organizing chair in the first edition of the BPM conference, back in 2003, in Eindhoven. I remember that there was a meeting towards the end of the conference in a small room of Eindhoven university about the event. The issue was how to continue with the conference after it turned out to be such a success. In the room where I was, all the more senior people involved in the event were gathered (I felt I was merely there as an observer). Wil raised the question: "Who wants to organize BPM 2004?" The room kept silent. I guess that everybody had on their mind what an effort it would be to set this up as an independent event, disconnected from the Petri Net conference of which it was part in 2003. Then Wil looked Mathias Weske in the eyes and said: "I think Potsdam would be the perfect location." I saw Mathias giving it some thought, taking his time, considering the options. He then responded, to my great relief: "Alright." So, BPM 2004 would indeed be held at HPI in Potsdam in the next year.
>
> It is my firm believe that this interaction between these two gentlemen was a defining moment for the success for the conference series. From that moment on, there has never been any doubt about the continuation of the conference and there have always been groups eager to organize the event.
> *Hajo Reijers*

Many colleagues emphasize Wil's vision and community-building role. Barbara Weber stresses:

> Wil was the founder of the BPM conference series and organized the first BPM conference in 2003 in Eindhoven. He was the first chair of the BPM SC and shaped the conference in this role for many years. Wil had an instrumental role not just in building the BPM community—without his vision and leadership, the field and its flagship conference series would not be where they are today. For me personally, Wil opened the door to

the community by inviting me to co-organize the BPI workshop which for many years was a highly successful workshop at BPM and a central venue for bridging research and practice in process mining. *Barbara Weber*

Others highlight his role in mentoring and inspiring younger researchers. Stefanie Rinderle-Ma recalls:

I first met Wil at the first BPM conference in Eindhoven in 2003. It was also my first paper presentation and I was quite nervous to present in front of all the superstars in the field. Wil asked a question after my presentation and provided me encouraging feedback. That moment left a strong impression on me and my motivation to pursue an academic career and I am sure that Wil has inspired many young colleagues in a similar way throughout the following 22 BPM conference editions. *Stefanie Rinderle-Ma*

For many, Wil's commitment went far beyond formal duties. Marlon Dumas remembers:

I first attended the BPM conference in 2005, when it was held in Nancy, France. At the time, I happened to be on a research stay in Wil's group in Eindhoven. Wil drove me personally from Eindhoven to Versailles for a workshop during the weekend preceding the BPM conference, and then from Versailles to Nancy on a Sunday. He was keen to drive me personally to introduce me to this young conference, which was in its third edition. At the conference, I met a young energetic Masters graduate, who was presenting a paper at one of the BPM workshops. That young man, who went by the name of Marcello La Rosa, convinced me to offer him a PhD place. That was the start of a long and fruitful trilateral cooperation. Wil was part of it, at every step. Since 2005, I have participated at every edition of the conference, including the 2025 edition in Sevilla, which I would mark as one of the most memorable in terms of food (both real food and scientific food). *Marlon Dumas*

Similarly, Jan Mendling reflects on Wil's mentoring [21]:

Wil van der Aalst is arguably the Pál Erdős of business process management. He invited me several times to Eindhoven, where we collaborated on papers in relation to my thesis. He played an important role for the verification part of my thesis and continued to be an important mentor for my career. *Jan Mendling*

Wil's influence also extended to broadening the horizons of the conference. Michael Rosemann recalls:

I am grateful to Wil as his love for and dedication to Brisbane meant we were able to host the BPM conference for the first time outside of Europe in 2007 here at QUT. *Michael Rosemann*

These testimonies confirm what Wil himself articulated in his 2012 reflection on the first decade of the BPM Conference [2]: that the event should be more than a venue for presenting papers. He stressed that the conference must serve as an anchor for the community, fostering debate, connecting diverse research concerns, and bridging the gap between theory and practice. Even at that stage, he emphasized that while BPM research had matured, adoption by vendors, consultants, and organizations was lagging, and he urged the community to face this challenge directly. This insistence on relevance and real-world uptake would become a hallmark of his vision.

Wil's influence on the BPM Conference cannot be separated from his broader vision for the discipline. As he has often stressed, his initial fascination was not only with how processes could be modeled in theory, but with how they actually unfolded in practice, including their deviations and inefficiencies. This realization, already clear in the 1990s, led him to pioneer process mining as a way to bridge the gap between formal models and organizational reality.

In his own words [28], "my interest in BPM arose from a fascination for processes: how they develop, how they deviate, and how we can analyze and improve them in a principled way. Although theory was elegant, I realized that most organizations did not actually know their real processes. This disconnection drove me to data-driven analysis, which eventually led to the development of process mining. From then on, process mining became not just a research topic, but a mission: to close the gap between models and reality."

This vision has been recently underscored [28]:

"Wil is not only the father of process mining, he is an architect of the bridge between science and business, between data and action, between today's BPM and its inevitable future in the age of AI. What is most inspiring is how he has combined three worlds that rarely align: academic rigor, industrial applicability, and a forward-looking vision of digital transformation."

Already in 2017, as he launched the Process and Data Science (PADS) group in Aachen, Wil made clear that the future of BPM lay in connecting data science with process management. He warned against the "death of BPM" narrative, emphasizing instead that BPM must embrace data-driven approaches [12]: "Data is connecting business and IT camps because it is real. Managers who did not care about models before are now interested in process mining, because it shows reality. IT specialists now have a way to feel the real challenges of managers and end-users. One of the dangers is thinking BPM is no longer needed because of advances in data science. It is crucial to connect both."

Equally important is Wil's recognition that the greatest challenges in BPM are not purely technical. While algorithms and tools function well, the bottlenecks lie in data quality, organizational resistance, and cultural change. As he put it in the interview in [28]: "The real Achilles' heel remains data management and cultural change. Sustainable improvement only happens when people trust the findings and are willing to act on them." This pragmatic awareness has guided the BPM community in balancing technical innovation with organizational realities.

His current advocacy for object-centric process mining [6] and for integrating AI into process intelligence demonstrates a consistent line of thought: BPM must remain rigorous, applicable, and visionary. His dual role as professor at RWTH Aachen and Chief Scientist at Celonis exemplifies his ability to move between academia and industry, embodying the idea that BPM research should not only advance science but also transform organizations.

Through these roles, reflections, and testimonies, a consistent picture emerges: Wil van der Aalst is not only the founder and long-time leader of the BPM Conference, but also its mentor, ambassador, and constant driving force. His vision has ensured the conference's continuity, his leadership has shaped its identity, and his personal commitment has inspired a generation of scholars to join and strengthen the BPM community.

## 6    Conclusions

Over more than two decades, the BPM Conference has established itself as the flagship venue of the field, balancing continuity in its scientific foundations with adaptability to emerging technologies, managerial perspectives, and societal concerns. Alongside advances in modeling, verification, and mining, the conference has provided a platform for discussing organizational adoption, governance, and cultural change, reminding us that BPM is not only about methods and tools but also about people, organizations, and their capacity to transform.

Wil van der Aalst's vision and leadership were instrumental in this journey. His ability to combine rigor with relevance not only anchored the conference in its early years but also ensured its evolution into a truly global and inclusive community. The BPM Conference today stands as both a premier scientific forum and a living example of how individual initiative and sustained community effort can create lasting impact. Thank you Wil!

**Acknowledgement.** The authors acknowledge the feedback of Jörg Desel on the 1998 Dagstuhl seminar and the respective proceedings, which are important aspects in the formation of the BPM conference series.

## References


1. van der Aa, H., Leopold, H., Reijers, H.A.: Detecting Inconsistencies Between Process Models and Textual Descriptions. In: Motahari-Nezhad, H.R., Recker, J., Weidlich, M. (eds.) BPM 2015. LNCS, vol. 9253, pp. 90–105. Springer, Cham (2015). https://doi.org/10.1007/978-3-319-23063-4_6
2. van der Aalst, W.M.P.: A decade of business process management conferences: Personal reflections on a developing discipline. In: Barros, A., Gal, A., Kindler, E. (eds.) Business Process Management. pp. 1–16 (2012)
3. van der Aalst, W.M.P., Best, E. (eds.): Applications and Theory of Petri Nets 2003, 24th International Conference, ICATPN 2003, Eindhoven, The Netherlands, June 23-27, 2003, Proceedings, Lecture Notes in Computer Science, vol. 2679. Springer, Cham (2003). https://doi.org/10.1007/3-540-44919-1

4. van der Aalst, W.M.P., Desel, J., Oberweis, A. (eds.): Business Process Management: Models, Techniques, and Empirical Studies, LNCS, vol. 1806. Springer, Cham (2000)

5. van der Aalst, W.M.P., ter Hofstede, A.H.M., Weske, M.: Business process management: a survey. In: van der Aalst, W.M.P., Weske, M. (eds.) Business Process Management. pp. 1–12 (2003)

6. Artale, A., Kovtunova, A., Montali, M., van der Aalst, W.M.P.: Modeling and Reasoning over Declarative Data-Aware Processes with Object-Centric Behavioral Constraints. In: Hildebrandt, T., van Dongen, B.F., Röglinger, M., Mendling, J. (eds.) BPM 2019. LNCS, vol. 11675, pp. 139–156. Springer, Cham (2019). https://doi.org/10.1007/978-3-030-26619-6_11

7. Chandrasiri, T., et al.: Beyond profit: the role of benevolent business processes in building long-term firm success. In: BPM 2025. LNCS, vol. 16044, pp. 489–504 (2025)

8. Ellis, C.A., Nutt, G.J.: Office information systems and computer science. ACM Comput. Surv. **12**(1), 27–60 (1980). https://doi.org/10.1145/356802.356805, https://doi.org/10.1145/356802.356805

9. Fahland, D., de Leoni, M., van Dongen, B.F., van der Aalst, W.M.P.: Conformance Checking of Interacting Processes with Overlapping Instances. In: Rinderle-Ma, S., Toumani, F., Wolf, K. (eds.) BPM 2011. LNCS, vol. 6896, pp. 345–361. Springer, Heidelberg (2011). https://doi.org/10.1007/978-3-642-23059-2_26

10. Golani, M., Pinter, S.S.: Generating a process model from a process audit log. In: van der Aalst, W.M.P., Weske, M. (eds.) Business Process Management. pp. 136–151 (2003)

11. Hammer, M., Champy, J.: Reengineering the Corporation: A Manifesto for Business Revolution. Harper Business (1993)

12. Harmon, P.: Wil van der aalst and a new bpm program (2017), bPM Trands Column, available at https://bptrends.info/wp-content/uploads/11-07-2017-COL-Harmon-on-BPM-Wil-Van-Der-Aalst.pdf

13. Hobeck, R., Klinkmüller, C., Bandara, H.M.N.D., Weber, I., van der Aalst, W.M.P.: Process Mining on Blockchain Data: A Case Study of Augur. In: Polyvyanyy, A., Wynn, M.T., Van Looy, A., Reichert, M. (eds.) BPM 2021. LNCS, vol. 12875, pp. 306–323. Springer, Cham (2021). https://doi.org/10.1007/978-3-030-85469-0_20

14. Hollingsworth, D.: The Workflow Reference Model. Tech. Rep. Document Number TC00-1003, Workflow Management Coalition (1995)

15. Kubrak, K., Botchorishvili, L., Milani, F., Nolte, A., Dumas, M.: Explanatory capabilities of large language models in prescriptive process monitoring. In: BPM 2024. LNCS, vol. 14940, pp. 403–420 (2024)

16. Leontjeva, A., Conforti, R., Di Francescomarino, C., Dumas, M., Maggi, F.M.: Complex symbolic sequence encodings for predictive monitoring of business processes. In: Business Process Management. pp. 297–313 (2015)

17. Leotta, F., Marrella, A., Mecella, M.: IoT for BPMers. Challenges, Case Studies and Successful Applications. In: Hildebrandt, T., van Dongen, B.F., Röglinger, M., Mendling, J. (eds.) BPM 2019. LNCS, vol. 11675, pp. 16–22. Springer, Cham (2019). https://doi.org/10.1007/978-3-030-26619-6_3

18. Ly, L.T., Rinderle, S., Dadam, P.: Semantic correctness in adaptive process management systems. In: Business Process Management. pp. 193–208 (2006)

19. Mansar, S.L., Reijers, H.A., Ounnar, F.: BPR implementation: A decision-making strategy. In: BPM 2005 Workshops. vol. 3812, pp. 421–431 (2005)

20. Martínez-Rojas, A., Ramirez, A.J., Enríquez, J.G., Reijers, H.A.: Analyzing variable human actions for robotic process automation. In: BPM 2022. LNCS, vol. 13420, pp. 75–90 (2022)
21. Mendling, J.: Everything is a process, even an academic career. In: Becoming an Organizational Scholar, pp. 198–211. Edward Elgar Publishing (2021)
22. Neiger, D., Churilov, L.: Structuring Business Objectives: A Business Process Modeling Perspective. In: van der Aalst, W.M.P., Weske, M. (eds.) BPM 2003. LNCS, vol. 2678, pp. 72–87. Springer, Heidelberg (2003). https://doi.org/10.1007/3-540-44895-0_6
23. Rafiei, M., van der Aalst, W.M.P.: Privacy-Preserving Data Publishing in Process Mining. In: Fahland, D., Ghidini, C., Becker, J., Dumas, M. (eds.) BPM 2020. LNBIP, vol. 392, pp. 122–138. Springer, Cham (2020). https://doi.org/10.1007/978-3-030-58638-6_8
24. Recker, J., Mendling, J.: The state of the art of business process management research as published in the bpm conference. Bus. Inf. Sys. Eng. **58**, 55–72 (2016)
25. Recker, J., Weidlich, M., Motahari-Nezhad, H.R.: Survey on bpm conference impressions (2014), qUT Survey Report, available at http://eprints.qut.edu.au/74555/
26. Resinas, M., del-Río-Ortega, A., van der Aa, H.: From text to performance measurement: Automatically computing process performance using textual descriptions and event logs. In: BPM 2023. LNCS, vol. 14159, pp. 266–283 (2023)
27. Rinderle, S., Reichert, M., Dadam, P.: Evaluation of Correctness Criteria for Dynamic Workflow Changes. In: van der Aalst, W.M.P., Weske, M. (eds.) BPM 2003. LNCS, vol. 2678, pp. 41–57. Springer, Heidelberg (2003). https://doi.org/10.1007/3-540-44895-0_4
28. Robledo, P.: Voces bpm. personas que inspiran: Wil van der aalst (2025), linkedIn post, available at https://www.linkedin.com/pulse/wil-van-der-aalst-pedro-robledo-bpm-ibcpf/
29. Schimm, G.: Mining Most Specific Workflow Models from Event-Based Data. In: van der Aalst, W.M.P., Weske, M. (eds.) BPM 2003. LNCS, vol. 2678, pp. 25–40. Springer, Heidelberg (2003). https://doi.org/10.1007/3-540-44895-0_3
30. Schmidt, K., Bannon, L.J.: Taking CSCW seriously. Comput. Support. Cooperative Work. **1**(1–2), 7–40 (1992). https://doi.org/10.1007/BF00752449, https://doi.org/10.1007/BF00752449
31. Teinemaa, I., Dumas, M., Maggi, F.M., Di Francescomarino, C.: Predictive Business Process Monitoring with Structured and Unstructured Data. In: La Rosa, M., Loos, P., Pastor, O. (eds.) BPM 2016. LNCS, vol. 9850, pp. 401–417. Springer, Cham (2016). https://doi.org/10.1007/978-3-319-45348-4_23
32. Weber, I., Xu, X., Riveret, R., Governatori, G., Ponomarev, A., Mendling, J.: Untrusted Business Process Monitoring and Execution Using Blockchain. In: La Rosa, M., Loos, P., Pastor, O. (eds.) BPM 2016. LNCS, vol. 9850, pp. 329–347. Springer, Cham (2016). https://doi.org/10.1007/978-3-319-45348-4_19
33. Weske, M., Montali, M., Weber, I., Brocke, J.: BPM: Foundations, Engineering, Management. In: Weske, M., Montali, M., Weber, I., vom Brocke, J. (eds.) BPM 2018. LNCS, vol. 11080, pp. 3–11. Springer, Cham (2018). https://doi.org/10.1007/978-3-319-98648-7_1

34. Wohed, P., van der Aalst, W.M.P., Dumas, M., ter Hofstede, A.H.M., Russell, N.: On the Suitability of BPMN for Business Process Modelling. In: Dustdar, S., Fiadeiro, J.L., Sheth, A.P. (eds.) BPM 2006. LNCS, vol. 4102, pp. 161–176. Springer, Heidelberg (2006). https://doi.org/10.1007/11841760_12
35. Zerbato, F., Soffer, P., Weber, B.: Process mining practices: Evidence from interviews. In: BPM 2022. LNCS, vol. 13420, pp. 268–285 (2022)

# A Theoretical Perspective for Process Science

Peter Fettke[1,2](✉) and Wolfgang Reisig[3]

[1] German Research Center for Artificial Intelligence (DFKI), Saarbrücken, Germany
[2] Saarland University, Saarbrücken, Germany
peter.fettke@dfki.de
[3] Humboldt-Universität zu Berlin, Berlin, Germany
reisig@informatik.hu-berlin.de

**Abstract.** Process science is a highly interdisciplinary field of research. Despite numerous proposals, there is still an inadequate understanding of the core concepts of the field, such as 'process', 'event', and 'system'. A more systematic framework is mandatory in order to cope with process science. We present such a framework by means of an example. This framework addresses three aspects: architecture, statics, and dynamics. The corresponding formal concepts, which are based on established scientific theories, provide an integrated framework for understanding processes in the world. We argue that our approach has positive implications for both theoretical and empirical research, as hypothesized relationships can be explicitly tested. Time has come to initiate a discussion on the foundations of our field.

**Keywords:** theory of modeling · discrete systems · behavior modeling · predicate logic · composition calculus · Petri nets · Tarski structure

## 1 Processes in the Digital World

Process science operates at the intersection of technology and human-centered fields, including (business) informatics, (management) information systems, social sciences, and mathematics. These disciplines all enhance our understanding of fundamental concepts in process science [9]. Consequently, the problems, solutions, and branches of business process management (BPM) draw insights from multiple academic areas. With this in mind, we seek to establish a strong theoretical foundation for process science. Specifically, we ask: what are the field's key concepts? What are the primary phenomena? What implicit or explicit assumptions does the scientific community hold? Which hypotheses about processes are currently under debate?

At first glance, the idea of a process seems simple. However, defining this idea precisely is challenging. For example, a process is often viewed as a completely ordered sequence of events that happen over time. Still, many real-world or

© The Author(s), under exclusive license to Springer Nature Switzerland AG 2026
J. Mendling et al. (Eds.): Wil van der Aalst Festschrift, LNCS 16480, pp. 65–81, 2026.
https://doi.org/10.1007/978-3-032-17618-9_6

imagined phenomena are better understood as events connected by cause-and-effect relationships. Cause-and-effect links are only partially ordered: usually, some events in a process are causally related, while others are not.

Furthermore, several related concepts need clarification, including process types, process instances, process cases, and process models. Although these terms are similar, it remains unclear how they are connected and what specifically distinguishes them.

In informatics, especially, the idea of "process" is related to the concept of "algorithm". In the digital world, the term "process" encompasses traditional mathematical algorithms as well as many other systems. Typical examples include:

- Euclid's algorithm for computing the greatest common divisor of two natural numbers;
- the bisection algorithm, taking three real numbers, $a$, $b$, and $\epsilon$, and a continuous function $f$ such that $f(a) < 0$ and $f(b) > 0$, returning a real number $c$ such that $f(c) < \epsilon$;
- the alternating bit protocol, detecting and correcting loss of messages;
- a cooking recipe;
- an apple sorter with a sloping plate that has holes of increasing size; the apples roll down the plate and eventually fall through a hole;
- organization of a stock exchange;
- a robot assembling a circuit board;
- the organization of a bakery;
- the hiring procedure for new staff in a company.

Moreover, the digital world encompasses large-scale systems such as embedded systems, business information systems, information infrastructures, the Internet of Things, cyber-physical systems, digital infrastructures in areas like health, mobility, industry, public services, and administration, digital ecosystems, digital twins, and Industry 4.0. Specifically, extensive business processes are also part of this world.

To better understand the digital world, it is often pointless to discuss the difference between an "algorithm" and a "process". Many systems in the digital world share the trait of being composed of cooperating components rather than being built as monolithic software. Therefore, a fundamental, unifying theory for understanding the digital world must include methods for describing real-world components and an overall framework for their integration.

Process science and business processes clearly belong to the digital world. A theoretical perspective on process science and business processes must align with a theoretical view of the digital world.

Our contribution proceeds as follows: Following the introduction, Sect. 2 considers the relationship between process science and the field of BPM. Section 3 investigates what kind of science process science is. Section 4 sketches the axiomatic method as a paradigmatic method for the science and engineering of processes. Section 5 introduces three important postulates for a theoretical perspective on process science. Section 6, the main part of the work, proposes a theoretical framework for this field by highlighting some aspects that are interesting for the theoretical foundation of process science. This general HERAKLIT approach is presented in the monograph [13]. Sections 7 and 8 then discuss related work and conclude the argumentation.

## 2 Process Science and Business Process Management

The term 'BPM' predates the term 'process science'. Clearly, both terms are related. But precisely how are process science and BPM connected? As with many terms in computing, the term 'BPM' can mean (1) a specific type of *problem*, (2) a possible *solution* to that problem, and (3) the *academic field* that studies the problem and its known solutions [12]:

1. BPM as a problem: People, organizations and systems execute processes in numerous fields, including manufacturing, healthcare, and logistics. It is an undeniable fact that resources are limited in these areas. Therefore, process management is essential in almost every domain. In other words, analyzing, planning, designing, implementing, and monitoring processes are active tasks in the daily work of many individuals across various organization.
2. BPM as a solution: Various ideas for tackling BPM have emerged in both academia and industry. The proposed solutions include: (a) general frameworks (such as the six core framework of [27]; (b) lifecycle models like [10]; (c) modeling approaches such as the *Business Process Model and Notation* (BPMN); (d) specific algorithms, including those for process discovery; and (e) available software tools. Each of these artifacts can be seen as a solution to a BPM problem.
3. BPM as an academic research field: BPM has a long research tradition [3,4,6,17,20,26]. Given the wide and heterogeneous spectrum of BPM problems and solutions, it is unsurprising that the field is interdisciplinary, rooted in various academic disciplines. Some important branches of the field and their main outlets for publishing results include: The *Business Process Management Journal* (established in 1995), the *International Conference on Business Process Management* (established in 2003), and the more specialized International *Conference on the Application and Theory of Petri Nets* (established in 1980) and the *International Conference on Process Mining* (established in 2019). Furthermore, many leading journals and conferences feature dedicated BPM sections, such as *Business and Information Systems Engineering*, the *International and European Conferences on Information Systems* and the *International Conference on Wirtschaftsinformatik*. The term 'process science' has recently been adopted as the name of the field of BPM [9] and of the newly founded journal *Process Science – Business Process Management and Process Mining*. In other words, 'process science' is used to refer to BPM as an academic field of research. As such, process science addresses the problems of process management, and provides solutions for the management of business processes.

## 3   What Kind of Science Is Process Science?

The term 'science' is often used narrowly, mainly referring to natural science. However, it can also be understood more broadly. This is especially clear when the term is translated into languages like French and German.

Based on considerations of McCloskey [21], Table 1 shows that the English term 'science' and its French and German translations, 'science' and 'Wissenschaft' respectively, are not used equivalently. In fact, the German and French terms have a wider usage: for example, the English term 'science' is not used for the disciplines named by the German term 'Geisteswissenschaft' or the French term 'les sciences humaines'. Conversely, the term 'computer science' is not generally considered to be a natural science. Indeed, some argue that computer science has *mathematical, engineering,* and *experimental* foundations [25]. Therefore, the question of whether process science is a kind of science should be discussed in more depth.

**Table 1.** Synopsis of terms denoting academic fields of inquiry in different languages based on [7, 21]

| English | French | German |
| --- | --- | --- |
| natural *sciences* | les *sciences* naturelles | die Natur*wissenschaften* |
| social *sciences* | les *sciences* sociales | die Sozial*wissenschaften* |
| humanities | les *sciences* humaines | die Geistes*wissenschaften* |
| engineering | l'ingénierie | die Ingenieur*wissenschaften* |

Several questions come up regarding these points: What kind of science is process science? How does it relate to the engineering and management of processes? A first hint to answer these questions is John von Neumann's remark [24]:

"The sciences do not try to explain, they hardly even try to interpret, they mainly make models. By a model is meant a mathematical construct which, with the addition of certain verbal interpretations, describes observed phenomena. The justification of such a mathematical construct is solely and precisely that it is expected to work – that is, correctly to describe phenomena from a reasonably wide area."

This quote emphasizes the importance of effective modeling techniques. In general, a good formal modeling approach enables a modeler to communicate their ideas as accurately and clearly as possible within a formal framework. When applied to specific examples, we typically understand what an 'adequate' description of a real-world or imagined system should include: it should cover all relevant aspects that need to be highlighted, while excluding those that are less important or better left out.

Given this context, the question arises whether informatics in general, and process science in particular, are truly scientific fields. What phenomena are actually observed and described? Informatics involves developing software for various domains, including business processes, technical production systems, and administration. There is no need to observe or describe this software for process automation. Instead, what must be observed and described are the systems in which the software operates – namely, the business processes, technical production systems, and administrations. A thorough understanding of the intended impact of software within the digital world is essential for its practical design. The semantics and properties of software are typically described using predicates over its input and output. This approach is too narrow and clearly insufficient for understanding the role of software in process automation. In this regard, informatics lacks strong conceptual foundations. There is no widely accepted or standardized basis for modeling techniques, and there is little willingness within the informatics community to develop and adopt one.

Existing techniques, such as the *Unified Modeling Language* (UML) and BPMN, are not expressive enough to capture all essential aspects of digital systems. Additionally, many modeling approaches lack solid theoretical foundations. In particular, there is a deficiency of applicable general concepts for components, composition, and refinement.

## 4 Theoretical Perspectives: Axioms, Structures, and Symbolic Representations

On the background of the general perspective on the theory of science as described in the section before, the well-proven axiomatic method of theory building is most promising, also for process management.

The axiomatic method helps create accurate models. You start with a set of basic assumptions (axioms) and then logically derive additional statements (theorems). The set of axioms should be as small as possible, with each one carefully justified. The idea of formalizing a body of knowledge through axioms is not new; it dates back at least $2,000$ years to Euclid, who established axiomatic foundations for geometry [31]. Since then, significant progress has been made; for example, geometry has branched into various areas, many with important applications, such as non-Euclidean geometry. Besides its specific role in geometry, the concept of axiomatization and formalization has evolved in many directions and is now understood in different ways. One common approach is known as informal axiomatization. This approach is called informal because it does not use a formal system to express the core principles of a body of knowledge; instead, it relies on an intuitive set theory that combines formal and informal ideas [30]. It is claimed that these ideas can be expressed within a first-order predicate logic formal system. However, in everyday scientific work, only informal language is used. This type of axiomatization can be traced back to model theory, as developed in logic and mathematics. Notably, the Bourbaki group applied this idea to address the fundamental crisis in mathematics at the start of the last century [8]. Since then, this approach has become standard in mathematics and has been widely adopted in the empirical sciences, as demonstrated by many examples. For instance, Patrick Suppes provides examples from physics, philosophy, psychology, computer science, economics, and semiotics [31].

We base models on well-established, general formal concepts that are standard in mathematics. In a systematic approach, real-world items are grouped into sets. These sets may be finite or infinite. They are related through functions. Properties are defined by predicates, which are subsets of Cartesian products of these sets. Since the 1950s, it has become standard to denote a finite collection of sets, distinguished elements, functions, and predicates as an "algebraic structure" [30]. Predicate logic interprets logical formulas within such structures. A structure is heterogeneous if its sets are of different types. Mathematical structures are usually small, containing a few sets, functions, and predicates. In contrast, informatics deals with richer, more complex structures. Conversely, the sets considered in mathematics are often uncountable, while informatics typically handles finite or, at most, countably infinite sets.

The core idea of informal axiomatization [31] is to introduce a structure $S$ consisting of finitely many:

- Basic sets: These sets define the fundamental objects of the structure $S$;
- Derived sets: Further sets can be derived from basic sets or already derived sets, as subsets, union, cartesian product, etc.;
- Distinguished elements from basic or derived sets;
- Functions: Mathematical functions over those sets;
- Predicates: Subsets of Cartesian products of sets of $S$.

Heterogeneous structures provide a smooth transition to symbolic representations: A signature of a structure $S$ assigns a symbol to each constant, function, and predicate of $S$. Along with a set of variables, the constant and function symbols generate (infinitely many) terms (symbol sequences). For example, with a constant symbol $a$, function symbols $f$ and $g$, and a variable $x$, the symbol sequence $f(g(a), x)$ would be a typical term. Each interpretation of the variable $x$ yields a value in one of the structure's sets.

Often, people focus on all structures with the same signature or those with specific properties, rather than just one structure. This is a widely accepted mathematical standard. Heterogeneous structures are used either explicitly or implicitly across various modeling techniques. As mentioned above, predicate logic examines properties of systems described by these structures.

Following the axiomatic method described earlier, heterogeneous structures use the fewest possible axioms: only those of the well-known elementary (Zermelo-Fraenkel) set theory, including basic operations such as union, intersection, set membership, tuples, functions, and predicates.

The axiomatic method is widely applied in process science. Most, if not all, computer science-oriented branches of process science use the axiomatic method. In addition, this idea is also used in management-oriented approaches, as emphasized by Nobel Laureate Paul Milgrom:

"Formalization is important to economics, because it allows readers and others to identify the precise assumptions that underpin any purported conclusion, to verify that the assumptions really do imply this conclusion, and to check how deviations from the assumptions might alter the conclusion." [23], page 3f.

## 5   Postulates and Axioms for Process Science

The challenge now is to develop an appropriate modeling approach for process science. Guided by the axiomatic method, we establish a theoretical perspective for process science. We begin with three postulates, which are simplified versions of axioms.

- Postulate 1: A model can include both data and real-life items, such as products, customers, machines, paper money and contracts. In a nutshell: *Objects matter!*
- Postulate 2: A model functions locally. Behavior cannot be viewed as a sequence of steps within a single 'global' state space. Instead, every change to the system has local causes and effects. Some events are causally connected, while others are not. In summary: *Causality matters!*
- Postulate 3: A comprehensive model of computer-integrated systems is structured. A large computer-integrated system is not amorphous; it is composed of a number of subsystems. In short: *Composition matters!*

Many of the ideas supporting these postulates have been published previously. However, it is now necessary to unify these so-far loosely connected concepts. This cannot be achieved simply by creating a new 'hyper model' of computation. Instead, fundamental questions about basic computing concepts must be asked and answered to establish a foundational framework for modeling discrete systems.

Meyer and Weber [22] highlight the benefits of starting a theory of programming languages in an axiomatic style. In fact, they begin solely with the axioms of Zermelo-Fraenkel set theory, as introduced in Sect. 4. Gurevich's abstract state machines [16] start with heterogeneous structures. We adopt this approach, with a small but crucial enhancement: dynamic behavior is modeled using predicates that may update their extensions. We carefully ensure that the behavior description is based on heterogeneous structures with fundamental axioms. We strictly avoid constructs common in programming language semantics, such as automata, grammars, type theories, assignment statements, and complex forms of composition and communication. This approach rules out any implicit or hidden assumptions and unjustified arguments.

Our proposal substantially differs from this approach, grounded in a fundamental concept: dynamics is represented as updates of predicates. In a state $s$, a predicate $p$ may apply to an item $a$; a step then may cease this fact. Vice versa, in a state $s$, the predicate $p$ may not apply to an item $a$; a step then may cease this fact. In general, in our proposal, a step locally updates a bounded set of predicates. This concept generates an amazing theory of models for discrete systems. The forthcoming section exemplifies details of the new theoretical perspective for process science.

# 6   An Example

In light of the above considerations, especially the previously mentioned postulates and epistemological arguments, we introduce the HERAKLIT modeling infrastructure. The monograph [13] describes the overall HERAKLIT approach. Here, we focus on aspects that stem from the considerations describe before.

## 6.1   Modeling Dynamics in Discrete Systems

As outlined before, in informatics, dynamics evolves in discrete steps. This is usually modeled in terms of transition systems, i.e. graph structures, with each node representing a state, and each arc a step. A single behavior is then a path through the graph. Specification- and analysis techniques of temporal logic usually assume a heterogeneous structure, including in particular some predicates, and provides logical formulae that are interpreted in single behaviors or in sets of behaviors.

In the rest of this paper, we concentrate on the smooth step from static to dynamic predicates. We do so by means of an every-day example.

## 6.2   Example: Elementary Steps in a Restaurant Organization

We start by identifying two predicates, *waiting clients* and *free tables*. Graphically, each predicate is represented as an ellipse in Fig. 1.

**Fig. 1.** Two predicates.

To express the proposition that a client is waiting, its name is inscribed into the ellipse. Likewise, the number of a free table may be inscribed into the ellipse of the free tables predicate in Fig. 2.

**Fig. 2.** Two propositions.

Predicates and propositions are nothing new: A predicate applies to an item, or does not apply to it. What's now new is a systematic capturing of steps: Whether or not a predicate applies to an item, may change in an evolving system.

In our running example, the so far waiting client *Alice* may enter the restaurant and sit down at Table 1. Then, the two propositions stated in Fig. 2 no longer hold. Graphically, this is expressed by means of a box, and arrows between the propositions and the box in Fig. 3.

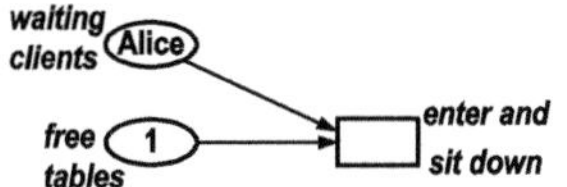


**Fig. 3.** Two predicates as preconditions of a step.

Intuitively stated, the arrows "remove" the items *Alice* and *1* from the predicates.

In an analogous manner, an item may "enter" a predicate. Here, *Alice* at Table 1 turns ready to order a meal in Fig. 4.

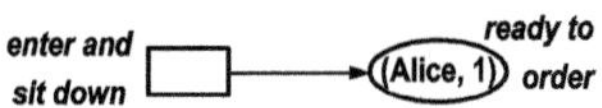


**Fig. 4.** One predicate as a postcondition of a step.

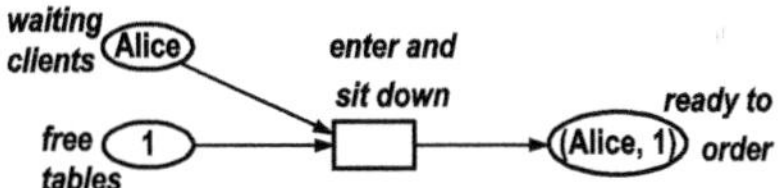


**Fig. 5.** One step with pre- and postconditions.

Finally, the steps in Fig. 3 and 4 are combined in Fig. 5. Intuitively formulated, Fig. 5 describes a simple step: In a situation where *Alice* is a waiting client, and Table 1 is free, *Alice* sits down at Table 1 and is ready to order a meal.

### 6.3   A More Complex Step: Subsets

The step of Fig. 5 is now followed by another, more complex step. In this step, the client *Alice* selects her meal in Fig. 6.

Here, the predicate menu represents the restaurant's menu card. The menu card contains rice, meat, and fish. In our example, the predicate menu does not apply to the single dishes, but to the entire set of dishes. The step *select* makes use of this set, without updating it. *Alice* selects the subset {*rice, meat*} from the menu and thus generates a purchase order for the kitchen. Coincidently, Alice remains sitting at Table 1, waiting for her meal.

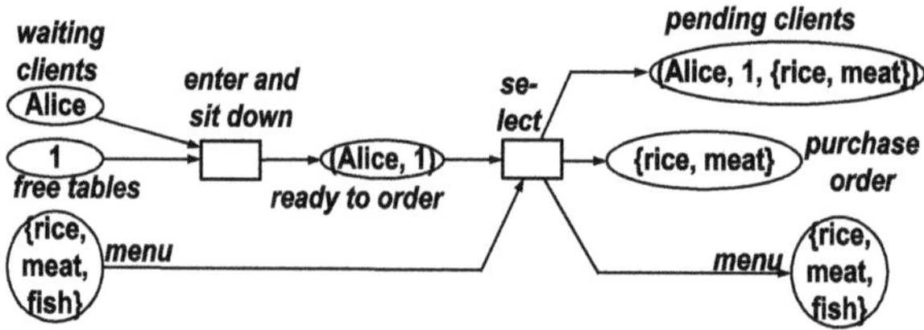


**Fig. 6.** Two steps.

In technical terms, what we have used so far are predicates over three sets *(clients, tables, menu)* with elements *Alice*, Table 1 and {*rice, meat, fish*}, as well as tuples and subsets. The next step employs another, the last, important concept: a function.

## 6.4   Functions

Here we model details of what is going on in the kitchen: The set {*rice, meat*} of Alice's purchase order is "unfolded", resulting in two independent orderings: one for meat and one for rice. Both are cooked independent of each other. As a notation, each cooked dish is underlined, e.g. "meat", to distinguish it from its ordering, e.g. "meat". More formally, we employ a function $f$ such that for each single ordering $x$ holds: $f(x) = \underline{x}$ in Fig. 7.

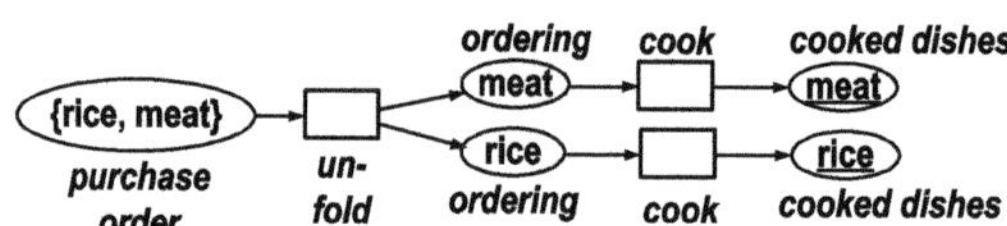


**Fig. 7.** A step with a function.

## 6.5   Putting It All Together

Now we extend the steps in Figs. 6 and 7 by two further events, hand over and eat and leave. This completes the modeling of Alice's restaurant visit in Fig. 8.

As a variant, the following models the meal of the hungry client Bob, sitting at table 2, ordering rice and fish in Fig. 9.

In addition, both Alice and Bob may eat at the restaurant. Consequently, steps in Figs. 8 and 9 together can be conceived as one behavior of the restaurant system.

Even a moderate increase of the number of clients, tables, and dishes significantly increases the number of potential runs of the system. For example, 2 clients, 3 tables, and 3 entries in the menu yields already $2 \times 3 \times 8 = 48$ potential

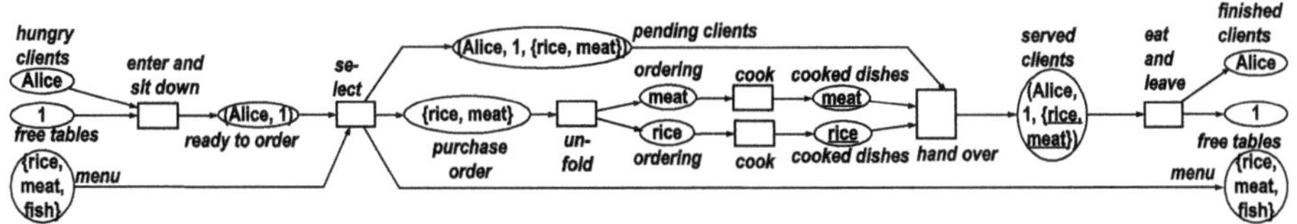

**Fig. 8.** All steps of Alice's restaurant visit.

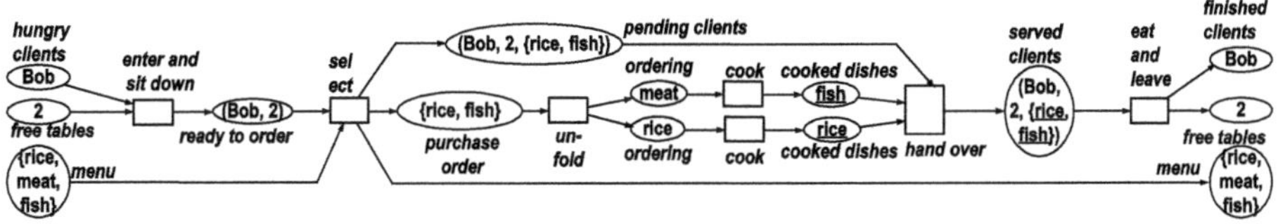

**Fig. 9.** All steps of Bob's restaurant visit.

meals of single persons! With a run consisting of meals of many persons, the number of potential meals is in the order of $10^{14}$. We want to model sets of behavior in a concise manner, with most elementary mathematical means. This is possible indeed, and predicate logic is helpful again.

## 6.6   Transition Schemata

As an example, we model all runs for the case of the clients *Alice* and *Bob*, the free tables 1, 2, 3, and the menu {*rice, meat, fish*}. We are interested in a characterization of all runs of the system, without explicitly representing each single run. This can be achieved by the following heterogeneous structure "restaurant", together with a set of variables in steps in Fig. 10.

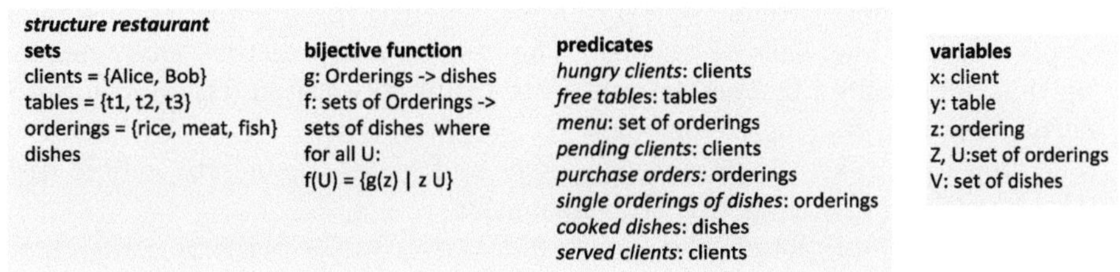

**Fig. 10.** The structure of the restaurant.

The central idea is now to parameterize the steps. For example, the step *enter and sit down* is parameterized by the variable $x$ for clients, and $y$ for tables. Valuating $x$ by *Alice* and $y$ by $t_1$, yields the step of Fig. 5. Technically, we represent the parameterized step as in Fig. 11.

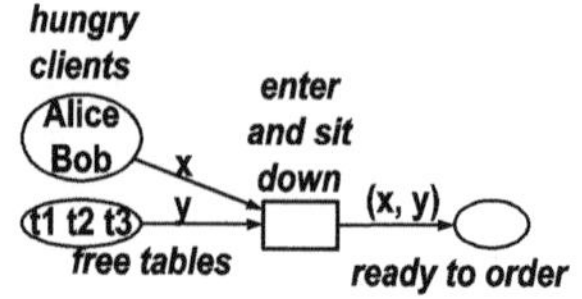



**Fig. 11.** A parameterized step.

Altogether, Fig. 11 represents six steps, among them the step in Fig. 5. Each step yields a different tuple for the predicate ready to order. We now extend the steps in Fig. 11 in the spirit of Figs. 8 and 9 in Fig. 12.

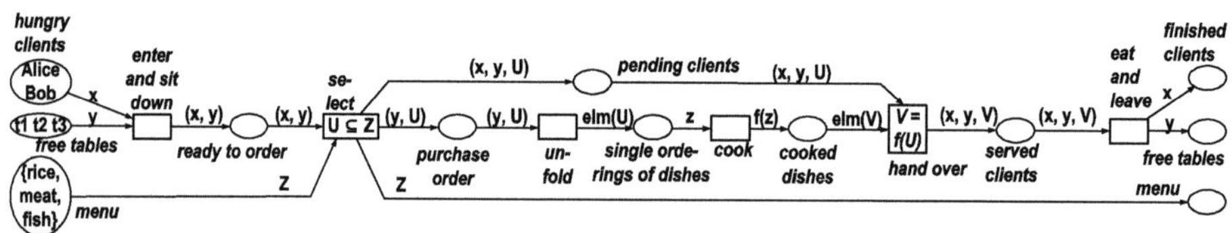



**Fig. 12.** The transition schema of a restaurant visit.

Some new concepts are required. They, however, remain in the world of elementary set operations:

- The step *select* comes with the additional requirement $U$ and $Z$. Both $U$ and $Z$ are variables for sets of offers. Intuitively stated, the client $x$ selects a subset of offers from the menu.
- A purchase order $P$ is a set of offers that must be unfolded into the single offers in $P$, to which the predicate single offers applies. In technical terms, the predicate purchase orders applies to a set, whereas the predicate single offers applies to the elements of the set. The step *unfold* executes this transformation, represented by the *elm*-notation. Intuitively stated, the *elm*-notation turns a set into its single elements.
- The step *cook* takes single ordered offers and yields a concrete, edible dish. The function $g$ describes this transformation.
- The step *hand over* hands the cooked dishes over to the corresponding client. Technically, with $U$ the set of orders of $x$, the corresponding set of dishes is $f(U)$. For convenience we write $f(U)$ as $V$. With the predicate cooked dishes applying to the single dishes of $V$, the set $V$ of dishes is handed over to the client $x$, sitting at table $y$.
- The step *eat and leave* is now obvious.

This completes the system in Fig. 12.

## 6.7   Predicate Schemata

The system of Fig. 12 does with fixed sets of clients, tables, and orders. But the behavior described by Fig. 12 can be applied to any sets of clients, tables, and orders. For example, for the predicate hungry clients, we need a symbolic representation to express "for any given set $C$ of clients, the predicate hungry clients applies to each element of $C$". In analogy to the steps *unfold* and *hand over*, we apply the *elm*-notation to a variable for sets of clients. The menu predicate anyway applies to sets of orders. This yields the following schematic, symbolic representation of infinitely many systems with initially different sets of hungry clients, free tables, and potential orders in Fig. 13.

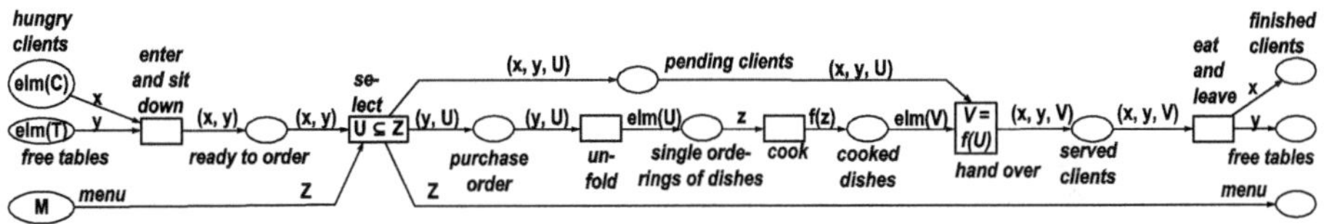


**Fig. 13.** The predicate schema of a restaurant visit.

This completes the example. Notice that a heterogeneous structure is the only mathematical concept used in this example.

# 7   Related Research

The aim of this Section is not to review all relevant prior work on the foundations of process science. Instead, we focus our discussion on a few key areas of research in the field.

The classical process framework distinguishes between the notions of a process $P$, sometimes also called system, and a model $M$, both are based on a set of activities or events, e.g. van der Aalst [1]. A trace, sometimes also called process instance, is defined as a finite sequence of activities; a model $M$ and a process $P$ are both subsets of the set of all possible traces. In other words, classical automata theory is used: $P$ and $M$ are understood as formal languages over an alphabet. This foundation is typically used to understand processes. Such a theoretical conceptualization has important advantages, e.g. it is well-known, intuitive, and simple to understand. However, on the other hand, this approach has significant shortcomings, since business processes contain further perspectives, e.g. objects, data, networked actions, (sub-) systems. Although there are already several alternative theoretical extensions of the classical framework, e.g. [2,11,32], it is an open question how these ideas can be used as a theoretical foundation for process science.

Houy et al. [18,19] review the theoretical foundations for empirical research in BPM. The framework introduced by [33], based on the philosophical work of

Bunge, is one of the most prominent theoretical foundations from the information systems discipline. Essentially, this approach follows the classical foundations of automata theory mentioned before.

In addition, there are many theoretical approaches which only offer ideas on a more or less intuitive level, e.g. Scheer [28], Frank [14], Winter [35]. Although these works offer a rich picture of theoretical ideas, it is open how they provide explicit theoretical foundations.

Another discussion focuses on what kind of theoretical foundations are important. Gregor (2006) introduces different types of theory [15]; Bichler et al. provide some general discussion on theoretical foundations of our field [7]. It is not always clear whether these ideas are based on the well-accepted axiomatic method in empirical science on which our proposal is based on. Note that, in philosophy of science, using set theory to shed light on the structure and dynamics of a theory, as well as to explain the implicit assumptions of theoretical terms and measurement theory, is a well-recognized approach [5,29,31,36].

We believe that, in the future, our introduced framework can serve as a foundation for several more specialized approaches in the field. For example, knowledge graphs and the Object-Centric Event Log (OCEL) are powerful existing approaches for modeling complex process data, while many variants of sophisticated Petri nets, such as Coloured Petri Nets (CPN), incorporate procedural and executable features, including changing attributes. In the future, such approaches can be based on the HERAKLIT framework as best practices and common process modeling patterns.

## 8    Conclusion

This contribution emphasizes two aspects: First, that process science should be given a solid theoretical footing. Second, that the role of modeling should be given more attention. We suggest heterogeneous algebraic structures, i.e. the mathematical basis of first order logic, as such a basis. We showed that this basis is quite expressive.

As a fundamentally new concept, we suggest a "dynamization" of heterogeneous structures. Similar ideas have been applied to *Abstract State Machines* [16] previously denoted as *Evolving Algebras*.

From an axiomatic point of view, this choice is most thrifty: it only assumes the axioms of first order logic. [22] emphasizes the advantages of such a starting point. Additionally, the close link to first order logic promises technically elegant and expressive means to deal with properties of digital systems.

This contribution describes the smooth path from classical, heterogeneous structures, to elementary steps of a dynamization. This is just a starting point; much more general constructs exploit the concept of predicates and a symbolic version of all this. Details can be found in [13].

This paper emphasizes the need for theoretical foundations of process science. We strongly agree with the positive aspects of formalization mentioned in the quote from Nobel Laureate Paul Milgrom (cp. Section 4). Furthermore, we fully share the surprise and wonder described by Weber at the use formalization in our field:

> "[W]e [Wand and Weber] have often been criticized for the formal approach we have used to articulate our models. I am perplexed by these criticisms because I cannot conceive of a discipline that is serious about its foundations if it proscribes use of mathematics to articulate these foundations." [34], page 33.

Looking back over the last decades, it is safe to say that many of the foundations introduced by Wand and Weber are well accepted and often empirically tested, especially in the information systems branch of process science. However, process science needs a broader discussion of foundations. Therefore, we believe that it is now time to intensify the discussion on the theoretical foundations of process science as a field of study. This is especially important in the context of the digital revolution of the twenty-first century. In particular, it is necessary to clarify what is meant by digital processes and process technology, including areas such as process mining, robotic process automation, and large process models. Since several branches of process science have already started the discussion on how our field can embrace digital transformation, a deeper discussion is now needed.

Despite the great advantages of the basic framework presented, we do not advocate abandoning other forms of scientific inquiry. The axiomatic method can easily be combined with other methods such as empirical approaches, e.g. experiments and case studies, as well as interpretation and speculation. In this sense, we strongly believe in a bright future for our field.

## References


1. van der Aalst, W.: Process mining. Commun. ACM **55**(8), 76–83 (2012)
2. van der Aalst, W., Berti, A.: Discovering object-centric petri nets. Fund. Inform. **175**(1–4), 1–40 (2020)
3. van der Aalst, W.M.P.: Business process management: a comprehensive survey. Int. Sch. Res. Not. **2013**(1), 507984 (2013). https://doi.org/10.1155/2013/507984, https://onlinelibrary.wiley.com/doi/abs/10.1155/2013/507984
4. van der Aalst, W.M.P., ter Hofstede, A.H.M., Weske, M.: Business process management: a survey. In: van der Aalst, W.M.P., ter Hofstede, A.H.M., Weske, M. (eds.) Business Process Management, International Conference, BPM 2003, Eindhoven, The Netherlands, June 26–27, 2003, Proceedings. Lecture Notes in Computer Science, vol. 2678, pp. 1–12. Springer (2003). https://doi.org/10.1007/3-540-44895-0_1, https://doi.org/10.1007/3-540-44895-0_1
5. Andreas, H.: Theoretical Terms in Science. In: Zalta, E.N. (ed.) The Stanford Encyclopedia of Philosophy. Metaphysics Research Lab, Stanford University, Fall 2021 edn. (2021)
6. Beverungen, D., et al.: Seven paradoxes of business process management in a hyperconnected world. Bus. Inf. Sys. Eng. **63**(2), 145–156 (2021)
7. Bichler, M., et al.: Theories in business and information systems engineering. Bus. Inf. Syst. Eng. **58**(4), 291–319 (2016)

8. Bourbaki, N.: The architecture of mathematics. Am. Math. Mon. **57**(4), 221–232 (1950)
9. Brocke, J., et al.: Process science: the interdisciplinary study of socio-technical change. Process Sci. **1**(1), 1 (2024). https://doi.org/10.1007/s44311-024-00001-5, https://doi.org/10.1007/s44311-024-00001-5
10. Dumas, M., Rosa, M.L., Mendling, J., Reijers, H.A.: Fundamentals of Business Process Management. Springer, 2 edn. (2018). https://doi.org/10.1007/978-3-662-56509-4
11. Fahland, D.: Artifact-centric process mining. In: Encyclopedia of Big Data Technologies, pp. 108–117. Springer (2019)
12. Fettke, P., Di Francescomarino, C.: Business process management and artificial intelligence. KI - Künstliche Intell. **39**(2), 67–79 (2025)
13. Fettke, P., Reisig, W.: Understanding the Digital World: Modeling with HERAKLIT. Springer (2024)
14. Frank, U.: Multi-perspective enterprise modeling: Foundational concepts, prospects and future research challenges. Soft. Sys. Model. **13**, 941–962 (2014)
15. Gregor, S.: The nature of theory in information systems. MIS Q. **30**(3), 611–642 (2006)
16. Gurevich, Y.: Sequential abstract-state machines capture sequential algorithms. ACM Trans. Comput. Logic (TOCL) **1**(1), 77–111 (2000)
17. Houy, C., Fettke, P., Loos, P.: Empirical research in business process management - analysis of an emerging field of research. Bus. Process. Manag. J. **16**(4), 619–661 (2010). https://doi.org/10.1108/14637151011065946, https://doi.org/10.1108/14637151011065946
18. Houy, C., Fettke, P., Loos, P.: On theoretical foundations of empirical business process management research. In: Daniel, F., Barkaoui, K., Dustdar, S. (eds.) Business Process Management Workshops - BPM 2011 International Workshops, Clermont-Ferrand, France, August 29, 2011, pp. 320–332. Part I, Revised Selected Papers (2011)
19. Houy, C., Fettke, P., Loos, P.: On the theoretical foundations of research into the understandability of business process models. In: Avital, M., Leimeister, J.M., Schultze, U. (eds.) 22nd European Conference on Information Systems, ECIS 2014, Tel Aviv, Israel, June 9–11, 2014 (2014)
20. Houy, C., Fettke, P., Loos, P., van der Aalst, W.M.P., Krogstie, J.: BPM-in-the-large – towards a higher level of abstraction in business process management. In: Janssen, M., Lamersdorf, W., Pries-Heje, J., Rosemann, M. (eds.) E-Government, E-Services and Global Processes – Joint IFIP TC 8 and TC 6 International Conferences, EGES 2010 and GISP 2010, Held as Part of WCC 2010, Brisbane, Australia, September 20-23, 2010. Proceedings. IFIP Advances in Information and Communication Technology, vol. 334, pp. 233–244. Springer, Berlin, Heidelberg (2010). https://doi.org/10.1007/978-3-642-15346-4_19
21. McCloskey, D.N.: The literary character of economics. Daedalus **113**(3), 97–119 (1984)
22. Meyer, B., Weber, R.: Programming really is simple mathematics (2025). https://arxiv.org/abs/2502.17149
23. Milgrom, P.: Discovering Prices – Auction Design in Markets with Complex Constraints. Columbia University Press (2017)
24. von Neumann, J.: Method in the physical sciences. In: Leary, L.G. (ed.) The Unity of Knowledge, pp. 157–183. Doubleday & Co. (1955)
25. Primiero, G.: On the Foundations of Computing. Oxford (2020)

26. Recker, J., Mendling, J.: The state of the art of business process management research as published in the BPM conference - recommendations for progressing the field. Bus. Inf. Syst. Eng. **58**(1), 55–72 (2016)
27. Rosemann, M., vom Brocke, J.: The six core elements of business process management. In: vom Brocke, J., Rosemann, M. (eds.) Handbook on Business Process Management 1, pp. 107–122. Springer (2010). https://doi.org/10.1007/978-3-642-45100-3_5
28. Scheer, A.W.: ARIS-Business Process Frameworks. Springer Science & Business Media, 3 edn. (2012)
29. Sneed, J.D.: The Logical Structure of Mathematical Physics. Dordrecht (1971)
30. Suppes, P.: Introduction to Logic. Dover Publications, Mineola, N.Y. (1957)
31. Suppes, P.: Representation and Invariance of Scientific Structures. CSLI Publications (2002)
32. Tour, A., Polyvyanyy, A., Kalenkova, A.: Agent system mining: vision, benefits, and challenges. IEEE Access **9**, 99480–99494 (2021)
33. Wand, Y., Weber, R.: An ontological model of an information system. IEEE Trans. Softw. Eng. **16**(11), 1282–1292 (1990)
34. Weber, R.: Ontological Foundations of Information Systems. Coopers & Lybrand (1997)
35. Winter, R.: Working for e-business - the business engineering approach. Int. J. Bus. Stud. **9**(1), 101–117 (2001)
36. Winther, R.G.: The Structure of Scientific Theories. In: Zalta, E.N. (ed.) The Stanford Encyclopedia of Philosophy. Metaphysics Research Lab, Stanford University, Spring 2021 edn. (2021)

# Leveraging the Status Graph in Predictive Process Monitoring Tasks

Giulia Ruffini[1], Riccardo Lo Bianco[2], Laura Genga[2(✉)], Emilio Sulis[1],
and Remco Dijkman[2]

[1] University of Turin, Turin, Italy
[2] Eindhoven University of Technology, Eindhoven, The Netherlands
`l.genga@tue.nl`

**Abstract.** Predictive Process Monitoring aims at forecasting how ongoing process executions will unfold. Recent advancements have shown the advantages of leveraging contextual and inter-case features for increasing the accuracy of the prediction. However, existing methodologies are based on feature engineering. This study introduces the novel concept of a Status Graph, a comprehensive graph representation of the status of all ongoing executions, incorporating all active cases and their interdependencies. By leveraging graph neural networks in predictive process monitoring tasks, the proposed approach eliminates the need for feature engineering, enabling the model to learn directly from graph structures. A proof-of-concept implementation shows improvements for the next activity and remaining completion time prediction tasks.

**Keywords:** Predictive Process Monitoring · Process Mining · Graph Neural Network

## 1 Introduction

Predictive Process Monitoring (PPM) is an emerging field within Process Mining aiming at predicting how ongoing process executions will unfold [8,15]. Traditionally, PPM has focused on intra-case features, which describe single process executions in isolation. In reality, however, business processes are usually not executed in isolation.

As an example, let us consider the scenario of an Emergency Department (ED). Table 1 provides an excerpt of an example event log tracking the trajectories of three patients at the ED. Each patient undergoes a series of medical activities, starting with a *Triage* activity (T), during which their medical history is recorded and initial examinations are conducted. Depending on the urgency code assigned, patients may proceed to further tests, such as *Blood Test* (BT), *Computed Tomography Scan* (CT), *Electrocardiogram* (EKG) or *Consultation* (C) with specialists. Depending on the test results and the consultation results, the patient will be either *admitted* (A) to the hospital or *discharged* (D). A critical challenge for the application of PPM in this scenario arises, for instance,


J. Mendling et al. (Eds.): Wil van der Aalst Festschrift, LNCS 16480, pp. 82–96, 2026.
https://doi.org/10.1007/978-3-032-17618-9_7

**Table 1.** Example Scenario Log

| Event | Case ID | Activity | Timestamp |
|-------|---------|----------|-----------|
| $e_1$ | A | Triage | 1 |
| $e_2$ | A | Blood Test | 6 |
| $e_3$ | A | EKG | 8 |
| $e_4$ | A | Discharge | 10 |
| $e_5$ | B | Triage | 2 |
| $e_6$ | B | Blood Test | 3 |
| $e_7$ | B | EKG | 4 |
| $e_8$ | B | CT Scan | 5 |
| $e_9$ | B | Blood Test | 7 |
| $e_{10}$ | B | Admission | 8 |
| $e_{11}$ | C | Triage | 3 |
| $e_{12}$ | C | Blood Test | 8 |
| $e_{13}$ | C | Consultation | 10 |
| $e_{14}$ | C | Discharge | 11 |

when shared resources, such as laboratory equipment or medical personnel, are required by multiple patients simultaneously, thereby influencing the completion time of the process.

In our example, Patient A, after T at time 1, waits until time 6 for the BT. A similar gap between these activities is observed for Patient C, which, with T at time 3, moves to BT at time 8. If we analyse Patient B's trace, however, we notice that the patient undergoes T at time 2, does the BT at time 3 and then the EKG at time 4, the CTS at time 5 and another BT at time 7. This might happen, for example, because Patient B has a more urgent code, and there are not enough nurses available to carry out the tests for multiple patients in parallel. Hence, Patient A waits for BT until Patient B is done. Then, Patient C waits for Patient A to finish. This simple scenario highlights the existence of interdependencies among different process executions caused, in this example, by shared resources, which result in one execution impacting the overall waiting time of the others. However, analysing patients' traces in isolation, as done by most state-of-the-art predictive process monitoring techniques, these interdependencies would go unnoticed.

To address this challenge, an emerging trend within PPM proposes to take these relations into account by considering also *inter-case* features for the prediction, which allow for capturing and accounting for potential interactions among different executions running concurrently. To this end, most state-of-the-art approaches have introduced a number of features describing different kinds of inter-execution properties. Examples include the number of active cases [17], or the number and the availability of shared resources [12]. While experiments did demonstrate the relevance of these features in obtaining accurate predictions, they are usually manually crafted within a feature engingeering step, which is far from trivial and whose results are challenging to generalize to different processes. Indeed, different execution contexts are likely to be affected differently by different inter-case features, which are challenging to grasp without an in-depth knowledge of the process.

A promising strategy to address this gap is to directly model the *comprehensive status* of a process, incorporating all ongoing activities for each active case, together with their properties. Leveraging such global representation when training a classifier would allow the latter to identify patterns and interdependencies between the status of the execution at hand and the status of all the other active executions without requiring explicit feature engineering. To the best of our knowledge, however, no existing approach has introduced such a representation.

To fill this gap, we introduce a novel concept, the *Status Graph*, which is a graph providing a snapshot of the state of the overall system at a given time, i.e., the state of all active process executions. This representation can directly be fed to a Graph Neural Network (GNN) for prediction, that can learn directly from raw graph structures. As a proof of concept, we test our approach on nine datasets previously used in literature. The experiments show improvements in both next-activity and remaining time prediction tasks when compared to a classifier and a regressor only relying on intra-case features.

To summarize, the main contributions of our work are as follows

1. **Definition of the Status Graph**: we formally define the Status Graph as a representation of the current state of a process.
2. **PPM with Status Graphs**: we propose a novel PPM approach that utilises Status Graphs as input to GNNs.
3. **Proof of concept**: we demonstrate how GNNs can learn from Status Graphs without requiring explicit feature engineering.

The remainder of the paper is organized as follows: Sect. 2 provides a review of related work; Sect. 3 presents the theoretical background; Sect. 4 presents the new definition of Status Graph; Sect. 5 outlines our proposed methodology; Sect. 6 presents and discusses our experimental results; and Sect. 7 concludes the paper.

## 2   Related Work

PPM has garnered significant attention in recent years, being applied to multiple tasks using various techniques across different domains [8,9,18]. A recent trend in PPM focuses on the types of features leveraged to improve predictions, particularly inter-case features. Table 2 provides an overview on recent related work, highlighting the inter-case features and the predictive models adopted. It should be noted that all of these approaches aim at predicting time-related KPIs, typically the remaining execution time. Only [11] also considered the next-activity prediction task.

**Table 2.** Summary of related works

| Study | Inter-Case Features | Predictive model |
|---|---|---|
| [17] | Number of active cases for each a-priori known type; distance from $K$ similar cases | Random forest, Gradient tree boosting |
| [12] | Activity frequencies and immediate predecessor; activity count per resource and resource group; averaged elapsed time of anchor events and average delta of end events; number of cases sharing common attribute values | Regression tree |
| [13] | Number of active cases in a location; number of cases processed at a location in an optimal time window | Random forest regressor |
| [14] | Time until batching; Batching partition | Random forest, XGBoost |
| [16] | Belonging to a segment with high prediction error; occurence of a predefined batching pattern; waiting time due to the batching pattern | Random forest, XGBoost |
| [6] | Concurrent cases and resource utilization | GNNs |
| [2] | Control-flow (e.g., previous and follow activity count), data-flow (e.g., aggregated previous data values), resource (e.g., the current resource workload and the total workload) performance (e.g., execution time, or waiting time) and objects (e.g., current total object count) inter-case features | Linear Regression, LSTM, GNN |
| [11] | Number of related objects | LSTM |
| [10] | Raw objects, Aggregator operators | CatBoost |
| [3] | Aggregator operators on object and on object connections | Tree regressor |
| [1] | Process Executions | GNNs |

Several previous works introduced different features to capture potential interdependencies among concurrent process executions. For instance, [17] proposes both a knowledge-driven and a data-driven approach. The former assumes cases to be a priori categorized in a set of types, then uses the number of active cases for each type as inter-case features. The latter employs a multidimensional distance metric considering the control-flow and the temporal dimensions, then computing these distances with respect to the $K$ closest executions and using them as inter-case features. [12] proposes a conceptual framework introducing different inter-case features for each process perspective, i.e., the control-flow, the resource, the time and the data perspective, computed over cases in the same time window. For their experiments, they consider for the control-flow the frequency of each activity in the trace in the peer cases and the most frequent immediate predecessor; for the resource, the activity count per resource and per resource group; for the time perspective, the average elapsed time of activities that correspond to a predefined anchor event, and the average delay or earliness of end events in peer cases; finally, for the data perspective, they count the number of cases that share some known attribute values. [13] enriches the events with information on the load state of one or more locations (i.e., activities) of interest. The load state can be computed by counting all currently active cases whose most recent event's activity label matches the defined location, or the number of cases which have passed through a specific location of interest during an optimized time window. Other approaches, like [14,16] leverage the performance spectrum of process segments, presented in [5], to enrich data with batching and inter-case dynamics. [14] leverages batch mining approaches and predictive models to estimate whether a current case will fall into a batching pattern and how long it will take to be processed, then converting this information in a batching feature, either in terms of absolute time before the batching ends or by considering a partition of the batching time. [16] follows a similar approach, leveraging a taxonomy describing batching behaviors and implementing predictive models to estimate whether a prefix belongs to an uncertain segment and the expected waiting time until batching. The work from Diamantini et al. [6] leverages graphs to represent process executions, and encodes the number of concurrent cases and the resource utilization as inter-case features. Recently, some works in the literature have proposed leveraging the Object-Centric paradigm to take into account interactions between different processes. [10,11] propose to flatten the event log and then deriving object-related features. The former enriches the flattened log with the number of related objects, in particular items in an order handling process. The latter considers both features modelling raw objects related to the main viewpoint chosen for flattening the log and aggregation operator. Authors in [2] introduce an object-centric definition of features previously defined for the case-centric perspective, considering the control-flow (e.g., previous and follow activity count), the data-flow (e.g., aggregated previous characteristic values), the resource (e.g., the current resource workload and the total workload) and the performance (e.g., execution time, or waiting time) and objects (e.g., current total object count) perspectives[1]. They advocate the use of a the native, graph structure of object-centric event log to avoid errors in feature extraction occurring when flattening the log. Authors in [3] propose different graphs modelling different relations among objects and propose a set of aggregator operators applied on the objects and on their connections. The approaches discussed so far rely on manual crafting of features representing inter-case dependencies. An approach closer to our work is discussed in [1], where process executions are encoded as graphs, thus encoding everything belonging to that execution, including objects and their relations with other objects and events. However, this notion is substantially different from our Status Graph: a single Process Execution is a single connected component of the entire state, thus implying the existence of different process executions non considered in prediction for the process execution considered. Our Status Graph, instead, represents the entire state of the process in the form of a disconnected union of execution graphs.

---

[1] We do not report the complete feature list here nor in Table 2 for the sake of space.

# 3   Background

In this section, we recall some definitions used throughout the paper, adapted from [4]. Executions of a process, so-called *process instances*, are recorded in *event logs*.

**Definition 1** (Event, Trace, Log). *Let $A$ be the set of all activity names, $C$ be the set of all case (aka, process instance) identifiers, $H$ be the set of all timestamps, $U$ a set of variable values, $V$ a set of variable names. An **event** $e = (a, D, c, t, v) \in A \times (V \nrightarrow U) \times C \times J \times H$ is a tuple consisting of an executed activity $a \in A$, a function $D$ which assigns a value to some process variables (possibly all of them), a case identifier $c \in C$ and a number $i \in J \in N$, where $J = \{i \in N : i = 1, 2, \ldots, k = length(case)\}$. A **case** corresponds to a single process execution; the number $i$ identifies the position of the event within the sequence of events that occurred within a case. The set of events is denoted by $E$. An **event trace** $\sigma_L \in E^*$ is a sequence of events with the same case id. An **event log** is a multi-set of event traces $L$.*

**Definition 2** (Prefix Trace). *A **prefix** of length $k$ of a trace $\sigma = \langle e_1, e_2, \ldots, e_n \rangle \in E^*$, is a trace $p_k(\sigma) = \langle e_1, e_2, \ldots, e_k \rangle \in E^*$ where $k \leq n$.*

A well known issue of log traces is that events are logged in a trace according to the timestamp of the corresponding activities, hiding possible concurrency among activities. To address this issue, Instance Graphs [7] can be used to convert log traces. Instance graphs are directed, acyclic graphs which represent the real execution flow of process activities, explicitly modelling concurrency.

**Definition 3** (Instance Graph). *Let $\sigma = \langle e_1, \ldots, e_n \rangle \in L$ be a trace of a case. The **Instance Graph (or IG)** $\gamma_\sigma$ of $\sigma$ is a directed acyclic graph $(E, W)$ where:*

- *$E = \{e \in \sigma\}$ is the set of nodes, corresponding to the events occurring in $\sigma$.*
- *$W = \{(e_h, e_k) \in E \times E \mid h < k \wedge act(e_h) \rightarrow act(e_k) \wedge (\forall e_q \in E(h < q < k \Rightarrow act(e_h) \nrightarrow act(e_q)) \vee \forall e_w \in E(h < w < k \wedge act(e_w) \nrightarrow act(e_k))\}$ is the set of edges, defining a partial order over $E$.*

Instance Graphs can be obtained from sequential traces using different strategies. This paper refers to the Building Instance Graphs (BIG) approach proposed in [7]. BIG takes as input an event log and a process model (either defined by domain experts or mined by well-known process discovery techniques). The latter is used to derive the ordering relations (i.e., dependency and concurrency) among the process activities. These relations are leveraged to convert sequential traces in IGs. BIG handles traces that do not conform to the model by using conformance checking techniques to detect deviations and implementing a repairing procedure to adjust the affected IGs (e.g., by manipulating the edges to properly connect nodes corresponding to activities executed in violations of the process model).

**Definition 4** (Prefix Instance Graph). *Let $(E, W)$ be the instance graph of some trace $\sigma$. Let $\tilde{E}_k$ be the set of events in the prefix trace $p_k(\sigma)$ of size $k$. We define the **prefix instance graph** of size $k$ of $\sigma$ as the graph $p_k((E, W)) = (\tilde{E}_k, W \cap (\tilde{E}_k \times \tilde{E}_k))$. Informally, a graph prefix $p_k(g_j)$ is a subgraph of $g_j$ involving only $k$ nodes of $g_j$, i.e., nodes included in the corresponding trace prefix.*

**Fig. 1.** Instance Graph Case A.　　**Fig. 2.** Instance Graph Case B

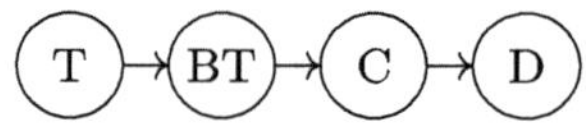


**Fig. 3.** Instance Graph Case C.

## 4　Status Graph

Let us consider the log provided in Table 1 and let us suppose that the Instance Graphs of cases A, B and C correspond to Fig. 1, 2, 3, respectively. The Status Graph for an event is the set of all prefix instance graphs of the concurrent cases at the event considered. Table 3 collects the Status Graphs for the first six events of Table 1. For example, consider $e_1$ in Table 1: since it happens at time 1, its Status corresponds to all prefix instance graphs of concurrent cases with events (and relations) happened before or at time of $e_1$, that is the first event of case A. For $e_2$, instead, since the time is 6, all three cases are active and the Status Graph is composed of the prefix instance graph of case A with activities *Triage* and *Blood Test*, the prefix instance graph of case B with activities *Triage*, *Blood Test*, *EKG* and *CT Scan*, and the prefix instance graph of case C with activity *Triage*. The Status Graph is created following a similar logic for all the remaining events. In other words, the Status Graph is the union of different graphs (a sub-instance graph for each active case) and represents the state of the process, as a panoramic view of all that is happening at a particular moment in time.

Formally:

**Definition 5** (Status Graph). *Let $L$ be an event log. Let $\sigma \in L$ be a trace of $L$. Let $e \in \sigma$ be an event of the trace $\sigma$ and $\pi_{time}(e) = v$ its timestamp. The status of the process for the event $e$, that is $S_e$, is the union of all prefix instance graphs $p_k(\gamma_j)$ with $\pi_{time}(e) \leq \pi_{time}(e_n^j)$ and $\pi_{time}(e_k^j) \leq \pi_{time}(e)$, if $p_k(\sigma_j) = \langle e_1^j, ..., e_k^j \rangle$ is the prefix traces of $p_k(\gamma_j)$ and $\sigma_j = \langle e_1^j, ..., e_n^j \rangle$ is the trace from which $p_k(\sigma_j)$ is extracted. More formally:*

$$S_e = \bigcup_{p_k(\gamma_j)} \{ p_k(\gamma_j) \mid \pi_{time}(e) \leq \pi_{time}(e_n^j) \wedge \pi_{time}(e_k^j) \leq \pi_{time}(e),$$

$$p_k(\sigma_j) = \langle e_1^j, ..., e_k^j \rangle, \sigma_j = \langle e_1^j, ..., e_n^j \rangle \}$$

**Table 3.** Status Graph for the first six events of Table 1

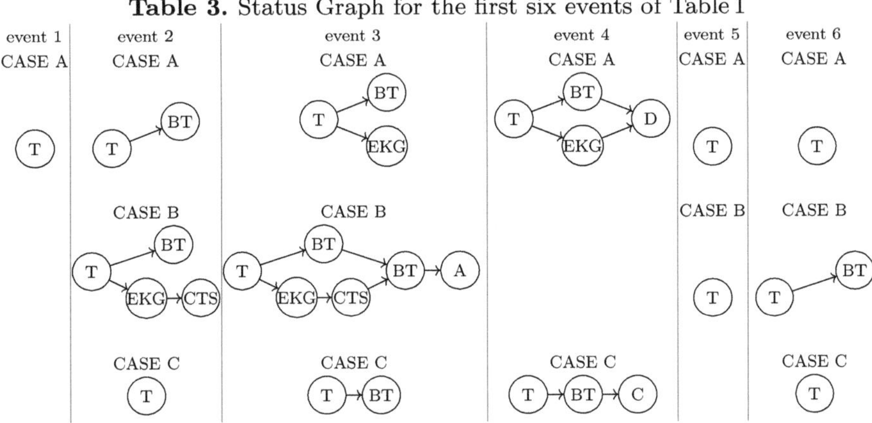

## 5    SG-GNN Methodology

Figure 4 provides an overview of our method, which starts from an event log and its process model expressed as a Petri Net. We first apply the BIG algorithm [7] to obtain the set of Instance Graphs. Then, we pre-process the event log to add the target features for the prediction. We then proceed to create the set of Status Graphs (one for each event in the log), which is finally used to train the GNN. The following paragraphs elaborate on each step of the approach.

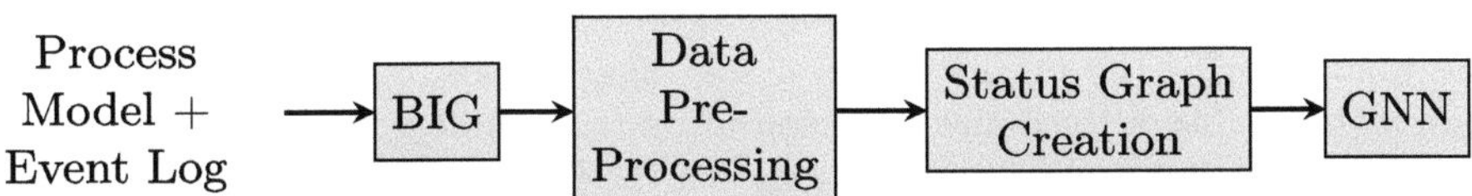

**Fig. 4.** The SG-GNN methodology pipeline.

*Building Instance Graphs.* The Building Instance Graph algorithm takes as input an event log and a process model and converts each sequential trace into a direct acyclic graph where nodes correspond to the trace events and edges correspond to the process ordering relations. If a trace includes events non-compliant with the provided process model, the algorithm includes a repair procedure to manipulate the graph to represent the ordering relations between compliant and non-compliant events while adhering to the original set of causal relations as much as possible. More information can be found in [7].

*Data Pre-processing.* This step annotates the original dataset with the target features necessary for the prediction tasks.

*Creating the Status Graph.* This step takes as input the event log and the instance graphs for each case in the log and produces as output the set of Status Graphs, one for each event. The procedure is as follows:

1. for each event in the log, we take all events that happened before, listed by case and timestamp. If a case is complete, it will be eliminated from the list.
2. with the list of ongoing cases and related activities, we can extract from Instance Graphs the prefix instance graph for each case. The Status Graph for the considered event is the union of all the so-created prefix instance graphs.

The implementation for the generation of the SG can be found at https://github. com/Djouck/statusGraph.

*Graph Neural Network Implementation.* The regression and classification tasks described in this work are performed using GNNs, similarly to [4]. The architectures devised for the two tasks follow the encoder-decoder paradigm, where an encoder is responsible for creating a hidden representation of the input data, and a decoder processes the hidden representation produced by the encoder to provide the desired output. The input data is the same for both tasks, namely, the status graph. Thus, we employ the same encoder architecture for both, which can be seen as the composition of two distinct encoders: the current graph encoder and the concurrent graphs encoder.

The current graph encoder is responsible for processing individual graphs. It employs a series of convolutional layers to transform the input features into a hidden representation. It initialises with a specified number of input channels and hidden channels, and it utilises three layers of convolution operations. Each layer applies a convolution operation followed by a ReLU activation function. The final layer of the encoder uses a sort aggregation mechanism to pool the node features into a fixed-size representation, to handle graphs of varying sizes.

The concurrent graphs encoder extends the functionality of the first encoder to handle sets of graphs. It processes each graph in the set individually through an encoder with the same structure as the current graph encoder. Then, it computes the mean representation of all encoded graphs. This approach allows the concurrent graphs encoder to aggregate information from multiple graphs, providing a fixed-size representation of the concurrent graphs.

The decoder structure depends on the prediction task. To handle the classification task, the decoder must transform the encoded graph representations into class predictions. One unidimensional convolutional layer processes the encoded current graph features, while another handles the features from additional graphs. The outputs of the convolutional layers are then concatenated and passed through two linear layers and a logarithmic softmax layer to produce the final class predictions. The network employs ReLU activations and dropout regularization to prevent overfitting. The loss function used for training is the negative log-likelihood.

To handle the regression task, the decoder must transform the encoded graph representations into continuous output values. One unidimensional convolutional

**Table 4.** Overview of benchmark dataset. $|\sigma|$ represents the trace length.

| Dataset | N.traces | Tot.Events | N.act.types | Min $|\sigma|$ | Max $|\sigma|$ | Avg $|\sigma|$ | n_months |
|---|---|---|---|---|---|---|---|
| Prepaid | 2099 | 18246 | 29 | 1 | 21 | 9 | 18 |
| RfP | 6886 | 50568 | 21 | 1 | 20 | 7 | 12 |
| TP | 7065 | 86581 | 51 | 3 | 90 | 12 | 6 |
| International | 6499 | 72151 | 34 | 3 | 27 | 11 | 5 |
| HelpDesk | 3804 | 13710 | 9 | 1 | 14 | 3 | All |
| BPI12_SE | 13087 | 262200 | 23 | 3 | 175 | 38 | All |
| BPIW12_SE | 9658 | 72413 | 6 | 1 | 74 | 20 | All |
| BPIC11 | 240 | 38854 | 142 | 2 | 1814 | 162 | 10 |
| BPI15 | 689 | 28504 | 280 | 2 | 101 | 41 | 6 |

layer processes the encoded current graph features, while another handles the features from additional graphs. The outputs of the convolutional layers are then concatenated and passed through additional linear layers to produce the final regression output. The network employs ReLU activations and dropout regularization in the same way as the classification decoder. The loss function used for training is the mean squared error.

## 6 Proof-of-Concept Implementation

This section describes the proof-of-concept we carried out on nine real-world datasets. We limit our analysis to the results obtained i) without any inter-case information, ii) with the number of active cases as inter-case feature (a commonly used feature in literature), and iii) with the Status Graph information. A comprehensive experimentation and benchmark are left to future research.

*Datasets.* We considered nine datasets well established in the literature. The *HelpDesk* dataset refers to a ticketing management process of an Italian company helpdesk. The BPI12 dataset refers to personal loan applications of a global financing organization. We considered BPI12 (BPI12_SE) and BPIW12 (BPIW12_SE) datasets, which relate to the work items associated with the application. *Prepaid Travel Cost* (Prepaid), *Travel Permit* (TP), *Request for Payment* (RfP), and *International Declaration* (International) belong to a reimbursement process at a Dutch university, focusing respectively on travel expense claims for prepayment, travel permit and declarations, cost declaration referred to expenses not related to trips, and international travel expense claims. BPIC11 contains cases from a Dutch Hospital and BPI15 refers to building permit application from a Dutch municipalities. Table 4 provides an overview of the datasets. In most datasets, we considered only a temporal fraction of the datasets to prevent an exponential increase in runtime, specified as *n_months* in the table.

**Table 5.** Experimental results: classification task

| Dataset | Accuracy | | | F1 Score | | |
|---|---|---|---|---|---|---|
| | GNN | GNNc | GNNs | GNN | GNNc | GNNs |
| Prepaid | 0.661 | 0.804 | **0.817** | 0.642 | 0.779 | **0.790** |
| RfP | 0.852 | **0.881** | 0.876 | 0.826 | 0.837 | **0.867** |
| TP | **0.633** | 0.516 | 0.573 | **0.572** | 0.485 | 0.504 |
| International | **0.885** | 0.547 | 0.764 | **0.872** | 0.473 | 0.721 |
| HelpDesk | 0.748 | 0.757 | **0.760** | 0.706 | **0.728** | 0.719 |
| BPIW12_SE | 0.682 | 0.692 | **0.710** | 0.644 | 0.664 | **0.695** |
| BPI12_SE | **0.430** | 0.365 | 0.413 | 0.366 | 0.286 | **0.374** |
| BPIC11 | **0.117** | 0.022 | 0.097 | **0.063** | 0.016 | 0.039 |
| BPI15 | 0.144 | 0.155 | **0.163** | 0.091 | **0.113** | **0.113** |

*Results.* We used a train-test split setting where 70% of the data is used for training, 15% for validation, and 15% for testing. The temporal order of samples is preserved to avoid data leakage. The maximum number of epochs is $10^2$, and early stopping with patience of 10 epochs is used to avoid overfitting.

In Table 5, we report the accuracy and F1 score obtained by the GNN with the entire status graphs (GNNs), and by the same GNN that is only fed with the current graph, without (GNN) and with (GNNc) the number of active cases as additional input feature, to assess the advantage of using the status graphs against the aggregate information regarding the number of active cases.

The next activity prediction task is a multiclass classification problem. In terms of accuracy, the GNNs outperforms the competitors for four datasets out of nine (Prepaid, HelpDesk, BPI15 and BPIW12_SE). The vanilla GNN also obtained the best results for four datasets (TP, International, BPIW12_SE and BPIC11), while GNNc was the winner approach only for RfP. Interestingly, the F1 score results show a similar trend, with a slight improvement for both the inter-case features models, which are now the winners for five (GNNs) and two (GNNc) datasets. It should be noted that for the last three datasets, all the models performed poorly, suggesting that no GNN was actually able to successfully learn a robust predictive model for these datasets. For the other datasets, the inter-case features models tend to perform better, suggesting the importance of inter-case dependencies for the prediction. GNNs tend to perform better than GNNc, though the performances are often close, suggesting that the number of cases is an impactful feature for the prediction. A notable excetion is represented by the International dataset, where the vanilla GNN significantly outperforms the other models, suggesting that considering inter-case features for this dataset has an overall detrimental effect for the classifier. It is worth noting that while GNNs still manages to score an overall good result, scoring higher than 70% both in terms of accuracy and F1score, GNNc performance drop to 54% and to

**Table 6.** Experimental results: regression task

| Dataset | MSE | | | R2 Score | | |
|---|---|---|---|---|---|---|
| | GNN | GNNc | GNNs | GNN | GNNc | GNNs |
| Prepaid | 0.774 | **0.633** | 0.846 | 0.276 | **0.294** | 0.159 |
| RfP | 1.661 | 0.801 | **0.254** | **0.256** | 0.175 | 0.171 |
| TP | **0.545** | 0.772 | 0.765 | **0.373** | 0.337 | 0.196 |
| International | 0.066 | **0.049** | 0.054 | 0.930 | **0.949** | 0.945 |
| HelpDesk | 0.824 | **0.794** | 0.805 | 0.208 | **0.237** | 0.227 |
| BPIW12_SE | 0.829 | **0.717** | **0.717** | 0.177 | **0.289** | **0.289** |
| BPI12_SE | 0.647 | 0.770 | **0.645** | 0.318 | 0.187 | **0.320** |
| BPIC11 | 0.216 | 0.016 | **0.004** | 0.790 | 0.984 | **0.996** |
| BPI15 | 1.114 | **1.092** | 1.111 | 0.111 | **0.128** | 0.113 |

47% respectively, suggesting that the number of active cases for this dataset is not relevant for the next-activity prediction task and it mostly adds noise.

The remaining time prediction task is a regression problem for targets whose variance is very high. To handle the high variance, the targets were normalized on the mean and variance of the targets in the training set. The results in Table 6 are expressed in terms of the mean square error (MSE) and the R2 score. Table 6 shows that GNN using inter-case features overall outperform the vanilla GNN, which obtains the best MSE only for the TP dataset and the best R2 Score for the TP and the RfP datasets. However, GNNc performs slightly better than GNNs, obtaining the best results for both metrics in four datasets (Prepaid, International, HelpDesk and BPI15), and matching GNNs for the BPIW12_SE dataset. GNNs performs better in one or the other metric for the remaining datasets, though it is worth noting that it achieves similar performance to GNNc even when it's not the best model. These results suggest that the number of running cases is important for predicting the remaining time, in line with observations in the literature. Nevertheless, our approach manages to obtain close or superior performance without the need for manually engineering inter-case features.

We would like to point out that the results for both the next-activity and the remaining time tasks were obtained without extensive parameter tuning, which could prove useful in further improving the results.

# 7   Conclusion

The paper has presented the concept of the Status Graph for capturing the whole state of a process, considering all active cases and their interdependencies. By leveraging GNNs and the Status Graph, the proposed approach eliminates the need for feature engineering, enabling the model to learn directly from the graph structure. Experimental results on benchmark datasets for next-activity and remaining time prediction tasks are promising, as they demonstrate the effectiveness of this method, which overall outperforms the model based on intra-case features only, while achieving comparable and often better performance than the tested competitor that leverages a manually engineered inter-case feature.

Given its proof-of-concept nature, this study comes with certain limitations. First, the current experimental set is too limited to draw general conclusions about the advantages of leveraging the status graph. We plan to tackle this challenge in future work through extensive experimentation on different datasets and different classifiers. Furthermore, the current implementation of the approach presents scalability issues, as the generation of the status graph is computationally expensive, and so is the training of the GNN. More sophisticated strategies can be implemented to improve the computational aspect. Another promising venue for future research is to investigate whether enriching the Status Graph with external or contextual data could improve prediction accuracy.

# References


1. Adams, J.N., Park, G., van der Aalst, W.M.P.: Preserving complex object-centric graph structures to improve machine learning tasks in process mining. Eng. Appl. Artif. Intell. **125**, 106764 (2023). https://doi.org/10.1016/J.ENGAPPAI.2023.106764
2. Adams, J.N., Park, G., Levich, S., Schuster, D., van der Aalst, W.M.P.: A framework for extracting and encoding features from object-centric event data. In: Troya, J., Medjahed, B., Piattini, M., Yao, L., Fernández, P., Ruiz-Cortés, A. (eds.) Service-Oriented Computing - 20th International Conference, ICSOC 2022, Seville, Spain, November 29 - December 2, 2022, Proceedings. Lecture Notes in Computer Science, vol. 13740, pp. 36–53. Springer (2022). https://doi.org/10.1007/978-3-031-20984-0_3
3. Berti, A., Herforth, J., Qafari, M.S., van der Aalst, W.M.: Graph-based feature extraction on object-centric event logs. Int. J. Data Sci. Anal. **18**(2), 139–155 (2023). https://doi.org/10.1007/s41060-023-00428-2
4. Chiorrini, A., Diamantini, C., Genga, L., Potena, D.: Multi-perspective enriched instance graphs for next activity prediction through graph neural network. J. Intell. Inf. Syst. **61**(1), 5–25 (2023). https://doi.org/10.1007/S10844-023-00777-1
5. Denisov, V., Fahland, D., van der Aalst, W.M.P.: Unbiased, fine-grained description of processes performance from event data. In: Weske, M., Montali, M., Weber, I., vom Brocke, J. (eds.) BPM 2018. LNCS, vol. 11080, pp. 139–157. Springer, Cham (2018). https://doi.org/10.1007/978-3-319-98648-7_9
6. Diamantini, C., Genga, L., Mele, A., Potena, D.: Impact of inter-case features on structure-aware next activity prediction. In: 2024 International Conference on AI x Data and Knowledge Engineering (AIxDKE), pp. 98–103 (2024). https://doi.org/10.1109/AIxDKE63520.2024.00025
7. Diamantini, C., Genga, L., Potena, D., van der Aalst, W.M.P.: Building instance graphs for highly variable processes. Expert Syst. Appl. **59**, 101–118 (2016). https://doi.org/10.1016/J.ESWA.2016.04.021
8. Francescomarino, C.D., Ghidini, C.: Predictive process monitoring. In: van der Aalst, W.M.P., Carmona, J. (eds.) Process Mining Handbook, Lecture Notes in

Business Information Processing, vol. 448, pp. 320–346. Springer (2022). https://doi.org/10.1007/978-3-031-08848-3_10

9. Francescomarino, C.D., Ghidini, C., Maggi, F.M., Milani, F.: Predictive process monitoring methods: which one suits me best? In: Weske, M., Montali, M., Weber, I., vom Brocke, J. (eds.) Business Process Management - 16th International Conference, BPM 2018, Sydney, NSW, Australia, September 9-14, 2018, Proceedings. Lecture Notes in Computer Science, vol. 11080, pp. 462–479. Springer (2018). https://doi.org/10.1007/978-3-319-98648-7_27

10. Galanti, R., de Leoni, M., Navarin, N., Marazzi, A.: Object-centric process predictive analytics. Expert Syst. Appl. **213**(Part), 119173 (2023). https://doi.org/10.1016/J.ESWA.2022.119173

11. Gherissi, W., El Haddad, J., Grigori, D.: Object-centric predictive process monitoring. In: Troya, J., et al. (eds.) Service-Oriented Computing – ICSOC 2022 Workshops, pp. 27–39. Springer Nature Switzerland, Cham (2023). https://doi.org/10.1007/978-3-031-26507-5_3

12. Grinvald, A., Soffer, P., Mokryn, O.: Inter-case properties and process variant considerations in time prediction: a conceptual framework. In: Augusto, A., Gill, A., Nurcan, S., Reinhartz-Berger, I., Schmidt, R., Zdravkovic, J. (eds.) Enterprise, Business-Process and Information Systems Modeling, pp. 96–111. Springer International Publishing, Cham (2021). https://doi.org/10.1007/978-3-030-79186-5_7

13. Gunnarsson, B.R., Weerdt, J.D., vanden Broucke, S.: A framework for encoding the multi-location load state of a business process. In: Giacomo, G.D., Guzzo, A., Montali, M., Limonad, L., Fournier, F., Chakraborti, T. (eds.) Proceedings of the Workshop on Process Management in the AI Era (PMAI 2022) co-located with 31st International Joint Conference on Artificial Intelligence and the 25th European Conference on Artificial Intelligence (IJCAI-ECAI 2022), Wien, Austria, July 23, 2022. CEUR Workshop Proceedings, vol. 3310, pp. 13–24. CEUR-WS.org (2022). https://ceur-ws.org/Vol-3310/paper2.pdf

14. Klijn, E.L., Fahland, D.: Identifying and reducing errors in remaining time prediction due to inter-case dynamics. In: van Dongen, B.F., Montali, M., Wynn, M.T. (eds.) 2nd International Conference on Process Mining, ICPM 2020, Padua, Italy, October 4-9, 2020, pp. 25–32. IEEE (2020). https://doi.org/10.1109/ICPM49681.2020.00015

15. Maggi, F.M., Francescomarino, C.D., Dumas, M., Ghidini, C.: Predictive monitoring of business processes. In: Jarke, M., Mylopoulos, J., Quix, C., Rolland, C., Manolopoulos, Y., Mouratidis, H., Horkoff, J. (eds.) Advanced Information Systems Engineering - 26th International Conference, CAiSE 2014, Thessaloniki, Greece, June 16-20, 2014. Proceedings. Lecture Notes in Computer Science, vol. 8484, pp. 457–472. Springer (2014). https://doi.org/10.1007/978-3-319-07881-6_31

16. Pourbafrani, M., Kar, S., Kaiser, S., van der Aalst, W.M.P.: Remaining time prediction for processes with inter-case dynamics. In: Munoz-Gama, J., Lu, X. (eds.) Process Mining Workshops - ICPM 2021 International Workshops, Eindhoven, The Netherlands, October 31 - November 4, 2021, Revised Selected Papers. Lecture Notes in Business Information Processing, vol. 433, pp. 140–153. Springer (2021). https://doi.org/10.1007/978-3-030-98581-3_11

17. Senderovich, A., Francescomarino, C.D., Maggi, F.M.: From knowledge-driven to data-driven inter-case feature encoding in predictive process monitoring. Inf. Syst. **84**, 255–264 (2019). https://doi.org/10.1016/J.IS.2019.01.007
18. Teinemaa, I., Dumas, M., Rosa, M.L., Maggi, F.M.: Outcome-oriented predictive process monitoring: review and benchmark. ACM Trans. Knowl. Discov. Data **13**(2), 17:1–17:57 (2019). https://doi.org/10.1145/3301300

# The Process of Process Science – Generating Actionable Insights from Digital Trace Data

Jan vom Brocke[1,2,3], Sandro Franzoi[1,2(✉)], Sophie Hartl[3], and Thomas Grisold[4]

[1] University of Münster, Münster, Germany
`sandro.franzoi@uni-muenster.de`
[2] European Research Center for Information Systems, Münster, Germany
[3] University of Liechtenstein, Vaduz, Liechtenstein
[4] Wirtschaftsuniversität Wien, Vienna, Austria

**Abstract.** Process science is an interdisciplinary field that concerns the study of socio-technical processes and their dynamics. While the field offers a compelling conceptual foundation outlining *what* process science is, concrete methodological guidance on *how* to conduct process science studies remains underdeveloped. In this paper, we present the *process of process science*, which conceptualizes critical activities on how to leverage the use of computational techniques, such as process mining, and digital trace data to generate meaningful insights. We frame process science studies as iterative inquiries guided by three core principles: (a) contextual grounding (b) iterative reasoning, and (c) the integration of computational and human sense-making. Building on these principles, we articulate three recursive cycles that constitute the process of process science: (1) a descriptive cycle, (2) an explanatory cycle and (3) a prescriptive cycle. For each cycle, we outline key activities that ensure rigor, relevance, and methodological transparency and illustrate them with the case of a financial institution. Together, these contributions offer methodological guidance for planning, conducting and communicating process science studies. This foundation enables future work to refine the recursive cycles of inquiry, develop tools that better support iterative sense-making, and extend process science across diverse organizational domains.

**Keywords:** Process Science · Methodology · Iteration · Process Mining · Digital Trace Data

## 1 Introduction

The emergence of process science builds on decades of research that have placed processes, rather than static entities, at the center of scientific and organizational inquiry [1, 2]. Within information systems, this development is closely tied to the groundbreaking work on process mining, pioneered by Wil van der Aalst and others, which has provided a computational backbone for studying how processes unfold in practice. Over the past two decades, process mining has matured into a vibrant field, enabling the discovery, conformance checking, and enhancement of real-world processes based on digital trace data [3]. Its success has demonstrated that event logs can serve as a powerful lens to

© The Author(s), under exclusive license to Springer Nature Switzerland AG 2026
J. Mendling et al. (Eds.): Wil van der Aalst Festschrift, LNCS 16480, pp. 97–111, 2026.
https://doi.org/10.1007/978-3-032-17618-9_8

understand and manage organizational change as it occurs. At the same time, process science draws on the broader intellectual foundation of process-oriented thought, from process ontology and philosophy to process organization studies [4, 5]. These traditions share the recognition that social and organizational phenomena are best understood as ongoing processes of becoming rather than as fixed states [6].

Process science thus emerges as an interdisciplinary field devoted to the systematic study of socio-technical processes and their change over time [7]. Socio-technical processes are coherent sequences of actions and events that involve both humans and digital technologies, unfolding across different levels of analysis and producing consequences at individual, organizational, and societal scales. By placing processes at the center of analysis, process science responds to the growing recognition that many of today's most pressing challenges, from digital transformation to sustainability transitions, are best understood as ongoing and continuous processes of change [5, 6].

The rise of process science is coupled with the increasing availability of digital trace data, growing computational power, and the evolution of computational techniques that make it possible to capture and analyze such data [3, 8]. Digital trace data, to this end, refer to records or evidence of activity generated whenever agents interact with digital technologies [9]. Their unique characteristics offer researchers unprecedented opportunities to study socio-technical change and to uncover dynamics that would otherwise remain invisible [10, 11]. Methods such as process mining [3], sequence analysis, and machine learning enable scholars to uncover patterns of activity, detect anomalies, and model temporal dynamics at scales previously unimaginable.

Yet, while computational methods excel at identifying *what* happens in processes, they are insufficient for explaining *why* and *how* processes unfold as they do. Without contextual information and interpretative reasoning, computational outputs remain descriptive snapshots, unable to generate explanatory or prescriptive insights. This understanding calls for a broader paradigm that combines computational techniques with human sense-making, thereby enabling scholars to move from description toward explanation and intervention. In line with vom Brocke et al. [7], process science therefore advances three types of activities: *descriptive process science*, which corresponds to developing visibility and descriptive accounts of how processes unfold; *explanatory process science*, which links observed patterns to their underlying drivers; and *prescriptive process science*, which builds and evaluates interventions for shaping processes in practice. A central challenge (and opportunity) for process science lies in moving iteratively within and between these levels of study.

Despite this conceptual clarity, there remains a lack of methodological support for conducting process science studies in practice. How should a process science study be conducted to generate meaningful and impactful results? While methodological guidance exists on how to technically conduct computational analysis, such as applying process mining techniques [e.g., 12], process scientists lack methodological support on how to combine different methods (e.g., qualitative and computational) and move from the application of such techniques to meaningful insight and relevant impact.

In this chapter, we present a structured account that details the *process of process science*: guidance on how researchers and analysts can navigate the iterative cycles of description, explanation, and prescription that characterize empirical process science studies. We frame the conduct of process science studies as an iterative progression through distinct but interconnected cycles of inquiry. Building on our research experiences from conducting process science studies in complex organizations as well as foundational literature from related fields, we highlight three core methodological principles of process science: *contextual grounding, iterative reasoning,* and the *integration of computational and human sense-making.* On this basis, we introduce the process of process science, a framework for planning, conducting, and communicating process science studies, and illustrate its application through the case of a customer onboarding process in a financial institution. In doing so, the chapter aims to provide both scholars and practitioners with methodological guidance, support them in positioning their work within the broader agenda of process science, and contribute to the interdisciplinary study of socio-technical change.

## 2 Core Principles of Process Science

Process science seeks to understand how socio-technical processes unfold over time, uncover patterns in these activities, and generate insights about underlying process structures [7]. We argue that three guiding principles are central to this endeavor: (1) *contextual grounding,* (2) *iterative reasoning* and (3) *the integration of computational and human sense-making.* These principles provide a conceptual and methodological foundation for studying processes in complex, data-rich organizational settings. Therefore, we outline those three principles in the subsequent sections.

### 2.1 Principle 1: Contextual Grounding

A first core principle of process science is contextual grounding. With *contextual grounding,* we refer to the systematic consideration of the socio-technical environment in which processes occur, ensuring that analyses and interpretations are anchored in the conditions, meanings, and interactions that shape process behavior. It entails recognizing that processes do not occur in isolation, but rather unfold within socio-technical environments that influence how activities are performed and how they manifest in digital trace data [7]. Context can be understood as "the situation within which something exists or happens, and that can help explain it" [13]. In process science, acknowledging context is essential, as it shapes how computational results are interpreted and connected to the realities they represent.

Digital trace data alone provide little information about the conditions in which they were produced. Taking shape through socio-technical activities, such as logging practices or activities within local work routines [14, 15], they showcase what is happening in a given process (or the event log that represents a process, thereof). Importantly, however, they do not explain how actors reasoned, thought or experienced at the time they performed the associated activities [16]. Hence, digital trace data must be looked at by accounting for the context in which they were produced. The study by Badakhshan et al. [17] is a case in point; they emphasize how successful value creation with process mining depends on the integration of contextual information. From a broader angle, then, contextual information is important to ascribe meanings to patterns that consider the settings in which they occur [18]. In other words, interpreting digital trace data requires understanding the environments and the conditions in which they originated [19].

Incorporating contextual awareness into every stage of the research process ensures that process science studies remain theoretically sound and practically relevant. But how can we do that? Existing research highlights approaches that can be helpful here. For instance, van der Aalst and Dustdar [20] distinguish between instance, process, social, and external context, each shaping process behavior in different ways. For process modeling and design, Rosemann et al. [21] distinguish contextual factors into four layers, immediate, internal, external, and environmental, depending on how 'close' they are to the process. Most recently, Franzoi et al. [18] proposed a process mining context taxonomy as a systematic lens for articulating contextual factors by distinguishing between process-immediate, organization-internal, and organization-external context. These perspectives can be helpful for process scientists as they identify how contextual dimensions interact with process dynamics over time.

## 2.2   Principle 2: Iterative Reasoning

Another defining feature of process science is its iterative nature. Hence, the second core principle, *iterative reasoning*, emphasizes a cyclical process of inquiry in which understanding evolves through successive rounds of observation, explanation, and validation. It reflects the recognition that knowledge about processes emerges progressively, as researchers continuously refine their interpretations in light of new evidence and contextual understanding. This principle is grounded in abductive reasoning. Following Sætre and van de Ven [22] the abductive theory-construction process can be understood as a cycle of four interrelated steps: (1) observing and identifying patterns or anomalies in data, (2), confirming these patterns or anomalies, (3) generating plausible explanatory hunches based on these observations, and (4) critically evaluating and refining these hunches against further evidence. In line with this, Lindberg [23] describes abduction as an "iterative alternation of discovery and justification" [23, p. 95], emphasizing that explanation emerges over time rather than being predetermined. At each iteration, emerging patterns in process data are discovered, provisional explanations are formulated, and these explanations are tested, justified, and refined. This aligns with Sahaym et al. [24], who describe understanding as a recursive process of generating inductive guesses and then performing deductive validation until 'no apparent absurdities' remain.

In the context of process science, computational methods, for example process mining, provide the foundation for iterative discovery. Here, techniques such as process discovery or conformance checking can reveal unexpected patterns in event logs [3]. Researchers or analysts then formulate abductive hypotheses to explain why these patterns occur; for instance, deviations from prescribed workflows, which may result from workarounds [25], or performance bottlenecks arising from resource constraints, as revealed by actor-centered analyses [26], among other things. Accounting for contextual information (Principle 1), these hypotheses are subsequently tested and refined through additional process mining analyses, cross-validation with other event logs, or qualitative contextual inquiry, such as interviews and document analysis [18].

Iterative reasoning can also extend across multiple levels of analysis. For example, at the instance level, individual enactments of processes are examined in detail to identify anomalies or localized patterns. These insights inform higher-level abstractions at the process or routine level, where generalized patterns can be formulated and tested. Importantly, the iterative cycle is bi-directional: insights at the aggregate level can prompt re-examination of individual enactments, while anomalies observed in individual cases may lead to revised abstractions at the broader process level. This facilitates a continuous zooming in and out of processes, enabling scholars to connect granular observations with more abstract process patterns [16].

This approach ensures that insights are not only empirically grounded but also explanatory and actionable, allowing scholars to uncover underlying process mechanisms, account for contextual variations, and generate knowledge that can create impact in both theory and practice.

## 2.3 Principle 3: Integration of Computational and Human Sense-Making

A third core principle of process science is the *integration of computational and human sense-making*, which captures the complementary interplay between algorithmic analysis and human interpretation in the generation of knowledge about processes. It emphasizes that understanding complex processes requires more than algorithmic pattern detection; rather, it demands the combination of computational insights with human interpretation to generate explanatory knowledge [23]. This principle is rooted in the emerging genre of computational theory construction within the information systems field [27, 28], where the iterative combination of computational methods and human interpretation is central to constructing theoretically meaningful insights [29].

Computational methods, such as process mining, provide a powerful lens to uncover hidden structures, deviations, and emergent patterns in process data [3]. However, these patterns rarely convey meaning on their own: without interpretive work, computational outputs remain descriptive snapshots, unable to explain the nuances of how and why processes are performed. In other words, process mining excels at revealing *what* organizations do, but, on its own, it does not explain *how* or *why* organizational processes unfold as they do.

Here, human sense-making, in combination with contextual grounding (Principle 1) and iterative reasoning (Principle 2), complements computational analysis by linking observed patterns to organizational context, goals, and practices [30]. Researchers or analysts can draw on domain knowledge, observations, and other knowledge sources to formulate plausible explanations for patterns detected in event logs. For example, a spike in throughput times revealed through process mining may be understood by considering contextual factors such as seasonal effects, temporary resource shortages, policy exceptions, or informal workarounds [31]. By iteratively combining computational insights with human interpretation, process scientists can refine their hypotheses, resolve ambiguities, and construct abductive explanations that are both data-driven and theoretically meaningful. This integration is often operationalized through triangulation, where multiple computational analyses are cross-validated against each other and interpreted alongside qualitative insights [29], supporting mixed-methods designs that combine computational and qualitative approaches [32].

By embedding the integration of computational and human sense-making into process science, scholars can move beyond descriptive analytics to explanatory insights. This principle enables the discovery of mechanisms, causes, and contingencies in processes, allowing for theoretically informed interpretations and actionable knowledge that can guide the design of interventions.

## 3   The Process of Process Science

Based on the principles of *contextual grounding, iterative reasoning,* and the *integration of computational and human sense-making,* we present a generalizable framework for conducting process science studies. Rather than following a linear procedure, *the process of process science* unfolds through three recursive cycles, each of which emphasizes a critical dimension of inquiry. Together, these cycles illustrate how descriptive, explanatory, and prescriptive process science can yield insights from the study of socio-technical processes. Figure 1 illustrates the process of process science and outlines how these three cycles are connected.

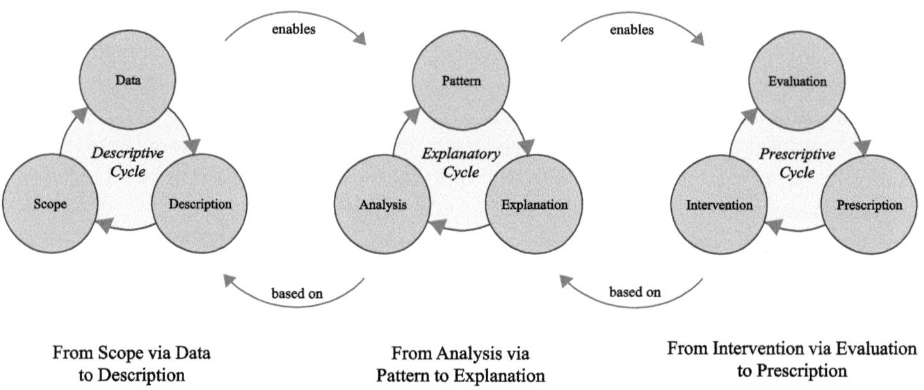


**Fig. 1.**  The Process of Process Science

In the following, we outline each of these cycles and describe important characteristics and considerations. We also demonstrate the process of process science using a real-life example: an analysis of digital trace data from a financial institution's digital customer onboarding process. Although the specific findings are context-dependent, the cycles are broadly applicable across domains.

### 3.1   From Scope via Data to Description

The foundation of process science lies in what has been referred to as *descriptive process science* [7], which focuses on developing data-based descriptions of processes. By grounding process measurement in data, process science enables researchers to observe processes as they emerge and unfold, going beyond traditional application domains and integrating diverse data sources. Within the process of process science, we conceptualize descriptive process science as an iterative progression from defining the scope, to collecting and representing data, to producing a description.

*Scoping* entails setting an objective of the study, defining the boundary conditions of a processual relevant phenomenon, deciding on data collection, and aligning these parameters in terms of both analytical feasibility and relevance for sense-making (Principle 3). A critical methodological consideration is how broad or narrow to set the initial scope. While a broader scope may lead to more general findings, a narrow scope might prematurely exclude relevant dynamics. Hence, effective iterative scoping involves balancing openness to discovery with given constraints such as data availability or stakeholder needs. Scoping should be done by considering contextual grounding (Principle 1) and iterative reasoning (Principle 2).

Another important aspect is the translation of the available *data* into meaningful *descriptions* of process behavior. In process science, this is not a purely technical step of cleaning and preparing data but a conceptual activity of representation: deciding how traces of activity are interpreted as events, how cases are delineated, and at what level of granularity actions are modeled. These choices are consequential, as they determine what aspects of a process become visible, and equally, what remains hidden [15]. This is also reflected in Kenneth Burke's assertion that 'a way of seeing is also a way of not seeing'. Researchers must remain aware that digital traces are not neutral reflections of reality. They are constructed artifacts, shaped by the design of the underlying information systems, the logging practices in place, and the partial digitalization of work [14]. As a result, they represent certain aspects of organizational activity while leaving others invisible. This makes iterating between data and description essential. Researchers often cycle between different ways of defining events (e.g., what counts as a 'case' or a 'completion'), adjusting levels of granularity, and testing alternative representations to evaluate whether they capture the process dynamics of interest. In sum, the development of descriptions should consider contextual grounding (Principle 1), iterative reasoning (Principle 2) and integrative sense-making (Principle 3).

**Case Illustration.** We present the case of a financial institutions of Central Europe that we have been analyzing within a research project [see e.g., 31]. In this case study, managers expressed concerns about long throughput times for onboarding cases in the onboarding process (i.e., a process where a potential customer applies for a loan, to the point where they are rejected to successfully open a bank account). As we defined the *scope* within the context of the study through conversations with employees and computational analyses of digital trace data stored in the onboarding platform, it became evident that delays were linked to frictions between roles and recurring IT changes in the digital onboarding tool. Users reported repeated loops with compliance, and compliance noted IT updates often introduced errors and work. These findings revealed that the initial problem scope was too narrow and needed to be refined. We iterated and shifted the research focus from measuring overall process duration to identifying which activities caused the greatest delays and determining how IT interventions and role tensions jointly shaped them, thereby redetermining the scope after data screening and initial descriptive insights.

Throughout the analysis of the onboarding process, *data* and *descriptions* were repeatedly aligned through cycles of experimentation. We tested for different event definitions, refined the notion of a case, and adjusted the level of granularity to find a balance between analytical feasibility and relevance for sense-making. For instance, focusing the analysis on successfully completed onboarding cases improved the coherence of the process description, but excluded disruptions caused by IT malfunctions. Including interrupted cases revealed how questionnaire updates or system errors introduced hidden loops and backlogs.

These iterations demonstrated that descriptions insights did not simply reside in digital traces but rather had to be constructed through decisions about data representation influenced by the overall scope. Decisions about what counted as an event or completion determined which aspects of the process became visible and which remained obscured, highlighting how process descriptions emerge through the interplay of computational analysis and interpretive reasoning.

### 3.2   From Analysis to Explanation

Once descriptive insights about socio-technical processes are established, computational analysis (e.g., process mining, AI-based pattern recognition) can reveal patterns such as frequent variants, rework loops, or bottlenecks. Identifying a pattern, however, does not yet explain it. Explanations require connecting observed traces to the underlying practices, organizational contexts, and stakeholder perspectives that generate them [18].

In this cycle, researchers iteratively move between computational outputs and interpretive reasoning to distinguish meaningful insights from superficial observations [23]. Importantly, this cycle does not always begin with computational discovery. Explanatory work can also be triggered by practitioner observations, suspicions, or contextual knowledge of problematic areas, which then guide targeted pattern detection in the data. This dual entry point underscores that process science relies on both machine-supported pattern recognition and human sense-making to move from 'what' to 'why' [23].

A critical methodological consideration in this cycle is knowing when explanations are 'good enough'. Following Schön's [33] notion of the reflective practitioner, explanations should be judged by their practical merits; or in other words, whether they provide stakeholders with a plausible and actionable understanding that can inform next steps. Perfection is neither possible nor worthwhile. Instead, explanations should aim to find a balance between further empirical analysis, plausibility, and usefulness.

Similarly, abductive reasoning emphasizes refining explanations until they are plausible and 'no apparent absurdities remain' [24]. But when is that point reached? When is an explanation 'plausible' enough? Here, the concept of 'stopping rules' from computationally intensive theory construction is instructive [27, 28]. Typical guiding questions are: "Is more data always better? When can I stop adding methods? Is my theoretical development adequate?" [29, p. 18]. Researchers can, in principle, always collect more data, use additional methods, or refine theoretical framing further. Stopping rules suggest that adequacy lies not in exhaustiveness but in whether the explanation offers novel, plausible, and situated insight that enables progress. In process science, this means that further iterations can be stopped when explanations sufficiently uncover plausible underlying drivers of process change to the degree necessary for intervention or for scholarly contribution. These observations taken together, this step strongly depends on contextual grounding (Principle 1), iterative reasoning (Principle 2) and integrative sense-making (Principle 3).

**Case Illustration.**  In the financial institution's onboarding process, initial process mining *analyses* revealed distinctive *patterns* of process complexity, extensive loops between relationship managers and the compliance department, and long delays in compliance checks [31]. Hunches linked these patterns of complexity to changes in the digital onboarding tool. However, only by integrating qualitative insights from stakeholders, we could uncover how and why these patterns emerged.

Specifically, further iterations relied on interviews and document analysis, which revealed that a recent update to the digital onboarding tool had introduced an error preventing account managers from continuing cases, forcing them to adopt workarounds that generated further loops and delays. With these insights in mind, we iterated and returned to conduct additional computational analyses by conducting detailed instance-level examinations through directly-follows graphs. This back-and-forth between computational detection and qualitative sense-making gradually refined our *explanations* until a convergence was reached: the combination of flaws in IT changes and the concomitant behavior changes of process participants explained the observed complexity and delays. Applying stopping rules, we realized that additional iterations would no longer produce substantially new insights, and the explanation was 'good enough' to inform both intervention design and theoretical contribution.

## 3.3  From Intervention via Evaluation to Prescription

The next cycle of the process of process science concerns moving from explanation toward intervention via evaluation to prescription. While descriptive and explanatory insights illuminate how processes unfold and why certain patterns arise, their practical value is realized when they inform interventions that impact practice. In this cycle, explanations serve as hypotheses for interventions, ranging from interventions of process redesigns to new governance mechanisms, or digital tool adjustments, which are subsequently implemented and evaluated. Crucially, this is an iterative process in which interventions are continuously tested, refined, and re-examined.

The prescriptive cycle can adopt principles of Design Science Research (DSR). DSR conceptualizes interventions as artifacts, such as prototypes, models, methods, or systems, that are purposefully built with the intent to solve problems [34–37]. A classical DSR approach is the build–evaluate loop, where artifacts are iteratively designed and assessed to ensure they are theoretically sound and practically useful [38]. Similarly, in process science, interventions are treated as provisional designs are subject to empirical evaluation. Here, evaluations can take various forms: qualitative feedback from stakeholders, experiments, or even new digital trace data generated after changes can provide the basis for assessing whether interventions produce the intended effects, surface unintended consequences, or reveal new challenges. Based on the evaluation results, process science in the prescriptive cycle intends arrive at normative statements. This means to make contributions to design knowledge, e.g. in form of design principles [39] to inform the design and management of processes. Here process science is to engage with existing design knowledge and argue how findings advance existing knowledge [36] to both add to theory and inform practice. Again, this step strongly depends on contextual grounding (Principle 1), iterative reasoning (Principle 2) and integrative sense-making (Principle 3).

**Case Illustration.** In the onboarding case, *interventions* were introduced through successive changes to the low-code platform, such as automating routine checks, refining questionnaires, or adjusting entry points for customer requests. These interventions were *evaluated* both computationally, by analyzing subsequent event logs, and qualitatively, by gathering stakeholder feedback [e.g., 31]. In several instances, improvements could be measured, including a reduction in the number of manual handovers due to automation and a shortening of certain approval steps thanks to revised questionnaires. However, other interventions produced unintended consequences. For example, fixing a bug in the KYC module led to new loops and delays before the process stabilized.

Each evaluation thus functioned as a build-evaluate cycle where digital trace data and practitioner insights revealed whether the changes addressed existing problems, introduced new ones, or required further refinement. Through these iterations, the interventions were treated as provisional designs that had to be empirically tested and repeatedly adjusted, not as final solutions. In consequence, we were able to gather *prescriptive* insights by unpacking process change in terms of types of change (sudden vs. incremental), strength of effect (bursts vs. bumps), temporal unfolding (immediate vs. delayed), and permanence of effect (persistent vs. ephemeral).

### 3.4   From Descriptive to Explanatory and Prescriptive Process Science

The three cycles of the process of process science are not discrete stages but interconnected movements within an iterative inquiry. Each cycle builds on the outcomes of the previous one, while also setting the stage for subsequent iterations. Scoping continues until the available data and organizational context provide a basis for meaningful descriptions. Analyses derived from such descriptions reveal patterns of activity, which in turn invite explanatory work to uncover the mechanisms and drivers underlying process dynamics. Explanations gain practical significance when they inform potential interventions, and interventions are refined through successive evaluations until they produce demonstrable improvements in process outcomes. This iterative movement is exemplified in the onboarding case described earlier: initial descriptive work revealed where delays occurred, explanatory analyses uncovered how IT-based changes shaped these delays, and prescriptive interventions were implemented to streamline the process. Across cycles, each step built directly on the previous one while reshaping the next.

Moving between cycles is rarely linear. Researchers may return to earlier cycles when new insights emerge, when explanations prove insufficient, or when interventions generate unanticipated consequences. Deciding when to move forward depends on methodological considerations such as stopping rules and reflective judgment. In the descriptive cycle, scoping continues until the problem space is sufficiently defined to guide analysis and process representations meaningfully capture behavior; in the explanatory cycle, analysis-informed patterns are refined until explanations are 'good enough' to support action [33]; and in the prescriptive cycle, interventions are pursued until evaluations indicate that the changes achieve the desired impact.

The process of process science conceptualizes and decomposes a complex process science research program into actionable parts. In this regard, the process of process science also calls for process science as a collaborative endeavor in which alternative descriptive cycles may be conducted, alternative explanatory cycles build on descriptive results and alternative prescriptive cycles build on explanatory results. Given the wide applicability of process science, our proposed process enables process scientists to position their work within a broader landscape of inquiry and make meaningful and impactful contributions.

Across all cycles, the three principles of process science, contextual grounding (Principle 1), iterative reasoning (Principle 2) and the integration of computational and human sense-making (Principle 3) remain central. Contextual grounding ensures that processes are studied within their specific environment, enabling sensitivity to specific conditions. Iteration ensures that process science studies are not one-off initiatives but continuous efforts that allow for adjustments and adaptations over time. Integrating computational analysis with human interpretation ensures that data-driven insights are triangulated to make sense of observations. Taken together, these principles anchor the process of process science as a structured yet flexible approach to studying and improving socio-technical processes.

## 4  Process Science and the Future of Process Mining

The emergence of process science is strongly linked to the ground-breaking work around process mining, driven by Wil van der Aalst and many other researchers in the process mining community. Over the past two decades, process mining has matured into a vibrant field with a wide range of techniques for discovery, conformance checking, and enhancement. Its success has also inspired large-scale adoption in practice, where organizations leverage process mining to improve efficiency, ensure compliance, and inform digital transformation initiatives [3, 40]. However, its impact lies not only in its computational advances, but also in the paradigm shift that comes with it: the fact that digital trace data in the form of event logs can serve as a lens to understand real-world processes as they unfold, and thus contribute to both better decision making [17] and further advancing science to understand and manage change [16]. We wish to close this chapter by reflecting on this connection, suggesting how process science can benefit from advancements in process mining, and how process mining can profit from approaches developed in process science.

Within the broader paradigm of process science, process mining provides the computational backbone for studying socio-technical processes [7]. Event logs are particularly suited for producing descriptive insights into how processes actually unfold across organizational settings [3]. However, process science highlights that such descriptive outputs represent only one part of a broader inquiry. We argue that iteratively moving from description to explanation and prescription requires embedding process mining into a broader set of qualitative and computational techniques. As such, process mining can become a powerful tool to uncover process dynamics, but it has to be integrated with contextual knowledge [19, 31] and human sense-making [23] to produce explanatory and prescriptive knowledge.

In doing so, process science extends the promise of process mining in two important ways. First, it emphasizes the iterative nature of inquiry. While process mining tools excel at descriptive discovery [3], process science highlights that insights rarely emerge from one-off analyses. Instead, descriptive, explanatory, and prescriptive insights evolve through iterative cycles of describing, explaining, and intervening. Embedding process mining into these cycles underscores its role not as a stand-alone analysis, but as part of a broader methodological process of inquiry towards a new evidence-based management paradigm. Second, process science emphasizes the integration of computational and human sense-making. Process mining can uncover patterns and anomalies in digital trace data, but these outputs require contextual interpretation to become meaningful [18, 19]. Process science, and the process of process science in particular, makes this integration explicit, providing a framework in which process mining results are iteratively validated, refined, and translated into explanations and interventions. Third, process science strengthens the role of process mining in theorizing about processes and organizations. Beyond its established applications in diagnosis and improvement, process mining provides a foundation for theoretical contributions. For example, it can reveal variations and dynamics in routines [16], enable abductive reasoning that connects computational outputs to emergent explanations [28], and support computationally intensive theory development through iterative refinement [29]. When embedded within socio-technical inquiries, these contributions can be situated within organizational contexts, thereby advancing context-sensitive theories of digital change [19]. Within the developed framework, theorizing emerges not as a separate task, but rather as the cumulative outcome of iteratively cycling through description, explanation, and prescription.

Seen through the lens of process science, the future of process mining can be envisioned as more than a computational technique. Rather, it can become a cornerstone of interdisciplinary inquiry into socio-technical change [7]. This perspective opens several avenues for future work. This requires embracing the iterative and integrative principles of process science, ensuring that computational analyses of digital trace data are continually triangulated, contextualized, interpreted, and refined to create even more meaningful impact in organizations and society.

Looking forward, several research opportunities arise for advancing process science. First, future research should develop methodological frameworks that operationalize the recursive cycles of description, explanation, and prescription at a more fine-grained level and across different domains. Second, there is a need to explore how human and computational sense-making can be systematically integrated to gain novel insights. Here, different computational methods, such as process mining or large language models, can be meaningfully combined with qualitative approaches or with each other. Third, process science studies should incorporate computational techniques that more effectively capture process dynamics, enabling fine-grained investigations of continuous change over time. Finally, a promising opportunity lies in deeply immersive empirical studies that combine digital trace data with qualitative data. Such studies can preserve rich contextual insights into organizational and processual dynamics, thereby enabling all three core principles and playing to the core strengths of process science. Together, these directions can help shape a more mature and methodologically grounded process science.

## 5  Conclusion

This chapter has outlined the process of process science as an iterative and integrative approach to studying socio-technical processes. Building on the principles of contextual grounding, iterative reasoning and the integration of computational and human sense-making, we presented a framework structured around three interconnected cycles: descriptive cycle (from scoping via data to description), explanatory cycle (from analysis via pattern to explanation), and prescriptive cycle (from intervention via evaluation to prescription). Together, these cycles illustrate how process science moves beyond isolated computational analyses toward the generation of descriptive, explanatory, and prescriptive knowledge and insights that are both rigorous and impactful. By situating computational techniques such as process mining within these cycles, process science emphasizes that computational outputs are not endpoints but starting points in an ongoing inquiry. Descriptive patterns become actionable when they are connected to contextual explanations, and explanations can create impact when they inform and are tested through interventions. Ultimately, the process of process science offers scholars a structured methodological grounding for conducting impactful studies of socio-technical change. By advancing our ability to understand, explain, and intervene into processes, it opens new opportunities for business process management and process mining research to contribute to the pressing challenges organizations and societies face today, specifically in dealing with change.

## References


1. March, J., Simon, H.: Organizations. Wiley, New York (1958)
2. Nelson, R., Winter, S.: An Evolutionary Theory of Economic Change. Harvard University Press, Cambridge (1982)
3. van der Aalst, W.M.P.: Process Mining. Springer Berlin Heidelberg, Berlin, Heidelberg (2016). https://doi.org/10.1007/978-3-662-49851-4
4. Rescher, N.: Process Philosophy: A Survey of Basic Issues. University of Pittsburgh Press (2000). https://doi.org/10.2307/j.ctt6wrc3b
5. Langley, A., Tsoukas, H.: The SAGE Handbook of Process Organization Studies. SAGE (2016)
6. Tsoukas, H., Chia, R.: On organizational becoming: rethinking organizational change. Organ. Sci. **13**, 567–582 (2002). https://doi.org/10.1287/orsc.13.5.567.7810
7. vom Brocke, J., et al.: Process science: the interdisciplinary study of socio-technical change. Process Sci. **1**, s44311–024–00001–00005 (2024). https://doi.org/10.1007/s44311-024-000 01-5
8. Lazer, D.M.J., et al.: Computational social science: obstacles and opportunities. Science **369**, 1060–1062 (2020). https://doi.org/10.1126/science.aaz8170
9. Howison, J., Wiggins, A., Crowston, K.: Validity issues in the use of social network analysis with digital trace data. JAIS **12**, 767–797 (2011). https://doi.org/10.17705/1jais.00282

10. Franzoi, S., Grisold, T., vom Brocke, J.: Studying dynamics and change with digital trace data: a systematic literature review. In: European Conference on Information Systems (ECIS) 2023 Proceedings (2023)
11. Akemu, O., Abdelnour, S.: Confronting the digital: doing ethnography in modern organizational settings. Organ. Res. Methods **23**, 296–321 (2020). https://doi.org/10.1177/1094428118791018
12. De Leoni, M., van Der Aalst, W.M.P., Dees, M.: A general process mining framework for correlating, predicting and clustering dynamic behavior based on event logs. Inf. Syst. **56**, 235–257 (2016). https://doi.org/10.1016/j.is.2015.07.003
13. Context. https://dictionary.cambridge.org/de/worterbuch/englisch/context. Accessed 05 Oct 2025
14. Aaltonen, A., Stelmaszak, M.: The performative production of trace data in knowledge work. Inf. Syst. Res. **35**, 1448–1462 (2024). https://doi.org/10.1287/isre.2019.0357
15. Grisold, T., Seidel, S., Heck, M., Berente, N.: Digital surveillance in organizations. Bus. Inf. Syst. Eng. **66**, 401–410 (2024). https://doi.org/10.1007/s12599-024-00866-7
16. Grisold, T., Wurm, B., Mendling, J., vom Brocke, J.: Using process mining to support theorizing about change in organizations. In: Hawaii International Conference on System Sciences (HICSS) 2020 Proceedings (2020). https://doi.org/10.24251/HICSS.2020.675
17. Badakhshan, P., Wurm, B., Grisold, T., Geyer-Klingeberg, J., Mendling, J., vom Brocke, J.: Creating business value with process mining. J. Strateg. Inf. Syst. **31**, 2023 (2022). https://doi.org/10.1016/j.jsis.2022.101745
18. Franzoi, S., Hartl, S., Grisold, T., van Der Aa, H., Mendling, J., vom Brocke, J.: Explaining process dynamics: a process mining context taxonomy for sense-making. Process Sci. **2**, 2 (2025). https://doi.org/10.1007/s44311-025-00008-6
19. Vaast, E.: Theorizing From Contexts in Research With Digital Trace Data. JAIS Preprints (Forthcoming) (2025). https://doi.org/10.17705/1jais.00955
20. van der Aalst, W.M.P., Dustdar, S.: Process mining put into context. IEEE Internet Comput. **16**, 82–86 (2012). https://doi.org/10.1109/MIC.2012.12
21. Rosemann, M., Recker, J., Flender, C.: Contextualisation of business processes. IJBPIM **3**, 47 (2008). https://doi.org/10.1504/IJBPIM.2008.019347
22. Sætre, A.S., Van De Ven, A.: Generating Theory by Abduction. AMR **46**, 684–701 (2021). https://doi.org/10.5465/amr.2019.0233
23. Lindberg, A.: Developing theory through integrating human and machine pattern recognition. JAIS 90–116 (2020). https://doi.org/10.17705/1jais.00593
24. Sahaym, A., Vithayathil, J., Sarker, S., Sarker, S., Bjørn-Andersen, N.: Value destruction in information technology ecosystems: a mixed-method investigation with interpretive case study and analytical modeling. Inf. Syst. Res. **34**, 508–531 (2023). https://doi.org/10.1287/isre.2022.1119
25. Bartelheimer, C., Löhr, B., Reineke, M., Aßbrock, A., Beverungen, D.: Workarounds as a cause of mismatches in business processes—: insights from a multiple case study. Bus. Inf. Syst. Eng. **67**, 339–356 (2025). https://doi.org/10.1007/s12599-025-00943-5
26. Klijn, E.L., Tentina, I., Fahland, D., Mannhardt, F.: Decomposing process performance based on actor behavior. In: 2024 6th International Conference on Process Mining (ICPM), pp. 129–136. IEEE, Kgs. Lyngby, Denmark (2024). https://doi.org/10.1109/ICPM63005.2024.10680657
27. Berente, N., Seidel, S., Safadi, H.: Research commentary—data-driven computationally intensive theory development. Inf. Syst. Res. **30**, 50–64 (2019). https://doi.org/10.1287/isre.2018.0774
28. Miranda, S., Berente, N., Seidel, S., Safadi, H., Burton-Jones, A.: Editor's comments: computationally intensive theory construction: a primer for authors and reviewers. MIS Quarterly **46**, iii–xviii (2022)

29. Berente, N., Lindberg, A., Miranda, S.M., Safadi, H., Seidel, S.: Computationally intensive theory construction. In: The Routledge Companion to Management Information Systems, pp. 14–27. Routledge, London (2025). https://doi.org/10.4324/9781032690483-4
30. Hartl, S., Franzoi, S., Grisold, T., vom Brocke, J.: Explaining change with digital trace data: a framework for temporal bracketing. In: Hawaii International Conference on System Sciences (HICSS-56) 2023 Proceedings (2023)
31. Franzoi, S., Hartl, S., Grisold, T., vom Brocke, J.: Effects of IT-based changes on the complexity of an organizational routine. Proceedings **2024**, 21034 (2024). https://doi.org/10.5465/AMPROC.2024.21034abstract
32. Whelan, E., Teigland, R., Vaast, E., Butler, B.: Expanding the horizons of digital social networks: Mixing big trace datasets with qualitative approaches. Inf. Organ. **26**, 1–12 (2016). https://doi.org/10.1016/j.infoandorg.2016.03.001
33. Schön, D.A.: The Reflective Practitioner: How Professionals Think in Action. Basic Books, New York (1983)
34. Gregor, S., Hevner, A.R.: Positioning and presenting design science research for maximum impact1. MIS Q. **37**, 337–355 (2013). https://doi.org/10.25300/MISQ/2013/37.2.01
35. Hevner, A.R., March, S.T., Park, J., Ram, S.: Design science in information systems research. MIS Q. **28**, 75 (2004). https://doi.org/10.2307/25148625
36. vom Brocke, J., Winter, R., Hevner, A., Maedche, A.: Special issue editorial –accumulation and evolution of design knowledge in design science research: a journey through time and space. JAIS **21**, 520–544 (2020). https://doi.org/10.17705/1jais.00611
37. Tuunanen, T., Winter, R., vom Brocke, J.: Dealing with complexity in design science research: a methodology using design echelons. MIS Q. **48**, 427–458 (2024). https://doi.org/10.25300/MISQ/2023/16700
38. March, S.T., Smith, G.F.: Design and natural science research on information technology. Decis. Support. Syst. **15**, 251–266 (1995). https://doi.org/10.1016/0167-9236(94)00041-2
39. vom Brocke, J., Maedche, A.: The DSR grid: six core dimensions for effectively planning and communicating design science research projects. Electron Markets. **29**, 379–385 (2019). https://doi.org/10.1007/s12525-019-00358-7
40. Reinkemeyer, L., Davenport, T.: Transform Business Operations with Process Mining. https://hbr.org/2023/10/transform-business-operations-with-process-mining (2023)

# Formal Foundations of Process Change

Stefanie Rinderle-Ma[(✉)]

Technical University of Munich, TUM School of Computation, Information and
Technology, Garching, Germany
`stefanie.rinderle-ma@tum.de`

**Abstract.** In a dynamic and uncertain world, processes are constantly
subject to change and adaptations, driven by factors such as changing
regulations and market conditions, implementing new strategic technologies such as AI, as well as process optimization efforts. Process change
has been investigated for a long time and several formal foundations are
provided including inheritance concepts and state-oriented compliance
verification mechanisms. This work revisits these formal foundations and
puts them into the context of current challenges and developments.

**Keywords:** Process Change · Process Evolution · Process
Adaptation · Formal Foundations · Concept Drift

## 1 Introduction

In 2012, in his reflections on a decade of the Business Process Management
Conference (BPM)[1], Wil van der Aalst concluded that *process flexibility* has
been one of the key concerns of the BPM conference and *"can be seen as the
ability to deal with both foreseen and unforeseen changes, by varying or adapting
those parts of the business process that are affected by them, while retaining the
essential format of those parts that are not impacted by the variations"* [1].

Business processes have been and are constantly subject to change due to
various reasons such as changing regulations and market conditions, implementing new strategic technologies such as AI, as well as process optimization efforts.
The major challenge is to enable adaptation and evolution of process models and
process instances while maintaining their soundness at any given point in time.
This challenge marks the starting point for research on process change in BPM
with foundational works on correctness verification of changes such as WASA$_2$
[51], inheritance in WF Nets [3], and ADEPT [38]. **The goal of this paper is
to provide an overview of the development of foundations of process
change over time in the BPM field, to highlight selected foundational
concepts, and to give a short outlook on future directions.**

Figure 1 depicts a timeline of foundations of process change starting with
the work by Wil van der Aalst on inheritance of workflows published in 2002.

---

[1] https://bpm-conference.org/.


J. Mendling et al. (Eds.): Wil van der Aalst Festschrift, LNCS 16480, pp. 112–125, 2026.
https://doi.org/10.1007/978-3-032-17618-9_9

Note that surveys and books in the field are put above the timeline (in blue color), core approaches are shown below the timeline marked by •, and research streams can be seen below the curly braces. The surveys [7,13,35,37,46,49] serve as yardsticks and are complemented by a lightweight literature search through all volumes of the BPM conference series. The keywords for the search are `change`, `evolution`, `adaptation`, `flexibility`, `variability/variants`, and `concept drift`, always in the context of a `process`. The search is also conducted the other way round, i.e., looking for `formal foundations` such as process languages that specifically enable or support `process change`. One example is the Refined Process Structure Tree [48] that based on its inherent block structure is well-suited for enable correct process change. Together with the literature search, also an update of the keywords was conducted, e.g., adding `uncertainty`, in order to consider new developments in the field.

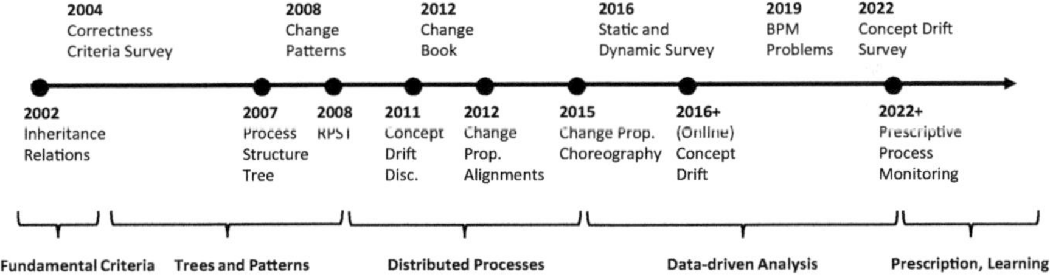


**Fig. 1.** Process change timeline with surveys (above timeline in blue color), foundational approaches (below timeline), and research streams (below curly braces). (Color figure online)

Selected results are clustered into research streams in certain time intervals and build the structure of the paper along the timeline. The first stream comprises fundamental correctness criteria for process change up to 2004 and is presented in Sect. 2. The stream between 2005 and 2008 discusses process trees, change patterns, and changes of process perspectives beyond control flow (cf. Sect. 3). The research stream between 2008 and 2015 covers formal foundations for multiple and distributed process models in Sect. 4. The research stream between 2015 and 2025 discusses data-driven methods for concept drift detection and prediction in Sect. 5. Section 6 discusses declarative and imperative process modeling in the context of process change and Sect. 7 concludes with a summary and outlook on future research directions.

## 2   Fundamental Correctness Criteria (up to 2004)

Change correctness of process models refers to the structural and behavorial soundness of the process model before and after applying a change. In the process change context, behavorial soundness means that after applying the process change, the running process instances can continue their execution in an

114     S. Rinderle-Ma

"undisturbed" way, without causing any undesired side effects such as missing data values or inconsistent execution states. As described in [37], formal change correctness criteria can be distinguished based on the underlying process meta model into models with TRUE/FALSE semantics such as WSM Nets, BPEL, and CPEE trees, and TRUE semantics such as Workflow Nets. Models with TRUE/FALSE semantics distinguish different execution states of activities such as ACTIVATED, RUNNING, and COMPLETED, i.e., typically have a duration what is also reflected in the corresponding execution traces by different life cycle events such as START and END events. For process models with **TRUE/FALSE** semantics, Def. 1 provides a state-based change compliance criterion.

**Criterion 1 (State-based Compliance, adapted from [37]).** *Let $P$ be a sound process model and $I$ be an instance running on $P$ reflected by its execution trace $\sigma_I$. Assume that $P$ is changed into process model $P'$ by applying change $\Delta$, i.e., $P[\Delta\rangle P'$. Then instance $I$ is compliant with $P'$ if $\sigma_I$ can be replayed on $P'$.*

A change $\Delta$ can be one of the change patterns proposed in [49], including adding, deleting, and moving tasks in a process model, adding and deleting process data elements, as well as change to the process hierarchy such as nesting process fragments. Figure 2 provides an example of two process models represented as CPEE trees (https://cpee.org) where process model P is changed into process model P' by applying change $\Delta$ =<insert after loop(P,A), insert into (P, loop, X), insert after (P, X, Y)> (in CPEE change notation). The CPEE tree is a textual representation of a Refined Process Structure Tree (RPST) as introduced in [48] with implicit flows, i.e., the correct flows are derived from the semantics of the nodes (cf. [40] for more details). We will describe RPSTs in more depth in Sect. 3 and provide an illustrating example in Fig. 4.

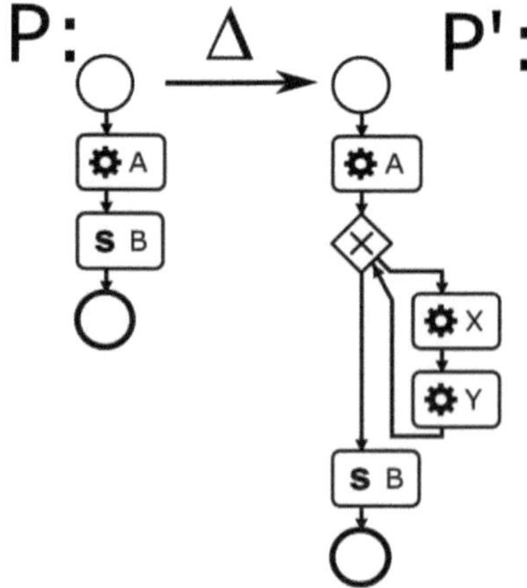


**Fig. 2.** Process Model P changed into Process Model P' by applying change $\Delta$, modeled using CPEE trees.

Structural soundness of the resulting CPEE tree P' is guaranteed by construction, i.e., only structurally correct CPEE trees can be designed and all change operations results in again structurally correct CPEE trees. Execution trace $\sigma_1$ =<START(A), END(D)> on P can be replayed on P', resulting in a sound execution state and hence behavioral soundness of $\Delta$. As a consequence, the corresponding process instance can be correctly *migrated* to P'.

The basic idea behind the formal soundness checks of Def. 1 is that a change $\Delta$ must not be applied if it is applied to instances that have already progressed too far, i.e., affect activities that are already in execution states RUNNING or COMPLETED.

An elegant approach for models with **TRUE-semantics** that is not based on any execution marking, but on the original and changed version of the process model, i.e., P and P' is the inheritance-based approach proposed by Wil van der Aalst [3]: four inheritance relations between original process model P and changed process model P' are defined where P' inherits from P. The inheritance is based on *blocking* and/or *hiding* activities in one model in order to generate the behavior of the other model. If P and P' are related under one of the inheritance relations, change $\Delta$ results in a structural sound process model P' and behavioral soundness of all running process instances.

**Criterion 2 (Compliance under inheritance relations, taken from [37]).** *Let P be a process model which is correctly transformed into another process model P'. Then instance I on P is compliant with P' if P and P' are related to each other under inheritance (for a more formal definition see [3]).*

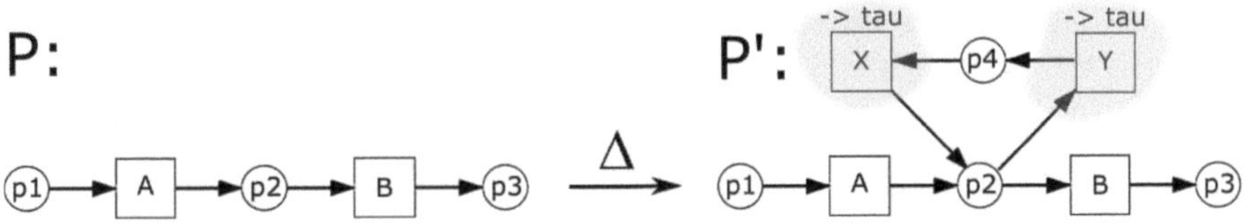


**Fig. 3.** Process Model P Changed to Process Model P'; P and P' are related under inheritance by hiding activities X and Y to silent activities $\tau$. Example taken and slightly adapted from [37].

Consider Fig. 3 for an example of two process models P and P'. The models are represented as Workflow Nets and are behaviorally equivalent to the CPEE trees depicted in Fig. 2. Change $\Delta$ can be represented by a sequence of operations $\Delta$ =<addTransition(P,X), addTransition(P, Y), addPlace(P,p4), addFlow(P,X,p2), addFlow(P,p2,Y,), addFlow(P,Y,p4), addflow(P,p4,X)>. P and P' are related under inheritance relations by hiding activities X and Y to silent activities $\tau$ in P'. After hiding, P and P' exhibit the same behavior, i.e., one execution trace $\sigma$ =< A, B > can be generated.

## 3  Process Trees, Change Patterns, and Changes Beyond Control Flow (2005–2008)

The time period between 2005 and 2012 was characterized by three developments, i.e., 1) elicitation and formalization of typical change patterns [49] (see short enumeration in Sect. 2), 2) development of a new tree-based formalism for process models, i.e., the (refined) process structure tree (R)PST which is block-structured and designed in a modular way such that *"a local change of the workflow graph can only cause a local change of the decomposition"* [48], and 3) development of correctness criteria for process perspectives beyond control flow such as the data [41] and the organizational [36] perspectives. Moreover, first approaches dealt with change of process choreographies [39], i.e., process orchestrations of different partners that are executed in a choreography, i.e., synchronized based on message exchanges between the partner orchestrations. We will discuss more approaches for formal foundations for process choreography change in Sect. 4.

*1) Change Patterns:* In [49], change patterns and change support features have been systematically collected and described. They range from inserting, deleting, replacing, and moving process fragments to the modification of control dependencies. Figure 2, for example, depicts an example for the insertion of a process fragment.

*2) Process Trees:* The (refined) process structure tree [48] can be seen as logical representation of processes with formal guarantees, comparable to Petri Net based formalisms. The core idea is to decompose a process model into single-entry-single exit (SESE) process fragments, ensuring the block structure of the process models. For the process structure tree, the SESE decomposition is based on the process activities and for the RPST on the edges of the process model.

Due to the block-structure, soundness of the models and their changes can be ensured by design. Especially, if a process fragment can be changed correctly, i.e., is structurally sound after the change, the resulting entire RPST is structurally sound. An example is depicted in Fig. 4: change $\Delta$ applied to process model P transforms it into P' (representation as Workflow Graphs in (a) and (b)). The representations as process structure trees of P and P' depicted in (c) and (d) show that $\Delta$ results in adaptation of process fragment F1 into F1'. F1' is structurally sound. This soundness (together with the unchanged structural soundness of the other fragments) can be propagated to the parent levels towards the root (e).

In addition to structural soundness, behavioral soundness after changes can be checked based on one of the criteria such as state-based compliance (cf. Def. 1) or inheritance-based compliance (cf. Def. 2).

*3) Perspectives beyond Control Flow:* Regarding formal approaches for changes of process perspectives beyond control flow, foundational compliance criteria such as in Defs. 1 and 2 already prevent severe data flow problems occuring after changes. In particular by not allowing to *"change the past"* [37], the unsupplied provision of mandatory data elements can be prevented. The data flow correctness has been further investigated in [41] where the original state-based compliance notion (cf. Def. 1) has been relaxed in order to allow

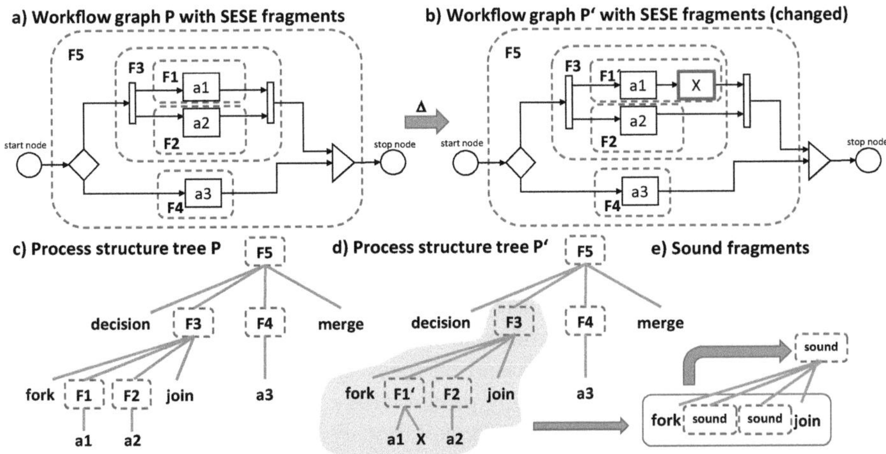


**Fig. 4.** Process model P represented as workflow graph (a), adapted into process model P' by applying change $\Delta$ (b); P and P' are represented as process structure trees in (c) and (d); soundness propagation of adapted fragment F1' is shown in (e) (example based on [48]).

more process instances to benefit from applying a change. Moreover, change of the organizational perspective has been investigated w.r.t. to a formal analysis of the impact on access rules which link organizational and process models [36]. Other approaches investigate change of further perspectives, e.g., ad-hoc changes of the devices used during process execution [10].

## 4  Formal Foundations for Multiple and Distributed Process Models (2008–2015)

Between 2008 and 2015 approaches developed from changes of single process orchestrations into changes and evolution of multiple (connected) models and process choreographies, including 1) change propagation between *alignments* of process models [50], 2) changes of services and their behavior [28], as well as 3) change and evolution of process choreographies [19]. This development coincides with the research on abstraction and alignment of process models as well as web services orchestration/choreographies.

*1) Change propagation between alignments of process models* [50] tackles the following problem. Assume two process models with commonalities, e.g., both describing a similar real-world process. The commonalities are expressed by correspondences between activities in both models with same or similar labels that have the same semantics, resulting in an alignment between the two models. If one of the models is changed, the question arises on how to propagate this change onto the alignment. The core idea is to determine a *change region* in the aligned model based on behavioral abstractions.

*2) Change of services and their behavior:* During runtime, process instances invoke endpoints such as services in order to execute the functionality connected to process tasks, e.g., booking a flight. It is required that the invoked service fulfills the requirements of the task, i.e., takes the expected parameters as input and delivers the expected data values back to the process as output. The expected input and output are referred to as service interface. The behavior of the service itself can be described as a process. In [28], it is investigated how service behavior can be migrated) by affecting as few interacting partners of the service as possible

3) Change and evolution of process choreographies: Process choreographies describe the synchronized modeling and execution of several process orchestrations owned and executed by different (business) partners that communicate and synchronize their execution based on message exchanges. Figure 5a) depicts a simplified book flight choreography model where three partners, i.e., the Travel Agency, the Acquirer, and the Airline, collaborate. A choreography task such as Notify is described by the sender (Acquirer), the task label (Notify), and the receiver (Airline).

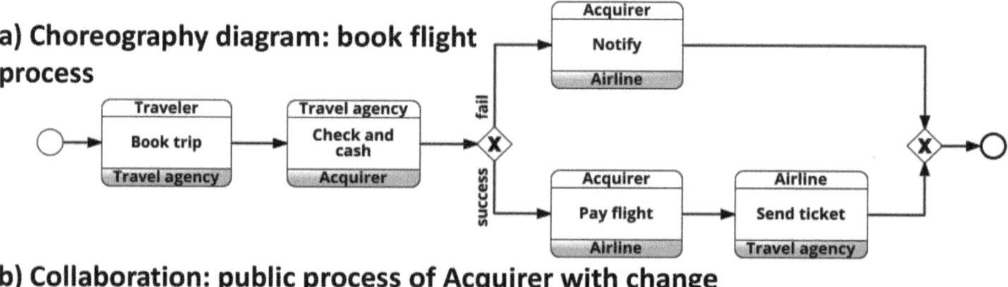


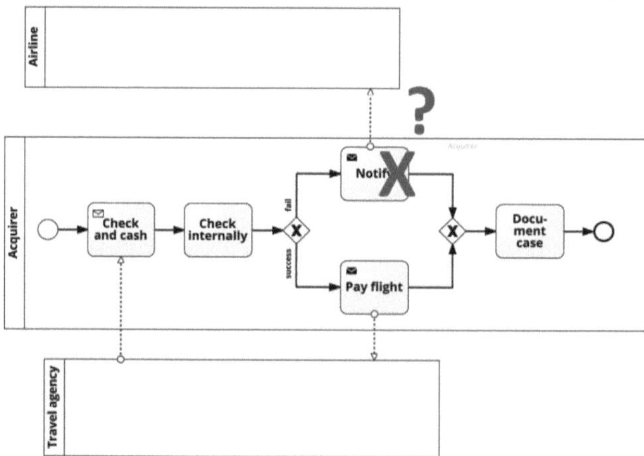


**Fig. 5.** Process choreography model (a) of a book trip example; private process model of partner Acquirer with message exchanges and deletion of task Notify; example simplified from [19], models created using SAP Signavio.

Each partner realizes the choreography by its public and private process orchestrations. A public process orchestration represents the process of message exchanging process activities (sending/receiving) with public process orchestrations of other partners. Private process orchestrations additionally contain private activities that remain invisible to the other partners due to confidentiality reasons. Examples are acvitities `Check internally` and `Document case` in Fig. 5b). Changing the process orchestration of one partner can be handled by soundness criteria as presented in Sect. 2. However, a change to one partner's orchestration might not only have local effects, but might be affecting other partners in the choreography, as well [19]. What are, for example, the consequences of deleting process activity `Notify` as it send a message to partner Airline? Receiving the message might be mandatory and hence could possibly block the execution at the Airline' side. The automatic detection and handling of change effects in process choreography is a hard problem because not all information about the partner processes is known and, if the choreography is executed in a fully decentralized way, transitive effects of change propagation are difficult to manage. Assume that, for example, the delection of an activity at one partner's side results in a cascading deletion of activities across several partners in, e.g., a supply chain. In the worst case, the transitive effects might occur in a circle, propagating back to orchestration that has initiated the change.

In [19], we proposed a structured algorithm to determine whether a change is only local or spreads to other partners in the choreography and if it spreads how to determine the effects in terms of change regions in the partner orchestrations. The partners can then check the change locally in the change region. The goal is to reduce the effort of change soundness verification and to keep the confidentiality of the partners. Overall, change regions are an important concept, already used in [18] for predictive change correctness verification, in [50] for change propagation in model alignments.

As change propagation might become expensive in large networks, in particular, if changes get rejected by partners during propagation and have to be, for example, rolled back, a pre-analysis of of the *change impact* might be useful. The core idea of change impact analysis presented in [20] is inspired by change spreading in large product networks such as the one of an airplane. We interpreted the change impact analysis problem as optimization problem change propagation and change logs and solved it using a memetic algorithm.

A data-driven approach to mine information about change from process data has gained traction already from 2006, more precisely discovering change process from change logs, refined into over discovering change processes from change logs in [22]. Another approach presented in [21] discovers reference process models from process variants [27]. The initial work to discover changes in the form of *concept drift* based on process event logs (not change logs) was presented in Bose et al. [11] in 2011, paving the way for a set of subsequent approaches in the BPM area (see next section).

## 5   From Model-Driven to Data-Driven Change Analysis: Concept Drift Detection and Prediction (2015–2025)

With the focus on process mining, BPM research shifted from model-oriented to data-driven methods. For research on process change this mainly resulted in several approaches addressing the detection of concept drifts (aka changes) from process event logs (not change logs). Process event logs store the process behavior that actually happened during execution time, i.e., for each process instance execution a trace is logged that captures the executed activities in the form of events. In a nutshell, process concept drift detection approaches aim at detecting deviations between trace cluster, using windows over the traces and statistical approaches [11,30]. Some of the approaches offer a characterization of the concepts drifts, e.g., [11] differentiate sudden, gradual, recurring, and incremental drifts and [15] differentiate into common, periodic, temporary, and anomalous drifts. The latter characterization shows the link to approaches for anomaly detection from process event logs, e.g., [8,25]. This raises the question if concept drift is the more neutreal term and anomaly already suggests some interpretation. This necessitates approaches for root cause analysis, visualization, and explainability of concepts drifts [5,9,12,53]. In addition to explainability, concept drift detection approaches should be accurate and robust [24,29] where robustness refers to differentiation between noise in the data and "real" drifts.

Another research direction is to analyze concept drift in process perspectives beyond control flow [16,53] and caused by context data such as sensor data [17,47]. Note the parallel development to the earlier process change research that has also started from the control flow perspective and then turned towards further perspectives such as process data and the organizational perspectives.

The categorization of existing concept drift detection approaches as sketched above is also reflected by the survey on concept drift presented in [43], including methods such as (trace) clustering, statistical, and visual and process perspective (control flow, data, time). An additional perspective is whether the drift detection is conducted during design time (offline) or runtime (online).

[47] is an online drift detection approach that exploits sensor data in order to predict a concept drift in the process as a consequence of preceding drifts in the sensor data. Actually, the approach is already going towards *drift prediction*, i.e., the prediction of deviating and possibly not yet observed process behavior (cf. predicting unseen behavior, e.g., in [14]).

## 6   Imperative and Declarative Process Models

The approaches introduced in Sects. 2 to 5 mostly work on imperative process models such as Petri Nets or Process Structure Trees, i.e., models which fully specify the process behavior. Another process modeling paradigm is declarative process modeling, e.g., [31,33,52], where flexibility is inherently built into the process models consisting of rules and constraints that provide a frame to possible behavior, but do not necessarily describe the exact process behavior.

Declarative approaches enable the adaptation and dynamic reconfiguration of process models represented as, e.g., Linear Temporal Logic (LTL) rules [31] or DCR graphs [32].

Despite the flexibility advantages of declarative models, they might be less understandable for users and in practice, predominantly, imperative process meta models such as Business Process Modeling and Notation (BPMN, https://bpmn.org) as the standard notation are used. However, for several application scenarios such as manufacturing or medicine, for example, a combination of imperative and declarative process models would describe the semantics of the processes well, demanding for a *multi model paradigm* [6] that covers hybrid processes, process orchestrations and choreographies as well as instance-spanning constraints. Research on how flexibility requirements can be met for different scenarios using multi models constitutes a promising research direction.

## 7   Conclusion

This work describes research on process change along a timeline starting from the fundamental work by Wil [3] on inheritance relations between process models in 2002 and concept drift detection and prediction in 2025 (cf. Fig. 1).

Process change remains to be a crucial challenge in practice, even more when facing rapidly changing conditions in which processes are modeled, mined, and executed, arising due to, e.g., exogeneous shocks [42]. Hence, research on process change has to continue, facing the transition from model-driven to data-driven research and the advent of (generative) AI methods.

A first research direction is how to determine which changes can be applied as mitigation actions to react to, e.g., unforeseen situations. Earlier work includes planning-based [26] and history-based adaptations [44]. In parallel, the development of techniques from detection, prediction, to prescription took place in process mining where **prescriptive process monitoring** techniques also aim to determine which changes can be prescribed to react on predicted process situations such as violating temporal deadlines, e.g., [13,45]. The implication of the advent of generative AI approaches on process change can be investigated, for example, its impact on automated process model redesign [7] which also connects back to the idea of self-healing processes [34] that could be revived with the new AI-based technologies. Including users, [23] looks into how the established change patterns [49] can be integrated into prompt engineering for supporting **conversational process model redesign**. Overall, we can see the development from model-driven to data-driven process change analysis as well as the development from change application to change detection and prescription.

Bringing current and future research streams together, processes can provide the operational grounding for AI [2] and the frame for autonomous agents in AI-augmented BPM systems [4] and Agentic AI. Combining this with process change, enables to balance control (process-based grounding and framing) and flexibility.

# References


1. van der Aalst, W.M.P.: A decade of business process management conferences: personal reflections on a developing discipline. In: Business Process Management, pp. 1–16 (2012). https://doi.org/10.1007/978-3-642-32885-5_1
2. van der Aalst, W.M.P.: No AI without PI ! Object-centric process mining as the enabler for generative, predictive, and prescriptive artificial intelligence. In: Intelligent and Fuzzy Systems, pp. 28–38 (2025)
3. van der Aalst, W.M.P., Basten, T.: Inheritance of workflows: an approach to tackling problems related to change. Theor. Comput. Sci. **270**(1-2), 125–203 (2002). https://doi.org/10.1016/S0304-3975(00)00321-2
4. Acitelli, G., Alman, A., Maggi, F.M., Marrella, A.: Achieving framed autonomy in AI-augmented business process management systems through automated planning. Inf. Syst. **133**, 102573 (2025). https://doi.org/10.1016/j.is.2025.102573
5. Adams, J.N., van Zelst, S.J., Quack, L., Hausmann, K., van der Aalst, W.M.P., Rose, T.: A framework for explainable concept drift detection in process mining. In: Business Process Management, pp. 400–416 (2021). https://doi.org/10.1007/978-3-030-85469-0_25
6. Alman, A., Maggi, F.M., Rinderle-Ma, S., Rivkin, A., Winter, K.: Towards a multi-model paradigm for business process management. In: Advanced Information Systems Engineering, pp. 178–194 (2024). https://doi.org/10.1007/978-3-031-61057-8_11
7. Beerepoot, I., et al.: The biggest business process management problems to solve before we die. Comput. Ind. **146**, 103837 (2023). https://doi.org/10.1016/j.compind.2022.103837
8. Böhmer, K., Rinderle-Ma, S.: Multi instance anomaly detection in business process executions. In: Business Process Management, pp. 77–93 (2017). https://doi.org/10.1007/978-3-319-65000-5_5
9. Böhmer, K., Rinderle-Ma, S.: Mining association rules for anomaly detection in dynamic process runtime behavior and explaining the root cause to users. Inf. Syst. **90**, 101438 (2020). https://doi.org/10.1016/j.is.2019.101438
10. Bokermann, D., Gerth, C., Engels, G.: Use your best device! Enabling device changes at runtime. In: Business Process Management, pp. 357–365 (2014). https://doi.org/10.1007/978-3-319-10172-9_23
11. Bose, R.P.J.C., van der Aalst, W.M.P., Zliobaite, I., Pechenizkiy, M.: Handling concept drift in process mining. In: Advanced Information Systems Engineering, pp. 391–405 (2011). https://doi.org/10.1007/978-3-642-21640-4_30
12. Busch, K., Kampik, T., Leopold, H.: xSemAD: explainable semantic anomaly detection in event logs using sequence-to-sequence models. In: Business Process Management, pp. 309–327 (2024). https://doi.org/10.1007/978-3-031-70396-6_18
13. Ceravolo, P., Tavares, G.M., Junior, S.B., Damiani, E.: Evaluation goals for online process mining: a concept drift perspective. IEEE Trans. Serv. Comput. **15**(4), 2473–2489 (2022). https://doi.org/10.1109/TSC.2020.3004532
14. Chen, Q., Rinderle-Ma, S.: Class incremental learning with drift detection and data augmentation for dynamic processes. In: Process Mining, pp. 1–8 (2025). https://doi.org/10.1109/ICPM66919.2025.11220682
15. Chouhan, S.G.R., Wilbik, A., Dijkman, R.M.: A real-time method for detecting temporary process variants in event log data. In: Business Process Management, pp. 197–214 (2021). https://doi.org/10.1007/978-3-030-85469-0_14

16. Cremerius, J., Weske, M.: Change detection in dynamic event attributes. In: Business Process Management Forum, pp. 157–172 (2022). https://doi.org/10.1007/978-3-031-16171-1_10
17. Ehrendorfer, M., Hebstreit, J., Mangler, J., Rinderle-Ma, S.: Interactive drift visualization in sensor data streams for explainable process outcome prediction. In: Business Process Management Forum, pp. 162–178 (2024). https://doi.org/10.1007/978-3-031-70418-5_10
18. Ellis, C.A., Keddara, K., Rozenberg, G.: Dynamic change within workflow systems. In: Organizational Computing Systems, pp. 10–21 (1995). https://doi.org/10.1145/224019.224021
19. Fdhila, W., Indiono, C., Rinderle-Ma, S., Reichert, M.: Dealing with change in process choreographies: design and implementation of propagation algorithms. Inf. Syst. **49**, 1–24 (2015). https://doi.org/10.1016/j.is.2014.10.004
20. Fdhila, W., Rinderle-Ma, S., Indiono, C.: Change propagation analysis and prediction in process choreographies. Int. J. Cooperative Inf. Syst. **24**(3), 1541003:1–1541003:33 (2015). https://doi.org/10.1142/S0218843015410038
21. Günther, C.W., Rinderle, S., Reichert, M., van der Aalst, W.M.P.: Change mining in adaptive process management systems. In: Cooperative Information Systems, pp. 309–326 (2006). https://doi.org/10.1007/11914853_19
22. Kaes, G., Rinderle Ma, S.: Mining and querying process change information based on change trees. In: Service-Oriented Computing, pp. 269–284 (2015). https://doi.org/10.1007/978-3-662-48616-0_17
23. Klievtsova, N., Kampik, T., Mangler, J., Rinderle-Ma, S.: Conversationally actionable process model creation. In: Cooperative Information Systems, pp. 39–55 (2024). https://doi.org/10.1007/978-3-031-81375-7_3
24. Kraus, A., van der Aa, H.: Looking for change: a computer vision approach for concept drift detection in process mining. In: Business Process Management, pp. 273–290 (2024). https://doi.org/10.1007/978-3-031-70396-6_16
25. Lee, Y., Kim, D., Kim, D., Bae, H.: Multi-task trained graph neural network for business process anomaly detection with a limited number of labeled anomalies. In: Business Process Management, pp. 361–378 (2025). https://doi.org/10.1007/978-3-032-02867-9_22
26. de Leoni, M., Mecella, M., Giacomo, G.D.: Highly dynamic adaptation in process management systems through execution monitoring. In: Business Process Management, pp. 182–197 (2007). https://doi.org/10.1007/978-3-540-75183-0_14
27. Li, C., Reichert, M., Wombacher, A.: Discovering reference models by mining process variants using a heuristic approach. In: Business Process Management, pp. 344–362 (2009). https://doi.org/10.1007/978-3-642-03848-8_23
28. Liske, N., Lohmann, N., Stahl, C., Wolf, K.: Another approach to service instance migration. In: Service-Oriented Computing, pp. 607–621 (2009). https://doi.org/10.1007/978-3-642-10383-4_44
29. Lu, Y., Chen, Q., Poon, S.K.: A robust and accurate approach to detect process drifts from event streams. In: Business Process Management, pp. 383–399 (2021). https://doi.org/10.1007/978-3-030-85469-0_24
30. Maaradji, A., Dumas, M., Rosa, M.L., Ostovar, A.: Fast and accurate business process drift detection. In: Business Process Management, pp. 406–422 (2015). https://doi.org/10.1007/978-3-319-23063-4_27
31. Maggi, F.M., Westergaard, M., Montali, M., van der Aalst, W.M.P.: Runtime verification of LTL-based declarative process models. In: Runtime Verification, pp. 131–146 (2011). https://doi.org/10.1007/978-3-642-29860-8_11

32. Nahabedian, L., Braberman, V.A., D'Ippolito, N., Kramer, J., Uchitel, S.: Dynamic reconfiguration of business processes. In: Business Process Management, pp. 35–51 (2019). https://doi.org/10.1007/978-3-030-26619-6_5
33. Pesic, M., Schonenberg, M.H., Sidorova, N., van der Aalst, W.M.P.: Constraint-based workflow models: change made easy. In: Cooperative Information Systems, pp. 77–94 (2007). https://doi.org/10.1007/978-3-540-76848-7_7
34. Pryss, R., Musiol, S., Reichert, M.: Handbook of Research on Architectural Trends in Service-Driven Computing, chap. A Self-Healing Approach. IGI Global, Integrating Mobile Tasks with Business Processes (2014)
35. Reichert, M., Weber, B.: Enabling Flexibility in Process-Aware Information Systems - Challenges, Methods, Technologies. Springer (2012). https://doi.org/10.1007/978-3-642-30409-5
36. Rinderle, S., Reichert, M.: A formal framework for adaptive access control models. J. Data Semant. **9**, 82–112 (2007). https://doi.org/10.1007/978-3-540-74987-5_3
37. Rinderle, S., Reichert, M., Dadam, P.: Correctness criteria for dynamic changes in workflow systems - a survey. Data Knowl. Eng. **50**(1), 9–34 (2004). https://doi.org/10.1016/j.datak.2004.01.002
38. Rinderle, S., Reichert, M., Dadam, P.: Flexible support of team processes by adaptive workflow systems. Distrib. Parallel Databases **16**(1), 91–116 (2004). https://doi.org/10.1023/B:DAPD.0000026270.78463.77
39. Rinderle, S., Wombacher, A., Reichert, M.: Evolution of process choreographies in DYCHOR. In: Cooperative Information Systems, pp. 273–290 (2006). https://doi.org/10.1007/11914853_17
40. Rinderle-Ma, S., Mangler, J., Ritter, D.: Fundamentals of Information Systems Interoperability - Data, Services, and Processes. Springer (2024). https://doi.org/10.1007/978-3-031-48322-6
41. Rinderle-Ma, S., Reichert, M., Weber, B.: Relaxed compliance notions in adaptive process management systems. In: Conceptual Modeling, pp. 232–247 (2008). https://doi.org/10.1007/978-3-540-87877-3_18
42. Röglinger, M., et al.: Exogenous shocks and business process management. Bus. Inf. Syst. Eng. **64**(5), 669–687 (2022). https://doi.org/10.1007/s12599-021-00740-w
43. Sato, D.M.V., Freitas, S.C.D., Barddal, J.P., Scalabrin, E.E.: A survey on concept drift in process mining. ACM Comput. Surv. **54**(9), 189:1–189:38 (2022). https://doi.org/10.1145/3472752
44. Schonenberg, H., Weber, B., van Dongen, B.F., van der Aalst, W.M.P.: Supporting flexible processes through recommendations based on history. In: Business Process Management, pp. 51–66 (2008). https://doi.org/10.1007/978-3-540-85758-7_7
45. Shoush, M., Dumas, M.: When to intervene? Prescriptive process monitoring under uncertainty and resource constraints. In: Business Process Management Forum, pp. 207–223 (2022). https://doi.org/10.1007/978-3-031-16171-1_13
46. Song, W., Jacobsen, H.: Static and dynamic process change. IEEE Trans. Serv. Comput. **11**(1), 215–231 (2018). https://doi.org/10.1109/TSC.2016.2536025
47. Stertz, F., Rinderle-Ma, S., Mangler, J.: Analyzing process concept drifts based on sensor event streams during runtime. In: Business Process Management, pp. 202–219. Springer (2020). https://doi.org/10.1007/978-3-030-58666-9_12
48. Vanhatalo, J., Völzer, H., Koehler, J.: The refined process structure tree. Data Knowl. Eng. **68**(9), 793–818 (2009). https://doi.org/10.1016/j.datak.2009.02.015
49. Weber, B., Reichert, M., Rinderle-Ma, S.: Change patterns and change support features - enhancing flexibility in process-aware information systems. Data Knowl. Eng. **66**(3), 438–466 (2008). https://doi.org/10.1016/j.datak.2008.05.001

50. Weidlich, M., Mendling, J., Weske, M.: Propagating changes between aligned process models. J. Syst. Softw. **85**(8), 1885–1898 (2012). https://doi.org/10.1016/j.jss.2012.02.044
51. Weske, M.: Formal foundation and conceptual design of dynamic adaptations in a workflow management system. In: Hawaii International Conference on System Sciences (2001). https://doi.org/10.1109/HICSS.2001.927082
52. Westergaard, M.: Better algorithms for analyzing and enacting declarative workflow languages using LTL. In: Business Process Management, pp. 83–98 (2011). https://doi.org/10.1007/978-3-642-23059-2_10
53. Wuyts, B., Weytjens, H., vanden Broucke, S., Weerdt, J.D.: DyLoPro: profiling the dynamics of event logs. In: Business Process Management, pp. 146–162 (2023). https://doi.org/10.1007/978-3-031-41620-0_9

# Data-Centric Support for Dynamic Processes

Manfred Reichert[1]([⊠])[iD], Shazia Sadiq[2][iD], and Barbara Weber[3][iD]

[1] University of Ulm, Ulm, Germany
`manfred.reichert@uni-ulm.de`
[2] The University of Queensland, Brisbane, Australia
[3] University of St. Gallen, St. Gallen, Switzerland

**Abstract.** From its roots in business process re-engineering, to current disruptions resulting from changes in processes and practices due to increasing adoption of Artificial Intelligence tools and systems, research on change management has been consistently prominent in the field of Business Process Management. In this paper, we summarize the foundational contributions made on the support of dynamic processes, covering ad-hoc changes, schema-level changes & instance migration, and approaches to achieve flexibility by design through loosely specified process schemes. Traditional activity-centric approaches, while effective for structured workflows, fall short in addressing the complexities of knowledge-intensive and increasingly automatized business environments. We outline the need for a paradigm shift to data- and object-centric process models, where business objects and their lifecycles drive process execution and coordination. We illustrate that this shift becomes necessary to tackle the challenges emerging from the convergence of AI and automation, and we highlight that effective change management must integrate data skills and human-in-the-loop support to ensure adaptability, safety, and continuous improvement. This paper positions data-centric BPM as essential for resilient and intelligent process management in dynamic organizational contexts.

**Keywords:** change management · data-centric · dynamic process support · augmented BPM

## 1 Introduction

It would not be unreasonable to argue that the emergence of Business Process Management (BPM) as a field was driven by the organizational need to continuously adapt, optimize, and improve business processes [22]. The historical reasons for adopting a process-centric approach were to seek process innovation that goes beyond control and efficiency objectives. A key motivation was to build the capacity in the organization to innovate and improve business operations at a cross-functional level. The need for and importance of cross-functional collaboration can be attributed to increasing scale and specialization of functional units


J. Mendling et al. (Eds.): Wil van der Aalst Festschrift, LNCS 16480, pp. 126–140, 2026.
https://doi.org/10.1007/978-3-032-17618-9_10

(e.g., procurement, sales, and HR), which led to the development of functional silos to the detriment of enterprise level benefits.

Decades of research in BPM have shown that the design of cross-functional processes represents only a small part of the overall challenge. Business processes remain exposed to change due to evolving market conditions, changing regulations, strategic redirection, operational constraints, and the continuous desire to improve business outcomes [35]. Although the pace of change varies across organizations and sectors, business processes are inherently dynamic, and stagnation remains a well-known risk. Technological support for modeling, execution, and monitoring of dynamic processes is a critical capability that organizations must cultivate. Without it, the core aims of BPM, especially continuous improvement, are unlikely to be fully achieved.

We first outline the key contributions to dynamic process support, celebrating the significant advancements made over the years [1,5,7,15,19,34,38,42,43,53]. We highlight the lessons learnt from these advancements motivating the need for a data-centric support for dynamic processes. Finally, we conclude the paper with a set of open challenges, emphasizing that supporting dynamic processes remains a compelling and important area for future BPM research.

## 2 Lessons Learnt from Dynamic Process Support

Technological support for continuous process improvement is grounded in a Process Aware Information System (PAIS) [50]. In general a PAIS can be viewed as a four-tier system (cf. Fig. 1) consisting of a *Persistence Layer* typically supported by database technology, but may include various forms of data repositories including multi-modal data. An *Application Layer* builds upon the persistence layer and may include enterprise applications, legacy systems, bespoke tools, web services, etc. A distinguishing characteristic of PAIS is a means to separate the process logic from application logic, and hence a PAIS has an explicit *Process Layer*, between the application and the *Presentation Layer*. The process layer on the one hand orchestrates and implements the process logic and constraints with the application layer and on the other hand works with the front end user interface through the final tier of the PAIS.

Today, this architecture often appears in more distributed deployments. Functionality is partitioned across domain services rather than centralized within a single process layer. Some services encapsulate local process logic, while others provide task-oriented capabilities. Despite this distribution, the four-tier separation of concerns–persistence, application, process, and presentation–remains conceptually intact.

Existing contributions from the BPM research community identify three main approaches to managing process changes within a PAIS:

- **Adaptation**, which refers to the ability of an implemented process to flexibly and dynamically handle exceptional cases.
- **Evolution**, which denotes the ability of the process to change in response to business transformation.

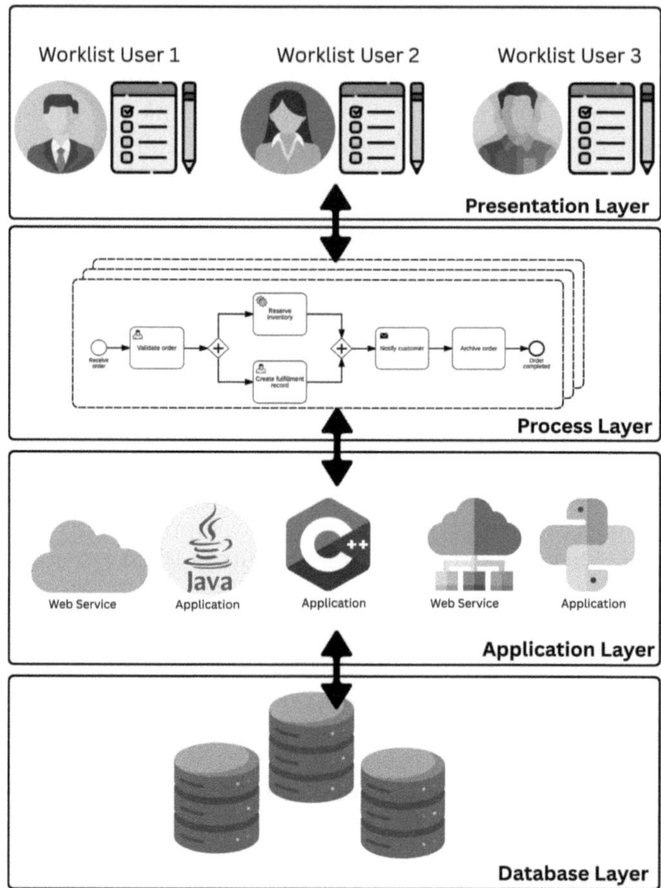


**Fig. 1.** PAIS Architecture.

– **Flexibility** which reflects the capacity of a process to execute on the basis of a loosely specified model.

This section summarizes key contributions to dynamic process support in PAIS in the areas of adaptation, evolution, and flexibility. To frame the discussion, we first introduce a running example. Consider a patient treatment process for cruciate ligament rupture. The process begins with activity `Patient Admission` followed by `Anamnesis & Clinical Examination`. Diagnostic activities `X-ray`, `MRT`, and `Sonography` may be performed in parallel in arbitrary order. If diagnostics indicate a cruciate rupture for which non-operative treatment is not viable, activities `Initial Treatment & Operation Planning` and `Operative Treatment` are executed; otherwise, activity `Non-Operative Therapy` is pursued. At process runtime, concrete instances follow the pre-specified schema but differ in chosen path and current state. For example, there may be a process instance for which the patient was admitted and examined, and then an X-ray was performed; moreover, activity Non-Operative Therapy was skipped, while activities MRT and Sonography have been concurrently activated. Each instance emits a trace of completed activities. Across many patients, multiple process instances in different states coexist for the same schema.

## 2.1  Adaptation: Ad-Hoc Changes at the Process Instance Level

Early work on process change emphasized ad-hoc changes, i.e., runtime changes to individual process instances without altering the underlying schema of other process instances. Frameworks such as ADEPTflex [34] pioneered support for dynamically inserting, skipping, or resequencing activities in running process instances to handle exceptional situations. However, such dynamic changes to a process instance can lead to dynamic change bugs (e.g., deadlocks, incorrect data flows, violated temporal constraints) if they are carried out in an uncontrolled manner. Early works on adaptation focused on ensuring the soundness of dynamically modified process instances. While ADEPTflex chose a proprietary and scalable approach with easily checkable correctness conditions for dynamic process adaptations, other works by van der Aalst & Basten dealt with the fundamental question of how to exterminate dynamic change bugs in existing formal languages such as Petri and Workflow Nets [1,5]. Finally, several works consider dynamic adaptations of aspects beyond control flow such as temporal constraints [26,42], and resources [41].

In the running example, adaptation may be required if a patient arrives at the health facility with a knee effusion. In this exceptional case, the physician may decide to perform an additional puncture, requiring a corresponding activity to be dynamically added to the process instance for this patient.

Although dynamic adaptations are vital in practice, they raise additional challenges around compliance, traceability, and reconciliation with the overarching process schema. To mitigate risks, Weber, Rinderle-Ma, and Reichert [48] introduced high-level change patterns. These semantically grounded operations– such as inserting an activity in parallel to a given process fragment or embedding a fragment within a loop– encapsulate behavioral guarantees and support correctness-by-design [16], thereby reducing the likelihood of introducing soundness errors during adaptation.

## 2.2  Evolution: Schema-Level Change and Instance Migration

In contrast to instance-level adaptations, process evolution focuses on modifications to the process schema itself [15,36]. Schema evolution raises the challenge of how to handle ongoing instances. A common strategy is process versioning [34,36], which allows old instances to complete under their original schema, while new instances start under the revised one. Although versioning avoids disruptive migrations, it introduces challenges related to consistency management, knowledge fragmentation, and governance across variants. Moreover, the nature of certain changes may require immediate compliance with the new requirement—in the running example, new legal regulations may require informing patients about alternative treatment options before any specific method is applied. This necessitates a change of the process schema, such as inserting activity `Inform Patient`). If the law requires that this rule is applied to ongoing treatment processes (where feasible), the schema of the process type must be updated, and the corresponding changes propagated to active instances of that type.

A more ambitious approach, particularly when dealing with long-running process instances, is instance migration, where running instances are transferred on the fly to the new process schema version. The seminal work by Rinderle, Reichert & Dadam [37, 38] in the ADEPT project formalized correctness criteria (e.g., compliance and soundness) and developed strategies to ensure that migrated instances remain sound. These approaches highlight the spectrum between co-existing versions and correctness-preserving migration, both essential in managing schema evolution. Certain approaches further enable the migration of instances that were previously subject to ad-hoc changes (i.e. adaptations) [39, 40], thereby reducing the overall exception handling load.

Commercial BPM tools have traditionally offered limited support for schema evolution and instance migration. Early systems like IBM FlowMark, IBM MQ Series Workflow, or SAP Workflow relied almost exclusively on versioning, letting old instances complete under their original schema while new ones followed the updated version. More recent platforms, such as Camunda 8, introduced migration plans, where administrators map activities between old and new schemes, such that running instances can continue under the revised schema. Other tools, like TIBCO BPM, restrict migration to predefined checkpoints. In contrast, AristaFlow [27], the commercial successor of ADEPTflex, stands out as one of the few systems that implemented formal correctness criteria from research, supporting both ad-hoc changes and correctness-preserving instance migrations.

## 2.3   Flexibility: Loosely Specified Models

Beyond adaptation and evolution, another line of research has explored flexibility through loosely specified models. Instead of prescribing all possible execution paths upfront, flexible process models allow for a range of behaviors that may be determined at runtime. Sadiq et al. [43] introduced the notion of Pockets of Flexibility, explicitly marking variability regions within a process where users may choose among alternative paths while still preserving overall correctness. A complementary stream investigated declarative approaches, where processes are not defined by pre-specified imperative activity sequences, but by constraints that specify what must or must not hold [44]. Languages such as DECLARE [8, 31, 32] support this paradigm by letting a process be executed in any way that satisfies the given set of constraints. Note that this approach eases the dynamic adaptation and evolution of processes [32].

In the running example, there may be different medical treatments. However, the exact ordering of the diagnostic and therapeutic procedures must be decided during patient treatment. Allowing the instance of a patient treatment process to be dynamically modeled or composed out of predefined activities without prescribed ordering removes a number of challenges in the outlined adaptation and evolution scenarios. Declarative models thus maximize flexibility by granting users freedom in choosing the actual execution path, while still ensuring compliance with required rules.

Together, these approaches shift the perspective from rigidly defined processes to constraint-guided execution, offering greater flexibility in dynamic and knowledge-intensive domains. However, this flexibility also shifts the burden of reasoning: while systems become more adaptable, users face harder cognitive challenges in understanding, maintaining, and applying changes. In other words, flexibility enables change, but only if it remains cognitively manageable.

Effective change management requires not only technical flexibility, but also cognitive manageability. If end-users cannot understand, maintain, or adapt declarative specifications, the promised flexibility risks becoming impractical. A growing body of empirical research has therefore examined how humans cope with declarative representations. Fahland et al. [20] showed that imperative notations are generally better for sequential reasoning, whereas declarative ones support circumstantial reasoning. They identified viscosity as a key maintainability issue and argued that sequential changes are easier in imperative models, while circumstantial changes are more demanding. Weidlich et al. [52] empirically confirmed this, showing that sequential modifications are applied more accurately in imperative models, whereas circumstantial changes are more difficult to implement. Pichler et al. [33] further reported that, overall, imperative notations yield better comprehension, even in tasks where declarative models might be expected to have an advantage. Finally, Haisjackl et al. [21] highlight recurring pitfalls: users tend to interpret DECLARE models sequentially, struggle with hidden dependencies and constraint combinations, and are often misled by graphical similarities to imperative notations. Collectively, these studies underscore that transitioning from sequential to constraint-based reasoning requires different cognitive strategies.

Despite these challenges, the DECLARE framework [8] spearheaded by van der Aalst and colleagues remains the most influential realization of declarative modeling, inspiring a rich body of follow-up research on how best to balance flexibility with usability. At the same time, empirical studies show that this flexibility comes with cognitive trade-offs for end-users, underscoring the need for strong guidance and change support when using declarative models in practice.


## 3  End-User Support for Process Change

Prior research on process change has emphasized the importance for end-user support. Such support must extend beyond merely ensuring the soundness of modified process instances, prompting considerable research into assisting end-users in managing process changes. As discussed earlier, the more flexibility and scope for change a system offers, the higher the cognitive burden on its users. Each additional option for adaptation or evolution can reduce rigidity, but it also increases the complexity of deciding the next steps, maintaining consistency, and avoiding errors. Accordingly, research on end-user support can be viewed as the natural complement to flexibility and change management: for processes to remain adaptable, they must also remain usable.

A central line of research has explicitly addressed this challenge by exploring how to enable users to perform changes themselves. For example, Weber et al. [49,51] introduced change reuse through case-based reasoning, allowing users to leverage past adaptations rather than starting from scratch and to elevate frequently occurring instance-level changes to the type level. This work established a user-centered vision of change management: empowering domain experts–not just system administrators–to adapt processes on the fly while avoiding inconsistencies. Complementing this, van der Aalst's work on process mining and conformance checking [2,4] provided the analytical foundation for evidence-driven guidance, enabling the detection of deviations, bottlenecks, and compliance issues, and explaining why a change might be necessary.

Expanding on this work, Schonenberg et al. [45] investigated the tension between flexibility and support in declarative process models. Declarative languages such as DECLARE permit numerous execution paths, providing users with freedom, while increasing the difficulty of determining the next activity. To mitigate this challenge, they proposed history-based recommendations: given the prefix of an ongoing execution, the system compares it with past traces to suggest plausible continuations. This work clearly illustrates the trade-off: flexibility multiplies potential behaviors, but without guidance, this freedom can overwhelm users. By leveraging execution data, Schonenberg and colleagues–drawing on van der Aalst's vision of process mining as a bridge between models and data–demonstrated how runtime recommendations could alleviate this cognitive burden. In this regard, their work can be seen as a precursor to predictive monitoring, where flexibility is preserved while users are actively guided through it. For example, van der Aalst, Schonenberg, and Song [9] introduced Annotated Transition Systems, in which each system state represents an execution prefix and is annotated with performance data, allowing for the prediction of remaining execution time for ongoing cases. Subsequent research expanded this approach to predicting compliance violations and outcomes [29], further advancing predictive monitoring as a runtime support mechanism for end-users.

Given the difficulties in understanding declarative models, test-driven development has been proposed as a remedy. Zugal, Pinggera & Weber [55] investigated the impact of test cases on the maintainability of declarative models, demonstrating that test-driven approaches enhance understandability and reduce modeling errors. In a follow-up study, Zugal, Haisjackl, Pinggera & Weber [54] provided an empirical evaluation of test-driven modeling, confirming that providing executable test cases alongside declarative specifications makes it easier for end-users to validate, maintain, and evolve process models over time.

Increasing flexibility requires equally powerful support mechanisms; without them, users are left to manage changes unaided. Across these strands, human-in-the-loop support remains central: systems should guide, recommend, and constrain, while leaving the final decisions to users.

# 4   Towards Data-Centric Support for Dynamic Processes

While end-user support mechanisms have alleviated much of the burden associated with managing process changes, interest is increasingly shifted toward (semi-)automated change management. A critical requirement in this context is explainability: when changes are derived from data, users must understand both why a change is necessary and the evidence supporting it. Van der Aalst's work on process mining has laid the groundwork for explainable process changes [2]. Conformance checking enables deviations, bottlenecks, and compliance issues to be identified and linked to event data, providing users with a clear rationale for potential adaptations [4]. Building on this foundation, action-oriented process mining advances from descriptive to prescriptive support by deriving concrete change actions– such as activity reordering or control insertion–directly from observed execution logs [30]. Importantly, these actions remain explainable, as they are backed by transparent evidence drawn from past behavior.

More recently, research on predictive process monitoring has extended this vision by proactively identifying risks in ongoing cases. The concept of the Digital Twin of an Organization [6] further integrates real-time data with process models to enable continuous monitoring, prediction, and simulation of alternative adaptations. A related capability is what-if analysis, which allows users to explore the potential consequences of a change before committing to it. These approaches show that even as process technologies advance towards increasing automation, human involvement remains essential. They highlight the critical role of data-driven insights in augmenting human decision-making, providing explainable recommendations, and enabling interactive simulations informed by domain expertise.

In the following, we will further highlight the necessity of data-centric approaches to supporting process change by first recapping the motivations and shortcomings that led to a paradigm shift from activity-centric to data and object-centric. We will then summarize key advancements in data and object-centric approaches for supporting process change.

## 4.1   From Activity to Data and Object-Centric Processes

The approaches discussed so far are activity-centric. What occurs during activity execution is often beyond the control of the PAIS, which treats activities as black boxes, managing application data solely through service invocations. This approach limits the ability of users to access processes and data in an integrated manner, creating a mismatch with preferred work practices [25]. Other drawbacks include context tunneling during the execution of individual activities [10] and the potential for missing data when interventions are needed in ongoing processes, such as adaptations in response to exceptions or emerging situations. Note that this applies to (semi-)automated interventions and adaptations as well.

While activity-centric approaches are appropriate for structured processes, semi-structured or unstructured processes cannot be rigidly confined to predefined activities. These processes are knowledge-intensive, with execution driven by both process participants and data [25]. Accordingly, a PAIS must provide users with direct access to the data necessary for making process-related decisions and performing process activities. Note that such integrated access to process and data is required in the context of (semi-)automated changes as well. For example, patient treatment involves a multitude of diagnostic and therapeutic procedures to be coordinated. The specific procedures to be performed are usually determined during treatment, taking into account clinical pathways, prior outcomes, the patient's condition, as well as considerations of cost, time, and invasiveness. Consequently, it is impossible to entirely model a treatment process a priori, as evidenced by the substantial research on flexible approaches to process change management (cf. Sect. 2).

To overcome the limitations of activity-centric approaches, data-centric PAIS have emerged [47]). Since data play a central role in process specification, execution, and evolution, data-centric approaches treat data as first-class citizens. Approaches such as case handling [10] have addressed this need by enabling more flexible, data-driven case enactment. Artifact- and object-centric processes [18,23,25], referred to here as *object-centric processes*, extend data-centric approaches introducing objects and their relations, thereby providing richer semantics and greater process flexibility. Regarding patient treatment, for example, doctors tend to think less in terms of processes and more in terms of interrelated business objects–along with their attributes and states–such as examinations, therapies, medical images, medical reports, medications, or patient problems [28]. In general, object-centricity in business processes is a key to richer semantics and thus to an improved assistance for end-users in the context of dynamic changes (cf. Sect. 3).

In object-centric processes, each business object of a business process is represented by a corresponding data object, which includes attributes (i.e., data) and a state-based process model [24,25] capturing the object's lifecycle [25,47]. Object processing is data-driven, meaning that the availability of specific object attributes governs the execution of its lifcycle. This fine-grained approach contrasts with the activity-centric paradigm, where the smallest unit of user action is an atomic black-box activity rather than an individual data attribute. Consequently, object-centric processes offer increased flexibility, as the granularity and sequencing of actions are largely determined by the user.

In general, object-centric processes may involve multiple objects, which together form the data model of an object-centric PAIS [25,46]. Beyond objects themselves, this model encompasses additional elements such as object relations, cardinalities, constraints, and roles. At runtime, each object can be instantiated multiple times in accordance with the constraints defined by the data model. The corresponding lifecycle process instances may then execute concurrently, except in states where their further execution depends on the states of other lifecycle instances. Overall, object-centric processes can include hundreds or even thousands of interacting business objects (i.e. object lifecycles), requiring synchronization at certain states to ensure correct concurrent processing [46].

## 4.2   Managing Change with Object-Centric Processes

The PHILharmonicFlows framework [25] developed by Reichert & Kuenzle is one of the few systems that implemented both design- and run-time support for object-centric processes. The framework covers the modeling, execution, monitoring, and evolution of object-centric processes, including data model, lifecycle processes, and coordination processes that synchronize the concurrent execution of multiple lifecycle processes. As objects publicly advertise their state information, states are used as an abstraction for monitoring lifecycle processes and for coordinating their execution with the lifecycle processes of other objects of the same business process. This coordination not only considers object relations and their cardinalities, but also other constraints set out by the respective coordination process. As examples consider a therapy stating that a medical report may only change to state Completed if more than 3 therapy cycles were performed.

Recently, PHILharmonicFlows was expanded by Andrews & Reichert [11], including advanced support for dynamic adaptation, evolution, context switch (i.e., dynamic changes of object relations), and a generic user interface component automatically generating process- and data-oriented views as well as personalized user forms at runtime based on the various models and a dynamic permission system. In several case studies, it could be shown that the integrated objec-centric access to process and data enable a richer semantics and better user assistance in the context of dynamic changes [11]. First techniques enabling the data-driven adaptation and evolution of object-centric processes at different abstraction levels were presented in [14].

Many information systems already implement object-centric processes, albeit not on the basis of a generic system such as PHILharmonicFlows. These systems store objects and their relationships in a relational DBMS, but implement the behaviour of objects and their state-based coordination (i.e., the interaction of objects lifecycles subject to certain constraints) in the context of a higher-level business process in the programme code. In general, such hard-coded approaches do not allow for the required flexibility and incur high maintenance costs, as process changes require interventions in the program code. On the positive side, the execution of object-centric processes is often reflected in database tables, from which object-centric event logs (OCEL) can be extracted, as shown by Berti, Park, and van der Aalst  [13]. This is precisely where object-centric process mining (OCPM) comes in. According to the vision drawn by van der Aalst, OCPM goes beyond the limitations of traditional case-centric process mining, which assumes that each event refers to a specific case, activity, and timestamp, whereas in reality, events may refer to multiple objects of different types [3]. OCPM relies on concepts such as objects, considered as the entities involved in events, object types, and events. An OCEL therefore considers two both event-to-object and object-to-object (O2O) relations [3]. As opposed to case-centric process mining, events may be related to multiple objects of different types, which allows organizations to better monitor, visualize and analyze the complexity and interconnectedness of their business operations [12].

Overall, OCPM better aligns event data and process models with the actual processes and data stored in information systems. In turn, this closer integration of process, objects, and events further can also contribute to an improved predictive process monitoring and real-time analytics.

## 5   Future Directions for Dynamic Process Support

The body of work on adaptation and evolution fundamentally reshaped the way process-aware information systems are conceived. Early contributions on ad-hoc changes and schema evolution with instance migration demonstrated that processes need not be rigid artifacts, but can be living entities that evolve in response to exceptions, regulatory updates, and organizational needs. Building on these foundations, research on end-user support introduced mechanisms such as change reuse, recommendations, and pockets of flexibility to ensure that human actors could manage change safely and effectively. More recently, the rise of process mining, predictive monitoring, and digital process twins points toward a future of semi-automated change, where data-driven insights and simulations propose and evaluate adaptations in real time. A key learning from these extensive contributions is the critical role data-centric approaches have played in overcoming a number of challenges for effective management of process change. Nonetheless, achieving data-driven process change and the corresponding PAIS adaptation demands holistic end-to-end support encompassing process modeling, execution, monitoring, mining, and evolution. This is particularly critical when changes are intended to be realized (semi-)automatically. While object-centric process management and object-centric process mining provide substantial potential in this direction, their tighter integration will be imperative to fully realize the vision of data-driven, automated process adaptation.

The inevitability of the need for change in business, makes change management an essential competency for process scientists. We have argued that this competency must be complemented with data skills and a data-driven mindset. Especially looking ahead, the emergence of Augmented BPM [17] highlights the convergence of automation and process mining. Advances in AI, predictive monitoring, and digital twins promise unprecedented capabilities for proactive adaptation, but further raise the importance of data-centric approaches to mitigate risks and pitfalls of automation. Capabilities for increasingly automated and AI-enabled BPM build directly on decades of foundational research on change management. The mechanisms developed for ad-hoc adaptations, correctness-preserving evolution, and flexible modeling remain essential, as they provide the theoretical and technical safeguards needed to ensure that automated interventions are explainable, compliant, and safe. The lasting impact of this line of research is a paradigm shift from static workflow enactment toward adaptive, intelligent process management.

# References


1. van der Aalst, W.M.P.: Exterminating the dynamic change bug: a concrete approach to support workflow change. Inf. Syst. Front. **3**(3), 297–317 (2001)
2. van der Aalst, W.M.P.: Process Mining - Data Science in Action, 2nd edn. Springer (2016). https://doi.org/10.1007/978-3-030-40172-6
3. van der Aalst, W.M.P.: Object-centric process mining: Unraveling the fabric of real processes. Mathematics **11**(12) (2023)
4. van der Aalst, W.M.P., Adriansyah, A., van Dongen, B.F.: Replaying history on process models for conformance checking and performance analysis. WIREs Data Min. Knowl. Discov. **2**(2), 182–192 (2012)
5. van der Aalst, W.M.P., Basten, T.: Inheritance of workflows: an approach to tackling problems related to change. Theor. Comp. Sci. **270**(1–2), 125–203 (2002)
6. van der Aalst, W.M.P., Hinz, O., Weinhardt, C.: Resilient digital twins: organizations need to prepare for the unexpected. BISE **63**(6), 615–619 (2021)
7. van der Aalst, W.M.P., Jablonski, S.: Flexible workflow technology driving the networked economy. Comp. Sys. Sci. Eng. **15**(5), 265–266 (2000)
8. van der Aalst, W.M.P., Pesic, M., Schonenberg, H.: Declarative workflows: balancing between flexibility and support. Comput. Sci. Res. Dev. **23**(2), 99–113 (2009)
9. van der Aalst, W.M.P., Schonenberg, M.H., Song, M.: Time prediction based on process mining. Inf. Syst. **36**(2), 450–475 (2011)
10. van der Aalst, W.M.P., Weske, M., Grünbauer, D.: Case handling: a new paradigm for business process support. Data Knowl. Eng. **53**(2), 129–162 (2005)
11. Andrews, K., Steinau, S., Reichert, M.: Enabling runtime flexibility in data-centric and data-driven process execution engines. Inf. Syst. **101**, 101447 (2021)
12. Berti, A., Jessen, U., Park, G., Rafiei, M., van der Aalst, W.M.P.: Analyzing interconnected processes: using object-centric process mining to analyze procurement processes. Int. J. Data Sci. Anal. **20**(2), 475–97 (2025)
13. Berti, A., Park, G., Rafiei, M., van der Aalst, W.M.P.: A generic approach to extract object-centric event data from databases supporting SAP ERP. J. Intell. Inf. Sys. **61**(3), 835–857 (2023)
14. Breitmayer, M., Arnold, L., Reichert, M.: Data-driven evolution of activity forms in object- and process-aware information systems. In: Proceedings of the CoopIS 2022, Bozen-Bolzano. LNCS, vol. 13591, pp. 186–204. Springer (2022). https://doi.org/10.1007/978-3-031-17834-4_11
15. Casati, F., Ceri, S., Pernici, B., Pozzi, G.: Workflow evolution. Data Knowl. Eng. **24**(3), 211–238 (1998)
16. Dadam, P., Reichert, M.: The ADEPT project: a decade of research and development for robust and flexible process support. Com. Sci. Res. Dev. **23**, 81–97 (2009)
17. Dumas, M., et al.: [AI-augmented business process management systems: a research manifesto. ACM Trans. Manag. Inf. Sys. **14**(1), 11:1–11:19 (2023)
18. Dumas, M., Hull, R., Patrizi, F.: Guest editorial: special issue on data and artifact-centric business processes. Computing **98**(4), 343–344 (2016). https://doi.org/10.1007/s00607-016-0486-9
19. Ellis, C.A., Keddara, K., Rozenberg, G.: Dynamic change within workflow systems. In: Comstock, N., Ellis, C.A. (eds.) Proceedings of the COOCS, pp. 10–21. ACM (1995)

20. Fahland, D., Lübke, D., Mendling, J., Reijers, H.A., Weber, B., Weidlich, M., Zugal, S.: Declarative versus imperative process modeling languages: the issue of understandability. In: Proceedings of the BPMDS 2009 and EMMSAD 2009, pp. 353–366 (2009)
21. Haisjackl, C., et al.: Understanding declare models: strategies, pitfalls, empirical results. Softw. Sys. Model. **15**(2), 325–352 (2016)
22. Hammer, M., Champy, J.: Reengineering the Corporation: A Manifesto for Business Revolution. HarperCollins (1993)
23. Heath, F.T., et al.: Barcelona: a design and runtime environment for declarative artifact-centric BPM. In: Basu, S., Pautasso, C., Zhang, L., Fu, X. (eds.) ICSOC 2013. LNCS, vol. 8274, pp. 705–709. Springer, Heidelberg (2013). https://doi.org/10.1007/978-3-642-45005-1_65
24. König, M., Gießler, R., Brandt, W., Seidel, A., Weske, M.: A unified view on data object states. In: Proceedings of the CAiSE 2025. LNCS, vol. 15702, pp. 259–276. Springer (2025). https://doi.org/10.1007/978-3-031-94571-7_15
25. Künzle, V., Reichert, M.: PHILharmonicFlows: towards a framework for object-aware process management. J. Softw. Maint. Res. Pract. **23**(4), 205–244 (2011)
26. Lanz, A., Reichert, M.: Dealing with changes of time-aware processes. In: Sadiq, S., Soffer, P., Völzer, H. (eds.) BPM 2014. LNCS, vol. 8659, pp. 217–233. Springer, Cham (2014). https://doi.org/10.1007/978-3-319-10172-9_14
27. Lanz, A., Reichert, M., Dadam, P.: Making business process implementations flexible and robust: Error handling in the aristaflow BPM suite. In: Proceedings of the CAiSE Forum2010, Hammamet, vol. 592. CEUR-WS.org (2010)
28. Lenz, R., Reichert, M.: IT support for healthcare processes - premises, challenges, perspectives. Data Knowl. Eng. **61**(1), 39–58 (2007)
29. Maggi, F.M., Di Francescomarino, C., Dumas, M., Ghidini, C.: Predictive monitoring of business processes. In: Jarke, M., et al. (eds.) CAiSE 2014. LNCS, vol. 8484, pp. 457–472. Springer, Cham (2014). https://doi.org/10.1007/978-3-319-07881-6_31
30. Park, G., van der Aalst, W.M.P.: Action-oriented process mining: bridging the gap between insights and actions. Progress Artif. Intell., 1–22 (2022)
31. Pesic, M., Schonenberg, H., van der Aalst, W.M.P.: DECLARE: full support for loosely-structured processes. In: Proceedings of the EDOC 2007, Annapolis, pp. 287–300. IEEE Comp Society (2007)
32. Pesic, M., Schonenberg, M.H., Sidorova, N., van der Aalst, W.M.P.: Constraint-based workflow models: change made easy. In: Meersman, R., Tari, Z. (eds.) OTM 2007. LNCS, vol. 4803, pp. 77–94. Springer, Heidelberg (2007). https://doi.org/10.1007/978-3-540-76848-7_7
33. Pichler, P., Weber, B., Zugal, S., Pinggera, J., Mendling, J., Reijers, H.A.: Imperative versus declarative process modeling languages: an empirical investigation. In: Proc BPM 2011 Workshops. LNBIP, vol. 99, pp. 383–394. Springer (2011). https://doi.org/10.1007/978-3-642-28108-2_37
34. Reichert, M., Dadam, P.: Adept$_{flex}$-supporting dynamic changes of workflows without losing control. J. Intell. Inf. Sys. **10**(2), 93–129 (1998)
35. Reichert, M., Weber, B.: Enabling Flexibility in Process-Aware Information Systems - Challenges, Methods. Springer, Technologies (2012). https://doi.org/10.1007/978-3-642-30409-5
36. Rinderle, S.: Schema evolution in process management systems. Ph.D. thesis, University of ULM (2004). https://d-nb.info/974021164

37. Rinderle, S., Reichert, M., Dadam, P.: Evaluation of correctness criteria for dynamic workflow changes. In: van der Aalst, W.M.P., Weske, M. (eds.) BPM 2003. LNCS, vol. 2678, pp. 41–57. Springer, Heidelberg (2003). https://doi.org/10.1007/3-540-44895-0_4

38. Rinderle, S., Reichert, M., Dadam, P.: Correctness criteria for dynamic changes in workflow systems - a survey. Data Knowl. Eng. **50**(1), 9–34 (2004)

39. Rinderle, S., Reichert, M., Dadam, P.: Disjoint and overlapping process changes: challenges, solutions, applications. In: Meersman, R., Tari, Z. (eds.) OTM 2004. LNCS, vol. 3290, pp. 101–120. Springer, Heidelberg (2004). https://doi.org/10.1007/978-3-540-30468-5_9

40. Rinderle, S., Reichert, M., Dadam, P.: On dealing with structural conflicts between process type and instance changes. In: Desel, J., Pernici, B., Weske, M. (eds.) BPM 2004. LNCS, vol. 3080, pp. 274–289. Springer, Heidelberg (2004). https://doi.org/10.1007/978-3-540-25970-1_18

41. Rinderle-Ma, S., Reichert, M.: Comprehensive life cycle support for access rules in information systems: the CEOSIS project. Enterp. Inf. Syst. **3**(3), 219–251 (2009)

42. Sadiq, S., Marjanovic, O., Orlowska, M.E.: Managing change and time in dynamic workflow processes. Int. J. Coop. Inf. Sys. **9**(1–2), 93–116 (2000)

43. Sadiq, S., Sadiq, W., Orlowska, M.: Pockets of flexibility in workflow specification. In: S.Kunii, H., Jajodia, S., Sølvberg, A. (eds.) ER 2001. LNCS, vol. 2224, pp. 513–526. Springer, Heidelberg (2001). https://doi.org/10.1007/3-540-45581-7_38

44. Sadiq, S.W., Orlowska, M.E., Sadiq, W.: Specification and validation of process constraints for flexible workflows. Inf. Sys. **30**(5), 349–378 (2005)

45. Schonenberg, H., Weber, B., van Dongen, B., van der Aalst, W.: Supporting flexible processes through recommendations based on history. In: Dumas, M., Reichert, M., Shan, M.-C. (eds.) BPM 2008. LNCS, vol. 5240, pp. 51–66. Springer, Heidelberg (2008). https://doi.org/10.1007/978-3-540-85758-7_7

46. Steinau, S., Andrews, K., Reichert, M.: The relational process structure. In: Krogstie, J., Reijers, H.A. (eds.) CAiSE 2018. LNCS, vol. 10816, pp. 53–67. Springer, Cham (2018). https://doi.org/10.1007/978-3-319-91563-0_4

47. Steinau, S., Marrella, A., Andrews, K., Leotta, F., Mecella, M., Reichert, M.: DALEC: a framework for the systematic evaluation of data-centric approaches to process management software. Soft. Sys. Model **18**(4), 2679–2716 (2019)

48. Weber, B., Reichert, M., Rinderle-Ma, S.: Change patterns and change support features - enhancing flexibility in process-aware information systems. Data Knowl. Eng. **66**(3), 438–466 (2008)

49. Weber, B., Reichert, M., Rinderle-Ma, S., Wild, W.: Providing integrated life cycle support in process-aware information systems. J. Coop. Inf. Sys. **18**(1), 115–65 (2009)

50. Weber, B., Sadiq, S., Reichert, M.: Beyond rigidity - dynamic process lifecycle support. Comput. Sci. Res. Dev. **23**(2), 47–65 (2009)

51. Weber, B., Wild, W., Breu, R.: CBRFlow: enabling adaptive workflow management through conversational case-based reasoning. In: Funk, P., González Calero, P.A. (eds.) ECCBR 2004. LNCS (LNAI), vol. 3155, pp. 434–448. Springer, Heidelberg (2004). https://doi.org/10.1007/978-3-540-28631-8_32

52. Weidlich, M., et al.: The impact of sequential and circumstantial changes on process models. In: Proceedings of the 1st Int Workshop on Empirical Research in Process-Oriented Information System, Hammamet, vol. 603, pp. 43–54. CEUR-WS.org (2010)

53. Weske, M.: Formal foundation and conceptual design of dynamic adaptations in a workflow management system. In: Proceedings of the HICSS 2001. IEEE Computer Society (2001)
54. Zugal, S., Haisjackl, C., Pinggera, J., Weber, B.: Empirical evaluation of test driven modeling. Int. J. Inf. Sys. Model Des. **4**(2), 23–43 (2013)
55. Zugal, S., Pinggera, J., Weber, B.: The impact of testcases on the maintainability of declarative process models. In: Proc BPMDS 2011 and EMMSAD 2011, London, UK, vol. 81, pp. 163–177. Springer (2011). https://doi.org/10.1007/978-3-642-21759-3_12

# Unusual Connections of Processes or Development Processes in Permanent Changes

Manfred Nagl[(⊠)]

RWTH Aachen University, 52054 Aachen, Germany
`nagl@i3.informatik.rwth-aachen.de`

**Abstract.** This paper has two goals. The first is to introduce the characteristics of processes we are discussing here: They are changing, rely on experience or upcoming knowledge and are not based on routine but on creative decisions. We find them for example in conceptual design, in knowledge acquisition, and in development of creative solutions.

In those processes we also have unusual connections between subprocesses, such as the development of a tool, which is directly used in the process. We introduce a notation for these subprocess connections, and we give examples, which show that complicated situations ca be handled.

**Keywords:** classification/characterization of processes · process modeling · process dependency · process aspects · interaction of different processes · change and dynamic processes · applications in informatics and engineering

## 1 Process Variety and Classification

There is a variety of *notations* for processes, which can be used for different kinds and levels of processes, [3, 16, 29] to name a few. They can be *classified* (i) along their main application (logistics, business processes, cooperative work in offices, mechanical production, building/maintaining software), (ii) where processes are used (knowledge acquisition, pre-development, development, preparation for production, production, maintenance, customer relationship), (iii) their granularity (from lifecycle or ERP to fine-grained tasks), or (iv) their characteristics (static, dynamic, etc.).

*Process research* can be classified into mining, analysis, formalization, classification, application, or evolution [3]. This can happen on single processes, on knowledge for processes, their change, on process type level, or knowledge for process classes.

Often processes connect mostly *output to input* (output of one process is the input of the next) corresponding to chain dependencies: The second process is dependent on the first and can only start when the first process has delivered a necessary result.

All these notations can be used to structure processes by composing them from simpler ones (subprocesses) and thereby building nets of these subprocesses by dependency relations. In graph theoretical terminology these nets are *transport networks* [10], which usually have a starting node (source) and an ending node (target). The networks are built


J. Mendling et al. (Eds.): Wil van der Aalst Festschrift, LNCS 16480, pp. 141–154, 2026.
https://doi.org/10.1007/978-3-032-17618-9_11

up from chains, splits, and joins. For organizational aspects of one specific process this may suffice.

In this paper, we look at how connections can be organized and denoted. Especially, we look at what aspects influence a process and take these aspects as targets of process dependency edges. Thereby, we *differentiate dependency* relations. We call the corresponding notation process interaction diagrams, in short PIDs, thereby adding another meaning to the abbreviation "PID". Roughly speaking, these diagrams distinguish incoming edges according to their purpose and thereby make these networks more semantical, corresponding to the different ways, how processes are connected.

The *paper* is *structured* as follows: After having introduced characterizations and the different aspects of a process, which influence the way processes can be connected in PIDs in Sect. 2 and 3, we discuss different examples of PID process interactions in Sect. 3. We present interesting and nontrivial examples of PIDs in Sect. 4. A summary and characterization of the results finish the paper.

## 2 Unusual Side of Processes: Changes and Flexibility

We *continue* the above *characterization* of processes:

A process can be *fixed*/determined, or it can *change*/be dynamic. Fixed processes we often find in business administration, e.g. a reservation. We find changing processes, for example in development depending on creativity. Even in fixed processes we can have changes, which are mostly solved by direct human interaction.

*Changes* can *happen* in a process itself, its embedding into a context, the integration with another process. Inside a process they may happen in modeling, in checking a process, when defining connections to other processes, or when executing a process.

*Where* do *changes* happen? When processes are modeled, when they are used for some time, from definition to redefinition of the process (next version), when processes are detected to belong to a family (detecting similarities), when processes are combined to company-cross processes or even families of such processes.

*Changes* are *due to* evolution (in the process implied by a decision) saying how to continue, or due to a detected error/failure (backtracking and deciding how to correct). Changes also appear when we reorganize processes to detect similarities and differences, organizing a family, or an extension of the underlying process knowledge.

Processes can be specific to an application area, or they are cross-disciplinary, or trying to find similarities corresponding to concepts and implemented tools.

We are working with *processes* for some time in an *unusual sense*. Most of the studies we have made are from informatics and from engineering and focus on creative development. We directly access the challenges of such creative processes as permanent changes and support them with intelligent tools. So, corresponding to process research activities, we work in an interesting and *challenging niche*.

*Processes* have 3 *levels*: lifecycle (e.g. design is only a node), organization (we organize design by assigning persons to parts, without looking into details of the persons' actions), and fine-grained (what are the detailed steps a developer takes). We only studied processes on middle-grained level. On fine-grained level we offered intelligent tools, complex actions of which can be regarded as process junks [19].

## 3   A Notation to Connect Processes

### *Aspects of a Process*

The process is influenced by different aspects, see Fig. 1. The process has an *input* and produces *output*, both can be of quite different kinds. The process has a *goal*, regards different *constraints*, and follows a certain *way to proceed*, expressed from rather vague to precise and determined. The process has an *actor*, usually a human, or a group of humans for a complicated task. The process uses *tools* or available *partial results/solutions* to be a part of the result of the process. Processes apply *knowledge* and/or *experience*. In [19, 22] other aspects of a process are discussed. We omit them here to keep the discussion simple.

The upper part of Fig. 1 corresponds to the *planning part* of the process (goal, constraints, way to proceed), the lower part determines the path in *direction* to the *solution* (partial solutions, tools, actor, experience/knowledge). One should distinguish between a task and the process to solve the task. In this paper a process stands for both. We have seven 'input' aspects and only one for the output.

Any of the corners of process P has a *specific semantic meaning*. So, it is important, at which corner an edge ends; the edge gets the semantics from that. To distinguish the corners, the topmost of them – the goal – is specifically marked to make orientation easier.

The *actor* of a development process is usually a *human*. In automatic processes, the actor can be a *machine* executing a program. Then, goals, constraints, and way to proceed are incorporated in the program. The same is true for experience/knowledge. The machine determines the level of the program (preciseness, degree of formality).

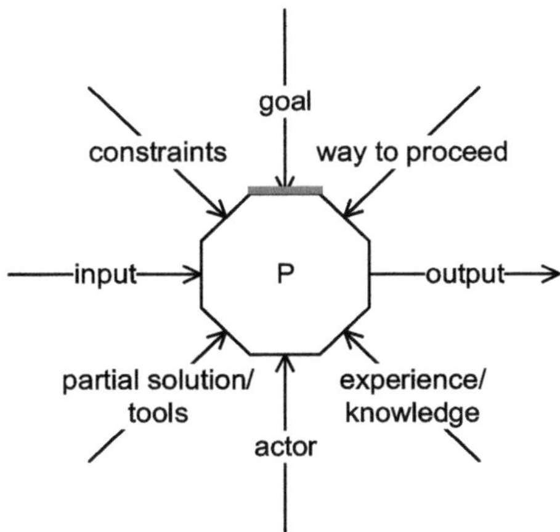


**Fig. 1.**  Different aspects influencing a process P and its output

A process corresponds to the solution of a task, which solves an underlying problem. The task may (a) demand *creativity*, as in acquisition or extension of knowledge, pre-development of a product, development of a novel and nontrivial product, extending a solution to a solution for a family, or detecting deep reuse for a class of solutions by remarkably changing the process. In all these cases, the process is not determined, it demands creativity and new ideas. The task may (b) be rather *determined*, like often executed processes in business administration, or in production of mechanical engineering. Finally, a process may (c) run *automatically*, as found in process automation & control. There, everything is running automatically, determined by software, eventually including interactions of an operator.

Processes can be found on different *granularity levels*: We find (i) *coarse-grained* processes, e.g. on lifecycle level, where we only distinguish subprocesses without looking into their structure. It can be (ii) *medium-grained*, where we go down to identify actions of single developers to manage these developers without regarding how they do their job, like the implementation of a certain component assigned to a developer, or how a subsystem is decomposed, and the parts are assigned to developers. Finally, processes can be (iii) *fine-grained*, e.g. how a designer solves the task assigned to him/her in detail. One further level down, (iv) we find the *actions* of a *tool* used by a developer to facilitate his/her job. Tools can be used on any granularity level.

Furthermore, development processes may be (1) *local* to a certain department, (2) happen inside a company but involving *different departments*, or may (3) spread over *different companies* (local, integrated, or inter-company processes).

What we have said is mostly *independent* from the *level* and *nature* of a *process*. It also applies to any kind of processes, from research, knowledge acquisition, pre-development, development, realization, preparation, production, to after sales and maintenance. In the last sentence we had mechanical engineering in mind. It could also be process engineering, material production, or anything else.

Development *processes* of teams of developers have a certain *structure*. This can be found in every engineering discipline [23, 29]: determining or changing the requirements, the design, and the realization. The latter in engineering is called detail engineering. The *product* of a process is a complex *configuration* of different and mutually dependent artifacts.

### *Process Interactions*

*Process Chain Dependency for Different Purposes*

In Fig. 2 we regard usual chains of processes; one process delivers a result which is handled by the following process. However, the *purpose of handling* is *different*. The examples are from development. In a), process $P_2$ makes the next step after $P_1$, e.g. in a computation. In b), $P_2$ produces a result consistent to the result of $P_1$. In c), $P_2$ formalizes a non-formal result of $P_1$. Further examples are possible.

These examples demonstrate that *chain dependency* between $P_1$ and $P_2$ can have *different semantics*. The examples are typical situations occurring in software development processes carried out by humans. The examples can also be from other domains, such as production or process engineering [21].

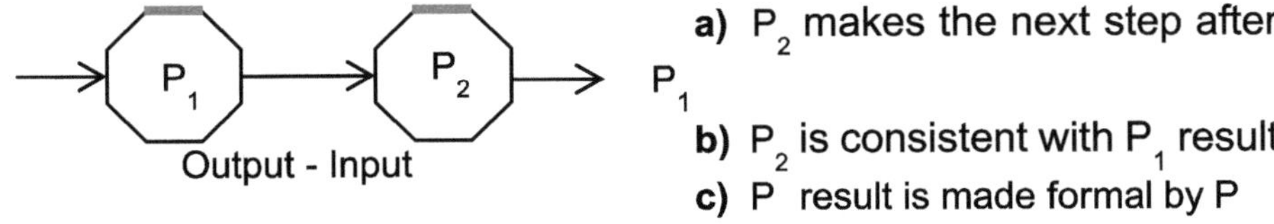



**Fig. 2.** Process chain relations for different purposes

*Processes Creating Components or Tools*

Please remember that the corners of the octagon have a specific meaning. Figure 3 shows that process $P_1$ can deliver a *result*, which makes *process $P_2$ easier*, as in Fig. 3a) $P_1$ delivers a *partial product* for $P_2$, or Fig. 3b) $P_1$ delivers a *tool*, which *helps* for $P_2$. These supports a), b) are possibly not restricted to $P_2$. If this were the case, process $P_1$ would deliver a part of the solution, then completed by $P_2$ (Fig. 2a).

In Fig. 3c, P1 delivers a result, which supports the process $P_2$ by delivering explicit knowledge or experience, helpful for $P_2$. This can be e.g. a checklist of items, which helps not to forget an important aspect for the actor of process $P_2$.

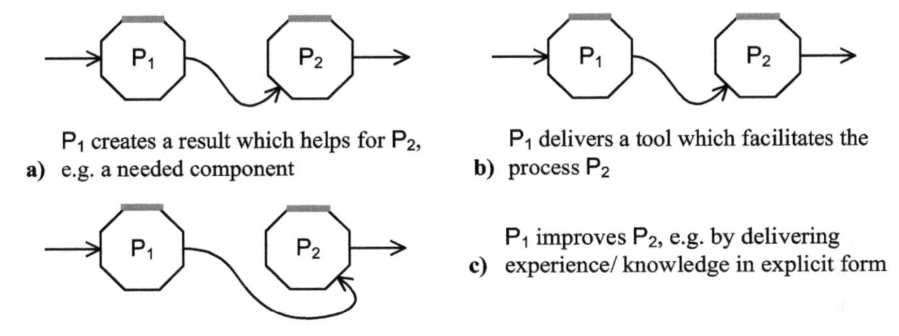



P₁ creates a result which helps for P₂,
**a)**  e.g. a needed component

P₁ delivers a tool which facilitates the
**b)**  process P₂

P₁ improves P₂, e.g. by delivering
**c)**  experience/ knowledge in explicit form

**Fig. 3.** Actor support: facilitating solution by a partial result, tool, experience/knowledge

*Clarifications for other Processes*

Process $P_1$ can *define*/make precise the *goals* of $P_2$ (Fig. 4a), or the *constraints* for $P_2$ (Fig. 4b), or the *way to proceed* in $P_2$ (Fig. 4c). The latter can be from vague and exemplary to formal and complete.

We see: Process $P_1$ can deliver a *helpful result* for *any* of the '*input*' aspects explained in Fig. 1, see Figs. 3 and 4. The composition of both processes $P_1$ and $P_2$ is different from those discussed in Fig. 2. In all cases, we have a dependency of process $P_2$ on process $P_1$. However, we recognize that the semantics of the dependency is different for all cases. Annotations may clarify these distinctions.

*Actors and Machines*

In all examples of above, we had *human actors*. A human actor is *intelligent* and *creative*. The actor can interpret constraints, evaluate a goal, compare a process result with its goal, can follow advice to proceed, can build, evaluate, apply partial results, or apply tools to facilitate or improve a solution. The person can use/apply experience or

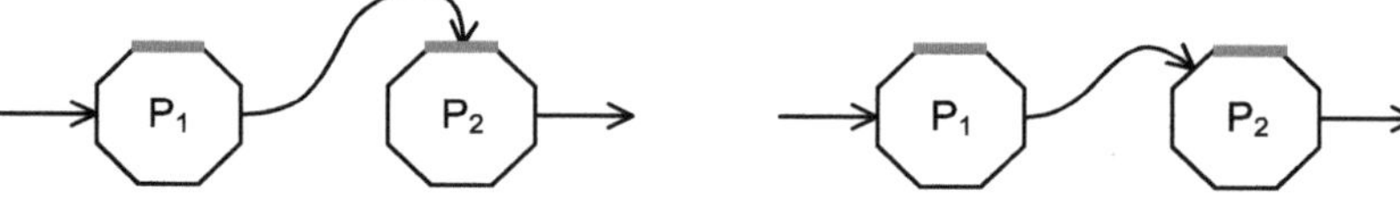

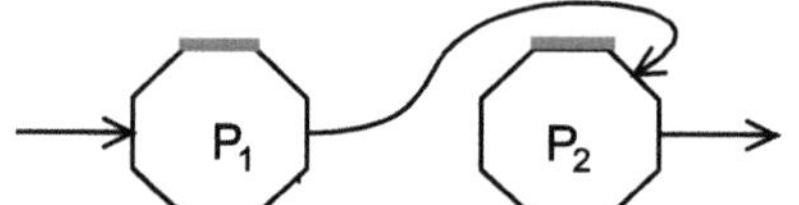

**a)** P₁ determines/ improves/ clarifies the goal of P₂

**b)** P₁ determines the constraints for P₂

**c)** P₁ determines / improves how P₂ should proceed, by giving the steps, a plan how to go, or a methodology

**Fig. 4.** Clarifications, P₁ delivers results for different aspects of P₂

knowledge. This is also true for a scientist, who extends knowledge, as well as for a worker, who carries out a fabrication process.

What is to recognize, if the *process* is *automatic*? And what to obey, if we switch from a human to an automatic process? In informatics terms, an automatic process is a *program* executed by a *machine*. The program may be an executable specification, or a program formulated in an interpreter language together with an interpreter. It can also be a program Pr of a programming language L, together with a machine M for this language (compiler, runtime system, and target machine).

Looking at Fig. 5 and P2, we now discuss that $P_2$ is an *automatic process*. Does this change the situation? $P_1$ can create the program, $P_1$' the machine. Both are human processes. The program with the machine is the automatic process, see Fig. 5a.

A different *explanation in our PID notation* is that $P_1$ creates the program, i.e. the way to proceed, and $P_1$' the actor of $P_2$. The program has been written to follow a goal, to regard restrictions, to use partial solutions or tools, or to adopt knowledge and experience. This, altogether, is incorporated and fixed in the program Pr. So, all the other aspects of $P_2$ (Fig. 1) are determined by the properties of the program (Fig. 5b).

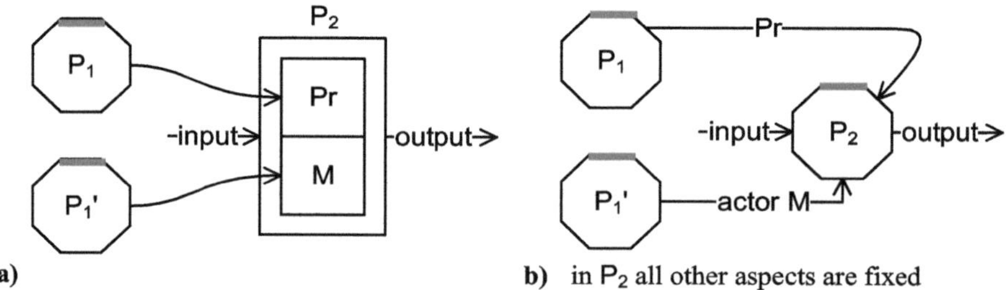

**a)**

**b)** in P₂ all other aspects are fixed

**Fig. 5.** Automatic actor P₂ by program Pr and machine M, in PID notation

# 4   Some Examples of Unusual Connections

### *Production Engineering*

We are now switching to *mechanical engineering*. That differs from software in two ways. (a) The products are produced in a production process after their development, which needs corresponding preparation after product development. Furthermore, (b) the facilities for production must be regarded. Production machinery is used for different products, in a novel product, it might be that the machinery is developed specifically. Both is usually not the case with *software*. In rare cases, there is something like a production of software. This production is mostly just configuration and delivery.

We now discuss the *interaction* of the three *processes* (i) development and production preparation, (ii) production and tool use, and (iii) production facility development [22]. The production of the facility is usually done by other companies, and the production machines in most cases serve for different production processes. The three processes are in *different dimensions*, see Fig. 6.

The example is on the level of *coarse processes* (lifecycle level), which means that the processes are not structured internally. For example, product *development* is usually done in steps belonging to *different levels* (requirements, conceptual and detailed design, detail engineering), which is not done in Fig. 6. These levels are structured internally to express that different people do different things, which must be consistent with each other. This we call middle-grained or *organizational level*, because it structures how the cooperation of different developers is organized. Figure 1 is repeated here as figure legend, as every corner of the octagon has a semantic meaning.

In Fig. 6 we see three process *chains*, which are *orthogonal* to each other:

(a) In the middle and drawn horizontally, there is the *physical product lifecycle*. A product is produced, later it is used and maintained (physical maintenance), and even later we see recycling. The production process uses parts, which are manufactured by suppliers. The chain has the usual output/input dependency relation.

(b) On top and drawn down, we find the *development lifecycle*, again presented in a coarse form with the usual output-input relation. We start with pre-development, to show that development is possible and results in a reasonable product (we build a prototype and decide to go further or stop). Then, we develop the product, using different internal steps. If successful, we start with production preparation, consisting of different internal steps. The results deliver know-how useful and necessary for the manufacturing process, or which corresponds to experience/knowledge. Production preparation also delivers constraints and ways to proceed (e.g. for NC programs).

(c) At the bottom and drawn upwards in Fig. 6, we find the process to *provide* the *platform for manufacturing*. The platform is developed in two parallel steps: (i) How the production platform is built up (determination of corresponding tool machines and how they are configured), and (ii) developing the corresponding automation and control programs. They are both combined in the manufacturing *plant*. Typically, the manufacturing tool machines are not specifically developed and built up (can happen if no corresponding machines are available on the market). However, the tool machines may need some adaptation. Also, the automation and control infrastructure is available, but specific programs must be written, adapted, or generated.

The production plant together with the corresponding personnel is the actor of the manufacturing process.

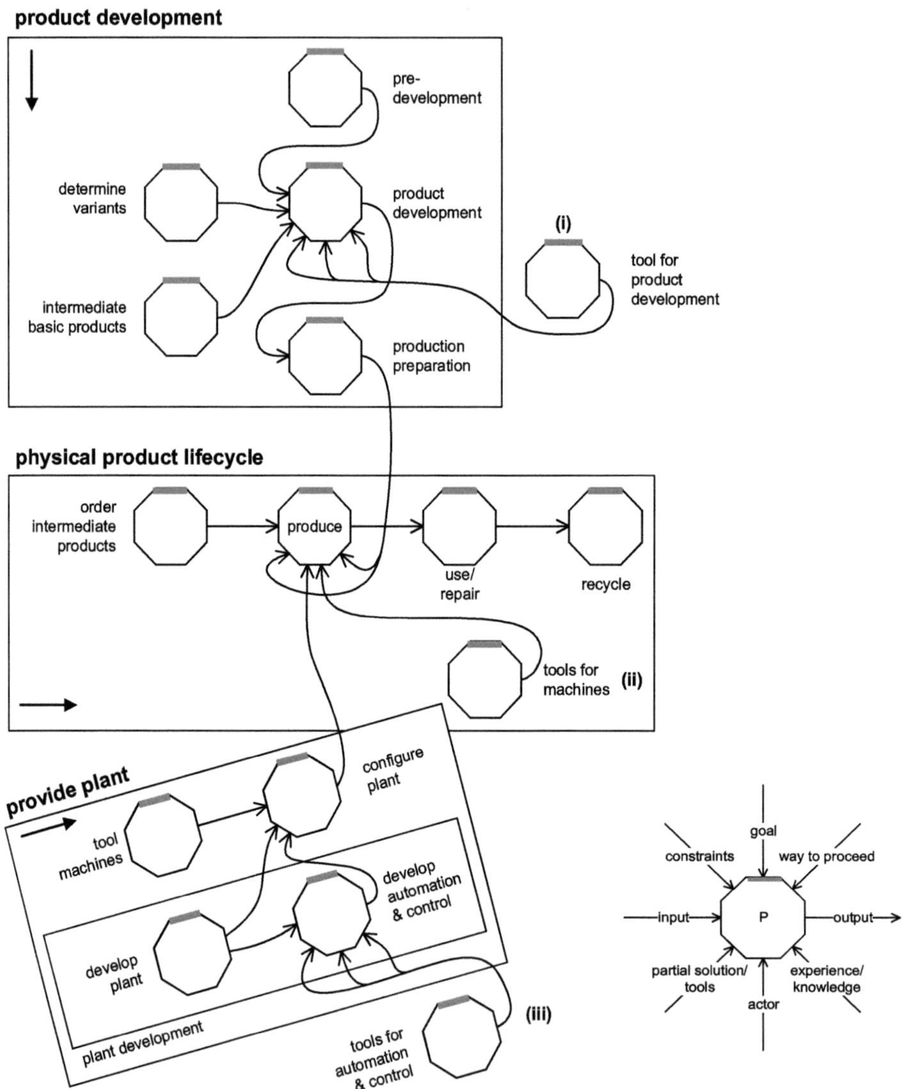



**Fig. 6.** Interleaved and orthogonal processes in production engineering

Summing up, we see that Fig. 6 consists of three coarse *processes* in *three dimensions*: physical production, development of the product to be later produced, and making the production infrastructure (plant) available. The processes are connected to the *business administration process* (ERP, not shown) for sales, production of several products, logistics, maintenance of products in a repair center, after sales relations.

Any of these processes is a cross-company process. The used intermediate products of them have a development and also need a manufacturing infrastructure. All processes *interact* in *different ways*. This was the main argument to sketch the situation.

Now, we introduce further new tools, which come up in the above three dimensions, see Fig. 6: (i) A new software *tool* is introduced which makes *product development* more efficient and helps to avoid mistakes/errors. Secondly, (ii) a new mechanical tool is needed for the *specific production* process. (iii) A new software tool helps in the *design* of the *automation and control* part, again for efficiency and quality improvement. These tools introduce further interaction dimensions.

The new tool for development (i) influences and changes the development process. Especially, it *changes* the *experience/knowledge*, and it also changes the *actors*. The change might be gradual or dramatic. The same is true (iii) for a new tool helping to develop the automation and control part. A tool helping for configuring the production plant (not shown) would influence the configuration process in the same way. Another role has (ii) the tool for a tool machine in the production process. It is produced (usually without development or production), and must be replaced, due to wear and tear.

Mostly production tool development is *not parallel* to product or facility development, or production. It is used for the next product cycle, rarely *in the running process*.

### Hierarchies in and Management of Software Development

We show some further process interactions, which are possible within *software development*, by sketching some of various situations in this subsection.

Firstly, we look at the dependency relations between *requirements engineering*, where the requirements for a future software system or the requirements for a change of an existing software system are made precise, and the following *realization* of the system, see Fig. 7a. In this activity area RE (requirements engineering, modeling and changing requirements), quite different results are produced.

One result of the requirements specification, which determines what the following system is going to do, is often called *functional requirements specification*. This part is (i) the *input* of the realization process. It is used to build up a system in several steps, which is consistent with the functional specification, see Fig. 2b. The requirements deliver *further determinations*: (ii) the goal of the system to be built/changed, (iii) the constraints of the future system, e.g. efficiency parameters, or (iv) they determine the ways to produce the result, e.g. the process shares similarities with other development processes already finished, or is in parallel (as ways to structure the interactive input, such that it is uniform to existing systems). Furthermore, it can (v) determine (v.a) some external components to be used, (v.b) tools to be applied. Furthermore, we (vi) predetermine the development process, e.g. by fixing the corresponding quality assurance procedures. Finally, the spec (vii) states which experience/knowledge is to be applied.

150     M. Nagl

We see that the requirements area produces quite *different results important* for the following development process which specify what to do (i, ii), the constraints for the future product and process (iii, iv), determining properties of the product (iv, v), and of the process (v, vi, vii). This can be separated and expressed by the *different facets* of a process (see Figs. 1 and 7a). This example is one of the rare cases, where *all forms of the dependency relations* occur between two processes, here DR and R of Fig. 7a.

The following process R (realization) is *structured internally*, Fig. 7b. It starts with A for *architecture modeling*. Most of the edges to R are directed to this process. Requirements influence the architecture of the system, or some component realizations.

We assume that the *architecture* process is simple; it can be carried out by one designer and need not be decomposed. For the following *realization* processes for components of the system we can only say that they appear. We do not know how many such processes will come up, as we do not know which components have to be realized. This is fixed in the result of process A, namely a part of/or the complete architecture.

In the *running process* R and the results of process A determine, how the *following processes look like*, see Fig. 7b. Furthermore, the dependency relations between these processes are also determined (e.g. the process for the component $P_{Cj}$ is dependent on that for $P_{Ci}$). Thus, a subnet of the process net is determined by the results of A, see again Fig. 7b. This was called *evolution dynamics* [17, 28].

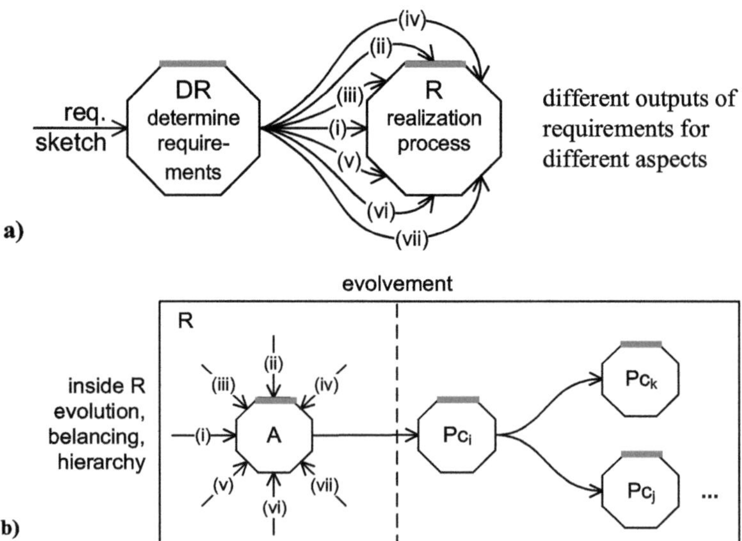


**Fig. 7.** Hierarchy, balancing, and evolution

It should be noted that the extension of the process net of R to get the processes for the components is done by another process, which does not appear in Fig. 7b. This *process* is usually done by a human, the *process manager* (or chief designer), who looks at the architecture (of the product of A), then makes the extension, possibly supported by a tool. The extension in Fig. 7b - a net of subprocesses with dependencies - is the result of this activity. There are *further* and more complex *dynamic situations* possible, some of which we sketch in the summary.

## 5  Summary and Conclusions

*What we have achieved*

We have generalized process notations to express different *influencing parameters* for a process, not only input and output, but to make *dependency relations* more specific.

That allows us to express the *interactions of processes more precisely*, especially the dependencies. We see that the output of one process has different influences on another process. These semantical dependency relations make the diagrams more *meaningful*.

In Sect. 4, we discussed *nontrivial examples*, such as *interleaving processes* (design of the product and planning its production; life cycle of the product, design/configuration of the producing infrastructure). Further examples are the relation between requirements and realization, changes due to process evolution, or showing that management and technical processes are intertwined. All examples profited from the extended notation of this paper. Section 4 also shows that the ideas are applicable to any domain.

*Example processes* can be on different levels: coarse (Figs. 6, 7a), middle (Fig. 7b), or even fine-grained (not used in this paper). We saw human and automatic processes, different situations of mechanical engineering, applications to software engineering, and software engineering in the systems development domain. So, the notation can be used in quite *different situations* wrt granularity, domains, characters of subprocesses.

There are *relations* to current activities in process *research*: In BPMN [2, 27] processes are modeled using parts usually connected by data and control flows. Process landscapes [3] connect processes in companies or other environments being separated but belonging together, as those of Fig. 6. Object-centric process approaches [4] connect related processes belonging to related objects and not only single objects. Finally, federated processes [4, 7] cooperate but nevertheless maintain their independence. So, all these different concepts have to do with integration problems of some sort. That is also the case with the concepts of this paper. They, however, concentrate on unusual and dynamic relations. They focus on some specific questions and do not compete with the abovementioned concepts.

*Our Activities in Process Research*

Some words on our *activities in process modeling*: Besides various tools for the fine-grained level, we have been active mostly on the middle-grained level, to organize development processes, where their parts are carried out by different persons [24, 29]. There, we specialized in models and tools. Especially, we focused on *dynamics* problems, i.e. changes that occur in a process in execution. The different aspects are (i) changes due to *evolution* (only in the running process do we see how to proceed [17], Fig. 7.). (ii) *Backtracking* (a mistake in the development implies that we go back in the process. However, we want to preserve useful results and minimize modifications of others). (iii) *Extending process knowledge* (new experience and knowledge in form of new process type definitions or workflow pieces) can happen in the running process [13, 28]. Finally, there are (iv) *cross-company processes* (where all the above problems occur and a grey-box model is needed, which allows cooperation (both sides know each other) but also protection (of subcontractor knowledge [12, 15]). Thus, the overall challenge was *changeability* even at *process runtime*.

There were many applications and studies. The most influential were in the IPSEN project dealing with new and tightly integrated tools for *software* development [20], in the SUKITS project on a-posteriori extension of tools in *mechanical engineering* [25], and in the IMPROVE project on new tools and furthermore on a posteriori extension of given tools in *chemical engineering* [23]. We developed novel tools, but also extensions of given tools [13, 30].

As indicated above, we concentrated our process research on the middle-grained processes (and on the coarse-grained processes, Figs. 6, 7a). Furthermore, we concentrated on the product part (the outcome) of processes, by building tools to make the product of a process faster or of a better quality to get, thereby supporting the process as well. We did not regard *fine-grained processes*, i.e. how a single developer is planning or doing his work, but we built a lot of tools for him. Fine-grained processes were studied in [19], where activity patterns were retrieved and used to build corresponding *tool actions*.

In this paper we specialized only in the process part and ignored the product, human actor, the support part, all on abstract and detailed level. The research we carried out included these parts [14, 24]. The results of this paper can be used to reformulate and *extend* the *process* part of the literature cited above. Therefore, this paper remains in the tradition of having a clear *focus* in the broad domain of process investigations.

**Acknowledgements and Best Wishes..** *Wil* is an extraordinary person: He is an extremely productive and well-known scientist with an outstanding record of success in process research and surrounding fields [1, 3, 5, 6, 26] as well as in applications [8, 9, 11, 18, 27]. He is well-decorated with prizes and honors. Nevertheless, he is completely unpretentious and friendly to everybody; he really is a friend. We are very proud to have him in the faculty. He should stay as he is. We wish him good health and continuing success, and all the best personally for him and his family. Thanks also go to the two *reviewers* of this paper for helpful and valuable remarks.

# References


1. Aalst, W., van Hee, K.: Workflow Management: Models, Methods and Systems, (in Chinese), Tsinghua University Press (2004)
2. Aalst, W., Hofstede, A., Weske, M. (eds.): BPM, LNCS 2678, Springer (2003). https://doi.org/10.1007/3-540-44895-0
3. Aalst, W.: Process Mining - Data Science in Action, Springer (2016). https://doi.org/10.1007/978-3-662-49851-4
4. Aalst, W.: Object-centric process mining: dealing with divergence and convergence in event data, in SESF 19, LNCS 11724, 1–23 (2019)
5. Aalst, W., Best, E. (eds.) Application and Theory of Petri Nets and Concurrency (PETRI NETS 2017), LNCS 10258 (2017)
6. Aalst, W., Stahl, C.: Modeling Business Processes: A Petri Net Oriented Approach, MIT Press (2011)
7. Buijs, J., van Dongen, B., Aalst, W.: Towards Cross-Organizational Process Mining in Collections of Process Models and their Executions, Intern. Workshop BPM 2011, pp. 2–13, Springer (2011). https://doi.org/10.1007/978-3-642-28115-0_2

8.  Brecher, C., Schuh, G., Aalst, W., Jarke, M., Piller, F., Padberg, M. (eds.): Internet of Production: Fundamentals, Methods, Applications, Springer (2023). https://doi.org/10.1007/978-3-031-44497-5

9.  Dumas, M., Aalst, W., Hofstede, A.: Process-Aware Information Systems: Bridging People and Software through Process Technology, Wiley (2005)

10. Deo, N.: Graph Theory with Applications to Engineering and Computer Science, Dover Publications (1974)

11. Hofstede, A., Aalst, W., Adams, M., Russell, N.: Modern Business Process Automation: YAWL and its Support Environment, Springer (2010). https://doi.org/10.1007/978-3-642-03121-2

12. Heller, M.: Dezentralisiertes, sichtenbasiertes Management übergreifender Entwicklungsprozesse, Doctoral Dissertation, RWTH Aachen (2008)

13. Heer, Th.: Controlling development processes, Doctoral Dissertation, RWTH Aachen, AIB SE 10 (2011)

14. Heller, M., Jäger, D., et al.: An adaptive and reactive management system for project coordination. LNCS **4970**, 300–366 (2008)

15. Jäger, D.: Unterstützung übergreifender Kooperation in komplexen Entwicklungsprozessen, Doctoral Dissertation RWTH Aachen, ABI 34 (2003)

16. Jablonski S., Bussler, C.: Workflow Management Modeling Concepts, Architecture and Implementation, International Thomson Computer Press (1996)

17. Krapp, K.A.: An adaptable environment for management of development processes, Doct. Diss. RWTH Aachen, ABI 22 (1998)

18. Mans, R., Aalst, W., Vanwersch, R.: Process Mining in Healthcare: Evaluating and Exploiting Operational Healthcare Processes, Springer (2015). https://doi.org/10.1007/978-3-319-160 71-9

19. Miatidis, M., Jarke, M. et al.: Using developers' experience in cooperative design processes. In: LNCS, vol. 4970, pp. 185–223 (2008). https://doi.org/10.1007/978-3-540-70552-9

20. Nagl, M. (ed.): Building tightly integrated software development environments - The IPSEN Project, LNCS 1170, Springer (1996). https://doi.org/10.1007/BFb0035684

21. Nagl, M.: Process Interaction Diagrams are more than Chains or Transport Networks, in Nagl, Westfechtel: Software Architectures: Topics Usually Missed in Textbooks, pp. 123–140, Springer (2024). https://doi.org/10.1007/978-3-031-51335-0

22. Nagl, M., Faneye, O.B.: Gemeinsamkeiten und Unterschiede von Entwicklungsprozessen in verschiedenen Ingenieurdisziplinen, vol. 24, pp. 311–324

23. Nagl, M., Marquardt, W. (eds.): Collaborative and distributed chemical engineering: from understanding to substantial design process support, LNCS 4970, Springer (2008). https://doi.org/10.1007/978-3-540-70552-9

24. Nagl, M., Westfechtel, B.: A Universal component for the administration in distributed and integrated development environments, TR AIB 94–8, Aachen (1994)

25. Nagl, M., Westfechtel, B. (Hrsg.): Integration von Entwicklungssystemen in Ingenieuranwendungen - Substanzielle Verbesserung der Entwicklungsprozesse, Springer (1999). https://doi.org/10.1007/978-3-642-59857-9

26. Russell, N., Aalst, W., Hofstede, A.: Workflow Patterns, The Definite Guide: MIT Press (2016)

27. Ruecker, B., Freund, J.: Real-Life BPMN. 5th edn. Independently published (2025)

28. Schleicher, A.: Roundtrip process evolution support in a wide spectrum process management system, Doctoral Dissertation RWTH Aachen, DUV (2002)

29. Westfechtel, B.: Models and tools for managing development processes, habilitation Thesis, RWTH Aachen, LNCS 1646 (1999)
30. Wörzberger, R.: Management dynamischer Geschäftsprozesse auf Basis statischer Prozessmanagementsysteme, Doctoral Dissertation, RWTH, ABI SE 2 (2010)

# Contributions of Wil van der Aalst to the Fundamentals of Business Process Management


Marlon Dumas[1], Marcello La Rosa[2], Jan Mendling[3,4]([✉]),
and Hajo A. Reijers[5]

[1] University of Tartu, Tartu, Estonia
[2] The University of Melbourne, Melbourne, Australia
[3] Humboldt-Universität zu Berlin, Department of Computer Science,
Berlin, Germany
jan.mendling@hu-berlin.de
[4] Weizenbaum Institute, Berlin, Germany
[5] Utrecht University, Department of Information and Computing Sciences,
Utrecht, The Netherlands



**Abstract.** The contributions by Wil van der Aalst to the fundamentals of business process management can be measured in different ways. A quantitative assessment can easily build on scientometrics. What is more difficult to grasp is the richness of topics that he has been working on so far. In this chapter, we use the business process management lifecycle as a map to structure the content of his research. Our analysis highlights the diversity of contributions that he has made to this field of research. His contributions on process mining, the workflow patterns, and soundness stand out.



**Keywords:** Business Process Management · Business Process
Lifecycle · Retrospective


## 1 Introduction

Wil van der Aalst is one of the most impactful computer scientists of our time. The quantity of Wil's work can be easily measured using scientometric analysis. He is co-author of more than 1,200 publications listed on the DBLP computer science bibliography. His publications have collectively received more than 160,000 citations according to Google Scholar, securing him a ranking as one of the ten top computer scientists worldwide of our time.[1] In the second edition of our

---

[1] https://research.com/scientists-rankings/computer-science.


Jan Mendling s research was supported by the Einstein Foundation Berlin under grant EPP-2019-524, by the Federal Ministry of Research, Technology and Space under the grant 16DII143, and by Deutsche Forschungsgemeinschaft under grants 496119880 (VisualMine), 531115272 (ProImpact), SFB 1404/2 (FONDA).





J. Mendling et al. (Eds.): Wil van der Aalst Festschrift, LNCS 16480, pp. 155–170, 2026.
https://doi.org/10.1007/978-3-032-17618-9_12

textbook on Fundamentals of Business Process Management [30], we cited 23 publications co-authored by Wil (out of around 200 citations), which reflects his imprint in the field.

Publications and citations have the advantage that they are easy to track. Often, they are too quickly considered as measures of productivity. In the end, they are reductionist and hardly able to reflect the personality and the content of the contributions of an eminent scholar. Also for Wil, these measures only capture the quantity of his contributions, but hardly their quality and richness in terms of topics and concepts.

The aim of this chapter is to capture the diversity of Wil's key contributions to the fundamentals of business process management (BPM). To this end, we use the BPM lifecycle as described in our textbook [30]. For each lifecycle phase, we highlight prominent examples of his work and discuss their impact. In this way, we provide transparency of how diverse Wil's contributions are. In particular, his contributions on process mining, the workflow patterns, and soundness stand out.

This chapter is structured as follows. Section 2 describes the business process management lifecycle as an aid to structure the overarching research field. Section 3 reflects specific contributions of Wil to the different lifecycle phases. Section 5 concludes the paper and gives an outlook on future research.

## 2    Business Process Management Lifecycle

The different management tasks of business process management are often described by help of a lifecycle. Lifecycle models are used in various textbooks such as those by Michael zur Muehlen [44] or by Mathias Weske [69]. The idea of a lifecycle can already be found in the textbook by Wil and Kees van Hee on Workflow Management from 2002 [11, p.213], though not very prominently. For the Fundamentals of Business Process Management textbook we use the BPM Lifecycle to organize the content. We also use it here to structure the spectrum of Wil's contributions.

An overview of the BPM lifecycle is provided in Fig. 1. In essence, there are six lifecycle phases that depend upon each other.

1. *Process identification* has the goal to construct a high-level description of a company from a process-oriented perspective. It often yields a process architecture and priorities that help to select processes for improvement.
2. *Process discovery* has the goal to describe a process systematically as an as-is model. To that end, information is collected about the current way a process operates.
3. *Process analysis* has the goal to obtain insights into current issues of the business process. Various analysis techniques exist, both qualitative and quantitative.
4. *Process redesign* has the goal to design an improved process that at least fixes the issues of the current process. Various methods support redesign including

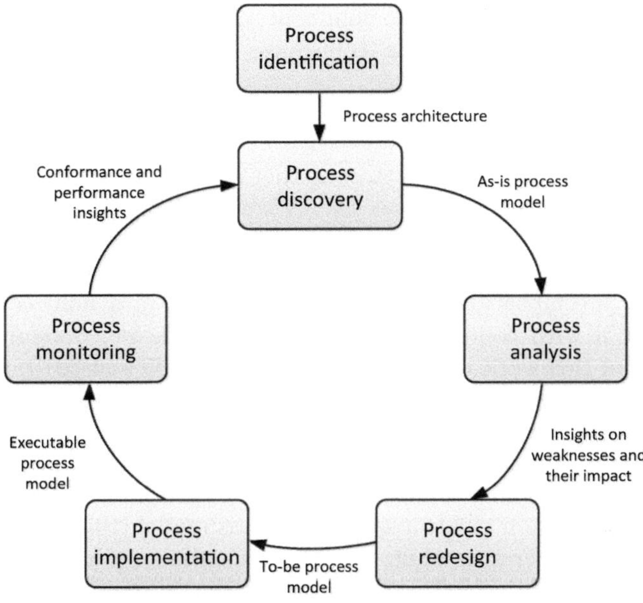


**Fig. 1.** BPM Lifecycle [30]

business process re-engineering [35], best practices [40] or the business process design space [33].

5. *Process implementation* has the goal to implement an executable business process model from a to-be process model specification. Such executable business process models can be executed by business process management systems (formerly known as workflow systems).

6. *Process monitoring* has the goal to monitor the performance and conformance of the implemented business process.

The BPM lifecycle is considered a useful aid for mapping contributions to BPM research. It has been used for literature reviews of different kind [23, 47] and for investigating the impact of new BPM-related technologies [42, 62]. The BPM lifecycle provides a comprehensive perspective on business process management. Therefore, we will also use it in the following.

## 3   Wil's Contributions to Different BPM Lifecycle Phases

This section presents important contributions by Wil in each of the six phases of the BPM lifecycle. At this stage, we will not conduct a systematic literature review. Instead, we will hand-pick those works that the authors have found to be most impactful for their work. In the typology of Paré et al., such a review is called a narrative review [45]. Such a review typically does not aim for generalization, but rather strives to comment on a specific part of the literature. Here, these are Wil's contributions to business process management.

## 3.1  Process Identification

Process identification has the goal to construct a high-level description of a company from a process-oriented perspective. A key challenge is to model a complex collection of business processes in a compact way. Typical concepts for process architecture design support the specification of sequences, decomposition, and specialization. Specialization is difficult to represent in a non-redundant way. To this end, Wil with co-authors developed concepts for configurable process models. Much of this work was published between 2005 and 2010.

The concept of configurable process models builds on the observation that enterprise systems are configurable in various ways and the such configuration modifies the business processes support by these systems [28]. Configurable process models offer mechanisms for describing reference models in a generic way, such that a configuration yields a specific process model [10]. Configuration can be expressed with operators that a) block execution paths and b) skip specific activities on execution paths. These operations have initially been formally defined for Configurable Event-Driven Process Chains (C-EPCs) [48,55].

The initial work on C-EPCs by Wil and co-authors inspired various techniques that help managing variability of process models. These other techniques include C-YAWL [32], ADOM [53], aEPC [51], PESOA [61], BPFN [43], or Provop [34]. The survey by Wil with Marcello La Rosa, Marlon Dumas, Frederik Milani summarizes this stream of research [38]. An extension of this work combines the concepts of configurable process models with specific techniques for process mining. As a result, reference models can be mined together with their configuration [25,31].

## 3.2  Process Discovery

Wil recognized already in the 1990s that Petri nets provide a solid foundation for modeling business processes. In a technical report from August 1995, he defines the class of business procedure nets (BP-nets) [1], which after dropping the free-choice restriction were renamed to workflow nets [3]. Why Petri nets? In 1998, he highlights three reasons [4]. First, Petri nets do not only offer a visual notation, but also formal semantics. Second, Petri nets provide an explicit notion of state. Third, a plethora of analysis techniques have been defined for Petri nets, which can be easily reused for process analysis. These reasons made Petri nets the reference for Wil's work on process modeling. Petri nets offered Wil all the required concepts for defining the notion of soundness [3,18,27], a formal correctness criterion that plausibly every meaningful process model should satisfy. This Petri net based approach to process modeling is presented in his books with Kees van Hee [11] and with Christian Stahl [17].

In practice, Wil and his colleagues found various languages for modeling processes. It was the ambition of the workflow patterns initiative, driven by him and Arthur ter Hofstede, to conquer this process tower of Babel. The original 20 workflow patterns [13] were a milestone on this journey. These patterns made the commonalities between various modeling languages explicit by the help of using Petri nets. They also strongly influenced the standardization of a modeling language that later became the Business Process Model and Notation (BPMN) [70]. The initial set of workflow patterns was just the start of a larger research program. It unfolded naturally, since there a patterns in various areas of workflow management: workflow data patterns [60], workflow resource patterns [60], workflow exception patterns [58], or service interaction patterns [15]. All these works have been integrated in the book published by MIT Press on Workflow Patterns: The Definitive Guide, co-authored by Nick Russell, Wil, and Arthur ter Hofstede [59]. This book discusses the fundamentals of business process modeling and business process management systems. Each set of patterns on control flow, data, and resources are discussed in a separate chapter. Also complementary pattern sets are presented, making this book a seminal reference for the work sparked by the workflow patterns initiative.

## 3.3  Process Analysis

The topic of quantitative analysis of business processes was a recurrent one in the early days of Wil's career. In his earliest paper according to the DBLP database [19], Wil reports on the development of ExSpect, a language for specifying discrete event systems. In the paper, he shows how ExSpect can support the modeling and specification of logistics processes, specifically a process where a producer receives orders, allocates products to the order from its inventory, and loads and dispatches trucks to take orders to multiple customers. This paper already contain many of the themes that will recur across Wil's career. Reading the paper, we can elicit elements of object-centric process modeling in it. The starting point in ExSpect is the identification of object types, such as suppliers, orders, products, and trucks, and the specification of relations between these objects. The ExSpect language is inspired by Coloured Petri nets, a discrete event modeling language that Wil would come to use many times during his career. In some of his other early papers, we see Wil using Interval Timed Coloured Petri Nets for temporal analysis of transportation processes.

In the mid-1990s, we see Wil realizing the potential of using Petri nets to model and analyze business processes. In this respect, we see Wil and his collaborators developing techniques to analyze the behavioral correctness of process models. This led a.o. things to Woflan [64], a tool for verification of behavioral correctness of process models, including soundness analysis of so-called workflow nets, a class of Petri nets that Wil defined to capture case-based processes.

On the other hand, we see Wil developing methods for business process simulation based on ExSpect. Along the way, Wil started to advocate for the use of data to enrich process models with simulation parameters for the purpose of short-term simulation (i.e. simulation starting from ongoing cases, for operational decision-marking) [49].

The topic of discovering simulation models based on execution data came back on several occasions during Wil's career. In 2007 during a visit to Queensland University of Technology (QUT), he instigated the development of a proof-of-concept data processing pipeline to enrich process models specified in the YAWL workflow language [12] to enable short-term simulations. He would then continue this route with his PhD student, Anne Rozinat, who developed a comprehensive method to discover simulation models from data [57]. Anne Rozinat would later go on to co-found one of the first companies in the field of process mining (Fluxicon) together with Christian Günther, another PhD student of Wil. Anne Rozinat's work would go on to inspire the development of various methods for simulation model discovery, e.g. Simod [26].

The first Handbook of Business Process Management came up in 2010. Naturally, Wil was invited to write a chapter for this handbook. Evidence of the fact that Wil considered simulation to be a key method for business process analysis is the fact that he accepted to lead the writing of the handbook's chapter on simulation [16]. His contributions to simulation did not stop there. We see Wil coming back to the topic, for example by advocating the use of system dynamics simulation models (discovered from data) for quantitative analysis of processes [46], and later on by proposing techniques to discover object-centric simulation models [36], thus combining three of his most recurrent research themes: process mining, object-centric processes, and simulation.

## 3.4  Process Redesign

Process redesign is an important phase of the BPM lifecycle, but typically an area for which it is difficult to develop generally usable artifacts. The reason for this is that redesign is a highly contextual task: it depends on the specific situation whether a process change is indeed an improvement. However, Wil did some pioneering work on this topic.

At an early stage, Wil identified the value of formal process models as an enabler for process redesign. In a workshop paper in 1995 – only a few years after Michael Hammer and Tom Davenport published their *magna opera* on Business Process Reengineering and Business Process Innovation, respectively – he and Kees van Hee described the value of Petri nets for specifying business processes in an understandable and precise way, with the added benefit that such models could also be simulated to compare *as-is* vs. *to-be* processes. Until now, Petri nets have been a popular model for these purposes.

From this early work, which set the stage for improving processes, Wil moved on to the development of redesign methods and techniques. Inspired by his knowledge of logistics, domains he studied in detail during his time as a PhD candidate, he came up with a remarkable idea: A product's bill-of-material could serve as an inspiration for the organization of the process to generate such a product. If a product component is composed of two smaller parts, then it is necessary that these parts need to be put together at some point. So, the bottom-up compositional hierarchy of process parts also indicates an order of generating these parts.

In 1997, Wil first introduced this idea [2], which was then extended for publication in Computers In Industry [5]. This was also the inspiration for follow-up work by two PhD candidates whom he supervised, namely Hajo Reijers and Irene Vanderfeesten. In this way, the spectrum of methods broadened with the development of the transformational redesign method of Product-Based Workflow Design [50], as well as with the automated and optimized executions of process designs generated in this way [63].

One process redesign problem that has intrigued Wil for some time is the so-called *knockout process*. In essence, this concerns a process that consists of a number of checks where a negative result for one check leads to immediate termination of the process. In case the checks can be freely ordered, there is an optimal way to do so. This idea and related design decisions form the subject of a single-authored paper by Wil in Decision Support Systems [6]. Interestingly, this idea became one of the elements in the set of 29 redesign heuristics [52], which also made its way to the Fundamentals book.

## 3.5 Process Implementation

Wil has often emphasized that his early work was inspired by the idea that better workflow systems are needed for better adoption in practice. He had investigated the specification of logistics processes already in the early 1990s.

The first contribution by Wil with the term *workflow* in the title appeared in 1996. This paper with Marc Voorhoeve discussed problems that arise when workflows are adapted [65]. Again, Wil makes use of his Petri net knowledge, in particular concepts of bisimilarity, extension and reduction. These support monitoring of adapted workflows at a higher level using views.

Wil's ambition to contribute to a better practice of workflow management created several circles of discussions with a diverse spectrum of researchers and practitioners. A first documentation of these discussions is the volume on Business Process Management from 2000 edited together with Jörg Desel and Andreas Oberweis [9]. The volume integrates works on process design, formalisms, and applications with contributions a.o. by Jörg Becker, Michael Rosemann, Anatol Holt, Clarence 'Skip' Ellis, Wolfgang Reisig, Mike Papazoglou, and August-Wilhelm Scheer. The success of this volume sparked the idea to launch a side-event co-located with the Petri Nets conference 2003 in Eindhoven: the International Conference on Business Process Management was born [14].

System support continued to be a key research area for this new business process management community. Where workflow technology was the initial focal point of his work on systems, he broadened this perspective to Process-Aware Information Systems [29]. In this way, the many enterprise systems that are not solely concerned with process orchestration yet are in some way capable of guiding processes were taken into account.

Arguably Wil's most influential work on the implementation of processes went through the work he carried out with Arthur ter Hofstede, Nick Russell and others on the identification, documentation, and formalization of a wide range of *patterns*. Most notably, the collection of control-flow patterns, describing the logical and logistical routing constructs that can be found in processes [13], made an enormous impact. Companies interested in acquiring process-aware systems started using these patterns to evaluate the completeness of available technologies; in turn, vendors started paying attention to incorporate missing constructs in their modeling languages. This line of research was successfully extended to also incorporate patterns in resource allocation, exception handling, data processing, and more[2].

Attesting to the success of the workflow patterns is the immediate spin-off of Wil's work into the development of YAWL [12]. What started as a specification language ("Yet Another Workflow Language") became over time an open-source BPM/Workflow system with advanced capabilities such as support for multiple instances (where at runtime a task may have multiple instances active at the same time), a generalized OR-join (where a construct only waits for further triggers if these can indeed arrive) and cancellation (where a collection of activities can be terminated through the execution of a certain task). In [22] a very nice overview can be found of the use of the system in other academic settings, which is only one of the many ways in which the work of Wil and his colleagues influenced the implementation of processes in the real world.

## 3.6   Process Monitoring

Process monitoring is the last phase of the BPM lifecycle. Wil was one of the first academics to recognize that monitoring business processes required more than dashboards and KPIs; it demanded a deep integration of process models with event data. His work on process mining provided the theoretical and technological underpinnings for process monitoring, enabling organizations not only to track activities as they unfold but also to detect deviations, bottlenecks, and compliance issues in real time. By combining work from automated discovery and conformance checking with performance analysis, Wil's contributions turned process monitoring from a purely descriptive practice into a diagnostic and predictive capability, shaping the way enterprises today monitor and improve their operations.

The automated discovery of process models from event logs has been one of the most impactful contributions of Wil and his research team, which inspired generations of academics to follow suit by extending and improving his seminal work. The pioneering Alpha Miner algorithm, introduced in the early 2000s, marked the first systematic attempt to automatically construct a Petri net from event logs [20]. While highly influential as a proof of concept, and improved in all forms and shapes (see e.g. Alpha Miner+, Alpha Miner++, Alpha Miner# [67,68]), this family of miners was limited by its sensitivity to noise and inability to handle short loops or incomplete information. This motivated the development of the Heuristics Miner, which incorporated frequency-based thresholds to better deal with noise and real-world variability, thereby making automated discovery more robust and practically usable in industry contexts [66].

---

[2] See http://www.workflowpatterns.com/patterns/ for an overview.

Building on these foundations, the Inductive Miner represented a conceptual leap forward. It introduced a recursive divide-and-conquer strategy to guarantee process models that are sound, block-structured, and easy to interpret [39]. This made it a landmark contribution to the field, ensuring a balance between theoretical rigor and practical usability. However, Inductive Miner's strict guarantees sometimes came at the cost of model flexibility, which led to the proposal of the Split Miner. This latter miner aimed for a middle ground: discovering models that balance fitness, precision, and simplicity, even if that means relaxing block-structuredness [24]. This distinction highlights the different philosophies in automated discovery—prioritizing formal soundness vs. pragmatic accuracy.

In recent years, Wil has further advanced the field by championing Object-Centric Process Mining (OCPM) to overcome the limitations of traditional case-centric discovery. Instead of assuming a single case notion, OCPM recognizes that modern processes are inherently object-centric, involving interactions between multiple entities such as orders, items, and payments. This paradigm shift addresses one of the most persistent criticisms of early automated discovery approaches: their reliance on artificially imposed case identifiers. By extending process mining with objects, Wil has paved the way for a new generation of discovery algorithms that better capture the complexity of real-world processes [7].

Conformance checking enables the comparison between observed behavior in event logs and normative models. Once again, Wil's work was seminal in this area. He and Anne Rozinat introduced the token-based replay technique, which provided one of the first systematic methods for diagnosing deviations by replaying event logs on a Petri net and identifying missing, consumed, or remaining tokens [56]. This framework not only quantified fitness, but also offered a clear diagnostic perspective that made it possible to explain deviations at the level of individual traces and activities. While highly intuitive and computationally efficient, token replay had limitations in terms of precision and its ability to fully capture all forms of behavioral deviations.

These challenges led to the development of alignment-based conformance checking, which reformulated conformance as a cost-based optimization problem [8]. Alignments ensure a one-to-one correspondence between log traces and model executions, offering a more precise foundation for evaluating fitness, precision, and generalization. This framework has since become widespread in the field of conformance checking, supporting not only diagnostics but also performance analysis and compliance monitoring, giving rise to many extensions and improvements, such as Daniel Reißner's work on reducing the computational complexity of alignment based on automata and S-Components [54].

## 4 "Wil, Do You Have 2 Minutes?"

### 4.1 Marlon's Memories

I first met Wil in 2002 in Brisbane, during one of his visits to QUT. It was the start of a long collaboration. There are three moments in this collaboration I vividly remember.

First moment was in 2004. Wil was incredibly enthusiastic about the topic of process mining. He was trying to convince me to get into it. At first, I did not pay much attention to it. A few years later, though, I jumped feet first into this topic. It led me to embark on the Apromore project with Marcello La Rosa, which eventually became a successful commercial process mining product. Few people know that Wil was the one who came up with the name Apromore. It's an acronym for Advanced PRocess MOdel REpository, reflecting its origins as a modeling tool before expanding into process mining and simulation.

The second moment came in 2007, when Wil and I, together with our QUT colleagues, co-authored a paper on data-driven, short-term simulation [71]. In it, we outlined a tool architecture that enriched a process model with simulation parameters derived from event logs, and incorporated the current state of ongoing cases. By running simulations from that live state, we could forecast how the process would unfold in the near future. This collaboration marked the beginning of one of my favorite lines of research—one that would eventually lead to the Simod method for automated discovery of simulation models from event logs [26]. Some of these ideas later found their way into Apromore as well.

The third moment was in 2012. I was working on the topic of object-centric process mining (OCPM).[3] I remember discussing this topic with Wil at a meeting. He was not overly enthusiastic about it at first. He would later tell me that he did not like the notations we were using to represent object-centric models back then, and that put him off. Years later, once he saw OCPM with the right notations, he became one of its most passionate champions.

Looking back, Wil and I shared countless passionate debates on all kinds of research questions. I often wish I had spent more time with him at the whiteboard, wrestling with ideas and chasing insights together.

### 4.2  Marcello's Memories

I've known Wil since 2005 and I have shared so many fantastic experiences with him. Looking back to the early days of my PhD, I will never forget the so-called two-minute meetings with Wil. Whenever he visited QUT in Brisbane, these meetings would often start in the late afternoon and, almost without us realizing it, continue well into the night. What was meant to be a quick check-in always turned into hours of deep discussion, where Wil—patient as ever—helped me grasp the foundations of process modeling and verification: Petri Nets, and their intricacies (and help me find elegant proofs to my theorems). I remember my first PhD paper came out of those nights; a paper that, interestingly, would only be published years later [37]. Those long evenings were more than academic guidance; they were formative experiences that fueled my passion and shaped my way of thinking about research. They remain some of my fondest memories of mentorship.

---

[3] We used to call it artifact-centric process mining back then.

### 4.3   Jan's Memories

In 2004, I had a tiny paper at a CAISE workshop [41], which gave me the opportunity to visit the conference in Riga, Latvia. At that occasion, I met some of my favorite writers in person, including Wil, Michael Rosemann, and Michael zur Muehlen. We ended up in a bar, Wil brought us one beer after the other and I have vague memories of some terrible shots in poisonous green. While everybody got more and more exhausted, it was Wil who got more and more awake. It must have been around 2am that he approached the disc jockey. The DJ looked at him in bewilderment: there was this tall Dutch guy asking him to let him check his emails on his DJ laptop! That night taught me a lesson on passion for your research and won me beautiful academic friends.

### 4.4   Hajo's Memories

My earliest memory of Wil goes back to 1994, when I was carrying out my master's project. In this project, I was investigating the impact of redesigning the intake process of a mental healthcare institute in Eindhoven, for which I needed to simulate this process under different conditions. The state of the art technology at that time was ExSpect, which was not an easy system to use. Rumors had it that there was a printed manual somewhere in the department and I pinned it down to the office of some young and brilliant assistant professor. When I knocked on his door and asked for the manual, he gave me a long, hard look after which he asked in a stern voice: "Will you bring it back?" I think that was the most tense moment I ever had with Wil, which says a lot about what a pleasure it was to work with him. Six years later, we would write a joint paper about ExSpect [21]. Way more unexpectedly, way more surprisingly: Wil would become the most influential person in my academic career.

## 5   Conclusion

There is a pattern in Wil's research: find a new topic, develop its core, then broaden and deepen it. He has done that with the adoption of Petri nets for process modeling and verification, for the workflow patterns, for configurable process modeling, for process mining, and more recently for object-centric process mining.

**Acknowledgements.** Jan: We proudly acknowledge that we managed with painful manual editing to have all first-author publications by Wil listed alphabetically under "A" like "Aalst", and not under "V" like "van". Marcello: But we must say it at least here: this is wrong. We are writing papers in English, not in Dutch. And in English your surname starts with "v" (not even "V"). You simply have to accept it, Wil! The truth is that no one ever wanted to argue with you. Hajo: I think the Dutch are right. Marlon: The correct English spelling with first name is "Wil van der Aalst" and without the first name "Van der Aalst".

# References


1. van der Aalst, W.M.P.: A class of petri nets for modeling and analyzing business processes. Tech. rep. (1995)
2. van der Aalst, W.M.P.: Designing workflows based on product structures. In: Proceedings of the ninth IASTED International Conference on Parallel and Distributed Computing Systems, IASTED/Acta press, Anaheim, pp. 337–342 (1997)
3. van der Aalst, W.M.P.: Verification of workflow nets. In: International conference on application and theory of petri nets, pp. 407–426. Springer (1997). https://doi.org/10.1007/3-540-63139-9_48
4. van der Aalst, W.M.P.: Three good reasons for using a petri-net-based workflow management system. In: Information and Process Integration in Enterprises: Rethinking Documents, pp. 161–182. Springer (1998). https://doi.org/10.1007/978-1-4615-5499-8_10
5. van der Aalst, W.M.P.: On the automatic generation of workflow processes based on product structures. Comput. Ind. **39**(2), 97–111 (1999)
6. van der Aalst, W.M.P.: Re-engineering knock-out processes. Decis. Support Syst. **30**(4), 451–468 (2001)
7. van der Aalst, W.M.P.: Object-centric process mining: Dealing with divergence and convergence in event data. In: Ölveczky, P.C., Salaün, G. (eds.) Software Engineering and Formal Methods - 17th International Conference, SEFM 2019, Oslo, Norway, 18-20 September 2019, Proceedings. LNCS, vol. 11724, pp. 3–25. Springer (2019). https://doi.org/10.1007/978-3-030-30446-1_1
8. van der Aalst, W.M.P., Adriansyah, A., van Dongen, B.F.: Replaying history on process models for conformance checking and performance analysis. WIREs Data Mining Knowl. Discov. **2**(2), 182–192 (2012)
9. van der Aalst, W.M.P., Desel, J., Oberweis, A. (eds.): Business Process Management, Models, Techniques, and Empirical Studies, LNCS, vol. 1806. Springer (2000). https://doi.org/10.1007/3-540-45594-9
10. van der Aalst, W.M.P., Dreiling, A., Gottschalk, F., Rosemann, M., Jansen-Vullers, M.H.: Configurable process models as a basis for reference modeling. In: International Conference on Business Process Management, pp. 512–518. Springer (2005). https://doi.org/10.1007/11678564_47
11. van der Aalst, W.M.P., van Hee, K.M.: Workflow Management: Models, Methods, and Systems. MIT Press, Cooperative information systems (2002)
12. van der Aalst, W.M.P., ter Hofstede, A.H.M.: YAWL: yet another workflow language. Inf. Syst. **30**(4), 245–275 (2005)
13. van der Aalst, W.M.P., ter Hofstede, A.H.M., Kiepuszewski, B., Barros, A.P.: Workflow patterns. Distrib. Parallel Datab. **14**(1), 5–51 (2003)
14. van der Aalst, W.M.P., ter Hofstede, A.H.M., Weske, M. (eds.): Business Process Management, International Conference, BPM 2003, Eindhoven, The Netherlands, 26-27 June 2003, Proceedings, Lecture Notes in Computer Science, vol. 2678. Springer (2003). https://doi.org/10.1007/3-540-44895-0
15. van der Aalst, W.M.P., Mooij, A.J., Stahl, C., Wolf, K.: Service interaction: Patterns, formalization, and analysis. In: International School on Formal Methods for the Design of Computer, Communication and Software Systems, pp. 42–88. Springer (2009). https://doi.org/10.1007/978-3-642-01918-0_2
16. van der Aalst, W.M.P., Nakatumba, J., Rozinat, A., Russell, N.: Business process simulation. In: Handbook on Business Process Management 1: Introduction, Methods, and Information Systems, pp. 313–338. Springer (2010). https://doi.org/10.1007/978-3-642-00416-2_15

17. van der Aalst, W.M.P., Stahl, C.: Modeling Business Processes - A Petri Net-Oriented Approach. Cooperative Information Systems series, MIT Press (2011). http://mitpress.mit.edu/books/modeling-business-processes
18. van der Aalst, W.M.P., et al.: Soundness of workflow nets: classification, decidability, and analysis. Formal Aspects Comput. **23**(3), 333–363 (2011)
19. van der Aalst, W.M.P., Waltmans, A.W.: Modelling logistic systems with ExSpect. In: van Hee, K.M., Sol, H.G. (eds.) Dynamic Modelling of Information Systems I, The First International Working Conference on Dynamic Modelling of Information Systems, Noordwijkerhout, The Netherlands, 9-10 April 1990, pp. 269–287. Elsevier/North Holland (1990)
20. van der Aalst, W.M.P., Weijters, A.J.M.M., Maruster, L.: Workflow mining: discovering process models from event logs. IEEE Trans. Knowl. Data Eng. **16**(9), 1128–1142 (2004)
21. van der Aalst, W.M., et al.: ExSpect 6.4 an executable specification tool for hierarchical colored petri nets. In: International Conference on Application and Theory of Petri Nets, pp. 455–464. Springer (2000). https://doi.org/10.1007/3-540-44988-4_26
22. Adams, M., Hense, A.V., ter Hofstede, A.H.M.: YAWL: an open source business process management system from science for science. SoftwareX **12**, 100576 (2020)
23. Ahmad, T., van Looy, A.: Business process management and digital innovations: a systematic literature review. Sustainability **12**(17), 6827 (2020)
24. Augusto, A., Conforti, R., Dumas, M., La Rosa, M., Polyvyanyy, A.: Split miner: automated discovery of accurate and simple business process models from event logs. Knowl. Inf. Syst. **59**(2), 251–284 (2019)
25. Buijs, J.C., van Dongen, B.F., van der Aalst, W.M.: Mining configurable process models from collections of event logs. In: Business Process Management: 11th International Conference, BPM 2013, Beijing, China, 26-30 August 2013. Proceedings, pp. 33–48. Springer (2013). https://doi.org/10.1007/978-3-642-40176-3_5
26. Chapela-Campa, D., López-Pintado, O., Suvorau, I., Dumas, M.: SIMOD: automated discovery of business process simulation models. SoftwareX **30**, 102157 (2025)
27. Dehnert, J., van der Aalst, W.M.P.: Bridging the gap between business models and workflow specifications. Int. J. Cooperat. Inf. Syst. **13**(03), 289–332 (2004)
28. Dreiling, A., Rosemann, M., van der Aalst, W.M.P., Sadiq, W.: From conceptual process models to running systems: a holistic approach for the configuration of enterprise system processes. Decis. Support Syst. **45**(2), 189–207 (2008)
29. Dumas, M., van der Aalst, W.M.P., ter Hofstede, A.H.M. (eds.): Process-Aware Information Systems: Bridging People and Software Through Process Technology. Wiley (2005). https://doi.org/10.1002/0471741442
30. Dumas, M., La Rosa, M., Mendling, J., Reijers, H.A.: Fundamentals of Business Process Management, Second Edition. Springer (2018). https://doi.org/10.1007/978-3-662-56509-4
31. Gottschalk, F., van der Aalst, W.M.P., Jansen-Vullers, M.H.: Mining reference process models and their configurations. In: OTM Confederated International Conferences on the Move to Meaningful Internet Systems, pp. 263–272. Springer (2008). https://doi.org/10.1007/978-3-540-88875-8_47
32. Gottschalk, F., van der Aalst, W.M.P., Jansen-Vullers, M.H., La Rosa, M.: Configurable workflow models. Int. J. Cooperat. Inf. Syst. **17**(02), 177–221 (2008)
33. Gross, S., Stelzl, K., Grisold, T., Mendling, J., Röglinger, M., vom Brocke, J.: The business process design space for exploring process redesign alternatives. Bus. Process. Manag. J. **27**(8), 25–56 (2021)

34. Hallerbach, A., Bauer, T., Reichert, M.: Capturing variability in business process models: the PROVOP approach. J. Softw. Maint. Evol. Res. Pract. **22**(6–7), 519–546 (2010)

35. Hammer, M., Champy, J.: Re-engineering the corporation: a manifesto for business revolution (1993)

36. Knopp, B., Pourbafrani, M., van der Aalst, W.M.P.: Discovering object-centric process simulation models. In: 5th International Conference on Process Mining, ICPM 2023, Rome, Italy, 23-27 October 2023, pp. 81–88. IEEE (2023)

37. La Rosa, M., van der Aalst, W.M.P., Dumas, M., ter Hofstede, A.H.M.: Questionnaire-based variability modeling for system configuration. Softw. Syst. Model. **8**(2), 251–274 (2009)

38. La Rosa, M., van der Aalst, W.M.P., Dumas, M., Milani, F.P.: Business process variability modeling: a survey. ACM Comput. Surv. (CSUR) **50**(1), 1–45 (2017)

39. Leemans, S.J.J., Fahland, D., van der Aalst, W.M.P.: Discovering block-structured process models from event logs - A constructive approach. In: Colom, J.M., Desel, J. (eds.) Application and Theory of Petri Nets and Concurrency - 34th International Conference, PETRI NETS 2013, Milan, Italy, 24-28 June 2013. Proceedings. LNCS, vol. 7927, pp. 311–329. Springer (2013). https://doi.org/10.1007/978-3-642-38697-8_17

40. Mansar, S.L., Reijers, H.A.: Best practices in business process redesign: validation of a redesign framework. Comput. Ind. **56**(5), 457–471 (2005)

41. Mendling, J., Strembeck, M., Neumann, G.: A motivation for multiple activity instantiation in BPEL4WS processes. In: Grundspenkis, J., Kirikova, M. (eds.) CAiSE 2004 Workshops in connection with The 16th Conference on Advanced Information Systems Engineering, Riga, Latvia, 7–11 June, 2004, Knowledge and Model Driven Information Systems Engineering for Networked Organisations, Proceedings, vol. 2, pp. 245–246. Riga Technical University, Riga, Latvia, Faculty of Computer Science and Information Technology (2004)

42. Mendling, J., et al.: Blockchains for business process management-challenges and opportunities. ACM Trans. Manage. Inf. Syst. (TMIS) **9**(1), 1–16 (2018)

43. Moon, M., Hong, M., Yeom, K.: Two-level variability analysis for business process with reusability and extensibility. In: 2008 32nd Annual IEEE International Computer Software and Applications Conference, pp. 263–270. IEEE (2008)

44. Muehlen, M.Z.: Workflow-Based Process Controlling: Foundation, Design, and Application of Workflow-driven Process Information Systems, vol. 6. Logos-Verlag (2004)

45. Paré, G., Trudel, M.C., Jaana, M., Kitsiou, S.: Synthesizing information systems knowledge: a typology of literature reviews. Inf. Manage. **52**(2), 183–199 (2015)

46. Pourbafrani, M., van der Aalst, W.M.P.: Discovering system dynamics simulation models using process mining. IEEE Access **10**, 78527–78547 (2022)

47. Recker, J., Mendling, J.: The state of the art of business process management research as published in the BPM conference: recommendations for progressing the field. Bus. Inf. Syst. Eng. **58**(1), 55–72 (2016)

48. Recker, J., Rosemann, M., van der Aalst, W.M.P., Mendling, J.: On the syntax of reference model configuration–transforming the C-EPC into lawful EPC models. In: International Conference on Business Process Management, pp. 497–511. Springer (2005). https://doi.org/10.1007/11678564_46

49. Reijers, H.A., van der Aalst, W.M.P.: Short-term simulation: bridging the gap between operational control and strategic decision making. In: Proceedings of the IASTED International Conference on Modelling and Simulation, pp. 417–421 (1999)

50. Reijers, H.A., Limam, S., van der Aalst, W.M.P.: Product-based workflow design. J. Manag. Inf. Syst. **20**(1), 229–262 (2003)
51. Reijers, H.A., Mans, R., van der Toorn, R.A.: Improved model management with aggregated business process models. Data Knowl. Eng. **68**(2), 221–243 (2009)
52. Reijers, H.A., Mansar, S.L.: Best practices in business process redesign: an overview and qualitative evaluation of successful redesign heuristics. Omega **33**(4), 283–306 (2005)
53. Reinhartz-Berger, I., Soffer, P., Sturm, A.: Extending the adaptability of reference models. IEEE Trans. Syst. Man Cybern. Part A Syst. Hum. **40**(5), 1045–1056 (2010)
54. Reißner, D., Armas-Cervantes, A., Conforti, R., Dumas, M., Fahland, D., La Rosa, M.: Scalable alignment of process models and event logs: an approach based on automata and s-components. Inf. Syst. **94**, 101561 (2020)
55. Rosemann, M., van der Aalst, W.M.P.: A configurable reference modelling language. Inf. Syst. **32**(1), 1–23 (2007)
56. Rozinat, A., van der Aalst, W.M.P.: Conformance checking of processes based on monitoring real behavior. Inf. Syst. **33**(1), 64–95 (2008)
57. Rozinat, A., Mans, R.S., Song, M., van der Aalst, W.M.P.: Discovering simulation models. Inf. Syst. **34**(3), 305–327 (2009)
58. Russell, N., van der Aalst, W.M.P., ter Hofstede, A.H.M.: Workflow exception patterns. In: International Conference on Advanced Information Systems Engineering, pp. 288–302. Springer (2006). https://doi.org/10.1007/11767138_20
59. Russell, N., van der Aalst, W.M.P., ter Hofstede, A.H.M.: Workflow Patterns: The Definitive Guide. MIT Press (2016)
60. Russell, N., ter Hofstede, A.H.M., Edmond, D., van der Aalst, W.M.P.: Workflow data patterns: Identification, representation and tool support. In: International Conference on Conceptual Modeling, pp. 353–368. Springer (2005). https://doi.org/10.1007/11568322_23
61. Schnieders, A., Puhlmann, F.: Variability mechanisms in e-business process families. In: Abramowicz, W., Mayr, H.C. (eds.) Business Information Systems, 9th International Conference on Business Information Systems, BIS 2006, May 31 - June 2, 2006, Klagenfurt, Austria. LNI, vol. P-85, pp. 583–601. GI (2006). https://dl.gi.de/handle/20.500.12116/24172
62. Schönig, S., Ackermann, L., Jablonski, S.: Internet of Things meets BPM: a conceptual integration framework. In: SIMULTECH, pp. 307–314 (2018)
63. Vanderfeesten, I., Reijers, H.A., van der Aalst, W.M.P.: Product-based workflow support. Inf. Syst. **36**(2), 517–535 (2011)
64. Verbeek, H.M.W., Basten, T., van der Aalst, W.M.P.: Diagnosing workflow processes using Woflan. Comput. J. **44**(4), 246–279 (2001)
65. Voorhoeve, M., van der Aalst, W.M.P.: Conservative adaption of workflow. In: Wolf, M.F., Reimer, U. (eds.) Proceedings of the First International Conference on Practical Aspects of Knowledge Management, PAKM 1996, Basel, Switzerland, 30-31 October 1996, pp. 8:1–8:20. Swiss Group for Artificial Intelligence and Cognitive Science (SGAICO) (1996)
66. Weijters, A.J.M.M., van der Aalst, W.M.P.: Rediscovering workflow models from event-based data using Little Thumb. Integr. Comput. Aided Eng. **10**(2), 151–162 (2003)
67. Wen, L., van der Aalst, W.M.P., Wang, J., Sun, J.: Mining process models with non-free-choice constructs. Data Min. Knowl. Discov. **15**(2), 145–180 (2007). https://doi.org/10.1007/S10618-007-0065-Y

68. Wen, L., Wang, J., van der Aalst, W.M.P., Huang, B., Sun, J.: Mining process models with prime invisible tasks. Data Knowl. Eng. **69**(10), 999–1021 (2010)
69. Weske, M.: Business Process Management: Concepts, Languages. Architectures, Springer Nature (2024)
70. White, S.A., et al.: Process modeling notations and workflow patterns. Workflow Handb. **2004**(265–294), 12 (2004)
71. Wynn, M.T., Dumas, M., Fidge, C.J., ter Hofstede, A.H.M., van der Aalst, W.M.P.: Business process simulation for operational decision support. In: ter Hofstede, A.H.M., Benatallah, B., Paik, H. (eds.) Business Process Management Workshops. LNCS, vol. 4928, pp. 66–77. Springer (2007). https://doi.org/10.1007/978-3-540-78238-4_8

# Business Process Support for Emergency Management

Thomas Rose[✉]

Fraunhofer FIT, Schloss Birlinghoven, 53757 Sankt Augustin, Germany
`Thomas.Rose@fit-extern.fraunhofer.de`

**Abstract.** Measures, tasks and procedures are pivotal elements of any rescue and relief operation in case of emergencies. Hence, process management appears certainly as attractive candidate for rescue and relief organizations by nature. Design, modelling, and assessment of emergency management processes may build upon concepts well established for business process management. Yet, the question arises whether emergency management processes differ from processes in business or software engineering. In this paper, we report on our experiences on transferring process management concepts and tools to emergency planning. It discusses whether rescue and relief organisations can capitalize on off-the-shelf business process management tools to prepare for disasters more effectively, and whether concepts of process modelling can be applied directly to standard operating procedures and vice versa. This paper will demonstrate why conventional business process means are inapplicable as planning tool in this domain. Smart checklists might be better suited both for the planning and during response phases of emergency episodes. Essentially, business process and emergency management often differ in their underlying governance.

**Keywords:** Emergency Management · Business Processes · Standard Operating Procedures · Check Lists · Cross-organizational Reference Models

## 1 Introduction

Business Process Management (BPM) comes with a record of methods and tools proven effective to enable organizations to design, model, assess, and optimize counter measures for emergency episodes. Once transferred successfully, measure and tasks for emergency episodes will be modelled as processes. Processes will mature and become optimized for better preparedness, response, and recovery from crises. By creating standardized procedures, enhancing communication and collaboration, and enabling real-time monitoring, BPM will enable relief and rescue organizations to reduce response times, improve coordination, and foster continuous learning and adaptation to challenging situations. The question arises whether the nature of the emergency management (EM) domain matches

This paper reports on experiences gained in national and international projects conducted by the author with colleagues at Fraunhofer FIT in Sankt Augustin and RWTH Aachen University, Germany.


J. Mendling et al. (Eds.): Wil van der Aalst Festschrift, LNCS 16480, pp. 171–182, 2026.
https://doi.org/10.1007/978-3-032-17618-9_13

with the perception of processes underlying prevailing tools for process management [18, 19].

Key to a successful capitalization on process management is the identification and modelling of processes [10]. Unfortunately, the authors found no adequate means for domain experts to grasp, to describe, or to formally model their courses of action themselves in daily work or for large-scale crisis. As far as we know no other research group investigated to date a modelling methodology custom-tailored to the emergency domain. Our objective is to support emergency experts in their modelling endeavours themselves. [34] discuss their ideas on customising a modelling language and on so-called activity templates, but do not elaborate on modelling concepts, tool support, and evaluation results. Flexibility with regard to the evolution of instances and schemas is supported technically by systems like Adept [23], while [15] present a reference framework for the different roles in emergency preparation and templates for specific design patterns [14]. Domain-oriented methods and tools are lacking although needs amplify due to a continuous increase of technical and natural risks.

Means for process modelling are well established for software and business processes with proven benefits. Essentially, we experienced that conventional business process modelling means are completely inappropriate to formalize standard operating procedures by emergency management organisations themselves. Consequently, BPM software is also unfitting as planning support in this domain [19].

However, the core objectives of business process modelling still provide vital contributions towards empowering rescue forces amid emergency preparation. On the one hand, process modelling is instrumental for establishing transparency inside and across organisations. A process model represents the activities planned as well as anticipated and their respective organisational units responsible for execution. Hence, courses of action can be communicated inside and across organisational boundaries. On the other hand, a process model can serve other purposes such as performance analysis, generation of checklists, simulation of counter measures, etc. These opportunities basically strive for quality improvement and rely on analysing patterns of the schema as well as simulation of admissible instantiations.

We present a critical reflection of deploying process modelling for the planning of counter measures for major disasters. And we discuss the objectives and concepts of process modelling, e.g., does the functional scope of tools for process modelling coincide with the objectives of rescue organisations and do the modelling concepts adequately address the objectives of rescue organisations.

## 2  Business Process Management

Industry intensively utilizes means for BPM to model, analyse, and execute recurrent and predictable business procedures. EPC (Event-driven Process Chain) [8] is one famous representative of graphical modelling languages for BPM. It describes the main concepts of a business process as: *functionalities*, triggered by *events*, executed by *organisational units* (referenced by *roles, positions*), passing and creating *information objects,* and linked by *connectors* allowing one to control the flow of functionalities, i.e. how functions are called (*and, or, xor*).

BPM typically distinguishes schemas and instances for the representation of processes, which is not always very familiar to rescue forces. They often talk about processes without distinguishing schema and case level. Yet, such distinction is an eye opener, because it unveils the difference between a capability such as ladder operator and available resources with required capabilities during operations.

EPC and their modelling methodology has been customized for an initial experiment with fire brigades to explore the potential of BPM for fire brigades. The customisation focused on the wording of control flows in first place. Functions turned to measures and events to notifications [24]. Further adaptations revolved around the use of resources. Fire brigades felt comfortable with the modelling methodology following these adaptations.

Additional exercises, e.g., process model for assessment by chief emergency physician on the scene, showed comparable results [27]. Domain oriented terminology is of pivotal importance for rescue and relief organisations as modelling incentive. Although processes are important, strategic objectives are at least of equal importance. Rescue forces think more in terms of strategic goals and objectives rather than tasks. Yet, modelling options for such strategy considerations are sparse in BPM environments. Modelling tools for strategic dependencies like i* seem to address different perspectives for modelling and analysis [33]. However, modelling of strategic rationales and an assessment of achievements appears more important than prevailing cost and performance indicators.

In parallel, emergency management organisations have discovered and promote the concept of *Standard Operating Procedures* (SOP) to describe commonly agreed courses of actions, which fire brigades, police departments, and rescue organisations should follow when in action (see for example [1], FW FfM 2011 [6]). Hence, the need of a modelling methodology for rescue and relief organisation is urging. Interestingly, emergency organisations also use the term algorithm to underpin the motivation for clearly defined structures and control flows. It seemed obvious for us to elaborate whether commercial business process modelling solutions might also be instrumental for the engineering of such SOP. Looking at the hierarchical structures in emergency management, e.g., city, county, state, SOP embody reference models serving as attractive means for scaling: *not everyone can prepare for anything*.


## 3   Our Background

Our assessment on BPM for crisis management is based on several projects with rescue and relief organisations. These projects examined different perspectives:

1. *Utilizing BPM tools for process capture* – Modelling the operational concept for cross-regional support of mass casualty incidents (MCI) with prevailing BPM methods [25]

   This project delivered a proof of concept for the use of business process means towards emergency preparation. We translated an already defined concept for the treatment of mass-casualties [28] into a formal process model, i.e. we transferred EM content into formal process models. This exercise demonstrated the virtues of formal process models, i.e. transparency inside and across organisations. Acceptance of models by domain experts has been high due to the domain-oriented terminology. This acceptance also translated into trust of the analysis.

2. *User-centred process assistance* – Risk management process support for small to medium-sized communities for planning of natural or man-made disasters (project ERMA) [17]

We strengthened the domain orientation by a modelling tool with a more intuitive interface directly tailored towards the terminology of the EM domain, but still founded in the look and feel of BPM tools (graphs with activities as nodes while edges presented the control flow). User acceptance was high due to the interface custom-tailored to domain expert's terminology. Yet, putting users on the driver seat for modelling is still a challenge.

3. *Re-engineering processes* – Mobile Data Capture and Communication for Emergency Medical Services [30]

Capturing patient data and an automation of information flows has been at the centre for a process improvement exercise. The process for data capture was re-engineered based on seamless information flows from the scene towards hospitals to improve situatedness of treatment. A mobile interface has been created built upon the processes optimized. However, the processes were not presented in detail but merely the services of the interface. Still, we faced the problem that domain experts were unable to change the process.

4. *Planning support for emergency preparedness* – Process support for emergency management organisations in case of a long-lasting power blackout (project InfoStrom) [20]

Power blackouts certainly call for procedures to be designed and coordinated in advance. We elaborated on a planning metaphor they already use and formalised it in order to provide IT support: checklist. A conceptual model of checklist has been designed and accompanied with editing services working in a network environment. Specific converters allowed one to translate into BPM tools.

Although we successfully employed BPM means –whether commercial or self-implemented– we could not enrapture our emergency management partners. To re-iterate, they liked the modelling results and usage perspectives, but disapproved planning process, tools and terminology. We undertook a critical follow-up research to find out why these projects felt a step short. Several indicators amid the projects were unveiled as potential reasons and are juxtaposed in Sect. 5.

## 4   Cross-Organisational Process Design – The ÜMANV

Our BPM journey for emergency episodes started with the ÜMANV (Überörtliche Unterstützung für den Massenanfall von Verletzten – *mass casualty incident* requiring supra-regional support). A specification of this operational concept, in which 500–1200 injured persons need treatment, was available [28] as starting point for modelling exercises.

The description encloses a text document of approximately 45 pages length, enriched by some graphics and visualization diagrams that already suggest a process-oriented view, yet do not go beyond it towards formalization. Objectives and requisites are described precisely in the specification although not explicitly exposed. The outcome of this research was a modelling methodology for emergency management processes, based on a commercial BP management tool and developed in collaboration with domain experts. It comprised several modelling views that illustrate the strategic level of the operational concept together with separate views on the services and the organizations that deliver them. The resulting model promoted an analytical evaluation of the procedures, thus boosting a high professional precision [25].

Our experience trying this modeling task was sobering. Most tools for process modeling use their own specific terms. These terms are usually fixed and do not adjust for new naming systems. For organizations focused on urgent response, like fire-fighting services, this situation proves unacceptable. These groups operate under their own specific rules, laws, and benchmarks; altering terms risks creating disorder and failure, especially regarding who tells whom what to do. Emergency medical services, fire services, and police services also use distinct terms. For cooperative planning to work, one must translate and explain the terms used. Furthermore, one needs to show the various aims and what happens because of them [29].

The core frameworks and review features in most process control programs fit business operations, not crisis response. For this reason, they usually assume the user wants financial gain. For instance, the programs examine important assets like hours and currency, yet overlook whether aims or targets were met. Consequently, the tools' foundational frameworks fail to properly address aims or targets. Still, police and fire services gauge success by whether they meet tactical and operational aims.

Other significant model differences center on how the organization and its sections appear. Businesses usually form around lasting organizational sections; emergency groups rely on temporary units, whose location, duties, capacity, and similar aspects change.

## 5  Discussion

Process management provides key support for designing and evaluating ways to reach objectives defined. Process management began with office automation, business informatics and software projects. Then, it extended into more application areas. Important fields still include manufacturing and production businesses, known for their clear processes. Supporting processes requiring much knowledge or complexity remains limited.

Process modeling primarily aims for three results: automation, quality, and transparency.

Many applications automate processes. This automation with information technology saves time and money. However, IT systems do not handle most tasks in emergency management. Information technology only improves information management and alert procedures. Therefore, automation tools for process management do not help to prepare or plan for emergencies.

Another reason to model a process is to improve a plan or course of action to achieve or assure objectives. A model helps make the plan better and more effective. Once a plan exists as a formal model, a team can analyze it. This analysis checks performance, resource use, and communication needs. For rescue organizations, many of these details are also important. However, the most important question for the plan's design often remains unanswered: Does this process truly help to manage the disaster? Does the process meet my strategic objectives?

To answer this question, first check and connect the main goals with the tasks. It is more important to align these goals than to change the steps in a work process. Unfortunately, most tools for planning processes do not help to define these goals. Some tools connect activities and processes with goals. But they do not show how these goals depend on each other.

Goals are very important, and we need to consider them carefully. Therefore, we must improve methods for process modeling. These methods should help find the right goals. They also need to explain the reasons for design choices and unveil design rationales [22]. Strategic design rationales might serve as additional means [33]. That makes it easier for people to reuse and share plans.

Improving process quality is a key reason for modeling processes. This ensures different users perform a task at a similar high standard. That is especially important for rescue organizations. For example, fire brigades and medical services show this by defining and using standard operating procedures.

Process models also make things clearer inside and between organizations. Organizations examine process models to understand their ways of working. They also grasp why other groups take certain steps. This deeper understanding lets them foresee upcoming actions, whether their own or someone else's, and make necessary arrangements.

To re-iterate, creating process models reveals both benefits and drawbacks for getting ready for emergencies. Rescue organizations gain from the clear view and better quality of action plans process modeling brings. A significant problem surfaces because most process modeling tools pay little attention to reaching goals, a major shortcoming when supporting rescue organizations' aims. Similarly, people find the language and functions of common tools too complex and unfocused for the purpose of planning for emergencies.

In an execution stance, additional concepts for dynamic control flow are required. A common adaption idea in handling emergencies involves increasing the alarm (moving from a lower alert to a higher one) along with lowering the alert afterward. Emergency planning also includes different ways to act, depending on the warning status. This status relates for instance to water levels in a flood, wind speed during a storm, or how fast rain falls. Actions for a higher status often contain tasks from lower statuses, add specific tasks or make existing ones bigger, and possibly swap out resources or tasks if you skip a level. The same applies when lowering the alert, where tasks "go backward" one step at a time (imagine people returning to a hospital or care facility after leaving). Right now, building models and carrying out these "alarm-raising" processes are neither put into practice nor studied in research, as far as we observe. These dynamic movements of control usually stay outside the usual tools for managing business processes.

Though an implementation with so-called worklets for different instances of a sub-process is possible in principle, more natural implementations are desirable.

The quest for completeness furnishes the most decisive impediment of process modelling. BPM typically claims a complete understanding of the intended course of action without any discrepancy. The philosophy of process modelling does not allow incomplete and partial models. Yet, action in emergencies often have to be prepared in a stepwise approach and call for customisation amid the event [10] since "effective response to a crisis is a combination of anticipation and improvisation" [12]. Incompleteness and flexibility are still open research issues in process management, although adaptive and ad-hoc workflows emerged.

The following table relates the characteristics of off-the-shelf BPM methods and tools with the requirements of emergency management organisations [21].

| Characteristics of BPM Tools | Requirements of emergency management organisations for planning |
|---|---|
| Concentration on automatic execution (office execution) | Concentration on planning, simulation, learning, and traceability |
| Analysis according to costs and time | Analysis according to fulfilment of goals and objectives<br>Analysis concerning overload of resources (staff) or double use of locations and rescue means |
| Expect complete model | Want to model skeletons of processes to be filled during operation based on situation, reusable process fragments |
| Large amount of functionalities, also for export, import, execution, database connection, etc. | Easy to use interface, scalable, i.e. only necessary functions visible |
| Fixed meta-model of processes | Change of meta-model to specific ones for different emergency management domain organisations |
| Rudimentary organisational meta-model, concentration on company terms and permanent units | Specific organisational meta-model with focus on non-permanent units, roles, capabilities, positions, ranks and the like<br>Support of organisational changes due to switch of alarm level or phases |
| Fixed terminology | Change of terminology to user-specific "language" |
| Mostly single user environment | Collaborative access by different organisations<br>Outlining of intersections between process models<br>Discussion groups for exchange of opinions<br>Translation features for interchange |
| Rare support of design patterns, no means for traceability of decisions | Support of design patterns and provision of means for traceability of decisions |
| Bilateral agreements for cross-organisational processes | Ad-hoc process interchanges between several different organisations with own models and terminology [10] |
| Predictable, foreseeable events triggering actions | Modelling of an unknown number as well as unpredictable timing and existence of events triggering actions |

(continued)

(*continued*)

| Characteristics of BPM Tools | Requirements of emergency management organisations for planning |
|---|---|
| No support for "escalation" of processes | Concepts for the planning of "escalation" processes |

## 6 Smart Checklists for Emergency Management

Project InfoStrom taught us the beauties of checklists. When existing BPM software or modelling methods are not successful, how to support emergency planning with a proper tool for modelling and analysing: not changing their way of working, by speaking their language, and by supporting their mind-set? How can several organisations plan collaboratively their courses of actions? And how can they possibly detect conflicts of resources and needs for co-ordination?

InfoStrom elaborated on the concept of *smart checklist* [20]. Checklists are well known in the aviation industry as well as emergency management domain (see e.g. [6]). But currently, IT-support for creating or using such checklists is mainly based on Microsoft Word or Excel and respective print outs. However, paper or Office documents cannot avoid conflicts on resources used and the like. Thus, a smarter approach is required for referencing resources from a common pool and by detecting location conflicts with checklists. Services and checks typical for BPM tools cannot help due to the lack of a formal model. Details of our checklist manager with editing and monitoring services are shown in [20]. A snapshot of checklists according to purpose is given below.

| A **Checklist** consists of several | Maybe sorted in hierarchical categories |
|---|---|
| **Items** describing | due to events, based on rules, in chronological order |
| • **Who** makes | Organisations with units/persons |
| • **What** | Measures with respective attributes |
| • **Where** and | Location |
| • **With What** | Material and Machines |
| • **Why** | Because of Event or by Rule |

The set of support services offered by our prototype has been limited to some essential functions such as visualisation and editing of check lists with various domain-oriented consistency checks, execution support on different devices and use of dictionaries for cross-organisational synchronisation. Collaborative and shared execution of check lists has been emphasised as innovative delegation and control feature by participating organisations because pending tasks can be shared among different units. In addition, version management demonstrated its benefits for organisational change management although it sounds purely technical in first place.

Typically, stakeholders from many different domains are involved in a large-scale crisis. Hence, plans to solve such a crisis must be created together with representatives of all domains. Unfortunately, terminologies in different domains are also dissimilar. This diversity is further compounded by using many acronyms in their internal communication. These acronyms shorten the duration of communication during an operation, but they also aggravate the communication to other organisations and external people, e.g., the public or private companies. Therefore, synchronization of terms from domains is required. Our initial prototype employed a kind of ontology roadmap for matching the terms. Language models might deliver better solutions today.

To re-iterate, a combination of the ease-of-use and effectivity experienced with smart checklist and the functional power of support services offered by BPM tools appears as attractive direction to follow.

## 7  Conclusion

Concepts and tools for process management have been instrumental for process capture, assessment, and cross-organizational communication. However, process management for emergency and relief episodes furnishes a biotope that comes with a special blend of governance [19]. Emergency and relief organization are founded in objectives that differ from economic businesses.

Process models certainly improve transparency inside and across organisation. On the one hand, organisations can learn their practices from process models. They also learn the reasons for actions conducted by others. Ultimately, they can also anticipate future actions by themselves or others and prepare for them.

Transparency and leveraged quality of courses of action is definitely a surplus of process modelling for rescue organisations. But the missing dedication to goal-orientation in most process modelling environments is felt as serious weakness for supporting the objectives of rescue organisations. By the same token, the complexity of terminology and functional scope of prevailing tools is considered as unfocused for the objectives of emergency planning.

In an execution stance, additional concepts for dynamic control flow are required. One typical control flow element in emergency management is escalation (going from a lower alarm level to a higher) with a corresponding de-escalation. Emergency management planning does also cover different procedures according to different warning levels, be it flooding, storm, or rain with respect to gauge levels, wind speed, or precipitation rate. Procedures of a higher level often include activities of lower levels, increased or extended specific measures, and possibly replacement of resources or activities, if a level is skipped. The same goes for de-escalation, where activities have to be "reversed" step by step (e.g., evacuation of a hospital or rest homes). Currently, modelling and execution of such "escalation" processes is neither implemented nor in research investigated as far as we know. Such dynamic control flows are typically not part of prevailing tools for business process management. Although they can be implemented with so-called worklets for different instances of a sub-process in principle, more natural implementations are desirable.

Once more process models are represented in terms of Standard Operating Procedures, an increase of overlapping concepts will unveil. Coordination and communication are typically spread across many process fragments. Concepts for modularisation and parameterized reference are required. Yet, such concepts must be usable for designers with an emergency management background. During our experiments with fire brigades in German counties we witnessed modularisation as a means for abstraction after several processes were captured.

**Acknowledgments.** The author sincerely thanks his colleague Gertraud Peinel for her fruitful contributions during the journey of our joint projects in the emergency management domain. The author is also indebted to Martin Sedlmayr for his contribution to processes in the medical domain, Alexander Wollert for the design of smart checklists, and Elmar Berger for developing customized tools for emergency experts.

# References


1. Cook, J.L.: Standard Operating Procedures and Guidelines. Fire Engineering Books & Videos (1998)
2. Becker, T., Lee, B.-S., Koch, R.: Effiziente Entscheidungsunterstützung im Krisenfall durch interaktive Standard Operating Procedures. Workshop "IT-Unterstützung von Einsatz- und Rettungskräften: Interdisziplinäre Anforderungsanalyse, Architekturen und Gestaltungskonzepte", Conference Software Engineering 2011, Karlsruhe, Germany (2011)
3. Bentivoglio, J.T.: SOPs and Liability. Fire Engineering. PennWell Corporation (1995)
4. de Leoni, M., Mecella, M.: Mobile process management through web services. In: 2010 IEEE International Conference on Services Computing (SCC), pp. 378–385. IEEE (2010). Franke, J., Charoy, F.: Design of a collaborative disaster response process management system. In: International Conference on the Design of Cooperative Systems (COOP 202020), Aix-en-Provence, France (2010)
5. Franke, J., Widera, A., Charoy, F., Hellingrath, B., Ulmer, C.: Reference process models and systems for inter-organizational Ad-Hoc coordination-supply chain management in humanitarian operations. In: Proceedings of the 8th International ISCRAM Conference (2011)
6. FW FfM: Standardeinsatzregeln, Standing Orders, Standard-Einsatz-Regeln. Feuerwehr- und Rettungsdienstakademie der Branddirektion Frankfurt am Main (2011)
7. Hoogendoorn, M., Jonker, C.M., Popova, V., Sharpaskykh, A., Xu, L.: Formal modelling and comparing of disaster plans. In: Proceedings of the Second International Conference on Information Systems for Crisis Response and Management ISCRAM 2005, pp. 97–107 (2005)
8. Keller, G., Nüttgens, M., Scheer, A.-W.: Semantische Prozeßmodellierung auf der Grundlage "Ereignisgesteuerter Prozeßketten (EPK)". Veröffentlichungen des Instituts für Wirtschaftsinformatik (IWi), Universität des Saarlandes 89 (1992)
9. Khalilbeigi, M., Bradler, D., Schweizer, I., Probst, F., Steimle, J.: Towards computer support of paper workflows in emergency management. In: Proceedings of the 7th International ISCRAM Conference (2010)
10. Kittel, K., Sackmann, S.: Gaining flexibility and compliance in rescue processes with BPM. In: Sixth International Conference on Availability, Reliability and Security (ARES) 2011, pp. 639–644. IEEE (2011)
11. Kunze, C., Rodriguez, D., Shammas, L., Chandra-Sekaran, A., Weber, B.: Nutzung von Sensornetzwerken und mobilen Informationsgeräten für die Situationserfassung und die Prozessunterstützung bei Massenanfällen von Verletzten. GI Jahrestagung 2009 (2009)

12. Lalonde, C.: Changing the paradigm of crisis management: how to put OD in the process. In: Buono, A.F., Grossmann, R., Lobnig, H., Mayer, K. (eds.) The Changing Paradigm of Consulting: Adjusting to the Fast-Paced World. United States of America: Information Age Publishing, inc. Department of Management, University Laval (2011)

13. Lasogga, F., von Ameln, F.: Kooperation bei Großschadensereignissen. Gr. Organ. **41**, 157–176 (2010)

14. Ludík, T., Pitner, T.: Process design patterns in emergency management. In: Proceedings Advances in Information and Communication Technology (IFIP) – Environmental Software Systems: Infrastructures, Services and Applications. (2015)

15. Ludík, T., Ráček, J.: Process methodology for emergency management. In: Proceedings Advances in Information and Communication Technology (IFIP) – Environmental Software Systems: Frameworks of eEnvironment (2011)

16. Paulheim, H., Döweling, S., Tso-Sutter, K., Probst, F., Ziegert, T.: Improving usability of integrated emergency response systems: the SoKNOS approach. In: Informatik 2009: Im Focus das Leben, Beiträge der 39. Jahrestagung der Gesellschaft für Informatik e.V. (GI), 28.9.-2.10.2009, pp. 1435–1449 (2009)

17. Peinel, G., Rose, T., Berger, E.: Process-oriented risk management for smaller municipalities. In: 4th International Conference on Information Systems for Crisis Response and Management (ISCRAM) (2007)

18. Peinel, G., Rose, T.: Deploying process management for emergency services - lessons learnt and research required. In: Future Security - 6th Security Research Conference, Berlin, Germany (2010)

19. Peinel, G., Rose, T.: Business processes and standard operating procedures: two coins with similar sides. In: Proc. IFIP e-Government 2013, Koblenz, 16th–19th September. Springer (2013). (Outstanding Paper Award)

20. Peinel, G., Rose, T., Wollert, A.: Cross-organizational preplanning in emergency management with IT-supported smart checklists. In: Aschenbruck, N., Martini, P., Meier, M., Tölle, J. (eds.) Future Security 2012. CCIS, vol. 318, pp. 497–508. Springer, Heidelberg (2012). https://doi. org/10.1007/978-3-642-33161-9_73

21. Peinel, G., Rose, T. Wollert, A.: The myth of business process modelling for emergency planning. In: Proceeding of the 9th Intl. ISCRAM Conference, Vancouver (2012)

22. Potts, C., Bruns, G.: Recording the Reasons for Design Decisions, pp. 418–427. IEEE Computer Society Press (1988)

23. Reichert, M., Rinderle-Ma, S., Kreger, U., Dadam, P.: Adaptive process management with ADEPT2. In: Proceedings of the 21st International Conference on Data Engineering (ICDA) (2005)

24. Reijers, H., Jansen-Vullers, M., Zur Muehlen, M., Appl, W.: Workflow management systems+ swarm intelligence= dynamic task assignment for emergency management applications. Business Process Manag., 125–140 (2007)

25. Rose, T., Peinel, G., Arsenova, E.: Process management support for emergency management procedures. In: eChallenges 2008 (2008)

26. Rüppel, U., Wagenknecht, A.: Improving emergency management by formal dynamic process-modelling. In: 24th Conference on Information Technology in Construction (2007)

27. Schafer, W.A., Carroll, J.M., Haynes, S.R., Abrams, S.: Emergency management planning as collaborative community work. J. Homel. Secur. Emerg. Manage. **5**, 10 (2008)

28. Schmidt, J.: Einsatzkonzept MANV Überörtlich. Rheinische Projektgruppe "MANV Überörtlich", Cologne, Germany (2007)

29. Smith, W., Dowell, J., Ortega-Lafuente, M.: Designing paper disasters: an authoring environment for developing training exercises in integrated emergency management. Cogn. Technol. Work **1**, 119–132 (1999)

30. Soboll, M., Binder, B., Quix, C., Geisler, S.: Prozessmodellierung der mobilen Datenerfassung für den Rettungsdienst bei einer Großschadenslage. Tagungsband zum 16. Workshop der Fachgruppe WI-VM der Gesellschaft für Informatik e.V. (GI), Düsseldorf (2009)
31. Soini, J., Polancic, G.: Toward adaptable communication and enhanced collaboration in global crisis management using process modeling. In: Kocaoglu, D.F., Anderson, T.R., Daim, T.U. (eds.) Proceedings of PICMET 2010, Portland International Center for Management of Engineering and Technology, Technology Management for Global Economic Growth, Phuket, Thailand, pp. 981–990 (2010)
32. United States Environmental Protection Agency: Guidance for Preparing Standard Operating Procedures (SOPs) In: Office of Environmental Information Washington, D. (ed.) vol. EPA QA/G-6, Washington, DC 20460 (2007)
33. Yu, E., Mylopoulos, J.: From E-R- to 'A-R' – modelling strategic actor relationships for business process reengineering. Int. J. Intell. Coop. Inf. Syst. 4(2/3) (1995)
34. Ziebermayr, T., Huber, J., Kollarits, S., Ortner, M.: A proposal for the application of dynamic workflows in disaster management: a process model language customized for disaster management. In: Proceedings of the 22 International Workshop on Database and Expert Systems Applications, pp. 284–288. IEEE (2011)

# An Overview on Predictive and Prescriptive Process Monitoring

Chiara Di Francescomarino[1], Chiara Ghidini[2(⊠)], Massimiliano Ronzani[3],
and Alessandro Sperduti[3,4]

[1] University of Trento, Trento, Italy
[2] Free University of Bolzano, Bolzano, Italy
`chiara.ghidini@unibz.it`
[3] Fondazione Bruno Kessler, Trento, Italy
[4] University of Padua, Padua, Italy

## 1  Introduction

While traditional Process Mining typically works on "post mortem" data, that is only complete cases are leveraged, operational support also takes into account "pre mortem" data, that is cases that are still running (ongoing cases) and can still be influenced and handled. Three main activities have been placed under the umbrella of the operational support in [2,3]: *detect, predict* and *recommend.*

The *detect* activity aims at detecting deviations or violations at runtime, as a form of on-line conformance checking. The *predict* activity focuses on predicting the future of individual cases and of the whole process in order to mitigate risks. Finally, the *recommend* activity moves towards providing guidance to achieve a certain goal.

In this chapter, we focus on these latter two activities, providing first an update of the Predictive Process Monitoring approaches presented in [20] (Sect. 2), then illustrating the novel works on object-centric Predictive Process Monitoring (Sect. 3, and finally concluding with offering an outline of the family of Prescriptive Process Monitoring approaches in Sect. 4.

While Predictive and Prescriptive Process Monitoring are not core topics in Wil van der Aalst research, notable is his contribution to the area. Indeed his push on providing a framework for operational support contributed in a significant manner to the start of the research in these fields [2,3,51]. Moreover, he contributed to start the investigation of Predictive Process Monitoring with early works that follow the Model-based approach (see Sect. 2.2 and [4,55]). Finally his work on object-centric Process Mining is at the basis of the new research stream on object-centric Predictive Process Monitoring.

## 2  Novelties in Trace-Based Predictive Process Monitoring

Following reference publications in literature [20], Predictive Process Monitoring approaches can be roughly classified along three main dimensions:


J. Mendling et al. (Eds.): Wil van der Aalst Festschrift, LNCS 16480, pp. 183–198, 2026.
https://doi.org/10.1007/978-3-032-17618-9_14

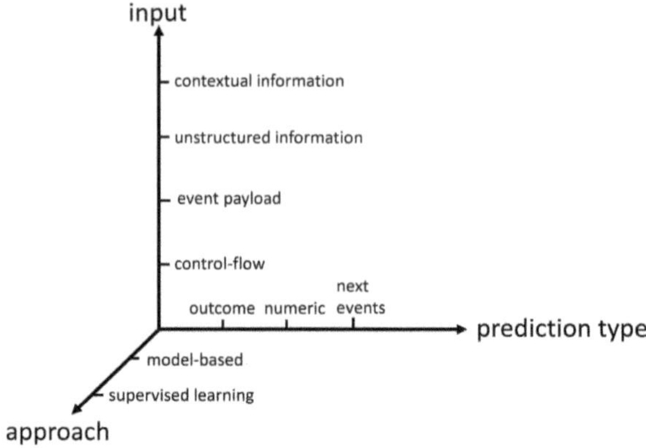



**Fig. 1.** The three dimensions of Predictive Process Monitoring.

- type of prediction provided as output;
- type of adopted approach and technique;
- type of information taken as input and exploited in order to get predictions.

## 2.1 Type of Prediction Provided as Output

Concerning the type of prediction, relevant work in literature [20,65], classify the existing prediction types into three main big categories:

- predictions related to the classification of the outcome in pre-defined categorical or boolean values (*outcome-based predictions*);
- predictions related to measures of interest taking numeric or continuous values (*numeric value predictions*);
- predictions related to sequences of future activities and related data payloads (*next event predictions*).

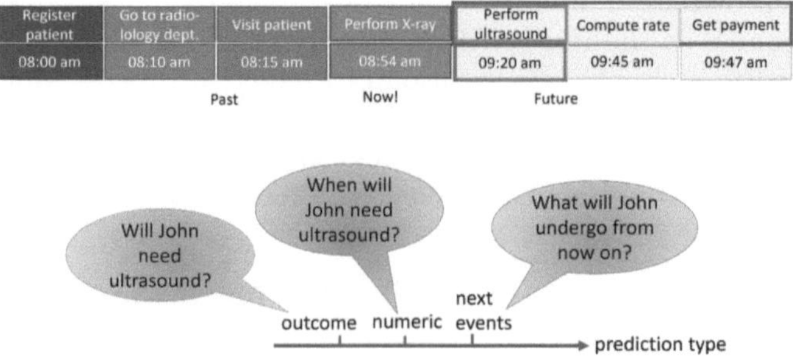



**Fig. 2.** Types of Prediction  (Figure taken from [20]).

We illustrate these dimensions with the help of an example originally introduced in [20], and graphically depicted in Fig. 2. The example pertains an execution trace describing the activities carried out by an hypothetical patient named John. Let us assume that it is 8:54 a.m. now and that John has undergone the first four activities depicted in the trace in Fig. 2. Predictive Process Monitoring would allow us to answer different types of questions on the future of John. For instance, we could predict whether John will undergo an ultrasound scan in the future. This is a typical example of a binary (a.k.a. true/false) outcome-based prediction. Outcome-based predictions can be extended to includes predictions assuming categorical values, that is, values that range in a limited and fixed number of possible options. For example, we could predict the specific exam that will be prescribed to John out of a fixed number of options. Another set of typical questions in Predictive Process Monitoring are questions about numeric answers. An example in our scenario could be how much time is needed for John to undergo an ultrasound, or how much will John care path cost to the public health service. Finally, we can predict what is the activity that John is going to do next, or the sequence of future activities that John is going to do from now on.

*Novelties in the Prediction Type.* By analysing the literature we notice that not many changes have happened on the type of prediction provided as output. Indeed, most recent papers still tackle one of the three types of prediction mentioned above. The innovations introduced by these works usually target secondary objectives rather than improving the accuracy of the predicted objective. For *outcome-based predictions*, recent works have explored aspects such as the fairness of predictive models [37], their robustness against adversarial attacks [62], and the stability of model performance during online prediction [40]. For *numeric value predictions*, and specifically for remaining time prediction, research has focused on quantifying prediction uncertainty [26] and improving training efficiency [58]. Finally, for *next event predictions*, recent studies have focused on leveraging model architectures (attention layers) to enhance explainability [36], and on predicting deviations with respect to the activities prescribed by the process model [32].

## 2.2 Type of Adopted Approach and Technique

Predictive Process Monitoring approaches are usually characterized by two phases. In a first phase, the *training or learning* phase (see the white upper part part in the two diagrams in Fig. 3), one or more models are built or enriched by leveraging the information contained in the execution log. In the second phase, the *runtime or prediction phase* (see the light brown part in Fig. 3), the learned model(s) is(are) exploited in order to get predictions related to an ongoing execution trace. We can identify two main groups of approaches dealing with the prediction problem:

- approaches relying on an explicit model (*model-based approaches*), e.g., annotated transition systems. The explicit model can either be discovered from

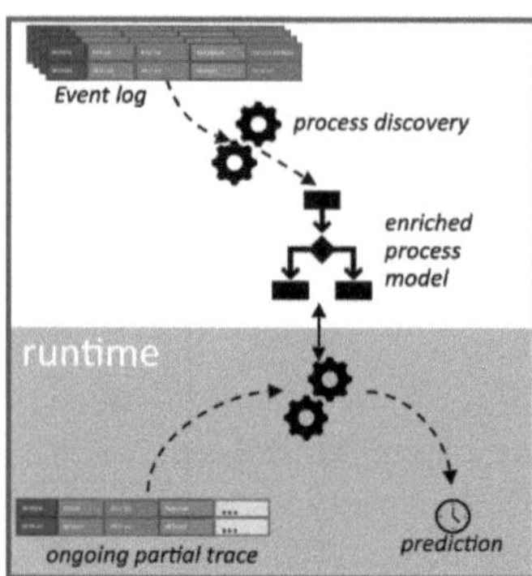


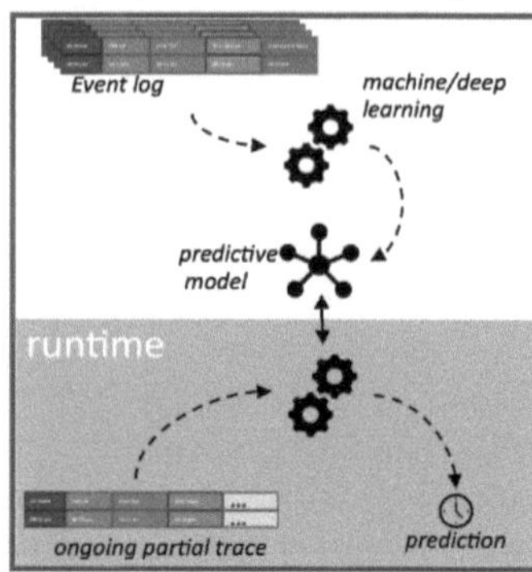


**Fig. 3.** Types of approach.

the event log and then enriched with the information the log contains or directly be enriched, if an explicit model is already available. In model-based approaches, the model that is then leveraged at runtime in order to get predictions is an (enriched) model in which the process control flow is somehow made explicit (see the left hand box in Fig. 3).

- approaches leveraging machine learning and statistical techniques, e.g., classification and regression models, as well as neural networks. These approaches only rely on (implicit) predictive models built by encoding event log information in terms of features to be used as input for machine/deep learning techniques (see the right hand box in Fig. 3).

*Novelties in the Approach and Technique.* Similarly to what was described in [20], most recent works exploit machine learning - and in particular supervised learning - techniques. Compared to the analysis made in [20], we can observe two novelties. The first concerns an increase of works that tackle the problem of next event(s) prediction and a widening of techniques employed to perform that type of prediction; the second concerns a novel approach that aims at combining Model-based and Machine Learning approaches.

Concerning the area of next event prediction, most of the approaches for early works on next event predictions did rely on Recurrent Neural Networks (RNN) and, more specifically, on LSTM (Long-Short Term Memory) architectures [14,43,63,64]. This type of deep learning approaches, by using recurrent connections in a single block (LSTM cell), was indeed considered particularly suitable to deal with sequence problems. More recently, the Transformer architecture [68], which has been successfully used for processing sequential inputs in NLP, has been adopted as a viable alternative to RNNs also in Predictive Process Monitoring; as an encoder-only architecture for next event and remaining time prediction tasks [11,49,53], and as a full encoderdecoder architecture for complete remaining trace (or suffix) prediction [38,71]. In a different direction, Graph Neural Networks (GNNs) have recently been leveraged in Predictive

Process Monitoring, mainly for their ability to encode process executions in a format different from the sequential vector representations required by RNNs and Transformers, allowing relations among different process execution perspectives (or modalities) to be explicitly represented as a graph. Graphs can be used to model relations between intracase attributes, as in [22], or intercase process relations, such as resource handover dependencies [33] or causal relations within the process model [15,57]. Finally pretrained Large Language Models (LLMs) [18,56] have been applied to Predictive Process Monitoring for the suffix prediction tasks, both in a zero-shot fashion [50] and in a fine-tuned setting [52]. Specifically, both methods transform process executions into semantic narratives, enabling them to be more easily associated with relatable implicit process executions that the LLM can identify and connect to its knowledge base, as derived from its training corpus in similar domains.

The combination of Model-based and Machine Learning approaches follows the recent stream of works on Integrative Artificial Intelligence (AI)[1] that aim at combining different techniques in order to exploit the different strengths they offer. When it comes to the approaches of Predictive Process Monitoring we can notice that Model-based approaches have the advantage of relying on an explicit model, and therefore of being transparent and explainable. Nonetheless, they are often used only for numeric prediction, as they struggle to represent complex patterns that one can find in the data. On the contrary, Machine Learning approaches are typically extremely effective in exploiting correlations and implicit patterns hidden in the data, but are often difficult to interpret. In [46], the authors propose the enhancement of simulation models discovered from data, by combining them with predictive models. The simulation of process executions becomes therefore an interleaving of simulation steps and prediction steps. These combined models can be used for simulation as well as for prediction. Another stream of work concerns the injection of domain knowledge, often in the form of Temporal Logic (on finite traces) [16,54] or Declare patterns [19], into machine learning architectures. These efforts follow the so-called neuro-symbolic Artificial Intelligence approach [34], which attempts to combine the open and transparent characteristics of symbolic (that is, logic based) AI and the flexibility and power of sub-symbolic (that is, data driven) AI into a unique framework. Domain knowledge can be considered here the formalization of certain aspects of a process model that one would like to enforce in the predictive one. In the early work of [21], the authors exploit Declare patterns to guide the prediction of sequences of next events. More recent efforts attempt to inject the domain knowledge logical formulae directly into the predictive model at training time [24] or in the computation of counterfactual explanations of predictive models [12,13]. If we look outside the Process Mining community and refer to the Artificial Intelligence area, we can observe the recent development of neuro-symbolic architectures for sequential data and temporal logic, that are being applied in particular to sequences of video frames [7,45,67]. These works can act as stimuli for the Process Mining community and foster the development of further hybrid approaches for Predictive Process Monitoring.

---

[1] https://www.ai4europe.eu/research/areas/integrative-ai.

## 2.3  Type of Information Taken as Input

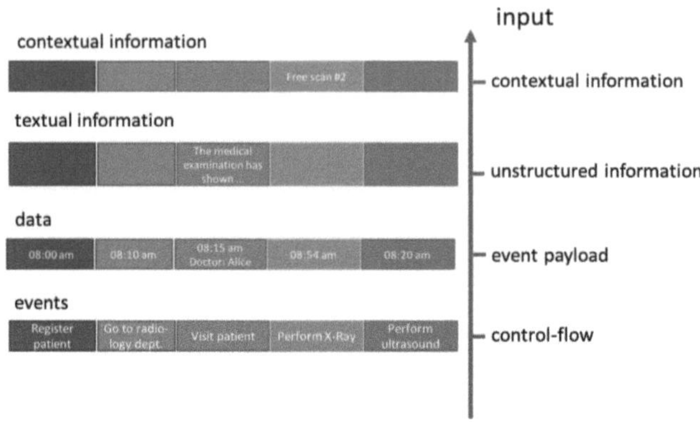


**Fig. 4.** Information used for making predictions  (Figure taken from [20]).

Concerning the information that can be used as input to the Predictive Process Monitoring approaches we do not observe any major change w.r.t., what was described in [20]. Namely, we can identify four different types of information that can be used as input to the Predictive Process Monitoring approaches, e.g., for building a model annotated with execution information or for building the features to be used by machine learning approaches:

- information related to the control flow - i.e., the sequence of events. As depicted in the fourth row of Fig. 4, in the example of our patient John introduced above, this is the information related to the activities carried out by John.
- information related to the structured data payload associated to the events. This information usually include the timestamp of the events, but it can also include other types of data attributes(see the third row in Fig. 4).
- information related to unstructured (textual) content, which can be available together with the event log. In John's example, for instance, the text of Alice's medical report is available together with the event "visit patient" (see the second row in Fig. 4) and could provide useful information on what John is going to do later on.
- information related to process context, such as workload or resource availability. In John's example, this kind of information could be related for instance to the availability of free ultrasound scan machines (first row in Fig. 4).

In several approaches, more than one of these types of information is used in order to learn from the past.

Even though the type of information taken as input has not changed in the last few years, the development of neuro-symbolic architectures that combine domain knowledge and data can contribute to widen the type of information used in the construction of Predictive Models. Indeed, together with the different types of information coming from data (process executions) described above, novel architectures may be able to incorporate domain knowledge in the form of logical formulae of different complexity. Knowledge could therefore become a novel and relevant input for the Predictive Process Monitoring models of the future.

## 3 Widening the Picture: Object-Centric Predictive Process Monitoring

One of the most significant recent innovations in the area of Process Mining consists in the observation that often process executions are not running independently but they refer to objects that are often shared among activities of different executions. This observation has lead to significant work by Wil van der Aalst [1] and Dirk Fahland [27], and on the rise of a new stream of works that aims at extending the typical services provided for case based Process Mining (e.g., process discovery, alignment, conformance checking, and so on) to scenarios where process executions are more naturally represented by graphs. This new trend is also true for Predictive Process Monitoring, and works are now appearing. A significant sample of recent works is provided by [5,6,29,30,41,61]. Here we briefly make an attempt to classify these new works in the diagram of Fig. 1. This classification provides a first overlook of how this new branch of Predictive Process Monitoring is developing.

One of the first works presented in literature is that of Gherissi et al., [30]. In this paper the authors tackle the problem of next activity and remaining time prediction by adapting the LSTM architecture used in [63] to tackle the challenge of next activity prediction in the more traditional process case setting. The work of Galanti et al., [29] aims at two types of predictions: first, whether a certain binary outcome (e.g., late payments) is happening in the future, and second a numeric prediction (e.g., about the delay of a certain activity). The models are obtained using Catboost (gradient boosting on decision trees) [25]. In [6], Adams et al., propose graphs and graph embeddings as a mechanism for preserving the graph structure of object-centric event data, and apply these embeddings, together with Graph Neural Network, to the prediction of next activity, next timestamp, and remaining time. A similar approach is taken in [61] and in [5], where graph encodings and Graph Neural Network architectures are used to address the problem of remaining time predictions. The recent work of de Leoni and Volpato [41], extends the graph based approach to integrate all concurrent process executions within a single structure, thus enabling to perform predictions of the process executions collectively. The work exploits Graph Attention Layers [69] and is used to perform remaining time predictions. Finally, Relational Graph Convolutional Network are used in [42] to tackle the problems of next activity prediction, next timestamp prediction, and remaining time prediction. Almost all the works above exploit information about events, payloads (typically, timestamps), objects, and the relationships between objects and events.

By looking at the dimensions shown in Fig. 1 we can easily notice that most works on object-centric Predictive Process Monitoring focus on numeric predictions, and in particular on the timing of events, or on single next event predictions. This is a clear difference with the development of trace-based Predictive Process Monitoring, where many efforts have been devoted to provide different types of predictions, and it is perhaps the clearest sign of the early days of this investigation. Concerning the techniques it is easy to notice that all works employ Machine Learning architectures, with a tendency to use the latest, and often sophisticated, ones. This fact can be partly due to the need of working with graph structures, which are inherently more complex than sequential traces. This can also be partly due to an increased adoption of sophisticated Machine Learning architectures in Predictive Process Monitoring, witnessed, for example, by the novel works on next event prediction described in Sect. 2.2. Concerning the type of information taken as input we can instead notice the unsuitability of the scheme provided in Fig. 4. The classification of this figure is, in fact, based on the notion of trace and does not scale to capture the input provided by object centric process executions. To sum up, the work on object-centric Predictive Process Monitoring is still in its very beginnings and does not provide a clear illustration of the directions it will explore. Nonetheless it presents already some clear differences with what has happened with trace-based Predictive Process Monitoring and will likely need a classification in terms of novel dimensions.

## 4   The Family of Prescriptive Process Monitoring Approaches

In this section, we provide a coarse classification of different Prescriptive Process Monitoring (PrPM) approaches. A systematic review of early PrPM techniques has been presented in [39]. In this section we include more recent works and we present them following a similar scheme to the one presented in [20] and reviewed in Sect. 2. In particular, for PrPM we focus on two main dimensions, as depicted in Fig. 5:

- the type of recommendation provided as output;
- the type of approach and technique adopted.

The two aspects are closely intertwined, as different approaches are more suitable for providing different types of recommendations. In the following, we present each type of recommendation together with the approaches that have been used to achieve it.

*Whether and When.* The first type of recommendation focuses on determining whether and when to intervene during a process execution in order to prevent or mitigate undesired outcomes. In this setting, both the possible interventions and

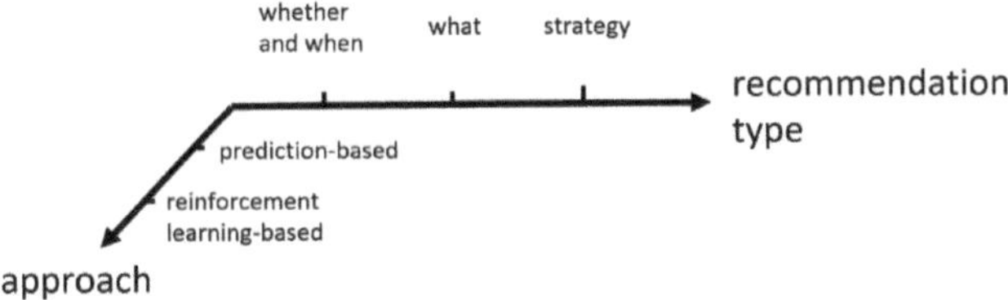


**Fig. 5.** Dimensions of Prescriptive Process Monitoring Approaches

their effects are predefined and known a priori. The effects are typically characterized by: the *intervention cost*; the *cost of undesired outcome*, incurred when the process execution ends negatively; the *cost of compensation*, representing the negative repercussions of performing an unnecessary intervention (i.e., when the process execution would have ended positively anyway); and the *mitigation effect*, which quantifies the proportion of the undesired outcome cost that can be avoided by performing the intervention. In this scenario, it is important to determine *whether* it is useful to intervene to prevent an undesired outcome, and when it is better not to intervene in order to save intervention and compensation costs. It is also crucial to decide *when* to intervene, since in many situations the mitigation effect may decrease if the intervention occurs too late. Many early works in PrPM have focused on this type of recommendation, mainly through prediction-based approaches [28,48,66], where a Predictive Process Monitoring model is designed to predict the risk of a case leading to an undesired outcome and to raise an alarm once a predefined threshold is exceeded, thereby triggering the intervention for that case.

Subsequent works in this direction have explored scenarios where the effect of an intervention is not deterministically known a priori. In such cases, *prediction-based* methods, and in particular causal estimators, have been employed to estimate the intervention effect. These approaches have been used to investigate the optimal timing for applying an intervention to achieve maximal impact [8,9], or to identify the most suitable subset of cases for which interventions should be applied when resources are limited [59].

A further step towards the automation of this type of recommendation has been achieved integrating *reinforcement learning* (RL) techniques. RL is applied to overcome the need for external user decisions in the previous methods, specifically the manual interpretation required to convert predictions into prescriptions: for example, setting thresholds to trigger the alarm that initiates an intervention. This approach has been applied both when the effect of the intervention is know a priori [47] and when it is estimated by prediction-based methods as in [60].

*What.* The second type of recommendation concerns not only when to apply an intervention, but also which intervention to select, that is, how to intervene. The intervention may be chosen from a predefined set of possible actions or determined in a more general manner. Pioneering works in this direction [31,44], leverage the structural transparency of the decision tree used as the *prediction model* to predict a case's risky outcome to extract recommendations. These recommendations correspond to alternative paths in the tree structure leading to a positive outcome. More recently, works as [23] have applied a similar approach with declarative encodings, so as to return recommendations in the form of declarative rules.

On another direction, research has focused on selecting interventions in the form of the next best activity (or set of activities) to perform in order to maximize a given KPI. Both [17,70] address this problem by combining a method for identifying feasible next-activity candidates with a *prediction-based* model, which essentially acts as a causal estimator to select the activity expected to yield the highest KPI.

*Strategy.* Finally, the third type of recommendation further broadens the notion of intervention by aiming not only to determine when or how to intervene, but also to provide the user with a complete intervention strategy: a policy that can be applied at any point during process execution to achieve the desired goal and can adapt to the erratic response of a dynamic environment [10,35]. Both these works minimize the knowledge known a priori or provided by the users. Indeed they do not require a priori knowledge on the possible interventions, on their effects, nor do they require user decision making for transforming what has been learned in prescriptions. By leveraging RL techniques for complex processes where the agent can perform only a subset of activities, they automatically learn the best strategy.

# References


1. Aalst, W.M.P.: Object-centric process mining: dealing with divergence and convergence in event data. In: Ölveczky, P.C., Salaün, G. (eds.) SEFM 2019. LNCS, vol. 11724, pp. 3–25. Springer, Cham (2019). https://doi.org/10.1007/978-3-030-30446-1_1
2. van der Aalst, W.M.P., Pesic, M., Song, M.: Beyond process mining: from the past to present and future. In: Pernici, B. (ed.) CAiSE 2010. LNCS, vol. 6051, pp. 38–52. Springer, Heidelberg (2010). https://doi.org/10.1007/978-3-642-13094-6_5
3. van der Aalst, W.M.P., Schonenberg, M.H., Song, M.: Time prediction based on process mining. Inf. Syst. **36**(2), 450–475 (2011)
4. van der Aalst, W.M.P., Schonenberg, M.H., Song, M.: Time prediction based on process mining. Inf. Syst. **36**(2), 450–475 (2011). https://doi.org/10.1016/J.IS.2010.09.001
5. Adams, J.N., Drescher, H., Swoboda, A., Günnemann, N., Park, G., van der Aalst, W.M.P.: Improving predictive process monitoring using object-centric process mining. In: Avital, M., Karahanna, E., Themistocleous, M., Constantiou, I.D., Fitzgerald, B., Seidel, S. (eds.) 32nd European Conference on Information Systems - People First: Constructing Digital Futures Together, ECIS 2024, Paphos, Cyprus, 13–19 June 2024 (2024)
6. Adams, J.N., Park, G., van der Aalst, W.M.P.: Preserving complex object-centric graph structures to improve machine learning tasks in process mining. Eng.

Appl. Artif. Intell. **125**, 106764 (2023). https://doi.org/10.1016/J.ENGAPPAI.2023.106764

7. Andreoni, R., Buliga, A., Daniele, A., Ghidini, C., Montali, M., Ronzani, M.: T-ILR: a neurosymbolic integration for LTLF. In: Gilpin, L.H., Giunchiglia, E., Hitzler, P., Krieken, E. (eds.) Proceedings of The 19th International Conference on Neurosymbolic Learning and Reasoning (NeSy 2025). Proceedings of Machine Learning Research, vol. 284. PMLR (2025)

8. Bozorgi, Z.D., Teinemaa, I., Dumas, M., Rosa, M.L., Polyvyanyy, A.: Prescriptive process monitoring for cost-aware cycle time reduction. In: Ciccio, C.D., Francescomarino, C.D., Soffer, P. (eds.) 3rd International Conference on Process Mining, ICPM 2021, Eindhoven, The Netherlands, October 31 – Nov. 4 2021, pp. 96–103. IEEE (2021). https://doi.org/10.1109/ICPM53251.2021.9576853

9. Bozorgi, Z.D., Teinemaa, I., Dumas, M., Rosa, M.L., Polyvyanyy, A.: Prescriptive process monitoring based on causal effect estimation. Inf. Syst. **116**, 102198 (2023). https://doi.org/10.1016/J.IS.2023.102198

10. Branchi, S., Di Francescomarino, C., Ghidini, C., Massimo, D., Ricci, F., Ronzani, M.: Learning to act: a reinforcement learning approach to recommend the best next activities. In: Business Process Management Forum - BPM 2022, Proc. LNBIP, vol. 458, pp. 137–154. Springer (2022). https://doi.org/10.1007/978-3-031-16171-1_9

11. Bukhsh, Z.A., Saeed, A., Dijkman, R.M.: Processtransformer: predictive business process monitoring with transformer network. CoRR **abs/2104.00721** (2021). https://arxiv.org/abs/2104.00721

12. Buliga, A., Francescomarino, C.D., Ghidini, C., Donadello, I., Maggi, F.M.: Guiding the generation of counterfactual explanations through temporal background knowledge for predictive process monitoring. Data Min. Knowl. Discov. **39**(5), 63 (2025). https://doi.org/10.1007/S10618-025-01117-3

13. Buliga, A., Francescomarino, C.D., Ghidini, C., Montali, M., Ronzani, M.: Generating counterfactual explanations under temporal constraints. In: Walsh, T., Shah, J., Kolter, Z. (eds.) AAAI-25, Sponsored by the Association for the Advancement of Artificial Intelligence, Philadelphia, PA, USA, February 25 - March 4 2025, pp. 15622–15631. AAAI Press (2025). https://doi.org/10.1609/AAAI.V39I15.33715

14. Camargo, M., Dumas, M., González-Rojas, O.: Learning accurate LSTM models of business processes. In: Hildebrandt, T., van Dongen, B.F., Röglinger, M., Mendling, J. (eds.) BPM 2019. LNCS, vol. 11675, pp. 286–302. Springer, Cham (2019). https://doi.org/10.1007/978-3-030-26619-6_19

15. Chiorrini, A., Diamantini, C., Genga, L., Potena, D.: Multi-perspective enriched instance graphs for next activity prediction through graph neural network. J. Intell. Inf. Syst. **61**(1), 5–25 (2023). https://doi.org/10.1007/S10844-023-00777-1

16. De Giacomo, G., Vardi, M.Y.: Linear temporal logic and linear dynamic logic on finite traces. In: Rossi, F. (ed.) IJCAI 2013, Proceedings of the 23rd International Joint Conference on Artificial Intelligence, Beijing, China, 3–9 August 2013, pp. 854–860. IJCAI/AAAI (2013). http://www.aaai.org/ocs/index.php/IJCAI/IJCAI13/paper/view/6997

17. de Leoni, M., Dees, M., Reulink, L.: Design and evaluation of a process-aware recommender system based on prescriptive analytics. In: 2nd Int. Conf. on Process Mining (ICPM 2020), pp. 9–16. IEEE (2020)

18. Devlin, J., Chang, M.W., Lee, K., Toutanova, K.: BERT: pre-training of deep bidirectional transformers for language understanding. In: Burstein, J., Doran, C., Solorio, T. (eds.) Proceedings of the 2019 Conference of the North American Chapter of the Association for Computational Linguistics: Human Language

Technologies, Volume 1 (Long and Short Papers), Minneapolis, Minnesota, pp. 4171–4186. Association for Computational Linguistics (2019). https://doi.org/10.18653/v1/N19-1423

19. Di Ciccio, C., Montali, M.: Declarative process specifications: reasoning, discovery, monitoring. In: Process Mining Handbook, vol. 448, p. 45. Springer (2022). https://doi.org/10.1007/978-3-031-08848-3_4

20. Di Francescomarino, C., Ghidini, C.: Predictive process monitoring. In: van der Aalst, W.M.P., Carmona, J. (eds.) Process Mining Handbook, LNBIP, vol. 448, pp. 320–346. Springer (2022). https://doi.org/10.1007/978-3-031-08848-3_10

21. Di Francescomarino, C., Ghidini, C., Maggi, F.M., Petrucci, G., Yeshchenko, A.: An Eye into the Future: Leveraging A-priori Knowledge in Predictive Business Process Monitoring, pp. 252–268. Springer, Cham (2017). https://doi.org/10.1007/978-3-319-65000-5_15

22. Dissegna, S., Francescomarino, C.D., Ronzani, M.: Multi-perspective next event prediction in PPM via heterogeneous graph neural networks. In: Grabis, J., Vos, T.E.J., Escalona, M.J., Pastor, O. (eds.) RCIS 2025, Part I. LNBIP, vol. 547, pp. 365–382. Springer (2025). https://doi.org/10.1007/978-3-031-92474-3_22

23. Donadello, I., Di Francescomarino, C., Maggi, F.M., Ricci, F., Shikhizada, A.: Outcome-oriented prescriptive process monitoring based on temporal logic patterns. Eng. Appl. Artif. Intell. **126**, 106899 (2023). https://doi.org/10.1016/j.engappai.2023.106899. https://www.sciencedirect.com/science/article/pii/S0952197623010837

24. Donadello, I., Ko, J., Maggi, F.M., Mendling, J., Riva, F., Weidlich, M.: Knowledge-driven modulation of neural networks with attention mechanism for next activity prediction. CoRR **abs/2312.08847** (2023). https://doi.org/10.48550/ARXIV.2312.08847

25. Dorogush, A.V., Ershov, V., Gulin, A.: CatBoost: gradient boosting with categorical features support (2018). https://arxiv.org/abs/1810.11363

26. Elyasi, K.A., van der Aa, H., Stuckenschmidt, H.: A simple and calibrated approach for uncertainty-aware remaining time prediction. In: Senderovich, A., Cabanillas, C., Vanderfeesten, I., Reijers, H.A. (eds.) BPM 2025. LNCS, vol. 16044, pp. 217–234. Springer (2025). https://doi.org/10.1007/978-3-032-02867-9_14

27. Fahland, D.: Process mining over multiple behavioral dimensions with event knowledge graphs. In: van der Aalst, W.M.P., Carmona, J. (eds.) Process Mining Handbook. LNBIP, vol. 448, pp. 274–319. Springer (2022). https://doi.org/10.1007/978-3-031-08848-3_9

28. Fahrenkrog-Petersen, S., et al.: Fire now, fire later: alarm-based systems for prescriptive process monitoring. Knowl. Inf. Syst. **64** (2022). https://doi.org/10.1007/s10115-021-01633-w

29. Galanti, R., de Leoni, M., Navarin, N., Marazzi, A.: Object-centric process predictive analytics. Expert Syst. Appl. **213**(Part), 119173 (2023). https://doi.org/10.1016/J.ESWA.2022.119173

30. Gherissi, W., Haddad, J.E., Grigori, D.: Object-centric predictive process monitoring. In: Troya, J., et al. (eds.) WESOACS 2022. LNCS, vol. 13821, pp. 27–39. Springer (2022). https://doi.org/10.1007/978-3-031-26507-5_3

31. Gröger, C., Schwarz, H., Mitschang, B.: Prescriptive analytics for recommendation-based business process optimization. In: Abramowicz, W., Kokkinaki, A. (eds.) BIS 2014. LNBIP, vol. 176, pp. 25–37. Springer, Cham (2014). https://doi.org/10.1007/978-3-319-06695-0_3

32. Grohs, M., Pfeiffer, P., Rehse, J.: Business process deviation prediction: predicting non-conforming process behavior. In: 5th International Conference on Process Mining, ICPM 2023, Rome, Italy, 23–27 October 2023, pp. 113–120. IEEE (2023). https://doi.org/10.1109/ICPM60904.2023.10271994
33. Hennig, M.C., Schmidt, R.: Leveraging temporal graphs for enhancing transformer-based predictive process monitoring. In: Senderovich, A., Cabanillas, C., Vanderfeesten, I., Reijers, H.A. (eds.) BPM 2025. LNCS, vol. 16044, pp. 291–307. Springer (2025). https://doi.org/10.1007/978-3-032-02867-9_18
34. Hitzler, P., Sarker, M.K., Eberhart, A. (eds.): Compendium of Neurosymbolic Artificial Intelligence, Frontiers in Artificial Intelligence and Applications, vol. 369. IOS Press (2023). https://doi.org/10.3233/FAIA369
35. Hundogan, O.A., Verhoef, B.J., Theeven, P., Reijers, H.A., Lu, X.: Reinforcement learning for optimizing responses in care processes. Data Knowl. Eng. **157**, 102412 (2025). https://doi.org/10.1016/J.DATAK.2025.102412
36. Käppel, M., Ackermann, L., Jablonski, S., Härtl, S.: Attention please: what transformer models really learn for process prediction. In: Marrella, A., Resinas, M., Jans, M., Rosemann, M. (eds.) BPM 2024. LNCS, vol. 14940, pp. 203–220. Springer (2024). https://doi.org/10.1007/978-3-031-70396-6_12
37. Käppel, M., Neuberger, J., Möhrlein, F., Weinzierl, S., Matzner, M., Jablonski, S.: A human-in-the-loop approach for improving fairness in predictive business process monitoring. In: Senderovich, A., Cabanillas, C., Vanderfeesten, I., Reijers, H.A. (eds.) BPM 2025. LNCS, vol. 16044, pp. 343–360. Springer (2025). https://doi.org/10.1007/978-3-032-02867-9_21
38. Ketykó, I., Mannhardt, F., Hassani, M., van Dongen, B.F.: What averages do not tell: predicting real life processes with sequential deep learning. In: Proceedings of the 37th ACM/SIGAPP Symposium on Applied Computing, SAC 2022, pp. 1128–1131. Association for Computing Machinery, New York (2022). https://doi.org/10.1145/3477314.3507179
39. Kubrak, K., Milani, F., Nolte, A., Dumas, M.: Prescriptive process monitoring: Quo vadis? PeerJ Comput. Sci. **8**, e1097 (2022). https://doi.org/10.7717/peerj-cs.1097
40. Lee, S., Comuzzi, M., Lu, X., Reijers, H.A.: Measuring the stability of process outcome predictions in online settings. In: 5th International Conference on Process Mining, ICPM 2023, Rome, Italy, 23–27 October 2023, pp. 105–112. IEEE (2023). https://doi.org/10.1109/ICPM60904.2023.10271960
41. de Leoni, M., Volpato, D.P.: Global predictive monitoring of object-centric processes. In: Senderovich, A., Cabanillas, C., Vanderfeesten, I., Reijers, H.A. (eds.) BPM 2025. LNCS, vol. 16044, pp. 255–272. Springer (2025). https://doi.org/10.1007/978-3-032-02867-9_16
42. Li, K., Fang, H., Xu, Y., Shao, C.: Multi-task prediction method based on GGCN for object centric event logs. IEEE Access **13**, 53949–53963 (2025). https://doi.org/10.1109/ACCESS.2025.3553618
43. Lin, L., Wen, L., Wang, J.: MM-Pred: a deep predictive model for multi-attribute event sequence. In: Berger-Wolf, T.Y., Chawla, N.V. (eds.) Proceedings of the 2019 SIAM International Conference on Data Mining, SDM 2019, Calgary, Alberta, Canada, 2–4 May 2019, pp. 118–126. SIAM (2019). https://doi.org/10.1137/1.9781611975673.14
44. Maggi, F.M., Di Francescomarino, C., Dumas, M., Ghidini, C.: Predictive monitoring of business processes. In: Jarke, M., et al. (eds.) CAiSE 2014. LNCS, vol. 8484, pp. 457–472. Springer, Cham (2014). https://doi.org/10.1007/978-3-319-07881-6_31

45. Manginas, N., Paliouras, G., Raedt, L.D.: NeSyA: neurosymbolic automata. In: Proceedings of the Thirty-Fourth International Joint Conference on Artificial Intelligence, IJCAI 2025, Montreal, Canada, 16–22 August 2025, pp. 5950–5958. ijcai.org (2025). https://doi.org/10.24963/IJCAI.2025/662
46. Meneghello, F., Francescomarino, C.D., Ghidini, C., Ronzani, M.: Runtime integration of machine learning and simulation for business processes: time and decision mining predictions. Inf. Syst. **128**, 102472 (2025). https://doi.org/10.1016/J.IS.2024.102472
47. Metzger, A., Kley, T., Palm, A.: Triggering proactive business process adaptations via online reinforcement learning. In: Fahland, D., Ghidini, C., Becker, J., Dumas, M. (eds.) BPM 2020. LNCS, vol. 12168, pp. 273–290. Springer, Cham (2020). https://doi.org/10.1007/978-3-030-58666-9_16
48. Metzger, A., Neubauer, A., Bohn, P., Pohl, K.: Proactive process adaptation using deep learning ensembles. In: Giorgini, P., Weber, B. (eds.) CAiSE 2019. LNCS, vol. 11483, pp. 547–562. Springer, Cham (2019). https://doi.org/10.1007/978-3-030-21290-2_34
49. Moon, J., Park, G., Jeong, J.: Pop-on: prediction of process using one-way language model based on NLP approach. Appl. Sci. **11**(2) (2021). https://doi.org/10.3390/app11020864. https://www.mdpi.com/2076-3417/11/2/864
50. Oved, A., Shlomov, S., Zeltyn, S., Mashkif, N., Yaeli, A.: SNAP: semantic stories for next activity prediction. In: Walsh, T., Shah, J., Kolter, Z. (eds.) AAAI-25, Sponsored by the Association for the Advancement of Artificial Intelligence, February 25 - March 4, 2025, Philadelphia, PA, USA, pp. 28871–28877. AAAI Press (2025). https://doi.org/10.1609/AAAI.V39I28.35153
51. Park, G., van der Aalst, W.M.P.: A general framework for action-oriented process mining. In: Del Río Ortega, A., Leopold, H., Santoro, F.M. (eds.) BPM 2020. LNBIP, vol. 397, pp. 206–218. Springer, Cham (2020). https://doi.org/10.1007/978-3-030-66498-5_16
52. Pasquadibisceglie, V., Appice, A., Malerba, D.: Lupin: A LLM approach for activity suffix prediction in business process event logs. In: 2024 6th International Conference on Process Mining (ICPM), pp. 1–8 (2024). https://doi.org/10.1109/ICPM63005.2024.10680620
53. Philipp, P., Jacob, R., Robert, S., Beyerer, J.: Predictive analysis of business processes using neural networks with attention mechanism. In: 2020 International Conference on Artificial Intelligence in Information and Communication (ICAIIC), pp. 225–230 (2020). https://doi.org/10.1109/ICAIIC48513.2020.9065057
54. Pnueli, A.: The temporal logic of programs. In: 18th Annual Symposium on Foundations of Computer Science, Providence, Rhode Island, USA, 31 October - 1 November 1977, pp. 46–57. IEEE Computer Society (1977). https://doi.org/10.1109/SFCS.1977.32
55. Polato, M., Sperduti, A., Burattin, A., de Leoni, M.: Data-aware remaining time prediction of business process instances. In: 2014 International Joint Conference on Neural Networks, IJCNN 2014, Beijing, China, 6–11 July 2014, pp. 816–823. IEEE (2014). https://doi.org/10.1109/IJCNN.2014.6889360
56. Radford, A., Narasimhan, K., Salimans, T., Sutskever, I.: Improving language understanding by generative pre-training (2018). https://cdn.openai.com/research-covers/language-unsupervised/language_understanding_paper.pdf. Accessed 06 Oct 2025
57. Rama-Maneiro, E., Vidal, J.C., Lama, M.: Embedding graph convolutional networks in recurrent neural networks for predictive monitoring. IEEE Trans. Knowl. Data Eng. **36**(1), 137–151 (2024). https://doi.org/10.1109/TKDE.2023.3286017

58. Roider, J., Zanca, D., Eskofier, B.M.: Efficient training of recurrent neural networks for remaining time prediction in predictive process monitoring. In: Marrella, A., Resinas, M., Jans, M., Rosemann, M. (eds.) BPM 2024. LNC, vol. 14940, pp. 238–255. Springer (2024). https://doi.org/10.1007/978-3-031-70396-6_14

59. Shoush, M., Dumas, M.: Prescriptive process monitoring under resource constraints: a causal inference approach. In: Munoz-Gama, J., Lu, X. (eds.) ICPM 2021. LNBIP, vol. 433, pp. 180–193. Springer, Cham (2022). https://doi.org/10.1007/978-3-030-98581-3_14

60. Shoush, M., Dumas, M.: Prescriptive process monitoring under resource constraints: a reinforcement learning approach. KI - Künstliche Intelligenz (2024). https://doi.org/10.1007/s13218-024-00881-6

61. Smit, T.K., Reijers, H.A., Lu, X.: HOEG: a new approach for object-centric predictive process monitoring. In: Guizzardi, G., Santoro, F.M., Mouratidis, H., Soffer, P. (eds.) CAiSE 2024. LNCS, vol. 14663, pp. 231–247. Springer (2024). https://doi.org/10.1007/978-3-031-61057-8_14

62. Stevens, A., Peeperkorn, J., Smedt, J.D., Weerdt, J.D.: Manifold learning for adversarial robustness in predictive process monitoring. In: 5th International Conference on Process Mining, ICPM 2023, Rome, Italy, 23–27 October 2023, pp. 17–24. IEEE (2023). https://doi.org/10.1109/ICPM60904.2023.10271991

63. Tax, N., Verenich, I., La Rosa, M., Dumas, M.: Predictive business process monitoring with LSTM neural networks. In: Dubois, E., Pohl, K. (eds.) CAiSE 2017. LNCS, vol. 10253, pp. 477–492. Springer, Cham (2017). https://doi.org/10.1007/978-3-319-59536-8_30

64. Taymouri, F., Rosa, M.L., Erfani, S.M.: A deep adversarial model for suffix and remaining time prediction of event sequences. In: Demeniconi, C., Davidson, I. (eds.) Proceedings of the 2021 SIAM International Conference on Data Mining, SDM 2021, Virtual Event, April 29–May 1 2021, pp. 522–530. SIAM (2021). https://doi.org/10.1137/1.9781611976700.59

65. Teinemaa, I., Dumas, M., Rosa, M.L., Maggi, F.M.: Outcome-oriented predictive process monitoring: review and benchmark. ACM Trans. Knowl. Discov. Data **13**(2) (2019). https://doi.org/10.1145/3301300

66. Teinemaa, I., Tax, N., de Leoni, M., Dumas, M., Maggi, F.M.: Alarm-based prescriptive process monitoring. In: Weske, M., Montali, M., Weber, I., vom Brocke, J. (eds.) BPM 2018. LNBIP, vol. 329, pp. 91–107. Springer, Cham (2018). https://doi.org/10.1007/978-3-319-98651-7_6

67. Umili, E., Licks, G.P., Patrizi, F.: Enhancing deep sequence generation with logical temporal knowledge. In: Giacomo, G.D., Fionda, V., Fournier, F., Ielo, A., Limonad, L., Montali, M. (eds.) Proceedings of the 3rd International Workshop on Process Management in the AI Era (PMAI 2024) co-located with 27th European Conference on Artificial Intelligence (ECAI 2024), Santiago de Compostela, Spain, 19 October 2024. CEUR Workshop Proceedings, vol. 3779, pp. 23–34. CEUR-WS.org (2024). https://ceur-ws.org/Vol-3779/paper4.pdf

68. Vaswani, A., et al.: Attention is all you need. In: Guyon, I., et al. (eds.) Advances in Neural Information Processing Systems, vol. 30. Curran Associates, Inc. (2017). https://proceedings.neurips.cc/paper_files/paper/2017/file/3f5ee243547dee91fbd053c1c4a845aa-Paper.pdf

69. Veličković, P., Cucurull, G., Casanova, A., Romero, A., Liò, P., Bengio, Y.: Graph attention networks (2018). https://arxiv.org/abs/1710.10903

70. Weinzierl, S., Dunzer, S., Zilker, S., Matzner, M.: Prescriptive business process monitoring for recommending next best actions. In: Fahland, D., Ghidini, C.,

Becker, J., Dumas, M. (eds.) BPM 2020. LNBIP, vol. 392, pp. 193–209. Springer, Cham (2020). https://doi.org/10.1007/978-3-030-58638-6_12
71. Wuyts, B., Vanden Broucke, S., De Weerdt, J.: SuTraN: an encoder-decoder transformer for full-context-aware suffix prediction of business processes. In: 2024 6th International Conference on Process Mining (ICPM), pp. 17–24 (2024). https://doi.org/10.1109/ICPM63005.2024.10680671

# From Constraint-Based Process Modeling to Framed Autonomy: A Historical Excursus

Fabrizio Maria Maggi$^{(\boxtimes)}$ , Anti Alman , and Paul Hermann Wittlinger

Free University of Bozen-Bolzano, Bolzano, Italy
`maggi@inf.unibz.it, {anti.alman,pwittlinger}@unibz.it`

**Abstract.** This paper presents a historical excursus from the initial introduction of the DECLARE Framework to its potential future applications within the context of AI-Augmented Business Process Management Systems (ABPMSs). On this path, we highlight how AI related techniques have intertwined with research on the DECLARE language, and how the core ideas of the original DECLARE Framework have become even more relevant with the conception of ABPMS. With the latter, we refer to the use of multiple interdependent models of different languages to express a business process – an idea now consolidated as the *multi-model paradigm*. Within this paradigm, we explore the use of Automated Planning for operational support in executing multi-faceted constraints that involve multiple models, timeline limitations, cost constraints, and resource optimization. We position this approach as a more expressive way of modeling the process frame of an ABPMS, with the goal of maximizing a KPI or finding a trade-off among several of them.

**Keywords:** Constraint Based Languages · Declarative Process Mining · Framed Autonomy · Multi-Model Paradigm · Automated Planning

## 1 Introduction

In 2006, Maja Pesic and Wil van der Aalst, building upon previous work by Dwyer et al. [24], introduced a subset of Linear Temporal Logic over finite traces ($\text{LTL}_f$) constraints that captured the most recurrent temporal relations used to model business processes [41,42]. This subset was formalized as the constraint-based language DECLARE. The core idea behind DECLARE was to support the execution of highly variable business processes without requiring overly rigid or complex process specifications. Instead of prescribing a single procedural flow, DECLARE adopted an *open-world assumption*, where a process could follow any execution path that complied with a given set of constraints. This approach represented the embryonic form of *process framing*, where the "frame" was defined solely by declarative constraints.


J. Mendling et al. (Eds.): Wil van der Aalst Festschrift, LNCS 16480, pp. 199–211, 2026.
https://doi.org/10.1007/978-3-032-17618-9_15

Only few years later, DECLARE became the key language in the emerging field of *declarative process mining*, which focused on data-driven analysis of process behavior. In this field, Wil van der Aalst inspired, and often lead, research on model discovery, compliance monitoring, conformance checking, and various other problems. As this research matured, the initial ad hoc algorithmic approaches gradually gave way to more robust Artificial Intelligence (AI)-based techniques, ranging from automata-based reasoning to SAT solvers, Automated Planning, and Answer Set Programming (ASP).

More recently, research has extended beyond pure constraint reasoning towards the concept of *framed autonomy* concerning the ability of AI-Augmented BPM Systems (ABPMS) to autonomously execute or suggest process behaviors within a predefined frame, while optimizing performance criteria such as the minimization of constraint violations [23]. This concept is further enhanced by the introduction of the *multi-model paradigm*, that advocates for the use of multiple interdependent specifications of different languages within a unified execution semantics to represent and reason about business processes [9].

Building upon earlier formalization of combining data-aware Petri nets with DECLARE [8], FRAIM [43] represents a further evolution of framed autonomy, where domain-specific algorithms are replaced by an *Automated Planning-based framework* that leverages established AI heuristics to optimize process execution. FRAIM supports process framing across different modeling languages, including Petri nets and DECLARE, and allows users to define cost models that assign different penalty values to constraint violations. The system is capable of generating process execution recommendations that minimize violation costs.

Future research will focus on extending FRAIM to support richer constraint types within the process frame, including MP-DECLARE and TIMED DECLARE constraints, and boundaries of different nature such as resource pools, probabilistic process models, and cost models. Another key direction is the incorporation of multi-objective optimization, enabling the system to balance multiple performance dimensions such as execution time, constraint violations, costs, and resource utilization. Finally, the integration of conversational AI components, such as Large Language Models (LLMs), could further enhance ABPMSs by allowing users to interactively adapt process frames based on system-generated execution suggestions.


## 2    The Declare Framework

In framed autonomy, a system operates under a heterogeneous set of constraints, declarative and procedural, resource-based, temporal, and cost-oriented, and suggests optimal actions while allowing continuous user interaction. The DECLARE Framework was developed based on a similar concept. In that early formulation, what is now called a "process frame" in framed autonomy, was defined exclusively through control-flow constraints, combining procedural and declarative perspectives: procedural through YAWL [28] workflows for structured, centrally controlled tasks, and declarative through DECLARE specifica-

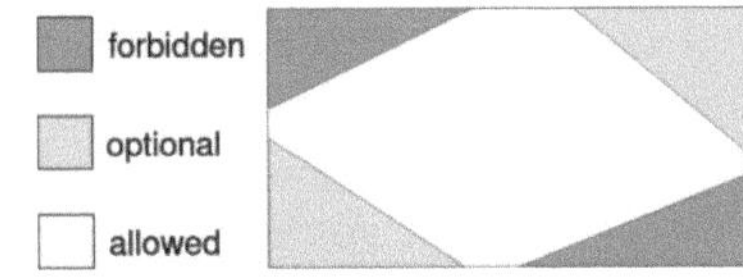


**Fig. 1.** Process scenarios in constraint-based process modeling (taken from [41]).

tions for flexible, constraint-driven sub-processes. Within this hybrid specification, the system continuously monitored constraint satisfaction, suggesting executions that avoided violations while leaving space for human decision-making.

The mechanisms in the original DECLARE Framework were basic but foundational. The system had no notion of goal optimization, it could not balance or maximize heterogeneous business objectives such as time, cost, or resource efficiency. Its only "objective function" was constraint satisfaction: maintaining a valid execution trace under the given procedural–declarative boundary. Although resource and data elements could be attached to DECLARE models, they were handled outside the formal $LTL_f$ semantics that governed process execution, meaning they lacked formal reasoning support. In addition, the integration of procedural and declarative models was achieved hierarchically rather than semantically. A single YAWL activity could be refined into a DECLARE sub-model, providing flexibility within a structured process; conversely, a single DECLARE activity could trigger a YAWL sub-workflow. However, there was no unified semantic model for hybrid reasoning: control passed between the declarative and procedural components, rather than being jointly reasoned about across them. At its core, the DECLARE Framework introduced constraint templates and models with mandatory and optional constraints, enabling a distinction between forbidden, optional, and allowed process behavior (cf. Figure 1). Optional constraints were particularly significant: they represented early forms of user-guided optimization and adaptive decision support. When an optional constraint risked violation, the system could alert the user, who could then choose whether to comply or deviate, mirroring the interaction loop of modern LLM-driven framed autonomy, where the system proposes optimized actions under multiple constraints and the human negotiates trade-offs among cost, time, resources, and satisfaction levels.

A further feature aligning DECLARE with framed autonomy was its support for dynamic instance adaptation. Tasks and constraints could be added, removed, or modified during execution while preserving instance consistency. Instances could even be migrated to updated models, allowing a process to evolve over time without restarting. This dynamic reconfiguration capability was a direct precursor to modern autonomous systems that adapt to evolving constraints and objectives while remaining human-in-the-loop.

Despite these anticipatory features, the DECLARE framework was not driven by AI in any substantial sense. Its reasoning mechanisms were entirely rule-based, with no integration of learning, perception, or adaptive autonomy. Moreover, the framework offered no explicit explainability mechanisms, even though individual constraints had relatively simple textual descriptions. Finally, it lacked any notion of environmental awareness: processes were modeled as self-contained systems, largely isolated from external contextual factors that modern frameworks now integrate through sensors, data streams, and situational logic.

## 3    Evolution of AI in Declarative Process Analysis

The verification semantics of the original DECLARE Framework, as defined in [40], relied purely on automata-theoretic reasoning to ensure compliance with a set of constraints. These early methods offered rigorous formal guarantees but lacked AI capabilities for learning, optimization, or adaptive reasoning. The real evolution toward AI-driven process analysis was driven by the development of *declarative process mining* techniques, one of the strongest and most investigated ties between AI and process analysis.

The first attempts to automate the discovery of declarative specifications applied Inductive Logic Programming (ILP) to infer DECLARE rules from positive and negative examples of process executions [12,30]. Subsequent approaches by Maggi et al. [34,36] introduced an unsupervised, two-phase algorithm: first, identifying frequent sets of correlated activities using an Apriori-based method; and second, verifying candidate constraints through the replay of logs on automata. The MINERful algorithm [21,22] advanced this direction from a knowledge-driven, statistical perspective. More recently, Agostinelli et al. [7] employed model learning to infer deterministic finite state automata directly from event logs, overcoming the limitations of approaches that required negative examples or pre-defined constraint candidates to carry on the discovery.

In parallel, *conformance checking* and *compliance monitoring* underwent a similar transformation. Early systems, such as [14,15], validated DECLARE constraints using ILP and automata-based verification. Alignment-based techniques [19,20] later mapped DECLARE models to automata and computed minimal deviations using A*-based search. Multi-perspective extensions like MP-DECLARE [13] further enriched declarative models with data and temporal reasoning. Complementary advances occurred in *runtime compliance monitoring* [32], with the development of reactive AI systems [31,33,35,37,39] capable of diagnosing, explaining, and anticipating violations in streaming settings.

More recently, *Automated Planning* has been used to enhance the scalability and optimality of trace alignment [17,18]. Other approaches employ *SAT solving* and *Answer Set Programming (ASP)*, encoding declarative problems as first-order theories and leveraging advanced AI solvers to efficiently compute bounded models. SAT-based methods formulate tasks such as conformance checking and query analysis as satisfiability problems, whereas ASP-based frameworks more effectively handle variants involving event payloads. Together, these methods achieve scalability and adaptability beyond traditional logic-based tools.

The latest advances focus on data- and time-aware declarative constraints through *numeric planning*. Within this paradigm, TIMED DECLARE extends

DECLARE with Metric Temporal Logic (MTL) to capture quantitative timing relationships between activities. The resulting problem, *Timed Trace Alignment (TTA)*, is formalized as a state-space search over one-clock deterministic timed automata (1-DTAs) [6]. By encoding TTA as a numeric AI planning task, optimal alignments can be efficiently computed, enabling systems not only to detect deviations but also to suggest corrective actions and optimize process executions with respect to activity timestamps.

## 4  Multi-model Paradigm

As evident from Sect. 3, the vast majority of research stemming from the original DECLARE Framework focuses on using constraints as a declarative representation of a business process. However, there are at least two other aspects of this framework that have not received as much explicit attention.

First, the combination of YAWL and DECLARE, as discussed in Sect. 2, positions the DECLARE Framework as an early example of what has now become known as *Hybrid Business Process Representations (HBPRs)* [10]. While limited to hierarchical compositions, it nevertheless opens up various interesting modeling possibilities. For example, one could use the cardinality constraints of the DECLARE language to impose how many times certain parts of the process can or must be repeated (e.g., *Absence3(A)*, where $A$ refers to another model), use a DECLARE model to define the rules for constructing (part of) a process instance from several procedural process fragments (e.g., *Alternate Response[A,B]*, *Absence3[B]*, where $A$ and $B$ refer to other models), or employ a top-level YAWL model to arrange declarative models into a procedural sequence.

Second, we highlight the use of multiple models itself. Analogous to the current motivation of HBPRs, the DECLARE Framework originally motivated this with the need to represent both procedural and declarative aspects of business processes. However, this can be extended further towards compartmentalization and modularization, which are common, for example, in software development. In general, larger software projects are not managed as single monolithic blocks. Instead, they are structured through phases, milestones, and deliverables; development tasks are organized through epics and stories; and software architectures may consist of components, packages, and classes. Examples include well-known methodologies such as Agile, Scrum, and Kanban, or software architectures such as service-oriented architecture and microservices. Similar concepts, although already partially enabled in the original DECLARE Framework, have not become equally common in the context of business processes.

Nevertheless, the use of multiple models is not unprecedented. For instance, customizable processes combine a base model with models capturing its variations [29], while guided process discovery uses (possibly interconnected) model fragments as an extra input [38]. In addition to his involvement in the aforementioned examples, Wil van der Aalst also kickstarted the development of object-centric process mining [1], which has a similar idea of using a collection of interdependent models, each modeling a specific type of object, at its core [3].

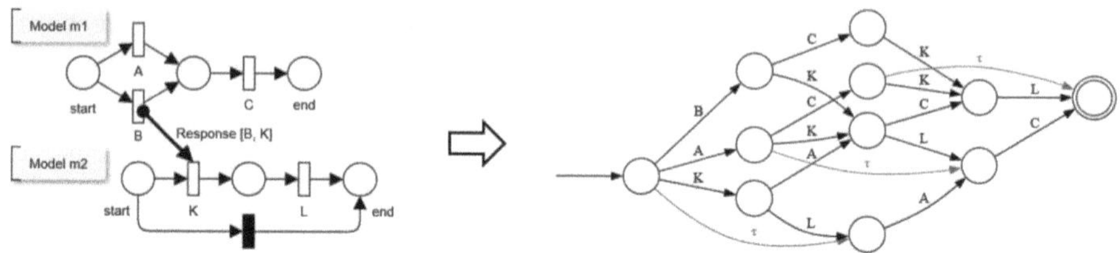

**Fig. 2.** An example of interdependent models on the left and the resulting state-space on the right (based on [8]).

Furthermore, object-centric process mining is, at least conceptually, not limited to a single process but, as also highlighted by Wil van der Aalst in [2], *"provides powerful insights to quickly determine the opportunities for improvement that are located at the intersection points of different business processes"*.

This leads us to the *multi-model paradigm* for BPM [9], which draws inspiration from all of the ideas and examples discussed above. The central tenet of this paradigm is the use of multiple interdependent models (possibly in different modeling languages) to represent a greater whole (i.e., a business process, a set of processes, or interactions between processes). Emphasis is placed on extensive reuse of existing languages, such that each aspect of a process (or their interactions) would be represented by the language best suited for that aspect (e.g., procedural models should not attempt to capture declarative knowledge in most cases). Of course, language extensions, or even new languages, may sometimes be required, but such cases should be clearly motivated. Crucially, semantics should be provided for the concurrent execution of individual models (possibly of different languages) rather than redefining the semantics of those models. For example, an individual Petri net that is created as part of a greater whole should behave as close to a normal Petri net as possible, even when viewed in isolation.

Consider, for instance, the example in Fig. 2. It consists of three individual models (two Petri nets and a single DECLARE constraint connecting them). For their concurrent execution, one could simply assume that each individual model progresses if and only if an activity referenced in that model occurs, and that activities referenced in multiple models progress all of these models concurrently. In that case, each individual model, when viewed in isolation, would continue to function as expected, while the state-space induced by their concurrent execution would effectively correspond to the intersection of their valid executions. Thus, in the given example, the activities in $m_2$ would become required if $B$ is executed, while $B$ can only be executed before $K$, since otherwise $K$ would become required in a state where another $K$ is no longer possible. For a deeper explanation of such examples, we refer the reader to [8], while operational support for HBPRs consisting of DECLARE and Petri net models is further discussed in Sect. 5.

Finally, we connect these ideas to ABPMS (cf. Sect. 1). Instead of relying strictly on process models, the concept of an ABPMS introduces a more general notion of the *process frame*, which defines the maximal permissible boundaries within which the system must operate to achieve its goals. The process frame is not limited to a single linguistic or symbolic formalism and is intended to incorporate heterogeneous knowledge ranging from predefined procedures to commonsense rules and best practices [23]. This makes the multi-model paradigm an ideal approach for representing the process frame.

## 5   Planning-Based Framed Autonomy

In Sect. 4, we traced our steps from the original DECLARE Framework to the multi-model paradigm, highlighting key ideas and related research topics along the way. In this section, we first take a deeper look at how DECLARE enables the formalization of component interactions in HBPRs, which represent the core foundation for process frames. We then expand upon this idea by providing operational support for HBPRs through *recommendations* on which actions to take next, as described by van der Aalst et al. [4].

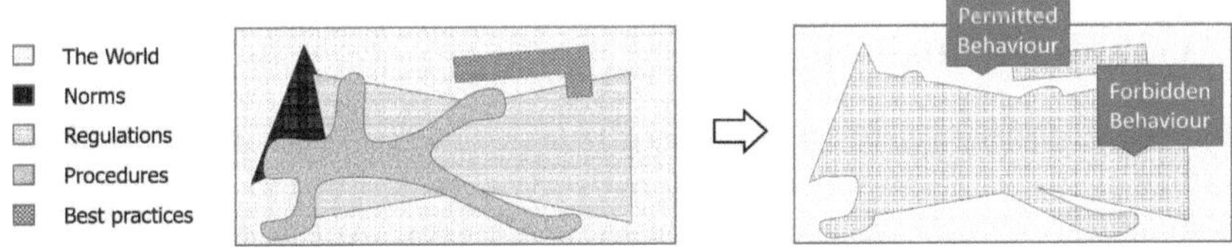


**Fig. 3.** A process frame consisting of multi-faceted constraints on the left and the resulting Behaviour on the right. Each constraint (implicitly) forbids part of the total state-space. The process frame allows any execution not forbidden by any constraint.

This idea, implemented in the publicly available tool FRAIM [43], reflects the capability of framed autonomy in ABPMSs, as discussed in [23]. An ABPMS should be able to operate *autonomously* within its permitted frame of action (i.e., its *process frame*). The required process frame can be specified through *multi-faceted constraints* that involve multiple models, timeline limitations, cost constraints, and resource optimization (see Fig. 3). As in the original DECLARE framework, HBPRs operate under the open-world assumption (i.e. every execution that is not explicitly forbidden is allowed). Each constraint either explicitly restricts part of the process space (i.e. ABSENCE of an activity), or implicitly restricts it through the inverse of the constraint (e.g., the EXISTENCE of an activity is equivalent to a negation of its ABSENCE). In this way, we can define the permitted behavior of the *process frame* as the union of the forbidden behavior defined by its constraint components. Current state-of-the-art techniques that achieve framed autonomy through Automated Planning are, however, limited to process frames expressed as HBPRs. As we emphasize in Sect. 6, future research should broaden this notion of HBPRs to encompass specifications that go beyond control-flow and integrate additional process perspectives.

Building on this foundation, the practical realization of framed autonomy involves providing intelligent operational support during process execution. Given an ongoing process instance, an agent (either human or artificial) interacting with an ABPMS should be guided toward the next actions that lead to an optimal outcome (e.g., in terms of cycle time, violation cost, or resource utilization). In the simplest case, i.e., for a consistent and non-conflicting process frame, the *Framed Autonomy Problem* can be reduced to a reachability problem. However, for more advanced scenarios, such as conflicting constraints or partial process executions that already violate certain limitations, existing reachability algorithms are insufficient. These cases require a dedicated *recovery strategy* to correctly recommend the best course of action.

To address this, we show how to operationalize framed autonomy by transforming it into an Automated Planning problem, following the approach presented in [5]. This formulation naturally supports the optimization of multiple objectives and can be further extended to incorporate temporal and constant-to-variable conditions, in line with earlier work on recommendation-based operational support [4].

### 5.1   Automated Planning

*Automated Planning* deals with the synthesis of *plans*, i.e., sequences of actions that solve a given state-space problem by transforming the *initial state* of a problem instance into an accepting *goal state* [26]. Automated Planning has found wide application across various domains, such as robotics, scheduling, and, as highlighted in Sect. 3, process verification tasks.

A planning task is typically defined as a tuple consisting of a *planning domain* and a corresponding *planning problem* (or instance). The planning domain provides an explicit representation of the system under consideration through a set of valid *propositions* and a set of applicable *operators* $\Omega$ that influence the current state of the system. Each *operator schema* $a \in \Omega$ defines the corresponding set of *parameters*, *preconditions*, and *effects* of $a$ [5]. The planning problem instance then specifies which propositions hold true initially (the *initial state*) and which propositions are desired at the end of the plan (the *goal state*).

### 5.2   Framed Autonomy as an Automated Planning Problem

The rationale for employing Automated Planning in the context of framed autonomy lies in the observation that the Framed Autonomy Problem can be formulated as a *state-space search problem*. The intuition is as follows. Let $\mathcal{F}$ be a process frame consisting of an HBPR with $m$ DECLARE specifications $(\mathcal{D}_1, \ldots, \mathcal{D}_m)$ and $n$ Petri nets $(\mathcal{P}_1, \ldots, \mathcal{P}_n)$. The alphabet of the frame is defined as:

$$\mathcal{E}_{\mathcal{F}} = \bigcup_{i=1}^{m} \mathcal{E}_{\mathcal{D}_i} \cup \bigcup_{j=1}^{n} \mathcal{E}_{\mathcal{P}_j},$$

where $\mathcal{E}_{\mathcal{D}_i}$ refers to the alphabet of the $i$-th DECLARE specification and $\mathcal{E}_{\mathcal{P}_j}$ denotes the alphabet of the $j$-th Petri net. In the initial step, each component (i.e., each DECLARE specification or Petri net) is transformed into a deterministic finite state automaton, where each DECLARE constraint yields a separate automaton. Subsequently, the (possibly empty) partial process execution is itself transformed into a finite state automaton. Then, the Automated Planning formulation we define allows us to monitor the conjunction of all individual components without explicitly constructing the product automaton, thereby avoiding the memory explosion that such a construction would entail. Furthermore, this enables the incorporation of *recovery strategies*, such as *(violated automaton) reset* or *(violated automaton) discard*, to resolve potential conflicts within the process frame.

Solving the framed autonomy problem then amounts to finding a sequence of applicable activities that leads all automata to an accepting state. Conceptually, the problem can be divided into two distinct phases:

1. replay a partial process execution (*prefix*) on the process frame, and
2. find the cost-optimal continuation (*suffix*) from the resulting state.

The final plan is obtained by concatenating the *prefix* and the *suffix*. It may consist of any number of activities from the process frame alphabet $\mathcal{E}_{\mathcal{F}}$, as well as recovery actions such as *reset* and *discard*.

## 6   Research Agenda

In this paper, we have presented the progression of constraint-based process models towards framed autonomy in ABPM. We conclude by outlining a set of research challenges that may inspire and drive future work in this area.

**C1. Data and Time.** In Sect. 5, we focused primarily on the control-flow, which can be handled with classical planning algorithms. Handling *data and temporal conditions* (i.e., MP-DECLARE constraints) in the same way through, for example, propositionalization exacerbates the state-explosion problem, thus requiring more suitable encoding approaches. As one alternative, *numeric planning* extends classical planning (STRIPS) by allowing real-valued state variables in the definition of operator schemas [27]. Additionally, there exists a fragment of the Planning Domain Definition Language, PDDL+ [25], specifically designed to model time-dependent effects within the planning domain.

**C2. Stochasticity.** To capture the inherent variability of real-world processes, *stochastic models* stochastic Petri nets and probabilistic DECLARE can be incorporated into the process frame, enabling explicit representation of uncertainty and probabilistic dependencies between events. This allows an ABPMS to assess the likelihood of constraint violations or performance degradation under varying operational conditions and to reason quantitatively about reliability and risk. Probabilistic and temporal constraints can also express common KPIs (e.g., 95% of applications reviewed within 3 days), serving as goal-setting mechanisms.

Since business processes rarely operate under complete certainty, *Fully Observable Non-deterministic (FOND) planning* can complement stochastic modeling by generating plans that satisfy business objectives despite uncertainty.

**C3. Business Goals.** BPM systems often need to balance multiple and, in many cases, conflicting objectives. *Trade-offs between business goals*, such as minimizing cycle time, avoiding constraint violations, reducing operational costs, and maximizing resource utilization, represent a fundamental challenge in process optimization. We can leverage advanced planning systems to find solutions that respect these goals in combination, considering the preferences of the users.

**C4. Real-time Sensor Data.** *Signal Temporal Logic (STL)-based constraints* can also extend the expressive power of BPM systems beyond the activity perspective. Traditional BPM tools typically exhibit limited or no awareness of their operating environment; they treat the process as an isolated, deterministic flow. STL introduces temporal and quantitative semantics that allow constraints to incorporate contextual and environmental factors, such as fluctuating demand, resource availability, or external sensor data, making the system more adaptive and situationally aware [16]. The first challenge in integrating STL stems from its continuous nature, i.e., the discrete state-space of traditional BPM tools is replaced by continuous signals which may gradually rise or fall over time. Overcoming this challenge would open up possibilities for creating a truly autonomous system that can track and react to changes in its environment in nearly real-time.

**C5. Object Perspective.** *Object-centric behavioral constraints (OCBC)* offer a way to represent rules and dependencies not only over activities, but also over the evolving states of business objects and their interactions [11]. An OCBC model consists of DECLARE-like constraints on the activity perspective, an UML class diagram on the relevant data objects, and the relations between the two, which can be seen as another example of combining models of different languages to describe a business process. Integrating this view in an ABPMS would enable, for example, multi-entity reasoning (such as linking customer orders, invoices, and deliveries within a single semantic frame), thereby enabling richer analytical capabilities than purely activity-centric approaches. Wil van der Aalst recently investigated an algorithm for discovering object-centric declarative patterns from event logs [44] that aligns with this direction, enabling the automated discovery and operationalization of declarative, synchronization-aware constraints that jointly capture activity semantics and inter-object dependencies, thereby supporting advanced multi-entity reasoning in ABPMS environments.

**C6. Conversational Autonomy.** Incorporating *Large Language Models (LLMs)* into framed autonomy enables a *conversational interface* to the system. Through natural-language interaction, users can query the state of the process, explore trade-offs, or request simulations under different contingencies. LLMs serve as mediators between human operators and the underlying formal models, translating intuitive questions into formal reasoning tasks and explaining results in accessible language. This synergy transforms traditional process optimization into conversational, context-aware autonomy, where human insight and algorithmic reasoning operate in a continuous feedback loop.

# References


1. van der Aalst, W.M.P.: Object-centric process mining: dealing with divergence and convergence in event data. In: Ölveczky, P.C., Salaün, G. (eds.) SEFM 2019. LNCS, vol. 11724, pp. 3–25. Springer, Cham (2019). https://doi.org/10.1007/978-3-030-30446-1_1
2. van der Aalst, W.M.P.: Object-Centric Process Mining: The Next Frontier in Business Performance. celon.is/OCPM-Whitepaper (2023)
3. van der Aalst, W.M.P.: Object-centric process mining: unraveling the fabric of real processes. Mathematics **11**(12) (2023)
4. van der Aalst, W.M.P., Pesic, M., Song, M.: Beyond process mining: from the past to present and future. In: Pernici, B. (ed.) CAiSE 2010. LNCS, vol. 6051, pp. 38–52. Springer, Heidelberg (2010). https://doi.org/10.1007/978-3-642-13094-6_5
5. Acitelli, G., Alman, A., Maggi, F.M., Marrella, A.: Achieving framed autonomy in AI-augmented business process management systems through automated planning. Inf. Syst. **133**, 102573 (2025)
6. Acitelli, G., De Bellis, E., Maggi, F.M., Marrella, A., Patrizi, F.: Aligning metric temporal constraints and event logs via numeric planning. In: BPM. vol. 16044, pp. 33–50. Springer (2025)
7. Agostinelli, S., Chiariello, F., Maggi, F.M., Marrella, A., Patrizi, F.: Process mining meets model learning: Discovering deterministic finite state automata from event logs for business process analysis. Inf. Syst. **114**, 102180 (2023)
8. Alman, A., Maggi, F.M., Montali, M., Patrizi, F., Rivkin, A.: A framework for modeling, executing, and monitoring hybrid multi-process specifications with bounded global-local memory. Inf. Syst. **119**, 102271 (2023)
9. Alman, A., Maggi, F.M., Rinderle-Ma, S., Rivkin, A., Winter, K.: Towards a multi-model paradigm for business process management. In: CAiSE, vol. 14663, pp. 178–194. Springer (2024)
10. Andaloussi, A.A., Burattin, A., Slaats, T., Kindler, E., Weber, B.: On the declarative paradigm in hybrid business process representations: A conceptual framework and a systematic literature study. Inf. Syst. **91**, 101505 (2020)
11. Artale, A., Kovtunova, A., Montali, M., van der Aalst, W.M.P.: Modeling and reasoning over declarative data-aware processes with object-centric behavioral constraints. In: Hildebrandt, T., van Dongen, B.F., Röglinger, M., Mendling, J. (eds.) BPM 2019. LNCS, vol. 11675, pp. 139–156. Springer, Cham (2019). https://doi.org/10.1007/978-3-030-26619-6_11
12. Bellodi, E., Riguzzi, F., Lamma, E.: Probabilistic declarative process mining. In: Bi, Y., Williams, M.-A. (eds.) KSEM 2010. LNCS (LNAI), vol. 6291, pp. 292–303. Springer, Heidelberg (2010). https://doi.org/10.1007/978-3-642-15280-1_28
13. Burattin, A., Maggi, F.M., Sperduti, A.: Conformance checking based on multi-perspective declarative process models. Expert Syst. Appl. **65**, 194–211 (2016)
14. Chesani, F., Lamma, E., Mello, P., Montali, M., Riguzzi, F., Storari, S.: Exploiting inductive logic programming techniques for declarative process mining. Trans. Petri Nets Other Model. Concurr. **2**, 278–295 (2009)
15. Chesani, F., Mello, P., Montali, M., Riguzzi, F., Sebastianis, M., Storari, S.: Checking Compliance of Execution Traces to Business Rules. In: Business Process Management Workshops, vol. 17, pp. 134–145. Springer (2008)

16. Corea, C., Alman, A., Maggi, F.M., Wittlinger, P.H.: Declarative process specifications over discrete/continuous event data. In: CAiSE, vol. 15702, pp. 277–294. Springer (2025)
17. De Giacomo, G., Maggi, F.M., Marrella, A., Patrizi, F.: On the disruptive effectiveness of automated planning for LTL$f$-based trace alignment. In: AAAI, pp. 3555–3561. AAAI Press (2017)
18. De Giacomo, G., Maggi, F.M., Marrella, A., Sardiña, S.: Computing trace alignment against declarative process models through planning. In: ICAPS, pp. 367–375. AAAI Press (2016)
19. de Leoni, M., Maggi, F.M., van der Aalst, W.M.P.: Aligning event logs and declarative process models for conformance checking. In: Barros, A., Gal, A., Kindler, E. (eds.) BPM 2012. LNCS, vol. 7481, pp. 82–97. Springer, Heidelberg (2012). https://doi.org/10.1007/978-3-642-32885-5_6
20. de Leoni, M., Maggi, F.M., van der Aalst, W.M.P.: An alignment-based framework to check the conformance of declarative process models and to preprocess event-log data. Inf. Syst. **47**, 258–277 (2015)
21. Di Ciccio, C., Mecella, M.: Mining constraints for artful processes. In: Abramowicz, W., Kriksciuniene, D., Sakalauskas, V. (eds.) BIS 2012. LNBIP, vol. 117, pp. 11–23. Springer, Heidelberg (2012). https://doi.org/10.1007/978-3-642-30359-3_2
22. Di Ciccio, C., Mecella, M.: On the Discovery of declarative control flows for artful processes. ACM Trans. Manag. Inf. Syst. **5**(4), 24:1–24:37 (2015)
23. Dumas, M., et al.: AI-augmented business process management systems: a research manifesto. ACM Trans. Manag. Inf. Syst. **14**(1), 11:1–11:19 (2023)
24. Dwyer, M.B., Avrunin, G.S., Corbett, J.C.: Patterns in property specifications for finite-state verification. In: ICSE, pp. 411–420. ACM (1999)
25. Fox, M., Long, D.: PDDL+: Modeling continuous time dependent effects. In: Proceedings of the 3rd International NASA Workshop on Planning and Scheduling for Space, vol. 4, p. 34 (2002)
26. Geffner, H., Bonet, B.: A Concise Introduction to Models and Methods for Automated Planning. Morgan & Claypool Publishers, Synthesis Lectures on Artificial Intelligence and Machine Learning (2013)
27. Haslum, P., Lipovetzky, N., Magazzeni, D., Muise, C.: Numeric planning, pp. 83–101. Springer (2019)
28. ter Hofstede, A.H.M., van der Aalst, W.M.P., Adams, M., Russell, N. (eds.): Modern Business Process Automation - YAWL and its Support Environment. Springer (2010)
29. La Rosa, M., van der Aalst, W.M.P., Dumas, M., Milani, F.: Business process variability modeling: a survey. ACM Comput. Surv. **50**(1), 2:1–2:45 (2017)
30. Lamma, E., Mello, P., Montali, M., Riguzzi, F., Storari, S.: Inducing declarative logic-based models from labeled traces. In: Alonso, G., Dadam, P., Rosemann, M. (eds.) BPM 2007. LNCS, vol. 4714, pp. 344–359. Springer, Heidelberg (2007). https://doi.org/10.1007/978-3-540-75183-0_25
31. Ly, L.T.: SeaFlows - a compliance checking framework for supporting the process lifecycle. Ph.D. thesis, University of Ulm (2013)
32. Ly, L.T., Maggi, F.M., Montali, M., Rinderle-Ma, S., van der Aalst, W.M.P.: Compliance monitoring in business processes: Functionalities, application, and tool-support. Inf. Syst. **54**, 209–234 (2015)
33. Ly, L.T., Rinderle-Ma, S., Knuplesch, D., Dadam, P.: Monitoring business process compliance using compliance rule graphs. In: Meersman, R., Dillon, T., Herrero, P., Kumar, A., Reichert, M., Qing, L., Ooi, B.-C., Damiani, E., Schmidt, D.C.,

White, J., Hauswirth, M., Hitzler, P., Mohania, M. (eds.) OTM 2011. LNCS, vol. 7044, pp. 82–99. Springer, Heidelberg (2011). https://doi.org/10.1007/978-3-642-25109-2_7

34. Maggi, F.M., Bose, R.P.J.C., van der Aalst, W.M.P.: Efficient discovery of understandable declarative process models from event logs. In: Ralyté, J., Franch, X., Brinkkemper, S., Wrycza, S. (eds.) CAiSE 2012. LNCS, vol. 7328, pp. 270–285. Springer, Heidelberg (2012). https://doi.org/10.1007/978-3-642-31095-9_18

35. Maggi, F.M., Montali, M., Westergaard, M., van der Aalst, W.M.P.: Monitoring business constraints with linear temporal logic: an approach based on colored automata. In: Rinderle-Ma, S., Toumani, F., Wolf, K. (eds.) BPM 2011. LNCS, vol. 6896, pp. 132–147. Springer, Heidelberg (2011). https://doi.org/10.1007/978-3-642-23059-2_13

36. Maggi, F.M., Mooij, A.J., van der Aalst, W.M.P.: User-guided discovery of declarative process models. In: Proceedings of the IEEE Symposium on Computational Intelligence and Data Mining, CIDM, pp. 192–199. IEEE (2011)

37. Maggi, F.M., Westergaard, M., Montali, M., van der Aalst, W.M.P.: Runtime verification of LTL-based declarative process models. In: Runtime Verification, vol. 7186, pp. 131–146. Springer (2011)

38. Mannhardt, F., de Leoni, M., Reijers, H.A., van der Aalst, W.M.P., Toussaint, P.J.: Guided process discovery - a pattern-based approach. Inf. Syst. **76**, 1–18 (2018)

39. Montali, M., Maggi, F.M., Chesani, F., Mello, P., van der Aalst, W.M.P.: Monitoring business constraints with the event calculus. ACM Trans. Intell. Syst. Technol. **5**(1), 17:1–17:30 (2013)

40. Montali, M., Pesic, M., van der Aalst, W.M.P., Chesani, F., Mello, P., Storari, S.: Declarative specification and verification of service choreographies. ACM Trans. Web **4**(1), 3:1–3:62 (2010)

41. Pesic, M.: Constraint-based workflow management systems: Shifting control to users. PhD thesis, Technische Universiteit Eindhoven (2008)

42. Pesic, M., van der Aalst, W.M.P.: A declarative approach for flexible business processes management. In: Eder, J., Dustdar, S. (eds.) BPM 2006. LNCS, vol. 4103, pp. 169–180. Springer, Heidelberg (2006). https://doi.org/10.1007/11837862_18

43. Wittlinger, P.H., Acitelli, G., Alman, A., Maggi, F.M., Marrella, A.: FrAIm: a what-if analysis tool enabling framed autonomy via automated planning. In: BPM (Demos / Resources Forum). CEUR Workshop Proceedings, vol. 4032, pp. 192–199. CEUR-WS.org (2025)

44. Küsters, A., van der Aalst, W.M.: August. OC-DECLARE: Discovering object-centric declarative patterns with synchronization. In: International Conference on Business Process Management, pp. 162–179. Cham: Springer Nature Switzerland (2025)

# Contextualized Storage of Process Models in a Process Database for Data-Driven Manufacturing

Christian Brecher[✉], Paul Weiler, Martin Krömer, Felix Fernholz, and Marcel Fey

Laboratory for Machine Tools and Production Engineering (WZL), RWTH Aachen University, Campus Boulevard 30, 52074 Aachen, Germany
`{c.brecher,p.weiler,m.kroemer,f.fernholz,m.fey}@wzl.rwth-aachen.de`

**Abstract.** Modern manufacturing systems are equipped with a multitude of sensors that continuously generate extensive time series data capturing the condition of production processes. A constant challenge is linking time series data to spatial product features or specific process states. The automated tape laying process exemplifies this challenge: defects are detected with high spatial resolution on the product surface, yet the defect origins must be traced back to corresponding segments in the time series data. Such a link can be achieved using process models. Process models describe the causal relationships of an underlying production process by connecting sensor signals with operating principles and provide these in the form of refined data. Beyond enabling the assignment of time series data to spatially resolved component features, process models also facilitate process analysis and optimization. Especially in data-driven modeling approaches, the core algorithms are often identical, while the resulting structure, parameterization, input, and output data vary depending on the application. Managing these models and their parameters in a systematic and reusable way is therefore critical for efficient process analysis and optimization. This paper proposes an extension of an existing process database to store process models along with their underlying algorithms. The approach aims at a semantic link between input and output data, the specific parameterization of a model, and the corresponding process context. By adhering to the FAIR principles, the approach not only enables effective model reuse and reproducibility but also facilitates the contextualization of parameterized models and their results within the underlying production processes.

**Keywords:** Data-driven manufacturing · Process modeling · Automated tape laying

## 1 Introduction

Manufacturing systems increasingly generate vast streams of time series data from heterogeneous production plants and sensor systems. Using both live and historical data enables data-driven optimization and monitoring, which reduces the need for a continuous expert inspection of workpiece quality. This proves particularly valuable in light of the ongoing shortage of skilled workers. To address this need, the Laboratory for Machine Tools and Production Engineering (WZL) at RWTH Aachen University has developed a digital infrastructure that stores and contextualizes process data in a central database. Contextualization links sensor signals to operational metadata, making the data broadly usable for monitoring and optimization across multiple machines and processes. Process data has a complex temporal structure, multiscale dynamics, and signals are often correlated. Extracting actionable insight therefore requires advanced modeling, including segmentation and clustering to discover regimes and patterns, as well as data-driven models such as regression to relate process signals to quality indicators. To make these models easily applicable, extensible, and customizable for different use cases, the WZL operates a framework that orchestrates the interdependent model execution on contextualized data. This framework supports reproducibility and rapid deployment of process models across machines. As a representative use case, we apply the infrastructure to automated tape laying (ATL). Data from an ATL process is recorded, contextualized, and analyzed by successive process models to establish a connection between process data and the resulting workpiece quality. In ATL, linking process data with spatially resolved tape placement is the key to identifying defects as patterns in the corresponding process data. This approach supports quality monitoring and process optimization without the need for continuous on-site expert supervision.

## 2  State of the Art

### 2.1  Data Acquisition and Storage in Manufacturing

Modern production systems are equipped with a wide range of sensors that are often used for monitoring and control purposes, providing valuable insights into the production state. Along the process chain of a part, datasets are thus generated, containing specific information about the underlying manufacturing processes [11]. Data sources include both external sensor systems and internal signals from a control system. Through proprietary or standardized interfaces, data can be retrieved from the control systems of a production plant. In this context, the Open Platform Communications Unified Architecture (OPC UA) is established as the widely used standard protocol in industrial applications [13]. The received data can be categorized according to their recording interval into time series data and event data [11]. In a technical context, time series data represent discrete recordings of time-dependent signals. The temporal nature of a time series arises from the ordered sequence of data points, which are typically spaced at equidistant intervals [1]. Event data, on the other hand, is output at irregular intervals and corresponds to a change in the condition of a defined signal. Both types of data are collectively referred to as raw or process data. To persist large amounts of raw data, relational databases are most commonly used. Relational databases organize data in tables with predefined columns and can model complex relationships by referencing data across different tables. To provide more flexible storage options, most relational databases also support JSON columns, which can hold any value that can be serialized in JSON format [12]. Because time series data are generated through repeated sensor measurements, it exhibits strong autocorrelation and predictable patterns, making it highly suitable for compression and indexing. For compression, both lossless and lossy methods can be employed. Lossless techniques, such as run-length encoding and delta encoding, leverage the redundancy in the data, while lossy methods, such as wavelet transforms, capture the underlying patterns and provide an approximation. Depending on the dataset, lossless methods can achieve compression ratios of approximately 10:1, whereas lossy methods can reach even higher compression ratios [4,5].

## 2.2   Data Processing and Contextualization

The vast array of high-frequency sensor signals in a production facility contains detailed information about the underlying manufacturing processes, yet remains largely unintelligible to humans in its entirety. To extract knowledge from large volumes of data, the concept of Knowledge Discovery in Databases (KDD) has been established. In data-driven manufacturing, KDD provides a structured framework for the systematic processing of data, thereby enabling a comprehensive understanding of production processes [5,6]. In the initial phase of data preparation, the completeness, consistency, and coherence of the raw data are ensured for subsequent analytical steps. Data preparation includes methods for data synchronization and data imputation. The datasets are subsequently transformed into a standardized format to facilitate data contextualization. In the field of production technology, data contextualization involves data enrichment with high-level system information (metadata), semantic segmentation of data, and data refinement using existing process models [10]. Semantic segmentation aims to automatically divide datasets into discrete intervals based on defined system states [8]. The underlying idea of segmentation is that transitions between system states are reflected by variations in values or patterns within the data. Numerous algorithms from the field of data mining have been developed for time series segmentation, including methods that detect changes in statistical characteristics or identify recurring patterns [11]. To obtain more detailed insights into production processes, data in manufacturing technology is supplemented with the aid of process models, as explained in Sect. 2.3. However, storing and processing high-frequency process data from numerous sources in a central database to provide it in a contextualized form remains a significant challenge. Approaches from production engineering are often tailored to specific use cases, making them difficult to scale [7]. Commercial providers often follow a platform-based approach. Although these platforms deliver comprehensive solutions, they primarily focus on optimizing compatibility and functionality within their own ecosystems, resulting in limited support for heterogeneous environments with sensor systems or controllers from multiple vendors. A centralized management of raw data, processed data including associated algorithms, and generated process models in a database holds the potential not only to contribute to a deeper understanding of production processes but also to enable efficient root cause analysis for the design of efficient process analysis and optimization.

## 2.3   Methods for Central Persistence of Process Models

Process models capture the interactions of production operations and predict process behavior and quality under varying conditions. Although many applications share common algorithmic families (e.g., clustering, regression, CNNs, autoencoders), each deployed model is uniquely defined by its architecture, learned parameters, training data, and runtime context according to the specific application. Since these elements evolve with incoming data and changing operating conditions, a centrally managed and semantically rich storage structure is essential for model reuse, reproducibility, and management in heterogeneous manufacturing environments. Appropriate frameworks and lifecycle tools provide key building blocks for the persistence of process models. TensorFlow Extended (TFX) offers a pipeline-centric architecture that enforces consistent data validation, feature transformation, training, and deployment, enabling continuous training and robust service [2]. MLflow complements this with experiment tracking and artifact management, logging parameters and metrics across runs, and maintaining a model registry for versioned promotion through stages (e.g., staging to production) [15]. ModelDB addresses centralized model metadata management, recording lineage relationships among datasets, features, code snapshots, and trained model versions to support reproducibility and auditability at scale [14]. Model Cards provide a human-readable description of a model's purpose, assumptions, limitations and performance across data groups, improving transparency and risk communication alongside machine-readable metadata. This helps stakeholders quickly assess fitness for a given use case, supports responsible deployment, and simplifies auditing and compliance [9].

Despite these capabilities, a critical gap persists: most solutions treat data and models as separate concerns, scattering raw and contextualized time series data in one system (e.g., files, object stores, data lakes) and models, weights as well as pipeline artifacts in another (e.g., registries, artifact stores). This fragmentation impedes end-to-end provenance, complicates the semantic linkage between model inputs, model parameterization, and physical processes, and restricts global accessibility for retraining and monitoring. Up to now, an approach for integrating process models into a database-centered architecture has been lacking, where raw data, contextualized segments, processed features, model specifications (architecture, weights, I/O schema), pipeline definitions, and evaluation results co-reside under a consistent schema and are accessible through standard APIs from anywhere. A central database structure allows direct queries across the data lineage and model history, supports reproducible retraining on selected segments, and make cross-site deployment easier by keeping models and data together as primary entities.

## 3    Approach

The approach for a central database implemented by the WZL expands an existing process database with a structural extension for the centralized storage, management, and deployment of process models. In this paper, "models" refers to both white-box approaches constructed from explicit process knowledge (e.g., the process parameter maps described in [3]) and black-box methods from data analysis and machine learning. These models can be applied across different machines sharing the same model type, while per-use-case parameterizations are persisted alongside each model instance to ensure a tailored, reproducible application. Models for preprocessing, monitoring, and optimization in manufacturing often rely on shared algorithmic primitives. Preprocessing uses segmentation and clustering algorithms to organize high-volume time series data into meaningful segments and groups, while monitoring and optimization use the resulting features and quality labels as input for prediction and decision-making. Across use cases, the underlying algorithms may be identical, while parameterization, selected input channels, and output targets vary. Linking model instances to contextualized data permits correct application and targeted retraining as process conditions evolve. To ensure continuous deployability and responsiveness, a centralized database persists data, model instances, and training pipelines. Each model instance is defined and stored within the database together with its full specification and current parameters (weights and biases), enabling reproducible retraining and consistent inference. Most importantly, explicit metadata clarify limitations and application range and facilitate safe reuse across machines and production lines. The approach integrates essential elements of existing frameworks such as TFX, MLflow, and ModelDB directly into the data analysis environment of the use case. This integration creates a seamless connection between process data and models, thereby enhancing the efficiency of analysis and application.

### 3.1    Introduction to the Existing Framework of a Production Database

To enable centralized data management, a production database framework is implemented by the WZL, the architecture of which is described below [3]. The framework is designed to be independent of any specific data source and can handle data from various systems, such as sensor systems, control units, or simulation software. The framework provides multiple interfaces to feed raw data into the process database (e.g., MQTT, CSV, JSON, REST API). The raw data are assigned to a *machine object* within the database according to their source. A *machine object* serves as the virtual abstraction of an entity within the production environment, such as a machine tool or a milling tool, and contains associated meta information. Through linking, multiple *machine objects* can be related to each other (e.g., associate the main spindle with the machine tool), which serves as the basis for data contextualization. To assign raw data to defined states, the framework is extended with automated segmentation. Segmentation is managed centrally through a *segmentation service* within the database. A *segmentation service* describes an algorithm to be used to segment the time series data into discrete segments. Each service has a unique name and descriptions of the parameters for running the algorithm and a description of the results calculated by the algorithm for each segment. Each service can be used in multiple contexts, such as different parameters or for different machine objects. This concrete parameterization of a segmentation service is stored as an instance in the *segmentation service instance* table in the database. This structure enables contextualized persistence of segmentation algorithms and their results while allowing flexible extensibility. An affiliated dashboard is used to display the raw data, including the calculated segments and the linked machine objects, enabling basic data analyzes to be performed. To perform more in-depth process analyzes, process models are required. Therefore, the framework is subsequently extended with a structure for the centralized management of process models, ensuring efficient and contextualized generation and persistence of process models and their associated results.

### 3.2  Database Structure for Centralized and Contextualized Storage of Process Models

The process database described in Sect. 3.1 allows experts to easily analyze individual manufacturing processes by combining process data with corresponding segments. However, for industrial applications, automated knowledge extraction and systematic feedback to the process are required. For this reason, the process database is extended by structures that support models that link process data with the underlying functional principles and generate derived or classified results. A simplified extended database structure is shown in Fig. 1. For model persistence, the process database is extended with a structure that mirrors the one already used for the services that create segments (*segmentation service*). The table *model type* specifies the model's parameter definitions and result structures in the form of JSON schemas. Based on this definition, each concrete realization of a model is stored as a model instance (*model instance*). An instance references its type, records the parameterization used, and stores the corresponding results. For many analytic models, parameterization requires manual tuning and must remain visible to the user. Therefore, these settings are stored in the *parameters* column of the *model instance* table. Conversely, blackbox such as ANNs, models utilize a separate *model data* BLOB column, leaving the definition of the internal structure to the specific model implementation. Because these models address specialized use cases, they are currently compact enough for direct database storage, however, should model sizes increase significantly, the use of dedicated storage solutions must be re-evaluated. Having an explicit model-type description provides a stable interface (via parameter and result schemas) and enables a generic UI for display and configuration without per model-type changes.

A key obstacle to generalized, large-scale ML models in manufacturing is the limited availability of high-quality labeled datasets. Large-scale annotation of

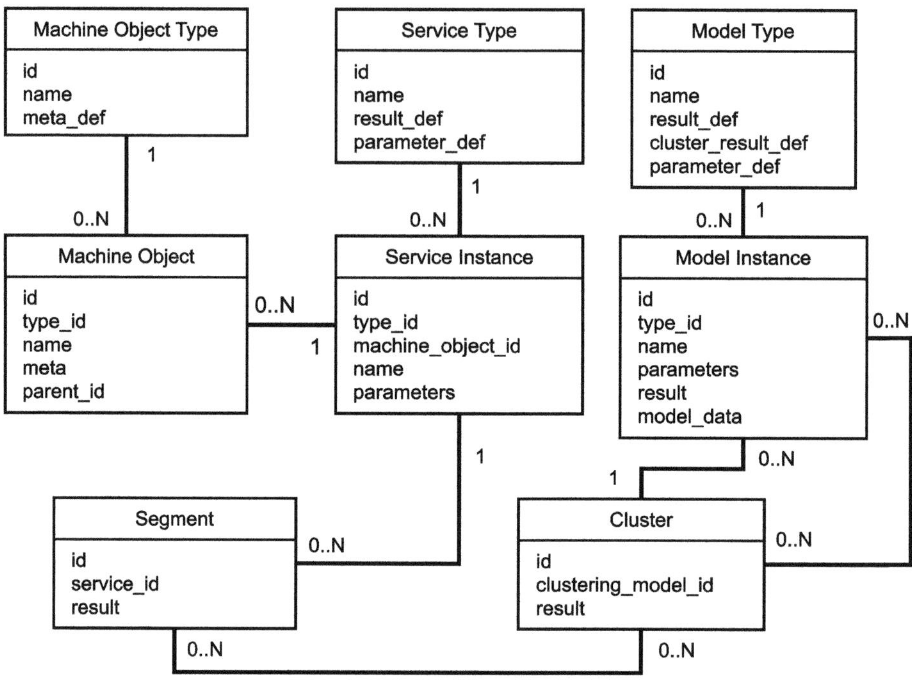

**Fig. 1.** Structure for the central persistence of process models in a process database.

new data for every application is typically not practical. A common approach is to develop specialized models that are validated for a restricted parameter space (e.g., specific combinations of material, machine, or settings). These models apply only within defined validity ranges and must be selected according to the context. To support this context-aware selection, a clustering step is performed first. The resulting clusters are persisted in the *cluster* table and linked to the segments calculated beforehand or are newly generated. Each entry in *cluster* stores a description produced by the clustering model, such as the centroid, density parameters, or labels. In a subsequent step, each model is configured to operate on specific clusters. When the model is executed again, it processes the newly added segments of the clusters that are assigned to the model. By explicitly storing the clusters and their references to the original segments, traceability is ensured.

The proposed structure satisfies key requirements for reproducibility and reusability of process models. First, all information relevant for inference is versioned and stored in machine-readable form. Second, the separation of type and instance enables targeted reuse of the same model class across applications without conflating specific parameterizations and validity ranges. Third, the explicit embedding into the service and segment context ensures end-to-end traceability of results back to the underlying data and process states.

# 4   Use Case and Outlook: Automated Tape Laying

Automated tape laying (ATL) systems are typically organized as production lines. The architecture considered in this work comprises one or more rotational stages that rotate the layup table, one or more application units, and one or more preheating units. Each station is instrumented with multiple sensors that record time series data such as the rotation of the table, the zone-wise heating power of the preheating unit, the compaction pressure of the roller, and the lateral displacement of the application unit.

The ATL process can be naturally segmented by the individual tapes placed over a discrete time interval. This property lends itself to a semi-automated storage procedure: for each tape and each rotation, a fixed time window is recorded and then batched as a packet to the MQTT broker. In detail, the data for each individual tape or rotation are bundled into a single JSON object, which is persisted in the central database; during ingestion, high-frequency time series and metadata are separated and saved in their respective locations and contextualized accordingly. The metadata, for example, include an identifier to associate the tape with a specific component and a layer index to indicate the ply height within the laminate. In the high-frequency raw data, the recorded signals include the current positions of the application roller and the underlying table, laser power, and roller compaction pressure.

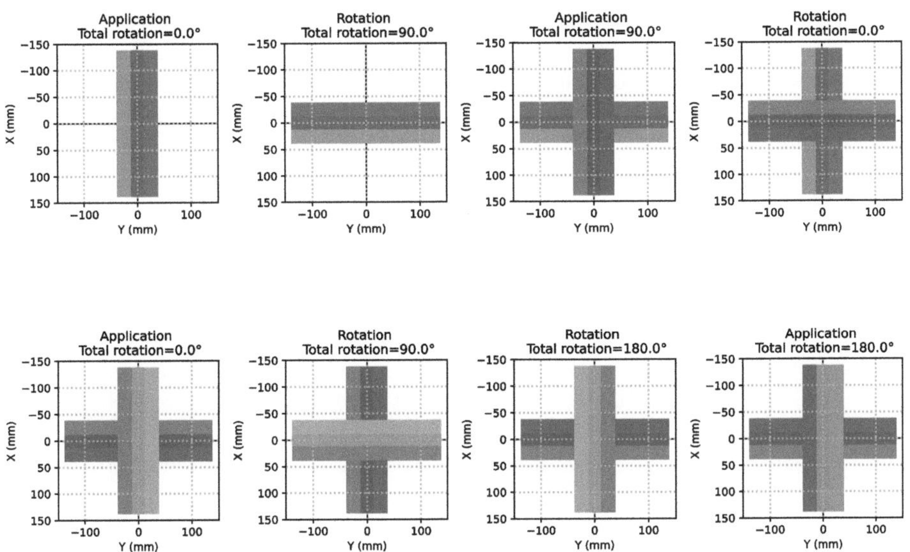

**Fig. 2.** Visualization of the tape laying process segments (from top left to bottom right).

Operations in the production line are inherently divided into discrete steps. Accordingly, input data are persisted as segments in a dedicated segments table in the database. This table also stores segments produced by algorithmic procedures (e.g., rule-based or change-point detection) and by machine learning models. For model training, segmentation is advantageous because it enables targeted selection of training examples consistent with the intended function of each model, thereby obviating manual preselection and improving reproducibility.

A key step toward establishing a causal relationship between recorded process signals and final part quality is the spatial registration of time series samples to their positions on the finished component. Before each tape placement, the orientation and precise position of the table, as well as the displacement of the tape laying head, must be known. These kinematic quantities allow computation of the final tape geometry and placement, enabling a bidirectional mapping that links local defects on the finished component to the corresponding time series windows of the layup process. Successful execution of this step depends on well-documented segment metadata and a gap-free acquisition of raw signals from the application unit.

An initial visualization of the recorded process segments can be observed in Fig. 2. This visualization allows for an overhead view of the laid laminate, providing a preliminary impression of the entire component. The figure shows individual steps of the tape laying process. The segments in which tapes are laid are labeled by *Application*, and the rotary segments are labeled by *Rotation*. In addition to these connections to the raw data segments, every plot shows the current cumulative rotation of the table on which the tapes are laid.

Following spatial registration, an artificial neural network (ANN) is trained to learn the relationship between process signals and quality outcomes. Defects must be identified and labeled prior to training. Only after this annotation step can the labeled regions be used as supervisory signals for the model. The trained ANN can then detect corresponding anomalies in the time series during operation and provide online feedback on part quality.

Models differ across machines due to variations in process states and machine characteristics. A single model is therefore insufficient. The resulting array of models requires the database structure described in Sect. 3.2 to version, extend, and deploy them at appropriate locations in the line. This structure ensures maintainability, scalability, and consistent application across heterogeneous stations.

To train models that capture specific defect modes in detail, defective segments are labeled in the *segments* table (Fig. 1). These segments can then be grouped by defect type, via a clustering algorithm, to form coherent training sets. Each training set is stored in the *cluster* table (Fig. 1). For each such group, a dedicated artificial neural network is trained to model the defect signature, and the resulting model is persisted as an entry in the *model instance* table (Fig. 1). From there, models are retrievable for application, extensible via incremental retraining with new data, and traceable through versioning and metadata.

# 5     Conclusion

This paper presents the extension of a process database to include a central persistence layer for process models. Until now, process data and process models have typically been managed separately, which impedes end-to-end provenance, complicates the semantic linkage between model inputs, model parameterization, physical processes, and restricts global accessibility for retraining and monitoring. To address this limitation, a new structure is integrated into an existing process database to centrally store process models. Central management of process models provides the advantage of reusing fundamental algorithms, particularly those from data-driven approaches, while linking derived or trained models to the input data of underlying production processes enables a semantic connection. Consequently, a comprehensive data pipeline is established, encompassing the storage of process data, data segmentation, and the subsequent derivation and application of process models to enable automated process analysis, actionable recommendations, and process optimization. In the automated tape laying (ATL) use case, centrally persisted models enable an end-to-end workflow that links process data to the finished part through spatial registration, derives quality labels for tapes and plies via segmentation, and trains artificial neural networks on the curated data to predict overall part quality. The framework consolidates models and data in a central persistence layer, ensuring reuse, reproducible retraining, and seamless deployment across similar production systems.

**Acknowledgments.** Funded by the Deutsche Forschungsgemeinschaft (DFG, German Research Foundation) TRR 402/1-525069572.

**Disclosure of Interests.** The authors have no competing interests to declare that are relevant to the content of this article.

# References


1. Charu C. Aggarwal.: Data mining: The textbook. Cham et al.: Springer (2015). ISBN: 978-3-319-14142-8
2. Baylor, D., et al.: TFX: A TensorFlow-Based Production-Scale Machine Learning Platform, pp. 1387–1395 (Aug 2017). https://doi.org/10.1145/3097983.3098021
3. Brecher, C., et al.: "Data usage in the internet of production: development of a process database for data-driven modeling". In: The International Journal of Advanced Manufacturing Technology (2025). ISSN: 0268-3768. https://doi.org/10.1007/s00170-025-15951-8
4. Chiarot, G., Silvestri, C.: "Time Series Compression Survey". In: ACM Computing Surveys, vol. 55(10), pp. 1–32 (2023). ISSN: 0360-0300. https://doi.org/10.1145/3560814
5. D'Onofrio, S., Meier, A., eds.: Big Data Analytics: Grundlagen, Fallbeispiele und Nutzungspotenziale. Springer eBook Collection. Wiesbaden: Springer Vieweg, 2021. ISBN: 978-3-658-32236-6. https://doi.org/10.1007/978-3-658-32236-6

6. Düsing, R.: Knowledge discovery in databases. In: Analytische Informationssysteme. Ed. by Chamoni, P., Gluchowski, P., Berlin, Heidelberg: Springer Berlin Heidelberg (2006), pp. 241–262. ISBN: 978-3-540-29286-9. https://doi.org/10.1007/3-540-33752-0

7. Eichelberger, H., et al.: Industry 4.0/IIoT Platforms for manufacturing systems — a systematic review contrasting the scientific and the industrial side. Inform. Softw. Technol. **179**, 107650 (2025). ISSN: 09505849. https://doi.org/10.1016/j.infsof.2024.107650

8. Gharghabi, S., et al.: Matrix Profile VIII: domain agnostic online semantic segmentation at superhuman performance levels. In: 2017 IEEE International Conference on Data Mining (ICDM). IEEE, pp. 117–126 (2017). ISBN: 978-1-5386-3835-4. https://doi.org/10.1109/ICDM.2017.21

9. Mitchell, M., et al.: Model Cards for Model Reporting. In: Proceedings of the Conference on Fairness, Accountability, and Transparency. FAT* '19. ACM, pp. 220–229 (Jan 2019). https://doi.org/10.1145/3287560.3287596

10. Ochel, J., Fey, M., Brecher, C.: Semantically meaningful segmentation of milling process data. In: Production at the Leading Edge of Technology. Ed. by Bernd-Arno Behrens et al. Lecture Notes in Production Engineering. Cham: Springer International Publishing (2022), pp. 319–327. ISBN: 978-3-030-78423-2. https://doi.org/10.1007/978-3-030-78424-9_36

11. Ochel, J.: "Datengetriebene Strukturierung von NC-Zerspanprozessen". Dissertation. Apprimus Verlag and Rheinisch-Westfälische Technische Hochschule Aachen (2023)

12. Petković, D.: JSON integration in relational database systems. Int. J. Comput. Appl. **168**(5), 14–19 (2017). https://doi.org/10.5120/ijca2017914389

13. Strutzenberger, D., et al.: An IoT architecture to integrate different machine tools into a compound OPC UA interface. It - Inform. Technol. **65**(3), pp. 76–91 (2023) ISSN: 1611-2776. https://doi.org/10.1515/itit-2023-0007

14. Vartak, M., et al.: ModelDB: a system for machine learning model management. In: Proceedings of the Workshop on Human-In-The-Loop Data Analytics. HILDA '16. San Francisco, California: Association for Computing Machinery, 2016. ISBN: 9781450342070. https://doi.org/10.1145/2939502.2939516

15. Zaharia, M.A., et al.: Accelerating the machine learning lifecycle with MLflow. In: IEEE Data Eng. Bull **41**, pp. 39–45 (2018). https://api.semanticscholar.org/CorpusID:83459546

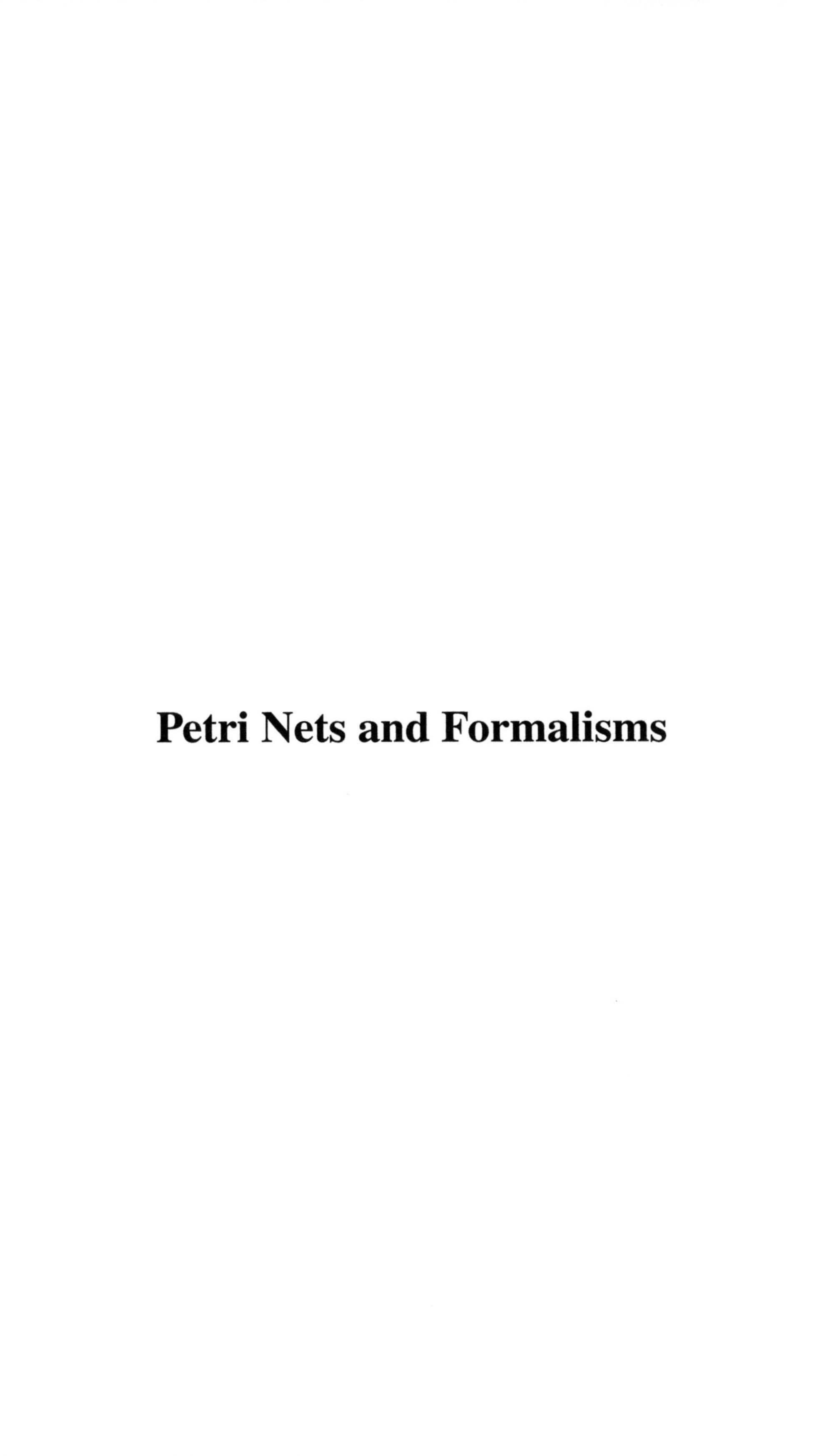

# Petri Nets and Formalisms

# Petri Net Encoding of Reaction Systems with Unspecified Durations

Maciej Koutny[1]([envelope]) [iD] and Łukasz Mikulski[2] [iD]

[1] School of Computing, Newcastle University, 1 Science Square,
Newcastle upon Tyne NE4 5TG, UK
`maciej.koutny@ncl.ac.uk`
[2] Faculty of Mathematics and Computer Science, Nicolaus Copernicus University in Toruń,
Chopina 12/18, 87-100 Toruń, Poland
`lukasz.mikulski@mat.umk.pl`

**Abstract.** Reaction systems, inspired by biochemical processes in living cells, form a computational model where system behaviour emerges from interactions of reactions governed by facilitation and inhibition. A distinctive feature of this model is the non-permanency of entities, which poses challenges for simulation using alternative frameworks such as Petri nets.

In this paper, we extend the standard semantical framework of reaction systems by introducing duration for reactions, while preserving the non-permanency assumption. We develop a modular Petri net encoding that supports a compositional construction and enables an accurate simulation of the new semantics. This framework is particularly well-suited for practical applications such as modelling of aneurysm, where structural variability, transient biochemical conditions, and uncertain process duration are critical factors.

**Keywords:** reaction system · reaction duration · Petri net · model transformation · theory of concurrency

## 1  Introduction

Reaction systems are inspired by biochemical processes in living cells, where behaviour is driven by interactions of reactions governed by facilitation and inhibition. Since their introduction in [3], they have evolved into a well-studied computational model with distinctive features and diverse applications.

Their classical semantical captures rely on system states defined by sets of entities and state transitions defined by sets of reactions. A key behavioural trait is the non-permanency of entities, requiring explicit mechanisms for data persistence. Such aspects must be carefully handled when simulating reaction systems using other frameworks, such as Petri nets [2, 11].

In this paper, we introduce explicit durations of reactions, putting more emphasis on reactions than entities, without losing the non-permanency assumption. Moreover, we present an efficient Petri net encoding of such reaction systems. The proposed method is modular and supports compositional construction, offering a flexible foundation for

© The Author(s), under exclusive license to Springer Nature Switzerland AG 2026
J. Mendling et al. (Eds.): Wil van der Aalst Festschrift, LNCS 16480, pp. 225–236, 2026.
https://doi.org/10.1007/978-3-032-17618-9_17

simulations. The practical applications include modelling the behaviour of aneurysms, where structural changes, non-permanent biochemical conditions, and unspecified duration of the whole process must be accurately represented.

*Contribution.* There are two main contributions of this paper:

- we introduce a new semantics of reaction systems (in the related work section we explain its novelty);
- we provide an efficient Petri net encoding (with proofs of soundness, deadlock-freeness, livelock-freeness, and polynomial size).

*Related Work.* The paper [1] defines reaction systems with (specified) durations. The idea is to introduce an additional function $d$ that assigns a non-negative integer to each entity and specifies its decay time. One might think of simulating the behaviour of reaction systems with durations proposed in this paper by duplicating each entity—providing an inactive version with large $d$-value and an active version which decays immediately (as in the original system). There are some subtle technical issues related to this approach; in particular, inactive entities are available until the decay time passes, and the decay time needs to be directly specified, making it impossible to postpone for an unspecified length of time.

Another paper that touches on similar topics is [4] which introduces time to reaction systems. Again, one can try to utilise the provided clocks with binary counters to postpone the effect of a reaction. The main technical problem is again a specified (or at least bounded) duration.

The effect of postponing the effect of an initiated reaction can also be observed in the distributed reaction systems introduced in [8]. In this model, part of the system (agents there are not pointed as active by the context sequence) can stay inactive for some (unspecified) time. However, in our approach, we introduce unspecified durations on the level of open systems (with trivial empty contexts).

The encoding itself is inspired by the fourth approach proposed in [6].

*Structure of this Paper.* In Sect. 2 we recall the basic notions related to Petri nets. We follow with the definition of reaction systems in two semantics: the standard one and a new one with unspecified reaction durations. After that, in Sect. 4, we provide a construction that allows us to simulate reaction systems with unspecified reaction durations using 1-safe Petri nets. We also prove the basic properties of this encoding. Section 5 concludes the paper.

## 2   Petri Nets

We use the standard model of 1-safe Place/Transition nets [10] which makes it possible to use a variety of tools and analytical techniques developed over the years for this class of Petri nets [5].

By a *Petri net* we mean a quadruple $\mathcal{N} = (P, T, F, M_0)$ such that $P$ and $T$ are finite disjoint sets of *places* and *transitions*, $F \subseteq (P \times T) \cup (T \times P)$ is the *flow relation*, and

$M_0 : P \rightarrow \{0,1,\dots\}$ is the *initial marking* satisfying $M_0(P) \subseteq \{0,1\}$ (in general, any mapping $M : P \rightarrow \{0,1,\dots\}$ is a *marking*).

For each transition $t \in T$, $\mathrm{pre}(t) = \{p \in P \mid (p,t) \in F\}$ are the *input* places of $t$, and $\mathrm{post}(t) = \{p \in P \mid (t,p) \in F\}$ are the *output* places of $t$.

We can denote $P$, $T$, and $F$ by $P_{\mathcal{N}}$, $T_{\mathcal{N}}$, and $F_{\mathcal{N}}$, respectively. Then, for a non-empty set of Petri nets $\mathfrak{N}$, we denote $P_{\mathfrak{N}} = \bigcup_{\mathcal{N} \in \mathfrak{N}} P_{\mathcal{N}}$, $T_{\mathfrak{N}} = \bigcup_{\mathcal{N} \in \mathfrak{N}} T_{\mathcal{N}}$, and $F_{\mathfrak{N}} = \bigcup_{\mathcal{N} \in \mathfrak{N}} F_{\mathcal{N}}$.

In the Petri nets constructed in this paper, $\rho_{\langle X \rangle}$ will denote a set of indexed places or transitions or sub-nets $\{\rho_x \mid x \in X\}$. For example, $1_{\langle \{s,r\} \rangle} = \{1_s, 1_r\}$ and $v_{\langle 1_{\langle \{s,r\} \rangle} \rangle} = \{v_{1_s}, v_{1_r}\}$.

*Execution Semantics.* A transition $t \in T$ is *enabled* at a marking $M$ if $M(p) \geq 1$, for every $p \in \mathrm{pre}(t)$. We denote this by $t \in \mathrm{enabled}(M)$.

In the diagrams, places are represented by circles, transitions by squares, and flow relations by directed arcs. A marking $M$ is indicated by placing $M(p)$ small black dots inside a circle representing the place $p$.

The standard interleaving execution semantics of a Petri net used in this paper is captured using sequences of alternating transitions and markings. A *(mixed) firing sequence* of $\mathcal{N}$ is

$$\sigma = M_0 t_1 M_1 t_2 M_2 \dots M_{n-1} t_n M_n \qquad (n \geq 0) \tag{1}$$

such that, for all $1 \leq i \leq n$, the following hold:

- $t_i \in \mathrm{enabled}(M_{i-1})$.
- $t_i$ is fired at $M_{i-1}$ and this leads to $M_i$, i.e., for every $p \in P$:

$$M_i(p) = \begin{cases} M_{i-1}(p) - 1 & \text{if } p \in \mathrm{pre}(t_i) \setminus \mathrm{post}(t_i) \\ M_{i-1}(p) + 1 & \text{if } p \in \mathrm{post}(t_i) \setminus \mathrm{pre}(t_i) \\ M_{i-1}(p) & \text{otherwise} . \end{cases}$$

Moreover, each $M_i$ is a *reachable* marking of $\mathcal{N}$, and the *length* of the sequence $\sigma$ is $1 + 2 \cdot n$.

$\mathcal{N}$ is *deadlock-free* if, for each firing sequence $\sigma$, there is a firing sequence $\sigma \sigma'$ of strictly greater length than $\sigma$.

A marking $M$ is *1-safe* if $M(P) \subseteq \{0,1\}$, and $\mathcal{N}$ itself is *1-safe* if all the reachable markings are 1-safe. Hence, reachable markings of 1-safe Petri nets can be represented as sets of places which contain tokens.

## 3  Reaction Systems

The definitions concerning the basic reaction systems we use are taken from the seminal paper [3].

A *reaction system* is a pair $\mathcal{R} = (S,A)$, where $S$ is a finite *background* set and $A$ is a set of *reactions* over $S$. Each reaction is a triple

$$a = (R,I,P) = (R_a, I_a, P_a),$$

where $R$, $I$, $P$ are non-empty subsets of $S$ such that $R \cap I = \varnothing$, called the *reactant*, *inhibitor*, and *product set*, respectively. In what follows, for a set of reactions $B$, we denote $P_B = \bigcup\{P_a \mid a \in B\}$.

*Standard Semantics.* Let $\mathscr{R} = (S,A)$ be a reaction system, $a = (R,I,P) \in A$, and $U \subseteq S$. Then:

- $a$ is enabled at $U$ if $R \subseteq U$ and $I \cap U = \varnothing$. We denote this by $a \in$ enabled$(U)$.
- The *result* of $a$ on $U$ is

$$res_a(U) = \begin{cases} P & \text{if } a \in \text{enabled}(U) \\ \varnothing & \text{otherwise} . \end{cases}$$

- The *result* of $A$ on $U$ is $res_A(U) = \bigcup\{res_b(U) \mid b \in A\}$.

The set $U$ above represents the current state of a biochemical system being modelled by listing all present biochemical entities. A reaction is enabled and can take place if all its reactants are present and none of its inhibitors is present. The system reaches the next state $res_A(U)$ by executing all the reactions enabled in $U$.

A reaction system is a finite state system as each state is a subset of the finite background set, and its state transformations are deterministic since there are no conflicts between enabled reactions.

The dynamic behaviour of a reaction system operating without external environment is captured by the state sequences of its processes.

A *process* in a reaction system $\mathscr{R} = (S,A)$ is a pair $\pi = (\gamma, \delta)$ such that:

- $\gamma = (C_0, C_1, \ldots, C_n)$ and $\delta = (D_0, D_1, \ldots, D_n)$      where $n \geq 0$
- $C_0, \ldots, C_n, D_0, \ldots, D_n \subseteq S$      where $D_0 = C_1 = \cdots = C_n = \varnothing$
- $D_i = res_A(D_{i-1} \cup C_{i-1})$      for $0 < i \leq n$

The *state sequence* of $\pi$ is $(C_0 \cup D_0, \ldots, C_n \cup D_n)$.

In the above definition, $(C_0, C_1, \ldots, C_n)$ is a context sequence which in this case consists of empty sets except for the first element which fixes the first state of the dynamic evolution.

*Semantics with Unspecified Reaction Durations.* In this paper, we propose to look at the behaviour of a basic reaction system not it terms of entities it can generate, but rather in terms of reactions which can extend over time and terminate at an unspecified point producing entities. With such an assumption, the meaning of the state of an evolving reaction system changes and it now comprises currently active reactions rather than non-permanent entities.

A *process with unspecified reaction durations* in a reaction system $\mathscr{R} = (S,A)$ is a pair $\pi = (\delta, \psi)$ such that:

- $\delta = (H_0, H_1, \ldots, H_n)$ and $\psi = (B_0, B_1, \ldots, B_n)$      where $n \geq 0$
- $H_0, H_1, \ldots, H_n, B_0, B_1, \ldots, B_n \subseteq A$
- $B_i \subseteq H_i$      for $0 \leq i \leq n$
- $H_{i+1} = (H_i \setminus B_i) \cup \text{enabled}(P_{B_i})$      for $0 \leq i < n$

The *reaction sequence* of $\pi$ is $(H_0, \ldots, H_n)$.

Intuitively, each set $H_i$ represents the currently executed reactions of $\mathscr{R}$. The set $B_i \subseteq H_i$ contains those active reactions which are now terminated and produce a set of entities $P_{B_i}$. These entities trigger the execution of all reactions enabled at $P_{B_i}$. After that, due to the non-permanence, $P_{B_i}$ vanish.

*Remark 1.* A reaction sequence $(H_0, \ldots, H_n)$ is composed of individual states $H_i$ which consists of active (reactions) rather than static (entities) elements of the reaction system with durations. Though counter-intuitive at the first glance, such a situation is perfectly understandable, as computation in the semantics with durations is close to an interval (rather than total) order of actions. A similar phenomenon can be observed in interval Petri nets with non-atomic transitions (see [7]), where reachable markings are enriched by pending transitions.

To emphasize the fact that we consider a reaction system $\mathscr{R}$ with the novel semantics supporting unspecified reaction durations, we will denote $\mathscr{R}$ by $\mathscr{RD}$, and refer to $\mathscr{RD}$ simply as a *reaction system with durations*.

## 4 Petri Net Encoding

In this section, we introduce a translation from a reaction system with durations $\mathscr{RD}$ to a behaviourally equivalent Petri net $\mathcal{N}_{\mathscr{RD}}$. The translation is compositional, and it will employ as building blocks a number of Petri nets (called modules) depicted in Figs. 2 and 3.

The *encoding* of a reaction system with durations $\mathscr{RD} = (S, A)$ is the Petri net $\mathcal{N}_{\mathscr{RD}} = (P, T, F, M_0)$ such that:

$$\begin{aligned} P &= P_{\mathfrak{N}} \cup 1_{\langle S \cup A \rangle} \cup 0_{\langle S \cup A \rangle} & T &= T_{\mathfrak{N}} \cup \{t_0, t_1, t_2, t_3\} \\ F &= F_{\mathfrak{N}} \cup F' & M_0 &= 2_{\langle A \rangle} \cup 0_{\langle S \cup A \rangle} \end{aligned} \tag{2}$$

where $\mathfrak{N} = \mathscr{I}_{\langle A \rangle} \cup \mathscr{T}_{\langle A \rangle} \cup \mathscr{E}_{\langle A \rangle} \cup \mathscr{C}_{\langle S \rangle}$ and

$$\begin{aligned} F' = \; &3_{\langle A \rangle} \times \{t_0\} \; \cup \; \{t_0\} \times 4_{\langle A \rangle} \; \cup \; 5_{\langle A \rangle} \times \{t_1\} \; \cup \; \{t_1\} \times 6_{\langle A \rangle} \; \cup \\ &7_{\langle A \rangle} \times \{t_2\} \; \cup \; \{t_2\} \times 8_{\langle S \rangle} \; \cup \; 9_{\langle S \rangle} \times \{t_3\} \; \cup \; \{t_3\} \times 4_{\langle A \rangle} \; . \end{aligned}$$

The encoding $\mathcal{N}_{\mathscr{RD}}$ of $\mathscr{RD}$ is illustrated by a high-level design diagram in Fig. 1. The diagram uses sub-nets (modules) depicted in Figs. 2 and 3 which implement some basic processing elements.

The places in $P_{data} = 1_{\langle S \cup A \rangle} \cup 0_{\langle S \cup A \rangle}$ and $P_{control} = P \setminus P_{data}$ will be called the *data* and *control* places of $\mathcal{N}_{\mathscr{RD}}$, respectively. The idea is that $0_{\langle A \rangle} \cup 1_{\langle A \rangle}$ are data places which hold record of the current execution of reactions, e.g., a token in $1_a$ indicates that $a$ is being executed whereas a token in $0_a$ indicates that $a$ is dormant. Moreover, $0_{\langle S \rangle} \cup 1_{\langle S \rangle}$ are data places used to record the entities which are currently available for being used to start reactions, e.g., a token in $1_s$ indicates that $s$ is currently available whereas a token in $0_s$ indicates that $s$ is currently not present.

The modules capturing basic processing elements have the following intended meaning:

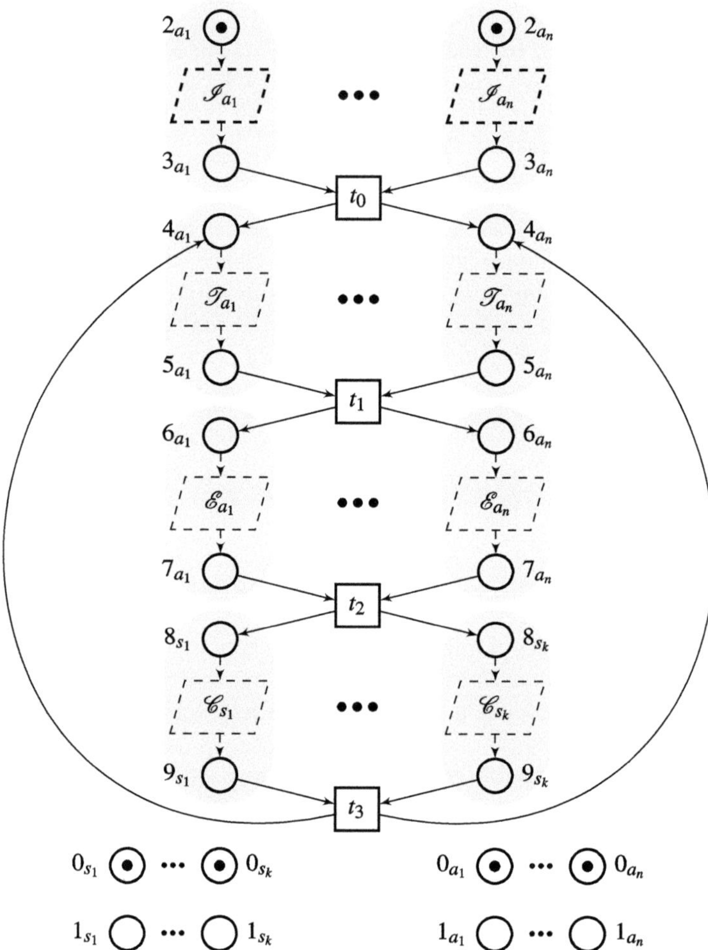



**Fig. 1.** Higher-level design diagram of the Petri net translation $\mathscr{N}_{\mathscr{R}\mathscr{D}}$ of a reaction system $\mathscr{R}\mathscr{D} = (\{s_1,\ldots,s_k\},\{a_1,\ldots,a_n\})$ $(k,n \geq 1)$.

- $\mathscr{I}_a = (\{0_a,1_a,2_a,3_a\},\{r_a^0,r_a^1\},F_{\mathscr{I}_a},\varnothing)$ where

$$F_{\mathscr{I}_a} = \{(2_a,r_a^0),(2_a,r_a^1),(0_a,r_a^1),(r_a^1,1_a),(r_a^0,3_a),(r_a^1,3_a)\}\,,$$

depicted in Fig. 2 sets the initial activity status of reaction $a$. Both outcomes, 'being executed' and 'being dormant', are possible and the choice is 'random'. Note that $\mathscr{I}_a$ is active at most once in any firing sequence of $\mathscr{N}_{\mathscr{R}\mathscr{D}}$.

- $\mathscr{C}_s = (\{8_s,9_s,1_s,0_s\},\{u_s,z_s\},F_{\mathscr{C}_s},\varnothing)$, where

$$F_{\mathscr{C}_s} = \{(8_s,u_s),(8_s,z_s),(u_s,9_s),(z_s,9_s),(1_s,u_s),(u_s,0_s),(0_s,z_s),(z_s,0_s)\}\,,$$

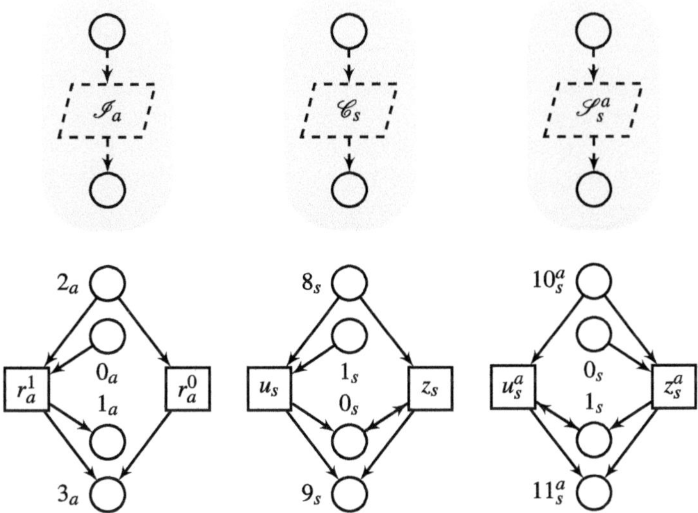

**Fig. 2.** Modules $\mathscr{I}_u$, $\mathscr{C}_s$, and $\mathscr{S}_s^a$.

depicted in Fig. 2 deletes entity $s$, i.e., after moving the initial token from the 'input' place $8_s$ down to the 'output' place $9_s$, it is guaranteed that there is a token in place $0_s$ and no token in place $1_s$.

- $\mathscr{S}_s^a = (\{10_s^a, 11_s^a, 1_s, 0_s\}, \{u_s^a, z_s^a\}, F_{\mathscr{S}_s^a}, \varnothing)$ where

$$F_{\mathscr{S}_s^a} = \{(10_s^a, u_s^a), (10_s^a, z_s^a), (u_s^a, 11_s^a), (z_s^a, 11_s^a),$$
$$(1_s, u_s^a), (u_s^a, 1_s), (0_s, z_s^a), (z_s^a, 1_s)\},$$

depicted in Fig. 2 makes sure that entity $s$ is present, i.e., after moving the initial token from the 'input' place $10_s^a$ down to the 'output' place $11_s^a$, it is guaranteed that there is a token in place $1_s$ and no token in place $0_s$. Note that this particular module does not appear in the diagram of Fig. 1, but is instead used inside the $\mathscr{T}_a$ module.

- $\mathscr{T}_a$ depicted in Fig. 3 'randomly' decides whether the currently executed reaction $a$ should be terminated or not (currently dormant reaction $a$ is not affected). If the decision is to terminate, the token residing in $1_a$ is moved to $0_a$ and all the products of $a$ are recorded as present using the data places $1_{\langle S \rangle} \cup 0_{\langle S \rangle}$.

- $\mathscr{E}_a$ depicted in Fig. 3 makes sure (if necessary) that the execution status of a currently enabled reaction $a$ is 'being executed'. If $a$ is not currently enabled, its execution status remains the same.

There are four distinct and non-overlapping phases, separated by global synchronisation transitions $t_0, t_1, t_2, t_3$, from which the the firing sequences of the encoding $\mathscr{N}_{\mathscr{R}\mathscr{D}}$ are assembled:

- *Phase I:* The initial state of the simulation of $\mathscr{R}\mathscr{D}$ by $\mathscr{N}_{\mathscr{R}\mathscr{D}}$ is set through a concurrent (in fact, independent) execution of the modules $\mathscr{I}_{\langle A \rangle}$, and the result is recorded in the data places $1_{\langle A \rangle} \cup 0_{\langle A \rangle}$.

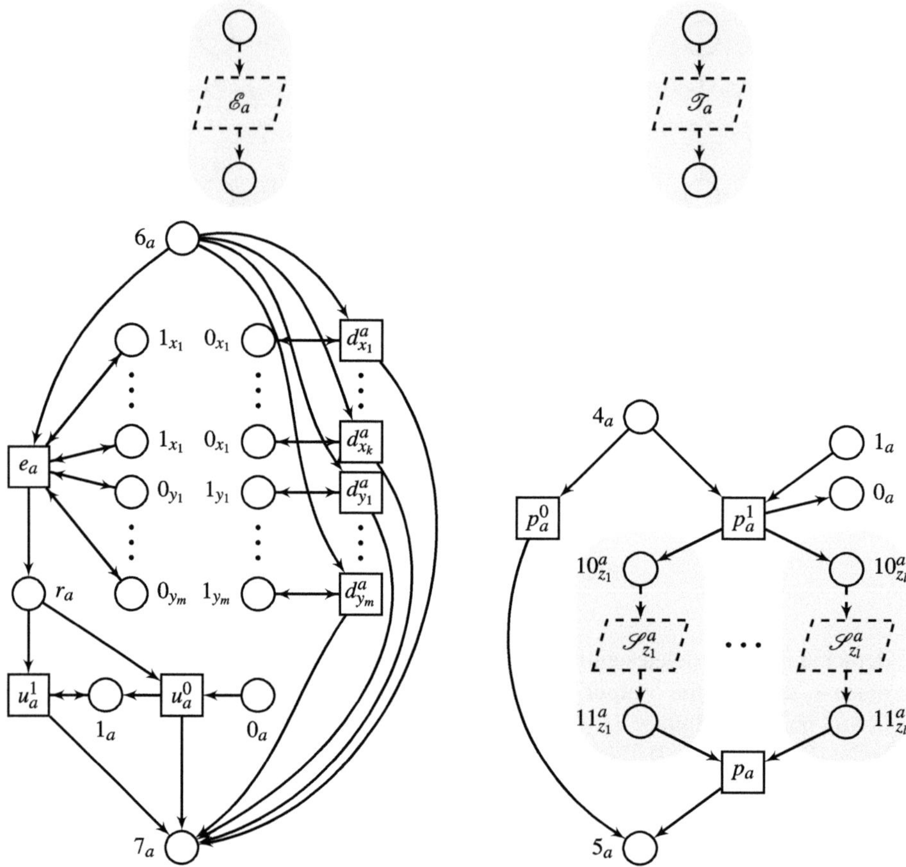

**Fig. 3.** Modules $\mathscr{E}_a$ and $\mathscr{T}_a$, where $R_a = \{x_1, \ldots, x_k\}$, $I_a = \{y_1, \ldots, x_m\}$ and $P_a = \{z_1, \ldots, z_l\}$.

- *Phase II:* A subset of currently active reaction is selected for termination by concurrently executing the modules $\mathscr{T}_{\langle A \rangle}$. The result is used to update the data places $1_{\langle A \rangle} \cup 0_{\langle A \rangle}$. Moreover, the products of terminated reactions are recorded in the data places $1_{\langle S \rangle} \cup 0_{\langle S \rangle}$.
- *Phase III:* Based on the record of the currently present entities in $1_{\langle S \rangle} \cup 0_{\langle S \rangle}$, all the enabled (and not currently active) reactions are activated by a concurrent execution of the modules $\mathscr{E}_{\langle A \rangle}$.
- *Phase IV:* The data stored in $1_{\langle S \rangle} \cup 0_{\langle S \rangle}$ is wiped out by a concurrent (in fact, independent) execution of the modules $\mathscr{C}_{\langle S \rangle}$. After this has been done, the whole simulation goes back to Phase II.

The number of reachable markings of the net $\mathscr{N}_{\mathscr{R}\mathscr{D}}$ is much greater than the number of the states of the reaction system with durations $\mathscr{R}\mathscr{D}$. We therefore need to single out those markings of $\mathscr{N}_{\mathscr{R}\mathscr{D}}$ which will correspond to the states of $\mathscr{R}\mathscr{D}$.

A reachable marking $M$ of $\mathcal{N}_{\mathcal{R}\mathcal{D}}$ is a *simulation point* if $4_{\langle A \rangle} \subseteq M$, i.e., if $M$ is a marking where the execution of Phase II begins (just after the firing of synchronisation transition $t_0$ or $t_3$). We then observe that for each firing sequence

$$\sigma = M_0 \; w_1 \; M_1 \; w_2 \; M_2 \; \ldots \; w_n \; M_n \; t_0 \; M_{n+1} \; w_{n+2} \; M_{n+2} \; w_{n+3} \; M_{n+3} \; \ldots \; w_k \; M_k \qquad (3)$$

of $\mathcal{N}_{\mathcal{R}\mathcal{D}}$ we have the following:

- $n = |A| + 1$ and $t_0 \notin \{w_1, \ldots, w_n, w_{n+2}, \ldots, w_k\}$.
- $M_{n+1}$ is a simulation point and $M_0, M_1, \ldots M_n$ are not simulation points.
- $|M_i \cap \{1_s, 0_s\}| = |M_i \cap \{1_a, 0_a\}| = 1$, for all $s \in S$ and $a \in A$ (*).

A firing sequence as in (3) (i.e., one which contains $t_0$) will be called *initialised*. Moreover, $simp(\sigma) = M_{i_1} M_{i_2} \ldots M_{i_m}$ is the subsequence of markings $M_0 M_1 \ldots M_k$ which are the simulation points of $\sigma$. Note that $m \geq 1$ and $i_1 = n+1$.

As a result, we can unambiguously associate with an initialised $\sigma$ (for which $simp(\sigma) = M_1 \ldots M_n$) a tuple $proj_{\mathcal{R}\mathcal{D}}(\sigma) = (G_1, \ldots, G_n)$ where each $G_i$ is a subset of $A$, such that, for all $a \in A$, $a \in G_i$ if $1_a \in M_i$ and $a \notin G_i$ if $0_a \in M_i$. The definition of $proj_{\mathcal{R}\mathcal{D}}(\sigma)$ is sound due to (*).

We then obtain the following correspondence result.

**Theorem 1.** *Let $\sigma$ be an initialised firing sequence of $\mathcal{N}_{\mathcal{R}\mathcal{D}}$, and $(H_0, H_1, \ldots, H_n)$ be the reaction sequence of a process of $\mathcal{R}\mathcal{D}$. Then the following hold:*

1. *$proj_{\mathcal{R}\mathcal{D}}(\sigma)$ is the reaction sequence of a process of $\mathcal{R}\mathcal{D}$.*
2. *$(H_0, H_1, \ldots, H_n) = proj_{\mathcal{R}\mathcal{D}}(\sigma')$ for some initialised firing sequence $\sigma'$ of $\mathcal{N}_{\mathcal{R}\mathcal{D}}$.*

*Proof.* Below, for every reachable marking $M$ of $\mathcal{N}_{\mathcal{R}\mathcal{D}}$, we denote $S_M = \{s \in S \mid 1_s \in M\}$ and $A_M = \{a \in A \mid 1_a \in M\}$.

(1) For a non-empty set of places $P$, let $Mar_P$ be the set of all reachable markings of $\mathcal{N}_{\mathcal{R}\mathcal{D}}$ such that $P \subseteq M$. We then define the following sets of markings:

$$Mar_1 = Mar_{2_{\langle A \rangle}} \qquad Mar_2 = Mar_{3_{\langle A \rangle}}$$
$$Mar_3 = Mar_{4_{\langle A \rangle}} \qquad Mar_4 = Mar_{5_{\langle A \rangle}}$$
$$Mar_5 = Mar_{6_{\langle A \rangle}} \qquad Mar_6 = Mar_{7_{\langle A \rangle}}$$
$$Mar_7 = Mar_{8_{\langle S \rangle}} \qquad Mar_8 = Mar_{9_{\langle S \rangle}} \; .$$

Note that $Mar_1 = \{M_0\}$ and $Mar_3$ is the set of simulation points.

It is then possible to show that if we consider an initialised firing sequence ending at a simulation point (it suffices to consider $\sigma$ satisfying such a property)

$$\sigma = M_0 w_1 M_1 w_2 M_2 \ldots w_n M_n \qquad (4)$$

and extract its subsequence $\mu$ consisting of all the markings belonging to the sets $Mar_i$ ($i = 1, \ldots, 8$) and the synchronisation transitions in the set $\{t_0, t_1, t_2, t_3\}$, then $\mu$ has the following form:

$$M \; M' \; t_0 \; M_3^1 M_4^1 \; t_1 \; M_5^1 M_6^1 \; t_2 \; M_7^1 M_8^1 \; t_3 \; \ldots \; M_3^k M_4^k \; t_1 \; M_5^k M_6^k \; t_2 \; M_7^k M_8^k \; t_3 \; M_3^{k+1}$$

where $M = M_0 \in Mar_1$, $M' \in Mar_2$, and $M_j^i \in Mar_j$ (for every $M_j^i$). Moreover, for $1 \leq i \leq k$, we have:

- $M_3^i \cap P_{control} = 4_{\langle A \rangle}$ and $S_{M_3^i} = \varnothing$.
- $M_4^i \cap P_{control} = 5_{\langle A \rangle}$ and there is $B_i \subseteq A_{M_3^i}$ such that $A_{M_4^i} = A_{M_3^i} \setminus B_i$ and $S_{M_4^i} = P_{B_i}$.
- $M_5^i \cap P_{control} = 6_{\langle A \rangle}$ and $M_5^i \cap P_{data} = M_4^i \cap P_{data}$.
- $M_6^i \cap P_{control} = 7_{\langle A \rangle}$ and $S_{M_6^i} = S_{M_5^i}$ and $A_{M_6^i} = A_{M_5^i} \cup enabled(P_{B_i})$.
- $M_7^i \cap P_{control} = 8_{\langle S \rangle}$ and $M_7^i \cap P_{data} = M_6^i \cap P_{data}$.
- $M_8^i \cap P_{control} = 9_{\langle S \rangle}$ and $A_{M_8^i} = A_{M_7^i}$ and $S_{M_8^i} = \varnothing$.
- $M_3^{i+1} \cap P_{control} = 4_{\langle A \rangle}$ and $M_3^{i+1} \cap P_{data} = M_8^i \cap P_{data}$.

As a result, $proj_{\mathscr{R}\mathscr{D}}(\sigma) = (A_{M_3^1}, \ldots, A_{M_3^{k+1}})$ is the state sequence of a process of $\mathscr{R}\mathscr{D}$.

(2) To show this part of the result by the induction on $n$ it suffices to prove the following two properties.

- *Property A:* Let $G \subseteq A$. Then there is an initialised firing sequence $\theta = \xi M$ such that $M$ is a simulation point and $proj_{\mathscr{R}\mathscr{D}}(\theta) = (G)$.
- *Property B:* Let $\sigma = \xi M$ be an initialised firing sequence such that $M$ is a simulation point. Moreover, let $B \subseteq A_M$ and $G = A_M \setminus B \cup enabled(P_B)$. Then there is a firing sequence $\sigma' = \sigma \xi' M'$ such that $M'$ is a simulation point, $G = A_{M'}$ and $proj_{\mathscr{R}\mathscr{D}}(\sigma')$ is $proj_{\mathscr{R}\mathscr{D}}(\sigma)$ extended by $G$.

We will prove that the above two properties hold by constructing sequences of transitions generating suitable $\theta$ and $\xi'$.

To show Property A, we proceed as follows. Let $A = \{a_1, \ldots, a_l, a_{l+1} \ldots, a_k\}$, where $a_1, \ldots, a_l \in G$ and $a_{l+1} \ldots, a_k \notin G$. Then $r_{a_1}^1 \ldots r_{a_l}^1 r_{a_{l+1}}^0 \ldots r_{a_k}^0 t_0$ generates the required $\theta$.

To show Property B, we construct $\xi'$ as $\kappa_1 t_1 \kappa_2 t_2 \kappa_3 t_3$, in the following way:

- Let $B = \{a_1, \ldots, a_m\}$ and $A \setminus B = \{a_{m+1}, \ldots, a_k\}$. Then, for $1 \le i \le m$, let $L_i = P_{a_i} \cap (P_{a_1} \cup \cdots \cup P_{a_{i-1}}) = \{b_1^i, \ldots, b_{h_i}^i\}$ and $K_i = P_{a_i} \setminus L_i = \{f_1^i, \ldots, f_{g_i}^i\}$. We then construct
$$\gamma_{a_i} = p_{a_i}^1 u_{b_1^i}^{a_i} \ldots u_{b_{h_1}^i}^{a_i} \ldots z_{f_1^i}^{a_i} \ldots z_{f_{g_1}^i}^{a_i} p_{a_i}.$$
Finally, we set $\kappa_1 = \gamma_{a_1} \ldots \gamma_{a_m} p_{a_{m+1}}^0 \ldots p_{a_n}^0$.
- Let $(A_M \setminus B) \cap enabled(P_B) = \{a_1, \ldots, a_m\}$ and $enabled(P_B) \setminus (A_M \setminus B) = \{a_{m+1}, \ldots, a_l\}$ and $A \setminus enabled(P_B) = \{a_{l+1}, \ldots, a_k\}$. Also, for $m+1 \le i \le n$, let $q_i \in (R_{a_i} \setminus P_B) \cup (I_{a_i} \cap P_B)$.
Then $\kappa_2 = e^{a_1} u_{a_1}^1 \ldots e^{a_m} u_{a_m}^1 \ e^{a_{m+1}} u_{a_{m+1}}^0 \ldots e^{a_l} u_{a_l}^0 \ d_{q_{m+1}}^{a_{l+1}} \ldots d_{q_n}^{a_n}$.
- Let $P_B = \{s_1, \ldots, s_m\}$ and $S \setminus P_B = \{s_{m+1}, \ldots, s_n\}$.
Then $\kappa_3 = u_{s_1} \ldots u_{s_m} z_{s_{m+1}} \ldots z_{s_n}$. $\qquad\qquad \square$

As far as other properties of the translation are concerned, one can show that each firing sequence of the Petri net resulting from the translation can be extended.

**Theorem 2.** $\mathscr{N}_{\mathscr{R}\mathscr{D}}$ *is deadlock-free.*

*Proof.* From the discussion in the proof of Theorem 1 and the construction of $\mathscr{N}_{\mathscr{R}\mathscr{D}}$ (including the definition of the various modules it uses), it follows that no deadlock can occur in any of the phases of the execution of $\mathscr{N}_{\mathscr{R}\mathscr{D}}$. $\qquad\qquad \square$

Moreover, it is the case that the Petri net resulting from the translation cannot 'idle'.

**Theorem 3.** *The maximum number of transitions executed between two consecutive simulation points of $\mathcal{N}_{\mathcal{RD}}$ is bounded by*

$$3 + |S| + 4 \cdot |A| + \sum_{a \in A} |P_a| < 10 \cdot |S|^4 \,.$$

*Moreover, the first simulation point is reached after exactly $|A| + 1$ transition firings.*
*Proof.* To show the first part of the result it suffices to observe that from the discussion in the proof of Theorem 1 and the construction of $\mathcal{N}_{\mathcal{RD}}$ it follows that no transition is executed more than once between two consecutive simulation points of $\mathcal{N}_{\mathcal{RD}}$.

The second part of the result follows from the construction of $\mathcal{N}_{\mathcal{RD}}$ and the definition of the modules $\mathcal{I}_{a_1}, \ldots, \mathcal{I}_{a_n}$. □

Finally, the size of the Petri net encoding $\mathcal{N}_{\mathcal{RD}}$ is polynomial.

**Theorem 4.** *Let $\mathcal{N}_{\mathcal{RD}} = (P, T, F, M_0)$. Then*

$$
\begin{aligned}
|P| &= 4 \cdot |S| + 9 \cdot |A| + \textstyle\sum_{a \in A} 2 \cdot |P_a| \\
|T| &= 4 + 2 \cdot |S| + 8 \cdot |A| + \textstyle\sum_{a \in A} |R_a| + |I_a| + 2 \cdot |P_a| \\
|P| + |T| &= 4 + 6 \cdot |S| + 17 \cdot |A| + \textstyle\sum_{a \in A} |R_a| + |I_a| + 4 \cdot |P_a| \\
&< 4 + 6 \cdot |S| + 17 \cdot |A| + 6 \cdot |S| \cdot |A| \qquad\qquad (5) \\
&< 33 \cdot |S|^4 \\
|M_0| &= 2 \cdot |A| + |S| \\
&< 3 \cdot |S|^3 \,.
\end{aligned}
$$

*Proof.* Follows from a straightforward inspection of the construction and the modules it involves. □

## 5    Concluding Remarks

The recent paper [6] provides a compositional Petri net encoding of the standard reaction systems with and without context automata. We plan to adapt some aspects of the latter to extend the results presented in this paper to reaction systems with durations in the presence of external contexts. It is also worth mentioning that [6] demonstrated that some simplistic translations of reaction systems into Petri nets result in nets of exponential size. With this in mind, the polynomial size result conveyed by Theorem 4 is essential to develop effective verification techniques for reaction systems with durations. A possible direction is to incorporate the proposed translation of reaction systems with durations in verification toolsets, such as WORKCRAFT [9].

The Petri net translation $\mathcal{N}_{\mathcal{RD}}$ can be modified by adding an input place and an output place, so that the result is a sound, 1-safe, and livelock-free resource-constrained workflow Petri net [12, 13] (with the data places acting as the resource places). We intend to investigate such a connection to develop effective analytical methods for reaction systems with durations.

**Acknowledgement.** Partial support by the Leverhulme Trust grant RPG-2022-025 is acknowledged. The authors are grateful to the anonymous referees, whose comments contributed to the revised version of this paper.

**Disclosure of Interests.** The authors have no competing interests to declare that are relevant to the content of this article.

# References


1. Brijder, R., Ehrenfeucht, A., Rozenberg, G.: Reaction systems with duration. In: Kelemen, J., Kelemenová, A. (eds.) Computation, Cooperation, and Life. LNCS, vol. 6610, pp. 191–202. Springer, Heidelberg (2011). https://doi.org/10.1007/978-3-642-20000-7_16
2. Desel, J., Reisig, W.: Place/transition Petri Nets. In: Reisig, W., Rozenberg, G. (eds.) ACPN 1996. LNCS, vol. 1491, pp. 122–173. Springer, Heidelberg (1998). https://doi.org/10.1007/3-540-65306-6_15
3. Ehrenfeucht, A., Rozenberg, G.: Reaction systems. Fundam. Informaticae **75**(1–4), 263–280 (2007)
4. Ehrenfeucht, A., Rozenberg, G.: Introducing time in reaction systems. Theor. Comput. Sci. **410**(4–5), 310–322 (2009)
5. Kordon, F., Hillah, L., Hulin-Hubard, F., Jezequel, L., Paviot-Adet, E.: Study of the efficiency of model checking techniques using results of the MCC from 2015 to 2019. Int. J. Softw. Tools Technol. Transf. **23**(6), 931–952 (2021)
6. Koutny, M., Mikulski, Ł.: Encoding reaction systems in Petri nets. Nat. Comput. (in press)
7. Koutny, M., Mikulski, Ł., Pietkiewicz-Koutny, M.: Interval order synthesis of EN-systems with read and mutex arcs. In: CEUR Workshop Proceedings. Newcastle University (2025)
8. Męski, A., Koutny, M., Penczek, W.: Model checking for temporal-epistemic properties of distributed reaction systems. School of computing technical report series (2019)
9. Poliakov, I., Khomenko, V., Yakovlev, A.: WORKCRAFT – a framework for interpreted graph models. In: Franceschinis, G., Wolf, K. (eds.) PETRI NETS 2009. LNCS, vol. 5606, pp. 333–342. Springer, Heidelberg (2009). https://doi.org/10.1007/978-3-642-02424-5_21
10. Reisig, W.: Petri Nets (An Introduction). EATCS Monographs on Theoretical Computer Science. Springer, Heidelberg (1985)
11. Reisig, W.: Understanding Petri Nets - Modeling Techniques, Analysis Methods, Case Studies. Springer, New York (2013)
12. Van Der Aalst, W.M.: Structural characterizations of sound workflow nets. Technische Universiteit Eindhoven, Technical report (1996)
13. Van Der Aalst, W.M., et al.: Soundness of workflow nets: classification, decidability, and analysis. Formal Aspects Comput. **23**, 333–363 (2011)

# Petri Nets for the Real World

Andreas V. Hense[(✉)] [iD]

Bonn-Rhein-Sieg University oAS, Sankt Augustin, Germany
`andreas.hense@h-brs.de`

**Abstract.** This paper presents twelve illustrative Petri nets developed for educational purposes to teach the fundamentals of system modeling. Inspired by an exercise by Wil van der Aalst on Brisbane's City-Cats, these models are grounded in realistic systems rather than purely abstract constructions. Each Petri net captures the dynamics of an everyday technical or social process – from radiator fans and digital clocks to espresso machines and population growth – and is characterized according to structural and behavioral properties such as free-choice, safety, boundedness, liveness, and sequentiality. The collection can be used for classroom exercises, examinations, and demonstrations of Petri net analysis techniques, including reachability and coverability graphs. All models were created using the WoPeD tool and are available in PNML format for download and reuse.

**Keywords:** Petri nets · Modeling · Education

## 1  Introduction

I first met Wil van der Aalst at the Queensland University of Technology in Brisbane while we were both visiting Arthur ter Hofstede. It was no coincidence that we met at "The University for the Real World" since we both share an interest in practical problems, Petri nets [1,4], and sushi. Most of the Petri nets that I have found in the literature are abstract in the sense that they are designed to illustrate mathematical properties rather than model real systems. Typically, their places are named $p_1$, $p_2$, etc., and transitions $t_1$, $t_2$, etc.

When I teach Petri nets to undergraduates, I always look for modeling problems that describe real systems and whose behaviour can be meaningfully analysed. The very limited expressiveness of pure Petri nets always makes this a challenge. Many of the real Petri nets that I have found were created by Wil, and it is his exercise about the Brisbane CityCats that I regularly use in my lectures. The CityCats are a catamaran service that goes up and down the Brisbane River. The 10 catamarans go upstream or downstream, and the constraint is that there can be only one catamaran at each of the stops A, B, C, D. The Petri net in Fig. 1 is a possible solution to this exercise, and its coverability graph is huge. The CityCats problem is suitable for a home assignment but too complex for an exam situation with very limited time. Therefore, I have designed minimalist Petri nets that can be used as solutions to problems that can be part of an exam. Here in this article, I present 12 of these Petri nets that have not been published on paper so far.


J. Mendling et al. (Eds.): Wil van der Aalst Festschrift, LNCS 16480, pp. 237–247, 2026.
https://doi.org/10.1007/978-3-032-17618-9_18

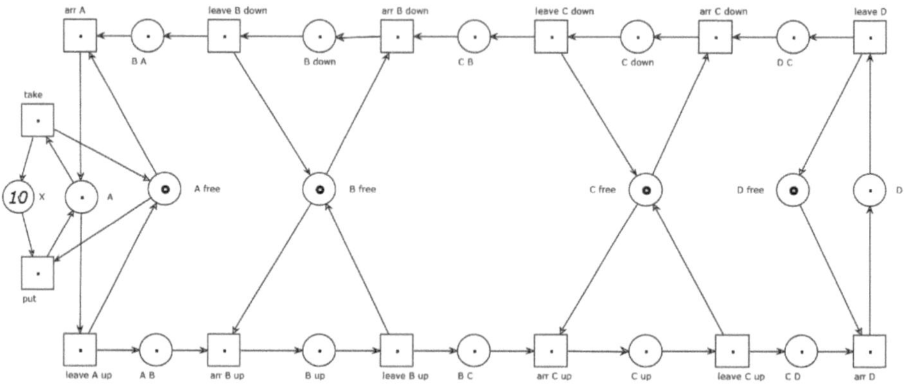


**Fig. 1.** CityCats according to an exercise by Wil van der Aalst.

## 2    Terminology Used Here

We assume that the reader is already familiar with the basic notions of Petri nets. In this section, we introduce the Petri net terminology without the mathematical formalism. Readers interested in these precise definitions and who want to know how Petri nets actually work, are referred to [5]. We only consider the most basic Petri nets – sometimes referred to as Place/Transition nets or P/T nets. P/T nets consist of places (circles), transitions (squares), and directed arcs between them. Arcs can be weighted and arc weights are positive integers, the default being 1. All Petri nets in this paper are shown with their initial marking. A marking is a function that assigns a number of tokens to each place in the net. Tokens are depicted as black dots. If there are more than 3 tokens in a place the dots are replaced by a number. If there are 100 tokens or more, this is depicted by an $\omega$. In this paper, we are using the following five properties for classifying our example nets:

**Free-choice** A Petri net is *free-choice* when the choice between alternative transitions depends solely on the tokens in their shared input places, and not on other tokens elsewhere in the net.
**Safety** A Petri net is called *safe* when no place can contain more than one token in any reachable marking.
**Boundedness** A Petri net is called *bounded* when the number of tokens in each place is limited by a finite number.
**Liveness** A Petri net is *live*, if from any reachable marking, it is always possible (perhaps after some further transitions fire) to eventually enable every transition again.
**Sequentiality** A Petri net is *sequential* if, for every reachable marking, at most one transition is enabled.

If we are interested in the number of states that a Petri net can reach from its initial marking we can look at the reachability graph if the Petri net is bounded or the coverability graph [2] if the Petri net is unbounded.

## 3   Overview of the 12 Petri Nets

The following table provides an overview of the twelve Petri nets discussed in this paper. The first three columns list the numbers of places, transitions, and arcs. The next five columns indicate the properties introduced in Sect. 2, where a value of 1 denotes that the net possesses the corresponding property. The final two columns show the numbers of vertices and edges of the coverability graph.

| Number | Name | # Places | # Transitions | # Arcs | Free-choice | Safety | Boundedness | Liveness | Sequentiality | CG # Vertices | CG # Edges |
|---|---|---|---|---|---|---|---|---|---|---|---|
| 1 | Radiator Fan | 5 | 6 | 20 | 0 | 1 | 1 | 1 | 0 | 6 | 10 |
| 2 | A Hotel Safe | 6 | 4 | 11 | 1 | 0 | 1 | 0 | 0 | 365 | 859 |
| 3 | Extractor Fan | 5 | 5 | 14 | 0 | 1 | 1 | 1 | 0 | 6 | 10 |
| 4 | Electric Roller Shutters | 9 | 8 | 24 | 0 | 0 | 1 | 1 | 0 | 15 | 56 |
| 5 | Landing Gear | 6 | 6 | 18 | 0 | 1 | 1 | 1 | 0 | 8 | 19 |
| 6 | Wind Farm | 11 | 12 | 32 | 0 | 1 | 1 | 1 | 0 | 48 | 233 |
| 7 | Digital Clock | 6 | 4 | 18 | 0 | 0 | 1 | 1 | 1 | 1440 | 1440 |
| 8 | Chain Saw Safety | 8 | 8 | 22 | 0 | 1 | 1 | 1 | 0 | 16 | 57 |
| 9 | Automatic Espresso Machine | 6 | 4 | 12 | 1 | 0 | 1 | 1 | 0 | 36 | 44 |
| 10 | Production of Hamburgers | 6 | 3 | 14 | 0 | 0 | 1 | 0 | 1 | 13 | 12 |
| 11 | All-Way Stop | 13 | 12 | 32 | 0 | 1 | 1 | 1 | 0 | 80 | 256 |
| 12 | Population Development | 2 | 5 | 9 | 1 | 0 | 0 | 0 | 0 | 2069 | 9528 |

Petri nets that are bounded and have a small coverability graph are well suited for exercises in which students manually construct the reachability graph. Although the collection includes a good mix of safe and non-safe models, it becomes immediately apparent that there is only one unbounded net and only a few that are not live. This observation can serve as a basis for extending the collection in the future.

## 4   Detailed Descriptions of the Petri Nets

### 4.1   Radiator Fan

The Petri net in Fig. 2 represents a radiator fan similar to those used in internal combustion engines. The fan can operate at two different speeds depending on the measured temperature. In reality, radiator fans are connected to temperature sensors, and their behavior is also influenced by time-dependent events. This example illustrates that Petri nets abstract away from time. The net is safe: each place represents a state, and at any given moment there are two tokens – one indicating the fan speed and the other the temperature.

### 4.2   A Hotel Safe

Hotel safes are notoriously tricky to handle. The one modeled in Fig. 3 features three buttons, each incrementing one of the three digits of a secret code.

The safe unlocks only with the combination 4-2-5, and there is no reset button.
It is therefore almost certain that hotel staff will eventually need to come to your
aid. The net is free-choice.

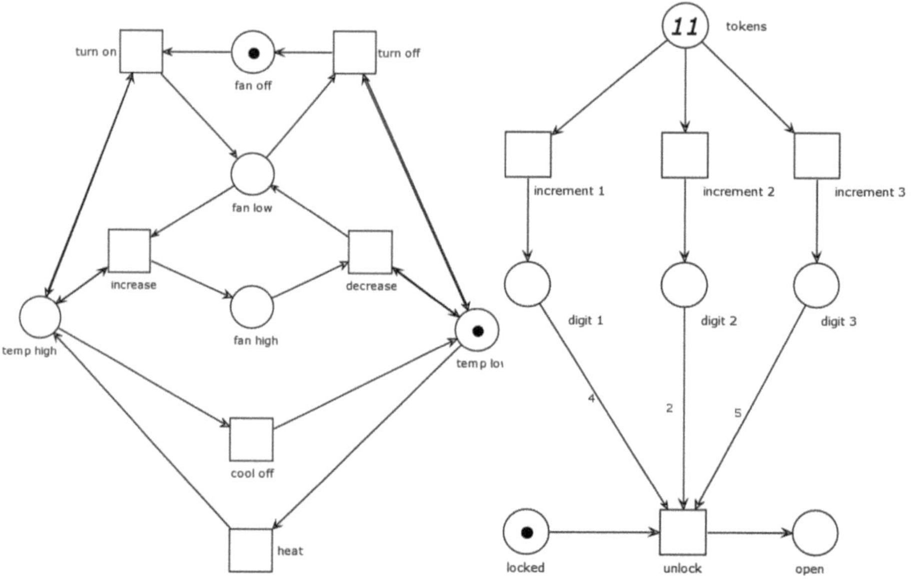



Fig. 2. Radiator Fan.
Fig. 3. A Hotel Safe.

### 4.3   Extractor Fan

Bathrooms without windows require an extractor fan to remove moist air. The
model in Fig. 4 represents a fan that is automatically triggered by the light
switch. When the light is turned off, the fan briefly increases its speed before
switching off again.

In reality, extractor fans include short time delays before each state change.
For instance, if you spend only a few seconds in the bathroom, the fan may
not start at all. This makes the example well suited to illustrate that Petri nets
abstract away from time. The net is live.

### 4.4   Electric Roller Shutters

Many electric roller shutters cannot be opened during a power failure. If all
windows are closed when a fire breaks out, such shutters can quickly become a
trap. The Petri net in Fig. 5 addresses this problem by ensuring that there is
always at least one escape route. This net provides a clear example of how four
identical components – the shutters – can be combined with a shared condition,
represented by the place "remaining", that links them all together.

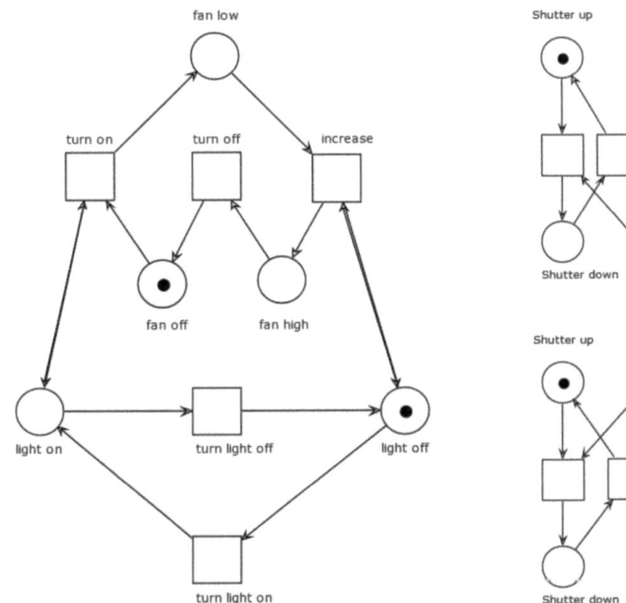


**Fig. 4.** Extractor Fan

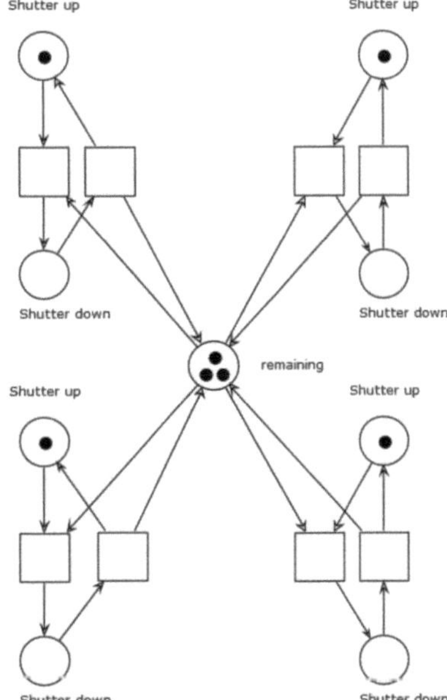


**Fig. 5.** Electric Roller Shutters

## 4.5  Landing Gear

According to the Petri net in Fig. 6, the landing gear of an airplane can only be extended at low speed. After takeoff, once a higher speed is reached, a warning light is activated. The net consists of three components: speed, gear, and warning. These components can be modeled individually and then combined according to the system's constraints.

One can imagine that the transition "start warning" is triggered by the airplane's computer, while the transition "ack" is triggered by the pilot pressing a button.

## 4.6  Wind Farm

Many wind turbines stand still even if there is wind. The Petri net in Fig. 7 lists a number of reasons why the wind turbine cannot start. The net consists of five components. At the top, there is the force of the wind that has three states. In the middle, there is the central information if the turbine is turning or not. At the bottom are three conditions that are all needed to turn the turbine on. When the turbine is in the state "turning" and one or more of the conditions for it to turn on are not given anymore, we need to assume that the system turns the turbine off and immediately on again to check the status. This can be used to start a discussion on Petri nets used in the implementation of complex systems.

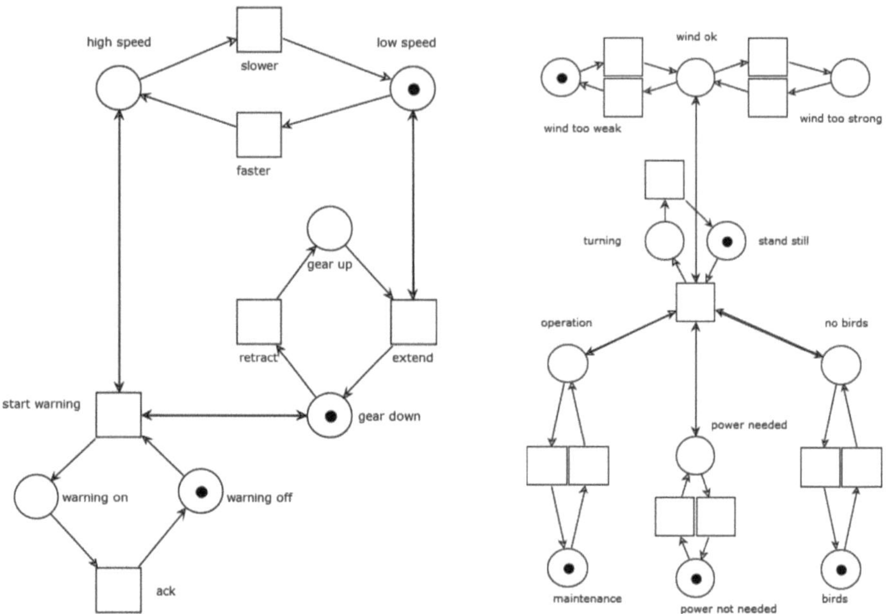



**Fig. 6.** Landing Gear.          **Fig. 7.** Wind Farm.

## 4.7   Digital Clock

The Petri net in Fig. 8 models a 24-h digital clock. The top three places represent the display of the clock. The "1 h" place displays the hours from 0 to 23. The "10 m" place the tens of minutes, and the "1 m" place the single minutes. The bottom three places contain the remaining tokens that guarantee that each of the three advancing transitions to the right cannot continue indefinitely. The net is sequential and therefore exactly one transition can be fired at any time. As a consequence, the number of vertices in the coverability graph, namely 1440, corresponds to the number of minutes in 24 h.

## 4.8   Chain Saw Safety

Chain saws are highly dangerous tools and, therefore, safety is very important. We have tried to adapt the design of the Petri net in Fig. 9 to an actual chain saw that has the chain on the right, the handle with the chain brake on top, and the dead man switch and the safety throttle on the left. The chain saw can only start when three conditions are met: the chain brake is off, the dead man switch is on, and the safety throttle is on. Similar to the wind turbine example, we have to imagine that once the chain is running, there is a permanent check if the three conditions are still met.

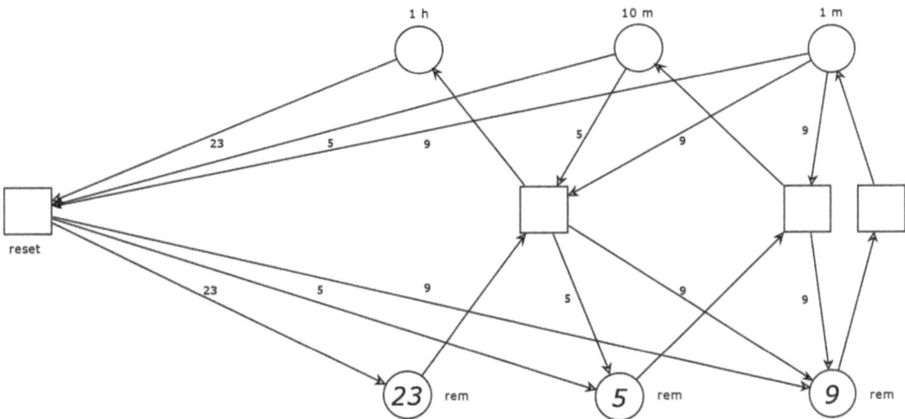



**Fig. 8.** Digital Clock.

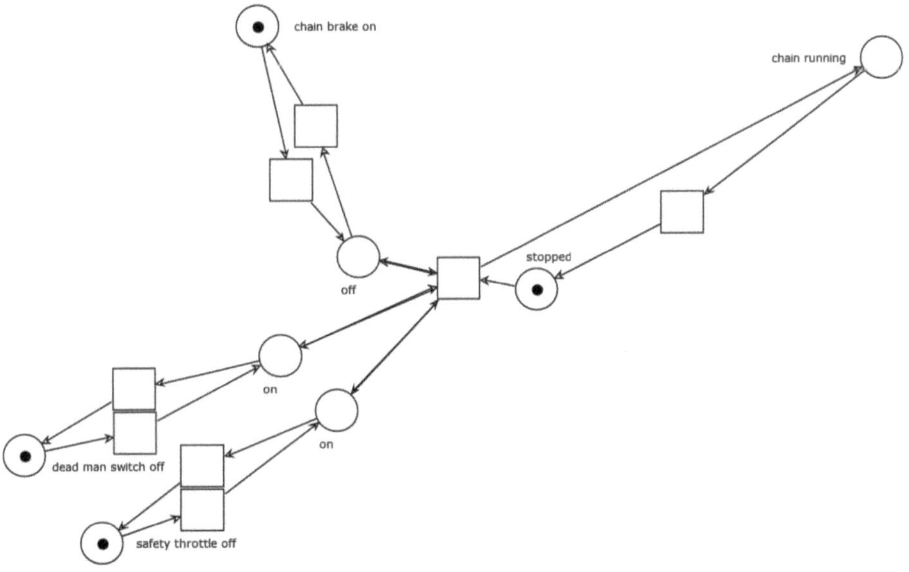



**Fig. 9.** Chain Saw Safety.

## 4.9   Automatic Espresso Machine

The Petri net in Fig. 10 was likely the first net in this series and was inspired by the fully automated espresso machine found at QUT's School of Information Systems. It models the various service tasks that must be carried out on an automatic espresso machine. This puts the supposed advantage of automation into perspective and explains why it always seems to be *you* who has to perform up to three service tasks before finally brewing a cup.

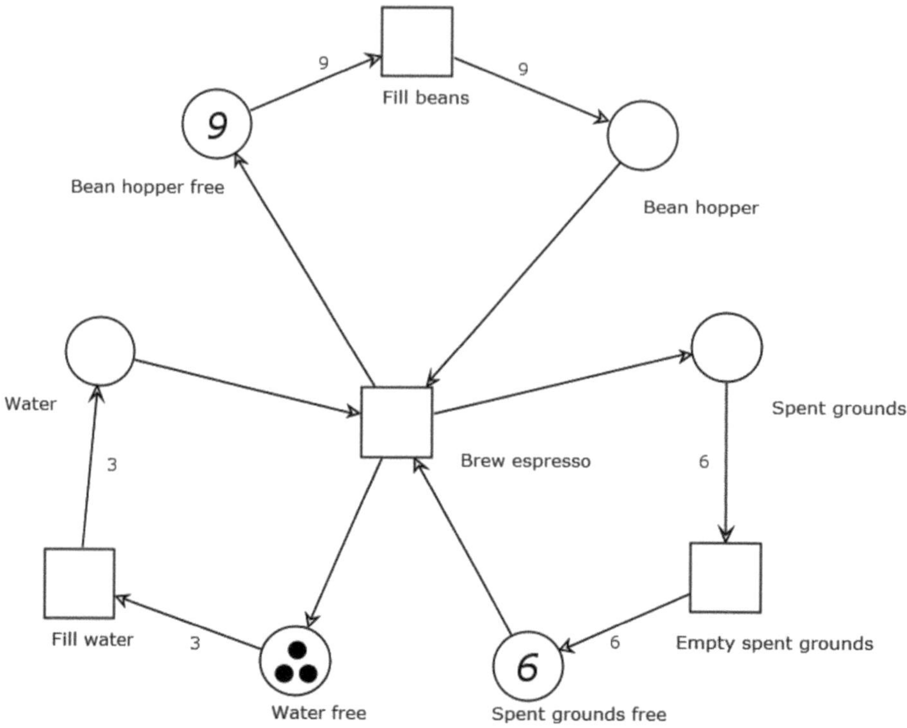


**Fig. 10.** Automatic Espresso Machine

The central transition "Brew espresso" consumes coffee beans and water while producing spent grounds. One might ask after how many espressos all three service actions in the surrounding transitions need to be executed. Interestingly, the espresso machine is also one of the few free-choice nets in this series.

### 4.10   Production of Hamburgers

The Petri net in Fig. 11 represents an imaginary machine for burger assembly. The meat must be placed between two slices of bread before a burger can be produced. With the available ingredients in the bread and meat places, three burgers can be assembled. The net is sequential. If you would like to add another place after the "produce burger" transition to indicate how many burgers have been produced so far, you can download the net and edit it accordingly. The procedure for doing so is explained in Sect. 5.

### 4.11   The All-Way Stop

The all-way stop is a traffic regulation commonly used in the United States. At such an intersection, all vehicles must come to a complete stop before proceeding.

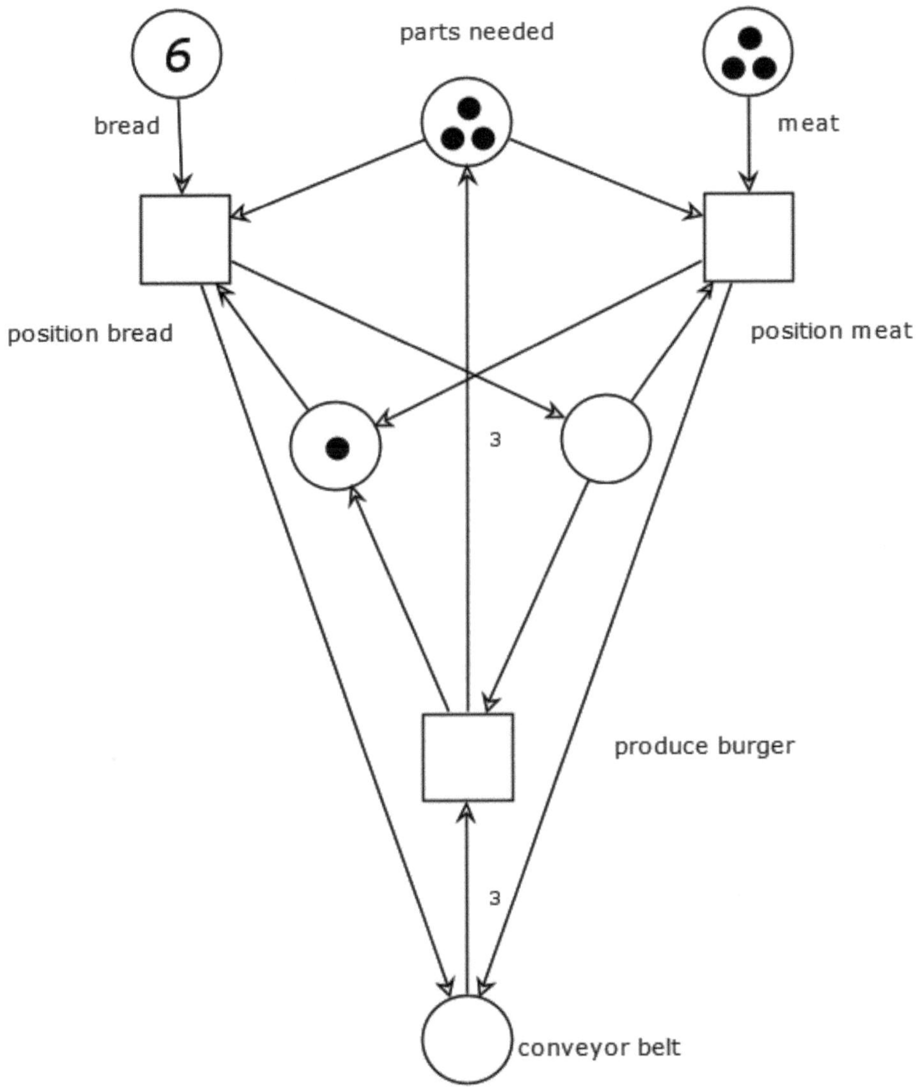


**Fig. 11.** Production of Hamburgers.

The vehicle that arrives first may enter the intersection first, following the FIFO (first in, first out) principle.

The Petri net in Fig. 12 illustrates a simplified version of this all-way stop, assuming that only one car can occupy the intersection at any given time.

When a new car approaches from the west-east direction, the transition "new car WE" fires. The place "1st WE free" ensures that only one car can wait in the pole position from that direction. To enter the intersection, a token must be

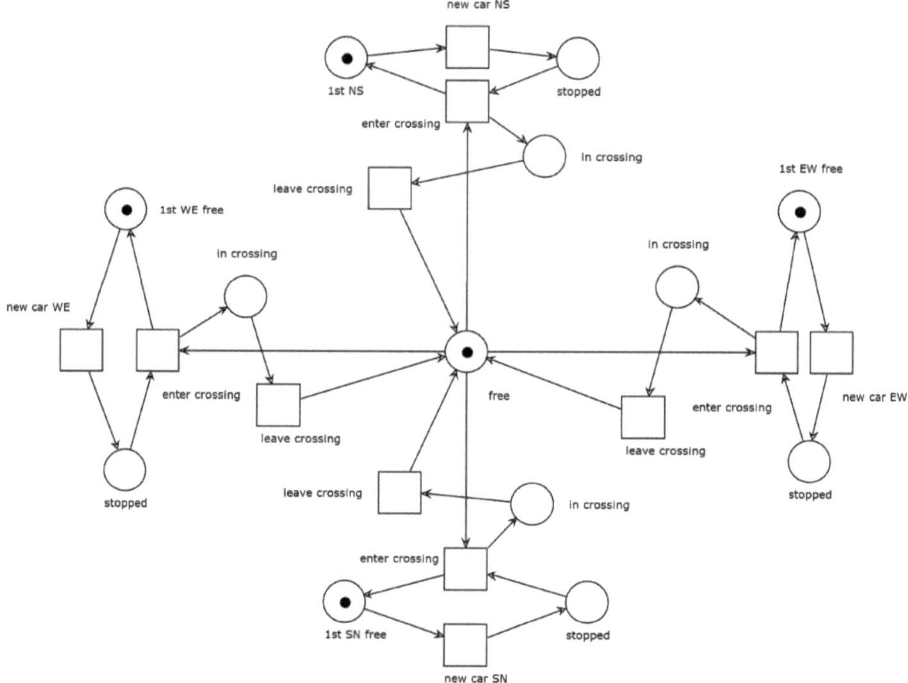



**Fig. 12.** The All-Way Stop.

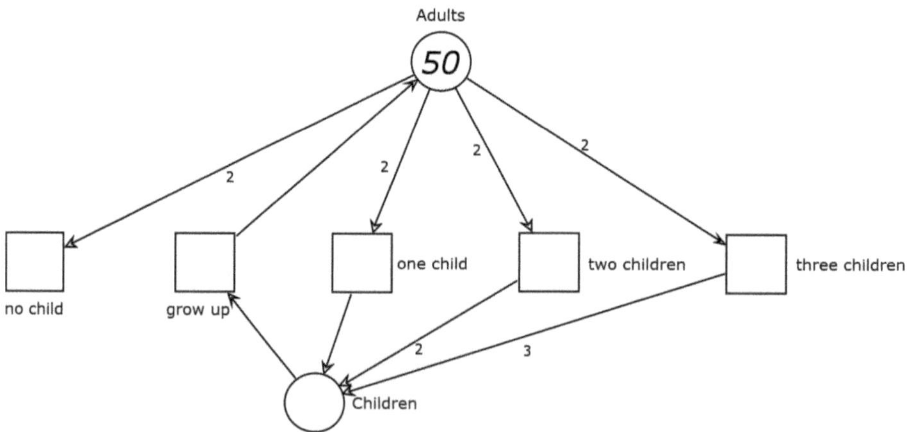



**Fig. 13.** Population Development.

available in the central place "free". When the car leaves, the token is returned – an arrangement typical for modeling a critical section.

As an exercise, you could extend this net by dividing the critical section of the intersection into four parts. This would yield a more realistic model, allowing two cars from opposite directions to pass straight through simultaneously.

### 4.12   Population Development

An extremely simplified model of population development is shown in Fig. 13. We begin with a population of 50 individuals. Two adults form a couple and may have between zero and three children. Over time, children grow up and become adults themselves. It is striking to observe how rapidly the population declines when the randomized autoplay is activated in the token game.

This model is so far removed from reality that it serves as an excellent starting point for discussing the correctness of models in general. Owing to the initial marking of 50 tokens, the model has an exceptionally large coverability graph. It is also the only unbounded net presented in this paper.

## 5   See the 12 Petri Nets in Action

All Petri nets were modeled using the WoPed [3] tool:

$$http://woped.org$$

The corresponding Petri nets in PNML format are available at:

$$https://doi.org/10.5281/zenodo.18615509$$

We would like to express our sincere gratitude to the anonymous reviewer for the detailed and constructive feedback, which has been invaluable in improving this contribution.

## References


1. van der Aalst, W.M.P., van Hee, K.: Workflow Management: Models, Methods, and Systems. MIT Press, Cambridge (2004)
2. Finkel, A.: The minimal coverability graph for Petri nets. In: Rozenberg, G. (ed.) ICATPN 1991. LNCS, vol. 674, pp. 210–243. Springer, Heidelberg (1993). https://doi.org/10.1007/3-540-56689-9_45
3. Freytag, T., Saenger, M.: WoPeD - An educational tool for workflow nets. In: Proceedings of the BPM Demo Sessions 2014 Co-located with the 12th International Conference on Business Process Management. CEUR Workshop Proceedings, vol. 1295. CEUR, Eindhoven, The Netherlands (2014). http://ceur-ws.org/Vol-1295/
4. Petri, C.A.: Kommunikation mit Automaten. PhD Thesis, Institutes für instrumentelle Mathematik an der Universität Bonn (1962)
5. Reisig, W.: Understanding Petri Nets: Modeling Techniques, Analysis Methods, 2013th edn. Case Studies. Springer, New York (2013). https://doi.org/10.1007/978-3-642-33278-4

# Variable Arc Nets: One-Dimensional Object-Centric Nets

Sebastiaan J. van Zelst[(✉)] and Sebastian Vaaßen

Celonis Labs GmbH, Munich, Germany
`{s.vanzelst,s.vaassen}@celonis.com`

**Abstract.** Wil introduced Object-Centric Petri Nets (OCPNs), i.e., a Petri net class that more explicitly reflects the control flow of different interacting business objects. However, the theoretical properties of these nets have not been extensively studied. In this paper, we define the one-dimensional equivalent of OCPNs, i.e., Variable Arc Nets (VAR-nets), and present corresponding foundational theoretical results. VAR-nets do not support different object types; however, they do allow for the consumption and production of an arbitrary number of tokens, effectively modeling 1:$n$ relationships between the execution of an event and related process instances. We extend the marking equation for VAR-nets and demonstrate that this extension provides the same guarantees as the regular marking equation. Furthermore, we derive a corresponding nonlinear optimization problem and show the existence of a linear relaxation. Our experiments indicate that adopting the proposed optimization problems as a heuristic in informed state space searches speeds up the general state space search of VAR-nets significantly, compared to uninformed search algorithms. Hence, our results, based on informed search algorithms, enable feasible state space search for VAR nets.

**Keywords:** Variable arc nets · marking equation · nonlinear optimization · linear relaxation

## 1 Introduction

In practice, various high-level process modeling notations are used to model processes, e.g., Business Process Model and Notation (BPMN) [4]. The majority of such modeling notations can be converted to *Petri nets* [9]. As such, many techniques proposed in the field of *business process management* [6], as well as *process mining* [1] (i.e., heavily utilizing process models in combination with *event data*), are (implicitly) based on Petri nets.

In [2], van der Aalst introduced *Object-Centric Petri Nets* (OCPNs), which extend regular Petri nets to more explicitly capture the joint control flow of different *business objects* in a process. For example, a typical sales process consists of different business objects like *Sales Orders*, *Sales Order Items*, and *Sales Quotations*. OCPNs allow for modeling the control flow of each object and its


J. Mendling et al. (Eds.): Wil van der Aalst Festschrift, LNCS 16480, pp. 248–261, 2026.
https://doi.org/10.1007/978-3-032-17618-9_19

interactions and synchronizations. In particular, OCPNs allow for expressing a novel type of arc, i.e., a *variable arc*, which allows for the consumption and production of an arbitrary amount of tokens.

Variable arcs introduce an additional factorial component to the general size of the net's state space. As such, the introduction of such arcs in Petri nets are an interesting topic of study in their own right. Therefore, in this paper, we define Variable Arc nets (VAR-nets), i.e., an extension of regular weighted Petri nets with arcs describing variable token consumption and production. We show that two types of semantics can be defined for variable arcs, i.e., a regular and a synchronizing semantic (of which the latter is usually assumed in combination with OCPNs). We also show that for both semantics, the marking equation can be extended, and, we show that we can derive corresponding generic heuristic functions that can be used in informed search algorithms on the net's state space.

We evaluate our approach based on different nets of varying complexity. Our results show that an informed search strategy significantly outperforms uninformed algorithms when solving the shortest path problem on the state space of VAR nets. Furthermore, our experiments show that our proposed linear heuristic outperforms the nonlinear heuristic when using a dedicated *linear solver*.

The remainder of this paper is structured as follows. In Sect. 2, we present background concepts. In Sect. 3, we present the notion of *Variable Arc Nets (VAR-Nets)*. In Sect. 4, we present the marking equation for VAR-nets. In Sect. 5, we show corresponding optimization problems that can be derived. In Sect. 6, we evaluate the performance impact of our derived heuristics, adopted in informed search algorithms. Section 7 concludes our work, including a personal note addressed to Wil.

## 2  Background

*Notation* Given a set $X$, $\mathcal{P}(X)=\{X'|X'\subseteq X\}$ denotes its *power set*. $\mathbb{N}=\{1,2,\dots\}$ denotes the set of positive integers and $\mathbb{N}_{\geq 0}=\mathbb{N}\cup\{0\}$. $\mathbb{R}$ denotes the set of real numbers and $\mathbb{R}_{\geq 0}=\{r\in\mathbb{R}|r\geq 0\}$. We assume general familiarity with the concepts *Cartesian products, relations, functions* and *(non)linear programming and optimization* [7]. A bag $b$ generalizes the notion of a set and allows for membership cardinality, i.e., $b\colon X\to\mathbb{N}_{\geq 0}$. We write a bag as $b=[x_1^i, x_2^j, \dots, x_n^k]$, where $b(x_1)=i$, $b(x_2)=j, \dots$. If $b(x_i)=0$, we omit $x_i$ from the bag notation, if $b(x_j)=1$, we omit the superscript. The set of all bags on $X$ is written as $\mathcal{B}(X)$. A sequence $\sigma$ of length $n$ over a set $X$ is a function $\sigma\colon \{1,\dots,n\}\to X$, written as $\sigma=\langle\sigma(1),\dots,\sigma(n)\rangle$. The set of all finite sequences over set $X$ is denoted $X^*$. The length of a sequence is written as $|\sigma|$; additionally, $|\sigma|_x$ denotes the number of occurrences of $x$ in $\sigma$. The empty sequence is written as $\epsilon$. Vectors are assumed to be column vectors. $\vec{0}$ denotes the null vector, $\vec{1}=(1,1,\dots,1)^\mathsf{T}$, and $\vec{1}_i=(0,0,\dots,1,0,\dots,0)^\mathsf{T}$ is a unit vector with value 1 at index $i$. Given $X=\{x_1,x_2,\dots,x_k\}$ and $\sigma\in X^*$, the *Parikh vector* is obtained by a function $\rho\colon X^*\to\mathbb{N}^k$, where $\rho(\sigma)=(|\sigma|_{x_1},|\sigma|_{x_2},\dots,|\sigma|_{x_k})^\mathsf{T}$. In the remainder, we let $\vec{\sigma}\equiv\rho(\sigma)$. Given an $n\times m$ matrix $\mathbf{A}$, e.g., $\mathbf{A}\in\mathbb{R}^{n\times m}$, and $i,j\in\{1,\dots,n\}$, we write $\mathbf{A}_{i,j}$ to access the matrix cell value at row $i$, column $j$.

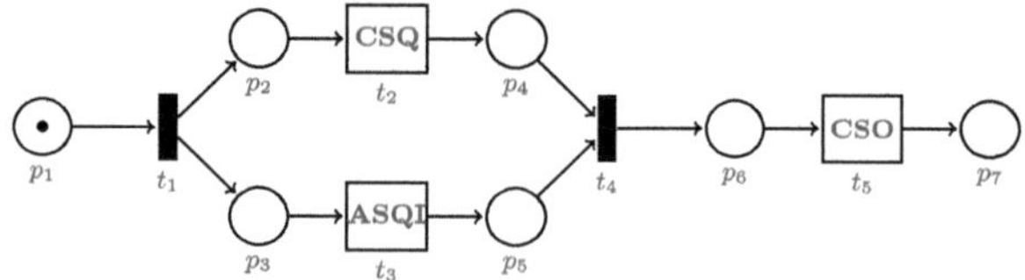


**Fig. 1.** Petri net $N_1$ depicting an example *Sales Quotation* process.

$\mathbf{A}_{i,*}$ denotes the row vector at index $i$, similarly, $\mathbf{A}_{*,j}$ denotes the column vector at index $j$.

*Petri Nets.* A *Petri net* is a bipartite graph that allows for compactly modeling concurrent systems. Without loss of generality, we exemplify the use of Petri nets for modeling *(business) process control flow*. For example, in Fig. 1, we depict a Petri net modeling a simplified *Sales Quotation* business process.

The Petri net describes that first, the *Create Sales Quotation (CSQ)* and the *Approve Sales Quotation Item (ASQI)* activities should be executed (in arbitrary order). Finally, the *Create Sales Order (CSO)* activity is executed. A Petri net consists of a set of *places* (visualized as circles) and a set of *transitions* (visualized as rectangles). Places allow for describing the *state* of the system modeled by the net; transitions manipulate the state of the net. Transitions may have an associated *label*, modeling the *activity* that the transition represents, e.g., in $N_1$ in Fig. 1, transition $t_2$ has label "CSQ", and transition $t_1$ has no label.[1] The arcs in the Petri have a weight value (a member of $\mathbb{N}$). In the example net $N_1$ in Fig. 1, all arc weights are 1; therefore, the weight values are omitted. We formally define a Petri net as follows.

**Definition 1 (Petri net).** *Let $P$ be a set of* places, *let $T$ be a set of* transitions *with $T \cap P = \emptyset$, let $F \subseteq (P \times T) \cup (T \times P)$ be a set of* arcs, *and let $w: (P \times T) \cup (T \times P) \to \mathbb{N}_{\geq 0}$ be an* arc weight function *with $w(x, y) > 0 \Leftrightarrow (x, y) \in F$ and $w(x, y) = 0 \Leftrightarrow (x, y) \notin F$. Tuple $N = (P, T, F, w)$ is a* Petri net.

Let $N = (P, T, F, w)$ be a Petri net. Given $x \in P \cup T$, we let $\bullet_N x = \{y \in P \cup T \mid (y, x) \in F\}$, and $x \bullet_N = \{y \in P \cup T \mid (x, y) \in F\}$ (we omit $N$ if it is clear from the context). We let $F^{\mathsf{C}} = ((P \times T) \cup (T \times P)) \setminus F$. Note that the arc weight function is defined on $F \cup F^{\mathsf{C}}$, i.e., for $(x, y) \in F$, $w(x, y) > 0$, and for $(x, y) \in F^{\mathsf{C}}$, $w(x, y) = 0$. A *marking* $m \in \mathcal{B}(P)$ of $N$ is a bag of its places; tuple $(N, m)$ is a *marked net*. A transition $t \in T$ is *enabled* in a marking $m$, written $(N, m)[t\rangle$, if $\forall p \in \bullet t \, (m(p) \geq w(p, t))$. Given some marking $m \in \mathcal{B}(P)$, an enabled transition $t$ can *fire*, yielding a marking $m' \in \mathcal{B}(P)$ with $m'(p) = m(p) - w(p, t) + w(t, p)$, $\forall p \in P$. We write the firing of a transition as $(N, m) \xrightarrow{t} (N, m')$. Similarly, for $\sigma \in T^*$, we write $(N, m) \xrightarrow{\sigma} (N, m')$ if $(N, m) \xrightarrow{\sigma(1)} (N, m_1), \ldots, (N, m_{|\sigma|-1}) \xrightarrow{\sigma(|\sigma|)} (N, m')$. We let $\mathcal{L}(N, m, m') = \{\sigma \in T^* \mid (N, m) \xrightarrow{\sigma} (N, m')\}$ denote the *language* of $(N, m)$

---

[1] Our work is independent of labels; hence, labels are omitted from definitions.

w.r.t. $m'$. $\mathcal{R}(N,m)=\{m'\in\mathcal{B}(P)|\exists\sigma\in T^*((N,m)\xrightarrow{\sigma}(N,m))\}$ denotes the reachable markings from marking $m$.

*The Marking Equation.* We assume that the places and transitions of a net are *indexed families* with bijective indexing functions of the form $f\colon\{1,\ldots,n\}\to P$ and $f'\colon\{1,\ldots,n\}\to T$. Correspondingly, matrices and vectors defined over places or transitions comply with the indexing. Given a matrix $\mathbf{A}$ with dimension $|P|\times|T|$, we write $\mathbf{A}_{p,t}$ instead of $\mathbf{A}_{f^{-1}(p),f'^{-1}(t)}$. Similarly, $\vec{1}_t$ denotes a *unit vector* with value 1 at index $f'^{-1}(t)$. Given a Petri net $N=(P,T,F,w)$, we let $\mathbf{C}^-\in\mathbb{N}_{\geq 0}^{|P|\times|T|}$ be its *consumption matrix*, with $\mathbf{C}^-_{p,t}=w(p,t)$. Similarly, we define the *production matrix* $\mathbf{C}^+\in\mathbb{N}_{\geq 0}^{|P|\times|T|}$, with $\mathbf{C}^+_{p,t}=w(t,p)$. The *incidence matrix* $\mathbf{C}$ of net $N$ is defined as $\mathbf{C}=-\mathbf{C}^-+\mathbf{C}^+$. Given markings $m,m'\in\mathcal{B}(P)$ and vector $\vec{x}\in\mathbb{N}_0^{|T|}$, the net's *marking equation* (MEQ) is a set of linear equations of the form $\vec{m'}=\vec{m}+\mathbf{C}\cdot\vec{x}$. The Parikh vector $\vec{\sigma}$ of a firing sequence $(N,m)\xrightarrow{\sigma}(N,m')$ is a solution to the MEQ (i.e., $\vec{x}=\vec{\sigma}$). The MEQ can alternatively be written as:

$$\forall p\in P\left(m(p)+\sum_{t\in\bullet p}w(t,p)\vec{x}_t-\sum_{t\in p\bullet}w(p,t)\vec{x}_t=m'(p)\right)\tag{1}$$

The MEQ has powerful practical applications. For example, consider solving a *shortest path problem* for a Petri net $N=(P,T,F,w)$ and markings $m_i,m_f$: *Given a cost function* $c\colon T\to\mathbb{R}_{\geq 0}$, *find* $\sigma\in\mathcal{L}(N,m_i,m_f)$ *that minimizes* $\sum_{t\in\sigma}c(t)$. A solution to the shortest path problem can be found by applying a *search algorithm*, e.g., Dijkstra [5], on the state space graph of the marked net $(N,m_i)$ (using $m_f$ as a goal state and $c$ as a cost function). A large class of search algorithms, i.e., *informed search algorithms*, uses additional domain-specific knowledge to speed up the search (e.g., the $A^*$ algorithm [8]). Such algorithms utilize a *heuristic function* $h$, which, in the context of the state space search problem, for any arbitrary marking $m\in\mathcal{R}(N,m_i)$, estimates the remaining distance to $m_f$. A heuristic must be *admissible*, i.e., it always underestimates the remaining distance. Ideally, it is also *consistent*, i.e., the estimate is always less than or equal to the estimated distance from any neighboring marking to the final marking, plus the cost of reaching that same neighboring marking. The MEQ allows us to define an admissible and consistent heuristic; i.e., we formulate a linear program based on the MEQ as follows.

**Definition 2 (Marking Equation LP).**  *Let* $N=(P,T,F,w)$ *be a Petri net, let* $m,m'\in\mathcal{B}(P)$ *be two markings of* $N$, *and let* $c\colon T\to\mathbb{R}_{\geq 0}$. *The marking equation-based linear programming problem is defined as follows.*

$$\text{minimize}\sum_{t\in T}c(t)x_t$$

$$\text{subject to: }m(p)+\sum_{t\in\bullet p}w(t,p)x_t-\sum_{t\in p\bullet}w(p,t)x_t=m'(p),\qquad\forall p\in P$$

$$x_t\in\mathbb{R}_{\geq 0},\qquad\qquad\forall t\in T$$

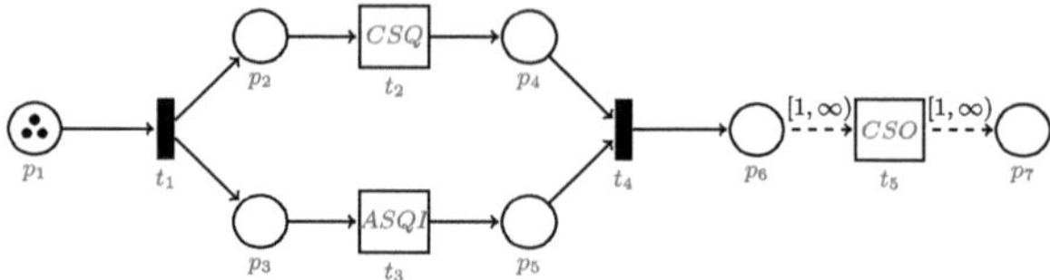

**Fig. 2.** Example VAR-net $\Lambda_1$, based on the Petri net $N_1$ in Fig. 1, consisting of two variable arcs, i.e., $(p_6, t_5)$ and $(t_5, p_7)$.

When adopting the linear program in Definition 2 in the $A^*$ algorithm, it is solved using $m_f$ as the target marking, yet with varying source marking, i.e., the currently visited marking in the search. The linear program is an admissible heuristic: a firing sequence is a solution, yet a cheaper solution may also exist. Consistency also holds since, if we can reach a marking $m'$ from marking $m$, the solution for $m'$ where we increase the $x_t$-value by one (for any transition $(N, m) \xrightarrow{t} (N, m'))$ is a solution for $m$. Observe that the *goal function* $\sum_{t \in T} c(t)x_t$ minimizes the cost of a firing sequence.

## 3   Variable Arc Nets

In various application scenarios, the tokens used in the execution semantics of a Petri net may refer to real-world phenomena, e.g., *Sales Orders* and *Sales Order Items*. The total amount of such phenomena manipulated or influenced by firing a transition may vary. For example, a *Sales Order* may typically consist of an arbitrary number of *Sales Order Items*. To model such variability, we define the notion of a *Variable ARc net* (VAR-net), in which we extend the notion of a conventional weighted labeled Petri net by specifying an additional type of arc, i.e., a *variable arc*. Such a variable arc allows for the consumption or production of an arbitrary number of tokens.

In a VAR-net we generalize the notion of a conventional weighted Petri net by letting the weight function map an arc to a set of non-negative weight values rather than a single weight value. An arc with a singleton weight set (excluding the singleton $\{0\}$) is a *regular* arc. Any other arc in the net, i.e., an arc $(x, y)$ with more than one weight value, is referred to as a *variable arc* and allows a variable amount of tokens to be consumed or produced upon firing a connecting transition. We visualize regular arcs with a solid line and variable arcs using a dashed line with the set of weight values specified on top. Consider Fig. 2, in which we depict an example VAR-net, based on the example Petri net in Fig. 1.

Since multiple quotation items belong to only one sales order, a variable arc connects from and to transition $t_5$, modeling the *CSO* activity and its variability in terms of token consumption. In the example, the weight functions for the variable arcs both describe the set of numbers characterized by the interval $[1, \infty)$. We formally define VAR-nets as follows.

**Definition 3 (Variable Arc net (VAR-net)).** *Let $P$ be a set of* places, *let $T$ be a set of* transitions, *s.t., $T \cap P = \emptyset$ and let $F \subseteq (P \times T) \cup (T \times P)$ be a corresponding set of* arcs. *Further, let $\omega \colon (P \times T) \cup (T \times P) \rightarrow \mathcal{P}(\mathbb{N}_{\geq 0})$ be an arc* weight *function, s.t. $(x,y) \in F \Leftrightarrow 0 \notin \omega(x,y)$ and $(x,y) \notin F \Leftrightarrow \omega(x,y) = \{0\}$. Tuple $\Lambda = (P, T, F, \omega)$ is a* Variable Arc net (VAR-net).

In the remainder, we let $F_r \subseteq F$ denote the set of regular arcs ($|\omega(x,y)| = 1$ for $(x,y) \in F_r$), and we let $F_v \subseteq F$ denote the set of variable arcs ($|\omega(x,y)| > 1$ for $(x,y) \in F_v$).[2] Additionally, given $z \in P \cup T$, we let $F|_z = \{(x,y) \in F \mid z \in \{x,y\}\}$. The sets $F_r|_z$ and $F_v|_z$ are defined similarly. Additionally, for $t \in T$, we let $\Omega(t) = \bigcap_{(x,y) \in F|_t} \omega(x,y)$. A transition for which all connected regular arcs describe the same singleton weight set is a *weight-consistent transition*. A VAR-net is *weight-consistent* if all its transitions are weight-consistent If a transition in a VAR-net only connects to regular or variable arcs (i.e., no mixtures of arc types), the transition is *variability-consistent*. A VAR-net is *variability-consistent* if all its transitions are variability-consistent[3].

The example VAR-net $\Lambda_1$ in Fig. 2 is both weight and variability consistent. Also, the often used Petri net class of *P/T-nets* [10], i.e., regular Petri nets in which all arc weights are equal to 1, is, by definition, weight-consistent. In a weight and variability-consistent net, a transition connects exclusively to regular or variable arcs. As such, the transitions themselves are either *regular* or *variable transitions*. We refer to the set of regular/variable transitions using $T_r \subseteq T$, and $T_v \subseteq T$, respectively. Observe that, if a VAR-net is variability-consistent and weight-consistent, then $\Omega(t)$ is either the empty set (in case $F|_t = \emptyset$), or, it is a singleton set only containing the single weight value associated to all regular arcs connected to the transition.

Finally, we present two *semantics* for VAR-nets, i.e., *regular* and *synchronizing semantics*, the latter of which is a strict subset of the former.

*Regular Semantics.* Under regular semantics, we apply the same principles as the semantics of regular weighted Petri nets. However, given a marking $m \in \mathcal{B}(P)$, and an arc $(p,t) \in F$, any number of $k \in \omega(p,t)$ tokens can be consumed, as long as $k \leq m(p)$. Similarly, we produce, for an arc $(t,p')$ any number $k \in \omega(p',t)$ tokens in $p'$. Since regular arcs describe a singleton weight set, token consumption/production is always the same value for these arcs. For example, reconsider the example VAR-net in Fig. 2, and assume we have marking $[p_6^3]$. After firing transition $t_5$, we can reach infinitely many markings. However, any of such markings either has either 2, 1, or 0 tokens in place $p_6$.

*Synchronizing Semantics.* In synchronizing semantics, we extend the regular semantics by requiring that, upon firing a transition, the number of tokens consumed and produced per connecting arc is equal. For example, in the marking $[p_6^3]$ in the VAR-net of Fig. 2, using the regular VAR-

---

[2] In [2] variable arcs can also be "ignored", i.e., no token is consumed/produced over a variable arc. In our work, we assume a variable arc to at least consume/produce one token.

[3] In [2], van der Aalsdt defines the variability consistency property as *well-formedness*.

net semantics, we obtain the following firings of $t_5$: $(\Lambda_1, [p_6^3]) \xrightarrow{t_5} (\Lambda_1, [p_6^2, p_7])$, $(\Lambda_1, [p_6^3]) \xrightarrow{t_5} (\Lambda_1, [p_6^2, p_7^2])$, $\ldots$, $(\Lambda_1, [p_6^3]) \xrightarrow{t_5} (\Lambda_1, [p_6, p_7])$, $(\Lambda_1, [p_6^3]) \xrightarrow{t_5} (\Lambda_1, [p_6, p_7^2])$, $\ldots$, $(\Lambda_1, [p_6^3]) \xrightarrow{t_5} (\Lambda_1, [p_7])$, $(\Lambda_1, [p_6^3]) \xrightarrow{t_5} (\Lambda_1, [p_7^2])$, $\ldots$. With synchronizing semantics, for the same marking, i.e., $[p_6^3]$, we only obtain three possible transition firings of $t_5$, i.e., $(\Lambda_1, [p_6^3]) \xrightarrow{t_5} (\Lambda_1, [p_6^2, p_7])$, $(\Lambda_1, [p_6^3]) \xrightarrow{t_5} (\Lambda_1, [p_6^1, p_7^2])$, and $(\Lambda_1, [p_6^3]) \xrightarrow{t_5} (\Lambda_1, [p_7^3])$. As such, the synchronizing semantic reduces the overall size of the VAR-net's state space. Any weight-inconsistent transition is, by definition, dead under synchronizing semantics. Similarly, the variable arcs of a variability-inconsistent transition act as regular arcs under synchronizing semantics (given that the transition is weight-consistent). Therefore, in the remainder, when synchronizing semantics are considered, we assume the VAR-net to be weight and variability-consistent. Regardless of the semantic adopted, the notation defined for regular Petri nets is also applicable to VAR-nets, e.g., $(\Lambda, m)[t\rangle$, $\mathcal{L}(\Lambda, m, m')$, etc.

## 4   Defining the Marking Equation

This section presents a set of nonlinear equations for net classes with variable token-flow semantics. The set of equations has the same property as the marking equation for regular weighted Petri nets: a firing sequence forms a solution to the set of nonlinear equations.

The incidence matrix for regular weighted Petri nets ($\mathbf{C}$) comprises two sub-matrices, $\mathbf{C}^+$ and $\mathbf{C}^-$, representing token production and consumption respectively. The individual entries of these matrices are based on the corresponding arc weights. For a VAR-net, we correspondingly define *variable production and consumption* matrices (dimensionality $|P| \times |T|$), i.e., $\mathbf{V}^+$ and $\mathbf{V}^-$. To this end, let $v_{x,y} \in \mathbb{R}_{\geq 0}$ for $(x, y) \in (P \times T) \cup (T \times P)$ denote arc-based real-valued variables, we let $\mathbf{V}^-_{p,t} = v_{p,t}$, and we let $\mathbf{V}^+_{p,t} = v_{t,p}$. In line with the definition of the regular incidence matrix, the variable incidence matrix $\mathbf{V}$ is characterized as $\mathbf{V} = -\mathbf{V}^- + \mathbf{V}^+$.

**Theorem 4 (Marking Equation for VAR-Nets).**  *Let $\Lambda = (P, T, F, \omega)$ be a VAR-net with corresponding variable incidence matrix $\mathbf{V}$, and let $m, m' \in \mathcal{B}(P)$ be two markings of $\Lambda$. Let $\vec{x} \in \mathbb{N}_0^{|T|}$ be a vector of transition variables, and let $\vec{m}, \vec{m'} \in \mathbb{N}_{\geq 0}^{|P|}$ be vector representations of markings $m, m' \in \mathcal{B}(P)$. If $m' \in \mathcal{R}(\Lambda, m)$, a solution exists to*

$$\vec{m'} = \vec{m} + \mathbf{V} \cdot \vec{x} \tag{2}$$

*Proof.* Let $\sigma \in T^*$ s.t. $(\Lambda, m) \xrightarrow{\sigma} (\Lambda, m')$, we prove that an assignment of $\mathbf{V}$ exists, such that $\vec{m'} = \vec{m} + \mathbf{V} \cdot \vec{\sigma}$.

**Case I** $\sigma = \epsilon$, then $m = m'$, $\vec{\sigma} = \vec{0}$, hence $\mathbf{V} \cdot \vec{\sigma} = \vec{0}$ for any feasible variable assignment in $\mathbf{V}$.

**Case II** $\sigma = \langle t \rangle$. Observe that we obtain $\vec{m'} = \vec{m} = \mathbf{V} \cdot \vec{1}_t$. Let $\vec{\Delta} = \vec{m} - \vec{m'}$. For any $p \notin \bullet t \cup t \bullet$, we observe $\vec{\Delta}_p = 0$. Clearly, for such $p$, $\mathbf{V}_{p,*} \cdot \vec{1}_t = 0$ for any arbitrary

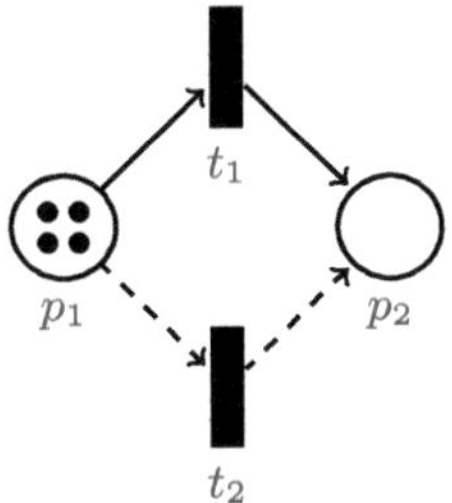


**Fig. 3.** Example VAR-net $\Lambda_2$.

*feasible variable assignment. For any $p\in\bullet t\cup t\bullet$, if no feasible variable assignment exists such that $\mathbf{V}_{p,*}\cdot\vec{1}_t=\vec{\Delta}_p$, this contradicts $(N,m)\xrightarrow{t}(N,m')$.*

*    **Case III**: $\sigma=\langle t_1,t_2,\ldots t_n\rangle$. We observe that we can iteratively apply **Case II** and derive $\vec{m}'=\vec{m}+\sum_{i\leftarrow 1}^{n}\mathbf{V}^i\cdot\vec{1}_{t_i}$, where each $\mathbf{V}^i$ is the step-based variable assignment as defined in **Case II**. However, $\mathbf{V}_{p,t}^i$ may be unequal to $\mathbf{V}_{p,t}^j$ for some $p\in P$, $t\in T$, and $1\leq i<j\leq n$. Yet, observe that we can combine the individual $\mathbf{V}^i$ matrices by assigning $\mathbf{V}_{p,t}=\dfrac{\sum_{i\leftarrow 1}^{n}\mathbf{V}_{p,t}^i b_i(t)}{|\sigma\downarrow t|}$, $\forall p\in P, t\in T$, where $b_i(t)=1$ if $t=t_i$ and $0$ otherwise, yielding a solution to $\vec{m}'=\vec{m}+\mathbf{V}\cdot\vec{\sigma}$.*    $\square$

The variable assignments in the entries of the $\mathbf{V}$ matrix generally correspond to *the average token-flow* over the arcs that the entry represents. For example, consider the VAR-net $\Lambda_2$ in Fig. 3, and firing sequence: $(\Lambda_2, [p_1^4])\xrightarrow{t_1}(\Lambda_2, [p_1^3, p_2^1])\xrightarrow{t_2}(\Lambda_2, [p_1, p_2^5])\xrightarrow{t_2}(\Lambda_2, [p_2^7])$. Equations 3-5 show the stepwise assignments of the incidence matrix $\mathbf{V}$ (i.e., **Case II** of the proof of Theorem 4). Equation 6 shows the assignment of the marking equation for the firing sequence $(\Lambda_2, [p_1^4])\xrightarrow{\langle t_1,t_2,t_2\rangle}(\Lambda_2, [p_2^7])$ (i.e., **Case III** of the proof of Theorem 4).

$$\begin{bmatrix}4\\0\end{bmatrix}+\begin{bmatrix}-1 & -1\\1 & 1\end{bmatrix}\cdot\begin{bmatrix}1\\0\end{bmatrix}=\begin{bmatrix}4\\0\end{bmatrix}+\begin{bmatrix}-1\\1\end{bmatrix}=\begin{bmatrix}3\\1\end{bmatrix} \tag{3}$$

$$\begin{bmatrix}3\\1\end{bmatrix}+\begin{bmatrix}-1 & -2\\1 & 4\end{bmatrix}\cdot\begin{bmatrix}0\\1\end{bmatrix}=\begin{bmatrix}3\\1\end{bmatrix}+\begin{bmatrix}-2\\4\end{bmatrix}=\begin{bmatrix}1\\5\end{bmatrix} \tag{4}$$

$$\begin{bmatrix}1\\3\end{bmatrix}+\begin{bmatrix}-1 & -1\\1 & 2\end{bmatrix}\cdot\begin{bmatrix}0\\1\end{bmatrix}=\begin{bmatrix}1\\3\end{bmatrix}+\begin{bmatrix}-1\\2\end{bmatrix}=\begin{bmatrix}0\\7\end{bmatrix} \tag{5}$$

$$\begin{bmatrix}4\\0\end{bmatrix}+\begin{bmatrix}-1 & -\frac{3}{2}\\1 & \frac{6}{2}\end{bmatrix}\cdot\begin{bmatrix}1\\2\end{bmatrix}=\begin{bmatrix}4\\0\end{bmatrix}+\begin{bmatrix}-4\\7\end{bmatrix}=\begin{bmatrix}0\\7\end{bmatrix} \tag{6}$$

## 5   Deriving Heuristic Functions

In this section, we present derived heuristic functions for search problems defined on the state space of VAR-nets, formulated as (non)linear optimization problems. The heuristics proposed stem from the marking equation in Sect. 4. We first show derived heuristics for *regular semantics* in Sect. 5.1, followed by the *synchronizing semantics* in Sect. 5.2. In Sect. 5.3, we present a general linear relaxation scheme that applies to both optimization problems.

### 5.1   Regular Semantics

Similar to the marking equation for regular Petri nets, we define a corresponding optimization problem by adopting the constraint body described by the marking equation with a transition firing cost function. In line with the marking equation for regular weighted Petri nets, we distill the following body of constraints.

$$\forall p \in P \left( m(p) + \sum_{t \in \bullet p} v_{t,p} \vec{x}_t - \sum_{t \in p \bullet} v_{p,t} \vec{x}_t = m'(p) \right) \tag{7}$$

Based on this, we define the corresponding optimization problem as follows.

**Optimization Problem 1 (Marking Equation NLP - Regular Semantics).** *Let* $\Lambda = (P, T, F, \omega)$ *be a VAR-net, let* $m, m' \in \mathcal{B}(P)$ *be two markings of* $\Lambda$, *and let* $c \colon T \to \mathbb{R}_{\geq 0}$. *The corresponding* Marking Equation-based Nonlinear Programming Problem *for regular semantics is defined as follows.*

$$
\begin{aligned}
\text{minimize} \quad & \sum_{t \in T} c(t) x_t \\
\text{subject to:} \quad & m(p) + \sum_{t \in \bullet p} v_{t,p} x_t - \sum_{t \in p \bullet} v_{p,t} x_t = m'(p), \forall p \in P \\
& v_{y,z} \in \omega(y, z), && \forall (y, z) \in F_r \cup F^{\mathsf{C}} \\
& \min(\omega(y, z)) \leq v_{y,z} \leq \max(\omega(y, z)), && \forall (y, z) \in F_v \\
& x_t \in \mathbb{N}_{\geq 0}, && \forall t \in T
\end{aligned}
$$

Observe that, in Optimization Problem 1, an arc variable that relates to a regular or non-existing arc is set to be $v_{y,z} \in \omega(y, z)$. Observe that this works as, in both cases, $\omega(y, z)$ is a singleton set (either $\{0\}$ or $\{k\}$ with $k > 0$). In line with Theorem 4, variables related to arcs with a variable arc weight are assigned any value $\min(\omega(y, z)) \leq v_{y,z} \leq \max(\omega(y, z))$, i.e., the average flow is in between the minimum and maximum number of tokens consumed/produced per transition firing. Observe that Theorem 4 guarantees that any solution to Optimization Problem 1 is an *admissible heuristic*, i.e., the cheapest firing sequence is an upper bound for the solution found by solving Optimization Problem 1.

## 5.2   Synchronizing Semantics

Observe that the results presented in Sect. 5.1 directly apply to synchronizing semantics, i.e., since the regular semantics are a strict superset of synchronizing semantics. However, a solution to the optimization problem presented in Sect. 5.1 does not enforce the synchronizing semantics. Enforcing synchronizing semantics on the optimization problems is expected to bring the solutions closer to realizable firing sequences.

As an example, reconsider Sect. 1. To embed synchronizing semantics in Sect. 1, we additionally enrich the optimization problem with the following four constraints: (i) $v_{t,p}{=}v_{t,p'}$, $\forall p, p' {\in} t{\bullet}$, (ii) $v_{t,p}{=}v_{p',t}$, $\forall p {\in} t{\bullet}, p' {\in} {\bullet}t$, (iii) $v_{p,t}{=}v_{p',t}$, $\forall p, p' {\in} {\bullet}t$, and (iv) $v_{p,t}{=}v_{t,p'}$, $\forall p {\in} {\bullet}t, p' {\in} t{\bullet}$ Hence, all variables related to arcs connecting to $t$ are equal. As a consequence, it suffices to use a single variable per transition to represent the corresponding arc-flow, rather than a variable per arc. We can thus (trivially) simplify Optimization Problem 1 as follows.

**Optimization Problem 2 (Marking Equation NLP - Synchronizing Semantics).**
*Let $\Lambda{=}(P, T, F, \omega)$ be a weight and variability-consistent VAR-net, let $m, m'{\in}\mathcal{B}(P)$ be two markings of $\Lambda$, and let $c\colon T{\to}\mathbb{R}_{\geq 0}$. The corresponding Marking Equation based Nonlinear Programming Problem is defined as follows.*

$$
\begin{aligned}
\text{minimize} \quad & \sum_{t\in T} c(t)x_t \\
\text{subject to:} \quad & m(p) + \sum_{t\in \bullet p} v_t x_t - \sum_{t\in p\bullet} v_t x_t = m'(p), \forall p \in P \\
& v_t \in \Omega(t), && \forall t \in T_r \\
& v_t \in \mathbb{R}_{\geq 0}, && \forall t \in T_v \\
& x_t \in \mathbb{N}_{\geq 0}, && \forall t \in T
\end{aligned}
$$

Adopting synchronizing semantics for identity-aware tokens can be achieved by the same simplification, i.e., a variable of the form $v_{t,p,i}$ is replaced by a variable of the form $v_{t,i}$, and, similarly $v_{p,t,i}$ is replaced by a variable of the form $v_{t,i}$. The same holds for the object-centric case, i.e., every variable that relates to an arc can be replaced by a variable that represents the connected transition (both for regular and identity-aware tokens).

## 5.3   Linear Relaxation

This section presents a general scheme to apply linear relaxation to the nonlinear optimization problems in Sect. 5.1 and Sect. 5.2. The key observation to apply linear relaxation is based on the fact that in the nonlinear formulations, multiplications of the form $v_{t,p}x_t$ and $v_{p,t}x_t$ exist (in various extensions) which represent the *total token flow* for the arcs that the variables represent. Therefore, in the core constraint body of the linear relaxation, we obfuscate the explicit differentiation of transition firings and corresponding token consumption/production by replacing all occurrences of $v_{t,p}x_t$ and $v_{p,t}x_t$ (or any extension thereof in other behavioral classes) by fresh variables $f_{t,p}$ and $f_{p,t}$ representing the total token flow over the corresponding arc. Observe that, for variable arcs, the lower bound of the flow is equal to the minimum corresponding arc weight value multiplied by the number of corresponding transition firings, e.g., $\min(\omega(t,p))x_t \leq f_{t,p}$. The upper-bound, symmetrically, is equal to $\max(\omega(t,p))x_t$, yielding $\min(\omega(t,p))x_t \leq f_{t,p} \leq \max(\omega(t,p))$ Observe that, for regular and non-existing arcs, $\min(\omega(t,p))x_t \leq f_{t,p} \leq \max(\omega(t,p))$ yields a single value.

**Optimization Problem 3 (Marking Equation LP - Regular Semantics).**
*Let $\Lambda=(P,T,F,\omega)$ be a VAR-net, let $m, m'\in\mathcal{B}(P)$ be two markings of $\Lambda$, and let $c\colon T\to\mathbb{R}_{\geq 0}$. The corresponding* Marking Equation based Linear Programming Problem *is defined as follows.*

$$
\begin{aligned}
\text{minimize} \quad & \sum_{t\in T} c(t)x_t \\
\text{subject to:} \quad & m(p)+\sum_{t\in\bullet p} f_{t,p}-\sum_{t\in p\bullet} f_{p,t}=m'(p), && \forall p\in P \\
& \min(\omega(y,z))x_t \leq f_{y,z} \leq \max(\omega(y,z))x_t, \forall(y,z)\in F\cup F^{C} \\
& x_t\in\mathbb{N}_{\geq 0}, && \forall t\in T \\
& f_{y,z}\in\mathbb{N}_{\geq 0}, && \forall(y,z)\in F\cup F^{C}
\end{aligned}
$$

Observe that the marking equation can also be defined on the basis of token flow. Assume we define *flow production and consumption* matrices (dimensionality $|P|\times|T|$), i.e., $\mathbf{F}^+$ and $\mathbf{F}^-$, with $\mathbf{F}^-_{p,t}=f_{p,t}$, $\mathbf{F}^+_{p,t}=f_{t,p}$, and we let $\mathbf{F}=\mathbf{F}^+-\mathbf{F}^-$. Observe that translating the core constraint body of Optimization Problem 3, i.e., $m(p)+\sum_{t\in\bullet p} f_{t,p}-\sum_{t\in p\bullet} f_{p,t}=m'(p)$, $\forall p\in P$, in matrix form yields:

$$\vec{m'}=\vec{m}+\mathbf{F}\cdot\vec{1} \tag{8}$$

Furthermore, if for some sequence $\sigma\in T^*$, we have $(N,m)\xrightarrow{\sigma}(N,m')$, then clearly, any feasible assignment of the VAR-net marking equation, i.e., $\vec{m'}=\vec{m}+\mathbf{V}\cdot\vec{x}$ (cf. Theorem 4), also satisfies Eq. 8, i.e., by assigning

$$\mathbf{F}_{p,t}=\mathbf{V}_{p,t}\cdot\vec{\sigma}_t \tag{9}$$

Hence, Eq. 9 allows us to deduce that Optimization Problem 3 can, similarly to Optimization Problem 1, serve as an *admissible search heuristic*, when combined with objective function $\sum_{t\in T} c(t)x_t$ for some given $c\colon T\to\mathbb{R}_{\geq 0}$. Finally, observe that substitution of the $v$ and $x$ variables by a flow variable $f$, is also applicable for the synchronizing semantics.

# 6    Evaluation

In this section we present the results of an evaluation of the usage of the presented marking equations for VAR-nets and their linear relaxation as a heuristic in the $A^*$ search algorithm. Section 6.1 presents the experimental setup. In Sect. 6.2, we present the results.

## 6.1    Experimental Setup

*Model Generation* Since few publicly available VAR-nets exist, we generated 30 models. We used **pm4py** [3] to generate random process trees with a size of 20 to 50 nodes, which we converted into Petri nets. To transform the Petri nets into VAR-nets we assigned each labeled transition a probability of 0.4 to replace its connected arcs with variable arcs. In all cases we allow any weight in $[1, \infty)$.

*Implementation.* The implementations of the proposed optimization problems, all process models, and corresponding results are available at https://osf. io/pav5m/?view_only=88177dfb771a4386bae79e71bad14dcf. We have implemented all proposed optimization problems in the dynamic optimization suite **GEKKO** (https://gekko.readthedocs.io) with the integrated **APOPT** (https://apopt. com/) solver. Additionally, for the linear relaxations, we use **Google OR tools** (https://developers.google.com/optimization) with the integrated **SAT solver** and **GLOP** (Google Linear Optimization Package). The number of tokens present in the initial marking is taken as the upper bound for variable arcs, as all models generated are bounded by that number.

*Experiments.* We assess the performance of using the linear relaxations as a heuristic in an $A^*$ search and compare it to the search performance with a Dijkstra-based search. The goal for both algorithms is to find the cheapest firing sequence considering the *synchronizing semantics* for the generated VAR-nets, leading from the initial to the final marking. We only consider the unit cost function: labeled transitions have cost 1; invisible transitions have cost 0. We use a timeout of *100 s* for each search. The search is conducted for different number of tokens in the initial and final marking, ranging from 1 to 5 tokens. The experiment was conducted on an Intel(R) Xeon(R) W-10855M CPU 2.80 GHz with 64 GB of RAM and repeated 10 times.

## 6.2    Results

In this section, we present the results of our experiments. Consider Fig. 4, in which we present the impact of using the proposed heuristic on state space search.

We observe that Dijkstra scales significantly worse with more initial tokens in the model. This is expected, since the corresponding state space grows factorially. Using $A^*$ with any of the proposed underestimating heuristics leads to consistently fast searches. This is also observable in the number of timeouts triggered after 100 seconds. Having just three tokens in the initial marking already causes Dijkstra to time out in 86.7% of all cases. Using the versions of the optimization

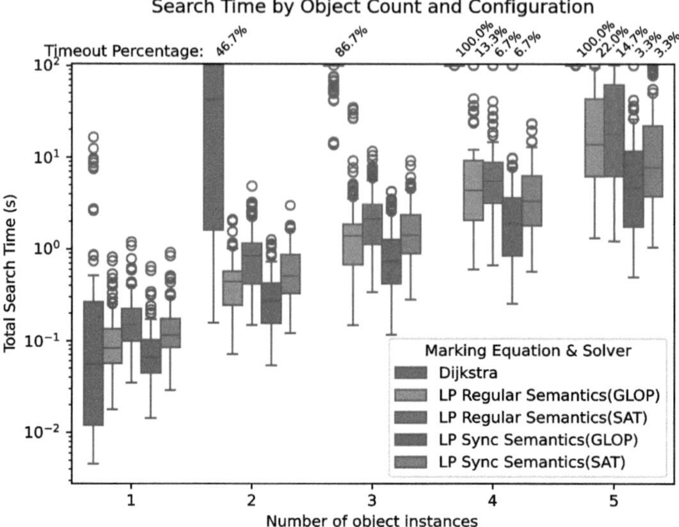


**Fig. 4.** Runtime and search-efficiency measurements of the use of search heuristics in shortest path search on the VAR-net state space.

problems, which do not restrict variables to integers and using the faster GLOP lp-solver leads to a faster search. This explained by a faster computation of the individual LP instances, which are computed for each state during the search. A less significant speed up can be observed for the Marking Equation for synchronizing semantics, compared to the regular semantics version. Generally, we observe that the differences between different optimization problems are small.

## 7    Conclusion

In this paper, we present Variable Arc nets (VAR-nets), an extension of regular weighted Petri nets supporting arcs with variable token consumption and production. Various applications, e.g., conformance checking, require a shortest path search on the state space of a process model. However, unlike classical Petri nets, no search heuristics exist for VAR-nets that enable us to traverse the state space more efficiently, i.e., by adopting informed search. To this end, in this paper, we presented several optimization problem formulations, i.e., both nonlinear and linear, that can serve as such a search heuristic. Our experiments confirm that using search heuristics within the state space search on VAR-nets greatly improves the search performance. Our experiments demonstrate that linear optimization problem formulations outperform their nonlinear counterparts. *Personal Note.* We acknowledge that this contribution, on behalf of all past and present members of the Celonis Engineering and Innovation Lab, may be dry for its purpose. Therefore, we conclude this paper with a personal note. The notion of VAR nets is based solely on Wil's foundational work on object-centric nets; without it, there would not be any of the results presented in this work. Furthermore, the authors would like to acknowledge that the results presented in this paper are entirely attributable to Wil's continuous guidance, support, and emphasis on mathematical and scientific rigor. It is therefore fair to say that this work is achieved by standing on the mighty shoulders of a true giant.

*Dear Wil, thank you for all your efforts and contributions in supporting our scientific, engineering, and personal growth throughout the past years. We sincerely hope you have enjoyed reading this contribution. Your ever-support, contributions, and love for the Petri net conference suggest to us that you would.*

# References


1. van der Aalst, W.M.P.: Process Mining - Data Science in Action, Second Edition. Springer (2016)
2. van der Aalst, W.M.P., Berti, A.: Discovering object-centric petri nets. Fundam. Informaticae **175**(1–4), 1–40 (2020)
3. Berti, A., van Zelst, S.J., Schuster, D.: Pm4py: a process mining library for python. Softw. Impacts **17**, 100556 (2023)
4. Chinosi, M., Trombetta, A.: BPMN: an introduction to the standard. Comput. Stand. Interfaces **34**(1), 124–134 (2012)
5. Dijkstra, E.W.: A note on two problems in connexion with graphs. Numer. Math. **1**, 269–271 (1959)
6. Fundamentals of Business Process Management. Springer, Heidelberg (2018). https://doi.org/10.1007/978-3-662-56509-4_9
7. Griva, I., Nash, S.G., Sofer, A.: Linear and Nonlinear Optimization (2. ed.). SIAM (2008)
8. Hart, P.E., Nilsson, N.J., Raphael, B.: A formal basis for the heuristic determination of minimum cost paths. IEEE Trans. Syst. Sci. Cybern. **4**(2), 100–107 (1968)
9. Murata, T.: Petri nets: Properties, analysis and applications. Proc. IEEE **77**(4), 541–580 (1989)
10. Reisig, W.: Petri Nets: An Introduction, EATCS Monographs on Theoretical Computer Science, vol. 4. Springer (1985)

# Is Quantum Mechanics Deterministic
or Non-deterministic?

Kees van Hee[✉] and Kees van Berkel

Department of Mathematics and Computer Science, Technical University Eindhoven,
P.O. Box 513, 5600 MB Eindhoven, The Netherlands
{k.m.v.hee,c.h.v.berkel}@tue.nl

**Abstract.** We first explore the role of (non-) determinism in various
modeling frameworks and zoom in on two of them: Markov processes and
quantum mechanics. A close and precise alignment of these two frameworks shows that quantum mechanics contains an embedded Markov
process. The well-known Bell experiment is used to show that quantum
mechanics is probabilistic and hence non-deterministic. We show that the
established model for the Bell experiment, based on four observables, is
wrong and leads to an apparent contradiction. An appropriate probability model, based on two observables and two detector settings, avoids
this paradox. We also offer a proof that there cannot exist a so-called hidden variable that makes our probability measure separable, in agreement
with Bell's main finding. Finally, we speculate whether at some deeper
level there may exist a deterministic theory for quantum mechanics.

## 1   Introduction

Physics may well be the first field where mathematical modeling was applied successfully. Since the second half of the twentieth century mathematical modeling
has spread to other fields including business processes, logistics, macro econom-
ical models, manufacturing processes, chemical processes, climate systems, and
biological systems. Although these fields posed new requirements, some of the
modeling frameworks proved applicable in widely different fields.

A *model* is a formal, mathematical description of a part of the universe,
commonly referred to as *system*. The typical objective of such a model is to
make *predictions* about the *evolution* of such a system. If the model makes good
predictions we can trust the model and we can claim to *understand* the world as
described by the model. Models in physics are good examples: Newton mechanics
for daily life, Einstein relativity for motion at extreme velocities (or energies),
and quantum mechanics at extremely small scales. A model does not need to be
perfect in order to make *useful* predictions. The degree of usefulness can only be
answered on the basis of *experiments* and the use of *statistical analysis*.

In physics there is no doubt that quantum mechanics is a useful description
of reality, because its predictions and the related experiments are extremely
close. These predictions are probabilistic in nature, because quantum mechanics


J. Mendling et al. (Eds.): Wil van der Aalst Festschrift, LNCS 16480, pp. 262–283, 2026.
https://doi.org/10.1007/978-3-032-17618-9_20

is a non-deterministic model. But does quantum mechanics describe reality? Is the quantum reality non-deterministic? Many physicists do not like this non-determinism: as if elementary particles make choices by themselves.

Einstein and others with him, claim that quantum mechanics is an incomplete theory, because he was convinced that the universe is deterministic ("God does not play dice"). We will revisit this point of view in Sect. 6. Even if the universe is deterministic, then non-deterministic models can still be useful, because the introduced non-determinism then hides our ignorance of details of reality. A non-deterministic model provides a set of possible evolutions (or scenario's) and in a probabilistic model each different evolution gets a probability (density) of occurrence. In models for business processes non-determinism often expresses our ignorance about human decision making, and the underlying assumption of the existence of a free will.

In Sect. 2 we provide a brief overview of common modeling frameworks. In Sect. 3 we focus on the differences and similarities between two of them: Markov processes and quantum mechanics. These two formalisms together offer a good vehicle for the study the of the (non)determinism in mathematical models. In Sect. 4 we describe the Bell experiment and offer a proof that quantum mechanics can be based on a proper probabilistic framework. In Sect. 5 we examine the role of (pseudo) random numbers in probabilistic models and chaotic models. In Sect. 6 we return to the question posed in the title: *Is quantum mechanics deterministic or non-deterministic?* The question will be addressed from two different perspectives, that of *superdeterminism* and that of *chaotic determinism*.

## 2    Modeling Frameworks

Most modeling frameworks share the notions of *state* space $S$, *time* domain $T$, and an *evolution mechanism $M$*. Here $S$ is either a countable set, or a subset of $\mathbb{R}^n$, or it has more structure like, for example, Petri nets. Time $T$ is an (open or closed) interval of the real numbers $\mathbb{R}$ or of the integers $\mathbb{Z}$. Evolution mechanism $M$ defines how the system transits from one state into a next state during a unit time step (if $T = \mathbb{Z}$) or during an infinitesimal time step (if time is real). An *evolution*, also called a *process* or path, is a mapping $s : T \to S$.

In a *discrete time* model the evolution mechanism $M$ can be represented by a *binary relation $M \subset S \times S$* with the meaning that if $(s_1, s_2) \in M$ then $s_2$ is a possible successor state of $s_1$. A process is then a sequence (finite or infinite) $(s_1, s_2, ....)$ such that for all relevant $(s_n, s_{n+1}) \in M$. A process is *deterministic* if $M$ is a *function*: $M : S \to S$.

In a *continuous time* model the evolution mechanism is typically represented by (partial) differential equations or by stochastic differential equations. Process $s(.)$ satisfies a differential equation of the form $ds(t)/dt = M(s(t), t)$. State $s(t)$ at time $t$ is supposed to contain all relevant information of the *history* of the process. The time derivative models the infinitesimal time step. The transformation of a model with discrete time into a model with continuous time is often conceptually straightforward: just let the time step go to zero, but it may require some heavy mathematical machinery. The other way around is easier. Such transformations for the state space are less obvious.

Modeling frameworks can be classified in many ways. We use the following characteristics. Not all characteristics are independent and some characteristics apply only to specific variations of the framework.

1. *Discrete vs continuous $S$.*
   If $S$ is a finite or countable (infinite) set, it is called discrete and if it is part of $\mathbb{R}^n$ for some $n \in \mathbb{N}$ it is called a continuous state space.
2. *Monolithic vs distributed $S$.*
   A state space is monolithic if we only know that $S$ is just a set or $\mathbb{R}^n$. States have no further structure and transitions affect the whole state. If a state space is distributed then states are *structured*, for instance a grid, or a graph endowed with one or more *tokens* that mark a *local state*. Tokens may have a data structure as well. So the state space can be divided into parts that behave as local sub-state spaces.
3. *Open vs closed.*
   An open model can have interaction with its environment, a closed model cannot. An open model may accept an input symbol (token) and/or produce an output symbol (token) during an evolution step.
4. *Discrete vs continuous $T$.*
   A model is discrete if $T$ is finite or countable infinite, ordered set. Often, $T = \mathbb{Z}$ or $T = \mathbb{N}$, but if $T$ is only ordered, then we can't measure time and we only have (partially) ordered events. If $T$ is an interval $\{t \in \mathbb{R} \mid t_0 \leq t \leq t_1\}$ where $t_1 = \infty$ is allowed, then the model is continuous.
5. *Sequential vs parallel $M$.*
   For distributed systems with more than one token, there can be *local transitions* that only affect a part of the state. If these local transitions always execute simultaneously, it is called *parallel* and if the local transitions occur one after another, it is called *sequential*. If the state space is monolithic there is one global transition per time step. If $T = \mathbb{Z}$ then a parallel system is called *synchronous*, because all parallel transitions occur simultaneously. Otherwise it is called *asynchronous*.
6. *Deterministic vs non-deterministic vs probabilistic $M$.*
   The evolution of a model is *deterministic* if, for every state $s \in S$, there is only *one* process starting at $s$. If it is not deterministic then there is for each starting state a set of possible processes starting in $s$. In *probabilistic* models there is a probability measure on this set, indicating that some futures are more probable than others. If this probability measure is unknown, we call the framework *non-deterministic*. Note that, if the probability measure for every $s \in S$ is one for only one future, then the model is also deterministic.

There is a plethora of process modeling frameworks, including many variations and extensions. Below we offer a non-exhaustive list of characteristic frameworks, including application domains and some variants. Table 1 summarizes these models in terms of the six characteristics listed above.

- *Finite automata*, with applications in control theory, digital systems, software engineering, network protocols, and more. Variants include, for example, Mealy and Moore automata, and UML state machines.
- *Turing machines*, with applications in the theory of computation.
- *Cellular automata* with applications in physics, theoretical biology, and cryptography. It has variants as Margolus, asynchronous, and stochastic cellular automata.
- *Petri nets* with original application domain concurrent information processing systems. It has variants as timed (deterministic or probabilistic) Petri nets, high-level Petri nets, coloured Petri nets, dataflow models, UML activity diagrams, and many business process modeling variants.
- *Process algebra* with applications in concurrent systems. Variants include CCS, CSP, ACP and $\pi$-calculus.
- *Neural networks* with applications in cognitive processes. Variants include convolution networks and transformers.
- *Markov processes* with applications in stochastic processes. Variants include hidden Markov processes, Markov decision processes and semi-Markov processes.
- *Differential equations*, with variants as partial differential equations, *stochastic* differential equations and the discrete variant, difference equations that are the basis of the finite elements method (FEM).
- *Quantum mechanics* with applications in solid-state physics, semiconductors, chemistry, materials science, and more. It has features of both Markov processes and of differential equations, as will be made clear in the next section.

**Table 1.** Examples of frameworks and their main characteristics.

| Framework | State space $S$ | | IO | Time $T$ | Evolution mechanism $M$ | |
|---|---|---|---|---|---|---|
| | discrete, continuous | monolithic, distributed | open, closed | discrete, continuous | sequential, parallel | deterministic, non-deterministic, probabilistic |
| Finite automata | d | m | o | d | s | n |
| Turing machines | d | m | c | d | s | n |
| Cellular automata | d | d | c | d | p | d |
| Petri nets | d | d | c | d | p | n |
| Process algebras | d | d | o | d | s | n |
| Neural networks | c | d | o | d | s | d |
| Markov processes | d, c | m | c | d, c | s | p |
| Differential equations | c | m | c | c | s | d, p |
| Quantum mechanics | c | m | o | c | s | p |

There are several reasons for this large variety of modeling frameworks. First, because real world systems are very different and very complex, so the extensions are necessary to cover specific characteristics of reality. Second, for modeling convenience, some frameworks should give better tractable models than others.

The various extensions of the frameworks offer additional features and lead to overlaps between different frameworks. Many applications can be addressed by multiple frameworks.

## 3    Quantum Mechanics Versus Markov Processes

Quantum mechanics and Markov processes are both probabilistic modeling frameworks. Although they are fundamentally different, they appear strikingly similar in some respects. We consider both continuous time and discrete time versions of each.[1] Because we are comparing frameworks of different fields of science here, we give a concise description of each. They are well-known, see for instance [20] and [24] for more detail. We sometimes use unconventional terminology, to make the frameworks comparable in Table 2.

### 3.1    The Basics of Probability Theory

The basics of probability theory can be summarized as follows.

- A *probability space* ([7,12], and [23]) is a 3-tuple $(\Omega, \mathcal{F}, \mathbb{P})$. Here $\Omega$ is an arbitrary set called the *outcome space* (or sample space), $\mathcal{F}$ is the *event space* (formally a $\sigma$-algebra). The last component $\mathbb{P}$ is a *probability measure* on $\mathcal{F}$.
- A *stochastic variable* is defined as a (measurable) function on a probability space $X : \Omega \to \Sigma$ ($\Sigma = \mathbb{R}$ or $\Sigma$ is countable). The probability $\mathbb{P}[\{\omega \in \Omega\} \mid X(\omega)=x]$ is abbreviated as $\mathbb{P}[X=x]$ and called the *distribution* of $X$.
- Given event $A \in \mathcal{F}$, the *conditional probability* of $X$ given $A$ is denoted by $\mathbb{P}[X|A]$ and is defined by $\mathbb{P}[X|A] := \mathbb{P}[X \cap A]/\mathbb{P}[A]$. (This notion can be generalized for conditioning on a sub-$\sigma$-algebra of $\mathcal{F}$.)
- Two events $A$ and $B$ are called *independent* if $\mathbb{P}[A \cap B] = \mathbb{P}[A] \cdot \mathbb{P}[B]$ and similarly two stochastic variables $X$ and $Y$ are *independent* if $\mathbb{P}[X \in A, Y \in B] = \mathbb{P}[X \in A] \cdot \mathbb{P}[Y \in B]$ for all events $A, B \in \mathcal{F}$.
- A *stochastic process* is a function $X : T \times \Omega \to \Sigma$, $X(.,\omega)$ is called a random function and $X(t,.)$ is a random variable.

The only relationship between probability theory and experimental observations is given by the *law of large numbers* and the *central limit theorem*. The first one says, that the *average* of $n$ independent and identical distributed, real-valued stochastic variables converges to a theoretical value, the so-called *expectation*. The second one says, that the distribution of this average (normalized by subtracting the average and divided by the variance of the average) converges to the *Gauss* distribution. Both laws have formal proofs and are empirically validated with high precision. Probability theory does not say anything about the mechanism that *selects* an element $\omega \in \Omega$. For physicists this fact is highly unsatisfactory.

---

[1] A discrete version of quantum mechanics assumes discrete space and time, with the Planck length and Planck time as units.

## 3.2   Markov Processes

We start with the continuous time domain $T = \mathbb{R}$ and a discrete *measurement space* $\Sigma$, i.e. the space where the measure the values of the random variables. For simplicity we assume $\Sigma = \{0, 1, ..., N - 1\}$. So a *state* is a distribution over the measurements. Here we deviate from the standard terminology of Markov processes, because we will show the analogy with quantum systems. The usual term for what we called here "measurement" is the "state" and so the measurement space $\Sigma$ is normally called "statespace".

We first define a *Markov kernel $P$* (see [21]) with the following properties:

$$P : \Sigma \times \Sigma \times T \to [0, 1], \ \text{such that} \ \sum_j P_{i,j}(t) = 1 \ \text{for all} \ i, j \in \Sigma \ \text{and} \ t \in T,$$
$$P_{i,j}(t + s) = \sum_k P_{i,k}(s).P_{k,j}(t) \ \text{for} \ i, j, k \in \Sigma \ \text{and} \ t, s \in T \ ,$$
$$P_{i,j}(h) = \delta_{i,j} + Q_{i,j}h + o(h) \ ,$$

$$(3.1)$$

where $Q$ is the *infinitesimal generator* with properties $Q_{i,j} \geq 0$ for $i \neq j$ and $Q_{i,i} = -\sum_{j,j \neq i} Q_{i,j}$, $\delta$ is the Kronecker delta function and $o(h)/h$ tends to zero if $h$ tends to zero.

The *evolution* is governed by the infinitesimal operator $Q$ via the *Kolmogorov (forward) equation:*

$$\frac{d}{dt} P_{i,j}(t) = \sum_k P_{i,k} \cdot Q_{k,j} \ , \tag{3.2}$$

which is easy to derive from the kernel definition (3.1).

A *Markov process* $X(t), t \in T$ is defined by:

$$\mathbb{P}[X(t_0) = i_0, ..., X(t_n) = i_n] = \pi_0(i_0) \prod_{k=0}^{n-1} P_{i_k, i_{k+1}}(t_{k+1} - t_k) \ , \tag{3.3}$$

where $i_k \in \Sigma, t_i \in T, t_i < t_{i+1}$ and $\pi_0$ is a probability measure on $\Sigma$. From this we derive the well-known *Markov property:*

$$\mathbb{P}[X(t_{n+1}) = i_{n+1} \mid X(t_0) = i_0, ..., X(t_n) = i_n] = \mathbb{P}[X(t_{n+1}) = i_{n+1} \mid X(t_n) = i_n] \ , \tag{3.4}$$

and similarly

$$\mathbb{P}[X(s + t) = j | X(s) = i] = P_{i,j}(t) \ \text{for} \ i, j \in \Sigma, s, t \in T \ . \tag{3.5}$$

If $T$ is *discrete* we assume $T = \mathbb{N}$ and then we define (using overloading) $P_{i,j} := P_{i,j}(\tau)$ for some fixed time step $\tau$ (e.g. $\tau = 1$). Then we get

$$\mathbb{P}[X_{m+n} = j | X_m = i] = P^n(i, j) \ \text{for all} \ i, j \in \Sigma, m, n \in \mathbb{N} \ , \tag{3.6}$$

where $P^n$ is the n-fold product of the matrix $P$. Given an initial probability measure or distribution $\pi_0$ on $\Sigma$ we can derive for $n \in T$ the distribution

$$\pi_n(j) = \sum_i \pi_0(i) \cdot P_{i,j}^n \ \text{or} \ \pi_n = \pi_0 \cdot P^n \ . \tag{3.7}$$

We see that the evolution in terms of the distribution $\pi_n, n \in T$ is purely *deterministic*. Only if we look at a *measurement* $X_n$, then we have a probabilistic effect. The relationship between the state and the measurement is given by

$$\mathbb{P}[X_n = i] = \pi_n(i) \ . \tag{3.8}$$

## 3.3   Quantum Mechanics

Quantum mechanics is a framework describing the behavior of nature at the smallest scale. Typical systems that are modeled by quantum mechanics include elementary particles, qubits, a harmonic oscillator, and a hydrogen atom.

The *state* of a quantum system is modeled by a *wave function* $\Psi$, which can be seen as a vector $|\Psi\rangle$ (Dirac notation) in a complex and separable *Hilbert space* $S$. There is an underlying *measurement* state $\Sigma$, such that $S$ is the set of all square integrable complex functions on $\Sigma$, i.e. $S = L^2(\Sigma)$. Typical examples are $\Sigma = \{0, 1, ..., N - 1\}$ for some $N \in \mathbb{N}$, or $\Sigma = \mathbb{R}^n$. For modeling a particle position $\Sigma = \mathbb{R}^3$ and for modeling a qubit measurement $\Sigma = \{0, 1\}$.

A separable Hilbert spaces has base $\{|e_x\rangle \in S \mid x \in \Sigma\}$ with at most countable many elements and the state as vector $|\Psi\rangle = \sum_{x \in \Sigma} \Psi(x) \cdot |e_x\rangle$. If $\Sigma = \mathbb{R}^n$ it is $|\Psi\rangle = \int_{x \in \Sigma} \Psi(x) \cdot |e_x\rangle dx$, where $x \in \mathbb{R}^n$, but for simplicity we use here the first notation. Note that $\Psi(x)$ is a complex number and it is the coordinate of the state vector $|\Psi\rangle$ at $x \in \Sigma$.

The Hilbert space $S$ has an inner product $\langle \Phi|\Psi\rangle := \sum_x \Phi(x)^* \cdot \Psi(x)$ , where $\Phi^*(x)$ is the complex conjugate of $\Phi(x)$. In fact, the states are all *unit vectors*, so $\langle \Psi|\Psi\rangle = 1$. When we consider the process of the system in time, we denote the state by $|\Psi(t)\rangle$ and the wave function by $\Psi(t, x)$.

The *evolution* mechanism of a quantum system has two parts. The first part is governed by a *unitary operator* $U(t)$, and is therefore purely *deterministic*. Unitarity means that $U^{-1} = U^\dagger$ where $U^\dagger$ is the conjugate transpose of $U$ and $U^{-1}$ its inverse. Operator $U(t)$ is derived from the *Schroedinger equation*, which is a partial differential equation:

$$\frac{d}{dt}|\Psi(t)\rangle = -\frac{i}{\hbar} H|\Psi(t)\rangle \ . \tag{3.9}$$

Here $H$ the so-called *Hamiltonian*, a Hermitian operator, i.e. $H^\dagger = H$. Further, $\hbar$ is the Planck constant. The Hamiltonian represents the *energy* of the system. There is a general solution to this equation:

$$|\Psi(t)\rangle \ = \ U(t)|\Psi(0)\rangle \ = \ e^{-\frac{i}{\hbar}Ht}|\Psi(0)\rangle \ , \tag{3.10}$$

where $|\Psi(0)\rangle$ is the initial state. Note that $U(t) = e^{-\frac{i}{\hbar}Ht}$ is continuous in $t$ and unitary. It is possible that $H$ depends on time as well, but we don't consider this here.

The second part of the quantum evolution mechanism describes the *collapse* of a quantum state, triggered by a so-called *measurement*. This collapse is governed by the so-called *Born rule*. When, why, or how such a collapse occurs is not part of quantum mechanics itself, but an environmental influence. That is why quantum mechanics is an open framework. A measurement is described by Hermitian operator $L$ and is called an *observable*. However, this operator is *not* applied to the state as a linear operation, like the evolution operator. Note that a Hermitian operators have a orthonormal basis of eigenvectors and all eigenvalues are reals. We assume the observables are *non-degenerate*, which means that for each eigenvalue there is only one eigenvector. Suppose the observable is $L$ with eigenvectors $|\lambda_i\rangle$ and corresponding eigenvalues $\lambda_i$. Then we can express the state $|\Psi(t)\rangle$ as $|\Psi(t)\rangle = \sum_i \alpha_i |\lambda_i\rangle$ with $\alpha_i = \langle\Psi(t)|\lambda_i\rangle$.

The Born rule states that the new state will be $|\lambda_i\rangle$ with probability $\alpha_i^*\alpha$. Note that $\sum_i \alpha_i^*\alpha_i = 1$, since all states are unit vectors. So, probability plays an essential role here. The state of a quantum system itself is not observable, but the result of a measurement is.

Quantum mechanics does not have an explicit probability model, but we will offer one below. To this end, we introduce a stochastic process $X(t)$ to describe measurements, related to the observables described above. Hence, the Born rule says:

$$\mathbb{P}[X(t) = \lambda_i] = \langle\lambda_i | \Psi(t)\rangle^*\langle\lambda_i | \Psi(t)\rangle = |\langle\lambda_i|\Psi(t)\rangle|^2 \ . \tag{3.11}$$

immediately after a measurement the state *collapses*, which means that the new state is $|\Psi(t)\rangle = |\lambda_i\rangle$, if $\lambda_i$ is measured. Stochastic variable $X(t)$ also determines the value of the measurement, the eigenvalue, but we sometimes neglect this.

Besides the probability, we can also compute the *expectation* of the measurement if $\Sigma = \mathbb{R}$ or $\Sigma = \mathbb{Z}$, with observable $L$:

$$\mathbb{E}[X(t)] = \langle\Psi | L | \Psi\rangle = \sum_i \lambda_i\mathbb{P}[X(t) = |\lambda_i\rangle] \ . \tag{3.12}$$

There are many familiar examples of observables. If we take the Hamiltonian of a system as observable, we measure the energy of the system. For a qubit we can measure its polarization, its angular velocity and its energy. For a single particle the *position* operator measures the position of the particle, and if we apply the *momentum* operator we measure its momentum. In many cases the observable is non-degenerate. Here the famous *Heisenberg* relation applies: it states that the product of the standard deviations of position $\sigma_x$ and momentum $\sigma_p$ satisfy: $\sigma_x.\sigma_p \geq \frac{\hbar}{2}$. This implies that we are not able to measure simultaneously position and momentum (velocity) with arbitrary precision.

So far, we have considered the evolution in continuous space and continuous time $U(t)$. A discrete version of quantum mechanics can be obtained by taking a small time step $\tau$, for instance the Planck time, and set $U = U(\tau)$.

By choosing $\tau = 1$ the discrete evolution becomes $|\Psi(t + 1)\rangle = U|\Psi(t)\rangle$. Combined with a discrete space, the Schroedinger equation becomes a difference equation. A straightforward approximation of the corresponding evolution mechanism appears to be non-unitary, and hence does not preserve probabilities. Using *cellular automata*, an evolution mechanism can be derived from the Schroedinger equation that is both unitary and local. (Locality means that the next state of each cell depends only on the current state of that cell and that of its immediate neighbors.) The evolution mechanism can then be described by a pair of unitary matrices, that are applied alternatingly to the state of the system as described by vector $\Psi(t)$. These so-called Schroedinger cellular automata were applied successfully to a wide range of quantum experiments [3].

## 3.4   Comparison

The similarities between the two formalisms are listed in Table 2. First note that both processes evolve deterministically until measurement is made. For the Markov process this means, as long as we do not observe the state by a measurement, we can compute the distribution by the evolution equation. As soon as we make a measurement of the Markov process the distribution of the state changes, except when the Markov process is in an steady state. Similarly the state of a quantum system evolves according to the evolution equation until a measurement and then the state becomes one of the eigen vectors of the measurement operator, the observable.

**Table 2.** A comparison of Markov processes and quantum mechanics.

| | Markov process | Quantum mechanics |
|---|---|---|
| Measurement space | $\Sigma$ | $\Sigma$ |
| State space | $S = \{\pi \mid \pi = \text{distribution on } \Sigma\}$ | $S = \text{Hilbert space over } \Sigma$ |
| State | $\pi(t) \in S$ | $\lvert\Psi(t)\rangle \in S$ |
| Differential equation | Kolmogorov $\frac{d}{dt}\pi(t) = \pi(t)Q$ | Schroedinger $\frac{d}{dt}\lvert\Psi(t)\rangle = -\frac{i}{\hbar}H\lvert\Psi(t)\rangle$ |
| Evolution | $\pi(t) = \pi(0)\exp(tQ)$ | $\lvert\Psi(t)\rangle = \exp\left(-\frac{i}{\hbar}Ht\right)\lvert\Psi(0)\rangle$ |
| Measurement | $X(t) \in \Sigma$ | $X(t) \in \Sigma$ by the Born rule |
| Probability | $\mathbb{P}[X(t) = i] = \pi_t(i)$ | $\mathbb{P}[X(t) = \lambda_n] = \lvert\langle\lambda_n\lvert\Psi(t)\rangle\rvert^2$ |

However, there are also essential differences. First of all, the imaginary $i$ in (3.9). This makes that the solutions are wave functions and not probability distributions as in (3.2). The Markov processes can be measured at any moment but, only if we observe it is we get a conditional distribution for the future based on it. Otherwise the distribution is given by the evolution equation like the quantum system. For the quantum system, the states are only probabilistic when a measurement is done.

Let's assume that we perform measurements at $n$ successive moments $(t_0, t_1, ...)$ with (non-degenerate) observables $L_1, L_2, ...$ In between these moments the process evolves deterministically based on unitary operator $U$. However, at these specified moments the processes is probabilistic. This deterministic evolution, interrupted by probabilistic measurement events, can be described by a Markov process, which is *embedded* in the evolution of the wave function. This is commonly called an embedded Markov process. If at $t_j$ a measurement is done with observable $L_j$ then the state is $|\lambda_j\rangle$ an eigenstate of $L_j$ and $\lambda_j$ the eigen valued is measured. Then until $t_{j+1}$ the system evolves according to the evolution equation and a new state $U^{t_{j+1}-t_j}|\lambda_j\rangle$ is reached just before the next measurement at $t_{j+1}$. According to the Born rule, the next state will be $|\lambda_{j+1}\rangle$ which is an eigenstate of observable $L_{j+1}$, with probability $|\langle\lambda_{j+1}|U^{t_{j+1}-t_j}|\lambda_j\rangle|^2$ and eigen value $\lambda_{j+1}$ will be measured. So, we derive:

$$\mathbb{P}\left[X(t_1) = \lambda_1, ..., X(t_n) = \lambda_n\right] = \prod_{i=0}^{n-1} |\langle\lambda_{j+1}|U^{t_{j+1}-t_j}|\lambda_j\rangle|^2 , \qquad (3.13)$$

where $|\lambda_0\rangle = |\psi_0\rangle$ is the initial state. Similar to the step from (3.3) to (3.4), we re-derive the Markov property.

$$\mathbb{P}\left[X(t_{k+1}) = \lambda_{k+1} \mid X(t_k) = \lambda_{k,}, ..., X(t_0) = \lambda_0\right] = \mathbb{P}\left[X(t_{k+1}) = \lambda_{k+1} \mid X(t_k) = \lambda_k\right] = \alpha^*\alpha ,$$
$$(3.14)$$

where $\alpha = \langle\lambda_{k+1}|U^{t_{k+1}-t_k}|\lambda_k\rangle$, which is the inner product of the eigenvector $|\lambda_{k+1}\rangle$ of $L_{k+1}$ and the state that is reached after the former measurement $U^{t_{k+1}-t_k}|\lambda_k\rangle$.[2] An example of an embedded Markov process with more than one step is the sequential Stern-Gerlach experiments discussed in Sect. 4.

Note that the Markov theory does not specify the Markov kernel $P$. It has to be determined by a model engineer, for example, a specific queuing system or a specific inventory system. Here we have a kernel that is determined by quantum mechanics. Hence, we conclude that quantum mechanics contains an embedded Markov process.

## 4  Sequential Stern-Gerlach Experiments

A sequential Stern-Gerlach experiment [25] offers a nice example of an embedded Markov process with more than one step. The original "single-step" experiment in 1922 decisively demonstrated that angular momentum (spin) at (sub-)atomic scale is quantized. The experiment is described in Fig. 1. The deflected silver atoms hit the detector screen at two distinct spots, corresponding to two discrete spin values: up and down.[3] According to classical physics, the condensed silver atoms on the screen should form a thin solid line, corresponding to a continuous range of possible spin values.

---

[2] In case we have also degenerate observables, we can't identify the eigenvectors and the eigenvalues. But we still have: $\mathbb{P}\left[X(t_1) = |\lambda_1\rangle, ..., X(t_n) = |\lambda_n\rangle\right] = \prod_{i=0}^{n-1}\langle\lambda_{j+1}|U^{t_{j+1}-t_j}|\lambda_j\rangle$. So, still a Markov process but now, the measurement space $\Sigma_M$ of the Markov chain is now an element of the Hilbert space over the measurement space $\Sigma_Q$.

[3] The deflection of the silver atoms is *not* the result of a Lorentz force that a moving *charged* particle would experience in a magnetic field. The silver atoms are neutral particles,.

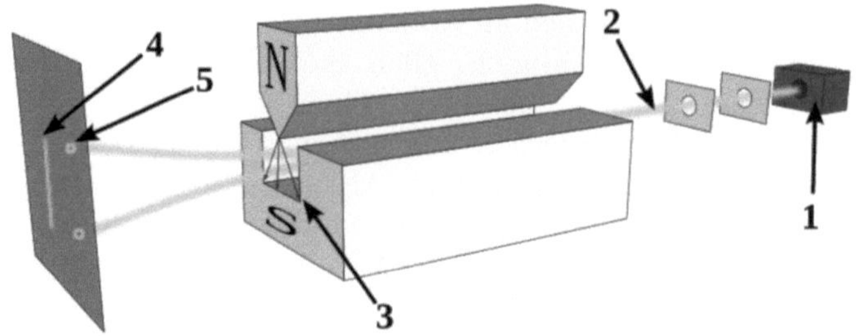

**Fig. 1.** The Stern-Gerlach experiment: Silver atoms travelling through an inhomogeneous magnetic field, and being deflected up or down depending on their spin; (1) furnace, (2) beam of silver atoms, (3) inhomogeneous magnetic field, (4) classically expected result, (5) observed result. Source: [25].

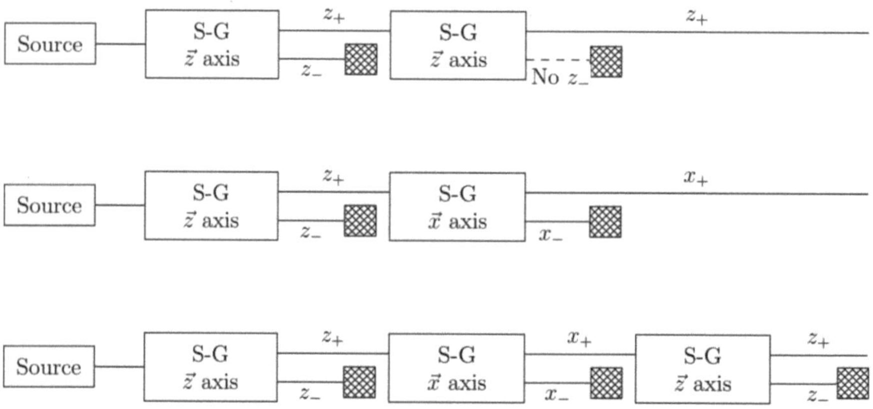

**Fig. 2.** Three sequential Stern-Gerlach experiments. Source: [25].

A sequential Stern-Gerlach experiment consists of a cascade of multiple SG apparatuses. Figure 2 shows three examples of sequential SG experiments. Each S-G box denotes an inhomogeneous magnetic field corresponding to a unitary operator $U^{t_{j+1}-t_j}$ in (3.13). Each cross-hatched box denotes a screen that blocks one of the two particle exits, and is part of a quantum measurement (observation) corresponding to a $\lambda_j, j > 0$ in (3.13). Note that for each stage only one of the two outputs has a detector, detecting only one of the two eigenstates. The other eigenstate is detected implicitly: if an incoming particle is not detected by the detector at lower output, it must have exit in the eigenstate corresponding the upper output.

The first stage of all three experiments detects the $z$ component of the spin. Observable $L_1$ has two eigenstates, labeled $z_-$ and $z_+$. The eigenstate with spin $z_-$ is detected explicitly, with probability of, say, $p_-$. By contrast, the probability $p_+$ for spin $z_+$ can be *inferred* as $p_+ = 1 - p_-$.

# 5   The Bell Experiment

Einstein often stated that quantum mechanics is incomplete. He based that statement on the EPR thought experiment [6]. He also argued that there have to be so-called *hidden variables*, yet unknown, in order to make quantum mechanics deterministic. Bell describes a variation of the EPR experiment [2], and presents a theorem that such hidden variables cannot exist. The Bell paper is cited over 16 thousand times, and debate on the Bell theorem and its consequences is *ongoing*.

The topic of the ongoing debate is whether or not quantum mechanics complies with probability theory. Below, we consider two probability models for the Bell experiment. A first model that is applied *implicitly* by most physicists leads to an artificial contradiction, and is a cause for much confusion. A second model, based on [10] is proposed as rigorous probability model that is fully consistent with all practical Bell experiments. We show that this model is *non-separable*, which implies that there cannot be any hidden variable that would make the model deterministic. Hence, the Bell experiment demonstrates that quantum mechanics is indeed probabilistic.

In the original Bell experiment an electron and a positron are formed in a *singlet spin state* and they move freely in opposite directions, one to the left and one to the right. On each side there are detectors to measure the *spin*, up or down also called -1 and +1. In a singlet spin state the spins of the two particles are maximal correlated, i.e. if one is up, then the other should be down and vice versa. The spins of the two particles are measured by detectors A (left) and B (right).

Here we focus on the more general CHSH version [5] of the Bell experiment: detector A has settings $a_0, a_1$ and detector B has $b_0, b_1$ and the selection among the available detector settings is possibly *random* and occurs possibly *after* the particle pair has been prepared and is on its way. (In Bell's original experiment there were in total only three detector settings). Furthermore, in the CHSH experiment the two entangled particles are a pair of photons, and the two detectors are so-called polarimeters.

## 5.1   A Model with Four Observables

Most researchers, including Bell, use an *implicit* probability model underlying the experiment. This model assumes four observables (or stochastic variables) $X_0, X_1, Y_0, Y_1$ corresponding to the four detector settings $a_0, a_1, b_0, b_1$. Although we observe in each experiment only two of them (one $X$ on the left-hand side and one $Y$ on the right-hand side) they assume that the others are there as well. This assumption is sometimes called *realism*. Note that these four random variables taking only values in $\{-1, 1\}$. The outcome space $\Omega$ for this experiment is given in Table 3.

The event space $\mathscr{F}$ is the power set of $\Omega$. We leave the probability measure unspecified, because the arguments we present hold for all possible probabilities measures. It is based on a simple, but famous, CHSH inequality [13]: if

**Table 3.** An outcome space for the CHSH experiment

|       | 1  | 2  | 3  | 4  | 5  | 6  | 7  | 8  | 9  | 10 | 11 | 12 | 13 | 14 | 15 | 16 |
|-------|----|----|----|----|----|----|----|----|----|----|----|----|----|----|----|----|
| $X_0$ | -1 | 1  | -1 | 1  | -1 | 1  | -1 | 1  | -1 | 1  | -1 | 1  | -1 | 1  | -1 | 1  |
| $X_1$ | -1 | -1 | 1  | 1  | -1 | -1 | 1  | 1  | -1 | -1 | 1  | 1  | -1 | -1 | 1  | 1  |
| $Y_0$ | -1 | -1 | -1 | -1 | 1  | 1  | 1  | 1  | -1 | -1 | -1 | -1 | 1  | 1  | 1  | 1  |
| $Y_1$ | -1 | -1 | -1 | -1 | -1 | -1 | -1 | -1 | 1  | 1  | 1  | 1  | 1  | 1  | 1  | 1  |

$Q, R, S, T \in \{-1, 1\}$ then

$$\left| QS + QT + RS - RT \right| \le 2 \ . \tag{5.1}$$

To prove the inequality for a more general case, the case, where the variables take values in $[-1, 1]$, we note that $\left| QS + QT + RS - RT \right| \le \left| Q(S+T) \right| + \left| R(S-T) \right| \le \left| S + T \right| + \left| S - T \right|$. The right-hand side equals $2|S|$ or $2|T|$, depending on the four cases of the signs of $S + T$ and $S - T$. So, for these four random variables we have:

$$\left| X_0 Y_0 + X_1 Y_0 + X_1 Y_1 - X_0 Y_1 \right| \le 2 \ . \tag{5.2}$$

Taking expectations we get:

$$\left| \mathbb{E}[X_0 Y_0] + \mathbb{E}[X_1 Y_0] + \mathbb{E}[X_1 Y_1] - \mathbb{E}[X_0 Y_1] \right| \le 2 \ . \tag{5.3}$$

Note that it holds for *any* probability measure on the outcome space of Table 3.

Next, we will summarize what quantum mechanics says about these quantities. For more details see [10]. The *quantum state* of an entangled photon pair can be described by

$$|\Psi\rangle = \frac{1}{\sqrt{2}} (\mathbf{e}_0 \otimes \mathbf{e}_1 - \mathbf{e}_1 \otimes \mathbf{e}_0) \ . \tag{5.4}$$

Here $\mathbf{e}_0 = (1, 0)^\top$ and $\mathbf{e}_1 = (0, 1)^\top$ are the two base vectors also known as up and down and $\otimes$ is the tensor operator. A detector setting with angle $\alpha$ is modeled by a Hermitian operator, $X_\alpha : \mathbb{C}^2 \to \mathbb{C}^2$, with $a \in [0, \pi)$ is the angle of the detector on the left side:

$$X_\alpha = \begin{bmatrix} \cos(2\alpha) & \sin(2\alpha) \\ \sin(2\alpha) & -\cos(2\alpha) \end{bmatrix} \ , \tag{5.5}$$

and an identical operator for $Y_\beta$ on the right side. The combined observation left and right means that the tensor product $X_\alpha \otimes Y_\beta$ is applied on the entangled state $|\Psi\rangle$. This operator is also Hermitian and is the observable of the experiment. In order to apply the Born rule, we need the eigenvectors of $X_\alpha \otimes Y_\beta$. They are the tensor products of the eigenvectors of $X_\alpha$ and $Y_\beta$ and the eigenvalues are the products of the eigenvalues of $X_\alpha$ and $Y_\beta$ and these are what we measure: 1 and $-1$ (or up and down). These can be calculated by standard methods (see

[10]). Applying the Born rule, see (3.11) we obtain:

$$\mathbb{P}[\,X_\alpha = i, Y_\beta = j] = \frac{1}{2}\sin^2(\alpha - \beta) \quad \text{if } i=j \tag{5.6}$$

$$= \frac{1}{2}\cos^2(\alpha - \beta) \quad \text{if } i \neq j,\ i,j \in \{-1,1\}\,. \tag{5.7}$$

In a similar way we can compute the expectations, using (3.12):

$$\mathbb{E}[X_\alpha Y_\beta] = \langle \Psi | X_\alpha \otimes Y_\beta | \Psi \rangle = \langle X_\alpha \otimes Y_\beta \rangle = -\cos(2(\alpha - \beta))\,. \tag{5.8}$$

Note that we use here the symbols $X$ and $Y$ for the random variables as well as for the operators $X$ and $Y$ they belong to.

Next, we will use the specific values for the detectors $\alpha : a_0, a_1$ and two for $\beta : b_0, b_1$. Also, we will re-introduce the four random variables belonging to outcome space of Table 3:

$$X_0 = a_0, X_1 = a_1, Y_0 = b_0, Y_1 = b_1\,. \tag{5.9}$$

Following [13], specific values for the detector settings will be chosen,

$$a_0 = 0, a_1 = \frac{1}{4}\pi, b_0 = \frac{5}{8}\pi, b_1 = \frac{7}{8}\pi\,. \tag{5.10}$$

They give the so-called Tsirelson's bound [14], where the Bell inequality allegedly is violated most. Use (5.8) to derive

$$\langle X_0 \otimes Y_0 \rangle = \langle X_1 \otimes Y_0 \rangle = \langle X_1 \otimes Y_1 \rangle = -\langle X_0 \otimes Y_1 \rangle = \frac{1}{2}\sqrt{2}\,, \tag{5.11}$$

which results in

$$\left| \langle X_0 \otimes Y_0 \rangle + \langle X_1 \otimes Y_0 \rangle + \langle X_1 \otimes Y_1 \rangle - \langle X_0 \otimes Y_1 \rangle \right| = 2\sqrt{2}\,, \tag{5.12}$$

which is clearly a *contradiction* with (5.8), using $\mathbb{E}[X_i Y_j] = \langle X_i \otimes Y_j \rangle$. The conclusion from this contradiction is that the probability model does not fit the quantum mechanical model of the experiment. The cause is that the assumption of four stochastic variables $X_0, X_1, Y_0, Y_1$ is wrong. There are only two observables and two detector settings, which means that $\langle X_i \otimes Y_j \rangle$ is a *conditional* expectation, and which implies that the step from (5.2) to (5.3) is not allowed, since the conditions are different. This will be explained in the next section.

### 5.2 A Model with Two Observables and Two Detector Settings

An appropriate probability model for the Bell experiment can be based on a different set of four stochastic variables: the two *observables* $X$ and $Y$ (who are also the measurements) and the two *settings* $A$ and $B$. Furthermore, the expressions $\langle X_\alpha \otimes Y_\beta \rangle$ is a *conditional* expectation:

$$\langle X_\alpha \otimes Y_\beta \rangle = \mathbb{E}[XY \mid A = \alpha, B = \beta]\,. \tag{5.13}$$

The corresponding (conditional) probability space is depicted in Table 4. Note that the outcomes of $A$ and $B$ should be known to compute the simultaneous probability of $X, Y$. This model is empirically validated, which means that repeated experiments for fixed $\alpha$ and $\beta$ give estimates for the four probabilities, that are very close to the computed values in Table 4.

**Table 4.** The conditional probability measure given $A = \alpha, B = \beta$.

|  |  | $\alpha$ | $A$ |
|---|---|---|---|
| $X$ | $Y$ | $\beta$ | $B$ |
| 1 | 1 | $\frac{1}{2}\sin^2(\alpha-\beta)$ | |
| $-1$ | 1 | $\frac{1}{2}\cos^2(\alpha-\beta)$ | |
| 1 | $-1$ | $\frac{1}{2}\cos^2(\alpha-\beta)$ | |
| $-1$ | $-1$ | $\frac{1}{2}\sin^2(\alpha-\beta)$ | |

When we fill in the specific parameters from (5.10) we obtain Table 5, which depicts the complete probability space: $\Omega = \{-1, 1\}^2 \times \{a_0, a_1\} \times \{b_0, b_1\}$ (a set of 16 cells), $\mathscr{F}$ is the power set of it and $\mathbb{P}[.]$ is represented by the content of the cells. It is easy to verify that $\mathbb{P}[A = a_i, B = b_j] = \frac{1}{4}$ for $i, j \in \{0, 1\}$, which means that $A$ and $B$ are *independent*.

**Table 5.** Probability measure with specific detector settings and all detector combinations the same probability

|  |  | $a_0$ | $a_1$ | $a_1$ | $a_0$ | $A$ |
|---|---|---|---|---|---|---|
| $X$ | $Y$ | $b_0$ | $b_0$ | $b_1$ | $b_1$ | $B$ |
| 1 | 1 | $\gamma^2/8$ | $\gamma^2/8$ | $\gamma^2/8$ | $\beta^2/8$ | |
| $-1$ | 1 | $\beta^2/8$ | $\beta^2/8$ | $\beta^2/8$ | $\gamma^2/8$ | |
| 1 | $-1$ | $\beta^2/8$ | $\beta^2/8$ | $\beta^2/8$ | $\gamma^2/8$ | |
| $-1$ | $-1$ | $\gamma^2/8$ | $\gamma^2/8$ | $\gamma^2/8$ | $\beta^2/8$ | |

$$\beta^2 = \sin^2\left(\tfrac{\pi}{8}\right) = \tfrac{1}{4}(2 - \sqrt{2})$$
$$\gamma^2 = \cos^2\left(\tfrac{\pi}{8}\right) = \tfrac{1}{4}(2 + \sqrt{2})$$

Note that the first three columns are identical, because $\sin^2(0 - \frac{5}{8}\pi) = \sin^2(\frac{1}{4}\pi - \frac{5}{8}\pi) = \sin^2(\frac{1}{4}\pi - \frac{7}{8}\pi) = \cos^2(\frac{1}{8}\pi) = \gamma^2$. Similarly, we derive for $(i, j) \in \{(0, 0), (1, 0), (1, 1)\}$:

$$\begin{aligned}
\mathbb{E}[XY \mid A = a_i, B = b_j] &= -\cos(2(a_i - b_j)) = \cos(\tfrac{1}{4}\pi) = \tfrac{1}{2}\sqrt{2}\,, \\
\mathbb{E}[XY \mid A = a_0, B = b_1] &= -\cos(\tfrac{1}{4}\pi) = -\tfrac{1}{2}\sqrt{2}\,.
\end{aligned} \tag{5.14}$$

So, this is consistent with (5.11) and (5.12) and therefore we don't have a contradiction. The step from (5.2) to (5.3) is allowed for expectations, but is incorrect for conditional expectations under different conditions. This is the cause of the earlier contradiction.

## 5.3   Some Consequences

With the appropriate probability model of Sect. 5.2 we got rid of the paradox. What does this probability model tell us about the existence of hidden variables? This question is addressed in detail in [10]. Here we summarize some of the results. From Table 5 it can be observed that $\mathbb{P}[X\!=\!x \mid A = \alpha, B\!=\!\beta] = \frac{1}{2}$. So, the outcome of detector A does *not* depend on the setting of detector B, and vice versa. This property is known as (statistical) locality [9] and also as no-signalling [4]. More precisely, the probability measure $\mathbb{P}$ is *statistically local* if

$$\mathbb{P}[X\!=\!x \mid A\!=\!\alpha, B\!=\!\beta] \;=\; \mathbb{P}[X\!=\!x \mid A\!=\!\alpha] \,, \tag{5.15}$$

and similarly for $Y$. From Table 5 we easily derive that $\mathbb{P}[X = x \mid A = \alpha, B = \beta] = \frac{1}{2}$. Hence $\mathbb{P}[X = x | A = \alpha] = \frac{1}{2}$ as well. Note that this property holds for all detector settings and for any probability $\mathbb{P}[A = \alpha, B = \beta]$, so also for any *arrangement* made by the observers, not withstanding that the particles are entangled. So, if an observer of one particle knows the outcome, he also knows what the other observer will see.

Next, we introduce a *hidden* variable in the probability model. In order to accommodate this hidden variable, the outcome space for the Bell experiment is extended with a random variable $L$, where the range of $L$ is $\Lambda$ which is assumed to be at most countable.

$$\Omega = \{-1,1\}^2 \times \{a_0, a_1\} \times \{b_0, b_1\} \times \Lambda \,. \tag{5.16}$$

Let random variable $L$ denote the *hidden variable* with $L(\omega) = \lambda$ if $\omega = (x, y, \alpha, \beta, \lambda)$ and probability distribution $\mathbb{P}[L = \lambda] = \rho(\lambda)$ (note that $\lambda$ is not an eigenvalue here). This model containing a hidden variable is *separable* [2,9] if, for all $x, y, \alpha, \beta$ :

$$p(x, y|\alpha, \beta) := \mathbb{P}[X\!=\!x, Y\!=\!y \mid A\!=\!\alpha, B\!=\!\beta] = \sum_{\lambda \in \Lambda} p_1(x|\alpha, \lambda).p_2(y|\beta, \lambda).\rho(\lambda) \,,$$

$$\tag{5.17}$$

where

$$p_1(x|\alpha, \lambda) \;:=\; \mathbb{P}[X\!=\!x \mid A\!=\!\alpha, L\!=\!\lambda] \quad \text{and} \quad p_2(y|\beta, \lambda) \;:=\; \mathbb{P}[Y\!=\!y \mid B\!=\!\beta, L\!=\!\lambda] \,. \tag{5.18}$$

Of course, the distribution should comply with the quantum-mechanical model, see Table (4). Critically, $L$ is *independent* of the detector settings $A$ and $B$. This assumption is known as *statistical independence* or *measurement independence*. See for example [9] for more detail.

If Bell separability holds, we derive:

$$\sum_{x,y} x.y.p(x,y|\alpha,\beta) \;=\; \sum_{\lambda\in\Lambda}(\sum_x x.p_1(x|\alpha,\lambda).\sum_y y.p_2(y|\beta,\lambda)).\rho(\lambda) \;, \qquad (5.19)$$

or, equivalently,

$$\mathbb{E}[XY|A=\alpha,B=\beta] \;=\; \sum_{\lambda\in\Lambda}\mathbb{E}[X|A=\alpha,L=\lambda].\mathbb{E}[Y|B=\beta,L=\lambda]).\rho(\lambda) \;.$$
$$(5.20)$$

We use this, by choosing the elements $a_0,a_1,b_0,b_1$ equal to (5.10) and we define

$$Q_\lambda := \mathbb{E}[X|A=a_0,L=\lambda], \; R_\lambda := \mathbb{E}[X|A=a_1,L=\lambda] \;, \qquad (5.21)$$

and

$$S_\lambda := \mathbb{E}[Y|B=b_0,L=\lambda], T_\lambda := \mathbb{E}[Y|B=b_1,L=\lambda] \;. \qquad (5.22)$$

Note that $Q_\lambda, R_\lambda, T_\lambda$, and $S_\lambda$, are all in $[-1,1]$.

So, by the assumption of separability, we obtain:

$$
\begin{aligned}
\mathbb{E}[XY|A=a_0,B=b_0] = \sum_\lambda Q_\lambda S_\lambda\rho(\lambda), \quad \mathbb{E}[XY|A=a_0,B=b_1] = \sum_\lambda Q_\lambda T_\lambda\rho(\lambda)\\
\mathbb{E}[XY|A=a_1,B=b_0] = \sum_\lambda R_\lambda S_\lambda\rho(\lambda), \quad \mathbb{E}[XY|A=a_1,B=b_1] = \sum_\lambda R_\lambda T_\lambda\rho(\lambda) \;.
\end{aligned}
\qquad (5.23)
$$

By (5.14) we have

$$\mathbb{E}[XY|A=a_0,B=b_0] = \frac{1}{2}\sqrt{(2)} \;, \qquad (5.24)$$

and similar for the others. So, on the one hand

$$
\begin{aligned}
\mathbb{E}[XY|A=a_0,B=b_0] + \mathbb{E}[XY|A=a_0,B=b_1]\\
+ \mathbb{E}[XY|A=a_1,B=b_1] - \mathbb{E}[XY|A=a_0,B=b_1]) = 2\sqrt{2} \;,
\end{aligned}
\qquad (5.25)
$$

and on the other hand the left-hand side of (5.25) equals:

$$\sum_\lambda (Q_\lambda S_\lambda + R_\lambda T_\lambda + R_\lambda S_\lambda - Q_\lambda T_\lambda)\rho(\lambda) \;. \qquad (5.26)$$

By the CHSH inequality (5.1) for each $\lambda\in\Lambda$:

$$|Q_\lambda S_\lambda + R_\lambda T_\lambda + R_\lambda S_\lambda - Q_\lambda T_\lambda| \le 2 \;. \qquad (5.27)$$

And therefore:

$$\sum_{\lambda\in\Lambda} (Q_\lambda S_\lambda + R_\lambda T_\lambda + R_\lambda S_\lambda - Q_\lambda T_\lambda)\rho(\lambda) \le 2 \;. \qquad (5.28)$$

Hence, now we do have a *contradiction*. Using the CHSH-inequality, we proved that the probability measure of our probability model is *not* separable. Our proof here for non-separability is similar to the proof in [4]. A different proof without the CHSH-inequality is given in [10].

In summary we conclude that there does not exist a hidden variable that makes our probability measure separable. (Note that we did not assume any structure of the hidden variable.) In [10] it is proved that such separability would *imply* determinism, i.e. the probability measure $\mathbb{P}[X=x, Y=y \mid A=\alpha, B=\beta] \in \{0,1\}$. Hence, we have proved here that quantum mechanics is probabilistic, and therefore also non-deterministic.

## 6   Random Versus Chaotic Behavior

Mainstream quantum mechanics is non-deterministic, as demonstrated in Sect. 4. Could it be that at some deeper level there exists a fully deterministic theory for quantum mechanics? This question has been addressed by Einstein, 't Hooft [8], Hossenfelder and Palmer [11] and others. As we have seen above, the extra assumption of a hidden variable does not make quantum mechanics deterministic. In this section we will show that it is possible in principle to extend the probabilistic framework with a mechanism to make it deterministic. However, it has no practical value as it does not make modeling or analysis simpler.

We start with the introduction of a *random process*. That is a stochastic process $R_n, n \in \mathbb{N}$ where $R_n$ and $R_m$ are *independent* for $n \neq m$ and $R_n$ is *uniformly distributed* for all $n \in \mathbb{N}$, i.e.

$$\mathbb{P}[a < R_n \leq b] = b - a \text{ for all } 0 \leq a \leq b \leq 1 . \tag{6.1}$$

From such a random process we can construct *every* discrete Markov process by a classical procedure for generation of random numbers from a distribution $\pi$, using a uniform distributed stochastic variable (see e.g. [19]).

We define a function $F : \Pi \times [0, 1] \to \Sigma$ where $\Pi$ is the set of all distributions on $\Sigma$. For a distribution $\pi$ on some measurement space $\Sigma$ by:

$$F(\pi, x) = k \text{ if and only if } \sum_{j=0}^{k-1} \pi(j) < x \leq \sum_{j=0}^{k} \pi(j)) , \tag{6.2}$$

It is easy to verify that for a uniformly distributed stochastic variable $R$:

$$\mathbb{P}[F(\pi, R) = k] = \pi(k) , \tag{6.3}$$

since

$$\mathbb{P}[F(\pi, R) = k] \; = \; \mathbb{P}[\sum_{j=0}^{k-1} \pi(j) < R \leq \sum_{j=0}^{k} \pi(j))] \; = \; \sum_{j=0}^{k} \pi(j)) - \sum_{j=0}^{k-1} \pi(j) = \pi(k) . \tag{6.4}$$

To construct a *Markov process* in this way, we define distribution $\pi_i$ on $\Sigma$ by:

$$\pi_i(j) = P_{i,j} \text{ for } i, j \in \Sigma . \tag{6.5}$$

Given a random process $R_n, n \in \mathbb{N}$ we define a Markov process $X_n, n \in T$:

$$X_0 := F(\pi_0, R_0)$$
$$X_n := F(\pi_{X_{n-1}}, R_n) \quad \text{for } n > 0 . \tag{6.6}$$

To verify the the Markov property still holds, note that $X_n$ is a function of $R_0, ..., R_n$ only, so it is independent of $R_{n+1}$:

$$\mathbb{P}[X_{n+1} = j \mid X_0 = i_0, ..., X_n = i] = \mathbb{P}[F(\pi_i, R_{n+1}) = j \mid X_0 = i_0, ..., X_n = i]$$
$$= \mathbb{P}[F(\pi_i, R_{n+1}) = j] = \pi_i(j) = P_{i,j} .$$
$$\tag{6.7}$$

For quantum mechanics we have a similar procedure, using the embedded Markov process as in (3.14). So, now the remaining problem is how to make such random processes? We consider two approaches.

The first approach is using a *chaotic* deterministic process [15]. These processes are often used as *random number generators*, [1]. Classical examples are *linear congruences* $R_{n+1} = (aR_n + b) \mod m$, where $m$ is a large number, often a Mersenne number $M_n := 2^n - 1$ for $n \in \mathbb{N}$. (If $n$ is prime then $M_n$ is prime as well). These generators are periodical, so not "random". There are much better random number generators with extremely large periods. For instance the Mersenne Twister (MT) [22] is a very good one. The MT(19937) has a period of $2^{19973} - 1$ what is ca $10^{6001}$. The age of the universe measured in nanoseconds is only $10^{26}$. There are other mechanisms to produce random sequences with extreme large periods, e.g. the cellular automaton with rule R30 (see [26]).

If we define a *random sequence* as the realization of a random process, then it is clear that an infinite periodical sequence with period $p$ is not random, since we know that, for $0 \le k \le p$: $\mathbb{E}[R_k.R_{k+np}] = \mathbb{E}[R_k^2]$ and so $\mathrm{cov}(X_k, X_{k+np}) = \mathbb{E}[R_k^2] - (\mathbb{E}[R_k])^2 > 0$ which should be zero if $R_k$ and $R_{k+np}$ are independent. It is easy to prove that every sequence of numbers, produced by a finite state machine, should be periodic in the long run. So, infinite random sequences can't be produced by finite state machines.

Turing machines with an unbounded tape could produce non periodic sequences. To verify this note that there is an algorithm and so a Turing machine, that can produce all the digits in the decimal development of the number $\pi$ (see [17]). This machine only needs a tape of finite length for any computed digit. And we know that the decimal developments of irrational numbers are aperiodic.

To *test* if a mechanism is producing random numbers, we only can use a *finite* sequence of these numbers. There are many good statistical tests for instance a test suite called Diehard Test (see [18]). However, there exists no statistical test that can formally decide whether or not a given finite sequence is produced by a random process. Accordingly, we can make the following assumption:

*There exist chaotic processes in the universe that can't be distinguished from a random processes.*

By this assumption there is a chaotic process $\{R_n | n \in \mathbb{N}\}$ that satisfies the properties of a random process as defined in (6.1).

With the construction of (6.2) and (6.3) we have argued that Markov processes, and by implication quantum mechanics, can be made deterministic. A hidden variable was not sufficient, but a chaotic process is. With this assumption we can say that the outcomes of a stochastic process are "computed" in stead of "sampled".

## 7 Conclusion

In this paper we analyzed and compared two probabilistic modeling frameworks in some detail, namely Markov processes and quantum mechanics. We found that quantum mechanics contains an embedded Markov process.

The Bell experiment shows that quantum mechanics is probabilistic. The evolution process itself is based on a deterministic (unitary) operator. However, each measurement converts the (complex) wave function into a probability density. It is this conversion that makes quantum mechanics non-deterministic. For the many practical applications of quantum mechanics this probabilistic and non-deterministic interpretation works very well. Furthermore, this model is fully compatible with all known experiments, including the Bell experiment. We also have seen that a hypothetical hidden variable does not make the framework deterministic.

However, this probabilistic *interpretation* does not rule out that quantum mechanics at some deeper level can be based on a fully deterministic theory. We consider and contrast two possible viewpoints on such a deterministic theory: 1) *superdeterminism* and 2) our *chaotic determinism*.

Hossenfelder and Palmer [11] present a good overview of *superdeterminism*, earlier proposed by 't Hooft and others to address a loophole in Bell's theorem. According to superdeterminism, the preparation of the entangled photon pair and the setting of the detectors have a common cause. This means that the outcomes of $A$ and $B$ are known already before the particles are prepared. So they give up *statistical independence*. They make this assumption in order to avoid the assumption of information transport faster than light.

Our proposal for a deterministic version of quantum mechanics relies on some form of chaotic processes [16]. It is open in the sense that the values of $A$ and $B$ are determined in the environment of the system after the preparation of the particles, computed by a chaotic process. But also we pay a price: we assume that the deterministic procedure somehow knows the values of $A$ and $B$ before it selects the outcomes $X$ and $Y$ from Table 4. As we have seen in (5.15), this does not mean that there is *information transfer* between the two detectors. But some "random mechanism" sees the information immediately.

This deterministic perspective does not offer any practical implications, does not give us new tools for prediction, and may even be seen as some artificial trick.

# References


1. Banks, J.: Handbook of simulation principles, methodology, advances, applications, and practice. Wiley online books, Wiley, New York (1998)
2. Bell, J.S.: On the einstein podolsky rosen paradox. Physics **1**, 195200 (1964). https://doi.org/10.1103/PhysicsPhysiqueFizika.1.195. https://cds.cern.ch/record/111654
3. van Berkel, K., de Graaf, J., van Hee, K.: Experiments with Schrödinger cellular automata. Quantum **9**, 1811 (2025). https://doi.org/10.22331/q-2025-07-23-1811
4. Brunner, N., Cavalcanti, D., Pironio, S., Scarani, V., Wehner, S.: Bell nonlocality. Rev. Mod. Phys. **86**, 419–478 (2014). https://doi.org/10.1103/RevModPhys.86.419. https://link.aps.org/doi/10.1103/RevModPhys.86.419
5. Clauser, J.F., Horne, M.A., Shimony, A., Holt, R.A.: Proposed experiment to test local hidden-variable theories. Phys. Rev. Lett. **23**, 880–884 (1969). https://doi.org/10.1103/PhysRevLett.23.880. https://link.aps.org/doi/10.1103/PhysRevLett.23.880
6. Einstein, A., Podolsky, B., Rosen, N.: Can quantum-mechanical description of physical reality be considered complete? Phys. Rev. **47**, 777–780 (1935). https://doi.org/10.1103/PhysRev.47.777
7. Feller, W.: An Introduction to Probability Theory and Its Applications, vol. 1. Wiley (1968). http://www.amazon.ca/exec/obidos/redirect?tag=citeulike04-20&path=ASIN/0471257087
8. Gerard 't Hooft: The Cellular Automaton Interpretation of Quantum Mechanics. Springer (2015)
9. Hall, M.J.W.: The significance of measurement independence for bell inequalities and locality. In: At the Frontier of Spacetime. Springer (2015)
10. van Hee, K., van Berkel, K., de Graaf, J.: An Appropriate Probability Model for the Bell Experiment (2023). https://arxiv.org/abs/2302.05174
11. Hossenfelder, S., Palmer, T.: Rethinking superdeterminism. Front. Phys. **8** (2020). https://doi.org/10.3389/fphy.2020.00139
12. Kolmogorov, A.N.: Grundbegriffe der Wahrscheinlichkeitsrechnung. Springer, Berlin (1933), second English Edition, *Foundations of Probability* 1950, published by Chelsea, New York
13. Nielsen, M.A., Chuang, I.L.: Quantum Computation and Quantum Information. Cambridge University Press (2000)
14. Pál, K.F., Vértesi, T.: Platonic Bell inequalities for all dimensions. Quantum **6**, 756 (2022). https://doi.org/10.22331/q-2022-07-07-756
15. Strogatz, S.H.: Nonlinear Dynamics and Chaos: With Applications to Physics, Biology. Chemistry and Engineering. Westview Press (2000)
16. Wikipedia contributors: Chaos theory — Wikipedia, the free encyclopedia (2025). https://en.wikipedia.org/wiki/Chaos_theory. Accessed Sept 2025
17. Wikipedia contributors: Chudnovsky algorithm—Wikipedia, the free encyclopedia (2025). https://en.wikipedia.org/wiki/Chudnovsky_algorithm. Accessed Sept 2025
18. Wikipedia contributors: Diehard tests—Wikipedia, the free encyclopedia (2025). https://en.wikipedia.org/wiki/Diehard_tests. Accessed Sept 2025
19. Wikipedia contributors: Inverse transforming sampling—Wikipedia, the free encyclopedia (2025). https://en.wikipedia.org/wiki/Inverse_transforming_sampling. Accessed Sept 2025

20. Wikipedia contributors: Markov chain— Wikipedia, the free encyclopedia (2025). https://en.wikipedia.org/wiki/Markov_chain. Accessed Sept 2025
21. Wikipedia contributors: Markov kernel — Wikipedia, the free encyclopedia (2025). https://en.wikipedia.org/wiki/Markov_kernel. Accessed Sept 2025
22. Wikipedia contributors: Mersenne twister — Wikipedia, the free encyclopedia (2025). https://en.wikipedia.org/wiki/Mersenne_Twister. Accessed Sept 2025
23. Wikipedia contributors: Probability space — Wikipedia, the free encyclopedia (2025). https://en.wikipedia.org/wiki/Probability_space. Accessed Sept 2025
24. Wikipedia contributors: Quantum mechanics — Wikipedia, the free encyclopedia (2025). https://en.wikipedia.org/wiki/Quantum_mechanics. Accessed Sept 2025
25. Wikipedia contributors: Stern–gerlach experiment — Wikipedia, the free encyclopedia (2025). https://en.wikipedia.org/wiki/Stern--Gerlach_experiment. Accessed Sept 2025
26. Wolfram, S.: A New Kind of Science. Wolfram Media (2002). http://www.amazon.com/exec/obidos/ASIN/1579550088/ref=nosim/rds-20

# Interaction of Petri Net Process Models

Jörg Desel[(✉)]

FernUniversität in Hagen, Universitätsstraße 1, 58097 Hagen, Germany
`joerg.desel@fernuni-hagen.de`

**Abstract.** The most common composition mechanism for Petri nets synchronizes transitions of two nets by merging them: two transitions are merged into one whose input places consists of all input places of the two transitions in their respective nets, and accordingly for the output places. This approach seems appropriate in applications where components are permanently connected, and therefore their models can be composed. However, it becomes very complex and even unsuitable when dealing with dynamically changing connection relations.

This contribution introduces a different composition mechanism tailored for the dynamic composition of Petri nets. We will call this *interaction*. The core idea is that when Petri net components interact, corresponding (interacting) transitions are merged, as is the case for composition, but the original transitions are preserved and available for further interactions.

The approach is motivated by various Petri net examples and applied to Workflow nets, where it incorporates several early concepts introduced by Wil van der Aalst.

**Keywords:** Petri net composition · Petri net interaction · Workflow nets

## 1 Introduction

Process modeling within the framework of Business Process Management is probably the most important application of Petri nets today. Process mining is largely based on algorithms that operate on Petri nets at their core. In this respect, Petri nets also form the basis of applications that are currently revolutionizing the process landscape in business. One can therefore state: Petri nets are very lucrative. Conversely, this application area has breathed new life into the aging world of Petri nets.

This entire branch of research is rightly attributed today to Wil van der Aalst. An AI-powered internet search yields the following:

> Professor Wil van der Aalst, a Dutch computer scientist at RWTH Aachen University, who is widely known as the "Godfather of Process Mining" for his foundational research and pioneering work in the field of analyzing and improving business processes.


J. Mendling et al. (Eds.): Wil van der Aalst Festschrift, LNCS 16480, pp. 284–297, 2026.
https://doi.org/10.1007/978-3-032-17618-9_21

Wil's success probably began with the publication of the definition of *Work-flow nets* [1,2] almost 30 years ago. This concept was accepted by the Petri net community at that time, but evaluated according to the then-prevailing criteria of mathematical difficulty and correctness. In fact, Wil established a connection between the *soundness* property of Workflow nets he introduced and well-behavedness (liveness and boundedness) prevalent in Petri nets, which saved his paper for the Petri net conference.

However, the groundbreaking concept of Workflow nets was not this (albeit beautiful) result. Rather, it was the perfectly suited abstraction of processes, which, in its simplification, not only enables the representation of business processes, but also their analysis. The diverse concepts and methods of Petri net theory could now be applied to process models.

Nowadays, the term "workflow" may seem somewhat old-fashioned. It was based on the then promising abstract concept that information systems have a workflow engine that reads syntactic representations of processes and then executes these processes. Other authors established a connection between workflow management and processes to Petri nets earlier or around the same time [14,15,17,18].

One of the key abstractions of Workflow nets is that they consider a process in isolation and only model its one-time execution. However, Wil also proposed an extension that allows a transition from the final state back to the initial state. This was motivated purely technically, to connect sound Workflow nets with well-behaved Petri nets. However, this feedback transition signifies much more: it abstracts the rest of the system to a single transition, while the level of abstraction of the depicted process is significantly lower. In the extended process model, this additional transition represents abstract behavior of the environment. It should not be viewed like other, process-internal transitions, but rather as a conceivable transition of the process environment.

Several years later, Wil and colleagues discovered that some essential processes were represented too inaccurately by Petri nets. In particular, Petri nets could not distinguish certain control structures of processes that express different behavior in the application context and especially when using tools. This was the birth of process pattern [4,6] and the more expressive process description language YAWL [3,5], which, roughly speaking, supplements Petri nets with meaningful annotations and introduces certain abbreviations. The aspect relevant to this article is the explicit introduction of transitions whose occurrence depend on the unmodeled external world. For example, an envelope symbol was used to illustrate that an action (modeled by a transition) depends on a message from the outside. Many of these concepts are found in BPMN, the leading process notation today.

Both the feedback transition in Workflow nets and the annotated transitions in YAWL are used to express external, unmodeled behavior that nevertheless influences the process under consideration. Somewhat surprisingly, the distinction between transitions with and without external influence is treated rather superficially in Petri nets. In this paper, we will argue that the interaction between multiple Petri nets with common transitions can occur in two fundamentally different ways, which we call *composition* and *interaction*. As we will show, both are relevant for process models and already for Workflow nets and YAWL nets.

We will not start with process models, but instead with the author's current favorite examples: a vending machine and chameleons that change their color according to certain rules, in sections two and three. The fourth section is devoted to a formal definition of interaction and some properties. In the fifth section, the introduced concepts are related to Workflow nets and YAWL nets.

Sections two to four can be viewed as an elaborated version of [12].

## 2  First Example: The Vending Machine

An introductory lecture on Petri nets often begins with Petri net models of vending machines, see e.g. [13,19]. Such a model (from the Petri Net Course at the Petri Net Conferences) is shown in Fig. 1.

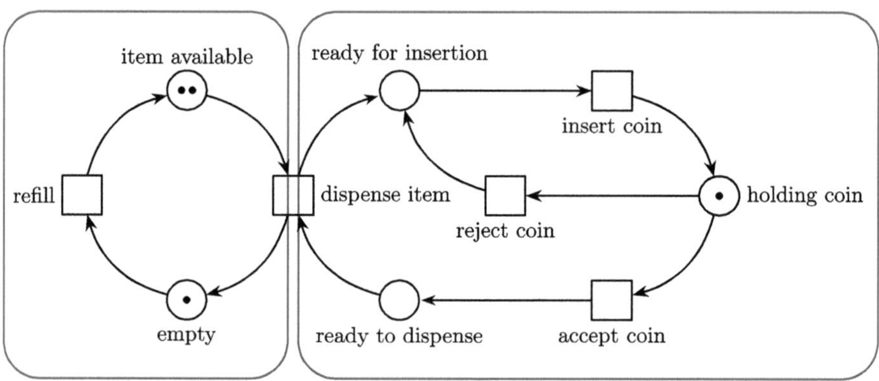


**Fig. 1.** Petri net model of a vending machine.

This example can explain a lot:

- There is a left hand component that describes the physical flow of goods and thus the physical part of a vending machine. This model is a place/transition Petri net. The number of tokens in a place indicates how many goods are located at that position.
- The right hand component models the internal logic of the automaton, represented by an elementary net system. Places of this component are therefore to be interpreted as conditions that can either be true or false.
- The example shows that both Petri net components, although they have different Petri net types, can be merged at the common transition "dispense item". The composed Petri net represents the overall behavior of the vending machine.

- The example was also created to represent alternatives (between "accept coin" and "reject coin") and little concurrency (for example between "refill" and "accept coin") in one figure.
- Considering the transitions "dispense item" separately in both components, both of them model an activity of the (hardware or software) system, that cannot occur without each other in the modeled composed system. No item can be dispensed without accepted money, and each signal "dispense item" should be accompanied by an actual dispense.
- There are further transitions of this Petri net that represent activities that also require an external partner. For example, one would not expect the system to insert a coin into itself. Therefore, the transition "insert coin" must merge with a transition from some customer model. The given model abstracts from this interaction, but we have to remember that the system cannot perform this activity on its own. The same applies to the transition "refill". We will call these two transitions *external*.
- For other activities, the responsibility lies solely with the modeled system. After a coin has been inserted, one can expect that the system proceeds without further interaction. The corresponding transitions "accept coin" and "reject coin" are said to be *internal*. Notice that the alternative between these two transitions is also considered internal. Although the criterion for coin acceptance is missing in the model and both transitions appear to occur randomly upon activation, the missing model of a coin acceptor is nevertheless internal.

Since almost every modeled system has some relations to the outside world which is not in the focus of the model, a Petri net is usually just a model of a system component that is potentially connected to models of other components. One could therefore assume that the transition "insert coin" is merged in a larger model with a transition of another Petri net – the model of a customer. However, this is not entirely true: while the two components of the vending machine model cooperate closely and permanently with each other, this is not the case when connecting to a model of a customer inserting a coin. A model composition with a customer model would represent that this would be the only customer forever; no other customer could dock to the "insert coin" transition. This is not the desired behavior. Instead, we need a dynamic composition operator where, in a single run (describing, for example, the behavior of a day), multiple customers use the machine, and thus multiple customer models can merge with the same transition of the vending machine model. We will call this operator *interaction*.

## 3   Second Example: The Chameleon Game

The chameleon game, originally found in [10] and [8], was modeled and analyzed with Petri nets in [11]. Although it is a rather unrealistic game, it deals with aspects of distributed systems with a high degree of concurrency, which is the favorite area of Petri nets. A description of the game reads as follows:

Some chameleons live quite happily in a large terrarium. There are $x$ red, $y$ blue, and $z$ green ones. These chameleons have a strange property: whenever two chameleons of different colors meet, both take on the third color. For example, when a blue and a green chameleon meet, they both turn red. And when a red and a green chameleon meet, they both turn blue.

In [11] termination and deadlock properties were studied, based on the respective initial numbers of red, blue and green chameleons. Now we want to focus on models of the chameleons that adequately describe their behavior.

Let us start with a correct model of one chameleon:

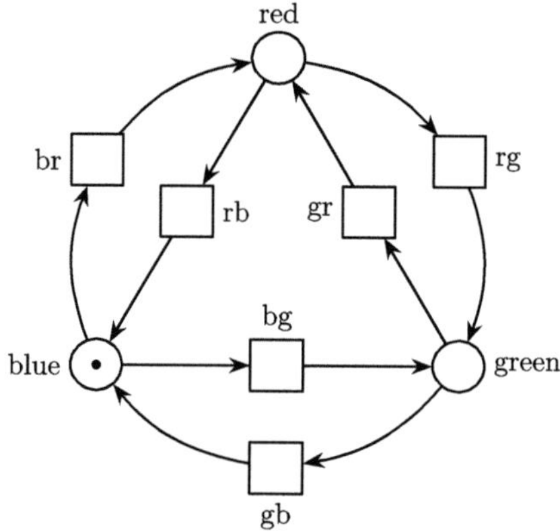


**Fig. 2.** Petri net model of one chameleon.

As Fig. 2 shows, a chameleon in a certain color can change to both other colors, resulting in a Petri net with three places (conditions) and six transitions. However, the rule of the chameleon game tells us that a chameleon cannot change color unless it contacts another chameleon. So, this model represents a single chameleon in some context, and all its transitions need to synchronize with transitions of other models representing other components of the assumed world. Referring to the terminology of the previous section, all six transitions are *external*.

Now let us look at a model for two chameleons, built by composition of two of the above Petri nets. Since every color change of one chameleon (say *red* $\rightarrow$ *blue*) corresponds to exactly one change of the other chameleon (here *green* $\rightarrow$ *blue*), there is a one-to-one match between the respective sets of transitions. The resulting net is shown in Fig. 3.

In this model, all transitions are *internal* because they cannot be composed with anything else. The net describes the complete behavior of two chameleons, provided that both will never contact a third one. However, its behavior is a bit boring: either both chameleons have the same color and therefore no transition is enabled (deadlock), or they have different colors (as depicted in the figure) and exactly one transition is enabled, the occurrence of which leads to a deadlock.

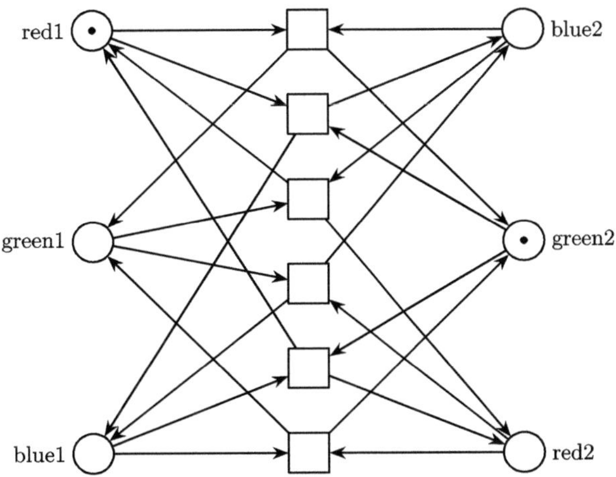

**Fig. 3.** Petri net model of two chameleons.

Instead, we are aiming for a model of two chameleons that is extendable. That is, the model should specify two chameleons that can interact as the ones modeled in Fig. 3, but can also encounter further chameleons. For this, the composition of two chameleon models should not "consume" all transitions (making them internal), because this interaction may occur only once, and then the same transition should be able to synchronize with another transition.

Figure 4 shows a Petri net model of two chameleons that interact as specified (internal transitions, annotated by $i$) but are also able to interact with other, unmodeled chameleons (external transitions, annotated with $e$).

## 4    The Interaction Operator

The considerations of the previous section leads to a new composition operator, called *interaction*. Figure 5 illustrates the classical composition operator and Fig. 6 the novel interaction operator.

The classical composition represents a fixed connection between two components at their interfaces, such as a plug and socket. Interaction, on the other hand, is suitable for representing non-permanent connections between components, such as communication via telephone. Consequently, composition reduces the available channels of the communicating partners, while this is not the case with interaction. Therefore, the two approaches are not in competition, but rather model different concepts.

While composition reduces the size of models (slightly) through transition merging, interaction increases it (slightly) through additional transitions. Therefore, the price for greater flexibility in interaction is a higher complexity of the models. At the end of this section, however, we will show how composition can be expressed through interaction and an additional unary operator that essentially hides external transitions.

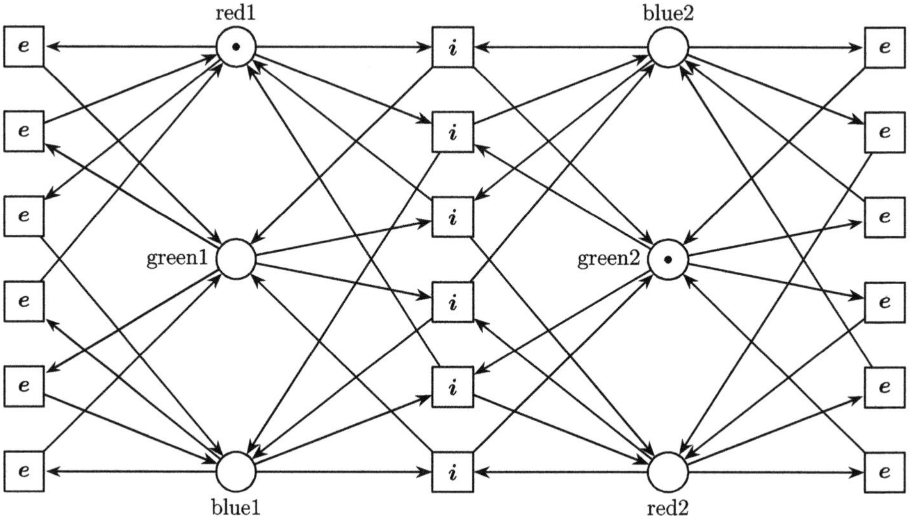

**Fig. 4.** A Petri net module for two chameleons, external transitions are marked by $e$, internal transitions are marked by $i$.

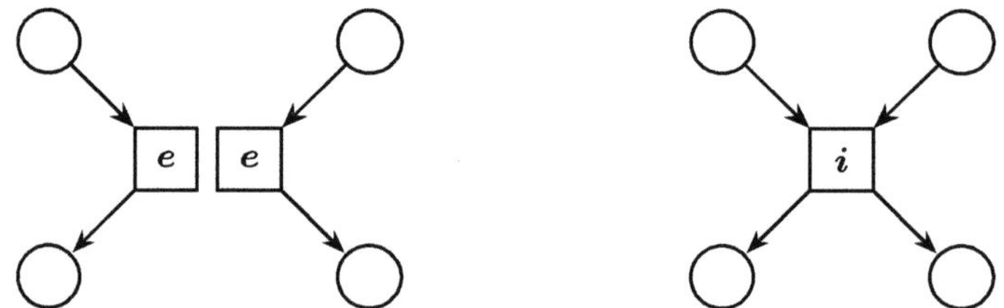

**Fig. 5.** The composition operator ($e$ and $i$ denote external and internal transitions).

**Definition 1.** *If an external transition $t_1$ of a Petri net $N_1$ interacts with an external transition $t_2$ of a Petri net $N_2$, then the resulting Petri net will have all the net elements and arcs of the nets $N_1$ and $N_2$ (in particular, $t_1$ and $t_2$ are still external transitions), and additionally a new internal transition $t$ satisfying* $^\bullet t = {}^\bullet t_1 \cup {}^\bullet t_2$ *and* $t^\bullet = t_1^\bullet \cup t_2^\bullet$.

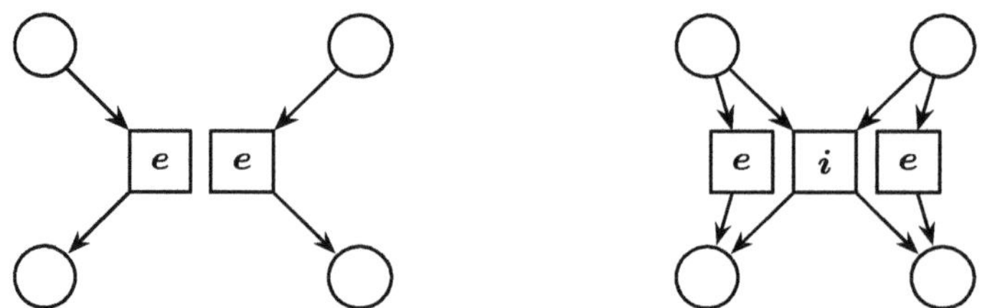

**Fig. 6.** The interaction operator ($e$ and $i$ denote external and internal transitions).

Merging two chameleon models by this interaction results in the Petri net shown in Fig. 4, which again has external transitions. The reader might argue that this Petri net interaction results in a Petri net with undesirable behavior: The internal transitions represent steps that are legal according to the rules of the chameleon game, whereas the external transitions represent illegal behavior, at least if the composed net is considered the final result.

So we distinguish the potential behavior of a Petri net given an arbitrary environment (*external behavior*) from the behavior of a Petri net which only uses its internal transitions (*internal behavior*). The internal behavior of the Petri net shown in Fig. 4 equals the behavior of the net of Fig. 3. It represents the behavior of two chameleons, which are the only ones, whereas the external behavior represents their potential behavior in a context.

**Definition 2.** *A Petri net module is a Petri net* $N = (S, T, F, M_0)$ *with a set* $T^e \subseteq T$ *of external transitions. If* $T^e \neq \emptyset$ *then we call the module* open Petri net, *otherwise* closed Petri net.

**Definition 3.** *Assume two Petri net modules* $N_1$ *and* $N_2$ *with disjoint sets of elements and a relation* $R \subseteq T_1^e \times T_2^e$. *Their interaction* $N_1 \circ N_2$ *is defined by the unions of places, transitions, arcs, markings (viewed as relations), plus additional transitions* $(x, y)$ *for each pair* $(x, y)$ *in* $R$. *For each* $(x, y) \in R$ *and each arc* $(s, x)$ *of* $N_1$ *or* $(s, y)$ *of* $N_2$ *we add an arc* $(s, (x, y))$, *and for each arc* $(x, s)$ *of* $N_1$ *or* $(y, s)$ *of* $N_2$ *we add an arc* $((x, y), s)$. *The set of external transitions of* $N_1 \circ N_2$ *is the union of external transitions of the component nets, i.e., the new transitions are internal.*

**Lemma 1.** *Petri net module interaction is commutative, i.e.* $N_1 \circ_R N_2 = N_2 \circ_{R^{-1}} N_1$, *where* $\circ_R$ *denotes interaction with respect to relation* $R$. *It is also associative, i.e.* $(N_1 \circ_{R_1} N_2) \circ_{R_2} N_3 = N_1 \circ_{R_1} (N_2 \circ_{R_2} N_3)$.

These rules follow immediately from the definition of Petri net module interaction. Notice that these properties are not trivial when it comes to a syntactical representation of the relation $R$, as discussed in detail in the HERAKLIT approach [16].

By associativity, repeated use of the interaction operator allows to build arbitrarily large net modules. Since we assume disjoint nets in the definition, we must take care to add always "new" net modules, although these might be copies of the same pattern. This is the case for the chameleon example – each chameleon model needs new names for places and transitions. Instead of this assumption, we could have shifted disjointness into the construction: if nets are not disjoint, then the operator distinguishes the elements of the components before performing the actual composition. This way we can specify large nets syntactically by e.g. $N \circ N \circ N \circ N \circ N$ or even $N^5$.

Interaction of net modules allows to specify sets of modules that can interact arbitrarily, just in the sense of [7]. In contrast, composition is used to restrict possible interactions. For example, we could model chameleons $c_0, c_1, \ldots, c_{n-1}$ such that chameleon $c_i$ can only interact with chameleons $c_{i-1(\mathrm{mod}\ n)}$ and $c_{i+1(\mathrm{mod}\ n)}$, i.e., with chameleons arranged in a cycle. This is done by composing each chameleon model with its neighboring models according to the cycle.

What is the "natural" behavior of a Petri net module? For the vending machine, one would consider external transitions as first-class citizens of the game: the usual considerations include "insert coin" etc. In contrast, for the chameleons, one would not consider chameleons that change color without a partner. So, it makes sense to consider both ways natural and to distinguish "internal behavior" (without external transitions) from "external behavior" (with external transitions). Considering the examples, we are interested in the external behavior of the vending machine model, but in the internal behavior of a model of the chameleon game.

The distinction between internal and external transitions also has consequences for the properties defined for Petri nets. As mentioned initially, liveness and boundedness are considered to define "well-behaved" Petri net models. Boundedness means that the number of tokens on places never exceeds a certain bound (or, equivalently for finite Petri nets, that the set of reachable markings is finite). Obviously, this property remains unaffected by the distinction between internal and external transitions. Liveness means that, whatever marking was reached, every transition can be enabled again. How does this translate to Petri net modules with external transitions? One obvious suggestion is:

**Definition 4.** *A Petri net module is* internally live *if, for each marking $m$ reached from the initial marking by firing internal or external transitions, and for each internal or external transition $t$, $m$ enables an occurrence sequence consisting of internal transitions only that leads to a marking $m'$ which enables $t$.*

According to this definition, the vending machine model of Fig. 1 is not internally live because it can get stuck without user cooperation - if nobody want's to buy something then there is nothing to be done. The chameleons, however, should be internally live because their survival should not depend on additional specimens that are not captured in the current model.

The reader might have noticed that interaction of open Petri net modules (modules with external transitions) always yields another open Petri net modul. So with this operator we never get closed modules. One way to fix this shortcoming is to combine the interaction operator with classical composition, sketched in Fig. 5. Another way is to add another, unary operator $\mathcal{I}$, which stands for "intern". Roughly speaking, $\mathcal{I}(N)$ is obtained from $N$ by deleting all external transitions and adjacent arcs.

**Definition 5.** *Given a Petri net module $N = (S, T, F, M_0)$ with a set of external transitions $T^e$, $\mathcal{I}(N)$ is defined as the net $(S, T \setminus T^e, F \setminus ((S \times T^e) \cup (T^e \times S)), M_0)$. The set of external transitions of $\mathcal{I}(N)$ is empty.*

Clearly, this operator is idempotent, i.e., $\mathcal{I}(\mathcal{I}(N)) = \mathcal{I}(N)$. We can redefine internal behavior of a Petri net module using the operator: the internal behavior of a Petri net module $N$ equals the (external) behavior of $\mathcal{I}(N)$.

## 5    Workflow Nets with External Transitions

Let us begin this section with the definition of Workflow nets and soundness.

**Definition 6.** *A Petri Net is a* Workflow net *if it has two places i (input) and o (output) such that i has no ingoing arc, o has no outgoing arc and every net element belongs to a directed path from i to o.*

As a consequence of the definition, $i$ is the only net element of the Workflow net without ingoing arc, and $o$ is the only net element without outgoing arc.

The standard interpretation of a Workflow net is that its behavior starts with the initial marking $m_i$ assigning one token to place $i$ and no token to all other places of the net. A regular run of the net should end with the final marking $m_o$ assigning one token to place $o$ and no token to all other places. $m_o$ does not enable any transition.

**Definition 7.** *A* Workflow net is sound *if it satisfies the following two conditions:*

*1. If a marking m is reachable from $m_i$ then $m_o$ is reachable from m.*
*2. Each transition is enabled by some marking reachable from $m_i$.*

The original definition of [1] had a third requirement stating that $m_o$ is the only reachable marking that assigns tokens to the place $o$. This requirement follows, however, from the other two requirements (every occurrence sequence from such a marking to $m_o$ has to end with an input transition of $o$, whence $o$ cannot be marked before).

Figure 7 shows a sound Workflow net. We refrain from an application-based interpretation of the net elements, as this would distract from our goals.

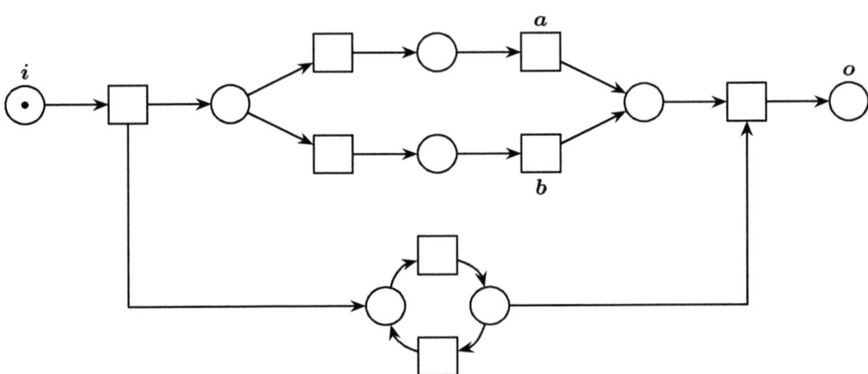


**Fig. 7.** A sound Workflow net.

The nice result of [1] is that a Workflow net is sound if and only if a related extended Petri net is live and bounded. This extension is given by an additional transition $t$ with input place $o$ and output place $i$, as shown in Fig. 8.

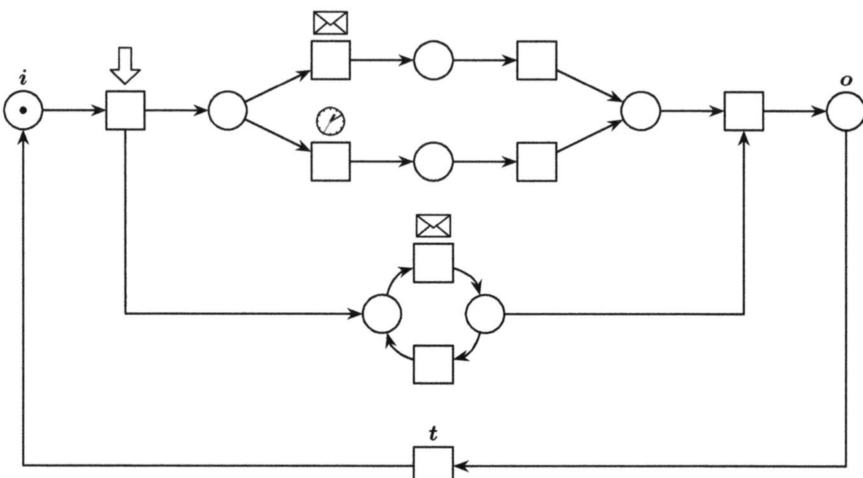

**Fig. 8.** Workflow net with additional transition $t$ from $o$ to $i$.

Workflow nets were extended in the YAWL language to include symbols at transitions [5], as is also shown in Fig. 8. There are three possibilities with the following meanings:

- An arrow means that the transition is user driven.
- A clock means that the transition fires after some time.
- An envelope means that the transition depends on an external event.

For our purposes, only the envelope symbol is relevant, because it specifies communication and thus interaction. It requires an additional system component (possibly modeled by another Petri net module) that interacts with the current module via this transition. Importantly, no composition is required here, since it is not specified that the event can only be triggered by a single other activity. So the envelope indicates an external transition in our setting.

Actually, YAWL also includes additional symbols for transition elements, allowing for different choices. We will not address this concept here.

Instead of the feedback transition $t$ representing the process environment, one could add a transition before the input place $i$ and another one after the output place $o$, as suggested e.g. in [14]. These transitions must, of course, be controlled, as the first transition could otherwise flood the net with tokens. This is done by composition (in the strict sense) with another, very simple Petri net, as shown in Fig. 9. This simple Petri net (at the bottom of the figure) represents a very abstract form of the process environment which is formally composed with the process net. It is straightforward to see that this composed net is live and bounded if and only if the one with a single transition from $o$ to $i$ is. Therefore, Wil's theorem applies to this net as well.

The same figure illustrates that the "envelope transitions" interact with transitions of some other modules.

It might be worth mentioning that interaction allows one to put together Workflow nets in a more general setting without destroying the soundness property. Any reachable marking of two interacting Workflow nets, projected to one of these Workflow nets, is a reachable marking of this Workflow net. Therefore, the interaction operator does not produce new markings. In particular, it does not destroy the boundedness property. Conversely, each occurrence sequence of a Workflow net continues to exist after the net is combined with another Workflow net using the interaction operator, thus ensuring that its liveness is not affected, too. Notice that this is not the case for the composition operator. An unfortunate composition of alternative branches of two Workflow nets can easily lead to a mutual blocking of these nets.

For example, assume two copies of the Workflow net of Fig. 7. Assume moreover that both transitions annotated by $a$ are connected by interaction, and the same for the transitions annotated by $b$. If the preceding alternatives were decided identically, the two $a$-transitions and the two $b$-transitions can synchronize or not. If the alternatives were decided differently, synchronization is not

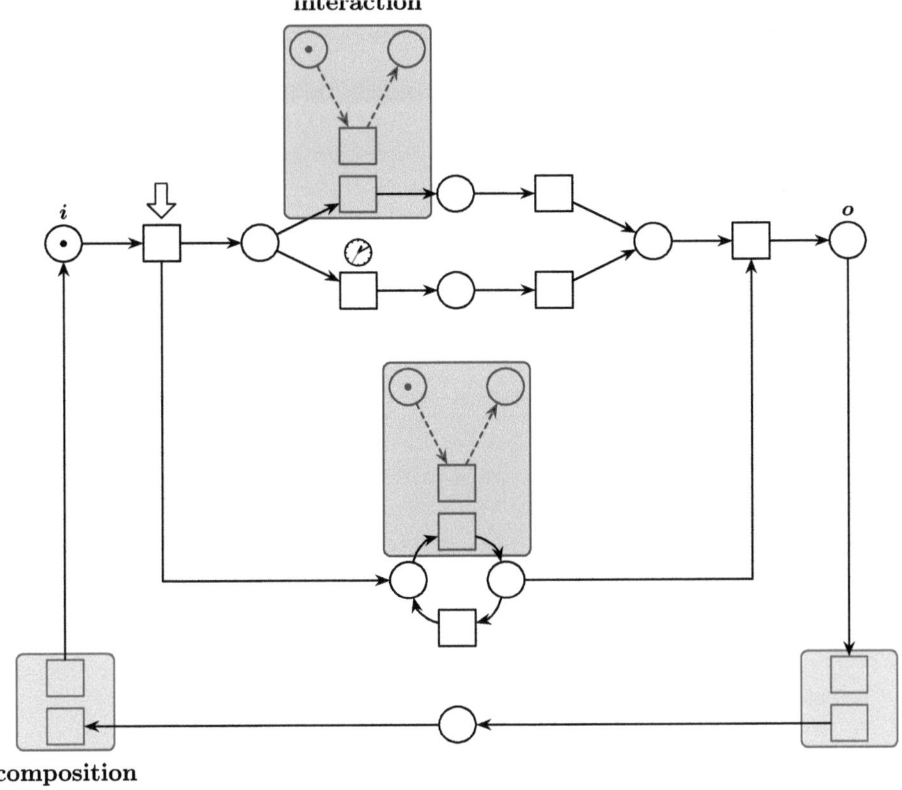


**Fig. 9.** Workflow net with composition and interaction.

possible, but both Workflow nets can continue without synchronization by firing their respective external transitions.

In contrast, if the two $a$-transitions are composed (and thus merged) and the two $b$-transitions are composed as well, then a mismatched decision of the previous alternatives leads to a marking of the composed net, where neither the composed $a$-transition nor the composed $b$-transition is enabled. Actually, the composed net reached a deadlock.

## 6    Conclusion

Since each model only models a section of the world, and this section has connections to other, unmodeled sections, each Petri net model can be understood as a module that has defined interfaces. We introduced the concept of interaction of Petri net modules and distinguished it from traditional composition. Both define different interpretations of behavior at interfaces. The distinction requires a distinction between internal and external transitions and between internal and external behavior. We have shown that these concepts already existed implicitly in Wil van der Aalst's Workflow nets and YAWL nets, which were invented more than 20 years ago, but still represent a vibrant field of research on Wil's 60th birthday.

As we have shown for the case of Workflow nets, applying the interaction operator to two Petri nets never leads to behavioral restrictions. This is because external transitions can always be used as a workaround. However, these external transitions must be interpreted as allowing other, unmodeled components to interact with them. Although the totality of all components in the model may be unknown, it is finite. Therefore, an arbitrary, and in the limiting case infinite, use of external transitions does not model reality. It will be necessary to introduce fairness assumptions in the sense of [9] to prevent infinite non-communication. Future research may investigate to what extent the interaction operator preserves properties such as liveness or deadlock-freeness, when fairness is assumed.

Another future research direction should uncover more about algebraic rules, as we have already demonstrated when introducing the interaction operator. Since interaction and composition serve different purposes and each has its own justification, considering both operators together is promising.

## References


1. van der Aalst, W.M.P.: Verification of Workflow nets. In: Azéma, P., Balbo, G. (eds.) Application and Theory of Petri Nets 1997. Lecture Notes in Computer Science, vol. 1248, pp. 407–426. Springer (1997)
2. van der Aalst, W.M.P.: The application of Petri nets to workflow management. J. Circuits Syst. Comput. **8**(1), 21–66 (1998)
3. van der Aalst, W.M.P., Aldred, L., Dumas, M., ter Hofstede, A.H.M.: Design and implementation of the YAWL system. In: Persson, A., Stirna, J. (eds.) CAiSE 2004. LNCS, vol. 3084, pp. 142–159. Springer, Heidelberg (2004). https://doi.org/10.1007/978-3-540-25975-6_12

4. van der Aalst, W.M.P., Barros, A.P., ter Hofstede, A.H.M., Kiepuszewski, B.: Advanced workflow patterns. In: Etzion, O., Scheuermann, P. (eds.) Cooperative Information Systems, 7th International Conference, CoopIS 2000, Eilat, Israel, 6–8 September 2000, Proceedings. Lecture Notes in Computer Science, vol. 1901, pp. 18–29. Springer (2000)
5. van der Aalst, W.M.P., ter Hofstede, A.H.M.: YAWL: yet another workflow language. Inf. Syst. **30**(4), 245–275 (2005)
6. van der Aalst, W.M.P., ter Hofstede, A.H.M., Kiepuszewski, B., Barros, A.P.: Workflow patterns. Distrib. Parallel Databases **14**(1), 5–51 (2003)
7. Berry, G., Boudol, G.: The chemical abstract machine. Theoret. Comput. Sci. **96**(1), 217–248 (1992)
8. Beutelspacher, A.: Das Geheimnis der zwölften Münze: Neue mathematische Knobeleien. C.H. Beck (2021)
9. Carstensen, H., Valk, R.: Infinite behaviour and fairness in Petri nets. In: Rozenberg, G., Genrich, H.J., Roucairol, G. (eds.) Advances in Petri Nets 1984. Lecture Notes in Computer Science, vol. 188, pp. 83–100. Springer (1984)
10. Dambeck, H., Niestedt, M.: Verwirrspiel im Terrarium (2021). https://www.spiegel.de/karriere/verwirrspiel-im-terrarium-raetsel-der-woche-a-404e0560-ca83-418c-a5f3-8acfa3167d3d. Accessed 01 Mar 2022
11. Desel, J.: The chameleon game. In: Köhler Bussmeier, M., Moldt, D., Rölke, H. (eds.) Petri Nets and Software Engineering 2022. CEUR Workshop Proceedings, vol. 3170, pp. 202–210 (2022)
12. Desel, J.: Composing chameleons. In: Köhler-Bussmeier, M., et al. (eds.) Joint Proceedings of the Workshops at the 46th International Conference on Application and Theory of Petri Nets and Concurrency (Petri Nets 2025), Paris, France, 24 June 2025. CEUR Workshop Proceedings, vol. 3998. CEUR-WS.org (2025)
13. Desel, J., Esparza, J.: Free choice Petri nets. Cambridge University Press, USA (1995)
14. Desel, J., Oberweis, A.: Petri-Netze in der angewandten Informatik - Einführung. Grundlagen und Perspektiven. Wirtschaftsinf. **38**(4), 359–367 (1996)
15. Ellis, C.A., Nutt, G.J.: Modeling and enactment of workflow systems. In: Marsan, M.A. (ed.) Application and Theory of Petri Nets 1993, 14th International Conference, Chicago, Illinois, USA, 21–25 June 1993, Proceedings. Lecture Notes in Computer Science, vol. 691, pp. 1–16. Springer (1993)
16. Fettke, P., Reisig, W.: Understanding the Digital World - Modeling with HERAKLIT. Springer (2024)
17. Oberweis, A.: An integrated approach for the specification of processes and related complex structured objects in business applications. Decis. Support Syst. **17**(1), 31–53 (1996)
18. Oberweis, A., Schätzle, R., Stucky, W., Weitz, W., Zimmermann, G.: INCOME/WF – a Petri net based approach to workflow management. In: Krallmann, H. (ed.) Wirtschaftsinformatik 1997, pp. 557–580. Physica-Verlag HD, Heidelberg (1997)
19. Reisig, W.: Elements of distributed algorithms: modeling and analysis with Petri nets. Springer (1998)

# On Free Choice and Wil(l):
# From Petri Net Theory to Process Mining


Christopher T. Schwanen[1]([✉])[iD] and Wied Pakusa[2][iD]

[1] Chair of Process and Data Science (PADS), RWTH Aachen University,
Aachen, Germany
`schwanen@pads.rwth-aachen.de`
[2] Faculty of Mathematics, Informatics and Technology, Koblenz University of
Applied Sciences, Koblenz, Germany
`pakusa@hs-koblenz.de`



**Abstract.** Workflow nets were introduced by Wil in the mid-90s as
a subclass of Petri nets tailored towards modelling business processes.
They are now the de-facto standard in process mining. We study the
complexity of the reachability problem on workflow net classes with the
varying properties of quasi-liveness, free-choice and the option to complete. This yields eight classes in total. A workflow net has the option
to complete if the final marking is reachable from every state and it is
quasi-live if every transition can be fired in some reachable marking. Our
main result is a strong dichotomy: on safe workflow nets, the reachability
problem is either in PTIME or PSPACE-complete (assuming PTIME and
PSPACE are different). This dichotomy becomes all the more apparent
when we drop safeness: then, the reachability problem is either in PTIME
or becomes at least PSPACE-hard or even Ackermann-complete. More
specifically, we show that the properties of being free-choice and having
the option to complete are necessary and sufficient to obtain PTIME-
complexity. Our proofs make strong use of several of Wil's results on the
structure theory of Petri nets, in particular of his work on lucency.

**Keywords:** Process Mining · Petri Net Theory · Free-Choice Petri
Nets · Workflow Nets · Reachability · Wil van der Aalst


## 1   Introduction

Algorithms are the technological backbone of process mining. In order to extract
insights from huge amounts of event data, efficient and scalable approaches are
required to make real-world process analyses possible. In process mining, the
de-facto standard for process modelling are *workflow nets*, which Wil introduced
in the mid-90s [1–4]. They are intended to describe business procedures by modelling the behaviour of a single case with a clear start and termination point.
Thereby, the behavioural concept of *soundness* arises naturally because every
case of the business procedure should (i) eventually terminate (*option to complete* (OC)), (ii) when terminating all other places of the workflow net should


© The Author(s), under exclusive license to Springer Nature Switzerland AG 2026
J. Mendling et al. (Eds.): Wil van der Aalst Festschrift, LNCS 16480, pp. 298–311, 2026.
https://doi.org/10.1007/978-3-032-17618-9_22

be empty (*proper completion*), and (iii) every task of the procedure should be executable (*quasi-liveness* (QL)).

Workflow nets yield a strong process modelling framework. In particular, their ability to express concurrency allows to succinctly encode exponential-sized state spaces, often referred to as the *state space explosion problem*. However, it has been observed that real-world processes do not require the full expressive power of workflow nets. In many cases, real-world processes bring extra structure that can be exploited to simplify the algorithmic analyses. Probably, the most well-studied of these restrictions is the so-called *free-choice* (FC) property. The intuition behind free-choice nets is that decisions are non-conflicting in the following sense: if two tasks require a common condition or resource, then they actually require precisely the same conditions or resources. In other words, whenever a condition precedes or a resource can be consumed by different tasks (i.e., we observe a choice), then such tasks can be performed in precisely the same situations (i.e., we can *freely choose* one among them). First heavily explored in the Petri net community, Wil recognised its huge potential for process mining applications very early, e.g., see [3]. Since then, the structure theory of free-choice workflow nets has been applied successfully to reduce the (algorithmic) complexity of many problems in process mining. As many real-world process models enjoy the free-choice property, this connection has a strong impact on everyday process mining applications.

Sound free-choice workflow nets enjoy a further structural property which Wil coined *lucency* [6–9]. A process model is *lucent* if its state is uniquely determined by the set of enabled transitions. In other words, if two reachable markings enable the same set of transitions, then they are identical. Here, the intuition is that a different state always comes with different actions enabled to perform, implying that states are fully observable by the possible behaviour. Wil also introduced the dual concept of *translucency* [7] for event logs, which requires that an event carries information about all enabled activities at the time it was recorded. Both properties are interesting concepts for academic investigation but, more importantly, they closely align with how processes behave in reality. It is surprising that Wil was the first one to discover and study lucency and translucency in depth and, from our point of view, this structural property deserves much more attention in the process mining and workflow management community.

In fact, Wil himself gave strong support for the applicability of these notions. He already proved in [6] that so-called *perpetual* free-choice nets are lucent. Here, a perpetual net is a live and bounded free-choice net which has a *home cluster*, i.e., a cluster such that in every reachable state it is possible to eventually mark the places of the home cluster and nothing more. Perpetual nets are a direct generalisation of sound workflow nets: the final marking of a sound workflow net induces a home cluster by the requirement of having the *option to complete* in combination with *proper completion*. While this earlier work mostly relied on the theory of live and bounded systems (most importantly, the Blocking Theorem [20]), Wil was later able to show that lucency holds for a much larger class of free-choice nets: he proved that a home cluster alone already implies lucency of

**Table 1.** Overview of complexity results for the reachability problem. Structural and behavioural properties of the considered workflow net classes are: quasi-liveness (QL), the option to complete (OC), free-choiceness (FC), and safeness (safe). Assumed properties are marked by •, thereby implied properties are marked by ○.

| Workflow Net Properties | | | | Complexity of the | |
|---|---|---|---|---|---|
| QL | OC | FC | safe | Reachability Problem | |
| | | | | Ackermann-complete | [16, 21] |
| • | | • | | Ackermann-complete | Corollary 7 |
| | • | | | $\in$ EXPSPACE | Corollary 6 |
| • | • | | | PSPACE-hard | Theorem 6 |
| | | | • | PSPACE-complete | [14, 15] |
| • | • | | • | PSPACE-complete | Theorem 6 |
| • | | • | • | PSPACE-complete | Corollary 8 |
| ○ | • | • | ○ | $\in$ PTIME | Corollary 5 |

proper free-choice systems and that the additional assumptions of liveness and boundedness are not needed [8]. In particular, this implies the uniqueness (but not the existence) of blocking markings in free-choice nets with a home cluster. This result is remarkable also because Wil could not rely on the theory of live and bounded systems anymore, but had to develop completely new techniques and concepts which are of independent interest. Again, we believe that this line of work deserves much more attention and further investigations.

In this article, we celebrate the success story of free-choice workflow nets and Wil! Specifically, we take up Wil's idea from almost 30 years ago and use the structure theory of Petri nets in order to reduce the algorithmic complexity of the *reachability problem* on workflow nets. Asking whether two given markings are reachable from one another, the reachability problem is one of the classic algorithmic benchmarks in Petri net theory. Almost all non-trivial questions about the behaviour of Petri nets are algorithmically at least as hard as reachability and in many cases exhibit equivalent complexity. Our main result is a dichotomy for sound free-choice workflow nets: we show that as soon as we drop one of the soundness criteria 'option to complete (OC)' (which implies proper completion) or the 'free-choice property (FC)', deciding reachability becomes at least PSPACE-hard. Only 'quasi-liveness (QL)' does not affect the complexity of the reachability problem. Table 1 highlights the main results of this paper.

## 2   Preliminaries

Let $\mathbb{N} := \{0, 1, 2, \dots\}$ denote the natural numbers.

**Definition 1 (Multiset).** A *multiset* $M$ over a set $A$ is a function $M \colon A \to \mathbb{N}$; thus, for any $a \in A$, $M(a)$ indicates how often $a$ is contained in the multiset $M$. The set of all multisets over $A$ is given by $\mathbb{N}^A$. We also use $[a^{M(a)} | a \in A]$ as notation for a multiset $M \in \mathbb{N}^A$. For multisets $M, M' \in \mathbb{N}^A$, we use the standard notation for functions, e.g., $M + M'$, $M \leq M'$, etc.

**Definition 2 (Sequence).** *Sequences* with index set $I$ over a set $A$ are denoted by $\sigma = \langle a_i \rangle_{i \in I} \in A^I$. The *length* of a sequence $\sigma$ is written as $|\sigma|$ and the set of all finite sequences over $A$ is denoted by $A^*$.

**Definition 3 (Petri Net).** A *Petri net* $N$ is a bipartite directed graph $N = (P, T, F)$ where $P$ and $T$, $P \cap T = \emptyset$ are disjoint finite sets of vertices and $F \subseteq (P \times T) \cup (T \times P)$ is the set of arcs. In a Petri net, $P$ is called the set of *places*, $T$ the set of *transitions*, and $F$ the *flow relation*. Given a vertex $v \in P \cup T$, its *pre-set* $\bullet v$ and *post-set* $v \bullet$ are defined by $\bullet v := \{u \in P \cup T | (u, v) \in F\}$ and $v \bullet := \{u \in P \cup T | (v, u) \in F\}$. With regard to a place (transition), its pre- and post-set are also called *input* and *output transitions (places)*.

**Definition 4 (Proper Petri Net).** A Petri net $N = (P, T, F)$ is *proper* if all transitions have input and output places, i.e., $\forall t \in T \colon \bullet t \neq \emptyset \neq t \bullet$.

**Definition 5 (Free-Choice Petri Net).** A Petri net $N = (P, T, F)$ is *free-choice* if any two transitions either share all or none of their input places, i.e., $\forall t, t' \in T \colon \bullet t = \bullet t' \vee \bullet t \cap \bullet t' = \emptyset$.

**Definition 6 (Marking, System, Firing Rule).** Given a Petri net $N = (P, T, F)$, a *marking* $M \in \mathbb{N}^P$ is a multiset where $M(p)$ is the number of *tokens* at place $p \in P$. A place $p \in P$ is *marked* at $M$ if $M(p) > 0$. The pair $(N, M)$ of a Petri net $N = (P, T, F)$ and a marking $M \in \mathbb{N}^P$ is called a *system*. A transition $t \in T$ is *enabled* in $M$, denoted by $(N, M)[t\rangle$, if and only if each of its input places $p \in \bullet t$ is marked, i.e., $\forall p \in \bullet t \colon M(p) > 0$. An enabled transition may *fire*, denoted by $(N, M)[t\rangle(N, M')$, and firing results in a new marking $M'$:

$$M'(p) = \begin{cases} M(p) - 1 & \text{if } p \in \bullet t \wedge p \notin t \bullet, \\ M(p) + 1 & \text{if } p \notin \bullet t \wedge p \in t \bullet, \\ M(p) & \text{otherwise.} \end{cases}$$

A sequence of transitions $\sigma = \langle t_i \rangle_{i=1}^n \in T^*$ is called a *firing sequence* of $(N, M)$ if for every transition $t_i$ of the sequence holds that $(N, M_{i-1})[t_i\rangle$ and $(N, M_{i-1})[t_i\rangle(N, M_i)$ where $M_0 = M$ and $M_n = M'$. Firing such a sequence is denoted by $(N, M)[\sigma\rangle(N, M')$. The empty sequence $\langle\rangle$ is always enabled and firing the empty sequence leaves the marking unchanged, i.e., $(N, M)[\langle\rangle\rangle(N, M)$. A marking $M'$ is *reachable* if a firing sequence $\sigma \in T^*$ exists such that $M'$ is the resulting marking, i.e., $(N, M)[\sigma\rangle(N, M')$. The set of all reachable markings of $(N, M)$ is denoted by $[N, M\rangle := \{M' \in \mathbb{N}^P | \exists \sigma \in T^* \colon (N, M)[\sigma\rangle(N, M')\}$.

**Definition 7 (Boundedness, Safeness).** Given some $k \in \mathbb{N}$, a system $(N, M_0)$ with $N = (P, T, F)$ is *k-bounded* if $k$ is a bound for any reachable marking, i.e., $\forall M \in [N, M_0\rangle \colon \forall p \in P \colon M(p) \leq k$. $(N, M_0)$ is *safe* if it is 1-bounded.

**Definition 8 ((Quasi-)Liveness).** Let $(N, M_0)$ with $N = (P, T, F)$ be a system. A transition $t \in T$ is *quasi-live* if there exists a reachable marking $M' \in [N, M_0\rangle$ which enables $t$. A transition $t \in T$ is *live* if it is quasi-live for every reachable marking $M \in [N, M_0\rangle$, i.e., $\forall M \in [N, M_0\rangle \colon \exists M' \in [N, M\rangle \colon (N, M')[t\rangle$. A system $(N, M_0)$ is *(quasi-)live* if every transition $t \in T$ is (quasi-)live.

**Definition 9 (Home Marking, Cyclic System).** Let $(N, M_0)$ be a system. A marking $M \in [N, M_0\rangle$ is a *home marking* if it can be reached from any reachable marking, i.e., $\forall M' \in [N, M_0\rangle \colon M \in [N, M'\rangle$. A system $(N, M_0)$ is *cyclic* if its initial marking $M_0$ is a home marking.

**Definition 10 (Cluster).** Let $N = (P, T, F)$ be a Petri net and let $v \in P \cup T$. The *cluster* of $v$, denoted by $[v]_C$, is the minimal set of places and transitions that includes $v$, i.e., $v \in [v]_C$, all output transitions of contained places, i.e., $\forall p \in [v]_C \cap P \colon p\bullet \in [v]_C$, and all input places of contained transitions, i.e., $\forall t \in [v]_C \cap T \colon \bullet t \in [v]_C$.

## 3   Workflow Nets and the Soundness Property

Wil introduced workflow nets [3] to describe business procedures and model the behaviour of a single case with a clear start and termination point.

**Definition 11 (Workflow Net).** A *workflow net* $N = (P, T, F, i, o)$ is a Petri net $(P, T, F)$ where $i, o \in P$ are special places, namely the single *source place* $i$ with $\bullet i = \emptyset$ and the single *sink place* $o$ with $o\bullet = \emptyset$, and the Petri net is strongly connected if a transition $\bar{t}$ with $\bullet\bar{t} = \{o\}$ and $\bar{t}\bullet = \{i\}$ is added, i.e., every vertex $v \in P \cup T$ of the Petri net is on a path from $i$ to $o$. Implicitly, in workflow nets, the initial marking is $[i]$ and the final marking is $[o]$.

As such, workflow nets serve as acceptors. This is a notable difference to standard Petri nets, which are indeed commonly considered with an initial marking, but rarely with any final states. Alongside workflow nets, Wil also introduced the soundness property [3] to describe their 'well-behavedness' as business procedures should terminate eventually with leaving no tokens behind and each task in the procedure should potentially be executable.

**Definition 12 (Soundness).** A workflow net $N = (P, T, F, i, o)$ is *sound* if and only if it satisfies the following requirements:

- option to complete,   i.e., $\forall M \in [N, [i]\rangle \colon [o] \in [N, M\rangle$,
- proper completion,   i.e., $\forall M \in [N, [i]\rangle \colon M \geq [o] \implies M = [o]$, and
- no dead transitions,   i.e., $\forall t \in T \colon \exists M \in [N, [i]\rangle \colon M[t\rangle$.

The requirement of having no dead transitions is the same as quasi-liveness, and in this definition, the option to complete also already implies proper completion. Although this is easy to see, we provide the corresponding proof which shows that there are no dominating markings in workflow nets with the option to complete.

**Theorem 1.** *Let $N = (P, T, F, i, o)$ be a workflow net with the option to complete, i.e., $\forall M \in [N, [i]\rangle : [o] \in [N, M\rangle$. There is no reachable marking dominating another reachable marking, i.e., $\forall M, M' \in [N, [i]\rangle : M \leq M' \implies M = M'$.*

*Proof.* Let $N = (P, T, F, i, o)$ be a workflow net with the option to complete. Now, let us assume that we have two reachable markings $M, M' \in [N, [i]\rangle$ with $M \leq M'$ and $M \neq M'$. Because of the option to complete, a firing sequence $\sigma$ with $(N, M)[\sigma\rangle(N, [o])$ exists. It is easy to see that $\sigma$ is also enabled in $M'$, i.e., $(N, M')[\sigma\rangle$, but firing results in a marking dominating the final marking $[o]$, i.e., $(N, M')[\sigma\rangle(N, [o] + M' - M)$. Again, because of the option to complete and the fact that $o\bullet = \emptyset$, there must exist a firing sequence $\sigma'$ removing all tokens in $M' - M$ from the net, i.e., $(N, M' - M)[\sigma'\rangle(N, [])$. This, however, is impossible because every transition has at least one output place and therefore some token always remains. Hence, $\forall M, M' \in [N, [i]\rangle : M \leq M' \implies M = M'$. $\qquad\square$

**Corollary 1.** *A workflow net with the option to complete has proper completion.*

It is a classic result from Petri net theory that reaching a dominating marking is equivalent to unboundedness, hence we further get:

**Corollary 2.** *A workflow net with the option to complete is bounded.*

The strongly-connected Petri net that we obtain by adding the transition $\bar{t}$ in Definition 11 which connects the sink place to the source place is now commonly referred to as the *short-circuited net*.

**Definition 13 (Short-Circuited Net).** Let $N = (P, T, F, i, o)$ be a workflow net. Its *short-circuited net* $\bar{N}$ is obtained by adding a transition $\bar{t} \notin T$ with $\bullet\bar{t} = \{o\}$ and $\bar{t}\bullet = \{i\}$, i.e., $\bar{N} := (P, T \cup \{\bar{t}\}, F \cup \{(o, \bar{t}), (\bar{t}, i)\})$. The system $(\bar{N}, [i])$ defines the *short-circuited system*.

Wil used the short-circuited net as an important tool to transfer well-known behavioural characteristics of Petri nets to workflow nets.

**Theorem 2** ([3, Theorem 11]). *A workflow net $N$ is sound if and only if the short-circuited system $(\bar{N}, [i])$ is live and bounded.*

Verifying soundness is equivalent to verifying whether the short-circuited system is live and bounded [3,4]. For safe workflow nets, this is equivalent to checking liveness of the short-circuited net and can be shown to be PSPACE-complete using a construction similar to the one in Theorem 6 based on [14,15]. Without safeness, deciding soundness on workflow nets has recently been shown to be EXPSPACE-complete [11]. Wil also co-authored a study on the complexity of deciding other soundness notions [10], which will not be elaborated further here.

We can also use the short-circuited system to draw a connection between the option to complete and cyclicity.

**Lemma 1.** *The short-circuited system of a workflow net with the option to complete is cyclic.*

*Proof.* Let $N = (P, T, F, i, o)$ be a workflow net. Adding a transition $\bar{t}$ with $\bullet\bar{t} = \{o\}$ and $\bar{t}\bullet = \{i\}$ to obtain the short-circuited system $(\bar{N}, [i])$ does not restrict any behaviour; thus, $[\bar{N}, [i]\rangle \supseteq [N, [i]\rangle$. Because of the option to complete, there is exactly one reachable marking enabling $\bar{t}$, namely $[o]$. Since $(\bar{N}, [o])[\bar{t}\rangle(\bar{N}, [i])$ and $[i] \in [N, [i]\rangle$, $[N, [i]\rangle = [\bar{N}, [i]\rangle$ follows. Hence, $(\bar{N}, [i])$ is cyclic. $\qquad\square$

But this shows that the general independence of boundedness, liveness, and cyclicity in Petri nets does not hold up in workflow nets.

**Corollary 3.** *A live and bounded short-circuited system is cyclic.*

Later on, Wil refined the structural and behavioural implications of soundness by introducing the notion of *perpetual* systems [6], i.e., systems that are live, bounded, and have a *home cluster*.

**Definition 14 (Home Cluster).** Let $(N, M_0)$ with $N = (P, T, F)$ be a system. A cluster $C \subseteq P \cup T$ of $N$ is a *home cluster* of $(N, M_0)$ if $[p|p \in C \cap P]$ is a home marking.

Obviously, the option to complete already implies the existence of a home cluster. While a home cluster itself does not imply boundedness, the option to complete does (cf. Theorem 1). Perpetual systems are considered a generalisation of sound workflow nets as their short-circuited systems clearly are perpetual [6, Lemma 2].

Wil additionally provided soundness-preserving transformation and composition rules for workflow nets [3,5,9]. In fact, every transformation that preserves liveness and boundedness would suffice. Hence, also well-known Petri net transformations (e.g., as shown in [22, p. 553]) are applicable to sound workflow nets.

## 4   Sound Free-Choice Workflow Nets

Early on, Wil recognised that the free-choice property has important implications in terms of soundness. With the free-choice property in the picture, he was able to use the Rank Theorem [13,17] to show that soundness can be verified efficiently.

**Theorem 3** ([3, Theorem 12]). *For a free-choice workflow net, soundness can be decided in polynomial time.*

He further showed that the option to complete alone suffices as a criterion for soundness because it already implies quasi-liveness:

**Proposition 1** ([3, Proposition 13]). *A free-choice workflow net with the option to complete is quasi-live.*

**Corollary 4.** *A free-choice workflow net with the option to complete is sound.*

But this is not the only relevant implication because another important result by Wil shows that free-choice workflow nets with the option to complete are always safe:

**Lemma 2** ([5, Lemma 1]). *A sound free-choice workflow net is safe.*

Therefore, it is not surprising that the reachability problem can be solved efficiently on this class, and although it would suffice to use Wil's results above and directly transfer the results of Desel and Esparza [18,19] on cyclic live and bounded free-choice systems, we take a small detour and investigate the reachability problem on another class, namely *proper free-choice systems with a home cluster* as it allows us to highlight some of Wil's more recent results.

Here, we briefly discuss classes with the structural property of *lucency* [6–9], meaning that each state is uniquely determined by its set of enabled transitions. Wil not only proved that *perpetual* free-choice nets are lucent [6], but the larger class of proper free-choice systems with home cluster in general [8]. This class is a strict generalisation of perpetual free-choice systems and it immediately applies to free-choice workflow nets which are not necessarily live, but guarantee proper completion of each process instance. Finally, we show that reachability can be solved efficiently for proper free-choice systems with a home cluster:

**Theorem 4.** *The reachability problem for proper free-choice systems with a home cluster is in* PTIME.

*Proof.* Let $(N, M_0)$ with $N = (P, T, F)$ be a proper free-choice system with a home cluster $C \subseteq P \cup T$. We use the short-circuited cleaned net polynomial-time construction from [8, Definition 6.4] with the added transition $t_C$ to obtain a cyclic live and bounded free-choice system for which reachability can be decided in polynomial time [19]. A small technicality remains: A firing sequence which starts in the initial marking $M_0$ and reaches a target marking $M$ might make use of the added transition $t_C$ which is not part of the original net. However, because $t_C$ reinitialises $M_0$, we can simply take the suffix of the firing sequence after $t_C$'s last occurrence to obtain a firing sequence in the original net.      □

**Corollary 5.** *Reachability for sound free-choice workflow nets is in* PTIME.

Dropping quasi-liveness alone as a requirement on free-choice workflow nets does not affect the complexity result for the reachability problem as the option to complete directly implies quasi-liveness (Proposition 1). Therefore, it remains to study classes of workflow nets without the free-choice property (Sect. 5) and without the option to complete (Sect. 6).

## 5   Classes Without the Free-Choice Property

The technically most challenging part concerns subclasses with missing free-choice property, i.e., sound workflow nets. We are going to show two things: first of all, as an upper bound, we show that the reachability problem is in EXPSPACE on the subclass of workflow nets with the option to complete. However, it remains open whether EXPSPACE also constitutes a lower bound for sound workflow nets. Instead, we are going to establish the weaker lower bound of PSPACE-hardness which positions the reachability problem for sound workflow nets somewhere in between of PSPACE and EXPSPACE.

### 5.1  Upper Bound for Workflow Nets with Option to Complete

The crucial observation is that workflow nets with the option to complete are cyclic and bounded. We can then apply the following result due to Bouziane and Finkel [12] which establishes an exponential bound on the representation size of reachable markings in bounded cyclic Petri nets.

**Lemma 3** ([12, Lemma 4.1]). *Let $(N, M_0)$ be a bounded cyclic Petri net of $size(N, M_0) = n$. Then, for every reachable marking $M \in [N, M_0\rangle$, we have $size(M) \leq 2^{cn \log n}$ for some fixed constant $c > 0$.*

This implies that all reachable markings in workflow nets with the option to complete can be represented in exponential space. This yields a simple non-deterministic EXPSPACE algorithm for the reachability problem on this class: just guess a firing sequence and keep track of the current marking. This is another great example of how structure-theoretic properties of Petri nets can be exploited for algorithmic purposes. Since by Savitch's Theorem EXPSPACE = NEXPSPACE, it follows:

**Theorem 5** ([12, Theorem 4.4]). *The reachability problem for cyclic bounded systems is in EXPSPACE.*

Actually the proof in [12] is more general and does not require boundedness, but for our purposes the above formulation suffices. Because (the short-circuited version of) each workflow net with the option to complete is cyclic and bounded, we can conclude:

**Corollary 6.** *The reachability problem for workflow nets with the option to complete is in EXPSPACE.*

### 5.2  Lower Bound for Sound Workflow Nets

We now turn our attention towards the PSPACE-lower bound. To this end we adapt a construction due to Wil and the authors which we recently used to establish PSPACE-hardness of the alignment problem for sound workflow nets [27]. It turns out that only minor changes are necessary, so we just sketch the main ideas and refer to the original paper for full details. The proof is based on simulating a PSPACE-Turing machine in terms of a sound workflow net. Depending on whether the Turing machine accepts or rejects, we can reach a designated accepting or rejecting marking respectively which proves PSPACE-hardness of the reachability problem on safe and sound workflow nets.

**Theorem 6.** *There is a polynomial-time algorithm which transforms a deterministic Turing machine $\mathcal{M}$ with polynomial space bound $p(n)$ and an input $w$ into a safe and sound workflow net $N = (P, T, F, i, o)$ together with a marking $M_{acc}$ such that $\mathcal{M}$ accepts $w$ if and only if $M_{acc} \in [N, [i]\rangle$.*

*Proof.* We here only sketch a proof that adapts the construction in [27, Theorem 8] which itself makes strong use of the ideas in [14, Theorem 4].

We assume the same Turing machine $\mathcal{M} = (K, \Sigma, \Gamma, \delta, q_0, q_+, q_-, \perp)$ as in [27, Theorem 8] with the same preprocessing to ensure the polynomial space bound, and exactly one accepting and one rejecting state. To encode the computation of $\mathcal{M}$ on input $w$, we define a workflow net $N = (P, T, F, i, o)$ where the set of places $P$ consists of $i$, $o$, and places to represent each possible state $(K)$, each head position $(\{0, \ldots, p(n)\})$, and each possible tape cell content $\{0, \ldots, p(n)\} \times \Gamma$, i.e., for each combination of a valid position and tape symbol. We construct the workflow net $N$ in such a way that reachable markings can be identified with configurations of $\mathcal{M}$ in the above sense. Thus the set of transitions $T$ consists of one initialising transition, one transition completing the computation when the (unique) accepting configuration is reached, one transition completing the computation when the (unique) rejecting configuration is reached, and a distinct transition for each possible local configuration $(q, a, j) \in K \setminus \{q_+, q_-\} \times \Gamma \times \{0, \ldots, p(n)\}$ that simulates the transition function $\delta$.

Because $\mathcal{M}$ is deterministic and the computation is acyclic, at each local configuration precisely one transition representing $\delta$ can fire and we eventually reach the unique accepting or rejecting configuration from which we can fire one of the completing transitions to end in the final marking $[o]$.

Finally, to ensure quasi-liveness of the workflow net $N$, additional transitions are added that can activate and deactivate each transition from above (by producing (consuming) exactly the required input (provided output) tokens). Thereby, additional places indicate whether the net operates in this auxiliary or in the standard mode. The above transitions therefore initialise and clear these places correspondingly.

The construction can be carried out in polynomial time, and the resulting workflow net $N$ is safe, has the option to complete, and is quasi-live. Asking whether the marking for the accepting configuration can be reached from $[i]$ is identical to asking whether $\mathcal{M}$ accepts $w$. $\qquad\square$

## 6   Classes Without the Option to Complete

If we drop the option to complete, then the remaining restrictions of being a quasi-live and free-choice workflow net do not provide any algorithmically useful structure. In fact, we are going to show that the reachability problem of general Petri nets can be reduced to the reachability problem of quasi-live free-choice workflow nets in polynomial time. Recall that the reachability problem for general Petri nets is decidable but Ackermann-complete [16, 21]. This clearly rules out any hope for efficient algorithms on this class and highlights the crucial role which the option to complete plays for process mining applications.

**Lemma 4.** *There is a polynomial time algorithm which reduces the reachability problem for general Petri nets to the reachability problem for quasi-live free-choice workflow nets.*

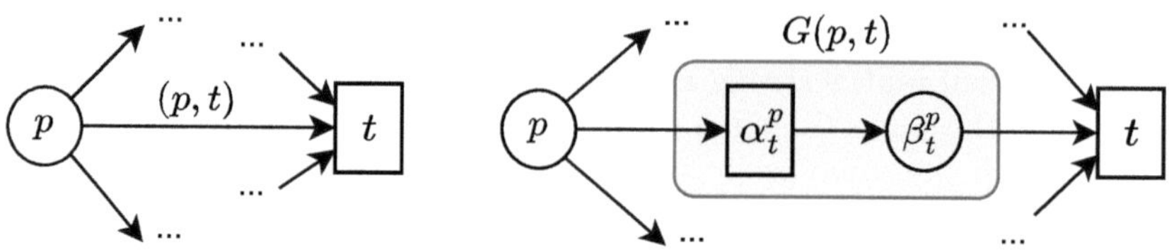

**Fig. 1.** Gadget $G(p,t)$ that replaces each flow relation $(p,t) \in F \cap (P \times T)$. The gadgets $G(p,t)$ separate choices and synchronisations explicitly.

*Proof.* Let $N$ be a general Petri net with $N = (P,T,F)$ and two markings $M_1, M_2 \in \mathbb{N}^P$. We can assume that $N$ is connected (otherwise, we can treat the components separately).

As a first step, we transform $N$ into a quasi-live workflow net. Therefore, we add two new places $i$ and $o$. Next, for each transition $t \in T$ we add two auxiliary transitions $t_+$ and $t_-$ with $\bullet t_+ = \{i\}$ and $t_+ \bullet = \bullet t$, and $\bullet t_- = t\bullet$ and $t_- \bullet = \{o\}$, respectively. This guarantees that every transition $t \in T$ can be fired from the initial marking $[i]$. Moreover, it also guarantees that each vertex is on a path from $i$ to $o$. Note that if there are other sink or source places (besides $i$ and $o$) in $N$ we can simply add a loop to make them non-sink or non-source. Hence, the resulting net $N'$ is a quasi-live workflow net. Clearly, this first step of the reduction can be carried out in polynomial time.

It remains to transform $N'$ into a free-choice net (while maintaining quasi-liveness and the worflow net structure). However, since we have no (strong) liveness requirement (due to the absence of the option to complete), this is quite easy. We simply substitute each flow relation $(p,t) \in F \cap (P \times T)$ by a small gadget $G(p,t)$ which is illustrated in Fig. 1.

This construction guarantees that synchronisations only occur for places that have precisely one output transition. The corresponding choices have to happen before and are separated from the synchronisations by the gadgets $G(p,t)$. This yields a free-choice net. If we call the resulting net $N''$, then it is clear that every firing sequence in $N'$ can be extended to a firing sequence in $N''$ (by pushing the required tokens through the gadgets $G(p,t)$) and that, vice versa, every firing sequence in $N''$ can be projected down to a firing sequence in $N'$ (by ignoring the transitions and places in the gadgets). In particular, the net $N''$ remains quasi-live (but the gadgets $G(p,t)$ might introduce new deadlocks). Hence, $M_2$ is reachable from $M_1$ in $N$ if and only if $M_2$ is reachable from $M_1$ in $N''$. The construction can be carried out in polynomial time. $\square$

Due to Lemma 4 and the Ackermann-completeness of the reachability problem for general Petri nets [16,21], we can conclude:

**Corollary 7.** *The reachability problem for quasi-live free-choice workflow nets is not primitive recursive but Ackermann-complete.*

It is easy to see that the construction of Lemma 4 preserves safeness. Due to the PSPACE-completeness of the reachability problem for general safe Petri nets [14,15], we can conclude:

**Corollary 8.** *The reachability problem for safe quasi-live free-choice workflow nets is* PSPACE-*complete.*

## 7  Beyond Reachability

We demonstrated that structural properties of workflow nets have a huge impact on the algorithmic complexity of the reachability problem. While for some classes standard linear-algebraic techniques combined with simple graph algorithms are sufficient, other classes touch the very limits of decidability and are way beyond any practical applicability. This highlights the great value of Petri net theory in general, and, in particular, of the theory of workflow nets developed by Wil in several seminal and highly influential works starting from [3–5]. As demonstrated, these results do not only provide clear orientation in the jungle of process models, but may even provide algorithmic pathways for seemingly intractable problems in practice.

Of course, reachability is only one of many relevant algorithmic problems in process mining. Along very similar lines, Wil and the authors recently classified the complexity of the alignment problem for several classes of workflow nets [24 27]. The results have a similar spirit in the sense that the FC and OC properties are key for algorithmic tractability. However, some details diverge from the case of the reachability problem as the alignment problem is generally harder to solve. Consequently, the present results immediately serve as a lower bound for the alignment problem.

These examples showcase how process mining algorithms can benefit from Petri net theory and, in particular, from Wil's extensive work on workflow nets. We believe that the potential here is far from being exhausted. First, there are many more algorithmic problems in process mining which could be studied from this perspective. For instance, the algorithmic complexity of model synthesis or model repair problems are completely open, yet these are fundamental problems in process mining. The same holds for model comparison problems, for example. Second, while free-choice is probably the most studied structural property which leads to efficient algorithms, there are many more patterns that we witness in real-life process models and which could be exploited for algorithmic purposes. One example is to add acyclicity: in many processes, actions are never repeated, and while of course still in PTIME, it allows for faster algorithms such as in [23] which decides reachability in quadratic time. Another example is Wil's notion of lucency: again, in many realistic processes, being in different states also implies being able to perform different actions. So one interesting question is the following: what happens to the algorithmic complexity of reachability (and other problems in process mining) if we consider other structural properties or replace the free-choice property by lucency?

This is not the end of the story! We should not forget that Wil's pioneering work on process mining was once rooted in Petri net theory. The huge success of our research field is also due to its beautiful theoretic foundation. Let us continue to foster the fruitful grounds out of which Wil once established a world full of notions that kept us busy and excited for already three decades. And more importantly, let us use our free choice, will and Wil to apply Petri net theory for solving real world problems!

# References


1. van der Aalst, W.M.P.: A class of Petri nets for modeling and analyzing business processes. Computing science reports 95/26. Technische Universiteit Eindhoven (1995). https://research.tue.nl/en/publications/76d57856-828b-49cd-ba84-7bfcd7042ee9
2. van der Aalst, W.M.P.: Structural characterizations of sound workflow nets. Computing science reports 96/23. Technische Universiteit Eindhoven (1996). https://research.tue.nl/en/publications/d7ac08f3-457f-449a-97bb-f6dc54cea668
3. van der Aalst, W.M.P.: Verification of workflow nets. In: Azéma, P., Balbo, G. (eds.) ICATPN 1997. LNCS, vol. 1248, pp. 407–426. Springer, Heidelberg (1997). https://doi.org/10.1007/3-540-63139-9_48
4. van der Aalst, W.M.P.: The application of petri nets to workflow management. J. Circ. Syst. Comput. **8**(1), 21–66 (1998). https://doi.org/10.1142/s0218126698000043
5. van der Aalst, W.M.P.: Workflow verification: finding control-flow errors using petri-net-based techniques. In: van der Aalst, W., Desel, J., Oberweis, A. (eds.) Business Process Management. LNCS, vol. 1806, pp. 161–183. Springer, Heidelberg (2000). https://doi.org/10.1007/3-540-45594-9_11
6. Aalst, W.M.P.: Markings in perpetual free-choice nets are fully characterized by their enabled transitions. In: Khomenko, V., Roux, O.H. (eds.) PETRI NETS 2018. LNCS, vol. 10877, pp. 315–336. Springer, Cham (2018). https://doi.org/10.1007/978-3-319-91268-4_16
7. van der Aalst, W.M.P.: Lucent process models and translucent event logs. Fund. Inform. **169**(1–2), 151–177 (2019). https://doi.org/10.3233/FI-2019-1842
8. van der Aalst, W.M.P.: Free-choice nets with home clusters are lucent. Fund. Inform. **181**(4), 273–302 (2021). https://doi.org/10.3233/FI-2021-2059
9. van der Aalst, W.M.P.: Reduction using induced subnets to systematically prove properties for free-choice nets. In: Buchs, D., Carmona, J. (eds.) PETRI NETS 2021. LNCS, vol. 12734, pp. 208–229. Springer, Cham (2021). https://doi.org/10.1007/978-3-030-76983-3_11
10. van der Aalst, W.M.P., et al.: Soundness of workflow nets: classification, decidability, and analysis. Formal Aspects Comput. **23**(3), 333–363 (2011). https://doi.org/10.1007/s00165-010-0161-4
11. Blondin, M., Mazowiecki, F., Offtermatt, P.: The complexity of soundness in workflow nets. In: Proceedings of the 37th Annual ACM/IEEE Symposium on Logic in Computer Science. LICS 2022. Association for Computing Machinery, New York (2022). https://doi.org/10.1145/3531130.3533341
12. Bouziane, Z., Finkel, A.: Cyclic petri net reachability sets are semilinear effectively constructible. Electron. Notes Theor. Comput. Sci. **9**, 15–24 (1997). https://doi.org/10.1016/S1571-0661(05)80423-2
13. Campos, J., Chiola, G., Silva, M.: Properties and performance bounds for closed free choice synchronized monoclass queueing networks. IEEE Trans. Automatic Control **36**(12), 1368–1382 (1991). https://doi.org/10.1109/9.106153

14. Cheng, A., Esparza, J., Palsberg, J.: Complexity results for 1-safe nets. In: Shyamasundar, R.K. (ed.) FSTTCS 1993. LNCS, vol. 761, pp. 326–337. Springer, Heidelberg (1993). https://doi.org/10.1007/3-540-57529-4_66

15. Cheng, A., Esparza, J., Palsberg, J.: Complexity results for 1-safe nets. Theoret. Comput. Sci. **147**(1–2), 117–136 (1995). https://doi.org/10.1016/0304-3975(94)00231-7

16. Czerwiński, W., Orlikowski, Ł.: Reachability in vector addition systems is Ackermann-complete. In: 62nd Annual Symposium on Foundations of Computer Science. FOCS 2021, pp. 1229–1240. IEEE (2022). https://doi.org/10.1109/FOCS52979.2021.00120

17. Desel, J.: A proof of the rank theorem for extended free choice nets. In: Jensen, K. (ed.) ICATPN 1992. LNCS, vol. 616, pp. 134–153. Springer, Heidelberg (1992). https://doi.org/10.1007/3-540-55676-1_8

18. Desel, J., Esparza, J.: Reachability in reversible free choice systems. In: Choffrut, C., Jantzen, M. (eds.) STACS 1991. LNCS, vol. 480, pp. 384–397. Springer, Heidelberg (1991). https://doi.org/10.1007/BFb0020814

19. Desel, J., Esparza, J.: Reachability in cyclic extended free-choice systems. Theoret. Comput. Sci. **114**(1), 93–118 (1993). https://doi.org/10.1016/0304-3975(93)90154-L

20. Gaujal, B., Haar, S., Mairesse, J.: Blocking a transition in a free choice net and what it tells about its throughput. J. Comput. Syst. Sci. **66**(3), 515–548 (2003). https://doi.org/10.1016/S0022-0000(03)00039-4

21. Leroux, J.: The reachability problem for petri nets is not primitive recursive. In: 62nd Annual Symposium on Foundations of Computer Science. FOCS 2021, pp. 1241–1252. IEEE (2022). https://doi.org/10.1109/FOCS52979.2021.00121

22. Murata, T.: Petri nets: properties, analysis and applications. Proc. IEEE **77**(4), 541–580 (1989). https://doi.org/10.1109/5.24143

23. Prinz, T.M., Schwanen, C.T., van der Aalst, W.M.P.: Deciding (sub-marking) reachability in O(P2 + T2) for sound acyclic free-choice workflow nets. In: Application and Theory of Petri Nets and Concurrency. Petri Nets 2025. LNCS, vol. 15714, pp. 366–387. Springer, Cham (2025). https://doi.org/10.1007/978-3-031-94634-9_18

24. Schwanen, C.T., Pakusa, W., van der Aalst, W.M.P.: A dynamic programming approach for alignments on process trees. In: Process Mining Workshops. ICPM 2024 International Workshops, Lyngby, Denmark, 14–18 October 2024, Revised Selected Papers. ICPM 2024. LNBIP, vol. 533, pp. 84–97. Springer, Cham (2025). https://doi.org/10.1007/978-3-031-82225-4_7

25. Schwanen, C.T., Pakusa, W., van der Aalst, W.M.P.: Alignments meet linear algebra. In: Algorithms & Theories for the Analysis of Event Data (ATAED 2025), vol. 3998, pp. 185–200. CEUR Workshop Proceedings. Aachen: CEURWS. org (2025). https://ceur-ws.org/Vol-3998/paper12.pdf

26. Schwanen, C.T., Pakusa, W., van der Aalst, W.M.P.: Process tree alignments. In: Enterprise Design, Operations, and Computing. EDOC 2024. LNCS, vol. 15409, pp. 300–317. Springer, Cham (2025). https://doi.org/10.1007/978-3-031-78338-8_16

27. Schwanen, C.T., Pakusa, W., van der Aalst, W.M.P.: Complexity of alignments on sound free-choice workflow nets. In: Application and Theory of Petri Nets and Concurrency. Petri Nets 2025. LNCS, vol. 15714, pp. 388–410. Springer, Cham (2025). https://doi.org/10.1007/978-3-031-94634-9_19

# Process Mining Foundations

# A Brief Overview of Process Trees

Sander J. J. Leemans[1(✉)], Sebastiaan J. van Zelst[2], and Xixi Lu[3]

[1] RWTH Aachen University, Aachen, Germany
`s.leemans@bpm.rwth-aachen.de`
[2] Celonis Gmbh, Munich, Germany
[3] Utrecht University, Utrecht, The Netherlands

**Abstract.** Process trees are a process modelling language for which inception and early development, like many other modelling languages, Wil van der Aalst played a pivotal role. The hierarchical nature of process trees provides many theoretical guarantees on which one can build. Therefore, unsurprisingly, process trees have often been used and applied in process mining techniques developed in recent years. Yet, a concise overview, combined with a solid formal foundation, is lacking. Therefore, in this paper, we provide a unified definition of process tree operators as defined in literature and discuss their applications and relation to Petri nets. It should not come as a surprise to the reader that the usage of process trees or related modelling formalisms, as well as other works relevant to this work, yielded a total of 60 references.

## 1 Introduction

Process mining analyses event data recorded by information systems to derive insights into how processes are actually executed. Process mining does so by discovering and analysing process models from event data. A key trade-off is selecting a model representation that is expressive enough to capture real-world behaviour while remaining suitable for the analyses to be conducted. Among the various modelling formalisms used in process discovery and analysis, **process trees** may be an attractive choice. Such trees are block-structured by syntax construction, support simple compositional semantics and can easily be converted to other modelling languages such as Petri nets and BPMN.

The idea of representing processes in a block-structured way, using a small set of well-nested control-flow operators such as sequence, choice, concurrency and loops, can be traced back to early workflow and service modelling languages. For example, Microsoft's XLANG language already emphasised block-structured modelling with operators for sequence, switch, while, parallel execution and race conditions [54]. Similarly, [13] compared graph-based notations (e.g., BPMN, Petri nets) with block-structured ones, highlighting the trade-off between modelling flexibility and analysability. These early contributions laid the ideas of block-structured models on which the process tree would later be based.

The term process trees was coined in the process mining literature by Wil van der Aalst and others [5,7], which selected a tree-based representation as the


J. Mendling et al. (Eds.): Wil van der Aalst Festschrift, LNCS 16480, pp. 315–332, 2026.
https://doi.org/10.1007/978-3-032-17618-9_23

modelling language for their Evolutionary Tree Miner (ETM). The tree structure guarantees soundness for all generated candidate models, while the evolutionary search optimises the quality of such models in terms of fitness, precision and simplicity. This property made process trees a suitable choice for the ETM.

Building on this idea, a team led by van der Aalst [21,25–27] introduced a formal definition of process trees and showed how process trees provide a direct, hierarchical representation of block-structured workflow nets, abstracting from Petri-net notations while preserving behaviour equivalence. The inductive discovery framework (the foundation for the later Inductive Miner family) exploits the process tree operators to ensure the discovery of sound and perfectly fitting models. Moreover, a proof was provided that under standard completeness assumptions, the algorithm rediscovers the original model from which the log was derived, if the model is block-structured. By formalising the semantics of process trees, this line of work established process trees as the standard representation for block-structured process discovery and related conformance techniques.

Building on these contributions, process trees have been widely used: as outputs of process discovery, as intermediate representations for translations to and from workflow nets, and as models for conformance checking and performance analysis. Their hierarchical nature enables scalable algorithms and modular, divide-and-conquer reasoning, while their extensible node types allow the expression of advanced constructs (e.g., cancellation, recursion) for more complex behaviour. These properties allow researchers and practitioners to strike a useful balance between expressive power and simplicity.

In this paper, we provide a brief overview of process trees, their applications, and their relation to Petri nets. Section 2 introduces the different types of process trees, ranging from basic operators to more advanced nodes. Section 3 discusses the main applications of process trees, focusing on their role in process discovery, conformance checking and other process mining tasks. Section 4 explores the relation between process trees and Petri nets. Section 5 concludes the paper.

## 2   Types of Process Trees

A *process tree* is a hierarchical structure over nodes, expressing a language of traces over an alphabet of activities $\Sigma$. A tree consists of *leaf* nodes and *operator* nodes. We define process trees in terms of their expressed language $\ell$.

### 2.1   Leaf Nodes

A leaf node has no children. Several flavours of leaf nodes have been proposed: the no-operation silent leaf $\tau$, the *activity* leaf $a$ and the non-atomic activity leaf $\bar{a}$. They can be defined as follows, assuming $a \in \Sigma$ and $\tau \notin \Sigma$ (the third column will be defined in Sect. 2.2):

$$\ell(\tau) = \{\langle\,\rangle\} \qquad\qquad\qquad = \ell(\times_{\text{start}\mapsto\text{end}}(\,))$$
$$\ell(a) = \{\langle a \rangle\}$$
$$\ell(\bar{a}) = \{\langle a_{\text{start}}, a_{\text{complete}} \rangle\} \qquad = \ell(\rightarrow(a_{\text{start}}, a_{\text{complete}}))$$

Two further leaf nodes, the recursive $\triangle$ and the cancellation $⩕$, will be explained with their corresponding operator nodes.

## 2.2 Operator Nodes

An operator node combines the languages of its children to express its own language. The way the children languages are combined depends on the operator $\oplus$, with a corresponding language combination function $\ell_\oplus$.

$$\ell(\oplus(P_1, \dots P_n)) = \ell_\oplus(P_1, \dots P_n) \qquad \text{with } P_1 \dots P_n \text{ process trees}$$

Several operators have been defined, of which we will provide a couple here.

$\times$  The exclusive choice operator $\times$ indicates that a trace from one of its children must be chosen. As such, its corresponding language combination function $\ell_\times$ takes the union of its children languages:

$$\ell_\times(P_1, \dots P_n) = \bigcup_{1 \leq i \leq n} \ell(P_i)$$
$$= \ell(\chi_{\{\text{start} \mapsto P_i \mapsto \text{end} | 1 \leq i \leq n\}}(P_1, \dots P_n))$$

$\circlearrowleft$  The loop operator $\circlearrowleft$ indicates a repeated execution of its children languages. Four syntactically different but expressivity-equivalent types have been defined, as well as a fifth completely different one.

(a) The $n$-nary loop operator $\circlearrowleft^n$ always executes a trace from its first child (the *body* child, and then there is a repeated choice to stop, or to execute another (*redo*) child followed by a trace from the body child, and be faced the same choice again. This implies that the $n$-ary loop operator must have at least two children.

$$\ell_{\circlearrowleft^n}(P_1, \dots P_n) = \ell(P_1) \cdot \left( \bigcup_{2 \leq i \leq n} \ell(P_i) \cdot \ell(P_1) \right)^*$$
$$= \ell(\circlearrowleft^1(\rightarrow(\times(P_2, \dots P_n), P_1)))$$

(b) The unary loop operator $\circlearrowleft^1$ has a single child. This child is always executed, after which it may be repeated.

$$\ell_{\circlearrowleft^1}(P_1) = \ell(P_1) \cdot \ell(P_1)^*$$
$$= \ell(\circlearrowleft^n(P_1, \tau)) = \ell(\circlearrowleft^2(P_1, \tau)) = \ell(\circlearrowleft^3(P_1, \tau, \tau))$$

(c) The binary loop operator $\circlearrowleft^2$ has two children. The first child is always executed, after which there is a repeated choice: either stop, or execute the second child and the first child again.

$$\ell_{\circlearrowleft^2}(P_1, P_n) = \ell(P_1) \cdot (\ell(P_2) \cdot \ell(P_1))^*$$
$$= \ell(\circlearrowleft^n(P_1, P_2))$$

(d) The ternary loop operator $\circlearrowleft^3$, in contrast, has precisely three children: a body, a redo and an exit child; the loop consists of a trace of the body child, and then an arbitrary number of traces of the redo child followed by a trace of the body child, and once the loop ends a trace from the exit child [5].

$$\ell_{\circlearrowleft^3}(P_1, P_2, P_3) = \ell(P_1) \cdot (\ell(P_2) \cdot \ell(P_1))^* \cdot \ell(P_3)$$
$$= \ell(\rightarrow(\circlearrowleft^n(P_1, P_2), P_3))$$

(e) The fixed-length loop $\circlearrowleft^k$ is unary and executes its only child exactly $k$ times [8], for a fixed $k$:

$$\ell_{\circlearrowleft^k}(P_1) = \bullet_{1 \le i \le k} \ell(P_1)$$
$$= \ell(\rightarrow(P_1, \ldots P_1))$$

$\rightarrow$ The sequence operator $\rightarrow$ executes a trace from all of its children in order.

$$\ell(\rightarrow(P_1, \ldots P_n)) = \ell(P_1) \cdot \ldots \cdot \ell(P_n)$$
$$= \ell(\prec_{\text{start} \mapsto P_1 \mapsto \ldots \mapsto P_n \mapsto \text{end}}(P_1, \ldots P_n))$$
$$= \ell(\chi_{\text{start} \mapsto P_1 \mapsto \ldots \mapsto P_n \mapsto \text{end}}(P_1, \ldots P_n))$$

$\leftarrow$ The reversed sequence operator $\leftarrow$ executes a trace from all of its children in reversed order.

$$\ell(\leftarrow(P_1, \ldots P_n)) = \ell(P_n) \cdot \ldots \cdot \ell(P_1)$$
$$= \ell(\rightarrow(P_n, \ldots P_1))$$

$\leftrightarrow$ The interleaved operator $\leftrightarrow$ includes a trace from all of its children, without overlap in these traces.

$$\ell(\leftrightarrow(P_1, \ldots P_n)) = \bigcup_{i_1 \ldots i_n \in \sim(n)} \ell(P_{i_1}) \cdot \ldots \cdot \ell(P_{i_n})$$
$$\text{with } \sim(n) \text{ all permutations of } \{1 \ldots n\}$$
$$= \times(\rightarrow(P_{i_1}, \ldots P_{i_n}), \ldots)$$

$\wedge$ The concurrent operator $\wedge$ takes one trace of each of its children, and shuffles these traces arbitrarily [24].

$$\ell(\wedge(P_1, \ldots P_n)) = \ell(P_1) \sqcup \ldots \sqcup \ell(P_n)$$
$$= \ell(\prec_{\{P_i | 1 \le i \le n\}}(P_1, \ldots P_n))$$

$\vee$ The inclusive choice operator $\vee$ operator must contain at least one trace from one of its children, but may contain a trace from any number of its children, concurrently.

$$\ell(\vee(P_1, \ldots P_n)) = \bigcup_{1 \leq j \leq n \wedge i_1, \ldots i_j \in \sim(j)} \wedge(\ell(P_{i_1}), \ldots \ell(P_{i_j}))$$

$$\text{with } \sim(j) \text{ all permutations of } \{1 \ldots j\}$$

$$= \begin{cases} \ell(\times(P_1, P_2, \wedge(P_1, P_2))) & \text{if } n = 2 \\ \ell(\times(P_1, \vee(P_2, \ldots P_n), \wedge(P_1, \vee(P_2, \ldots P_n))) & \text{if } n > 2 \end{cases}$$

$\prec$ The partially ordered operator $\prec$ generalises over the sequence and concurrent operators, by including one trace from all of its children, while enforcing a partial order $G$ between these traces [18].

$$\ell(\prec_G(P_1, \ldots P_n)) = \{\sigma \mid \forall_{1 \leq i,j \leq n} \sigma_i \in \ell(P_i) \wedge \sigma_j \in \ell(P_j) \wedge$$

$$\sigma \downarrow_{\sigma_i \cup \sigma_i} = \begin{cases} \sigma_i \cdot \sigma_j & \text{if } P_i \rightsquigarrow_G P_j \\ \sigma_i \sqcup \sigma_j & \text{otherwise} \end{cases} \}$$

Without loss of generality, in this definition we assume each event to project to a unique child $P_i$.

$\chi$ The arbitrary choice operator $\chi$ generalises over the exclusive choice and sequence operators by allowing arbitrary choices between children. That is, using a directed acyclic graph $G$ with indicated start and end nodes, every child on a path from start to end is executed in the order of the path.

$$\ell(\chi_G(P_1, \ldots P_n)) = \bigcup_{\text{start} \mapsto_G P_{i_1} \mapsto_G \ldots \mapsto_G P_{i_m} \mapsto_G \text{end}} \ell(P_{i_1}) \cdot \ldots \cdot \ell(P_{i_m})$$

To ensure that every child is on a path from start to end, we define the directed acyclic graph $G$ as follows: let $\langle \text{start}, P_1, \ldots P_n, \text{end} \rangle$ be a sequence of the start node, all process tree children and the end node. Then, $G$ is a directed acyclic graph if and only if for every child $i$ it holds that (i) for every edge $X \mapsto P_i$ it holds that $X$ is either the start node or a child $P_{x<i}$, (ii) for every edge $P_i \mapsto X$ it holds that $X$ is either the end node or a child $P_{i<x}$, (iii) the start node and every child $P_i$ have an outgoing edge and (iv) every child $P_i$ and the end node have an incoming edge.

$\nabla$ The recursion operator $\nabla$ has exactly one child and executes this child transparently. However, if the child executes a $\triangle$ leaf node, execution jumps back up to the corresponding $\nabla$ node [20]. Each $\nabla$ must be uniquely labelled in its subtree, and thus the label $q$ of a $\triangle$ node links it to a single $\nabla$ node.

Intuitively, the $\nabla$ operator node indicates that a function is entered. The $\triangle$ leaf node indicates a recursive step into the $\nabla$ node. Figure 1a provides an example. The corresponding language definition is therefore also recursive:

$$\ell(\nabla_q(P_1)) = \ell(P_1)$$

$$\ell(\triangle_q) = \begin{cases} \ell(\nabla_q) & \text{if } \triangle_q \text{ is a descendant of } \nabla_q \wedge \mathrm{rfp}(\nabla_q) \\ \{\langle\,\rangle\} & \text{otherwise} \end{cases}$$

Note that by design, a recursive leaf node $\triangle_q$ only recurses if there is a corresponding $\nabla_q$ of which it is a descendant, and in this operator node $\nabla_q$, it must be possible to avoid $\triangle$ leaves, in order to not have infinite recursion (rfp). If these conditions are not satisfied, the $\triangle_q$ leaf behaves as a silent leaf $\tau$. A node has a $\triangle$-free path if:

$$\mathrm{rfp}(\tau) = \text{true}$$
$$\mathrm{rfp}(a) = \text{true} \qquad\qquad \text{for } a \in \Sigma$$
$$\mathrm{rfp}(\circlearrowright^n(P_1, \ldots P_n)) = \mathrm{rfp}(P_1)$$
$$\mathrm{rfp}(\circlearrowright^3(P_1, P_2, P_n)) = \mathrm{rfp}(P_1) \wedge \mathrm{rfp}(P_3)$$
$$\mathrm{rfp}(\circlearrowright^k(P_1)) = \mathrm{rfp}(P_1)$$
$$\mathrm{rfp}(\otimes(P_1, \ldots P_n)) = \mathrm{rfp}(P_1) \vee \ldots \vee \mathrm{rfp}(P_n) \qquad \text{for } \otimes \in \{\times, \vee\}$$
$$\mathrm{rfp}(\oplus(P_1, \ldots P_n)) = \mathrm{rfp}(P_1) \wedge \ldots \wedge \mathrm{rfp}(P_n) \qquad \text{for } \oplus \in \{\rightarrow, \leftrightarrow, \wedge, \prec\}$$
$$\mathrm{rfp}(\nabla(P_1)) = \mathrm{rfp}(P_1)$$
$$\mathrm{rfp}(\triangle_r) = \text{false} \qquad\qquad \text{for any label } r$$

↯ Cancellation in process trees involves a leaf and two operators. First, a cancellation leaf $↯_E$ either executes an activity $a \in \Sigma$ or triggers an error of the set $E \subseteq \Sigma$. Second, there are two cancellation handling operator nodes $↯_{e,\rightarrow}$ and $↯_{e,\circlearrowright}$. Each of these operators has at least two children, and, on normal execution, executes its first child. If during that execution an error occurs, a non-first child will handle the error $e$, if the child's language contains a trace that starts with $e$. In that case, the remaining execution of the first child is halted, and one of such $e$-handling non-first children is executed. Afterwards, the $↯_\rightarrow$ operator ends its execution, while the $↯_\circlearrowright$ operator attempts to execute its first child again. Figure 1b shows an example.

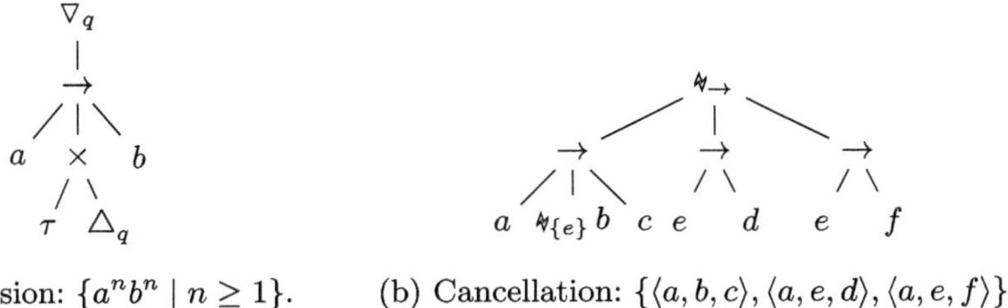

(a) Recursion: $\{a^n b^n \mid n \geq 1\}$.        (b) Cancellation: $\{\langle a, b, c\rangle, \langle a, e, d\rangle, \langle a, e, f\rangle\}$.

**Fig. 1.** Examples of process trees with their languages.

$$\ell(⩕_E\, a) = \{\langle a\rangle\} \cup \bigcup_{e \in E} \{\langle e^⩕\rangle\}$$

$$\ell(⩕_\rightarrow(P_1, \ldots P_n)) = \{\sigma \mid \sigma \in \ell(P_1) \wedge \sigma \cap \{e^⩕ \mid \langle e, \ldots\rangle \in \ell(P_i) \wedge 2 \leq i \leq n\} = \emptyset\}$$
$$\cup \{\sigma_1 \cdot \langle e\rangle \cdot \sigma_2 \mid$$
$$\sigma_1 \cdot \langle e^⩕\rangle \cdot \sigma_1' \in \ell(P_1) \wedge e^⩕ \notin \sigma_1 \wedge \langle e\rangle \cdot \sigma_2 \in \bigcup_{2 \leq i \leq n} \ell(P_i)\}$$

$$\ell(⩕_\circlearrowleft(P_1, \ldots P_n)) = \{\sigma \mid \sigma \in \ell(P_1) \wedge \sigma \cap \{e^⩕ \mid \langle e, \ldots\rangle \in \ell(P_i) \wedge 2 \leq i \leq n\} = \emptyset\}$$
$$\cup \{\sigma_1 \cdot \langle e\rangle \cdot \sigma_2 \cdot \sigma_3 \mid$$
$$\sigma_1 \cdot \langle e^⩕\rangle \cdot \sigma_1' \in \ell(P_1) \wedge e^⩕ \notin \sigma_1 \wedge$$
$$\langle e\rangle \cdot \sigma_2 \in \bigcup_{2 \leq i \leq n} \ell(P_i) \wedge \sigma_3 \in \ell(⩕_\circlearrowleft(P_1, \ldots P_n))\}$$

To the best of our knowledge, these leaves and operators are all that have been used in context of process trees. Nevertheless, there are still operators in formal languages to be explored, such as the $k$-times-concurrent-with-itself (iterated shuffle) [57] operator and the concatenation operator.

## 2.3   Summary and Expressivity

Table 1 gives an overview of the usage of process tree leaves and operators in a selection of literature. In total, we identified 5 types of leaves and 16 operators.

For most leaves and operators in Sects. 2.1 and 2.2, alternative definitions were provided in terms of other operators. First, the operators $\circlearrowleft^1$, $\circlearrowleft^2$, $\circlearrowleft^3$ and $\circlearrowleft^n$ can be rewritten into one another and are thus equally-expressive. Second, using the alternative definitions, the leaf node $\tau$ and the operator nodes $\times$, $\circlearrowleft^k$, $\rightarrow$, $\leftarrow$, $\leftrightarrow$, $\wedge$ and $\vee$ can be language-equivalently rewritten into a process tree using only the nodes $a$, $\circlearrowleft^n$, $\chi$, $\prec$, $\nabla$ and $⩕$. Thus, this set of leaf and operator nodes forms a **minimal process tree** definition. The non-minimal operators an be considered as convenience operators to express languages more elegantly.

However, as every regular language can be represented by the regex-operators choice, sequence and Kleene-star, every regular language can also be represented by the nodes $a$, $\to$, $\times$ and $\circlearrowright^1$. Conversely, as no process tree operator except $\nabla$ induces an infinite state space, every process tree without the recursion operator $\nabla$ expresses a regular language. The recursion operator $\nabla$ brings the expressivity of process trees to context-free languages, as witnessed by Fig. 1a, in which a model with an infinite state space is shown.

**Table 1.** Process tree operators used in literature.

| Application | | $\tau$ | $a$ | $\bar a$ | $\times$ | $\circlearrowright^n$ | $\circlearrowright^1$ | $\circlearrowright^2$ | $\circlearrowright^3$ | $\circlearrowright^k$ | $\to$ | $\leftarrow$ | $\leftrightarrow$ | $\wedge$ | $\vee$ | $\prec$ | $\chi$ | $\nabla$ | ↯ |
|---|---|---|---|---|---|---|---|---|---|---|---|---|---|---|---|---|---|---|---|
| discovery | [4,10,25–27,29,31,35,43][1] | $\tau$ | $a$ | | $\times$ | $\circlearrowright^n$ | | | | | $\to$ | | | $\wedge$ | | | | | |
| discovery | [23] | $\tau$ | $a$ | | $\times$ | $\circlearrowright^n$ | | | | | $\to$ | | $\leftrightarrow$ | $\wedge$ | $\vee$ | | | | |
| discovery | [5] | | $a$ | | $\times$ | | $\circlearrowright^1$ | | | | $\to$ | | | $\wedge$ | | | | | |
| discovery | [16–18] | $\tau$ | $a$ | | $\times$ | | | $\circlearrowright^2$ | | | | | | | | $\prec$ | | | |
| discovery | [15] | $\tau$ | $a$ | | | | | $\circlearrowright^2$ | | | | | | | | $\prec$ | $\chi$ | | |
| discovery | [20] | $\tau$ | $a$ | | $\times$ | $\circlearrowright^n$ | | | | | $\to$ | | | $\wedge$ | | | | $\nabla$ | |
| discovery | [19] | $\tau$ | $a$ | | $\times$ | $\circlearrowright^n$ | | | | | $\to$ | | | $\wedge$ | | | | | ↯ |
| configurable models | [7] | | $a$ | | $\times$ | | | | $\circlearrowright^3$ | | $\to$ | $\leftarrow$ | | $\wedge$ | | | | | |
| in-database discovery | [55] | | $a$ | | $\times$ | $\circlearrowright^n$ | | | | | $\to$ | | | $\wedge$ | | | | | |
| life-cycle discovery | [30] | $\tau$ | | $\bar a$ | $\times$ | $\circlearrowright^n$ | | | | | $\to$ | | $\leftrightarrow$ | $\wedge$ | | | | | |
| stochastic tree discovery | [8] | $\tau$ | $a$ | | $\times$ | | $\circlearrowright^1$ | | | $\circlearrowright^k$ | $\to$ | | | $\wedge$ | | | | | |
| conformance checking | [31,41,42] | $\tau$ | $a$ | | $\times$ | $\circlearrowright^n$ | | | | | $\to$ | | | $\wedge$ | | | | | |
| conformance checking | [3,46,50,51][2] | $\tau$ | $a$ | | $\times$ | | | $\circlearrowright^2$ | | | $\to$ | | | $\wedge$ | | | | | |
| model quality | [6] | $\tau$ | $a$ | | $\times$ | | | $\circlearrowright^2$ | | | $\to$ | $\leftarrow$ | | $\wedge$ | $\vee$ | | | | |
| abstraction rediscoverability | [24] | $\tau$ | $a$ | | $\times$ | $\circlearrowright^n$ | | | | | $\to$ | | $\leftrightarrow$ | $\wedge$ | $\vee$ | | | | |
| concept-drift detection | [38] | $\tau$ | $a$ | | $\times$ | | | $\circlearrowright^2$ | | | $\to$ | | | $\wedge$ | | | | | |
| translation from workflow-nets | [59] | $\tau$ | $a$ | | $\times$ | | | $\circlearrowright^2$ | | | $\to$ | | | $\wedge$ | | | | | |
| translation from workflow-nets | [14] | $\tau$ | $a$ | | $\times$ | | | $\circlearrowright^2$ | | | | | | | | $\prec$ | | | |
| reduction rules | [22,23] | $\tau$ | $a$ | | $\times$ | $\circlearrowright^n$ | | | | | $\to$ | | $\leftrightarrow$ | $\wedge$ | $\vee$ | | | | |
| process redesign | [60] | | $a$ | | $\times$ | | | $\circlearrowright^2$ | | | $\to$ | | | $\wedge$ | | | | | |
| process redesign | [40] | $\tau$ | $a$ | | $\times$ | $\circlearrowright^n$ | | | | | $\to$ | | | $\wedge$ | | | | | |

[1] [10,43] use binary trees, "without loss of generality".

[2] [50] assumes that every activity $a \in \Sigma$ appears only once in a process tree.

## 2.4  Extensions

Process trees have been extended in several directions to broaden their expressiveness, beyond a sole focus on control-flow. Configurable process trees were introduced by Wil and his colleagues [7] to allow the definition of *families of related process trees* by introducing configuration nodes in the tree. This supports variability management, for instance, in organisations or product lines where processes share a common core but differ in specific steps. Another line of research focuses on object-centric process trees [11], which move from the traditional, single-case notion to model processes involving multiple interacting objects. Queue-extended process trees [53] enrich the tree with explicit queuing semantics, allowing the modelling of buffering and processing-time behaviour. In a different direction, hybrid approaches such as Declare-trees [32] combine the strict block-structuredness of process trees with the flexibility of declarative models.

Process trees have also been adapted to prefix trees with data attributes [33], which incorporate data perspectives into the process model. By linking behaviour to case-level properties (e.g., cost, priority, or region), these models support more context-aware analyses and facilitate the discovery of behaviour conditioned by data. Finally, process trees have been extended with likelihoods of choices made in their execution, making them stochastic process trees [3,8].

## 3   Applications

### 3.1   Discovery

As shown in Table 1, several process tree discovery techniques have been proposed, which aim to construct a process tree automatically, given only an event log of recorded behaviour. These can be categorised into genetic algorithms, reduction algorithms, recursive algorithms, and random algorithms.

Genetic algorithms start with an initial population of process trees, which is evolved using cross-over, random mutations and selection. The Evolutionary Tree Miner [5,7] is an example of a genetic algorithm. Reduction algorithms start from a process tree that trivially represents the entire event log, after which reduction rules are applied that lower the complexity of the tree, while preserving its behaviour as much as possible. The Toothpaste Miner [8] is an example of a reduction algorithm. Recursive approaches work in a top-down fashion, in which they first identify the most important tree operator in an event log, then split the log according to this operator and recurse, until a base case ends the recursion. The Inductive Miner family [4,10,15–20,23,25–27,29–31,35,43,55] is an example of recursive approaches. Finally, random algorithms construct a process tree by selecting operators and activities randomly, which leverages the structure that a process tree provides. In a study of model quality [9], random process trees were leveraged.

### 3.2   Conformance Checking

The structure of process trees is also leveraged in conformance checking, that is, the study of to what extent a process model (a process tree) coincides with an event log.

An alignment is a sequence of edit operations that transform a trace from an event log into a path through a process model, which to some extent provides an explanation of the deviations between the trace and the model, which can in turn be used as a measure for fitness and precision. Obtaining an alignment with a minimal number of edit operations is PSPACE-complete [52].

To address this, derivative measures on sub-sets of activities [31] or sub-traces [41] have been proposed. This first technique projects process trees to sub-sets of activities, which is hard on Petri nets but easy on process trees, using reduction rules [22]. Computing a minimal alignment has been approximated [46], again leveraging the structure that process trees provide. Recently, finding a minimal alignment has been translated to mixed integer linear programming [51], and finding a minimal alignment on a process tree in which each activity appears at most once is polynomial [50]. In [58], the authors propose an alignment repair approach for process trees. Given an existing alignment for a process tree, the authors propose a technique that repairs the alignment, i.e., on the basis of a given slight modification of the original process tree. Finally, in [42], an approach is discussed to find an alignment in case one does not completely trust the log and/or the process tree, and in [3], all optimal alignments are computed to avoid having to make an arbitrary choice between them.

For model-model comparisons, the formal results of process discovery can be leveraged: for certain classes of process trees, it suffices to reduce both trees exhaustively using reduction rules [22], after which the resulting trees can be compared on syntactical equivalence to decide language equality [23].

### 3.3   Other

Beyond foundational extensions to the process tree definition (Sect. 2.4), a variety of tools, visualisations and applications have been developed, and a multitude of case studies have been conducted to evaluate their accessibility and practical usefulness. A prominent example is the Inductive Visual Miner [28], which provides an interactive environment to explore process trees. It supports the operators $\times$, $\to$, $\circlearrowright^n$, $\wedge$, $\leftrightarrow$ and $\vee$. In addition, it combines tree editing with enhancing the tree with time performance measures. Another notable tool is Cortado [49], based on a variety of incremental process tree-based discovery and conformance checking approaches [44,45,47,48], which supports interactive and incremental process discovery using process trees as the modelling language.

Complementing tool support, process trees have also been used frequently in case studies due to their block-structured, easy-to-understand, and sound nature. For example, the $PM^2$ project, led by Wil [12], conducted a case study using the Inductive Visual Miner and process tree discovery in real-life business settings, demonstrating both its scalability and interpretability for practitioners.

In practice, process tree–based approaches have also been adopted in commercial tools. For instance, Celonis' Process Adherence Manager implements a variant of the Inductive Miner and provides functionalities that uses the discovered process trees as reference models for conformance checking and deviation analysis.[1]

On the analytical side, several approaches build upon process trees to advance specific forms of analysis. Under Wil's leadership, process trees have also been used as the modelling language for local process models (LPMs) to express and discover frequent behavioural patterns in event logs [56]. Process trees have also been used for causal analysis [34], providing more fine-grained insights into causal dependencies between activities. Other work has focused on pre-processing event logs to further extend the practical usability of process trees. Examples include handling the discovery of process trees with duplicated tasks [36] and embedding process trees into hierarchical activity trees to support multi-level abstraction [37].

## 4    Relation with Petri Nets

In this section, we explore the relationship between process trees in Petri nets. We show, for the basic process tree operators $\rightarrow$, $\times$, $\wedge$ and $\circlearrowleft^2$, how a corresponding sound WF-net can be obtained. Furthermore, we explore the reverse, i.e., deciding whether a given sound WF-net corresponds to a process tree, and, if so, discover the tree.

### 4.1    Translating Process Trees Into Petri Nets

Recall that, with the exception of the recursion operator, a process tree expresses a regular language. Translation to a Petri net is therefore trivial. However, such a translation may yield an overly large Petri net.

To retain a compact model, when translating a process tree to a Petri net, one is often interested in utilising the same number of *labelled transitions* as there are *activity leaves* in the tree. Still, under this constraint, translating a process tree to a Petri net is straightforward. For each basic operator, a simple schematic construct can be defined that describes the same behaviour, as shown schematically in Fig. 2. A leaf (either visible or not) is translated to a single transition with one connecting pre- and one connecting post-place. A token resides in the pre-place, which also serves as the source place of the WF-net.

Process tree operators are translated into a Petri net fragment by inserting the (recursively computed) Petri net representations of their children into a predefined fragment corresponding to the operator's nature. In this context, we let $\lambda(Q)$ represent the Petri net representation of some process tree $Q$. We assume $\lambda(Q)$ to be a WF-net, and thus, to describe a unique source and a unique sink place. We let $\hat{\lambda}(Q)$ be the Petri net that is obtained by removing the unique source and sink from $\lambda(Q)$. For a sequence construct $\rightarrow(Q_1, \ldots, Q_n)$, we compute the WF-net representation $\lambda(Q_i)$ of each of its children $Q_1, \ldots, Q_n$ and then form a sequential Petri net structure that includes each of the WF-net structures

---

[1] https://docs.celonis.com/en/process-adherence-manager.html.

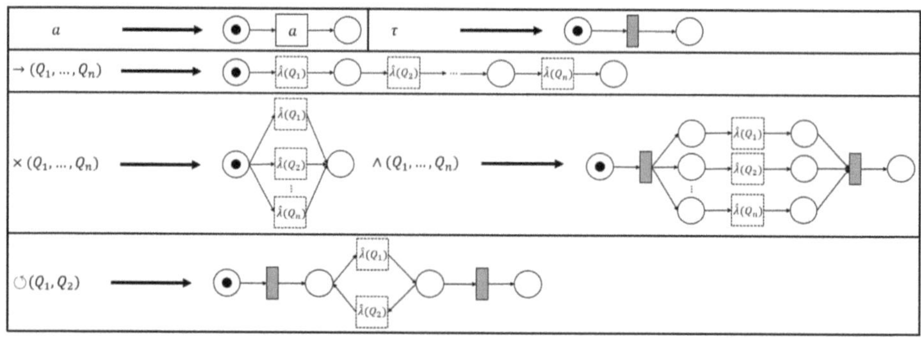

**Fig. 2.** Schematic overview of the translation of process tree structures into sound WF-net fragments (borrowed from [59]). $\lambda(Q_i)$ refers to the (recursively) constructed patterns as shown, $\hat{\lambda}(Q_i)$ corresponds to said net in which the unique source and sink place are removed.

of its children. When inserting the subnets computed for the children of the operator (i.e., nets $\hat{\lambda}(Q_1), \ldots, \hat{\lambda}(Q_n)$), we do so by connecting the source place of the operator's fragment to the transitions that connect to the source place of the fragment computed for the subtree. Symmetrically, the same procedure is performed on the transitions that connect to the sink place of the net fragment computed for the subtree. In Fig. 2, patterns for the other operators are depicted as well. Note that as each pattern describes a sound WF-net fragment, the final recursively composed WF-net of a process tree is sound by construction.[2]

### 4.2   Translating Petri Nets into Process Trees

Translation of a Petri net to a process tree is useful, since, if a process tree can be defined that is language-equivalent to a given Petri net, the discovered tree structure can be exploited, e.g., *alignments* can be computed more efficiently. Like in the translation from process trees to Petri nets, if a Petri net describes a finite language, a process tree of the form $\times(\rightarrow(\sigma_1(1), \ldots, \sigma_1(|\sigma_1|)), \ldots \rightarrow(\sigma_n(1), \ldots \sigma_n(|\sigma_n|)))$ can be constructed, assuming that the net's language consists of $n$ members. However, to utilise the tree hierarchy effectively, one ideally finds a process tree that has the same number of activity leaves as there are labelled transitions in the net.

In [59], a method is proposed to detect a process tree representation of a given WF-net. The core idea of this work is to identify subnets in the main net that can be mapped to a process tree structure. When such a subnet is identified, the subnet is replaced by a single transition, carrying the process tree representation as its label. This procedure is repeated until (i) no pattern can be found, or, (ii) a net with a single transition remains. If case (i) applies, the algorithm cannot

---

[2] Interestingly, the basis for this proof, provided in [59], is based on [1], published by van der Aalst in 2000, long before process trees were studied.

construct a language-equivalent process tree, if (ii) applies, the label of the single remaining transition is a language-equivalent process tree to the original input net. The authors note that the work bears great similarity to the work by van der Aalst and Lassen on the translation of unstructured Workflow processes to BPEL [2].

An alternative, under-explored, direction toward the problem of detecting tree structures in Petri nets is by identify whether a WF-net is *block-structured*. We present an informal characterisation of this class of nets, i.e., for acyclic WF-nets. In a block-structured acyclic net, a choice/parallel construct (i.e., source place/transition) introduces sub-regions that cannot interact with one another. Consider Fig. 3, in which we depict a schematic example of a WF-net containing a place-bordered block. From a formal perspective, a place-bordered block is formed by two places $p$, $p'$ with the same outdegree and indegree, for which a bijection $b$ on the arcs exists such that any path from the source to the sink that visits $(p, t)$ also visits $b(p, t)$, with $b=(t', p')$. Observer that, if such a path exists, indeed, the transitions in one sub-net of a place/transition bordered block cannot consume/produce tokens in the other sub-nets of a block. As an example, consider Fig. 4, in which we depict the above described notion on an example Petri net.

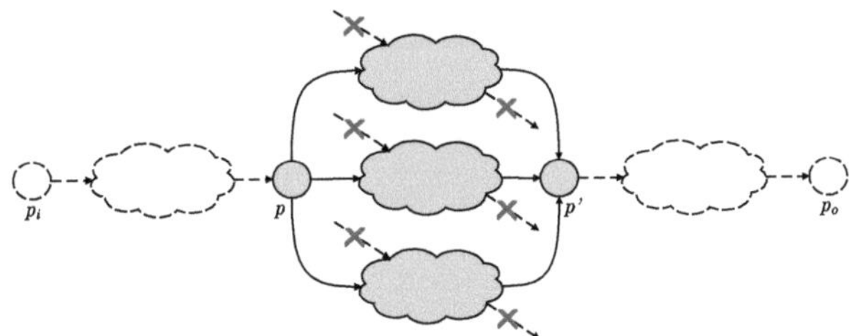



**Fig. 3.** Schematic overview of a place-bordered block in a WF-net.

For nets with cycles, the above-described definition requires an extension since places that can act as the source place of the do part of a loop act as the target place of the redo-part of a loop. However, one of the incoming arcs of said source place is used to activate the loop, and hence, needs to be excluded from the mapping. Additionally, the definition of paths from the source to the sink place is not applicable to WF-nets containing cycles.

Finally, note that the detection of process tree structures in arbitrary Petri nets bears significant similarity with respect to the detection of Refined Process Structure Tree (RPST) decomposition [39]. However, since RPST decomposition is defined for Workflow-graphs (i.e., a predecessor of BPMN), which do not have a visual entity representing a process state (such as places), detection of the RPST decomposition on an arbitrary Petri net does not yield a corresponding process tree structure. As a consequence, a proper RPST decomposition can be discovered on unsound (not well-handled) WF-nets (see also Fig. 18 of [59]).

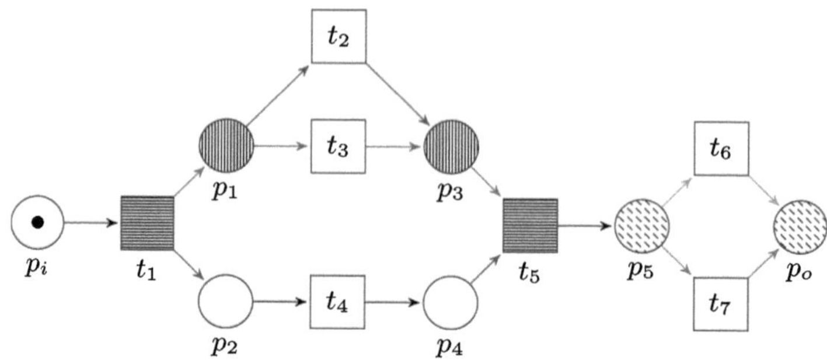

**Fig. 4.** Example Petri net $N_1$ where each pair of the block has a dedicated visual pattern. The colored arc pairs represent the corresponding arc bijection.

## 5    Conclusion

This paper reiterated several process tree operators and combined them in a single formal framework, and we identified a minimal set of process tree operators and leaves that can express any process tree of any formalism we encountered. The applications of process trees, including process discovery, conformance checking and various others, were discussed. We illustrated the relation between process trees and Petri nets by translating trees to nets and vice versa.

As future work, we foresee that process trees have the potential to assist in process-based reasoning, for instance in process mining with stochasticity or time performance. To this end, the hierarchical block-structured nature may be leveraged to structurally compute probabilities and timing. Furthermore, current techniques may see even wider application if translations of Petri nets to process trees for all operators would be established.

## References


1. Aalst, W.M.P.: Workflow verification: finding control-flow errors using petri-net-based techniques. In: van der Aalst, W., Desel, J., Oberweis, A. (eds.) Business Process Management. LNCS, vol. 1806, pp. 161–183. Springer, Heidelberg (2000). https://doi.org/10.1007/3-540-45594-9_11
2. van der Aalst, W.M.P., Lassen, K.B.: Translating unstructured workflow processes to readable BPEL: theory and implementation. Inf. Softw. Technol. **50**(3), 131–159 (2008)
3. Bär, P., Wynn, M.T., Leemans, S.J.J.: A full picture in conformance checking: efficiently summarizing all optimal alignments. In: Senderovich, A., Cabanillas, C., Vanderfeesten, I., A. Reijers, H. (eds.) BPM. LNCS, vol. 16044, pp. 69–87. Springer, Cham (2025). https://doi.org/10.1007/978-3-032-02867-9_6
4. Brons, D., Scheepens, R., Fahland, D.: Striking a new balance in accuracy and simplicity with the probabilistic inductive miner. In: ICPM, pp. 32–39. IEEE (2021)
5. Buijs, J.C.A.M., van Dongen, B.F., van der Aalst, W.M.P.: A genetic algorithm for discovering process trees. In: IEEE Congress on Evolutionary Computation, pp. 1–8. IEEE (2012)

6. Buijs, J.C.A.M., van Dongen, B.F., van der Aalst, W.M.P.: On the role of fitness, precision, generalization and simplicity in process discovery. In: Meersman, R., Panetto, H., Dillon, T., Rinderle-Ma, S., Dadam, P., Zhou, X., Pearson, S., Ferscha, A., Bergamaschi, S., Cruz, I.F. (eds.) OTM 2012. LNCS, vol. 7565, pp. 305–322. Springer, Heidelberg (2012). https://doi.org/10.1007/978-3-642-33606-5_19

7. Buijs, J.C.A.M., van Dongen, B.F., van der Aalst, W.M.P.: Mining configurable process models from collections of event logs. In: Daniel, F., Wang, J., Weber, B. (eds.) BPM 2013. LNCS, vol. 8094, pp. 33–48. Springer, Heidelberg (2013). https://doi.org/10.1007/978-3-642-40176-3_5

8. Burke, A., Leemans, S.J.J., Wynn, M.T.: Discovering stochastic process models by reduction and abstraction. In: Buchs, D., Carmona, J. (eds.) PETRI NETS 2021. LNCS, vol. 12734, pp. 312–336. Springer, Cham (2021). https://doi.org/10.1007/978-3-030-76983-3_16

9. Burke, A.T., Leemans, S.J.J., Wynn, M.T., van der Aalst, W.M.P., ter Hofstede, A.H.M.: A chance for models to show their quality: stochastic process model-log dimensions. Inf. Syst. **124**, 102382 (2024)

10. van Detten, J.N., Schumacher, P., Leemans, S.J.J.: An approximate inductive miner. In: ICPM, pp. 129–136. IEEE (2023)

11. van Detten, J.N., Schumacher, P., Leemans, S.J.J.: Discovering compact, live and identifier-sound object-centric process models. In: ICPM, pp. 113–120. IEEE (2024)

12. van Eck, M.L., Lu, X., Leemans, S.J.J., van der Aalst, W.M.P.: PM$^2$: a process mining project methodology. In: Zdravkovic, J., Kirikova, M., Johannesson, P. (eds.) CAiSE 2015. LNCS, vol. 9097, pp. 297–313. Springer, Cham (2015). https://doi.org/10.1007/978-3-319-19069-3_19

13. Kopp, O., Martin, D., Wutke, D., Leymann, F.: The difference between graph-based and block-structured business process modelling languages. Enterp. Model. Inf. Syst. Archit. Int. J. Concept. Model. **4**(1), 3–13 (2009)

14. Kourani, H., Park, G., van der Aalst, W.M.P.: Translating workflow nets into the partially ordered workflow language. In: Amparore, E., Mikulski, Ł. (eds.) Petri Nets. LNCS, vol. 15714, pp. 242–264. Springer, Cham (2025). https://doi.org/10.1007/978-3-031-94634-9_12

15. Kourani, H., Park, G., van der Aalst, W.M.P.: Unlocking non-block-structured decisions: inductive mining with choice graphs. CoRR abs/2505.07052 (2025)

16. Kourani, H., Schuster, D., van der Aalst, W.M.P.: Scalable discovery of partially ordered workflow models with formal guarantees. In: ICPM, pp. 89–96. IEEE (2023)

17. Kourani, H., van Zelst, S.J.: POWL: partially ordered workflow language. In: Di Francescomarino, C., Burattin, A., Janiesch, C., Sadiq, S. (eds.) BPM. LNCS, vol. 14159, pp. 92–108. Springer, Cham (2023). https://doi.org/10.1007/978-3-031-41620-0_6

18. Kourani, H., van Zelst, S.J., Schuster, D., van der Aalst, W.M.P.: Discovering partially ordered workflow models. Inf. Syst. **128**, 102493 (2025)

19. Leemans, M., van der Aalst, W.M.P.: Modeling and discovering cancelation behavior. In: Panetto, H., Debruyne, C., Gaaloul, W., Papazoglou, M., Paschke, A., Ardagna, C.A., Meersman, R. (eds.) OTM 2017. LNCS, vol. 10573, pp. 93–113. Springer, Cham (2017). https://doi.org/10.1007/978-3-319-69462-7_8

20. Leemans, M., van der Aalst, W.M.P., van den Brand, M.G.J.: Recursion aware modeling and discovery for hierarchical software event log analysis. In: SANER, pp. 185–196. IEEE Computer Society (2018)

21. Leemans, S.J.J.: Process discovery and exploration. In: Fournier, F., Mendling, J. (eds.) BPM 2014. LNBIP, vol. 202, pp. 582–585. Springer, Cham (2015). https://doi.org/10.1007/978-3-319-15895-2_52
22. Leemans, S.J.J.: Language-preserving reduction rules for block-structured workflow nets. CoRR abs/2203.10410 (2022)
23. Leemans, S.J.J.: Robust process mining with guarantees - process discovery, conformance checking and enhancement. In: LNBIP, vol. 440. Springer, Cham (2022). https://doi.org/10.1007/978-3-030-96655-3
24. Leemans, S.J.J., Fahland, D.: Information-preserving abstractions of event data in process mining. Knowl. Inf. Syst. **62**(3), 1143–1197 (2020)
25. Leemans, S.J.J., Fahland, D., van der Aalst, W.M.P.: Discovering block-structured process models from event logs - a constructive approach. In: Colom, J.-M., Desel, J. (eds.) PETRI NETS 2013. LNCS, vol. 7927, pp. 311–329. Springer, Heidelberg (2013). https://doi.org/10.1007/978-3-642-38697-8_17
26. Leemans, S.J.J., Fahland, D., van der Aalst, W.M.P.: Discovering block-structured process models from event logs containing infrequent behaviour. In: Lohmann, N., Song, M., Wohed, P. (eds.) BPM 2013. LNBIP, vol. 171, pp. 66–78. Springer, Cham (2014). https://doi.org/10.1007/978-3-319-06257-0_6
27. Leemans, S.J.J., Fahland, D., van der Aalst, W.M.P.: Discovering block-structured process models from incomplete event logs. In: Ciardo, G., Kindler, E. (eds.) PETRI NETS 2014. LNCS, vol. 8489, pp. 91–110. Springer, Cham (2014). https://doi.org/10.1007/978-3-319-07734-5_6
28. Leemans, S.J.J., Fahland, D., van der Aalst, W.M.P.: Exploring processes and deviations. In: Fournier, F., Mendling, J. (eds.) BPM 2014. LNBIP, vol. 202, pp. 304–316. Springer, Cham (2015). https://doi.org/10.1007/978-3-319-15895-2_26
29. Leemans, S.J.J., Fahland, D., van der Aalst, W.M.P.: Scalable process discovery with guarantees. In: Gaaloul, K., Schmidt, R., Nurcan, S., Guerreiro, S., Ma, Q. (eds.) CAISE 2015. LNBIP, vol. 214, pp. 85–101. Springer, Cham (2015). https://doi.org/10.1007/978-3-319-19237-6_6
30. Leemans, S.J.J., Fahland, D., van der Aalst, W.M.P.: Using life cycle information in process discovery. In: Reichert, M., Reijers, H.A. (eds.) BPM 2015. LNBIP, vol. 256, pp. 204–217. Springer, Cham (2016). https://doi.org/10.1007/978-3-319-42887-1_17
31. Leemans, S.J.J., Fahland, D., van der Aalst, W.M.P.: Scalable process discovery and conformance checking. Softw. Syst. Model. **17**(2), 599–631 (2018)
32. Leemans, S.J.J., Goel, K., van Zelst, S.J.: Using multi-level information in hierarchical process mining: Balancing behavioural quality and model complexity. In: ICPM, pp. 137–144. IEEE (2020)
33. Leemans, S.J.J., Partington, A., Karnon, J., Wynn, M.T.: Process mining for healthcare decision analytics with micro-costing estimations. Artif. Intell. Medicine **135**, 102473 (2023)
34. Leemans, S.J.J., Tax, N.: Causal reasoning over control-flow decisions in process models. In: Franch, X., Poels, G., Gailly, F., Snoeck, M. (eds.) Advanced Information Systems Engineering. CAiSE 2022. LNCS, vol. 13295, pp. 183–200. Springer, Cham (2022). https://doi.org/10.1007/978-3-031-07472-1_11
35. Leemans, S.J.J., Tax, N., ter Hofstede, A.H.M.: Indulpet miner: combining discovery algorithms. In: Panetto, H., Debruyne, C., Proper, H.A., Ardagna, C.A., Roman, D., Meersman, R. (eds.) OTM 2018. LNCS, vol. 11229, pp. 97–115. Springer, Cham (2018). https://doi.org/10.1007/978-3-030-02610-3_6

36. Lu, X., Fahland, D., van den Biggelaar, F.J.H.M., van der Aalst, W.M.P.: Detecting deviating behaviors without models. In: Business Process Management Workshops. LNBIP, vol. 256, pp. 126–139. Springer, Cham (2015)

37. Lu, X., Gal, A., Reijers, H.A.: Discovering hierarchical processes using flexible activity trees for event abstraction. In: ICPM, pp. 145–152. IEEE (2020)

38. Ostovar, A., Leemans, S.J.J., Rosa, M.L.: Robust drift characterization from event streams of business processes. ACM Trans. Knowl. Discov. Data **14**(3), 30:1–30:57 (2020)

39. Polyvyanyy, A., Vanhatalo, J., Völzer, H.: Simplified computation and generalization of the refined process structure tree. In: Bravetti, M., Bultan, T. (eds.) WS-FM 2010. LNCS, vol. 6551, pp. 25–41. Springer, Heidelberg (2011). https://doi.org/10.1007/978-3-642-19589-1_2

40. Pourbafrani, M., van der Aalst, W.M.P.: Interactive process improvement using simulation of enriched process trees. In: Hacid, H., et al. ICSOC Workshops. LNCS, vol. 13236, pp. 61–76. Springer, Cham (2021). https://doi.org/10.1007/978-3-031-14135-5_5

41. Rocha, E.G., van der Aalst, W.M.P.: Polynomial-time conformance checking for process trees. In: Di Francescomarino, C., Burattin, A., Janiesch, C., Sadiq, S. (eds.) BPM. LNCS, vol. 14159, pp. 109–125. Springer, Cham (2023). https://doi.org/10.1007/978-3-031-41620-0_7

42. Rogge-Solti, A., Senderovich, A., Weidlich, M., Mendling, J., Gal, A.: In log and model we trust? a generalized conformance checking framework. In: La Rosa, M., Loos, P., Pastor, O. (eds.) BPM 2016. LNCS, vol. 9850, pp. 179–196. Springer, Cham (2016). https://doi.org/10.1007/978-3-319-45348-4_11

43. Schröder, C., van Detten, J.N., Leemans, S.J.J.: Locally optimized process tree discovery. In: ICPM Workshops. LNBIP, vol. 533, pp. 389–401. Springer (2024)

44. Schuster, D., Föcking, N., van Zelst, S.J., van der Aalst, W.M.P.: Conformance checking for trace fragments using infix and postfix alignments. In: Sellami, M., Ceravolo, P., Reijers, H.A., Gaaloul, W., Panetto, H. (eds.) CoopIS. LNCS, vol. 13591, pp. 299–310. Springer, Cham (2022). https://doi.org/10.1007/978-3-031-17834-4_18

45. Schuster, D., Föcking, N., van Zelst, S.J., van der Aalst, W.M.P.: Incremental discovery of process models using trace fragments. In: Di Francescomarino, C., Burattin, A., Janiesch, C., Sadiq, S. (eds.) BPM. LNCS, vol. 14159, pp. 55–73. Springer, Cham (2023). https://doi.org/10.1007/978-3-031-41620-0_4

46. Schuster, D., van Zelst, S., van der Aalst, W.M.P.: Alignment approximation for process trees. In: Leemans, S., Leopold, H. (eds.) ICPM 2020. LNBIP, vol. 406, pp. 247–259. Springer, Cham (2021). https://doi.org/10.1007/978-3-030-72693-5_19

47. Schuster, D., van Zelst, S.J., van der Aalst, W.M.P.: Incremental discovery of hierarchical process models. In: Dalpiaz, F., Zdravkovic, J., Loucopoulos, P. (eds.) RCIS 2020. LNBIP, vol. 385, pp. 417–433. Springer, Cham (2020). https://doi.org/10.1007/978-3-030-50316-1_25

48. Schuster, D., van Zelst, S.J., van der Aalst, W.M.P.: Freezing sub-models during incremental process discovery. In: Ghose, A., Horkoff, J., Silva Souza, V.E., Parsons, J., Evermann, J. (eds.) ER 2021. LNCS, vol. 13011, pp. 14–24. Springer, Cham (2021). https://doi.org/10.1007/978-3-030-89022-3_2

49. Schuster, D., van Zelst, S.J., van der Aalst, W.M.P.: Cortado: a dedicated process mining tool for interactive process discovery. SoftwareX **22**, 101373 (2023)

50. Schwanen, C.T., Pakusa, W., van der Aalst, W.M.P.: A dynamic programming approach for alignments on process trees. In: Delgado, A., Slaats, T. (eds.) ICPM

Workshops. LNBIP, vol. 533, pp. 84–97. Springer, Cham (2024). https://doi.org/10.1007/978-3-031-82225-4_7
51. Schwanen, C.T., Pakusa, W., van der Aalst, W.M.P.: Process tree alignments. In: Borbinha, J., Prince Sales, T., Da Silva, M.M., Proper, H.A., Schnellmann, M. (eds.) EDOC. LNCS, vol. 15409, pp. 300–317. Springer, Cham (2024). https://doi.org/10.1007/978-3-031-78338-8_16
52. Schwanen, C.T., Pakusa, W., van der Aalst, W.M.P.: Complexity of alignments on sound free-choice workflow nets. In: Amparore, E., Mikulski, Ł. (eds.) Petri Nets. LNCS, vol. 15714, pp. 388–410. Springer, Cham (2025). https://doi.org/10.1007/978-3-031-94634-9_19
53. Senderovich, A., Leemans, S.J.J., Harel, S., Gal, A., Mandelbaum, A., van der Aalst, W.M.P.: Discovering queues from event logs with varying levels of information. In: Reichert, M., Reijers, H.A. (eds.) BPM 2015. LNBIP, vol. 256, pp. 154–166. Springer, Cham (2016). https://doi.org/10.1007/978-3-319-42887-1_13
54. Staab, S., van der Aalst, W.M.P., Benjamins, V.R., Sheth, A.P., Miller, J.A., Bussler, C., Maedche, A., Fensel, D., Gannon, D.: Web services: been there, done that? IEEE Intell. Syst. **18**(1), 72–85 (2003)
55. Syamsiyah, A., Leemans, S.J.J.: Process discovery using in-database minimum self distance abstractions. In: SAC, pp. 26–35. ACM (2020)
56. Tax, N., Sidorova, N., Haakma, R., van der Aalst, W.M.P.: Mining local process models. J. Innov. Digit. Ecosyst. **3**(2), 183–196 (2016)
57. Warmuth, M.K., Haussler, D.: On the complexity of iterated shuffle. J. Comput. Syst. Sci. **28**(3), 345–358 (1984)
58. van Zelst, S.J., Buijs, J.C.A.M., Vázquez-Barreiros, B., Lama, M., Mucientes, M.: Repairing alignments of process models. Bus. Inf. Syst. Eng. **62**(4), 289–304 (2020)
59. van Zelst, S.J., Leemans, S.J.J.: Translating workflow nets to process trees: an algorithmic approach. Algorithms **13**(11), 279 (2020)
60. van Zelst, S.J., Santos, L.F.R., van der Aalst, W.M.P.: Data-driven process performance measurement and prediction: a process-tree-based approach. In: Nurcan, S., Korthaus, A. (eds.) CAiSE 2021. LNBIP, vol. 424, pp. 73–81. Springer, Cham (2021). https://doi.org/10.1007/978-3-030-79108-7_9

# Challenges and Contests in Process Mining

Boudewijn F. van Dongen[(✉)] and Eric Verbeek

Process Analytics, Eindhoven University of Technology, Eindhoven, The Netherlands
`b.f.v.dongen@tue.nl`

**Abstract.** Around the turn of the century, when the first process mining papers started appearing, researchers across the world started reaching out to the group of Wil van der Aalst. They were looking for help finding real-life data. Data that would allow them to prove that their algorithms, techniques, tools or simply ideas would also work in practice.

Using the connections of his department in Eindhoven and his industry contacts from previous years, Wil was very active in finding real-life data for personal use by his group members, but sharing this data with the world proved one step too far for many companies.

Nonetheless, Wil pursued this direction and by 2011 the first BPI Challenge dataset was publicly released. This challenge consisted of a dataset that contained real-life data from a real hospital. Researchers worldwide were challenged to showcase their work and this first challenge sparked a series of BPI Challenges and Process Discovery Contests which we outline in this paper.

**Keywords:** BPI Challenges · Process Discovery Contests · Process Mining

## 1 Introduction

From the start of process mining research, executing proper case studies to show the practical applicability and relevance of process mining results has been a challenge. In the early papers on process discovery algorithms, the focus was very much on "rediscoverability", i.e. given that an event log was generated by a model from a specific model class and that the log was complete, the generating model could be rediscovered. For the alpha-algorithm, for example, rediscoverability is guaranteed for locally complete event logs generated by structured workflow nets [19].

However, for process mining to be truly relevant, there was a need for proper real-life data, i.e. event logs, taken from practice, where researchers could show that their work actually works outside of the academic setting. Unfortunately, obtaining data from companies for the sole purpose of validating research was proving difficult.


J. Mendling et al. (Eds.): Wil van der Aalst Festschrift, LNCS 16480, pp. 333–348, 2026.
https://doi.org/10.1007/978-3-032-17618-9_24

While across the community, many studies were performed inside companies, there was no true benchmark, i.e. a public collection of event logs which would allow any researcher to compare his or her work against that of colleagues. For this reason, the group in Eindhoven, led by Wil van der Aalst, started a series of challenges and contests.

In this paper, we present the BPI Challenges and the Process Discovery Contests. The BPI Challenges provide real-life data, in anonymous form, to be used for testing all kinds of process mining technology. However, in practice, they often proved difficult for process discovery due to the high variability in the processes. The Process Discovery Contest was therefore started to assess process discovery tools in a controlled setting.

## 2   Business Process Intelligence Challenge

The efforts to obtain, anonymize and publish real event data started around 2010 with the search of a company willing to participate in this. This led to the first Business Process Intelligence challenge, or BPI Challenge, in **2011**. We published a dataset [20] from a Dutch academic hospital containing over 150,000 events pertaining to the treatment of 1,100 gynecology patients. The data was provided almost as-is, without any specific questions and this proved challenging for the community. We received three submissions and it may not come as a surprise that the best report was co-authored by J.C. Bose, who was a PhD student at the time, and Wil van der Aalst, his supervisor.

The next year, **2012**, we found a Dutch financial institute willing to share their data [21]. They provided us with 262,200 events pertaining to 13,087 loan applications and little did we know that this event log would become the most studied dataset in process mining. The log proved to be very structured, with three intertwined processes: the life cycle of the applications, the life cycle of the offers and the workflow of the call agents in the process. One cannot attend a BPM or ICPM conference today without seeing this log appear in at least a handful of papers as a benchmark for process prediction techniques or discovery techniques.

The winner in 2012 was a US based consultancy company called CKM advisors and they became a regular participant in the challenges. One of the most striking results they presented in 2012 was a simple chart, showing that the amount of person hours spent on loan applications in the last week before the automatic cancellation did not pay off in terms of approved loans and they suggested the company to automatically cancel applications after three weeks instead of one month.

Many participants in 2012 noticed that the event log was a bit messy, because of the system not allowing for more than one offer being made at any point in time, while customers would ask for multiple offers. To accommodate the customer, call agents would cancel offers immediately to be able to create a new one, while still talking to the customers, only to recreate them later if the customer preferred the first offer anyway. They suggested to allow for the system to create multiple offers per application.

In **2013**, the data came from Volvo IT Belgium [16–18]. They included data from their incident and problem management system and on top of the event logs, the original CSV files were provided, together with extensive documentation on the VINST system the data originated from. The company also provided specific analysis questions and could be reached by participants for help. The winner in 2013 was a team of Korean students who joined us in China, where they received a handcrafted award trophy, made by the German artist Felix Güther.

In **2014** the ICT department of Rabobank The Netherlands provided the data [22–26]. Similar to the year before, the data came from a ticketing system and it was provided in the form of four event logs. And again, CKM advisors submitted the best analysis of the data.

In **2015**, the BPI Challenge consisted of five event logs, from five different Dutch municipalities [27–32]. Each event log contained data of the same process, but executed differently in these municipalities. To keep it interesting, there was some exchange of staff visible in the data. While the number of events was not too high, approximately 250,000, the number of activities was very high: around 400. This meant that the data was challenging to analyze. As the data was in Dutch, it was not too surprising that the best analysis was performed by a Dutch consultant from Meijer & Van der Ham Management Consultants in Amsterdam.

In **2016**, we stayed in the field of government agencies, but now we obtained click-data from a website of the Dutch unemployment agency [4–9]. Obtaining this data was a challenge, since governments have strict protocols about data. In this case, the protocol dictated that data should leave the building in encrypted form, hence, despite having all written permissions to publish the data, we had to physically go to the building, put the encrypted data on a USB drive, leave the building and then decrypt and publish the dataset.

The sheer size of the data made this a true challenge and we decided to allocate two winners. One professional, not surprisingly the same as in 2015, but also an academic team with academics from Saarbrücken, Germany and Newfoundland, Canada.

In **2017**, we contacted the same company as in 2012. Following up on some of the recommendations made in 2012, they updated their systems, such that now more offers could be made per application. For the challenge, we obtained a new event log from them, this time with over a million events and 31,509 loan applications [33, 41]. With the number of submissions steadily growing over the years, we now introduced three categories: professional submissions, academic submissions and student submissions and winners were selected by the Jury in three categories: A student team from Moscow, Russia, an academic team from Rio de Janeiro, Brasil and a team of professionals from Brussels, Belgium.

Like the 2012 edition, the event data of the 2017 edition is still heavily used today as a benchmark set, particularly because of the structured processes that it describes. However, this was also the first dataset where it became clear that sometimes, data is not clearly structured in cases. In fact, the two sets look at the same events from a different perspective, namely that of the application and of the offer.

In **2018**, the challenge dataset doubled in size again to 2.5 million events. This time, the data was provided by a company supporting German agencies processing applications of farmers for EU subsidies from the European Agricultural Guarantee Fund [42]. Again, three teams were declared as the winners, a student team from the Honors academy in Eindhoven, the Netherlands, an academic team from the University of Antwerp, Belgium and a professional team from Cognitio Analytics, based in Short Hills, USA. The latter team was led by a frequent participant, formerly working for CKM advisors and a member of the winning team in 2012.

**2019** became a very special year for the BPI Challenge as for the first time, the challenge was no longer part of a workshop at the BPM Conference, but it was co-located with the first International Conference on Process Mining, hosted by Wil van der Aalst in Aachen, Germany.

We gathered data from a purchasing process of a large multinational coatings and paint company in the Netherlands [34]. The dataset of 1.5 million events of a well known purchase-to-pay process was analyzed by fifteen teams worldwide. This dataset became the most downloaded BPI Challenge, probably as it is used in trainings. Winners were selected in the student and non-student categories and both were German teams. The students came from the Rhine-Waal University of Applied Sciences, Kamp-Lintfort and the non-student team from The Hasso Plattner Institute in Potsdam.

One of the most interesting findings in 2019 was that one of the vendors (Vendor 0550) found a way to get their invoices paid 17 days faster on average, simply by creating an invoice before a purchase order was created. Another interesting observation in this year was the sheer amount of cases with compliance issues, i.e. payment blocks being removed before goods are received or violations of four-eyes principles.

In **2020**, for the tenth edition of the BPI Challenge, our own university shared data from their travel declaration process [35–40]. They just implemented a new system and they were interested in the overall performance of this system. With only a quarter of a million events, the dataset was definitely not too large and this led to a record number of 37 submitted reports. However, only two could be declared the winner in the two categories. The best student submission came from Utrecht University in the Netherlands, whereas the best non-student submission was partly authored by the same authors as in 2019, but this time working in a different university in Berlin, Germany.

Unfortunately, after ten editions of the BPI Challenge, the series came to an end. While many researchers have contacted us since, asking for new challenges, it has proven increasingly difficult to convince companies to share their data, even in anonymized form.

### 2.1   From Cases to Objects

In recent years, process mining research has become increasingly object centric. Where previously processes were considered from the perspective of a single object type which defined the notion of a case, now event data is considered to refer to many interacting objects. And as many BPI Challenges come from database tables referring to different objects, some researchers have tried to reconstruct the original data in an object centric way. This led to the BPI Challenges of 2014 [10], 2015 [10], 2016 [12], 2017 [13] and 2019 [14] to be republished in object-centric form.

## 2.2  Wrapping up

The original aim of the BPI Challenges was to provide benchmark datasets for the community to test and validate their process mining work. To some extent, this has proven successful as shown by the many, many papers that use these datasets in some form. In Table 1, we listed the views, proper citations and downloads per dataset. The citations are an underestimate of the actual papers using these datasets as citing BPI Challenge datasets is rarely done properly using the DOI's. Instead, the datasets are mostly cited using footnotes which the 4TU Center for Research Data (which hosts the data) cannot track. However, it can be seen that the downloads of all datasets are consistently very high, while three stand out. The related BPI Challenges of 2012 and 2017 are both downloaded and cited very often. These datasets are used in process mining education due to their clear structure and their nice relation. The purchase to pay process of the BPI Challenge 2019 however is the most downloaded dataset overall. The four object centric versions were published more recently, but they too are gathering views and downloads.

However, the datasets soon proved unsuitable for validating or testing process discovery algorithms. Such algorithms were typically not able to produce meaningful models from the challenge data, simply because real-life data proved to be much more unstructured than anticipated by researchers. More than once, Wil and his colleagues would receive an e-mail stating that the data was not good because algorithm x cannot produce a nice Petri net. Therefore, in 2016, we also started a series of Process Discovery Contests on synthetic data, rather than on real data.

## 3  Process Discovery Contests

### 3.1  Introduction

The Process Discovery Contest (PDC) is dedicated to the assessment of tools and techniques that discover business process models from event logs. The objective is to compare the efficiency of techniques to discover process models that provide a proper balance between *overfitting* and *underfitting*. A process model is overfitting (the event log) if it is too restrictive, disallowing behavior which is part of the underlying process. This typically occurs when the model only allows for the behavior recorded in the event log. Conversely, it is underfitting (the reality) if it is not restrictive enough, allowing behavior that is not part of the underlying process. This typically occurs if it overgeneralizes the example behavior in the event log.

**Table 1.** Downloads and views of the BPI Challenge datasets (October 2025)

| Year | Dataset | Views | Citations | Downloads |
| --- | --- | --- | --- | --- |
| 2011 | [20] | 22,153 | 58 | 8,376 |
| 2012 | [21] | 29,880 | 151 | 10,288 |
| 2013 | [17] | 11,562 | 36 | 4,052 |
| 2013 | [18] | 6,031 | 6 | 2,034 |
| 2013 | [16] | 6,599 | 12 | 3,038 |
| 2014 | [26] | 5,782 | 1 | 1,527 |
| 2014 | [22] | 7,690 | 5 | 3,034 |
| 2014 | [23] | 3,991 | 0 | 1,026 |
| 2014 | [25] | 7,223 | 0 | 2,216 |
| 2014 | [24] | 3,239 | 35 | collection |
| 2015 | [28] | 8,520 | 8 | 4,870 |
| 2015 | [29] | 4,895 | 0 | 2,517 |
| 2015 | [30] | 4,079 | 1 | 2,225 |
| 2015 | [31] | 5,662 | 0 | 2,569 |
| 2015 | [32] | 4,561 | 0 | 2,353 |
| 2015 | [27] | 4,603 | 41 | collection |
| 2016 | [9] | 5,857 | 0 | 1,851 |
| 2016 | [7] | 7,359 | 0 | 2,306 |
| 2016 | [8] | 6,664 | 0 | 2,391 |
| 2016 | [4] | 6,570 | 1 | 4,587 |
| 2016 | [5] | 6,054 | 0 | 3,857 |
| 2016 | [6] | 2,970 | 4 | collection |
| 2017 | [33] | 30,775 | 73 | 12,169 |
| 2017 | [41] | 9,420 | 0 | 3,337 |
| 2018 | [42] | 15,389 | 26 | 6,194 |
| 2019 | [34] | 66,779 | 35 | 14,123 |
| 2020 | [39] | 5,962 | 0 | 3,259 |
| 2020 | [36] | 5,127 | 7 | 2,395 |
| 2020 | [37] | 5,210 | 2 | 3,461 |
| 2020 | [40] | 5,477 | 2 | 2,599 |
| 2020 | [38] | 7,191 | 2 | 3,258 |
| 2020 | [35] | 9,528 | 20 | collection |
| 2014 OCEL | [10] | 464 | 0 | 436 |
| 2015 OCEL | [11] | 548 | 0 | 597 |
| 2016 OCEL | [12] | 392 | 0 | 238 |
| 2017 OCEL | [13] | 733 | 0 | 679 |
| 2019 OCEL | [14] | 868 | 0 | 463 |

**Table 2.** Characteristics of the different PDC datasets (October 2025)

| Year | Dataset | Logs | | | Models | Views | Citations | Downloads |
|---|---|---|---|---|---|---|---|---|
| | | Training | Test | Base | | | | |
| 2016 | [2] | 10 | 10 | | 10 | 2,950 | 0 | 1,252 |
| 2017 | [3] | 10 | 10 | | 10 | 1,972 | 0 | 1,148 |
| 2019 | [1] | 10 | 10 | | 10 | 2,573 | 0 | 1,216 |
| 2020 | [43] | 192 | 192 | | 96 | 3,465 | 0 | 3,015 |
| 2021 | [44] | 480 | 96 | | 96 | 3,453 | 1 | 2,004 |
| 2022 | [45] | 480 | 96 | 96 | 96 | 3,120 | 0 | 1,594 |
| 2023 | [46] | 384 | 96 | 96 | 96 | 2,319 | 0 | 1,692 |
| 2024 | [47] | 288 | 96 | 96 | 96 | 300 | 0 | 197 |
| 2025 | [48] | 288 | 96 | 96 | 96 | 0 | 0 | 0 |

The Process Discovery Contest is different from the BPI Challenges as its focus is on process discovery. Synthetic datasets are used to have objectified *proper* answers. Process discovery becomes a classification task with a training set and a test set. First, a process model is discovered from a training log. Second, the discovered process model is used to decide whether a first (test) trace fits the model better than a second (base) trace. The idea here is that a better discovered model will classify better.

## 3.2    Datasets

Table 2 shows the characteristics of the different datasets that exist today, including the number of times they have been viewed, cited, and downloaded on 2 October 2025. The models for the 2016[1], 2017[2] and 2019[3] editions were 10 entirely different models generated by hand. From the 2020 edition onward, a configurable model was used to generate all models and all event logs. The classification for the 2020 and 2021 editions had to determine whether a test trace fits, while from the 2022 edition onward, the classification had to determine whether a test trace fits the discovered model better than a corresponding base trace.

The dataset for an edition of the PDC will only become available after the deadline for submission has passed. This is done to prevent any submitted discovery algorithm from being tailored specifically towards the dataset. As a result, contestants do not know the actual dataset, but can still use the datasets from previous editions to test their discovery algorithm.

---

[1] Download available at https://www.tf-pm.org/competitions-awards/discovery-contest/2016.

[2] Download available at https://www.tf-pm.org/competitions-awards/discovery-contest/2017.

[3] No download available.

### 3.3   Configurable Model

As an example of a configurable model, Fig. 1 shows the configurable model for PDC 2025. This model contains as its backbone two parallel branches that each have two binary choices. The model also contains six stacks of three sibling transitions that carry the same name. These transitions appear in an exit path of a (possible) loop, and the only reason for having three sibling transitions is to achieve a higher probability of exiting the loop (75% instead of 50%).

The configurable model shown in Fig. 1 allows for the following seven configuration options:

A Long-term dependencies ( red fill ). The corresponding nodes will be included in the configured model if and only if option A is selected.
B1 Simple loops ( orange fill ). The corresponding notes will be included in the configured model if and only if option B1 or option B2 is selected.
B2 Extension to complex loops ( magenta fill ). The corresponding nodes will be included in the configured model if and only if option B2 is selected.
C Or constructs ( green fill ). The corresponding nodes will be included in the configurable model if and only if option C is selected.
D Routing constructs ( cyan fill ). The corresponding nodes will be included in the configurable model, but they will be made silent (no associated activity) if and only if option D is selected.
E Optional tasks (**bold border**). The corresponding nodes will be included in the configurable model, but a bypassing invisible transition will be added if and only if option E is selected.
F Duplicate tasks ( yellow fill , one has an orange fill, as it is also included in a cycle). The corresponding nodes will be included in the configurable model, but the transition labels will be changed to the alternative (duplicate) labels (third line) if and only if option F is selected.

As a result, we have five configuration options that can be selected or not, and one configuration option (loops) that can be selected as simple, selected as complex, or not selected, leading to $2^5 \times 3 = 96$ different configured models.

The node names in Fig. 1 may contain up to three lines, which provide the necessary information to configure a model provided the selected configuration options:

1. The (default) label. This label will be used if options D and F are not selected.
2. The selected configuration options (in any order) that affect this node.
3. The (duplicate) alternative label. This label will be used if option F is selected.

As an example, the configured model when selecting the options B1, D, E, and F is shown in Fig. 2.

### 3.4   Pipeline for Creating a Dataset

From a configurable model, we can generate an entire dataset using the following pipeline:

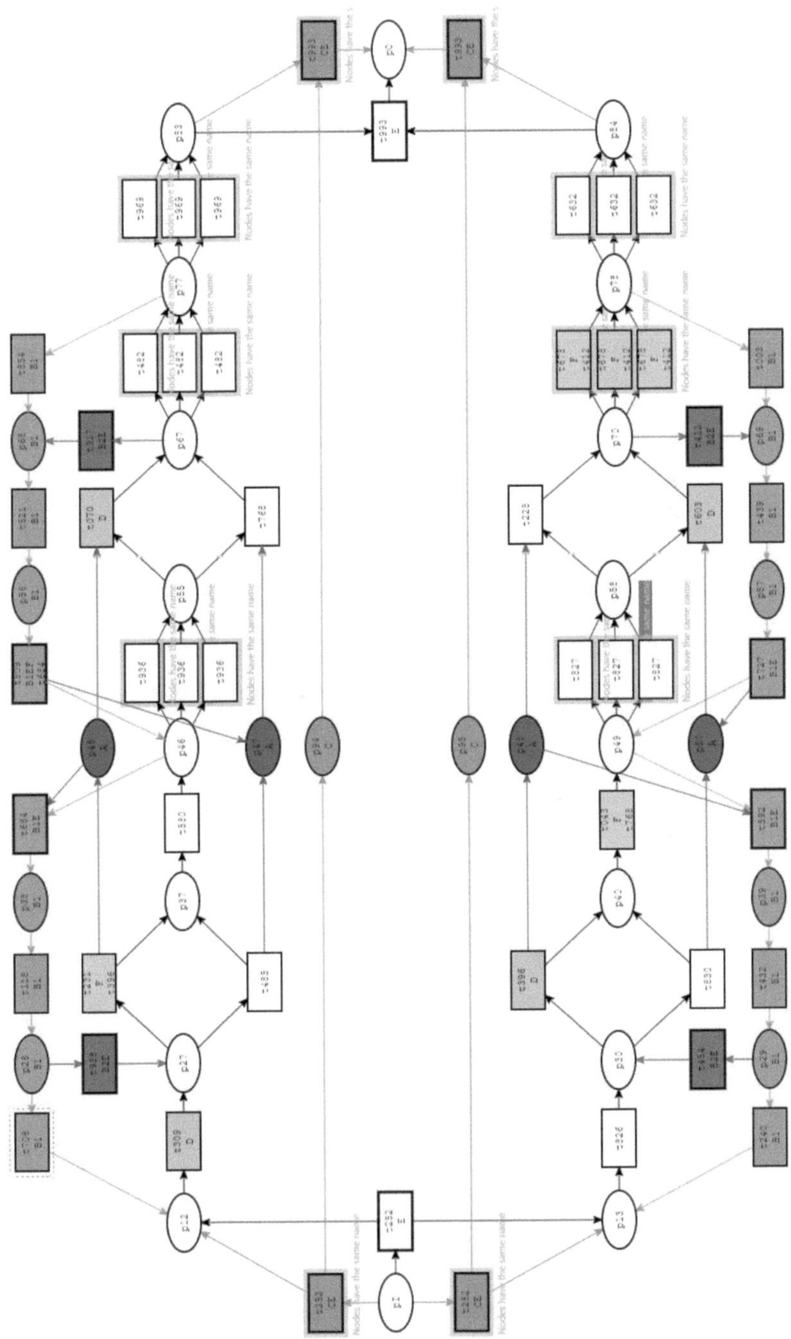

**Fig. 1.** The configurable model used for PDC 2025

1. Create all configured models from the configurable model.
2. Create three training logs for every configured model[4]:
   (a) Create a noise-free training log with only unclassified traces by generating 1000 random traces for the configured model.
   (b) Create a noisy training log with only unclassified traces by generating 1000 random traces for the configured model while injecting some noise for some traces: in about 20% of the traces one event will be either removed (8%), moved to another position in the trace (4%) or copied to another position in the trace (8%).
   (c) Create a noisy training log with 20 positively classified traces and 20 negatively classified traces by replaying the noisy training log on the configured model.
3. Create a master log by generating 500 random traces for every configured model.
4. Create a test log and a base log from the master log for every configured model:
   (a) Replay every trace from the master log on the configured model.
   (b) Use trace-repair on the trace and the configured model to create a trace that fits the model better (about half of the model moves and half of the log moves will be repaired).
   (c) Select 1000 random pairs of traces and repaired traces and distribute them over a test log and a base log such that exactly 500 traces in the test log fit better than the corresponding trace in the base log.
5. Create a ground-truth log for every configured model:

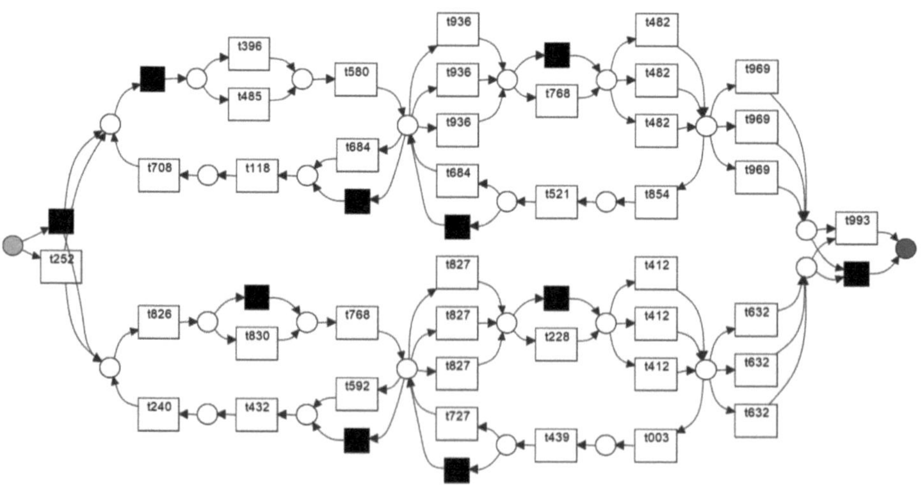

**Fig. 2.** The model obtained from the configurable model shown in Fig. 1 when selecting the options B1, D, E, and F

---

[4] The developer should make sure that every possible configured model is sound, as a result of which creating these logs is possible.

(a) Replay both the corresponding test log and the corresponding base log on the configured model,
(b) Classify every test trace by checking whether it fits the configured model better than the corresponding base trace and
(c) Add this classification to a copy of the test log.

This pipeline has been implemented using ProM CLI[5] plugins and JavaScript files. As an example, to create all configured models from the configuration model, a JavaScript file is called that (i) iterates over all possible configurations and (ii) calls in every iteration the `Configure Petri net` plugin[6] to create a configured model from the configurable model and the current configuration. As a result, the entire pipeline can be run from a terminal using a single command.

## 3.5  Pipeline for Calculating a Submission Score

A submission contains a fully functional discovery tool that can be called through a `Discovery.bat` file. If the model discovered by the discovery tool is a Petri net stored in PNML format or a BPMN diagram stored as a BPMN 2.0 file, then a classification tool provided by the PDC organizers may be used. Otherwise, the submission should also contain a fully functional classification tool that can be called through a `Classify.bat` file.

To score a submitted discovery tool, we use the following pipeline for every training log in the dataset:

1. Run the `Discovery.bat` script, which discovers a model from the training log.
2. Run the `Classify.bat` script to:
   (a) determine for every trace from the test log whether it fits the discovered model better than the corresponding trace in the base log and
   (b) export a copy of the test log with the obtained classification.
3. Compare the classified test log with the ground-truth log and report the numbers of true positives $(t_p)$, true negatives $(t_n)$, false positives $(f_p)$ and false negatives $(f_n)$.

For a single training log, we can then calculate the positive accuracy $a_p = t_p/(t_p + f_n)$ and the negative accuracy $a_n = t_n/(t_n + f_p)$, after which we can calculate the score for this log as the F-score for both accuracies: $s = (2 \times a_p \times a_n)/(a_p + a_n)$. For the entire submission, we then can calculate the score as the average of the scores of all training logs in the dataset.

Table 3 shows the winning submissions for the different contests, including the type of model that was used by the submission and (where applicable) the submission score. This overview indicates that the earlier contests have been dominated by using Petri nets, whereas the later contests have been dominated by using DCR graphs.

---

[5] Command Line Interface, these plugins run in any context as they do not require a graphical context.
[6] This plugin can be found in the **PDC2021 ProM** package.

**Table 3.** Winning submissions of the different PDC datasets

| Year | Winning submission | Model type | Winner(s) | Score |
|---|---|---|---|---|
| 2016 | The DrFurby Classifier | Petri nets | Eric Verbeek and Felix Mannhardt | NA |
| 2017 | Interactive Process Discovery | Petri nets | Alok Dixit and Humberto Garcia Caballero | NA |
| 2019 | Discovery using the Log Skeleton Filter and Browser | Log skeletons converted by hand to Petri nets | Eric Verbeek | NA |
| 2020 | Directly Follows Model Miner | Directly Follows graphs converted to Petri nets | Sander Leemans | 76.2% |
| 2021 | DisCoverRJS RINet | DCR graphs converted to Petri nets | Axel Christfort and Tijs Slaats | 96.2% |
| 2022 | UiPath_PIM_PDC2022 | BPMN diagrams | Dennis Brons | 89.5% |
| 2023 | 2.a.DisCoveRJS-Filtering-SimpleClassification-18 | DCR graphs | Axel Christfort and Tijs Slaats | 84.0% |
| 2024 | 3.c.FuzzyLogAbstraction (aka Pyrrhus) | DCR graphs | Axel Christford, Yibin Xu and Tijs Slaats | 90.9% |
| 2025 | 3.c.FuzzyLogAbstraction (aka Pyrrhus) | DCR graphs | Tijs Slaats | 91.8% |

## 3.6   Wrapping up

For a new Process Discovery Contest, creating a new dataset is done by creating a new configurable model and then running this model through the automated pipeline as described in Sect. 3.4. This dataset can then be used to assess the quality of a process discovery tool by using the pipeline as described in Sect. 3.5.

The Process Discovery Contest does not prescribe which kind of model should be discovered; this is left open to the contestants. However, if a contestant decides to submit a discovery tool that discovers models different from Petri nets in PNML format and BPMN diagrams in BPMN format, the submission should also include a classification tool to allow the organizers to assess the quality of the discovery tool.

Possibly, the datasets could also be used for a Conformance Checking Contest, especially in combination with some of the submitted discovery tools, as most of the time spent computing the score for some submissions is spent performing the classification. As an example, for one of the PDC submissions that discovered BPMN diagrams in BPMN format, the discovery tool took a total of 38 min, the conversion from BPMN diagrams to Petri nets took a total of 22 min, while the (alignment-based) classification tool took a total of over 19 h. As such, the Process Discovery Contests could benefit from having faster classification tools and hence faster conformance checking algorithms.

# 4   Conformance Checking Contest

Next to discovery and overall process analysis, conformance checking is an important topic in process mining. Interestingly enough, only one true conformance checking contest has ever been organized, co-located with the first International Conference on Process Mining in 2019. The challenge provided participants with data from a real medical process [15] and invited them to analyze the conformance between the observed and expected behavior of the process, with an emphasis on providing process owners with interpretable and understandable conformance results. Several reports were submitted and the winners came from the German company Mehrwerk AG, Karlsruhe, Germany.

# 5   Conclusion and Outlook

The discovery contests show that even when taking a purely algorithmic view on process mining, there is still no perfect solution for process discovery. The question: "can we discover a model of a process given a set of traces" turns out to be a challenging one, even 25 years after the $\alpha$-algorithm was presented. At the same time, the ten BPI Challenges held between 2011 and 2020 have proven to the community that there is more to process mining than developing new discovery algorithms. Next to the data and the process models the community strives to discover, there is the illusive "process". A real-world phenomenon that is often hard to fully capture in a model and any analysis of a real dataset, like any of the BPI Challenges, shows that in the real world, processes are never as simple as a Petri net. The fact that the BPI Challenges are, still today, used as benchmarks for all kinds of process mining papers shows that they served their purpose. Interestingly, there is even a recent trend of researchers revisiting the old BPI Challenges, trying to reconstruct the underlying tables from which the data was produced in order to republish these in an object-centric fashion.

We expect the Process Discovery Contests to continue some time into the future, however the BPI Challenges are a different story. Finding companies willing to publicly share their data has become increasingly difficult. Nonetheless, in 2024 and 2025, the ICPM conference organizers managed to organize a process mining hackaton. This hackaton is in the same spirit as the BPI Challenges, but the data is not publicly available for non-participants, which makes their use as benchmarks limited.

We would like to conclude with an explicit call to the reader: publish data! Make your data available for a large audience and challenge the community to analyze it. If you have an idea for a challenge or contest, do not hesitate to contact members of the Task Force on Process Mining for help.

# References


1. Carmona, J., de Leoni, M., Depaire, B.: Process Discovery Contest 2019 (2021) https://doi.org/10.4121/14625996.V1. https://icpmconference.org/2019/process-discovery-contest/
2. Carmona, J., de Leoni, M., Depaire, B., Jouck, T.: Process Discovery Contest 2016 (2021). https://doi.org/10.4121/14625912.V1. https://www.tf-pm.org/competitions-awards/discovery-contest/2016
3. Carmona, J., de Leoni, M., Depaire, B., Jouck, T.: Process Discovery Contest 2017 (2021). https://doi.org/10.4121/14625948.V1. https://www.tf-pm.org/competitions-awards/discovery-contest/2017
4. Dees, M., van Dongen, B.: BPI challenge 2016: clicks logged in 2016. https://doi.org/10.4121/uuid:01345ac4-7d1d-426e-92b8-24933a079412. https://data.4tu.nl/articles/dataset/BPI_Challenge_2016_Clicks_Logged_In/12674816/1
5. Dees, M., van Dongen, B.: BPI challenge 2016: clicks not logged in 2016. https://doi.org/10.4121/uuid:9b99a146-51b5-48df-aa70-288a76c82ec4. https://data.4tu.nl/articles/dataset/BPI_Challenge_2016_Clicks_NOT_Logged_In/12708596/1
6. Dees, M., van Dongen, B.: BPI challenge 2016: collection (2016). https://doi.org/10.4121/uuid:360795c8-1dd6-4a5b-a443-185001076eab. https://data.4tu.nl/collections/ea85f19e-26a9-497a-9ac8-06afb069d6a7
7. Dees, M., van Dongen, B.: BPI challenge 2016: complaints (2016). https://doi.org/10.4121/uuid:e30ba0c8-0039-4835-a493-6e3aa2301d3f. https://data.4tu.nl/articles/dataset/BPI_Challenge_2016_Complaints/12717647/1
8. Dees, M., van Dongen, B.: BPI challenge 2016: questions (2016). https://doi.org/10.4121/uuid:2b02709f-9a84-4538-a76a-eb002eacf8d1. https://data.4tu.nl/articles/dataset/BPI_Challenge_2016_Questions/12687320/1
9. Dees, M., van Dongen, B.: BPI challenge 2016: werkmap messages (2016). https://doi.org/10.4121/uuid:c3f3ba2d-e81e-4274-87c7-882fa1dbab0d. https://data.4tu.nl/articles/dataset/BPI_Challenge_2016_Werkmap_Messages/12714569/1
10. Khayatbashi, S., Hartig, O., Jalali, A.: BPI challenge 2014 (OCEL) (2023). https://doi.org/10.4121/7d097cec-7304-4b85-9e78-a3ca1cc44c40.v1
11. Khayatbashi, S., Hartig, O., Jalali, A.: BPI challenge 2015 (OCEL) (2023). https://doi.org/10.4121/110d2fcf-b5e1-494a-a588-896a0a21e60a.v1
12. Khayatbashi, S., Hartig, O., Jalali, A.: BPI challenge 2016 (OCEL) (2023). https://doi.org/10.4121/95613fb2-29a5-49dc-b196-0948cf96cd7c.v1
13. Khayatbashi, S., Hartig, O., Jalali, A.: BPI challenge 2017 (OCEL) (2023). https://doi.org/10.4121/6889ca3f-97cf-459a-b630-3b0b0d8664b5.v1
14. Khayatbashi, S., Hartig, O., Jalali, A.: BPI challenge 2019 (OCEL) (2023). https://doi.org/10.4121/46a7e15b-10c7-4ab2-988d-ee67d8ea515a.v1
15. Munoz-Gama, J., de la Fuente, R., Sepúlveda, M., Fuentes, R.: Conformance checking challenge 2019 (CCC19) (2019). https://doi.org/10.4121/uuid:c923af09-ce93-44c3-ace0-c5508cf103ad. https://data.4tu.nl/articles/dataset/Conformance_Checking_Challenge_2019_CCC19_/12714932/1
16. Steeman, W.: BPI challenge 2013, closed problems (2013). https://doi.org/10.4121/uuid:c2c3b154-ab26-4b31-a0e8-8f2350ddac11. https://data.4tu.nl/articles/dataset/BPI_Challenge_2013_closed_problems/12714476/1
17. Steeman, W.: BPI challenge 2013, incidents (2013). https://doi.org/10.4121/uuid:500573e6-accc-4b0c-9576-aa5468b10cee. https://data.4tu.nl/articles/dataset/BPI_Challenge_2013_incidents/12693914/1

18. Steeman, W.: BPI challenge 2013, open problems (2013). https://doi.org/10.
    4121/uuid:3537c19d-6c64-4b1d-815d-915ab0e479da. https://data.4tu.nl/articles/
    dataset/BPI_Challenge_2013_open_problems/12688556/1
19. van der Aalst, W., Weijters, T., Maruster, L.: Workflow mining: discovering process
    models from event logs. IEEE Trans. Knowl. Data Eng. **16**(9), 1128–1142 (2004).
    https://doi.org/10.1109/TKDE.2004.47
20. van Dongen, B.F.: Real-life event logs - hospital log (2011). https://
    doi.org/10.4121/uuid:d9769f3d-0ab0-4fb8-803b-0d1120ffcf54. https://data.4tu.nl/
    articles/dataset/Real-life_event_logs_-_Hospital_log/12716513/1
21. van Dongen, B.: BPI challenge 2012 (2012). https://doi.org/10.4121/uuid:
    3926db30-f712-4394-aebc-75976070e91f.       https://data.4tu.nl/articles/dataset/
    BPI_Challenge_2012/12689204/1
22. van Dongen, B.: BPI challenge 2014: activity log for incidents (2014). https://
    doi.org/10.4121/uuid:86977bac-f874-49cf-8337-80f26bf5d2ef. https://data.4tu.nl/
    articles/dataset/BPI_Challenge_2014_Activity_log_for_incidents/12706424/1
23. van Dongen, B.: BPI challenge 2014: change details (2014). https://doi.org/10.
    4121/uuid:d5ccb355-ca67-480f-8739-289b9b593aaf.   https://data.4tu.nl/articles/
    dataset/BPI_Challenge_2014_Change_details/12716234/1
24. van Dongen, B.: BPI challenge 2014: collection (2014). https://doi.org/10.4121/
    uuid:c3e5d162-0cfd-4bb0-bd82-af5268819c35.    https://data.4tu.nl/collections/_/
    5065469/1
25. van Dongen, B.: BPI challenge 2014: incident details (2014). https://doi.org/10.
    4121/uuid:3cfa2260-f5c5-44be-afe1-b70d35288d6d.   https://data.4tu.nl/articles/
    dataset/BPI_Challenge_2014_Incident_details/12692378/1
26. van Dongen, B.: BPI challenge 2014: interaction details (2014). https://doi.org/10.
    4121/uuid:3d5ae0ce-198c-4b5c-b0f9-60d3035d07bf.   https://data.4tu.nl/articles/
    dataset/BPI_Challenge_2014_Interaction_details/12692411/1
27. van Dongen, B.: BPI challenge 2015 collection (2015). https://doi.org/10.4121/
    uuid:31a308ef-c844-48da-948c-305d167a0ec1.     https://data.4tu.nl/collections/
    f929dc43-b588-404b-8d2c-be4903622913
28. van Dongen, B.: BPI challenge 2015 municipality 1 (2015). https://doi.org/10.
    4121/uuid:a0addfda-2044-4541-a450-fdcc9fe16d17.   https://data.4tu.nl/articles/
    dataset/BPI_Challenge_2015_Municipality_1/12709154/1
29. van Dongen, B.: BPI challenge 2015 municipality 2 (2015). https://doi.org/10.
    4121/uuid:63a8435a-077d-4ece-97cd-2c76d394d99c.  https://data.4tu.nl/articles/
    dataset/BPI_Challenge_2015_Municipality_2/12697349/1
30. van Dongen, B.: BPI challenge 2015 municipality 3 (2015). https://doi.org/10.
    4121/uuid:ed445cdd-27d5-4d77-a1f7-59fe7360cfbe.   https://data.4tu.nl/articles/
    dataset/BPI_Challenge_2015_Municipality_3/12718370/1
31. van Dongen, B.: BPI challenge 2015 municipality 4 (2015). https://doi.org/10.
    4121/uuid:679b11cf-47cd-459e-a6de-9ca614e25985.   https://data.4tu.nl/articles/
    dataset/BPI_Challenge_2015_Municipality_4/12697898/1
32. van Dongen, B.: BPI challenge 2015 municipality 5 (2015). https://doi.org/10.
    4121/uuid:b32c6fe5-f212-4286-9774-58dd53511cf8.   https://data.4tu.nl/articles/
    dataset/BPI_Challenge_2015_Municipality_5/12713285/1
33. van Dongen, B.: BPI challenge 2017 (2017). https://doi.org/10.4121/uuid:
    5f3067df-f10b-45da-b98b-86ae4c7a310b.      https://data.4tu.nl/articles/dataset/
    BPI_Challenge_2017/12696884/1
34. van Dongen, B.: BPI challenge 2019 (2019). https://doi.org/10.4121/uuid:
    d06aff4b-79f0-45e6-8ec8-e19730c248f1. https://data.4tu.nl/articles/dataset/BPI_
    Challenge_2019/12715853/1

35. van Dongen, B.: BPI challenge 2020: collection (2020). https://doi.org/10.4121/ uuid:52fb97d4-4588-43c9-9d04-3604d4613b51.     https://data.4tu.nl/collections/ 6bcb71ec-6e2e-4837-a899-624367f1c36b

36. van Dongen, B.: BPI challenge 2020: domestic declarations (2020). https://doi. org/10.4121/uuid:3f422315-ed9d-4882-891f-e180b5b4feb5.     https://data.4tu.nl/ articles/dataset/BPI_Challenge_2020_Domestic_Declarations/12692543/1

37. van Dongen, B.: BPI challenge 2020: ldeclarations (2020). https://doi.org/10.4121/ uuid:2bbf8f6a-fc50-48eb-aa9e-c4ea5ef7e8c5.  https://data.4tu.nl/articles/dataset/ BPI_Challenge_2020_International_Declarations/12687374/1

38. van Dongen, B.: BPI challenge 2020: prepaid travel costs (2020). https://doi. org/10.4121/uuid:5d2fe5e1-f91f-4a3b-ad9b-9e4126870165.     https://data.4tu.nl/ articles/dataset/BPI_Challenge_2020_Prepaid_Travel_Costs/12696722/1

39. van Dongen, B.: BPI challenge 2020: request for payment (2020). https://doi. org/10.4121/uuid:895b26fb-6f25-46eb-9e48-0dca26fcd030.     https://data.4tu.nl/ articles/dataset/BPI_Challenge_2020_Request_For_Payment/12706886/1

40. van Dongen, B.: BPI challenge 2020: travel permit data (2020). https://doi. org/10.4121/uuid:ea03d361-a7cd-4f5e-83d8-5fbdf0362550.     https://data.4tu.nl/ articles/dataset/BPI_Challenge_2020_Travel_Permit_Data/12718178/1

41. van Dongen, B.: BPI challenge 2017 - offer log (2021). https://doi.org/ 10.4121/12705737.v2. https://data.4tu.nl/articles/dataset/BPI_Challenge_2017_-_ Offer_log/12705737/2

42. van Dongen, B.F., Borchert, F.: BPI challenge 2018 (2018). https://doi.org/ 10.4121/uuid:3301445f-95e8-4ff0-98a4-901f1f204972. https://data.4tu.nl/articles/ dataset/BPI_Challenge_2018/12688355/1

43. Verbeek, H.M.W.: Process Discovery Contest 2020 (2021). https://doi.org/10. 4121/14626020.V1. https://icpmconference.org/2020/process-discovery-contest/

44. Verbeek, H.M.W.: Process Discovery Contest 2021 (2021). https://doi.org/10. 4121/16803232.V1. https://icpmconference.org/2021/process-discovery-contest/

45. Verbeek, H.M.W.: Process Discovery Contest 2022 (2022). https://doi.org/10. 4121/21261402.V2. https://icpmconference.org/2022/process-discovery-contest/

46. Verbeek, H.M.W.: Process Discovery Contest 2023 (2023). https://doi.org/ 10.4121/AFD6F608-469E-48F9-977D-875B45840D39.V1. https://icpmconference. org/2023/process-discovery-contest/

47. Verbeek, H.M.W.: Process Discovery Contest 2024 (2024). https://doi.org/10. 4121/3CFCDBB7-C909-4F60-8BEC-62C780598047.V1.     https://icpmconference. org/2024/process-discovery-contest/

48. Verbeek, H.M.W.: Process Discovery Contest 2025 (2025). https://doi.org/10. 4121/7212A73A-1EAC-4A08-8C01-973DCA020822.V1.     https://icpmconference. org/2025/process-discovery-contest/

# There's no Process Mining without Conformance Checking

Boudewijn F. van Dongen[1(✉)] and Josep Carmona[2]

[1] Eindhoven University of Technology, Eindhoven, The Netherlands
`b.f.v.dongen@tue.nl`
[2] Universitat Politècnica de Catalunya, Barcelona, Spain

**Abstract.** When the first process discovery algorithms were being developed, the question arose whether the result was actually any good. Algorithms, such as Little Thumb and the Alpha Miner were shown to be able to reproduce the model used to generate data, but in a realistic setting, that model would not be available (otherwise, why would you use process mining?)

This simple question: "Is my model a good model for this dataset?" sparked an entire research area, known today as conformance checking.

**Keywords:** Conformance Checking · Process Mining

## 1   Introduction

"Conformance checking is an important - but also challenging - topic in process mining". With these words, Wil van der Aalst started the foreword of the book "Conformance Checking, relating Processes and Models" [8]. In the book, we, together with Matthias Weidlich and Andreas Solti, provided an introduction to conformance checking, we presented the ins and outs of alignments and an overview of conformance checking applications at the time.

Conformance checking can be seen in the broader context of compliance, i.e. organizations can, by comparing event logs and process models, analyze when and where their day to day operations may differ from the rules, processes, procedures or even logic that governs the same operations. Through conformance checking, one can for example identify the three loan applications in the BPI Challenge 2012 where the loan was paid to the customer, without the customer ever accepting an offer.

Conformance checking has received a lot of attention in the process mining community. Rule checking techniques [18,30], for example, are used to check if specific business rules are respected while case-replay techniques developed in the research groups led by Wil van der Aalst aim to identify specific deviations between modeled and observed behavior on the control flow level [5,27,37,40]. More advanced techniques consider resources and data on top of the control flow [3,19]. Here, authorization (which resource can perform which activity) and


J. Mendling et al. (Eds.): Wil van der Aalst Festschrift, LNCS 16480, pp. 349–367, 2026.
https://doi.org/10.1007/978-3-032-17618-9_25

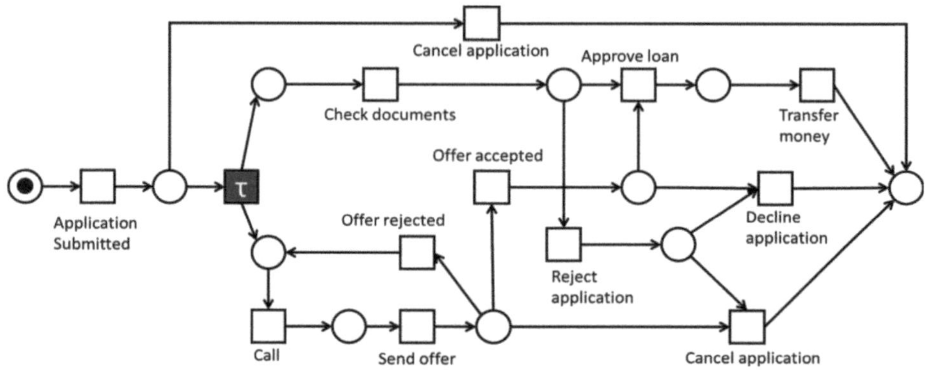


**Fig. 1.** Process model of a fictive financial institute.

data dependencies (higher-value cases take a different route) play a role. More recently, a technique was proposed to consider all perspectives at once [4,41]. For a full literature review, we refer to [12,13].

In this paper, we look at conformance checking from the data-science perspective. We focus on the three main quality metrics that the process mining community has defined for the relation between a process model and an event log, namely fitness, precision and generalization. To this end, we use an example process of a fictive financial institute, not much different from the BPI Challenge 2012, depicted in Fig. 1. Applications are submitted, after which they can immediately be canceled. If they are not canceled, they are taken into processing where two things happen in parallel. There is a document check and contact with the customer. The latter consists of a loop of calling the customer, providing an offer which can be rejected or accepted. Once an offer is accepted and the document check is positive, the loan can be approved and money transferred. Should the document check fail, the application is either declined or canceled, depending on whether the customer has already accepted an offer or not.

In the remainder of the paper, we investigate conformance checking using a couple of example traces.

## 2    Fitness

Fitness measures the ability of a model to explain the recorded execution of a process as recorded in an event log. In that sense, fitness is comparable to recall in classical data mining, i.e. to what extent is the discovered model able to explain the behavior observed in the log. It is therefore the main measure to assess whether a model is well-suited to explain the recorded behavior. One of the first techniques to compute fitness was a technique called token replay.

**Token Replay.** In essence, token replay assumes that each trace in the event log corresponds to a valid execution sequence of the process model. This is verified

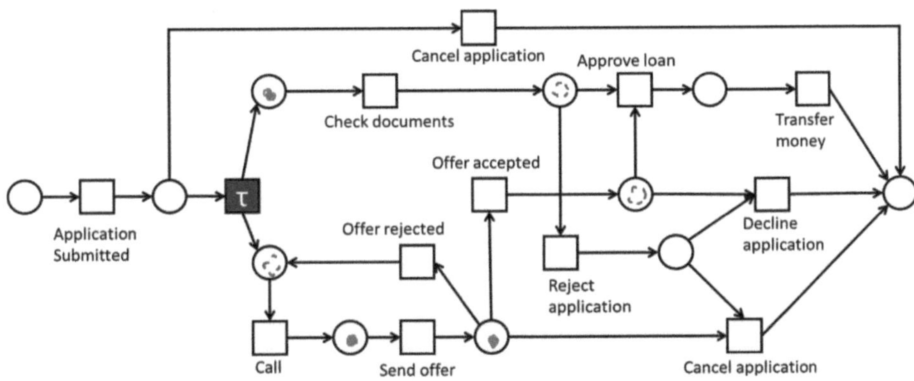


**Fig. 2.** State reached after replaying the full trace $\langle As, Cc, So, Cc, Al, Tm \rangle$. One can see that there are three remaining tokens (denoted in blue), and three missing tokens (denoted by dashed red lines).

by step-wise executing tasks of the process model, according to the order of the respective events in the trace. During this replay, we may observe two cases that hint at non-conformance (see Fig. 2):

(i) the execution of a task requires the consumption of a token on the incoming arc, but the arc is not assigned any token in the current state, i.e. a token is *missing* during replay;

(ii) the execution of a task produces a token at an outgoing arc, but this token is not consumed eventually, i.e. a token is *remaining* after replay.

By exploring whether the replay of a trace yields missing or remaining tokens, replay-based conformance checking focuses mainly on the fitness dimension. That is, the ability of the model to explain the recorded behavior is the primary concern. Traces are fitting if their replay does not yield any missing or remaining tokens, and non-fitting otherwise:

$$\text{fitness}(L, M) = \frac{1}{2}\left(1 - \frac{\sum_{t \in L} \mathit{missing}(t, M)}{\sum_{t \in L} \mathit{consumed}(t, M)}\right) + \frac{1}{2}\left(1 - \frac{\sum_{t \in L} \mathit{remaining}(t, M)}{\sum_{t \in L} \mathit{produced}(t, M)}\right) \qquad (1)$$

Although token replay is still perceived today as a useful technique to measure the fitness of a log with respect to a model, the assumption on the traces to be fitting may be too restrictive in real-world scenarios. The following technique overcomes this limitation by quering the model for the best run that can mimic an observed trace.

**Alignments.** Many conformance checking techniques use *alignments* to expose where the behavior recorded in a log and the model agree, which activities are missing in the log and which events should not be performed according to the model [8,37]. The usual focus is on the control flow of the process. In more advanced techniques [3,4,11,19], data and/or resource information is additionally incorporated in the alignments. In this paper, we focus on the control flow.

Alignments take a symmetric view on the relation between modeled and recorded behavior. Specifically, they can be seen as an evolution of token replay. Instead of establishing a link between a trace and sequences of task executions in the model through replay, alignments directly connect a trace with a model run.

An alignment connects a trace of the event log with a run of the process model. It is represented by a two-row matrix, where the first row consists of activities as their execution is signaled by the events of the trace and a special symbol $\gg$ (jointly denoted by $e_i$ below), and the second row consists of the activities that are captured by task executions of a run of the process model and a special symbol $\gg$ (jointly denoted by $a_i$):

| log trace | $e_1$ | $e_2$ | ... | $e_n$ |
|---|---|---|---|---|
| model run | $a_1$ | $a_2$ | ... | $a_m$ |

Each column in this matrix, a pair $(e_i, a_i)$, is a *move* of the alignment, meaning that an alignment can also be understood as a sequence of moves. There are different types of such moves, each encoding a different situation that can be encountered when comparing modeled and recorded behavior. We consider three types of moves:

- *Synchronous move*: A step in which the event of the trace and the task in the run correspond to each other. Synchronous moves denote the expected situation that the recorded events in the trace are in line with the tasks of a run of the process model. In the above model, a synchronous move means that it holds $e_i = a_i$ and $e_i \neq \gg$ (and thus $a_i \neq \gg$).
- *Model move*: When a task should have been executed according to the model, but there is no related event in the trace, we refer to this situation as a model move. As such, the move represents a deviation between the trace and the run of the process model in the sense that the execution of an activity has been skipped. In the above model, a model move is denoted by a pair $(e_i, a_i)$ with $e_i = \gg$ and $a_i \neq \gg$.
- *Log move*: When an event in the trace indicates that an activity has been executed, even though it should not have been executed according to the model, the alignment contains a log move . Being the counterpart of a model move, a log move also represents a deviation in the sense of a superfluous execution of an activity. A log move is denoted by a pair $(e_i, a_i)$ with $e_i \neq \gg$ and $a_i = \gg$.

Alignments are constructed only from these three types of moves (see an in-depth explanation on this in [8]).

For instance, let us use the running example (see Fig. 2) and the trace $\langle As, Cc, So, Cc, Al, Tm \rangle$. A possible alignment with this trace is:

| log trace | $As$ | $\gg$ | $Cc$ | $So$ | $Cc$ | $\gg$ | $\gg$ | $Al$ | $Tm$ |
|---|---|---|---|---|---|---|---|---|---|
| model run | $As$ | $\tau$ | $Cc$ | $So$ | $\gg$ | $Oa$ | $Cd$ | $Al$ | $Tm$ |

This alignment comprises six synchronous moves, one log move, $(Cc, \gg)$, and two model moves, $(\gg, Oa)$ and $(\gg, Cd)$. The log move $(Cc, \gg)$ indicates that the customer was contacted, even though this was not expected in the current state of processing (as this had just been done before sending the offer). The model move $(\gg, Oa)$ indicates that the customer never accepted the offer in writing (but maybe s/he did during the unexpected call). The model move $(\gg, Cd)$ indicates that the documents were not properly checked before approving the loan and transfering the money.

One can easily extract the original trace by projecting away the special symbol for skipping from the top row. Applying the projection to the bottom row yields the run of the model $(\langle As, Cc, So, Cc, Al, Tm \rangle)$ (Fig. 3).

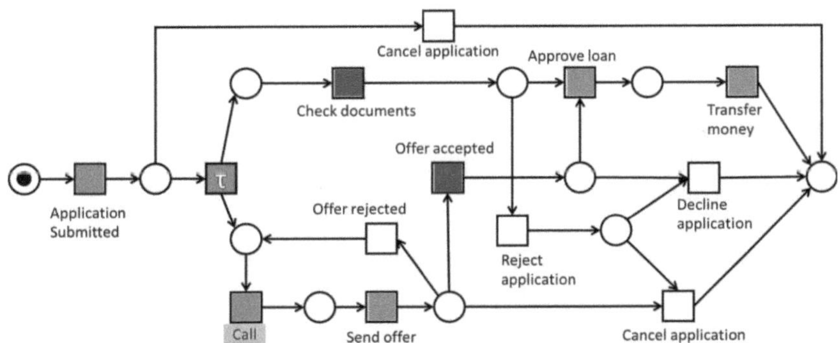


**Fig. 3.** Loan application process model with highlighted path corresponding to the same trace $\langle As, Cc, So, Cc, Al, Tm \rangle$ used in Fig. 2. One can see that "Check documents" and "Offer accepted" are marked as move on model in purple, whereas the second "Call" is marked as a log move in yellow. The other green transitions are synchronous moves.

In general, *optimal alignments*, i.e. alignments with a minimal number of model or log moves, are preferred. The alignment shown above is optimal since there is no other alignment with fewer deviations. Computing (optimal) alignments is a hot research topic, which has been addressed in many papers in the last years $[1, 6, 10, 15, 22, 25, 26, 32\text{--}35, 39, 40]$. In this paper, however, we refrain from describing all state-of-the-art methods for alignment computation, and refer the interested reader to the aforementioned papers, or to $[8]$.

Remarkably, alignments provide a simple means to quantify fitness. Again, this may be done based on the level of an individual trace or the event log as a whole. However, the aggregated cost of log moves and model moves may be a misleading measure, though, as it is not normalised. A common approach, therefore, is to normalise this cost by dividing it by the worst-case cost of a aligning the trace with the given model. Under a uniform assignment of costs to log and model moves, such a worst-case cost originates from an alignment in which each event of the trace $T_i$ relates to a log move, whereas all task executions of a run $\sigma$ of the model relate to a model move and $\sigma$ is as short as possible.

Since the cost induced by the model moves of a model run depends on its length, the shortest possible model run leading from the initial state to a final state in the model is considered for this purpose.

Realising the above idea, we obtain two ratios that denote the relative share of non-fitness in the alignments of a trace or an event log, respectively. Let $M$ be a model and $L$ an event log. Then, we denote by $cost(t, M)$ the cost of an optimal alignment of a trace $t \in L$ with respect to the model. Furthermore, let $cost(t, \langle \rangle)$ and $cost(\langle \rangle, x)$ be the costs of aligning a trace $t$ with an empty model run, or some run $x \in M$ of the model with an empty trace, respectively. Then, fitness based on alignments is quantified for a trace or an event log:

$$\text{fitness}(L, M) = 1 - \left( \frac{\sum_{t \in L} cost(t, M)}{\sum_{t \in L} \left( cost(t, \langle \rangle) \right) + |L| \times \min_{x \in M} cost(\langle \rangle, x)} \right) \quad (2)$$

Fitness, as discussed in this section, is often considered as a comparison of traces, i.e. to what extend is a model able to reproduce traces observed in the log. However, it is trivial to obtain a process model with perfect fitness for any given event log. In process mining, the so-called "flower model" is a model that essentially allows for all possible traces over a set of activity labels and is therefore always perfectly fitting.

Therefore, when comparing process models and event logs, more than fitness is needed and the first dimension we discuss here is precision.

## 3   Precision

Precision measures how much more behavior a model has that has not been observed in an event log. A very precise model allows for exactly the behavior observed in the event log, while a very imprecise model allows for much more behavior. Here, it is important to understand what 'behavior' means. In the context of precision in process mining, behavior is often understood as possible sequences and again, there are token-replay and alignment based techniques for estimating precision.

In [21] the authors estimate precision using token replay, but unfortunately, the corresponding technique strongly relies on the assumption that traces are fitting. If they are not, then the estimation of precision can be significantly degraded [2].

**Escaping Edges.** A simple precision metric based on alignments is grounded in the general idea of *escaping edges* [21]. To give the intuition, we assume that (i) the event log fits the process model; and (ii) that the process model is deterministic. The former means that we simply exclude non-fitting traces, for which the optimal alignment contains log moves or model moves, from the assessment of the precision of the model. The latter refers to a process model not being able to reach a state, in which two tasks that capture the same activity of the process are enabled.

For the activity of each event of a trace of the event log, we can determine a state of the process model right before the respective task would be executed. Under the above assumptions, this state is uniquely characterised. What is relevant when assessing precision, is the number of tasks enabled in this state of the process model. Let $M$ be a process model and $L$ an event log, with $t \in L$ as a trace and, overloading notation, $e \in t$ as one of the events of the trace. Then, by $enabled_M(e)$, we denote the number of tasks and, due to determinism of the process model also the number of activities that can be executed in the state right before executing the task corresponding to $e$.

Similarly, we consider all traces of the log that also contain events related to the activity of event $e$, say $a$, and have the same prefix, i.e. events that indicate that the same sequence of activities has been executed before an event signalling the execution of activity $a$. Then, we determine the number of activities for which events signal the execution directly after this prefix, i.e. the set of activities that have been executed in the same context as the activity $a$ as indicated by event $e$. Let this number of activities be denoted by $enabled_L(e)$, which, under the above assumptions, is necessarily less than or equal to $enabled_M(e)$. Then, the ratio of both numbers captures the amount of 'escaping edges' that represent modeled behavior that has not been recorded. As such, precision of log $L$ and $M$ is quantified as follows:

$$\text{precision}(L, M) = \frac{\sum_{t \in L, e \in t} enabled_L(e)}{\sum_{t \in L, e \in t} enabled_M(e)} \tag{3}$$

While escaping edge precision can provide an estimate of the amount of behavior the model may have which is not visited in the event log, it has a drawback that it does not consider whether this behavior is similar or dissimilar to the behavior found in the log[1].

To overcome this, precision can also be estimated using a technique called anti-alignments [9].

**Anti-alignments.** Since precision aims to quantify how much behavior of the model is not observed in the log, one could argue that precision can be estimated by using the model as a predictor for unseen behavior in the following way: A maximally precise model should not be able to generate any traces not observed in the event log and as such, if you remove one trace from the event log, the model should be able to perfectly predict which trace that was. This is the basis for anti-alignment based precision [9].

Contrary to an alignment, an anti-alignment is an execution sequence of the model that is as different as possible from the observed traces in the event log. The term "different" can be quantified using typical distance metrics on strings, such as hamming distance or edit distance. As process models typically contain

---

[1] Still, in [2] an extension for escaping edges-based precision using alignments was introduced.

loops, the length of the anti-alignment needs to be bounded, for example by the length of the removed trace.

$$\text{precision}_{\text{trace}}(L, M) = 1 - \sum_{\sigma \in L} \frac{d(\text{anti-alignment}(M, |\sigma|, L \setminus \{\sigma\}), \sigma)}{|\sigma|}. \qquad (4)$$

The assumption is made here that all traces in the log fit the model, but that is easy to guarantee by using the aligned traces rather than the original traces.

Consider our example again and let's suppose the event log contains all possible sequences of events where the loop is executed at most three times. This event log has 187 different traces (1 where the application is immediately cancelled, 21 where the loan is approved, 93 where the application is declined and 72 where the application is eventually cancelled).

In this case, the provided model is almost maximally precise. If one trace is removed from the event log and the model is asked to provide a trace that fits the model, but is different from anything already observed, then the removed trace will be provided. The model is not maximally precise though, since the model as a whole allows for traces never observed as there is a loop which may be executed more than three times. We therefore also define log-based precision where an anti-alignment is sought between the model and the log as a whole. For such an alignment, some maximal length N needs to be decided on upfront. N should be larger than the longest trace in the model, but not much larger.

$$\text{precision}_{\text{log}}(L, M) = 1 - \frac{1}{|L|} \cdot \sum_{\sigma \in L} d(\text{anti-alignment}(M, N, L), \sigma). \qquad (5)$$

Interestingly, using both fitness and precision as metrics, one can still obtain process models that are undesirable. The flower model mentioned earlier is not precise at all. In fact, this model should lead to a precision score of 0 as it is unable to predict which trace was removed from the log regardless of the removed trace. A perfectly fitting and perfectly precise model also always exist for any event log. This is the log itself, i.e. a process model where each trace is represented by a series of appropriately labeled transitions, possibly with similar prefixes merged into one.

We therefore introduce the final metric, called generalization.

## 4   Generalization

It was Buijs et al. who showed, using genetic algorithms, that focusing on fitness and precision, next to simplicity in process discovery, is simply not sufficient to discover good process models from an event log [7]. Instead, they showed that at least one more dimension is needed, i.e. generalization. However, while the process mining community understands this to be a necessary dimension in process mining, for which metrics should be developed, it is an open discussion what (proper) generalization actually means.

Buijs' generalization metric depended on the 'frequency of use' per model element. A model generalizes properly, in his work, when each part of the model plays an equally important role in explaining observed behavior. Hence in his work, he relies on alignments to count frequency of use per model element, asserting that for such a model, it is unlikely that it would produce new, previously unseen behavior. While his metric proved to be working well in the context of genetic algorithms, it fails to bridge the gap between process discovery and process modeling, where generalization plays an important role to minimize routing paths per element and to minimize the number of elements in a model, both important modeling guidelines [20].

When modeling a process, the modeler often resorts to specific modeling constructs as parallelism and loops to describe parts of a process in a generic way. Think of the example: the checking of documents and possibly rejecting the application is modeled in parallel with contacting the customer. However, in practice, it is unlikely that the customer is called to provide an offer if the document check was already negative. While this can be modeled, it would complicate the structure significantly. Instead, the modeler generalized from this behavior. Similarly, the loop around contacting the customer is a generalization of reality, since no process instance will ever continue with thousands of calls, while the model allows for this.

Interestingly, loops and parallel constructs in process models have something in common. They both introduce many different traces without introducing many new reachable markings in the model. Loops do not add any markings, while adding infinitely many traces, while parallel constructs of $n$ transitions introduce $2^n$ states with $n!$ sequences and $n! > 2^n$ for $n \geq 4$.

Using the concept of anti-alignments again, we can now define generalization based on anti alignments by keeping track of the so-called "recovery distance" $rc$, i.e. what is the (undirected) graph-distance between the markings reached in the anti-alignment and the markings reached in the actual event log in the statespace of the process model. A model that has very few states, but many traces will have a low recovery distance, i.e. any marking reached in the anti-alignment will be close to a marking reached in the original trace, but a model in which each anti-alignment is part of an almost fully separate part of the statepace will have a high recovery distance and hence a low generalization score.

$$\text{generalization}_{\text{trace}}(L, M) = 1 - \sum_{\sigma \in L} \frac{rd(\text{anti-alignment}(M, |\sigma|, L \setminus \{\sigma\}), \sigma)}{|\sigma| - 1} \quad (6)$$

$$\text{generalization}_{\log}(L, M) = 1 - \frac{1}{|L| * (N - 1)} \cdot \sum_{\sigma \in L} rd(\text{anti-alignment}(M, N, L), \sigma)$$

$$(7)$$

**Table 1.** Example event log.

| Trace | Frequency |
|---|---|
| $\langle A, B, C, D, B, C, E \rangle$ | 1,000 |
| $\langle A, B, C, D, C, B, E \rangle$ | 800 |
| $\langle A, C, B, D, B, C, E \rangle$ | 50 |
| $\langle A, C, B, E \rangle$ | 10 |

## 5   Examples

To illustrate that both precision and generalization as presented in this paper
are needed to evaluate the quality of models, we now discuss two examples. The
first is an example with a set of sound workflow models that have perfect fitness
for the log under consideration. Then, we show three models that do not have
perfect fitness and we show how using alignments as a foundation may lead to
counter-intuitive results.

### 5.1   Fitting Models

Let's consider the event log that is shown in Table 1. It's a small log with 1,860
traces in there.

As indicated before, there are two trivial models we can construct for any
event log: the flower model and the log itself. These are depicted in Fig. 4 and
Fig. 5. Both models are perfectly fitting, but in terms of precision and generalization they are opposites.

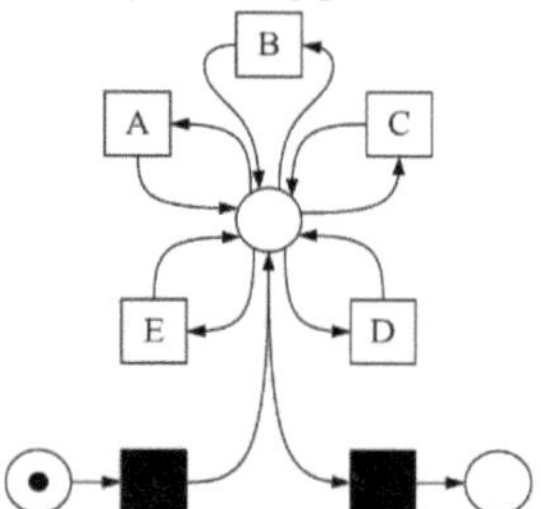

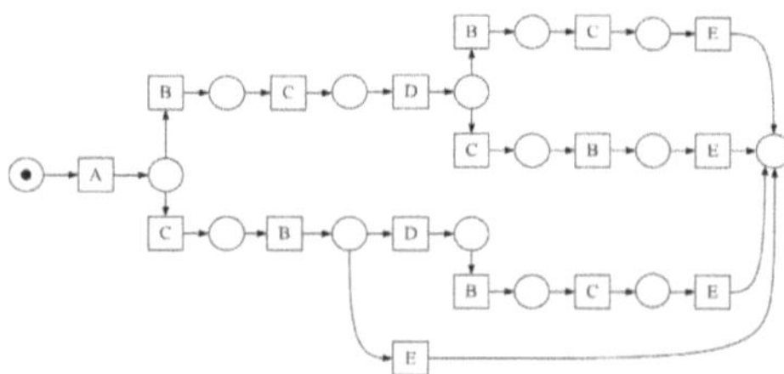

**Fig. 4.** Flower model for the event log of Table 1. The model is minimally precise and maximally generalizing.

**Fig. 5.** Trace model for the event log of Table 1. The model is maximally precise and minimally generalizing.

To show that precision and generalization are not each others' complement,
we developed the round-robin model, shown in Fig. 6. This model, like the flower
model, can be constructed for any event log and it consists of a circle of the
labels in the log. The process starts at one point and ends at another. The
labeled transitions can be fired in one direction, the unlabeled transitions in the
other. This means that the model allows for all sequences of labels, just like the

flower model does (they are language-equivalent models). However, where the process starts, determines where it ends. In this case, it can start with any of the five labeled transitions. Because of that, and the fact that each trace in the log starts with $A$ and ends with $E$, only 20% of the statespace of the model will be visited by the event log in Table 1, at least when aligning this event log using state-of-the-art alignment techniques.

When looking for anti-alignments, those will most likely start with different labels and therefore visit previously unseen parts of the statespace, maximizing the recovery distance as the path from any new state to a state visited before, will be a path to the initial (or final) marking. The model is therefore both minimally precise and minimally generalizing.

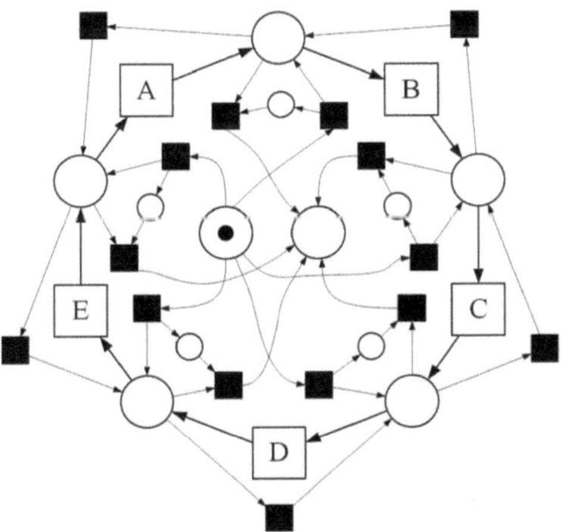

**Fig. 6.** Sound, fitting process model for the event log of Table 1. The model is minimally precise and minimally generalizing. Furthermore, despite its appearance, it is a sound workflow net.

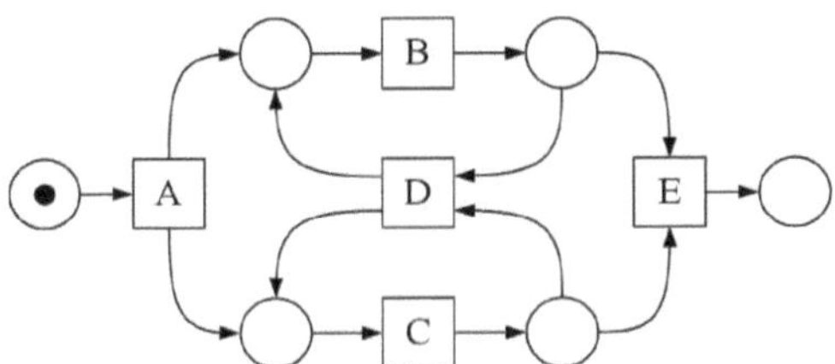

**Fig. 7.** Sound, fitting process model for the event log of Table 1. The model is almost maximally precise and maximally generalizing.

Fortunately, even the most basic process discovery techniques can discover the process model shown in Fig. 7. This model was produced using the $\alpha$-

algorithm [38] and it is almost maximally precise (one can execute more loops) and maximally generalizing (one cannot find states not previously seen) for this event log.

## 5.2   Non Fitting Models

In this section, we consider a different event log and three non-fitting process models. The event log is shown in Table 2 and the models, with their full state-spaces in Figs. 8, 9, 10, 11 and 12.

**Table 2.** Example event log.

| Trace | Frequency |
|---|---|
| $\langle a, b, d, f, e \rangle$ | 200 |
| $\langle a, d, b, g, e \rangle$ | 50 |
| $\langle a, d, d, g, e \rangle$ | 5 |
| $\langle a, g, e \rangle$ | 2 |

It is clear that none of the models are actually fitting. When calculating the fitness using alignments, models A and B can be shown to be equally fitting (with a fitness of 0.88) and model C is less fitting as it has more deviations. It's also relatively easy to see that the language of model C, consisting of only 20 possible traces, is fully contained in the infinite language of model B and the language of model B is contained in model A. Furthermore, in terms of states, model A has a statespace with 6 states, model B has 11 states and model C has 18 states.

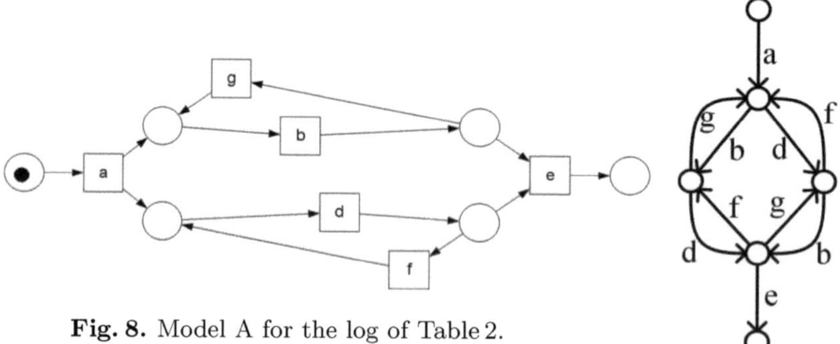


**Fig. 8.** Model A for the log of Table 2.

**Fig. 9.** Behavior model A.

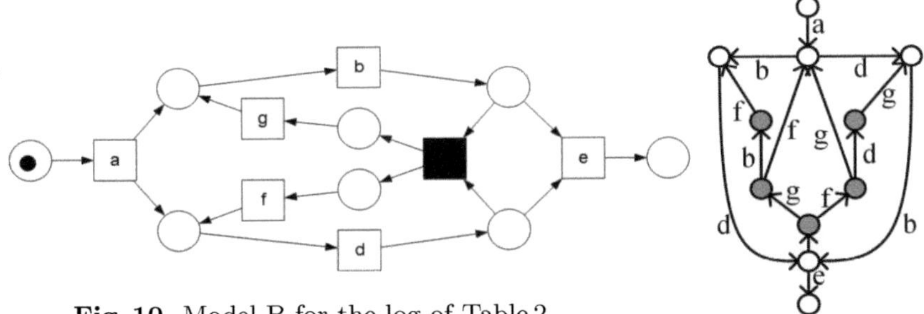

**Fig. 10.** Model B for the log of Table 2.

**Fig. 11.** Behavior model B.

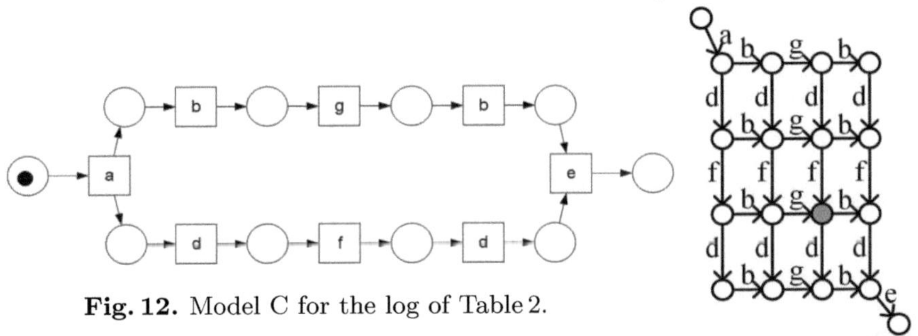

**Fig. 12.** Model C for the log of Table 2.

**Fig. 13.** Behavior model C.

To determine fitness, the traces in the log should be aligned to the model. This leads to a total of twelve alignments shown in Table 3. Note that for most of the traces, multiple optimal alignments exist. We opted to show the simplest ones. Using the alignments and the commonly used default cost function assigning cost 1 to deviations, one can compute fitness to be 0.88 for the first two models A and B and 0.77 for model C.

**Table 3.** All alignments for event log of Table 2 onto the models of Figs. 8, 9, 10, 11, 12 and 13.

| model | $\langle a,b,d,f,e\rangle^{200}$ | $\langle a,b,d,g,e\rangle^{50}$ | $\langle a,d,d,g,e\rangle^{5}$ | $\langle a,g,e\rangle^{2}$ |
|---|---|---|---|---|
| A | trace: $a\,b\,d\,f\,e$ <br> run: $a\,b\,d\,\gg\,e$ | trace: $a\,d\,b\,g\,e$ <br> run: $a\,d\,b\,\gg\,e$ | trace: $a\,d\,d\,g\,e$ <br> run: $a\,d\,\gg\,\gg\,e$ | trace: $a\,g\,\gg\,\gg\,e$ <br> run: $a\,\gg\,b\,d\,e$ |
| B | trace: $a\,b\,d\,f\,e$ <br> run: $a\,b\,d\,\gg\,e$ | trace: $a\,d\,b\,g\,e$ <br> run: $a\,d\,b\,\gg\,e$ | trace: $a\,d\,d\,g\,e$ <br> run: $a\,d\,\gg\,\gg\,e$ | trace: $a\,g\,\gg\,\gg\,e$ <br> run: $a\,\gg\,b\,d\,e$ |
| C | trace: $a\,b\,d\,f\,\gg\,\gg\,\gg\,e$ <br> run: $a\,b\,d\,f\,d\,g\,b\,e$ | trace: $a\,d\,b\,g\,\gg\,\gg\,\gg\,e$ <br> run: $a\,d\,b\,g\,b\,f\,d\,e$ | trace: $a\,d\,\gg\,d\,\gg\,g\,\gg\,e$ <br> run: $a\,d\,f\,d\,b\,g\,b\,e$ | trace: $a\,\gg\,g\,\gg\,\gg\,\gg\,\gg\,e$ <br> run: $a\,b\,g\,b\,d\,f\,d\,e$ |

When reasoning about precision and generalization, it is important to reason about the behavior of the model observed in the event log. However, since traces are non-fitting, we may not know what the actual behavior is that is observed in the event log. Therefore, fitness and generalization metrics are best defined over the aligned logs, rather than the original log. This gives us three new event logs to reason about as shown in Table 4 that we can use to determine precision.

**Table 4.** Three aligned event logs.

| Trace | Frequency |
| --- | --- |
| $\langle a, b, d, e \rangle$ | 202 |
| $\langle a, d, b, e \rangle$ | 55 |

log A

| Trace | Frequency |
| --- | --- |
| $\langle a, b, d, e \rangle$ | 202 |
| $\langle a, d, b, e \rangle$ | 55 |

log B

| Trace | Frequency |
| --- | --- |
| $\langle a, b, d, f, d, g, b, e \rangle$ | 200 |
| $\langle a, d, b, g, b, f, d, e \rangle$ | 50 |
| $\langle a, d, f, d, b, g, b, e \rangle$ | 5 |
| $\langle a, b, g, b, d, f, d, e \rangle$ | 2 |

log C

In Sect. 3, we defined trace precision as the ability to predict which trace was removed from the log. It's easy to see that models A and B are perfectly able to do this. Removing any of the two traces from the aligned logs and asking the model which trace of length 4 from the aligned log was removed, you will obtain the correct answer. In other words, they are maximally precise in this regard. Log-based precision is the ability to find a new trace maximally different from the existing traces in the log, up to a length $N$. Here, both models would be able to produce similar traces, depending on the parameter $N$ since all traces in model A are of length $4 + 2 \cdot X$, for some integer X, while all traces in model B are of length $4 + 4 \cdot X$ for some X. In other words, depending on the choice of $N$, model A would be considered as precise as, or less precise than model B.

Model C is a different story. The event log contains only four traces of length 8, while the model allows for twenty traces of that length. In other words, when removing one trace from the log, predicting which one was removed will prove challenging. The trace precision is therefore lower than that of models A and B. The log precision, on the other hand, is higher, since the model can only produce those 20 traces of length 8. Depending on how you weigh log vs trace precision, the overall precision score may be higher or lower than that of models A and B.

For generalization, we consider the recovery distance, i.e. the distance from states visited by traces not observed in the log to states visited by traces in the log and again, we distinguish trace and log generalization. Model A has very few states that are all visited by the event log. Any anti-alignment for a removed trace will not visit states not visited by the original log. The trace generalization is therefore perfect and so is the log generalization.

In model B, there are five states, indicated in grey in Fig. 11, that are never visited by the aligned event log. For trace generalization, these traces will also not be visited when looking for anti-alignments of length 4, hence trace generalization is perfect. However, log generalization is not. Any anti-alignment of length $N > 4$ will visit at least 2 of the new states, leading to a recovery distance of at least 2. Therefore, log generalization is not perfect.

In model C, the alignments chosen in the aligned log visit all but one of the 18 states in the statespace. It's likely that this state will be visited by an anti-alignment of length 8 for trace generalization and certain that this is the case for log-generalization. In both cases the recovery distance is however limited to 1. As with precision, it depends on the weighing of trace and log generalization to decide whether model C is better or worse than B in terms of generalization.

Overall, model A is the best fitting, the most precise and the most generalizing model for the event log under consideration and this is what we expect as model A is indeed a model that we could see being discovered for the event log under consideration, where the others are less likely candidates and after all, the holy grail in process mining is still to develop process discovery techniques that result in fitting, yet precise and properly generalizing process models.

## 6   Conclusion and Outlook

In this paper, we showed that conformance checking is a very relevant topic for process mining. It can be used for identifying differences between event logs and process models, and it is simply needed to assess the quality of a process model given an event log. We argued that fitness forms the basis of conformance checking, but we also showed that both precision and generalization are important measures. Through examples, we argue that precision and generalization are independent of each other and that any good process mining result should result in a fitting, yet precise enough and properly generalizing process model.

The discussion also shows that there is still a lot to be done in the area of conformance checking. There are many different metrics for fitness, precision and generalization and some researchers tried to provide desirable properties these metrics should have [31]. Interestingly enough, none of the metrics in this paper have all desired properties and the authors may even disagree on the desirability of them. Therefore, there is still room to develop clear ideas around the notions of fitness, precision and generalization.

In this paper we focused on essential algorithms and metrics, although we want to acknowledge interesting variations and specializations of the core techniques. One interesting body of work started by Leemans and Polyvyanyy, and which Wil also joined, is the stochastic version of conformance checking which aims for a more realistic view on the likelihood of the relation of model run and log traces [16,17].

Next to the fundamental challenges around conformance checking, there are also computational challenges. Finding an alignment, for example, is a reachability question and from Petri net theory, we know that these questions are computationally challenging. Therefore, there is work needed on fast approximation of alignments. First steps have been made in this direction by several researchers [28,34], but the field lacks a proper set of benchmarks with ground truth to properly compare techniques. Furthermore, as shown elegantly in [13], there is potential for using, applying or simply learning from developments in artificial intelligence in the context of conformance checking.

Finally, with the shift in process mining from trace centric to object centric, there is also a need for conformance checking techniques at the level of a system rather than a case. Initial work in this direction is promising [14, 23, 24, 29, 36, 41], but computationally even more challenging as reachability in system models, as opposed to in process models, may even be undecidable when including case identifiers.

**Acknowledgements.** Supported by MCIN/AEI/10.13039/501100011033 under grant PID2020-112581GB-C21 (MOTION).

# References


1. Adriansyah, A.: Aligning observed and modeled behavior. Ph.D. thesis, Technische Universiteit Eindhoven (2014)
2. Adriansyah, A., Munoz-Gama, J., Carmona, J., van Dongen, B.F., van der Aalst, W.M.P.: Measuring precision of modeled behavior. Inf. Syst. E-Bus. Manag. **13**(1), 37–67 (2015). https://doi.org/10.1007/s10257-014-0234-7
3. Alizadeh, M., Lu, X., Fahland, D., Zannone, N., van der Aalst, W.M.P.: Linking data and process perspectives for conformance analysis. Comput. Secur. **73**, 172–193 (2018). https://doi.org/10.1016/j.cose.2017.10.010
4. Mozafari Mehr, A.S., de Carvalho, R.M., van Dongen, B.: Detecting privacy, data and control-flow deviations in business processes. In: Nurcan, S., Korthaus, A. (eds.) CAiSE 2021. LNBIP, vol. 424, pp. 82–91. Springer, Cham (2021). https://doi.org/10.1007/978-3-030-79108-7_10
5. Berti, A., van der Aalst, W.M.P.: A novel token-based replay technique to speed up conformance checking and process enhancement. In: Koutny, M., Kordon, F., Pomello, L. (eds.) Transactions on Petri Nets and Other Models of Concurrency XV. LNCS, vol. 12530, pp. 1–26. Springer, Heidelberg (2021). https://doi.org/10.1007/978-3-662-63079-2_1
6. Bloemen, V., van de Pol, J., van der Aalst, W.M.P.: Symbolically aligning observed and modelled behaviour. In: 18th International Conference on Application of Concurrency to System Design, ACSD 2018, Bratislava, Slovakia, 25–29 June 2018, pp. 50–59 (2018)
7. Buijs, J.C.A.M., van Dongen, B.F., van der Aalst, W.M.P.: Quality dimensions in process discovery: the importance of fitness, precision, generalization and simplicity. Int. J. Cooperative Inf. Syst. **23**(1), 1440001 (2014). https://doi.org/10.1142/S0218843014400012
8. Carmona, J., van Dongen, B.F., Solti, A., Weidlich, M.: Conformance Checking - Relating Processes and Models. Springer, Cham (2018). https://doi.org/10.1007/978-3-319-99414-7
9. Chatain, T., Carmona, J.: Anti-alignments in conformance checking - the dark side of process models. In: Proceedings of the Application and Theory of Petri Nets and Concurrency - 37th International Conference, PETRI NETS 2016, Toruń, Poland, 19–24 June 2016, pp. 240–258 (2016)

10. de Leoni, M., Marrella, A.: Aligning real process executions and prescriptive process models through automated planning. Expert Syst. Appl. **82**, 162–183 (2017)
11. de Leoni, M., van der Aalst, W.M.P.: Aligning event logs and process models for multi-perspective conformance checking: an approach based on integer linear programming. In: Daniel, F., Wang, J., Weber, B. (eds.) BPM 2013. LNCS, vol. 8094, pp. 113–129. Springer, Heidelberg (2013). https://doi.org/10.1007/978-3-642-40176-3_10
12. Dunzer, S., Stierle, M., Matzner, M., Baier, S.: Conformance checking: a state-of-the-art literature review. In: Betz, S. (ed.) Proceedings of the 11th International Conference on Subject-Oriented Business Process Management, S-BPM ONE 2019, Seville, Spain, 26–28 June 2019, pp. 4:1–4:10. ACM (2019). https://doi.org/10.1145/3329007.3329014
13. Genga, L., Winter, K.: Artificial intelligence in conformance checking: state of the art and research agenda. Process Sci. **2**(1), 9 (2025). https://doi.org/10.1007/s44311-025-00015-7
14. Leemans, S.J.J., Brockhoff, T., van der Aalst, W.M.P., Polyvyanyy, A.: Partially ordered stochastic conformance checking. Knowl. Inf. Syst. **67**(3), 2291–2319 (2025). https://doi.org/10.1007/s10115-024-02280-7
15. Leemans, S.J.J., Fahland, D., van der Aalst, W.M.P.: Scalable process discovery and conformance checking. Softw. Syst. Model. **17**(2), 599–631 (2016). https://doi.org/10.1007/s10270-016-0545-x
16. Leemans, S.J.J., Polyvyanyy, A.: Stochastic-aware conformance checking: an entropy-based approach. In: Dustdar, S., Yu, E., Salinesi, C., Rieu, D., Pant, V. (eds.) CAiSE 2020. LNCS, vol. 12127, pp. 217–233. Springer, Cham (2020). https://doi.org/10.1007/978-3-030-49435-3_14
17. Leemans, S.J.J., van der Aalst, W.M.P., Brockhoff, T., Polyvyanyy, A.: Stochastic process mining: earth movers' stochastic conformance. Inf. Syst. **102**, 101724 (2021). https://doi.org/10.1016/j.is.2021.101724. https://www.sciencedirect.com/science/article/pii/S0306437921000041
18. Letia, I.A., Goron, A.: Model checking as support for inspecting compliance to rules in flexible processes. J. Vis. Lang. Comput. **28**, 100–121 (2015). https://doi.org/10.1016/j.jvlc.2014.12.008
19. Mannhardt, F., de Leoni, M., Reijers, H.A., van der Aalst, W.M.P.: Balanced multi-perspective checking of process conformance. Computing **98**(4), 407–437 (2015). https://doi.org/10.1007/s00607-015-0441-1
20. Mendling, J., Reijers, H., van der Aalst, W.M.P.: Seven process modeling guidelines (7PMG). Inf. Softw. Technol. **52**(2), 127–136 (2010)
21. Muñoz-Gama, J., Carmona, J.: A fresh look at precision in process conformance. In: Hull, R., Mendling, J., Tai, S. (eds.) BPM 2010. LNCS, vol. 6336, pp. 211–226. Springer, Heidelberg (2010). https://doi.org/10.1007/978-3-642-15618-2_16
22. Padró, L., Carmona, J.: Computation of alignments of business processes through relaxation labeling and local optimal search. Inf. Syst. **104**, 101703 (2022). https://doi.org/10.1016/j.is.2020.101703
23. Park, G., Adams, J.N., van der Aalst, W.M.P.: Conformance checking and performance analysis using object-centric directly-follows graphs. In: Marrella, A., Resinas, M., Jans, M., Rosemann, M. (eds.) BPM 2024. LNBIP, vol. 526, pp. 179–196. Springer, Cham (2024). https://doi.org/10.1007/978-3-031-70418-5_11
24. Rafiei, M., Pourbafrani, M., van der Aalst, W.M.P.: Federated conformance checking. Inf. Syst. **131**, 102525 (2025). https://doi.org/10.1016/J.IS.2025.102525

25. Reißner, D., Conforti, R., Dumas, M., La Rosa, M., Armas-Cervantes, A.: Scalable conformance checking of business processes. In: OTM CoopIS, Rhodes, Greece, pp. 607–627 (2017)

26. Reißner, D., Armas-Cervantes, A., Conforti, R., Dumas, M., Fahland, D., La Rosa, M.: Scalable alignment of process models and event logs: an approach based on automata and s-components. Inf. Syst. **94**, 101561 (2020). https://doi.org/10.1016/j.is.2020.101561. http://www.sciencedirect.com/science/article/pii/S0306437920300545

27. Rozinat, A., van der Aalst, W.M.P.: Conformance checking of processes based on monitoring real behavior. Inf. Syst. **33**(1), 64–95 (2008). https://doi.org/10.1016/j.is.2007.07.001

28. Sommers, D., Sidorova, N., van Dongen, B.: Exact and approximated log alignments for processes with inter-case dependencies. In: Gomes, L., Lorenz, R. (eds.) PETRI NETS 2023. LNCS, vol. 13929, pp. 99–119. Springer, Cham (2023). https://doi.org/10.1007/978-3-031-33620-1_6

29. Sommers, D., Sidorova, N., van Dongen, B.: Conformance checking with model projections. In: Kristensen, L.M., van der Werf, J.M. (eds.) PETRI NETS 2024. LNCS, vol. 14628, pp. 61–82. Springer, Cham (2024). https://doi.org/10.1007/978-3-031-61433-0_4

30. Taghiabadi, E.R., Gromov, V., Fahland, D., van der Aalst, W.M.P.: Compliance checking of data-aware and resource-aware compliance requirements. In: Meersman, R., et al. (eds.) OTM 2014. LNCS, vol. 8841, pp. 237–257. Springer, Heidelberg (2014). https://doi.org/10.1007/978-3-662-45563-0_14

31. Tax, N., Lu, X., Sidorova, N., Fahland, D., van der Aalst, W.M.P.: The imprecisions of precision measures in process mining. Inf. Process. Lett. **135**, 1–8 (2018). https://doi.org/10.1016/j.ipl.2018.01.013. http://www.sciencedirect.com/science/article/pii/S0020019018300280

32. Taymouri, F., Carmona, J.: Model and event log reductions to boost the computation of alignments. In: Proceedings of the 6th International Symposium on Data-driven Process Discovery and Analysis (SIMPDA 2016), Graz, Austria, 15–16 December 2016, pp. 50–62 (2016). http://ceur-ws.org/Vol-1757/paper4.pdf

33. Taymouri, F., Carmona, J.: A recursive paradigm for aligning observed behavior of large structured process models. In: 14th International Conference of Business Process Management (BPM), Rio de Janeiro, Brazil, 18–22 September 2016

34. Taymouri, F., Carmona, J.: An evolutionary technique to approximate multiple optimal alignments. In: Weske, M., Montali, M., Weber, I., vom Brocke, J. (eds.) BPM 2018. LNCS, vol. 11080, pp. 215–232. Springer, Cham (2018). https://doi.org/10.1007/978-3-319-98648-7_13

35. Taymouri, F., Carmona, J.: Structural computation of alignments of business processes over partial orders. In: 19th International Conference on Application of Concurrency to System Design, ACSD 2019, Aachen, Germany, 23–28 June 2019, pp. 73–81. IEEE (2019). https://doi.org/10.1109/ACSD.2019.00012

36. van der Aalst, W.M.P.: Lifting process discovery and conformance checking to the next level: a general approach to object-centric process mining (invited talk). In: Köhler-Bussmeier, M., Moldt, D., Rölke, H. (eds.) Proceedings of the International Workshop on Petri Nets and Software Engineering 2024 co-located with the 45th International Conference on Application and Theory of Petri Nets and Concurrency (PETRI NETS 2024), 24–25 June 2024, Geneva, Switzerland. CEUR Workshop Proceedings, vol. 3730 , pp. 1–12. CEUR-WS.org (2024). https://ceur-ws.org/Vol-3730/keynote.pdf

37. van der Aalst, W.M.P., Adriansyah, A., van Dongen, B.F.: Replaying history on process models for conformance checking and performance analysis. Wiley Interdiscip. Rev. Data Min. Knowl. Discov. **2**(2), 182–192 (2012). https://doi.org/10.1002/widm.1045

38. van der Aalst, W.M.P., Weijters, T., Maruster, L.: Workflow mining: discovering process models from event logs. IEEE Trans. Knowl. Data Eng. **16**(9), 1128–1142 (2004). https://doi.org/10.1109/TKDE.2004.47

39. van Dongen, B., Carmona, J., Chatain, T., Taymouri, F.: Aligning modeled and observed behavior: a compromise between computation complexity and quality. In: Dubois, E., Pohl, K. (eds.) CAiSE 2017. LNCS, vol. 10253, pp. 94–109. Springer, Cham (2017). https://doi.org/10.1007/978-3-319-59536-8_7

40. Dongen, B.F.: Efficiently computing alignments - using the extended marking equation. In: Weske, M., Montali, M., Weber, I., vom Brocke, J. (eds.) BPM 2018. LNCS, vol. 11080, pp. 197–214. Springer, Cham (2018). https://doi.org/10.1007/978-3-319-98648-7_12

41. Dongen, B.F.: Conformance checking: a systemic view. In: Marrella, A., Weber, B. (eds.) BPM 2021. LNBIP, vol. 436, pp. 61–72. Springer, Cham (2022). https://doi.org/10.1007/978-3-030-94343-1_5

# Notes of a Process Scientist: Process Discovery

Artem Polyvyanyy[(✉)][iD]

The University of Melbourne, Melbourne, Australia
artem.polyvyanyy@unimelb.edu.au

**Abstract.** Process discovery uses event data generated by information systems to construct process models that describe system behavior. This paper revisits the problem from a conceptual standpoint and clarifies its core elements, including the nature of the input event data, the intended characteristics and purposes of the resulting models, the variants of the discovery problem, the key challenges associated with solving it, and the principles that guide the evaluation of the quality of discovered models. We further position process discovery in relation to related problems in adjacent research areas and identify open issues and research opportunities. Through this analysis, the paper aims to provide a solid reference point for future methodological and tool developments in process discovery.

**Keywords:** Process mining · process discovery · variants · challenges · related problems · quality · future directions

## 1 Introduction

Process mining is a discipline that bridges data science and process science. It studies how processes executed by systems in the real world can be discovered, monitored, and improved by analyzing event data recorded during their execution [2]. At its core, process mining seeks to answer how a system actually behaves, including which activities occur, how often and in what order they are executed, under which conditions and by whom they are performed, and what outcomes they produce. Over the past two decades, process mining has evolved into a mature research field, influencing both academia and industry, with techniques now applied across domains such as business operations, healthcare, manufacturing, and software engineering. Among the key problems in process mining, process discovery stands as the foundational one. Given event data, *process discovery* aims to construct a process model that meaningfully represents the behavior of the system that generated the data [8].

This paper is the first in a series of opinion pieces under the heading *Notes of a Process Scientist*, in which we examine foundational problems in process science. Here, we focus on the problem of process discovery as it should be understood in light of its purpose and scientific roots. The goal is to contribute to the discussion about what process discovery aims to achieve, what its results should explain, and how its success should be evaluated. In this sense, the paper is not a survey of existing methods, but a conceptual reflection on the essence and future direction of process discovery.


J. Mendling et al. (Eds.): Wil van der Aalst Festschrift, LNCS 16480, pp. 368–383, 2026.
https://doi.org/10.1007/978-3-032-17618-9_26

The remainder of the paper proceeds as follows. The next section introduces the fundamental concepts underlying process discovery and provides a formal definition of the problem. Section 3 then outlines important variants of the conventional problem formulation that differ in the behavioral aspects of the system they capture in discovered models. Section 4 discusses the main challenges associated with discovering process models from event data. Subsequently, Sect. 5 reviews related problems explored in adjacent research areas. Finally, Sect. 6 examines how the quality of discovered models can be evaluated, before Sect. 7 concludes the paper.

## 2   Process Discovery

This section presents key concepts relevant to process discovery, namely systems (Sect. 2.1), event data (Sect. 2.2), processes (Sect. 2.3), and process models (Sect. 2.4), and gives a formal definition of the process discovery problem (Sect. 2.5).

### 2.1   Systems

A dynamical system, or simply a *system*, consists of interacting components whose behavior changes over time. The behavior of a system can be described by its states and by rules that determine how it transitions between states. A state is a collection of attributes and their values that characterize the condition of the system at a given point in time. A state can be a global snapshot that abstracts away the internal complexity of individual components and captures only the information needed to describe the system as a whole. Alternatively, the global state of a system can be understood as the aggregation of the local states of its interacting components [35].

The state of a continuous-time system evolves smoothly at every instant, whereas in a discrete-time system, state updates occur at distinct time steps. Discrete systems are particularly relevant in the context of information systems. An information system consists of interacting software components that perform activities by consuming, producing, and manipulating information. Its states change at identifiable, discrete events.

### 2.2   Event Data

In the context of systems, *data* refers to the measured and recorded values that describe the observed states of a system, the inputs it consumes, the outputs it produces, the activities that trigger state changes, or the characteristics of the environment in which the system is embedded. To associate each measurement with a specific moment in the life of the system, it is timestamped and represented as an *event*. Whereas states and state-transition rules define the principles that govern how the system evolves, data form the observed and recorded traces of that evolution. In this way, data provide empirical evidence of how the system behaves in the real world.

Let $\mathcal{A}$ be a universe of *attributes* and let $\mathcal{V}$ be a universe of *values*, such that $timestamp \in \mathcal{A}$ is a special timestamp attribute. Then, an *event e* is a partial function $e : \mathcal{A} \rightharpoonup \mathcal{V}$ that assigns a value to the timestamp attribute; that is, $timestamp \in dom(e)$ and $e(timestamp) \in \mathcal{T}$, where $\mathcal{T} \subset \mathcal{V}$ is a set of timestamps totally ordered by $\leq$. The value *e*(*timestamp*) specifies the point in time at which event *e* was observed and/or recorded. Finally, *event data* is a collection of events.

Table 1 presents an example of event data comprising twenty events. Each row in the table defines a single event with three attributes: *case*, *activity*, and *timestamp*. For instance, the last row defines the event with the values of case, activity, and timestamp attributes set to 3, d, and 20, respectively. This event was triggered at timestamp 20 by activity d executed as part of process case 3.

### 2.3   Processes

A *process instance* is a sequence or ordering of activities that a system performs, or is capable of performing, in pursuit of achieving a specific goal. Each activity transforms the system by inducing a state transition, and the entire process instance leads the system from an initial state to a final state. A *process* is a collection of such instances that (aim to) accomplish the same goal. For example, an information system may automate the process of handling customer orders, involving activities such as receiving requests, checking inventory, processing payments, and shipping products. In computing more broadly, a process instance may refer to the execution of a workflow, program, or algorithm. The processes a system can perform collectively define its *behavior*.

Events that record which activity generated them, that is, events with a value for the attribute *activity* $\in \mathcal{A}$, can be associated with the process instances in which those activities occurred. In conventional process discovery [8], the attribute *case* $\in \mathcal{A}$ is used to correlate events with their corresponding process instances. Specifically, all events that share the same *case identifier* form the complete set of events for a single process instance, or *case*. Ordering these events by their timestamps using the total order $\leq$ yields a *trace*. A collection of traces is commonly referred to as an *event log*.

Table 1. Example event data.

| Case | Activity | Timestamp |
|------|----------|-----------|
| 1 | a | 1 |
| 2 | a | 2 |
| 3 | a | 3 |
| 3 | c | 4 |
| 4 | b | 5 |
| 2 | b | 6 |
| 5 | b | 7 |
| 5 | a | 8 |
| 1 | b | 9 |
| 2 | d | 10 |
| 1 | c | 11 |
| 3 | b | 12 |
| 2 | c | 13 |
| 4 | a | 14 |
| 4 | c | 15 |
| 5 | d | 16 |
| 5 | c | 17 |
| 4 | d | 18 |
| 1 | d | 19 |
| 3 | d | 20 |

For instance, the events in Table 1 define five traces that can be grouped into event log $L = [\langle a,b,c,d \rangle, \langle a,b,d,c \rangle, \langle a,c,b,d \rangle, \langle b,a,c,d \rangle, \langle b,a,d,c \rangle]$. For simplicity, we denote each trace as a sequence of activities without explicitly showing timestamps or case identifiers. In this example, these attributes can be inferred unambiguously from the activity sequences. In general, an event log may contain multiple traces that yield the same activity sequence. Hence, event logs are commonly conceptualized as multisets of activity sequences. More recently, object-centric process discovery [7] has been introduced, where events are grouped into process instances based on sets of attribute values that identify the objects involved in the activities that triggered the events.

## 2.4   Process Models

A *process model* describes the possible orderings of activities, providing a simplified representation of a process constructed for a specific purpose and target audience. It captures multiple process instances that aim to achieve a specific goal by following common activity patterns. For example, Petri nets [31] offer a formal modeling framework capable of representing concurrency, choice, and synchronization between activities, whereas directly-follows graphs (DFGs) [5] and stochastic directed action graphs (SDAGs) [10] provide abstract representations that emphasize directly-follows relations observed between recorded activities.

Figure 1 depicts an example Petri net consisting of eleven places (circles $p_0$ to $p_{10}$) and eight transitions (squares $t_0$ to $t_7$). Among these, four transitions ($t_1$, $t_2$, $t_5$, and $t_6$) are observable and represent the activities a, b, c, and d, respectively. These are the transitions whose execution is visible to an external observer. The remaining four transitions are silent, capturing internal activities that are not visible to observers. By projecting execution sequences of transitions described by the net onto the activities associated with the observable transitions, one obtains the activity sequences of the traces supported by the net. The Petri net shown in Fig. 1 supports exactly the five activity sequences induced by the traces in the event log $L$ introduced in Sect. 2.3.

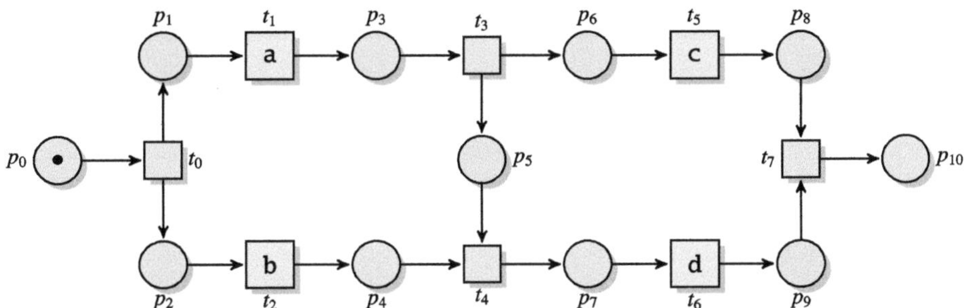

**Fig. 1.** A Petri net.

## 2.5   Definition

Let $\mathcal{E}$ be a universe of events and let $\mathcal{M}$ be a universe of process models. A technique that solves the process discovery problem can be conceptualized as a function $d$ that maps collections of events and configurations $C$ to process models, that is:

$$d : \mathcal{P}(\mathcal{E}) \times C \to \mathcal{M}. \tag{1}$$

A *configuration* of a discovery technique customizes the construction of the resulting process model. Most often, the configuration specifies the level of detail about the process that generated the input data that should be preserved in the discovered process model. In many cases, the configuration determines the level of detail from the process that generated the input data that should be retained in the discovered model. This level of detail can be adjusted by the user, for example, by using a slider control [30].

Discovered process models serve as a starting point for understanding and improving the processes of the system that produced the event data. They provide valuable insights for diverse stakeholders, including system analysts diagnosing inefficiencies, managers optimizing operations, and domain experts ensuring compliance and quality, as they uncover how the system behaves in the real world.

For example, Fig. 2 shows a Petri net discovered from the event log $L$ introduced in Sect. 2.3. The model was obtained using the implementation of the Inductive Miner infrequent algorithm [22] in ProM 6.11 [37], configured with a noise threshold of 0.0.

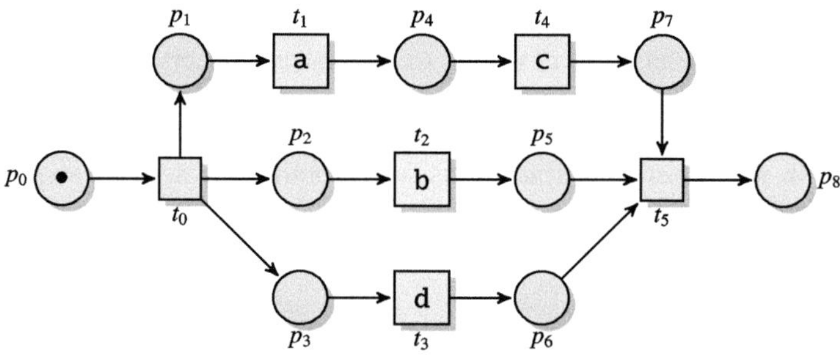

**Fig. 2.** A Petri net discovered from event log $L$ introduced in Sect. 2.3 using the implementation of the Inductive Miner infrequent algorithm in ProM 6.11.

## 3 Variants

A process model constructed as a solution to the original process discovery problem described in Sect. 2.5 aims to capture the full behavior of the system that produced the data, including behavior that has not been observed but is allowed by its rules. Such a model is useful for comprehensive system analysis. It enables analysts and engineers to reason about system behavior, identify design deficiencies, and verify that the system supports its intended functionalities. This section discusses several common variants of the conventional process discovery problem that differ in the representational focus of the models derived from the input event data.

### 3.1 Relevant Behavior Discovery

Often, only a portion of the system's behavior that is actively used and likely to be used in the future is of practical interest. Different organizations may use the same system in different ways, depending on their operational needs. Consequently, they may also have no practical interest in certain process instances that the system supports but that do not occur in their day-to-day operations. The focus of the *relevant behavior discovery* variant of the discovery problem is therefore on constructing models that represent this operationally active subset of behavior. As a result, the discovered models exclude obsolete or infrequent behavior and provide a clearer reflection of how the system functions in practice. Such models are useful for process optimization, resource planning, and continuous improvement because they emphasize dominant and recurring behavior patterns supported by empirical evidence.

### 3.2 Observed Behavior Discovery

The *observed behavior discovery* variant of the discovery problem emphasizes the importance of the recorded event data. When discovering the observed system's behavior, the objective is to construct process models that accurately reproduce the system's behavior as captured in the event data, without inferring unobserved or hypothetical behavior. Such models are especially valuable for auditing, compliance checking, and retrospective analysis, where the focus is on verifying that actual executions conform to expectations or regulations. Observed behavior discovery prioritizes descriptive accuracy and minimizes assumptions beyond what is explicitly present in the data.

### 3.3 Process Forecasting

The *process forecasting* variant of the process discovery problem aims to construct models that describe the system's expected behavior in a given future period [27,43], for example, in the next year. Rather than focusing on historical operations or on unconstrained generalizations of what the system can do in principle, this approach generalizes from historical data to predict how the system will behave under future conditions. Process forecasting enables proactive decision-making, supporting the preparation, adaptation, or redesign of processes before they take place. Such models are instrumental for capacity planning, risk management, and process evolution, where anticipating future trends and deviations is critical.

## 4 Challenges

Process discovery presents a range of challenges. Event data are often heterogeneous, incomplete, or noisy, while the underlying processes can be complex and subject to change over time. The main categories of challenges in process discovery are outlined below in an order that reflects their perceived importance.

### 4.1 Data Quality

Real world event data often contain missing attribute values, duplicate or spurious events, incorrect timestamps, or inconsistently named attributes. These data quality issues are commonly grouped under the broad umbrella of *noise* in event data. Typical sources of noise include human errors or deviations from prescribed behavior, asynchronous logging across distributed system components, and inconsistencies introduced by heterogeneous system integrations. The corresponding manifestations of noise include insertion, absence, ordering, and substitution noise [21]. Poor data quality undermines the reliability of discovered process models, potentially leading to misleading interpretations of the underlying system and, consequently, to suboptimal redesign and improvement decisions. Therefore, data cleaning, filtering, imputation, and semantic alignment constitute essential data preprocessing steps for meaningful discovery. Addressing noise in event data remains a non-trivial task, as effective mitigation strategies are often domain-specific and dependent on contextual process knowledge.

## 4.2 Data Incompleteness

An event log typically captures only a fraction of all process instances the system can perform. Specific instances or exceptional behaviors may be absent because they occur rarely or were not recorded. In additionevent data does not naturally contain information about negative process instances, that is, instances that are known not to belong to the process, as they never occur and hence are not recorded. Consequently, discovered models risk undergeneralization, failing to represent legitimate but unseen process paths. In addition, the absence of negative examples is known to prevent the exact inference of many interesting classes of behavior [18]. Addressing incompleteness, therefore, requires designing discovery algorithms that generalize well from limited evidence while avoiding overfitting. Techniques such as probabilistic inference [10], simulation [3], and bootstrapping [29] can improve robustness by estimating or sampling plausible, yet unseen, behavior.

## 4.3 Representational Bias

Each discovery algorithm embodies assumptions about how processes should be represented, e.g., as imperative models, declarative rules, agent-based models, or causal graphs. These assumptions determine which behavioral patterns can be expressed in the discovered models and which are inherently excluded. On the one hand, restricting the set of admissible model patterns narrows the solution space of the discovery problem; on the other hand, it prevents the modeling of certain classes of processes [1]. Distinguishing concurrency from alternative choices, or rework loops from routine repetitions, is often difficult based solely on observed event data, since logs may not provide sufficient evidence to support a particular interpretation. Certain behavioral patterns, such as the one shown in Fig. 1, do not admit block-structured imperative representations that preserve the original concurrency relations, while other concurrency patterns require duplicate activities to obtain an equivalent block-structured form [28]. Moreover, free-choice models are unable to adequately capture long-term dependencies among activities [20,38]. Selecting an appropriate process representation and paradigm, therefore, strongly influences both the interpretability and the utility of the discovered models and constitutes a non-trivial design decision in process discovery that needs to account for the concrete discovery technique and the characteristics of the discovered process.

## 4.4 Evaluation and Benchmarking

Assessing the performance of process discovery techniques remains a non-trivial task. Metrics for precision, fitness, generalization, and simplicity are well established for procedural models [34], but are far less mature for object-centric [9], data- and resource-aware [25], stochastic [11,24], or agent-based [36] representations. Moreover, existing benchmark datasets are often limited to a few domain-specific logs, which limits the generalizability of empirical findings. Inconsistent log formats, preprocessing choices, and configuration settings across studies further hinder reproducibility. A key challenge for the community is, therefore, to establish standardized evaluation frameworks and open benchmarks that enable fair, transparent, and repeatable assessments across diverse modeling paradigms.

### 4.5  Multiple Perspectives

Modern event logs contain far more than control-flow information. They also record resource involvement, data attributes that influence process decisions, and case-level contextual information. Integrating these perspectives to discover models that jointly explain who performs activities, under which conditions, and with what outcomes remains a substantial challenge. Simple extensions of control-flow discovery often fail to capture complex data dependencies, conditional routing, or resource interactions. Multi-perspective discovery aims to unify (subsets of) behavioral, stochastic, organizational, informational, and transactional aspects within a single model, but achieving this requires richer semantics and more expressive modeling formalisms.

### 4.6  Scalability

Process discovery must increasingly handle event data that span millions of cases and billions of events. Efficient algorithms and scalable infrastructures are therefore essential, particularly when discovery results are expected to be produced close to real time. As data volume and complexity grow, both model discovery and quality assessment become more computationally demanding in terms of runtime and memory usage. Techniques such as data sampling, distributed processing, and incremental or streaming discovery can mitigate scalability challenges, although often at the cost of reduced accuracy or completeness. Balancing scalability with analytical depth thus remains an ongoing research problem. Finally, only a limited number of existing discovery techniques explicitly report their runtime requirements, which further complicates systematic comparison and evaluation.

### 4.7  Concept Drift

Real world processes evolve over time due to policy changes, system updates, or organizational adaptations. This phenomenon is known as concept drift. Concept drift causes event data to reflect a mix of outdated and current behaviors. Discovering a single static model from such data may obscure important temporal dynamics. Detecting and handling drift requires identifying change points, comparing models across time windows, and supporting incremental updates [32,40]. Adaptive and online discovery techniques are increasingly crucial to ensure that models remain accurate and relevant.

## 4.8   Historical Dependencies

Event data often contain historical dependencies, where the execution of an activity depends on conditions or events that occurred far earlier in the process. Such dependencies may span long intervals, be mediated through data attributes, or arise from implicit business rules that are not directly observable in the data. Identifying these relationships from raw event data is challenging because the evidence needed to justify them may be sparse, weakly correlated, or confounded by unrelated, unregistered behavior. As a result, traditional discovery techniques that rely primarily on local or short-range patterns may overlook long-term interactions, leading to models that underrepresent the true constraints of the process. Accurately capturing historical dependencies, therefore, remains an open research problem that requires richer representations, more expressive analysis techniques, and stronger statistical foundations [23].

## 4.9   Event Correlation

Identifying which events belong to the same process instance, or case, is a fundamental challenge in process mining. While traditional event logs provide explicit case identifiers, many modern information systems generate multi-object or object-centric data in which activities involve several interacting entities, e.g., orders, customers, and invoices. Inferring the correct correlations between events and process instances in such settings requires reasoning about object relationships, shared attributes, and temporal dependencies [14]. Wrong event correlation can lead to fragmented traces or the merging of unrelated behaviors, both of which severely distort the outcomes of process discovery and subsequent analyses.

## 4.10   Data Granularity

Data granularity may vary substantially within and across data sources, complicating its interpretation. Some systems record fine-grained technical events, while others capture only high-level business activities, and changes in system configuration or process implementation can further alter what is recorded. Such variability can lead to incomplete, inconsistent, or ambiguous behavioral evidence, making it challenging to reconstruct precise execution paths or infer accurate control-flow relationships. Discovery algorithms that assume consistent event abstraction may misinterpret coarse-grained data or fragment already fine-grained ones, resulting in distorted or misleading models. Managing heterogeneity in logging granularity, therefore, requires techniques that adapt to different levels of abstraction and reason robustly under partial or unevenly detailed observations [41], including techniques for multi-level, hierarchical discovery across abstraction layers.

## 4.11   Semantic and Contextual Interpretation

Event data typically record observed activities while omitting the contextual and semantic information that explains why those activities occur. Consequently, discovered models often describe processes syntactically but may lack interpretability for domain experts. Bridging this gap requires the incorporation of semantic knowledge, such as domain ontologies, goal hierarchies, and data dependencies, into the discovery process. Automatically linking low-level events to higher-level concepts or organizational semantics remains difficult when only conventional event logs are available. Effective integration of contextual knowledge would enable models that accurately represent the process and are semantically meaningful, improving their usefulness for explanation, compliance, and reasoning tasks.

### 4.12  Human-in-the-Loop and Explainability

While process discovery aims to automate model construction, human expertise remains essential for interpreting, validating, and refining the resulting models. Many existing algorithms operate as black boxes, producing complex models whose structure and underlying assumptions are difficult to understand or justify. Incorporating user feedback during discovery, for instance, through interactive visual analytics, constraint specification, or iterative model refinement, can improve both accuracy and user trust [33]. Designing explainable discovery techniques that make their reasoning transparent, for example, by exposing intermediate decisions or highlighting evidence supporting discovered patterns, is an emerging and increasingly important research direction.

## 5  Related Problems

This section examines related inference problems studied in adjacent fields, highlighting conceptual parallels and methodological insights relevant to process discovery.

### 5.1  Grammatical Inference

Grammatical inference and process discovery share striking conceptual similarities [10, 19]. Both aim to reconstruct an underlying generative system from observed examples. These examples are words or sentences in grammatical inference and process traces in process discovery. In each setting, the observed data provide positive evidence of system behavior, from which the learner seeks to infer a compact and general model capable of reproducing and predicting similar observations. Both fields must cope with noise and exceptional instances that deviate from the dominant patterns, and they develop techniques to mitigate such deviations without overfitting. They also emphasize representational parsimony. The inferred grammar or process model should capture the observed examples with high fidelity while remaining as simple as possible, in line with the Occam's razor principle. Similarly, both seek predictive power. Grammatical inference estimates the probability of the next character or word, while process discovery forecasts the likelihood of the next activity, trace suffix, or entire trace. Finally, both aspire to generalization by moving beyond the finite samples in the training data and characterizing the broader, unseen language or process that produced them. The main differences arise from the nature and structure of the input data, which are natural language text for grammatical inference and business process event traces for discovery.

## 5.2  Specification Discovery

Specification discovery in software engineering shares many conceptual foundations with process discovery [12,26]. Both seek to reconstruct a formal description of system behavior from observed executions. In specification discovery, the input consists of program traces or logs of software runs, from which the goal is to infer behavioral specifications, such as temporal properties, state machines, or pre- and post-conditions, that characterize how the software behaves. Like process discovery, specification discovery learns from positive examples, identifies and filters out noise or outlier traces, and aims to derive concise, human-interpretable models that generalize beyond the observed executions. Inferred specifications can also support predictive reasoning, for example, by signaling likely future violations or anticipating potential deviations. Both fields value simplicity and explanatory clarity, favoring minimal models that remain faithful to the data. Ultimately, both process and specification discovery aim to transform empirical observations into formal and generalizable descriptions that capture the essential behavior of the underlying system.

## 5.3  Model Synthesis

Model synthesis encompasses a family of techniques that aim to construct formal system models from behavioral observations. Within this paradigm, region theory in Petri nets [13,15] and automata synthesis [16] in formal methods represent two prominent approaches. Both start from an observed behavior, for example, a transition system, execution log, or collection of traces, and infer a structural model that could have generated it. The goal is to reverse-engineer the causal or ordering relations underlying the observed behavior and express them as an interpretable and verifiable model. Region theory provides the mathematical foundation for synthesizing Petri nets from labeled transition systems. It identifies subsets of states, called regions, that correspond to potential places in the resulting net, ensuring that the constructed model reproduces the behavior of the original system. Automata synthesis follows a similar logic by deriving state machines or temporal automata from examples, formal specifications, or observed executions, often guided by constraints of consistency and minimality.

## 5.4  Other Inference Problems

Several other problems share conceptual foundations with process discovery. Automata learning studies how to construct behavioral models from observations and has produced influential techniques for learning regular and symbolic automata. Inductive logic programming and constraint mining aim to infer declarative rules from examples, a setting closely related to the discovery of declarative process models. In data mining, sequential pattern mining and episode mining identify frequent behavioral patterns that serve as the basis for some process discovery methods. System identification in control theory similarly seeks to infer state-based dynamic models from time-series observations and addresses issues of noise, generalization, and prediction. Finally, causal discovery investigates how to recover causal dependencies from observational data, an increasingly important concern in predictive and prescriptive process analytics.

## 6  Quality

The success of process discovery depends on the quality of the resulting models. Thus, discovered models should be assessed against well-defined and practically meaningful quality criteria that determine their adequacy for analysis and decision-making.

In the conventional process discovery, where discovered process models aim to describe event traces the system can generate, four interrelated quality dimensions are widely accepted [17]. A discovered model should allow as few traces as possible that are not present in the log (good *precision*), should describe as many as possible of the traces recorded in the log (good *recall*, also known as *fitness*), should allow traces that may stem from the same process but are not present in the log (good *generalization*), and should be as simple as is consistent with the other goals (good *simplicity*). Many desirable properties for the measurements of these quality dimensions [4] and techniques to implement the measurements [34] have been proposed.

These dimensions are not independent. For instance, increasing precision often comes at the expense of generalization, while maximizing fitness can lead to unnecessarily complex models. Process discovery is fundamentally a multi-objective optimization problem [17,42] that shapes both algorithm design and the interpretation of discovered models. The relative weighting of these quality dimensions depends on the purpose and audience of the model. Managers may prioritize simplicity and generalization for decision support (that is, relevant behavior discovery and process forecasting, cf. Sects. 3.1 and 3.3), whereas system engineers may prefer fitness and precision for system diagnostics (that is, observed behavior discovery, cf. Sect. 3.2). Each quality dimension is usually measured on a scale from zero to one, where larger values indicate better model quality.

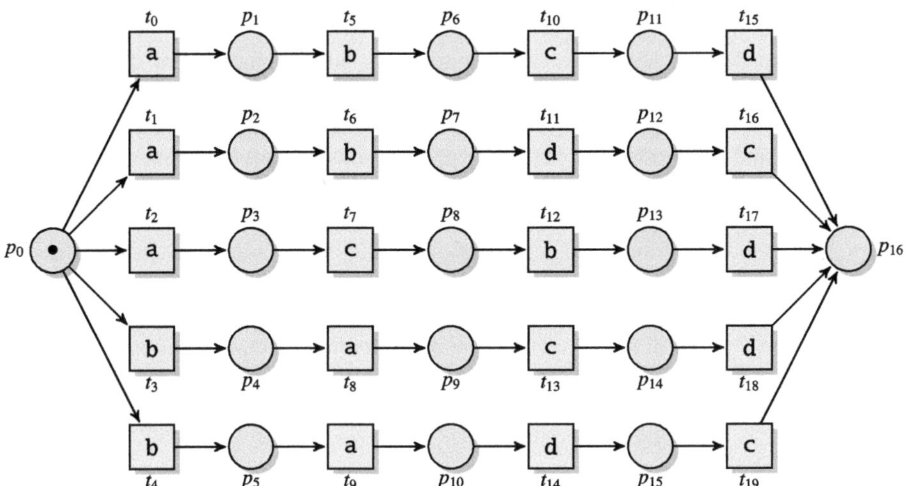

**Fig. 3.** All traces Petri net.

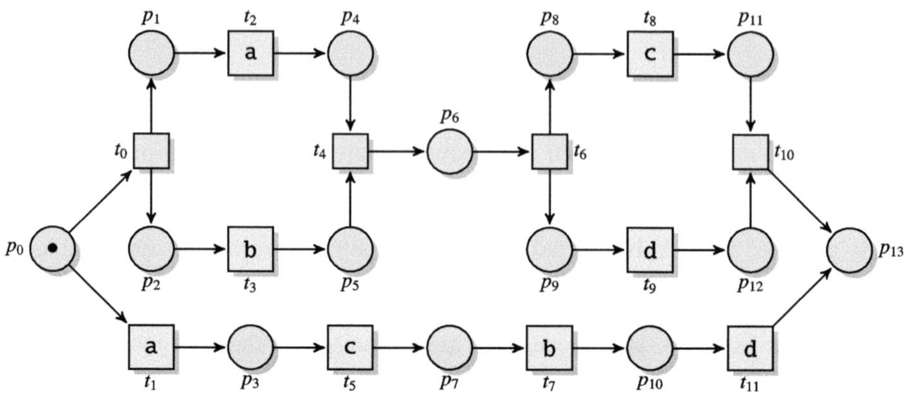

**Fig. 4.** A block structured Petri net with duplicate activities.

Figures 3 and 4 illustrate two additional models that can be discovered from the event log $L$. All models shown in Figs. 1, 2, 3 and 4 exhibit perfect recall with respect to $L$, since each of them describes all the traces recorded in this event log. The models depicted in Figs. 1, 3 and 4 also exhibit perfect precision, since they do not allow for any traces that are absent from $L$. In contrast, the model in Fig. 2 does not have perfect precision, as it allows for traces that do not occur in the event log, namely $\langle a,c,d,b \rangle$, $\langle a,d,b,c \rangle$, $\langle a,d,c,b \rangle$, $\langle b,d,a,c \rangle$, $\langle d,a,b,c \rangle$, $\langle d,a,c,b \rangle$, and $\langle d,b,a,c \rangle$. The models depicted in Figs. 1, 2 and 4 are simpler than the one in Fig. 3 if the number of nodes and arcs is used as a measure of model complexity. Finally, the additional traces permitted by the model in Fig. 2 can be interpreted as instances of generalization.

Alignments are diagnostic artifacts that describe how a process model explains the traces recorded in an event log [6]. An alignment provides a step-by-step correspondence between a log trace and a model execution, identifying where the model can reproduce the observed activities and where deviations occur. Optimal alignments minimize the cost of deviation steps. Intuitively, the lower the cost of alignments between the log traces and the model, the better the precision and recall of the model.

The SOLID-M framework provides an ontology-aware approach to assessing the quality of conceptual models discovered from event data [36]. It extends traditional quality measures grounded in log and model traces to support new process discovery types studied within Object-Centric Process Mining and Agent System Mining. SOLID-M supports the assessment of model quality by how well the model describes the structure and behavior of the system that generated the data, where correspondences between the model, system, and data elements are traced through a shared ontology.

## 7   Conclusion

Process discovery has made significant progress over the past two decades. Advances in algorithms, tools, and theoretical foundations have expanded the range of systems that can be analyzed based on their event data. Despite this progress, many open gaps remain. Comprehensive benchmarks that integrate both real world and synthetic datasets are lacking. As a result, process discovery results are rarely comparable, since they are evaluated on different datasets using diverse quality measures. Current discovery techniques tend to exhibit strong representational biases, most notably toward block-structured models without duplicate activities, which limits their ability to reconstruct more complex process behaviors, such as those illustrated in Figs. 1 and 4. Moreover, the community lacks large-scale, publicly available event logs for systematic evaluation, and there is little agreement on which model quality measures should be adopted for broad use [34]. Among the standard quality dimensions, generalization remains perhaps the least understood and most neglected aspect of discovery quality. Empirical evaluations involving ground-truth systems, where algorithms are assessed based on their ability to rediscover known processes, are exceedingly rare [39]. Equally underexplored are the qualities of the discovery algorithms themselves, including their robustness and scalability, rather than merely the quality of their outputs. As the field continues to mature, addressing these open issues will be essential for establishing process discovery as a rigorous, reproducible, and insightful scientific discipline. The years ahead will bring research that narrows these gaps and deepens our understanding of how systems can be accurately discovered from the traces of their behavior.

# References


1. van der Aalst, W.M.P.: On the representational bias in process mining. In: WETICE, pp. 2–7. IEEE Computer Society (2011). https://doi.org/10.1109/WETICE.2011.64
2. van der Aalst, W.M.P.: Process Mining—Data Science in Action, 2nd edn. Springer, Heidelberg (2016). https://doi.org/10.1007/978-3-662-49851-4
3. van der Aalst, W.M.P.: Process mining and simulation: a match made in heaven! In: SummerSim, pp. 4:1–4:12. ACM (2018)
4. van der Aalst, W.M.P.: Relating process models and event logs—21 conformance propositions. In: Proceedings of the International Workshop on Algorithms & Theories for the Analysis of Event Data, CEUR Workshop Proceedings, vol. 2115, pp. 56–74. CEUR-WS.org (2018). http://ceur-ws.org/Vol-2115/ATAED2018-56-74.pdf
5. van der Aalst, W.M.P.: A practitioner's guide to process mining: limitations of the directly-follows graph. Procedia Comput. Sci. **164**, 321–328 (2019). https://doi.org/10.1016/j.procs.2019.12.189
6. van der Aalst, W.M.P., Adriansyah, A., van Dongen, B.F.: Replaying history on process models for conformance checking and performance analysis. Wiley Interdisc. Rev.: Data Min. Knowl. Discov. **2**(2), 182–192 (2012). https://doi.org/10.1002/WIDM.1045
7. van der Aalst, W.M.P., Berti, A.: Discovering object-centric Petri nets. Fund. Inform. **175**(1–4), 1–40 (2020). https://doi.org/10.3233/FI-2020-1946
8. van der Aalst, W.M.P., Weijters, T., Maruster, L.: Workflow mining: discovering process models from event logs. Trans. Knowl. Data Eng. **16**(9), 1128–1142 (2004). https://doi.org/10.1109/TKDE.2004.47
9. Adams, J.N., van der Aalst, W.M.P.: Precision and fitness in object-centric process mining. In: ICPM, pp. 128–135. IEEE (2021)
10. Alkhammash, H., Polyvyanyy, A., Moffat, A.: Stochastic directly-follows process discovery using grammatical inference. In: CAiSE. LNCS, vol. 14663, pp. 87–103. Springer, Cham (2024). https://doi.org/10.1007/978-3-031-61057-8_6

11. Alkhammash, H., Polyvyanyy, A., Moffat, A., García-Bañuelos, L.: Entropic relevance: a mechanism for measuring stochastic process models discovered from event data. Inf. Syst. **107**, 101922 (2022). https://doi.org/10.1016/J.IS.2021.101922

12. Ammons, G., Bodík, R., Larus, J.R.: Mining specifications. In: POPL, pp. 4–16. ACM (2002). https://doi.org/10.1145/503272.503275

13. Badouel, É., Bernardinello, L., Darondeau, P.: Petri Net Synthesis. Texts in Theoretical Computer Science. An EATCS Series. Springer, Cham (2015). https://doi.org/10.1007/978-3-662-47967-4

14. Bayomie, D., Ciccio, C.D., Mendling, J.: Event-case correlation for process mining using probabilistic optimization. Inf. Syst. **114**, 102167 (2023)

15. Bergenthum, R., Desel, J., Lorenz, R., Mauser, S.: Process mining based on regions of languages. In: Alonso, G., Dadam, P., Rosemann, M. (eds.) BPM 2007. LNCS, vol. 4714, pp. 375–383. Springer, Heidelberg (2007). https://doi.org/10.1007/978-3-540-75183-0_27

16. Biermann, A.W., Feldman, J.A.: On the synthesis of finite-state machines from samples of their behavior. IEEE Trans. Comput. **21**(6), 592–597 (1972). https://doi.org/10.1109/TC.1972.5009015

17. Buijs, J.C.A.M., van Dongen, B.F., van der Aalst, W.M.P.: Quality dimensions in process discovery: the importance of fitness, precision, generalization and simplicity. Int. J. Cooperative Inf. Syst. **23**(01), 1440001 (2014). https://doi.org/10.1142/S0218843014400012

18. Gold, E.M.: Language identification in the limit. Inf. Control **10**(5), 447–474 (1967). https://doi.org/10.1016/s0019-9958(67)91165-5

19. de la Higuera, C.: Grammatical Inference: Learning Automata and Grammars. Cambridge University Press (2010)

20. Kalenkova, A.A., Carmona, J., Polyvyanyy, A., Rosa, M.L.: Automated repair of process models with non-local constraints using state-based region theory. Fund. Inform. **183**(3–4), 293–317 (2021). https://doi.org/10.3233/FI-2021-2089

21. Karunaratne, A., Polyvyanyy, A., Moffat, A.: The effects of log noise in process mining. IEEE Access **13**, 198540–198563 (2025). https://doi.org/10.1109/access.2025.3635682

22. Leemans, S.J.J., Fahland, D., van der Aalst, W.M.P.: Discovering block-structured process models from event logs containing infrequent behaviour. In: Lohmann, N., Song, M., Wohed, P. (eds.) BPM 2013. LNBIP, vol. 171, pp. 66–78. Springer, Cham (2014). https://doi.org/10.1007/978-3-319-06257-0_6

23. Leemans, S.J.J., Mannel, L.L., Sidorova, N.: Significant stochastic dependencies in process models. Inf. Syst. **118**, 102223 (2023). https://doi.org/10.1016/J.IS.2023.102223

24. Leemans, S.J.J., Polyvyanyy, A.: Stochastic-aware precision and recall measures for conformance checking in process mining. Inf. Syst. **115**, 102197 (2023). https://doi.org/10.1016/J.IS.2023.102197

25. de Leoni, M., van der Aalst, W.M.P., van Dongen, B.F.: Data- and resource-aware conformance checking of business processes. In: Abramowicz, W., Kriksciuniene, D., Sakalauskas, V. (eds.) BIS 2012. LNBIP, vol. 117, pp. 48–59. Springer, Heidelberg (2012). https://doi.org/10.1007/978-3-642-30359-3_5

26. Lo, D., Khoo, S.C., Han, J., Liu, C.: Mining Software Specifications: Methodologies and Applications. CRC Press, Inc. (2017)

27. Poll, R., Polyvyanyy, A., Rosemann, M., Röglinger, M., Rupprecht, L.: Process forecasting: towards proactive business process management. In: Weske, M., Montali, M., Weber, I., vom Brocke, J. (eds.) BPM 2018. LNCS, vol. 11080, pp. 496–512. Springer, Cham (2018). https://doi.org/10.1007/978-3-319-98648-7_29

28. Polyvyanyy, A.: Structuring process models. Ph.D. thesis, University of Potsdam (2012). http://opus.kobv.de/ubp/volltexte/2012/5902/

29. Polyvyanyy, A., Moffat, A., García-Bañuelos, L.: Bootstrapping generalization of process models discovered from event data. In: CAiSE, pp. 36–54. Springer, Cham (2022). https://doi.org/10.1007/978-3-031-07472-1_3
30. Polyvyanyy, A., Smirnov, S., Weske, M.: Process model abstraction: a slider approach. In: EDOC, pp. 325–331. IEEE Computer Society (2008). https://doi.org/10.1109/EDOC.2008.17
31. Reisig, W.: Understanding Petri Nets – Modeling Techniques, Analysis Methods, Case Studies. Springer, Cham (2013). https://doi.org/10.1007/978-3-642-33278-4. ISBN 978-3-642-33277-7
32. Sato, D.M.V., Freitas, S.C.D., Barddal, J.P., Scalabrin, E.E.: A survey on concept drift in process mining. ACM Comput. Surv. **54**(9), 189:1–189:38 (2022)
33. Schuster, D.: Incremental Process Discovery. LNBIP, vol. 540. Springer, Cham (2025)
34. Syring, A.F., Tax, N., van der Aalst, W.M.P.: Evaluating conformance measures in process mining using conformance propositions. Trans. Petri Nets Other Model. Concurr. **14**, 192–221 (2019). https://doi.org/10.1007/978-3-662-60651-3_8
35. Tour, A., Polyvyanyy, A., Kalenkova, A.A.: Agent system mining: vision, benefits, and challenges. IEEE Access **9**, 99480–99494 (2021). https://doi.org/10.1109/ACCESS.2021.3095464
36. Tour, A., Polyvyanyy, A., Kalenkova, A.A.: SOLID-M: an ontology-aware quality framework for conceptual models discovered from event data. Inf. Syst. **137**, 102641 (2026). https://doi.org/10.1016/J.IS.2025.102641
37. Verbeek, E., Buijs, J.C.A.M., van Dongen, B.F., van der Aalst, W.M.P.: ProM 6: the process mining toolkit. In: BPM Demonstration Track. CEUR Workshop Proceedings, vol. 615. CEUR-WS.org (2010)
38. Wen, L., van der Aalst, W.M.P., Wang, J., Sun, J.: Mining process models with non-free-choice constructs. Data Min. Knowl. Disc. **15**(2), 145–180 (2007). https://doi.org/10.1007/S10618-007-0065-Y
39. van der Werf, J.M.E.M., Polyvyanyy, A., van Wensveen, B.R., Brinkhuis, M.J.S., Reijers, H.A.: All that glitters is not gold: Four maturity stages of process discovery algorithms. Inf. Syst. **114**, 102155 (2023). https://doi.org/10.1016/J.IS.2022.102155
40. Yeshchenko, A., Ciccio, C.D., Mendling, J., Polyvyanyy, A.: Visual drift detection for event sequence data of business processes. IEEE Trans. Vis. Comput. Graph. **28**(8), 3050–3068 (2022)
41. van Zelst, S.J., Mannhardt, F., de Leoni, M., Koschmider, A.: Event abstraction in process mining: literature review and taxonomy. Granular Comput. **6**(3), 719–736 (2020). https://doi.org/10.1007/s41066-020-00226-2
42. Zhian, H., Buyya, R., Polyvyanyy, A.: Multi-objective metaheuristics for effective and efficient stochastic process discovery. In: BPM. LNCS, vol. 16044, pp. 469–486. Springer, Cham (2025). https://doi.org/10.1007/978-3-032-02867-9_28
43. Zhou, W., Polyvyanyy, A., Bailey, J.: Event data and process model forecasting. In: CAiSE Forum. LNBIP, vol. 520, pp. 3–10. Springer, Cham (2024). https://doi.org/10.1007/978-3-031-61000-4_1

# Process-Data Quality Management Lifecycle: Building Strong Data Foundations for Process Mining

Moe Thandar Wynn[(✉)] [iD], Robert Andrews [iD], and Sareh Sadeghianasl [iD]

Centre for Data Science, Queensland University of Technology,
Brisbane, QLD 4000, Australia
`{m.wynn,r.andrews,s.sadeghianasl}@qut.edu.au`

**Abstract.** Process Mining relies on historical event data as its single source of truth. Using such event data, process mining techniques visualise and analyse the behaviour and performance of organisational processes. To generate actionable recommendations from process mining, the event data must be of high quality. Over the past decade, there has been increasing recognition in the field of 1) the need for high-quality data and 2) the significant time and effort being spent on data pre-processing tasks. This paper provides an overview of the state-of-the-art in process data quality management research, proposes a four-phase data quality management lifecycle for a systematic treatment of data quality challenges and positions its role among recent advances in process mining, e.g., streaming process mining and object-centric process mining.

**Keywords:** Process Mining · Data Quality · Event Data · Process Intelligence

## 1   Introduction

Process mining techniques use historical event data captured by IT systems to analyse the behaviour and performance of organisational processes [59]. To generate actionable data-driven recommendations from process mining, the event data must be of high quality. This crucial dependence of the quality of process mining results on the quality of event data was first acknowledged in the Process Mining Manifesto [60]. The manifesto also made the first attempt to describe a model of data quality suitable for process mining. This model included dimensions by which event data quality could be measured (trustworthiness, completeness, well-defined semantics, safe in terms of privacy and security) as well as a 1–5 'star' rating by which overall event log quality could be quantified. Subsequent event data quality models, such as those in [10, 21, 41, 54], went so far as to recognise the quality aspects specific to process-event data.

Over the past decade, the field of process mining has matured from fundamental research studies which develop novel process mining algorithms for process


J. Mendling et al. (Eds.): Wil van der Aalst Festschrift, LNCS 16480, pp. 384–397, 2026.
https://doi.org/10.1007/978-3-032-17618-9_27

discovery, conformance and performance to the emergence of applied research studies which are concerned with how process mining techniques could be utilised in organisations. The global process mining community is now made up of many process mining enthusiasts from academia and industry. Among the community, there has been increasing recognition of the need for high-quality data and the significant time and effort being spent on data pre-processing tasks [47,65]. A 2021 survey of the process mining community [65] found that 75% of respondents report expending more than 40% of effort on data pre-processing tasks for process mining. Other studies (e.g., [47]) also note that pre-processing is frequently time-consuming, manual and *ad hoc*.

There is a growing community of process mining researchers who explore new methods, techniques and solutions to address the research question: *what are the essential elements of a data pre-processing pipeline that ensures event logs are fit for purpose?*. This paper takes a holistic view of the research topic, proposes a four-phase lifecycle (PDQM) to position the work to date.

The rest of the paper is organised as follows. Section 2 describes what is typically captured in event data and how the data is extracted and used for process mining. Section 3 proposes a four-phase lifecycle for process data quality management and positions the state-of-the-art in research papers against these phases. Section 4 concludes the paper by providing a future outlook for this area.

## 2 Process Data Foundations

This section positions the critical role of historical event data for process mining and describes the core steps involved in generating event logs.

### 2.1 Event Data as 'the' Source of Truth

Process mining requires data that supports the notion of 'events'. Event data captures, at the minimum, the *when, what,* and *to whom* of actions that occurred during the execution of some process. A collection of such event data forms an event log, the main input for process mining. Event logs provide precise, time-stamped details about activities, such as who performed what action, when, and in what sequence. This granularity makes them invaluable for reconstructing process flows and identifying bottlenecks, deviations, or inefficiencies. The data used to generate event logs is often generated automatically during process executions by (process-aware) information systems. Thus, the event data objectively reflects actual process behaviour, reducing possible human bias included in other data sources such as observations, reports or interviews. Further, event logs are scalable and can handle large volumes of data, enabling process mining tools to analyse complex, high-frequency processes across organisations and for long time horizons. Event logs, then, are the critical foundation for process mining, and are often regarded as 'the' source of truth.

However, non-critically accepting any event log as 'the' source of truth is naive. Event logs often contain data quality issues and are only as reliable as the systems generating them. Incomplete logs, missing attributes (e.g., case IDs, timestamps), inconsistent formats, or errors in data extraction and subsequent pre-processing (for example, combining/correlating logs from different sources with different formats or levels of granularity) can undermine their accuracy and negatively affect the reliability of insights generated through process mining.

If a system fails to log certain events or logs them ambiguously, the resulting process model may be incomplete and somewhat misleading. Logs often lack qualitative context, such as why certain actions were taken or how external factors influenced some/all process executions. This can limit their ability to fully explain process behaviour without supplementary data sources (e.g., user feedback, business rules, or external events). While logs generated from systems are potentially objective, such logs only reflect what the system records, not necessarily the entire real-world process. For instance, workarounds or manual activities outside the system (e.g., phone calls, emails) may not be captured, leading to incomplete or skewed process models.

Thus, robust data governance and pre-processing pipelines are critical to generating, cleaning, and enriching logs, and to providing some level of assurance as to the log actually being 'the' source of truth for any given analysis.

## 2.2   Event Data Extraction and Pre-processing

Generating an event log is a foundational step in process mining, involving the transformation of raw data into a structured format for analysis. Event logs for process mining should consist of event data that is relevant to the study's aims and questions of interest. Towards this end, log generation is a step-wise process usually involving: identifying relevant data sources, extracting data, transforming data to a standard format, dealing with (identifying and repairing) data quality issues, and taking relevant steps to preserve privacy.

Typical event data sources, as identified in [21], include BPMS, Case management and ticketing systems, ERP/CRM, Operational databases, Project management software, Data warehouses and lakes, web data, and IoT. Wynn et al. [65] in a survey of 289 international process mining community members, identified SAP ECC, SAP S/4 HANA and Salesforce as the top three most analysed source systems. Interestingly, [65] also found that plain text file format (txt or csv) is the most commonly available source data format. It is worth noting that the majority of these data sources consist of structured data. Recently, König et al. [36] report an increasing number of studies exploiting unstructured data (mainly text) as sources of event data. Extracted event data may be further enriched by adding supplementary attributes to enhance analysis, such as organisational roles, resources, costs, or external context. Also in this step is abstracting events to a level of granularity appropriate for the analysis. This may involve aggregating (combining multiple low-level events into a single higher level event) or filtering events to match the analysis scope. Abstraction ensures the log is neither too detailed (causing noise) nor too coarse (missing insights), and is often guided by domain knowledge.

Apart from data recorded in Process Aware Information Systems (PAIS), the source data for process mining is not in a form directly usable by process mining algorithms. Conceptual and practical steps to construct event logs for process mining are discussed in [18]. Techniques exist for extracting event data from various data sources, including *XESame* [63] and *RDB2Log* [4] for relational databases, [20,58] for ERP redo logs, and [27] for text, [62] for IoT sensor data, and [43] for extracting logs from blockchain. [37] describe techniques for extracting logs in eXtensible Object-centric (XOC) format, while [13] describes an approach for extracting object-centric logs from textual data. [17] reviews 21 tools for event log extraction, and [47] provides a review of 50 techniques, none of which are completely automated, for event log building from the various data sources mentioned earlier.

Event data has been represented in various standard, structured formats such as the XML-based Mining eXtensible Markup Language (MXML) which emerged in 2003, and eXtensible Event Stream (XES), which was adopted by the IEEE in 2010 and is an official IEEE standard (with IEEE 1849-2023 being the latest version) [64]. Both MXML and XES take a *case-centric* view of event data. The recently released Object-Centric Event Log (OCEL 2.0) [1] provides a means of overcoming the limitation, explicit in case-based event logs, that any event is relevant to only a single primary object, i.e., the *case*. In an object-centric log, an event can be associated with any number of objects. Thus, OCEL captures the interactions and relationships between the various business objects as they occur in a process. There is also an ongoing initiative to develop an object-centric meta-model by the IEEE Taskforce on Process Mining [24].

General process mining methodologies such as PDM [11], L* [29], PMPM [48], and $PM^2$ [61] refer to the importance of good data quality, but do not include explicit steps to identify data quality issues. In [31], the authors describe the ClearPath methodology which extends $PM^2$ to include steps to address issues of poor quality and missing data through the use of CP-DQF (Care Path Data Quality Framework) [26] designed for process mining of electronic health record (EHR) data. In [5], the authors adapt the CRISP-DM (Cross Industry Standard Process for Data Mining) to systematically identify data quality issues, link identified data quality issues to effects on process mining, and inform data extraction in such a way that identified quality issues can be addressed in the data that is extracted for use in event logs.

Where event data contains personally identifying information or other private data, such data should be anonymised to obfuscate sensitive information (e.g., personal data like names or IDs) using techniques like filtering (to remove attributes not directly related to the anlaysis at hand), (pseudo)anonymisation (encrypting personally identifying or private information so that users can't correlate it to real data), or differential privacy [40]. This step may be required to comply with regulations such as the EU's General Data Protection Regulation (GDPR) or Health Insurance Portability and Accountability Act(HIPAA), and document privacy measures to prevent data breaches during log sharing or analysis.

# 3    Process Data Quality Management Lifecycle

This section provides an overview of process data quality management research and positions it in the context of a four-phase Process Data Quality Management (PDQM) lifecycle which is, in turn, a part of the overall process mining journey (see Fig. 1). In each of the subsections, we discuss key activities and techniques developed to support each phase of the PDQM lifecycle, and point out open research questions relevant to each phase.

## 3.1    PDQM Lifecycle

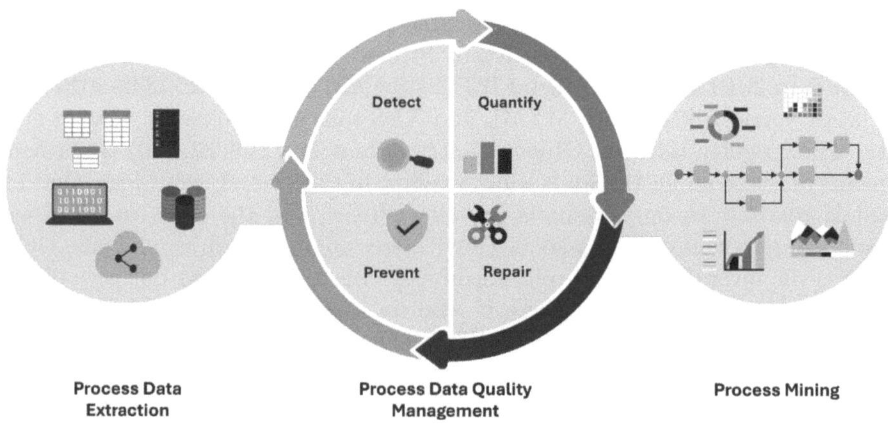



**Fig. 1.** The process mining journey.

Figure 1 illustrates the process mining journey from source data to process mining insights, with particular focus on the lifecycle. The PDQM lifecycle is structured to maximise the likelihood that process mining delivers reliable insights by maintaining high-quality data throughout the process mining journey. Process data quality management should not be viewed as a 'one-off' activity. It is iterative, requiring continuous attention to the key phases of detecting quality issues, quantifying the impact of quality issues on process analysis, repairing identified issues, and modifying systems and process participant behaviour in response to identified issues and changes to the environment in which the process executes to prevent data quality issues.

## 3.2    Detect

As the name suggests, this phase of the PDQM lifecycle focuses on detecting data quality issues in the event log. The purpose of the detection phase is to facilitate log cleaning by guiding cleaning and repair activities. A convenient way to discuss approaches to detecting event log data quality issues is by using one or other of the frameworks that classify data quality issues, e.g., log imperfection patterns [54], or the framework proposed by Bose et al. [10], or the recent variation of the Bose et al. framework in Basmer et al. [6], designed to capture object-centric event data quality issues. Some techniques that explicitly or implicitly refer to log imperfection patterns include (i) Form-based Event Capture [25], (ii) Inadvertent Time Travel [38,67], (ii) Polluted Label [50,67], (iii) Synonymous Labels [50], (iv) Distorted Label [51], (v) Homonymous Labels [39] (vi) Elusive Case [55,66]. It should be noted that log imperfection patterns such as Scattered Case, Scattered Event, and Elusive Case remain under-researched. Some techniques that address categories in the framework in [10] include *missing* data [7,22], *incorrect* data [53], *imprecise* data [16], and *irrelvant data* [15].

It is important to note that while so far, little research has been conducted into detecting quality issues specific to object-centric logs, some approaches for 'anomaly detection' in object-centric logs are beginning to emerge. Niro and Werner [44] report on an approach using a graph convolutional autoencoder architecture to detect anomalous events. The approach can detect anomalies at the activity type and attributes level, with a lesser ability to detect anomalies in the temporal order of events. Abb and Rehse [2] propose a method limited to identifying event-level anomalies in object-centric logs (i.e., does not detect object-level anomalies), and [8] proposes three methodologies for explainable anomaly detection in object-centric logs.

### 3.3   Quantify

The problem of quantifying the suitability of an event log to satisfy the aims and objectives of a given study remains an open question. Techniques to quantify event log suitability would, at a minimum, need metrics to (i) determine that the log, trace, and event data are *complete* i.e., contain all mandatory log elements and adequately *spans* the process execution space, (ii) determine the presence and suitability of contextual data attributes necessary to answer the questions of interest, (iii) assess the quality of the log and event data, and (iv) determine that the granularity of the log is appropriate for the questions of interest.

Techniques exist to address some of these aspects. For instance, log completeness is addressed in [32,46], spanning the process execution space is addressed in [35], log quality is addressed in [42]. While multiple techniques exist to detect/repair event data quality issues, few, if any, provide means for quantifying the pervasiveness or impact on process mining analysis of the quality issues considered. Goel et al. [28] partially addresses this issue by proposing an extension to the XES standard to include data quality annotations, which provide a means for recording, in the event log, the fraction of traces and events affected by imprecise, missing, or inaccurate values for any attribute. In [57], the authors describe an approach that assesses the impact on process elements that are related to a given data change. Deleoni et al. [19] propose a framework that correlates process characteristics with some standard process mining analyses with a view to determining log suitability.

## 3.4  Repair

The repair phase of the PDQM lifecycle aims to correct identified quality issues in event data to ensure it is accurate and fit for its intended purpose. There have been several techniques proposed to deal with the range of data quality issues already discussed. Suriadi et al. [54], as well as describing event log imperfection patterns, suggest possible repair approaches (without providing implementations) for each pattern. Label repair approaches are suggested in [50,51]. Timestamp and consequent event ordering repair actions are described in [23,25]. Several techniques exist for noise-related imperfections, including incorrect, missing, and incomplete data [7,22]. Techniques to filter noise due to infrequent behaviours include [15,52].

It is important to note that not all data quality issues can be sensibly repaired. For instance, the Elusive Case (missing case identifier) in [54] has proven difficult to repair. Recent attempts using transformer architecture with human-in-the-loop domain knowledge achieved only partial success [66]. Unlogged manual steps discovered through conformance checking [56] or some domain knowledge expert review of the log can't be recovered from the log itself, as they were never captured.

Further, an open question is how best to structure and order repair operations so as to arrive at the best possible log for its intended purpose. Consider a simple example of a log which contains some missing timestamps. Timestamps are generally considered essential for process mining. Possible repair actions include (i) filtering the log to remove records with missing timestamps, or (ii) imputing values for missing timestamps. Both options will result in a log that meets the quality criteria of all rows having a timestamp. The first option will result in a log where some activities have been removed from the log, but all timestamps are accurate (or, at least, are 'as recorded'), the second option will result in a log where all recorded activities occur in the log, but the timing of activities cannot be guaranteed.

## 3.5  Prevent

Given the extensive effort involved in cleaning event logs in preparation for process mining, preventing data quality issues from occurring in the first place is preferable to cleaning up afterwards. Capiello et al. [14] distinguishes between improving the quality of logs already collected (through cleaning) and modifying the information systems supporting the process to improve the quality of logs collected in the future. The ODIGOS framework [3] points the way to identifying the root causes of data quality issues beyond only system changes. The ODIGOS framework [3] describes the process management ecosystem in terms of the interactions between three worlds, the *social* world (e.g., organisational policies), the *material* world (e.g., computer systems and interfaces), and the *personal* world (e.g., behavioural traits of process participants). These interactions can help explain the root causes of process-data quality problems that emerge. Andrews et al., [3] describe the RC-Network, the first structured approach to linking observed quality issues to their root causes and a mechanism for preventing identified data quality issues from recurring in future process analysis.

### 3.6  Tool Support

There are varying levels of support to detect, qualify, and repair data quality issues within process mining tools. Commercial process mining platforms differ in the extent and sophistication of their data pre-processing capabilities. For example, Disco[1] offers a variety of filtering options based on case attributes, performance indicators, and process variants, along with tools for reformatting timestamps. Celonis[2] provides support for filtering, converting data types, and executing basic transformation tasks. ETL functionalities are also available through integration with business intelligence tools in platforms such as Mindzie[3], Signavio[4], and Apromore[5]. Additionally, the open-source process mining framework ProM[6] includes a range of plug-ins designed for pre-processing tasks, including noise reduction, removal of incomplete traces, formatting adjustments, and data type conversions.

There are several standalone tools dedicated to providing support for high-quality event log generation. Konekti[7] serves as a standalone solution focused on data transformation for process mining, enabling operations such as filtering, type validation, table joining, and event log generation. PraeclarusPDQ[8] is an open-source framework dedicated to process data quality management, and it offers detection and repair techniques for event log imperfection patterns, such as synonymous and distorted labels.

## 4  Future Outlook and Conclusion

In the age of Artificial Intelligence (AI) combined with Process Intelligence (PI), the importance of maintaining the quality of underlying data that drives decisions has never been higher. Redman [49] found that "Poor data quality costs approximately \$3.1 trillion annually, affecting productivity and decision-making. Businesses face an average annual loss of \$15 million due to poor data quality."

To date, many process mining initiatives still spend a large portion of the project time identifying relevant data sources and preparing the input data for process mining. The landscape of event data extraction is changing rapidly, now with more and more organisations expecting near real-time analysis. Thus, it is

---

[1] www.fluxicon.com.

[2] www.celonis.com.

[3] www.mindzie.com.

[4] www.signavio.com.

[5] www.apromore.com.

[6] www.promtools.org.

[7] www.getkonekti.io.

[8] github.com/praeclaruspdq/PraeclarusPDQ.

essential to move away from a post-hoc and ad-hoc approach to data quality management to a more systematic, proactive, timely, and transparent way to address data quality management issues, leading to more certain data lineage of process event data.

It was reported that 80–90% of the data we generate today is unstructured[9]. Thus, if process mining techniques were to limit themselves to structured data, only a small part of a potentially complex process would be analysed by these techniques, and most of the process context that might be critical for a true understanding of the end-to-end process would be missing. Therefore, future work on process data quality management should focus not only on how to improve structured data but also on how to incorporate non-structured/semi-structured data. Several papers have attempted to incorporate unstructured textual data into events and event logs [13,34,36], but more research is needed to systematically incorporate non-structured text as part of the analysis.

Recent advances in the field of process mining, such as object-centric process mining, streaming process mining [12], and the use of uncertain event data [45] further increases the urgency of a systematic approach to address event data quality issues, preferably at the source. With streaming process mining, there is a need to undertake data quality assurance activities for streaming data. Some recent papers have investigated data quality issues associated with streaming data. For instance, [9] reviews 17 papers that discuss data quality issues in (streamed) IoT data, and synthesises 5 patterns to classify quality issues. Further [9] also mentions two main strategies to improve sensor data - retroactive cleaning and proactively improving logging practices. In [33], the authors propose an approach to detect and repair activity label quality issues in event streams. With the complexity increasing with object-centric event data, there is a need to identify new challenges and remedies to address them. For instance, the events may be correlated to incorrect object(s), objects may have attributes that are inconsistent with the attributes of their correlated events, or object-to-object relations might not align with event-to-object relations.

A research agenda [30] that advocates for a paradigm shift in process mining from reactive data cleaning to proactive data quality management has been published. It outlines nine key directions to advance the field: leveraging domain expertise to improve detection and repair of data quality issues; establishing robust process-data governance frameworks to ensure the availability and reliability of data; providing methodological and visual guidance to stakeholders during data cleaning; enabling cleaning techniques to handle diverse data types and log formats; quantifying the impact of cleaning operations on analytical outcomes; maintaining detailed provenance of data transformations; prioritising prevention and mitigation of data quality issues over post-hoc repairs; monitoring data quality throughout its lifecycle to detect emerging issues; and abstracting and logging repair actions to support future reuse and root-cause analysis. These directions aim to enhance the reliability, interpretability, and efficiency of pro-

---

[9] www.cio.com/article/220347/ai-unleashes-the-power-of-unstructured-data.html.

cess mining analyses by embedding data quality considerations throughout the entire process mining lifecycle.

With this paper, we call for more researchers, tool vendors, and industry practitioners to co-create fast and effective data quality assurance solutions for process mining together.

**Acknowledgments.** The authors would like to acknowledge all our collaborators from the international BPM and PM communities who share the same vision and contribute to this topic - too many to name them individually here. We would like to especially acknowledge the significant contributions of Emeritus Professor Arthur ter Hofstede to the field of process data quality management.

**Disclosure of Interests.** The authors have no competing interests to declare that are relevant to the content of this article.

# References


1. Object-centric event log 2.0 (2024). https://ocel-standard.org/
2. Abb, L., Rehse, J.R.: Multivariate anomaly detection in object-centric event data. In: International Conference on Business Process Management, pp. 20–36. Springer, Cham (2024)
3. Andrews, R., Emamjome, F., ter Hofstede, A.H., Reijers, H.A.: Root-cause analysis of process-data quality problems. J. Bus. Anal. **5**(1), 51–75 (2022)
4. Andrews, R., van Dun, C.G.J., Wynn, M.T., Kratsch, W., Röglinger, M.K.E., ter Hofstede, A.H.M.: Quality-informed semi-automated event log generation for process mining. Decis. Support Syst. **132**(3) (2020)
5. Andrews, R., Wynn, M.T., Vallmuur, K., et al.: Leveraging data quality to better prepare for process mining: an approach illustrated through analysing road trauma pre-hospital retrieval and transport processes in Queensland. Int. J. Environ. Res. Public Health **16**(7), 1138 (2019)
6. Basmer, M., Kabierski, M., Sahling, K., et al.: A classification of data quality issues in object-centric event data. In: International Conference on Process Mining, pp. 311–323. Springer, Cham (2024)
7. Bernard, G., Andritsos, P.: Truncated trace classifier. In: Removal of Incomplete Traces from Event Logs. LNBIP, vol. 387, pp. 150–165. Springer, Cham (2020)
8. Berti, A., Jessen, U., van der Aalst, W.M., Fahland, D.: Explainable object-centric anomaly detection: the role of domain knowledge. In: Best Dissertation Award, 22nd International Conference on Business Process Management, pp. 162–168 (2024)
9. Bertrand, Y., Van Belle, R., De Weerdt, J., Serral, E.: Defining data quality issues in process mining with IoT data. In: International Conference on Process Mining, pp. 422–434. Springer, Cham (2022)
10. Bose, R.P.J.C., Mans, R.S., van der Aalst, W.M.P.: Wanna improve process mining results? In: 2013 IEEE Symposium on Computational Intelligence and Data Mining (CIDM), pp. 127–134. IEEE (2013)
11. Bozkaya, M., Gabriels, J., Van der Werf, J.M.: Process diagnostics: a method based on process mining. In: 2009 International Conference on Information, Process, and Knowledge Management, pp. 22–27. IEEE (2009)

12. Burattin, A.: Streaming process mining. Process Min. Handb. **349**, 3–10 (2022)
13. Buss, A., Kecht, C., Kratsch, W., et al.: From words to workflows: extracting object-centric event logs from textual data. In: International Conference on Advanced Information Systems Engineering, pp. 37–44. Springer, Cham (2025)
14. Cappiello, C., Comuzzi, M., Plebani, P., Fim, M.: Assessing and improving measurability of process performance indicators based on quality of logs. Inf. Syst. **103**, 101874 (2022)
15. Conforti, R., La Rosa, M., ter Hofstede, A.H.: Filtering out infrequent behavior from business process event logs. IEEE Trans. Knowl. Data Eng. **29**(2), 300–314 (2017)
16. Conforti, R., La Rosa, M., ter Hofstede, A.H.M., Augusto, A.: Automatic repair of same-timestamp errors in business process event logs. In: Fahland, D., Ghidini, C., Becker, J., Dumas, M. (eds.) BPM 2020. LNCS, vol. 12168, pp. 327–345. Springer, Cham (2020). https://doi.org/10.1007/978-3-030-58666-9_19
17. Dakic, D., Stefanovic, D., Lolic, T., et al.: Event log extraction for the purpose of process mining: a systematic literature review, pp. 299–312. Springer Proceedings in Business and Economics. Springer, Cham (2019)
18. Dani, S., Leopold, H., van der Werf, J.M.E., et al.: Towards understanding the role of the human in event log extraction. In: International Conference on Business Process Management, pp. 86–98. Springer, Cham (2021)
19. De Leoni, M., van der Aalst, W.M., Dees, M.: A general process mining framework for correlating, predicting and clustering dynamic behavior based on event logs. Inf. Syst. **56**, 235–257 (2016)
20. de Murillas, E.G.L., van der Aalst, W.M.P., Reijers, H.A.: Process mining on databases: unearthing historical data from redo logs. In: Motahari-Nezhad, H.R., Recker, J., Weidlich, M. (eds.) BPM 2015. LNCS, vol. 9253, pp. 367–385. Springer, Cham (2015). https://doi.org/10.1007/978-3-319-23063-4_25
21. De Weerdt, J., Wynn, M.T.: Foundations of process event data. In: Process Mining Handbook, pp. 193–211. Springer, Cham (2022)
22. Denisov, V., Fahland, D., van der Aalst, W.M.P.: Repairing event logs with missing events to support performance analysis of systems with shared resources. In: Janicki, R., Sidorova, N., Chatain, T. (eds.) PETRI NETS 2020. LNCS, vol. 12152, pp. 239–259. Springer, Cham (2020). https://doi.org/10.1007/978-3-030-51831-8_12
23. Dixit, P.M., et al.: Detection and interactive repair of event ordering imperfection in process logs. In: Krogstie, J., Reijers, H.A. (eds.) CAiSE 2018. LNCS, vol. 10816, pp. 274–290. Springer, Cham (2018). https://doi.org/10.1007/978-3-319-91563-0_17
24. Fahland, D., Montali, M., Lebherz, J., et al.: Towards a simple and extensible standard for object-centric event data (OCED) – Core model, design space, and lessons learned (2024). https://arxiv.org/abs/2410.14495
25. Fischer, D.A., Goel, K., Andrews, R., van Dun, C.G.J., Wynn, M.T., Röglinger, M.: Enhancing event log quality: detecting and quantifying timestamp imperfections. Inf. Syst. **109**, 102039 (2022)
26. Fox, F., Aggarwal, V.R., Whelton, H., Johnson, O.: A data quality framework for process mining of electronic health record data. In: 2018 IEEE International Conference on Healthcare Informatics (ICHI), pp. 12–21. IEEE (2018)
27. Geeganage, D.T.K., Wynn, M.T., ter Hofstede, A.H.: Text2EL: expert guided event log enrichment using unstructured text. ACM J. Data Inf. Qual. **16**(1), 8:1–8:28 (2024)

28. Goel, K., Leemans, S.J., Martin, N., Wynn, M.T.: Quality-informed process mining: a case for standardised data quality annotations. ACM Trans. Knowl. Discov. Data **16**(5), 1–47 (2022)

29. Van der Heijden, T.: Process mining project methodology: Developing a general approach to apply process mining in practice. Master of Science in Operations Management and Logistics. Technische Universiteit Eindhoven, School of Industrial Engineering, Netherlands (2012)

30. ter Hofstede, A.H.M., Koschmider, A., Marrella, A., et al.: Process-data quality: the true frontier of process mining. ACM J. Data Inf. Qual. **15**(3), 29:1–29:21 (2023)

31. Johnson, O.A., Ba Dhafari, T., Kurniati, A., Fox, F., Rojas, E.: The ClearPath method for care pathway process mining and simulation. In: International Conference on Business Process Management, pp. 239–250. Springer, Cham (2018)

32. Kabierski, M., Richter, M., Weidlich, M.: Quantifying and relating the completeness and diversity of process representations using species estimation. Inf. Syst. **130**, 102512 (2025)

33. Kalukapuge, S., ter Hofstede, A.H.M., Wynn, M.T.: Swiftmend: an approach to detect and repair activity label quality issues in process event streams. In: Cooperative Information Systems, pp. 131–149. Springer, Cham (2025)

34. Kapugama Geeganage, D.T., Wynn, M.T., ter Hofstede, A.H.M.: Text2EL+: expert guided event log enrichment using unstructured text. J. Data Inf. Qual. **16**(1) (2024)

35. Knols, B., van der Werf, J.M.E.: Measuring the behavioral quality of log sampling. In: 2019 International Conference on Process Mining, pp. 97–104. IEEE (2019)

36. König, F., Egger, A., Kratsch, W., Röglinger, M., Wördehoff, N.: Unstructured data in process mining: a systematic literature review. ACM Trans. Manag. Inf. Syst. **16**(3), 1–34 (2025)

37. Li, G., de Murillas, E.G.L., de Carvalho, R.M., van der Aalst, W.M.P.: Extracting object-centric event logs to support process mining on databases. In: Mendling, J., Mouratidis, H. (eds.) CAiSE 2018. LNBIP, vol. 317, pp. 182–199. Springer, Cham (2018). https://doi.org/10.1007/978-3-319-92901-9_16

38. Lu, X., et al.: Semi-supervised log pattern detection and exploration using event concurrence and contextual information. In: Panetto, H., et al. (eds.) OTM 2017. LNCS, vol. 10573, pp. 154–174. Springer, Cham (2017). https://doi.org/10.1007/978-3-319-69462-7_11

39. Lu, X., Fahland, D., van den Biggelaar, F.J.H.M., van der Aalst, W.M.P.: Handling duplicated tasks in process discovery by refining event labels. In: La Rosa, M., Loos, P., Pastor, O. (eds.) BPM 2016. LNCS, vol. 9850, pp. 90–107. Springer, Cham (2016). https://doi.org/10.1007/978-3-319-45348-4_6

40. Mannhardt, F., Koschmider, A., Baracaldo, N., Weidlich, M., Michael, J.: Privacy-preserving process mining: differential privacy for event logs. Bus. Inf. Syst. Eng. **61**(5), 595–614 (2019)

41. Mans, R., van der Aalst, W.M.P., Vanwersch, R.J.B., Moleman, A.J.: Process mining in healthcare: Data challenges when answering frequently posed questions. In: Process Support and Knowledge Representation in Health Care. LNCS, vol. 7738, pp. 140–153. Springer, Heidelberg (2012)

42. Martin, N., Van Houdt, G., Janssenswillen, G.: DaQAPO: supporting flexible and fine-grained event log quality assessment. Expert Syst. Appl. **191**, 116274 (2022)

43. Mühlberger, R., Bachhofner, S., Di Ciccio, C., García-Bañuelos, L., López-Pintado, O.: Extracting event logs for process mining from data stored on the blockchain. In: International Conference on Business Process Management, pp. 690–703. Springer, Cham (2019)

44. Niro, A., Werner, M.: Detecting anomalous events in object-centric business processes via graph neural networks. In: International Conference on Process Mining, pp. 179–190. Springer, Cham (2023)

45. Pegoraro, M., van der Aalst, W.M.: Mining uncertain event data in process mining. In: International Conference on Process Mining, pp. 89–96. IEEE (2019)

46. Pei, J., Wen, L., Yang, H., Wang, J., Ye, X.: Estimating global completeness of event logs: a comparative study. IEEE Trans. Serv. Comput. **14**(2), 441–457 (2018)

47. Pradhan, S.K., Jans, M., Martin, N.: Getting the data in shape for your process mining analysis: an in-depth analysis of the pre-analysis stage. ACM Comput. Surv. **57**(6), 1–37 (2025)

48. Rebuge, Á., Ferreira, D.R.: Business process analysis in healthcare environments: a methodology based on process mining. Inf. Syst. **37**(2), 99–116 (2012)

49. Redman, T.C.: Bad data costs the us \$3 trillion per year. Harv. Bus. Rev. **22**(2016), 11–18 (2016)

50. Sadeghianasl, S., ter Hofstede, A.H.M., Wynn, M.T., Suriadi, S.: A contextual approach to detecting synonymous and polluted activity labels in process event logs. In: Panetto, H., Debruyne, C., Hepp, M., Lewis, D., Ardagna, C.A., Meersman, R. (eds.) OTM 2019. LNCS, vol. 11877, pp. 76–94. Springer, Cham (2019). https://doi.org/10.1007/978-3-030-33246-4_5

51. Sadeghianasl, S., ter ofstede, A.H., Suriadi, S., Turkay, S.: Collaborative and interactive detection and repair of activity labels in process event logs. In: International Conference on Process Mining, pp. 41–48. IEEE (2020)

52. Sani, M.F., van Zelst, S.J., van der Aalst, W.M.P.: Improving process discovery results by filtering outliers using conditional behavioural probabilities. In: BPM Workshops. LNBIP, vol. 308, pp. 216–229. Springer, Cham (2017)

53. Shirali, M., Ahmadi, Z., Fernández-Llatas, C., Bayo Montón, J.L., Di Federico, G.: An interactive error-correcting approach for IoT-sourced event logs. ACM Trans. Internet Things **5**(4), 1–30 (2024)

54. Suriadi, S., Andrews, R., ter Hofstede, A.H.M., Wynn, M.T.: Event log imperfection patterns for process mining: towards a systematic approach to cleaning event logs. Inf. Syst. **64**, 132–150 (2017)

55. Swevels, A., Dijkman, R.M., Fahland, D.: Inferring missing entity identifiers from context using event knowledge graphs. In: International Conference on Business Process Management. LNCS, vol. 14159, pp. 180–197. Springer, Cham (2023)

56. Syring, A.F., Tax, N., van der Aalst, W.M.: Evaluating conformance measures in process mining using conformance propositions. In: Transactions on Petri Nets and Other Models of Concurrency XIV, pp. 192–221. Springer, Cham (2019)

57. Tsoury, A., Soffer, P., Reinhartz-Berger, I.: Data impact analysis in business processes: automatic support and practical implications. Bus. Inf. Syst. Eng. **62**(1), 41–60 (2020)

58. van der Aalst, W.M.P.: Extracting event data from databases to unleash process mining. In: vom Brocke, J., Schmiedel, T. (eds.) BPM - Driving Innovation in a Digital World. Management for Professionals, pp. 105–128. Springer, Cham (2015)

59. van der Aalst, W.M.P.: Process Mining: Data Science in Action, 2nd edn. Springer, Heidelberg (2016)

60. van der Aalst, W., et al.: Process mining manifesto. In: Daniel, F., Barkaoui, K., Dustdar, S. (eds.) BPM 2011. LNBIP, vol. 99, pp. 169–194. Springer, Heidelberg (2012). https://doi.org/10.1007/978-3-642-28108-2_19
61. Van Eck, M.L., Lu, X., Leemans, S.J., Van Der Aalst, W.M.: PM$^2$: a process mining project methodology. In: International Conference on Advanced Information Systems Engineering, pp. 297–313. Springer, Cham (2015)
62. Van Eck, M.L., Sidorova, N., van der Aalst, W.M.: Enabling process mining on sensor data from smart products. In: International Conference on Research Challenges in Information Science, pp. 1–12. IEEE (2016)
63. Verbeek, H.M.W., Buijs, J.C.A.M., van Dongen, B.F., van der Aalst, W.M.P.: XES, XESame, and ProM 6. In: Soffer, P., Proper, E. (eds.) CAiSE Forum 2010. LNBIP, vol. 72, pp. 60–75. Springer, Heidelberg (2011). https://doi.org/10.1007/978-3-642-17722-4_5
64. Wynn, M.T., Van Der Aalst, W., Verbeek, E., Di Stefano, B.: The IEEE XES standard for process mining: experiences, adoption, and revision [Society Briefs]. IEEE Comput. Intell. Mag. **19**(1), 20–23 (2024)
65. Wynn, M.T., et al.: Rethinking the input for process mining: insights from the XES Survey and Workshop. Technical report, IEEE Task Force on Process Mining (2021). https://www.tf-pm.org/upload/1637134004497.pdf. Accessed 29 Sept 2025
66. Zetzsche, F., Andrews, R., ter Hofstede, A.H., Röglinger, M., Schmid, S.J., Wynn, M.T.: Case ID revealed HERE: hybrid elusive case repair method for transformer-driven business process event log enhancement. Bus. Inf. Syst. Eng. 1–27 (2025)
67. Ziolkowski, T., Brandt, L., Koschmider, A.: ElogQP: an event log quality pointer. In: Proceedings of the 13th European Workshop on Services and Their Composition. CEUR Workshop Proceedings, vol. 2839, pp. 42–45. CEUR (2021)

# What is an Object-Centric Case? An Exploration

Dirk Fahland[1]([✉])(iD) and Marco Montali[2](iD)

[1] Eindhoven University of Technology, Eindhoven, The Netherlands
d.fahland@tue.nl
[2] Free University of Bozen-Bolzano, Bolzano, Italy
montali@inf.unibz.it

**Abstract.** The concept of a *case* describing all information relevant for one execution of a process is fundamental to process science. It is *the* conceptual lens through which process behavior is studied. The implicit assumption that cases partition behavior into distinct and separate executions hinders transferring established methods and techniques for process analysis and mining to *object-centric* settings. Here, processes operate over shared objects and hence behavior cannot easily be separated. To enable such a transfer, we need a suitable notion of *object-centric case*. This paper explores possible definitions for object-centric cases and executions grounded in object-centric event data. We propose formal definitions that generalize the classical setting. We specifically illustrate that, on one hand, any object-centric case notion has to break with the assumption of partitioning behavior, and on the other hand, this break enables new use cases. We conclude with a critical analysis of our proposal highlighting gaps and deficiencies that need to be addressed.

**Keywords:** Object-Centric Processes · Object-Centric Process Mining · Object-Centric Event Data · Case

## 1 Introduction

The concept of a *case* describing one execution, or *instance*, of a process [1] is fundamental to process science. It is an important conceptual lens through which the discipline studies all aspects contributing to a start-to-end behavior that is meaningful in the domain-context of the process, such as treating a patient or handling an order. It also is the lens through which process behavior is structured into separately handled executions in mathematical models of processes [1], data models for event logs [47], and in the architecture of Workflow/BPM systems [7] and Case Handling systems [5,8].

While ubiquitously relied-upon, the case concept is neither exactly defined in the process science literature but rather illustrated through examples and a general intuition, see [1]. Nor is it universally applicable to all process behaviors – specifically those where a process handles multiple, possibly shared objects [4].

© The Author(s), under exclusive license to Springer Nature Switzerland AG 2026
J. Mendling et al. (Eds.): Wil van der Aalst Festschrift, LNCS 16480, pp. 398–425, 2026.
https://doi.org/10.1007/978-3-032-17618-9_28

The discipline studied processes over multiple, shared objects conceptually and empirically since the early 2000's under various approaches grounded on business artifacts/objects [17,19,20,30,36,39,41,43], relational databases [16,31], Petri nets [4,6,14,24,29,32], and temporal logics [13,37]. Building on these, the paradigm of *object-centric processes* is grounding the concepts for modeling and analyzing such process behavior empirically in *event data* over multiple objects [3]. However, despite 20 years of research and some first proposals [12], no notion of an *object-centric case* has emerged that serves the same function for the discipline as the classical notion of a case: *a generally applicable conceptual lens to study start-to-end behavior over multiple objects* that is meaningful in the domain of the process. We detail this problem in Sect. 2.

In this paper, we explore a possible definition of an object-centric case that is grounded in object-centric event data, yet aims to stay in spirit close to the original case concept and its function for the discipline. Section 3 provides a simple mathematical definition of object-centric event data on which we build our argumentation. In contrast to previous attempts to define cases via objects, e.g., [12], we approach the problem from the angle of *events*.

In Sect. 4 we define and study *object-centric start-to-end executions* comprising all events between a chosen start event and a chosen end event. We then explore how to define *object-centric case notions* that correspond to such executions without having to actually know about the underlying events. We observe that – due to the nature of object-centric behavior – any object-centric process inevitably gives rise to *multiple* object-centric case notions and that – unlike in the classical situation – cases inevitably *overlap* in the general case. Yet, we argue that these traits are essential for revealing and studying relevant properties of object-centric processes.

Our discussion in Sect. 6 reflects both on new use cases and applications enabled by this case concept observed in industrial case studies and on the inherent assumptions limitations of our proposal. Although our exploration is not complete, the suggested ideas may help the discipline form new abstractions for methods and algorithms that can handle the complexity of object-centric processes in a meaningful way, which we outline in Sect. 7.

## 2 The Role of Cases and the Challenge to Generalize Them

Business Process Management and Process Mining are disciplines that developed methods and techniques for modeling, analyzing, and improving (business) processes. Thereby, adequate abstractions of actual process behavior provide these disciplines with concepts to structure problems and to develop models and techniques that are applicable to a wide range of processes and analysis tasks. One such central abstraction is the notion of *case*, which represents all information and behavior related to a single execution of a process, that is, a process instance [1]. Examples of cases are an insurance claim or a loan request. Every case results in a distinct process execution, focused on the application of the process to that particular object. In this light, a case can be seen as a "basket" in which all process-relevant data and information related to the case object are placed, and the process execution is essentially determined by "what is in the basket". Structuring behavior into such cases provides well-defined units of reasoning over process behavior that can be addressed and inspected individually, compared, or grouped.

These notions are central even in the most fundamental formal models of processes. *Workflow nets* and their executions define the *trace* of a case as the sequence of activities executed in the process instance [1]. Event logs group events into traces based on a chosen *case identifier* [2,47]. Workflow Management Systems, which laid the technical foundations for BPM systems, define the case as one dimension for structuring and organizing the system architecture and operation [7,48]. Case Handling systems are literally conceptualized and built around managing a "case" as a unit of information [5,8,44]. Notably, none of the works that build on the case concept provide a precise definition of a case, but rather characterize it through enumerating examples [1] or by describing general properties of case, just as we did at the beginning of this section.

Yet, while being arguably one of the most important concepts in process modeling and analysis, not all process behavior of interest can be naturally *separated* into cases, even for those processes where it appears quite clear what a natural case notion actually is.

In fact, some information or behavior may belong into multiple, distinct "baskets", or put differently, information in the "basket" of one case may influence how the process execution of another case can/must proceed. A typical example showing this phenomenon is that of a hiring process to fill a vacancy. The process calls for handling multiple applications, each being an execution of the same process with reviewing documents and interviewing applicants, i.e., representing distinct cases. Yet, at some point only one of the cases may proceed to the step where the candidate receives a job offer, while the other candidates are either declined or have to wait until the first candidate accepts or rejects this offer. Such cross-dependencies among cases manifest in many processes and for different reasons. Past research on "artifact-centric" [19,41] and "object-aware" [36] or early "object-centric" approaches [43] have identified two main "culprits".

- Processes where different executions synchronize on a number of shared business or data objects [16,20–22,29–31,42,49], such as the vacancy that is shared by several applicants.
- Process behavior that can be conceptualized as a bundle of two or more distinct processes interacting with each other through shared business or data objects and their mutual relationships [4,14,24,26,29,30,32], such as an order being put into multiple packages, and multiple packages of different customers being grouped into a delivery.


**Running Example.** The following example, taken from [25], illustrates these two types of dynamics of processes over shared objects described above.

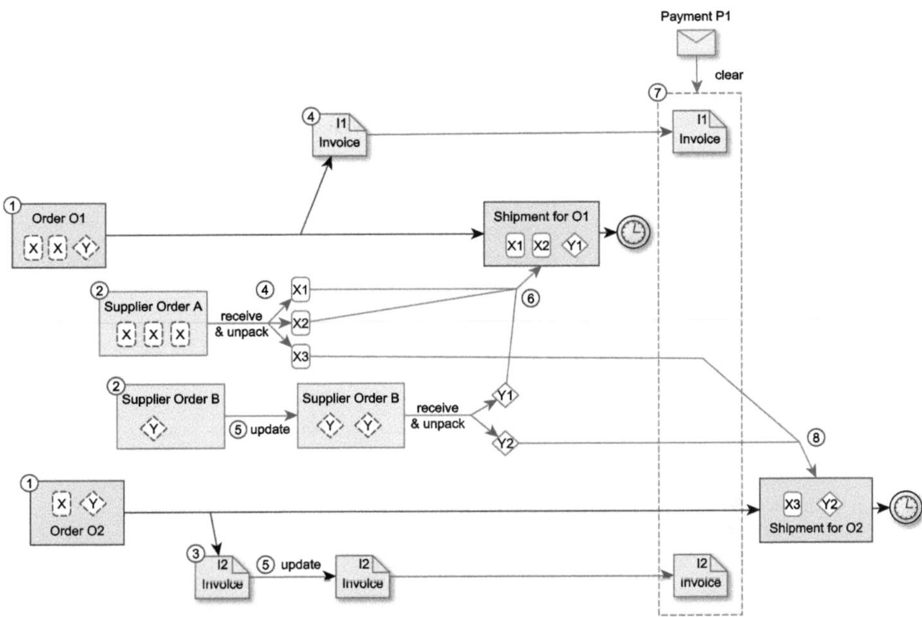


**Fig. 1.** Illustration of a multi-entity process: a retailer handles two orders for multiple items by placing and receiving supplier orders for specific items.

1. Consider a retailer who took two *Orders* for multiple *Items* from the same customer: the customer first places Order $O1$ for 2 items $X$ and 1 item $Y$, and shortly afterwards Order $O2$ for 1 item $X$ and 1 item $Y$.

The retailer handles both orders as explained next and illustrated in Fig. 1.

2. Items $X$ are provided by supplier $A$ while items $Y$ are provided by supplier $B$. To save costs, the retailer bundles the orders for the items and place two *Supplier Orders*, one at $A$ for 3 items $X$ and one at $B$ for 1 item $Y$.
3. Invoice $I2$ for Order $O2$ is created right after placing the supplier order at $B$.
4. When the retailer receives the Supplier Order from $A$, three Items $X$ are unpacked and await shipment. At this point, also *Invoice* $I1$ is created for $O1$.
5. Around the time of receiving the supplier order from $A$, the retailer notices their mistake: they ordered only one item $Y$ from $B$ while $O1$ and $O2$ both require one item $Y$ *each*. The Supplier Order $B$ and invoice $I2$ are updated accordingly.
6. When finally the supplier order from $B$ is received, the items $Y$ are unpacked. One item $Y$ is packed together with two items $X$ into the shipment for $O1$ which is then shipped.
7. In the meantime, the customer sends a single *Payment* $P1$ which covers the amount for both invoices $I1$ and $I2$.

**Table 1.** Event data of the process of Fig. 1 with events referring to multiple objects.

| EventID | Activity | Time | Order | Supplier Order | Item | Invoice | Payment |
|---|---|---|---|---|---|---|---|
| e1 | Create Order | 01-05 09:05 | O1 | | | | |
| e2 | Create Order | 01-05 09:30 | O2 | | | | |
| e3 | Place SO | 01-05 11:25 | | A | | | |
| e4 | Place SO | 02-05 11:55 | | B | | | |
| e5 | Create Invoice | 03-05 16:15 | O2 | | | I2 | |
| e6 | Receive SO | 00-01 10:00 | | A | X1,X2,X3 | | |
| e7 | Update SO | 04-05 10:25 | O2 | B | | | |
| e8 | Unpack | 00-01 10:30 | | A | X3 | | |
| e9 | Update Invoice | 04-05 10:50 | | | | I2 | |
| e10 | Unpack | 04-05 11:00 | | A | X1 | | |
| e11 | Unpack | 04-05 11:15 | | A | X2 | | |
| e18 | Create Invoice | 06-05 14:35 | O1 | | | I1 | |
| e19 | Receive SO | 07-05 10:10 | | B | Y1,Y2 | | |
| e20 | Unpack | 07-05 10:45 | | B | Y1 | | |
| e21 | Unpack | 07-05 11:00 | | B | Y2 | | |
| e27 | Pack Shipment | 07-05 17:00 | O1 | | X1,X2,Y1 | | |
| e28 | Ship | 08-05 15:00 | O1 | | | | |
| e29 | Receive Payment | 09-05 08:30 | | | | | P1 |
| e30 | Clear Invoice | 09-05 08:45 | | | | I1,I2 | P1 |
| e33 | Pack Shipment | 09-05 11:45 | O2 | | X3,Y2 | | |
| e34 | Ship | 09-05 15:00 | O2 | | | | |

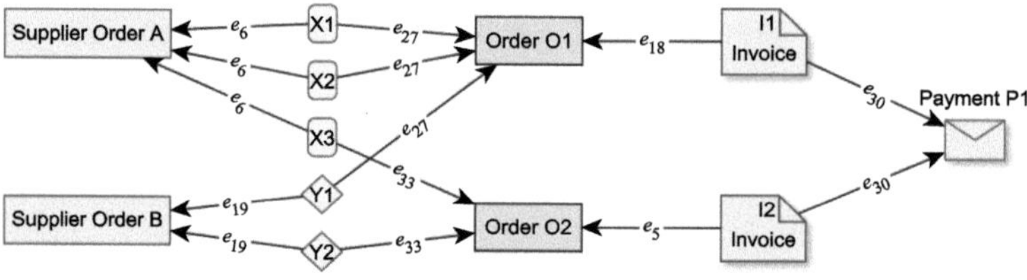


**Fig. 2.** Objects and relations in Table 1.

8. Finally, another item $X$ and the second $Y$ are packed in the shipment for order $O2$.

This process handles 5 types of objects: *Orders, Supplier Orders, Items, Invoices, Payments*. The behavior above could be recorded as events referring to these object types as shown in Table 1. The data pertain the objects and relations as shown in Fig. 2, where we can assume that two objects are related if they are referred to by the same event [25].[1]

---

[1] Notice that this indicates the existence of a relationship, but does not provide domain-specific knowledge on its nature. We will come back to this point in the discussion part.

**Where the Conceptual Lens of Cases Fails.** What makes the transfer of the case concept to object-centric processes challenging is that it is not a mathematically precise notion, but rather a "conceptual lens" through which the field conceives mathematically precise notions. Such consequent mathematically precise notions, specifically that of a *trace* of a case describing the events associated to the case ordered by time, rely on the implicit assumption that two cases do not overlap in behavior, i.e., do not share events.

Research on artifact-centric processes and object-aware processes side-stepped the problem by structuring the process behavior in terms of object life-cycles only, i.e., defining a trace per object [26,45] and then devising means to express relations between object traces on the model level [27,40], through enriching events [21,22], or by deriving traces describing interactions between two related objects [39]. This way of structuring behavior in terms of individual objects is too fine grained compared to a "basket" of related behavior involving multiple objects. And hence, no reliable case notion emerged from this angle that would also resonate with the notion of a trace.

However, this research ultimately led to the definition of *object-centric event logs* [15] and *object-centric event data* [28]. Adams et al. [12] explored how to generalize the case concept with this implicit assumption to an object-centric setting. Their proposal defines an object-centric case as a connected component of related objects and their associated events. This notion has been used to introduce (alignment-based) conformance checking techniques for object-centric processes [32,38].

However, most object-centric data cannot be separated into multiple "meaningful" connected components as already our simple example shows. The behavior in our example cannot be divided into multiple connected components of objects: all objects in our example are (transitively) related to each other as Fig. 2 shows. Thus, by [12] we would have to treat all behavior as a single case.

In contrast, a classical view or interpretation of cases would, for instance, focus on the processing of the two *Order* objects $O1$ and $O2$, i.e., argue for the existence of two cases. The cases themselves then should comprise all related information, i.e., related objects and events relevant for handling these. Various methods and heuristics are available [11,34] to scope which information is related to a case over such data. For example, the case for $O1$ would contain information about $O1, I1, P1, X1, X2, Y1, A, B$ and the case for $O2$ would contain information about $O2, I2, P1, X3, Y2, A, B$ [25]. However this view for structuring the behavior has several drawbacks:

- Both cases $O1$ and $O2$ share information and hence events – violating the implicit assumption that cases structure process behavior into distinct and *separate* executions.
- The cases are also overly complex as they do not just describe the behavior of $O1$ and $O2$ respectively: the included *Supplier Orders A* and $B$ are largely independent of $O1$ and $O2$, and interleaved with the *Invoices I1* and $I2$, which are in turn semantically unrelated to $A$ and $B$.

In extracted classical, sequential event logs, the first drawback manifests as *convergence* of cases: information related to multiple cases is extracted repeatedly, leading to false statistics. The second drawback manifests as *divergence* of cases, i.e., event orderings of unrelated objects are patched together, giving the false impression of behavioural patterns that do not actually exist. [3, 39]

From a formal angle, representing event data in an object-centric model [28], instead of sequential logs, avoids convergence and divergence in the data model [3, 25]. Yet, any attempt to identify subsets of objects and events that form a "case" fundamentally resurfaces both issues conceptually:

- How to choose objects and events in a way that it only contains information that is relevant to some "meaningful" start-to-end dynamics? This question is related to avoiding "conceptual divergence".
- How to handle the fact that start-to-end dynamics are overlapping with each other? This question is related to avoiding or dealing with "conceptual convergence."

In the following, we explore these questions through the specific model of object-centric event data, which we present in Sect. 3. We then propose in Sect. 4 a new notion of "start-to-end" dynamics in terms of object-centric event data and discuss how it relates to the issues of "conceptual divergence" and "conceptual convergence". We will argue that our proposal addresses conceptual divergence, but that conceptual convergence is inevitable – explicitly noting that this should not be considered as a limitation, but rather a useful tool to structure process behavior in an object-centric setting.

## 3   Object-Centric Event Data

We base our exploration for an object-centric case notion on the proposed core model for object-centric event data (OCED) [28]. We first provide a formal definition for OCED. We then define two behavioral views on OCED: as partially-ordered object-centric event log, and as an OCED-graph. both views rely on a suitable lifting of the classical directly-follows relation among events, now defined on a per-object basis.

We assume the following universes: attribute names *Attr*, values *Val*, object types *OType*, and event types *EType* (e.g., activities), and timestamps $\mathcal{T}$.

**Definition 1 (Object-Centric Event Data set).**   *An* object-centric event data set *(OCED-set)* $D = (O, E, type, corr, rel, \#)$ *defines*

1. *finite sets of* objects $O$ *and of* events $E$, $O \cap E = \emptyset$;
2. *a* type *for each object and each event,* $type : (O \rightarrow OType) \cup (E \rightarrow EType)$;
3. *the event-to-object (E2O) relation* $corr \subseteq E \times O$ *stating which events are correlated to which objects;*
4. *the object-to-object (O2O) relation* $rel \subseteq O \times O$ *stating which objects are related to each other; and*

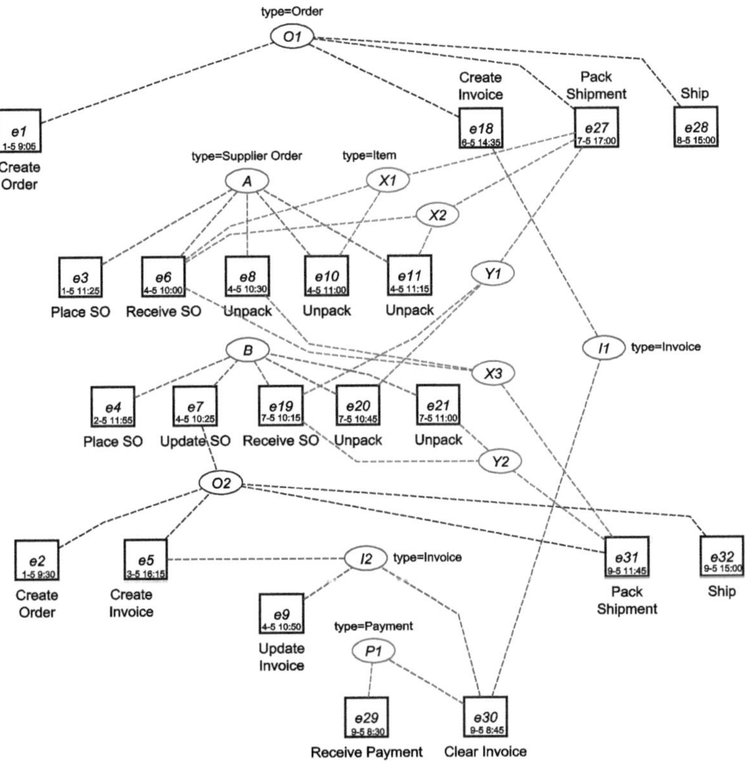

**Fig. 3.** OCED-set of the data of the running example in Table 1.

5. *a number of* attribute-value pairs *for each object and event,* $\# : (O \cup E) \times Attr \nrightarrow Val$ *s.t. each event carries a* timestamp, *i.e.,* $\forall e \in E : \#_{time}(e) \in \mathcal{T}$.

Each $o \in O$ and $e \in E$ can be interpreted as unique *object identifier* and unique *event identifier*, respectively. The *corr* relation and the *rel* relation describe *which* events and objects are related to each other, but they do *not* impose a particular semantics, e.g., "create object" or "child of". However, OCED-sets impose the following consistency constraint on *corr* and *rel*.

**Definition 2 (Relation-consistent OCED).** *An OCED set $D$ is* relation-consistent *wrt. its events iff any two objects $o, o' \in O$ correlated to the same event $e \in E$, $(e, o), (e, o') \in corr$ are also related to each other: $(o, o') \in rel$ or $(o', o) \in rel$.*

Figure 3 visualizes the OCED-set of our running example based on Table 1: a square represents an event, an ellipsis represents an object, and a dashed edge represents a *corr* relation. Table 1 translates to Fig. 3 by simple rules [25]: each event id in Table 1 maps to an event, so that the activity column provides the event type, and the time column the event timestamp; each unique object id in

Table 1 maps to an object, so that the name of the column it belongs to provides its object type; in addition, a row containing an event id $e$ and an object id $o$ maps to $(e, o) \in corr$. To make the OCED-set relation-consistent, we add $(o, o') \in rel$ whenever $\exists e \in E : (e, o), (e, o') \in corr$; these O2O relations are shown in Fig. 2.

**Event Ordering in OCED.** The basis of behavioral analysis of object-centric processes is describing the order of events per object: an event $e'$ *directly follows* an event $e$ from the perspective of $o$ if both $e$ and $e'$ are correlated to $o$, and no other event $e''$ correlated to $o$ occurs temporally between $e$ and $e'$:

**Definition 3 (Directly-follows per object).** *Let $D$ be an OCED-set. The local directly follows relation inferred from $D$ is $< \,\subseteq E \times O \times E$ with $e <_o e'$, i.e., $e'$ directly-follows $e$ from the perspective of object $o$ iff*

- *$(e, o), (e', o) \in corr$ (e and e' are correlated to o),*
- *$\#_{time}(e) < \#_{time}(e')$ (e occurs temporally before e'), and*
- *there exists no other event $e'' \in E$ with $(e'', o) \in corr$ (e'' correlated to o), such that $\#_{time}(e) < \#_{time}(e'') < \#_{time}(e')$.*

For example, in Fig. 3, $e_6 <_A e_8, e_6 <_{X1} e_{10}$ but $e_6 \not<_o e_7$ for any $o \in O$.

We reason over $<$ in two complementary views: turning $<$ into a partial order, and treating $<$ as edges in a graph. We present both views next.

**Partial-Order View on OCED.** We can extend an OCED-set $D$ into a partially-ordered object-centric event log by turning $<$ into a partial order $\leq$ over the events (where $\leq$ hides for which object(s) the relation holds).

**Definition 4 (Partially-Ordered OCEL (po-OCEL)).** *Let $D = (O, E, type, corr, rel, \#)$ be an OCED-set.*

1. *The partial order over $E$ is $\leq \,\subseteq E \times E$ with $\leq \,= (\{(e, e') \mid \exists o \in O : e <_o e'\})^*$, i.e., we build the transitive closure of $<$ where we ignore per $e <_o e'$ the object for which "e' directly follows e" was observed.*
2. *The partially-ordered object-centric event log (po-OCEL) of $D$ is $L = (D, \leq)$ which we may also write as $L = (O, E, type, corr, rel, \#, \leq)$.*

In the log $L$ of the OCED-set of Fig. 3, we have, for instance, $e_3 \leq e_{28}$, because $e_3 <_A e_6 <_{X1} e_{10} <_{X1} e_{27} <_{O1} e_{28}$; instead, $e_6 \not\leq e_7$ and $e_7 \not\leq e_6$, i.e., $e_6$ and $e_7$ are concurrent.

It is easy to show that $\leq$ is indeed a partial order (reflexive, transitive, anti-symmetric) over the events of $D$.

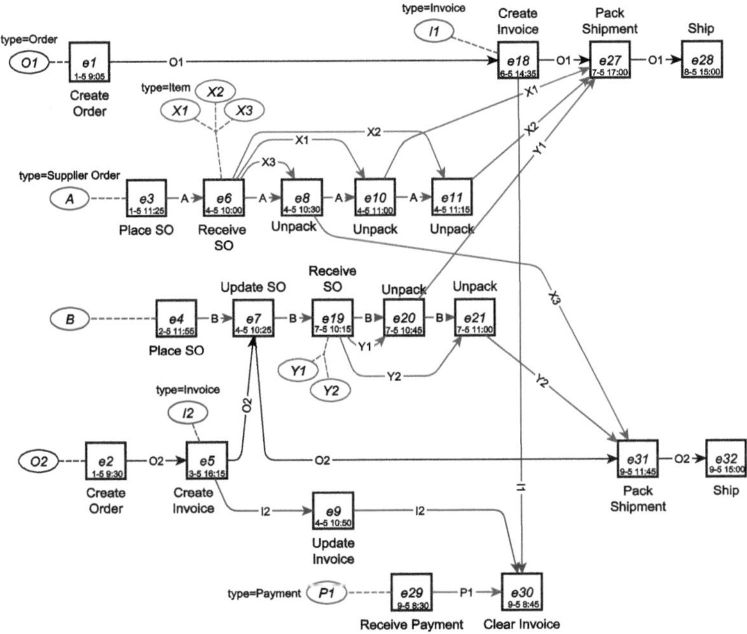

**Fig. 4.** OCED-Graph of the OCED-set of Fig. 3.

**Graph View on OCED.** We can also interpret each event as a node and each $e <_o e'$ as a directed edge from $e$ to $e'$ (annotated with the object $o$). This interpretation gives rise to the following graph-view on an OCED, where we also treat objects as nodes, and *corr* and *rel* as edges.

**Definition 5 (OCED-Graph).** *Let* $D = (O, E, type, corr, rel, \#)$ *be an OCED-set. The OCED-Graph* $G = (N, R, type, \#)$ *of* $D$ *has*

*1. nodes* $N = E \cup O$,
*2. edges (or relationships)* $R = corr \cup rel \cup <$, *and*
*3. type specifies the type of the node while* $\#$ *specifies properties of the nodes.*

Figure 4 shows the OCED-graph for the OCED-set of Fig. 3 where only the *corr* edge to the first event of each object is shown and *rel* edges are omitted.

This definition of $G$ as a graph relies on $E \cap O = \emptyset$, on *type* clearly assigning each node a unique type, and on the fact that each edge in $R$ gets a type through the distinct signatures of $corr \subseteq E \times O$, $rel \subseteq O \times O$, and $< \subseteq E \times O \times E$. Note that $G$ is a actually a hyper-graph, as $<$ may contain multiple edges $(e, o_1, e'), (e, o_2, e')$ between the same pair of events.

An OCED-Graph can also be seen as a labeled property graph (LPG) or *Event Knowledge Graph*, see [23,25], allowing implementation and querying in graph databases.

Seeing $D$ as a graph $G$ enables reasoning over *paths*. In general, a path in $G$ is a sequence $\langle n_1, \ldots, n_k \rangle \in N^*$ of nodes (events and/or objects) in $G$, connected by edges $(n_i, n_{i+1}) \in R$ or $(n_i, o, n_{i+1}) \in R$ for $1 \leq i < k$. We are specifically interested in paths over events.

**Definition 6 (Directly-Follows Path).** *Let $D$ be an OCED-set and let $G$ be the OCED-Graph of $D$. Let $O' \subseteq O$ be a subset of objects. A* directly-follows path *(df-path) in $G$ wrt. $O'$ is a sequence $\langle e_1, \ldots, e_k \rangle \in E^*$ of events connected by directly-follows edges only involving objects $O'$, i.e., there exist $o_1, \ldots, o_{k-1} \in O'$ s.t. $e_i <_{o_i} e_{i+1}$ for $1 \leq i < k$. We write $\langle e_1, \ldots, e_k \rangle \in df(D, O')$ in this case.*

Generally, we consider df-paths over all objects $O$ and then just write "a df-path" in $G$. For example, $\langle e_3, e_6, e_{10}, e_{27}, e_{28} \rangle$ is a df-path in Fig. 4.

An event $e$ is a *start event* wrt. objects $O' \subseteq O$ in $D$ iff no event precedes $e$ from the perspective of any object in $O'$, i.e., there exists no $o \in O'$ and no event $e' \in E$ with $e' <_o e$; we write $start(O')$ for the set of all start events wrt. $O'$. *End events* and $end(O')$ are defined correspondingly. A df-path $\langle e_1, \ldots, e_k \rangle$ wrt. $O'$ is *maximal* iff it cannot be extended with another df-edge for an object from $O'$, i.e., $e_1 \in start(O')$ and $e_k \in end(O')$.

**Views are Equivalent.** As $<$ is fully determined by an OCED-set $D$, i.e., we can compute it from $D$ alone, both the po-OCEL $L$ of $D$ and the OCED-graph $G$ of $D$ are just different "materialized views" of $D + <$. This is confirmed by the following lemma.

**Lemma 1.** *Let $D$ be an OCED-set and let po-OCEL $L = (D, \leq)$ of $D$ and the OCED-graph $G$ of $D$. Then $e < e'$ in $L$ iff there exists a df-path from $e$ to $e'$ in $G$.*

In the following, we therefore treat $D$, $L$, and $G$ interchangeably and just write $D$ when reasoning over $\leq$ in $D$ or df-paths in $D$.

## 4    Object-Centric Start-to-End Executions

The traditional approach to defining cases as concepts for process executions is to first identify a set of objects forming a case, and then retrieving the related events forming the execution or trace [11, 12, 34]. We explore what happens when we invert this approach: we identify a set of events that form what we typically would consider an execution or (partially-ordered) trace, and then retrieve the objects associated. We first introduce some relations and operations on OCED-sets and then provide a formal definition for this idea.

**Operations on OCED.** Let $D = (O, E, type, corr, rel, \#)$ be an OCED-set. Let $E' \subseteq E$ be a subset of events and let $O' \subseteq O$ be a subset of objects.

The set of events correlated to $O'$ is the set $E[O'] = \{e \in E \mid \exists o \in O' : (e, o) \in corr\}$. The set of objects correlated to $E'$ is the set $O[E'] = \{o \in O \mid \exists e \in E' : (e, o) \in corr\}$.

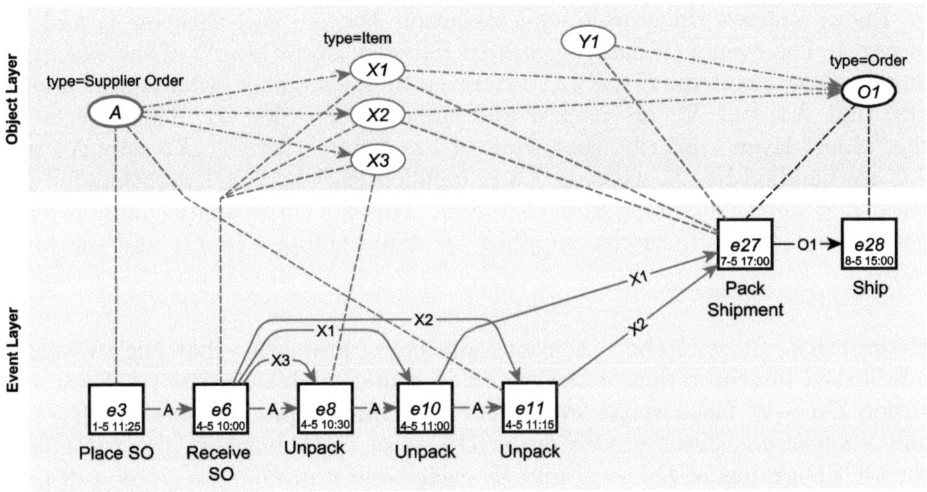


**Fig. 5.** The start-to-end execution $D[e_3 \rightarrow e_{28}]$ between $e_3$ and $e_{28}$ of Fig. 4.

The *restriction* of $D$ to objects $O'$ and events $E'$ is $Res_{O',E'}D = (O', E', type|_{O' \cup E'}, corr|_{E' \times O'}, rel|_{O' \times O'}, \#|_{O \cup E'})$. We use two special restrictions. The **selection of objects** $O'$ **from** $D$ [25], written $Sel_{O'}D = Res_{O',E[O']}D$, is the restriction of $D$ to the objects $O'$ and their correlated events $E[O']$. The **projection of** $D$ **onto events** $E'$ [25], written $Proj_{E'}D = Res_{O[E'],E'}D$, is the restriction of $D$ to the events $E'$ and the objects $O[E']$ correlated to $E'$. Notice that projection may alter the directly-follows relation $<$, as events are removed.

Let $D'$ be another OCED-set. $D'$ is a *subset* of $D$, written $D' \subseteq D$, iff $D'$ is an element-wise subset of $D$. Note that $Res_{O',E'}D \subseteq D$ for any $O' \subseteq O, E \subseteq E$. We write $D \cup D'$ for the element-wise union of $D$ and $D'$. For a finite set $\mathcal{D} = \{D_1, \ldots, D_n\}$ of OCED-sets, we write $\bigcup \mathcal{D} = D_1 \cup \ldots \cup D_n$.

**Start-to-End Execution.** The existing literature [11,12,34] defines cases and executions via the selection operation: pick a set of objects $O'$ that form a case, and then retrieve the associated events $E[O']$.

We explore the inverse. We pick events $E'$ that form an execution and then retrieve the objects $O[E']$, i.e., the projection operation. However, to succeed we have to choose $E'$ in a way that it is conceptually aligned with our understanding of a process execution or classical notions of (partially-ordered) traces: a set of events that is closed wrt. event ordering $\leq$.

**Definition 7 (Start-to-End Execution).** *Let $D$ be an OCED-set. Let $i, o \in E$ be two events. Let $E_i^o = \{e \in E \mid i \leq e \leq o\}$ be the events between $i$ and $o$. The object-centric start to end execution from $i$ to $o$ is $D[i \rightarrow o] = Proj_{E_i^o}D$, i.e., the projection of $D$ to the events between $i$ and $o$ and their correlated objects.*

Figure 5 shows the start-to-end execution $D[e_3 \rightarrow e_{28}]$ between $e_3$ and $e_{28}$ of Fig. 4. The events (visually separated into the "event layer") of the execution describe how the items $X1, X2, X3$ received by the supplier order $A$ are handled and that $X1$ and $X2$ are packed and shipped for order $O1$. The objects (in the "object layer") describe that while $A$ has 3 items $X1, X2, X3$ only $X1$ and $X2$ are handled by $O1$ whereas $X3$ is handled elsewhere. $O1$ additionally also packs and ships $Y1$ coming from elsewhere. This is a surprisingly comprehensive description of how the items supplied by $A$ are shipped by $O1$ and its direct context.

**Properties.** Start-to-end executions also enjoy properties that align with the established interpretation of executions in sound workflows nets [1]. Each execution $D[i \rightarrow o]$ has a *single start event $i$* (having no predecessors in $D[i \rightarrow o]$) and a *single end event $o$*. Obviously, $D[i \rightarrow o] \subseteq D$, but this also extends to the OCED-graphs of $D[i \rightarrow o]$ and $D$: each event $e$ in $D[i \rightarrow o]$ is on a df-path $\langle i, \ldots, e, \ldots, o \rangle$ in $D[i \rightarrow o]$ and in $D$. Thus, we can also rewrite $E_i^o$ in Definition 7 as $E_i^o = \{e \in E \mid i \leq e \leq o\} = \{e \in E \mid \langle i, \ldots, e \rangle, \langle e, \ldots, o \rangle \in df(D, O)\}$, i.e., each $e$ that is reachable via a df-path from $i$ in $D[i \rightarrow o]$ has a continuing df-path to $o$ in $D[i \rightarrow o]$.

## 5 Object-Centric Case Notions

A start-to-end execution is similar to a classical trace as both describe process behavior. However, the case concept is not defined in terms of behavior, but in terms of the information or data being processed, see [1]. Although the proposed start-to-end execution has an "object-layer", a case is typically characterized by a single key data object, e.g., "*the* order being processed".

We argue that in an object-centric setting we have to be a bit more precise regarding what characterizes a case. We begin in Sect. 5.1 with the simple idea that an object-centric case is defined by a start object $o_{st}$ and an end object $o_{end}$ containing all information (events and objects) between the start event of $o_{st}$ to the end event of $o_{end}$. Applying this idea on our running example in Sect. 5.2 reveals multiple case notions that complement each other but also clarify which choices we (have to) make when defining object-centric cases. We finally outline in Sect. 5.3 ideas to generalize this case notion and to provide more "control" of what information is part of a case.

### 5.1 Cases Defined by Start and End Objects

In the following, we assume that each object $o \in O$ has a single start event $start(o) = \{e_{st}\}$ and a single end event $end(o) = \{e_{end}\}$, and we write $start(o) = e_{st}$ and $end(o) = e_{end}$.

**Definition 8 (Object-Centric Start-to-End Case).** *Let $D$ be an OCED-set. The* object-centric start-to-end case *from $o_{st} \in O$ to $o_{end} \in O$ is $D[o_{st} \rightarrow o_{end}] = D[start(o_{st}) \rightarrow end(o_{end})]$.*

Figure 5 shows the start-to-end case $D[A \rightarrow O1]$ from $A$ to $O1$. We can interpret such a start-to-end case as a description of how the creation of the start object, here supplier order $A$, is resolved by the conclusion of the end object, here order $O1$.

Now, to structure process behavior into cases, we need to conceptualize a "case notion" from which we can unambiguously derive the individual cases to study separately. Similar to how we can classically study the processing of all orders (each individual order being a case), we here can study the processing from all supplier orders to all orders. Thus, we can conceptualize an object-centric case notion as a start object type and an end object type.

**Definition 9 (Object-Centric Start-to-End Case Notion).** *Let $D$ be an OCED-set. The* start-to-end cases *from objects of type $T_{st} \in Type$ to objects of type $T_{end} \in Type$ are $\mathcal{D}[T_{st} \rightarrow T_{end}] = \{D[o_{st} \rightarrow o_{end}] \mid o_{st}, o_{end} \in O, type(o_{st}) = T_{st}, type(o_{end}) = T_{end}\}$. We call $D[T_{st} \rightarrow T_{end}] = \bigcup \mathcal{D}[T_{st} \rightarrow T_{end}]$ the behavior defined by $\mathcal{D}[T_{st} \rightarrow T_{end}]$.*

A case notion $\mathcal{D}[T_{st} \rightarrow T_{end}]$ is a collection of start-to-end cases, similar to a classical log being a collection of classical cases. However, in contrast to classical logs, the start-to-end cases in $\mathcal{D}[T_{st} \rightarrow T_{end}]$ may overlap. For example, $\mathcal{D}[SupplierOrder \rightarrow Order]$ defines 4 cases $D[A \rightarrow O1], D[A \rightarrow O2], D[B \rightarrow O1], D[B \rightarrow O2]$. Figure 6 shows the event layer of their behavior.

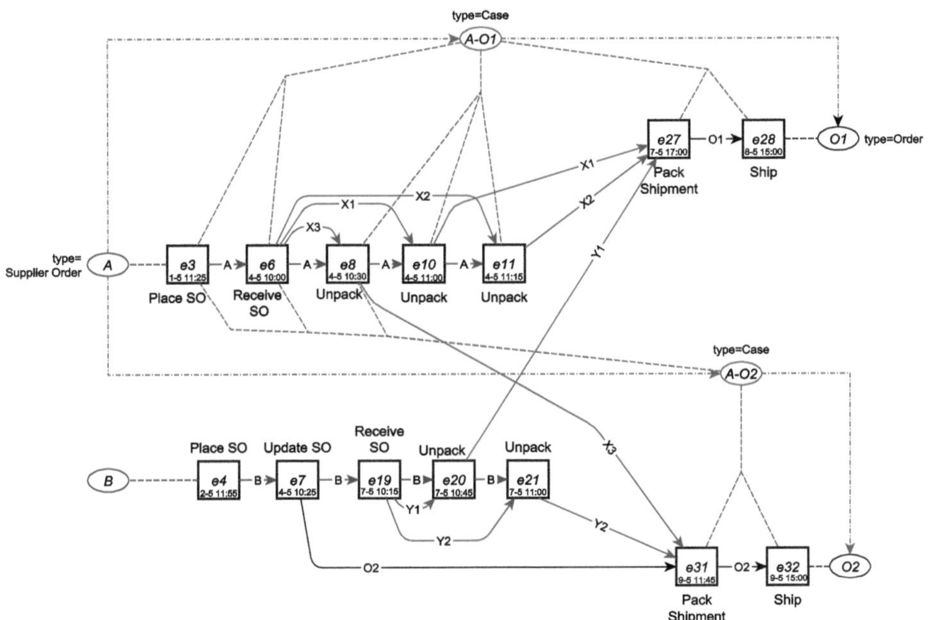


**Fig. 6.** All object-centric cases $D[SupplierOrder \rightarrow Order]$ with cases $D[A \rightarrow O1]$ and $D[A \rightarrow O2]$ modeled explicitly.

For example, $D[A \rightarrow O1]$ and $D[A \rightarrow O2]$ overlap on $e_3, e_6, e_8$ whereas $D[A \rightarrow O1]$ and $D[B \rightarrow O1]$ overlap on $e_{27}, e_{28}$. The use of OCED formally avoids event duplication (convergence) and false behavioral relations (divergence) compared to the classical setting. Yet, cases (conceptually) do overlap. We argue that such overlap of different cases is inevitable in processes where various dynamics of the same kind share objects, e.g., $A$ providing items to $O1$ and to $O2$ causes overlap in $D[A \rightarrow O1]$ and $D[A \rightarrow O2]$.

As cases overlap, we need another way to distinguish different cases from each other within OCED. One possibility is to materialize an object-centric case $D[start(o_{st}) \rightarrow end(o_{end})]$ in $D$ by introducing a new object node $c = (o_{st}, o_{end}) \in O$ of $type(c) = case$ with $(o_{st}, c), (c, o_{end}) \in rel$ and $(e, c) \in corr$ for each event $e$ in $D[start(o_{st}) \rightarrow end(o_{end})]$. Figure 6 shows the materialization of $D[A \rightarrow O1]$ and $D[A \rightarrow O2]$ as red nodes.

**How Meaningful is this Case Notion?** Overall, we can see how the items provided by *Supplier Orders* are later used to fulfill *Orders*. Note that we do not see the full *Order* traces, but only the part of each *Order* trace that is influenced or affected by *Supplier Orders*. We also see that each *Order* depends on *Items* from two different *Supplier Orders*. Furthermore, we see that all executions generally have the same structure or order of activities: *Place SO, Receive SO, Unpack* a number of items, *Pack Shipment* and *Ship*.

## 5.2 OCED Contains Multiple Start-to-End Case Notions

Having established that the proposed concept of start-to-end case has some utility in partitioning the process behavior, we now explore the consequence of applying this concept to the entire running example. We consider all possible start-to-end case notions as possible pairs of distinct object types. But we restrict start object types to those where objects have a global start event, i.e., are not preceded by another event of another object, correspondingly for end object types. Thus, we consider *Order, Supplier Order* and *Payment* as start object types and *Order, Invoice,* and *Payment* as end object types.

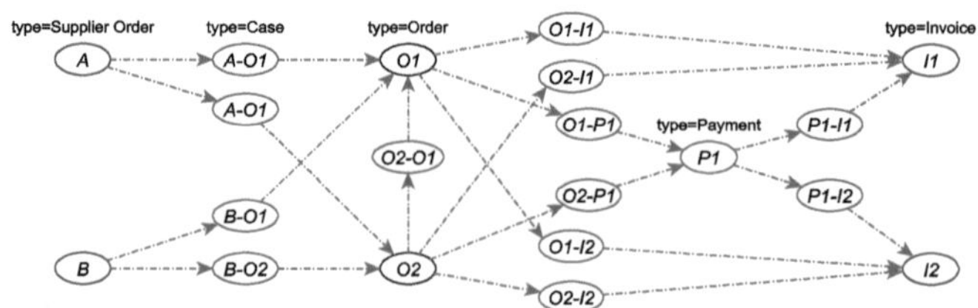


**Fig. 7.** All start-to-end cases of the running example of Fig. 4.

**A High-Level Summary of the Process.** Figure 7 shows the resulting cases and their corresponding start and end objects that already give us a *high-level summary of the process*: On the left, we see the four cases for $\mathcal{D}[SupplierOrder \rightarrow Order]$ that we already discussed in Sect. 5.1. On the right, we see two executions for $\mathcal{D}[Order \rightarrow Payment]$ indicating that both orders $O1$ and $O2$ end in the *same* payment $P1$, and two executions for $\mathcal{D}[Payment \rightarrow Invoice]$ indicating that the same payment $P1$ concludes both invoices $I1$ and $I2$. We also see four executions for $\mathcal{D}[Order \rightarrow Invoice]$, and one execution for $\mathcal{D}[Order \rightarrow Order]$ that we need to better understand.

Finally, we note that there are *no executions* for $\mathcal{D}[Order \rightarrow SupplierOrder]$ and $\mathcal{D}[SupplierOrder \rightarrow Invoice]$ or $\mathcal{D}[SupplierOrder \rightarrow Payment]$. We now discuss the individual case notions in more detail.

**How Meaningful are the Different Case Notions?** In our example, the case notions $\mathcal{D}[Order \rightarrow Invoice]$ and $\mathcal{D}[Order \rightarrow Payment]$ yield the same cases and executions because the invoices $I1$ and $I2$ and the payment $P1$ share the same end event $e_{30}$. Their start-to-end executions (event and object layer) are shown in Fig. 8 (left).

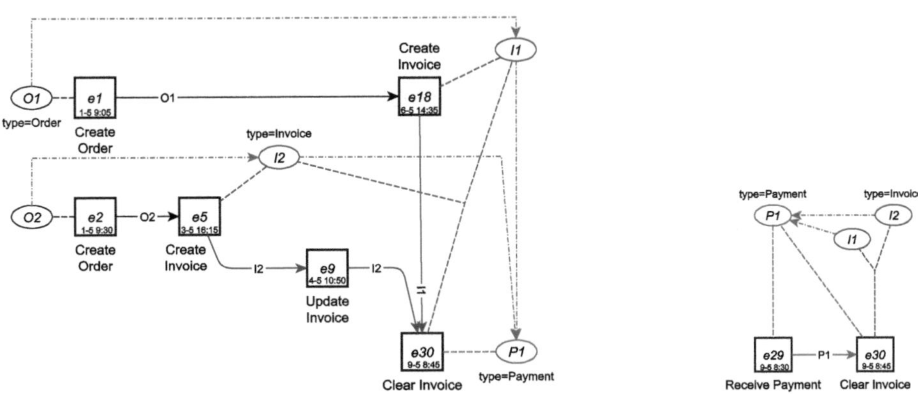


**Fig. 8.** Cases from Order to Payment/Invoice (left) and from Payment to Invoice (right).

We see that all orders, i.e., orders $O1$ and $O2$, each have their own invoice $P1$ and $P2$, respectively, and are settled by the same payment $P1$. We also see their executions differ as the intermediate invoices $I1$ and $I2$ are handled differently: $I2$ has an additional *Update Invoice* event. Because $e_{30}$ is a shared end event for $I1$ and $I2$, we also have the cases $D[O1 \rightarrow I2]$ and $D[O2 \rightarrow I1]$. On one hand, $D[O1 \rightarrow I2]$ and $D[O2 \rightarrow I1]$ do not represent an "intended" start-to-end behavior in the process as $I2$ and $I1$ are not the invoices of (created by) $O1$ and $O2$, respectively. On the other hand, these cases show an "emergent" start-to-end behavior in the process within the case notion of $\mathcal{D}[Order \rightarrow Invoice]$: the conclusion of the order $O1$ wrt. the invoices is also dependent on $I2$ which can be relevant from an auditing perspective [35] or from a performance perspective (i.e., delays in $I2$ may possibly also delay the invoice-flow starting in $O1$).

The case $\mathcal{D}[Payment \rightarrow Invoice]$ shown in Fig. 8(right) is behaviorally simple as it only contains the df-path for $P1$ but the object context clearly shows that payment $P1$ starts on its own with *Receive Payment* and clears (and ends) both invoices $I1$ and $I2$ together.

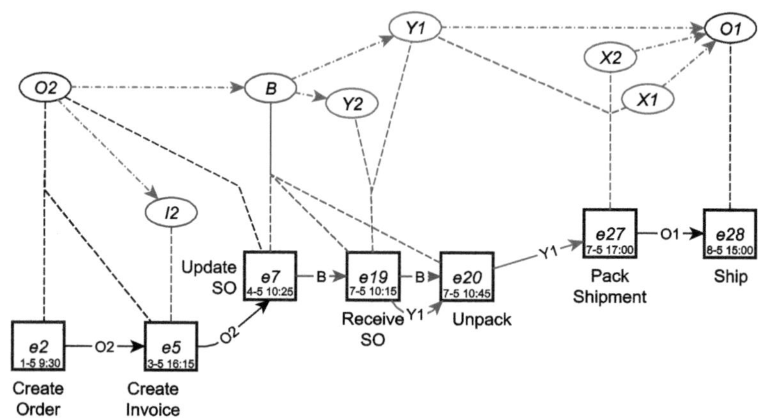



**Fig. 9.** Cases from Order to Order

The unusual case notion $\mathcal{D}[Order \rightarrow Order]$ contains a single execution $\mathcal{D}[O2 \rightarrow O1]$ shown in Fig. 9. It is unusual to find executions between different objects of the same type. Like $\mathcal{D}[O1 \rightarrow I2]$, $\mathcal{D}[O2 \rightarrow O1]$ is an "emergent" start-to-end behavior and not an "intended" one: in the example data, $O2$ synchronized with supplier order $B$ in the *Update SO* event. As a result, an execution from $O2$ to $O1$ forms that consists of two parts: $\mathcal{D}[e_2 \rightarrow e_7]$ from *Create Order* at $O2$ to *Update SO* at $B$ and $\mathcal{D}[e_7 \rightarrow e_{28}]$ from *Update SO* at $B$ to *Ship* at $O1$, which largely overlaps with the execution $\mathcal{D}[B \rightarrow O1]$ that we already discussed above. This execution clearly is an outlier compared to all other executions we found and reveals a surprising dependency between $O2$ and $O1$ due to the *Update SO* event, which can also be seen as undesired.

**What do Absent Case Notions Explain?** The data contains no executions from *Order* to *Supplier Order*, from *Supplier Order* to *Payment* or to *Invoice*, or between any objects of the same type (except for $O2$ to $O1$ discussed above).

This suggests that *Supplier Orders* are indeed created and managed independently of *Orders*, that is, there is no directly recorded control-flow dependency between the incoming *Orders* and the replenishment of the inventory through *Supplier Orders*. Inventory replenishment through *Supplier Orders* is independent and unrelated to financial transactions related to orders (i.e., *Invoices* and

*Payments*). Lastly, different *Supplier Orders* are independent of each other, and different *Invoices* are independent of each other.

## 5.3  Generalized OCED Cases

Not all process behaviors of interest fit the start-to-end case notion as we defined it. For example, none of the discussed case notions allows us to study how an *Order* is handled in its entirety. While $D[O1 \to O1]$ and $D[O2 \to O2]$ give the behavior of each order object, they are arguably too limited in scope to describe the *process* of handling an order.

We discuss a more general case notion defined by just the start (or just the end) of an object type. However, doing so will raise the need to also *filter* behavior from cases and executions. We discuss both aspects.

Instead of defining a case $D[o_{st} \to o_{end}]$ between two specific objects, we can make one of the end points a wildcard '$*$'. Let $O_{end} = \{o \in O \mid end(o) \subseteq end(O)\}$ the set of objects whose end event is also a "global" end event in $O$, i.e., their end events have no successor in $D$ at all. $O_{start}$ is defined correspondingly.

**Definition 10 (Start Case, End Case).** *The start case for the start object* $o$ *in* $D$ *is* $D[o \to *] = \bigcup\{D[o \to o_{end}] \mid o_{end} \in O_{end}\}$. *The end case for* $o$ *in* $D$ *is* $D[* \to o] = \bigcup\{D[o_{st} \to o] \mid o_{st} \in O_{start}\}$.

A start case is simply the union of cases that start in the single object $o$ and end in any of the end objects that are reachable from $o$. An end case is the union of cases that start somewhere and end in the single object $o$. Note that start cases are conceptually similar to the "leading type extraction" proposed in [12].

Both notions lift to start- and end-object types. For example, the *start case notion* $\mathcal{D}[Order \to *]$ defines two cases $D[O1 \to *]$ and $D[O2 \to *]$ whose joint behavior is shown in Fig. 10.

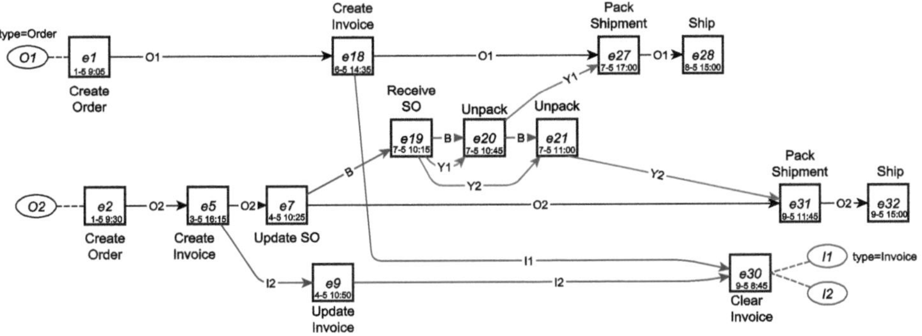

**Fig. 10.** Object-centric cases $\mathcal{D}[Order \to *]$ that begin at *Order* objects.

The execution shows the completion of $O1$ and $O2$ and their associated invoices $I1$ and $I2$ that are cleared together in $e_{30}$, but also behavior wrt. $B$ and items $Y1$ and $Y2$. We already explained in Sect. 5.2 that this emergent behavior is part of $D[O2 \rightarrow O1]$. Yet its inclusion in $D[O2 \rightarrow *]$ is problematic as it is incomplete wrt. the supplier order and the item object types: it does not contain (behavior of) all items involved in $O1$ and in $O2$, and it shows one supplier order ($B$) but not the other one ($A$). This case notion mirrors an undesired property of the "leading type extraction" [12] which includes all associated objects reachable from a start object, even if they are not conceptually contributing to the case.

Such incomplete representation of behavior is undesirable as it likely leads to wrong interpretations and conclusions. We should either show all involved items and both supplier orders in the same way or none. One possibility is to filter the df-paths used to build the start-to-end executions wrt. the allowed objects.

**Definition 11 (Filtered Start-to-End Execution).** *Let $D$ be an OCED-set. Let $X \subseteq O$ be a set of excluded objects. Let $i, o \in E$ be two events. Let $E_i^o|_{\bar{X}} = \{e \in E \mid \langle i, \ldots, e, \ldots, o \rangle \in df(D, O \setminus X)\}$ be the events on a df-path from $i$ to $o$ without df-edges involving excluded objects $X$. The* object-centric start to end execution *from $i$ to $o$ filtered by objects $X$ is $D[i \rightarrow o \setminus X] = Proj_{E_i^o|_{\bar{X}}} D$, i.e., the projection of $D$ to the events between $i$ and $o$ without $X$ and their correlated objects.*

Filtered start-to-end executions lift canonically to all previous definitions.

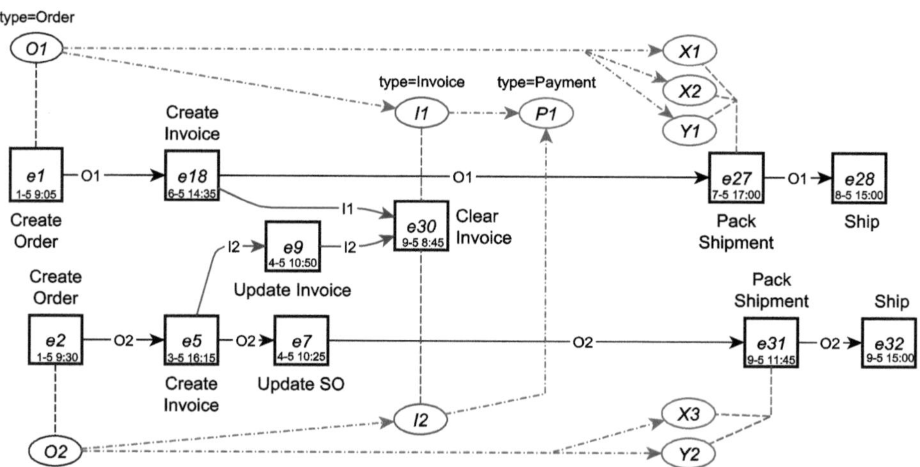



**Fig. 11.** Object-centric cases $D[Order \rightarrow * \setminus \{SupplierOrder\}]$ that begin at *Order* objects and do not involve any behavior of a *Supplier Order* object.

**What do Filtered Start/End Case Notions Explain?** For example, the filtered start case notion $\mathcal{D}[Order \rightarrow * \setminus \{SupplierOrder\}]$ contains the object-centric cases that begin at *Order* objects and do not involve any behavior of a

*Supplier Order* object; the cases are shown in Fig. 11. We obtain two simple and clear cases starting in *Place Order* that show the handling of each order and the fact that their invoices are both cleared by the same payment.

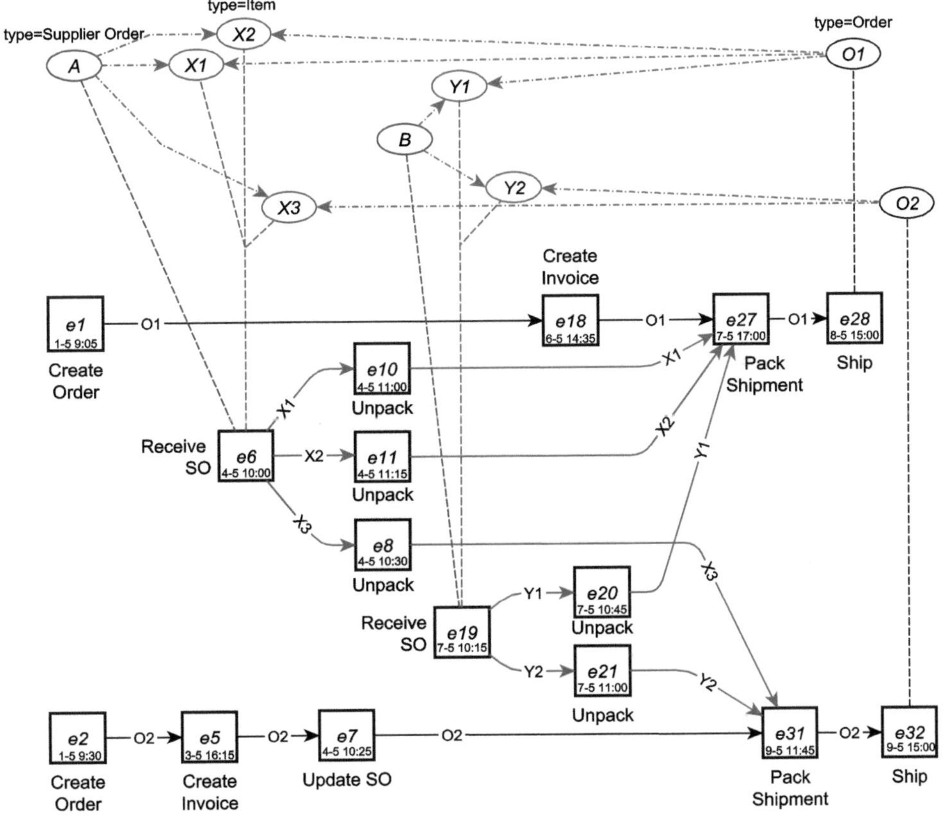


**Fig. 12.** Object-centric cases $D[* \rightarrow Order \setminus \{SupplierOrder\}]$ that end at *Order* objects and do not involve any behavior of a *Supplier Order* object.

The corresponding filtered end case notion $\mathcal{D}[* \rightarrow Order \setminus \{SupplierOrder\}]$ is shown in Fig. 12. The executions show what it takes to complete each order. This obviously involves creating the *Order* and packing the individual *Items*, but it also shows that the execution of the orders are independent of each other (as classical cases would be), while being dependent on the same *Receive SO* events that provide their *Items*. Notably, the executions do not contain any invoices or payments as these are not involved in completing an order.

**A Case Algebra?** The examples discussed show that multiple case notions can (and have to) be considered in OCED, and that different case notions convey different information. This suggests that analysts and domain experts should be given more control over how to pick and scope a case notion of interest. We also have shown that case notions can be combined (see Definition 10) and filtered (see Definition 11). These could possibly be the tools to allow analysts and experts derive new case notions. For example, an analyst could define the case $D[O1 \rightarrow * \setminus \{SupplierOrder\}] \cup D[* \rightarrow O1 \setminus \{SupplierOrder\}]$ showing the complete behavior that originates from $O1$ and that is needed to complete $O1$ (up to a certain "radius" of interest) – without having to perform complex data modeling or transformation.

## 6    Discussion

We reflect on the properties of the start-to-end case notion and its underlying assumptions and limitations.

**Utility as a Concept.** We argue that the start-to-end case notion demonstrated in Sect. 5 has utility in structuring object-centric process behavior in line with the classical notion. Similarly to classical cases, it can be explained in terms of one or two objects that define the "scope" of the behavior. It is accompanied by a formal notion of object-centric start-to-end behavior that generalizes the notion of a trace. We also argue that we have to give up the property of partitioning behavior into disconnected components, simply because the behaviors of interest are overlapping due to shared objects. Notice, though, that our proposal also abandons the "perceived objectivity" of how behavior of a process is defined: object-centric processes have multiple start-to-end case notions, and we have to make an explicit subjective choice about the case notion when modeling and analyzing object-centric processes. Arguably, that subjective choice is also present in the classical case notion, just hidden in the assumption of naming the case notion or defining it during event log extraction [11,34]. Explicitly allowing multiple case notions and understanding how they relate to each other in turn allows understanding an object-centric process at a higher level of abstraction, see Fig. 7, and allows one to relate reasoning and analysis from multiple different perspectives to each other, which applies for instance in an auditing context [35].

**Technical Feasibility.** The definitions proposed in Sect. 4 and Sect. 5 have been implemented using standard graph queries[2] over event knowledge graphs that implement the OCED-graph view.

**Variations and New Use Cases.** While applicable and feasible, the proposed concept is not complete. For instance, in industrial processes that handle physical objects, process behavior is not determined by the creation/conclusion of an

---

[2] https://github.com/multi-dimensional-process-mining/eventgraph_tutorial.

object, but by an object entering/leaving a particular area. Here, the object-centric case is rather defined by start- and end- activities while the object layer of the case is defined by physical locations or processing stations. We discuss 3 examples.

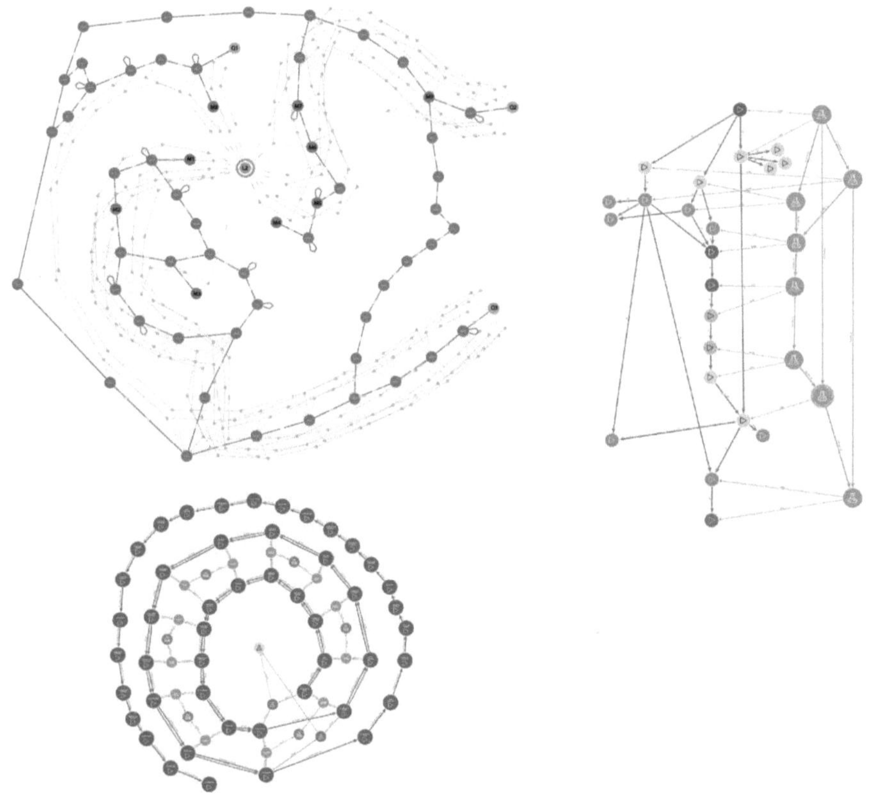

**Fig. 13.** Industrial use cases of object-centric case concept; top left: object-centric case of moving multiple yellow tubs to 3 loader queues (Q1, Q2, Q3); bottom left: circular process of medical kit sterilization consisting of multiple consecutive object-centric cases (red edges); right: object-centric start-to-end case in chemical processing from blue process (top) to red process (bottom) with splitting and merging over intermediate processes and associated material batches (light blue). (Color figure online)

Figure 13(top left) shows a case of an airport baggage handling system, where yellow tubs are loaded with a bag, transport it to their destination, and after unloading are free to be loaded with the next bag. This requires to move empty tubs from where they are to a "loader queue". The corresponding case begins with the orange-highlighted *request* activity that causes 16 tubs to move; it ends per tub that arrives at one of the three loader queues Q1 (top), Q2, Q3 (right). [18]

Figure 13(bottom left) shows multiple *consecutive cases* of the same medical kit undergoing a cycle of sterilization and usage in a hospital in a circular process [9]. Each case (shown as a red node and red df-path alongside the black kit df-path) starts when being *received* in the sterilization center and ends when being *put into storage* for usage by the hospital.

Figure 13(right) shows a case in a chemical PET recycling process involving multiples batches of material (light-blue nodes on the right) being separated, processed, and merged [10]. The case starts at the blue process activity at the top and involves multiple intermediate process activities (orange, yellow, green) and ends in the red activity at the bottom. This case is part of a larger dynamics as material batches are processed in other continuations, i.e., other cases (indicated by the orange and yellow leaf nodes).

**Assumptions and Limitations.** Our proposal builds on a number of assumptions. First, it assumes that the OCED-set available has been modeled in terms of all relevant domain concepts [46], allowing one to define case notions of relevance merely looking into the object types in the OCED-set. Second, it assumes that all relevant behavior "across different objects" has been modeled as otherwise start-to-end executions between two different objects do not exist. This assumption is in principle satisfied if any two related objects also share an event that refers to both objects (c.f. Definition 2). If related objects do not share events, then behavior between two objects can be derived by reifying the relation between both objects into a derived objects, which now shares events with either of the objects resulting in DF-edges between the two related objects [23,24].

However, in either case, using shared events as surrogate for relations has several non-trivial assumptions in itself.

First, events correlated to multiple objects are assumed to correctly represent when two related objects synchronize. This could, for instance, be violated when objects are only related to each other in a "create" event while subsequent events are only correlated to a single object. For example, the "create" event of an order line item object is also correlated to the order header while events that update the amount are only correlated to the order line item object, suggesting no changes occur on the header. Yet, the domain semantics of the "update" event on an order line item object state that updating amounts in order line items lead to subsequent changes in the order header, i.e., that both objects are involved in the "update" event. Conversely, it is assumed that events relating to two objects indeed signify a relevant interaction; event $e_7$ in our running example may not satisfy this assumption.

Second, the notion assumes that object relations are *rigid*, i.e., that they hold when they have been observed for the first time and do not change. This is not true in general. In our running example, imagine that item $X3$ is initially by accident also packed into the shipment for order $O1$ (i.e., correlated to $e_{27}$) but then taken out (in another event $e'_{27}$) and only afterwards packed into the shipment for order $O2$ (i.e., correlated to $e_{31}$). Now $X3$ is related to two orders $O1$ and $O2$, but $X3$ was never related to two orders *at the same time*. Instead,

$X3$ first was related to $O1$; then this relation was changed to relate $X3$ to $O2$. One hand, the OCED data model used here cannot naturally express changes of relations between objects, see [28]. On the other hand, our approach is not aware that relations may only hold for a certain period of time. Retrieving the case $D[X3 \rightarrow *]$ in this fictitious variation would wrongly suggest that $X3$ was packed and shipped twice (once by following the path to the end of $O1$ and once by following the path to the end of $O2$).

Another open challenge pertains the possibility of further exploring domain knowledge when defining object-centric cases. Specifically, while OCED-sets abstractly deal with generic object-to-object relationships (induced from their co-participation to events), clarifying the meaning and properties of such relationships can be instrumental to support and guide domain experts in singling out meaningful cases. For example, as pointed out in Sect. 5.2, looking into temporal dependencies induced by common events helps filtering out meaningless pairs of start-end object types. However, this is not enough to filter out pairs that show some potentially meaningful temporal dependencies, which are instead resulting from spurious relations. Such issues have to be manually disentangled. The presence (or absence) of domain-specific object-to-object relationships may help the user in this process, provided that the user comes up with an explicit, detailed account about the questions to be answered. Consider, for example, the classical object-to-object relationship of ownership, linking every order to the person who created it. When dealing with spatiotemporal questions (such as how far orders have to be shipped, and what is the average delivery time), navigating this relationship from the order to the owner is essential, as the owner is in turn linked to the physical address to which the order must be shipped. At the same time, navigating this relationship back – to obtain all orders owned by the same person – may be relevant only for those orders that share packages, while disconnected orders of the same customer may be filtered out. Importantly, exploiting this domain-specific knowledge requires not only to elicit object-to-object relationships, but also to qualify their properties. This calls for investigating how foundational ontologies, in particular those dealing with events [33], can be exploited in defining and scoping suitable object-centric case notions.

While the aforementioned limitations do not prevent further exploring and applying the case concept, they do indicate the need for a more systematic study of the semantic co-dependency between events and relationships when defining object-centric cases.

## 7   Conclusion

We explored how to transfer the case notion as a conceptual lens to structure process behavior to the object-centric setting. While the case concept classically is defined in terms of the information objects that define the case, we approached the problem by first defining start-to-end executions as "units of behavior" and then lifted these to the level of objects. The accompanying formal definitions and implementations in graph databases show surprising versatility in defining and deriving various case notions. Both our running example and industrial case studies suggest that start-to-end cases have utility in taking a "relevant slice" of behavior for analysis.

Our bottom-up proposal accommodates behaviors where different dynamics or executions inherently overlap due to shared objects, allowing to study executions both individually and together. Further, our proposal is inherently tied to the idea that any (sufficiently complex) object-centric processes gives rise to different case notions that overlap and describe different yet relevant dynamics of the process. Together, these properties indicate the need to explicitly allow subjective choices in choosing and defining case notions depending on the analysis interests. We believe our proposal allows such flexibility but requires further exploration and validation in practical settings to become robust.

**Acknowledgments.** The research underlying this paper was partially supported by AutoTwin EU GA n. 101092021. The idea of a start-to-end dynamic was conceived in discussions with Mitchel Brunings.

# References


1. Aalst, W.M.P.: Verification of workflow nets. In: Azéma, P., Balbo, G. (eds.) ICATPN 1997. LNCS, vol. 1248, pp. 407–426. Springer, Heidelberg (1997). https://doi.org/10.1007/3-540-63139-9_48
2. van der Aalst, W.M.P.: Process Mining - Data Science in Action, 2nd edn. Springer, Cham (2016). https://doi.org/10.1007/978-3-662-49851-4
3. Aalst, W.M.P.: Object-centric process mining: dealing with divergence and convergence in event data. In: Ölveczky, P.C., Salaün, G. (eds.) SEFM 2019. LNCS, vol. 11724, pp. 3–25. Springer, Cham (2019). https://doi.org/10.1007/978-3-030-30446-1_1
4. van der Aalst, W.M.P., Barthelmess, P., Ellis, C.A., Wainer, J.: Proclets: a framework for lightweight interacting workflow processes. Int. J. Cooperative Inf. Syst. **10**(4), 443–481 (2001). https://doi.org/10.1142/S0218843001000412
5. van der Aalst, W.M.P., Berens, P.J.S.: Beyond workflow management: product-driven case handling. In: GROUP 2001, pp. 42–51. ACM (2001). https://doi.org/10.1145/500286.500296
6. van der Aalst, W.M.P., Berti, A.: Discovering object-centric petri nets. Fundam. Informaticae **175**(1–4), 1–40 (2020). https://doi.org/10.3233/FI-2020-1946
7. van der Aalst, W.M.P., van Hee, K.M.: Workflow Management: Models, Methods, and Systems. Cooperative Information Systems. MIT Press (2002)
8. van der Aalst, W.M.P., Weske, M., Grünbauer, D.: Case handling: a new paradigm for business process support. Data Knowl. Eng. **53**(2), 129–162 (2005). https://doi.org/10.1016/J.DATAK.2004.07.003
9. Abu Sbeit, A.: Developing a digital twin for discrete event processes using event knowledge graphs and process mining techniques. Master thesis, Eindhoven University of Technology (2024)
10. Abu Sbeit, A., Cavadini, F., Fahland, D.: Enabling object-centric process mining from time-series. In: 6th Workshop on Event Data and Behavioral Analytics (EdbA 2025) at ICPM, Montevideo, Uruguay, 20 October 2025. LNBIP (2025, to appear)

11. Accorsi, R., Lebherz, J.: A practitioner's view on process mining adoption, event log engineering and data challenges. In: Process Mining Handbook. LNBIP, vol. 448, pp. 212–240. Springer, Cham (2022). https://doi.org/10.1007/978-3-031-08848-3_7

12. Adams, J.N., Schuster, D., Schmitz, S., Schuh, G., van der Aalst, W.M.P.: Defining cases and variants for object-centric event data. In: ICPM 2022, pp. 128–135. IEEE (2022). https://doi.org/10.1109/ICPM57379.2022.9980730

13. Artale, A., Kovtunova, A., Montali, M., van der Aalst, W.M.P.: Modeling and reasoning over declarative data-aware processes with object-centric behavioral constraints. In: Hildebrandt, T., van Dongen, B.F., Röglinger, M., Mendling, J. (eds.) BPM 2019. LNCS, vol. 11675, pp. 139–156. Springer, Cham (2019). https://doi.org/10.1007/978-3-030-26619-6_11

14. Barenholz, D., Montali, M., Polyvyanyy, A., Reijers, H.A., Rivkin, A., van der Werf, J.M.E.M.: There and back again - on the reconstructability and rediscoverability of typed Jackson nets. In: PETRI NETS 2023. LNCS, vol. 13929, pp. 37–58. Springer, Cham (2023). https://doi.org/10.1007/978-3-031-33620-1_3

15. Berti, A., et al.: OCEL (object-centric event log) 2.0 specification. CoRR abs/2403.01975 (2024). https://doi.org/10.48550/ARXIV.2403.01975

16. Calvanese, D., Giacomo, G.D., Montali, M.: Foundations of data-aware process analysis: a database theory perspective. In: PODS 2013, pp. 1–12. ACM (2013). https://doi.org/10.1145/2463664.2467796

17. Calvanese, D., Montali, M., Estañol, M., Teniente, E.: Verifiable UML artifact-centric business process models (extended version). CoRR abs/1408.5094 (2014). http://arxiv.org/abs/1408.5094

18. Chu, V.: Using event knowledge graphs to model multi-dimensional dynamics in a baggage handling system. Master thesis, Eindhoven University of Technology (2022)

19. Cohn, D., Hull, R.: Business artifacts: a data-centric approach to modeling business operations and processes. IEEE Data Eng. Bull. 32(3), 3–9 (2009). http://sites.computer.org/debull/A09sept/david.pdf

20. Deutsch, A., Hull, R., Li, Y., Vianu, V.: Automatic verification of database-centric systems. ACM SIGLOG News 5(2), 37–56 (2018). https://doi.org/10.1145/3212019.3212025

21. van Eck, M.L., Sidorova, N., van der Aalst, W.M.P.: Multi-instance mining: discovering synchronisation in artifact-centric processes. In: Daniel, F., Sheng, Q.Z., Motahari, H. (eds.) BPM 2018. LNBIP, vol. 342, pp. 18–30. Springer, Cham (2019). https://doi.org/10.1007/978-3-030-11641-5_2

22. van Eck, M.L., Sidorova, N., van der Aalst, W.M.P.: Guided interaction exploration and performance analysis in artifact-centric process models. Bus. Inf. Syst. Eng. 61(6), 649–663 (2019). https://doi.org/10.1007/S12599-018-0546-0

23. Esser, S., Fahland, D.: Multi-dimensional event data in graph databases. J. Data Semant. 10(1–2), 109–141 (2021). https://doi.org/10.1007/S13740-021-00122-1

24. Fahland, D.: Describing behavior of processes with many-to-many interactions. In: Donatelli, S., Haar, S. (eds.) PETRI NETS 2019. LNCS, vol. 11522, pp. 3–24. Springer, Cham (2019). https://doi.org/10.1007/978-3-030-21571-2_1

25. Fahland, D.: Process mining over multiple behavioral dimensions with event knowledge graphs. In: Process Mining Handbook. LNBIP, vol. 448, pp. 274–319. Springer, Cham (2022). https://doi.org/10.1007/978-3-031-08848-3_9

26. Fahland, D., de Leoni, M., van Dongen, B.F., van der Aalst, W.M.P.: Behavioral conformance of artifact-centric process models. In: Abramowicz, W. (ed.) BIS 2011. LNBIP, vol. 87, pp. 37–49. Springer, Heidelberg (2011). https://doi.org/10.1007/978-3-642-21863-7_4

27. Fahland, D., de Leoni, M., van Dongen, B.F., van der Aalst, W.M.P.: Conformance checking of interacting processes with overlapping instances. In: Rinderle-Ma, S., Toumani, F., Wolf, K. (eds.) BPM 2011. LNCS, vol. 6896, pp. 345–361. Springer, Heidelberg (2011). https://doi.org/10.1007/978-3-642-23059-2_26

28. Fahland, D., et al.: Towards a simple and extensible standard for object-centric event data (OCED) - core model, design space, and lessons learned. CoRR abs/2410.14495 (2024). https://doi.org/10.48550/ARXIV.2410.14495

29. Ghilardi, S., Gianola, A., Montali, M., Rivkin, A.: Petri net-based object-centric processes with read-only data. Inf. Syst. **107**, 102011 (2022). https://doi.org/10.1016/J.IS.2022.102011

30. Ghilardi, S., Gianola, A., Montali, M., Rivkin, A.: Safety verification and universal invariants for relational action bases. In: IJCAI 2023, pp. 3248–3257. ijcai.org (2023). https://doi.org/10.24963/IJCAI.2023/362

31. Gianola, A.: Verification of Data-Aware Processes via Satisfiability Modulo Theories. LNBIP, vol. 470. Springer, Cham (2023). https://doi.org/10.1007/978-3-031-42746-6

32. Gianola, A., Montali, M., Winkler, S.: Object-centric processes with structured data and exact synchronization - formal modelling and conformance checking. In: CAiSE 2025. LNCS, vol. 15702, pp. 185–202. Springer, Cham (2025). https://doi.org/10.1007/978-3-031-94571-7_11

33. Guizzardi, G., Benevides, A.B., Fonseca, C.M., Porello, D., Almeida, J.P.A., Sales, T.P.: UFO: unified foundational ontology. Appl. Ontology **17**(1), 167–210 (2022). https://doi.org/10.3233/AO-210256

34. Jans, M., Soffer, P.: From relational database to event log: decisions with quality impact. In: Teniente, E., Weidlich, M. (eds.) BPM 2017. LNBIP, vol. 308, pp. 588–599. Springer, Cham (2018). https://doi.org/10.1007/978-3-319-74030-0_46

35. Klijn, E.L., Preuss, D., Imeri, L., Baumann, F., Mannhardt, F., Fahland, D.: Event knowledge graphs for auditing: a case study. In: ICPM 2023 Workshops. LNBIP, vol. 503, pp. 84–97. Springer, Cham (2023). https://doi.org/10.1007/978-3-031-56107-8_7

36. Künzle, V., Weber, B., Reichert, M.: Object-aware business processes: fundamental requirements and their support in existing approaches. Int. J. Inf. Syst. Model. Des. **2**(2), 19–46 (2011). https://doi.org/10.4018/JISMD.2011040102

37. Li, G., de Carvalho, R.M., van der Aalst, W.M.P.: Object-centric behavioral constraint models: a hybrid model for behavioral and data perspectives. In: Proceedings of SAC, pp. 48–56. ACM (2019). https://doi.org/10.1145/3297280.3297287

38. Liss, L., Adams, J.N., van der Aalst, W.M.P.: Object-centric alignments. In: Almeida, J.P.A., Borbinha, J., Guizzardi, G., Link, S., Zdravkovic, J. (eds.) Conceptual Modeling - 42nd International Conference, ER 2023, Lisbon, Portugal, 6–9 November 2023. LNCS, vol. 14320, pp. 201–219. Springer, Cham (2023). https://doi.org/10.1007/978-3-031-47262-6_11

39. Lu, X., Nagelkerke, M., van de Wiel, D., Fahland, D.: Discovering interacting artifacts from ERP systems. IEEE Trans. Serv. Comput. **8**(6), 861–873 (2015). https://doi.org/10.1109/TSC.2015.2474358

40. Müller, D., Reichert, M., Herbst, J.: Data-driven modeling and coordination of large process structures. In: Meersman, R., Tari, Z. (eds.) OTM 2007. LNCS, vol. 4803, pp. 131–149. Springer, Heidelberg (2007). https://doi.org/10.1007/978-3-540-76848-7_10

41. Nigam, A., Caswell, N.S.: Business artifacts: an approach to operational specification. IBM Syst. J. **42**(3), 428–445 (2003). https://doi.org/10.1147/sj.423.0428

42. Popova, V., Dumas, M.: Discovering unbounded synchronization conditions in artifact-centric process models. In: Lohmann, N., Song, M., Wohed, P. (eds.) BPM 2013. LNBIP, vol. 171, pp. 28–40. Springer, Cham (2014). https://doi.org/10.1007/978-3-319-06257-0_3

43. Redding, G., Dumas, M., ter Hofstede, A.H.M., Iordachescu, A.: A flexible, object-centric approach for business process modelling. Serv. Oriented Comput. Appl. **4**(3), 191–201 (2010). https://doi.org/10.1007/S11761-010-0065-4

44. Reijers, H.A., Rigter, J.H.M., van der Aalst, W.M.P.: The case handling case. Int. J. Cooperative Inf. Syst. **12**(3), 365–391 (2003). https://doi.org/10.1142/S0218843003000784

45. Ryndina, K., Küster, J.M., Gall, H.: Consistency of business process models and object life cycles. In: Kühne, T. (ed.) MODELS 2006. LNCS, vol. 4364, pp. 80–90. Springer, Heidelberg (2007). https://doi.org/10.1007/978-3-540-69489-2_11

46. Swevels, A., Fahland, D., Montali, M.: Implementing object-centric event data models in event knowledge graphs. In: ICPM 2023 Workshops. LNBIP, vol. 503, pp. 431–443. Springer, Cham (2023). https://doi.org/10.1007/978-3-031-56107-8_33

47. Verbeek, H.M.W., Buijs, J.C.A.M., van Dongen, B.F., van der Aalst, W.M.P.: XES, XESame, and ProM 6. In: Soffer, P., Proper, E. (eds.) CAiSE Forum 2010. LNBIP, vol. 72, pp. 60–75. Springer, Heidelberg (2011). https://doi.org/10.1007/978-3-642-17722-4_5

48. Weske, M.: Business Process Management - Concepts, Languages, Architectures, 3rd edn. Springer, Cham (2019). https://doi.org/10.1007/978-3-662-59432-2

49. Winter, K., Rinderle-Ma, S.: Defining instance spanning constraint patterns for business processes based on proclets. In: Dobbie, G., Frank, U., Kappel, G., Liddle, S.W., Mayr, H.C. (eds.) ER 2020. LNCS, vol. 12400, pp. 149–163. Springer, Cham (2020). https://doi.org/10.1007/978-3-030-62522-1_11

# Towards Object-Centric and Translucent Process Mining


Lukas Liss[(✉)] and Harry H. Beyel

RWTH Aachen University, Aachen, Germany
`{liss,beyel}@pads.rwth-aachen.de`



**Abstract.** Event data is the starting point for most process mining methods. In traditional process mining, events are assumed to belong to a single case identifier. Recently, concepts emerged that lift this assumption and extend the information captured in event data. Two of them are: object-centric process mining and translucent process mining. In object-centric process mining, events can be connected to multiple objects from different object types. This allows for capturing inter-object dependencies that are present in most real-world processes. In translucent process mining, each event also contains information on which activities could have been performed—besides the executed activity. Both approaches have proven to improve process mining tasks, such as process discovery and conformance checking. So far, they have only been investigated in isolation. In this paper, we propose a way to combine object-centric and translucent process mining. We provide a formalization for event data that is both object-centric and translucent. Also, we propose a research agenda for further investigating object-centric translucent process mining.

**Keywords:** Object-Centric Process Mining · Translucent Process Mining · Research Agenda


## 1   Introduction

*Process mining* deals with analyzing event logs, which can be extracted from organizations' databases [18,35]. A traditional case-centric event log, the data source for these techniques, is a collection of events, and each event consists of at least three attributes: a *case identifier*, an *activity*, and a *timestamp*. In process mining, event data are analyzed to gain insights into processes, with the overall goal of understanding and improving them [35]. Important to note is that such analyses are domain independent—the developed techniques can be applied to domains ranging from the healthcare sector, auditing, production, and the Internet of Things [32].

For many years, the assumption about event data was that it is case-centric and not translucent. This means that each recorded event belongs to exactly one case and only activities that actually happened are recorded. For example,



J. Mendling et al. (Eds.): Wil van der Aalst Festschrift, LNCS 16480, pp. 426–439, 2026.
https://doi.org/10.1007/978-3-032-17618-9_29

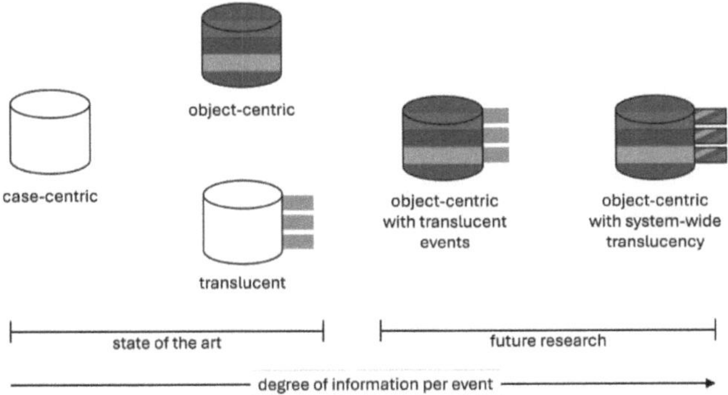


**Fig. 1.** Spectrum that captures the different degrees of adoption of object-centricity and translucency, annotated with the current state of the art and future research. Event data on the left of the spectrum allows for less information per event than event data concepts on the right side of the spectrum.

in a hospital, the sequence of events concerning patient treatment is investigated in isolation, without considering relationships to the involved physicians or machines. Moreover, information on what else could have been done besides the performed activity of an event is not utilized. This can be related to other treatment options that were available or the use of different machines. In recent years, two ideas emerged that extend the information that can be stored in event data. One of them is object-centric process mining [37] and another one is translucent process mining [36]. Event data that contains alternative options for the performed activities in the event data is called translucent event data [36]. For example, in the hospital process, information about other treatment steps that could have been taken at a given point in time would be considered, enabling the discovery of a better process model from the data [10]. Event data that includes other entities involved in the process, such as the physicians' event in the hospital example, is called object-centric event data [21]. Prof. Wil van der Aalst contributed significantly to both object-centric process mining [39] and translucent process mining [36]. Both ideas have proven to improve the performance across all common steps of a process mining analysis pipeline: process discovery [4], conformance checking [14], and process enhancement [16]. So far, the two ideas have only been investigated in isolation.

While both object-centric process mining and translucent process mining have individually shown improvements in process discovery, conformance checking, and enhancement, their benefits address different types of incompleteness in event data. Object-centric event data resolves issues arising from multi-entity behavior by capturing relations between objects and their dynamic attributes. Translucent event data, in contrast, provides information on enabled but not executed activities, allowing the derivation of more representative models from fewer observed events. Combining both ideas allows not only to track which objects were involved in an event, but also to understand what these objects could have done at that moment. This integration opens new possibilities for analyzing alternative behaviors of interacting objects, improving discovery in settings with sparse or incomplete data, and increasing the precision of conformance checking when object interactions or alternative paths are not fully observable. Hence, a unified perspective on object-centric and translucent event data offers analytical capabilities that extend beyond existing approaches.

In this paper, we propose a research agenda that combines these two ideas, working towards object-centric, translucent process mining. As a foundation, we define a spectrum that captures different degrees of adoption of the two concepts and propose a formal definition for the types of event logs that can result from integrating object-centricity and translucency. Figure 1 shows the spectrum with event data types on the left of the spectrum, allowing for less information per event, compared to those on the right side of the spectrum. Three of the five mentioned types of event data are already part of the current state-of-the-art research. These are case-centric, object-centric, and translucent event data. We introduce them formally in Sect. 3. The two remaining types of event data in Fig. 1 combine object-centric event data with translucency. They represent future research. We give formal definitions of the two types of object-centric translucent event data in Sect. 4. Based on the spectrum, we identified future research challenges that are described in Sect. 5. The conclusion is given in Sect. 6.

## 2   Related Work

Process mining covers analysis tasks such as process discovery, conformance checking, enhancement, and prediction [35]. Process discovery tries to derive a process model given event data that captures the process behavior [4]. In conformance checking, a normative process model is given as well as an event log that describes the real behavior. The algorithms investigate the degree to which actual behavior aligns with the desired normative behavior [14]. In enhancement tasks, the goal is to improve a given process model with additional information from a given event log [16]. The discovered or enhanced process models can then be used to predict future process behavior. All of these tasks incorporate event data in some form. The information contained in the event data influences the results that can be obtained [2,10].

Initially, event data was assumed to be case-centric, meaning that each event is connected to exactly one case of the process. There exists a standardized event data format for case-centric event logs, which is called XES [24]. Publicly accessible event logs enable benchmarking and algorithm evaluation. One prominent source of publicly accessible case-centric event data is the BPI challenges, which are used frequently within the community to compare and evaluate approaches [41]. Also, a variety of extraction [17] and simulation [31] approaches for case-centric event data exist, thereby increasing its accessibility. Over the years, many algorithms based on case-centric event data have been proposed for all tasks within process mining. The Alpha Miner [40] was the first discovery algorithm, which was followed by many more discovery algorithms like the Inductive Miner [26], Region-based Miner [5,19,20], and many more. Some of these discovery algorithms come with guarantees, such as fitness or soundness guarantees. To evaluate the result models, quality measures like fitness, precision, simplicity, and generalization are used [14]. Many algorithms in conformance checking are based on token-based replay [38] or alignments [3], with numerous approaches enhancing their runtime or capabilities [42]. All these algorithms assume case-centric event data.

In reality, it is often challenging to identify a single case notion because events involve multiple entities, such as the patient treated by a physician with the assistance of a nurse. To address this issue, object-centric process mining gained traction in recent years. This multiperspective view on processes allows tracking the behavior of multiple objects of different types throughout the process [21]. Different data formats have emerged. Object-centroc event log 2.0 format (OCEL 2.0) allows the capture of event-to-object relations with qualified relationships as well as objects with dynamic attribute values and qualified object-to-object relations [6]. Event knowledge graphs store object-centric event data in a graph structure, modeling the relations as arcs in the graph [34]. A subset of common object-centric characteristics emerged as the object-centric event data (OCED) standard [22]. The lack of publicly accessible object-centric event logs has been addressed recently by work about object-centric simulation [25] and extraction [30] This resulted in some publicly accessible object-centric event logs[1] that are commonly used to evaluate and benchmark algorithms. But there is still a lack of real-world object-centric event data. So far, initial approaches exist for most process mining tasks involving object-centric event data. For example, there are object-centric discovery approaches [15,29,39], and conformance checking methods [23,28].

The field of translucent process mining provides approaches for getting access to translucent event data and using information on enabled activities in process discovery and conformance checking. In [9], two approaches for accessing translucent event data are presented. One approach deals with using domain knowledge to add the information of enabled activities to a case-centric event log. The other approach involves recording user interactions in a desktop environment. By creating labeled templates and using template matching [13], the recordings are transformed into a translucent event log. This approach has been refined in [7], where no user input is required to transform the logs. In [36], the first discovery algorithm using a translucent event log is presented. Using information on events' enabled and executed activities, a transition system is created, used as input for region-based mining. In [10], translucent activity relationships are derived from a translucent event log. These are used to enhance directly-follows graphs used in the Inductive Miner [26]. In [12], the approach is extended to also work with the Inductive Miner—infrequent [27]. In [11], a precision-measuring technique using translucent event logs based on escaping edges is presented. In [8], translucent

---

[1] https://www.ocel-standard.org/event-logs/overview/.

alignments are presented, using information on enabled activities in the log and model.

Besides case-centric, object-centric, and translucent event data, further domains have proposed event data models that capture rich contextual information. User Interaction Event Data (UIED) describes low-level interaction events between a user and a hierarchical UI structure, linking each event to exactly one user and one UI target object, thereby emphasizing fine-grained interaction context rather than multi-object process relations [1]. Agent System Event Data (ASED) provides a complementary perspective by explicitly modeling agents, roles, and roleplays as first-class concepts, enabling events to be triggered by multiple agents acting in different organizational roles [33]. While these models capture multi-entity interaction structures, they fundamentally differ from object-centric event data, which organizes events around business objects and their qualified relations, and from translucent event data, which additionally stores information about enabled but non-executed activities. In contrast to object-centric event data's object-relation focus and the partial-visibility perspective of translucent logs, UIED is centered on userâĂŞinterface interactions, and ASED is centered on agentâĂŞroleâĂŞorganization structures.


## 3   Preliminaries

We define the universes needed to formalize the different types of event logs using the universe of strings $\mathbb{U}_\Sigma$ to be consistent with the OCEL 2.0 standard.

**Definition 1 (Universes [6]).** *Let $\mathbb{U}_\Sigma$ be the universe of strings. We define the following pairwise disjoint universes:*

- $\mathbb{U}_{ev} \subseteq \mathbb{U}_\Sigma$ *is the universe of events*
- $\mathbb{U}_{etype} \subseteq \mathbb{U}_\Sigma$ *is the universe event types (i.e. activities)*
- $\mathbb{U}_{obj} \subseteq \mathbb{U}_\Sigma$ *is the universe of objects*
- $\mathbb{U}_{otype} \subseteq \mathbb{U}_\Sigma$ *is the universe of object types*
- $\mathbb{U}_{attr} \subseteq \mathbb{U}_\Sigma$ *is the universe of attribute names*
- $\mathbb{U}_{val}$ *is the universe of attribute values*
- $\mathbb{U}_{time}$ *is the universe of timestamps*
- $\mathbb{U}_{qual} \subseteq \mathbb{U}_\Sigma$ *is the universe of qualifiers*


Given these universes, we can define a case-centric event log as a set of events, each with an activity and timestamp, mapped to exactly one case identifier. Additionally, the events can have attributes. Note that there exist other (also more compact) definitions for case-centric event logs, but the one presented here is harmonized with the definition of OCEL 2.0 event logs, which are a generalization of case-centric event logs.

**Definition 2 (Case-Centric Event Log).** *A case-centric event log is a tuple* $EL = (E, C, EA, \pi_{case}, \pi_{time}, \pi_{evtype}, \pi_{eatype}, \pi_{eaval})$ *where*

- $E \subseteq \mathbb{U}_{ev}$ *is a set of events*

- $C \subseteq \mathbb{U}_{obj}$ *is a set of case identifiers*
- $EA \subseteq \mathbb{U}_{attr}$ *is a set of event attributes*
- $\pi_{case} : E \to C$ *maps each event to one case identifier*
- $\pi_{time} : E \to \mathbb{U}_{time}$ *maps each event to a timestamp*
- $\pi_{evtype} : E \to \mathbb{U}_{etype}$ *maps each event to an activity*
- $\pi_{eatype} : EA \to \mathbb{U}_{etype}$ *maps each event attribute to an activity*
- $\pi_{eaval} : (E \times EA) \nrightarrow \mathbb{U}_{val}$ *maps an event attribute to a value*

An example of a case-centric event log is shown in Table 1. Each row represents an event. The first column shows the case identifier of the event, the second the activity, and the third the timestamp. There are no attributes in the example. This data format allows tracking what happens to the patients. The first case (patient *p01*) has first *admission, checkup,* and then *treatment B.* Out of this data, we can not derive what other treatments were possible or which doctor performed the treatment. Both types of information can be useful, as shown in the following.

**Table 1.** Example excerpt of a case-centric event log.

| case | activity | timestamp |
|---|---|---|
| p01 | admission | 01.01.25 13:15 |
| p02 | admission | 01.01.25 13:20 |
| p01 | checkup | 01.01.25 14:00 |
| p02 | checkup | 01.01.25 14:05 |
| p02 | treatment A | 01.01.25 14:10 |
| p01 | treatment B | 01.01.25 15:00 |

An object-centric event log lifts the assumption of a single case notion and enables events to be connected to multiple objects of different types. These objects can have attribute values that change over time. We used the OCEL 2.0 [6] definition here, which includes the object-centric characteristics defined in the OCED standard [22].

**Definition 3 (Object-Centric Event Log [6]).** *An Object-Centric Event Log (OCEL 2.0) is a tuple* $OCEL = (E, O, EA, OA, E2O, O2O, \pi_{time}, \pi_{evtype}, \pi_{objtype}, \pi_{eatype}, \pi_{oatype}, \pi_{eaval}, \pi_{oaval})$ *where*

- $O \subseteq \mathbb{U}_{obj}$ *is a set of objects*
- $OA \subseteq \mathbb{U}_{attr}$ *is a set of object attributes*
- $E2O \subseteq E \times \mathbb{U}_{qual} \times O$ *is a set of qualified event-to-object relations*
- $O2O \subseteq O \times \mathbb{U}_{qual} \times O$ *is a set of qualified object-to-object relations*
- $\pi_{objtype} : O \to \mathbb{U}_{otype}$ *maps each object to an object type*
- $\pi_{oatype} : OA \to \mathbb{U}_{otype}$ *maps each object attribute to an object type*

- $\pi_{oaval} : (O \times OA \times \mathbb{U}_{time}) \nrightarrow \mathbb{U}_{val}$ *maps an object attribute to a value*

*such that*

- $dom(\pi_{eaval}) \subseteq \{(e, ea) \in E \times EA \mid \pi_{evtype}(e) = \pi_{eatype}(ea)\}$ *and*
- $dom(\pi_{oaval}) \subseteq \{(o, oa, t) \in O \times OA \times \mathbb{U}_{time} \mid \pi_{objtype}(o) = \pi_{oatype}(oa)\}.$

An object-centric event log for the example process can be seen in Table 2. This representation allows for capturing object interactions. For example, one can see that the *chekup* event of patient *p01* involved doctor *d1* whereas patient *p02* was checked by doctor *d2*. The object-to-object relations show that doctor *d2* is authorised for machine *m1*, which is involved in *treatment A* and *treatment B* events. Also one can see that the doctors can change between checkup and the treatment, as they did for patient *p01*.

**Table 2.** Example excerpt of an object-centric event log. The event-to-object relations are shown on the left and the object-to-object relations are shown on the right.

| activity | timestamp | object types | | | source | qualifier | target |
|---|---|---|---|---|---|---|---|
| | | patient | doctor | machine | | | |
| admission | 01.01.25 13:15 | p01 | | | d2 | authorised | m1 |
| admission | 01.01.25 13:20 | p02 | | | | | |
| checkup | 01.01.25 14:00 | p01 | d1 | | | | |
| checkup | 01.01.25 14:05 | p02 | d2 | | | | |
| treatment A | 01.01.25 14:10 | p02 | d2 | m1 | | | |
| treatment B | 01.01.25 15:00 | p01 | d2 | m1 | | | |

Translucent event logs also extend traditional case-centric event data by storing enabled activities for each event.

**Definition 4 (Translucent Event Log [36]).** *A translucent event log is a tuple* $EL = (E, C, EA, \pi_{case}, \pi_{time}, \pi_{evtype}, \pi_{eatype}, \pi_{eaval}, \pi_{en})$ *where*

- $\pi_{en} : E \to \mathcal{P}(\mathbb{U}_{etype})$ *maps an event to the set of enabled activities such that the executed activity is part of the enabled activities* $\forall e \in E : \pi_{evtype} \in \pi_{en}.$

An example of a translucent event log is shown in Table 3. For the same hospital process, we denote that the patient could also have been declined in the beginning, although we did not see that happening in the excerpt. Also, it can be observed that the patient *p02* could have also been treated with *treatment B* and *treatment C*.

**Table 3.** Example excerpt of a translucent event log.

| case | activity | timestamp | enabled activities |
|------|----------|-----------|--------------------|
| p01 | admission | 01.01.25 13:15 | admission, decline |
| p02 | admission | 01.01.25 13:20 | admission, decline |
| p01 | checkup | 01.01.25 14:00 | checkup |
| p02 | checkup | 01.01.25 14:05 | checkup |
| p02 | treatment A | 01.01.25 14:10 | treatment A, treatment B, treatment C |
| p01 | treatment B | 01.01.25 15:00 | treatment A, treatment B, treatment C |

# 4  Object-Centric Translucent Process Data

In this section, we introduce how the concept behind the translucent event logs can be merged with object-centric events. We showed that object-centric event data is connected to multiple objects. Based on this, we introduce two approaches to extend object-centric data with translucency. The first one deals with introducing translucency to the objects in isolation. The second one is about introducing multi-object translucent events.

## 4.1  Object-Centric Event Data with Object-Based Translucency

While object-centric event data highlights which objects are used together in an event, it is unclear what the involved objects would have done otherwise. Object-based translucency bridges this gap by adding what activities could have been done for each object in isolation.

**Definition 5 (OCEL with object translucency).** *An object-centric event log with event-translucency is a tuple $EL_{obj-transl} = (OCEL, \pi_{obj-transl})$ with an object centric event log $OCEL = (E, O, EA, OA, E2O, O2O, \pi_{time}, \pi_{evtype}, \pi_{objtype}, \pi_{eatype}, \pi_{oatype}, \pi_{eaval}, \pi_{oaval})$ where:*

- *$\pi_{obj-transl} : E \rightarrow \mathcal{P}(O \times \mathcal{P}(\mathbb{U}_{etype}))$ such that $\forall e \in E : \{o \mid (e, q, o) \in E2O\} = \{o \mid (o, X) \in \pi_{obj-transl}(e)\}$ maps an event to a mapping from each objects of the event to its enabled activities.*

An example is shown in Table 4. For each object, enabled activities are listed that a specific object could have performed besides the one performed. When comparing to the data shown in Table 2, we can observe that physicians can leave. In addition, *d1* can perform *treatment C* instead of performing no treatment at all. Additionally, the excerpt indicates that *d1* is the only one to perform this treatment, as it is not possible to do this for *d2*. In general, object-based translucency allows for inspecting enabled activities for objects independent of an event's associated objects. At the same time, it is unclear which objects are involved in each possible action.

**Table 4.** Example excerpt of an object-centric event log with object-based translucency.

| activity | timestamp | object types | | doctor | | machine | |
|---|---|---|---|---|---|---|---|
| | | patient | | | | | |
| | | E2O | enabled | E2O | enabled | E2O | enabled |
| admission | 01.01.25 13:15 | p01 | p01: decline | | | | |
| admission | 01.01.25 13:20 | p02 | p02: decline | | | | |
| checkup | 01.01.25 14:00 | p01 | | d1 | d1: treatment C, leave | | |
| checkup | 01.01.25 14:05 | p02 | | d2 | d2: treatment A, treatment B, leave | | |
| treatment A | 01.01.25 14:10 | p02 | p02: treatment B, treatment C | d2 | d2: checkup, treatment B, leave | m1 | m1: treatment B |
| treatment B | 01.01.25 15:00 | p01 | p01: treatment A, treatment C | d2 | d2: checkup, treatment A, leave | m1 | m1: treatment A |

## 4.2 Object-Centric Event Data with Event-Based Translucency

Event-based translucency highlights which other activities the objects involved could have performed for each event. It is important to note that other object-centric events are highlighted there; i.e., all objects involved in the execution of an activity are known. The following captures this.

**Definition 6 (OCEL with event translucency).** *An object-centric event log with event-translucency is a tuple $EL_{ev-transl} = (OCEL, \pi_{ev-transl})$ with object centric event log $OCEL = (E, O, EA, OA, E2O, O2O, \pi_{time}, \pi_{evtype},$ $\pi_{objtype}, \pi_{eatype}, \pi_{oatype}, \pi_{eaval}, \pi_{oaval})$ where:*

- $\pi_{ev-transl} : E \to \mathcal{P}(\mathbb{U}_{etype} \times \mathcal{P}(\mathbb{U}_{obj}))$ *maps an event to a set of tuples that represent enabled object-centric events.*

An example is shown in Table 5. In the third row, it is shown that another object-centric event would involve *p01*, *d1*, and the activity *treatment C (tr C)* or a *leave* activity that involves only doctor *d1*.

In general, the scope of enabled events can be restricted based on the event's objects. Event-based translucency can be divided into three categories:

- *Closed*: For each object-centric event, associated enabled object-centric events can only cover the objects present in the event,
- *Partially-closed*: For each object-centric event, associated enabled object-centric events have to cover at least one object present in the event, and can also include other objects,
- *Open*: For each object-centric event, associated enabled object-centric events can include arbitrary objects

The object-centric event data with event-based translucency in Table 5 is partially-closed because the last event does not involve *d1*, but some of its enabled events do. The first four events can also be considered closed.

**Table 5.** Example excerpt of an object-centric event log with event-aware translucency.

| activity | timestamp | object types | | | enabled |
|---|---|---|---|---|---|
| | | patient | doctor | machine | |
| admission | 01.01.25 13:15 | p01 | | | (decline, {p01}) |
| admission | 01.01.25 13:20 | p02 | | | (decline, {p02}) |
| checkup | 01.01.25 14:00 | p01 | d1 | | (tr C, {p01, d1}),<br>(leave, {d1}) |
| checkup | 01.01.25 14:05 | p02 | d2 | | (tr C, {p02, d2}),<br>(leave, {d2}) |
| tr A | 01.01.25 14:10 | p02 | d2 | m1 | (tr B, {p02, d2, m1}),<br>(tr C, {p02, d1}),<br>(leave, {d2}) |
| tr B | 01.01.25 15:00 | p01 | d2 | m1 | (tr A, {p01, d2, m1}),<br>(tr C, {p01, d2}),<br>(leave, {d2}) |

# 5  Challenges

In this section, we present challenges that are related to combining object-centric
event data with the concept of translucency. For each challenge, we highlight
its importance and discuss potential solutions. Addressing these challenges is
worthwhile because integrating object-centricity and translucency provides complementary information: object-centric event data reveals how multiple objects
jointly contribute to process behavior, while translucent event data captures
alternative activities and object-centric events that were possible but unobserved. Together, these dimensions enable more informed discovery and conformance techniques, particularly in settings where behavior is only partially
visible or where object interactions drive process variability.

## 5.1  Data Availability

Data availability is essential for a vast majority of process mining techniques.
As discussed, classic translucent event data can be assessed from screenshots
in a desktop environment or by utilizing domain knowledge. The extraction
of object-centric event data with event-based translucency iterates on this. As
shown in Fig. 2, such data can be accessed by tracking objects visible on the
screen. Examples are the course name in the heading, the username, and the
document. By considering the layout information in the UI, one can derive which
objects are involved in certain events that are triggered by clicks in the UI. Thus,
there exists a need to extend existing approaches for extracting real-life object-
centric event data with object- and event-based translucency. This is a necessary
foundation for developing techniques that can handle this type of data.

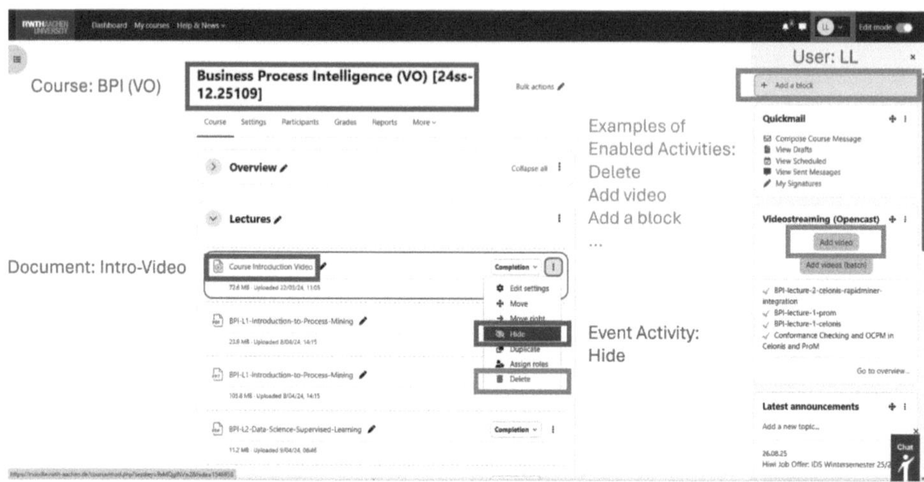

**Fig. 2.** Example of object-centric and event-based translucent event data extraction.

## 5.2 Data Format

As demonstrated in the past, having a standardized data format that enables interoperability and collaboration has led to advances in the field, resulting in unified efforts. Hence, having a standard data format for object-centric translucent event data allows for an acceleration in research and industry applications.

## 5.3 Process Discovery

Process discovery is an important field in process mining. As shown before, both fields have isolated approaches for discovering process models from their event data. In [10], it is demonstrated that fewer events are required to discover a more representative process model when the event contains information about enabled activities. Hence, a discovery approach for object-centric event data with translucency seems a right follow-up. However, until such an approach exists, it remains open whether the individual advantages of each field are also visible when they are combined.

## 5.4 Conformance Checking

Conformance checking is an essential field in process mining for quantifying a process model's quality with respect to an event log. The individual efforts of the field enabled better quantification. When a new type of data is available, there is a need for techniques that can use these data to quantify how well the model represents them.

# 6    Conclusion

As discussed, translucent event logs and object-centric event logs extend traditional process mining in meaningful ways. By combining these areas, more representative process models can be discovered, and the quantification of their quality can be improved. In addition, organizations' processes can be better understood, leading to actionable insights. At the same time, the data for these techniques has to be made available, a data format has to be developed, and techniques in the area of process discovery and conformance checking have to be developed.

# References


1. Abb, L., Rehse, J.R.: A reference data model for process-related user interaction logs. In: Di Ciccio, C., Dijkman, R., del Río Ortega, A., Rinderle-Ma, S. (eds.) BPM 2022. LNCS, vol. 13420, pp. 57–74. Springer, Cham (2022). https://doi.org/10.1007/978-3-031-16103-2_7
2. Adams, J.N., et al.: Discovering high-quality process models despite data scarcity. In: ER Forum. CEUR-WS.org (2023)
3. Adriansyah, A.: Aligning observed and modeled behavior. Technische Universiteit Eindhoven (2014)
4. Augusto, A., et al.: Automated discovery of process models from event logs: review and benchmark. IEEE Trans. Knowl. Data Eng. **31**(4), 686–705 (2019)
5. Bergenthum, R., Desel, J., Lorenz, R., Mauser, S.: Process mining based on regions of languages. In: Alonso, G., Dadam, P., Rosemann, M. (eds.) BPM 2007. LNCS, vol. 4714, pp. 375–383. Springer, Heidelberg (2007). https://doi.org/10.1007/978-3-540-75183-0_27
6. Berti, A., et al.: OCEL (object-centric event log) 2.0 specification. CoRR, abs/2403.01975 (2024)
7. Beyel, H.H., Manuel, S., van der Aalst, W.M.P.: Activitygen: extracting enabled activities from screenshots. In: ECAI, pp. 712–720. IOS Press (2024)
8. Beyel, H.H., Schwanen, C.T., van der Aalst, W.M.P.: Translucent alignments. In: Krogstie, J., Rinderle-Ma, S., Kappel, G., Proper, H.A. (eds.) CAiSE 2025. LNCS, vol. 15702, pp. 167–184. Springer, Cham (2025). https://doi.org/10.1007/978-3-031-94571-7_10
9. Beyel, H.H., van der Aalst, W.M.P.: Creating translucent event logs to improve process discovery. In: Montali, M., Senderovich, A., Weidlich, M. (eds.) ICPM 2022. LNBIP, vol. 468, pp. 435–447. Springer, Cham (2023). https://doi.org/10.1007/978-3-031-27815-0_32
10. Beyel, H.H., van der Aalst, W.M.P.: Improving process discovery using translucent activity relationships. In: Marrella, A., Resinas, M., Jans, M., Rosemann, M. (eds.) BPM 2024. LNCS, vol. 14940, pp. 146–163. Springer, Cham (2024). https://doi.org/10.1007/978-3-031-70396-6_9
11. Beyel, H.H., van der Aalst, W.M.P.: Translucent precision: exploiting enabling information to evaluate the quality of process models. In: Araújo, J., de la Vara, J.L., Santos, M.Y., Assar, S. (eds.) RCIS 2024. LNBIP, vol. 514, pp. 29–37. Springer, Cham (2024). https://doi.org/10.1007/978-3-031-59468-7_4
12. Beyel, H.H., van der Aalst, W.M.P.: Using translucent activity relationships frequencies to enhance process discovery. Process Sci. **2**(1) (2025)

13. Brunelli, R.: Template Matching Techniques in Computer Vision: Theory and Practice. Wiley, Hoboken (2009)
14. Carmona, J., van Dongen, B.F., Solti, A., Weidlich, M.: Conformance Checking - Relating Processes and Models. Springer, Cham (2018)
15. Christfort, A.K., Rivkin, A., Fahland, D., Hildebrandt, T.T., Slaats, T.: Discovery of object-centric declarative models. In: ICPM, pp. 121–128. IEEE (2024)
16. de Leoni, M.: Foundations of process enhancement. In: van der Aalst, W.M.P., Carmona, J. (eds.) Process Mining Handbook. LNBIP, vol. 448, pp. 243–273. Springer, Cham (2022). https://doi.org/10.1007/978-3-031-08848-3_8
17. Diba, K., Batoulis, K., Weidlich, M., Weske, M.: Extraction, correlation, and abstraction of event data for process mining. WIREs Data Mining Knowl. Discov. **10**(3) (2020)
18. Dumas, M., La Rosa, M., Mendling, J., Reijers, H.A.: Fundamentals of Business Process Management, 2nd edn. Springer, Cham (2018)
19. Ehrenfeucht, A., Rozenberg, G.: Partial (set) 2-structures. Part I: basic notions and the representation problem. Acta Informatica **27**(4), 315–342 (1990)
20. Ehrenfeucht, A., Rozenberg, G.: Partial (set) 2-structures. Part II: state spaces of concurrent systems. Acta Informatica **27**(4), 343–368 (1990)
21. Fahland, D.: Process mining over multiple behavioral dimensions with event knowledge graphs. In: van der Aalst, W.M.P., Carmona, J. (eds.) Process Mining Handbook. LNBIP, vol. 448, pp. 274–319. Springer, Cham (2022). https://doi.org/10.1007/978-3-031-08848-3_9
22. Fahland, D., et al.: Towards a simple and extensible standard for object-centric event data (OCED) - core model, design space, and lessons learned. CoRR, abs/2410.14495 (2024)
23. Gianola, A., Montali, M., Winkler, S.: Object-centric conformance alignments with synchronization. In: Guizzardi, G., Santoro, F., Mouratidis, H., Soffer, P. (eds.) CAiSE 2024. LNCS, vol. 14663, pp. 3–19. Springer, Cham (2024). https://doi.org/10.1007/978-3-031-61057-8_1
24. Gunther, C.W., Verbeek, H.M.W.: XES-standard definition (2014)
25. Knopp, B., Pourbafrani, M., van der Aalst, W.M.P.: Discovering object-centric process simulation models. In: ICPM, pp. 81–88. IEEE (2023)
26. Leemans, S.J.J., Fahland, D., van der Aalst, W.M.P.: Discovering block-structured process models from event logs - a constructive approach. In: Colom, J.-M., Desel, J. (eds.) PETRI NETS 2013. LNCS, vol. 7927, pp. 311–329. Springer, Heidelberg (2013). https://doi.org/10.1007/978-3-642-38697-8_17
27. Leemans, S.J.J., Fahland, D., van der Aalst, W.M.P.: Discovering block-structured process models from event logs containing infrequent behaviour. In: Lohmann, N., Song, M., Wohed, P. (eds.) BPM 2013. LNBIP, vol. 171, pp. 66–78. Springer, Cham (2014). https://doi.org/10.1007/978-3-319-06257-0_6
28. Liss, L., Adams, J.N., van der Aalst, W.M.P.: Object-centric alignments. In: Almeida, J.P.A., Borbinha, J., Guizzardi, G., Link, S., Zdravkovic, J. (eds.) ER 2023. LNCS, vol. 14320, pp. 201–219. Springer, Cham (2023). https://doi.org/10.1007/978-3-031-47262-6_11
29. Liss, L., Adams, J.N., van der Aalst, W.M.P.: TOTeM: temporal object type model for object-centric process mining. In: Marrella, A., Resinas, M., Jans, M., Rosemann, M. (eds.) BPM 2024. LNBIP, vol. 526, pp. 107–123. Springer, Cham (2024). https://doi.org/10.1007/978-3-031-70418-5_7
30. Liss, L., Elbert, N., Flath, C.M., van der Aalst, W.M.P.: Framework for extracting real-world object-centric event logs from game data. In: Delgado, A., Slaats, T.

(eds.) ICPM 2024. LNBIP, vol. 533, pp. 363–375. Springer, Cham (2025). https://doi.org/10.1007/978-3-031-82225-4_27
31. Martin, N., Depaire, B., Caris, A.: The use of process mining in a business process simulation context: overview and challenges. In: CIDM, pp. 381–388. IEEE (2014)
32. Reinkemeyer, L.: Process mining in action. In: Process Mining in Action Principles, Use Cases and Outloook, vol. 11, no. 7, pp. 116–128 (2020)
33. Shen, Q., Polyvyanyy, A., Lipovetzky, N., Kampik, T.: Agent system event data: concepts, dimensions, applications. In: Maass, W., Han, H., Yasar, H., Multari, N. (eds.) ER 2024. LNCS, vol. 15238, pp. 56–72. Springer, Cham (2025). https://doi.org/10.1007/978-3-031-75872-0_4
34. Swevels, A., Fahland, D., Montali, M.: Implementing object-centric event data models in event knowledge graphs. In: De Smedt, J., Soffer, P. (eds.) ICPM 2023. LNBIP, vol. 503, pp. 431–443. Springer, Cham (2024). https://doi.org/10.1007/978-3-031-56107-8_33
35. van der Aalst, W.M.P.: Process Mining - Data Science in Action, 2nd edn. Springer, Cham (2016)
36. van der Aalst, W.M.P.: Lucent process models and translucent event logs. Fundam. Informaticae **169**(1–2), 151–177 (2019)
37. Aalst, W.M.P.: Object-centric process mining: dealing with divergence and convergence in event data. In: Ölveczky, P.C., Salaün, G. (eds.) SEFM 2019. LNCS, vol. 11724, pp. 3–25. Springer, Cham (2019). https://doi.org/10.1007/978-3-030-30446-1_1
38. van der Aalst, W.M.P., Adriansyah, A., van Dongen, B.F.: Replaying history on process models for conformance checking and performance analysis. WIREs Data Mining Knowl. Discov. **2**(2), 182–192 (2012)
39. van der Aalst, W.M.P., Berti, A.: Discovering object-centric petri nets. Fundam. Informaticae **175**(1–4), 1–40 (2020)
40. van der Aalst, W.M.P., Weijters, T., Maruster, L.: Workflow mining: discovering process models from event logs. IEEE Trans. Knowl. Data Eng. **16**(9), 1128–1142 (2004)
41. van Dongen, B.: Real-life event logs - hospital log (2011)
42. Dongen, B.F.: Efficiently computing alignments. In: Weske, M., Montali, M., Weber, I., vom Brocke, J. (eds.) BPM 2018. LNCS, vol. 11080, pp. 197–214. Springer, Cham (2018). https://doi.org/10.1007/978-3-319-98648-7_12

# Bridging the Granularity Gap: From Fine-Grained Events to Coarse-Grained Process Models

R. P. Jagadeesh Chandra Bose[✉]

Skan Inc., Menlo Park, CA, USA
jcbose@gmail.com

**Abstract.** Event logs obtained from modern information systems often record data at a very fine level of granularity. This can lead to traces containing hundreds of distinct low-level activities, resulting in process models that are far too complex for human comprehension. Empirical evidence suggests that analysts can effectively interpret models with at most a few dozen nodes, highlighting the need for higher-level abstractions. This challenge is even more pronounced in task mining, where detailed user click streams are analyzed. Bridging the gap between fine-grained events and meaningful process activities and/or tasks is therefore crucial for generating actionable insights. In this paper, we propose an iterative, hierarchical framework that combines pattern based activity-interaction graphs with community detection algorithms for clustering coherent sets of activities. These clusters are automatically labeled with concise, human-readable task names using LLMs, bridging the gap between structural abstraction and semantic interpretability. The resulting abstractions not only reduce model complexity but also enhance interpretability, enabling process mining to provide more meaningful and business-relevant insights.

## 1 Introduction

Process mining has emerged as a powerful paradigm for uncovering, analyzing, and improving business processes based on event data captured from enterprise information systems. Most organizations routinely collect massive volumes of digital traces from modern information systems each recording a multitude of activities (in the order of hundreds and thousands) executed during process execution [16]. Although such fine-granular data offers greater visibility into process behavior, it also poses a significant challenge; the resulting process models often become overwhelmingly complex, spaghetti-like, and hard to comprehend, thereby limiting their practical value for stakeholders [16].

This issue reflects what we term the *granularity gap*, the disconnect between the fine-grained nature of recorded event data and the coarse-grained abstractions needed for effective process understanding and decision support. Bridging


J. Mendling et al. (Eds.): Wil van der Aalst Festschrift, LNCS 16480, pp. 440–453, 2026.
https://doi.org/10.1007/978-3-032-17618-9_30

this gap is crucial for transforming data-level observations into meaningful process knowledge. Traditional techniques such as activity filtering or manual aggregation are often ad hoc and insufficient to systematically reduce this complexity while preserving behavioral and semantic coherence.

The challenge has become even more pronounced with the rise of task mining, an emerging discipline that extends process mining to the user-interaction level or *clickstream* data [16]. Task mining captures detailed, low-level events generated through human-computer interactions, such as mouse clicks, keystrokes, and window switches, during task execution. Although this opens new opportunities to analyze operational work patterns, it also aggravates the granularity problem: task mining logs may contain hundreds or thousands of unique low-level actions. This calls for the need for robust abstraction mechanisms that can transform raw interactions into semantically meaningful process representations.

Existing event abstraction methods effectively reduce model complexity and, in some cases, preserve behavioral fidelity. However, they often rely on domain knowledge [1,9,10], manual labeling, or supervised training [13], limiting scalability and generalizability. Moreover, most approaches struggle to provide semantically meaningful, human-readable task labels and rarely support iterative or hierarchical abstraction for logs with very large activity vocabularies.

In this paper, we extend our earlier work [2,3] and propose a framework for bridging the granularity gap—from fine-grained events (as found in both traditional process logs and user-interaction logs) to coarse-grained, interpretable process models. The proposed approach discovers common execution patterns in event data and represents them as pattern-activity graph. Graph-based community detection techniques are then applied to identify clusters of closely related activities that correspond to higher-level process tasks. Each discovered cluster is then semantically labeled using large language models (LLMs), which combine a linguistic and contextual understanding to generate concise, human-readable task names. Through iterative abstraction, the framework produces hierarchical representations improving comprehensibility. Furthermore, the proposed approach acts as a unifying bridge between process mining and task mining, helping organizations move from fragmented, low-level observations to coherent, high-level process insights.

The remainder of the paper is structured as follows. Section 2 reviews the related work, while Sect. 3 presents our proposed iterative framework. Section 4 reports experimental results, and Sect. 5 concludes the paper.

## 2 Related Work

Despite significant progress in process mining, event abstraction remains a challenging problem in deriving human-understandable models from fine-grained event data. One of the earliest works, notably by Bose and van der Aalst [2,3], characterized the manifestation of process model constructs (sequence, choice, loop) in the event log and proposed patterns to form abstractions. It uses subsumption based grouping of patterns. This approach doesn't address the semantic relevance of the groups and an automated naming of the tasks. Bridging abstraction layers in process mining [1] relies on domain knowledge and process documentation to map low-level events to high-level activities. Knowledge-based trace abstraction [10] and multi-level semantic labeling in medical processes [11] demonstrate the benefits of semantic enrichment. However, they often rely on pre-defined ontologies or domain expertise, reducing generalizability across heterogeneous logs or task-mining datasets and are difficult to scale to dynamic, poorly documented, or evolving processes. Information-preserving methods [9] and trace correlation approaches [7] focus on maintaining behavioral fidelity but do not provide human-readable, semantically meaningful task labels. Supervised methods [13] can infer semantic mappings but require extensive labeled data, limiting applicability to new domains or high-activity logs. Recent advancements have explored hierarchical and unsupervised abstractions to enhance scalability and interpretability. Li et al. [12] introduced an activity instance-based hierarchical framework that iteratively abstracts logs by grouping similar event classes using earth mover's distance and extracting instances via oracles for class identification and case segmentation. Empirical studies have further illuminated trade-offs in these techniques. Van Houdt et al. [15] evaluated unsupervised methods, such as local process model-based and session-based abstractions, on 400 artificial logs, revealing a fitness-precision-complexity trade-off where abstractions improve comprehensibility but may distort behavioral fidelity.

Van Zelst et al. [16] conducted a comprehensive literature review of 21 techniques, introducing a multi-dimensional taxonomy that classifies methods by supervision strategy (supervised vs. unsupervised), event interleaving (sequential vs. concurrent), probabilistic outcomes, data nature (discrete vs. continuous), use of alternative perspectives (e.g., time or resources), and mappings between event and activity classes/instances (e.g., n:1 or n:m). Their analysis underscores the prevalence of supervised methods, which leverage domain knowledge for accuracy but limit scalability, while highlighting gaps in unsupervised approaches for continuous data and online mining. Despite advances in process mining, existing event abstraction techniques face three major limitations: (i) reliance on domain knowledge or manual labeling, which limits applicability in dynamic or poorly documented processes, (ii) lack of semantic interpretability, with most methods producing structurally correct but human-unreadable abstractions, and (iii) limited scalability for logs with very large activity vocabularies, including task-mining traces capturing fine-grained user interactions.

To address these gaps, this paper builds upon our earlier work [2,3] and proposes a unified, iterative framework that combines behavioral abstraction via activity-interaction graphs and community detection with semantic labeling using large language models (LLMs). By recursively applying this approach, the framework generates hierarchical, coarse-grained process models that preserve essential behavioral semantics while remaining interpretable and compact.

# 3   Iterative Event Abstraction Framework

Our approach to bridging the granularity gap in event logs, summarized in Fig. 1, draws inspiration from the hierarchical organization of biological systems, where individual cells form tissues, tissues combine into organs, and organs collectively create functional systems. In this analogy, fine-grained event logs, capturing individual activities or user actions, act as the "cells" of a process. These atomic events can be grouped into recurring patterns that correspond to tasks or sub-processes, forming "microstructures" akin to tissues. Aggregating these microstructures based on their interrelationships and co-occurrence across traces produces higher-level *macro-processes*, analogous to organs, which capture functional coherence and support interpretability. By systematically abstracting event logs across these layers, from low-level events to tasks, to patterns of task interactions (sub-processes), and finally to high-level macro-process structures, our framework allows analysts to transition seamlessly from raw, complex event data to clear, actionable insights into process behavior.

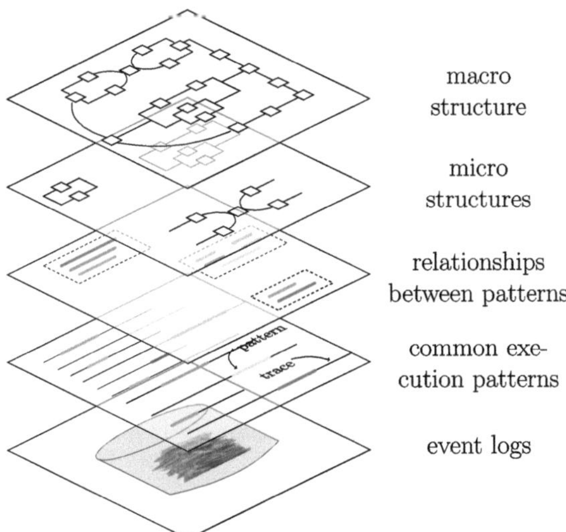


**Fig. 1.** Bridging the granularity gap: event logs are systematically aggregated from atomic actions to interpretable process structures.

## 3.1   Discovering Higher Level Tasks Using Patterns and Communities

This section presents our abstraction framework from event logs based on common execution patterns. The building blocks of the framework are shown in Fig. 2.

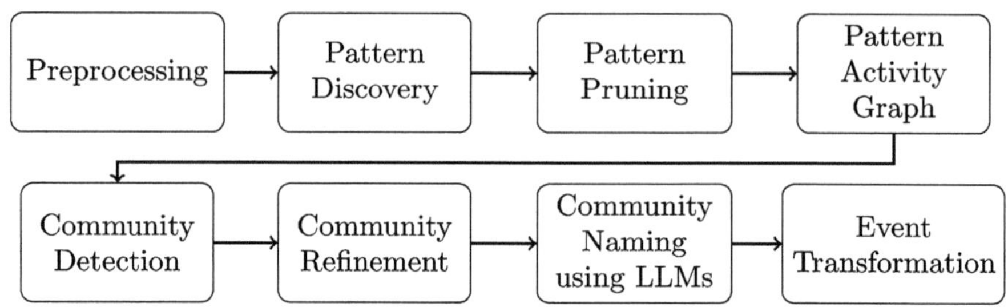

**Fig. 2.** Building blocks of the event abstraction framework.

– **Preprocessing:** This stage aims to enhance the quality, consistency, and usability of raw event logs by addressing issues such as data noise, sparsity, and heterogeneity. It includes the following steps:
  - *Activity filtering:* Activities that are statistically insignificant or introduce noise are removed. Specifically, activities whose relative frequency (that is, total number of occurrences in the log) or case coverage (i.e., proportion of unique traces or cases in which the activity appears) falls below a predefined threshold $\theta$ are filtered. This step reduces noise and computational complexity. Additionally, activities identified as purely technical or non-essential to the main process logic (e.g., frequent returns to a landing or home page in task mining) are also excluded.
  - *Loop reduction:* Repeated consecutive occurrences of the same event within a case are replaced by a single instance, thus simplifying the trace while preserving behavioral semantics.
  - *Data partitioning (for heterogeneous logs):* When the event log captures diverse behaviors, such as traces from different user groups or functionalities, trace clustering methods have been shown to be effective [4,6]. Trace clustering divides the log into several homogeneous sublogs. This ensures that subsequent pattern discovery is performed on more coherent and comparable datasets.
– **Pattern Discovery:** This stage identifies patterns (recurrent sequences of activities) within the preprocessed logs. A pattern is a regularity in an event log. Such a regularity implies a sense of strong correlation between the elements (e.g., activities) involved in the pattern. We define two types of patterns
  - *Maximal repeats:* These are the longest sequences of activities that appear repeatedly within the log. They represent stable, recurring behavioral blocks. These can be efficiently discovered in linear time and space (over the length of the event log) using suffix trees. For a more formal definition, the user is referred to [2]
  - *Navigation patterns:* These patterns are particularly relevant in contexts like task mining. They are typically defined by a change of context e.g., transition between application screens such as the different tabs within an application or the navigation through menu items or a change of appli-

cation or a change of user within a single trace, signaling a boundary or shift in the executed task.

Once the patterns are discovered, we merge similar patterns based on the pattern alphabets. Patterns are considered similar and merged if they are defined over the exact same set of underlying activities, regardless of their precise sequence or length. For example, both the patterns abdc and abcd are defined over the same alphabet (i.e., set of activities) {a, b, c, d}. This abstracts the specific pattern instance to its constituent activity set, enabling analysis on a common vocabulary. We compute pattern frequencies both for patterns and pattern alphabets. The occurrence of each pattern is quantified using two principal metrics:

- *Overlapping count:* counts every instance of the pattern, even if it overlaps with a preceding or succeeding instance.
- *Non-Overlapping count:* counts only independent, non-overlapping occurrences, providing a more conservative measure of discrete task executions.

- **Pattern Pruning:** This step refines the set of discovered patterns by removing those deemed insignificant or overly specific, ensuring focus on robust, meaningful behaviors. We adopt two pruning strategies:
  - *Infrequent pattern filtering:* patterns whose frequency (e.g., overlapping count) or whose case percentage falls below a threshold $\theta_{\text{pat\_freq}}$ are discarded.
  - *Short Pattern Filtering:* patterns or pattern alphabets shorter than a specified minimum length $l_{\text{min}}$ are removed, as they often lack the necessary detail to represent a complete, meaningful sub-task.

- **Pattern Activity Graph:** The retained patterns are used to construct a Pattern Activity Graph (PAG), $G = (V, E)$ where $V$, the set of nodes, is defined over *only* the activities involved in the patterns and the edges represent the direct or sequential flow observed in the patterns. An edge between $a_1$ and $a_2$ is drawn if the subsequence $a_1 a_2$ is involved in a pattern with the edge weights indicating the frequency that this subsequence manifests in the preprocessed log.

- **Community Detection:** The fundamental principle of community detection is to partition a graph such that connections within groups are denser than connections between groups. A dense cluster of activities (nodes) in the PAG implies that these activities are executed repeatedly in close proximity or consecutively within the overall process flow, i.e., they exhibit a high degree of cohesion. We recommend two community detection algorithms, e.g.: Louvain and Leiden [14] for their proven scalability, speed, and high modularity yield. The communities form the basis of our abstractions and each community defines a higher-level task (or sub-process).

- **Community Refinement:** This stage refines the output of the community detection step by addressing two critical issues: (a) statistical insignificance and (b) the rigid, non-overlapping nature of most modularity-based algorithms (Fig. 3).

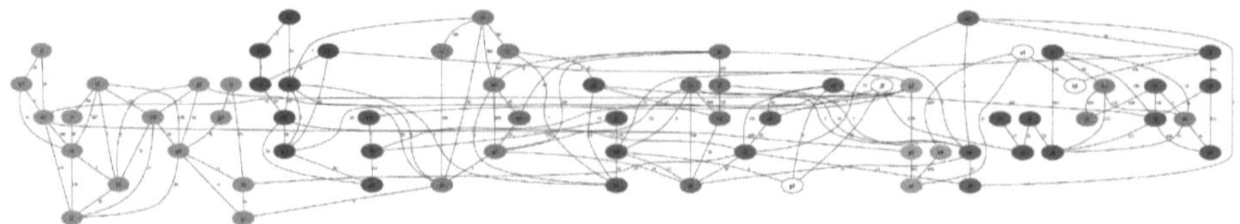

**Fig. 3.** The pattern activity graph and the communities formed. Each community is depicted in a different color.

- *Community pruning:* Communities that are deemed statistically or structurally insignificant are removed. This typically includes communities that contain too few activities (nodes) or whose aggregate frequency (the sum of all edge frequencies within the community) falls below a minimal threshold $\theta_{\mathrm{comm_{freq}}}$. This ensures that the resulting high-level groups are based only on well-supported, frequent behaviors.
- *Handling context-dependent activities:* Community detection algorithms produce non-overlapping clusters (an activity belongs to exactly one community). However, real-world processes often contain context-dependent activities or "bridge" activities that participate in multiple, distinct high-level tasks. To address this, a post-processing analysis is implemented during the pruning stage. We identify activities that show strong sequential ties (high edge weights in the PAG) to activities belonging to multiple distinct communities. The activity is analyzed against the functional definition (community name) of its top N connected communities. If the activity is semantically or structurally relevant to more than one high-level task, it is intentionally assigned to multiple communities. For example, the activity `Save Document` might be a valid component of both the `Approve Loan` community and the `Close Account` community. This yields a more functionally accurate set of community definitions for the subsequent naming and transformation stages.

– **Community Naming:** This crucial step in the framework provides human-interpretable context to the discovered communities. We leverage the capabilities of Large Language Models (LLMs), which combine extensive linguistic and domain knowledge, to generate concise, descriptive, and semantically coherent names for entire communities. Specifically, the LLM is provided with the list of activities contained within each community and tasked with inferring an appropriate and comprehensible task label, such as "Customer Onboarding" or "Order Submission". Any activity in the community that do not semantically fit can also be filtered out using LLMs. Figure 4 provides a prompt curated for this purpose. We can refine the prompt with any additional process context we have at hand e.g., if we know that the event log corresponds to handling building permits of a municipality, we can add that as context in the prompt.

```
You are a senior business process analyst.
Your task is to examine groups of low-level activity labels
    and assign a single, high-level task name to each group.

### Naming Requirements:
1. Task names must use a consistent pattern: "<Verb> <Object
    >".
2. Each name should reflect the dominant intent or shared
    purpose of the group.
3. Be domain-agnostic: infer meaning only from the activity
    labels themselves.
4. Avoid domain-specific jargon unless the activity labels
    explicitly imply it.
5. Names must be concise, intuitive, stable, and reusable
    across similar logs.
6. Do NOT invent activities; infer strictly from what is
    provided.
7. If any activity does not semantically fit within the
    dominant meaning of its group, filter it out and report
    it explicitly.
8. Prefer verbs that describe actions (e.g., Review, Validate
    , Register, Assess, Prepare, Approve).
9. Prefer objects that broadly match business actions (e.g.,
    Application, Data, Request, Case, Decision, Document).
10. Output strictly in JSON.

### Output Format:
Return a JSON array with the following structure:

[
  {
    "group_index": <index starting at 1>,
    "activities_used": [ ... activities kept for naming ...
        ],
    "activities_filtered": [ ... activities removed because
        they did not fit ... ],
    "task_name": "<Verb> <Object>"
  }
]

### Input:
Below are the groups of activities. Assign a high-level task
    name to each group.

{{groups}}
```

**Fig. 4.** Prompt for naming tasks from activities involved in a community.

Community detection is performed on the Pattern Activity Graph (PAG) rather than the entire event log because the PAG provides a noise-reduced, semantically coherent view of the process. The raw event log produces a dense, noisy graph capturing rare behaviors, and low-level transitions, making communities unstable and meaningless. By first discovering and pruning patterns, we retain only activities that repeatedly co-occur in meaningful behavioral fragments, and edges represent high-frequency subsequences rather than incidental adjacency. This yields a sparse but strong graph that preserves multi-step context, enhances modularity, and aligns community structure with true subprocesses. As a result, communities extracted from the PAG are significantly more robust, interpretable, and reflective of actual tasks than those derived directly from the full event log. Furthermore, from a computational perspective, performing community detection on the Pattern Activity Graph (PAG) is substantially more efficient than running it on the full event-log graph. Community detection algorithms such as Louvain or Leiden run in approximately $O(|E|)$ per iteration and thus become significantly more expensive on such dense structures [14].

Upon completion of the stages mentioned above, the fine-grained activities are mapped to their corresponding higher-level tasks. These mappings are subsequently used to transform the event log.

### 3.2  Event Log Transformation

The high-level intuition of the event log transformation is depicted in Fig. 5. The original activity log is transformed into a new, higher-level log. Here the elements W, Y and Z correspond to three communities/tasks. The consecutive sequence of activities corresponding to an instance of a community is replaced by the community's assigned name (the task name). At the same time, each consecutive run of the activities is created as an instance of the sub-log for the task. It could be the case that not all activities present in the event log are involved in communities. We can keep those activities as is or can merge with its neighboring communities (tasks) depending on their semantic relevance.

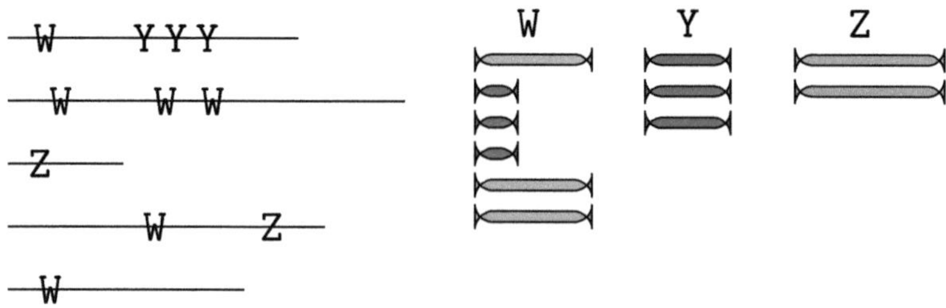

**Fig. 5.** The replacement of fine-granular activities with high-level tasks and the creation of sub-logs for each task.

### 3.3   Iterative Refinement

The transformation explained above can be applied iteratively as depicted in Fig. 6. In each iteration, the transformed event log from the current step serves as the input for the subsequent one. This iterative transformation proceeds until a termination condition is satisfied (at iteration $k$) or until no new meaningful communities emerge. For example, in Fig. 6, in the first iteration, we find three communities, viz., X, Y and Z. After substituting the sequence of activities involved in these communities with their respective names, in the second iteration, we find a new community involving the earlier formed community X along with its surrounding activities, which is named as W. The communities identified in the later iterations can be interpreted as sub-processes (communities formed over patterns of higher-level tasks). The final outcome is a significantly simplified event log, in which long sequences of original fine-grained activities are replaced by a concise sequence of abstract, semantically rich, high-level tasks or sub-processes.

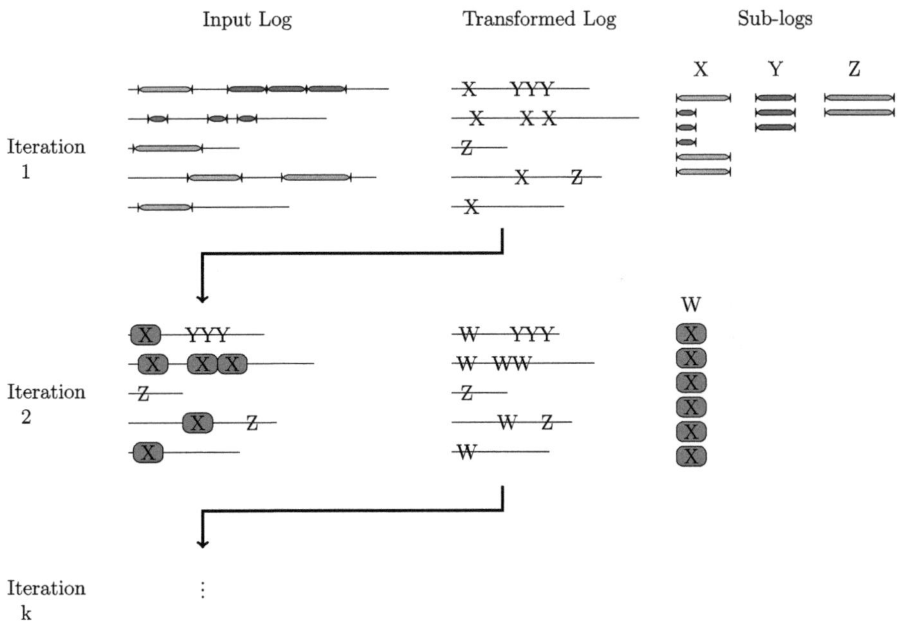


**Fig. 6.** The iterative refinement of event logs with abstractions and the creation of sub-logs for each abstraction.

## 4   Experiments and Discussion

In this section, we present selected experimental results. The proposed approach has been applied to several real-world datasets, including both process mining event logs (e.g., BPI Challenge datasets) and task mining event data. Due to space limitations, we focus on the results for Municipality Log 1 from the BPI Challenge 2015 [8]. This event log comprises 1,199 cases and 52,217 events spanning 398 distinct event classes (activities). The large number of activities, on the order of hundreds, renders any directly discovered process model extremely difficult to interpret.

We began with exploratory data analysis to examine the heterogeneity in the event log and subsequently applied trace clustering using a bag-of-activities representation combined with the k-means algorithm. The optimal number of clusters was determined automatically via the elbow method, resulting in the log being partitioned into 14 clusters. Here, we present results from one cluster, which contains 47 cases and 124 distinct activities. It is worth noting that, even within this cluster, the number of activities remains relatively large. We then filtered the infrequent activities using the thresholds of the case percentage less than 2 and cumulative percentage >95 and further removed self-loops. This resulted in a log with 68 prominent activities, the process map of which using the directly-follows-graph is depicted in Fig. 7. As can be seen, the map is complex and incomprehensible.

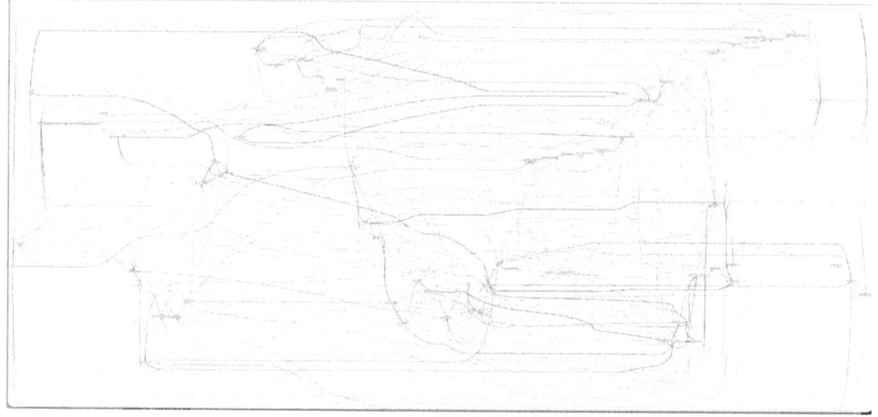

**Fig. 7.** The process map obtained with directly-follows-graph on the filtered event log.

We discovered the repeating patterns, generated the pattern activity graph, and formed communities using Louvain algorithm [14]. This resulted in 12 communities covering 64 of the 68 activities, indicating a good coverage of activities in the communities. We subjected each of these communities through LLMs (OpenAI GPT-4o) for a meaningful name. Table 1 depicts three of the communities with the activities involved in the community and the task name obtained. As we can see that the communities are formed with a coherent set of activities, e.g., the second community pertains to the extension related activities while the third community pertains to the environmental decision. It is noteworthy that the LLM is able to understand the intent behind these activity groups and give a relatable high-level task/sub-process name.

**Table 1.** Mapping of Communities to Task Names

| Community | Task Name |
| --- | --- |
| – regular procedure without MER<br>– registration date publication<br>– forward to the competent authority<br>– send procedure confirmation<br>– enter senddate procedure confirmation | Initiate Regular Procedure and Confirm Receipt |
| – phase procedure extended<br>– create decision procedure term extension<br>– enter senddate decision procedure term extension<br>– enter senddate procedure term extension<br>– enter date decision procedure term extension<br>– copy decision to extend procedure to stakeholders<br>– start decision phase extension granted | Extend Procedure Term and Notify Stakeholders |
| – enter senddate decision environmental permit<br>– generate publication document decision environmental permit<br>– phase decision taken<br>– transcript decision environmental permit to stakeholders<br>– register date environmental permit decision<br>– record date of decision environmental permit<br>– submit decision<br>– continue or abort mutation BAG objects<br>– enter date publication decision environmental permit<br>– generating decision environmental permit<br>– register objection and appeal periods | Issue and Publish Environmental Permit Decision |

We then used these activity mappings to tasks and transformed the event log. Figure 8 depicts the directly-follows process map on the transformed event log obtained after applying the greedy edge-filtering [5]. As can be seen the map is pretty easy to comprehend. We can use the sub-logs to zoom-in on any of the tasks to see the process maps of the underlying activities. This clearly illustrates the strength and potential of our proposed approach.

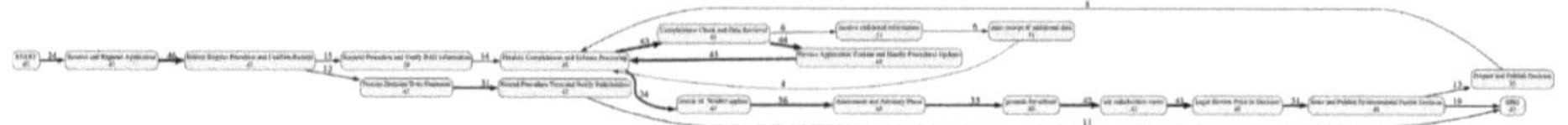

**Fig. 8.** The simplified process map obtained with directly-follows-graph on the transformed event log after one iteration after applying greedy simplification.

## 5    Conclusions and Future Directions

This paper tackled a persistent challenge in process mining viz., the granularity gap between fine-grained event data and the coarse-grained, semantically meaningful models needed for effective analysis. As enterprise systems capture increasingly detailed interactions, event logs have grown exponentially, often producing syntactically correct yet semantically opaque process models.

To address this, we proposed a framework that progressively abstracts event logs into higher-level representations. By identifying recurring execution patterns, representing them as activity-interaction graphs, and applying graph-based community detection, fine-grained activities are consolidated into meaningful tasks and sub-processes. The use of large language models (LLMs) for semantic labeling further enhances interpretability, turning structural clusters into human-aligned process concepts. Through iterative abstraction, the framework yields hierarchical models that preserve behavioral fidelity while significantly reducing complexity.

Future work will explore several promising directions. One is the integration of domain ontologies and contextual knowledge to further refine semantic abstraction, enabling automated alignment of discovered task clusters with known business concepts. Another is to develop interactive, human-in-the-loop mechanisms, allowing analysts to guide or validate abstraction decisions dynamically. Finally, we aim to extend the framework toward online abstraction for streaming event data, allowing continuous simplification and monitoring of processes in real time.

## References


1. Baier, T., Mendling, J., Weske, M.: Bridging abstraction layers in process mining. Inf. Syst. **46**, 123–139 (2014)
2. Bose, R.P.J.C.: Process mining in the large: preprocessing, discovery, and diagnostics. Ph.D. thesis, Eindhoven University of Technology (2012)
3. Jagadeesh Chandra Bose, R.P., van der Aalst, W.M.P.: Abstractions in process mining: a taxonomy of patterns. In: Dayal, U., Eder, J., Koehler, J., Reijers, H.A. (eds.) BPM 2009. LNCS, vol. 5701, pp. 159–175. Springer, Heidelberg (2009). https://doi.org/10.1007/978-3-642-03848-8_12
4. Bose, R.P.J.C., van der Aalst, W.M.P.: Context aware trace clustering: towards improving process mining results. In: Proceedings of the 2009 SIAM International Conference on Data Mining, pp. 401–412. SIAM (2009)
5. Chapela-Campa, D., Dumas, M., Mucientes, M., Lama, M.: Efficient edge filtering of directly-follows graphs for process mining. Inf. Sci. **610**, 830–846 (2022)

6. De Weerdt, J., Vanden Broucke, S., Vanthienen, J., Baesens, B.: Active trace clustering for improved process discovery. IEEE Trans. Knowl. Data Eng. **25**(12), 2708–2720 (2013)
7. Diba, K., Batoulis, K., Weidlich, M., Weske, M.: Extraction, correlation, and abstraction of event data for process mining. Wiley Interdisc. Rev. Data Min. Knowl. Discov. **10**(3), e1346 (2020)
8. Dongen, B.: BPI challenge 2015 (2015). https://doi.org/10.4121/uuid: 31a308ef-c844-48da-948c-305d167a0ec1. https://www.win.tue.nl/bpi/doku. php?id=2015:start. http://www.win.tue.nl/bpi/doku.php?id=2015:challenge& redirect=1id=2015/challenge, 11th International Workshop on Business Process Intelligence (BPI 2015), BPI 2015; Conference date: 31-08-2015 Through 31-08-2015
9. Leemans, S.J., Fahland, D.: Information-preserving abstractions of event data in process mining. Knowl. Inf. Syst. **62**(3), 1143–1197 (2020)
10. Leonardi, G., Striani, M., Quaglini, S., Cavallini, A., Montani, S.: Towards semantic process mining through knowledge-based trace abstraction. In: Ceravolo, P., van Keulen, M., Stoffel, K. (eds.) SIMPDA 2017. LNBIP, vol. 340, pp. 45–64. Springer, Cham (2019). https://doi.org/10.1007/978-3-030-11638-5_3
11. Leonardi, G., Striani, M., Quaglini, S., Cavallini, A., Montani, S.: Leveraging semantic labels for multi-level abstraction in medical process mining and trace comparison. J. Biomed. Inform. **83**, 10–24 (2018)
12. Li, C.Y., van Zelst, S.J., van der Aalst, W.M.: An activity instance based hierarchical framework for event abstraction. In: 2021 3rd International Conference on Process Mining (ICPM), pp. 160–167. IEEE (2021)
13. Tax, N., Sidorova, N., Haakma, R., van der Aalst, W.M.: Event abstraction for process mining using supervised learning techniques. In: Proceedings of SAI Intelligent Systems Conference, pp. 251–269. Springer, Cham (2016)
14. Traag, V.A., Waltman, L., van Eck, N.J.: From Louvain to Leiden: guaranteeing well-connected communities. Sci. Rep. **9**(1), 5233 (2019). https://doi.org/10.1038/ s41598-019-41695-z
15. Van Houdt, G., de Leoni, M., Martin, N., Depaire, B.: An empirical evaluation of unsupervised event log abstraction techniques in process mining. Inf. Syst. **121**, 102320 (2024)
16. van Zelst, S.J., Mannhardt, F., de Leoni, M., Koschmider, A.: Event abstraction in process mining: literature review and taxonomy. Granular Comput. **6**(3), 719–736 (2021)

# Forward-Looking Process Mining: Simulation-Based Approaches, Challenges, and Research Directions

Mahsa Pourbafrani[(✉)]

RWTH Aachen University, Aachen, Germany
Mahsa.pourbafrani@rwth-aachen.de

**Abstract.** Forward-looking process mining enables organizations to anticipate future process behavior and support decision-making beyond retrospective analysis by using simulation to model alternative scenarios and perform what-if analysis. Existing simulation approaches, however, are often limited to fine-grained event logs. They rely on ad hoc assumptions, and lack integration across different levels of analysis. This paper presents recent advances in the mining of simulation-based processes and places them within a unified research framework. We highlight key gaps, including the absence of systematic design principles for data-driven business process simulation, the neglect of aggregated perspectives, and the lack of interplay between coarse- and fine-grained models, and propose methods to address these issues. Our contributions include a reference meta-model for simulation design, systematic transformation of event logs into coarse-grained representations, data-driven system dynamics models, hybrid simulation approaches, and tool support. We conclude with a discussion of open challenges and future research directions, intending to establish simulation as a core pillar of forward-looking process mining.

**Keywords:** Forward-looking process mining · Data-driven simulation · Business process simulation

## 1 Introduction

Process mining, a data-driven discipline at the intersection of process science and data science, has transformed the way organizations analyze, monitor, and improve their processes [1]. Process mining techniques primarily focus on backward-looking approaches, using historical event data to discover process models, verify conformance, and diagnose performance or compliance issues [3]. Although valuable, these methods are inherently limited to describing the past and present.

The real advantage lies in forward-looking capabilities: predicting, simulating, and proactively managing future process outcomes. Forward-looking process mining enables organizations to assess potential actions, evaluate the impact of


J. Mendling et al. (Eds.): Wil van der Aalst Festschrift, LNCS 16480, pp. 454–470, 2026.
https://doi.org/10.1007/978-3-032-17618-9_31

changes, and make data-driven decisions. Two main approaches dominate here: predictive models, which forecast future process states using machine learning, and simulation models, which explicitly reenact process behavior under various scenarios.

Despite progress in predictive process mining, existing simulation models often rely on ad hoc assumptions, lack systematic integration with process mining insights, and focus narrowly on operational details [2]. As a result, organizations lack robust, multi-level simulation frameworks that connect fine-grained event data with strategic, aggregated analysis to support both operational and high-level decision-making.

*Process Mining: From Description to Prescription.* Business processes are structured activities to achieve organizational goals. Their execution generates rich event data that backward-looking process mining uses to uncover flows, bottlenecks, and deviations. Forward-looking process mining extends this by enabling the prediction of outcomes and simulating scenarios. Predictive models estimate metrics such as remaining time or deviation chance, while simulation models allow transparent, explainable what-if analyses that consider resources, process flows, and environmental factors.

*The Need for a Systematic, Multi-Level Simulation Framework.* Current simulation approaches face several limitations: ad hoc assumptions, neglect of quality and resource effects, obscured causal relationships, lack of strategic aggregation, and weak integration across operational and strategic levels. This paper introduces a holistic, multi-level framework grounded in process mining insights. It supports the transformation of detailed event logs into aggregated data, enables both discrete event and system dynamics simulations, and facilitates hybrid modeling that links operational and strategic perspectives.

This paper addresses this gap by presenting the missing aspects and challenges, and by proposing a comprehensive data-driven framework as a baseline for forward-looking process mining with an emphasis on simulation. By integrating process mining insights with simulation techniques, it provides a reference architecture and methods that extend from descriptive analytics to prescriptive, future-oriented process management. While building on results presented in the PhD thesis[1], this paper focuses on establishing a foundation for subsequent work and on positioning simulation as a forward-looking technique.

## 2   Proposed Approaches and Contributions

A key challenge in data-driven simulation for process mining lies mainly in the reliance on detailed-level models and various ad hoc design choices, as well as the neglect of external and contextual factors. Current approaches often emphasize detailed event representations, while overlooking broader systemic perspectives. This paper outlines the problem and proposes a forward-looking framework that

---

[1] https://publications.rwth-aachen.de/record/973806/files/973806.pdf.

can serve as a basis for further developments in simulation techniques for process mining.

We propose a framework that transforms fine-grained event logs into coarse-grained, time-aware representations, enabling both predictive and diagnostic simulation. By integrating discrete event simulation and system dynamics, the framework supports multi-level modeling and advanced analysis such as causal diagnostics and forecasting. Figure 1 provides an overview; the following subsections detail the main contributions.

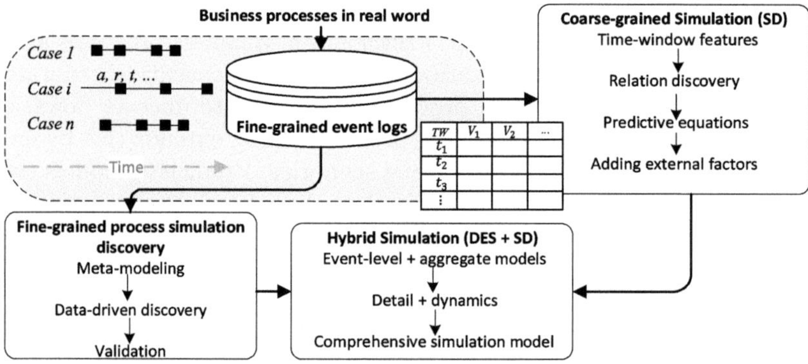


**Fig. 1.** Simulation framework including generating coarse-grained process logs, two types of process mining simulation, and the interaction between these types,

## 2.1 Fine-Grained Simulation (DES)

Fine-grained simulation in process mining is based predominantly on discrete event simulation (DES), where individual events, activities, and resource interactions are explicitly represented. Event logs provide the basis for such models, yet existing approaches frequently depend on manual, ad hoc decisions during model construction. This results in inconsistent design practices, weak reproducibility, and limited comparability between studies.

To overcome these issues, there should be a reference model for the design, execution and evaluation of DES models derived from event data to position the role of data, users, goal and simulation results. The modeling workflow should be structured into phases in Table 1.

This structured pipeline transforms fragmented practices into a systematic methodology for fine-grained simulation. By integrating process mining techniques with DES, the reference phases ensure reproducibility, facilitates model validation, and provides a reference for benchmarking.

**Meta Model for Simulation:** The reference model is introduced to formalize the design and execution of simulation models in process mining [13]. The

**Table 1.** Forward-Looking Process Simulation Framework Phases

| Phase | Description |
| --- | --- |
| Design | **Input**: Event log with control-flow, performance, attributes, resources, plus the user and simulation purpose<br>**Approach**: Automated discovery plus manual input<br>**Outcome**: Parameterized simulation (routing, durations, resources, arrivals) |
| Execution | **Implementation**: Simulations via rules, predictive models, or empirical distributions<br>**Outcome**: Event streams replicating process behavior |
| Validation & Verification | Check internal correctness<br>Compare outputs to logs (throughput, waiting, utilization) |
| Benchmark | Compare models to assess accuracy, robustness, and interpretability |

reference model distinguishes between the *design phase* (model discovery, parameter extraction) and the *execution phase* (simulation run, value regeneration). Extractable process aspects include activity flow, resource assignment, scheduling, queuing strategies, decision logic, and interruption handling. Simulation parameters can be derived automatically via process mining techniques or manually via domain expertise. The meta model supports various regeneration mechanisms: fixed values, rule-based programming, predictive models, and random function generators (e.g., Poisson arrival rates), see Fig. 2.

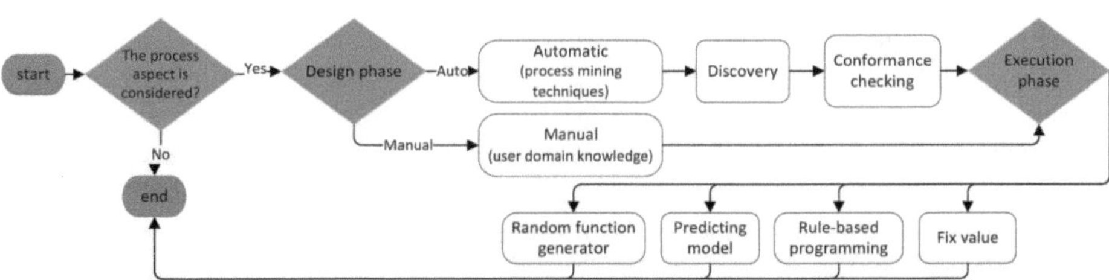


**Fig. 2.** The designed flowchart, for creating each aspect of a simulation model of a process, is based on two required phases: design and execution [13].

Formally, let $L$ be an event log and $PT$ the process model, e.g., a process tree, discovered via a process discovery technique. For each activity $a \in PT_a$, properties such as probability of occurrence, processing time, and resource assignment are attached. For XOR operators, the probability $w_a$ of activity $a$ in a trace is explicitly modeled. Resource and activity blocks are enriched with attributes: organization, role, type, schedule, cost, count, interruption, and queue strategy [13].

By following the steps and phases in Fig. 2, data-driven simulation models can be clearly derived, allowing for the comparison of different models and techniques regardless of their focus solely on DES.

**Reference Model Sample Realization:** To show how the operationalization of the reference model is, here is a simplified example of generating simulation models from enriched process trees [15] and event logs. Automatically discoverable parameters (e.g., activity flow, resource capacity, business hours) are extracted, while user-defined parameters (e.g., arrival rates, case generator functions) enable scenario management. The simulation engine executes the process model, updating the system clock and handling events according to the specified execution configuration [11,15].

**Evaluation and Comparison:** To assess simulation quality, both model and result validation are performed. For two event logs $L$ and $L'$, let $L_A$ and $L'_A$ denote the multisets of traces projected on activities. The behavioral difference is quantified by the sets of unique traces $e_{L_A}$ and $e_{L'_A}$, with metrics for newly generated and removed behaviors:

$$New\ Behavior\ Ratio = \frac{|e_{L'_A} \setminus e_{L_A}|}{|e_{L_A} \cup e_{L'_A}|}, \quad Removed\ Behavior\ Ratio = \frac{|e_{L_A} \setminus e_{L'_A}|}{|e_{L_A} \cup e_{L'_A}|}$$

Stochastic conformance checking is performed using Earth Mover's Distance (EMD), where the reallocation function $r(\sigma, \sigma')$ maps frequencies between traces, and the trace distance $d(\sigma, \sigma')$ is computed via normalized string edit distance [7]. The overall EMD is:

$$\text{EMD}(L_A, L'_A) = \min_{r \in R} \sum_{\sigma \in L_A} \sum_{\sigma' \in L'_A} r(\sigma, \sigma') \cdot d(\sigma, \sigma')$$

This represents one possible approach for demonstrating the use of a systematic model for model generation, as well as for validation and verification of results. The techniques applied here can be replaced or complemented by others.

The reference model and framework enable automatic, data-driven simulation model generation and rigorous evaluation. However, challenges remain: lack of generic standards for executable models, limited tool interoperability, and incomplete extraction of process aspects (e.g., queuing strategies, accurate timing). Future work should address these gaps by developing standardized model formats (e.g., XML), service-based simulation engines, and improved backward-looking techniques for process discovery and performance analysis. Fine-grained simulation in process mining, grounded in a formal meta model and robust evaluation techniques, provides a powerful approach for digital process shadows, scenario analysis, and process improvement [14,16].

## 2.2 Coarse-Grained Process Log Generation and Data-Driven Simulation Modeling

Traditional process mining approaches primarily rely on fine-grained event logs, focusing on detailed analyses of process instances [4]. While effective for diagnostics and instance-level predictions, such granularity restricts high-level modeling and long-term strategic analysis, particularly when environmental and contextual factors are relevant.

Most simulation approaches in process mining face three main limitations: (1) lack of systematic design and validation, often relying on ad hoc modeling choices; (2) overemphasis on fine-grained event data, which obscures cause–effect relations and neglects quality-related factors such as resource expertise; and (3) insufficient support for decision-making, with few data-driven models addressing both operational and strategic levels, and little interaction between fine- and coarse-grained perspectives.

These gaps highlight the need for comprehensive, data-driven simulation models and aggregated views of event logs. To overcome these limitations, we propose a framework for transforming detailed, instance-level event logs into aggregated, coarse-grained process logs, enabling higher-level analysis and simulation.

Among the simulation techniques suited for aggregated modeling, System Dynamics is particularly promising. It allows simulation over time, incorporating contextual and external factors in a quantifiable manner. In this paper, we use System Dynamics to demonstrate its potential for process mining simulation. As shown in Fig. 3, we transform detailed event logs into more aggregated data over time, which can be used to design higher-level aggregated data for process simulation.

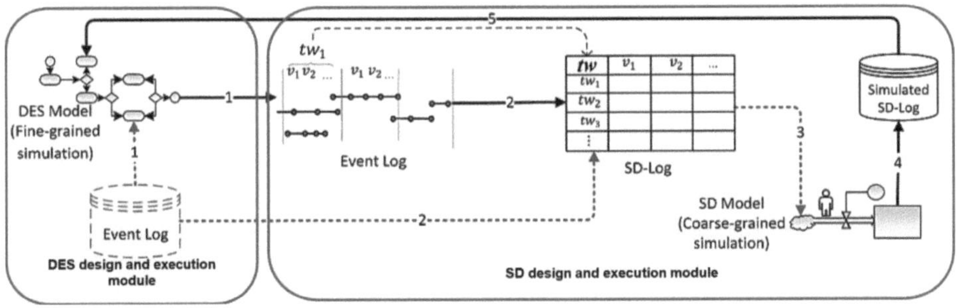

**Fig. 3.** Process mining, simulation, and data analysis techniques are used to gain insights and knowledge.

## 2.3   System Dynamics

System dynamics models complex systems with interacting variables and feedback loops to support strategy-level decision-making [21]. Conceptually, Causal-Loop Diagrams (CLDs) (Fig. 4) show variables as nodes and causal effects as signed arcs. For simulation, CLDs are translated into Stock-Flow Diagrams (SFDs) (Fig. 5), where variables are mapped to stocks, flows, or auxiliaries, and relations are either information dependencies or material flows. The system's behavior over time is computed using underlying equations; for example, a stock variable updates based on its previous value and influencing flows (1).

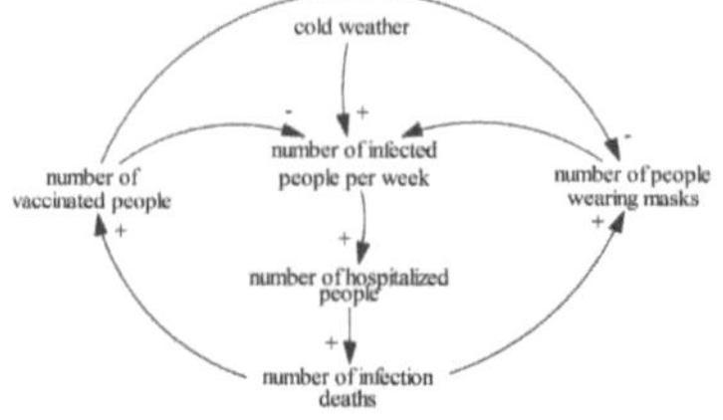

**Fig. 4.** An example of a Causal-Loop Diagram (CLD).

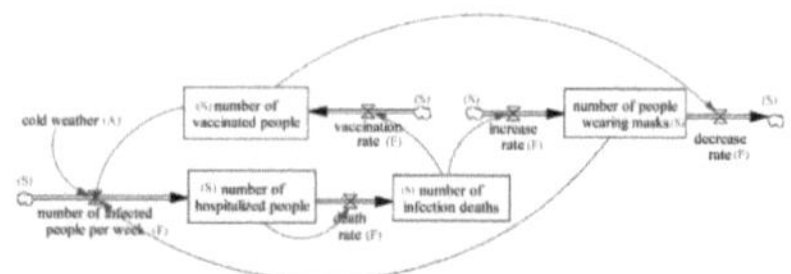

**Fig. 5.** The designed SFD for the CLD of the infection situation in Fig. 4.

$$number\ of\ hospitalized\ people_i = number\ of\ hospitalized\ people_{i-1}$$
$$+\ (number\ of\ infected\ people\ per\ week_i - death\ rate_i) \tag{1}$$

## 2.4  Fine-Grained vs Coarse-Grained Process Logs(SD)

Fine-grained process logs capture individual events as they occur within process instances, providing detailed information on activities, resources, timestamps, and case-level behavior. While this granularity enables precise diagnostics, it constrains high-level modeling and long-term analysis because the data remains tied to single events and isolated instances. Coarse-grained logs, in contrast, aggregate fine-grained events over predefined time windows (e.g., hours, days, weeks) and transform them into a set of higher-level process variables. These variables summarize broader characteristics such as case volume, average processing time, queue lengths, or resource utilization, enabling analysis that incorporates both process context and environmental context.

A coarse-grained process log is therefore an abstraction layer that describes process behavior per time step rather than per event. Instead of recording one row per event, a coarse-grained log contains one row per time window, and each row holds the values of aggregated process variables for that period. This representation makes it possible to study system-wide dynamics that affect all process instances collectively. For example, aggregating raw sensor data from vehicles into hourly traffic intensity reveals congestion patterns that cannot be inferred from individual car-pass events.

Formally, a coarse-grained log consists of one or more process variables and a sequence of time steps, where each process variable has exactly one aggregated value for each time step. Each process variable is defined by three components: an aggregation function (e.g., count, sum, average), a process aspect (e.g., cases, activities, resources), and a performance indicator (e.g., throughput, waiting time). When system dynamics simulation models are later applied, their outputs naturally take the form of coarse-grained logs, values of simulation variables over

**Table 2.** Sample event log (left) and corresponding SD-Log (coarse-grained process log for System Dynamics simulation) of the running example (right).

| Case ID | Activity | Age | Start Timestamp | Complete Timestamp | Resource |
|---|---|---|---|---|---|
| 116 | Registration | 28 | 1/1/2020 10:29 | 1/1/2020 10:47 | John |
| 117 | Registration | 65 | 1/1/2020 10:29 | 1/1/2020 10:29 | Sarah |
| 116 | First visit | 35 | 1/1/2020 10:30 | 1/1/2020 10:50 | Sam |
| 118 | Registration | 78 | 1/1/2020 10:31 | 1/1/2020 10:49 | Sarah |
| 116 | Examine | 54 | 1/1/2020 10:31 | 1/1/2020 10:31 | Carl |
| ... | ... | ... | ... | ... | ... |

| Time Window (Daily) | Arrival rate of cases | Number of resources | Average service time | Average waiting time in process |
|---|---|---|---|---|
| 1 | 180 | 6 | 0.359 | 0.609 |
| 2 | 147 | 6 | 0.415 | 0.540 |
| 3 | 160 | 6 | 0.401 | 0.596 |
| ⋮ | ⋮ | ⋮ | ⋮ | ⋮ |

successive time steps. These simulation-generated logs are referred to as SD-logs and serve as the foundation for the coarse-grained simulation and diagnostics [17].

## 2.5   Approach

The framework for aggregated event log generation comprises three principal modules: **Design Choices Selection**, **Event Log Projection**, and **Variable Extraction**. Initially, process mining insights including process discovery, conformance checking, and performance analysis, are leveraged to select relevant subsets of cases, activities, and resources for aggregation. Formally, given an event log $L \subseteq \xi$, the *Design Choice Projection* function $\Pi_{C,A,R}(L)$ projects events onto selected sets $C \subseteq \mathcal{C}$, $A \subseteq \mathcal{A}$, and $R \subseteq \mathcal{R}$, where $C$, $A$, $R$ denote cases, activities, and resources, respectively [10].

Subsequently, the *Time Window Projection* partitions the projected event log into non-overlapping intervals of fixed duration $\delta$, generating a sequence of event logs $\{L_1, L_2, \ldots, L_k\}$ corresponding to each time window. This enables aggregation of process variables over time, facilitating analysis of process behavior at different temporal resolutions [17].

The final step, *Variable Extraction*, systematically defines process variables as combinations of process aspects (case, activity, resource), performance indicators (service time, waiting time, count, value), and aggregation functions (average, median, sum). The set of process variables $V = DC \times F$ is computed, where $DC$ denotes design choices and $F$ denotes process features. For each time window, the *Performance Function* $\Phi : V \times 2^{\xi} \to \mathbb{R}_{\geq 0}$ calculates the value of each process variable, resulting in a coarse-grained process log $PL_{L,\delta} : \{1, \ldots, k\} \times V \to \mathbb{R}_{\geq 0}$.

The generated coarse-grained process logs, referred to as **SD-Logs**, serve as the foundation for data-driven simulation modeling using system dynamics [18]. An example of generated coarse-grained logs is shown next to the event log in Table 2 and Table 2.

Unlike discrete event simulation, which operates at the fine-grained level, system dynamics models require aggregated, time-series data to capture strategic and environmental influences. The modeling pipeline comprises four key steps:

1. **Time Window Stability Assessment**: Pattern detection (via partial autocorrelation) and inactivity detection are applied to SD-Logs to select the

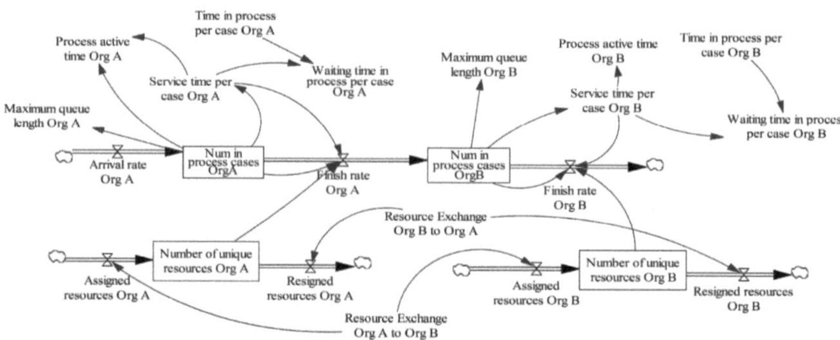

**Fig. 6.** The designed model for two organizations in the process which hand-over the tasks. Assessing possible scenarios such as how to share the resources between two organizations A and B for smaller queues is possible [9].

optimal time window size, ensuring stable and meaningful process variable behavior for simulation.

2. **Relation Detection**: Statistical and machine learning techniques (e.g., regression, ARIMA) are employed to discover linear and nonlinear relationships among process variables, including temporal shifts and causal dependencies.

3. **Model Generation**: Detected relations are translated into Causal-Loop Diagrams (CLDs) and subsequently into Stock-Flow Diagrams (SFDs), with process variables labeled as stocks, flows, or auxiliaries based on their semantic roles and aggregation types.

4. **Simulation and Validation**: The executable SFD models are simulated over the selected time windows, and the results are validated against real process variable values from SD-Logs. This enables strategic what-if analysis, scenario evaluation, and the incorporation of external factors (e.g., resource efficiency, advertising effects).

Figure 6 shows an example of the implementation of the approach for the data-driven, aggregated and higher-level design of a simulation model of a process using its event log, where the system dynamics model can be executed, changes are observed over time, as well as the effect of a variable or aspect on other aspects of the process.

This approach enables systematic, data-driven aggregation and simulation of business processes at higher abstraction levels, supporting strategic decision-making and forward-looking analysis. By formalizing the transformation from fine-grained event logs to coarse-grained SD-Logs and integrating statistical relation detection, the framework overcomes limitations of ad hoc feature extraction and domain-dependent modeling. The methodology is extensible to various process mining scenarios, including diagnostics, anomaly detection, and organizational modeling, and provides a robust foundation for future research in automated, context-aware process simulation.

## 2.6  Hybrid Business Simulation

In process mining and business process simulation, most approaches adopt a technique-specific perspective, with discrete event simulation (DES) as the dominant paradigm. These approaches usually operate at a single level of abstraction. In contrast, hybrid models allow the integration of multiple levels, combining detailed and aggregated perspectives to leverage the strengths of both.

***Hybrid Simulation of Processes Using SD and DES.*** DES and system dynamics (SD) are complementary paradigms: DES captures fine-grained operational behavior from event logs, while SD models higher-level dynamics and external factors. DES provides execution-level accuracy, whereas SD delivers strategic insights, motivating their integration. The proposed framework is shown in Fig. 7.

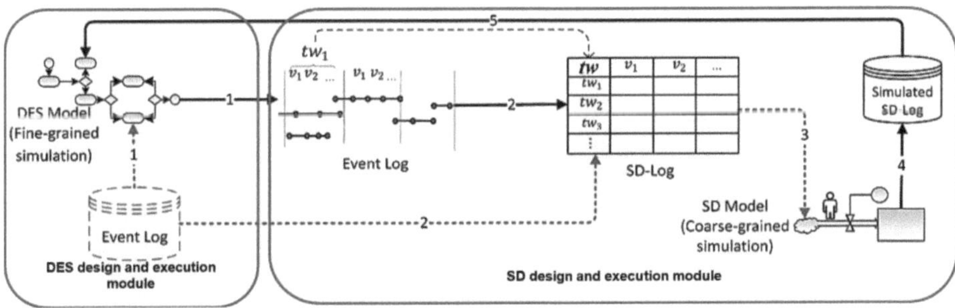


**Fig. 7.** Hybrid simulation framework: event logs from DES are aggregated into SD-Logs, used to build and update the SD model, which in turn influences subsequent DES runs.

The framework integrates DES and SD through three modules: (1) DES design and execution, (2) SD design and execution, and (3) a connection module that synchronizes shared variables. DES models are instantiated as Colored Petri Nets (CPNs), where tokens represent cases and transitions correspond to activities, producing fine-grained event logs. SD models are constructed from aggregated SD-Logs, extracted over time windows $\delta$, and populated with process variables and external factors.

Integration is achieved via gateway variables shared between both models (e.g., arrival rates, service times, resource counts). The iterative procedure is: (i) run the DES model $M_{DES}$ to generate an event log $L$, (ii) aggregate $L$ into an SD-Log $sd_{L,\delta}$, (iii) simulate the SD model $M_{SD}$ to obtain updated values, and (iv) propagate these to $M_{DES}$ for subsequent runs. This feedback loop enables DES to reflect the strategic influences captured by SD [12].

***Proof of Concept: Hybrid Simulation.*** The proposed framework aims to demonstrate the feasibility of integrating two data-driven process simulations: Discrete Event Simulation (DES) and System Dynamics (SD). This proof of concept validates the applicability and importance of jointly executing both simulation types in practice (Fig. 8).

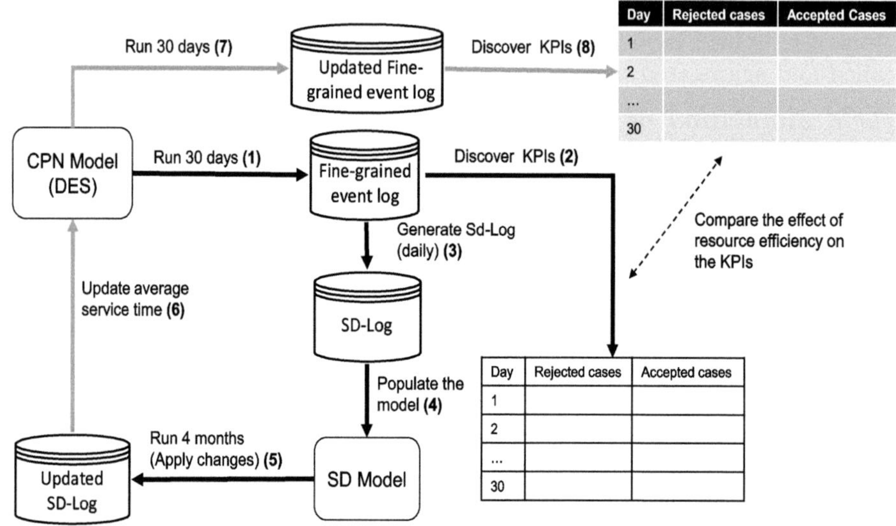

**Fig. 8.** Overview of the designed scenario for combining DES and SD in practice. Black arrows represent model creation steps, and gray arrows indicate execution and what-if analysis [9].

### *Experimental Setup*

A business process model was implemented in CPN Tools using Colored Petri Nets (CPN). The simulation generates a fine-grained event log, from which relevant KPIs (e.g., handled and rejected cases) are extracted. Using the approach for coarse-grained simulation, a coarse-grained process log referred to as SD-Log is generated and used to design and execute an SD model, e.g., in Vensim as one of the supporting platforms.

Common variables across models, such as average service time, are automatically detected and updated dynamically. The CPN simulation continues execution while the SD model provides updated parameter values. A Python Jupyter Notebook coordinates all data exchanges and executions.

### *Case Description*

The example models a company processing two types of customer requests (new and existing). Requests arrive every five minutes during standard working hours (9 am–5 pm). Each of two departments has three resources. If the queue exceeds 20 requests, new arrivals are rejected. Processing time depends nonlinearly on queue length (faster service under high load) (Figs. 9 and Fig. 10).

Table 3 and 4 show samples of the generated event log and SD-Log.

### *Execution and Results*

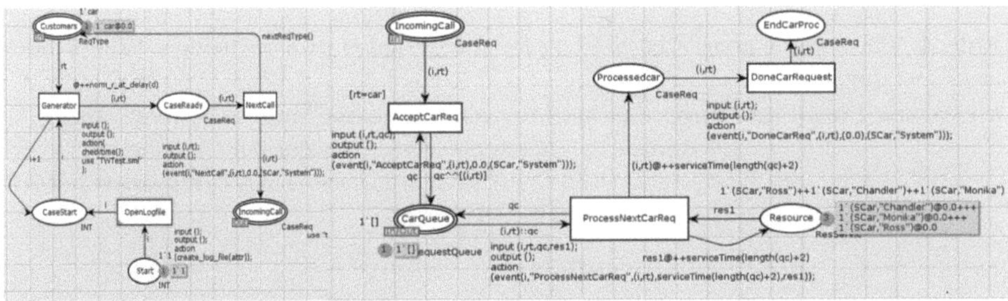

**Fig. 9.** The designed CPN simulation model using CPN Tools for handling customer requests in a sample company.

**Table 3.** A part of the generated event log for the designed process using CPN Tools.

| Case ID | Activity | type | StartTime | CompleteTime | Resources |
|---|---|---|---|---|---|
| ⋮ | ⋮ | ⋮ | ⋮ | ⋮ | ⋮ |
| 5 | ProcessNewReq | NewCustomerRequest | 5/20/2022 11:42 | 5/20/2022 11:59 | Monika |
| 1 | DoneNewReq | NewCustomerRequest | 5/20/2022 11:42 | 5/20/2022 11:42 | System |
| 32 | NextRequesst | NewCustomerRequest | 5/20/2022 11:42 | 5/20/2022 11:42 | System |
| 32 | RejectRequest | NewCustomerRequest | 5/20/2022 11:42 | 5/20/2022 11:42 | System |
| 2 | DoneNewReq | NewCustomerRequest | 5/20/2022 11:43 | 5/20/2022 11:43 | System |
| 6 | ProcessNewReq | NewCustomerRequest | 5/20/2022 11:43 | 5/20/2022 12:00 | Ross |
| 33 | NextRequesst | NewCustomerRequest | 5/20/2022 11:44 | 5/20/2022 11:44 | System |
| 33 | RejectRequest | NewCustomerRequest | 5/20/2022 11:44 | 5/20/2022 11:44 | System |
| 3 | DoneNewReq | NewCustomerRequest | 5/20/2022 11:44 | 5/20/2022 11:44 | System |
| 9 | ProcessNewReq | NewCustomerRequest | 5/20/2022 11:44 | 5/20/2022 12:02 | Chandler |
| 34 | NextRequesst | CurrentCustomerRequest | 5/20/2022 11:45 | 5/20/2022 11:45 | System |
| 34 | StartCurrentReq | CurrentCustomerRequest | 5/20/2022 11:45 | 5/20/2022 12:05 | System |
| 8 | ProcessCurrentReq | CurrentCustomerRequest | 5/20/2022 11:46 | 5/20/2022 12:06 | Joe |
| ⋮ | ⋮ | ⋮ | ⋮ | ⋮ | ⋮ |

The integrated simulation runs for 30 days, with the SD model capturing the long-term effect of training (300 h) on resource efficiency, assumed to improve service speed by 20% on average. Updated efficiency values from the SD model are fed into the CPN simulation through automated parameter updates.

The results (Fig. 11) show that improvements in training gradually reduce service times and the number of rejected cases after approximately two months, confirming that SD can effectively capture aggregate, time-dependent effects and feed them back into fine-grained DES for more realistic performance estimation.

## 3 Challenges and Research Directions

Despite advances in simulation-based process mining, several challenges hinder its systematic adoption and scalability.

**Table 4.** The sample generated SD-Log for the designed process using a time window size of one day.

| Arrival rate | Finish rate | Num of unique resources | Avg service time per case | Avg time in process per case | Avg waiting time in process per case |
|---|---|---|---|---|---|
| ⋮ | ⋮ | ⋮ | ⋮ | ⋮ | ⋮ |
| 180 | 180 | 6 | 0.359012 | 0.968992 | 0.609981 |
| 147 | 147 | 6 | 0.415646 | 0.956576 | 0.54093 |
| 160 | 160 | 6 | 0.401146 | 0.997292 | 0.596146 |
| 116 | 116 | 6 | 0.445546 | 0.936351 | 0.490805 |
| 94 | 94 | 6 | 0.502482 | 0.825887 | 0.323404 |
| 147 | 147 | 6 | 0.442123 | 0.98984 | 0.547717 |
| 117 | 117 | 6 | 0.399715 | 0.895726 | 0.496011 |
| 117 | 117 | 6 | 0.435613 | 0.960256 | 0.524644 |
| ⋮ | ⋮ | ⋮ | ⋮ | ⋮ | ⋮ |

**Standardization and Interoperability.** A major obstacle is the lack of standardized methodologies for designing simulation models. While reference meta-models and frameworks exist, no universally accepted standards for simulation input or model representation, particularly for discrete event simulation (DES), are available. This limits interoperability, complicates automated model extraction from event logs, and impedes integration with process mining tools.

**Aggregation and Abstraction.** Converting fine-grained logs into meaningful coarse-grained representations requires sophisticated feature engineering and variable extraction. Computational complexity grows with log size and temporal granularity, making real-time or large-scale applications difficult. Relevant process variables often require domain-specific, partially manual identification, limiting automation and generalizability.

**Hybrid Simulation Models.** Combining DES and system dynamics (SD) enables more comprehensive process analysis but introduces challenges. Synchronizing models at different abstraction levels, defining interface variables, and ensuring consistent execution semantics are non-trivial. Existing frameworks often support only unidirectional updates, and evaluation is typically restricted to proof-of-concept studies or synthetic data. Large-scale, real-world benchmarks are lacking, slowing broader validation.

**User Involvement.** The role of the user remains critical in the design phase, scenario selection, and model configuration. Expert knowledge ensures meaningful variable selection, scenario relevance, and validation, and should not be

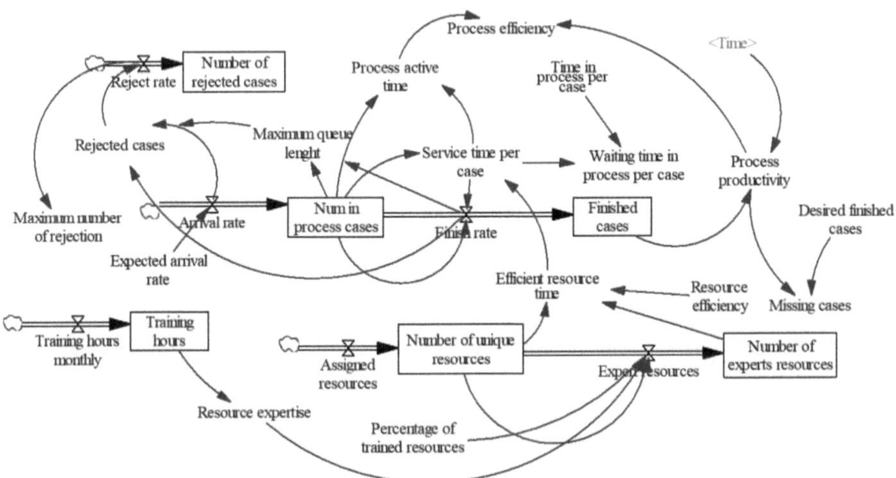

Fig. 10. Refined stock-flow diagram (SFD) capturing the effect of training on resource efficiency over time.

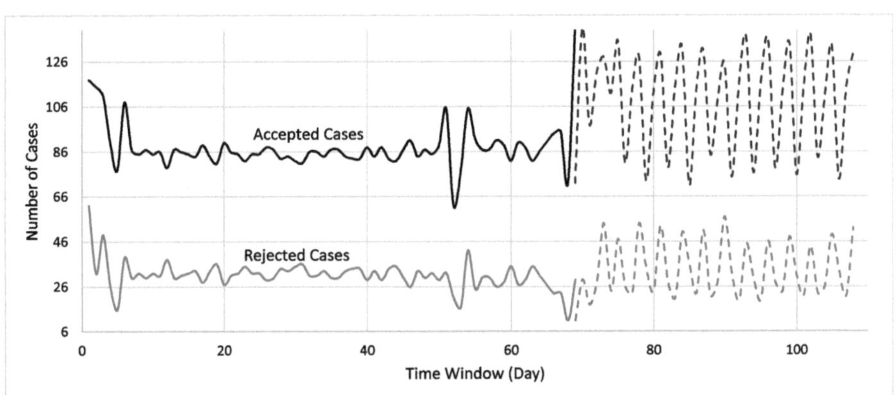


Fig. 11. Number of handled and rejected requests per day over four months. Dotted lines indicate updated DES results after incorporating SD outcomes.

neglected even with automated or AI-assisted modeling. *Emerging research directions include*:

- **Adaptive hybrid simulations:** Real-time models integrating streaming event data and responding dynamically to process changes to support operational and strategic decisions.
- **Machine learning integration:** Deep learning for pattern discovery, predictive modeling, and automated feature extraction to improve simulation accuracy and reduce manual effort.

- **Industry-scale evaluation:** Frameworks and benchmarks to validate scalability, including digital twins and object-centric process mining [6], application in different domains such as healthcare [20].
- **Generative AI for scenario synthesis:** Creating realistic event streams and alternative process scenarios for extensive what-if analyses, ensuring data validity and reliability.
- **Resource modeling:** Capturing dynamic availability, multitasking, and interactions in large-scale, multi-instance environments [19], the combination of resource availability and multitasking [8], and multi-agent deployment using event logs [5].
- **Standardization:** Open, extensible standards for model representation and exchange to foster interoperability, reproducibility, and community adoption.

## 4   Discussion

By introducing a systematic, data-driven framework for simulation-based forward-looking process mining, this research addresses several longstanding gaps in the field. The proposed approaches enable the automated extraction of simulation models from event logs, support multi-level analysis through fine- and coarse-grained modeling, and facilitate hybrid simulation scenarios that bridge operational and strategic perspectives.

A key strength of the framework lies in its generality and extensibility: it is applicable to a wide range of event logs and process domains, and the implemented tools are open source and modular, supporting further research and integration. The systematic transformation of event logs into aggregated process logs provides a foundation for diagnostics, prediction, and simulation at multiple levels of abstraction. The hybrid modeling approach, which enables the interaction between DES and SD models, opens new avenues for comprehensive process analysis and what-if scenario evaluation.

Nevertheless, several limitations remain. The scope of empirical validation is constrained by the availability of real-world event logs and the complexity of implementing large-scale, industry-grade scenarios. The reliance on user intervention for model specification and scenario design, particularly in coarse-grained and hybrid simulations, highlights the need for more automated and user-friendly interfaces. Scalability challenges persist in the processing of large event logs and the execution of complex simulation models. Future work should focus on addressing these limitations by expanding the range of tested domains, improving automation in model generation, and developing scalable, interactive simulation environments.

The presented framework provides a robust foundation upon which the community can build. Researchers and practitioners are encouraged to extend the tools, apply the methodologies to new domains, and contribute to the development of standards and benchmarks for simulation-based process mining.

## 5   Conclusion

This paper has presented a unified framework for simulation-based forward-looking process mining, integrating fine-grained and coarse-grained simulation models and enabling hybrid scenarios that combine operational and strategic analysis. The main contributions include systematic model extraction from event logs, automated aggregation and variable extraction for coarse-grained simulation, and the design of hybrid simulation frameworks that synchronize DES and SD models. Despite these advances, significant challenges remain, including the need for standardized model representations, scalable aggregation techniques, and real-time, adaptive hybrid models. Future research should focus on integrating machine learning for automation, developing industry-scale evaluation platforms, and fostering community standards. In summary, simulation is positioned as a core pillar of forward-looking process mining, providing the analytical foundation for predictive, prescriptive, and adaptive business process management in the era of digital transformation.

## References


1. van der Aalst, W.M.P.: Process Mining - Data Science in Action, 2nd edn. Springer, Cham (2016). https://doi.org/10.1007/978-3-662-49851-4
2. van der Aalst, W.M.P.: Process mining and simulation: a match made in heaven! In: Computer Simulation Conference (SummerSim 2018), pp. 1–12. ACM Press (2018)
3. van der Aalst, W., et al.: Process mining manifesto. In: Daniel, F., Barkaoui, K., Dustdar, S. (eds.) BPM 2011. LNBIP, vol. 99, pp. 169–194. Springer, Heidelberg (2012). https://doi.org/10.1007/978-3-642-28108-2_19
4. van der Aalst, W.M., Carmona, J.: Process Mining Handbook. Springer, Cham (2022)
5. Kirchdorfer, L., Blümel, R., Kampik, T., Van der Aa, H., Stuckenschmidt, H.: Agentsimulator: an agent-based approach for data-driven business process simulation. In: 2024 6th International Conference on Process Mining (ICPM), pp. 97–104 (2024). https://doi.org/10.1109/ICPM63005.2024.10680660
6. Knopp, B., Pourbafrani, M., van der Aalst, W.M.P.: Discovering object-centric process simulation models. In: 2023 5th International Conference on Process Mining (ICPM), pp. 81–88 (2023). https://doi.org/10.1109/ICPM60904.2023.10271944
7. Leemans, S.J.J., Syring, A.F., van der Aalst, W.M.P.: Earth movers' stochastic conformance checking. In: Hildebrandt, T., van Dongen, B.F., Röglinger, M., Mendling, J. (eds.) BPM 2019. LNBIP, vol. 360, pp. 127–143. Springer, Cham (2019). https://doi.org/10.1007/978-3-030-26643-1_8
8. López-Pintado, O., Dumas, M.: Business process simulation: probabilistic modeling of intermittent resource availability and multitasking behavior. Inf. Syst. **127**, 102471 (2025)
9. Pourbafrani, M.: Forward-Looking Process Mining : Data-Driven Simulation. Dissertation, RWTH Aachen University, Aachen (2023). https://doi.org/10.18154/RWTH-2023-11014

10. Pourbafrani, M., van der Aalst, W.M.P.: Extracting process features from event logs to learn coarse-grained simulation models. In: La Rosa, M., Sadiq, S., Teniente, E. (eds.) CAiSE 2021. LNCS, vol. 12751, pp. 125–140. Springer, Cham (2021). https://doi.org/10.1007/978-3-030-79382-1_8

11. Pourbafrani, M., van der Aalst, W.M.P.: Interactive process improvement using enriched process trees. In: The 2nd International Workshop on AI-enabled Process Automation, ICSOC Conference 2021 (2021)

12. Pourbafrani, M., van der Aalst, W.M.P.: Hybrid business process simulation: updating detailed process simulation models using high-level simulations. In: Research Challenges in Information Science, pp. 177–194. Springer, Cham (2022). https://doi.org/10.1007/978-3-031-05760-1_11

13. Pourbafrani, M., van der Aalst, W.M.P.: Data-driven simulation in process mining: introducing a reference model. In: Communications of the ECMS, Volume 37, Issue 1, June 2023 - The ECMS2023 Proceedings, pp. 136–143 (2023)

14. Pourbafrani, M., Balyan, S., Ahmed, M., Chugh, S., van der Aalst, W.M.P.: GenCPN: automatic generation of CPN models for processes (2021)

15. Pourbafrani, M., Jiao, S., van der Aalst, W.M.P.: SIMPT: process improvement using interactive simulation of time-aware process trees. In: Cherfi, S., Perini, A., Nurcan, S. (eds.) RCIS 2021. LNBIP, vol. 415, pp. 588–594. Springer, Cham (2021). https://doi.org/10.1007/978-3-030-75018-3_40

16. Pourbafrani, M., Rafiei, M., Berti, A., van der Aalst, W.M.P.: Interactive business process comparison using conformance and performance insights - a tool. In: Research Challenges in Information Science - 16th International Conference, RCIS 2022, Barcelona, Spain, 17–20 May 2022. LNBIP, vol. 446, pp. 735–743. Springer, Cham (2022). https://doi.org/10.1007/978-3-031-05760-1_50

17. Pourbafrani, M., van Zelst, S.J., van der Aalst, W.M.P.: Semi-automated time-granularity detection for data-driven simulation using process mining and system dynamics. In: Dobbie, G., Frank, U., Kappel, G., Liddle, S.W., Mayr, H.C. (eds.) ER 2020. LNCS, vol. 12400, pp. 77–91. Springer, Cham (2020). https://doi.org/10.1007/978-3-030-62522-1_6

18. Pourbafrani, M., van Zelst, S.J., van der Aalst, W.M.P.: Supporting automatic system dynamics model generation for simulation in the context of process mining. In: Abramowicz, W., Klein, G. (eds.) BIS 2020. LNBIP, vol. 389, pp. 249–263. Springer, Cham (2020). https://doi.org/10.1007/978-3-030-53337-3_19

19. Rubensson, C., Pufahl, L., Mendling, J.: A conceptual framework for resource analysis in process mining. In: Enterprise Design, Operations, and Computing. EDOC 2024 Workshops, pp. 183–202. Springer, Cham (2025)

20. Salas, E., Arias, M., Aguirre, S., Rojas, E.: Combining process mining and process simulation in healthcare: a literature review. IEEE Access (2024)

21. Sterman, J.D.: Business Dynamics: Systems Thinking and Modeling for a Complex World. McGraw-Hill (2000)

# What is the Problem?
## Process Mining with a Control Theory Perspective


Andrea Burattin$^{(\boxtimes)}$ and Ekkart Kindler

Technical University of Denmark, Kgs. Lyngby, Denmark
`{andbur,ekki}@dtu.dk`



**Abstract.** Process mining aims to discover and monitor business processes from event data, traditionally evaluated using criteria such as simplicity, generalization, fitness, and precision. But, these criteria mostly assess how well the discovered model reflects the observed event data; they do not assess how well the discovered model serves its purpose. Looking at business process management and process mining from a control theory point of view, led us to including business goals and key performance indicators into the feedback loop; which gives feedback on how well a discovered process model serves its purpose. In this paper, we propose a framework for process mining and business process management with a control theory perspective. This framework helps us identifying additional quality dimensions on the level of business goals, such as stability, robustness and responsiveness. In addition, this framework identifies the sources of disturbances on a more detailed level than the traditional notions of noise and incompleteness in process mining. This perspective not only enriches process mining evaluation but also offers a deeper understanding of the discipline.

**Keywords:** Process Mining · Control Theory · Stability · Robustness


## 1 Introduction

Process Mining (PM) emerged from the vision of Wil van der Aalst [8], who not only conceived a new way of thinking about processes in combination with corresponding execution data, but also developed the theoretical, methodological, and technological foundations that enabled the discipline to flourish. Over the past few decades, what started as a discipline within Business Process Management (BPM) has matured into a very active area of research, combining conceptual rigor and advanced data-driven methodologies. Its impact has been expanding beyond academia, and Process Mining has achieved remarkable relevance in industry as well.

Process Mining is concerned with deriving process models from the observations of the execution of these processes in some IT system (event traces) and in monitoring such processes based on these observations [7,14]. The first is called process discovery, and the second is called conformance checking.


© The Author(s), under exclusive license to Springer Nature Switzerland AG 2026
J. Mendling et al. (Eds.): Wil van der Aalst Festschrift, LNCS 16480, pp. 471–484, 2026.
https://doi.org/10.1007/978-3-032-17618-9_32

For assessing the quality of a discovered process model and the underlying process mining algorithm, there exist four well-established quality criteria: simplicity, generalization, fitness, and precision. These criteria determine how well a discovered process model captures the behaviour of the observations and the quality of the discovered model itself.

These well-established quality criteria, however, only indirectly assess the quality of the mining algorithm itself. Therefore, additional analysis includes the behaviour of the mining algorithm in the presence of noise, i.e., incomplete and inaccurate observations in event traces.

Therefore, we asked ourselves how we could capture some quality criteria like stability, robustness, speed, or responsiveness of process mining algorithms, and looked at how some of these notions are defined and formalized in other disciplines like mathematics, numerics, and control theory. And, in particular, control theory as a classical engineering discipline dealing with feedback loops and avoiding instability due to positive feedback loops seemed to provide a good starting point.

Our first attempts at adapting some of the concepts and frameworks of control theory to the area of business process management and process mining were failing. We could not figure out what the concepts of set points, input and output values, and disturbances and errors actually should be in the world of BPM and PM. Only after we added the concepts of *goals* and *key performance indicators* (KPI), things started to fall into place. In addition, goals and KPIs do not only allow us to adopt the control theory framework for process mining; they make sure that the process goals are a target value of the feedback loop, which will keep the process model *fit for its purpose*. Even though goals had been mentioned as a crucial part in BPM for a long time [6, 12], they often did not get the attention they deserve. The control theoretic approach made them a necessity.

In this paper, we present a framework for business process management, process-aware information systems, and workflow-management inspired by control theory. And we show how it can help define criteria for the quality of such a system, which include stability, robustness, and performance. In addition, this framework allows us to identify different kinds of disturbances and their sources. Lastly, it emphasizes once again the goals of a process as a crucial part of defining and managing processes, and means to honestly measure whether or to which degree these goals are achieved.

We claim that having this framework in the back of our minds will help us to better understand what we are doing in process mining.


## 2   Background

To position our control-theoretic perspective on process mining, we first revisit the core ideas from these disciplines. This includes an overview of process mining concepts within BPM, a brief recap of control theory notions, and a discussion on how process mining projects are typically structured in practice. Together, these provide the conceptual basis for the rest of the paper.

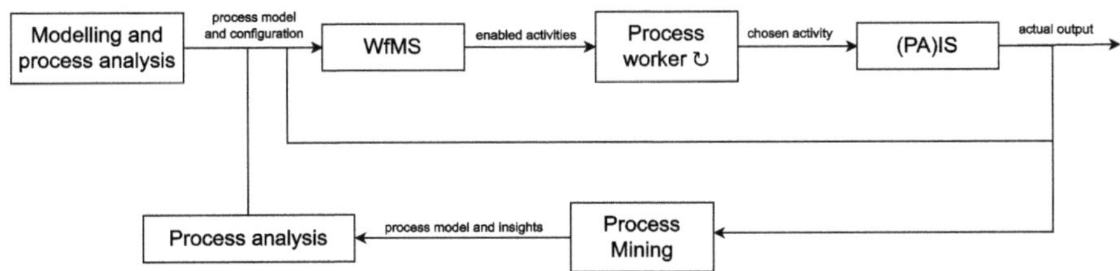



**Fig. 1.** Business Process Management and Process Mining.

*Business Process Management and Process Mining.* Figure 1 shows the traditional and slightly simplified version of the life cycles of business processes in workflow management systems (WfMS) and process-aware information systems (PAIS) [5,9,16]. The diagram already includes some process mining activities for monitoring the processes and for updating and configuring the processes. The life cycle starts with the creation of a model of a process. This model is then used by a workflow management system for coordinating the work on these processes: showing which activities the agents can choose. The agents or process workers can be human actors or software agents, that pick activities, which, in the traditional view of the Workflow Management Coalition, would be done by the work item handler [6]. The agents (human actors or software agents) would pick and then perform the respective activity by adding and changing data, and eventually finishing the activity. The data would be stored and changed in some information system, but also trigger the workflow system to update the available activities, which the agents can choose from. And this would leave a trace of what has happened in the different processes, which is called the *event stream* or *event log.*

At the bottom of Fig. 1, it is shown how process mining techniques use these event logs for monitoring the process and also for discovering new and better fitting models of the process. These can be used to change the model or the configuration of the processes—either automatically or by human intervention—based on insights obtained by process mining. For this, the event log could either be processed offline as a section of the event log at certain points in time, or the event stream could be processed online while the system is running. We call the latter case "streaming process mining" [1].

*Control Theory.* For later reference, we briefly recapitulated some of the core concepts of control theory, picked from the introduction of Dorf's and Bishop's book on Modern Control Systems [4]. Control theory is about controlling a system, where the system is typically a *dynamic system* with continuous signals and variables. In control systems, there are several systems under consideration, the system that is to be controlled, the actual *controller*, and the overall system consisting of both together, which is called the *control system*. In order to make this distinction clear and to avoid confusion, the system to be controlled is

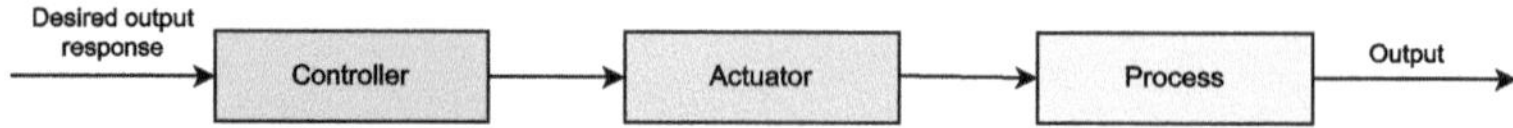



**Fig. 2.** Open-loop control system (after Fig. 1.2 from [4]). The different blocks are colored to simplify their identification.

often called the *process*, which nicely aligns with business processes management anyway.

Control theory distinguishes between two different types of control systems: *open-loop control systems* and *closed-loop control systems*. Figure 2 shows a block diagram of an open-loop control system. It consists of the process (i.e. the system to be controlled), for example, this could be a car, where the gas pedal or accelerator would be pressed down to a certain level to run the car at a certain speed, called the target or the set speed. Dorf and Bishop call this the "Desired output response" of the process. And there are a controller and an actuator that will affect the process to reach the desired output value. In our car example, this would be pressing the accelerator to a certain point for setting the desired speed; the controller would be all the mechanical (and digital) contraptions that open some valve in the combustor to a certain level to let in the right amount of gas to run the engine at certain rotation per minutes, and this would bring the car to run at a certain speed—hopefully close to the set target speed.

As you might have already guessed, this is not really how it works. Pressing the accelerator of a car to a certain level does not immediately correlate to the car's speed, even after the steady state is reached. There are many other factors that directly or indirectly affect the speed of the car, such as weight, wind, and, most importantly, the slope of the road. We would need to press the accelerator a bit more when the road goes up and a bit less when the road goes down. In general, these other factors are called *disturbances*.

In order to take care of these uncontrollable and unpredictable factors, control theory introduced control systems with a feedback loop or closed-loop control systems, as shown in Fig. 3. In a closed-loop control system, the actual output value (in our example, the speed of the car) is measured by a sensor, and the difference between the set target value and the actual output value (the error) is fed to the controller. This way, the speed can be controlled more accurately in spite of disturbances, noise in the measurement and even unknown factors.

In the real world, there are always disturbances. Therefore, the block diagram for closed-loop systems from Fig. 3, in addition to the feedback loop, shows the points where disturbances and noise might come into the system, or at least which sources of disturbances there are in the overall system.

Closed-loop control systems and the concept of feedback loops are at the core of control theory. They allow to take the actual output value into account for controlling the system, and this way are able to closely reach the desired output value even in the presence of disturbances and noise.

In spite of these advantages, the feedback loop introduces some additional problems: when not carefully designed, it could happen that the output value

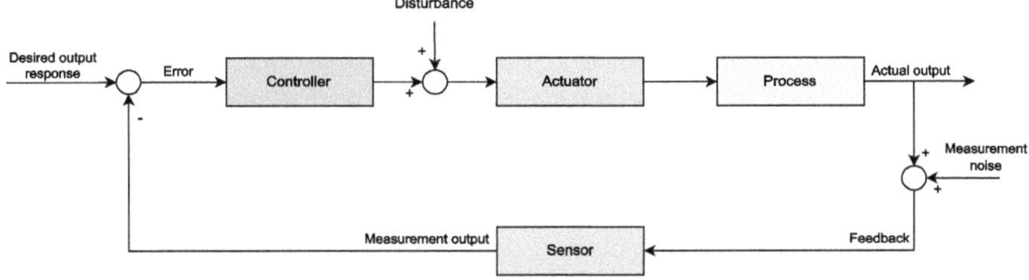


**Fig. 3.** Closed-loop control system with disturbances and noise (after Fig. 1.4 from [4]). The different blocks are colored to simplify their identification.

of such a system starts oscillating even when the desired output value is not changing and when there are no disturbances and noise at all; and the amplitude of the oscillation might steadily increase over time. The best-known example from daily life is the acoustic feedback loop, which results in howling loudspeakers when a microphone picks up the sound from the loudspeakers of a sound system again and is fed back to the sound system and its loudspeakers. This effect is also known as the Larsen effect.[1] Such systems are called *unstable* in control theory.

Control theory has developed different quality criteria for such closed-loop systems. Most prominently, stability, which would avoid the above-mentioned acoustic feedback, i.e., the Larsen effect. Even though the precise definitions vary depending on the context, in a nutshell, stability means that if the target value is not changed and there are no disturbances, the system will reach an equilibrium again; or if the input value is changed by a finite value, the output value will only change by a finite amount (bounded-input-bounded-output). Control theory provides a whole body of theories for analysing and guaranteeing the stability of closed-loop control systems under certain assumptions. See the book of Dorf and Bishop [4] for examples.

In addition to stability, control theory researchers came up with several other important quality criteria: Concerning performance, there are *accuracy* and *speed*: how accurate and fast is the desired output value obtained; and there is *robustness*, which captures how well the desired properties are achieved even in the presence of other unplanned errors, which include disturbances (that were not made explicit), but also the presence of design errors.

*Process Mining Project Methodologies.* After a brief introduction to control theory, let's move back to process mining. In practice, process mining projects are typically organized according to established methodologies. A prominent example is the PM$^2$ methodology [14,15], which provides a phased approach covering

---

[1] This effect is named after the Danish scientist Søren Absalon Larsen, professor of electrical engineering at Danmarks Tekniske Højskole, which now is the Technical University of Denmark (DTU). Examples of such effects can be listened to at https:// en.wikipedia.org/wiki/Larsen_effect.

project planning, data extraction and preparation, analysis and evaluation, and the implementation of improvements. $PM^2$ emphasizes iterative cycles and the involvement of stakeholders to ensure that process mining results are actionable and aligned with organizational needs.

Similarly, the L* family of life cycles models [13,14] conceptualizes process mining as a recurring set of activities comprising discovery, enhancement, and operational support. These models are closely tied to the business process management life cycle, highlighting the iterative nature of process monitoring and adjustment.

Although these approaches provide valuable guidance on structuring process mining projects, they are largely procedural in nature: they do not explicitly incorporate or foresee aspects such as stability or robustness of the results. For example, $PM^2$ includes an evaluation step, but it does not really emphasize the stability of the outcomes, but relates them to previous iterations. And there are no feedback loops assessing whether the processes are fit for purpose, meaning whether they are actually achieving their goals.

Recent literature [17] shows that the involvement of human analysts and the choices they make, as well as the interpretative steps, remain a critical aspect of process mining projects. Without explicitly talking about stability and robustness, process mining projects risk yielding insights that are fragile. A control-theoretic approach can complement existing methodologies by providing a structural lexicon to discuss new quality dimensions and feedback concepts. In this way, the strength of structured project management approaches can be combined with a more rigorous system-level evaluation of the outcomes.

Two important phenomena in process mining and the representativeness of event logs are *noise* and *incompleteness* [14, Sect. 6.4.2]: *noise* refers to rare and infrequent behaviour not representative of the typical behaviour of the process, and *incompleteness* refers to event logs with too few events for process discovery. In the control theory setting, these are two particular kinds of disturbances. Our framework enables us to pinpoint this notion of noise, as well as other disturbances.

## 3   Aligning Process Mining and Control Systems

In this section, we revisit the concepts of business process management and process mining in light of control theory, as shown in Fig. 1 and discussed in Sect. 2. First and foremost, in BPM, the values between the different components are not continuous signals as they would be in control theory, but they are sequences of discrete values; and the values themselves can be composite and more complex than a single signal, such as events with many attributes, and even complete process models or trace alignments. This renders most of the mathematics of dynamic continuous systems of control theory not immediately applicable in our BPM and PM setting.

Figure 1 shows that there are some feedback loops, so we can already guess that we are in a *closed loop* scenario. Some of the performance criteria of control theory, like accuracy, are also used in process mining—even though with a slightly different meaning. In particular, for process mining, we would expect a notion of stability similar to the one in control theory. However, there are only a few papers that mention it or even go into details of a definition in the context of process mining [2,11]. What stands out even more is that the input and output of this "loop" do not match on the type level: the input is the process model—ignoring the configuration information for a moment—and the output is event data in the form of an event log. We could, of course, cut up the loop after the process mining block. If process mining were in the discovery setting, where the output would be another process model, the input and output would be of the same type: process models. In the setting of workflow management systems and process mining, however, this would be, at large, a bit trivial since, by the setup without any disturbances, the output model would always be the same[2] of the input model. Only disturbances would ever lead to a significant change in the process model—even when the process model is far from meeting its goals (cf. "rediscovery problem"). In addition, from the control theory setting of closed-loop systems, we have the feeling that the input and output of the controlled system should be on a more abstract level than a detailed model, like on the level of "business goals" and "key performance indicators" (KPIs). Process models would just be a *way* to accomplish these goals, and KPIs would be a way to measure the extent to which the goals have been achieved by a certain model and its executions (in a WfMS and PAIS). Therefore, we would need to have a closed loop, which involves setting goals and measures to determine the extent to which these goals have been achieved as input and output. It is at this level that the performance, stability, and robustness criteria should be applied.

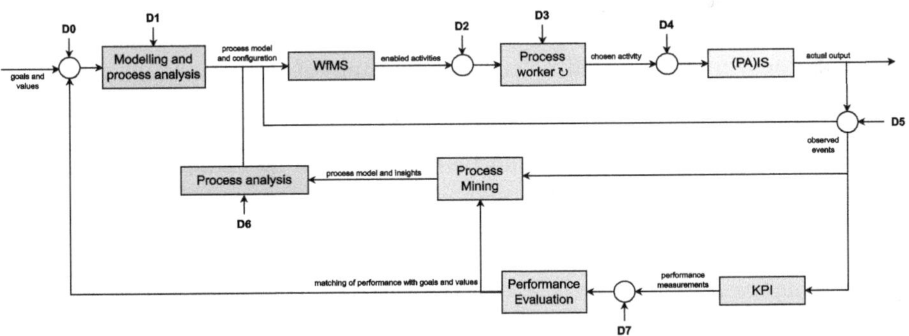


**Fig. 4.** Conceptual Framework with a Control Theory Angle. The background colours of the different components refer to the type reported in Fig. 3: blue are controllers, green is the actuator, yellow is the process, and orange are sensors (Color figure online).

Most closed-loop control systems, in control theory, make explicit at which point disturbances are coming in, as shown in the block diagram of Fig. 3.

---

[2] Or, when the agents choose to use only a subset of available behaviour, a subset.

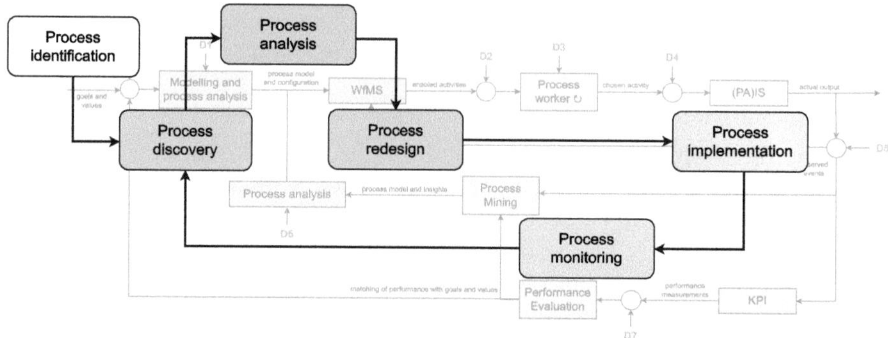


**Fig. 5.** The BPM life cycle overlaid on top of the proposed conceptual framework. The background colours of the different components refer to the type reported in Fig. 3: blue are controllers, green is the actuator, yellow is the process, and orange are sensors. (Color figure online)

Figure 4 shows an extension of the diagram in Fig. 1 and provides a more coherent and comprehensive picture of how control theory could be used to express where process mining "lives" in an organizational setting. The first extension comprises the modelling of the input of the system: "goals and values". In business process management, goals are typically formulated as text, if at all; and, unfortunately, there are often no metrics for measuring how well a process actually fits its purpose. The goals could, however, be broken down to features and formulated as metrics that capture the extent to which the goal was achieved. These metrics would need to be formulated in a way that allows them to be applied to the event logs and produce a numeric value. Then, the values for these metrics would be the output value of the system (at some point in time); in contrast to classical control flow theory, however, they would not be continuous signals.

Typically, the overall goals would be broken down into some quality features and sub-features, which in turn could be formulated as metrics for measuring these features and aggregating them into the KPIs; these are the basis to formulate desired properties of such systems like stability, robustness, and performance, which will be discussed later in Sect. 5.

Altogether, the explicit formulation of the set goals and corresponding metrics form a closed-loop control system with set values and target values, and a feedback loop to ensure that the KPIs are actually achieved. Actually, Fig. 4 models a "multiloop feedback system" [4] where the outer-most loop verifies the achievement of the goals and values via the KPIs; and the innermost loop is focused on the process level, ensuring that the executions are happening according to the designed process model, regardless of whether this serves its purpose. The picture also highlights disturbances that could occur and disrupt the organization, which are be discussed in detail in Sect. 5. Please also note that the different blocks are coloured according to the block's meanings specified in Fig. 3:

blue components refer to controllers, green to the actuator, yellow to the process, and orange to sensors.

It is also relevant to mention that the "feedback loop" aspect of the proposed control system had to some extent already been identified in the literature and is called the "BPM life cycle" [5]. We believe that the framework presented in Fig. 4 can be useful in making the BPM life cycle more tangible and, in particular, in establishing a more explicit link between process mining and such life cycle. Figure 5 presents the BPM life cycle on top of the proposed framework, where the different components of the BPM life cycle have been coloured according to the block meanings specified in Fig. 3.

## 4   The Need for Metrics in Process Mining

The evaluation of process mining algorithms is a central topic in the field. Traditionally, the quality of a discovered process model is assessed along four well-established dimensions: fitness, precision, generalization, and simplicity [14]. Fitness captures the extent to which the model reproduces the observed event traces, while precision measures whether the model allows for behaviour not present in the log. Generalization aims to avoid overfitting to a specific log by considering unseen but possible behaviour, and simplicity rewards models that are understandable and not overly complex. Together, these criteria provide a balanced view of how well a process model reflects the recorded events and whether it is usable for analysis and decision making.

Despite their widespread acceptance, these metrics capture only certain aspects of model quality. They are primarily focused on the outcome of the process mining and only indirectly assess the underlying algorithms and the more general insights. In addition, these metrics do not directly evaluate how a mining algorithm performs under realistic conditions, such as the presence of noise, incomplete logs, or changes in the process. For example, two algorithms might achieve high fitness and precision, but one may be highly sensitive to small perturbations in the input data, while the other produces more stable results. This difference remains unnoticeable under the traditional evaluation framework.

In addition, the existing evaluation criteria are inherently *static* in nature: they assume the availability of a fixed event log and do not easily extend to scenarios where data arrives in a continuous fashion. However, process mining outcomes, in order to be useful, should have consequences on the actual process being executed, thus creating a dynamic environment. In such dynamic contexts, additional qualities become relevant, such as stability of the mining results over time, robustness to missing or noisy events, and responsiveness to newly arriving information. Without appropriate metrics, these aspects remain unassessed.

Finally, current process mining metrics focus on the internal validity with respect to the *process model* rather than the general *process* and its *goals*. In practice, organizations apply process mining to improve precise metrics, such as process performance, compliance, and customer satisfaction [7, 10]. Therefore, process mining evaluations should not only focus on structural model qualities, but also on whether the insights generated are reliable, actionable, and generally aligned with the organizational goals and key performance indicators.

## 5   Metric, Disturbances and Noise in Process Mining

The control theory framework presented in Sect. 2 provides a well-established vocabulary for analysing the behaviour of dynamic systems with feedback. As discussed, process mining can indeed be seen as such a type of system; therefore, when we transfer control-theory notions to process mining, it is also important to transfer the quality concepts and metrics into this new domain.

Specifically, concepts like *stability*, *robustness*, and *disturbance* offer a valuable perspective for evaluating process mining algorithms beyond the traditional dimensions.

*Disturbances.* As mentioned previously, in control theory, disturbances represent unexpected external inputs that affect the behaviour of the system [3]. Analogously, disturbances can happen in organizations too, and they can affect the smoothness of operations. Referring to Fig. 4, disturbances can happen essentially in any possible stage of the processing; some of these disturbances are well-known and investigated, others are less explored.

As mentioned at the end of Sect. 2, please remember that there is only a partial overlap between the concept of "disturbance" in control theory and "noise" in process mining. Let's explore the meaning of the disturbances in Fig. 4:

**D0:** Disturbances in this case can cause a misinterpretation of the goals and the values of the organization, for example, due to a cognitive bias. Examples:
  - In a healthcare scenario, the primary focus of the organization is on the social media presence instead of being on the treatment of the patients.
  - In an educational organization, there is little focus on the actual quality of education, compared to the recreational activities.

**D1:** Disturbances in the modelling phase cause the goals and the values of an organization to not be properly captured and described in the process model. Examples of such a situation are:
  - An emergency room models "patient admission" without considering a triage, treating patients on a first-come-first-served basis.
  - In a bank, the process model assumes that all loan requests follow a uniform approval flow, but in reality, a VIP customer may skip steps, leading to mismatches.

**D2:** Disturbances in this case are happening when the process worker does not perceive the correct set of activities to perform from the workflow management system. Examples of such a situation are:
  - A doctor's task list doesn't update after a nurse finishes a prerequisite activity due to system lag.
  - An agent follows a direct supervisor's ad-hoc instruction rather than the recommended protocol.

**D3:** The actual process worker, in certain scenarios, may decide to overrule the workflow management system and simply proceed in executing a different activity (e.g., knowledge-intensive situations). For example:
- A doctor, during a medical procedure, makes the conscious decision to deviate from the clinical protocol due to specific circumstances not previously known.
- Upon delivery of a package at an address, the delivery person realizes that the recipient of a second package, originally scheduled for a different address, is there, and they deliver the second package to the same place.

**D4:** In this setting, a disturbance is represented by the misalignment between what the process worker executed and what is reported into the (PA)IS. This could happen due to communication issues. Examples:
- A nurse administers medication but forgets to log it in the system, leading to an incomplete event trace.
- A worker forgets scanning a barcode on a package, so the system shows the item as "in storage" while it has already been shipped.

**D5:** Disturbances in this case indicate that the output of the (PA)IS is not observed correctly. Examples of such a situation are:
- During a system crash, some of the appointment visits in a hospital are not logged.
- In an online store, order confirmation emails are sent, but the event log fails to record the corresponding "order placed".

**D6:** Disturbances in this setting typically refer to the wrong interpretation of process mining results and the effect that these have in implementing resolutions. Examples of such a situation are:
- A department is flagged as "slow" but, in reality, it handles high-complexity cases (e.g., fraud detection team).
- An analyst discards results referring to "rare cases" from the model, though they are critical to ensure compliance.

**D7:** This disturbance, similar to D5, can be caused by a faulty communication channel. This can be due to a delay in communication or just an incomplete view of the situation. Examples:
- A hospital's dashboard shows reduced waiting times, but it excludes emergency patients who were logged in a separate system.
- Customer reports are not yet available from a key region (due to a different time zone), biasing the evaluation.

Please note that the characterization of disturbances described in this section is not complete, and new disturbances may be identified in specific scenarios.

*Stability.* In control theory, stability refers to the ability of a system to return to a desired equilibrium state after small perturbations. Translated to process mining, stability can be understood as the consistency of discovered models and analysis results under small changes in the input event data. For example, if a few traces are removed, perturbed, or slightly altered, the process mining/evaluation algorithms should still produce models that are structurally and behaviourally close to the original one. When tailoring this concept to the terminology depicted in Fig. 4, stability can actually refer to the results of process mining (i.e., the models being discovered) or, more importantly, to the "outer" feedback loop involving performance evaluation. The latter case refers, essentially, to the stability of the entire organization to disturbances that can occur throughout.

*Robustness.* Robustness in control theory refers to the ability of a system to maintain certain quality criteria under a variety of operating conditions, including noise and disturbances. Translated to process mining, robustness can be understood as the extent to which discovered models and analytical insights remain meaningful and useful when the data is incomplete, noisy, or, more generally, non-ideal. Unlike stability, which focuses on the sensitivity to small perturbations, robustness is about maintaining reliable analysis results under adverse conditions. Anchoring robustness in Fig. 4 means that an organization is capable of delivering good performance (i.e., resulting from the KPI measurements with respect to the goals) despite challenges in the modelling or in how agents are behaving.

*Performance (accuracy and speed/latency).* In addition to stability and robustness, our framework can be characterized by at least two performance dimensions: accuracy and speed/latency, similar to those in control theory. Accuracy here refers to how closely the results of the process mining and the general KPIs evaluation approximate the true values (resp. the original process and the goal/values of the organization). Speed or latency, on the other hand, becomes critical in a closed-loop setting as the feedback loop should allow the system to adjust itself in order to reach the desired goals. A process mining system that is highly accurate but suffers from delivering results very slowly may fail to provide timely insights for operational interventions, while a system that is fast but inaccurate risks producing misleading guidance. Therefore, evaluating the performance means to assess the balance of different aspects: algorithms should be benchmarked not only on how correct their results are, but also on how efficiently they can be deployed and how reactive their results can become actionable.

Considering all these aspects, we can conclude that following the analogy with control theory, process mining deployments that are stable (resistant to small perturbations), robust (able to operate under imperfect conditions), and performant (delivering accurate and fast results) will provide more reliable and actionable insights in real-world environments.

## 6  Conclusion and Outlook

Drawing from the ancient insights often attributed to Heraclitus that *"the only constant is change"* we argue that when deploying process mining techniques, we must consider that execution and behaviour evolve over time. In this paper, we propose a perspective on process mining that is enriched by concepts from control theory. While the traditional evaluation of process discovery has been dominated by quality criteria such as fitness, precision, generalization, and simplicity, our idea emphasizes additional qualities such as stability and robustness. By framing process mining as a feedback closed-loop system, we highlighted the importance of explicitly considering disturbances, their sources, and their impact on the reliability of results—including fitness for purpose. The alignment with control theory does not replace existing evaluation criteria but complements them, offering a more dynamic lens that is better suited for modern process mining applications where data arrives continuously and organizations evolve rapidly.

Looking ahead, we see several avenues for future research. First, the proposed mapping of stability, robustness, and performance needs to be formalized into metrics that can be systematically applied across different algorithms and scenarios. Second, empirical validation is required to test whether these metrics capture meaningful differences in practice and whether they correlate with business outcomes. Third, integrating these concepts into existing process mining methodologies (e.g., $PM^2$, $L^*$) could help practitioners to pay adequate attention to performance, stability, and robustness of the results. Finally, making the disturbances more concrete can help in devising techniques and algorithms that will better cope with them.

By embracing these directions, process mining research and practice can move closer to an engineering discipline that is not only about understanding process models, but also about actively steering them towards organizational goals, thus properly answering the question: *"What is the problem?"*

# References


1. Andrea, B.: Streaming Process Mining. In: van der Aalst, W.M.P., Josep, C., (eds.) Process Mining Handbook, pp. 349–372. Springer, Cham (2022)
2. Pieter, D.K., Jochen, D.W.: A stability assessment framework for process discovery techniques. In: Proceedings of BPM, pp. 57–72. Springer, Cham (2016)
3. Pieter, D.K., Jochen, D.W.: A stability assessment framework for process discovery techniques. In: Proceedings of BPM, pp. 57–72. Springer, Cham (2016)
4. Richard, D.D., Robert, H.B.: Modern Control Systems. Pearson, $12^{th}$ edition, (2011)
5. Marlon, D., Marcello, L.R., Jan, M., Hajo, A.R.: Fundamentals of Business Process Management. Springer, 2 edn. (2018)
6. David, H.: The workflow reference model. Technical Report TC00-1003, The Workflow Management Coalition (WfMC), (1995)
7. IEEE Task Force on Process Mining. Process Mining Manifesto. In: Proc. of BPM Workshops, pp. 169–194. Springer, (2011)
8. Laura, M., Antal, B., Ton, A.J.M., Weijters, M., van der Aalst, W.M.P.: Process mining: discovering direct successors in process logs. In: Lange, S., Satoh, K., Smith, C.H. (eds.) Discovery Science. DS 2002, pp. 364–373. Springer, Berlin, Heidelberg (2002). https://doi.org/10.1007/3-540-36182-0_37
9. Reichert, M., Weber, B.: Enabling Flexibility in Process-Aware Information Systems. Springer, Berlin Heidelberg (2012)

10. Lars, R.: Process mining in action. Process Min. Action Principles Uuse Cases and Outloook **11**(7), 116–128 (2020)
11. Anne Rozinat, M.V., Van der Aalst, W.M.P.: Evaluating the quality of discovered process models. In: Conference ECML/PKDD 2008 Workshop on the Induction of Process Models, 15 September 2008, pp. 45–52 (2008)
12. Scheer, A. W.: ARIS — Business Process Modeling. Springer Science & Business Media (2000)
13. van der Aalst, W.M.P.: Process mining: discovering and improving Spaghetti and Lasagna processes. In In 2011 IEEE symposium on computational intelligence and data mining (CIDM), pages 1–7. IEEE, 4 (2011)
14. van der Aalst, W.M.P.: Process Mining. Springer, second edition (2016)
15. van Eck, M.L., Lu, X., Leemans, S.J.J., van der Aalst, W.M.P.: PM2: A Process Mining Project Methodology. In: International Conference on Advanced Information Systems Engineering, pp. 297–313 (2015)
16. Weske, M.: Business Process Management: Concepts, Languages. Architectures, Springer Nature (2024)
17. Zerbato, F., Zimmermann, L., Vrotsou, K., Weber, B.: From analysis to findings: How do process mining analysts discover results? Inf. Syst. **135**, 1 (2026)

# DisCoveR and Beyond: Exploring Recent Advances in Declarative Process Discovery

Tijs Slaats[(✉)], Paul Cosma, and Thomas Hildebrandt

Department of Computer Science (DIKU), University of Copenhagen,
Copenhagen, Denmark
**slaats@di.ku.dk**

**Abstract.** Declarative process mining has emerged as a powerful paradigm for modelling, analysing, and improving knowledge-intensive processes, offering flexibility and expressiveness beyond traditional procedural approaches. In this paper, we present a comprehensive overview of recent advances in declarative process discovery, with particular emphasis on Dynamic Condition Response (DCR) Graphs and the DisCoveR algorithm. We present a high-level overview of the base algorithm, discuss important extensions and successors that allow the mining of hierarchy, the use of labelled event logs, the mining of object-centric models, and the mining of probabilistic models, and provide a short overview of important enabling technologies such as a mapping to Petri nets and algorithms for model-log alignment. Finally, we briefly outline a number of key open questions and future research directions.

**Keywords:** Process Discovery · Alignment · Declarative Models · DCR Graphs

## 1  Introduction

Process modelling notations are commonly categorised into two paradigms: flow-based and constraint-based. The flow-based paradigm [3] represents control flow explicitly, usually via token-based semantics in notations such as Petri nets or BPMN. Tokens traverse activities according to predefined routing constructs such as sequences, choices, and parallelism. In contrast, the constraint-based paradigm [31,46] specifies the permissible behaviour declaratively through constraints over activities, enforcing aspects such as the ordering, co-occurrence, and mutual exclusion of activities. The set of allowed executions emerges from the satisfaction of these constraints rather than from an enumerated process graph. Conceptually, the former prescribes particular paths, whereas the latter describes the rules of the processes within which any execution conforming to the rules is valid.

Constraint-based techniques are often regarded as well-suited to knowledge-intensive processes conducted by professionals such as clinicians and legal practitioners. These processes exhibit high variability, substantial actor discretion,

© The Author(s), under exclusive license to Springer Nature Switzerland AG 2026
J. Mendling et al. (Eds.): Wil van der Aalst Festschrift, LNCS 16480, pp. 485–505, 2026.
https://doi.org/10.1007/978-3-032-17618-9_33

and case- and context-dependent decisions. Under such conditions, imperative flow-based models can suffer from combinatorial explosion: an attempt to encode many alternative paths often leads to "spaghetti" models that are difficult to validate, analyse, and maintain. Declarative specifications often allow this to be mitigated by modelling at the level of business rules, and avoiding over-specification of the various ways these rules can be realised whenever possible. Under the right circumstances, this has been noted to yield models that are more compact under high variability while still enabling rigorous reasoning about temporal dependencies.

As in many other areas of BPM, seminal work on constraint-based notations for flexible business process management was carried out by Wil van der Aalst and his co-workers, in particular Pesic who worked on the ConDec [45] language, the *Declarative Service Flow Language* (DecSerFlow [1,2]) and DECLARE [46] language, all based on the idea of introducing a graphical syntax for constraint patterns formalized in Linear-time Temporal Logic (LTL). The work brought constraint-based languages onto the scene of BPM, demonstrated their advantages for flexible and adaptable processes and was the start of declarative languages becoming more and more recognized in the field of BPM.

Independently of the work by Aalst, Pesic and co-workers, the declarative Dynamic Condition Response (DCR) Graphs [31,41] language came out of the collaboration with an industrial partner in a research project on Trustworthy Pervasive Healthcare Services[1] (TrustCare) research project, aiming to develop a formal, executable declarative language for distributed, flexible and adaptable workflow processes. DCR Graphs was both inspired by the the Process Matrix [36], an industrial declarative workflow language, developed by one of the industrial partners, and by prime event structures [61]. Relative to alternatives such as Declare [46] and DPIL [51], DCR Graphs are notable for their industrial adoption [27,28,40,44,55]. DCR Graphs provide an operational semantics based on a marking that tracks, for each activity, whether it is currently included, has been executed, or has pending responses. Four core relations, condition, response, include, and exclude, govern the dynamic availability of activities and obligations across the execution. Whereas the declarative nature of these relations enables the specification and enforcement of business rules, the use of a marking-based operational semantics allows for straightforward visualisation, analysis, and adaptation of processes at runtime. This semantic foundation is supported by mature modelling and simulation tools [24], as a process mining library [29], a range of documented industrial applications [27,32], and the deployment of DCR execution engines within commercial case management and workflow platforms widely used in Danish public-sector organizations [30,44].

Process mining [58,59] leverages historical executions, captured as event logs, to analyse and improve processes. Event logs typically consist of traces (cases) formed by timestamped activity events, often enriched with life-cycle transitions, resources, and data attributes. More recently, there has been a shift in the community towards *object-centric* process mining [5], which broadens the scope of

---

[1] https://pure.itu.dk/en/projects/trustworthy-pervasive-healthcare-services.

event logs and process models from capturing independent cases to capturing the interactions of various objects (including e.g. actors, resources, documents, physical items, etc.) within a single case, and across multiple cases. Key tasks include discovery (deriving models from logs) [4], conformance checking (quantifying agreement between logs and models) [48], and enhancement (refining models using log evidence) [60]. Evaluation commonly considers fitness, precision, generalisation, and simplicity [14,56], and techniques may operate offline on complete logs or online for operational monitoring [15,63].

Although early work on declarative process mining focused predominantly on Declare [20,37], research specific to DCR Graphs has accelerated in recent years. A central challenge has been the non-orthogonal nature of DCR relations [53]: whereas in Declare and other approaches grounded in formal logics the addition of a constraint to a model strictly limits the possible behaviour, this is not the case for DCR Graphs. The reason for this is quite intuitive: the inclusion relation allows the re-introduction of previously excluded behaviour, and when introduced to a model typically introduces new possible paths. This means that common pruning techniques used to reduce the search space of potential logical models that satisfy a log cannot be applied in the case of DCR Graphs.

This challenge was first made tractable by the introduction of DisCoveR, a discovery algorithm that learns DCR Graphs from event logs and has been reported to achieve high accuracy and runtime efficiency [13]. Empirical studies indicate that it performs competitively not only against other declarative miners but also relative to state-of-the-art imperative discovery techniques, suggesting that DCR-based models can capture complex behaviour compactly without sacrificing empirical quality measures. In particular, it has performed very well in international process discovery competitions, achieving first place in the Process Discovery Contest (PDC) at the International Conference on Process Mining in 2021 and 2023 [17].

After briefly addressing related work on declarative process mining in Sect. 2, we will in the following sections review recent advances in DCR-based process discovery. We first provide in Sect. 3 a short informal introduction to DCR Graphs. We then present in Sect. 4 a high-level overview of the DisCoveR algorithm, including an extension for mining hierarchical models, and a short discussion on techniques for mapping to Petri nets and computing model-log alignment. We then discuss in Sect. 5–7 three key successors to DisCoveR, which respectively allow binary mining on labelled data, mining on object-centric data, and producing probabilistic models. Finally, we provide in Sect. 8 a brief overview of the most important open research questions that we expect to be addressed in the field of DCR mining in the coming years and conclude the paper.

## 2   Related Work

A substantial body of work has addressed declarative process discovery, predominantly in the Declare family of languages.

The DECLARE MINER learns declarative patterns based on Linear Temporal Logic on finite traces (LTLf) or, in more recent work, regular expressions.

It checks an event log for a set of constraints instantiated over the activities in the log and counts activations and violations to select constraints that best describe observed behaviour [7,38]. MINERFUL improves on this work by introducing an efficient, language-agnostic pipeline to discover (and rank) Declare-style constraints by exploiting frequency, support, and confidence measures computed over log abstractions [21]. The first stages of the development of DisCoveR were heavily inspired by this approach of first abstracting the log to a smaller set of basic declarative patterns. Multi-perspective Declare (MP-Declare) extends declarative discovery to incorporate data, resource, and time perspectives by enriching templates with activation and correlation conditions mined from event attributes [50].

A key difference between these miners and the DCR-oriented techniques surveyed in this paper is the fact that they operate in a purely logical setting without non-orthogonal relations such as dynamic include/exclude. While this makes analysis of the log more straightforward, it also limits what models can be found, as there are limits on the formal expressiveness of the output language that are not present for DCR Graphs. In addition, mined DCR Graphs benefit heavily from extensive tool support not only from academic tools but also from commercial solutions, and the marking-based operational semantics allows for intuitive simulation of mined models, improving their explainability.

Process discovery has also been explored for the Declarative Process Intermediate Language (DPIL) [51,62], a textual, multi-perspective, declarative modelling language. The DPIL approach distinguishes itself from both the work on DCR Graphs and Declare by focusing on the organizational perspective of processes [49], as opposed to the control-flow perspective.

## 3   Dynamic Condition Response Graphs

Dynamic Condition Response (DCR) Graphs provide a declarative semantics for processes based on a runtime *marking* $M = (Ex, Re, In)$ that tracks, respectively, executed activities, pending responses (obligations), and included (currently relevant) activities [31,41,52]. An activity is enabled iff it is included and all its *conditions* are satisfied. When an enabled activity executes, the marking is updated: it is recorded as executed; triggered *responses* are added as pending obligations; and *include/exclude* effects may change which activities are considered as relevant in subsequent steps.

Figure 1 illustrates a simplified thesis writing process, using the four core relations:

(1) **Condition** ($a\bullet\!\!\leftarrow b$): while $b$ is included, $a$ can execute only after $b$ has executed at least once. In the example, conditions constrain the writing activities, so that they occur only after papers have been selected.

(2) **Response** ($a\bullet\!\!\rightarrow b$): executing $a$ creates a pending obligation to eventually execute $b$, unless $b$ is eventually permanently excluded instead. In the example, *Write introduction & related work* and *Write conclusion & future work* generate obligations to *Write Abstract*, ensuring that the abstract is always checked and

updated after changes are made to the other sections, even if an abstract had already been written before. Activities can also be initially pending, as denoted by the blue exclamation marks. This means that they must be done at least once from the start of the process, without the need for a response relation. By having several activities as initial pending obligations, we ensure that the process requires some form of execution. In contrast, a DCR Graph without initial pending responses will always accept the empty language.

(3) **Exclude** ($a\rightarrow\%b$): executing $a$ removes $b$ from the included set, making it ineligible for future execution (unless it is included again). Notably, it also makes constraints imposed by $b$ irrelevant, meaning that as long as the activity remains excluded, they do not have to be upheld. In the example, *Select papers* excludes itself, meaning that in normal circumstances this activity is only performed once.

(4) **Include** ($a\rightarrow+b$): executing $a$ returns $b$ into the included set, making it eligible for future execution if other constraints are satisfied. In the example, *New papers* includes *Select papers*, allowing the author to re-open the selection step if they publish new works. This also makes constraints imposed on and by the target activity relevant again. Note that both the exclude and include relations are dynamic: if we exclude an activity $e$ that imposes a condition on some activity $e'$, then execute $e'$, and later include $e$ again, it does not mean that the former execution of $e'$ was invalid. However, we cannot execute $e'$ again before we satisfy the condition by executing $e$, as it is now considered relevant again.

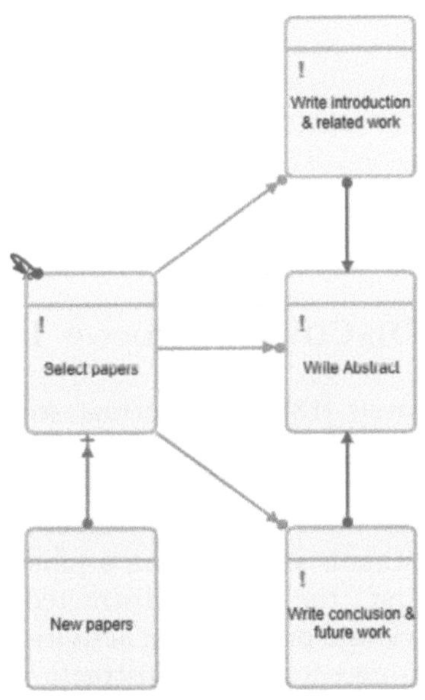



**Fig. 1.** Example DCR graph for a thesis-writing workflow.

Together, these relations define the behaviour of a process: any execution that satisfies all constraints, respects the intermediate markings, and eventually clears all responses is compliant with the model [31]. Interestingly, it has been shown formally that the combination of this small set of relations captures all regular and omega-regular languages [42]. In addition, Turing completeness can be achieved through the introduction of a single additional relation capturing dynamic instantiation of unique activity instances that have their own life cycle [25] (for example a "Write chapter" activity which can be instantiated with a separate marking for each chapter in the thesis). This shows us that essentially, any process, algorithm, or computer program can be modelled using DCR Graphs (Fig. 2).

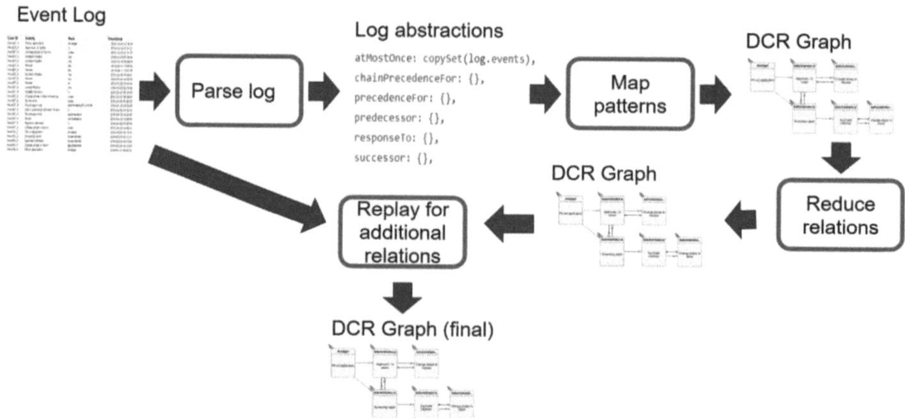

**Fig. 2.** High-level overview of the DisCoveR miner.

# 4    DISCOVER: Process Discovery for DCR Graphs

DisCoveR [13] is the current state-of-the-art discovery algorithm for inferring DCR Graphs from event logs. Following the constraint-based paradigm, it starts from an empty specification and incrementally adds relations that are consistent with all observed traces, thereby ensuring perfect fitness by construction. The algorithm is structured as a pipeline with four main phases.

First, the log is abstracted into lightweight data structures capturing behavioural properties of activities. Besides direct-adjacency information such as chain-precedence, the abstractions summarize trace-spanning correlations such as precedence and response relations, (indirect) successor/predecessor sets, and single-execution invariants (e.g., at-most-once). This emphasis on long-range dependencies, rather than only directly-follows relations, distinguishes DisCoveR from typical imperative miners and supports the inference of declarative obligations that need not correspond to local control-flow patterns.

Second, the algorithm maps these abstractions to DCR relations by checking entailment conditions derived from DCR execution semantics. For instance, if all occurrences of $a$ are eventually followed by $b$, we can add the relation $a \bullet\!\!\to b$ to the model, while systematic absence of $b$ before $a$ suggests a condition $a \bullet\!\!\leftarrow b$. Both of these can be derived directly from the abstractions resulting from the first stage. Co-occurrence and activation observations provide candidates for inclusion and exclusion. For example, the at-most-once abstraction maps directly to self-exclusions $(a \to\% a)$, and additional exclusions can be derived from the predecessor and successor sets by checking which activities never follow others. Finally, more imperative patterns such as chain-precedence are often representable through more complex patterns made up of multiple relations, which may also encompass the include relation. This approach produces exclusively perfectly fitting models, but may create a significant number of redundant relations.

In the third phase, to maintain model simplicity, DisCoveR applies reduction heuristics, primarily based on the removal of transitively entailed relations. Usually, this results in a significantly smaller set of relations that preserves fitness while improving readability.

Finally, the current model is analysed through log replay under DCR semantics. This enables the detection of additional conditions that cannot be inferred from static abstractions alone. This step has demonstrated significant potential for improving precision on various real-life logs, while maintaining the guarantee of perfect fitness.

The abstractions and the replay procedure can be implemented in time linear in the number of events, supporting scalability to large logs. Several optimized implementations leverage bitvector encodings for sets and relation matrices, enabling cache-friendly, vectorized operations and near-second run times on sizeable datasets [13,57]. Empirical evaluations on public benchmarks demonstrate competitive precision and overall accuracy [13,43], and the approach won the Process Discovery Contest (PDC) at ICPM 2021 and 2023 [17].

### 4.1  Mining Hierarchical DCR Graphs

Despite the simplicity gains achieved through relation reduction, the readability of models mined by DisCoveR remains a key challenge. Recent work addresses this by discovering hierarchical DCR Graphs, which enhance readability while preserving behavioural semantics [22].

In this approach, nested groups are used to gather activities that share the same relations in a shared syntactic and semantic construct, making it easier to spot similarities in behaviour between activities, and reducing the number of relations that need to be drawn, as a single arrow may denote a relation between all activities in groups. Notably the approach was evaluated on a large benchmark of real-life and synthetic event logs, measuring the size, density, separability, and constraint variability of mined models with and without grouping of activities showing a reduction in complexity on 3 of the 4 measures. The approach employs two separate algorithms, which can be used individually or in sequence. Each algorithm first mines a flat DCR model with DisCoveR [13], which is then analysed syntactically.

The first algorithm detects the well-known choice pattern, which captures that at most one activity from a designated set executes in a given process instance. In DCR, this is expressed with nested groups by placing the activities in a single group and adding a self-exclude relation from the group to itself. Operationally, when any member executes, the group is excluded and, by propagation, all members (including the one just executed) become excluded for the remainder of the case. We prioritize isolating this pattern because (a) it is widely understood by modellers, including novices; (b) it occurs frequently across domains; and (c) it typically yields a substantial reduction in visible inter-activity relations, materially improving readability.

The second algorithm greedily explores the space of possible groupings in order to optimize a configurable metric, for example, the total number of

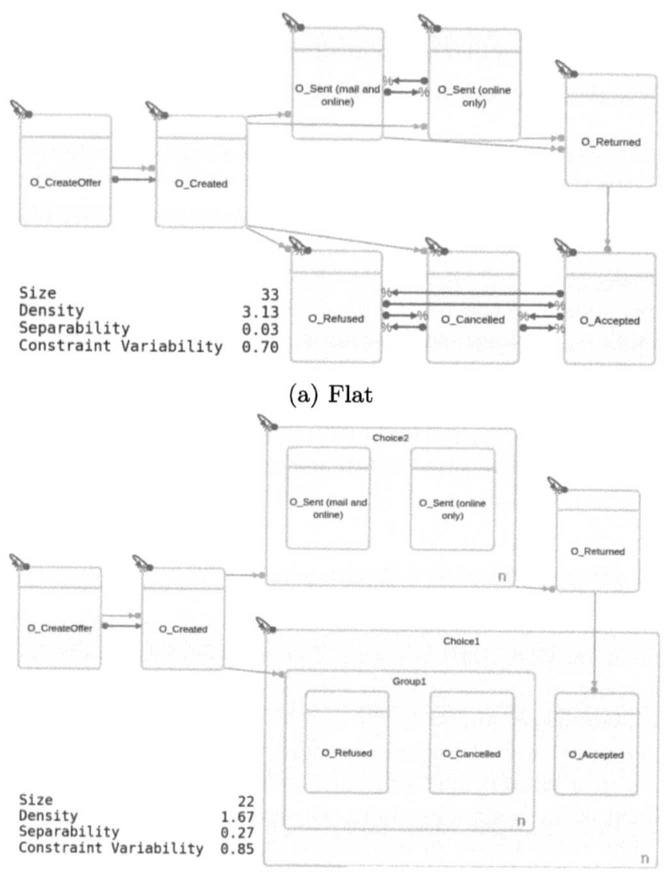


(a) Flat



(b) Both Choice & Group algorithms

**Fig. 3.** Hierarchical DCR Graphs for the BPIC17 Offer log. As presented in [22].

relations in the graph. This approach is significantly more general than the former, allowing the discovery of all kinds of possible reductions in structural complexity. As a result, it had the largest impact on the complexity metrics in the evaluation, but this comes with the caveat that it does not focus on identifying combinations of relations that are particularly intuitive to users, an equally important factor in the understandability of models which was not evaluated for this approach.

Figure 3 shows the results of running this approach on the BPIC17 log, as previously reported in [22].

## 4.2   Mining Petri Nets with DisCoveR

A recent line of work shows how specifications in Dynamic Condition Response (DCR) Graphs can be transformed into safe Petri nets equipped with inhibitor and read arcs, together with an acceptance criterion that mirrors DCR's notion of eventually discharging pending responses [23]. This bridge allows us to use DisCoveR [13] as a front end for Petri net discovery: first mine a perfectly fitting DCR model from an event log, then translate that model into a Petri net for downstream analysis with standard Petri net tool chains.

Intuitively, the translation encodes the DCR *marking* in Petri net *places* and represents each *activity* as one or more *transitions* having the same label. Inclusion is tracked by control places that enable or disable the corresponding transition via read arcs. Conditions employ control places that track whether prerequisite activities have (at least once) been executed. Responses are captured by producing tokens in obligation places upon firing the source activity; those tokens must eventually be consumed, reflecting that the corresponding targets need to occur or be justifiably made irrelevant. The main complication in the mapping is the fact that excluding events can make other relations irrelevant. To capture this correctly, we may need to duplicate transitions and places to correctly capture that the effect of executing an activity may depend on the current marking, which in the worst case can lead to significant state-space explosion.

Because the mapping preserves marking equivalence, enablement, and obligations, across activity executions, the DCR model and its Petri-net image are behaviourally equivalent up to bisimulation under the stated acceptance criterion [23]. This yields a practical mining pipeline: (i) apply DisCoveR to obtain a DCR model that fits the log by construction; (ii) translate the result to a safe Petri net; (iii) use mature PN analysis (e.g. reachability, coverability, invariant or model-checking analyses) to reason about the discovered behaviour. In effect, DisCoveR can be used to mine Petri nets via a declarative intermediate representation.

An important characteristic of the resulting nets is that they inherit the declarative nature of DCR. Rather than prescribing a single control-flow skeleton, the net may enable a large set of transitions concurrently, constrained only by current inclusion, satisfied conditions, and outstanding obligations. Consequently, the nets are often less block-structured than those produced by imperative miners, which may make them harder to read. On the other hand, in this way the mapping does preserve the full observed behaviour of the process, including all possible variations. Using a more declarative style of Petri nets may in such cases improve precision by avoiding cases where imperative miners would yield flower models. In early experiments, we have also noted that for some logs this approach actually yields smaller models if the block-structured miner employs multiple transitions for the same activities in order to improve precision. The declarative style, and making use of inhibitor and read arcs, appears to allow for increased conciseness in models as compared to approaches that mimic the underlying transitions system of the process. This is highlighted by the DisCoveR mined Petri net in Fig. 4 from the Road Traffic Fine Management Process log [39]. The net consists of 16 places, 11 transitions and 56 arc (of which 15 are inhibitor arcs). In comparison the imperative Inductive Miner [35],

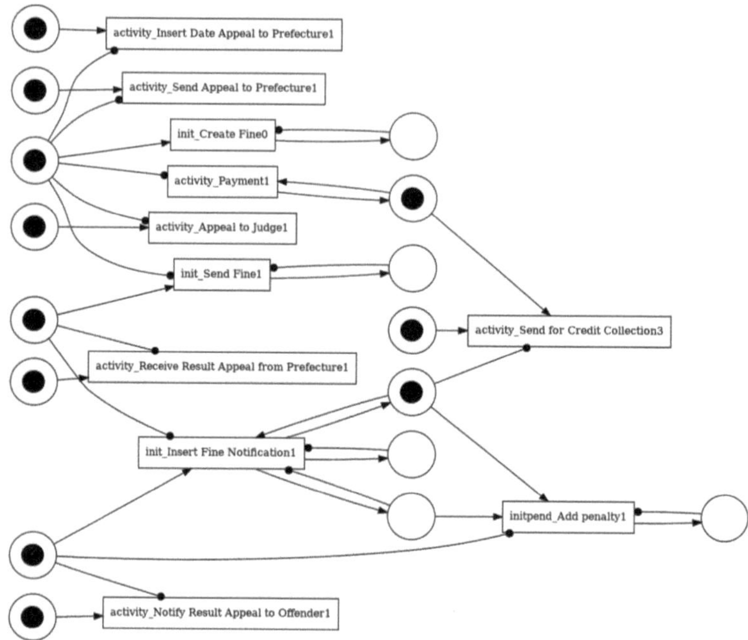


**Fig. 4.** DisCoveR mined Petri net from the Road Traffic Fine log.

with the noise threshold at 0, produces 29 places, 35 transitions (of which 24 are silent) and 84 arcs.

In conclusion, while the original declarative model may in many cases be better suited to visual descriptive tasks, the mapping enables the benefits of the extensive Petri-net analysis ecosystem and provides a general bridge between the two paradigms.

### 4.3   Conformance Checking and Trace Alignment

While this work focusses on process discovery, we add a few notes regarding conformance checking and trace alignment, as these often play an important part in checking the quality of mined models.

Because of the marking-based semantics of DCR Graphs, basic conformance checking through trace-replay is fairly straightforward to implement. However, trace replay is commonly seen as a relatively poor indicator of the conformance of a log [6,16]. It does not distinguish between the number and types of deviations occurring in a trace, and simply records each trace as either satisfying the model or not. Trace alignment has been proposed as a more accurate measure of fitness and conformance [6]. It allows some deviations between the log and the model to be considered less serious than others by using a cost function parametrised by type of deviation and computing the optimal alignment between a trace and the model that minimises this cost. In recent work [19] we have developed an algorithm for computing trace alignment for DCR Graphs which uses several optimisations to allow for the efficient computation of alignments on complex models.

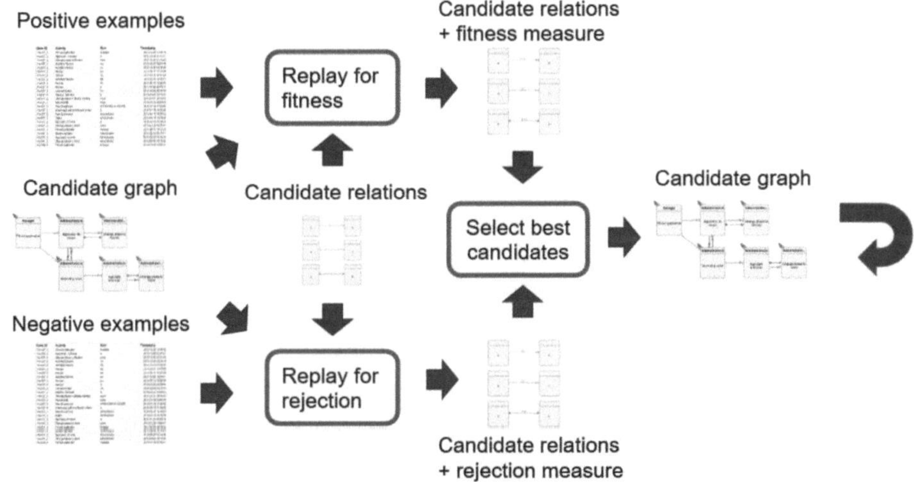


**Fig. 5.** High-level overview of the Rejection DCR Miner.

## 5  REJECTION DCR MINER: Binary Process Discovery

Classical discovery treats the log as a set of positive examples and searches for a model that reproduces these traces (up to noise), which frames the task as unary classification. Prior studies have argued that this makes discovery—especially for declarative notations—more difficult because many distinct models can fit the same positive-only evidence while differing in how they generalize [34,47,54]. The Rejection DCR Miner addresses this issue by using *labelled* logs with both desirable (positive) and undesirable (negative) examples, turning discovery into a binary classification problem [53]. Intuitively, negative traces act as counterexamples that expose which constraints are necessary to exclude behaviour that should not occur.

The miner iterates over four high-level steps (Fig. 5). It maintains a candidate DCR graph $G$ and a pool of candidate relations derived from log abstractions, similarly to DisCoveR [13]. For each iteration: (i) the miner replays the positive log $L^+$ on $G$ to measure *fitness* (how well the model accepts intended behaviour); (ii) it replays the negative log $L^-$ to measure *rejection* (how well the model rejects unintended behaviour); (iii) it evaluates the *marginal effect* of adding each candidate relation to $G$, estimating improvements in fitness and/or rejection via fast incremental replay; and (iv) it selects and adds the best-scoring relation(s), then repeats. Iteration is required because DCR relations are not orthogonal:

adding one relation can change the behaviour of the process in unexpected ways, e.g. by removing a condition.

Candidate generation follows the same principle as in DisCoveR: from statistics over the event log (e.g., precedence, response, at-most-once, successor/predecessor sets), the miner proposes syntactically valid DCR relations (conditions, responses, includes, excludes). In the binary setting, however, candidates are not accepted merely because they perfectly fit $L^+$; instead, they are ranked by a configurable objective score, for example one that requires perfect fitness, or one that allows for losses in positive fitness if this is balanced versus a greater gain in precision through the rejection of negative traces.

Replay is central to both evaluation and scoring. To scale to large candidate sets, the implementation uses: (a) bitvector encodings of markings and relation matrices; (b) caching of intermediate replay states to reuse work across candidates; and (c) early termination heuristics when a candidate cannot improve the current score. These optimisations keep each round close to linear in the size of the logs, despite re-evaluating candidates after every addition. The binary approach yields two primary benefits:

**Increased Accuracy:** incorporating negative evidence reduces overgeneralization, improving the model's ability to distinguish intended from unintended behaviour on held-out data. In our experiments we observed that replacing DisCoveR by the rejection miner either resulted in almost exactly the same accuracy for some logs, and significantly improved accuracy for other logs. In none of the examples we studied was accuracy reduced by the use of the rejection miner.

**Improved Simplicity:** by preferring relations that exclude many negative traces while retaining positive ones, the miner tends to select fewer, more impactful constraints. Empirical evaluation of the miner showed order-of-magnitude reductions in the number of relations compared to positive-only discovery.

## 6    OCDISCOVER: Object-Centric Process Discovery

Traditional discovery assumes a single *case notion* and produces a model that does not consider interactions that span multiple cases. Object-centric logs (OCEL) capture such interactions explicitly by linking each event to one or more objects of different types. Objects may be shared between multiple cases, or one may forgo the notion of a case altogether and instead consider the process as the culmination of the interactions between the various objects. Recent work on discovering *object-centric declarative models* [18] exploits this perspective to mine object-centric DCR Graphs, which can describe an overall process consisting of object types allowing unbounded instantiation, the internal constraints governing their individual life cycles, and cross-cutting constraints capturing the rules over the interactions between single or multiple instances of different object types.

The approach takes an event knowledge graph where events are associated with instances of object types (e.g., Order, Item, Delivery), and requires the following additional domain knowledge: (1) For each activity we identify a primary object type. This is the type under which the activity will be grouped (visually) in the mined model. Not all activities need to be assigned a primary object type, and this step does not limit activities from being involved in the execution of multiple objects. (2) The dynamic instantiation (*spawn*) relation between activities and object types. For example, a Create Order activity might instantiate new objects of type Order. The OCDISCOVER miner takes this input and finds three primary types of relations:

**Object Life-Cycles:** First, for each object type in the event knowledge graph we project a log capturing the traces for each of the objects of a type. We do not mine a DCR Graph directly, but instead use the initial phase of DisCoveR to mine a declarative log abstraction (consisting of e.g., existence, response, precedence, etc.). Afterwards we merge these abstractions through set union on the individual patterns. We maintain the multi-dimensionality of the event knowledge graph by including information on the relation between activities and object types. The usual guarantees of DisCoveR still hold, and if an abstraction is found for events belonging to a particular object type, then we can deduce the usual DCR relations and generate a model that captures the internal life-cycle of this object type.

**One-to-Many Interactions:** Next we check the abstractions for interactions between different objects. We disregard relations between pairs of activities that are both instantiated; these will be captured in the next step. The remaining relations can be seen as one-to-one and one-to-many interactions, where a single instance of an activity affects one or more instances of another activity.

**Many-to-Many Interactions:** In the final step of the algorithm we mine relations between the instantiable activities of different objects. These can be seen as a kind of synchronisation constraint on interactions: for example one can use a condition to capture that before an activity $a$ in any object of type $T$ can be executed, the activity $b$ must have been executed in all of the objects of type $T'$. The added complexity in this step comes from the fact that it is no longer sufficient to consider constraint satisfaction from a global perspective. Instead we need to mine with the added knowledge of which instances an event belongs to and consider the interactions between the traces of each instance. For the full details of the resulting algorithm we refer to [18].

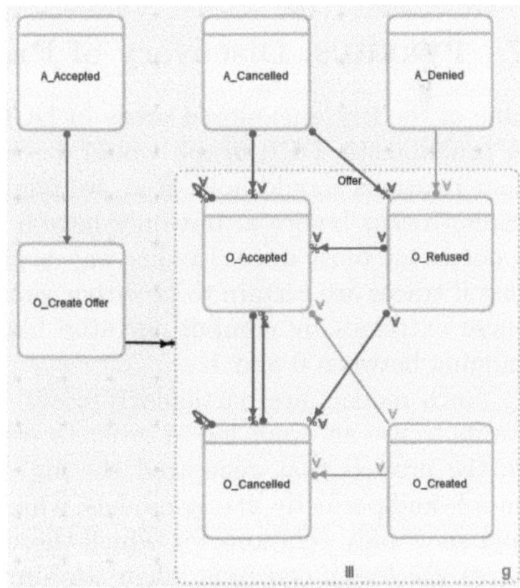

**Fig. 6.** Partial OC-DCR graph as mined from the BPIC 2017 dataset. As presented in [22].

Figure 6 shows a partial model mined by this algorithm from the BPIC 2017 dataset. Note that this example still uses the notion of a case to some degree: at the parent level each process instance captures a loan application, but within each loan application several objects interact. The types shown in the example are the application itself (A), of which there is only one instance, and loan offers (O) of which there can be multiple instances. In the figure we can see that this is modelled as a multi-instance sub-process OFFER.

We can see several life-cycle constraints, for example for every individual instance of an offer accepting (O_ACCEPTED) and cancelling the offer (O_CANCELLED) are mutually exclusive. Such constraints can also occur at the level of the process instance life cycle: accepting an application (A_ACCEPTED) requires eventually making an offer (O_CREATE OFFER). Examples of one-to-many relations include several constraints from the main process towards the offers, such as the fact that cancelling the application (A_CANCELLED) removes the possibility to accept or refuse all offers (O_ACCEPTED, O_REFUSED). We also see an example of a one-to-many relation between offers: accepting any single offer (O_ACCEPTED) excludes the ability to accept all other offers (O_ACCEPTED). Finally, we also see a number of many-to-many relations between offer instances. For example, we see that all instances of creating an offer (O_CREATED) occur before all instances of accepting or cancelling an offer (O_ACCEPTED, O_CANCELLED). The former is the most intuitive and to be expected: once an offer has been accepted, it is no longer necessary to create new offers for the same loan application. The latter may be an artefact of how the process was executed - possibly offers are never individually cancelled, but only as part of a cancelled application.

## 7    PYRRHUS: Discovery of Probabilistic Predictive Models

One of the key unexplored areas in DCR mining is to use probabilistic models. A probabilistic DCR graph would describe a process in terms of the likelihood that relations should hold. E.g., we might be absolutely certain ($p = 1.0$) that $b$ cannot occur before $a$, but only have a strong suspicion ($p = 0.9$) that activity $b$ occurs at most once. In this way a probabilistic process model captures not just if traces are certain to be either valid or invalid, but instead ranges between these extremes by computingÂăthe likelihood of a trace's validity, as a value ranging between 0 and 1.

Such models are particularly useful for predictive tasks, for example if one wants to use an event log in order to predict the likelihood that a trace belongs to the process that generated the log. Whereas descriptive tasks benefit from simple and perfectly fitting models, which can be easily understood by an analyst and show only relations for which there is conclusive evidence of their validity, these are lesser concerns when we aim for predictive accuracy. When aiming for accuracy, being able to denote the likelihood that a relation holds usually increases the predictive power of a mined model, as it allows for a more detailed evaluation of traces by weighing the cost of broken constraints (as a function of the probability of the constraint).

While there have been some initial attempts at formalizing the syntax and semantics of probabilistic DCR graphs, these are still at an early, unpublished, stage. Similarly there have been early attempts at designing algorithms that mine DCR graphs with a probabilistic perspective. Here the results are both similar and dissimilar: while the algorithms are in a very early stage and unpublished, they were submitted to the Process Discovery Contest [17] in 2024.

Essentially two approaches were investigated: first we formalized a basic probabilistic DCR Graph notation and extended DisCoveR to mine these. This miner did not score particularly well, but we realised that we captured a significant amount of probabilistic information in the initial log abstractions that was lost in the translation to DCR relations, in particular in the steps necessary to ensure correctness of the underlying (marking-based) semantics. We thus decided to create a new miner that simply uses the probabilistic log abstractions to create a set of traditional declarative patterns. This miner scored significantly higher, achieving the highest accuracy out of all submissions and winning the contest. The miner also managed to repeat this success for the 2025 edition of the contest.

The new miner is extremely straightforward in its design. It checks the log for a number of basic declarative patterns, counts the number of times that the pattern is broken versus the number of times that it might have held (i.e. the activations), and computes from this the probability of the pattern being a part of the generating process. When evaluating a trace, we check for each event if any patterns are broken, and from this compute a total cost for that trace. Patterns with a high likelihood contribute more to this cost than patterns with a low likelihood. Depending on the scenario, one may want to normalise these costs, but for the Process Discovery Contest this was not needed; the contest requires us to evaluate two traces against each other and predict which of the two best fits the model, therefore a simple comparison of the costs for each trace is sufficient. Because of the relative simplicity of the algorithm, and the mixed experience of outperforming our own flagship miner, we decided to aptly name it **Pyrrhus**.

## 8    Open Challenges and Future Work

In this section we briefly discuss a number of research questions which we expect will be at the centre of DCR-related process mining research in the coming years. Many of these also underline important more general challenges in the area of Declarative process discovery. These should not be seen as a conclusive list of open topics in this area, but rather a look under the hood of the directions our group expects to pursue and an invitation for collaboration. Concretely, the topics will be explored in two new larger national research projects initiated in 2025 with support from Innovation Fund Denmark. The first project, *Predictive and Prescriptive Process Analytics for Industry 4.0* (P3AI4) focus on the use of DCR process mining for human-centric, explainable predictive and prescriptive maintenance in the industry, with partners providing real-time data from the domains of train services and maintenance of large diesel engines on ships.

The second project, *Explainable Hybrid AI for Computational Law and accurate Legal Chatbots*[2] (XHAILE) aims to explore the combination of rule-based DCR Graph models of the law with large language models for case management and citizen-centric services in the public sector. Here process mining will play a more indirect role as a means to support continuous improvement in the public sector administration.

RQ 1: *How well do DCR-based process mining tools work in practice?* While there have been many case studies [26–28,30,31,55] and a number of empirical investigations [8–12,33] on the understandability and practical use of DCR Graphs as a modelling notation, the use of process mining tools has not been studied in a structured empirical manner yet. Because several of these algorithms have already been adopted by industry, there are clear opportunities to study their use in a business setting. Such studies would not only measure the business value of the algorithms, but also reveal their strengths and weaknesses, thereby guiding future research in improving these tools.

RQ 2: *How can the results of Pyrrhus be presented in an understandable manner, so that the miner can be used also for descriptive tasks?* As part of this question we expect that we will investigate better ways to map these results to more mature Declarative models (e.g. DCR Graphs). Such a mapping would on the one hand enable the use of mature modelling and analysis tools, and on the other provide increased accuracy in the discovery of DCR Graphs.

RQ 3: *What is the predictive power of various declarative constraints, and how does this shift between models and domains?* This question is driven by an observation made on the PDC dataset: the combination of the condition and response patterns was almost as accurate at making predictions as more complex combinations of patterns. We do not yet know if this is an artefact of the process used for the challenge, or a deeper observation that generalises to other event logs. Finding this answer will be an important first step towards identifying what makes for a good declarative predictive process model.

RQ 4: *How can we integrate methods for mining (contextual) data into DCR Discovery?* While we have recently made significant progress on including the time perspective in mined models, we have yet to develop a conclusive technique including data as well. This is of particular relevance as we are moving further into object-centric mining approaches, as object life cycles are often data-driven.

RQ 5: *Can probabilistic declarative process discovery be combined with recent advances in neural machine learning in order to offer a neuro-symbolic approach towards predictive and prescriptive monitoring?* This question underpins a recently started research project where we will investigate if declarative mining, and in particular DCR Graphs, can be integrated

---

[2] https://di.ku.dk/english/research/research-projects/xhaile/.

with statistical methods in order to better capture the process perspective, improve the integration of domain knowledge, and offer more explainable recommendations in predictive maintenance applications. We expect that answering the earlier questions will help progress towards this larger overall goal.

## 9   Conclusion

In this paper we presented recent advances in process discovery for DCR Graphs and provided a high-level overview of the different algorithms, aiming to equip the reader with a general intuition of their approach, while leaving the full technical details to the individual research papers. We hope that this provides a general impression of the state-of-the-art in DCR mining, which we believe has caught up with, and moved to the forefront of, the field of process discovery. This notion is somewhat supported by recent success in the process discovery contest, with the caveat that the contest primarily considers predictive accuracy as a metric.

In future work we are driven in particular by this success and aim to investigate the use of these techniques in areas where predictive accuracy is an important success criterion. We hope that in fields which currently rely heavily on black-box machine learning approaches, we can provide a bridge to the strong descriptive and usability focus of process science. DCR discovery algorithms seem particularly promising for this approach as they combine the accuracy typically required in such applications with the descriptive aspects of process modelling notations, and are supported by many academic and commercial tools that enhance their understandability, allow for further analysis, and allow model maintenance by domain experts.

## References


1. van der Aalst, W., Pesic, M.: DecSerFlow: towards a truly declarative service flow language. In: Leymann, F., Reisig, W., Thatte, S.R., van der Aalst, W. (eds.) The Role of Business Processes in Service Oriented Architectures. Dagstuhl Seminar Proceedings (DagSemProc), vol. 6291, pp. 1–23. Schloss Dagstuhl – Leibniz-Zentrum für Informatik, Dagstuhl, Germany (2006). https://doi.org/10.4230/DagSemProc.06291.10. https://drops.dagstuhl.de/entities/document/10.4230/DagSemProc.06291.10
2. van der Aalst, W.M.P., Pesic, M.: DecSerFlow: towards a truly declarative service flow language. In: Bravetti, M., Núñez, M., Zavattaro, G. (eds.) WS-FM 2006. LNCS, vol. 4184, pp. 1–23. Springer, Heidelberg (2006). https://doi.org/10.1007/11841197_1
3. van der Aalst, W.M.P., Stahl, C.: Modeling Business Processes - A Petri Net-Oriented Approach. Cooperative Information Systems Series. MIT Press (2011). http://mitpress.mit.edu/books/modeling-business-processes
4. van der Aalst, W.M.: Process discovery: capturing the invisible. IEEE Comput. Intell. Mag. **5**(1), 28–41 (2010)

5. Aalst, W.M.P.: Object-centric process mining: dealing with divergence and convergence in event data. In: Ölveczky, P.C., Salaün, G. (eds.) SEFM 2019. LNCS, vol. 11724, pp. 3–25. Springer, Cham (2019). https://doi.org/10.1007/978-3-030-30446-1_1

6. Adriansyah, A.: Aligning observed and modeled behavior. Ph.D. thesis, Mathematics and Computer Science (2014)

7. Alman, A., Di Ciccio, C., Haas, D., Maggi, F.M., Nolte, A.: Rule mining with rum. In: 2020 2nd International Conference on Process Mining (ICPM), pp. 121–128. IEEE (2020)

8. Abbad Andaloussi, A., Buch-Lorentsen, J., López, H.A., Slaats, T., Weber, B.: Exploring the modeling of declarative processes using a hybrid approach. In: Laender, A.H.F., Pernici, B., Lim, E.-P., de Oliveira, J.P.M. (eds.) ER 2019. LNCS, vol. 11788, pp. 162–170. Springer, Cham (2019). https://doi.org/10.1007/978-3-030-33223-5_14

9. Andaloussi, A.A., Burattin, A., Slaats, T., Kindler, E., Weber, B.: Complexity in declarative process models: Metrics and multi-modal assessment of cognitive load. Expert Syst. Appl. **233**, 120924 (2023)

10. Abbad Andaloussi, A., Burattin, A., Slaats, T., Petersen, A.C.M., Hildebrandt, T.T., Weber, B.: Exploring the understandability of a hybrid process design artifact based on DCR graphs. In: Reinhartz-Berger, I., Zdravkovic, J., Gulden, J., Schmidt, R. (eds.) BPMDS/EMMSAD -2019. LNBIP, vol. 352, pp. 69–84. Springer, Cham (2019). https://doi.org/10.1007/978-3-030-20618-5_5

11. Abbad Andaloussi, A., Davis, C.J., Burattin, A., López, H.A., Slaats, T., Weber, B.: Understanding quality in declarative process modeling through the mental models of experts. In: Fahland, D., Ghidini, C., Becker, J., Dumas, M. (eds.) BPM 2020. LNCS, vol. 12168, pp. 417–434. Springer, Cham (2020). https://doi.org/10.1007/978-3-030-58666-9_24

12. Andaloussi, A.A., Zerbato, F., Burattin, A., Slaats, T., Hildebrandt, T.T., Weber, B.: Exploring how users engage with hybrid process artifacts based on declarative process models: a behavioral analysis based on eye-tracking and think-aloud. Softw. Syst. Model. **20**(5), 1437–1464 (2021)

13. Back, C.O., Slaats, T., Hildebrandt, T.T., Marquard, M.: Discover: accurate and efficient discovery of declarative process models. Int. J. Softw. Tools Technol. Transfer **24**(4), 563–587 (2022)

14. Buijs, J.C., van Dongen, B.F., van der Aalst, W.M.: Quality dimensions in process discovery: the importance of fitness, precision, generalization and simplicity. Int. J. Coop. Inf. Syst. **23**(01), 1440001 (2014)

15. Burattin, A.: Streaming process mining. Process Mining Handbook **349**, 3–10 (2022)

16. Carmona, J., van Dongen, B., Solti, A., Weidlich, M.: Conformance checking. Springer (2018)

17. Carmona, J., de Leoni, M., Depaire, B., Jouck, T., Verbeek, E.: Process discovery contest (PDC) (2016-2025). https://www.tf-pm.org/competitions-awards/discovery-contest

18. Christfort, A.K.F., Rivkin, A., Fahland, D., Hildebrandt, T.T., Slaats, T.: Discovery of object-centric declarative models. In: 6th International Conference on Process Mining, ICPM 2024, Kgs. Lyngby, Denmark, 14–18 October 2024, pp. 121–128. IEEE (2024). https://doi.org/10.1109/ICPM63005.2024.10680680

19. Christfort, A.K.F., Slaats, T.: Efficient optimal alignment between dynamic condition response graphs and traces. In: Accepted for the 21st International Conference on Business Process Management (BPM 2023) (2023)

20. Ciccio, C.D., Mecella, M.: On the discovery of declarative control flows for artful processes. ACM Trans. Manage. Inf. Syst. **5**(4), 24:1–24:37 (2015)
21. Ciccio, C.D., Mecella, M.: On the discovery of declarative control flows for artful processes. ACM Trans. Manag. Inf. Syst. (TMIS) **5**(4), 1–37 (2015)
22. Cosma, V.P., Christfort, A.K.F., Hildebrandt, T.T., Lu, X., Reijers, H.A., Slaats, T.: Improving simplicity by discovering nested groups in declarative models. In: Guizzardi, G., Santoro, F.M., Mouratidis, H., Soffer, P. (eds.) Advanced Information Systems Engineering - 36th International Conference, CAiSE 2024, Limassol, Cyprus, 3–7 June 2024, Proceedings. Lecture Notes in Computer Science, vol. 14663, pp. 440–455. Springer (2024)
23. Cosma, V.P., Hildebrandt, T.T., Slaats, T.: Transforming dynamic condition response graphs to safe petri nets. In: Gomes, L., Lorenz, R. (eds.) Application and Theory of Petri Nets and Concurrency - 44th International Conference, PETRI NETS 2023, Lisbon, Portugal, 25–30 June 2023, Proceedings. Lecture Notes in Computer Science, vol. 13929, pp. 417–439. Springer (2023)
24. Debois, S., Hildebrandt, T.T., Marquard, M., Slaats, T.: The DCR graphs process portal. In: BPM (Demos), pp. 7–11 (2016)
25. Debois, S., Hildebrandt, T.T., Slaats, T.: Replication, refinement & reachability: complexity in dynamic condition-response graphs. Acta Informatica **55**(6), 489–520 (2018)
26. Debois, S., Slaats, T.: The analysis of a real life declarative process. In: IEEE Symposium Series on Computational Intelligence, SSCI 2015, Cape Town, South Africa, 7–10 December 2015, pp. 1374–1382. IEEE (2015)
27. Debois, S., Hildebrandt, T., Marquard, M., Slaats, T.: Bridging the valley of death - a success story on danish funding schemes paving a path from technology readiness level 1 to 9. In: Accepted for 2nd International Workshop on Software Engineering Research and Industrial Practice (SER&IP 2015) (2015)
28. Debois, S., Hildebrandt, T., Slaats, T., Marquard, M.: A case for declarative process modelling: agile development of a grant application system. In: 2014 IEEE 18th International Enterprise Distributed Object Computing Conference Workshops and Demonstrations, pp. 126–133 (2014). https://doi.org/10.1109/EDOCW.2014.27
29. Hermansen, S.V., Jónsson, R., Kjeldsen, J.L., Slaats, T., Cosma, V.P., López, H.A.: Dcr4py: a pm4py library extension for declarative process mining in python. In: 6th International Conference on Process Mining. CEUR-WS (2024)
30. Hildebrandt, T.T., et al.: Ecoknow: engineering effective, co-created and compliant adaptive case management systems for knowledge workers. In: Proceedings of the International Conference on Software and System Processes, pp. 155–164 (2020)
31. Hildebrandt, T.T., Mukkamala, R.R.: Declarative event-based workflow as distributed dynamic condition response graphs. In: Proceedings Third Workshop on Programming Language Approaches to Concurrency and communication-cEntric Software, PLACES 2010, Paphos, Cyprus, 21st March 2010, pp. 59–73 (2010)
32. Hildebrandt, T.T., Mukkamala, R.R., Slaats, T.: Declarative modelling and safe distribution of healthcare workflows. In: Foundations of Health Informatics Engineering and Systems - First International Symposium, FHIES, pp. 39–56 (2011)
33. Jalali, A.: Evaluating perceived usefulness and ease of use of CMMN and DCR. In: Augusto, A., Gill, A., Nurcan, S., Reinhartz-Berger, I., Schmidt, R., Zdravkovic, J. (eds.) BPMDS/EMMSAD -2021. LNBIP, vol. 421, pp. 147–162. Springer, Cham (2021). https://doi.org/10.1007/978-3-030-79186-5_10
34. Lamma, E., Mello, P., Montali, M., Riguzzi, F., Storari, S.: Inducing declarative logic-based models from labeled traces. In: BPM, pp. 344–359 (2007)

35. Leemans, S.J.J., Fahland, D., van der Aalst, W.M.P.: Discovering block-structured process models from event logs - a constructive approach. In: Colom, J.-M., Desel, J. (eds.) PETRI NETS 2013. LNCS, vol. 7927, pp. 311–329. Springer, Heidelberg (2013). https://doi.org/10.1007/978-3-642-38697-8_17

36. Lyng, K.M., Hildebrandt, T., Mukkamala, R.R.: From paper based clinical practice guidelines to declarative workflow management. In: Ardagna, D., Mecella, M., Yang, J. (eds.) BPM 2008. LNBIP, vol. 17, pp. 336–347. Springer, Heidelberg (2009). https://doi.org/10.1007/978-3-642-00328-8_34

37. Maggi, F.M., Mooij, A.J., van der Aalst, W.M.P.: User-guided discovery of declarative process models. In: 2011 IEEE Symposium on Computational Intelligence and Data Mining (CIDM), pp. 192–199 (2011)

38. Maggi, F.M.: Declarative process mining with the declare component of prom. In: Proceedings of the BPM Demo sessions 2013, Co-located with 11th International Conference on Business Process Management (BPM2013), Beijing, China, 26–30 August 2013, vol. 1021. CEUR-WS (2013)

39. Mannhardt, F., De Leoni, M., Reijers, H.A., Van Der Aalst, W.M.: Balanced multi-perspective checking of process conformance. Computing **98**(4), 407–437 (2016)

40. Marquard, M., Shahzad, M., Slaats, T.: Web-based modelling and collaborative simulation of declarative processes. In: Motahari-Nezhad, H.R., Recker, J., Weidlich, M. (eds.) BPM 2015. LNCS, vol. 9253, pp. 209–225. Springer, Cham (2015). https://doi.org/10.1007/978-3-319-23063-4_15

41. Mukkamala, R.R.: A Formal Model For Declarative Workflows: Dynamic Condition Response Graphs. Ph.D. thesis, IT University of Copenhagen (2012)

42. Mukkamala, R.R., Hildebrandt, T.T.: From dynamic condition response structures to büchi automata. In: Liu, J., Peled, D.A., Wang, B., Wang, F. (eds.) 4th IEEE International Symposium on Theoretical Aspects of Software Engineering, TASE 2010, Taipei, Taiwan, 25–27 August 2010, pp. 187–190. IEEE Computer Society (2010). https://doi.org/10.1109/TASE.2010.22

43. Nekrasaite, V., Parli, A.T., Back, C.O., Slaats, T.: Discovering responsibilities with dynamic condition response graphs. In: Giorgini, P., Weber, B. (eds.) CAiSE 2019. LNCS, vol. 11483, pp. 595–610. Springer, Cham (2019). https://doi.org/10.1007/978-3-030-21290-2_37

44. Norgaard, L.H., Andreasen, J.B., Marquard, M., Debois, S., Larsen, F.S., Jeppesen, V.: Declarative process models in government centric case and document management. In: Brambilla, M., Hildebrandt, T.T. (eds.) Proceedings of the BPM 2017 Industry Track co-located with the 15th International Conference on Business Process Management (BPM 2017), Barcelona, Spain, 10–15 September 2017. CEUR Workshop Proceedings, vol. 1985, pp. 38–51 (2017)

45. Pesic, M., van der Aalst, W.M.P.: A declarative approach for flexible business processes management. In: Eder, J., Dustdar, S. (eds.) BPM 2006. LNCS, vol. 4103, pp. 169–180. Springer, Heidelberg (2006). https://doi.org/10.1007/11837862_18

46. Pesic, M., Schonenberg, H., van der Aalst, W.M.P.: DECLARE: full support for loosely-structured processes. In: 11th IEEE International Enterprise Distributed Object Computing Conference (EDOC 2007), 15–19 October 2007, Annapolis, Maryland, USA, pp. 287–300 (2007)

47. Ponce de León, H., Nardelli, L., Carmona, J., vanden Broucke, S.K.: Incorporating negative information to process discovery of complex systems. Inf. Sci. **422**, 480–496 (2018)

48. Rozinat, A., Van der Aalst, W.M.: Conformance checking of processes based on monitoring real behavior. Inf. Syst. **33**(1), 64–95 (2008)

49. Schönig, S., Cabanillas, C., Jablonski, S., Mendling, J.: A framework for efficiently mining the organisational perspective of business processes. Decis. Support Syst. **89**, 87–97 (2016)
50. Schönig, S., Di Ciccio, C., Maggi, F.M., Mendling, J.: Discovery of multi-perspective declarative process models. In: Sheng, Q.Z., Stroulia, E., Tata, S., Bhiri, S. (eds.) ICSOC 2016. LNCS, vol. 9936, pp. 87–103. Springer, Cham (2016). https://doi.org/10.1007/978-3-319-46295-0_6
51. Schönig, S., Zeising, M.: The DPIL framework: tool support for agile and resource-aware business processes. BPM (Demos) **1418**, 125–129 (2015)
52. Slaats, T.: Flexible Process Notations for Cross-organizational Case Management Systems. Ph.D. thesis, IT University of Copenhagen (2015)
53. Slaats, T., Debois, S., Back, C.O., Christfort, A.K.F.: Foundations and practice of binary process discovery. Inf. Syst. **121**, 102339 (2024). https://doi.org/10.1016/J.IS.2023.102339
54. Slaats, T., Debois, S., Back, C.O.: Weighing the pros and cons: process discovery with negative examples. In: Polyvyanyy, A., Wynn, M.T., Van Looy, A., Reichert, M. (eds.) BPM 2021. LNCS, vol. 12875, pp. 47–64. Springer, Cham (2021). https://doi.org/10.1007/978-3-030-85469-0_6
55. Slaats, T., Mukkamala, R.R., Hildebrandt, T., Marquard, M.: Exformatics declarative case management workflows as DCR graphs. In: Daniel, F., Wang, J., Weber, B. (eds.) BPM 2013. LNCS, vol. 8094, pp. 339–354. Springer, Heidelberg (2013). https://doi.org/10.1007/978-3-642-40176-3_28
56. Tax, N., Lu, X., Sidorova, N., Fahland, D., van der Aalst, W.M.: The imprecisions of precision measures in process mining. Inf. Process. Lett. **135**, 1–8 (2018)
57. Tijs Slaats: Discover (2021). https://github.com/tslaats/DisCoveR
58. Van Der Aalst, W.: Process mining: data science in action, vol. 2. Springer (2016)
59. van der Aalst, W., et al.: Process mining manifesto. In: Daniel, F., Barkaoui, K., Dustdar, S. (eds.) BPM 2011. LNBIP, vol. 99, pp. 169–194. Springer, Heidelberg (2012). https://doi.org/10.1007/978-3-642-28108-2_19
60. Van Der Aalst, W.M., La Rosa, M., Santoro, F.M.: Business process management: don't forget to improve the process! Bus. Inf. Syst. Eng. **58**(1), 1–6 (2016)
61. Winskel, G.: Event structures. In: Brauer, W., Reisig, W., Rozenberg, G. (eds.) ACPN 1986. LNCS, vol. 255, pp. 325–392. Springer, Heidelberg (1987). https://doi.org/10.1007/3-540-17906-2_31
62. Zeising, M., Schonig, S., Jablonski, S.: Towards a common platform for the support of routine and agile business processes. In: 2014 International Conference on Collaborative Computing: Networking, Applications and Worksharing (CollaborateCom), pp. 94–103. IEEE (2014)
63. van Zelst, S.J., van Dongen, B.F., van der Aalst, W.M.: Event stream-based process discovery using abstract representations. Knowl. Inf. Syst. **54**(2), 407–435 (2018)

# Leveraging Meta-Properties of Petri Net Classes to Efficiently Enforce Formal Guarantees in Bottom-Up Process Discovery

Marco Pegoraro[(✉)] and Lisa Luise Mannel[(✉)]

Chair of Process and Data Science (PADS), Department of Computer Science,
RWTH Aachen University, Ahornstr. 55, 52074 Aachen, Germany
{pegoraro,mannel}@pads.rwth-aachen.de
http://mpegoraro.net/

**Abstract.** Process discovery refers to the task of learning a process model on the basis of data about historical executions of process operations, in the form of an event log. Recently, a new family of bottom-up discovery techniques known as eST mining has been established: the eST miner is able to flexibly produce Petri nets from event data, to represent long-term dependencies, and to guarantee a certain output quality. In this paper, we provide formal proofs for meta-properties of selected Petri net classes, and we propose an extension pattern for bottom-up discovery methods able to produce Petri nets of chosen classes more efficiently, by leveraging meta-properties results to prune the search space of model components. We show how this pruning method can aid bottom-up discovery by applying it to the candidate places search of the eST miner.

**Keywords:** Process Mining · Process Discovery · Petri Nets

## 1  Introduction

*Process discovery*—the act of automatically learning a process model from event data—has historically been the catalyst for the development and success of the discipline of process mining, and it has characterized the field to the point of becoming, at times, conflated with it. After its introduction in the mid '90s by Cook and Wolf [10], process discovery was popularized through the term *workflow mining* between the late '90s and early '00s by Wil van der Aalst and co-authors [6], as part of what will become process mining [5].

Driven by success in academic circles and industry applications, process discovery has since then flourished in a vast array of diverse techniques and methods [4,7]. Of these, many favor Petri nets as formalism of choice to represent

The authors contributed equally to this work. The order of authorship was determined via a cook-off.


J. Mendling et al. (Eds.): Wil van der Aalst Festschrift, LNCS 16480, pp. 506–524, 2026.
https://doi.org/10.1007/978-3-032-17618-9_34

behavior, due to their flexibility, the simplicity of their semantics, and the ability to effectively represent concurrency. A recently introduced discovery technique for Petri nets is the *eST miner*. Begotten from a contribution by Van der Aalst to Farhad Arbab's Festschrift[1] introducing the concepts of quality scores of single places in a net, monotonicity properties of such scores, and viewing the places in a Petri net as a set of constraints [3], the eST miner approaches process discovery with a bottom-up strategy, by assembling a Petri net on the basis of evidence about single places and their quality [17]. This search and selection methodology across the available space of places allows the eST miner to capture elusive control-flow constructs, such as long-term dependencies, while remaining robust to low-frequency behavior. Practical efficiency comes from aggressive pruning: thanks to monotonic properties on place quality, results on earlier candidates cut large swaths of the search space, avoiding the combinatorial blow-up that dogs naïve exhaustive search methods. Subsequent improved versions broaden the scope: extensions target the class of *uniwired Petri nets* to improve model simplicity and readability [18], engineering work speeds up the state-space traversal [20], while extensions able to work with partially-ordered event data are now available [12].

Inspired by [3], in this paper we propose a framework describing the discovery of Petri nets with desirable formal properties from event logs in settings where bottom-up process discovery is performed. This effect, which extends the proposal of [18], can be obtained with little impact on overall computing time. We will discuss the effects of such a framework on the eST family of algorithms, which we selected for their high flexibility. In some cases, thanks to closure meta-properties akin to the monotonic properties shown in [3], we will be able to further prune the search space of candidate places of the eST miner, therefore inducing a speed-up of the computation.

The remainder of the paper is structured as follows. Section 2 contains preliminary formal definitions. Section 3 defines meta-properties for Petri net classes, and illustrates their interaction with eST discovery. Section 4 contains formal proofs for the results introduced in Sect. 3. Lastly, Sect. 5 comments the results, discusses future work, and closes the paper.

## 2    Preliminaries

First, let us briefly revisit some fundamental concepts and notations.

A *multiset* is a set that allows for multiple instances of the same member. We indicate with $\mathcal{B}(X)$ the set of all multisets built over the elements of the set $X$. We denote with $m(x)$ the multiplicity of the element $x \in X$ in the multiset $m \in \mathcal{B}(X)$.

---

[1] The development of the eST miner has been propelled in no small part by the request of implementing the theory in [3] as interview assignment for aspiring doctoral candidates in the early days of Wil van der Aalst's Chair of Process and Data Science. The authors fondly remember their subsequent sparring sessions at the whiteboard—the first of their careers.

A *sequence*, denoted $s := \langle x_1, x_2, \ldots, x_n \rangle$, is a totally ordered collection of (non-necessarily unique) elements. The *Kleene star* $X^*$ indicates the set of all sequences of finite length obtainable by using the elements in the set $X$. We denote the length of a sequence as $|s| := n$, and we access elements with $s[i] := x_i$. We overload set operators on sequences: for instance, for $s_1 = \langle a, b, b, c \rangle$ and $s_2 = \langle b, b, c, d \rangle$, we have that $a \in s_1$ but $a \notin s_2$, $s_1 \cup s_2 = \{a, b, c, d\}$, and $s_1 \cap s_2 = \{b, c\}$.

In the next section, we will introduce the basic building blocks of process mining.

## 2.1   Event Logs and Petri Nets

Process mining is based on the interplay between event data—in the form of events, traces, and event logs—and process models. Let us define event data constructs, and our modeling formalism of choice: the Petri net.

**Definition 1 (Activities, Traces, Logs).** *Let $A$ be the universe of* activity identifiers, *with* $\blacktriangleright \in A$ *being a designated* start activity, *and* $\blacksquare \in A$ *being a designated* end activity. *A* trace *is a sequence* $\sigma := \langle \blacktriangleright, a_1, a_2, \ldots, a_n, \blacksquare \rangle$, *with* $\{a_1, a_2, \ldots, a_n\} \subseteq A \setminus \{\blacktriangleright, \blacksquare\}$. *We denote with* $\Sigma$ *the set of all such traces. A* log $L \in \mathcal{B}(\Sigma)$ *is a multiset of traces.*

**Definition 2 (Petri Nets).** *A* Petri net *is a tuple* $N := (P, T, F)$ *where $P$ is the set of* places, $T$ *is the set of* transitions, *and* $F \subseteq (P \times T) \cup (T \times P)$ *is the* flow relation, *which defines a set of* edges. *Let $\mathcal{N}$ be the set of all Petri nets.*

*Given a node of the net $n \in P \cup T$, we denote* $\bullet n := \{n' \in P \cup T \mid (n', n) \in F\}$ *(the* preset *of $n$), and $n \bullet := \{n' \in P \cup T \mid (n, n') \in F\}$ (the* postset *of $n$).*

At times, Petri nets appear in literature with the inclusion of arc weights, typically expressed through a weighting function $w \colon F \to \mathbb{N}$. In this paper, as is common in process mining, we disregard $w$, and we assume all arcs in $F$ are equally weighted at one unit.

While the previous definition reflects Petri nets as they are traditionally formalized, the representational bias of current versions of the eST miner induces a subset of Petri nets for which all places have some inbound and outbound arcs, and for which all places may be uniquely identified by their preset and postset.

**Definition 3 (Domain of eST Discovery).** *A* Petri net $N := (P, T, F) \in \mathcal{N}$ *is a member of the* domain of eST discovery *if and only if:*

- $T := A$ *(see Definition 1);*
- $i \in P$, *with* $\bullet i = \varnothing$ *and* $i \bullet = \{\blacktriangleright\}$;
- $o \in P$, *with* $\bullet o = \{\blacksquare\}$ *and* $o \bullet = \varnothing$;
- *for* $p \in P \setminus \{i, o\}$, $\bullet p \neq \varnothing$ *and* $p \bullet \neq \varnothing$.

*The set $\mathcal{E} \subsetneq \mathcal{N}$ is the* domain of eST discovery.

For $N := (P, T, F) \in \mathcal{E}$, we will alternatively denote the place $p \in P$ as $(I \mid O)$, where $I := \bullet p$ and $O := p\bullet$. Note that, given a fixed reference set of activity identifiers $A$, we have $N = (P, A, F) \in \mathcal{E}$ for all the nets in $\mathcal{E}$. Section 2.2 will provide an introduction to eST discovery.

Note that Definition 3 presents a very general definition of the Petri net space considered in the eST family of algorithms, though in specific contexts, additional refinements are possible. For example, if guaranteeing fitness with respect to the input log is a priority, it is trivial to see that forcing $\blacksquare \notin \bullet p$ and $\blacktriangleright \notin p\bullet$ for all $p \in P$ is desirable.

We now present a number of Petri net classes, selected by their notoriety, their desirability in process discovery, and the formal guarantees they induce on the behavior of the corresponding Petri nets.

**Definition 4 (Petri Net Classes).** *Let $N := (P, T, F) \in \mathcal{N}$ be a Petri net.*

*Marked Graphs and Generalized Marked Graphs. The net $N$ is a* marked graph *[9] (or T-system) if and only if all places connect to and from exactly one transition: for all $p \in P$, $|\bullet p| = |p\bullet| = 1$. Let $\mathcal{MG} \subsetneq \mathcal{N}$ be the set of all marked graphs. The net $N$ is a* generalized marked graph *[8] if and only if all places connect to and from at most one transition: for all $p \in P$, $|\bullet p| \leqslant 1$ and $|p\bullet| \leqslant 1$. Let $\mathcal{GMG} \subsetneq \mathcal{N}$ be the set of all generalized marked graphs.*

*State Machines and Generalized State Machines. The net $N$ is a* state machine *[15] (or S-system) if and only if all transitions connect to and from exactly one place: for all $t \in T$, $|\bullet t| = 1$ and $|t\bullet| = 1$. Let $\mathcal{SM} \subsetneq \mathcal{N}$ be the set of all state machines. The net $N$ is a* generalized state machine *[13] if and only if all transitions connect to and from at most one place: for all $t \in T$, $|\bullet t| \leqslant 1$ and $|t\bullet| \leqslant 1$. Let $\mathcal{GSM} \subsetneq \mathcal{N}$ be the set of all generalized state machines.*

*Well-Structured Petri Nets. A* path *in a net $N := (P, T, F)$ is a sequence $\rho := \langle n_1, n_2, \ldots, n_n \rangle \in (P \cup T)^*$ where, for $1 \leqslant i \leqslant n - 1$, $(n[i], n[i+1]) \in F$. The path $\rho$ is* elementary *if no nodes appear multiple times: for $1 \leqslant i < j \leqslant n$, $n_i \neq n_j$. The net $N$ is a* well-structured Petri net *[1] if and only if, for any two elementary paths $\rho := \langle n, n_1, n_2, \ldots, n_n, n' \rangle$ and $\rho' := \langle n, m_1, m_2, \ldots, m_m, n' \rangle$ in $N$ such that $\rho \neq \rho'$, it holds that*

$$\rho \cap \rho' = \varnothing \Rightarrow \{n, n'\} \subseteq P \vee \{n, n'\} \subseteq T.$$

*Let $\mathcal{WS} \subsetneq \mathcal{N}$ be the set of all well-structured Petri nets.*

*Uniwired Petri Nets. The net $N$ is a* uniwired Petri net *[18] if and only if any two transitions are connected through at most one place: for $t \in T$ and $t' \in T$, it holds that $t\bullet \cap \bullet t' \leqslant 1$. Let $\mathcal{U} \subsetneq \mathcal{N}$ be the set of all uniwired Petri nets.*

*Workflow Nets. The net $N$ is a* workflow net *[2] if and only if*

- *there exist a place $i \in P$ such that $\bullet i = \varnothing$ (the* source *place);*
- *there exist a place $o \in P$ such that $o\bullet = \varnothing$ (the* sink *place);*
- *for any node $n \in P \cup T$, there exist a path $\rho$ in $N$ such that $\rho[1] = i$, $\rho[|\rho|] = o$, and $n \in \rho$.*

*Let $\mathcal{WF} \subsetneq \mathcal{N}$ be the set of all workflow nets.*

**Structured Workflow Nets.** *The net $N$ is a* structured workflow net *[6] if and only if it is a workflow net and the following hold:*

- *$N$ has no implicit places (removing any of the places changes the behavior of the Petri net);*
- *for any $p \in P$ and $t \in T$ with $p \in {\bullet}t$ we have that*
  - *$|p{\bullet}| > 1 \Rightarrow |{\bullet}t| = 1$ (choice and synchronization are separated);*
  - *$|{\bullet}t| > 1 \Rightarrow |{\bullet}p| = 1$ (only synchronize a fixed set of transitions).*

*Let $\mathcal{SWF} \subsetneq \mathcal{N}$ be the set of all structured workflow nets.*

**Free-choice Petri Nets.** *The net $N$ is a* free-choice Petri net *[14] if and only if any two transitions share either all or none of their input places: ${\bullet}t \cap {\bullet}t' \neq \varnothing \Rightarrow {\bullet}t = {\bullet}t'$. Let $\mathcal{FC} \subsetneq \mathcal{N}$ be the set of all free-choice Petri nets.*

*Let us also define the complement sets $\neg\mathcal{MG} := \mathcal{N} \setminus \mathcal{MG}$, $\neg\mathcal{GMG} := \mathcal{N} \setminus \mathcal{GMG}$, $\neg\mathcal{SM} := \mathcal{N} \setminus \mathcal{SM}$, $\neg\mathcal{GSM} := \mathcal{N} \setminus \mathcal{GSM}$, $\neg\mathcal{WS} := \mathcal{N} \setminus \mathcal{WS}$, $\neg\mathcal{U} := \mathcal{N} \setminus \mathcal{U}$, $\neg\mathcal{WF} := \mathcal{N} \setminus \mathcal{WF}$, $\neg\mathcal{SWF} := \mathcal{N} \setminus \mathcal{SWF}$ and $\neg\mathcal{FC} := \mathcal{N} \setminus \mathcal{FC}$.*

*The sets $\mathcal{MG}, \mathcal{GMG}, \mathcal{SM}, \mathcal{GSM}, \mathcal{WS}, \mathcal{U}, \mathcal{WF}, \mathcal{SWF}, \mathcal{FC}, \neg\mathcal{MG}, \neg\mathcal{GMG}, \neg\mathcal{SM}, \neg\mathcal{GSM}, \neg\mathcal{WS}, \neg\mathcal{U}, \neg\mathcal{WF}, \neg\mathcal{SWF}$, and $\neg\mathcal{FC}$ are collectively known as* Petri net classes *(or* Petri net properties*).*

The Petri net classes defined here have been extensively studied in Petri net theory and entail desirable properties or behavior well-documented in literature. The token conservation ability of state machines and conflict-free characteristic of marked graphs allow for decidable and scalable checks of, e.g., liveness and boundedness [11,21]. The same two properties may be determined for the more complex classes of well-structured and free-choice Petri nets in polynomial time and, under workflow conditions, they imply soundness [1].

## 2.2 Bottom-Up Discovery: The eST Miner

In process discovery, we aim at automatically extracting a process model from event data. Let us now informally recall some process discovery concepts, focusing in particular on those related to the discovery of Petri nets.

Discovered models need to offer execution capabilities through their behavioral properties, which are built over their structural properties. Petri nets obtained through discovery need to have a starting state (the *initial marking*), a final state (the *final marking*), and a *labeling function* mapping the firing of transitions to the execution of a corresponding activity in the process.

A labeled Petri net $N$ obtained through discovery from a log $L$ should ideally be able to *replay* most of the traces in $L$: that is, given a trace $\sigma \in L$, there should exist a *complete firing sequence* of the transitions of $N$ such that the corresponding sequence of labels matches $\sigma$. If this is the case, $N$ *perfectly fits* $\sigma$. If the fitness is not perfect, there may be extra tokens (not belonging to the final marking) in the net at the end of the execution (*remaining tokens*), or some

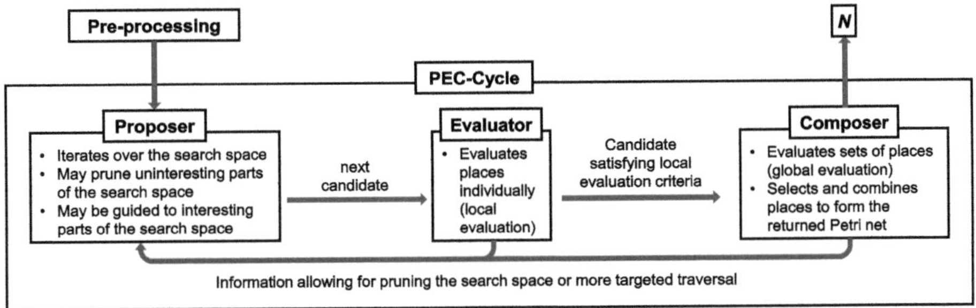

**Fig. 1.** Overview of the eST miner framework.

places might be empty although a transition in its postset needs to fire (*missing tokens*).

The ideas we present in this paper can be applied to *bottom-up discovery*, a style of process discovery where a model (for instance, a Petri net) is obtained by aggregating a selection of components such that each selected component scores well with respect to some quality measures. As example of bottom-up discovery method, we will consider the eST miner. The eST miner family is formed by a variety of approaches based on the same underlying framework, as visualized in Fig. 1. The standard input is an event log $L$. In a pre-processing step, we add the designated start and end activities ($\blacktriangleright$, $\blacksquare$) to $L$ and set up an initial Petri net with one uniquely labeled transition for each activity in the event log. A unique initial place ($\varnothing \mid \blacktriangleright$) and unique final place ($\blacksquare \mid \varnothing$) are added. Then, a set of desirable intermediate places is computed and added to this Petri net by applying the so-called PEC-Cycle.

Each iteration of this cycle is started by the Proposer selecting the next candidate place from the complete candidate space. This candidate place is then considered in isolation, i.e., locally, by the Evaluator and may or may not pass the set of evaluation criteria. Places that pass individual evaluation are collected by the Composer. Here, they are considered in relation to other discovered places, i.e., globally, and may or may not be used to extend the Petri net under construction. When the cycle terminates due to the Proposer completing the candidate space traversal, the Composer returns the discovered net as the final result.

Depending on the instantiation chosen for the three main modules, the behavior of the algorithm may differ significantly and can be tailored towards a user's specific needs. In the context of this work we are specifically interested in instantiations where the Proposer may leverage information obtained from previous iterations of the PEC-Cycle to increase efficiency by pruning undesirable parts of the search space or by guiding the search towards particularly desirable candidates. The details are, obviously, dependent on what is considered desirable.

As an example, consider individual place fitness. Every Evaluator instantiation proposed so far requires each place to satisfy a (user-definable) minimal fitness threshold, i.e., to allow for replay of a certain number of traces in the event log without missing or left-over tokens. If a place fails to satisfy this require-

ment, we may apply the following monotonicity results to prune large parts of
the search space:

**Theorem 1 (Monotonicity Properties [3]).** *Consider an event log $L$ and a place $p = (\,I \mid O\,)$. Let $p' = (\,I' \mid O'\,)$ and $p'' = (\,I'' \mid O''\,)$ be two places such that $I \supseteq I' \wedge O \subseteq O'$ and $I \subseteq I'' \wedge O \supseteq O''$. Then the following holds for any $\sigma \in L$:*

- *$p''$ is missing tokens during replay of $\sigma \Rightarrow p$ is missing tokens during replay of $\sigma$*
- *$p'$ has remaining tokens after replay of $\sigma \Rightarrow p$ has remaining tokens after replay of $\sigma$*

*Proof (Theorem 1).* See [3, Defs. 5–7, 10, 11, Th. 1].                    $\square$

An example for the use of information on relations between places is the search for uniwired Petri nets. Once a set of transitions is connected by a place, all places expressing the same connections may be skipped during candidate space traversal.

## 3 Meta-Properties of Petri Net Classes

In this section, we introduce the concept of *meta-properties* of Petri net classes, features that characterize Petri net classes and that allow to prove that the corresponding class is a closed set with respect to specific graph operations. We will then show how meta-properties of Petri net classes may be used to guide the evaluation of place quality during the state space traversal.

### 3.1 Classification of Petri Nets Properties

As mentioned earlier, Petri nets belonging to the classes of Definition 4 are desirable in process discovery, since such classes entail various formal guarantees on the behavior and language of the corresponding models. To aid their discovery, we introduce *closure* meta-properties: class invariants that apply under modification of Petri nets—either the addition of new elements (*expansion*), or the removal of existing elements (*contraction*).

**Definition 5 (Expansion and Contraction).** *Let $N := (P, T, F) \in \mathcal{N}$ be a Petri net. We can expand the net $N$ by adding places, transitions or arcs. An* expansion *of $N$, denoted $N^E$, is a net obtained from $N$ by adding elements: $N^E := (P' \supseteq P, T' \supseteq T, F' \supseteq F)$.*

*We can contract the net $N$ by removing places, transitions or arcs. A* contraction *of $N$, denoted $N^C$, is a net obtained from $N$ by removing elements: $N^C := (P'' \subseteq P, T'' \subseteq T, F'' \subseteq F)$.*

Note that any Petri net is both an expansion and a contraction of itself; also, if the net $N$ is an expansion of the net $N'$, then $N'$ is a contraction of $N$.

We then define two closure meta-properties of Petri net classes as follows.

**Definition 6 (Closure Meta-Properties).** *Let $C$ be a Petri net class, and let $N := (P, T, F) \in \mathcal{N}' \subseteq \mathcal{N}$ be a Petri net. Furthermore, let $N^E \in \mathcal{N}'$ be an expansion of $N$, and let $N^C \in \mathcal{N}'$ be a contraction of $N$.*

*The class $C$ is*

- *closed under expansion in $\mathcal{N}'$, denoted $C \in clE(\mathcal{N}')$, if $N \in C \Rightarrow N^E \in C$;*
- *closed under contraction in $\mathcal{N}'$, denoted $C \in clC(\mathcal{N}')$, if $N \in C \Rightarrow N^C \in C$.*

Given a subset of Petri nets $\mathcal{N}' \subseteq \mathcal{N}$, if the class $C$ is closed over expansion in $\mathcal{N}'$, it holds that any expansion $N^E \in \mathcal{N}'$ of any net $N \in \mathcal{N}'$ will still belong to the class $C$. Analogously, if the class $C$ is closed over contraction in $\mathcal{N}'$, it holds that any contraction $N^C \in \mathcal{N}'$ of any net $N \in \mathcal{N}'$ will still belong to $C$.

These closure meta-properties have, in turn, some noteworthy properties. First, it is important to notice that $C \in clE(\varnothing)$ and $C \in clC(\varnothing)$ hold for any Petri net class $C$; informally, a larger subset $\mathcal{N}'$ for which a meta-property holds for $C$ implies a stronger meta-property. A closure meta-property for the class $C$ is maximally strong if it holds for the entire universe of Petri nets $\mathcal{N}$.

It is also the case that, regardless of the choice of $\mathcal{N}' \subseteq \mathcal{N}$, both $C \in clE(\mathcal{N}')$ and $C \in clC(\mathcal{N}')$ trivially hold for both $C := \varnothing$ (the empty Petri net class) and $C := \mathcal{N}$ (the class including all Petri nets). Intuitively, it is in general more unusual for a closure meta-property to hold for very narrow (but non-empty) Petri net classes—that is, classes bound by many restrictive conditions. Conversely, permissive Petri nets classes will exhibit stronger and/or more common closure properties.

Lastly, it is trivial that both closure under expansion and contraction hold if we expand and contract within a class itself. For any Petri net class $C$, both $C \in clE(C)$ and $C \in clC(C)$ are true.

For the (non-exhaustive) set of Petri net classes introduced in Definition 4, Table 1 provides an overview of the meta-properties satisfied by each class: every cell indicates the subset $\mathcal{N}' \subseteq \mathcal{N}$ for which the closure holds. For instance, the row for generalized marked graphs contains $\mathcal{N}$ for the row $clC(\cdot)$, since it holds that $\mathcal{GMG} \in clC(\mathcal{N})$.

Formal proofs for the results of Table 1 are given later in the paper, in Sect. 4.

### 3.2   Petri Net Classes and Meta-Properties in eST Discovery

The eST miner may be immediately extended to only allow for output models belonging to a given class of Petri nets $C$, by altering the behavior of the Composer accordingly. Given the current net $N := (P, T, F)$ and a new place to be evaluated $p := (I \mid O) \notin P$, we may naïvely check whether $N' := (P \cup \{p\}, T, F \cup (I \times \{p\}) \cup (\{p\} \times O)) \in C$. If it does not, the Composer simply discards the place $p$.

**Table 1.** Overview of known subsets of Petri nets for which meta-properties are satisfied, by selected Petri net classes. The subsets in the cells represent the argument of the corresponding meta-property (column) that has been shown to hold for a given class (row). These results clearly highlight the symmetries of meta-properties, proven in Theorem 2.

| Petri net class $\mathcal{C}$ | $\mathcal{C} \in \texttt{clE}(\cdot)$ | $\mathcal{C} \in \texttt{clC}(\cdot)$ | $\neg\mathcal{C} \in \texttt{clE}(\cdot)$ | $\neg\mathcal{C} \in \texttt{clC}(\cdot)$ |
|---|---|---|---|---|
| Marked graphs (T-systems) | $\varnothing$ | $\varnothing$ | $\varnothing$ | $\varnothing$ |
| Generalized marked graphs | $\varnothing$ | $\mathcal{N}$ | $\mathcal{N}$ | $\varnothing$ |
| State machines (S-systems) | $\varnothing$ | $\varnothing$ | $\varnothing$ | $\varnothing$ |
| Generalized state machines | $\varnothing$ | $\mathcal{N}$ | $\mathcal{N}$ | $\varnothing$ |
| Well-structured Petri nets | $\varnothing$ | $\mathcal{N}$ | $\mathcal{N}$ | $\varnothing$ |
| Uniwired Petri nets | $\varnothing$ | $\mathcal{N}$ | $\mathcal{N}$ | $\varnothing$ |
| Workflow nets | $\mathcal{E}$ | $\varnothing$ | $\varnothing$ | $\mathcal{E}$ |
| Structured workflow nets | $\varnothing$ | $\varnothing$ | $\varnothing$ | $\varnothing$ |
| Free-choice Petri nets | $\varnothing$ | $\varnothing$ | $\varnothing$ | $\varnothing$ |

It is relevant to note that this may be done in a very efficient way for many of the Petri net classes of Definition 4: if we know that $N \in \mathcal{C}$, it is sufficient to check whether the new place $p$ causes $N' \notin \mathcal{C}$. This may be checked in $\mathcal{O}(I+O)$ time—which in most settings may be considered constant time—for the $\mathcal{MG}$, $\mathcal{GMG}, \mathcal{SM}, \mathcal{GSM}, \mathcal{U}, \mathcal{WF}, \mathcal{FC}$ Petri net classes. Mannel et al. [18] implemented this principle for the class $\mathcal{U}$ of uniwired Petri nets, of which this paper may be considered an extension. The class $\mathcal{SWF}$ of structured workflow nets additionally requires an implicitness check on the new place $p$, an approach which is already viable and implemented in previous work [19]. Note that the check on connectedness on classes $\mathcal{WF}$ and $\mathcal{SWF}$ is not needed, provided we begin the eST discovery with $(\{\blacktriangleright\} \cup T \mid T \cup \{\blacksquare\}) \in P$ (see Sect. 2.2). Lastly, the class $\mathcal{WS}$ of well-structured Petri nets needs a more complex check—on paths, rather than arcs. Since we need to keep track of new paths formed by the insertion of a place, the problem coincides with dynamic transitive closure, which is known to have a complexity of $\mathcal{O}((I+O) \cdot (P \cup T)^2)$ [16]. Since we only need to keep track of the paths that violate well-structuredness, we can disregard the update of all paths from place to place and from transition to transition, improving the complexity by a constant factor of at least 4, to $\mathcal{O}((I+O) \cdot P \cdot T)$.

Following this same principle, it is easy to further extend this framework to a version of the eST miner that guarantees the output to be in multiple Petri net classes, by checking if the addition of the place $p$ violates $N' \in \mathcal{C}_1 \cap \mathcal{C}_2 \cap \cdots \cap \mathcal{C}_n$. In some cases, we may even be interested in obtaining an output net belonging to at least one of a selection of classes: for instance, since well-structured Petri nets and free-choice Petri nets have shared formal guarantees [1], we may aim to discover a net $N \in \mathcal{WS} \cup \mathcal{FC}$.

Known closure meta-properties of the Petri net class we intend to discover may be used to prune the search space. In fact, there is an evident relation

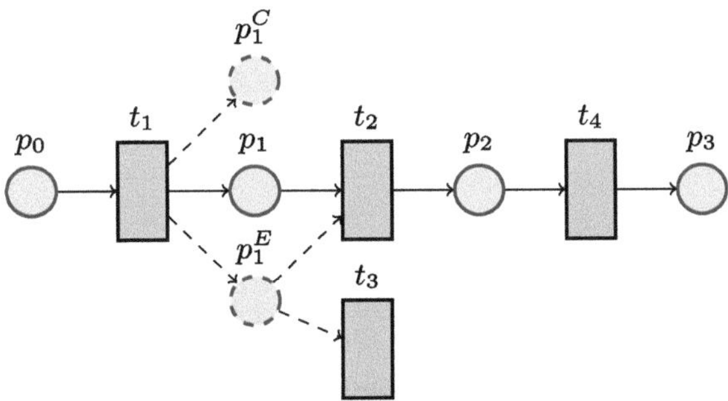

**Fig. 2.** An example showcasing the possible application of closure results within bottom-up discovery of generalized marked graphs. Consider the Petri net $N$ drawn in solid lines. The net obtained by adding the place candidate $p_1^E$ violates the properties of general marked graphs. We can derive from $\neg \mathcal{GMG} \in \mathtt{clE}(\mathcal{N})$ that any possible Petri net containing a place that extends $p_1$, i.e., any place $(I \mid O)$ with $I \supseteq \{t_1\}, O \supseteq \{t_2, t_3\}$, also violates the properties of marked graphs. In contrast, since $N$ satisfies the properties of generalized marked graphs and $\mathcal{GMG} \in \mathtt{clC}(\mathcal{N})$, we can apply any arbitrary contraction and remain in the class of generalized marked graphs. For example, we may replace $p_1$ with any place $(I \mid O)$ with $I \subseteq \{t_1\}, O \subseteq \{t_2\}$, e.g. $p_1^C$.

between the monotonicity properties of places in Theorem 1, and the closure meta-properties of net classes in Definition 6. While the Composer tests the new place $p$ against the class $\mathcal{C}$, the Proposer is able to leverage meta-properties of $\mathcal{C}$ to discard places derived from $p$ in the search. For instance, if $N' \notin \mathcal{C}$, and $\neg \mathcal{C} \in \mathtt{clE}(\mathcal{N})$, we know that the addition of any place $p' := (I' \supseteq I \mid O' \supseteq O)$ will also cause the net to violate $\mathcal{C}$, and therefore we can prune all places in that form from the candidate set. This is due to the fact that any net $(P \cup \{p'\}, T, F \cup I \times \{p'\} \cup \{p'\} \times O)$, obtained by adding $p'$ to $N$, will be a valid expansion $N^E$ of $N$. Figure 2 shows an example of this pruning strategy applied to generalized marked graph. Note that this simplistic example showcases the idea, but closure results on more complex Petri net classes can be used in practice within eST discovery.

Since the Petri net classes considered in this paper are based on structural properties, and thus may be verified very efficiently by the Composer, the pruning induced by their closure meta-properties results in an overall speed-up of the eST discovery, by way of reduction of the search space. Experiments are currently underway to verify whether this remains the case for harder-to-check Petri net classes, such as $\mathcal{WS}$.

## 4    Proofs and Guarantees

This section contains formal proofs for the statements given in previous sections of the paper related to closure meta-properties for certain Petri net classes. However, before showing these results it is important to prove an important feature of closure meta-properties: as heavily hinted by Table 1, $\mathtt{clE}(\cdot)$ and $\mathtt{clC}(\cdot)$ are symmetric with respect to a Petri net class and its negation.

**Theorem 2 (Meta-Properties are Symmetric).** *For any Petri net class $\mathcal{C}$ and any set $\mathcal{N}' \in \mathcal{N}$, it holds that*

$$\mathcal{C} \in \mathtt{clE}(\mathcal{N}') \Leftrightarrow \neg\mathcal{C} \in \mathtt{clC}(\mathcal{N}') \tag{1}$$
$$\mathcal{C} \in \mathtt{clC}(\mathcal{N}') \Leftrightarrow \neg\mathcal{C} \in \mathtt{clE}(\mathcal{N}') \tag{2}$$

*Proof (Theorem 2).* Equation (1): Assume $\mathcal{C} \in \mathtt{clE}(\mathcal{N}')$ holds. If $\neg\mathcal{C} \in \mathtt{clC}(\mathcal{N}')$ does not hold, then there must be a Petri net $N \in \neg\mathcal{C}$ and a series of contraction steps $\rho$ resulting in a Petri net $N_\rho \in \mathcal{C}$. This implies that by applying a series of expansion steps inverting $\rho$ the Petri net $N$ can be obtained from $N_\rho$, contradicting the initial assumption.

The reverse direction follows from a symmetric argument.

Equation 2: The second equivalence can be derived by applying the same reasoning to $\neg\mathcal{C}$ rather than $\mathcal{C}$. $\qquad\square$

We may now proceed in proving the closure meta-properties of the Petri nets classes considered in this paper and characterized in Definition 4, of which the results are summarized in Table 1 of Sect. 3. These lemmata largely argue for the invariance to expansion or contraction of the conditions defining a Petri net class where closures hold; and provide counterexamples for the cases where closure properties do not hold.

**Lemma 1 (Meta-Properties of Marked Graphs).** $\mathcal{MG}$ *is the class of marked graphs (Definition 4). It holds that* $\mathcal{MG} \notin \mathtt{clE}(\mathcal{N})$, $\mathcal{MG} \notin \mathtt{clC}(\mathcal{N})$, $\neg\mathcal{MG} \notin \mathtt{clE}(\mathcal{N})$ *and* $\neg\mathcal{MG} \notin \mathtt{clC}(\mathcal{N})$.

*Proof (Lemma 1).* Consider the example Petri nets presented in Fig. 3. $N := (P, T, F) \in \mathcal{N}, N \in \mathcal{MG}$ with $\{t_1, t_2, t_3\} \subseteq T$, $p \in P$ and $\{(t_1, p), (p, t_2)\} \subseteq F$ is a marked graph. For the Petri nets $N^E := (P, T, F^E)$ obtained by adding an arc $F^E := F \cup \{(p, t_3)\}$ and $N^C := (P, T, F^C)$ obtained by removing an arc $F^C := F \setminus \{(p, t_2)\}$, it holds that $N^E \notin \mathcal{MG}$ and $N^C \notin \mathcal{MG}$. Thus, $\mathcal{MG} \notin \mathtt{clE}(\mathcal{N})$ and $\mathcal{MG} \notin \mathtt{clC}(\mathcal{N})$. By Theorem 2 we also conclude that $\neg\mathcal{MG} \notin \mathtt{clE}(\mathcal{N})$ and $\neg\mathcal{MG} \notin \mathtt{clC}(\mathcal{N})$. $\qquad\square$

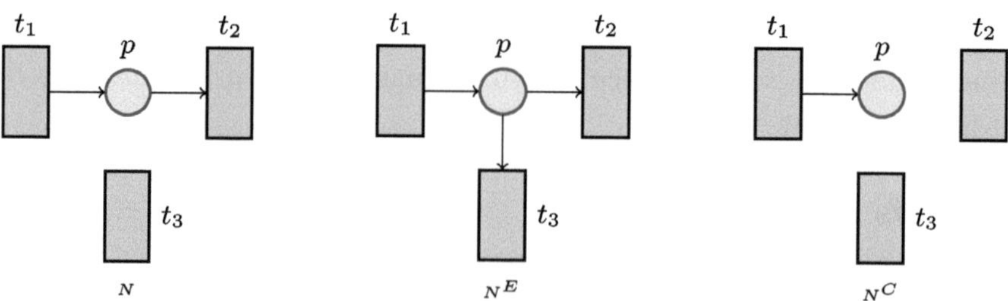


**Fig. 3.** Illustration of counterexamples used in proving Lemma 1 and Lemma 2.

**Lemma 2 (Meta-Properties of Generalized Marked Graphs).** $\mathcal{GMG}$ *is the class of generalized marked graphs (Definition 4). It holds that* $\mathcal{GMG} \in$ *$clC(\mathcal{N})$ and $\neg\mathcal{GMG} \in clE(\mathcal{N})$. Furthermore, we have that $\mathcal{GMG} \notin clE(\mathcal{N})$ and $\neg\mathcal{GMG} \notin clC(\mathcal{N})$.*

*Proof (Lemma 2).* Consider the example Petri nets presented in Fig. 3. Consider $N := (P, T, F) \in \mathcal{N}, N \in \mathcal{GMG}$ such that $\{t_1, t_2, t_3\} \subseteq T$, $p \in P$ and $\{(t_1, p), (p, t_2)\} \subseteq F$. For the Petri net $N^E := (P, T, F^E)$ obtained by adding an arc $F^E := F \cup \{(p, t_3)\}$ it holds that $N^E \notin \mathcal{GMG}$. Thus, $\mathcal{GMG} \notin clE(\mathcal{N})$ and, by Theorem 2, $\neg\mathcal{GMG} \notin clC(\mathcal{N})$.

Now, consider $N := (P, T, F) \notin \mathcal{GMG}$, implying the existence of a place $p \in P$ with $\bullet p \geqslant 2$ or $p\bullet \geqslant 2$. The number of transitions connected to $p$ cannot be decreased by adding more transitions, places or arcs. Thus, $\neg\mathcal{GMG} \in clE(\mathcal{N})$ holds and, by Theorem 2, $\mathcal{GMG} \in clC(\mathcal{N})$ holds as well. $\qquad\square$

**Lemma 3 (Meta-Properties of State Machines).** $\mathcal{SM}$ *is the class of state machines (Definition 4). It holds that* $\mathcal{SM} \notin clE(\mathcal{N})$, $\mathcal{SM} \notin clC(\mathcal{N})$, $\neg\mathcal{SM} \notin$ *$clE(\mathcal{N})$ and $\neg\mathcal{SM} \notin clC(\mathcal{N})$.*

**Lemma 4 (Meta-Properties of Generalized State Machines).** $\mathcal{GSM}$ *is the class of generalized state machines (Definition 4). It holds that* $\mathcal{GSM} \in$ *$clC(\mathcal{N})$ and $\neg\mathcal{GSM} \in clE(\mathcal{N})$. Also, $\mathcal{GSM} \notin clE(\mathcal{N})$ and $\neg\mathcal{GSM} \notin clC(\mathcal{N})$.*

*Proof (Lemma 3, Lemma 4).* The proofs follow the exact same arguments as the proofs for Lemma 1 and Lemma 2 with places and transitions inverted. $\qquad\square$

**Lemma 5 (Meta-Properties of Well-Structured Petri Nets).** $\mathcal{WS}$ *is the class of well-structured Petri nets (Definition 4). It holds that* $\mathcal{WS} \in clC(\mathcal{N})$ *and $\neg\mathcal{WS} \in clE(\mathcal{N})$. Also, $\mathcal{WS} \notin clE(\mathcal{N})$ and $\neg\mathcal{WS} \notin clC(\mathcal{N})$.*

*Proof (Lemma 5).* Consider $N := (P, T, F) \in \mathcal{N}, N \notin \mathcal{WS}$, i.e., there are two non-overlapping elementary paths connecting two nodes $n_1, n_2$ such that $n_1 \in P$ and $n_2 \in T$ or $n_1 \in T$ and $n_2 \in P$. By expanding $N$, it is not possible to remove these two paths (even though additional paths may be added), nor is it possible to change the type of node for $n_1, n_2$. Thus, for any expansion of $N$ we have $N^E \in \mathcal{WS}$ and thus $\neg\mathcal{WS} \in clE(\mathcal{N})$. By Theorem 2, $\mathcal{WS} \in clC(\mathcal{N})$.

Now consider the example presented in Fig. 4. $N := (P, T, F) \in \mathcal{N}$ with $P := \{p_1, p_2\}$, $T := \{t_1, t_2\}$ and $F := \{(p_1, t_1), (p_1, t_2), (t_1, p_2)\}$. Since there are no two non-overlapping, elementary paths between any two nodes, the net is well-structured. The expansion obtained by adding an arc from $p_2$ to $t_2$, $N^E(P, T, F \cup (p_2, t_2))$, is not well-structured: the two distinct, non-overlapping, elementary paths $(p_1, t_2)$ and $(p_1, t_1, p_2, t_2)$ connect the place $p_1$ with the transition $t_2$. Thus, $\mathcal{WS} \notin clE(\mathcal{N})$, and by Theorem 2, $\neg\mathcal{WS} \notin clC(\mathcal{N})$. $\qquad\square$

**Lemma 6 (Meta-Properties of Uniwired Petri Nets).** $\mathcal{U}$ *is the class of uniwired Petri nets (Definition 4). It holds that* $\mathcal{U} \in clC(\mathcal{N})$ *and $\neg\mathcal{U} \in clE(\mathcal{N})$. Also, $\mathcal{U} \notin clE(\mathcal{N})$ and $\neg\mathcal{U} \notin clC(\mathcal{N})$.*

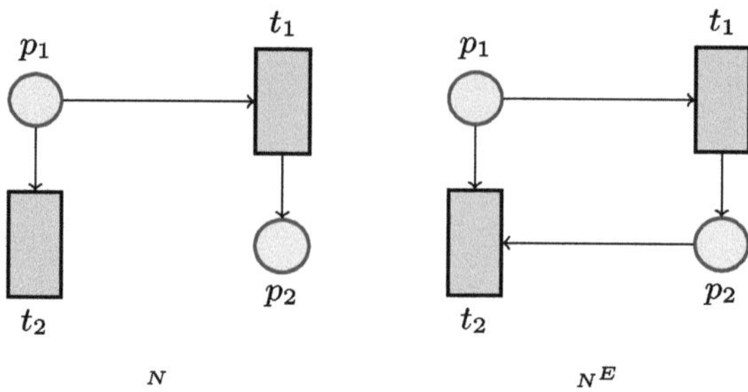

**Fig. 4.** Illustration of counterexamples used in proving Lemma 5.

*Proof (Lemma 6).* Consider the example Petri nets presented in Fig. 5. The Petri net $N := (P, T, F) \in \mathcal{N}$ with $T = \{t_1, t_2\}$, $P = \{p_1, p_2\}$ and $F = \{(t_1, p1), (p_1, t_2), (t_1, p_2)\}$ is uniwired. The expansion of $N$ obtained by adding an arc connecting $p_2$ to $t_2$, $N^E := (P, T, F \cup \{(p_2, t_2)\})$ is no longer uniwired. Thus, $\mathcal{U} \notin \texttt{clE}(\mathcal{N})$, and, by Theorem 2, $\neg\mathcal{U} \notin \texttt{clC}(\mathcal{N})$.

Now consider a Petri net $N := (P, T, F) \in \mathcal{N}$ that is not uniwired, i.e., there exist two transitions that are connected by at least two places. This connection cannot be removed by adding places, transitions or arcs. Thus, $\neg\mathcal{U} \in \texttt{clE}(\mathcal{N})$ holds, and, by Theorem 2, $\mathcal{U} \in \texttt{clC}(\mathcal{N})$ holds as well. $\square$

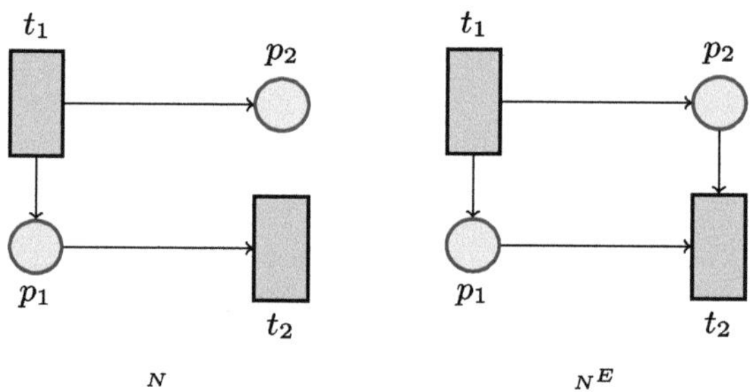

**Fig. 5.** Illustration of counterexamples used in proving Lemma 6.

Even though the class of workflow nets is not closed under neither expansion nor contraction in the context of general Petri nets $\mathcal{N}$, interestingly, we were able to obtain some closure results in the restricted context of the domain of eST discovery, i.e., $\mathcal{E}$.

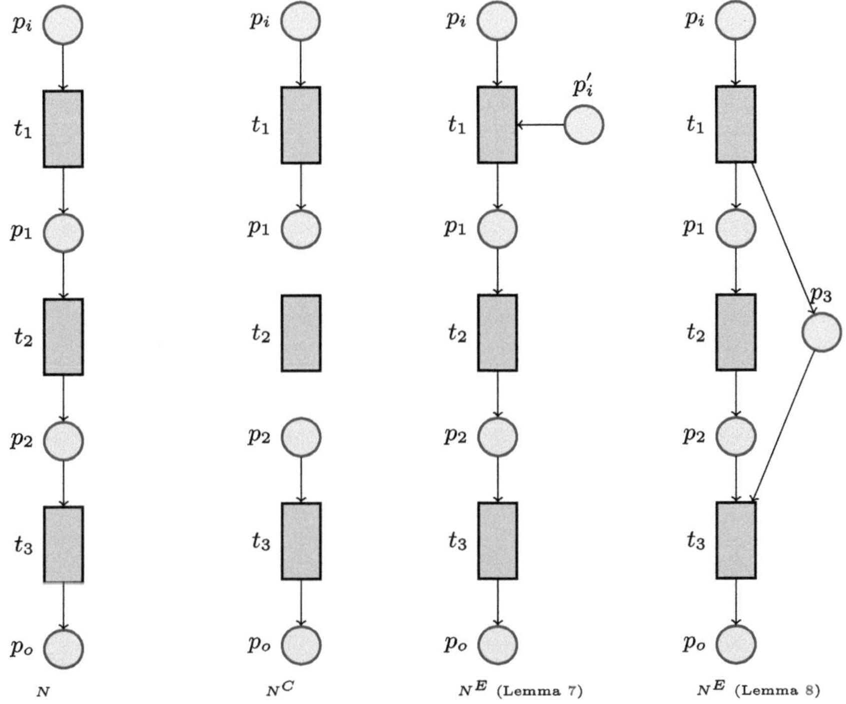

**Fig. 6.** Illustration of counterexamples used in proving Lemma 7 and Lemma 8.

**Lemma 7 (Meta-Properties of Workflow Nets).** $\mathcal{WF}$ *is the class of workflow nets (Definition 4). Then it holds that*

1. $\mathcal{WF} \notin clE(\mathcal{N})$ *and* $\neg\mathcal{WF} \notin clC(\mathcal{N})$, *as well as* $\mathcal{WF} \notin clC(\mathcal{N})$ *and* $\neg\mathcal{WF} \notin clE(\mathcal{N})$,
2. $\mathcal{WF} \in clE(\mathcal{E})$ *and* $\neg\mathcal{WF} \in clC(\mathcal{E})$, *as well as* $\mathcal{WF} \notin clC(\mathcal{E})$ *and* $\neg\mathcal{WF} \notin clE(\mathcal{E})$.

*Proof (Lemma 7).* We prove Item 1 by counterexample. Consider the example Petri nets shown in Fig. 6. $N := (P, T, F) \in \mathcal{N}$, with $P = \{p_i, p_1, p_2, p_o\}$, $T = \{t_1, t_2, t_3\}$ and $F = \{(p_i, t_1), (t_1, p_1), (p_1, t_2), (t_2, p_2), (p_2, t_3), (t_3, p_o)\}$ is a workflow net. The expansion $N^E := (P \cup \{p_i'\}, T, F \cup \{(p_i', t)\})$ violates the requirement for a unique source place. Thus, $\mathcal{WF} \notin clE(\mathcal{N})$, and, by Theorem 2, $\neg\mathcal{WF} \notin clC(\mathcal{N})$. The contraction $N^C := (P, T, F \setminus \{(p_1, t_2), (t_2, p_2)\})$ violates the requirement of all nodes being part of a path from source to sink ($t_2$ is disconnected) and is, therefore, not a workflow net. Thus, $\mathcal{WF} \notin clC(\mathcal{N})$, and thus, by Theorem 2, $\neg\mathcal{WF} \notin clE(\mathcal{N})$. The same argument can be applied to prove $\mathcal{WF} \notin clC(\mathcal{E})$ and $\neg\mathcal{WF} \notin clE(\mathcal{E})$ (Item 2).

To show the remainder of Item 2, consider a Petri net $N := (P, T, F) \in \mathcal{E}$ that is not a workflow net. $N \in \mathcal{E}$ implies that $N$ has a unique source and sink place

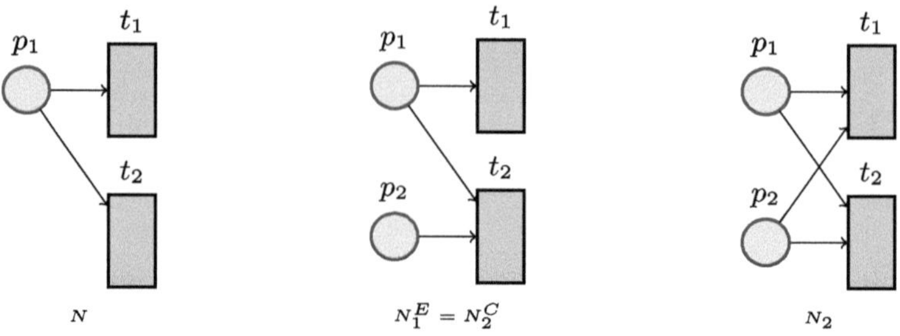

**Fig. 7.** Illustration of counterexamples used in proving Lemma 9.

and that all other places do not have an empty preset or postset. Thus, for $N$ not to be a workflow net, it must contain at least one transition $t$ that is not on a path from source to sink. Any contraction of $N$ within the domain $\mathcal{E}$ must be obtained by removing (intermediate) places or arcs, since the set of transitions is fixed in $\mathcal{E}$. Applying only these operations, $t$ cannot become included into a path from source to sink. We conclude that $\neg\mathcal{WF} \in \mathtt{clC}(\mathcal{E})$, and, by Theorem 2, $\mathcal{WF} \in \mathtt{clE}(\mathcal{E})$. □

**Lemma 8 (Meta-Properties of Structured Workflow Nets).** $\mathcal{SWF}$ *is the class of structured workflow nets (Definition 4). It holds that that* $\mathcal{SWF} \notin \mathtt{clE}(\mathcal{N})$, $\mathcal{SWF} \notin \mathtt{clC}(\mathcal{N})$, $\neg\mathcal{SWF} \notin \mathtt{clE}(\mathcal{N})$ *and* $\neg\mathcal{SWF} \notin \mathtt{clC}(\mathcal{N})$.

*Proof (Lemma 8).* Using the same argument as for workflow nets, the contraction of a structured workflow net may cease to be a (structured) workflow net by becoming disconnected due to removing all arcs connecting a transition. Thus, $\mathcal{SWF} \notin \mathtt{clC}(\mathcal{N})$, and thus, by Theorem 2, $\neq \mathcal{SWF} \notin \mathtt{clE}(\mathcal{N})$.

Now, reconsider the structured workflow net $N := (P, T, F) \in \mathcal{N}$ presented in Fig. 6. The expansion obtained by adding the place $p_3$, i.e., $N^E := (P \cup \{p_3\}, T, F \cup \{(t_1, p_3), (p_3, t_3)\})$, violates the requirement of not having implicit places ($p_3$ does not change the behavior of this Petri net). Thus, $\mathcal{SWF} \notin \mathtt{clE}(\mathcal{N})$, and, by Theorem 2, $\neg\mathcal{SWF} \notin \mathtt{clC}(\mathcal{E})$. □

**Lemma 9 (Meta-Properties of Free-Choice Petri Nets).** $\mathcal{FC}$ *is the class of free-choice Petri nets (Definition 4). It holds that* $\mathcal{FC} \notin \mathtt{clE}(\mathcal{N})$, $\mathcal{FC} \notin \mathtt{clC}(\mathcal{N})$, $\neg\mathcal{FC} \notin \mathtt{clE}(\mathcal{N})$ *and* $\neg\mathcal{FC} \notin \mathtt{clC}(\mathcal{N})$.

*Proof (Lemma 9).* We use the counterexamples presented in Fig. 7.

Consider the free-choice Petri net $N_1 := (P, T, F) \in \mathcal{N}$, with $T = \{t_1, t_2\}$, $P = \{p_1\}$ and $F = \{(p_1, t_1), (p_1, t_2)\}$. Its expansion $N_1^E := (P \cup p_2, T, F \cup \{(p_2, t_1)\})$ is not free-choice. Thus, $\mathcal{FC} \notin \mathtt{clE}(\mathcal{N})$, and, by Theorem 2, $\neg\mathcal{FC} \notin \mathtt{clC}(\mathcal{N})$.

Now, consider the free-choice Petri net $N_2 := (P, T, F) \in \mathcal{N}$ with $T = \{t_1, t_2\}, P = \{p_1, p_2\}, F = \{(p_1, t_1), (p_1, t_2), (p_2, t_1), (p_2, t_2)\}$. Its contraction $N_2^C := (P, T, F \setminus \{(p_2, t_1)\})$ is not free-choice. Thus, $\mathcal{FC} \notin \mathtt{clC}(\mathcal{N})$, and, by Theorem 2, $\neg\mathcal{FC} \notin \mathtt{clE}(\mathcal{N})$. □

In future work, we resolve to improve these preliminary results by (i) finding tighter bounds, (ii) studying relationships between Petri net classes, and (iii) considering multiple and narrower expansion and contraction operations.

## 5   Conclusion

In this paper, we discussed a general framework to extend Petri net class-guarantees beyond uniwiredness in eST discovery. Given a set of defined Petri nets classes, we defined the meta-properties of closure, we formally proved closure results over said classes, and illustrated how closures may be embedded in the eST miner pipeline to obtain a set of new pruning strategies for the search space of candidate places. This sets the stage for the next stages in this research project, of which the realization is ongoing: the implementation of the verification and pruning principles shown here in a version of the eST miner, complete with an experimental evaluation of effectiveness, feasibility and efficiency, and a more extensive presentation of the asymptotic computational complexity required to check whether the addition or removal of a Petri net component violates the property of given classes.

The present work intends to lay the theoretical grounds for new research in the domain of bottom-up discovery; therefore, there are many aspects—both theoretical and practical—of which the details remain to investigate.

First, the general results in Table 1 do not represent tight bounds. For some of the selected Petri net classes, it is likely that closure properties hold for some currently unknown set $\varnothing \subsetneq \mathcal{N}' \subsetneq \mathcal{N}$. Similarly, restricted versions of the expansion and contraction operations (e.g., component-wise, obtaining place-expansion, place-contraction, arc-expansion, etc.) may induce the discovery of meaningful bounds for the corresponding closure notions. Relations between Petri net classes (e.g., if $\mathcal{C}_1 \subsetneq \mathcal{C}_2$) may also be used to better describe closure bounds.

While in this paper we focus on eST discovery as example of application, other bottom-up discovery approaches may benefit from closure results. For instance, in the Alpha family of algorithms, if maximal input and output sets for candidate places are computed incrementally from the empty set, violations w.r.t. the class $\mathcal{C}$ indicate we may stop the search for candidate places with larger input or output sets, if $\neg \mathcal{C}$ is closed under expansion. Since $\mathcal{SWF}$ is the Petri net class induced by the representational bias of the Alpha algorithm, meta-properties of subsets of $\mathcal{SWF}$ or intersections of $\mathcal{SWF}$ with other classes would be of particular interest.

Lastly, in this paper we only consider *structural properties* of Petri nets, i.e., classes of nets only defined by their places, transitions, and connections. However, the framework hereby illustrated may also be applied to *behavioral* properties of Petri nets, i.e., classes defined by the structure of the net as well as initial and final markings. Several desirable behavioral properties exist in process mining— *soundness* probably being the most notorious [1]. While behavioral properties are harder and more complex to check, and are less connected to the meta-properties described here, the Composer of the eST miner may nonetheless grant them.

Here, speed-up may be related to connections between structural and behavioral properties, e.g., the connection of free-choiceness and well-structuredness with soundness [2].

**Acknowledgments.** This paper tributes the scientific achievements and the lifelong commitment to research and education of Wil van der Aalst.

Many know that Wil is particularly fond of a quote by English mountaineer George Mallory (1886–1924) who, in response to being asked why he wanted to climb Mount Everest, answered:

"Because it's there."

While this quote excellently reflects Wil's spirit, grit, determination and curiosity in taking on tough scientific challenges, we believe that another quote, attributed to American novelist William Faulkner (1897–1962), brilliantly illustrates his attitude towards doing research:

"I only write when inspiration strikes. Fortunately, it strikes at nine o'clock sharp every morning."

# References


1. van der Aalst, W.M.P.: Structural characterizations of sound workflow nets. Comput. Sci. R. **9623** (1996). https://research.tue.nl/files/2454992/9712195.pdf
2. van der Aalst, W.M.P.: Verification of workflow nets. In: Azéma, P., Balbo, G. (eds.) Application and Theory of Petri Nets 1997, 18th International Conference, ICATPN '97, Toulouse, France, June 23-27, 1997, Proceedings. Lecture Notes in Computer Science, vol. 1248, pp. 407–426. Springer (1997). https://doi.org/10.1007/3-540-63139-9_48
3. van der Aalst, W.M.P.: Discovering the "glue" connecting activities - exploiting monotonicity to learn places faster. In: de Boer, F.S., Bonsangue, M.M., Rutten, J. (eds.) It's All About Coordination - Essays to Celebrate the Lifelong Scientific Achievements of Farhad Arbab. Lecture Notes in Computer Science, vol. 10865, pp. 1–20. Springer (2018). https://doi.org/10.1007/978-3-319-90089-6_1
4. van der Aalst, W.M.P.: Foundations of process discovery. In: van der Aalst, W.M.P., Carmona, J. (eds.) Process Mining Handbook, Lecture Notes in Business Information Processing, vol. 448, pp. 37–75. Springer (2022). https://doi.org/10.1007/978-3-031-08848-3_2
5. van der Aalst, W.M.P., Weijters, A.J.M.M.: Process mining: a research agenda. Comput. Ind. **53**(3), 231–244 (2004). https://doi.org/10.1016/J.COMPIND.2003.10.001
6. van der Aalst, W.M.P., Weijters, T., Maruster, L.: Workflow mining: Discovering process models from event logs. IEEE Trans. Knowl. Data Eng. **16**(9), 1128–1142 (2004). https://doi.org/10.1109/TKDE.2004.47
7. Augusto, A., Carmona, J., Verbeek, E.: Advanced process discovery techniques. In: van der Aalst, W.M.P., Carmona, J. (eds.) Process Mining Handbook, Lecture Notes in Business Information Processing, vol. 448, pp. 76–107. Springer (2022). https://doi.org/10.1007/978-3-031-08848-3_3
8. Brauer, W., Reisig, W., Rozenberg, G. (eds.): Petri Nets: Central Models and Their Properties, Advances in Petri Nets 1986, Part I, Proceedings of an Advanced Course, Bad Honnef, Germany, 8-19 September 1986, Lecture Notes in Computer Science, vol. 254. Springer (1987). https://doi.org/10.1007/978-3-540-47919-2

9. Commoner, F.G., Holt, A.W., Even, S., Pnueli, A.: Marked directed graphs. J. Comput. Syst. Sci. **5**(5), 511–523 (1971). https://doi.org/10.1016/S0022-0000(71)80013-2

10. Cook, J.E., Wolf, A.L.: Automating process discovery through event-data analysis. In: Proceedings of the 17th International Conference on Software Engineering. pp. 73–82. ICSE '95, Association for Computing Machinery, New York, NY, USA (1995). https://doi.org/10.1145/225014.225021

11. Desel, J., Esparza, J.: Free Choice Petri Nets. Cambridge Tracts in Theoretical Computer Science, Cambridge University Press (1995). https://doi.org/10.1017/CBO9780511526558

12. Folz-Weinstein, S., Rennert, C., Mannel, L.L., Bergenthum, R., van der Aalst, W.M.P.: eST$^2$ miner - process discovery based on firing partial orders. In: Krogstie, J., Rinderle-Ma, S., Kappel, G., Proper, H.A. (eds.) Advanced Information Systems Engineering - 37th International Conference, CAiSE 2025, Vienna, Austria, June 16-20, 2025, Proceedings, Part II. Lecture Notes in Computer Science, vol. 15702, pp. 59–75. Springer (2025). https://doi.org/10.1007/978-3-031-94571-7_4

13. Hack, M.H.T.: Extended state-machine allocatable nets (ESMA), an extension of free choice Petri net results. Computation Structures Group Memo 78-1, Massachusetts Institute of Technology, Project MAC, Computation Structures Group, Cambridge, MA, USA (1974). https://csg.csail.mit.edu/pubs/publications.html, revised from Computation Structures Group Memo 78 (1973)

14. Hack, M.H.T.: Analysis of production schemata by Petri nets. Master's thesis, Massachusetts Institute of Technology, Cambridge, Massachusetts (1972)

15. Holt, A.W., Commoner, F.G.: Events and conditions: state machines and information. In: Dennis, J.B. (ed.) Record of the Project MAC Conference on Concurrent Systems and Parallel Computation, Woods Hole, Massachusetts, USA, June 2–5, 1970. pp. 33–52. ACM (1970). https://doi.org/10.1145/1344551.1344556

16. King, V., Sagert, G.: A fully dynamic algorithm for maintaining the transitive closure. In: Vitter, J.S., Larmore, L.L., Leighton, F.T. (eds.) Proceedings of the Thirty-First Annual ACM Symposium on Theory of Computing, May 1–4, 1999, Atlanta, Georgia, USA. pp. 492–498. ACM (1999). https://doi.org/10.1145/301250.301380

17. Mannel, L.L., van der Aalst, W.M.P.: Finding complex process-structures by exploiting the token-game. In: Donatelli, S., Haar, S. (eds.) Application and Theory of Petri Nets and Concurrency - 40th International Conference, PETRI NETS 2019, Aachen, Germany, June 23–28, 2019, Proceedings. Lecture Notes in Computer Science, vol. 11522, pp. 258–278. Springer (2019). https://doi.org/10.1007/978-3-030-21571-2_15

18. Mannel, L.L., van der Aalst, W.M.P.: Finding uniwired petri nets using eST-miner. In: Francescomarino, C.D., Dijkman, R.M., Zdun, U. (eds.) Business Process Management Workshops - BPM 2019 International Workshops, Vienna, Austria, September 1–6, 2019, Revised Selected Papers. Lecture Notes in Business Information Processing, vol. 362, pp. 224–237. Springer (2019). https://doi.org/10.1007/978-3-030-37453-2_19

19. Mannel, L.L., Bergenthum, R., van der Aalst, W.M.P.: Removing implicit places using regions for process discovery. In: van der Aalst, W.M.P., Bergenthum, R., Carmona, J. (eds.) Proceedings of the International Workshop on Algorithms & Theories for the Analysis of Event Data 2020 Satellite event of the 41st International Conference on Application and Theory of Petri Nets and Concurrency Petri Nets 2020, virtual workshop, June 24, 2020. CEUR Workshop Proceedings, vol. 2625, pp. 20–32. CEUR-WS.org (2020). https://ceur-ws.org/Vol-2625/paper-02.pdf

20. Mannel, L.L., Epstein, Y., van der Aalst, W.M.P.: Improving the state-space traversal of the eST-miner by exploiting underlying log structures. In: del-Río-Ortega, A., Leopold, H., Santoro, F.M. (eds.) Business Process Management Workshops - BPM 2020 International Workshops, Seville, Spain, September 13–18, 2020, Revised Selected Papers. Lecture Notes in Business Information Processing, vol. 397, pp. 334–347. Springer (2020). https://doi.org/10.1007/978-3-030-66498-5_25

21. Murata, T.: Petri nets: Properties, analysis and applications. Proc. IEEE **77**(4), 541–580 (1989). https://doi.org/10.1109/5.24143

# Automated Conformance Checking Between Process Models and Their Generalized Reference Process Models

Judith Michael[1], Bernhard Rumpe[2], Max Stachon[2(✉)],
Sebastian Stüber[2], and Valdes Voufo[2]

[1] Programming and Software Engineering, University of Regensburg,
Regensburg, Germany
`judith.michael@ur.de`
[2] Software Engineering, RWTH Aachen University, Aachen, Germany
`{rumpe,stachon,stueber}@se-rwth.de, valdes.voufo@rwth-aachen.de`
`https://www.se-rwth.de/`

**Abstract.** Reference process models are normative and prescriptive models that encapsulate best practices and standards for reuse and are thus essential for ensuring quality and consistency in concrete processes. Conformance checks are required to verify the adherence between a concrete process model of a system and its reference model.

This paper explores automated conformance checks using causal dependency analysis of tasks and events. Current methods primarily focus on verifying execution traces, lacking the necessary expressiveness and automation for semantic model-to-model comparison. Our approach is integrated into a broader semantic framework for defining reference model conformance. We present an algorithm for conformance checking, evaluate its implementation, and discuss its strengths and limitations. Our research offers a tool-assisted automated solution that enhances accuracy and flexibility in process model conformance verification.

**Keywords:** Reference Models · Process Models · Denotational Semantics · Conformance Checking · BPMN · Model-Driven Engineering

## 1 Introduction

Process models are crucial in various domains, providing structured representations of workflows. They standardize processes [5,63], optimize performance [36], and ensure compliance with industry standards [32,39]. As organizations increasingly rely on these models [19], robust mechanisms for verifying adherence of concrete implementations to reference models are essential.

Reference models are normative and prescriptive models that serve as benchmarks and encapsulate standardized processes and best practices [20,29]. However, their usage remains mostly informal, since formal conformance verification


J. Mendling et al. (Eds.): Wil van der Aalst Festschrift, LNCS 16480, pp. 525–550, 2026.
https://doi.org/10.1007/978-3-032-17618-9_35

methods for effective model-to-model comparisons are lacking. Current conformance checking approaches focus primarily on the alignment of execution logs [1,4,9,18,51,53,54,58,59,62] with process models, overlooking the often critical preservation of semantic properties from reference to concrete models.

Conformance checks [34] are vital to ensure that concrete process models align with reference models, facilitating adherence to best practices and timely identification of deviations. This alignment is essential for regulatory compliance and operational efficiency. However, the complexity and variability of real-world processes complicate conformance checking, as frequent changes in process structures challenge validation efforts. Existing methods of semantic model-to-model comparison often struggle with limited expressiveness and scalability, impeding effective validation in diverse environments [31,41,42,56,60].

This paper is a revised and extended version of an existing arXiv-preprint [61]. It introduces a novel algorithmic approach for tool-assisted model-to-model conformance checking, leveraging causal relations analysis to improve process verification automation. Our goal is to provide a more accurate and flexible solution for verifying the conformance of complex process structures to reference models.

**Objective:** We aim to develop a method that systematically analyzes causal dependencies in reference process models and compares them to the causal relation between corresponding elements in concrete models, advancing the state-of-the-art in process model verification.

**Contributions:**

- A semantic framework for reference process models and conformance
- An abstract description of a conformance checking algorithm
- A publicly available Java implementation for conformance checking
- An evaluation of the tool's validity and performance using constructed models
- A discussion of the capabilities and limitations of or approach

Please note that our perspective on this topic is coming from the software engineering community, more concretely, the model-driven engineering community. Thus, we might use terms different from those of the process mining community. However, our aim is to bridge research from these communities.

**Structure:** In Sect. 2, we present a motivating example that illustrates key concepts. Section 3 discusses related work in the field. We introduce our conformance checking algorithm in Sect. 4, addressing its complexity, soundness, and completeness. Section 5 outlines the implementation and provides an evaluation of the tool. In Sect. 6, we discuss precision, limitations, and potential threats to validity, concluding with a summary of findings and future work directions.

## 2   Motivating Example

Consider the process model displayed in Fig. 1, a reference process for scientific writing. After starting the process, the first task is **Research**. After **Research**

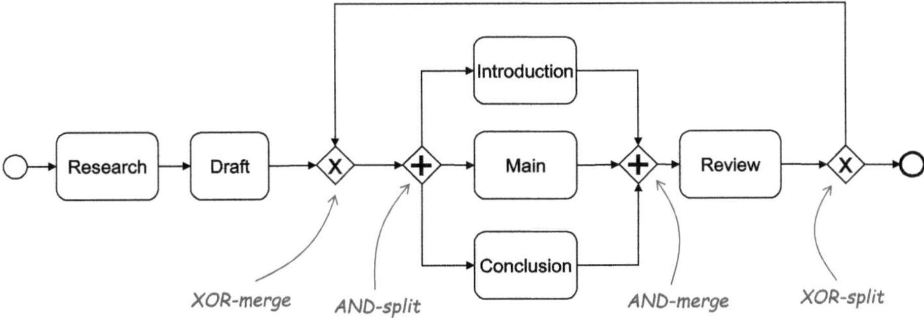



**Fig. 1.** Reference process model for scientific writing.

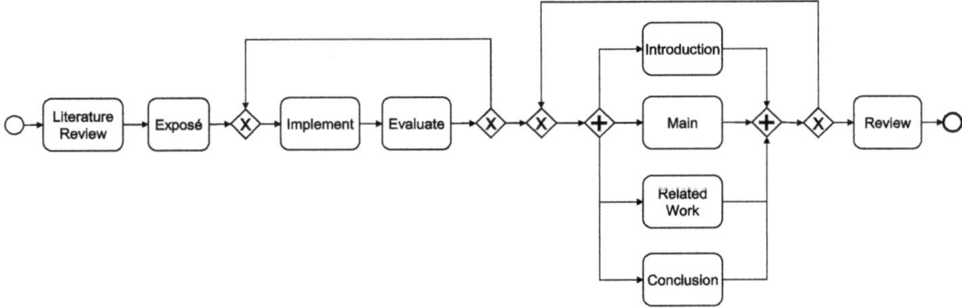



**Fig. 2.** Concrete process model for writing a thesis; the `Review` task is incorrectly placed after the final loop.

is completed, the next task is to write an initial `Draft`. Following that `Introduction`, `Main`, and `Conclusion` have to be completed. These three can be worked on in parallel. Next up is the task `Review`, after which the process either ends or the tasks `Introduction`, `Main`, and `Conclusion` are repeated.

Based on this reference model, we want to develop a more refined version of the model for the concrete case of writing a thesis. This model is displayed in Fig. 2: The thesis starts with a `Literature Review` instead of `Research`, followed by writing an `Exposé` instead of a `Draft`. Afterwards, the tasks `Implement` and then `Evaluation` have to be completed. Both may have to be repeated. Following that `Introduction`, `Main`, `Conclusion`, as well as `Related Work` have to be written. After a `Review` of the work, these tasks may have to be repeated, as well. Otherwise, the process ends.

This is the intended specification of the process. However, the modeler made a mistake and placed the `Review` task after the final loop. As a consequence, the execution behavior of the model does not *conform* to the reference model, *i.e.*, its semantics were not properly preserved.

A mistake such as this becomes harder to discover the larger the model grows, increasing the chances that the model will be implemented and executed when the corresponding software system is deployed. The severity of the impact such a mistake has can vary, but if compliance to the reference model is legally required, it is best to avoid this situation in the first place by utilizing tool-assisted model-to-model conformance checks.

## 3  Background and Related Work

We outline necessary background information and discuss related work.

### Process Modeling with BPMN

Business Process Model and Notation (BPMN) [50] is an internationally recognized standard developed by the Object Management Group (OMG). Its primary aim is to furnish a notation for business process design that is easily comprehensible to all stakeholders across various levels of the development process, from initial drafts to implementation, and extending to the management and monitoring of these processes. BPMN serves as a synthesis of best practices from the business modeling community, delineating the notation and semantics for collaboration, process, and choreography diagrams.

In this paper, we focus on the process design aspects of BPMN, specifically addressing the order and interdependencies of task executions within a business process. Consequently, we restrict our analysis to a subset of the BPMN syntax and features. Our focus encompasses process definitions that involve *events*, *tasks*, *gateways*, and *sequence flows* that interconnect these elements. For our purposes, we categorize gateways into two types: *split* and *merge*. Each gateway can further be classified as an AND gateway, an XOR gateway, or an OR gateway.

According to the BPMN standard, the following execution semantics apply to gateways: All sequence flows following an AND-split gateway are executed in parallel. In contrast, after an XOR-split gateway, only one of the subsequent sequence flows is executed. OR-split gateways permit the parallel execution of multiple subsequent sequence flows. An AND-merge waits for the completion of all preceding sequence flows, while an XOR-merge requires the completion of just one preceding sequence flow. Notably, other active flows are not terminated and may continue to pass through the gateway. Lastly, an OR-merge awaits the completion of all active preceding sequence flows.

### Conformance to a Reference Model

In the context of process mining, the terms *conformance checking* or *conformance testing* usually refer to a comparison of actual process executions recorded in event logs with the behavior specified by a process model, *i.e.*, the intended or required procedure [1,4,9,18,51,53,54,58,59,62]. We aim to extend this notion of conformance to a semantic model-to-model comparison between a reference model and a concrete model. Now, the focus shifts from determining whether a process execution trace represents a legal instance of a model to verifying whether all legal executions of the concrete model conform to the reference model.

A reference model is an abstract model within a given modeling language that captures domain concepts and their domain-specific relations. It specifies properties that must be maintained for any conformant concrete model, *e.g.,* which model elements may or must exist, and how they interrelate [33]. Thus, from a model-driven engineering perspective, a reference model presents a template-solution for a class of concrete problems, or in the case of reference process models, a family of business processes.

An alternative approach to this notion of a reference model is the concept of configurable process models, which capture multiple variants of a process model in a consolidated manner [37,57].

Conformance to a reference model is crucial, especially in cases where the reference model encodes compliance constraints. To formally specify conformance, a conformance relation is used. A robust conformance relation must guarantee that all relevant semantic properties are preserved by conformant concrete models [34]. Specifically, a conformant concrete model must contain appropriate *incarnations* of relevant elements from the reference model. These incarnations are concrete model elements that correspond to reference elements while preserving their interrelations in the concrete model.

To ensure this formally, we require semantic refinement of the reference model by the concrete model in the context of incarnation. This process is crucial to maintain the intended semantics of the reference model and ensure integrity in the relationships among model elements.

Incarnations are specified via an incarnation mapping—a formal specification that defines how elements in the reference model correspond to elements in the concrete model—or automatically derived by a conformance checking algorithm. Conformance checking algorithms implement these conformance relations. Such algorithms have been developed for various modeling paradigms, including class diagrams, feature models, and statecharts [34]. They evaluate how well a concrete model adheres to its reference model and determine conformance violations that occur in the concrete model.

The incarnation mappings for these algorithms were either specified using stereotypes [21,28], which annotate model elements with additional semantics, or through custom mapping languages that provide a flexible way to define relationships between model elements. In cases where explicit mappings are incomplete or ambiguous, name-equality serves as a fall-back option, allowing the algorithm to infer correspondences based on the similarity of element names.

In this paper, we present a novel conformance checking algorithm specifically designed for process models. Our approach leverages stereotypes for encoding the incarnation mapping while also employing name-equality as a fall-back option to enhance the robustness of the conformance checking process.

With our conformance checking approach, we aim to address process compliance at design time. Runtime compliance, which is ensured through compliance monitoring [55], is beyond the scope of this paper.

## Semantic Differencing

Conformance checking requires a formal notion of semantics. We employ a denotational semantics definition $sem : M \rightarrow 2^D$ which assigns each syntactically correct model of a modeling language $M$ a set of valid instances within a well-defined and comprehensible semantic domain $D$ [26]. In this context, refinement is characterized as a subset relation between sets of instances; specifically, a model $A$ is said to refine a model $B$ if and only if $sem(A) \subseteq sem(B)$. For process models, valid instances correspond to process execution traces.

Denotational semantics is employed in a variety of semantic differencing operators for multiple modeling languages [10, 11, 15, 16, 30, 31, 38, 40, 42, 56, 60]. These operators compare two input models with respect to their legal instances and can be extended with incarnation mappings to allow for conformance checking [34].

For concrete models to meaningfully extend reference models, it is generally more appropriate to adopt an open-world assumption regarding model semantics for conformance relations, rather than a closed-world assumption. This perspective allows a concrete model to incorporate additional elements that do not have counterparts in the reference model while still maintaining conformance. In terms of process model semantics, this implies that the execution trace of the concrete model may include additional tasks and events, provided that the causal relations among tasks and events in the reference model are preserved by their incarnations. It is essential to note that we assume tasks and events are uniquely identified by names within a process model, ensuring that each appears only once.

One approach to formalizing the execution semantics of process models, particularly Business Process Model and Notation (BPMN), is to translate them into Petri nets [3, 14]. For example, Medeiros et al. [45] utilize a Petri net representation to evaluate the precision of process models derived from event logs via a genetic algorithm. They compare the execution behavior of the derived model with that of the original process model used to build the synthetic event log. However, this comparison only considers the traces contained within the event log, which is insufficient to guarantee a refinement of the original model. In general, comparing Petri nets based on their execution traces is undecidable [27], so a simpler model would be preferable.

Existing semantic differencing operators for process models [31, 40] convert activity diagrams into state machines, where the state space is represented by the power set of activities, and the transition function encodes all potential process execution steps, namely, transitions from one set of active tasks to another. In this context, [40] employs this translation to perform bisimulation of the models, while [31] utilizes language inclusion checking algorithms for finite word automata.

The translation to state machines significantly increases the state space compared to the original activity diagram, leading to scalability issues due to the power-set automaton construction necessary for capturing the semantics of concurrent activities. Although it should be noted that state space reduction is possible and alternative concurrency models, such as partially ordered multisets (pomsets) and Mazurkiewicz traces [6,44,52] exist, which address this issue by utilizing partial orders and equivalence classes that maintain causal dependencies and independence. However, these models introduce additional mathematical complexity and require specialized algorithms for determining behavioral equivalences, such as concurrency-aware bisimulation.

Another complicating factor in using bisimulation for conformance checking is the handling of multiple and composite incarnations of reference tasks and events. Multiple incarnations occur when a single reference element is incarnated multiple times in the concrete model, while composite incarnations involve a single reference element being represented by a configuration multiple elements in the concrete model or vice versa. For example, in process models, multiple incarnations may appear as inclusive or exclusive alternatives of tasks or events, whereas composite incarnations require the parallel or sequential execution of these tasks and/or events.

The challenge lies in bisimulation's requirement for a one-to-one correspondence between states in the reference and concrete models. This requirement becomes problematic with multiple and composite incarnations, as they introduce complexity that cannot be easily reconciled with the strict nature of bisimulation. Additionally, due to our open-world assumption regarding process model semantics, extra tasks and events may be added to the concrete model, further complicating the conformance checking process. Unlike these additional elements, multiple and composite incarnations cannot simply be deleted or ignored in the concrete model, as they are integral to its structure and behavior.

Our approach circumvents the need for full bisimulation by focusing exclusively on local causal dependencies, accepting a trade-off in completeness. Initially, we construct two propositional formulas for each task and event in the reference model: one formula captures the causal dependencies to its direct predecessor tasks and events, while the other addresses the dependencies to its direct successors. We then verify whether these dependencies are maintained for the corresponding incarnations in the concrete model.

This approach is in principle similar to the compliance analysis based on behavioral profiles developed by Weidlich et al. [64]. A behavioral profile considers binary order relations between activities in a process log or model. It can be extended to a causal behavioral profile by adding a binary causal relation. These relations can be efficiently computed for sound process models without OR gateways as well as process logs. From there several metrics for compliance of a process log to a process model can be derived.

However, we believe that the causal behavioral profile is unsuited to serve as the semantic basis for our notion of reference process model conformance, as the addition of further alternatives to an already existing set of exclusive alternatives would not violate any of the existing relations, despite being contrary to our notion of refinement and causal dependency preservation.

This might not have been an issue if we were simply computing a compliance metric, but we are interested in identifying (potential) violations of conformance in a concrete model, so that they may be addressed by the modeler.

## 4    Conformance Checking Approach

We define the open-world semantics of a process model as the collection of process execution traces that uphold the local causal dependencies of tasks and events as specified by the process model. In this context, each instance of a task or event is permitted to occur only after a suitable configuration of its predecessor instances has taken place and before an appropriate configuration of its successor instances is realized. Furthermore, these configurations of predecessor and successor instances must also be maintained between instances of the same task or event. In other words, loops that disrupt the local dependency structure of tasks and events are explicitly disallowed.

Our conformance checking algorithm operates under the assumption that an incarnation mapping exists which relates each incarnation in the concrete process model to a corresponding reference task or event in the reference model. Notably, each reference element may have multiple incarnations. We analyze each reference element and its incarnations individually, scrutinizing its local causal dependencies with respect to both its predecessor and successor tasks and events as encoded in the graph structure and gateways of the reference process model. This analysis is then juxtaposed with the causal dependencies of the corresponding incarnations in the concrete model.

This approach bears similarity to our conformance checking method for class diagrams as described in [34], where an incarnation is deemed conformant to its corresponding reference element if its properties and relationships with other elements are preserved. However, in the context of concrete process models, it is inadequate to limit our examination to neighboring tasks and events. For example, consider the following scenarios:

- **Insertion of New Tasks or Events:** A new task or event may be introduced between two incarnations of subsequent reference elements. This situation reflects a refinement in accordance with our open-world semantics, as it allows for the evolution of the process model without violating causal dependencies.
- **Sequential Execution of Parallel Tasks:** In the concrete model, the incarnations of two parallel tasks might need to be executed sequentially. This represents a refinement, since it alters the execution order while still preserving the underlying dependencies defined in the reference model.
- **Violation of Exclusive Alternatives:** The relationships defined by exclusive alternatives among reference tasks may be contravened in the concrete model if their incarnations are executed sequentially. In such cases, the concrete model fails to be a refinement of the reference model and thus does not conform to it.


### Algorithm

The conformance checking algorithm is divided into two distinct phases. In the first phase, we identify the local causal dependencies of tasks and events within the reference model and encode these dependencies into propositional logic formulas, one for all direct predecessors and another for all direct successors. In the second phase, we perform the conformance check on the concrete model by analyzing the causal relation of each incarnation to its predecessors and successors in the concrete model and subsequently comparing these relations to the local causal dependencies expressed in the corresponding formulas.

**Phase 1: Construct the Formula** In this phase, we compute the direct predecessors and successors of a task or event in the reference model and represent its interrelations as formulas in propositional logic, treating each task and each event as a Boolean variable. This process involves executing a depth-first search both forwards and backwards from the reference element.

During the forward search, we branch out at each split gateway, while in the backward search, we branch out at each merge gateway, continuing until we encounter the first task or event on each branch. Each gateway is interpreted as a corresponding logical operation applied to the sub-formulas derived from the branches. The pseudocode for the forward direction is presented in Algorithm 1.

---

**Algorithm 1.** A recursive algorithm for computing the successor formula of $n$

---

**Require:** $x$.suc are the predecessor nodes of $x$
  **return** SUCFORM($n$.suc)
  **function** SUCFORM($x$)
    **if** $x$ is an AND-split gateway **then**
      **return** $AND(\{\text{SUCFORM}(s)\colon s \in x.\text{suc}\})$
    **else if** $x$ is an XOR-split gateway **then**
      **return** $XOR(\{\text{SUCFORM}(s)\colon s \in x.\text{suc}\})$
    **else if** $x$ is an OR-split gateway **then**
      **return** $OR(\{\text{SUCFORM}(s)\colon s \in x.\text{suc}\})$
    **else if** $x$ is an event or task of the reference model **then**
      **return** $x$
    **else**
      **return** SUCFORM($x.suc$)
    **end if**
  **end function**

---

In the backward direction, we treat XOR-merge gateways identically to OR-merge gateways, reflecting the execution semantics of BPMN. Specifically, multiple preceding sequence flows can be concurrently active and reach the gateway. The corresponding pseudocode for this process can be found in Algorithm 2.

**Example:** Consider the task `Draft` in the reference process model from Fig. 1. Its only predecessor is `Research`, so the formula for the backward direction consists only of the Boolean variable of the same name. For successors, we find `Introduction`, `Main`, and `Conclusion` after an AND-split gateway, which means that the formula for the forward direction is the following:

`Introduction AND Main AND Conclusion`

---

**Algorithm 2.** A recursive algorithm for computing the predecessor formula of $n$

---

**Require:** $x$.pred are the successor nodes of $x$
  **return** PREFORM($n$.pred)
  **function** PREFORM($x$)
    **if** $x$ is an AND-merge gateway **then**
      **return** $AND(\{\text{PREFORM}(p) : p \in x.\text{pred}\})$
    **else if** $x$ is an XOR- or OR-merge gateway **then**
      **return** $OR(\{\text{PREFORM}(p) : p \in x.\text{pred}\})$
    **else if** $x$ is an event or task of the reference model **then**
      **return** $x$
    **else**
      **return** PREFORM($x.pred$)
    **end if**
  **end function**

---

If we consider the task `Review`, instead, we get an identical formula but for the backward direction. As for the forward direction, `Review` is assigned the formula:

$$(\texttt{Introduction AND Main AND Conclusion}) \texttt{ XOR Done}$$

with `Done` being the end event.

**Phase 2: Check Conformance** After constructing the two formulas encoding the local causal dependency of the reference task or event to either its direct predecessors and its direct successors, we perform a quasi-simulation of the concrete model—both forward and backward—using breadth-first search, starting with the incarnation of the reference element. The forward search aims to determine whether the incarnations of the successors can be located in a configuration that satisfies the corresponding formula, while the backward search serves a similar purpose for the predecessors.

In the following, we focus solely on the forward direction, as the backward direction follows a largely analogous approach. A simplified version of our algorithm for the forward direction is presented as pseudocode in Algorithm 3. We initiate the process with the incarnation $n$ and establish the initial branch $b$. Each branch comprises a set of visited nodes $N$, a set of active nodes $A$, and a result $r$. Additionally, we maintain the current execution trace, although this detail is omitted from the pseudocode for simplicity.

---

**Algorithm 3.** Simplified conformance checking algorithm for an incarnation $n$

---

**Require:** $x$.suc are the successor nodes of $x$ and $x$.pred the predecessors
1: $\mathcal{B} \leftarrow \{(\emptyset, \{n\}, \text{not conformant})\}$
2: **while** $\exists b = (N, A, r) \in \mathcal{B}$ with $A \neq \emptyset$ **do**
3:     **for all** $b = (N, A, r) \in \mathcal{B}$ with $A \neq \emptyset$ **do**
4:         **for all** $x \in A$ **do**
5:             **if** $x$ is an event, a task, an AND-split gateway, or an XOR- or OR-merge gateway **then**
6:                 $A \leftarrow (A \backslash \{x\}) \cup (x.\text{suc} \backslash N)$
7:                 $N \leftarrow N \cup x.\text{suc}$
8:                 UPDATERESULT($b$)
9:             **end if**
10:         **end for**
11:         **if** $\exists x \in A : x$ is an XOR- or OR-split gateway **then**
12:             **if** $x$ is an XOR gateway **then**
13:                 **for all** $s \in x.\text{suc}$ **do**
14:                     $b_s \leftarrow (N \cup \{s\}, (A \backslash \{x\}) \cup (\{s\} \backslash N), r)$
15:                     UPDATERESULT($b_s$)
16:                     $\mathcal{B} \leftarrow \mathcal{B} \cup \{b_s\}$
17:                 **end for**
18:             **else if** $x$ is an OR gateway **then**
19:                 **for all** $S \subseteq x.\text{suc}$ with $S \neq \emptyset$ **do**
20:                     $b_S \leftarrow (N \cup S, (A \backslash \{x\}) \cup (S \backslash N), r)$
21:                     UPDATERESULT($b_s$)
22:                     $\mathcal{B} \leftarrow \mathcal{B} \cup \{b_S\}$
23:                 **end for**
24:             **end if**
25:             $\mathcal{B} \leftarrow \mathcal{B} \backslash b$
26:         **else if** $A \neq \emptyset$ **then**
27:             **while** $A$ contains only AND-gateways **do**
28:                 **if** $\exists m \in A : m.\text{pred} \subseteq N$ **then**
29:                     $x \leftarrow m$
30:                 **else**
31:                     $x \in A$
32:                 **end if**
33:                 $A \leftarrow (A \backslash \{x\}) \cup (x.\text{suc} \backslash N)$
34:                 $N \leftarrow N \cup x.\text{suc}$
35:                 UPDATERESULT($b$)
36:             **end while**
37:         **else if** $n \notin N$ and $N$ contains no end event **then**
38:             $\mathcal{B} \leftarrow \mathcal{B} \backslash b$
39:         **end if**
40:     **end for**
41: **end while**
42: **return** $\mathcal{B}$
43: **function** UPDATRESULT($b = (N, A, r)$)
44:     **if** $r = $ not conformant and $N$ satisfies the formula **then**
45:         $r = $ conformant
46:     **else if** $r = $ conformant and $N$ does not satisfies the formula **then**
47:         $r = $ unknown
48:     **end if**
49: **end function**

---

The algorithm proceeds iteratively until no branches with active nodes remain. In each iteration, for every event, task, AND-split gateway, and XOR- or OR-merge gateway present in $A$, we perform the following steps to progress:

1. Remove the current node from $A$.
2. Add all successor nodes that are not already included in $N$ to $A$.
3. Update the result of the branch by checking whether the current set of tasks and events in $N$ satisfies the encoded formula.

Due to the presence of exclusive alternatives, we may encounter situations where a branch previously marked as *conformant* no longer satisfies the formula, leading us to designate its status as *unknown*. This does not necessarily imply that the execution trace represented by this branch is non-conformant.

When encountering an XOR-split gateway in $A$, a new branch is created for each successor node, updating the sets of visited and active nodes for each new branch, after which the current branch is deleted. Similarly, if an OR-split gateway is encountered, a new branch is created for each subset of successor nodes before deleting the current branch. Conversely, if the set of active nodes $A$ contains only AND-merge gateways, we can progress through one of these gateways if all its predecessor nodes are included in $N$; otherwise, we will advance through another available AND-merge gateway.

If no active nodes remain and we have not yet reached an end event or returned to nn, we delete the branch. Once all branches with active nodes have been exhausted, we return the set of branches that were not deleted to examine their results. If any non-conformant branch exists, we conclude that the incarnation is *not conformant*, returning the execution trace as a diff witness. Conversely, if a branch with the status *unknown* exists, the conformance status of the incarnation is designated as *unknown*, and we return the trace for potential manual verification. Lastly, if all remaining branches are conformant, we classify the incarnation as *conformant*.

**Example:** Going back to our previous example, we now consider the concrete process model from Fig. 2, where we start the forward search for the task Review. We branch out in our search because of the subsequent XOR-split gateway. One branch terminates in the next step as we reach the end event Done. Having visited Done, the branch satisfies the successor formula:

$$(\text{Introduction AND Main AND Conclusion}) \text{ XOR Done}$$

The other branch finds an AND-split gateway after the loop and adds the tasks Introduction, Main, Related Work, and Conclusion to its list of visited nodes. In the next step, we reach the starting point Review and terminate the search in this branch. This branch also satisfies the successor formula, having visited:

$$[\text{Introduction, Main, Related Work, Conclusion, Review}]$$

Since all branches satisfy the formula, the task Review is conformant with respect to its successors. However, this is not the case with regard to its predecessors.

If we backtrack, we immediately encounter an XOR-split and branch out. One of the branches will now, before terminating, visit:

```
[Related Work, Evaluate, Implement, Exposé, Literature Review,
                        Start]
```

This does not satisfy the predecessor formula:

```
Introduction AND Main AND Conclusion
```

As such, the task `Review` is not conformant.

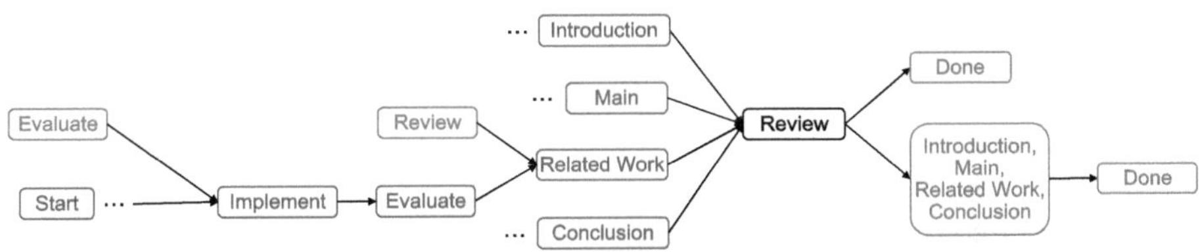


**Fig. 3.** Abbreviated search tree for forward and backward search for the task `Review` in the concrete model in Fig. 2 with satisfying branches in green, non-satisfying in red, and branches deleted due to loops/idleness in gray.

The abbreviated search tree for both the forward and backward search is illustrated in Fig. 3. The nodes contain the tasks and events visited in that step and are colored green if the formula is satisfied in this step, red if not, and gray if an already visited element was visited once again and the branch will be ignored.

**Complexity:** If no inclusive OR gateways are utilized, both parts of the algorithm can be executed in polynomial time. Specifically, we first employ depth-first search to construct the formula, followed by breadth-first search for the conformance checking. However, the complexity increases exponentially with the number of inclusive decision branches. Notably, this represents an improvement over previous approaches that relied on power-set automaton construction [31,40], as our method does not require interleaving concurrent tasks and events.

**Soundness:** A conformance relation must ensure semantic refinement in the context of incarnations. For process models, this means that every execution trace of the concrete model must align with the reference model. To enable process extension in the concrete case, we operate under an open-world assumption. As such, the relative order of elements in a trace must correspond to the causal dependencies of reference elements.

Our algorithm checks for the preservation of causal dependencies under incarnation, which serves as a sufficient condition for semantic refinement under the open-world assumption: At any point during the concrete process's execution, it guarantees for each active incarnation that all predecessor incarnations can ultimately be identified through backtracking, and a suitable configuration of successor incarnations will eventually be established if the execution is continued. Consequently, the resulting execution trace must align with the reference model.

**Completeness:** The reduced complexity of our approach compared to previous semantic differencing methods for process models [31,41] comes at a cost. In certain cases, a branch may reach a configuration that violates the formula concerning an XOR-constraint after having satisfied the formula in a prior step. This circumstance does not necessarily indicate that the model is non-conformant, as illustrated by the process model depicted in Fig. 4.

For instance, when checking the conformance of this model against itself, the algorithm first derives the formula B XOR C for the successors of A. During the conformance check of A as an incarnation of itself, the algorithm will branch in the first step due to the XOR-split and will successfully identify satisfying configurations B and C, respectively. However, in the subsequent step, the configuration [B,C] is encountered, which no longer satisfies the formula. Consequently, the branch is unable to reach a satisfying configuration thereafter.

As a result, the algorithm indicates that it cannot ascertain whether A is conformant, outputting the configuration [B,C]. Nevertheless, this task sequence [B,C] can be extended to form a legal run [start,A,B,C,end], as the reference model is identical to the concrete model. This allows for manual verification, confirming that the model is indeed conformant.

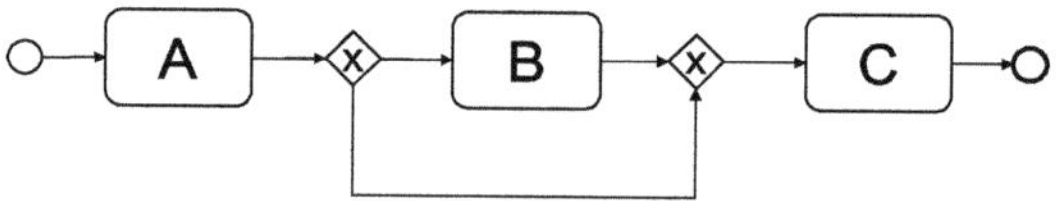

**Fig. 4.** Example of a process model with a skippable task.

## 5    Implementation and Tool

For our implementation, we use a textual variant of BPMN [17] developed with the MontiCore[1] language workbench [22,28]. To encode the incarnation mapping, we have extended the grammar of the language to allow the annotation of tasks and events with stereotypes [21,28]. Similar to our previous conformance checking approach of class diagrams [34], incarnations are identified via stereotypes that specify the name of the incarnation mapping as well as the name of the corresponding reference element. If for a given reference element no incarnation is specified, a concrete element of the same name is considered as incarnation.

Listing 1.1 shows a process model in the textual BPMN syntax that describes a sequential writing process. The tasks Concept and Implementation are each

---

[1] https://monticore.github.io/monticore/.

annotated with a stereotype indicating that both tasks are mapped via the incarnation mapping `ref` to a task in a reference model with the name `Main`. This process does in fact conform to our reference model for scientific writing displayed in Fig. 1, since the order of tasks has simply been sequentialized.

The conformance-checking tool has been integrated into the `BPMN` language project of the `MontiCore` language family and is publicly available on GitHub[2]. After building the project the BPMN conformance check can be executed via the `BPMN.jar`. The tool takes as input a path to the reference model, specified via the option $-r$ and a path to the concrete model, specified via the option $-c$. Both must be in the form of a `.wfm`-file containing the textual specification. Finally, the name of the incarnation mapping used in the concrete model is specified via the option $-m$. An example command as well as examples of potential outputs are presented in the Appendix.

```
1  process SequentialWriting {
2     event start Start;
3     event end Done;
4
5     task Research;
6     task Draft;
7     task Introduction;
8     <<ref="Main">> task Concept;
9     <<ref="Main">> task Implementation;
10    task Conclusion;
11    task Review;
12
13    Start -> Research -> Draft -> Introduction -> Concept
14       -> Implementation -> Conclusion -> Review -> Done;
15 }
```

**Listing 1.1.** Example – BPMN in textual syntax.


**Evaluation**

We evaluated both the validity of our approach and the output and performance of our implementation using constructed process models. The tests for the case study and performance analysis—including the algorithm for constructing the performance test model—can be found in the BPMN project at [49] with the corresponding model-files for the case studies at [48].

**Validation:** In order to validate our approach and evaluate the output of our implementation, we constructed a small case study, in which we consider conformant and non-conformant extensions and modifications of reference models using the reference process model for scientific writing displayed in Fig. 1 as our initial model. Noticeably, we have included ten changes that we consider conformant, and ten that are non-conformant.

---

[2] https://github.com/MontiCore/bpmn.

We consider the following modifications refining, *i.e.,* the resulting models should conform to the original model:

1. sequentializing parallel tasks
2. removing a loop
3. adding new tasks
4. removing alternatives
5. parallelizing inclusive alternatives
6. transforming inclusive into exclusive alternatives
7. incarnating a task multiple times in parallel
8. incarnating a task multiple times in sequence
9. incarnating a task multiple times as inclusive alternatives
10. incarnating a task multiple times as exclusive alternatives

We consider the following modifications non-refining, *i.e.,* the resulting models should not conform to the original model:

1. switching the order of tasks
2. removing or not incarnating a task
3. incarnating a task at a correct and incorrect position
4. transforming an XOR-split into an AND-split
5. transforming an AND-split into an XOR-split
6. transforming an AND-merge into an XOR-merge
7. transforming an AND-split into an OR-split
8. parallelizing exclusive alternatives
9. turning exclusive alternatives into inclusive alternatives
10. sequentializing exclusive alternatives

We perform a conformance check to compare the modified model to the original and verify the results. In all cases the tool identifies the non-conformant nodes and outputs a corresponding diff witness in the form of a run or backtrack sequence.

**Performance and Scalability:** For our performance test, we designed the process model shown in Fig. 5. It contains ten tasks, two branches of parallel activities, two branches with exclusive alternatives, and a loop. We then implemented an algorithm that automatically constructs duplicates of this model and concatenates them. For our approach, it is also necessary to relabel the tasks so that their names remain unique. This is done by adding indices to the task names.

Each concatenation increases the size of our model by ten tasks. For each concatenated model, we also produced a duplicate with a small modification: the task $G1$ is moved to the other branch right after $H1$. As a result, the modified model does not conform to the original.

We used our conformance checking tool to compare ten pairs of models, starting with the base model in Fig. 5 and iteratively increasing the size by ten tasks each step through concatenation. We validated the results of the conformance

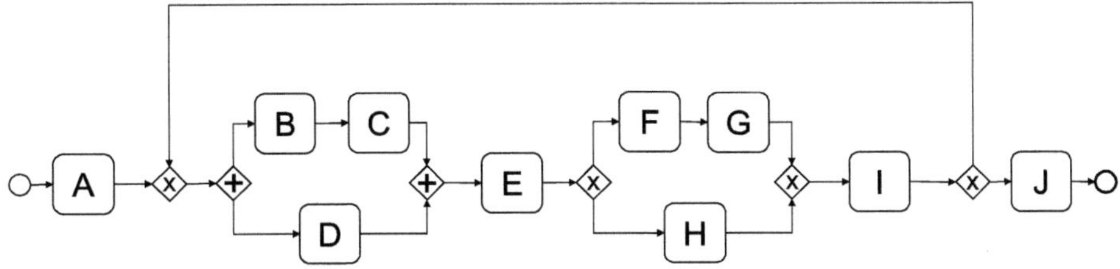

**Fig. 5.** Process model used as the basis for the performance test.

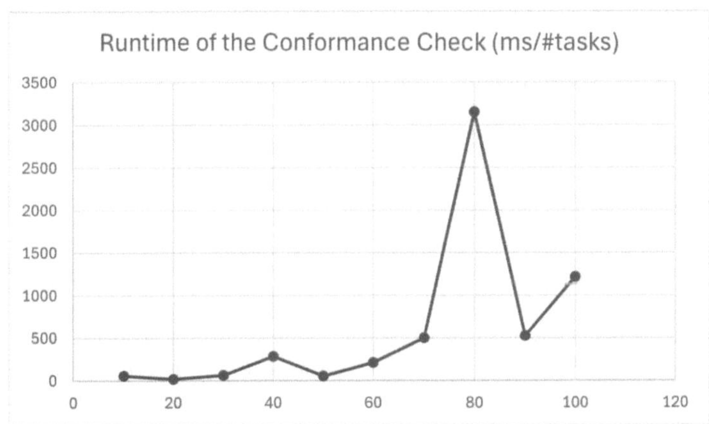


**Fig. 6.** Runtime of the conformance checking procedure in milliseconds (y-axis) compared to the size of the model/number of tasks (x-axis).

check and measured the performance of our tool in milliseconds. All experiments were performed on an 11th Gen Intel Core i7-1185G7 CPU, 3.0 GHz, with 32 GB RAM, running Windows 11. The results are displayed in Fig. 6.

The runtime of our conformance check remains under half a second until we reach a size of 70 tasks in our model. We see a sudden spike in the runtime at 80 tasks, where the conformance check takes more than 3 s to terminate.

Despite this sudden spike in runtime, our approach seems, at least at first glance, to scale significantly better than our original semantic differencing operator for activity diagrams [43].

Moreover, further optimization is possible through parallelization. For example, each incarnation can be independently checked, and the branches produced by our algorithm can be parallelized as well.

## 6   Discussion

In this paper, we explored conformance checking between concrete and reference process models, developing an approach that preserves causal dependencies among tasks and events in their incarnations. This section addresses aspects of uncertainty, limitations, and potential threats to validity within our approach.

**Uncertainty:** The algorithm we developed ensures that during the execution of a conformant concrete model, tasks and events from the reference model can only occur if their predecessor incarnations have been executed, and suitable configurations of successor incarnations follow. This design guarantees that the execution trace remains aligned with the reference model in the context of incarnation under the open-world assumption.

When the algorithm identifies a non-conformant incarnation, it reveals a path that violates local dependencies as specified by the reference model. If the incarnation is reachable and a path to an end event exists, this path can be expanded into a *diff witness*, representing a process execution trace not permitted by the reference model. Uncertainty arises only from incarnations with undetermined conformance status, labeled as *unknown*. This occurs when a satisfying configuration is followed by a non-satisfying one in the same search branch, often due to exclusive alternatives among successors.

Unlike previous model-to-model conformance checking approaches that exhibit uncertainty regarding semantic refinement [34], our method cannot categorically label these cases as non-conformant, as reflexivity is essential in a conformance relation (cf. Fig. 4). Thus, we acknowledge our approach as somewhat incomplete, requiring manual review of these ambiguous instances. Fortunately, our algorithm provides the name of the individual incarnation and the execution trace flagged as potentially non-conformant, aiding this review process.

**Limitations:** A significant limitation of our current approach is that it only considers a subset of BPMN language features [50]. Specifically, we focus on basic tasks, start and end events, and the logical gateways XOR, OR, and AND, which together represent a rudimentary foundation for process modeling. However, certain features, such as lanes, are not integrated into our current trace-based semantics definition and may therefore be overlooked.

Future work should explore additional BPMN features and their implications for process semantics. In particular, executable formal expressions play a crucial role in defining flow and loop conditions, as well as event triggers. Our textual process model syntax supports such expressions, and we could extend our approach to include conformance checks for them by utilizing SMT-solving to verify the refinement of individual reference expressions by their concrete counterparts.

Moreover, sub-processes and call activities could be managed through a hierarchical conformance check, while data and message flows represent another critical aspect for consideration. In our BPMN variant's implementation, we can define usable data types using class diagrams [24,25], enabling us to leverage our existing conformance checks [34]. If behaviors are specified through operation constraints in OCL [13,60], operations declared in a class diagram and referenced in a task of the process model could also be subjected to conformance verification.

To enhance our approach further, it is essential to enable a more precise encoding of incarnation mappings—not only to support additional features but also to facilitate more complex incarnations of currently supported features, such as tasks. The existing mapping mechanism, which relies on stereotypes, lacks sufficient expressiveness; for example, it does not allow a task in the reference model to be represented as a sequence of tasks. To overcome these limitations, we propose developing a custom mapping language to enhance the expressiveness and versatility of our incarnation mappings.

In addition, we will need to address compatibility and integration with existing tools in the business process management and process mining communities. Luckily, the conformance check itself is not directly tied to our textual BPMN variant and we have already begun work on an XML-translation.

**Threats to Validity:** Our current interpretation of open-world semantics views any extension of the original model as a refinement that preserves local causal dependencies between tasks and events, ensuring that our approach is effectively correct by construction. However, this definition may not apply universally; alternative interpretations could be more suitable in certain contexts.

For instance, we disallow adding loops that involve tasks and events present in the model by requiring suitable configurations of direct successors and predecessors between two instances of the same task or event within an execution trace. However, in some scenarios, these loops may represent necessary refinement steps, and it might suffice for the predecessor and successor configurations to occur just once, before and after all instances of the task or event within the trace.

To further validate our approach, we plan to enhance our evaluation by identifying relevant example cases from business, industry, and scientific literature for a comprehensive analysis.

## 7    Conclusion

This paper introduces an innovative approach to reference process model conformance checking, providing an algorithmic solution that leverages causal dependency analysis. Our motivation was to improve the expressiveness and automation of conformance checks, enabling more precise verification of complex process structures. We developed a method that systematically examines the causal interdependency of reference model elements and compares it with the causal relation between corresponding elements in concrete models, thus providing a comprehensive framework for conformance verification.

Our contributions include establishing a semantic concept for reference process models and conformance, providing an abstract description of the conformance checking algorithm, releasing a publicly accessible Java implementation, and evaluating the tool with multiple examples. These efforts advance the field by offering a robust methodology and toolset for improving conformance checks.

Future work will involve conducting industry case studies to validate our approach in real-world scenarios, extending our BPMN feature support to cover a broader range of elements and language variants [12, 23], and integrating our algorithm into existing toolsets, *e.g.*, via plugin. Additionally, we intend to make further improvements to our tool's performance by leveraging parallelization. These efforts aim to enhance the practical applicability and robustness of our method across diverse industrial contexts.

**Acknowledgments.** Funded by the Deutsche Forschungsgemeinschaft (DFG, German Research Foundation) - 250902306. All authors contributed equally.

**Disclosure of Interests.** The authors have no competing interests to declare that are relevant to the content of this article.

## Traces of Thought: In Honor of Wil van der Aalst

In the ever-evolving landscape of computer science, there are figures who do more than advance a field. They shape it, define it, and inspire generations of scientists through their vision and perseverance. Among these rare individuals stands Professor Wil van der Aalst, a pioneer whose contributions to process and workflow modeling, and process mining have left a lasting intellectual and institutional legacy.

As a result, Wil has left an indelible mark on colleagues, students, the broader academic community, but also industry, where even a Decacorn has meanwhile created to a large extent on his ideas. As colleagues privileged to witness his impact firsthand within RWTH Aachen University, we are deeply impressed, by his career and the impact he produced.

Wil van der Aalst's scientific journey is nothing short of monumental. With over 1,000 publications, countless keynote addresses, and the creation of process mining as a field in its own right, he has shown that innovation requires both precision and imagination. His seminal works—from the introduction of the $\alpha$-algorithm [2] (together with colleagues Weijters and Maruster) to the foundational texts on specifying, identifying or mining workflow nets (again with colleagues) have become cornerstones for students and researchers alike.

But beyond the theorems and algorithms, what sets Wil apart is his unwavering commitment to relevance: bridging the gap between theory and application, ensuring that process science remains grounded in real-world systems and societal needs. He reminds us that research should not only be rigorous, but purposeful. He lives by the advice he is giving PhD students (see for his interview in [46]): Not to follow the crowd, do something original while still being able to explain what you do in the real world.

Wil's intellectual influence extends far beyond his papers. He has mentored many of doctoral students, many of whom now lead their own research groups across the world. He has built institutions—both formal and informal—where inquiry flourishes. Finally, his leadership at RWTH Aachen's Process and Data Science (PADS) Group has turned it into a global nucleus for process mining research. It was a pleasure to work with him and his great team for several years in the Cluster of Excellence Internet of Production on topics such as Models-in-the-Moddle [35], digital shadows [47], process prediction with digital twins [8], and further topics that Computer Science can contribute to the digital transformation of production [7].

In conference halls, classrooms, and informal lunch discussions, Wil has continuously cultivated a spirit of generosity and collaboration. He listens as attentively as he lectures, and he engages as rigorously with a first-year student as with a senior peer. This rare humility in a scholar of his stature only deepens the respect he commands.

To Wil: Your intellectual rigor, your boundless curiosity, and your commitment to building a scholarly community are a guiding light. This paper is only a small gesture to honor a career whose influence cannot be quantified. Thank you for showing us how to think deeply, collaborate generously, and lead with integrity.

*Bernhard Rumpe, Max Stachon, Judith Michael*
(now or formerly at RWTH Aachen University)

## Appendix

```
java -jar BPMN.jar                                          \
          -i Concrete.wfm -ref Reference.wfm        \
          -m "ref"
```

**Listing 1.2.** Example command for executing the BPMN conformance checker.

```
Checking Conformance of [Concrete:AntiPattern] to
[Reference:PaperAuthoring]

--- Final Result of Conformance Checking ---
The following nodes do not conform: [Main, Introduction,
Conclusion]

-------- Explanations --------:

Result: Node [MotivatingExample:Main] does not conform to
Node [PaperAuthoring:Main]
Counter example: The following run [Conclusion,
    Introduction,
Main] is possible in [MotivatingExample] but not in
[PaperAuthoring].

Result: Node [MotivatingExample:Introduction] does not
conform to Node [PaperAuthoring:Introduction]
Counter example: The following run [Conclusion,
    Introduction,
Main] is possible in [MotivatingExample] but not in
[PaperAuthoring].
```

```
21
22  Result: Node [MotivatingExample:Conclusion] does not
        conform
23  to Node [PaperAuthoring:Conclusion]
24  Counter example: The following run [Conclusion,
        Introduction,
25  Main] is possible in [MotivatingExample] but not in
26  [PaperAuthoring].
```

**Listing 1.3.** Example output in case of non-conformance, using the concrete model from fig. 2 and reference model from fig. 1.

```
1  Checking Conformance of [Concrete:Sequential] to
2  [Reference:PaperAuthoring]
3
4  --- Final Result of Conformance Checking ---
5  --- All nodes conform to their reference ---
```

**Listing 1.4.** Example output in case of conformance, using the concrete model from listing 1.1 and reference model from fig. 1.

```
1  Checking Conformance of [Concrete:Skip] to [Reference:
        Skip]
2
3  --- Final Result of Conformance Checking ---
4  The status of the following nodes is unknown: [A]
5
6  -------- Explanations --------:
7
8  Result: Node [Skip:A] may not conform to Node [Skip:A]
9  Counter example: The following run [B, C, Done] is
        possible
10 in [Skip] but may not be possible in [Skip].
```

**Listing 1.5.** Example output in case of potential non-conformance, using the model in fig. 4 as both concrete and reference model.

# References


1. Van der Aalst, W., Adriansyah, A., Van Dongen, B.: Replaying history on process models for conformance checking and performance analysis. Wiley Interdisc. Rev. Data Min. Knowl. Discov. **2**(2), 182–192 (2012)
2. Van der Aalst, W., Weijters, T., Maruster, L.: Workflow mining: discovering process models from event logs. IEEE Trans. Knowl. Data Eng. **16**(9), 1128–1142 (2004)
3. Van der Aalst, W.M.: The application of petri nets to workflow management. J. Circuits Syst. Comput. **8**(01), 21–66 (1998)

4. Adriansyah, A., van Dongen, B.F., van der Aalst, W.M.: Conformance checking using cost-based fitness analysis. In: 2011 IEEE 15th International Enterprise Distributed Object Computing Conference, pp. 55–64. IEEE (2011)

5. Allweyer, T.: BPMN 2.0: introduction to the standard for business process modeling. BoD–Books on Demand (2016)

6. Bloom, B., Kwiatkowska, M.: Trade-offs in true concurrency: pomsets and mazurkiewicz traces. In: Brookes, S., Main, M., Melton, A., Mislove, M., Schmidt, D. (eds.) MFPS 1991. LNCS, vol. 598, pp. 350–375. Springer, Heidelberg (1992). https://doi.org/10.1007/3-540-55511-0_18

7. Brauner, P., et al.: A computer science perspective on digital transformation in production. J. ACM Trans. Internet Things **3**, 1–32 (2022). https://doi.org/10.1145/3502265

8. Brockhoff, T., et al.: Process prediction with digital twins. In: International Conference on Model Driven Engineering Languages and Systems Companion (MODELS-C), pp. 182–187. ACM/IEEE (2021)

9. Burattin, A., Maggi, F.M., Sperduti, A.: Conformance checking based on multi-perspective declarative process models. Expert Syst. Appl. **65**, 194–211 (2016). https://doi.org/10.1016/j.eswa.2016.08.040

10. Butting, A., Kautz, O., Rumpe, B., Wortmann, A.: Semantic differencing for message-driven component & connector architectures. In: International Conference on Software Architecture (ICSA 2017), pp. 145–154. IEEE (2017)

11. Butting, A., Kautz, O., Rumpe, B., Wortmann, A.: Continuously analyzing finite, message-driven, time-synchronous component & connector systems during architecture evolution. J. Syst. Softw. (JSS) **149**, 437–461 (2019). https://doi.org/10.1016/j.jss.2018.12.016

12. Cengarle, M.V., Grönniger, H., Rumpe, B.: Variability within modeling language definitions. In: Schürr, A., Selic, B. (eds.) MODELS 2009. LNCS, vol. 5795, pp. 670–684. Springer, Heidelberg (2009). https://doi.org/10.1007/978-3-642-04425-0_54

13. Cook, S., Kleppe, A., Mitchell, R., Rumpe, B., Warmer, J., Wills, A.: The Amsterdam manifesto on OCL. In: Clark, T., Warmer, J. (eds.) Object Modeling with the OCL. LNCS, vol. 2263, pp. 115–149. Springer, Heidelberg (2002). https://doi.org/10.1007/3-540-45669-4_7

14. Dijkman, R.M., Dumas, M., Ouyang, C.: Semantics and analysis of business process models in BPMN. Inf. Softw. Technol. **50**(12), 1281–1294 (2008)

15. Drave, I., Eikermann, R., Kautz, O., Rumpe, B.: Semantic differencing of statecharts for object-oriented systems. In: Hammoudi, S., Pires, L.F., Selić, B. (eds.) 7th International Conference on Model-Driven Engineering and Software Development (MODELSWARD 2019), pp. 274–282. SciTePress (2019)

16. Drave, I., Kautz, O., Michael, J., Rumpe, B.: Semantic evolution analysis of feature models. In: Berger, T., et al. (eds.) International Systems and Software Product Line Conference (SPLC 2019), pp. 245–255. ACM (2019)

17. Drave, I., Michael, J., Müller, E., Rumpe, B., Varga, S.: Model-driven engineering of process-aware information systems. Springer Nature Comput. Sci. J. **3** (2022)

18. Dunzer, S., Stierle, M., Matzner, M., Baier, S.: Conformance checking: a state-of-the-art literature review. In: 11th International Conference on Subject-Oriented Business Process Management, S-BPM ONE 2019. ACM, New York (2019). https://doi.org/10.1145/3329007.3329014

19. Fernandes, J., Reis, J., Melão, N., Teixeira, L., Amorim, M.: The role of industry 4.0 and BPMN in the arise of condition-based and predictive maintenance: a case study in the automotive industry. Appl. Sci. **11**(8), 3438 (2021)

20. Gamma, E., Helm, R., Johnson, R.E., Vlissides, J.: Design Patterns: Elements of Reusable Object-Oriented Software. Prentice Hall (1997)
21. Gogolla, M., Henderson-Sellers, B.: Analysis of UML Stereotypes within the UML Metamodel, pp. 84–99. Springer, Heidelberg (2002). https://doi.org/10.1007/3-540-45800-x_8
22. Grönniger, H., Krahn, H., Rumpe, B., Schindler, M., Völkel, S.: MontiCore 1.0: Ein Framework zur Erstellung und Verarbeitung domänspezifischer Sprachen. Informatik-Bericht 2006-04, CFG-Fakultät, TU Braunschweig (2006)
23. Grönniger, H., Rumpe, B.: Modeling language variability. In: Workshop on Modeling, Development and Verification of Adaptive Systems. (16th Monterey Workshop). Redmond, Microsoft Research (2010)
24. Haber, A., et al.: Composition of heterogeneous modeling languages. In: Desfray, P., Filipe, J., Hammoudi, S., Pires, L.F. (eds.) MODELSWARD 2015. CCIS, vol. 580, pp. 45–66. Springer, Cham (2015). https://doi.org/10.1007/978-3-319-27869-8_3
25. Haber, A., et al.: Integration of heterogeneous modeling languages via extensible and composable language components. In: Model-Driven Engineering and Software Development Conference (MODELSWARD 2015), pp. 19–31. SciTePress (2015)
26. Harel, D., Rumpe, B.: Meaningful modeling: what's the semantics of "semantics"? IEEE Comput. J. **37**(10), 64–72 (2004)
27. Hirshfeld, Y.: Petri nets and the equivalence problem. In: Börger, E., Gurevich, Y., Meinke, K. (eds.) CSL 1993. LNCS, vol. 832, pp. 165–174. Springer, Heidelberg (1994). https://doi.org/10.1007/BFb0049331
28. Hölldobler, K., Kautz, O., Rumpe, B.: MontiCore Language Workbench and Library Handbook: Edition 2021. Aachener Informatik-Berichte, Software Engineering, Band 48, Shaker Verlag (2021)
29. ITU-T: Information technology – Open Systems Interconnection – Basic Reference Model: The basic model. ITU-T X.200, Int. Telecommunication Union (1994)
30. Kautz, O.: Model Analyses Based on Semantic Differencing and Automatic Model Repair. Aachener Informatik-Berichte, Software Engineering, Band 46, Shaker Verlag (2021)
31. Kautz, O., Rumpe, B.: Semantic differencing of activity diagrams by a translation into finite automata. In: MODELS 2018. Workshop ME (2018)
32. Knuplesch, D., Reichert, M., Pryss, R., Fdhila, W., Rinderle-Ma, S.: Ensuring compliance of distributed and collaborative workflows. In: 9th IEEE International Conference on Collaborative Computing: Networking, Applications and Worksharing, pp. 133–142. IEEE (2013)
33. Konersmann, M., Michael, J., Rumpe, B.: Towards Reference Models with Conformance Relations for Structure, pp. 247–269. Logos Verlag Berlin (2024)
34. Konersmann, M., Rumpe, B., Stachon, M., Stüber, S., Voufo, V.: Towards a semantically useful definition of conformance with a reference model. J. Object Technol. (JOT) **23**(3), 1–14 (2024). https://doi.org/10.5381/jot.2024.23.3.a5
35. Koren, I., et al.: Navigating the data model divide in smart manufacturing: an empirical investigation for enhanced AI integration. In: van der Aa, H., Bork, D., Schmidt, R., Sturm, A. (eds.) Enterprise, Business-Process and Information Systems Modeling, pp. 275–290. Springer, Cham (2024). https://doi.org/10.1007/978-3-031-61007-3_21
36. Kougka, G., Gounaris, A., Simitsis, A.: The many faces of data-centric workflow optimization: a survey. Int. J. Data Sci. Anal. **6**, 81–107 (2018). https://doi.org/10.1007/s41060-018-0107-0

37. La Rosa, M., Dumas, M., ter Hofstede, A.H., Mendling, J.: Configurable multi-perspective business process models. Inf. Syst. **36**(2), 313–340 (2011). https://doi.org/10.1016/j.is.2010.07.001. Special Issue: Semantic Integration of Data, Multimedia, and Services

38. Langer, P., Mayerhofer, T., Kappel, G.: Semantic model differencing utilizing behavioral semantics specifications. In: Dingel, J., Schulte, W., Ramos, I., Abrahão, S., Insfran, E. (eds.) Model-Driven Engineering Languages and Systems, pp. 116–132. Springer, Cham (2014)

39. Lim, H.W., Kerschbaum, F., Wang, H.: Workflow signatures for business process compliance. IEEE Trans. Dependable Secure Comput. **9**(5), 756–769 (2012)

40. Maoz, S., Ringert, J.O., Rumpe, B.: ADDiff: semantic differencing for activity diagrams. In: Conference on Foundations of Software Engineering (ESEC/FSE 2011), pp. 179–189. ACM (2011)

41. Maoz, S., Ringert, J.O., Rumpe, B.: An Operational Semantics for Activity Diagrams using SMV. Technical Report AIB-2011-07, RWTH Aachen University (2011)

42. Maoz, S., Ringert, J.O., Rumpe, B.: CDDiff: semantic differencing for class diagrams. In: Mezini, M. (ed.) ECOOP 2011 - Object-Oriented Programming, pp. 230–254. Springer, Heidelberg (2011)

43. Maoz, S., Ringert, J.O., Rumpe, B.: Modal object diagrams. In: Mezini, M. (ed.) ECOOP 2011. LNCS, vol. 6813, pp. 281–305. Springer, Heidelberg (2011). https://doi.org/10.1007/978-3-642-22655-7_14

44. Mazurkiewicz, A.: Trace theory. In: Brauer, W., Reisig, W., Rozenberg, G. (eds.) ACPN 1986. LNCS, vol. 255, pp. 278–324. Springer, Heidelberg (1987). https://doi.org/10.1007/3-540-17906-2_30

45. de Medeiros, A.K.A., Weijters, A.J., van der Aalst, W.M.: Genetic process mining: an experimental evaluation. Data Min. Knowl. Disc. **14**(2), 245–304 (2007)

46. Michael, J., Bork, D., Wimmer, M., Mayr, H.C.: Quo Vadis modeling? Findings of a community survey, an ad-hoc bibliometric analysis, and expert interviews on data, process, and software modeling. J. Softw. Syst. Model. (SoSyM) **23**(1), 7–28 (2024). https://doi.org/10.1007/s10270-023-01128-y

47. Michael, J., et al.: A digital shadow reference model for worldwide production labs. In: Brecher, C., Schuh, G., van der Aalst, W., Jarke, M., Piller, F., Padberg, M. (eds.) Internet of Production: Fundamentals, Applications and Proceedings, pp. 1–28. Springer, Cham (2023). https://doi.org/10.1007/978-3-030-98062-7_3-2

48. Michael, J., Rumpe, B., Stachon, M., Stüber, S., Voufo, V.: Workflow conformance test resources (2025). WorkflowConformance/src/test/resources/de/monticore/bpmn/conformance. Accessed 23 Sept 2025

49. Michael, J., Rumpe, B., Stachon, M., Stüber, S., Voufo, V.: Workflow conformance tests (2025). WorkflowConformance/src/test/java/de/monticore/bpmn/-conformance. Accessed 23 Sept 2025

50. Business process model and notation (2014)

51. Pegoraro, M., Uysal, M.S., van der Aalst, W.M.: Conformance checking over uncertain event data. Inf. Syst. **102**, 101810 (2021)

52. Pratt, V.: Modeling concurrency with partial orders. Int. J. Parallel Prog. **15**(1), 33–71 (1986)

53. Rafiei, M., van der Aalst, W.M.P.: Mining roles from event logs while preserving privacy. In: Di Francescomarino, C., Dijkman, R., Zdun, U. (eds.) BPM 2019. LNBIP, vol. 362, pp. 676–689. Springer, Cham (2019). https://doi.org/10.1007/978-3-030-37453-2_54

54. Rafiei, M., Pourbafrani, M., van der Aalst, W.M.: Federated conformance checking. Inf. Syst. **131**, 102525 (2025)
55. Rinderle-Ma, S., Winter, K., Benzin, J.V.: Predictive compliance monitoring in process-aware information systems: state of the art, functionalities, research directions. Inf. Syst. **115**, 102210 (2023)
56. Ringert, J.O., Rumpe, B., Stachon, M.: On implementing open world semantic differencing for class diagrams. J. Object Technol. (JOT) **22**(2), 2:1–14 (2023). https://doi.org/10.5381/jot.2023.22.2.a11
57. Rosemann, M., Van der Aalst, W.M.: A configurable reference modelling language. Inf. Syst. **32**(1), 1–23 (2007)
58. Rozinat, A., van der Aalst, W.M.P.: Conformance testing: Measuring the fit and appropriateness of event logs and process models. In: Bussler, C.J., Haller, A. (eds.) Business Process Management Workshops, pp. 163–176. Springer, Heidelberg (2006)
59. Rozinat, A., Van der Aalst, W.M.: Conformance checking of processes based on monitoring real behavior. Inf. Syst. **33**(1), 64–95 (2008)
60. Rumpe, B., Stachon, M., Stüber, S., Voufo, V.: Semantic difference analysis with invariant tracing for class diagrams extended by OCL. In: WS on Model Driven Engineering, Verification and Validation (MoDeVVa), MODELS Companion 2024. ACM (2024). https://doi.org/10.1145/3652620.3687818
61. Rumpe, B., Stachon, M., Stüber, S., Voufo, V.: Tool-assisted conformance checking to reference process models. arXiv (2025). https://doi.org/10.48550/arXiv.2508.00738
62. Schuster, D., Kolhof, G.J.: Scalable online conformance checking using incremental prefix-alignment computation. In: Hacid, H., et al. (eds.) ICSOC 2020. LNCS, vol. 12632, pp. 379–394. Springer, Cham (2021). https://doi.org/10.1007/978-3-030-76352-7_36
63. Ungan, M.C.: Standardization through process documentation. Bus. Process. Manag. J. **12**(2), 135–148 (2006). https://doi.org/10.1108/14637150610657495
64. Weidlich, M., Polyvyanyy, A., Desai, N., Mendling, J., Weske, M.: Process compliance analysis based on behavioural profiles. Inf. Syst. **36**(7), 1009–1025 (2011). https://doi.org/10.1016/j.is.2011.04.002. Special Issue: Advanced Information Systems Engineering (CAiSE 2010)

# Threats to Validity of Process Mining Research

Benoît Depaire[1], Henrik Leopold[2], and Jan Mendling[3,4,5]

[1] Digital Future Lab, Hasselt University, Hasselt, Belgium
benoit.depaire@uhasselt.be
[2] Kühne Logistics University, Hamburg, Germany
henrik.leopold@klu.org
[3] Department of Computer Science, Humboldt-Universität zu Berlin,
Berlin, Germany
jan.mendling@hu-berlin.de
[4] Department of Information Systems and Operations Management, Vienna
University of Economics and Business, Vienna, Austria
[5] Weizenbaum Institute, Berlin, Germany

**Abstract.** Process mining has grown into a mature research field with a wide range of techniques and applications. Much of this development builds on the pioneering work of Wil van der Aalst, whose contributions have shaped both the foundations and the growth of the discipline. Today, the field's breadth raises the need for systematic methodological reflection to ensure that findings are robust and meaningful. In this paper, we provide a comprehensive discussion of threats to validity in process mining research. Building on the methodological framework of algorithm engineering, we analyze nine distinct validity concerns and examine how they apply across different streams of process mining. Our analysis highlights both established strengths and recurring challenges, drawing on examples from seminal contributions in the field, many inspired by Wil's work.

**Keywords:** Process Mining · Methodology · Algorithm engineering · Evaluation · Validity

## 1 Outline

Few scholars have shaped an entire research field as profoundly as Wil van der Aalst. From his early work on workflow mining to his far-reaching vision of process mining as a bridge between data science and business process management, Wil and his collaborators have provided both the conceptual foundations and

Research by Jan Mendling was supported by the Einstein Foundation Berlin under grant EPP-2019-524, by the Federal Ministry of Research, Technology and Space under the grant 16DII143, and by Deutsche Forschungsgemeinschaft under grants 496119880 (VisualMine), 531115272 (ProImpact), SFB 1404/2 (FONDA).


J. Mendling et al. (Eds.): Wil van der Aalst Festschrift, LNCS 16480, pp. 551–568, 2026.
https://doi.org/10.1007/978-3-032-17618-9_36

the practical tools that define the discipline today. Based on these foundations, process mining has become a mature research field with industrial applications across various sectors.

The field's very success, with its broadening scope and increasingly sophisticated algorithms, now brings new opportunities for *methodological reflection*. With more competing algorithmic designs and diverse real-world applications, the challenge is to draw on a wider set of research methods, particularly empirical ones, to ensure meaningful evaluation. Early contributions have already begun to discuss validity concerns systematically. For example, Rehse et al. highlight the relevance of classical notions of validity and reliability [57]. More recently, Van der Waal et al. explicitly examine threats to validity in process mining research [66]. These studies raise important general concerns that apply to empirical research at large, yet they do not fully capture the specific challenges of evaluating process mining algorithms.

In this paper, we contribute to the ongoing methodological reflection in process mining by illustrating how the nine validity notions from the methodological framework for algorithm engineering [50] relate to prominent streams of process mining research. Rather than offering a full formal or exhaustive systematic assessment, our goal is to make these validity concerns more concrete by discussing them through representative examples from the process mining literature. This perspective highlights recurring strengths as well as areas where further methodological attention may be beneficial. In this way, the paper provides orientation on how considerations of validity can be embedded into research designs in process mining and points to practices that authors may draw upon when reflecting on potential threats to validity.

This paper is structured as follows. Section 2 discusses the methodological framework for algorithm engineering upon which we build our analysis. Section 3 presents the findings of our analysis for each of the nine validity concerns. Section 4 concludes the paper with a summary and an outlook on future research.

## 2    Background

Algorithms can be examined from several complementary perspectives. In this paper, we follow the framework of the methodology of algorithm engineering, [50], which distinguishes three perspectives: ontological, epistemological, and methodological. The ontological perspective asks what the key entities are when we speak of an algorithm, i.e., how real-world problems are turned into algorithmic tasks, designs, and implementations. The epistemological perspective considers what we can know about an algorithm. To this end, we introduce the notion of knowledge of and about tasks as well as knowledge of and about designs. Finally, the methodological perspective reflects on how we can proceed when designing, testing, and refining algorithms with a particular focus on threats to validity. Together, these perspectives provide a structured lens for understanding and studying algorithms in a scientific context.

Figure 1 provides an overview of the three perspectives of algorithm engineering, ontological, epistemological, and methodological, and their relationships to the different forms of knowledge and the associated validity concerns. This schematic serves as a conceptual roadmap for the sections that follow. The figure summarizes how real-world problems are abstracted into algorithmic tasks, how designs and implementations instantiate these tasks, and how various validity concerns arise along these relationships. We draw on this framework throughout Sects. 2 and 3.

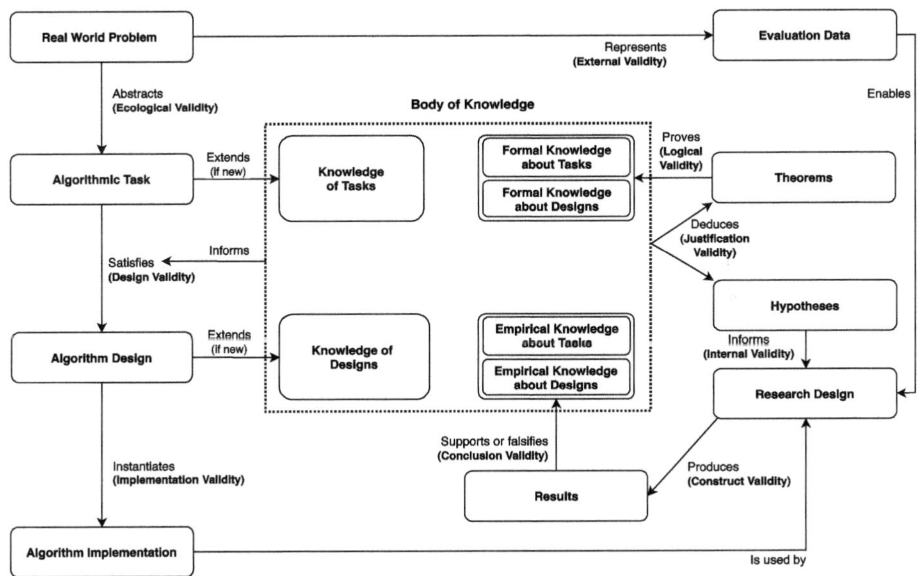


**Fig. 1.** Overview of the algorithm engineering framework, showing the ontological, epistemological, and methodological perspectives and their associated validity concerns (adapted from [50]).

## 2.1  Ontological Perspective

Building on the ontological model of [62], our framework characterizes algorithm engineering through four ontological entities and their relations: 1) a real-world problem situated in a concrete context, 2) an algorithmic task that abstracts this problem by making its assumptions explicit and setting a goal, 3) an algorithm design that satisfies the task through principled design choices, and 4) an algorithm implementation that instantiates the design and produces concrete results when executed on data. This view highlights that algorithms are engineered artifacts whose identity and value depend on their relationship to the real world. We illustrate this view for process mining.

The starting point is always a *real-world problem*. In process mining, for example, an organization may want to understand how its business processes actually unfold, beyond what is described in manuals or imagined by managers.

The complex and messy reality of system logs, exceptions, and human behavior provides the raw situation. To tackle such a problem, one first defines an *algorithmic task*: a carefully delimited abstraction that captures the essence of the practical need. For process mining this might be "discover a process model that reflects the behavior recorded in the event logs." The task makes explicit what counts as a good outcome and what constraints must be respected. The next step is developing an *algorithm design* that will address or solve that task. In our example, scientists lay out the steps that are taken to transform a given event log into a structured process model, deciding, for instance, how to detect the order of activities or how to handle noise in the data. Finally, the *algorithm implementation* realizes the design in a concrete piece of software. Only at this stage, the algorithm as implemented can be executed on actual logs, producing a tangible model that allows researchers to evaluate how well it meets the original need. Here, we can distinguish two dimensions of performance: effectiveness, meaning the discovered model truly captures the organization's behavior, and efficiency, meaning the program runs with acceptable time and resource use.

This example illustrates that the ontological perspective clarifies how real-world needs are transformed into algorithmic artifacts. It provides a vocabulary for reasoning about where scientific claims belong, whether about the problem, the algorithmic task, the algorithmic design choices, or the final implementation.

### 2.2   Epistemological Perspective

While the ontological perspective clarifies what entities exist in algorithm engineering, the epistemological perspective asks what we know about these entities. We distinguish between *knowledge of* a task or design and *knowledge about* them, resulting in four types of knowledge:

*Knowledge of tasks* captures what tasks exist and how they are structured. This notion of knowledge is important since algorithmic tasks are not connected with a real-world problem via a simple isomorphic mapping. Real-world problems are often "wicked problems" [58], meaning that they are complex and can be addressed in various ways. To illustrate this, reconsider the problem of an organization that would like to understand how its business processes actually unfold. One task that might be derived from this problem is indeed process discovery based on event logs, as described above. However, there exist numerous other tasks that could be derived. One example could be to derive a process model from a set of video recordings. While many tasks are already known, researchers might also come up with new ones for a given real-world problem. What the example above highlight is that algorithmic tasks explicate assumptions regarding the input, the processing of the input, and the goal the algorithm is meant to achieve in terms of output.

*Knowledge about tasks* relates to insights into the properties of specific algorithmic tasks. Such analysis can yield both formal and empirical knowledge. Formal knowledge has been established for a wide range of tasks, often described as computational problems. A classical example is the classification of problems by complexity. Many well-known problems have been shown to belong to the class NP, the set of problems that can be solved in polynomial time on a non-deterministic Turing machine. An important subclass is the set of NP-complete problems, whose members are, loosely speaking, at least as difficult to solve as any other problem in NP. In the domain of process mining, for instance, the task of simplifying a directly-follows graph has been shown to be NP-complete [13]. Empirical knowledge, in contrast, is obtained through experimentation. It emerges from observing patterns in typical input data that can be exploited when designing algorithms. Improvements for many algorithmic tasks have been inspired by the availability of benchmark data sets. In the process-mining community, for instance, experiments with the various BPI challenge logs have helped researchers both to understand and to refine algorithm designs for key tasks such as process discovery and conformance checking via alignments.

*Knowledge of designs* refers to understanding what an algorithm design is, how it operates, and how it addresses a given algorithmic task. This kind of knowledge is prescriptive: it enables humans to implement concrete algorithms by following the design's blueprint. Established designs range from concrete designs that address specific tasks to more general procedures that are applicable for a wide range of tasks. In process mining, for example, highly focused designs include the alpha-miner [4], which discovers a Petri-net model from event logs, and the inductive miner [41], which recursively partitions logs to obtain a sound, block-structured workflow model. At the same time, these and other designs draw on broader principles, such as divide-and-conquer strategies or heuristic search, that guide the construction of solutions for a wide variety of algorithmic problems. Whether narrow or general, knowledge of designs captures the "recipe" that allows an algorithm to be realized in code and used to solve the intended task. It is important to note that knowledge of a concrete algorithm design can be expressed at varying levels of abstraction, ranging from pseudocode to visually oriented diagrams to formal mathematical specifications. Each offers different trade-offs in terms of clarity, detail, and suitability for re-implementation.

*Knowledge about designs* concerns the properties and characteristics of an algorithmic design and can be substantiated in both formal and empirical ways. Building on Santner at al. [61] on the design and analysis of computer experiments, we differentiate four broad types of such knowledge: performance, sensitivity, uncertainty, and explanatory knowledge. Performance knowledge addresses how well the algorithm design meets its task requirements. It can be framed as a question of satisfaction: Does the design fulfill the requirements? or to what extent does the design satisfy the requirements better than alternative designs [28,62,70]? In process mining, for example, comparative studies of process mining algorithms have assessed which discovery algorithms produce models with higher fitness or precision or which predictive process monitoring techniques are most accurate in terms of accuracy. Sensitivity knowledge examines how robust an algorithm's performance is to changes in internal design decisions, such as parameter settings. It also assesses whether the algorithm remains effective when these parameters are not optimally chosen. For example, one may test how noise-threshold settings in the Inductive Miner influence the quality of the discovered model. Uncertainty knowledge considers the performance of the algorithm relative to the assumptions of the task environment and seeks to determine how expected performance varies across different problem instances, such as event logs of varying size or with incomplete traces. Finally, explanatory knowledge provides insight into the mechanisms by which task assumptions and design decisions interact to influence performance, often by comparing alternative configurations, such as using different sequence encoding mechanisms in predictive process monitoring. Together these four types of knowledge make explicit what can be claimed and justified about an algorithm design and provide the basis for its scientific evaluation.

### 2.3  Methodological Perspective

The methodological perspective focuses on how the body of knowledge in algorithm engineering can be systematically extended. Research contributes in four broad ways: 1) by creating new or improved knowledge of tasks, 2) by developing new or improved knowledge of designs, 3) by establishing new or stronger formal knowledge about tasks and designs, and 4) by generating new or stronger empirical knowledge about tasks and designs. As illustrated by Fig. 1, these contributions are typically part of iterative processes in which new tasks or designs expand their respective knowledge categories: new theorems and proofs establish formal insights about algorithms and new experimental results enrich the empirical understanding of algorithmic behavior. Each type of knowledge is associated with characteristic research methods, such as inductive methods for identifying and formulating tasks, design methods for crafting new algorithms, formal methods for deriving theorems and proofs, and empirical methods for experimentation and evaluation. Across all of these methods, careful attention to validity concerns is essential to ensure that the generated knowledge is sound. The next section takes a look at these validity concerns in more detail (Table 1).

## 3  Validity and Process Mining Research

This section introduces nine validity concerns that each correspond to a specific relationship within the algorithm engineering framework [50] and that help evaluate the soundness of knowledge claims made at different stages of the algorithm engineering process. We review recent discussions in process mining for each concern.

### 3.1  Ecological Validity

In his reflection on writing papers from 2022 [2], Wil van der Aalst emphasizes that a paper has to clearly state: What is the problem and why is it relevant? The initial real-world problem that inspired process mining related to workflow system implementation: "One of the problems is that these systems require a workflow design, i.e., a designer has to construct a detailed model accurately

**Table 1.** Validity concerns in algorithm engineering, excerpt from [50].

| Validity Concern | Explanation |
| --- | --- |
| Ecological validity | The extent to which an algorithmic task or setup reflects real-world conditions and problem contexts (based on [7,30]) |
| Design validity | The degree to which the internal structure and logic of an algorithm design is coherent, justified, and explainable [40] |
| Implementation validity | The extent to which an algorithm implementation faithfully instantiates the intended design and behaves as expected (based on [43,44]) |
| External validity | The degree to which results generalize across data sets of interest (based on [16]) |
| Justification validity | The degree how convincingly a hypothesis or theorem is supported by a deductive argument (based on [39]) |
| Logical validity | The degree to which the syllogisms used in a proof preserve truth (based on Aristotle and reflection in [21]) |
| Internal validity | The extent to which observed effects can be attributed to the treatment rather than to confounding factors [71] |
| Construct validity | The degree to which the measure of a construct accurately measures the intended property [52] |
| Conclusion validity | The degree to which the results can reasonably be regarded as revealing the hypothesized connection [15,26] |

describing the routing of work" [5]. The algorithmic task of automatic process discovery assumed that execution sequences are available and that a structured process description can be generated.

Ecological validity refers to the extent to which an algorithmic task reflects real-world problems. When new real-world problems attract academic attention, initial algorithmic tasks are often highly abstract and simplify real-world complexity. This makes the problem tractable. Wil van der Aalst's seminal paper from 2004 on the alpha-miner [4] introduced one of the first process discovery algorithms. The alpha-algorithm was developed under several simplifying assumptions, such as completeness in terms of directly-follows relations and the absence of short loops or duplicate tasks. These assumptions helped the authors to prove the algorithm's capacity to rediscover a large class of sound WF nets from event logs. However, they also acknowledged the algorithm's limited ecological validity. Early application studies with real-life data showed substantial challenges, among others, because of noise, which inspired the development of heuristic approaches [18]. Nevertheless, the alpha-algorithm served as a catalyst for the development of the field. Over time, the definitions of algorithmic tasks have been refined to enhance ecological validity, resulting in algorithmic designs that are increasingly applicable to practical settings.

Beyond the example of the alpha-algorithm, ecological validity also depends on how well algorithmic tasks in process mining reflect the broader landscape of practical BPM problems. In this sense, the evolution of process discovery within the BPM lifecycle and the emergence of new empirical studies provide important context for understanding how ecological validity has developed in the field. In general, process discovery can be related to the BPM Lifecycle [20] and the set of real-world problems of business process management. Wil has worked on the specification of various other algorithmic tasks and corresponding algorithm designs, most prominently conformance checking [59]. He also contributed to taxonomies of algorithmic tasks for process mining. The paper with Ailenei et al. from 2012 describes 19 use cases related to discovery, conformance checking, and enhancement [6]. Wil's reflection on the first decade of the BPM conference presents 20 BPM use cases [1]. In our terminology, both papers describe algorithmic tasks. Others have extended these lists, for example, with 25 additional tasks that relate to semantic process models [51].

Today, research at the intersection of real-world problems and algorithmic tasks is conducted using empirical methods. One example of such empirical research on process mining is the interview study by Zimmermann, Zerbato and Weber [72] that looks at challenges that process analysts face who use process mining tools. Such works reveal hidden assumptions of process mining tasks and highlight real-world challenges. In this way, such empirical research contributes to an increased ecological validity by the new identification and appropriate refinement of algorithmic tasks for process mining. For a long time, however, the process mining community has focused quite strongly on discovery. Wil has criticized that already in 2013 [1] and echoed by Recker and Mendling in 2016 [56]. As Wil and co-authors coined it in 2016 [63]: "Don't forget to improve the process!". Over the last years, we have witnessed a shift towards analytical methods, such as predictive process monitoring. Nevertheless, it is important to keep in mind that we need a profound understanding of the real-world problems of process analysts and operations managers together with a broad corresponding set of algorithmic tasks with high ecological validity that can inspire our algorithmic designs.

### 3.2  Design Validity

Wil has often emphasized the importance of keeping design and implementation separate [2]: "We rarely want to discuss implementation details. Of course, there are exceptions, e.g., to prove the complexity of an algorithm. When it is possible to formalize things in a few lines, it is better to avoid pseudo-code. Pseudo-code is often ambiguous and non-declarative." This statement reflects the importance of design validity as the degree to which the internal structure and logic of an algorithm design is coherent, justified, and explainable [40]. While Wil's remark highlights that declarative specifications can often express algorithmic ideas more precisely and concisely than pseudocode, this does not preclude the use of pseudocode when it serves a different purpose. In practice, pseudocode plays an important role in supporting empirical evaluation, implementation, and reproducibility, and is therefore complementary rather than contradictory to declarative specifications.

Declarative specification has often helped Wil to define guarantees and proof their correctness. The papers introducing the alpha-algorithm [5] and the inductive miner [41] are testament to this ambition. The paper on the alpha-algorithm provides proofs that the presented algorithm rediscovers structured workflow nets and explicitly states limitations. The paper on the inductive miner proofs formal properties and the recovery of process models for sufficiently large directly-follows complete logs.

The compactness of declarative design specification is a strong foundation for formal analysis and performance guarantees. Research on algorithm engineering highlights the benefits of additionally providing implementation details by help of pseudocode [60]. Often, such pseudocode facilitates empirical evaluation and reuse by help of implementation libraries. An example from Wil's work is the paper on the inductive miner [41]. It combine formalizations and pseudocode to achieve complementary goals. The former provide the foundation for proofs of relevant properties, while the latter facilities easy implementation, dissemination, and replication. Such a design specification at different levels is specifically useful for contributions that go beyond isolated algorithms, but cover chains of processing or overall system designs [29]. Split miner is an example [9]. The paper presents a high-level chart and description of the processing pipeline with six steps, followed by nine pseudocode algorithms. Furthermore, the complexity of the overall processing pipeline is theoretically analyzed and a theorem of the soundness of the resulting process model is proven.

Today, both declarative specifications for formal analysis and pseudocode are established in process mining, often complemented with system architecture or charts of processing pipelines. The availability of libraries provides additional credibility of design validity as they allow to understand how an algorithm can be implemented.

## 3.3  Implementation Validity

Many evaluations in process mining build on the comparison of different implementations of competing algorithmic designs. These implementations are run with evaluation data as input to produce performance measurements of the computational process and of the generated output. Implementation validity is the extent to which an algorithm implementation faithfully instantiates the intended design and behaves as expected [43,44,50].

Designs do not simply map to an implementation. Any implementation uses a specific programming language on a specific operating system running on a specific microprocessor family, which all affect the performance of the algorithm [50]. We also know that there are bugs in machine learning code with a negative effect on statistical analysis properties [14]. Kriegel et al. demonstrate that implementations of the same algorithm design can drastically vary in performance [38].

They find run time differences of DBScan implementations of four orders of magnitude. Even different versions of the same frameworks like ELKI and WEKA yielded substantial performance differences.

While only a few works have paid attention to implementation validity in process mining so far, a good example that stands out is the ProM framework[1] that was initiated at TU Eindhoven under Wil's supervision. In order to manage the various plug-ins, there was the option to include unit tests. Every ProM package came with a default test file. Another good example is research on trace alignment [31]. The conceptual foundations of alignment are known to be computationally expensive. Advances in this area focus not only on algorithmic designs, but also on efficient implementation strategies. González-Montesino and Grass-Boada use various optimization strategies to improve the speed of alignment by three orders of magnitude [27]. This example highlights the need to reflect on implementation concerns whenever empirical evaluation is the primary source of knowledge about algorithmic performance.

Today, comparative evaluation has become a prominent strategy to provide evidence that a new algorithm improves performance. Both the BPM and the ICPM conference call for making implementations available in order to foster reproducibility. Publishing code is generally recommended to establish implementation validity [38]. This is even more important for research that increasingly uses AI-based techniques, for example, for process prediction where formal guarantees cannot be devised. As Kriegel et al. observe that implementations strongly differ in quality, authors should find the fastest implementation of an algorithm, debug and optimize it before conducting comparative evaluations [38].

## 3.4  External Validity

Already the article introducing the alpha-algorithm discusses, though only very briefly, the application of the algorithm for mining practically relevant processes in hospitals in Tilburg and Maastricht and at a Dutch authority in Leeuwarden [5]. Wil's early article on the industrial application of process mining demonstrates the benefits and challenges of working with realistic data. External validity refers to the extent to which empirical research findings can be generalized beyond a specific study context to other datasets, problem instances, populations, and conditions.

The introduction of the BPI challenge logs significantly facilitated a shift toward the use of real-life data. On the one hand, this shift enhanced external validity by ensuring the data more accurately reflected actual processes. On the other hand, these logs often represent a convenience sample and are likely subject to selection bias, which limits their representativeness. Recent research showed that the available real-life event logs indeed only cover a limited set of possible process variants [45]. To address these limitations, Jouck et al. [34] introduced a methodology for sampling synthetic event logs from a predefined population of processes. By defining such a population, researchers can randomly generate an

---

[1] https://promtools.org.

unlimited number of event logs, thus improving representativeness and external validity with respect to that population. Recent research has further extended this approach to ensure that synthetic data covers a broad range of possible process populations [45].

A key takeaway from neighboring research communities is the strategic focus on the creation of benchmark data sets. Entire research projects in areas such as computer vision or time-series modeling have evolved around the systematic construction of large and publicly available data collections. Well-known examples include ImageNet [19] and TSM-Bench [36]. In these fields, it is common practice to publish dedicated "data set papers", whose primary contribution is the careful design and open release of a data resource that others can use for evaluation and comparison. Such an option exists at the BPM conference and its call for demonstrations and resources. Although there is still a way to go to match other fields, there have been several submissions of resource papers over the past years, with multiple contributions by Wil leading the way [22,53].

Today, many process mining papers use BPI Challenge datasets for their evaluation. It has also become good practice to conduct evaluations using both synthetic data and available BPI data. Generators like GEDI support the construction of synthetic data [45]. Furthermore, event logs are always preprocessed and involve a potentially large number of selection choices. It is therefore worth investigating how datasets can be constructed from real databases, like the MIMIC-III clinical database [33], and how pre-analysis event construction like surveyed in [55] affects algorithmic performance.

### 3.5  Justification Validity

Justification validity concerns the strength of the deductive argument that supports a hypothesis or theorem. It asks whether the reasoning offered genuinely warrants the claimed conclusion [39]. Depending on the type of hypothesis, this justification may draw on established theory, on previously proven results, or on a clearly articulated chain of logical implications. When such a theoretical basis is available, it provides the explanatory foundation for why the hypothesized effect should hold.

Many new algorithms are designed with justification from phenomena discussed in the natural sciences. These include simulated annealing [37], particle swarm optimization [35], or backpropagation for artificial neural networks [69]. Genetic algorithms are inspired by the process of natural selection [25]. They build on the concepts of mutation, crossover, and selection to iteratively generate high-quality solutions to optimization and search problems. In their article on genetic process mining, Wil and co-authors justify the choice with the benefits of global search provided by genetic algorithms [48].

An alternative to a justification by theory or general principles is a justification by empirical observation. An illustrative example of such justification from process mining are the alpha-algorithm and its various extensions [47,67,68]. Each extension builds on an observed limitation and inductively develops a solution that addresses this limitation. For instance, handling short loops requires considering triplets instead of pairs in the discovery algorithm. Claims about the suitability of an algorithm design can also be formulated empirical in a deductive way. For example, Camargo et al. [12] justify the use of deep learning methods for learning simulation models by pointing to prior empirical studies showing that such methods often outperform traditional approaches in process prediction tasks. They provide the required justification why plausibly this choice should provide the expected benefits in this case.

Today, process mining research builds on all these strategies for providing justification validity. These works build on transparent argumentation that makes explicit how prior knowledge, theoretical insights, or well-motivated assumptions underpin the hypothesis or theorem. Whether the claim is a result of formal correctness or an empirically grounded performance conjecture, the persuasive power of its justification is an important aspect of its scientific contribution.

### 3.6  Logical Validity

Logical validity is a key concern when it comes to proofs for theorems. Following Aristotle, it can be defined as the degree to which the syllogisms used in a proof preserve truth [21]. Logical validity ensures that, if the premises of a proof are true, the conclusion must also be true. Crafting proofs is a careful, intellectual exercise performed by researchers.

Wil has made substantial contributions in this regard. In his papers, he rigorously formalizes and proves fundamental properties of his algorithms. Early work on the alpha-algorithm [4] exemplifies his approach. The introduction of the algorithm is accompanied by theorems and proofs that provide guarantees of its ability to rediscover a large class of sound workflow nets under clearly specified assumptions [4]. As more recent examples, his work on object-centric Petri nets [3] and object-centric alignments [42] continues this tradition by establishing formal properties of these approaches, again supported by explicit theorems and proofs. These efforts illustrate how logical validity serve as a practical foundation for trustworthy algorithmic innovations in process mining.

Today, many contributions on process mining follow Wil's example. His text on how to write beautiful papers [2] describes a repertoire of key notations for process mining research. How to prove theorems is covered in complementary textbooks like [64]. Both elegant notations and correct proofs provide the foundations for logical validity.

### 3.7  Internal Validity

Process mining research increasingly builds on empirical evaluations. Internal validity is the extent to which observed effects can be attributed to the treatment rather than to confounding factors [71]. In process mining, this often concerns knowledge about algorithm designs. Here, we have to distinguish studies that focus on performance and sensitivity analysis for a comparative set of algorithms from studies that investigate uncertainty and explanatory claims.

For studies dealing with knowledge claims of performance and sensitivity, different algorithms or their variants are typically applied to the same set of event logs [8]. Here, observed performance differences can be directly attributed to the algorithms under comparison, since they are the only element changing in the experimental setup. In essence, such a setup is a within-subject design. While challenges with human subjects such as carryover, learning effects, or fatigue [71] do not apply for computer experiments, we have to carefully consider implementation validity.

For studies dealing with knowledge claims about uncertainty or explanation, more caution is necessary. These studies often focus on effects obtained from combinations of algorithm designs and corresponding input data. They require a systematic variation of both algorithms and data features. When operating on real-life event logs, a systematic controlled variation of input data is not possible. Such a study is therefore observational, suffering from challenges associated with measured and unmeasured confounding factors. One method proposed to address these challenges is the use of synthetic event logs. Systematic variation of synthetic input data transforms the study into a controlled experiment, thereby allowing researchers to manage confounding factors more effectively [11,32].

Today, various studies in process mining conduct comparative evaluations using a large set of BPI Challenge datasets. It is important to bear in mind that some algorithms perform better on input data with specific characteristics [10,32]. Therefore, it is a good idea to perform focused evaluations with synthetic data for internal validity and additionally with real-world data for external validity, as for example done in Wil's article on genetic process mining [48].

## 3.8    Construct Validity

Various characteristics of business processes and corresponding models or of event data are important to measure, because they have an impact on process performance and process improvement. The definition of such measures in an appropriate way is not trivial [23]. Construct validity describes the degree to which the measure of a construct accurately captures the intended property [52]. Intuitively, it asks whether the metric genuinely reflects the concept it is meant to represent—for example, whether a measure of process model complexity captures meaningful structural complexity rather than merely counting elements. In other words, the chosen indicators must provide a valid and reliable operationalization of the underlying concept.

Three important types of measures from the domain of process mining and modeling illustrate the challenge of maintaining construct validity: (i) fitness between a process model and an event log, (ii) process complexity, and (iii) understanding of a process model.

First, there is a diverse spectrum of fitness measures for assessing conformance [54]. A persistent difficulty is the absence of a formal ground truth and of a universally accepted definition of conformance, which makes it challenging to ensure that these metrics truly reflect the intended concept. Second, process complexity can be assessed both for event logs [10] and for process models [49]. Here, construct validity hinges on demonstrating that the selected complexity metrics indeed capture the aspects of structural or behavioral complexity that matter for analysis and comparison. Third, the comprehension of a process model has been investigated from a cognitive perspective [24,46]. Measures of model understanding must be carefully designed so that the recorded outcomes, such as accuracy of answers to comprehension questions, can legitimately be interpreted as indicators of the underlying construct of "process model comprehension."

Today, these three and other measures are extensively used in process mining research. Ensuring construct validity therefore requires more than the mere use of established measures. Researchers must argue explicitly that the selected measures faithfully represent the theoretical concepts under investigation and that they do so consistently across different contexts. This can lead to the definition of new measures if established ones do not fit. Empirical findings in process mining can only be considered valid evidence of the intended constructs if the links between concepts and measures are made explicit.

### 3.9  Conclusion Validity

Conclusion validity concerns the degree to which the results of a study can reasonably be regarded as revealing the hypothesised relationship [15,26]. While often associated with statistical analysis, it also includes qualitative considerations [17]. Conclusions drawn from statistical tests are credible only when the assumptions of those tests hold and appropriate significance levels are achieved. In addition, careful examination of outliers or other anomalous data points can strengthen or qualify the conclusions and help explain unexpected findings [29].

In process mining, for example, researchers frequently compare the predictive accuracy of alternative process monitoring techniques [65]. A claim that one method outperforms another is valid only if the underlying statistical tests are applied correctly and the evaluation data are representative of the intended application context. Similar care is needed when interpreting comparisons of discovery algorithms or alignment techniques: unexplained anomalies or untested assumptions can weaken the credibility of the stated performance differences.

Today, conclusion validity is not always explicitly discussed in process mining research. Maintaining high conclusion validity therefore requires both rigorous statistical practice and transparent discussion of limitations. In a way, it is an integrated assessment of the other validity concerns. Whether the evidence is quantitative or qualitative, authors should make explicit how their analysis supports, or fails to support, the hypothesized connection and acknowledge limitations and the assumptions under which their conclusions remain warranted.

## 4  Conclusion

Process mining research has matured since its inception 25 years ago. In this paper, we addressed the need for a broad and systematic discussion of validity for process mining research. To this end, we used the methodological framework for algorithm engineering [50]. We analyzed its nine validity notions for various streams of process mining research and identified various best practices to address each concern. In particular, Wil's works provide good examples of how process mining research can be conducted with methodological rigor and an eye on validity.

**Acknowledgments.** This research was supported by the Einstein Foundation Berlin under grant EPP-2019-524, by the Federal Ministry of Research, Technology and Space under the grant 16DII143, and by Deutsche Forschungsgemeinschaft under grants 496119880 (VisualMine), 531115272 (ProImpact), SFB 1404/2 (FONDA).

# References


1. van der Aalst, W.M.P.: Business process management: a comprehensive survey. Int. Sch. Res. Not. **2013**(1), 507984 (2013)
2. van der Aalst, W.M.P.: How to write beautiful process-and-data-science papers? arXiv preprint arXiv:2203.09286 (2022)
3. van der Aalst, W.M.P., Berti, A.: Discovering object-centric petri nets. Fund. Inform. **175**(1–4), 1–40 (2020)
4. van der Aalst, W.M.P., Weijters, T., Maruster, L.: Workflow mining: discovering process models from event logs. IEEE Trans. Knowl. Data Eng. **16**(9), 1128–1142 (2004)
5. van der Aalst, W.M.P., Weijters, T., Maruster, L.: Workflow mining: discovering process models from event logs. IEEE Trans. Knowl. Data Eng. **16**(9), 1128–1142 (2004)
6. Ailenei, I., Rozinat, A., Eckert, A., van der Aalst, W.M.P.: Definition and validation of process mining use cases. In: Daniel, F., Barkaoui, K., Dustdar, S. (eds.) BPM 2011. LNBIP, vol. 99, pp. 75–86. Springer, Heidelberg (2012). https://doi.org/10.1007/978-3-642-28108-2_7
7. Ashcraft, M.H., Radvansky, G.A.: Cognition. Pearson Education India (2010)
8. Augusto, A., et al.: Automated discovery of process models from event logs: review and benchmark. IEEE Trans. Knowl. Data Eng. **31**(4), 686–705 (2018)
9. Augusto, A., Conforti, R., Dumas, M., La Rosa, M., Polyvyanyy, A.: Split miner: automated discovery of accurate and simple business process models from event logs. Knowl. Inf. Syst. **59**(2), 251–284 (2019)
10. Augusto, A., Mendling, J., Vidgof, M., Wurm, B.: The connection between process complexity of event sequences and models discovered by process mining. Inf. Sci. **598**, 196–215 (2022)
11. vanden Broucke, S.K.L.M., Delvaux, C., Freitas, J., Rogova, T., Vanthienen, J., Baesens, B.: Uncovering the relationship between event log characteristics and process discovery techniques. In: Lohmann, N., Song, M., Wohed, P. (eds.) BPM 2013. LNBIP, vol. 171, pp. 41–53. Springer, Cham (2014). https://doi.org/10.1007/978-3-319-06257-0_4
12. Camargo, M., Báron, D., Dumas, M., González-Rojas, O.: Learning business process simulation models: a hybrid process mining and deep learning approach. Inf. Syst. **117**, 102248 (2023)

13. Chapela-Campa, D., Dumas, M., Mucientes, M., Lama, M.: Efficient edge filtering of directly-follows graphs for process mining. Inf. Sci. **610**, 830–846 (2022)
14. Cheng, D., Cao, C., Xu, C., Ma, X.: Manifesting bugs in machine learning code: an explorative study with mutation testing. In: 2018 IEEE International Conference on Software Quality, Reliability and Security (QRS), pp. 313–324. IEEE (2018)
15. Cook, T.D., Campbell, D.T.: The design and conduct of true experiments and quasi-experiments in field settings. In: Reproduced in part in Research in Organizations: Issues and Controversies. Goodyear Publishing Company (1979)
16. Cook, T.D., Campbell, D.T., Shadish, W.: Experimental and quasi-experimental designs for generalized causal inference, vol. 1195. Houghton Mifflin, Boston (2002)
17. Cozby, P.C.: Methods in Behavioral Research. McGraw-Hill (2007)
18. De Medeiros, A.A.: Business process mining: an industrial application. Inf. Syst. **32**(5), 713–732 (2007)
19. Deng, J., Dong, W., Socher, R., Li, L.J., Li, K., Fei-Fei, L.: Imagenet: a large-scale hierarchical image database. In: 2009 IEEE Conference on Computer Vision and Pattern Recognition, pp. 248–255 (2009)
20. Dumas, M., La Rosa, M., Mendling, J., Reijers, H.A.: Process-aware information systems. In: Fundamentals of Business Process Management, pp. 341–369. Springer, Heidelberg (2018). https://doi.org/10.1007/978-3-662-56509-4_9
21. Durand-Guerrier, V.: Truth versus validity in mathematical proof. ZDM **40**(3), 373–384 (2008)
22. Engelberg, G., Hadad, M., Pegoraro, M., Soffer, P., Hadar, E., van der Aalst, W.M.: An uncertainty-aware event log of network traffic. In: BPM (Demos/Resources Forum), pp. 67–71 (2023)
23. Fenton, N.: Software measurement: a necessary scientific basis. IEEE Trans. Software Eng. **20**(3), 199–206 (2002)
24. Figl, K.: Comprehension of procedural visual business process models: a literature review. Bus. Inf. Syst. Eng. **59**(1), 41–67 (2017)
25. Forrest, S.: Genetic algorithms. ACM Comput. Surv. (CSUR) **28**(1), 77–80 (1996)
26. García-Pérez, M.A.: Statistical conclusion validity: some common threats and simple remedies. Front. Psychol. **3**, 325 (2012)
27. González-Montesino, L., Grass-Boada, D.H.: Trace alignment algorithm optimization. Data Min. Knowl. Disc. **39**(5), 59 (2025)
28. Hall, J.G., Rapanotti, L.: A design theory for software engineering. Inf. Softw. Technol. **87**, 46–61 (2017)
29. Hernández-Orallo, J.: Evaluation in artificial intelligence: from task-oriented to ability-oriented measurement. Artif. Intell. Rev. **48**(3), 397–447 (2017)
30. Holleman, G.A., Hooge, I.T.C., Kemner, C., Hessels, R.S.: The 'real-world approach' and its problems: a critique of the term ecological validity. Front. Psychol. **11** (2020)
31. Jagadeesh Chandra Bose, R.P., van der Aalst, W.: Trace alignment in process mining: opportunities for process diagnostics. In: Hull, R., Mendling, J., Tai, S. (eds.) BPM 2010. LNCS, vol. 6336, pp. 227–242. Springer, Heidelberg (2010). https://doi.org/10.1007/978-3-642-15618-2_17
32. Janssenswillen, G., Donders, N., Jouck, T., Depaire, B.: A comparative study of existing quality measures for process discovery. Inf. Syst. **71**, 1–15 (2017)
33. Johnson, A.E., et al.: MIMIC-III, a freely accessible critical care database. Sci. Data **3**(1), 1–9 (2016)
34. Jouck, T., Depaire, B.: Generating artificial data for empirical analysis of control-flow discovery algorithms: a process tree and log generator. Bus. Inf. Syst. Eng. **61**(6), 695–712 (2019)

35. Kennedy, J., Eberhart, R.: Particle swarm optimization. In: Proceedings of ICNN'95-International Conference on Neural Networks, vol. 4, pp. 1942–1948. IEEE (1995)

36. Khelifati, A., Khayati, M., Dignös, A., Difallah, D., Cudré-Mauroux, P.: TSMbench: benchmarking time series database systems for monitoring applications. Proc. VLDB Endow. **16**(11), 3363–3376 (2023)

37. Kirkpatrick, S., Gelatt, C.D., Jr., Vecchi, M.P.: Optimization by simulated annealing. Science **220**(4598), 671–680 (1983)

38. Kriegel, H.P., Schubert, E., Zimek, A.: The (black) art of runtime evaluation: are we comparing algorithms or implementations? Knowl. Inf. Syst. **52**(2), 341–378 (2017)

39. Lannin, J.K.: Generalization and justification: the challenge of introducing algebraic reasoning through patterning activities. Math. Think. Learn. **7**(3), 231–258 (2005)

40. Larsen, K.R., et al.: Validity in design science research. In: Hofmann, S., Müller, O., Rossi, M. (eds.) DESRIST 2020. LNCS, vol. 12388, pp. 272–282. Springer, Cham (2020). https://doi.org/10.1007/978-3-030-64823-7_25

41. Leemans, S.J.J., Fahland, D., van der Aalst, W.M.P.: Discovering block-structured process models from incomplete event logs. In: Ciardo, G., Kindler, E. (eds.) PETRI NETS 2014. LNCS, vol. 8489, pp. 91–110. Springer, Cham (2014). https://doi.org/10.1007/978-3-319-07734-5_6

42. Liss, L., Adams, J.N., van der Aalst, W.M.P.: Object-centric alignments. In: International Conference on Conceptual Modeling, pp. 201–219. Springer (2023)

43. Lukyanenko, R., Evermann, J., Parsons, J.: Guidelines for establishing instantiation validity in IT artifacts: a survey of IS research. In: Donnellan, B., Helfert, M., Kenneally, J., VanderMeer, D., Rothenberger, M., Winter, R. (eds.) DESRIST 2015. LNCS, vol. 9073, pp. 430–438. Springer, Cham (2015). https://doi.org/10.1007/978-3-319-18714-3_35

44. Lukyanenko, R., Parsons, J.: Design theory indeterminacy: what is it, how can it be reduced, and why did the polar bear drown? J. Assoc. Inf. Syst. (2020)

45. Maldonado, A., Frey, C.M., Tavares, G.M., Rehwald, N., Seidl, T.: Gedi: generating event data with intentional features for benchmarking process mining. In: International Conference on Business Process Management, pp. 221–237. Springer (2024)

46. Malinova Mandelburger, M., Mendling, J.: Cognitive diagram understanding and task performance in systems analysis and design. MIS Q. **45**(4), 2101–2157 (2021)

47. de Medeiros, A.K.A., van Dongen, B.F., van der Aalst, W.M.P., Weijters, A.J.M.M.: Process mining for ubiquitous mobile systems: an overview and a concrete algorithm. In: Baresi, L., Dustdar, S., Gall, H.C., Matera, M. (eds.) UMICS 2004. LNCS, vol. 3272, pp. 151–165. Springer, Heidelberg (2004). https://doi.org/10.1007/978-3-540-30188-2_12

48. de Medeiros, A.K.A., Weijters, A.J., van der Aalst, W.M.P.: Genetic process mining: an experimental evaluation. Data Min. Knowl. Disc. **14**(2), 245–304 (2007)

49. Mendling, J.: Metrics for Process Models: Empirical Foundations of Verification, Error Prediction, and Guidelines for Correctness. LNBIP, vol. 6. Springer, Heidelberg (2008). https://doi.org/10.1007/978-3-540-89224-3

50. Mendling, J., Leopold, H., Meyerhenke, H., Depaire, B.: Methodology of algorithm engineering. ACM Comput. Surv. (2025)

51. Mendling, J., Leopold, H., Pittke, F.: 25 challenges of semantic process modeling. Int. J. Inf. Syst. Softw. Eng. Big Companies **1**(1), 78–94 (2015)

52. O'Leary-Kelly, S.W., J. Vokurka, R.: The empirical assessment of construct validity. J. Oper. Manag. **16**(4), 387–405 (1998)
53. Pohl, T., Berti, A., Qafari, M.S., van der Aalst, W.M.P.: A collection of simulated event logs for fairness assessment in process mining. arXiv preprint arXiv:2306.11453 (2023)
54. Polyvyanyy, A., Solti, A., Weidlich, M., Ciccio, C.D., Mendling, J.: Monotone precision and recall measures for comparing executions and specifications of dynamic systems. ACM Trans. Softw. Eng. Methodol. (TOSEM) **29**(3), 1–41 (2020)
55. Pradhan, S.K., Jans, M., Martin, N.: Getting the data in shape for your process mining analysis: an in-depth analysis of the pre-analysis stage. ACM Comput. Surv. **57**(6), 1–37 (2025)
56. Recker, J., Mendling, J.: The state of the art of business process management research as published in the bpm conference: Recommendations for progressing the field. Bus. Inf. Syst. Eng. **58**(1), 55–72 (2016)
57. Rehse, J.R., Leemans, S.J., Fettke, P., van der Werf, J.M.E.: On process discovery experimentation: addressing the need for research methodology in process discovery. ACM Trans. Softw. Eng. Methodol. **34**(1), 1–29 (2024)
58. Rittel, H.W., Webber, M.M.: Dilemmas in a general theory of planning. Policy Sci. **4**(2), 155–169 (1973)
59. Rozinat, A., Van der Aalst, W.M.: Conformance checking of processes based on monitoring real behavior. Inf. Syst. **33**(1), 64–95 (2008)
60. Sanders, P.: Algorithm engineering–an attempt at a definition. In: Efficient Algorithms, pp. 321–340. Springer (2009)
61. Santner, T.J., Williams, B.J., Notz, W., Williams, B.J.: The design and analysis of computer experiments, vol. 1. Springer (2003)
62. Staples, M.: Critical rationalism and engineering: ontology. Synthese **191**(10), 2255–2279 (2014). https://doi.org/10.1007/s11229-014-0396-3
63. Van Der Aalst, W.M.P., La Rosa, M., Santoro, F.M.: Business process management: don't forget to improve the process! Bus. Inf. Syst. Eng. **58**(1), 1–6 (2016)
64. Velleman, D.J.: How to Prove It: A Structured Approach, 2nd edn. Cambridge University Press (2019)
65. Verenich, I., Dumas, M., Rosa, M.L., Maggi, F.M., Teinemaa, I.: Survey and cross-benchmark comparison of remaining time prediction methods in business process monitoring. ACM Trans. Intell. Syst. Technol. (TIST) **10**(4), 1–34 (2019)
66. van der Waal, W., van de Weerd, I., Beerepoot, I., Lu, X., Kappen, T., Haitjema, S., Reijers, H.A.: Putting the sword to the test: finding workarounds with process mining. Bus. Inf. Syst. Eng. **67**(2), 171–190 (2025)
67. Wen, L., van der Aalst, W.M.P., Wang, J., Sun, J.: Mining process models with non-free-choice constructs. Data Min. Knowl. Disc. **15**(2), 145–180 (2007)
68. Wen, L., Wang, J., van der Aalst, W.M.P., Huang, B., Sun, J.: Mining process models with prime invisible tasks. Data Knowl. Eng. **69**(10), 999–1021 (2010)
69. Werbos, P.J.: The Roots of Backpropagation: From Ordered Derivatives to Neural Networks and Political Forecasting, vol. 1. Wiley (1994)
70. Wieringa, R.J.: Design Science Methodology for Information Systems and Software Engineering. Springer (2014)
71. Wohlin, C., Runeson, P., Höst, M., Ohlsson, M.C., Regnell, B., Wesslén, A.: Experimentation in Software Engineering. Springer (2012)
72. Zimmermann, L., Zerbato, F., Weber, B.: What makes life for process mining analysts difficult? A reflection of challenges. Softw. Syst. Model. **23**(6), 1345–1373 (2024)

# A Semantic Encoding of Object Centric Event Data


Saba Latif[1] , Fajar J. Ekaputra[2] , Maxim Vidgof[2] , Sabrina Kirrane[2] ,
and Claudio Di Ciccio[3](✉) 

[1] Sapienza University of Rome, Rome, Italy
`saba.latif@uniroma1.it`
[2] Wirtschaftsuniversität Wien, Vienna, Austria
`{fajar.ekaputra,maxim.vidgof,sabrina.kirrane}@wu.ac.at`
[3] University of Utrecht, Utrecht, The Netherlands
`c.diciccio@uu.nl`



**Abstract.** The Object-Centric Event Data (OCED) is a novel meta-model aimed at providing a common ground for process data records centered around events and objects. One of its objectives is to foster both interoperability and process information exchange. In this context, the integration of data from different providers, the combination of multiple processes, and the enhancement of knowledge inference are novel challenges. Semantic Web technologies can enable the creation of a machine-readable OCED description enriched through ontology-based relationships and entity categorization. In this paper, we introduce an approach built upon Semantic Web technologies for the realization of semantic-enhanced OCED, with the aim to strengthen process data reasoning, interconnect information sources, and boost expressiveness.

**Keywords:** Object centric event log · OCED · Semantic web · Ontology · Knowledge graphs · Process mining


## 1 Introduction

Process mining is the discipline aimed at extracting, analyzing, and enhancing knowledge of business processes from event data stored by information systems in the form of event logs [2]. Over the last few years, the focus of process mining has experienced a gradual drift from the historically established activity-centric view, interpreting process execution logs as sequences of actions [34]. The spotlight is moving towards the information artifacts, namely *objects*, that activity executions alter or read. This viewpoint shift is testified by the surge of object-centric process mining [3] and object-centric event log formats [24].

The IEEE Task Force on Process Mining leads the standardization process for a new event data paradigm, with the aim to overcome the previous established format of XES (eXtensible Event Stream, [34]): The Object Centric Event Data (OCED) meta-model [22]. An accurate semantic ontology of the novel meta-model is still under discussion. Ontologies function as explicit conceptual models



J. Mendling et al. (Eds.): Wil van der Aalst Festschrift, LNCS 16480, pp. 569–582, 2026.
https://doi.org/10.1007/978-3-032-17618-9_37

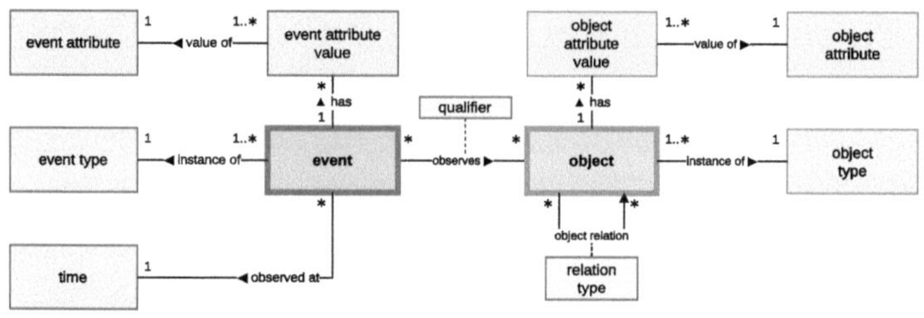

**Fig. 1.** The OCED meta-model core [22]

representing domain knowledge, making it accessible to information systems. They are essential to the vision of the semantics, offering the semantic vocabulary needed to annotate websites so that machines can meaningfully interpret [25].

In this paper, we provide a framework that defines the semantics of OCED to endow the new standard with a consistent, extensible, and interoperable representation. We achieve this by leveraging the body of knowledge of the semantic web [11]. On top of that, we introduce an approach inspired by the literature in information integration [15] that resorts to semantic web description languages to establish links between the model at the meta-level (described by the OCED Ontology, OCEDO), customizable and domain-specific representations at an intentional level (via Domain-specific extensions of OCED, OCEDD), and the data at an extensional level (as knowledge graphs of OCED Resources, OCEDR). We provide a demonstration of how raw process data can be automatically endowed with machine-readable semantics in an object-oriented fashion through a proof-of-concept prototype that automatically extracts OCEDR knowledge graphs from activity-centric XES logs. Our semantic framework encoding and tools are openly available at github.com/wu-semsys/ocedo.

Our long-term goal is manifold. Among others, the foreseeable opportunities opened up by our approach range from an improvement of OCED data reasoning, to the knowledge inference from semantically enriched data, from an increase in expressiveness, to the interconnection of information sources. Regarding the last point, we remark that under our semantic umbrella, other (not necessarily process-specific) existing datasets can be linked with the resulting potential of unleashing unprecedented contextual enrichment for (semantic reasoning in) process mining.

The remainder of the paper is as follows. Section 2 outlines the notions and technical bases of our investigation. Section 3 proposes our three-layered conceptual framework for the semantic encoding of OCED. Section 4 discusses the implications of our endeavor. Section 5 overviews related work. Section 6 draws conclusions for this work.

## 2   Background

Our investigation aims to forge semantic layers for object-centric event data using the OCED standard as the anvil, and the conceptual tools and frameworks provided by semantic web technologies as the hammer. In this section, we provide a description of our conceptual forgery's items.

## 2.1   The OCED Meta Model

OCED aims to overcome the limitations of the well-established IEEE standard XES [1], which emerged in its ultra-decennial adoption at the time of writing. These limitations include lack of generalizability, complexity of the data structure, and memory expensiveness of the storage format [34]. Unlike XES, OCED shifts the focus from sequences of activities recorded in information systems, trace after trace, to the lifecycle and conceptual interconnection of business objects that these systems handle.

A clear example of how semantically-aware object-centric formats can be useful to the representation of process execution records comes a public real-world event log tracing the process for incident and problem management at Volvo [33]. Although the event log is natively stored in XES, it comes endowed with several pieces of information pertaining to the treated business objects, and rich documentation for the data representation and contents.[1] Furthermore, it demonstrates how raw, activity-centric event logs can be turned into semantically rich, object-centric information stores. We shall use it as a running example in this paper, revisited under the lens of object-centric representations.

Figure 1 graphically depicts the key elements of the OCED meta-model and their interrelation. Events and objects (marked with a thick bounding box in the figure) represent the first-class citizens of OCED. An *event* represents a point-in-time occurrence of an action. The *objects* are entities of which the event may report the creation, change, deletion, or mere reading (i.e., that the object *observes* in a way that the *qualifier* clarifies). For example, every status change of an incident (e.g., the one identified by the ticket number 1-364285768) is an event (e.g., signaling that it closes the incident by acquiring a `Completed` status and `Closed` sub-status [32]). The reported incident, and hence the event, pertains to a product (e.g., `PROD582`). The status change is operated by a responsible (e.g., `Siebel`) of a support team (e.g., `V5 3rd`) within an IT function division (e.g., the one of `A2_5`). of a service center (e.g., the one of `Org line A2`). The incident, the product, the responsible, and the team are all objects in OCED. Notice that there are relations between two objects in this example (`Siebel` works in a team, which is part of an IT function division, which is in turn within a service center). In OCED, the concept of *object relation*, labelled by a *relation type* (*works in*, *is part of* and *is within*, in our example) bears this notion.

Both events and objects can come endowed with attributes. In OCED, attributes are akin to name-value pairs; therefore, an object (like the incident) is associated to an *object attribute value* for an *object attribute* (e.g., `High` for the `Impact` of the problem), and an event (like the status change) is associated to an *event attribute value* for an *event attribute* (e.g., *Completed* for the new incident's *status* and *Closed* for its *sub_status*). A *time*-stamp is a special

---

[1] https://ais.win.tue.nl/bpi/2013/challenge.html. Accessed: 26/09/2025.

attribute since, unlike the other attributes, it has fixed semantics: In particular, it indicates when the event was registered (e.g., 2012-05-11T01:26:15+02:00).

## 2.2  Semantic Web Technologies

Semantic web technologies provide a comprehensive set of standards for the representation, linking, and processing of semantically explicit information. For our intents and purposes, of particular relevance in the semantic web technology stack is the Resource Description Framework (RDF), which we use as a uniform model to represent object-centric event logs and the information they bear. RDF is a data representation model published by the World Wide Web Consortium (W3C) as a set of recommendations and working group notes.[2] It provides a standard model for expressing information about *resources*, which in our paper represent events, objects, attributes, relations, etc. An RDF dataset consists of a set of statements about these resources, expressed in the form of triples $(s, p, o)$ where $s$ is an RDF-*subject*, $p$ is a *predicate*, and $o$ is an RDF-*object*; $s$ and $o$ represent the two resources being related whereas $p$ represents the nature of their relationship. For instance, with RDF we can declare that $ev_1$ (RDF-subject) is *observed at* (predicate) 2012-05-11T01:26:15+02:00 (RDF-object). A key advantage of RDF as a data model is its extensible nature, i.e., additional statements about $s$, $p$, and $o$ can be added to link concepts and predicates from various additional, potentially domain-specific vocabularies. To this end, the encoding of a resource is associated to a Uniform Resource Identifier (URI), and grouped into namespaces that are used as prefixes to clarify the vocabulary they belong to. The notion of RDF-object itself, for instance, is encoded as `rdf:object`, whereby the namespace `rdf` is associated to the URI `http://www.w3.org/1999/02/22-rdf-syntax-ns#`. New vocabularies can be defined and connected.

Notice that RDF can cross the boundaries of information integration levels. The triple $(ev_1,$ *observed at*, 2011-02-03T08:28:58+01:00) is exerted on RDF-subject and RDF-object at the extensional level, whilst *observed at* is a meta-model element. We can also claim that $ev_1$ *is a*n event, having the RDF-object at the meta-level. The RDF Schema (RDF/S)[3] is built upon the RDF vocabulary and predicates over resources, classes categorizing resources, and the relations among classes. For instance, with RDF/S we can express that *observes* relates events (*domain*) to objects (*range*). It is thus possible to automatically deduce that if $(ev_1,$ *observes*, $obj_1)$ is a declared triple, then $ev_1$ is an event and $obj_1$ an object. Ontology specification languages such as the Web Ontology Language (OWL)[4] can be used to more closely describe the semantic characteristics of terms in use. For example, with RDF and OWL we can clarify that *event* is a `owl:Class`, and that *observed at* is an `owl:DataTypeProperty`. RDF can be serialized via different formats, including RDF/XML, JSON-LD, and the text-

---

[2] http://www.w3.org/TR/rdf11-primer/. Accessed: 30/09/2025.

[3] RDF/S: www.w3.org/TR/rdf-schema. Accessed: 30/09/2025.

[4] OWL: www.w3.org/TR/owl2-primer. Accessed: 30/09/2025.

based Terse RDF Triple Language (Turtle).[5] Without loss of generality, we adopt Turtle in the remainder of the paper due to its compactness.

A clear benefit of the aforementioned technologies is interoperability: information expressed in RDF using shared vocabularies and ontologies can be exchanged between applications without loss of meaning. Furthermore, it makes it possible to apply a wide range of general purpose RDF parsing, mapping, transformation, and query processing tools. Once transformed into RDF, information assumes the form of *Knowledge Graphs* that can be published online, interlinked, and shared between applications and organizations, which is particularly interesting in the context of collaborative processes. Next, we will see how we use semantic web technologies as a building block for a semantic encoding of OCED that allows for an explicit stratification of domain-specific intensional layers over the meta-model.

## 3   A Semantic Stratification of OCED

The OCED meta-model allows for flexibility in data representation, as it is meant to be *domain-agnostic*. Notice, e.g., that no restrictions are exerted on the possible relations that an object of a given type may or may not have with other objects, the values that attributes can take, or what (types of) objects are observed by which events. For example, OCED does not natively provide users with means to enforce that each incident pertains to a product, enumerate what the possible status changes can be, or indicate that every status change event affects an incident. It is also worth noticing that this meta-model removes a constraint that activity-centric standards like XES exerted, i.e., that every event be associated to a case, namely a process instance [10,31]. In the OCED meta-model, the case is not considered as a relevant, let alone mandatory, concept –however, it can be represented as an object.

While this structural looseness is desirable to encompass the amplest plethora of process data in a meta-model, domain experts should be allowed to inject knowledge on top of the meta-model, to provide additional details on the structure of the recorded data, promote traceability of process information provenance, and help the linkage of different data sources [14,16,30]. With this paper, we thus advocate the adoption of an overarching ontological approach to cover three conceptual layers, following a well-known approach in the field of information integration [15]: From the *meta-level* (represented by the *OCED Ontology*, OCEDO) to the *intensional level* (the *OCED Domain*-specific extension, OCEDD) to the *extensional level* (the *OCED Resources'* knowledge graph, OCEDR). To define and interconnect the three levels, we resort to semantic web technologies, as we describe in the remainder of this section.

---

[5] RDF/XML: w3.org/TR/rdf-syntax-grammar; JSON-LD: w3.org/TR/json-ld; Turtle: w3.org/TR/turtle. Accessed: 30/09/2025.

## 3.1   The Meta-level: OCED Ontology (OCEDO)

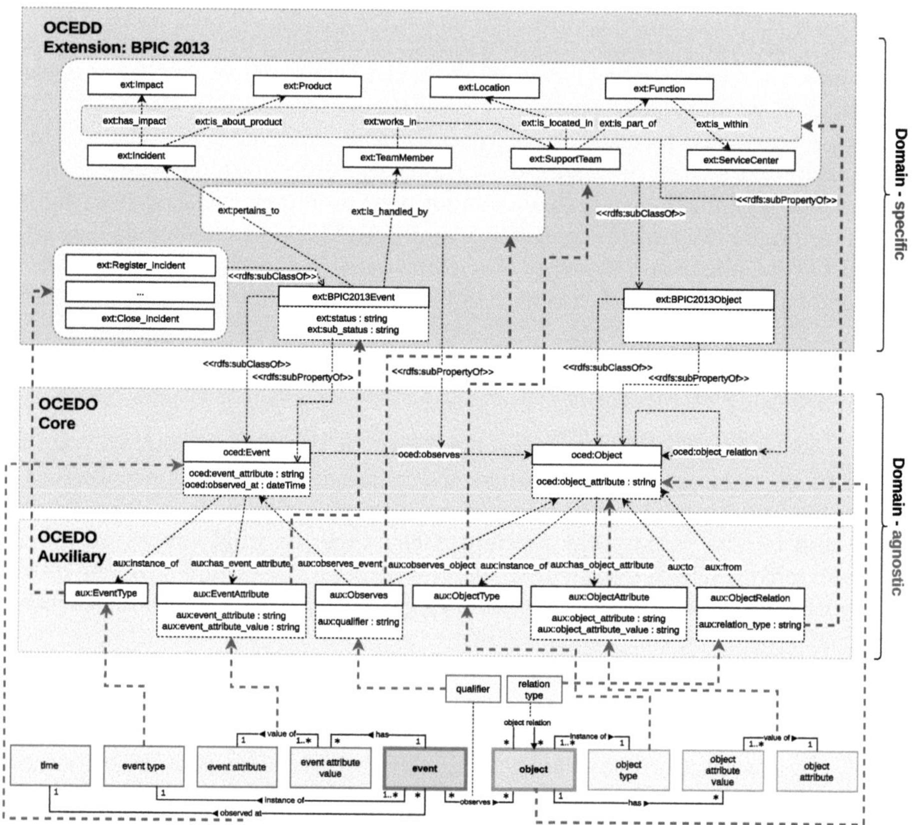

**Fig. 2.** OCED meta-model with RDF representation and additional domain-specific layer

Figure 2 depicts our reference implementation of OCED's meta-model and intensional level in the form of an RDF semantic network. The OCED original meta-model entities and relations from Fig. 1 occur below in the figure, as a reference. With dashed blue lines, we link those to the corresponding semantic encodings in our new OCED Ontology (OCEDO, in the middle). OCEDO is split in two parts. *OCEDO Core* (prefixed with `oced`, namespace https:// w3id.org/ocedo/core#) encompasses the first-class citizens of OCED, namely `oced:Event` and `oced:Object`.[6] *OCEDO Auxiliary* (`aux` prefix, namespace https://w3id.org/ocedo/aux#) contains the representations of the other entities and relations in the original meta-model, namely the event type, event attribute,

---

[6] Notice that the prefix linked to URIs allows for disambiguation: The notion of the `rdf:object`, defined by W3C, does not match that of an `oced:Object`.

```
 1  @prefix rdf: <http://www.w3.org/1999/02/22-rdf-
        syntax-ns#> .
 2  @prefix rdfs: <http://www.w3.org/2000/01/rdf-schema#
        > .
 3  @prefix owl: <http://www.w3.org/2002/07/owl#> .
 4  @prefix xsd: <http://www.w3.org/2001/XMLSchema#> .
 5  @prefix oced: <https://w3id.org/ocedo/core#> .
 6  @prefix aux: <https://w3id.org/ocedo/auxiliary#> .
 7  # [...] OCED core
 8  oced:Event a owl:Class ;
 9    rdfs:label "Event" ;
10    rdfs:comment "Representation of the concept of
            Event" .
11  oced:Object a owl:Class ;
12    rdfs:label "Object" ;
13    rdfs:comment "Representation of the concept of
            Object" .
14  # [...] OCED core - data properties
15  oced:observed_at a owl:DatatypeProperty ;
16    rdfs:label "observed_at" ;
17    rdfs:comment "timestamp of an event" ;
18    rdfs:domain oced:Event ;
19    rdfs:range xsd:dateTime .
20  # [...] OCED auxilary - classes
21  aux:Observe a owl:Class ;
22    rdfs:label "Observe" .
23  aux:ObjectAttribute a owl:Class ;
24    rdfs:label "Object Attribute" .
25  aux:ObjectRelation a owl:Class ;
26    rdfs:label "Object Relation" .
27  # [...] OCED auxilary - object properties
28  aux:has_object_attribute a owl:ObjectProperty ;
29    rdfs:label "has_object_attribute" ;
30    rdfs:domain oced:Object ;
31    rdfs:range aux:ObjectAttribute .
32  aux:from a owl:ObjectProperty ;
33    rdfs:label "from" ;
34    rdfs:domain aux:ObjectRelation ;
35    rdfs:range oced:Object ;
36    rdfs:comment "source Object" .
37  aux:to a owl:ObjectProperty ;
38    rdfs:label "to" ;
39    rdfs:domain aux:ObjectRelation ;
40    rdfs:range oced:Object ;
41    rdfs:comment "target Object" .
42  aux:observe_object a owl:ObjectProperty ;
43    rdfs:label "observe_object" ;
44    rdfs:domain aux:Observe ;
45    rdfs:range oced:Object ;
46    rdfs:comment "Relation between Observe and related
            Object" .
47  aux:observe_event a owl:ObjectProperty ;
48    rdfs:label "observe_event" ;
49    rdfs:domain aux:Observe ;
50    rdfs:range oced:Event ;
51    rdfs:comment "Relation between Observe and related
            Event" .
            # [...]
```

**Listing 1.** A Turtle representation of the OCEDO ontology (excerpt)

object type, object attribute, and the reified relations between objects, and from events to objects (*observe*).

Here we provide a brief overview of the OCED meta-model's encoding with semantic web technologies. A full specification is available in our open code repository.[7] Listing 1 shows an excerpt of the OCEDO schema serialized in Turtle. In the listing, we colored the background of keywords compatibly with the color scheme of Fig. 2 for understandability purposes. After the import of existing ontologies via prefixes and namespaces (like the aforementioned RDF, RDF/S, OWL, see Sect. 2.2) we declare that what is preceded by `oced:` and `aux:` identifies concepts for our core and auxiliary ontology parts of the meta-model, respectively. Thereafter, starting from line 8, we state that `oced:Event` is a class to be `labeled` "Event", to be regarded as a representation of the event class (see the `comment` directive; both `label` and `comment` are terms of the `rdfs` vocabulary). Similarly, we introduce the concept of `oced:Object` (line 11).

Among the concepts of the auxiliary section of OCEDO, we report here that of `aux:ObjectAttribute`, and of the reified relation types `aux:ObjectRelation` and `aux:Observe` (see lines 23, 25 and 21, respectively). Notice that the mappings from objects to their attributes, from objects to the relation to other objects, and from events to the observation of objects are all defined in the form of an `owl:ObjectProperty`, specifying the `rdfs:domain` and `rdfs:range` of such mappings (see Sect. 2.2), as can be noticed on lines 28-31, 32-41, and 42-51. Since the timestamp of an event is a scalar value of a type provided by the well-established XML-schema (`xsd`) vocabulary, we indicate that `observed_at` is an `owl:DataTypeProperty` and specify that the RDF/S domain and range of it are the `oced:Event` class and the `xsd:dateTime` datatype, respectively (see the block starting on lines 15-19).

---

[7] https://semsys.ai.wu.ac.at/ocedo. Accessed: 30/09/2025.

```
 1  @prefix ext: <https://w3id.org/ocedo/domain#> .        16  ext:pertains_to a owl:ObjectProperty ;
 2  # [...] Domain-specific event and object types          17    rdfs:label "ext:pertains_to" ;
 3  ext:BPIC2013Event a owl:Class ;                          18    rdfs:domain oced:Event ;
 4    rdfs:subClassOf oced:Object .                          19    rdfs:range ext:Incident .
 5  ext:BPIC2013Object a owl:Class ;                         20  ext:is_handled_by a owl:ObjectProperty;
 6    rdfs:subClassOf oced:Object .                          21    rdfs:label "ext:is_handled_by" ;
 7  ext:Incident a owl:Class ;                               22    rdfs:domain oced:Event ;
 8    rdfs:subClassOf ext:BPIC2013Object .                   23    rdfs:range ext:TeamMember .
 9  ext:TeamMember a owl:Class ;                             24  ext:works_in a owl:ObjectProperty ;
10    rdfs:subClassOf ext:BPIC2013Object .                   25    rdfs:label "ext:works_in" ;
11  ext:SupportTeam a owl:Class ;                            26    rdfs:domain ext:TeamMember ;
12    rdfs:subClassOf ext:BPIC2013Object .                   27    rdfs:range ext:SupportTeam .
13  ext:Completed_Resolved a owl:Class ;                     28  # [...] Domain-specific event-attribute relations
14    rdfs:subClassOf ext:BPIC2013Event .                    29  ext:status a owl:DatatypeProperty ;
15  # [...] Domain-specific event-object and object-         30    rdfs:subPropertyOf oced:event_attribute .
        object relations                                     31  ext:substatus a owl:DatatypeProperty ;
                                                             32    rdfs:subPropertyOf oced:event_attribute .
```

**Listing 2.** A Turtle representation of an OCEDD extension for BPIC 2013 (excerpt)

## 3.2    The Intensional Level: Domain-Specific Extension (OCEDD)

OCEDO is domain-agnostic. Regardless of the organization registering the process data, and the structure thereof, it does not vary. The members of the OCED Working Group encourage work for enriching process data semantics with domain-specific knowledge in their white paper [22]. To cater for this, we leverage the extensibility of RDF to postulate the addition of another semantic layer at the intensional level: The domain-specific extensions which we collectively name as OCEDD (henceforth prefixed with ext). The abstraction step is akin to the passage from the notion of entity and relationship types as modeling concepts to the conceptual schema of a relational database, with actual entities and relationships representing the business domain of data. Notice, however, that our modeling objective is descriptive and not normative like an ER diagram.

While OCEDO is meant to encode the semantics of the OCED meta model based on the directives of the XES/OCED working group [22], OCEDD is intended as a customizable addendum to create dialects of OCED that are domain- or case-specific. OCEDD extensions allow domain experts, analysts, but also data mining tools, to enrich the information brought by recorded process data with additional knowledge tailored for the situation in use in a controlled fashion, thus propelling *extensibility*. However, OCEDD classes are intended to extend the existing, domain-agnostic OCEDO counterparts, so as to foster retro-compatibility and *interoperability*.

Let us consider again the example of BPIC 2013. Some concepts therein solely pertain to the domain-specific nomenclature of the terms (like incidents, products, responsible person, support teams) and to the constraints binding the concepts the information system reports on (every incident pertains a product, and every status update thereof is handled by a responsible person who works in a support team). Therefore, they do not apply to OCED as a whole, but to the specific extension thereof to use in this case. In what follows, we provide an example of a possible domain-specific encoding of the BPIC 2013 data linked with OCEDO. Our reconstruction is tentative and based on the dataset documentation[4] and the analysis of the challenge submissions like [32] for exemplification purposes. It is by no means intended to be comprehensive or devoid

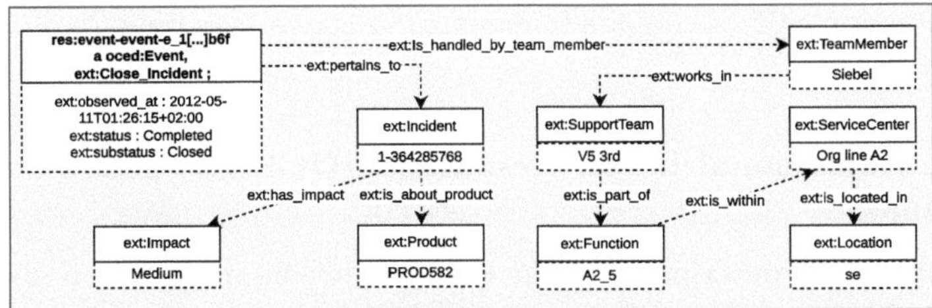



**Fig. 3.** A section of the OCEDD knowledge graph from BPIC2013

```
1  @prefix res : <https://w3id.org/ocedo/resource/> .
2  # [...] An event
3  res : event -e_1[...]b6f a oced : Event , ext :
          Close_Incident ;
4      oced : observed_at "2012-05-11T01:26:15+02:00"^^
              xsd:dateTime ;
5      ext : status "Completed" ;
6      ext : pertains_to res : object -o_5[...]374 ;
7      ext : is_handled_by res : object -o_e[...]011 ;
8      ext : substatus "Closed" .
9  # [...] An object of type Incident
10 res : object -o_5[...]374 a oced : Object , ext :
          Incident ;
11     ext : ticket_number "1-364285768" .
12     ext : is_about_product res : object -o_T[...]040 ,
13 # [...] An object of Type TeamMember
14 res : object -o_e[...]011 a oced : Object , ext :
          TeamMember ;
15     ext : team_member_name "Siebel" ;
16     ext : works_in res : object -o_8[...]430,
17 # [...] An object of Type SupportTeam
18 res : object -o_b[...]430 a oced : Object ,
19     ext : SupportTeam ;
20     ext : team "V5 3rd" ;
21 # [...] An object of type Product
22 res : object -
          o_7cb5c41b1041559e8f4b2d1286c58459145ac846 a
          oced : Object , ext : Product ;
23     ext : product_number "PROD582" .
```

**Listing 3.** A Turtle representation of an OCEDR knowledge graph for the BPIC 2013 datastore (excerpt)

of interpretation mistakes, but serves the purpose of clarifying the rationale of OCEDD.

Listing 2 shows an excerpt of an OCEDD extension for the BPIC2013 log. An overview of it is graphically depicted in the topmost layer of Fig. 2, with dashed green arcs highlighting some implicit connections between OCEDD elements and the related OCEDO concepts below whenever entailed, but not explicitly enforced, by RDF primitives. The full encoding is publicly available in our codebase.[10] Here we focus on a few salient characteristics. We begin defining a sub-class of `oced:Event` and `oced:Object` to characterize the concepts of pertinence for the specific log, here `ext:BPIC2013Event` (line 3) and `ext:BPIC2013Object` (line 5), respectively. Event types categorize the possible `ext:BPIC2013Events` via `rdfs:subClassOf` (see line 13 for the status transition of the incident to being completed and resolved). Objects of interest in this domain include `ext:Incident`, `ext:TeamMember`, and `ext:SupportTeam` (the names recall the ones mentioned in Sect. 2.1; see lines 7, 9 and 11 in Listing 2).

In our example scenario, all events are bound to an incident. We express this concept by means of the `owl:ObjectProperty` we adopted in OCEDO (see Sect. 3.1): thereby, the `pertains_to` relationship binds `oced:Events`, the domain, to an `ext:Incident` (range; see lines 16-19). Similarly, we indicate that an `oced:Event` is handled by an `ext:TeamMember` (lines 20-23),and that an `ext:TeamMember` works in an `ext:SupportTeam` (lines 24-27). Through the aforementioned `owl:DatatypeProperty`, we can associate events to given attributes like the `ext:status` and `ext:substatus` by declaring those as an `rdfs:subPropertyOf` of the `oced:event_attribute` (see lines 29-30 and 31-32, respectively).

### 3.3  The Extensional Level: Resources' (OCEDR) Knowledge Graphs

Equipped with the description of the domain-specific information about events and objects in the process data, we proceed with the third and last, extensional level. To this end, we introduce the OCEDR layers.

Figure 3 shows an excerpt of the BPIC2013 event log turned into an OCEDR knowledge graph, revolving around a specific event from our running example in Sect. 2.1. In Listing 3, we show a fragment of the corresponding Turtle encoding. In the latter, we refer to the entries instantiating the concepts in OCEDO and OCEDD generically as resources (prefixed with `res`). On line 3, e.g., we indicate that `event-e_1[...]b6f` is an event of type `ext:Close_Incident`. In the indented lines that follow (till 8), we specify its status and substatus attributes, its timestamp, and the relations to two more resources instantiating objects: among others, the `ext:Incident` it pertains to (namely the one with ticket number 1-364285768, see line 10), and the `ext:TeamMember` (whose name attribute is `Siebel`, see line 14). Some relations among objects are shown on lines 16 (to indicate that Siebel works in team `V5 3rd`, see line 19) and 12 (to indicate that the incident pertains to product number `PROD582`, see line 22).

Thus far, we have discussed with examples the core concepts underpinning our three-layered conceptual framework for the semantic description of OCED data. Next, we discuss ongoing work and future implications for its possible adoption and enhancement.

## 4  Potential Impact and Future Work

Our proposed framework is a first building block, on which diverse research endeavors can be based. The core contribution here is the systematization of semantic object-centric process data modeling with distinct strata: Meta-level, intensional level, and extensional level. To generate the examples in this paper, and have a preliminary proof-of-concept testing our framework, we created a tool for the automated extraction of OCEDR knowledge graphs out of flattened event logs in XES format. It is openly available at github.com/wu-semsys/ocedo. It takes as input an XES event log, an OCEDD document, and a tabular descriptor linking XES entry names to OCEDO and OCEDD concepts. The descriptor, e.g., dictates that the `org:resource` and `org:group` XES event attributes respectively contain the values of the `name` attribute of an `ext:TeamMember` in `ext:is_handled_by` relation with that `oced:Event`, and the `team` attribute of an `ext:SupportTeam` object in `ext:works_in` relation with the latter. The tool leverages RDF Mapping language (RML)[8] for the mapping from input to output resources. Further tests conducted with other real-world event logs in the

---

[8] https://rml.io/specs/rml/. Accessed: 30/09/2025.

financial and governmental domains can be found there. A description of the tool goes beyond the scope of this paper. However, it serves as a clarion call for further implementations that link not only XES but other formats including raw CSVs, relational databases, OCEL files to OCEDR graphs. The more the connectors, the higher the impact that a semantic framework can yield. Furthermore, they can allow for the linkage of heterogeneous data repositories from multiple sources, enhancing knowledge inference capabilities, and enriching expressiveness. Information integration is indeed a driving factor that motivates our work.

The idea underneath our proof of concept takes inspiration from noticeably sophisticated approaches proposed for the automated extraction of activity-centric event logs like ONPROM [17]. Our vision is that the transfer of knowledge from those notable endeavors to the object-centric paradigm intertwined with our semantic encoding can unleash unprecedented results. Among those, we foresee a novel holistic mining approach: While object-centric process mining stands out as the natural extension towards information extraction from OCEDR knowledge graphs, an intriguing direction points at the use of machine learning approaches to automatically infer event-to-object and object-to-object relations based on raw event data. It is also worth mentioning that RDF datastores cater for query engines that retrieve, aggregate and manipulate semantically rich information via SPARQL Protocol and RDF Query Language (SPARQL),[9] opening up the opportunity for an advanced intermediate layer between data and process mining algorithms.

While the creation of OCEDD documents can be a way to encode the knowledge of knowledge experts, visual languages and model-driven approaches should be developed so as to allow their definition without necessarily being fluent in RDF and derivatives. Furthermore, OCEDD documents could be complemented with normative specifications dictating the structure of process data (e.g., dictating that every team member *must be* associated to exactly one support team). To this end, existing standardized languages like Shapes Constraint Language (SHACL) could come handy (a first attempt in this direction was shown in [19] for compliance checking). Reasoning on description and prescription documents looking for redundancies and contradictions, as well as to deduce connections among concepts, is a core task for semantic web and the foundational track of process management.

## 5    Related Work

Our investigation relates with the semantic enrichment of process data, and to object-centric approaches to process mining. Next, we overview some notable pieces of work investigating those two areas.

---

[9] https://www.w3.org/TR/sparql11-query/. Accessed: 30/09/2025.

The efforts to standardize an exchange format for event logs began in 2003[10] with the XML-based format MXML (Mining eXtensible Markup Language) [20]. The well-known open-source process mining toolkit ProM [5] used MXML as the language of choice for input event logs. In their paper, the authors postulated key concepts for process mining data treatment: The instantaneous nature of an event, without duration, the typing of events to classify the activity they report on, the association of data to a process, and the association of a process instance (case) to an event. Soon after, Alves de Medeiros et al. [29] advocated the need for a semantic stratum to lay on data to allow mining techniques to consolidate, link and reason on concepts rather than strings. Hence their proposal: Semantically Annotated Mining eXtensible Markup Language (SA-MXML), annotating MXML entries with ontology references. We share their goal of semantically enriching the notions included in an event log, although we aim to operate at a deeper level by representing the whole standard as a multi-layered extensible knowledge graph. Bertoli et al. [13] use an OWL knowledge base to represent business processes with semantic annotations. They advance prior research by encoding data artifacts, integrating execution traces, and enhancing semantic modeling. Furthermore, they improve on collaborative modeling and execution analysis using semantic reasoning techniques [26]. The cross-fertilization of those disciplines has already brought about fruitful results (cf. [8,9,19]), which we seek to further spur.

Object-centric process mining has been gaining traction in recent years [6]. Several approaches to object-centric process mining have been proposed, by enhancing techniques for imperative [4,28] and declarative languages [18], or for completely new paradigms like the Object-Centric Behavioral Constraints (OCBC) [7,27]. Interestingly, the notion of knowledge graph was presented in the process mining community for a more comprehensive view on multi-dimensional analyses, covering control flow, data flow, resources, and time, with the event knowledge graphs [21]. By adding a semantic layer to the event data network introduced thereby, we approach can be integrated with that.

Before and concurrently to OCED, other object-centric event log languages have been introduced, such as eXtensible Object-Centric (XOC) logs [28], and Object-Centric Event Logs (OCEL) [24]. Especially OCEL has observed a production of several utilities to handle and process it, including a visualization tool [23], case and variant comparison [6], filtering and sampling [12]. Our framework could amply leverage this body of knowledge to promote semantic web reasoning tasks on OCED datastores.


# 6   Conclusion

Recent advances in object-centric process mining underscore the need for a formal semantic definition of Object-centric Event Data (OCED) to ensure con-

---

[10] Quoting the words of the initiator, Wil van der Aalst, on the occasion of the 10th anniversary of XES: https://www.tf-pm.org/newsletter/newsletter-stream-4-12-2020/10-years-of-xes. Accessed: 28/09/2025.

sistency, extensibility, and interoperability. By leveraging semantic web technologies, we presented a machine-readable semantic framework that enhances ontology-based relationships and entity categorization for OCED. Our approach involves a three-level knowledge representation, having OCEDO at the meta-level, OCEDD domain-specific extensions at the intensional level, and OCEDR knowledge graphs at the extensional level. We demonstrated how our framework can be employed to automatically endow raw event logs with data semantics, with the help of a proof-of-concept tool we implemented to this end. Through iterative refinements, we seek to build upon the presented results and deliver new techniques to improve OCED data reasoning, link heterogeneous data sources, and enhance knowledge inference and expressiveness.

# References


1. IEEE Standard for eXtensible Event Stream (XES) for achieving interoperability in event logs and event streams (2023)
2. van der Aalst, W.M.P.: Process Mining - Data Science in Action, Second Edition. Springer (2016)
3. van der Aalst, W.M.P.: Object-centric process mining: dealing with divergence and convergence in event data. In: SEFM 2019, vol. 17, pp. 3–25. Springer (2019). https://doi.org/10.1007/978-3-030-30446-1_1
4. van der Aalst, W.M.P., Berti, A.: Discovering object-centric petri nets. Fundam. Informaticae **175**(1–4), 1–40 (2020)
5. van der Aalst, W.M.P., van Dongen, B.F., Günther, C.W., Rozinat, A., Verbeek, E., Weijters, T.: ProM: The process mining toolkit. In: BPM Demos (2009). http://ceur-ws.org/Vol-489/paper3.pdf
6. Adams, J.N., Schuster, D., Schmitz, S., Schuh, G., van der Aalst, W.M.P.: Defining cases and variants for object-centric event data. In: ICPM, pp. 128–135 (2022)
7. Artale, A., Kovtunova, A., Montali, M., van der Aalst, W.M.P.: Modeling and reasoning over declarative data-aware processes with object-centric behavioral constraints. In: The 17th International Conference on Business Process Management (BPM 2019), pp. 139–156 (2019)
8. Bachhofner, S., Kiesling, E., Revoredo, K., Waibel, P., Polleres, A.: Automated process knowledge graph construction from BPMN models. In: DEXA (1), pp. 32–47 (2022)
9. Baumann, N., Hinkelmann, K., Montecchiari, D.: Supporting reuse of business process models by semantic annotation. In: CAiSE, pp. 29–35 (2023)
10. Bayomie, D., Di Ciccio, C., Mendling, J.: Event-case correlation for process mining using probabilistic optimization. Inf. Syst. **114**, 102167 (2023)
11. Berners-Lee, T., Hendler, J., Lassila, O.: The semantic web. Sci. Am. **284**(5), 34–43 (2001)
12. Berti, A.: Filtering and sampling object-centric event logs. CoRR abs/arXiv:2205.01428 (2022)
13. Bertoli, P., Corcoglioniti, F., Di Francescomarino, C., Dragoni, M., Ghidini, C., Pistore, M.: Semantic modeling and analysis of complex data-aware processes and their executions. Expert Syst. Appl. **198**, 116702 (2022)
14. Calegari, D., Delgado, A.: A model-driven engineering perspective for the object-centric event data (OCED) metamodel. In: BPM Workshops, pp. 508–520 (2023)

15. Calvanese, D., De Giacomo, G., Lenzerini, M., Nardi, D., Rosati, R.: Information integration: Conceptual modeling and reasoning support. In: CoopIS. pp. 280–291 (1998,

16. Calvanese, D., Kalayci, T.E., Montali, M., Tinella, S.: Ontology-based data access for extracting event logs from legacy data: The onprom tool and methodology. In: BIS, pp. 220–236 (2017)

17. Calvanese, D., Kalayci, T.E., Montali, M., et al.: Conceptual schema transformation in ontology-based data access. In: EKAW, pp. 50–67 (2018)

18. Christfort, A.K., Rivkin, A., Fahland, D., Hildebrandt, T.T., Slaats, T.: Discovery of object-centric declarative models. In: ICPM, pp. 121–128 (2024)

19. Di Ciccio, C., Ekaputra, F.J., Cecconi, A., Ekelhart, A., Kiesling, E.: Finding non-compliances with declarative process constraints through semantic technologies. In: CAiSE Forum 2019, pp. 60–74 (2019)

20. van Dongen, B.F., van der Aalst, W.M.P.: A meta model for process mining data. In: EMOI-INTEROP (2005). https://ceur-ws.org/Vol-160/paper11.pdf

21. Fahland, D.: Process mining over multiple behavioral dimensions with event knowledge graphs. In: van der Aalst, W.M.P., Carmona, J. (eds.) Process Mining Handbook, pp. 274–319. Springer (2022). https://doi.org/10.1007/978-3-031-08848-3_9

22. Fahland, D., Montali, M., Lebherz, J., et al.: Towards a simple and extensible standard for Object-Centric Event Data (OCED) - Core model, design space, and lessons learned. CoRR abs/ arXiv:2410.14495 (2024)

23. Ghahfarokhi, A.F., van der Aalst, W.M.P.: A python tool for object-centric process mining comparison. CoRR abs/ arXiv:2202.05709 (2022)

24. Ghahfarokhi, A.F., Park, G., Berti, A., van der Aalst, W.M.P.: OCEL: a standard for object-centric event logs. In: ADBIS Short Papers, pp. 169–175 (2021)

25. Grimm, S., Abecker, A., Völker, J., Studer, R.: Ontologies and the semantic web. In: Handbook of Semantic Web Technologies, pp. 507–579. Springer (2011)

26. Kampik, T., et al.: Governance of autonomous agents on the web: challenges and opportunities. ACM Trans. Internet Technol. **22**(4), 1–31 (2022)

27. Li, G., de Carvalho, R.M., van der Aalst, W.M.P.: Automatic discovery of object-centric behavioral constraint models. In: BIS, pp. 43–58 (2017)

28. Li, G., de Murillas, E.G.L., de Carvalho, R.M., van der Aalst, W.M.P.: Extracting object-centric event logs to support process mining on databases. In: CAiSE Forum, vol. 30, pp. 182–199 (2018)

29. Alves de Medeiros, A.K., van der Aalst, W.M.P., Pedrinaci, C.: Semantic process mining tools: core building blocks. In: ECIS, pp. 1953–1964 (2008)

30. Piccirilli, E., Di Ciccio, C., Montali, M., Peñaloza, R., Pontieri, L., Ricca, F.: Explainable knowledge-aware process intelligence. KI - Künstliche Intelligenz (2025)

31. Pourmirza, S., Dijkman, R.M., Grefen, P.: Correlation miner: mining business process models and event correlations without case identifiers. Int. J. Cooperative Inf. Syst. **26**(2), 1742002:1–1742002:32 (2017)

32. Van den Spiegel, P., Dieltjens, L., Blevi, L.: Applied process mining techniques for incident and problem management. In: BPI (2013). https://ceur-ws.org/Vol-1052/paper12.pdf

33. Steeman, W.: BPI Challenge 2013 (2013). https://doi.org/10.4121/uuid:a7ce5c55-03a7-4583-b855-98b86e1a2b07

34. Wynn, M.T., et al.: Rethinking the input for process mining: Insights from the XES survey and workshop. In: ICPM Workshops, pp. 3–16 (2021)

# Ten Years After Our Framework for Correlating and Clustering Process Behavior: A Reflection on the Journey, Legacy and Outlook

Massimiliano de Leoni[(✉)]

University of Padua, Padua, Italy
`deleoni@math.unipd.it`

**Abstract.** This chapter revisits a general framework for correlating, predicting, and clustering process behavior based on event logs, which Wil van der Aalst and I designed more than one decade ago. After a brief summary of the framework and showcasing its application, the revisiting focuses on the historical and personal context in which it was designed and reflects on its legacy in current and future research in the BPM field. The framework's structured approach anticipated later developments in predictive and prescriptive process monitoring, causal and stochastic process mining, and business process simulation. The rise of object-centric process paradigm introduces new challenges, as processes are increasingly modeled as interacting networks of objects rather than single case flows. The chapter also discusses the promising future work to adjust the framework according to this new paradigm, where tabular data are conceptually replaced by graph-shaped data structures, thereby moving toward graph-based learning models.

**Keywords:** Event log Preprocessing · Process Analytics · Predictive and Prescriptive Analytics · Causal Process Mining · Object-centric Process Management

## 1 Opening Words

When I was invited to contribute to a *festschrift* celebrating Wil's 60th birthday, I immediately knew that I wanted to focus my chapter on revisiting the framework for analyzing and predicting process behavior, one decade after it was initially presented at the 12th International Conference on Business Process Management (BPM 2014) [1].

This framework was conceived during my time as a postdoctoral researcher, and later as an Assistant Professor, in Wil's group at TU Eindhoven (TU/e). Being part of his research group and collaborating with him was, without doubt, the most formative period of my career. What I particularly admired, and sought to learn, was his constant commitment to combining technical rigor with practical applicability and industrial relevance in every piece of research he undertook.

Our general framework formalizes many analytical and predictive tasks as instances of a more general problem: how to generate predictive or analytical models from event


J. Mendling et al. (Eds.): Wil van der Aalst Festschrift, LNCS 16480, pp. 583–596, 2026.
https://doi.org/10.1007/978-3-032-17618-9_38

logs through structured steps of event selection, feature enrichment, and identification of dependent and independent variables. By providing this methodology, the framework serves as a reusable template applicable to a broad spectrum of questions. The idea of developing this framework stemmed from the observation at the time – and unfortunately still true today – that several problems were addressed by developing very similar research solutions that were all based on ad hoc selection of features, often reimplementing mechanisms for feature extraction and event selection.

Working on this framework was not only extremely formative, but also very rewarding. The significance of the framework and the quality of our contribution were immediately recognized: the conference paper [1] received the Best Paper Award at BPM 2014 and was subsequently invited for a special issue featuring extended versions of the best conference papers, leading to the journal article [2].

According to Google Scholar, as of the end of October 2025, the conference paper [1] and its journal extension [2] have been cited 99 and 360 times, respectively. The large number of citations testifies to the recognition of our framework's relevance, and their annual steady number even after a decade indicates the lasting relevance of the framework within the BPM community. This recognition was further reinforced by the prestigious Test-of-Time Award, which recognize the papers that have had a significant, lasting impact on the field, that we received at the 23rd International Conference on Business Process Management (BPM 2023), as well as by the inclusion of [2] in a virtual special issue of *Information Systems* to celebrate the journal's 50th anniversary, which incorporates the most influential articles of the past decade (see [3]).

## 2    Context

My first encounter with Wil took place during my Ph.D. studies, when I was visiting Arthur ter Hofstede at QUT in Brisbane (Australia) between September 2007 and April 2008. Wil had been appointed as an adjunct professor at QUT and regularly visited the university each year. I was particularly fortunate that my stay coincided with a special year: in addition to his usual visit, Wil came to Brisbane in September to participate in the 2007 BPM edition. During those six months, Arthur, Wil, and I collaborated on a visual work-list handler for YAWL, which was later accepted at BPM 2008 [4]. I still vividly remember how intimidated I felt during our first meetings: after all, he was the author of the book [5] that had inspired my Master's thesis and shaped the early path of my Ph.D. journey!

I very much enjoyed the collaboration with Wil, and thus I contacted him after I defended my Ph.D. work at SAPIENZA - University of Rome to verify whether he had some postdoctoral positions in his group at TU/e, and whether I could be a suitable candidate. I was eventually hired and started my position that was financially supported by the EU's FP7 project ACSI. The TU/e contribution in the project was along two main directions: object-centric process mining (at the time, known as artifact-centric), and multi-perspective process mining. Another postdoctoral researcher was hired to carry out the first research direction – Dirk Fahland – while I largely focused on multi-perspective process mining. In 2013, Wil and I published a paper that focused on conformance checking by building multi-perspective alignments to pinpoint deviations and correlating them with the observed process-instance behavior via decision-tree discovery [6]. Decision-tree discovery was also employed in a second paper published during the same year where we devised an alignment-based technique to mine activities' guards at decision points [7].

After publishing [6] and [7], we realized we had essentially come up with the same framework skeleton where a certain feature was used as the dependent feature, a set of other features as independent features and certain events were used to create the training set and to assign values to these features: the only difference was in a different event filtering and ad hoc selection of features. In fact, the same could be observed in other works that were published up to that time [8–13].

Therefore, we asked ourselves: can we devise a framework that could address the various predictive and analytical tasks, of which those mentioned above are just specific instances? To answer the question, we designed such a unifying framework, which is also extensible enough to tackle a broad spectrum of questions. The motivation behind defining this framework was to encourage researchers to move beyond an excessive focus on feature engineering, and instead concentrate on formulating problems in AI terms, so that appropriate AI techniques could be systematically selected. Feature engineering, while necessary, is inherently less interesting from a methodological perspective because the superiority of a given approach largely depends on the data and underlying assumptions, and the relevant features are naturally domain-specific.

The framework's usefulness was ultimately assessed with the help of Marcus Dees, who was a data analyst at the Dutch Employee Insurance Agency (UWV) when we designed the framework. Marcus joined the research team because he was directly confronted with the same problems. At least at the time, many information systems at UWV were custom-built, and the extraction of a proper data set for the analysis has been hard to achieve: a significant effort was necessary to integrate data across these systems. Moreover, because those systems were continuously evolving, the data format was subject to frequent changes. Our framework is designed to accommodate such settings: its extensible and configurable nature enables it to quickly adjust to dataset changes. The help from Marcus was invaluable because he came with valid, concrete business questions from its application domain, which allowed us to assess the practical usefulness of the framework.

## 3   Structure and Rationale of the Framework

Process mining has traditionally focused on two main capabilities: (1) *process discovery*, i.e., extracting process models directly from event logs, and (2) *conformance checking*, i.e., replaying logs on models to detect deviations, bottlenecks and other issues. These techniques provide powerful insights into compliance and performance problems. However, to fully understand why deviations or bottlenecks occur, analysts must *correlate* different process perspectives, such as control-flow, data, time, organization.

It was mentioned above that this has been the first work to propose a *unified framework* that addresses a broad range of analytical and predictive tasks under a single methodological umbrella.  The framework builds around the concept of *characteristics*, which are the observable or derived properties of events or traces that can be used

**Table 1.** Types of Characteristics Defined in the Framework

| Perspective | Example Characteristics | Meaning/Purpose |
| --- | --- | --- |
| Control-flow | Previous activity; next activity; number of times an activity occurred; trace length so far | Captures the position or structure of an event within the process flow. |
| Data-flow | Current value of case variables; aggregated numerical attributes; differences between data values | Reflects the evolution of business data and its correlation with control-flow. |
| Time | Timestamp; elapsed time since case start; activity duration; remaining time; inter-arrival time | Captures temporal aspects of process execution and supports predictive performance analysis. |
| Resource and Organizational | Resource performing the event; workload at event time; role; hand-over frequency | Describes human or system actors and the organizational context of events. |
| Conformance | Fitness score; number of violations; deviation count w.r.t. model or LTL rules | Indicates how closely a trace adheres to the expected or normative process behavior. |

to analyze, correlate, or predict process behavior. These can be directly available in the event log (e.g., activity name, timestamp, resource), derived from event-log manipulations or enriched from external services (e.g., remaining time, workload, number of activities executed, deviations, weather). Table 1 reports on examples of characteristics for different perspectives, illustrating their meaning. The framework is summarized in Fig. 1 and is based on a structured, methodology of three steps, depicted in red in the figure, to conduct correlation and prediction analyses:

1. **Define the Analysis Use Case.** Specify a dependent characteristic (the variable to be explained), a set of independent characteristics (explanatory variables), and an event filter to select relevant events.
2. **Manipulate and Enrich Event log.** Derive additional characteristics from the log or external sources (e.g., remaining time, workload, process models, conformance information). This ensures that all relevant variables are available for analysis.
3. **Make analysis.** Treat the problem as a supervised learning task, e.g. using classification or regression trees to model relationships between variables. The framework is independent of the specific algorithm used to discover the relationships.

If the analysis result after the third step (e.g., the decision tree) is not satisfactory, the analysis use case be refined through, e.g., adding new independent characteristics or varying the dependent characteristic. This means that the three steps can be iteratively repeated. Once the result is satisfactory, the framework provides an additional optional step *4. Cluster* to cluster traces and split the event logs in sub-logs. The independent characteristics can be used as clustering dimensions, with the support of the dependent characteristics to help define the clusters.

This step was not present in the original framework discussed in [1], and was later introduced in the journal extension [2]. This was inspired by Wil's interest in *Process Cubes* at the time [14,15]. A process cube is a multidimensional data structure that organizes event data along multiple dimensions, which correspond to our characteristics, allowing users to slice, dice, roll up, and drill down on process-related data,

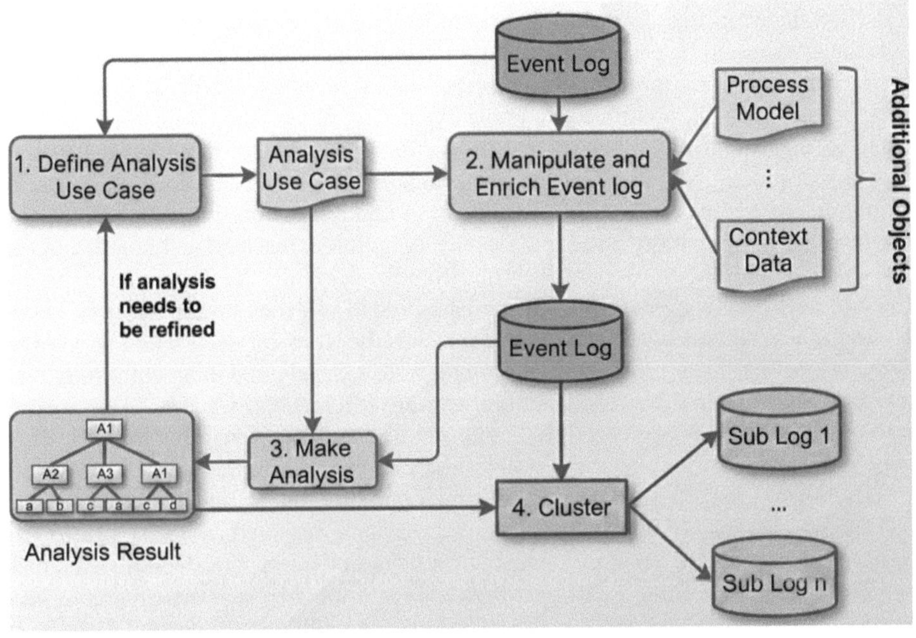


Fig. 1. The structure of our framework (Adjusted from [2])

analogously to an OLAP cube (Online Analytical Processing) in data warehousing but adapted to process mining. In fact, clustering techniques provide support to define how to slice the event logs. Both process cubes and the clustering step of our framework share the same goal: to decompose an event log into sublogs that capture more homogeneous process behavior. By subsequently applying the same analytical pipeline to each sublog, one can obtain clearer and more meaningful insights for individual subgroups, rather than deriving aggregated findings, which can even be conflicting because of stemming from a single heterogeneous log.

The framework was implemented as a plug-in for different PROM versions, including PROM Lite 1.4.[1] PROM is an open-source, extensible platform for process mining developed at TU/e. It is based on a plug-in architecture where researchers and practitioners can implement, integrate, and apply a wide range of process mining algorithms, such as for discovery, conformance checking, and predictive analysis. This extensibility allows our framework to be easily integrated with the output produced by other plug-ins to support a larger set of potential characteristics.

Note how the framework is *technology-agnostic*, and one could operationalize it for any Machine or Deep Learning techniques, as well as one could also potentially use pure, statistical methods. The first PROM implementation was also made public at the 12th International Conference on Business Process Management (BPM 2014), for which we wrote a demonstration paper [16]. This first implementation only focused

---

[1] PROM Lite 1.4 can be downloaded at https://promtools.org/prom-lite-1-4/.

on the J48 decision-tree discovery algorithm for classification tasks. To illustrate how the framework could be easily extended with additional features from sources external to the event log, we connected the implementation with the PROM's conformance-checking plug-in [17], and illustrated how events can be enriched with characteristics related to, e.g., the trace's fitness w.r.t. the normative models, or the number of deviations (log or model moves). Later the operationalization was extended with clustering and regression-tree discovery [2]. Classification and regression trees were chosen for their inherent explainability and for their wide adoption in research and practice during 2014-2016, namely when we published our framework. While the first practical models of neural networks were deployed in the late 1950s [18], they became widely known only in the second half of the2010 s Note that Java libraries for deep learning were not yet mature before those years: Deeplearning4j was, e.g., released in an alpha version at the end of 2014, while Python and its libraries were still niche. If we were to propose the same framework today, we certainly would not overlook deep learning models, likely coupled with post-hoc explanation techniques or surrogate models.

In summary, the framework enables a methodology that provides a reusable template for a wide range of analytical questions, replacing repeated ad hoc solutions with a consistent procedure. The key contribution does not lie in introducing new analysis types, but in *integrating existing capabilities* into a *coherent, extensible, and user-friendly framework*, where analysis use cases, trace manipulation and event filtering are well formalized. As mentioned, the specific techniques used in the implementation were only meant to provide a concrete showcase for the framework's application. Unfortunately, this has often been misinterpreted: many recent research works have focused on comparing their approaches to the specific techniques used in the original implementation, rather than recognizing that the main contribution was the framework itself, not the choice of algorithms. The central message of the work is to move away from developing solutions that rely on a fixed set of features, which are naturally tailored to a single domain. Instead, the relevant features to consider should be configured on a case-by-case basis, and new frameworks should be designed to support a *flexibility* similar to what our framework supports.

## 4    Framework Implementation and Case Study

The practical effectiveness can be showcased through the application to the seventh International Business Process Intelligence Challenge (BPIC'17).[2] It pertains to a loan application process of a Dutch financial institute. The data contains all applications filed through an online system in 2016 and their subsequent events until February 1st 2017, 15:11. The BPIC'17 web site indicates that the process consists of three types of activities: those starting with 'A' and 'O' are respectively related to the changes in customer's application states or offer states, while those starting with 'W' refer to workflow activities performed by the 149 originators, namely employees or systems of the company, to work on the applications.

---

[2] The BPIC'17 page is available at https://ais.win.tue.nl/bpi/2017/challenge.html.

The remainder of this section shows how some of the questions that the process owners asked can quickly be answered through our framework. Space limitation prevented from the framework's illustration to answer more business questions. In discovering these decision trees, we set a pruning confidence of 0.1, which roughly corresponds to a 90% confidence level for keeping decision-tree splits.

*Question 1. The influence on the incompleteness frequency to the final outcome.* The BPIC'17 web site indicates that the company's stakeholders hypothesized that if applicants are confronted with more requests for completion, they are more likely to not accept the final offer. The focus is thus to find correlations, if any, between the execution of workflow activities and whether the applicant is going to cancel the offer.

The framework was instantiated as follows:

**Independent characteristics.** The number of events for activities starting with 'W'.

**Dependent characteristic.** The number of events for activity *A_Cancelled*

**Event filtering.** Retain the last event of each log trace.

**Decision Tree.** Regression tree.

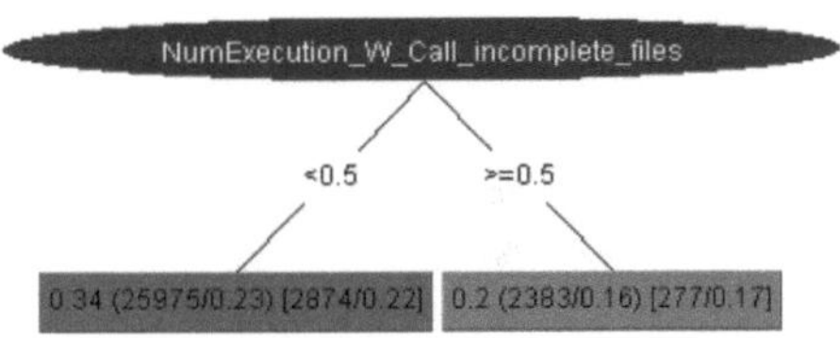


**Fig. 2.** Regression tree correlating BPIC'17 workflow activities to application cancellation.

The results are shown in Fig. 2, where a split is observed for the number of occurrences of *W_Call_incomplete_files*. The leaves' labels as:

```
value (number_of_instances / error) [number_of_instances_prune / error_prune]}
```

where `value` is the expected value, `number_of_instances` is the number of instances that are associated with the leaf, and `error` is the root mean square error, while the values in squared parentheses indicate the same quantities computed over the pruning set of that leaf. The results in Fig. 2 show that the stakeholders' hypothesis of a negative correlation between the number of completion requests and offer acceptance is not supported by the data. When applicants were not contacted, the expected value of *A_Cancelled* is 0.32, compared to 0.22 when they were contacted. Although the RMSE values indicate that these results may not be statistically reliable, they nonetheless suggest a weak trend toward a *positive* correlation, rather than the hypothesized negative one.

*Question 2. How many customers ask for more than one offer?* This question aimed to determine if a correlation exists between the characteristics of the applicant and of the loan request (e.g., the credit score, the number of terms, the offered amount) and the number of occurrences of *O_Created*. The framework was consequently set as follows:

**Independent characteristics.** CreditScore, FirstWithdrawalAmount, MonthlyCost, NumberOfTerms, OfferedAmount.

**Dependent characteristic.** The number of events for *O_Created*

**Event filtering.** Retain the last event of each log trace.
**Decision Tree.** Regression tree.

In this case, the output was a tree with one leaf with expected value 1.36 (i.e., the average number of offers per application), which basically indicates that no correlation was found.

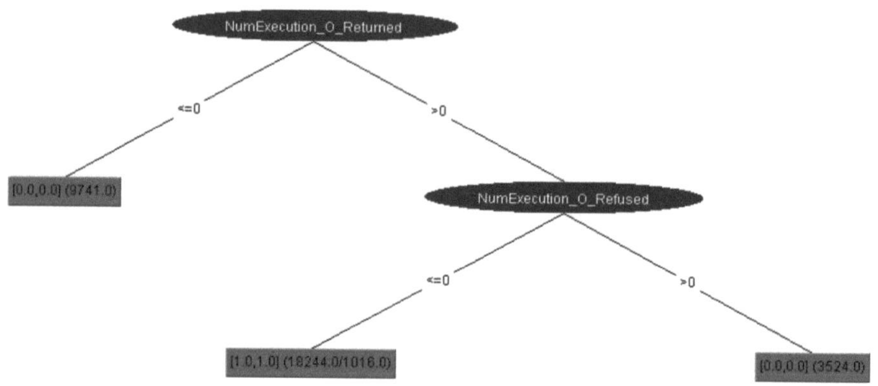


**Fig. 3.** Classification tree correlating BPIC'17 offer-related activities with application success.

*Question 3. How does the customer behavior w.r.t. offers correlate to a (un)successful application?* This question was answered as classification problem with value 0 or 1 if the application wasn't or was ultimately successful, respectively. We excluded the number of events for *O_Accepted* from the set of independent characteristics, because trivially each accepted offer leads to a successful application.

**Independent characteristics.** The number of events for activities starting with 'O', excluding *O_Accepted*
**Dependent characteristic.** The number of occurrences of events for *A_Pending*.
**Event filtering.** Retain the last event of each log trace.
**Decision Tree.** Classification tree.

The analysis produced the classification tree in Fig. 3. If no offer is returned to the credit institute with an amendment request (event *O_Returned*), the application is ultimately unsuccessful in 100% of cases; if an amendment is conversely requested, if the offer is finally refused by the applicant, the application is not going to be successful (100% accuracy), otherwise it is generally successful (ca. 95% accuracy).

## 5   Recent Directions and Future Trends

The current BPM research is increasingly focusing on predictive and prescriptive process analytics, business process simulation, anomaly detection, conformance checking, and related topics. The challenges addressed by the framework have naturally become even more urgent: it remains fundamental to provide a lens that turns raw event data into the input required by mainstream AI approaches, without an excessive focus on engineering specific features, which are naturally domain-dependent. The remainder focuses on a personal reflection on recent direction and future trends that are related to the framework.

### 5.1   Process Simulation and Stochastic Process Mining

Over the years, process simulation model discovery has been a fertile field where several techniques have been put forward that address problems that can be linked to instances of the framework discussed here. The goal has been to characterize the run-time aspects of process simulation to ensure high fidelity. For instance, Camargo et al. used control-flow characteristics similar to those introduced in Table 1 as independent character-istics to predict dependent characteristics related to the start and end timestamps of events [19]. López-Pintado et al. have similarly used process characteristics related to the data-flow to predict the values of process attributes (namely the independent charac-teristics) and to predict what the next activity in process is going to be when a process' branching point is reached [20]. RIMS is an alternative approach to simulation model discovery: it uses activity labels, timestamps, weekdays, and some intercase features related to queues and resource occupations, which serve as the independent character-istics, to estimate waiting and execution times of activities, which act as the dependent characteristics. These works certainly laid solid foundations for discovering accurate simulation models, but the set of independent characteristics are fixed. For instance, the choice at a branching point might depend on the resource performing the preced-ing activity rather than on specific process attribute values. This observation motivates the need for the set of independent characteristics used to predict the next activity at a branching point to be customizable on a case-by-case basis (cf. the discussion at the end of Sect. 3). The customization principle is, e.g., exemplified in de Leoni et al. [21] where the prediction of the next activity is made from a configurable set of independent characteristics, collectively referred to as *process state*. It is important to however note that, in all such settings, identical values of the selected independent characteristics do not always lead to the same predicted value. If they otherwise did, the simulation would exhibit limited generation, generating executions that are all very similar. It follows that deterministic models, such as classification or regression trees or even certain classes of neural networks, are inadequate for this purpose. Instead, one must employ proba-bilistic models that return values of the dependent characteristics in accordance to an appropriate probability distribution.

The discussion on probabilistic approaches to, e.g., discover the branching proba-bilities offers a natural bridge between our framework and the emerging area of *stochas-tic process mining*. This line of research has been gaining momentum within the BPM community for its capacity to capture system and process performance with high fidelity (and is closely related to business process simulation, of course). Notably, Wil began exploring this topic more than a decade ago, when it was still a niche area [22]. Most existing studies, including recent ones, have concentrated on estimating the probability of activity occurrences based solely on the sequence of preceding activities [23,24].

The work by Mannhardt et al. [25] represents the first step beyond this limitation, introducing a configurable notion of state, in line with the principle of flexibility of our correlation framework. Given the stochastic nature of the process models, a probabilistic predictor was employed, specifically a simple logistic regressor.

## 5.2  Predictive Process Monitoring

Predictive process monitoring (PPM) extends classical process mining from descriptive and diagnostic analytics to a predictive analytics [26]. Our framework is able to provide a methodological foundation on which PPM is building. The definition of the analysis use case and the event-log enrichment directly correspond to feature engineering in PPM, while the performance of the analysis is close to model-building phase in PPM. It is thus straightforward to define PPM frameworks that are configurable in terms of the independent characteristics, on the one hand, and the dependent characteristics that one aims to predict, on the other hand. Traditionally, PPM techniques have been differentiated, depending on whether the dependent characteristic is temporal (e.g., the remaining time to completion), or related to the next activity, or to some KPI-related outcome [26], but, in fact, there is no methodological or technical ground to treat them differently. Indeed, besides considering whether the specific prediction problem is a classification or regression one, the choice of the most suitable Machine or Deep Learning technique is likely mainly driven by the data present in the log, and the specific process behavior recorded therein. Last, our framework's clustering step is very close to the proposal by Di Francescomarino et al. [27] whether one extracts segments from event logs (e.g., process variants) on which one applies different PPM techniques, or even the same technique with different hyper-parameter settings.

## 5.3  Causal Process Mining

The original framework and operationalization were designed to find correlations, rather than causations. Finding real causations is often more insightful from a business viewpoint, than correlations. For example, consider the case study discussed in Sect. 4 and, more specifically, Question 1: a correlation is found between the number of executions of *W_Call_incomplete_files* in each process execution and the expected number of *A_Cancelled*. However, it is not clear whether the occurrence of the first activity triggers the application's cancellation (causation), or if the application's cancellation is, e.g., due to other factors that also cause more completion requests (correlation). Extending our framework towards causation is relatively easy: once the dataset is prepared through the pipeline to determine dependent and independent characteristics, and filtering, causal discovery methods can be applied as part of the third step of our framework. Note that typical causations represented through knowledge graphs do not work when the process characteristics are numerical, and converting numerical variables into categorical bins for using knowledge graphs can result in significant information loss. Numerical characteristics must not be converted into categorical ones. Wil has indeed worked on bringing causal discovery into our framework, through various proposals. Hompes et al. [28] build on very similar concepts of dependent and independent process characteristics, filtering, etc. to ensure generality and extensibility: once the event log is processed through a pipeline similar to what our framework proposes, it generates a graph of causal factors that explain the dependent characteristics, combining time-series aggregations with the notion of Granger causality. A similar proposal with the same structure was also proposed in a paper by Qafari and Wil [29] through structural equation models, which estimate the magnitude with which each independent characteristic X influences the dependent Y, offering insight into *"if we changed X, how would Y be affected?"*. One can easily notice that this approach shares the same causal interface framework, from Pearl's causal model theory, as that used for counterfactual explanations [30]. The core difference is in the use: structural equations models are employed to quantify causal relationships to build the model at phenomenon level, while counterfactual explanations are meant to explain the model and work at instance level. Other researchers have worked on applying causal theory to event data. For instance, Polyvyanyy et al. [31] propose a method to discover latent causal dependencies within extensive event data, or Narendra et al. [32] leverage the Pearl's causal model theory to confirm hypotheses of causeâĂŞeffect relations that had been identified during an analyst's preliminary investigation.

## 5.4 Object-Centric Process Management and Mining

A promising avenue for extending our framework concerns adapting to the object-centric process paradigm. In this paradigm, process execution is no longer represented as a single, linear flow of activities, but rather as a choreography of interacting object instances of different types. These objects synchronize and exchange information at well-defined points through bridging events [33]. Within this paradigm, object-centric event logs record both events and objects, as well as their relations through Event-to-Object (E2O) and Object-to-Object (O2O) links. The resulting network of many-to-many associations between process instances creates a level of structural complexity that makes a direct application of our framework infeasible, since it was originally conceived for traditional, single-identifier event logs. To illustrate, consider the question of whether a particular customer order will be delivered on time and in full. In an object-centric setting, this question extends far beyond the order itself: it may involve interactions among production, logistics, procurement, and sales objects. Whereas classical event logs can naturally be transformed into tabular data suitable for Machine and Deep Learning models, object-centric logs are provided with an inherently graph-like structure. This structure must be explicitly accounted for when defining dependent and independent characteristics, filtering events (and possibly objects?) and designing suitable predictive models. When extending our framework towards object-centric event logs, an unexplored research direction is towards the use of graph-based neural networks. It would be particularly valuable to investigate whether graph neural networks can yield better correlation/prediction analyses. This stems from the hypothesis that transforming the graph-like structure of object-centric logs into flat, tabular data may cause an explosion in the number of features, and/or may lead to substantial information loss. I have recently discussed this framework with Wil, I am confident that he shares my view on the importance of adapting our framework to this emerging paradigm, enabling its use within the rapidly expanding field of object-centric process mining.

## 6    Conclusion

If I look back at the framework that we designed more than one decade ago, I am impressed by how the framework is still contemporary, in the questions that it aims to answer, and in the motivation that led to its design. At that time, we noticed that several scattered solutions were provided - including by ourselves - to answer questions that were fundamentally the same, except for using different dependent and independent characteristics, and different predictive models. The goal was to signal the community to not pay attention to feature-engineering aspects and to not fixate on specific process characteristics and predictive models, which are more or less relevant depending on the specific case study, but rather to focus on the fundamental problems that can be answered through such frameworks as what we proposed.

Our framework anticipated the methodological needs of business process simulation, predictive and prescriptive process analytics, in which similar notions of feature enrichment and identification have become fundamental building blocks. Recently, many causal and counterfactual-driven approaches have emerged to rightfully move from correlation to causation, some of which are based on our framework. This important step allowed the framework to move from a mere descriptive and predictive focus to defining actionable business process improvement. Within the scope of BPM, object-centric process mining has emerged as a major step forward, which requires to rethink the framework's assumptions. Processes are no longer simple linear sequences, but rather they are intricate choreographies of interacting objects, whose relationships are best captured through graph-like structures rather than traditional tabular data. Our framework certainly needs to be adapted to embrace graph-shaped process characteristics, and graph-based deep learning architectures, to remain relevant and up-to-date.

The relative simplicity of this framework, along with its high effectiveness, is a great example of Wil's scientific vision: process mining should be a rigorous scientific field and open to innovation, while it needs to be rooted into real-world problems and have practical applicability in industry. This is in fact the main lesson that I have learned and keep learning from past, present and hopefully future collaborations with him.

## References


1. de Leoni, M., van der Aalst, W.M.P., Dees, M.: A general framework for correlating business process characteristics. In: Sadiq, S., Soffer, P., Völzer, H. (eds.) BPM 2014. LNCS, vol. 8659, pp. 250–266. Springer, Cham (2014). https://doi.org/10.1007/978-3-319-10172-9_16
2. de Leoni, M., van der Aalst, W.M.P., Dees, M.: A general process mining framework for correlating, predicting and clustering dynamic behavior based on event logs. Inf. Syst. **56** (2016)
3. de Leoni, M., van der Aalst, W.M.P., Dees, M.: Nine years later: reflecting on our article: A general process mining framework for correlating, predicting, and clustering dynamic behavior based on event logs. Inf. Syst. **137**, 102644 (2026)
4. de Leoni, M., van der Aalst, W.M.P., ter Hofstede, A.H.M.: Visual support for work assignment in process-aware information systems. In: Dumas, M., Reichert, M., Shan, M.-C. (eds.) BPM 2008. LNCS, vol. 5240, pp. 67–83. Springer, Heidelberg (2008). https://doi.org/10.1007/978-3-540-85758-7_8

5. van der Aalst, W.M.P., van Hee, K.M.: Workflow Management: Models, Methods, and Systems. Cooperative Information Systems. MIT Press (2002)
6. de Leoni, M., van der Aalst, W.M.P.: Aligning event logs and process models for multi-perspective conformance checking: an approach based on integer linear programming. In: Daniel, F., Wang, J., Weber, B. (eds.) BPM 2013. LNCS, vol. 8094, pp. 113–129. Springer, Heidelberg (2013). https://doi.org/10.1007/978-3-642-40176-3_10
7. de Leoni, M., van der Aalst, W.M.P.: Data-aware process mining: discovering decisions in processes using alignments. In: Proceedings of the 28th Annual ACM Symposium on Applied Computing (SAC 13), pp. 1454–1461. Association for Computing Machinery (2013)
8. Kim, A., Obregon, J., Jung, J.-Y.: Constructing decision trees from process logs for performer recommendation. In: Lohmann, N., Song, M., Wohed, P. (eds.) BPM 2013. LNBIP, vol. 171, pp. 224–236. Springer, Cham (2014). https://doi.org/10.1007/978-3-319-06257-0_18
9. Metzger, A., et al.: Comparing and combining predictive business process monitoring techniques. IEEE Trans. Syst. Man Cybernet. Syst. 45(2), 276–290 (2015)
10. Ghattas, J., Soffer, P., Peleg, M.: Improving business process decision making based on past experience. Decis. Support Syst. 59, 93–107 (2014)
11. Folino, F., Guarascio, M., Pontieri, L.: Discovering context-aware models for predicting business process performances. In: Meersman, R., et al. (eds.) OTM 2012. LNCS, vol. 7565, pp. 287–304. Springer, Heidelberg (2012). https://doi.org/10.1007/978-3-642-33606-5_18
12. Lakshmanan, G., Shamsi, D., Doganata, Y., Unuvar, M., Khalaf, R.: A markov prediction model for data-driven semi-structured business processes. Knowl. Inform. Syst., 1–30 (2013)
13. Sutrisnowati, R.A., Bae, H., Park, J., Ha, B.H.: Learning bayesian network from event logs using mutual information test. In: Proceedings of the 6th International Conference on Service-Oriented Computing and Applications (SOCA 2013), pp. 356–360 (2013)
14. Aalst, W.M.P.: Process cubes: slicing, dicing, rolling up and drilling down event data for process mining. In: Song, M., Wynn, M.T., Liu, J. (eds.) AP-BPM 2013. LNBIP, vol. 159, pp. 1–22. Springer, Cham (2013). https://doi.org/10.1007/978-3-319-02922-1_1
15. Bolt, A., van der Aalst, W.M.P.: Multidimensional process mining using process cubes. In: Gaaloul, K., Schmidt, R., Nurcan, S., Guerreiro, S., Ma, Q. (eds.) CAISE 2015. LNBIP, vol. 214, pp. 102–116. Springer, Cham (2015). https://doi.org/10.1007/978-3-319-19237-6_7
16. de Leoni, M., van der Aalst, W.M.P.: The FeaturePrediction package in prom: Correlating business process characteristics. In: Proceedings of the BPM Demo Sessions 2014. CEUR Workshop Proceedings, vol. 1295, p. 26. CEUR-WS.org (2014)
17. van der Aalst, W.M.P., Adriansyah, A., van Dongen, B.F.: Replaying history on process models for conformance checking and performance analysis. WIREs Data Min. Knowl. Discovery 2(2), 182–192 (2012)
18. Rosenblatt, F.: Perceptron simulation experiments. Proc. IRE 48(3), 301–309 (1960)
19. Camargo, M., Dumas, M., González-Rojas, O.: Learning accurate business process simulation models from event logs via automated process discovery and deep learning. In: Proceedings of the 34th International Conference on Advanced Information Systems Engineering (CAiSE 2022). LNCS, vol. 13295, pp. 57–72. Springer (2022). https://doi.org/10.1007/978-3-031-07472-1_4
20. López-Pintado, O., Murashko, S., Dumas, M.: Discovery and simulation of data-aware business processes. In: Proceedings of the 6th International Conference on Process Mining (ICPM), pp. 105–112. IEEE (2024)
21. de Leoni, M., Vinci, F., Leemans, S.J.J., Mannhardt, F.: Investigating the influence of data-aware process states on activity probabilities in simulation models: does accuracy improve? In: Proceedings of 21st International Conference on Business Process Management (BPM 2023). pp. 129–145. Springer (2023). https://doi.org/10.1007/978-3-031-41620-0_8

22. Rogge-Solti, A., van der Aalst, W.M.P., Weske, M.: Discovering stochastic petri nets with arbitrary delay distributions from event logs. In: Proceedings of 2013 Business Process Management Workshops. LNBIP, vol. 171, pp. 15–27. Springer (2014)

23. Alman, A., Maggi, F.M., Montali, M., Peñaloza, R.: Probabilistic declarative process mining. Inf. Syst. **109**, 102033 (2022)

24. Burke, A., Leemans, S.J.J., Wynn, M.T.: Discovering stochastic process models by reduction and abstraction. In: Buchs, D., Carmona, J. (eds.) PETRI NETS 2021. LNCS, vol. 12734, pp. 312–336. Springer, Cham (2021). https://doi.org/10.1007/978-3-030-76983-3_16

25. Mannhardt, F., Leemans, S.J., Schwanen, C.T., de Leoni, M.: Modelling data-aware stochastic processes – discovery and conformance checking. In: Proceedings of 44th International Conference on Application and Theory of Petri Nets and Concurrency (Petri Nets 2021). LNCS, vol. 13929, pp. 77–98. Springer (2023). https://doi.org/10.1007/978-3-031-33620-1_5

26. Ceravolo, P., Comuzzi, M., De Weerdt, J., Di Francescomarino, C., Maggi, F.M.: Predictive process monitoring: concepts, challenges, and future research directions. Process Sci. **1**(2) (2024)

27. Di Francescomarino, C., Dumas, M., Maggi, F.M., Teinemaa, I.: Clustering-based predictive process monitoring. IEEE Trans. Serv. Comput. **12**(6), 896–909 (2019)

28. Hompes, B.F.A., Maaradji, A., La Rosa, M., Dumas, M., Buijs, J.C.A.M., van der Aalst, W.M.P.: Discovering causal factors explaining business process performance variation. In: Dubois, E., Pohl, K. (eds.) CAiSE 2017. LNCS, vol. 10253, pp. 177–192. Springer, Cham (2017). https://doi.org/10.1007/978-3-319-59536-8_12

29. Qafari, M.S., van der Aalst, W.: Root cause analysis in process mining using structural equation models. In: Del Río Ortega, A., Leopold, H., Santoro, F.M. (eds.) BPM 2020. LNBIP, vol. 397, pp. 155–167. Springer, Cham (2020). https://doi.org/10.1007/978-3-030-66498-5_12

30. Molnar, C.: Interpretable Machine Learning. The third edn. (2025). https://christophm.github.io/interpretable-ml-book

31. Polyvyanyy, A., Pika, A., Wynn, M.T., ter Hofstede, A.H.: A systematic approach for discovering causal dependencies between observations and incidents in the health and safety domain. Saf. Sci. **118**, 345–354 (2019)

32. Narendra, T., Agarwal, P., Gupta, M., Dechu, S.: Counterfactual reasoning for process optimization using structural causal models. In: Hildebrandt, T., van Dongen, B.F., Röglinger, M., Mendling, J. (eds.) BPM 2019. LNBIP, vol. 360, pp. 91–106. Springer, Cham (2019). https://doi.org/10.1007/978-3-030-26643-1_6

33. van der Aalst, W.M.P.: Object-centric process mining: unraveling the fabric of real processes. Mathematics **11**(12), 2691 (2023)

# Process Applications

# Shaping the Digital Transformation in Production: An Information and Network-Centric Perspective

Jan Pennekamp[1]([⊠])[iD], Ike Kunze[1][iD], Liam Tirpitz[2][iD], Benedikt Bode[1][iD], Constantin Sander[1][iD], Sandra Geisler[2][iD], and Klaus Wehrle[1][iD]

[1] Communication and Distributed Systems, RWTH Aachen University, Aachen, Germany
`{pennekamp,kunze,bode,sander,wehrle}@comsys.rwth-aachen.de`
[2] Data Stream Management and Analysis, RWTH Aachen University, Aachen, Germany
`{tirpitz,geisler}@cs.rwth-aachen.de`

**Abstract.** The Internet of Production exemplifies the ongoing digital transformation in production by holistically approaching the creation of data-to-knowledge pipelines—from the initial collaborative collection of data from various, possibly competing entities up to the final knowledge generation and exploitation. Primary envisioned benefits include process optimization and resilience improvement to advance sustainability—addressing today's most pressing challenge. In this paper, we outline the current state of the digital transformation, highlighting research achievements across various layers of interest, namely application, data modeling, and the underlying infrastructure. Based on this assessment, we identify critical information- and network-centric questions that help guide the industrial domain to an even more collaborative and sustainable future.

**Keywords:** secure industrial collaboration · decentralized information dissemination · ad-hoc compute orchestration · process mining

## 1 Introduction

The digital transformation in production is an ongoing process, as exemplified by the Internet of Production (IoP) [8,38] and other large-scale initiatives. Aiming to improve data exploitation and the transition from data to knowledge, the IoP has made focused advances that enable sharing and jointly leveraging data and knowledge, partially even on a global scale and incorporating multiple, potentially competing stakeholders [5,29,35]. These advancements provide a solid foundation for evolving the industrial domain. However, corresponding

---

Dedicated to *Wil van der Aalst*.

© The Author(s), under exclusive license to Springer Nature Switzerland AG 2026
J. Mendling et al. (Eds.): Wil van der Aalst Festschrift, LNCS 16480, pp. 599–615, 2026.
https://doi.org/10.1007/978-3-032-17618-9_39

developments face new fundamental research challenges that greatly impact the ongoing transformation.

Aiming to establish a knowledge-fused distributed business ecosystem that considers various forms of sustainability, several dimensions become important. First, while our previous work has demonstrated that secure industrial collaboration is possible, we initially only targeted designing use case-specific solutions, leaving universally applicable concepts still missing. Second, the IoP primarily focuses on creating well-defined collaboration environments and sourcing information from these interactions, limiting responsiveness to world-wide events and overall flexibility. Third, current initiatives tend to concentrate on fundamentally building pipelines without adequately addressing their sustainability; holistic solutions could utilize available resources more efficiently. Given this context, we identify three information- and network-centric questions:

▶ *How to conceptualize, evolve, and standardize secure industrial collaboration?*
▶ *Which approaches promise a successful signaling mechanism for global use?*
▶ *What is needed to enable and optimize a novel federated cloud continuum?*

Tackling these currently-overlooked research questions is crucial for reliably, safely, securely, and sustainably providing the right information with appropriate expressiveness to the right party at the right time—aspects that are essential for higher-layer analyses, decision-making, and operation in the context of production.

In this paper, we derive a corresponding research agenda that strives for a truly interconnected production landscape while simultaneously incorporating sustainability considerations in knowledge-fused distributed business ecosystems. For this, we first outline the status quo of the digital transformation in production, which has evolved considerably due to the emergence of approximated close-to-edge control loops, Models-in-the-Middle, and secure industrial collaboration [5,29,35,58]. Specifically, we recap key conceptual considerations of the IoP in Sect. 2 and distill its research impact concerning the realization of a World-Wide Lab from an information- and network-centric perspective with a focus on the data-to-knowledge approach in Sect. 3. In this context, we also highlight corresponding implications for higher-layer applications and decision-making. This summary serves as a point of origin for deriving a concrete agenda that further evolves the production landscape (Sect. 4), i.e., continues the digital transformation. We focus our presentation on an information- and network-centric viewpoint to create the foundation for higher-layer data-to-knowledge pipelines and improved decision-making, as we outline in Sect. 5. Finally, Sect. 6 concludes this paper.

## 2   Premise and Concepts of the Internet of Production

The Internet of Production (IoP) pursues the vision of setting up world-wide data-driven, cross-domain, and interorganizational collaboration by providing semantically adequate and context-aware data to relevant stakeholders in real time and at a reasonable level of granularity [38]. These dataflows are then embedded and orchestrated with the World-Wide Lab (WWL) [8], introducing significant benefits in terms of costs, productivity, flexibility, innovation, and product quality, among others [33], to participating organizations and society alike. Brauner et al. [8] classify corresponding developments for transforming production into four layers, which we visualize in Fig. 1.

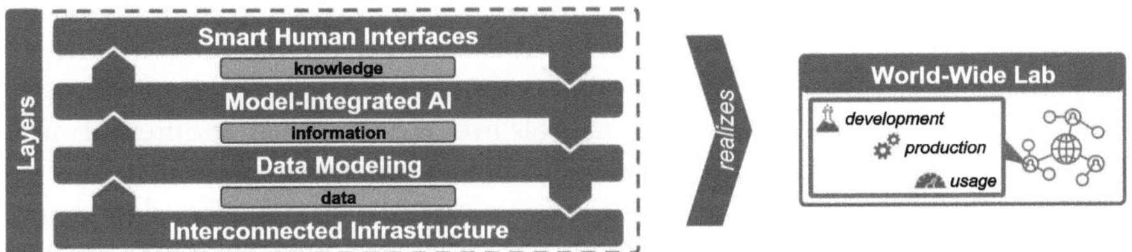


**Fig. 1.** In 2022, Brauner et al. [8] defined four research layers that shape the digital transformation in production, as the IoP exemplifies, and collectively realize the WWL.

In essence, data processed in the lowest layer is turned into information, which is then translated into knowledge, ready for communication to humans and organizations. This processing joins data, information, and knowledge from previously organizationally-isolated phases, i.e., development, production, and usage, and builds on data abstraction, aggregation, and refinement [8]. The WWL complements these layers by facilitating seamless integration of data, information, and knowledge across stakeholders, while the layers contribute the following functionality:

- **Smart Human Interfaces:** Evolved interfaces enable both experts and non-experts to interact adaptively with generated knowledge and their environments. They are specifically tailored to tasks, contexts, and users, enhancing engagement and efficiency, for instance, by applying multi-faceted visual process analytics and multi-layer frameworks such as Tiramisù [2,3].
- **Model-Integrated Artificial Intelligence (AI):** Using abstraction and aggregation, this layer proposes novel (foundational) models that offer tailored insights into production environments and their dependencies based on data, metadata, and (structured) information representations. It provides the knowledge basis for the smart human interfaces above. These interfaces can operationalize model outputs via layered, on-demand visual dimensions [2,3].
- **Data Modeling:** This layer features abstraction and aggregation of data, which is pivotal for transforming raw data into information and actionable knowledge, including the abstraction of raw IoT sensor streams into discrete events for process mining [9]. As such, it fuels the AI models situated on top.
- **Interconnected Infrastructure:** The underlying infrastructure serves as the backbone of the IoP and WWL by ensuring reliable data sensing, retrieval, sharing, and processing, thus providing the basis for any data modeling. Systematic approaches to transform sensor data into event logs are particularly critical for IoT-rich environments [9], as prevalent in the interconnected IoP.

With organizational changes [27,40] that enable the underlying exchange of information and data, these layers create the basis for collaboration-based value creation and facilitate the aforementioned cost, flexibility, and quality benefits.

Here, as a central layer, *Model-Integrated AI* is crucial for achieving the objectives because it is responsible for outputting findings for improved decision-making. Apart from machine learning, leveraging methodologies known from process mining promises to bridge the gap between model-based process analyses and data-oriented analyses [54]. Respective research activities on data-to-knowledge pipelines [15] are particularly valuable for complex environments with high concurrency. An early idea in this context covers the concept of process cubes [53], where events and process models are organized using different dimensions to discover, analyze, and improve (business) processes based on event data. Complementary approaches on visual process analytics explicitly address multi-faceted event data and interactive analytical abstraction [12]. While the *Smart Human Interfaces* layer utilizes this information to communicate derived knowledge to the stakeholders, the *Data Modeling* layer is particularly of interest for efficiently and reliably providing models to the environment that bridge data to knowledge and vice versa, i.e., connecting the surrounding layers.

By design, said layer builds upon the availability of information and, thus, initial data for its successful operation. Consequently, the *Interconnected Infrastructure* layer is essential for creating, providing, and maintaining added value in higher-level layers and applications like process mining. Specifically, the availability of rich data from diverse and potentially distributed yet broadly dependable data sources enables global optimization of processes by converting data into knowledge. Reviews of process mining on sensor data detail these pipelines and common pitfalls [9]. Beyond standardization of (secured) dataflows, we see a great demand for mature signaling and optimization approaches within this layer, as we substantiate and detail in Sect. 4. Thus, we emphasize the need to focus on this information- and network-centric perspective to establish a robust foundation for reliably collecting, handling, and sharing data safely and securely. Contrary actions will otherwise impair achieving the full potential of the IoP.

Having these overarching conceptual considerations of the IoP in mind, we next examine how its progress has shaped the digital transformation in production since the publication by Brauner et al. [8] in 2022.

## 3    Status Quo: Research Contributions and Achievements

Research within the IoP has made significant strides in advancing the understanding and application of digital shadows [4,26], the WWL, and related concepts. In this section, we highlight key research contributions to the fundamental conceptualization and realization of the IoP and leave aside research on individual production processes or similar topics with a narrower scope. Specifically, we focus on innovations in three key domains that advance the overarching objective of the IoP of turning data into knowledge [58]: (a) data-to-knowledge pipelines, (b) interoperable data models, and (c) data communication and dataflows.

**Data-to-Knowledge Pipelines** [5]. The development of robust data-to-knowledge pipelines is a cornerstone component of the IoP. At their core, these pipelines rely on integrating real-time manufacturing data, simulations, and mathematical models, which yield the basis for communication and data sharing within the WWL. Specifically, autonomous AI agents can query the WWL for machine-level and process-level information, subsequently transforming the standalone raw (production) data into actionable insights. The focus is on creating systematic approaches that leverage machine learning and model-based AI methods to enhance decision-making processes for operators and managers alike, ultimately leading to the realization of validated self-adaptive production systems. For instance, utilizing these pipelines for predictive maintenance can significantly reduce downtime by enabling proactive adjustments based on real-time analytics. At the same time, these pipelines have the ability to analyze even complex process chains using process mining techniques. They can further complement data-driven approaches with manufacturing-specific structural information to generate comprehensive views of shop-floor processes. With this domain-oriented application, the IoP can focus on time-dependent metrics over traditional control-flow perspectives, hence, creating the foundation for instantiating object-centric process mining (OCPM) [55,57] in production.

**Interoperable Data Models** [29]. Another critical area of advancement and driver of a successful IoP is the establishment of interoperable data models that promote seamless communication across diverse systems within the ecosystem. Specifically, the IoP focuses on conceptualizing an adequate set of data modeling techniques and transformations that link to metamodels to appropriately capture their semantics and cover the entire product life cycle. These interoperable models not only support cross-domain collaboration but simultaneously enhance the reusability of existing knowledge across different applications in manufacturing processes. The such-generated foundation for data modeling is essential for enabling higher-layer activities, including process mining methods such as process discovery and prediction, but also for ensuring interoperability of data, information, and knowledge. Key for the successful interfacing between the different models and the higher-layer applications is the Model(s)-in-the-Middle concept [21,49], which bridges semantic gaps between stakeholders and ultimately fosters a more cohesive ecosystem where insights are shared efficiently between organizations, enabling various stakeholders to interpret data consistently.

**Advances to Data Communication and Dataflows** [35]. Third, providing the underlying infrastructure for enabling data models and the WWL, prior work has also focused on improving the fundamental dataflows and data processing capabilities on different levels. For instance, researchers have studied and analyzed dataflows in the IoP [39] and within supply chains [34,40]. Secure industrial collaborations (SICs) and deployable information security are prime examples of such new forms of industrial data sharing [33]. Even though several designs were proposed, including an approach [41] that can collect the confidentiality requirements of the involved stakeholders in a structured manner, additional dimensions, including organizational security as well as legal and economic aspects, must still be considered when fully maturing the concept of SICs [33]. On a lower level, research has studied how data stream processing can be orchestrated in a scalable manner, for example, proposing a distributed, locality-aware data stream processing architecture that provides a framework for flexibly distributing and scaling compute tasks [47]. At the same time, work on in-network computing (INC) has opened up networking devices as new resources for executing compute tasks, e.g., showing that bandwidths can be reduced by leveraging process semantics [52] and response times can be shortened by transforming data [22] or analyzing the process state [23] in the network. These contributions have also helped shape the overall research agenda for INC beyond industrial scenarios [24].

**Main IoP Achievements.** Overall, the pointed out IoP achievements encompass a holistic approach to transforming traditional manufacturing paradigms and production into agile, interconnected ecosystems capable of adapting swiftly to dynamically-changing demands. Specifically, the focus was on mitigating the trade-off between agility, cost efficiency, and quality, and enabling a new level of cross-domain collaboration in production. By combining process mining with simulation and machine learning at both event and aggregate levels, novel solutions allow for the proactive anticipation of production issues, improving operational planning and control [43]. Similarly, the Model(s)-in-the-Middle concept standardizes data-sharing structures across domain silos and has proven to be a critical step in enhancing data exchange mechanisms and facilitating interoperability [21,49], and also enabling large-scale data interoperability that builds upon the FAIR principles [13]. Finally, first communication system and information security realizations [33] as well as network security considerations [11] establish crucial building blocks for the establishment of a WWL that enables communication among numerous, heterogeneous stakeholders across the world.

**Important Areas for Improvement.** Despite these promising and broad advances, three relevant capabilities remain underdeveloped and limit the scalable, trustworthy realization of the WWL: (i) *Standardized Large-Scale Secure Industrial Collaborations:* Prior work has proposed several designs for SIC, but many solutions have been tailored to specific use cases, limiting the widespread adoption of the concept as such; consequently, universally-applicable, interoperable frameworks and standards for modeling, establishing, and operating SICs have yet to be developed and adopted. (ii) *Decentralized Information and Event Dissemination:* While research has described dataflows in the IoP and supply chains, today's established messaging channels lack support for automatically and securely setting up cross-domain channels, thereby constraining the utilization of valuable data and information. (iii) *Ad-hoc Compute Orchestration within the Cloud Continuum:* Locality-aware stream processing and INC provide building blocks for ad-hoc compute orchestration, but policy-aware placement, migration, and monitoring across the edge-network-cloud continuum and across domains are not yet fully explored. By advancing the WWL, these areas for improvement promise to significantly realize the vision of the IoP in practice.

# 4 An Information and Network-Centric Research Agenda for Shaping the Digital Transformation in Production

After establishing the status quo of the digital transformation in production, we now dive into its consecutive research agenda. Specifically, we still focus on information- and network-centric aspects, i.e., the lowest layer of the transformation (cf. Fig. 1)—the interconnected infrastructure—but now turn our attention toward future lines of research. Building upon the first successes related to SICs, we discuss the next steps in maturing and standardizing this technology in Sect. 4.1. In an effort to further evolve these collaborations, we present our vision for a global signaling approach in Sect. 4.2 that eases and maintains information flows in the WWL. We then examine the challenges of holistically co-optimizing computation, its placement across compute nodes, the corresponding data transmissions, and the concurrent selection of algorithms in Sect. 4.3. Finally, in Sect. 4.4, we summarize our information- and network-centric research directions and highlight shared sustainability considerations and goals.

## 4.1 Standardized Large-Scale Secure Industrial Collaborations

The industrial landscape, participating organizations, and their security and privacy requirements are very diverse. As such, different industrial scenarios and information flows usually require individual solutions as we also showed with our work on use case-specific SICs [33]. In particular, we relied on different technical building blocks [39], applying both software- and hardware-based ones, to provide organizations with reliable (security) guarantees. At the same time, research best practices [20,36] encourage the reuse of previous work, and we showed that reuse across domains or use cases may still be possible, potentially with minor adaptations (e.g., exchanging production process parameters or milling tool specifications [37]). These considerations motivated us to develop ConfMod [41], a middleware that simplifies and standardizes a fine-grained modeling of confidentiality requirements.

Based on these observations, the next step of the transformation is to standardize SICs. To this end, one way may be to create a toolbox that captures different (conceptual) approaches for collaborating securely among multiple, potentially even mutually distrusting, organizations in a reliable and interoperable manner. This toolbox can effectively hold approaches for various use cases and settings, showcasing the breadth of SICs. By applying ConfMod, stakeholders can then model their confidentiality requirements in a standardized and reusable representation to identify other use cases with similar constraints and eventually apply (and adapt if needed) a well-known approach for their respective deployment. In the future, ConfMod could (a) further contribute to ensuring that derived deployments comply with competition laws and data protection regulations, and even (b) derive accurate, legally-binding cooperation agreements that additionally safeguard SICs. Both measures are likely to accelerate the real-world use of SICs.

Certainly, this SIC toolbox needs to evolve over time to account for the most recent developments in terms of scale (with a growing WWL, approaches need to scale accordingly [18,48]), technology (large-scale federated approaches are only beginning to emerge [25,56]), and level of automation (while early collaborations focused on comparing information, more sophisticated ones will autonomously control processes [35]). For instance, we expect an evolution from bilateral SICs, whose data is processed manually, to massively-federated, potentially cloud-based SICs that exploit information more broadly—sourcing the entire ecosystem—in an automated manner. Given the lack of dependable reliability guarantees so far, organizations are still concerned with utilizing information from third parties without prior validation [35]. More advanced SICs may alleviate these concerns and thus have the potential of increasing the share of autonomously utilizing third-party-sourced information. We already see first attempts at utilizing and advancing federated machine learning [10,19] and federated process mining [16,44].

Despite the shift toward large-scale SICs, considering the resource footprint of collaborating (securely) is crucial. In particular, the security and communication overhead is immense, such that stakeholders should carefully weigh whether the additional resource usage is beneficial on a global scale. This question thus calls for benchmarking criteria that capture this trade-off timely and accurately.

## 4.2  Global Signaling and Decentralized Information Dissemination

While the envisioned SIC toolbox will ease and secure collaborations, getting notified of and finding relevant information is increasingly difficult due to the exponential growth of global data. Additionally, increasing interdependencies resulting from globalization can easily lead to ripple effects felt around the world, as was evident when the Suez Canal was blocked by a ship in 2021 [31]. To realize a truly global, sustainable, and adaptable WWL, efficient information exchange is crucial to meet the growing demand for meaningful information flows. This demand extends beyond merely establishing the flows but requires sharing signals and information within rapidly changing networks of entities with increasing scale and a high need for reliability and federation. Given these complexities, we argue that current approaches, such as popular message brokers like Kafka or basic data-sharing platforms, are inadequate: they lack semantic interoperability, scale poorly across sovereign domains, and provide limited support for federation. New methods are therefore required to enable a truly global, yet sovereign and adaptable, exploitation of knowledge through massively networked information.

We propose to address the identified need via decentralized information and event dissemination that can globally connect "data silos" and enable new information flows, even across domains. In particular, we envision a meaningful interweaving of information from diverse sources and stakeholders to ensure all entities receive appropriate and up-to-date information at the right time. Central to this concept is an embedded, decentralized signaling system inspired by the human nervous system, offering two complementary modes of operation: push (afferent) and pull (efferent). Unlike conventional message brokers, where producers push opaque messages into a centralized system, our approach enables semantically aware dissemination across sovereign domains. Information providers can push updates into the system, which then dynamically routes them to relevant recipients while accounting for transitive dependencies and potential ripple effects. At the same time, entities are able to pull relevant information as needed, ensuring both adaptability and sovereignty in global-scale information flows.

From a technical perspective, our dissemination framework relies on key conceptual ideas of information-centric networking (ICN) [1], an approach that fundamentally shifts networking to an information-centered view [30], enabling hosts to query specific information from the network without needing to know where exactly the information resides. Similarly, peer-to-peer-based approaches that utilize distributed hash tables, e.g., Chord [46], provide decentralized and scalable structures that help in realizing the system in a sovereign and fault-proof way. Beyond the fundamental signal and information exchange, we also consider additional important aspects, such as security and information protection. For example, we envision making use of attribute-based encryption (ABE) [7,60] to safeguard information in flows and provide confidentiality. ABE allows for selectively granting access without the need to specify individual recipients (per message), instead relying on assigned attributes and carefully-crafted policies. Similarly, we intend to use such concepts to restrict the spread of information and to limit interests as much as possible. Overall, additional consideration of various network and security attacks (and how to securely embed security protocols) is needed to develop a system that protects against these threats.

### 4.3  Ad-hoc Compute Orchestration in Federated Cloud Continuum

The described signaling and information dissemination framework provides the foundation for a vision of dynamic (ad-hoc), large-scale coordination across the cloud–edge continuum. Rather than limiting its role to transporting raw data and notifications in a globally-distributed network of independent organizations, the framework can act as a control fabric that enables both information flows and computational workloads to be steered to the right place at the right time. By integrating computation into global data exchange, such an approach can reduce unnecessary data movement, preserve privacy, and optimize the use of limited compute and network resources distributed across the whole network [50].

In the cloud-edge continuum, workloads may be orchestrated vertically, across heterogeneous edge environments and centralized cloud infrastructures, or federated horizontally, across independent organizations and providers, forming a WWL. Deciding where and when to execute computation depends on multiple criteria: proximity to data sources, availability of compute and network resources, local energy conditions, and compliance with regulatory or organizational data sharing policies [51]. All these conditions can be signaled and acted upon through our event dissemination framework.

Globally-distributed workload placement offers several opportunities for advancing the federated cloud-edge continuum. For instance, computation can be

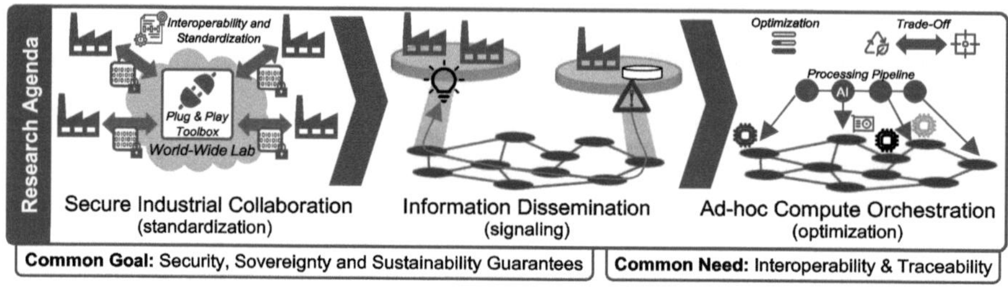



**Fig. 2.** The three research directions directly build on each other. Standardized collaboration methods enable dynamic and interoperable signaling across organizational boundaries, which is, in turn, the foundation for globally distributed processing pipelines.

shifted closer to data sources to uphold sovereignty and security, or redirected to regions with greener energy to minimize environmental impact [32], albeit at the cost of increased network utilization and reduced control. Considering the data-quality and quality-of-service requirements of applications, we can tune different dimensions, including resource utilization, accuracy and timeliness of results, and processing locality. For instance, through time-shifting execution, operators can align workloads with fluctuations in renewable energy availability. As a result, the carbon footprint can be reduced and different forms of efficiency, including energy efficiency and resource utilization, can be jointly optimized, although timeliness is lost [59]. Dynamic adjustments of the forwarding frequency and data resolution can be used to allow for more specific runtime trade-offs. Additionally, by reducing data volumes on the edge close to the data source, e.g., by placing data stream synopses on the data path [42], the utilization of network links toward the cloud can be reduced and, depending on the context, latency can be improved. In this way, ad-hoc compute orchestration helps to dynamically balance performance, sustainability, and sovereignty.

At a global scale, our signaling framework enables independent systems to interoperate in flexible and spontaneous ways. Its capabilities allow participants to advertise resources, data availability, or sustainability attributes, while simultaneously discovering and engaging with partners that meet their own quality, trust, or policy objectives. As conditions evolve, e.g., when energy mixes change or new data sources appear, our framework supports reconfiguring pipelines and migrating workloads in an ad-hoc, on-demand fashion.

This vision positions our event dissemination framework as the backbone of a vertically and horizontally integrated cloud–edge ecosystem. Coupling dynamic data exchange with distributed workload orchestration enables global environments in which compute is actively steered toward globally optimal trade-offs across performance, sustainability, quality, and sovereignty.

## 4.4  Continued Transformation: Converging Global Collaboration, Signaling, and Optimization Through Interoperable Data

In this section, we have highlighted a research agenda for the continued digital transformation in production based on three directions, as we also summarize in Fig. 2. An interoperable toolbox with adaptable methods for different settings can provide the foundation for large-scale, standardized secure industrial collaborations. These methods may be instantiated to move from rigid data exchange between selected organizations within the WWL to dynamic and distributed ad-hoc collaborations. The signaling of our event dissemination framework provides the necessary communication infrastructure to dynamically connect independent organizations at scale through interoperable information flows. Further, by building on cross-domain dataflows of our framework, we can globally distribute and orchestrate workloads in a federated cloud-edge continuum. Here, exchanging signals on available compute resources allows for ad-hoc optimization of global, collaborative processing pipelines.

Across all these efforts, two core themes emerge: First, sovereign infrastructures are a core pillar for globally-collaborative environments, safeguarding sensitive processes and information in computation and sharing, building trust between decentralized entities, and enabling secure and interoperable information flows and processing pipelines. Second, the ability to dynamically adapt setups based on given requirements is paramount for global optimization. A constant trade-off between sustainability, information availability, and sovereignty across independent systems is required to reduce energy consumption. For example, data quality can be reduced through local processing, which also reduces the communication frequency compared to centralized computation in the cloud. Locally computing approximated results or offloading compute to a third party can also optimize resource usage, including carbon emissions.

Through the previously described layers of industrial collaboration, event dissemination, and compute orchestration, we identified key common objectives.

**Common Goal:** *Providing security, sovereignty, and sustainability guarantees through trust, adaptability, and optimization in knowledge-fused distributed business ecosystems to improve production.*

Realizing interoperability and trust in these global ecosystems requires common data formats and traceability of physical and digital resources, as well as any applied transformations [6,14]. The Model(s)-in-the-Middle concept [21,49] can contribute to standardized data-sharing structures and therefore interoperable understanding of data across organizations. Building on top of these data models, data structures like the digital shadows [29] or digital product records [45] can contribute to the vision of a WWL in the future, by capturing traceable data through the entire life cycle of physical and digital products across organizations. In the future, such evolving records could log information on the initial manufacturing process and provenance of raw materials and their sustainability, but also continuously collect usage and reuse information, integrating data sources from various organizations along the supply and usage chain. Through standardized data models, the proposed event dissemination framework could base forwarding decisions on the content of product records and enable federated records by signaling updates and usage information across organizations, providing the foundation for higher-level applications built on a dynamic communication infrastructure and interoperable and traceable data records.

**Common Need:** *Interoperable data exchange formats and provenance information relating to the history and origin of physical and digital goods.*

## 5   Interplay with Higher-Layer Research Directions

By design (cf. Fig. 1), the research directions discussed in Sect. 4, concerning the information- and network-centric perspective, influence higher layers and vice versa. Specifically, we identify four main aspects of interplay.

First, information flows and relationships within the distributed business ecosystem provide diverse input for sophisticated process mining activities. For example, recent advances like OCPM [55,57] allow for conducting more accurate and holistic analyses concerning the design, maintenance, and evaluation of data-to-knowledge pipelines, as required for the IoP. Relatedly, SIC, our event dissemination framework, ad-hoc compute orchestration, and their associated information flows add new deployment areas for state-of-the-art approaches of the model-integrated AI layer, including federated process mining [56].

Second, compared to more traditional (process) optimization goals like productivity, product quality, or cost, the ongoing digital transformation in production adds another dimension—sustainability (cf. Sect. 4.4). Applying this dimension to process mining research could introduce a new optimization goal when looking at processes and event logs [17], thereby shifting the focus away from traditional control-flow perspectives. Made findings may even point out optimization potential for the lower layers as well. Ongoing activities already showcase the amplitude of this dimension in general [17]. Any efforts taken should be equally translatable to the lower layers, including the discussed future research directions.

Third, primarily concerning the data modeling layer, research should look into how (matured) concepts known from process mining can help track where information originates (and exploit this tracking), how it transforms, and where it flows, ensuring end-to-end provenance within the entire business ecosystem. In terms of our discussed research focus, corresponding activities are mainly related to SIC and data ownership questions and their legal implications. By addressing legal concerns and resolving uncertainties related to ownership and liability in distributed data-to-knowledge pipelines, advances in this direction may strengthen the perceived benefits of participating in the envisioned WWL.

Four, general feedback from and demands communicated by higher-layer applications within this distributed ecosystem in terms of deadlines, quality (e.g., resolution or approximation potential), and all sorts of information security and data sovereignty needs, including safeguarding data in transit and in use [28], introduce requirements for the lower layers. Accordingly, all concepts, designs, and implementations need to take them into account as part of their evolution.

To conclude, we observe direct interplay of the different layers that we introduced in Sect. 2 with varying implications for research and operation.

## 6   Conclusion

Based on the research roadmap by Brauner et al. [8], we set out to assess the state of digital transformation in production. In this context, the Internet of Production (IoP) is a prime example of a research initiative with strong ties to computer science research, ranging from improved process-mining applications over the conceptualization of Models-in-the-Middle to the application of novel processing paradigms like in-network computing. Even though our assessment of the status quo revealed significant advances (since 2022) in the ongoing transformation, we still identified three major challenges that result in a call for action on information- and network-centric research. First, we see the benefits of standardizing secure industrial collaborations to eventually deploy it on a large scale within the WWL. Second, we derive the need for a novel signaling mechanism that is able to reliably distribute information and knowledge among distributed stakeholders. Third, we call for an improved cloud continuum concept that optimizes the placement of computations. Thus, to continue the digital transformation in production, these research directions must consider the trade-off between the availability of data and sustainable operation while introducing diverse reliability, security, and sovereignty guarantees into knowledge-fused distributed business ecosystems.

**Acknowledgments.** Funded by the Deutsche Forschungsgemeinschaft (DFG, German Research Foundation) under Germany's Excellence Strategy – EXC-2023 Internet of Sustainable Production – 390621612. We further thank all contributors to the *Internet of Production (IoP)* and *Internet of Sustainable Production (IoSP)* proposals, as well as all researchers who contribute(d) to their research objectives.

## References


1. Ahlgren, B., Dannewitz, C., Imbrenda, C., Kutscher, D., Ohlman, B.: A Survey of Information-Centric Networking. IEEE Commun. Mag. **50**(7) (2012). https://doi.org/10.1109/MCOM.2012.6231276
2. Alman, A., et al.: Tiramisù: a recipe for visual sensemaking of multi-faceted process information. In: Process Mining Workshops (2023). https://doi.org/10.1007/978-3-031-56107-8_2
3. Alman, A.: Tiramisù: making sense of multi-faceted process information through time and space. J. Intell. Inf. Syst. (2024). https://doi.org/10.1007/s10844-024-00875-8
4. Becker, F., et al.: A conceptual model for digital shadows in industry and its application. In: ER (2021). https://doi.org/10.1007/978-3-030-89022-3_22
5. Behery, M., et al.: Actionable artificial intelligence for the future of production. In: Internet of Production: Fundamentals, Methods and Applications. Interdisciplinary Excellence Accelerator Series, Springer (2023). https://doi.org/10.1007/978-3-031-44497-5_4

6. Belova, A., Revenko, A., Gallina, V., Bachlechner, D., Sowe, S.K.: Bringing the digital product passport to life: requirements analysis for a carbon footprint tracking system using knowledge graphs and data spaces. In: ACM SAC (2025). https://doi.org/10.1145/3672608.3707971

7. Bethencourt, J., Sahai, A., Waters, B.: Ciphertext-Policy attribute-based encryption. In: IEEE SP (2007). https://doi.org/10.1109/SP.2007.11

8. Brauner, P., et al.: A computer science perspective on digital transformation in production. ACM Trans. Internet Things **3**(2) (2022). https://doi.org/10.1145/3502265

9. Brzychczy, E., Aleknonytė-Resch, M., Janssen, D., Koschmider, A.: Process mining on sensor data: a review of related works. Knowl. Inf. Syst. **67**(6) (2025). https://doi.org/10.1007/s10115-024-02297-y

10. Choudhary, S.K., Kar, A.K., Dwivedi, Y.K.: How does federated learning impact decision-making in firms: a systematic literature review. Commun. Assoc. Inf. Syst. **54**(1) (2024). https://doi.org/10.17705/1CAIS.05419

11. Dahlmanns, M.: Identifying Security Issues in the Industrial Internet of Things. Ph.D. thesis, RWTH Aachen University (2025)

12. van den Elzen, S., et al.: Towards multi-faceted visual process analytics. Inf. Syst. **133** (2025). https://doi.org/10.1016/j.is.2025.102560

13. Gleim, L., et al.: FactDAG: Formalizing data interoperability in an internet of production. IEEE Internet Things J. **7**(4) (2020). https://doi.org/10.1109/JIOT.2020.2966402

14. Gleim, L., Tirpitz, L., Pennekamp, J., Decker, S.: Expressing FactDAG Provenance with PROV-O. In: MEPDaW (2020)

15. Gorißen, L., et al.: Demonstrating data-to-knowledge pipelines for connecting production sites in the World Wide Lab. arXiv:2412.12231 (2024). https://doi.org/10.48550/arXiv.2412.12231

16. Graves, N., Koren, I., Rafiei, M., van der Aalst, W.M.P.: From identities to quantities: introducing items and decoupling points to object-centric process mining. In: COMINDS (2023). https://doi.org/10.1007/978-3-031-56107-8_35

17. Graves, N., Koren, I., van der Aalst, W.M.P.: ReThink your processes! a review of process mining for sustainability. In: ICT4S (2023). https://doi.org/10.1109/ICT4S58814.2023.00025

18. Hazra, A., Adhikari, M., Amgoth, T., Srirama, S.N.: A comprehensive survey on interoperability for IIoT: taxonomy, standards, and future directions. ACM Comput. Surv. **55**(1) (2021). https://doi.org/10.1145/3485130

19. Hirt, R., Kühl, N., Martin, D., Satzger, G.: Enabling inter-organizational analytics in business networks through meta machine learning. Inf. Technol. Manag. **26**(1) (2025). https://doi.org/10.1007/s10799-023-00399-7

20. Kim, S.Y., Tirpitz, L., Wagels, M., Arnold, B.T., et al.: Dataspaces for collaborative research. In: IEEE BigData (2025)

21. Koren, I., et al.: Navigating the data model divide in smart manufacturing: an empirical investigation for enhanced AI integration. In: EMMSAD (2024). https://doi.org/10.1007/978-3-031-61007-3_21

22. Kunze, I., et al.: Investigating the applicability of in-network computing to industrial scenarios. In: IEEE ICPS (2021). https://doi.org/10.1109/ICPS49255.2021.9468247

23. Kunze, I., Scheurenberg, D., Tirpitz, L., Geisler, S., Wehrle, K.: In-Situ model validation for continuous processes using in-network computing. In: IEEE ICPS (2024). https://doi.org/10.1109/ICPS59941.2024.10639999

24. Kunze, I., Wehrle, K., Trossen, D., Montpetit, M.J., et al.: Use cases for in-network computing. IRTF RFC 9817 (2025). https://doi.org/10.17487/RFC9817
25. Li, T., Sahu, A.K., Talwalkar, A., Smith, V.: Federated learning: challenges, methods, and future directions. IEEE Signal Process. Mag. **37**(3) (2020). https://doi.org/10.1109/MSP.2020.2975749
26. Liebenberg, M., Jarke, M.: Information systems engineering with digitalshadows: concept and case studies. In: CAiSE (2020). https://doi.org/10.1007/978-3-030-49435-3_5
27. Lohmöller, J., Jeon, H., Hentschel, J., Wehrle, K., Pennekamp, J.: Between promise and practice: challenges and misperceptions of applying privacy enhancing technologies in business contexts. In: HICSS (2026)
28. Lohmöller, J., et al.: The unresolved need for dependable guarantees on security, sovereignty, and trust in data ecosystems. Data Knowl. Eng. **151** (2024). https://doi.org/10.1016/j.datak.2024.102301
29. Michael, J., Koren, I., Dimitriadis, I., Fulterer, J., et al.: A digital shadow reference model for worldwide production labs. In: Internet of Production: Fundamentals, Methods and Applications. Interdisciplinary Excellence Accelerator Series, Springer (2023). https://doi.org/10.1007/978-3-031-44497-5_3
30. Morelli, A., Tortonesi, M., Stefanelli, C., Suri, N.: Information-Centric Networking in next-generation communications scenarios. J. Comput. Appl. **80** (2017). https://doi.org/10.1016/j.jnca.2016.12.026
31. Özkanlisoy, Ö., Akkartal, E.: The effect of suez canal blockage on supply chains. Dokuz Eylül Üniversitesi Denizcilik Fakültesi Dergisi **14**(1) (2022). https://doi.org/10.18613/deudfd.933816
32. Patel, Y.S., Townend, P.: A stable matching approach to energy efficient and sustainable serverless scheduling for the green cloud continuum. In: IEEE SOSE (2024). https://doi.org/10.1109/SOSE62363.2024.00010
33. Pennekamp, J.: Secure Collaborations for the Industrial Internet of Things. Ph.D. thesis, RWTH Aachen University (2024). https://doi.org/10.18154/RWTH-2024-03585
34. Pennekamp, J., et al.: PRepChain: a versatile privacy-preserving reputation system for dynamic supply chain environments. Future Gener. Comput. Syst. **175** (2026). https://doi.org/10.1016/j.future.2025.108024
35. Pennekamp, J., et al.: Evolving the digital industrial infrastructure for production: steps taken and the road ahead. in: internet of production: fundamentals, methods and applications. Interdisciplinary Excellence Accelerator Series. Springer (2023). https://doi.org/10.1007/978-3-031-44497-5_2
36. Pennekamp, J., et al.: Collaboration is not Evil: a systematic look at security research for industrial use. In: LASER (2021). https://doi.org/10.14722/laser-acsac.2020.23088
37. Pennekamp, J., Buchholz, E., Lockner, Y., Dahlmanns, M., et al.: Privacy-Preserving Production Process Parameter Exchange. In: ACSAC (2020). https://doi.org/10.1145/3427228.3427248
38. Pennekamp, J., Glebke, R., Henze, M., Meisen, T., et al.: Towards an infrastructure enabling the internet of production. In: IEEE ICPS (2019). https://doi.org/10.1109/ICPHYS.2019.8780276
39. Pennekamp, J., et al.: Dataflow Challenges in an Internet of production: a security and privacy perspective. In: ACM CPS-SPC (2019). https://doi.org/10.1145/3338499.3357357
40. Pennekamp, J., et al.: An interdisciplinary survey on information flows in supply chains. ACM Comput. Surv. **56**(2) (2024). https://doi.org/10.1145/3606693

41. Pennekamp, J., et al.: ConfMod: a simple modeling of confidentiality requirements for inter-organizational data sharing. In: MFI5.0 (2025). https://doi.org/10.1109/NOMS57970.2025.11073722

42. Poepsel-Lemaitre, R., Kiefer, M., von Hein, J., Quiané-Ruiz, J.A., Markl, V.: In the land of data streams where synopses are missing, one framework to bring them all. Proc. VLDB Endow. **14**(10) (2021). https://doi.org/10.14778/3467861.3467871

43. Pourbafrani, M., van Zelst, S.J., van der Aalst, W.M.P.: Supporting automatic system dynamics model generation for simulation in the context of process mining. In: BIS (2020). https://doi.org/10.1007/978-3-030-53337-3_19

44. Rafiei, M., van der Aalst, W.M.P.: An abstraction-based approach for privacy-aware federated process mining. IEEE Access **11** (2023). https://doi.org/10.1109/ACCESS.2023.3263673

45. Schuh, G., et al.: Green re-assembly upgrade factory. In: Proceedings of the 31st Aachener Machine Tool Colloquium (AWK '23) (2023). https://doi.org/10.24406/publica-952

46. Stoica, I., Morris, R., Karger, D., Kaashoek, M.F., Balakrishnan, H.: Chord: a scalable peer-to-peer lookup service for internet applications. ACM SIGCOMM Comput. Commun. Rev. **31**(4) (2001). https://doi.org/10.1145/964723.383071

47. Stolz, T., Koren, I., Tirpitz, L., Geisler, S.: GALOIS: a hybrid and platform-agnostic stream processing architecture. In: BiDEDE (2023). https://doi.org/10.1145/3579142.3594287

48. Sun, D., et al.: A comprehensive survey on collaborative data-access enablers in the IIoT. ACM Comput. Surv. **56**(2) (2023). https://doi.org/10.1145/3612918

49. Unterberg, T.G.L., Koren, I., van der Aalst, W.M.P.: Maximizing reuse and interoperability in industry 4.0 with a minimal data exchange format for machine data. In: Modellierung (2024). https://doi.org/10.18420/modellierung2024_011

50. Tirpitz, L.: Towards FAIR data stream processing ecosystems. In: ACM DEBS (2024). https://doi.org/10.1145/3629104.3672434

51. Tirpitz, L., Gentges, L.: Process model-based access control policies for cross-organizational data sharing. In: QBD (2024)

52. Tirpitz, L., et al.: Reducio: data aggregation and stability detection for industrial processes using in-network computing. In: ACM DEBS (2025). https://doi.org/10.1145/3701717.3730547

53. van der Aalst, W.M.P.: Process cubes: slicing, dicing, rolling up and drilling down event data for process mining. In: AP-BPM (2013). https://doi.org/10.1007/978-3-319-02922-1_1

54. van der Aalst, W.M.P.: Process Mining: Data Science in Action. Springer, 2nd edn. (2016). https://doi.org/10.1007/978-3-662-49851-4

55. van der Aalst, W.M.P.: Object-Centric process mining: dealing with divergence and convergence in event data. In: SEFM (2019). https://doi.org/10.1007/978-3-030-30446-1_1

56. van der Aalst, W.M.P.: Federated process mining: exploiting event data across organizational boundaries. In: IEEE SMDS (2021). https://doi.org/10.1109/SMDS53860.2021.00011

57. van der Aalst, W.M.P.: Object-Centric process mining: unraveling the fabric of real processes. Mathematics **11**(12) (2023). https://doi.org/10.3390/math11122691

58. van der Aalst, W.M.P., Jarke, M., Koren, I., Quix, C.: Digital shadows: infrastructuring the internet of production. In: Internet of Production: Fundamentals, Methods and Applications. Interdisciplinary Excellence Accelerator Series, Springer (2023). https://doi.org/10.1007/978-3-031-44497-5_25

59. Wiesner, P., Behnke, I., Scheinert, D., Gontarska, K., Thamsen, L.: Let's Wait awhile: how temporal workload shifting can reduce carbon emissions in the cloud. In: Middleware (2021). https://doi.org/10.1145/3464298.3493399
60. Zhang, Y., et al.: Attribute-based encryption for cloud computing access control: a survey. ACM Comput. Surv. **53**(4) (2021). https://doi.org/10.1145/3398036

# Process Mining for Heavy Industries: Lessons Learned from Mining Use Cases

Edyta Brzychczy$^{(\boxtimes)}$ 

AGH University of Krakow, Mickiewicza Av. 30, 30-059 Krakow, Poland
`brzych3@agh.edu.pl`

**Abstract.** Process Mining (PM) has shown great potential in business domains; however, its application in heavy industries remains limited. The main reasons are the dominance of raw sensor data, which requires preprocessing and abstraction, and the variability of industrial process execution. Based on mining cases studied in various research teams, this paper presents lessons that illustrate both the challenges and opportunities of applying PM in industrial contexts. We identified two key challenges: (1) constructing suitable event logs from heterogeneous sensor data, supported by domain knowledge, and (2) selecting modeling approaches that cope with process complexity and variability while serving the analytical objective. Our research focused on event log creation through case identification, event abstraction, and labeling techniques, including recent advances in utilizing Large Language Models (LLMs) for event abstraction. We also compared imperative, declarative, and hybrid modeling paradigms, highlighting their different capacities to represent variability of real-life processes. Based on mining experiences, the paper presents lessons transferable to other heavy industry sectors, demonstrating the potential of PM to analyze complex processes and support data-driven decision-making.

**Keywords:** Process mining · Heavy industry · Sensor data · Event abstraction · Case identification · Process modeling

## 1 Introduction

Process Mining (PM) has become a recognized analytics in Business Process Management (BPM), offering effective techniques for discovering, analyzing, and monitoring processes on the basis of event data [1]. Its usefulness has been demonstrated in various domains, such as finance, healthcare, logistics, and administrative processes [2]. In these areas, data is typically generated by IT systems in the form of structured event logs, which include three basic attributes: a case identifier (case ID), an activity name, and a timestamp. The availability of such logs has enabled the widespread adoption of PM for business process modeling and analysis.

In the context of heavy industries, however, the application of process mining is still in its early stages. Domains such as mining, steel production, or chemical


J. Mendling et al. (Eds.): Wil van der Aalst Festschrift, LNCS 16480, pp. 616–630, 2026.
https://doi.org/10.1007/978-3-032-17618-9_40

industries generate vast amounts of operational data, but this data is predominantly collected in the form of low-level sensor readings [4]. These signals, often continuous or binary in nature, are stored in monitoring systems and describe the physical states of equipment rather than abstract process activities [5,19,20]. In many cases, this data often lacks two essential components of an event log: the case ID and the activity label. Without these, raw sensor data cannot be directly applied in process mining [15].

This gap between industrial low-level data reality and process analytics requirements is one of the main challenges for BPM based on Internet of Things (IoT) technologies [3,16–18].

This challenge is particularly evident in underground mining. First of all, process data are captured as low-level sensor readings by no process-aware monitoring systems (e.g., *Supervisory Control And Data Acquisition* - SCADA), and no explicit case identifiers are provided. When the process exhibits a clearly cyclic nature, case identification can be derived from this assumption by detecting recurring dependencies in the data. However, for more acyclic processes, identifying suitable case IDs becomes significantly more difficult.

The identification of activities from sensor data is also demanding, closely linked to the level of data granularity [22]. Low-level signals reflect basic machine states or physical measurements, making direct mapping to high-level activities non-trivial. If the granularity is too fine, activities become fragmented and difficult to interpret; if too coarse, specific process variations may be lost.

Another challenge concerns the variability of industrial process execution. For example, mining processes are typically cyclical and, at least in theory, can be described by well-defined operational stages. In practice, however, their execution is subject to considerable variation, resulting from geological conditions, machine performance, and organizational factors [8]. Consequently, the theoretical process model frequently fails to capture the complexity and diversity of real execution traces [11]. This difference has a strong impact on the choice of modeling paradigm, as heavy industrial processes rarely follow the same workflow, and the selected approach must balance precision with flexibility to capture both regular patterns and acceptable deviations in execution.

Therefore, for heavy industries, there are two main challenges of applying process mining:

1. Construction of suitable event logs from heterogeneous sensor data, which requires addressing issues related to data quality, and the absence of explicit case identifiers or activity labels.
2. Selection of a modeling approach suitable for the purpose of analysis, able to cope with the complexity and variability of real process execution. The chosen modeling paradigm should balance precision and generalization in order to capture both regular patterns and acceptable deviations in execution.

An additional but equally important issue for applying PM in heavy industry is access to domain knowledge, which is essential for process understanding and for interpreting analysis results. Domain experts are often not easily available, as their time is primarily devoted to operational tasks rather than analytical activities. Even when experts are accessible, their knowledge may be fragmented or focused on narrow aspects of the process, which limits its direct applicability to broader PM studies. In some cases, experts may also be reluctant to share knowledge, either due to organizational constraints or concerns about the use of their insights. These limitations highlight the need for systematic approaches to capturing, formalizing, and reusing domain knowledge in conjunction with data-driven analysis, as well as for developing tools that support collaboration between experts and analysts.

The contribution of this paper is to present lessons learned from mining use cases as relevant insights for the application of process mining in heavy industries in the presented contexts. By analyzing studies on longwall shearer operation, roof bolter, load-haul-dump (LHD) machine, we highlight both practical experiences and methodological implications.

The structure of this paper is as follows. Section 2 describes the specific characteristics of heavy industry processes, using the mining example. Section 3 presents case studies from the mining industry in relation to defined challenges. Section 4 presents the lessons learned and discusses open challenges and future directions. Section 5 concludes with recommendations for transferring the insights from mining to other heavy industry domains.

## 2   Mining Processes as Industrial Reality

One of the main features of mining processes, as a typical heavy industry example, is high variability and uncertainty. Unlike administrative or service-oriented processes, which typically follow structured workflows supported by information systems, mining processes take place in dynamic environments shaped by physical, mechanical, and environmental factors. In underground mining, geological and mining conditions could vary along the excavation, directly affecting the behavior of machines such as the longwall shearer [21]. As a result, process execution often differs from theoretical models that assume a repetitive, cyclical structure of operations (e.g., cutting at the beginning of the longwall, stoppage, return to the drive, stoppage, cutting in the middle and at the end of the longwall, stoppage, moving). Variations stem from rock hardness, natural hazards, equipment failures, or operational decisions made by machine operators due to the occurring conditions. Consequently, very often no two cycles are identical, and the number of process variants may be equal to the total number of cases - a situation rarely encountered in business domains [8]. This raises important questions about how to interpret deviations and what constitutes *normal* versus *abnormal* behavior.

The data reality in heavy industries further complicates matters. Monitoring systems used in underground mining, which could be useful for process analysis, are dominated by low-level sensor data - continuous time series (e.g., currents, temperatures, pressures, speeds) and binary signals (e.g., switches, on/off states). Such data are often incomplete due to technical problems in data transfer from the machinery to the surface or sensor malfunctions. Thus, significant preprocessing is required: data cleaning, imputation of missing values, discretization of continuous variables, and often dimensionality reduction (e.g., based on correlation analysis or Principal Component Analysis - PCA) [13]. Only after these steps sensor data can be transformed into event logs suitable for PM.

Another specificity of mining processes is their spatial and contextual nature. For example, the performance of a shearer differs depending on whether it operates at the beginning, middle, or at the end of the excavation, and whether it moves in the *along* or *return* direction. Some activities are considered normal only in specific spatial contexts; the same action in another part of the excavation could be classified as a deviation. Contextual attributes such as location, speed, or load play a decisive role in interpreting the execution of industrial processes [12].

Finally, analysis of the industrial processes, especially in mining, demands close collaboration with domain experts. Sensor data alone rarely have sufficient meaning to identify activities or interpret process deviations, especially regarding the definition of *normal* and *abnormal* behavior in the spatial context. Expert knowledge is often required for case ID detection and labeling activities during event abstraction. Even with advances in machine learning and LLM-supported labeling, expert validation remains essential.

Described characteristics make mining a particularly demanding but also highly instructive domain for process mining research. In the following section, we present these aspects and potential solutions through examples from different mining processes, including the longwall shearer operation, anchoring process, and load–haul–dump (LHD) process.

## 3  Case Studies from Mining Industry

Presented studies conducted on various mining use cases illustrate how raw sensor data can be transformed into event logs, how different modeling paradigms perform in the industrial process contexts, and how advanced AI methods such as Large Language Models (LLMs) may assist in event abstraction for heavy industry purposes.

### 3.1  Event Log Creation PM4LMP Method and Its Extensions

A basic prerequisite for process mining is the availability of an event log. In underground mining, however, monitoring systems do not produce logs in the traditional sense. Instead, they record time-stamped sensor readings. To transform this raw data into an event log, two basic elements must be reconstructed: the case identifier (case ID) and the activity label. For this purpose, the PM4LMP (Process Mining for Longwall Mining Process) method was designed by structuring the analytical workflow into three phases: data preprocessing, case ID detection, and activity identification (event abstraction).

The PM4LMP method was applied to the longwall shearer operation process [14]. The main challenge related to this process is that the case ID, besides the standard requirement for PM, has crucial meaning for event abstraction. Without a case ID, e.g., we will not be able to label low-level sensor data with rules describing technological stages. This situation is opposite to the most typical case, i.e., when we use a set of events to correlate with a known case ID [10].

In the longwall mining process context, the natural case ID is the cycle of the shearer, which reflects one complete traversal of the machine across the longwall (Fig. 1). Cycles are not explicitly marked in the data, but they can be derived from the shearer location variable. The main challenge in this task is that real cycles have various executions (Fig. 2). Early attempts to use local minima and maxima of the location variable proved insufficient due to local variability and noise. Therefore, a heuristic method was developed, dividing the longwall face into zones (beginning, middle, end) and identifying cycle boundaries based on position thresholds. This approach enables the detection of cycle start and end points; however, its accuracy depends heavily on data quality [12]. This fact motivated us to further research. In subsequent work on case ID detection, we addressed this limitation by developing a more robust approach that uses time-series segmentation [10], which significantly improved case ID detection for shearer data, raising accuracy from approximately 70% with the heuristic method to over 90%.

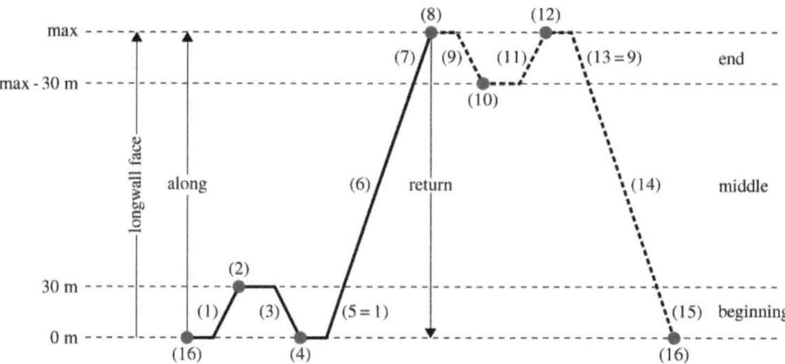


**Fig. 1.** Theoretical cycle of the longwall shearer. Numbers denote prescribed activities. Source: [21]

In the case of activity identification (event abstraction), the PM4LMP transformed raw sensor readings into events associated with meaningful process stages with two complementary approaches:

1. Supervised, rule-based labeling, grounded in expert knowledge of the theoretical cycle. Rules used thresholds and logical conditions on selected variables such as drum currents, movement direction, and speed,
2. Unsupervised, clustering-based labeling, which groups sensor states into clusters using distance measures suitable for mixed data (e.g., Gower distance) and hierarchical methods with Ward's linkage. The clusters are subsequently interpreted and labeled by experts.

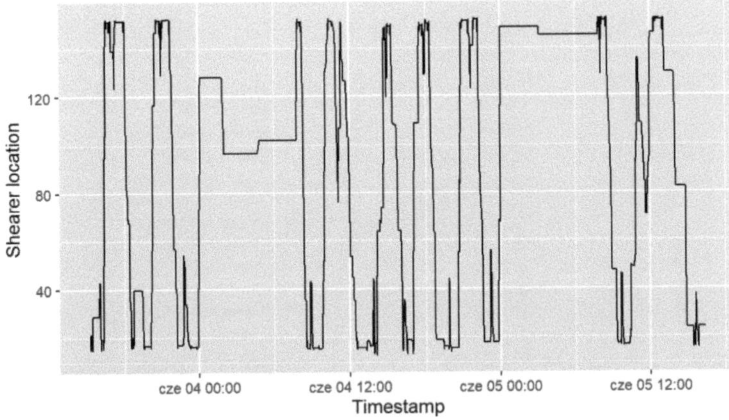

**Fig. 2.** Real cycles in longwall shearer dataset

This dual approach led to the creation of parallel event logs - one grounded in expert knowledge, the other in clustering results. The combination proved valuable for extensive process analysis: while rule-based labeling provided interpretability and adherence to the prescribed theoretical process model, clustering revealed previously undefined by experts states, e.g., "Moving Middle Overloading", "Moving Middle Cooling down", "Stoppage Quick Stop" which are potentially interesting from a process analysis and machine maintenance points of view.

An example of an identified cycle with the developed heuristic and activities abstracted with expert rules is presented in Fig. 3.

The outcome of the PM4LMP method is a structured event log containing case IDs, activity names, and timestamps, which satisfies the formal requirements of process mining. Importantly, log creation is not a one-time step but an iterative process: preprocessing decisions, choice of abstraction methods, and expert validation all strongly influence the final event log and, by extension, the quality of discovered models and conformance results.

### 3.2 Mining Process Modeling

With event logs available, the next step is to apply process modeling techniques. The choice of a formal modeling paradigm is a critical step in process mining for heavy industries, as it determines how variability in execution is represented and interpreted. The longwall shearer operation, a highly cyclical process with recurring cutting and return phases, provides an instructive example.

First of all, on the basis of an expert-labeled event log, we created a Petri net to represent the cyclical nature of the shearer operation and to perform conformance checking. Conducted experiments showed that due to the high variability of execution, discovered models often were too complex and unreadable, with low fitness when compared against a theoretical process model. Conformance

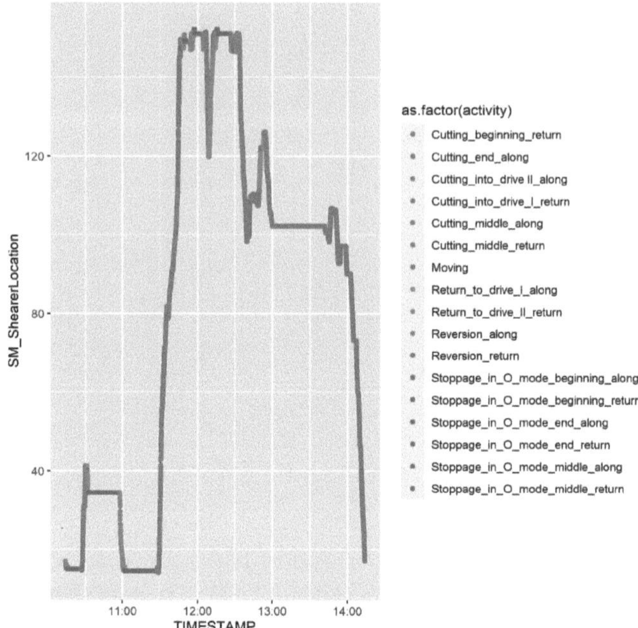


**Fig. 3.** Identified cycle with labeled activities

checking revealed numerous deviations (Fig. 4), many of which reflected not true anomalies but natural adaptations to geological or organizational conditions.

Therefore, as the second approach to modeling, we chose declarative models (Declare), which capture behavior through constraints rather than explicit paths [11]. This proved advantageous in tolerating natural variability and unforeseen sequences. Nevertheless, experiments revealed a counterintuitive finding: in certain cases, Declare models reported more deviations than Petri nets, as a single irregular trace could simultaneously breach multiple constraints.

To overcome these limitations, we introduced a hybrid model generated by Fusion Miner [8]. This model combined procedural fragments with declarative constraints. In the longwall shearer use case, the hybrid model (HybM) consistently reduced the number of deviations compared to purely imperative or declarative models (e.g., HybM with 9,039 violations vs. Declare with 14,420 and Petri net with 17,610 on the same log). A reduced number of violations must be interpreted with caution, since hybrid models may relax certain constraints and make deviations less apparent. Expert validation is therefore essential to verify whether better conformance reflects real operational behavior or increased model tolerance. Nevertheless, the ability of hybrid models to balance rigidity and flexibility makes them a promising approach for industrial processes.

Alongside these formal paradigms, simpler approaches such as Directly-Follows Graphs (DFGs) can also be highly valuable. As shown in the other mining example - anchoring process with roof bolter machine [6], DFGs provide

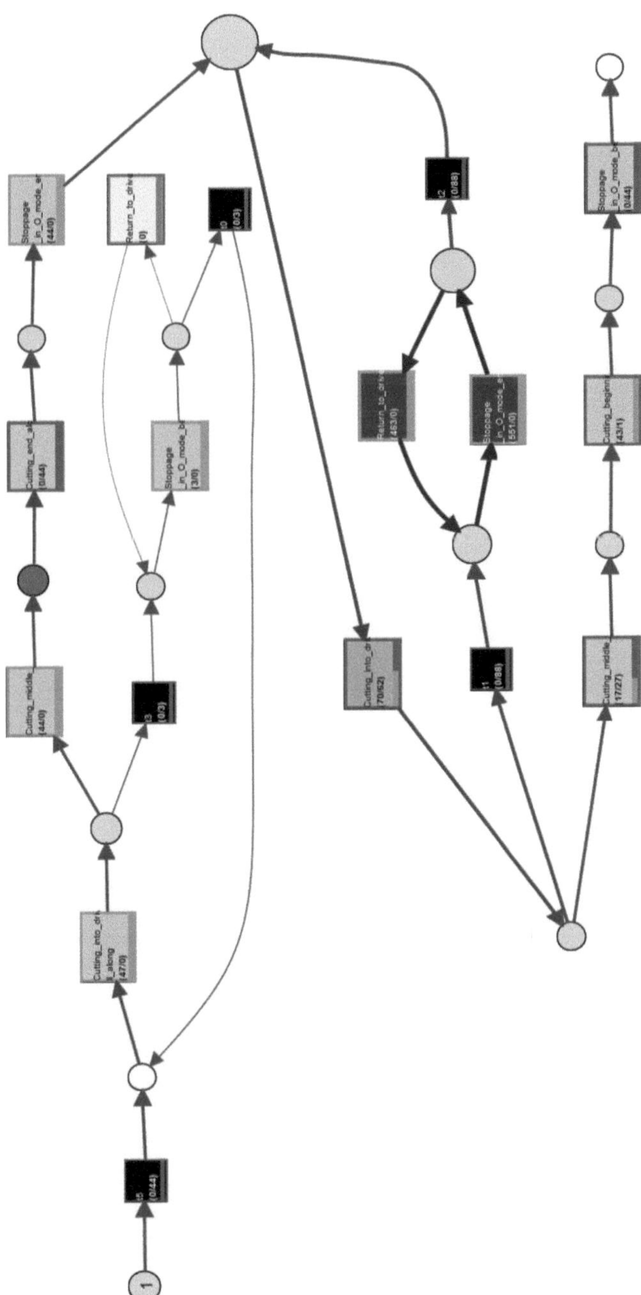

**Fig. 4.** Conformance checking of abstracted event log vs ideal process model

an easily interpretable overview of operational states and their dependencies. By quantifying the frequency and duration of activities, it was possible to detect bottlenecks where the roof bolter spent excessive time in non-productive states, i.e. 3 h in the transitional delay state (Fig. 5). By comparing the DFGs across shifts, differences in operator practices were also observed, highlighting the role of human factors. DFGs can serve as a first layer of process analysis in industrial contexts, allowing practitioners to quickly identify inefficiencies and irregularities without the complexity of formal modeling.

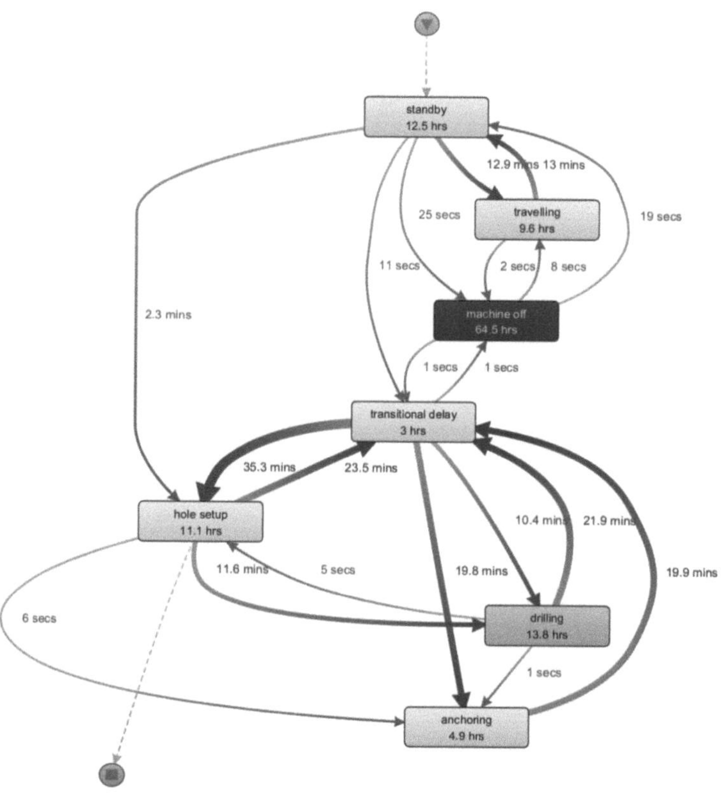


**Fig. 5.** DFG model of roof bolter operation (total duration view)

The choice of modeling paradigm for industrial processes should be guided by the analytical goal, as different approaches emphasize different aspects of process behavior (more strict and more relaxed parts of process execution). However, even simple representations such as Directly-Follows Graphs can reveal valuable insights into machine utilization and irregularities, making them a useful complement to more advanced modeling techniques.

## 3.3   New Directions in Event Abstraction

The dependence on domain experts in event abstraction remains one of the main challenges to wider adoption of process mining in heavy industries. Expert knowledge is required for process understanding, interpreting sensor data, and defining what constitutes normal and abnormal behavior. However, sometimes expert rules are prone to inconsistencies and may fail to capture atypical but operationally meaningful states. Also, manual labeling is time-consuming and difficult to scale when dealing with a large volume of heterogeneous data. To address this bottleneck, AI-based approaches have been investigated to support or partially automate the abstraction task. Among them, LLMs have recently attracted attention due to their ability to generate textual content based on analytical engines (using, e.g., Python libraries).

The first attempt to use LLM for raw sensor data labeling was presented in [9]. The dataset contained raw operational variables from the longwall shearer monitoring system, such as haulage currents (HL, HR), drum currents (OL, OR), movement direction, speed, and location, which together characterize the machine's operational phases. Instead of relying on expert rules or clustering techniques, we applied LLM in an unsupervised labeling setting. Using structured prompts with variable descriptions and sample sensor records, the LLM generated Python labeling functions that mapped raw sensor readings into four process phases: Stoppage, Move, Cutting, and Idle. We repeated the experiment 31 times and evaluated the results against expert-labeled ground truth. The obtained functions achieved promising performance, with some iterations reaching high accuracy, precision, recall, and Cohen's Kappa values (above 0.85 in well-performing runs), while maintaining interpretability due to their simple rule-based form. Moreover, the LLM-generated rules were often more concise and understandable than those derived from decision tree classifiers, making validation by domain experts easier. At the same time, variability in results across runs highlighted the sensitivity of prompt-based approaches, pointing to the need for expert-in-the-loop validation and careful selection of generated rules. These experiments confirmed that LLMs can serve as a support assistant in event abstraction.

The obtained results motivated us to further work on the use of LLMs in event log creation based on an unsupervised approach (clustering). Traditionally, clustering requires extensive expert involvement to interpret and name discovered clusters. This task is time-consuming and cognitively demanding, especially in domains with many variables and atypical states. For this purpose, we created the IoT Miner framework [7]. IoT Miner uses a four-stage pipeline consisting of preprocessing, clustering, LLM-based labeling, and event log construction (Fig. 6).

After cleaning and normalizing the raw data, unsupervised clustering methods (K-means, DBSCAN) are applied to detect recurring operational states. According to clustering quality measures, the optimal clustering results are selected and passed to the labeling phase. For each cluster, statistical profiles (min, max, quartiles, standard deviation) are automatically generated and

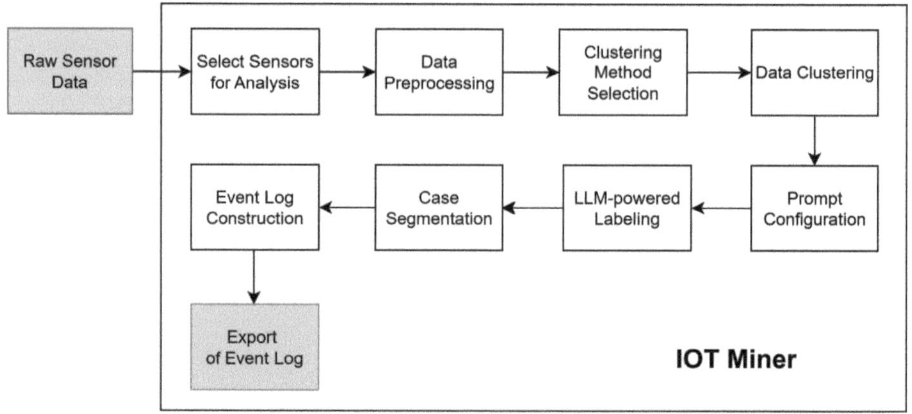



**Fig. 6.** IoT Miner pipeline. Based on [7]

provided to an LLM via structured prompts enriched with domain context. We test IoT Miner on load–haul–dump process with a dataset consisting of raw sensor data collected from the LHD's machine Controller Area Network (CAN) bus, including variables such as engine speed, torque, fuel rate, oil pressure, and accelerator pedal position. The LLM proposed activity labels such as Idling, Loading, Hauling, and Dumping, which aligned closely with expert-defined operational phases. To evaluate the quality of labeling, we introduced the Similarity-Weighted Accuracy (SWA) metric, which accounts for both correctness and semantic proximity of labels. Results showed that enriched prompts improved label accuracy and consistency. This experiment confirmed that integrating LLMs with clustering and preprocessing provides a scalable and interpretable method for abstracting industrial sensor data into event logs.

The presented use cases, from event log creation with PM4LMP, through the evaluation of modeling approaches for mining processes, to new advancements in event abstraction, demonstrate both the feasibility and the complexity of applying process mining in mining contexts, and provide lessons discussed in the next section.

## 4   Lessons Learned and Future Directions

The analysis of mining use cases confirms that applying process mining in heavy industries is both feasible and valuable, but it requires substantial adaptation compared to business domains. Several lessons can be distilled from the presented case studies, each pointing to open research directions and practical improvements:

1. *Unlike in business IT systems, where case identifiers and activity labels are available in event logs, in mining they must be engineered from low-level sensor streams.* The PM4LMP method demonstrated that constructing event

logs requires a multi-stage pipeline including preprocessing, case ID detection, and event abstraction. This lesson underlines that event log creation is not a trivial preparatory step, but a central analytical task in industrial PM. Future research should focus on generalizing such frameworks beyond mining and supporting their deployment across different industrial contexts.

2. *Data quality remains a bottleneck because noisy, incomplete, and heterogeneous signals (continuous and binary) dominate mining logs.* Techniques such as imputation, normalization, and dimensionality reduction are indispensable to ensure that the resulting logs are usable. Still, parameterization of preprocessing steps often requires expert input, limiting scalability. Further developments should include automated quality assessment and adaptive preprocessing methods that can adjust to varying sensor conditions. One of the attempts we made in IoT Miner.

3. *Event abstraction is decisive and transforming raw sensor data into meaningful activities is the key to revealing the value of process mining for industry.* The case studies confirmed that combining expert rules with unsupervised clustering yields complementary event logs that extend the scope of process analysis. Rule-based logs remain closely aligned with the theoretical process model and thus can be directly applied to discovery and conformance checking. In contrast, logs obtained from clustering do not have a prescribed reference model for conformance checking analysis; instead, they serve as exploratory resources that reveal operational states and behavioral patterns not present in expert models. The process models derived from such logs provide an alternative perspective for the identification of atypical but meaningful behaviors. In this way, clustering-based abstraction does not replace expert-driven logs but complements them, enriching process analysis with insights from different points of view.

4. *Modeling paradigms should follow the process variability.* The longwall shearer example confirmed that imperative Petri nets over-penalize natural deviations, while declarative models may overestimate violations. Hybrid models reduced deviations and offered a more realistic balance, but at the cost of interpretability, requiring careful validation by experts. Simpler paradigms, such as DFGs applied to the roof bolter process, also proved useful for quick insights and communication with practitioners. Future research should focus on hybrid modeling with guardrails, ensuring that flexibility does not obscure critical operational constraints, and integrating simpler models for exploratory analysis.

5. *Deviations are not always errors.* Many deviations in heavy processes reflect legitimate adaptations to environmental or organizational conditions rather than anomalies. Treating all deviations as violations risks misinterpretation. Reference models should explicitly account for variability, and conformance analysis must be contextualized with domain knowledge. This lesson directly motivates the need for human-centered PM in heavy industries.

6. *Human expertise is crucial, but can be supported by AI.* Experts remain central in process understanding, event abstraction, and interpreting deviations. Also, knowledge acquisition or manual abstraction is slow and difficult to

scale. AI-based methods, such as IoT Miner with its combination of clustering and LLM-based labeling, show how automation can support event abstraction. Future directions should explore AI as an assistant rather than a human replacement, offering candidate labels and explanations that experts can refine.

Presented studies were conducted retrospectively, but industrial processes are safety-critical and time-sensitive, thus transitioning from offline analysis to real-time or quasi-online monitoring is another future direction of research. This will require scalable streaming abstractions, incremental conformance checking, and integration with predictive maintenance dashboards.

The success of PM in heavy industries depends on producing results that are interpretable for engineers, operators, and decision-makers. Transparent connections between raw data, abstracted activities, and process models are of high importance to ensure trust and wider adoption of PM in heavy industrial domains.

## 5    Conclusions

This paper presented a summary of the research work on process mining in heavy industries, with mining processes serving as the use cases source. Firstly, the paper outlined the specificity of industrial processes with their complexity, variability, and data heterogeneity. Further case studies demonstrated concrete approaches: event log construction with the PM4LMP method, the use of Directly-Follows Graphs for roof bolter analysis, the comparison of modeling paradigms for the longwall shearer, and the application of AI-supported labeling with IoT Miner for the load–haul–dump process.

Lessons learned from the presented use cases include the need to engineer event logs from heterogeneous sensor data, handling existing issues of data quality, designing abstraction pipelines that balance expert input with automation, and selecting modeling paradigms that reflect process variability without disregarding operational meaning. These insights point to promising future directions: developing more robust case identification methods, advancing AI-supported abstraction with LLMs, introducing wider usage of hybrid models, and moving towards real-time analysis.

Although this work has focused on mining, the challenges and solutions identified are not unique to this sector. Other heavy industries such as construction engineering, steel production, and chemicals also rely on sensor-rich environments characterized by variability, uncertainty, and contextual dependencies. The experiences gained in mining provide useful lessons for event log creation, model selection, and AI-assisted event abstraction in these domains. The presented use cases and methods proposed in this work may serve as a motivation for developing systematic frameworks for IoT-based PM and for advancing its adoption in other heavy industry domains.

**Acknowledgments.** I would like to thank Prof. Wil van der Aalst for his work, which inspired me to expand analytics of real mining processes with process mining based on low-level data and for the opportunity to collaborate in this area.

# References


1. van der Aalst, W.M.P.: Process Mining - Data Science in Action. 2nd edn. Springer (2016). https://doi.org/10.1007/978-3-662-49851-4
2. Accorsi, R., Lebherz, J.: A practitioner's view on process mining adoption, event log engineering and data challenges, pp. 212–240. Springer International Publishing, Cham (2022). https://doi.org/10.1007/978-3-031-08848-3_7
3. Bertrand, Y., De Weerdt, J., Serral, E.: A bridging model for process mining and IoT. In: Munoz-Gama, J., Lu, X. (eds.) Process Mining Workshops, pp. 98–110. Springer International Publishing, Cham (2022)
4. Bertrand, Y.: Approaches for IoT-enhanced predictive process monitoring. Process Sci. **2**(1), 7 (2025). https://doi.org/10.1007/s44311-025-00011-x
5. Brock, J., Rempe, N., von Enzberg, S., Kühn, A., Dumitrescu, R.: A framework for the domain-driven utilization of manufacturing sensor data in process mining: an action design approach. ESSN: 2701-6277, pp. 771–781 (2023). https://doi.org/10.1016/j.engappai.2023.106748
6. Brzychczy, E., Gackowiec, P., Liebetrau, M.: Data analytic approaches for mining process improvement—machinery utilization use case. Resources **9**(2) (2020). https://doi.org/10.3390/resources9020017
7. Brzychczy, E., Jessen, U., Kluza, K., Sriram, S., Nettelnstroth, M.V.: IoT miner: Intelligent extraction of event logs from sensor data for process mining (2025). https://arxiv.org/abs/2509.05769
8. Brzychczy, E., Kluza, K., Gdowska, K.: Exploring hybrid modelling of industrial process - mining use case. In: De Weerdt, J., Pufahl, L. (eds.) Business Process Management Workshops, pp. 302–313. Springer Nature Switzerland, Cham (2024)
9. Brzychczy, E., Kluza, K., Szała, L.: Enhancement of low-level event abstraction with large language models (LLMs). In: Gdowska, K., Gómez-López, M.T., Rehse, J.R. (eds.) Business Process Management Workshops, pp. 209–220. Springer Nature Switzerland, Cham (2025)
10. Brzychczy, E., Pełech-Pilichowski, T., Dworakowski, Z.: Case id detection based on time series data – the mining use case (2024). https://arxiv.org/abs/2410.23846
11. Brzychczy, E., Szpyrka, M., Korski, J., Nalepa, G.J.: Imperative vs. declarative modeling of industrial process. the case study of the longwall shearer operation. IEEE Access **11**, 54495–54508 (2023). https://doi.org/10.1109/ACCESS.2023.3281304
12. Brzychczy, E., Trzcionkowska, A.: Creation of an event log from a low-level machinery monitoring system for process mining purposes. In: Yin, H., Camacho, D., Novais, P., Tallón-Ballesteros, A.J. (eds.) Intelligent Data Engineering and Automated Learning - IDEAL 2018 - 19th International Conference, Madrid, Spain, November 21–23, 2018, Proceedings, Part II. Lecture Notes in Computer Science, vol. 11315, pp. 54–63. Springer (2018). https://doi.org/10.1007/978-3-030-03496-2_7
13. Brzychczy, E., Trzcionkowska, A.: Process-oriented approach for analysis of sensor data from longwall monitoring system. In: Burduk, A., Chlebus, E., Nowakowski, T., Tubis, A. (eds.) Intelligent Systems in Production Engineering and Maintenance, pp. 611–621. Springer International Publishing, Cham (2019)

14. Brzychczy, E., Żuber, A., Aalst, W.v.d.: Process mining of mining processes: analyzing longwall coal excavation using event data. IEEE Trans. Syst. Man Cybern. Syst. **54**(5), 2723–2734 (2024). https://doi.org/10.1109/TSMC.2023.3348496

15. De Weerdt, J., Wynn, M.T.: Foundations of process event data. In: Process Mining Handbook, pp. 193–211. Springer International Publishing Cham (2022)

16. Janiesch, C., et al.: The internet of things meets business process management: a manifesto. IEEE Syst. Man Cybern. Mag. **6**(4), 34–44 (2020). https://doi.org/10.1109/MSMC.2020.3003135

17. Koschmider, A., et al.: Process mining for unstructured data: challenges and research directions. arXiv preprint arXiv:2401.13677 (2023)

18. Mangler, J., et al.: From internet of things data to business processes: challenges and a framework (2024)

19. Mayr, M., Luftensteiner, S., Chasparis, G.C.: Abstracting process mining event logs from process-state data to monitor control-flow of industrial manufacturing processes. In: Longo, F., Affenzeller, M., Padovano, A. (eds.) Proceedings of the 3rd International Conference on Industry 4.0 and Smart Manufacturing (ISM 2022). Procedia Computer Science, vol. 200, pp. 1442–1450. Elsevier (2021). https://doi.org/10.1016/j.procs.2022.01.345

20. Seiger, R., Franceschetti, M., Weber, B.: An interactive method for detection of process activity executions from IoT data. Future Internet **15**(2) (2023). https://doi.org/10.3390/fi15020077, https://www.mdpi.com/1999-5903/15/2/77

21. Szpyrka, M., Brzychczy, E., Napieraj, A., Korski, J., Nalepa, G.: Conformance checking of a longwall shearer operation based on low-level events. Energies **13**(24) (2020). https://doi.org/10.3390/en13246630

22. van Zelst, S.J., Mannhardt, F., de Leoni, M., Koschmider, A.: Event abstraction in process mining: literature review and taxonomy. Granular Comput. **6**(3), 719–736 (2020). https://doi.org/10.1007/s41066-020-00226-2

# Diagnosing LLM Hallucinations in Process Mining Tasks: a Taxonomy and a Benchmark

Alessandro Berti[1(✉)] and Humam Kourani[1,2]

[1] RWTH Aachen University, Ahornstraße 55, 52074 Aachen, Germany
a.berti@pads.rwth-aachen.de
[2] Fraunhofer Institute for Applied Information Technology FIT, Schloss Birlinghoven, 53757 Sankt Augustin, Germany
humam.kourani@fit.fraunhofer.de

**Abstract.** Large language models (LLMs) are increasingly used to support process mining tasks, yet their answers may contain *hallucinations*, content that is unfaithful to the prompt, unsupported by evidence, or invalid with respect to PM formalisms. The PM-LLM-Benchmark evaluates model answers with an expert LLM-as-a-judge that assigns a numeric score and a short explanation. This paper introduces a complementary *hallucination audit* that reads the judge's explanation and converts it into structured annotations about the answering model. We map issues mentioned by the judge onto a PM-tailored taxonomy (four families, twelve sub-types) with severities, aggregate them per model and task family, and analyze their relationships with benchmark performance and model characteristics. Across models, higher PM-LLM-Benchmark scores align with fewer hallucinations; reasoning-oriented and newer models show more favorable profiles; and hallucination families tend to co-occur rather than trade off. We discuss safeguards (reinforce context fidelity, disciplined reasoning, and validate structured outputs), that directly target the dominant failure modes.

**Keywords:** Process Mining · Large Language Models · Hallucination Detection · Benchmarking

## 1 Introduction

Process mining significantly benefits from Large Language Models (LLMs) capable of interpreting, explaining, and synthesizing domain-specific artifacts such as event logs, process models, and diagrams [6]. To systematically assess these capabilities, the PM-LLM-Benchmark provides a structured evaluation framework where candidate models respond to process mining prompts [5]. Each response is then evaluated by an expert judge, who assigns a numerical score along with a brief explanatory rationale. While these scores effectively summarize the overall performance of the models, practitioners additionally require detailed insights

© The Author(s), under exclusive license to Springer Nature Switzerland AG 2026
J. Mendling et al. (Eds.): Wil van der Aalst Festschrift, LNCS 16480, pp. 631–647, 2026.
https://doi.org/10.1007/978-3-032-17618-9_41

into the specific ways models fail [7]. Understanding these failure modes is crucial for implementing effective safeguards and making informed decisions about model selection and deployment.

To bridge this gap, we introduce a structured *hallucination audit* grounded in the judges' feedback narratives. Assuming the accuracy and faithfulness of the judge's qualitative assessments, we systematically analyze these narratives, categorizing identified issues according to a clearly defined hallucination taxonomy tailored explicitly for process mining applications. This taxonomy includes four primary categories (*input misalignment, factual errors, logical errors,* and *technical errors*) further subdivided into twelve specific sub-types. By classifying hallucination occurrences and assigning severity ratings, we transform the judges' qualitative comments into structured diagnostics.

The contribution of this paper is a structured auditing framework that systematically translates PM-LLM-Benchmark rationales into detailed hallucination annotations for model responses, publicly available at https://github.com/ fit-alessandro-berti/pm-llm-benchmark/tree/main/hallucinations. We propose a comprehensive process-mining-specific hallucination taxonomy, complete with illustrative examples. Furthermore, we provide an aggregated analysis linking hallucination patterns to benchmark scores and model characteristics, uncovering robust trends that can guide model selection and deployment strategies. Finally, we offer recommendations for practitioners in the form of practical guidelines, alongside openly accessible resources to ensure reproducibility and facilitate community-driven enhancements.

The paper is organized as follows. Section 2 introduces the base PM-LLM-Benchmark. Section 3 details the auditing benchmark and hallucination taxonomy. Sections 4 and 5 present and interpret the analysis results and their implications. We discuss related work in Sect. 6 and conclude the paper in Sect. 7.

## 2   Preliminaries: The PM-LLM-Benchmark

The PM-LLM-Benchmark [5] https://github.com/fit-alessandro-berti/pm-llm-benchmark assesses the capability of LLMs in addressing various process mining tasks. Each evaluated task comprises a prompt to which the candidate LLM provides a response. Subsequently, an expert judge evaluates the answer, assigning a numerical score between 1.0 and 10.0 along with a concise explanatory justification. These individual scores are aggregated across all prompts, generating an overall performance score for each model, where a higher score indicates superior performance. The benchmark includes eight distinct categories of process mining tasks: (**C1**) context understanding, (**C2**) conformance and anomaly detection, (**C3**) model generation and modification, (**C4**) process querying, (**C5**) hypothesis and question generation, (**C6**) fairness analysis, (**C7**) visual diagram interpretation, and (**C8**) optimization.

Table 1 presents the top-performing LLMs in the date 2025-08-15 along with their average scores across the eight task categories of the PM-LLM-Benchmark. Additionally, the leaderboard clearly indicates whether each listed model is open source and whether it explicitly emphasizes reasoning capabilities. This detailed breakdown enables informed comparisons of model performance across different PM tasks and provides insights into the influence of model characteristics such as openness and reasoning orientation on overall effectiveness.

**Table 1.** Top models on the PM-LLM-Benchmark leaderboard, available at https://github.com/fit-alessandro-berti/pm-llm-benchmark, with category breakdown (higher is better).

| | Model | Score | OS | Reasoning | C1 PCo | C2 CC | C3 PMo | C4 PQ | C5 HG | C6 FA | C7 VI | C8 OPT |
|---|---|---|---|---|---|---|---|---|---|---|---|---|
| 1 | Qwen3-235B-A22B-Thinking-2507 | 45.4 | Yes | Yes | 6.9 | 8.0 | 6.9 | 6.3 | 6.2 | 6.4 | 0.0 | 4.8 |
| 2 | gpt-5-2025-08-07-HIGH | 43.3 | No | Yes | 6.8 | 8.3 | 4.6 | 6.0 | 6.5 | 6.2 | 4.9 | 4.8 |
| 3 | gpt-5-2025-08-07 | 43.0 | No | Yes | 7.1 | 8.4 | 5.2 | 5.8 | 6.0 | 6.0 | 4.0 | 4.6 |
| 4 | gemini-2.5-pro-thinkhigh | 42.4 | No | Yes | 6.4 | 8.3 | 5.2 | 5.6 | 6.2 | 6.0 | 4.7 | 4.6 |
| 5 | gpt-5-mini-2025-08-07 | 42.3 | No | Yes | 6.3 | 8.6 | 4.9 | 5.9 | 6.1 | 5.8 | 3.8 | 4.8 |
| 6 | gemini-2.5-pro-thinklow | 42.2 | No | Yes | 5.7 | 8.4 | 5.3 | 5.5 | 6.1 | 6.5 | 5.4 | 4.7 |
| 7 | gemini-2.5-flash-thinkhigh | 41.0 | No | Yes | 6.1 | 8.3 | 4.8 | 5.4 | 6.2 | 5.5 | 5.1 | 4.7 |
| 8 | o3-pro-2025-06-10-search | 40.1 | No | Yes | 6.9 | 8.4 | 4.2 | 4.5 | 6.3 | 5.3 | 5.0 | 4.7 |
| 9 | grok-4-0709 | 40.1 | No | Yes | 6.0 | 8.7 | 5.4 | 4.3 | 5.6 | 5.4 | 3.1 | 4.6 |
| 10 | o3-pro-2025-06-10 | 39.9 | No | Yes | 6.2 | 7.7 | 5.3 | 5.2 | 5.3 | 5.9 | 5.0 | 4.3 |
| 11 | Qwen3-30B-A3B-2507-Thinking | 39.7 | Yes | Yes | 6.2 | 7.7 | 4.8 | 4.8 | 5.7 | 6.0 | 0.0 | 4.6 |

# 3 Hallucinations Benchmark

To bridge the limitations of numeric scores in revealing actionable insights into model failures, we develop a hallucination auditing benchmark that parses the judge's qualitative rationales into a taxonomy of error types, severities, and task associations.

## 3.1 Scope and Availability

This study enhances the *PM-LLM-Benchmark* by translating the qualitative feedback provided by the judge LLM into structured, process-mining-specific hallucination annotations. The key contribution is the introduction of an auditing layer utilizing a lightweight classifier LLM (*gpt-4.1-mini*) to systematically interpret the judge's narrative, mapping identified issues to a defined process-mining-oriented hallucination taxonomy. An overview of the end-to-end evaluation pipeline is shown in Fig. 1.

To facilitate transparency, reproducibility, and practical usage, all artifacts associated with the hallucinations benchmark for process mining have been made openly accessible. The main repository of the hallucinations benchmark, including comprehensive documentation, data, and analysis resources, can be found at https://github.com/fit-alessandro-berti/pm-llm-benchmark/tree/main/hallucinations.

Within this repository, several core files are particularly important to the analyses presented in this paper:

– `hallucination_report.md`: per-model hallucination breakdown by taxonomy (counts and brief notes).

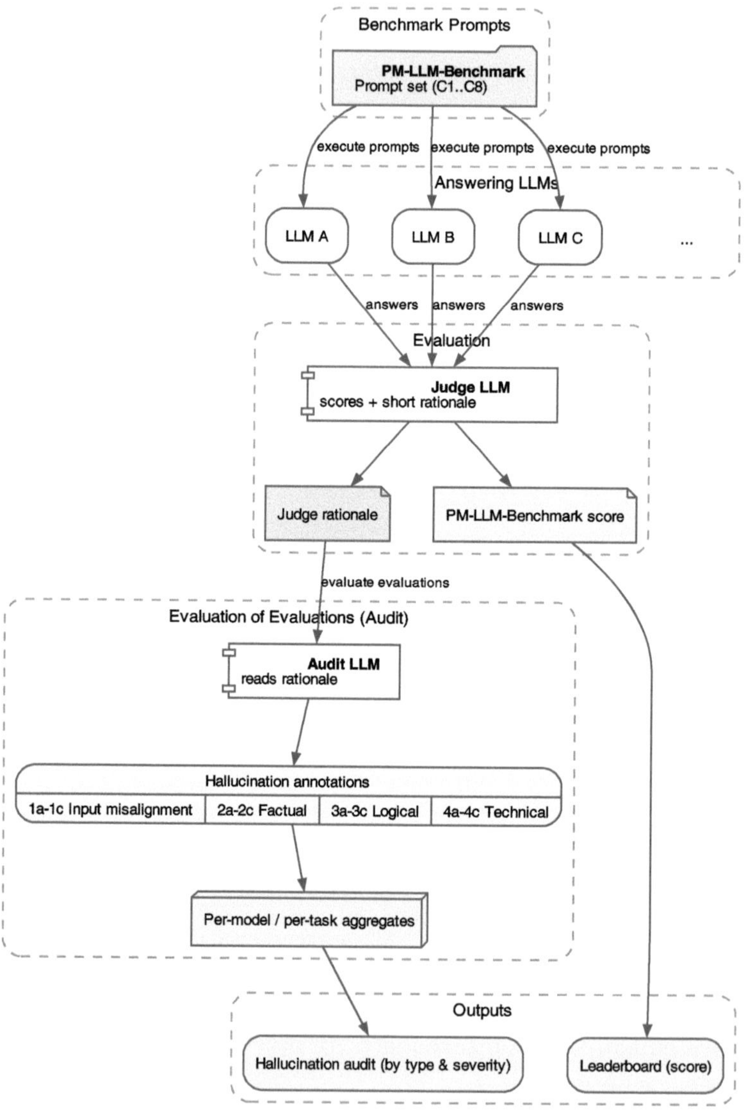


**Fig. 1.** Execution flow of the PM-LLM-Benchmark and the evaluation-of-evaluations audit. For each answering LLM, the shared PM prompt set (C1–C8) is run; an expert Judge LLM assigns a numeric score with a short rationale; a lightweight Audit LLM then reads the judge's rationale to produce structured hallucination annotations (1a–4c) that are aggregated per model and task, yielding a hallucination audit alongside the standard leaderboard score.

- `pm_llm_category_table.md`: cross-tab mapping sub-types to PM task families (C1–C8).
- `CORRELATION.md`: summary of correlations between hallucination rates, benchmark scores, and model attributes.

## 3.2  Hallucination Taxonomy

We employ a comprehensive hallucination taxonomy adapted from broader hallucination categories established in existing literature. The taxonomy is structured into four main categories, each containing specific subcategories explicitly designed for process mining tasks. The taxonomy is exemplified in Listing 1. Below we describe each category and its respective subcategories:

**Category 1: Input Misalignment.** This category addresses issues where the generated response does not correctly adhere to the provided prompt instructions and context. It comprises:

- *1a. Instruction Override:* Occurs when the model ignores explicit constraints specified by the prompt. Example: Prompt states, "List only activity names, no explanation", but the answer returns a narrative with recommendations and metrics.
- *1b. Context Omission:* Refers to situations where the model silently omits necessary contextual information from the prompt, leading to incomplete or irrelevant responses. Example: The prompt provides a rework loop between *Review* and *Fix*; the answer ignores it and discusses unrelated steps.
- *1c. Prompt Contradiction:* Happens when the model explicitly provides responses opposite to the requirements stated in the prompt. Example: Prompt instructs,"Assume conformance and explain why", but the answer claims compliance violations.

**Category 2: Factual Errors.** This category identifies inaccuracies related to factual correctness and grounding within the responses. It includes:

- *2a. Concept Fabrication:* Involves the invention or fabrication of process mining concepts, methods, or KPI definitions that are not established within the PM literature. Example: The answer cites a non-existent algorithm like "Quantum BPM Miner" or invents a KPI definition not used in PM literature.
- *2b. Spurious Numeric:* Refers to numeric claims or quantitative assertions presented without support from the prompt or provided data. Example: The answer states, "throughput improved by 20%", although no numbers were provided or derivable from the prompt.
- *2c. False Citation:* Occurs when the model incorrectly attributes statements to non-existent or incorrect sources. Example: Attributes a claim to a paper or standard that does not exist or misquotes a real source.

**Category 3: Logical Errors.** This category covers errors related to flawed or inconsistent reasoning within generated responses. It consists of:

**Listing 1.** Judge evaluation annotated with hallucination tags (about the *answering model*). Tags follow the PM-specific taxonomy: 1a–1c (Input Misalignment), 2a–2c (Factual Errors), 3a–3c (Logical Errors), 4a–4c (Technical Errors).

```
Prompt (excerpt): "Assume the process conforms to the provided model. List ONLY the
    activity names in order. Do NOT explain or recommend."
Context (excerpt): Event log summary states 18% rework from "Review" back to "Fix"; no
    resource data provided. The BPMN shows Start -> Register -> Review -> Fix (optional
    rework) -> Approve -> End; no decision gateways.

--- Judge Evaluation (score + narrative) ---

Score: 4.3 / 10. The answer does not meet the prompt constraints and includes several
    issues.
(1) Format and scope. The prompt requires listing activity names only; the answer adds
    analysis and recommendations.
    [1a Instruction override]
(2) Use of provided context. The BPMN and context include an optional "Fix" step and 18%
    rework; the answer omits "Fix" and claims there is no rework.
    [1b Context omission]
(3) Consistency with prompt intent. Despite "assume conformance," the answer asserts non-
    conformance without basis.
    [1c Prompt contradiction][3a Unsupported leap]
(4) Quantitative claims. The answer states throughput improved by "20%" and reports "92%
    precision / 95% recall" without sources or derivation.
    [2b Spurious numeric]
(5) References. The answer cites a non-existent 2021 journal article ("X Algorithm") as
    evidence.
    [2c False citation]
(6) Internal coherence. The answer first claims "no bottlenecks" then calls "Approval" the
    main bottleneck; the justification is tautological.
    [3b Self-contradiction][3c Circular reasoning]
(7) Causal attribution. The answer attributes delays to a "back-office resource shortage"
    although no resource data are provided.
    [3a Unsupported leap]
(8) Domain concepts. The answer introduces a fictitious metric ("case convergence ratio")
    and tool ("Quantum BPM Miner 3000").
    [2a Concept fabrication]
(9) Structured output. The requested JSON is malformed (missing bracket/quote), so it
    cannot be parsed.
    [4a Syntax error]
(10) Modeling and visuals. The proposed BPMN "two Start Events merging at an AND before
    Register" violates notation semantics, and the described decision gateway after "
    Review" does not appear in the provided diagram.
    [4b Modeling-semantics breach][4c Visual-description mismatch]

Overall rationale: the score reflects multiple high-impact issues across alignment, logic,
    and structure. A corrected answer should (only) list activities in order, cite the
    rework loop, avoid unsupported numerics/claims, and provide valid JSON if requested.
```

**Legend.** *1a* Instruction override; *1b* Context omission; *1c* Prompt contradiction; *2a* Concept fabrication; *2b* Spurious numeric; *2c* False citation; *3a* Unsupported leap; *3b* Self-contradiction; *3c* Circular reasoning; *4a* Syntax error; *4b* Modeling-semantics breach; *4c* Visual-description mismatch. Tags refer to hallucinations *in the answering model*, extracted from the judge's rationale.

- *3c. Unsupported Leaps:* Pertains to conclusions made without sufficient logical or factual backing from preceding statements. Example: Infers that "delays are caused by resource shortage" without any resource information in the provided data.

- *3b. Self-Contradiction:* Describes instances where the model generates conflicting statements within the same response, undermining internal consistency. Example: Initially claims, "no bottlenecks are present", but later asserts, "*Approval* is the main bottleneck".
- *3c. Circular Reasoning:* Refers to cases where the model uses a claim as its own justification, resulting in logically circular arguments. Example: "Activity X is a bottleneck because it slows the process, which makes it a bottleneck".

**Category 4: Technical Errors.** This category addresses issues arising from generating structured outputs, adherence to modeling conventions, or accuracy in interpreting visual materials. Subcategories include:

- *4a. Syntax Error:* Occurs when the model produces invalid structured outputs such as JSON, code, or other structured formats that cannot be parsed or executed. Example: Emits malformed JSON, code, or query that cannot be parsed or executed as requested.
- *4b. Model Semantics Breach:* Involves generating outputs that violate established modeling notation rules or semantic conventions in process mining. Example: Describes a BPMN fragment violating semantics, like two start events merging directly at a gateway.
- *4c. Visual Description Mismatch:* Refers to descriptions of diagrams or images that reference components or aspects not present in the provided visuals. Example: Describes a gateway and extra path not shown in the provided process diagram.


## 3.3   Evaluation Metrics

We introduce an approach to measuring hallucinations based explicitly on the judge's textual feedback. The following aspects are evaluated:

- *Incidence by Type:* For each evaluated answer, we record the presence or absence of specific hallucination sub-types, as identified by the judge. These sub-types fall within a comprehensive taxonomy of 12 categories grouped into four broader families.
- *Severity Levels:* Each identified hallucination sub-type is assigned a severity rating (*low*, *medium*, *high*, or *critical*), indicating its potential impact on practical PM tasks.
- *Aggregated Summaries:* We generate aggregated summaries at both per-prompt and per-model levels. These summaries include total counts, frequency distributions, and severity distributions, allowing comparative analysis across the eight task categories of the PM-LLM-Benchmark: context understanding, conformance/anomalies, model generation/modification, querying, hypothesis generation, fairness, diagram interpretation, and optimization.

These metrics, derived solely from the judge's explanations, provide interpretable signals about the reliability of each answering LLM.

## 3.4  Measurement Procedure

The evaluation process involves several sequential steps:

1. *Ingestion:* We begin by collecting the narrative feedback from the judge.
2. *Normalization:* The judge's narrative feedback is passed to the classifier LLM, instructed explicitly to produce structured annotations based on the judge's descriptions.
3. *Taxonomy Tagging:* The classifier identifies and tags each hallucination subtype present, assigns corresponding severity levels, and extracts brief textual examples (trigger spans) from the judge's narrative as supporting evidence.
4. *Consolidation and Aggregation:* Identified tags are de-duplicated for each response, and aggregated across models and PM task categories to generate summarized metrics.

The structured annotations derived from the judge's feedback facilitate an understanding of each LLM's error patterns and associated risks. Specifically, the annotations clarify *where* (error types), *how often* (frequency), and *how severely* (impact) each model fails.

## 4  Results

In this section, we summarize the key outcomes of the hallucination audit and their relationship to benchmark scores, model characteristics, and process mining task families.

**Overall Alignment Between Scores and Hallucinations.**
Across models, higher PM-LLM-Benchmark scores are strongly associated with fewer hallucinations. The total hallucination incidence exhibits a pronounced negative correlation with the benchmark score ($r = -0.866$), confirming that the numeric evaluation offered by the judge LLM is a reliable summary of answer fidelity. The effect is especially marked for *logical errors* ($r = -0.800$) and *input misalignment* ($r = -0.767$), while *factual* and *technical* errors also decrease, albeit more moderately ($r = -0.543$ and $r = -0.533$, respectively), as shown in Table 2.

**Where the Reductions Come From.**
Within families, the largest improvements for better-scoring LLMs concentrate on high-impact subtypes. *Unsupported leaps* in reasoning drive the logical family and show the strongest single correlation with score ($r = -0.811$). On the alignment side, *context omission* is the most prevalent subtype and declines with score ($r = -0.666$), followed by *instruction override* ($r = -0.629$). Among factual errors, *spurious numeric claims* decrease with performance ($r = -0.522$), whereas fabricated citations are comparatively rare and weakly linked to score. Technical reliability improves mainly through fewer *model-semantics breaches* ($r = -0.546$) and some reduction of *syntax errors*. By contrast, *circular reasoning* is infrequent and shows no meaningful relationship with score. These patterns, summarized in Table 2, indicate that gains in disciplined inference and faithful use of context account for most of the aggregate reduction.

**Table 2.** Pearson correlations between model features and hallucination categories/-types. *Coloring:* blue = negative correlation (feature increases as hallucinations decrease), red = positive; darker shade marks $|r| \geq 0.70$, lighter shade marks $0.50 \leq |r| < 0.70$. Bold = strongest absolute correlation in each row.

| Category / Type | PM-LLM-Benchmark Score | Is Open Source | Is Reasoning Model | Model Size | Days Since 2024-01-01 |
|---|---|---|---|---|---|
| Overall (Total Hallucinations) | **−0.866** | 0.225 | −0.601 | −0.174 | −0.334 |
| Category 1: Input Misalignment | **−0.767** | 0.196 | −0.559 | −0.168 | −0.582 |
| Category 2: Factual Errors | **−0.543** | 0.232 | −0.160 | −0.134 | 0.030 |
| Category 3: Logical Errors | **−0.800** | 0.170 | −0.699 | −0.129 | −0.322 |
| Category 4: Technical Errors | **−0.533** | 0.124 | −0.225 | −0.129 | −0.016 |
| 1a Instruction Override | **−0.629** | 0.238 | −0.277 | −0.131 | −0.269 |
| 1b Context Omission | **−0.666** | 0.123 | −0.547 | −0.142 | −0.644 |
| 1c Prompt Contradiction | **−0.591** | 0.311 | −0.343 | −0.159 | 0.053 |
| 2a Concept Fabrication | **−0.410** | 0.190 | −0.161 | −0.047 | 0.109 |
| 2b Spurious Numeric | **−0.522** | 0.257 | −0.157 | −0.150 | −0.008 |
| 2c False Citation | **−0.141** | −0.046 | 0.030 | −0.075 | −0.047 |
| 3a Unsupported Leap | **−0.811** | 0.173 | −0.701 | −0.125 | −0.376 |
| 3b Self-Contradiction | **−0.430** | 0.078 | −0.415 | −0.111 | 0.075 |
| 3c Circular Reasoning | 0.023 | 0.045 | −0.016 | 0.037 | **0.243** |
| 4a Syntax Error | **−0.421** | 0.210 | 0.077 | −0.144 | 0.026 |
| 4b Model Semantics Breach | **−0.546** | 0.162 | −0.319 | −0.195 | −0.040 |
| 4c Visual Description Mismatch | 0.023 | **−0.245** | −0.194 | 0.220 | −0.023 |

Notes: Negative correlations with the benchmark score indicate that higher PM-LLM-Benchmark performance is associated with fewer detected hallucinations. Only cells with $|r| \geq 0.50$ are tinted.

**Impact of Reasoning Orientation and Model Recency.** Reasoning-oriented models exhibit systematically lower hallucination rates, particularly for logical errors ($r = -0.699$ with the "reasoning model" indicator) and input misalignment ($r = -0.559$). At the subtype level, the reductions are most visible for *unsupported leaps* and *context omissions*. Model recency also helps: newer models show fewer input-alignment issues overall ($r = -0.582$) and fewer context omissions specifically ($r = -0.644$), with a moderate reduction of logical errors. In contrast, recency yields limited changes for factual and technical subtypes, and circular reasoning does not improve, suggesting a residual challenge that persists across generations (Table 2).

**Size and Openness Effects.** Model size correlates only weakly with hallucination counts, and the open-source indicator shows mixed associations. Open-source models tend to have slightly higher rates in alignment and logic on average, while exhibiting somewhat fewer *visual-description mismatches*. These differences are small compared to the advantages conferred by reasoning specialization and recency, reinforcing that architectural and training choices targeting reasoning quality matter more than raw scale alone (Table 2).

**Task-Family Hotspots.** Hallucination profiles concentrate in specific PM task families. *Unsupported leaps* peak in model generation and modification (C3: 2155 counts), with substantial incidence also in process querying and context understanding; overall, logical errors sum to 10,550 occurrences across tasks. *Context omission* dominates input misalignment (total 4926), with the highest counts in context understanding (C1: 957), optimization (C8: 849), and process querying (C4: 790). Factual errors are led by *spurious numerics*, most prominent in conformance and anomaly detection (C2: 716) and also elevated in modeling (C3: 501) and optimization (C8: 403). Technical errors show two clear hotspots: *model-semantics breaches* concentrate in modeling tasks (C3: 791), while *syntax errors* are most frequent during hypothesis and question generation (C5: 200). Visual interpretation (C7) has comparatively fewer total hallucinations but the highest concentration of *visual-description mismatches* (249). Aggregates per family, reported in Table 3, confirm that C3 contributes the largest share of hallucinations overall, followed by C1 and C4.

**Table 3.** Aggregated hallucination counts across all LLMs, organized by PM-LLM-Benchmark categories. *Bold numbers* indicate, for each hallucination type, the PM category with the highest count in that row (ties are bolded). The *Total* row is fully bolded for readability.

| Hallucination Type | C1 PCo | C2 CC | C3 PMo | C4 PQ | C5 HG | C6 FA | C7 VI | C8 OPT | Total |
|---|---|---|---|---|---|---|---|---|---|
| 1a. Instruction Override | **304** | 86 | 156 | 147 | 113 | 121 | 1 | 43 | 971 |
| 1b. Context Omission | **957** | 724 | 286 | 790 | 377 | 592 | 351 | 849 | 4926 |
| 1c. Prompt Contradiction | **179** | 84 | 95 | 91 | 22 | 38 | 13 | 8 | 530 |
| 2a. Concept Fabrication | 95 | 45 | 105 | 205 | 47 | 113 | 55 | **220** | 885 |
| 2b. Spurious Numeric | 361 | **716** | 501 | 153 | 191 | 177 | 108 | 403 | 2610 |
| 2c. False Citation | 12 | 21 | 6 | **37** | 6 | 15 | 0 | 9 | 106 |
| 3a. Unsupported Leap | 1406 | 1384 | **2155** | 1711 | 1227 | 1098 | 449 | 1120 | 10550 |
| 3b. Self Contradiction | **317** | 186 | 309 | 183 | 56 | 128 | 26 | 30 | 1235 |
| 3c. Circular Reasoning | 6 | 4 | 5 | 0 | 3 | 1 | 0 | **14** | 33 |
| 4a. Syntax Error | 39 | 12 | 186 | 77 | **200** | 63 | 0 | 14 | 591 |
| 4b. Model Semantics Breach | 151 | 61 | **791** | 156 | 95 | 165 | 123 | 7 | 1549 |
| 4c. Visual Description Mismatch | 105 | 26 | 39 | 68 | 21 | 20 | **249** | 20 | 548 |
| **Total** | **3932** | **3349** | **4634** | **3618** | **2358** | **2531** | **1375** | **2737** | **24534** |

**Co-occurrence of Failure Modes.** Hallucination families tend to co-occur rather than trade off. The strongest off-diagonal association links input misalignment with logical errors ($r = 0.717$), indicating that answers that underuse or contradict context often also contain unjustified inferences. Factual and technical errors are likewise coupled ($r = 0.572$), and logical errors correlate moderately with technical issues ($r = 0.553$). These relationships, summarized in Table 4, suggest shared underlying causes: improving context fidelity and enforcing disciplined reasoning are likely to reduce several error families simultaneously.

**Table 4.** Inter-category correlation matrix. Cell shading encodes magnitude (white = 0, blue = 1); diagonal cells (1.000) are shown in gray; bold marks the strongest off-diagonal correlation per row.

| Category | Cat. 1 Input Misalign. | Cat. 2 Factual Errors | Cat. 3 Logical Errors | Cat. 4 Technical Errors |
| --- | --- | --- | --- | --- |
| Cat. 1 Input Misalignment | 1.000 | 0.236 | **0.717** | 0.290 |
| Cat. 2 Factual Errors | 0.236 | 1.000 | 0.489 | **0.572** |
| Cat. 3 Logical Errors | **0.717** | 0.489 | 1.000 | 0.553 |
| Cat. 4 Technical Errors | 0.290 | **0.572** | 0.553 | 1.000 |

**Practical Reading of the Audit.** Taken together, the results indicate that the judge's numeric score is a strong first filter for reliability, while the hallucination audit pinpoints the residual risks that persist even at moderate scores. Emphasis on reasoning-oriented configurations and recent model versions yields the largest risk reductions, especially for the dominant pairs of failure modes— context omissions and unsupported leaps—whereas technical and factual hygiene require complementary safeguards in tasks that demand structured outputs or quantitative claims.

## 5   Discussion

The analysis presented in this study provides an interpretable and structured risk profile for each evaluated LLM by translating the judge's qualitative feedback into quantitative hallucination metrics. Two key insights emerge clearly: first, models that score higher on the PM-LLM-Benchmark demonstrate significantly fewer hallucinations, especially regarding logical reasoning and alignment with prompt instructions. Second, hallucination categories tend to co-occur, suggesting common underlying mechanisms that produce errors. These findings underscore that improving contextual understanding and reasoning abilities can mitigate multiple categories of hallucinations simultaneously, thus enhancing overall model reliability [30,32,33].

**Practical Consequences** We identify three main suggestions for practical use. First, use the PM-LLM-Benchmark score as a coarse filter and the hallucination audit as a fine-grained risk profile for deployment. In practice, teams should (i) shortlist models by overall score to ensure baseline task competence, then (ii) gate deployment on *per-category* and *per-severity* thresholds from the audit (e.g., no high/critical "unsupported leap" or "context omission" events in C2–C4, no syntax or modeling-semantics breaches in C3). Because our results show that newer, reasoning-oriented models reduce input-misalignment and logical errors more than size alone, practitioners should prefer recent, reasoning-focused models when two candidates tie on the headline score. This two-step selection reduces the chance that seemingly "good" answers still carry high-impact failure modes. Second, map safeguards directly to the dominant failure modes revealed by the audit and to the PM task family at hand. To reinforce *context fidelity*, structure prompts and outputs so claims are explicitly tied to provided artifacts (log/model/diagram snippets or retrieved evidence) [4,20,34]. To enforce *disciplined reasoning*, require structured justifications and self-checks to prevent unsupported leaps and contradictions [21,24,30,32]. To ensure *structured-output hygiene*, validate JSON/queries with grammars or constrained decoding and check BPMN/Petri-net semantics automatically [1,2,8,12,13,15,26]. Make these controls task-specific: e.g., for C3 (model generation/modification) run notation/semantics validators; for C7 (visual interpretation) require that textual references correspond to nodes/edges present in the diagram; for C2 (conformance/anomalies) forbid causal attributions that are not grounded in the supplied evidence. Targeting the audit's top error types yields broad gains because these categories frequently co-occur.

Third, operationalize continuous monitoring and governance around the same taxonomy used for selection. Periodically re-run the hallucination audit on production samples and model updates; track counts by type and severity, set alert thresholds, and route high-severity cases to human review. Maintain a living regression suite of prompts per process mining category (with expected structured outputs and validator checks) [28], and record drift when providers roll new versions. Because improvements to context fidelity and reasoning tend to reduce multiple error families simultaneously, focus monitoring and remediation on these levers first, then address rarer but impactful issues (e.g., fabricated citations) through targeted checks. This closes the loop from benchmark to deployment, keeps risk visible, and prevents silent degradation over time.

**Model Selection:** When selecting models, prioritizing reasoning capabilities and recent advancements yields substantial improvements in reducing hallucinations compared to merely selecting larger models. While larger models offer incremental improvements, reasoning-oriented and newly developed models significantly outperform older or general-purpose models, regardless of their open-source or proprietary status [23,30,32,33].

**Limitations**: Our analysis carries inherent limitations. The annotations rely solely on the judge's narrative completeness and accuracy [9,16,22,31,35]. Consequently, any oversight or omission by the judge directly affects the taxonomy's comprehensiveness. Additionally, the automated extraction process, while efficient, may blur subtle distinctions between certain error types, such as circular versus unsupported reasoning. Finally, correlation-based findings demonstrate associations rather than causal relationships.

**Future Work:** Looking ahead, the robustness of hallucination detection can be enhanced through multi-judge evaluations of LLM answers [10,22,35], which would help assess the stability and generalizability of risk profiles. Additionally, integrating structured guardrails directly into PM workflows (such as mandatory evidence referencing, structured reasoning prompts, and automated validation tools) can further elevate the reliability of LLM-generated answers [4,15,20, 21,26]. Together, these measures provide a practical framework for managing and mitigating hallucination risks in process mining tasks using large language models.

## 6    Related Work

In this section, we situate our hallucination audit within prior work on LLM hallucinations and BPM/PM evaluation, highlighting how our taxonomy, cross-task scope, and empirical findings extend and generalize existing approaches.

### 6.1    Hallucination Taxonomies

**General Taxonomies and Surveys.** Recent syntheses organize hallucinations into a small set of recurring families: *input misalignment/faithfulness, factual errors, logical errors,* and *technical or domain-specific errors.* These surveys argue for sub-types that make failure modes actionable and comparable across tasks, which we adopt and tailor to process mining use cases [17,25].

**Faithfulness and Input Use.** Work on faithfulness distinguishes instruction inconsistency (violating explicit task constraints) and context inconsistency (ignoring or contradicting supplied evidence) [17,25]. In PM prompts, these map directly to *instruction override, context omission,* and *prompt contradiction,* which we use to flag when answers drift from format requirements or fail to use provided logs, models, or diagrams.

**Factual Fabrication and References.** Factual hallucinations include invented concepts, ungrounded numbers, and fabricated or misattributed citations [17]. Our *concept fabrication, spurious numeric,* and *false citation* sub-types reflect these patterns; the last one is motivated by studies showing models can produce authoritative-sounding but non-existent references [3].

**Logical Consistency and Reasoning Errors.** Surveys also emphasize internal coherence: models may make unsupported inferences, contradict themselves within one answer, or argue in circles [17,18]. We capture these as *unsupported leap*, *self-contradiction*, and *circular reasoning*, which are particularly harmful in analytic PM tasks (e.g., causal claims without evidence in the log or model).

**Technical and Domain-Specific Violations.** As LLMs emit structured outputs or describe visuals, additional failure modes arise: malformed JSON/code, notation/schema breaches (e.g., BPMN/Petri-net),
and visual misreadings [11,14,27,36]. These motivate *syntax error*, *model-semantics breach*, and *visual-description mismatch*, which we audit explicitly in PM settings.

**Process-Mining-Oriented Frameworks.** Domain treatments for PM consolidate these ideas into practical taxonomies and pipelines that combine automatic checks (format/schema validators, factual spot checks) with model- or human-in-the-loop review of subtler reasoning flaws [29]. Our work follows this line but extracts the signals from the judge's narratives in PM-LLM-Benchmark [5], producing per-model hallucination profiles aligned with PM task families.

## 6.2    Existing Hallucination Benchmarks in BPM

Empirical studies of hallucinations in Business Process Management (BPM) are limited. A recent line of work on process *modeling* introduces *knowledge-driven hallucinations*, where an LLM's domain priors override the provided specification, yielding plausible but unsupported elements (e.g., extra activities/gateways/flows) ( [19]). These errors primarily reflect *Input Misalignment* (ignoring or contradicting the given model: 1b/1c) and *Logical Errors* (unsupported leaps: 3a), and often co-occur with *Technical Errors* when invented fragments violate notation semantics (4b).

Our audit generalizes this perspective across eight process mining task families (C1–C8). We observe the same prior-over-evidence mechanism beyond modeling: large counts for *context omission* in context understanding and optimization, *spurious numerics* in conformance/anomaly detection, and concentration of *unsupported leaps* and *model-semantics breaches* in model generation/modification (see Tables 3-4). Moreover, reasoning-oriented and newer models show fewer omissions and unsupported leaps (Table 2), suggesting that disciplined inference reduces these prior-driven deviations. Practically, safeguards that enforce context fidelity, structured reasoning, and notation/schema validation operationalize the main lesson from prior BPM work: do not trust domain priors over authoritative artifacts (logs, reference models, diagrams).

## 7    Conclusion

This paper introduced a structured hallucination audit that converts the judge narratives of the PM-LLM-Benchmark into process-mining–specific annotations.

By mapping issues to a four-family taxonomy and aggregating them across models and task families, we obtain an interpretable risk profile that complements the benchmark score.

Our analysis shows that although higher PM-LLM-Benchmark scores generally correlate with fewer hallucinations, non-zero, and often co-occurring, hallucinations remain across input alignment and logical reasoning (Table 2 and 4). This residual error profile is not merely cosmetic: in high-stakes PM scenarios such as conformance checking and anomaly detection (C2), fairness assessment (C6), and optimization or change recommendations (C8), hallucinations can translate into regulatory misstatements, unfair decisions, or costly operational actions. Consequently, hallucinations are a primary factor limiting the applicability of current LLMs as *autonomous* decision-makers in these settings. Until incidence and severity are demonstrably low for the specific deployment distribution, LLM outputs should be treated as *untrusted suggestions* that require verification before action.

**Implications for High-Stakes Deployment.** The audit suggests a risk-driven deployment pattern in which model autonomy is conditioned on measured hallucination risk:

1. *Classify task criticality and cap autonomy.* Use LLMs in assistive or propose-and-review modes for high-impact tasks; reserve autonomous actions for low-risk utilities (e.g., drafting, retrieval).
2. *Enforce evidence grounding.* Require answers to explicitly reference provided logs, models, or diagrams; suppress unverifiable numbers and claims; prefer prompts that elicit structured citations to the given context.
3. *Validate structure and semantics.* Gate outputs through schema/grammar checks (e.g., JSON, queries) and domain validators (e.g., BPMN/Petri-net semantics), rejecting or auto-correcting malformed content.
4. *Add disciplined reasoning and self-checks.* Use structured justifications, self-consistency/reflection, and cross-checking judges; trigger abstention or escalation when checks disagree or confidence is low.
5. *Mandate human-in-the-loop and auditability.* Require expert review for high-stakes actions, maintain logs, and continuously sample for hallucination audits post-deployment.

**Outlook.** All artifacts are openly released to enable replication, extension, and continuous monitoring. Future work should (i) incorporate multi-judge setups to improve robustness, (ii) calibrate severities to downstream harm for task- and domain-specific risk limits, and (iii) integrate the audit into PM toolchains as a standing safety layer. In summary, while recent models reduce hallucinations, the remaining failure modes identified by our audit currently bound the safe applicability of LLMs in high-stakes process mining; rigorous verification and risk-aware deployment are therefore prerequisites, not add-ons.

## References


1. Business Process Model and Notation (BPMN), Version 2.0.2 (2013). oMG Document Number: formal/13-12-09
2. van der Aalst, W.M.: Data science in action. In: Process Mining: Data Science in Action, pp. 3–23. Springer (2016)
3. Agrawal, A., Suzgun, M., Mackey, L., Kalai, A.: Do language models know when they're hallucinating references? In: EACL (Findings), pp. 912–928. Association for Computational Linguistics (2024)
4. Asai, A., Wu, Z., Wang, Y., Sil, A., Hajishirzi, H.: Self-RAG: learning to retrieve, generate, and critique through self-reflection (2023)
5. Berti, A., Kourani, H., van der Aalst, W.M.P.: PM-LLM-Benchmark: evaluating large language models on process mining tasks. In: ICPM Workshops. Lecture Notes in Business Information Processing, vol. 533, pp. 610–623. Springer (2024)
6. Berti, A., Kourani, H., Häfke, H., Li, C., Schuster, D.: Evaluating large language models in process mining: capabilities, benchmarks, and evaluation strategies. In: BPMDS/EMMSAD@CAiSE. Lecture Notes in Business Information Processing, vol. 511, pp. 13–21. Springer (2024)
7. Berti, A., Kourani, H., Park, G., van der Aalst, W.M.: Configuring large reasoning models using process mining: a benchmark and a case study. authorea preprints (2025)
8. Beurer-Kellner, L., Fischer, M., Vechev, M.: Prompting is programming: a query language for large language models. Proc. ACM Program. Languages **7**(PLDI), 1946–1969 (2023)
9. Chen, G.H., Chen, S., Liu, Z., Jiang, F., Wang, B.: Humans or LLMs as the judge? a study on judgement biases (2024)
10. Chiang, W.L., et al.: Chatbot arena: an open platform for evaluating LLMs by human preference (2024)
11. Cossio, M.: A comprehensive taxonomy of hallucinations in large language models. arXiv preprint arXiv:2508.01781 (2025)
12. Dijkman, R.M., Dumas, M., Ouyang, C.: Semantics and analysis of business process models in BPMN. Inf. Softw. Technol. **50**(12), 1281–1294 (2008)
13. Dong, Y., et al.: XGrammar: flexible and efficient structured generation engine for large language models (2025)
14. Dugar, R.: Crafting structured JSON responses: ensuring consistent output from any LLM, updated 2024-10-26
15. Geng, S., Josifoski, M., Peyrard, M., West, R.: Grammar-constrained decoding for structured NLP tasks without finetuning (2024)
16. Gu, J., et al.: A survey on LLM-as-a-judge (2025)
17. Huang, L., et al.: A survey on hallucination in large language models: principles, taxonomy, challenges, and open questions. ACM Trans. Inf. Syst. **43**(2), 42:1–42:55 (2025)
18. Ji, Z., et al.: Survey of hallucination in natural language generation. ACM Comput. Surv. **55**(12), 248:1–248:38 (2023)
19. Kourani, H., Antonov, A., Berti, A., van der Aalst, W.M.: Knowledge-driven hallucination in large language models: an empirical study on process modeling (2025)
20. Lewis, P., et al.: Retrieval-augmented generation for knowledge-intensive NLP tasks (2021)
21. Lightman, H., et al.: Let's verify step by step (2023)

22. Liu, Y., Iter, D., Xu, Y., Wang, S., Xu, R., Zhu, C.: G-Eval: NLG evaluation using GPT-4 with better human alignment (2023)
23. Madaan, A., et al.: Self-Refine: iterative refinement with self-feedback (2023)
24. Manakul, P., Liusie, A., Gales, M.J.F.: SelfCheckGPT: zero-resource black-box hallucination detection for generative large language models (2023)
25. Maynez, J., Narayan, S., Bohnet, B., McDonald, R.T.: On faithfulness and factuality in abstractive summarization. In: ACL, pp. 1906–1919. Association for Computational Linguistics (2020)
26. Rajpal, S.: Guardrails AI (2023), guardrails AI Framework
27. Ravuri, C., Amarasinghe, S.: Eliminating hallucination-induced errors in LLM code generation with functional clustering. CoRR abs/2506.11021 (2025)
28. Ribeiro, M.T., Wu, T., Guestrin, C., Singh, S.: Beyond accuracy: behavioral testing of NLP models with CheckList (2020)
29. Shankar, S., Zamfirescu-Pereira, J.D., Hartmann, B., Parameswaran, A.G., Arawjo, I.: Who validates the validators? aligning LLM-assisted evaluation of LLM outputs with human preferences. In: UIST, pp. 131:1–131:14. ACM (2024)
30. Wang, X., et al.: Self-consistency improves chain of thought reasoning in language models (2023)
31. Wataoka, K., Takahashi, T., Ri, R.: Self-Preference Bias in LLM-as-a-Judge (2025)
32. Wei, J., et al.: Chain-of-thought prompting elicits reasoning in large language models (2023)
33. Yao, S., et al.: Tree of thoughts: deliberate problem solving with large language models (2023)
34. Ye, X., Sun, R., Arik, S., Pfister, T.: Effective large language model adaptation for improved grounding and citation generation (2024)
35. Zheng, L., et al.: Judging LLM-as-a-Judge with MT-Bench and Chatbot Arena (2023)
36. Zhou, Y., et al.: Analyzing and mitigating object hallucination in large vision-language models. In: ICLR. OpenReview.net (2024)

# Uncharted Workflows: Process Mining Perspectives in Health


Natalia Sidorova[(✉)] and Renata Medeiros de Carvalho

Department of Mathematics and Computer Science, Eindhoven University of
Technology, Eindhoven, The Netherlands
`{n.sidorova,r.medeiros.de.carvalho}@tue.nl`



**Abstract.** Why do patients experience delays or encounter deviations
from care protocols? Where do bottlenecks, inefficiencies, or errors arise
in complex clinical workflows? How can healthcare organizations better understand and optimize processes that are flexible, adaptive, and
context-dependent? Process mining (PM) provides methods to illuminate
hidden pathways in these uncharted workflows integrating heterogeneous
data—structured, semi-structured, and unstructured—as well as multiple perspectives reflecting differences between roles in care processes and
between individual clinicians, to uncover patterns and actionable insights
often missed by conventional analytics. This paper reviews the contributions of PM in healthcare, highlighting its ability to interpret flexible processes, connect system-level and human-level perspectives, and support
improvements in care delivery and operational efficiency. We also discuss
seminal work by Wil van der Aalst and colleagues, situating PM within
the evolving field of healthcare analytics and illustrating its methodological foundations.

**Keywords:** Process Mining · Process Analytics · Healthcare ·
Business Insights


## 1  Introduction

How can healthcare organizations make sense of huge volumes of clinical data
generated daily and ranging from laboratory tests and imaging to patient charts
and bedside notes, when these data are heterogeneous, fragmented, and often
incomplete? Why do established data mining and AI techniques, while powerful, face challenges in explaining the underlying causes of bottlenecks, deviations
from protocols, or delays in patient care? And what makes process-oriented analysis distinct for a domain where workflows are uncharted, flexible, and continuously shaped by both systemic constraints and human judgment and choices?
These questions are central to understanding why process mining (PM) and its
broader evolution into process intelligence provide a unique lens for healthcare.

Healthcare data is often spread across silos that rarely interoperate seamlessly. Laboratory results may reside in one system, diagnostic images in another,



J. Mendling et al. (Eds.): Wil van der Aalst Festschrift, LNCS 16480, pp. 648–661, 2026.
https://doi.org/10.1007/978-3-032-17618-9_42

and physician notes in yet another, often with incompatible identifiers and inconsistent time stamps. For instance, a clinician may order and perform an urgent blood test immediately, while the corresponding note explaining the reasons is entered into the electronic record hours later, creating a mismatch between the recorded timestamps and the actual sequence of care. *Semi-structured* forms and *free-text* narratives capture essential clinical reasoning but remain difficult to reconcile with transactional records. Even when data sources are technically integrated, missing entries, ambiguities and undocumented deviations from care protocols limit their reliability. This patchwork of structured, semi-structured, and unstructured data creates a distorted view of actual care delivery that can obscure the view on the dynamics that healthcare organizations most urgently need to understand.

It is not only the diversity of its data, which makes healthcare challenging. Unlike manufacturing or logistics, where processes can often be specified in advance in great detail, clinical pathways evolve dynamically: treatments are adjusted to patient responses, diagnostic work-ups follow branching decisions, and coordination across departments requires constant adaptation. Exceptions are the rule rather than the anomaly. Moreover, the same process appears differently depending on perspective: a physician may describe a pathway in terms of diagnoses and treatments, while a nurse may emphasize handovers, monitoring, and resource availability. Each *perspective* is valid yet incomplete, and none alone captures the full complexity of care delivery.

Conventional analytics, even when powered by advanced AI, often simplify the complexity of healthcare processes into correlations and predictions detached from the underlying processes. They answer what is likely to happen but rarely why it happens in the way it does. For example, a machine learning model may predict high readmission risk for a patient, but it cannot trace how variations in ward routines, diagnostic timing, or interdepartmental coordination contribute to that outcome. In healthcare, where workflows[1] evolve through context-sensitive decisions and real-time adaptations, such process blindness is a critical limitation. What is needed are methods that reconstruct and analyze the flows of activities themselves, making visible the latent structures and deviations within clinical practice.

Another distinctive aspect of healthcare processes is the complexity of process goals. *Key performance indicators* (KPIs) are often multidimensional and conflicting: improving throughput may compromise patient safety, reducing costs may affect care quality, and optimizing one department's efficiency may create bottlenecks elsewhere. Traditional analytics often reduce performance to single metrics or simple trade-offs, which can obscure these tensions. Process mining, in contrast, aims at supporting the analysis of multiple KPIs simultaneously, enabling the identification of Pareto-optimal pathways and revealing where compromises occur in practice. By mapping outcomes to the underlying sequences of

---

[1] *Workflows* refer to the structured sequences of clinical activities and decision points that define patient care processes, which can adapt dynamically to context and real-time conditions.

activities, PM provides actionable insights that account for both the variability of care and the multiple objectives that define healthcare quality.

Process mining responds to these challenges by treating processes themselves as the object of analysis [31]. Rather than imposing rigid models, it reconstructs the actual flows of activities from event data, revealing both common pathways and the many deviations that occur in practice. It can integrate structured logs with semi-structured records and even signals from unstructured sources, thereby capturing a more complete picture of care delivery. Importantly, PM has methods which do not collapse multiple perspectives into a single view but allows them to coexist, tracing the same patient journey from the standpoint of different roles, or contrasting team-level practices with system-wide performance. This capacity to embrace variability and reconcile perspectives makes PM suited to healthcare's uncharted workflows.

The methodological foundations of process mining have been shaped to a large extent by the pioneering work of Wil van der Aalst and colleagues. Their contributions established the theoretical basis for discovering, checking, and enhancing processes from event data, and they continue to inspire applications in domains where variability and complexity are the norm. In healthcare, this perspective has proven particularly valuable: it enables the systematic analysis of patient journeys, the identification of inefficiencies, and the bridging of system-level objectives with human-level practices.

In this paper, we review process mining contributions that highlight the unique challenges of healthcare data, the flexible and adaptive nature of clinical workflows, the need to capture multiple perspectives and multi-dimensional KPIs. The remainder of the paper is organized as follows: Sect. 2 discusses the challenges of heterogeneous healthcare data, approaches for extracting events from structured, semi-structured, and unstructured sources and organizing them into event logs, and the use of conformance checking to fill in gaps in healthcare logs. Section 3 reviews approaches suited to the flexible and adaptive nature of clinical workflows, focusing on local process models and declarative process models. Section 4 addresses multi-dimensional KPIs and the analysis of trade-offs in healthcare performance. Finally, Sect. 5 concludes with reflections on the implications of these approaches and perspectives on future directions for process mining in healthcare.

## 2   From Data to Event Logs

Healthcare processes unfold in ways that are flexible and adaptive, these are only partially specified and documented. To analyze these uncharted workflows, process mining requires high-quality event logs, but clinical data rarely comes in a form that is ready to use. Instead, records are distributed across electronic health records, laboratory systems, imaging archives, and nursing documentation platforms, each with its own conventions, level of granularity, and temporal precision. Mobile health (mHealth) applications add more streams of sensor and app data, which are semi-structured and asynchronous [50]. The result is a heterogeneous patchwork of traces that must be abstracted, integrated, and validated before they can serve as the basis for process-oriented analysis [25,31].

In this section we highlight several challenges and approaches for constructing event logs from such heterogeneous and partially observed data, focusing on event extraction from patients' charts, event log reconstruction, and context-sensitive refinement.

## 2.1  Extracting Events from Clinical Text

Structured records such as lab results or billing transactions can often be transformed into events with relatively straightforward mappings. But the richer details of care, like medication responses, symptoms, or daily activities, are typically captured in free-text nurse and doctor notes [16,18]. Extracting events from them requires addressing variability, ambiguity, abbreviations, and negations that are inherent to clinical narratives [8,9,36]. This raises a fundamental question: how can meaningful events be reliably extracted from unstructured text so that the realities of care become accessible to process mining?

Finding an answer to this question has become increasingly feasible due to the rapid development of natural language processing (NLP) technologies, including transformer-based models and large language models (LLMs). Recent research has explored multiple approaches for event extraction in clinical text. Keyword matching (KM) remains popular due to its transparency, low cost, and ease of implementation, but it struggles with implicit mentions or variations in phrasing [39,49,51,53]. Embedding similarity (EM) methods, such as those leveraging Sentence Transformers (ST), improve recall by capturing sentence-level semantic similarity to predefined event types [9,34]. Nevertheless, EM methods may suffer from precision issues and require careful calibration [39].

Large language models (LLMs) offer strong semantic understanding and can perform zero-shot event extraction or augment training datasets for traditional models [4,15,40]. However, their high computational cost and environmental impact limit scalability in clinical applications [38,39]. To reconcile the trade-offs between accuracy, interpretability, and efficiency, hybrid approaches have been proposed. For example, the method in [39] applies KM and EM to detect candidate events, identifies sentences with conflicting predictions, and selectively applies LLMs only to these ambiguous cases. This selective strategy reduces computational cost while maintaining performance comparable to full LLM-based extraction. Additionally, LLMs can refine keyword sets by suggesting additions or removals, further improving the performance of KM-based methods [39].

Evaluation study [41] shows that a combination of semantic embeddings, selective LLM usage for ambiguous cases, and expert-defined event schemas forms a basis of effective event extractions. This approach enables event extraction from clinical text, reducing computational cost and environmental impact while preserving interpretability and clinical relevance.

Overall, these approaches demonstrate that unstructured clinical text can be transformed into structured event logs suitable for process mining, while balancing the trade-offs between automation, interpretability, and computational cost.

## 2.2 Recovering Missing Data with Process Mining Techniques

In addition to heterogeneity and ambiguity, healthcare data frequently suffers from incomplete documentation [26]. Activities are often performed but not recorded in the hospital information system, which reduces the reliability of event logs and may even lead to direct revenue losses when billing is tied to documentation. To address this issue, a probabilistic repair technique proposed in [35] leverages process knowledge to insert missing events into event logs. Their approach combines stochastic Petri nets, alignments, and Bayesian networks to identify the most likely missing activities and to estimate their timestamps based on historical traces. Evaluations using synthetic data and real hospital records from a Dutch hospital demonstrated that such repair mechanisms can significantly improve the quality and completeness of healthcare event logs, thereby supporting more reliable process mining and safeguarding compliance and revenue.

Another approach [2] aimed to quantify and subsequently estimate patient care acuity in daily clinical nursing care – the quantification of individual patient's need for nursing care. They also dealt with events not recorded, especially regarding the activities in the *Activities of Daily Living* (ADL) category, such as helping the patient to take a shower. To mitigate non-recorded events, the approach analyzes the patient situation (based on the cognitive and mobility status of the patient, but also on measurements from medical devices and medications that are connected to, inserted in, or administered to the patient) and classifies the patient into three categories: completely independent, partial support, and full support. For example, patients who are classified into the first scenario need no or little help with the nursing care activities contained in the ADL category and can carry out the activities independently. Furthermore, after the classification of patients, domain knowledge of the process allows for the estimation of such non-recorded activities, its quantification in terms of care, and better predictions on the amount of care acuity expected for the next day. This helped a Dutch hospital adjust the standard nurse-to-patient ratios and nurse staffing norms accordingly and improve decision making in terms of the number of nursing staff per shift, leading to an equal distribution of care acuity among nurses.

## 2.3 Context and Abstraction in Event Reconstruction

Even when activities are recorded, their interpretation can depend heavily on context and the level of abstraction chosen for analysis [54]. For instance, consider a nurse treating a patient's wound when an alarm indicates that another patient needs attention. If the wound is still open, leaving it unattended could be unsafe; if the dressing is complete, the nurse may respond immediately. From a raw data perspective, whether in the EHR, care log, or patient trace, both situations might appear identical: "nurse treating wound, alarm rings". Without considering the activity's state or context, analyses could misinterpret care behavior, potentially leading to inaccurate conclusions or unsafe recommendations.

Addressing this challenge requires multi-level event abstraction, where high-level activities such as "wound care" are linked to finer-grained tasks (e.g., cleaning, evaluating, dressing) and the corresponding context. By distinguishing between interrupting and non-interrupting alarms, based on response time thresholds, temporal overlap with ongoing tasks, and whether the activity was resumed shortly after, the approach in [3] demonstrates how layered modeling enables more accurate interpretation of nurses' decisions and workflow dynamics. Incorporating such context-sensitive reconstruction into event logs enhances the reliability and clinical relevance of subsequent process mining analyses, allowing analysts to capture both the sequence and the state of care activities.

The idea that context and abstraction levels affect the interpretation of events is also frequently used for label refinements, increasing the precision of event logs. An automated time-based label refinement framework proposed in [44] distinguishes behaviorally different instances of the same event type using the timestamp of each event. Applied to assisted living setting, this method showed that refining low-level events based on temporal context yields more precise and interpretable process models. In healthcare, such refinements are particularly relevant, as seemingly identical actions, like routine measurements or interventions, may have different implications depending on their timing and the patient's condition.

In short, constructing event logs in healthcare is not a mere act of data transformation. It is a process of reconstruction: extracting events from unstructured text, integrating heterogeneous systems, and even repairing what was never documented. This layered reconstruction turns fragmented pieces of clinical data into a usable basis for revealing uncharted workflows of healthcare.

## 3  Modeling Flexible and Adaptive Clinical Workflows

Clinical workflows are inherently complex, variable, and context-sensitive. Traditional imperative modeling approaches often struggle to accommodate the dynamic nature of healthcare processes, where deviations from standard pathways are not exceptions but the norm. To address these challenges, researchers have developed more flexible paradigms that have shown promise in healthcare contexts. In these section we discuss four of them: local process models (LPMs), declarative process models, multi-perspective and object-centric models, which have become key topics in the process mining community, largely due to Wil van der Aalst's efforts in developing and promoting them.

### 3.1  Local Process Models

Capturing highly flexible processes with global process models often leads to highly complex "spaghetti" models that are difficult to interpret and act upon.

This realization led to the first ideas of local process models in different contexts: managing decentralized, multi-perspective enactment of software development processes [21], deriving local models from clusters of manufacturing process instances to reveal context-specific patterns [20], or verification that organizational workflows conform to global collaborative rules [19]. These works highlighted the value of focusing on local, interpretable fragments of process behavior as a practical alternative to modeling entire complex workflows.

In the context of process mining, the concept of local process models (LPMs) was formalized and studied in [43, 46, 47], providing a systematic framework for discovering frequent, interpretable patterns directly from event data and building on the rigorous methodological foundations established by van der Aalst. The LPM approach allows to choose most interesting LPMs based on different metrics coming from the data minimg field, like support and confidence, at the same time handling concurrency, loops, and branching, brought in from process minimg [45]. LPMs also serve as a useful instrument for event abstraction, lifting raw, low-level events to higher-level behavioral patterns, especially in the context of health monitoring and ambient assisted living [42].

In healthcare, LPMs have proven particularly valuable for uncovering hidden pathways and bottlenecks [10, 17, 33]. Rather than forcing a single global view, LPMs reveal recurring, clinically meaningful fragments, such as diagnostic procedures, treatment steps, or coordination activities, that appear across many patient journeys but in diverse orders and contexts. Studies have shown that LPMs enables the extraction of major treatment stages in otherwise flexible clinical pathways, supports evidence-based evaluation and uncovers high-frequency sub-paths together with contributing risk factors in care procedures.

## 3.2  Declarative Process Models

Declarative process modeling defines constraints on activity execution rather than prescribing exact orderings, focusing on what is forbidden instead of what must be done. Models based on the Declare language, introduced by Pesic and van der Aalst [32], allow the expression of temporal and logical relationships (e.g., "a lab test must precede a diagnosis" or "a follow-up must occur within 7 days of discharge") without enforcing a fixed execution order. Logically, healthcare became a natural application area for the declarative paradigm: the declarative language for modeling clinical guidelines CIGDec [30] used constraint-based specifications to define permissible behaviors while allowing clinicians to adapt workflows in real time. Like many other declarative languages, CIGDec models are built using Linear Temporal Logic (LTL) templates, enabling representation of complex dependencies between tasks and supporting runtime flexibility in unpredictable clinical environments.

Interactive declarative process discovery frameworks, such as I-PALIA [7], allow clinicians to guide model construction using declarative expressions. Features like milestones, circuits, and protected regions help isolate clinically significant trajectories and differentiate repetitive tasks, enhancing both interpretability and relevance of the resulting workflow models.

Further extending the capabilities of declarative modeling, the DeciClareMiner tool [28] integrates decision logic into process discovery. This method captures not only the control-flow constraints but also the data-driven conditions under which specific actions are triggered. Using a combination of association rule mining and genetic algorithms, DeciClareMiner identifies decision-dependent constraints that reflect the tacit knowledge of clinicians. Applied to the emergency care process of a Belgian hospital [29], the tool successfully uncovered patterns of clinical decision-making and enabled the construction of executable models for process automation. The resulting models support both operational execution and strategic analysis, offering insights into variations in care delivery and potential deviations from clinical guidelines.

LPMs and declarative models have complementary strengths for modeling clinical workflows. LPMs uncover recurring low-level activity patterns, providing interpretable building blocks, while declarative models specify high-level constraints that govern how these fragments may combine, ensuring compliance with clinical guidelines. Integrating the two could yield multi-level process representations that are both detailed and flexible, supporting adaptive, policy-compliant workflow modeling in healthcare.

### 3.3  Multi-perspective and Object-Centric Approaches

Healthcare processes involve diverse stakeholders and dynamic interactions crossing organizational boundaries, making traditional case-centric process models insufficient to capture their full complexity. Ignoring these multiple perspectives or the interactions between key entities can lead to incomplete or misleading insights, misaligned interventions, and suboptimal decisions.

To address these challenges, several projects initiated by Wil van der Aalst and his colleagues laid the groundwork for multi-perspective approaches [5,6] and object-centric process mining  [1,22,23]. Both paradigms aim to overcome the limitations of traditional, case-centric process mining, recognizing that a single "case" view (e.g., a patient admission) often fails to capture the full scope of interactions among entities such as patients, clinicians, medical devices, and administrative systems. Still these approaches are not interchangeable and should be clearly distinguished in both theory and application:

- *Multi-Perspective Approaches* integrate separate process views, e.g., doctor, nurse, dietitian, or patient perspectives, into a unified analytical model. By mining each perspective from its relevant data sources (EHRs, sensors, patient-reported outcomes), these approaches focus on understanding process behavior in the context of a particular actor, enabling nuanced interpretations and targeted interventions. This approach enables the use of complementary methods such as qualitative analysis [24], statistical modeling [5], and domain-specific ontologies [27].
- *Object-Centric Process Mining* formalizes the process model around interacting objects (e.g., patients, lab tests, medications), each with its own lifecycle. Here, the focus is on explicitly modeling interactions between objects, allowing the discovery and analysis of concurrent and interrelated process flows.

Multiple applications of both approaches in the healthcare domain deliver evidence of their value (see e.g. [6,14,48,52]). The inherent diversity of these approaches can lead to methodological confusion and misaligned expectations. Looking forward, there is strong potential for a unified framework that combines both paradigms: leveraging object-centric structures to rigorously capture interactions between entities, while simultaneously applying multi-perspective analyses to contextualize behavior from the viewpoints of different stakeholders.

## 4 Defining Multi-dimensional KPIs in Healthcare

Defining Key Performance Indicators (KPIs) correctly is essential for prediction tasks in process mining, as KPIs define what constitutes success and guide both model evaluation and optimization. Recent reviews [13] emphasize that a comprehensive set of KPIs should include not only input, process, and output measures, but also outcome and impact indicators that reflect the real-world effects of care on patients and the healthcare system. There is a need to design KPIs that are context-sensitive, patient-centered, and inclusive of multiple stakeholder perspectives [37]. The study of discharge planning [11,12] illustrates why conventional ways of defining KPIs in healthcare may be insufficient in healthcare and need to be reconsidered.

Consider the discharge planning process. Efficient discharge planning remains a critical challenge in hospital operations, particularly when post-discharge care must be arranged externally. In [12], the discharge process of a Dutch hospital was investigated. In particular, for this process, the misalignment between the medical discharge and the transfer process for aftercare leads to substantial inefficiencies. Between 2021 and 2024, nearly 800 patients experienced prolonged hospital stays due to delays in aftercare arrangements, resulting in over 4,500 excess hospital days. These delays not only strain hospital resources but also compromise patient outcomes. Current practice relies on daily expert estimations of remaining length of stay (RLOS) and aftercare needs, yet these predictions are accurate only 46% and 58% of the time, respectively.

To address this, the authors propose a framework to predict RLOS and aftercare needs from electronic helath records (EHRs). The novelty of the approach lies in the evaluation methodology. Rather than optimizing models for conventional metrics such as accuracy or mean absolute error (MAE), the study introduces a multi-perspective evaluation framework based on the Adaptive Discharge Evaluation Metric (ADEM) [11]. ADEM defines scenarios of prediction outcomes, each associated with specific operational and clinical consequences, including unnecessary administrative work and prolonged hospital stays. These scenarios are quantified using both financial penalties and expert-defined clinical impact scores, allowing a more nuanced assessment of model performance.

Importantly, the study demonstrates that standard performance metrics are insufficient KPIs for evaluating predictive models in healthcare contexts where operational and clinical consequences are tightly coupled. The joint evaluation approach not only captures the interdependencies between RLOS and aftercare predictions, which are essential for effective discharge planning. It also considers the multidimensional goal of the process: on one hand, staying longer in the hospital is not beneficial for the patient, as he/she will not receive the specialized necessary care; and on the other hand, such optimization cannot burden transfer nurses with too many false alarms to arrange unnecessary aftercare placements.

## 5 Conclusion

Healthcare processes pose unique challenges for data-driven analysis and optimization due to its dynamic and flexible nature. This paper has reflected on how process mining offers a powerful lens to illuminate these uncharted workflows by integrating heterogeneous data sources, embracing multiple perspectives, and supporting flexible modeling paradigms. From reconstructing event logs using structured and unstructured data, to modeling adaptive clinical pathways through declarative and local process models, process mining enables a nuanced understanding of care delivery that goes beyond conventional analytics.

We have highlighted the importance of multi-perspective and object-centric approaches in capturing the richness of healthcare interactions, and emphasized the need for multi-level abstraction to accurately reflect clinical decision-making. Furthermore, we discussed the limitations of traditional KPIs and the novelty of multi-dimensional evaluation frameworks that align better with the operational and clinical realities of healthcare.

The methodological foundations laid by Wil van der Aalst and colleagues continue to inspire innovations in healthcare process analysis, and the field is now at an exciting stage of growth. Many traditional research areas remain open for exploration, offering rich opportunities to advance both theory and practice. At the same time, rapid progress in artificial intelligence, especially in machine learning, natural language processing, and generative models, provides opportunities for further enriching process mining approaches. Promising directions include developing more robust object-centric process mining algorithms, integrating clinical decision logic into adaptive models, and designing more mature, explainable, and clinician-friendly tools capable of supporting real-time decision-making. Continued methodological innovation and interdisciplinary collaboration will strengthen the applicability and clinical relevance of process mining, contributing to a deeper understanding of complex care processes and supporting safer, more responsive, context-aware and patient-centered healthcare systems.

## References

1. van der Aalst, W.M.P.: Object-centric process mining: unraveling the fabric of real processes. Mathematics **11**(12) (2023)
2. Bekelaar, J.W.R., Luime, J.J., de Carvalho, R.M.: Predicting patient care acuity: an LSTM approach for days-to-day prediction. In: Montali, M., Senderovich, A., Weidlich, M. (eds.) Process Mining Workshops, pp. 378–390. Springer Nature Switzerland, Cham (2023)

3. de Carvalho, R.M., Nguyen, H., Heetveld, M., Luime, J.: An insight to nurse workload: predicting activities in the next shift and analyzing bedside alarms influence. In: Proceedings of the 55th Hawaii International Conference on System Sciences (2022)

4. Chen, R., Qin, C., Jiang, W., Choi, D.: Is a large language model a good annotator for event extraction? Proc. AAAI Conf. Artif. Intell. **38**(16), 17772–17780 (2024)

5. van Eck, M.L., Sidorova, N., van der Aalst, W.M.P.: Discovering and exploring state-based models for multi-perspective processes. In: La Rosa, M., Loos, P., Pastor, O. (eds.) Business Process Management, pp. 142–157. Springer International Publishing, Cham (2016)

6. Erdogan, T.G., Tarhan, A.K.: Multi-perspective process mining for emergency process. Health Inf. J. **28**(1) (2022)

7. Fernández-Llatas, C., Martínez-Salvador, B., Marcos, M.: A declarative approach for interactive process discovery in the clinical domain. J. Biomed. Inform. **168**, 104862 (2025)

8. Geeganage, D.T.K., Wynn, M.T., ter Hofstede, A.H.: Text2el: exploiting unstructured text for event log enrichment. In: 2022 16th Int. Conf. on Signal-Image Technology & Internet-Based Systems (SITIS), pp. 1–8. IEEE (2022)

9. Geeganage, D.T.K., Wynn, M.T., ter Hofstede, A.H.: Text2el+: expert guided event log enrichment using unstructured text. ACM J. Data Inf. Quality **16**(1), 1–28 (2024)

10. Guo, R., et al.: A data-driven framework for improving clinical managements of severe paralytic ileus in ICU: from path discovery, model generation to validation. In: Juarez, J.M., et al., (eds.) Explainable Artificial Intelligence and Process Mining Applications for Healthcare, pp. 87–94. Springer Nature Switzerland, Cham (2024)

11. van der Haas, Y.J., de Carvalho, R.M., van Dijk, T., van Dongen, B.F., Plas, R.L.C.: A novel way to evaluate medical discharge predictions: a research paper. In: 2nd International Workshop on Process Mining Applications for Healthcare (PM4H25), 23rd International Conference on Artificial Intelligence in Medicine (AIME 2025) (2025)

12. van der Haas, Y.J., de Carvalho, R.M., van Dongen, B.F., Plas, R.L.C., van Dijk, T.: Optimizing the discharge planning process in a dutch hospital. In: 7th International Conference on Process Mining, ICPM 2025. IEEE (2025)

13. Hadian, S., Rezayatmand, R., Shaarbafchizadeh, N., Ketabi, S., Pourghaderi, A.: Hospital performance evaluation indicators: a scoping review. BMC Health Serv. Res. **24** (05 2024)

14. Heidemeyer, H., et al.: A pipeline for the usage of the core data set of the medical informatics initiative for process mining–a technical case report. In: German Medical Data Sciences 2024, pp. 30–39. IOS Press (2024)

15. Huang, F., Huang, Q., Zhao, Y., Qi, Z., Wang, B., Huang, Y., et al.: A three-stage framework for event-event relation extraction with large language model. In: Neural Information Processing. vol. 1968, pp. 434–446. Springer (2024)

16. Johnson, A., Pollard, T., Mark, R.: MIMIC-III clinical database (version 1.4). PhysioNet **10**(C2XW26), 2 (2016)

17. Kirchner, K., Marković, P.: Unveiling hidden patterns in flexible medical treatment processes - a process mining case study. In: Dargam, F., Delias, P., Linden, I., Mareschal, B. (eds.) Decision Support Systems VIII: Sustainable Data-Driven and Evidence-Based Decision Support, pp. 169–180. Springer International Publishing, Cham (2018)

18. Korach, Z.T., Yang, J., Rossetti, S.C., Cato, K.D., Kang, M.J., Knaplund, C., et al.: Mining clinical phrases from nursing notes to discover risk factors of patient deterioration. Int. J. Med. Inf. **135**, 104053 (2020)
19. Kwantes, P.M., Van Gorp, P., Kleijn, J., Rensink, A.: Towards compliance verification between global and local process models. In: Parisi-Presicce, F., Westfechtel, B. (eds.) Graph Transformation, pp. 221–236. Springer International Publishing, Cham (2015)
20. Lee, S., Kim, B., Huh, M., Cho, S., Park, S., Lee, D.: Mining transportation logs for understanding the after-assembly block manufacturing process in the shipbuilding industry. Expert Syst. Appl. **40**(1), 83–95 (2013)
21. Leonhardt, U., Kramer, J., Nuseibeh, B.: Decentralised process enactment in a multi-perspective development environment. In: Proceedings of the 17th International Conference on Software Engineering, pp. 255–264 (1995)
22. Li, G., M. de Carvalho, R., Aalst, W.: Automatic discovery of object-centric behavioral constraint models. In: Lecture Notes in Business Information Processing, pp. 43–58 (2017)
23. Li, G., de Carvalho, R.M., van der Aalst, W.M.P.: Object-centric behavioral constraint models: a hybrid model for behavioral and data perspectives. In: Proceedings of the 34th ACM/SIGAPP Symposium on Applied Computing, pp. 48–56. SAC '19, Association for Computing Machinery, New York (2019)
24. Mannhardt, F., De Leoni, M., Reijers, H.A.: The multi-perspective process explorer. In: 13th International Workshops on Business Process Management Workshops (BPM 2015), pp. 130–134 (2015)
25. Mans, R.S., van der Aalst, W.M.P., Vanwersch, R.J.B., Moleman, A.J.: Process mining in healthcare: data challenges when answering frequently posed questions. In: Lenz, R., Miksch, S., Peleg, M., Reichert, M., Riaño, D., ten Teije, A. (eds.) Process Support and Knowledge Representation in Health Care, pp. 140–153. Springer, Berlin Heidelberg, Berlin, Heidelberg (2013)
26. Martin, N., et al.: Recommendations for enhancing the usability and understandability of process mining in healthcare. Artif. Intell. Med. **109**, 101962 (2020)
27. Mayrhuber, E., Helm, E., Ehrlinger, L.: Ontology-based multi-perspective process mining in laboratories: a case study. In: De Smedt, J., Soffer, P. (eds.) Process Mining Workshops, pp. 283–295. Springer Nature Switzerland, Cham (2024)
28. Mertens, S., Gailly, F., Poels, G.: Discovering health-care processes using declareminer. Health Syst. **7**(3), 195–211 (2018)
29. Mertens, S., Gailly, F., Van Sassenbroeck, D., Poels, G.: Integrated declarative process and decision discovery of the emergency care process. Inf. Syst. Front. **24**(1), 305–327 (2022)
30. Mulyar, N., Pesic, M., van der Aalst, W.M.P., Peleg, M.: Declarative and procedural approaches for modelling clinical guidelines: addressing flexibility issues. In: ter Hofstede, A., Benatallah, B., Paik, H.Y. (eds.) Business Process Management Workshops, pp. 335–346. Springer, Berlin Heidelberg, Berlin, Heidelberg (2008)
31. Munoz-Gama, J., et al.: Process mining for healthcare: characteristics and challenges. J. Biomed. Inform. **127**, 103994 (2022)
32. Pesic, M., Schonenberg, H., van der Aalst, W.M.: Declare: full support for loosely-structured processes. In: 11th IEEE International Enterprise Distributed Object Computing Conference (EDOC 2007), pp. 287–287 (2007)
33. Pijnenborg, P., Verhoeven, R., Firat, M., Laarhoven, H.v., Genga, L.: Towards evidence-based analysis of palliative treatments for stomach and esophageal cancer patients: a process mining approach. In: 2021 3rd International Conference on Process Mining (ICPM), pp. 136–143 (2021)

34. Remy, F., Demuynck, K., Demeester, T.: BioLORD-2023: semantic textual representations fusing large language models and clinical knowledge graph insights. J. Am. Med. Inform. Assoc. **31**(9), 1844–1855 (2024)
35. Rogge-Solti, A., Mans, R.S., van der Aalst, W.M.P., Weske, M.: Improving documentation by repairing event logs. In: Grabis, J., Kirikova, M., Zdravkovic, J., Stirna, J. (eds.) The Practice of Enterprise Modeling, pp. 129–144. Springer, Berlin Heidelberg, Berlin, Heidelberg (2013)
36. Rokach, L., Romano, R., Maimon, O.: Negation recognition in medical narrative reports. Inf. Retrieval **11**, 499–538 (2008)
37. Santana, M.J., Ahmed, S., Lorenzetti, D., Jolley, R.J., Manalili, K., Zelinsky, S., Quan, H., Lu, M.: Measuring patient-centred system performance: a scoping review of patient-centred care quality indicators. BMJ Open **9**(1) (2019)
38. Solovyeva, L., Weidmann, S., Castor, F.: AI-powered, but power-hungry? energy efficiency of LLM-generated code. In: 2025 IEEE/ACM 2nd Int. Conf. on AI Foundation Models and Software Engineering (Forge), pp. 49–60. IEEE (2025)
39. Susaiyah, A., Sidorova, N.: Extracting events from nursing notes: a MIMIC-III case study. In: Proceedings of GenAI4PM 2025 (2025)
40. Susaiyah, A., Sidorova, N.: Zero-shot approaches for the extraction of event logs from medical notes. In: RCIS. LNBIP, vol. 547, pp. 435–451. Springer (2025)
41. Susaiyah, A., Sidorova, N.: Zero-shot approaches for the extraction of event logs from medical notes. In: Grabis, J., Vos, T.E.J., Escalona, M.J., Pastor, O. (eds.) Research Challenges in Information Science, pp. 435–451. Springer Nature Switzerland, Cham (2025)
42. Tax, N., Sidorova, N., Haakma, R., van der Aalst, W.: Mining process model descriptions of daily life through event abstraction. In: Bi, Y., Kapoor, S., Bhatia, R. (eds.) Intelligent Systems and Applications, pp. 83–104. Springer International Publishing, Cham (2018)
43. Tax, N.: Mining insights from weakly-structured event data, phd thesis (2019)
44. Tax, N., Alasgarov, E., Sidorova, N., Haakma, R., van der Aalst, W.M.: Generating time-based label refinements to discover more precise process models. J. Ambient Intell. Smart Environ. **11**(2), 165–182 (2019)
45. Tax, N., Dalmas, B., Sidorova, N., van der Aalst, W.M., Norre, S.: Interest-driven discovery of local process models. Inf. Syst. **77**, 105–117 (2018)
46. Tax, N., Sidorova, N., van der Aalst, W.M.P., Haakma, R.: Heuristic approaches for generating local process models through log projections. In: 2016 IEEE Symposium Series on Computational Intelligence (SSCI), pp. 1–8 (2016)
47. Tax, N., Sidorova, N., Haakma, R., van der Aalst, W.M.: Mining local process models. J. Innov. Digital Ecosyst. **3**(2), 183–196 (2016)
48. Tripathi, A., Aneesh, Shivam, Y., Pandey, S., Vyas, A., Vyas, O.P.: Exploring object centric process mining with mimic iv: Unlocking insights in healthcare. In: Almeida, J.P.A., Di Ciccio, C., Kalloniatis, C. (eds.) Advanced Information Systems Engineering Workshops, pp. 360–372. Springer Nature Switzerland, Cham (2024)
49. Wang, Y., Wang, L., Rastegar-Mojarad, M., Moon, S., Shen, F., Afzal, N., et al.: Clinical information extraction applications: a literature review. J. Biomed. Inform. **77**, 34–49 (2018)
50. Winter, M., Langguth, B., Schlee, W., Pryss, R.: Process mining in mHealth data analysis. NPJ Digit. Med. **7**, 299 (2024)
51. Wu, P.-H., Yu, A., Tsai, C.-W., Koh, J.-L., Kuo, C.-C., Chen, A.L.P.: Keyword extraction and structuralization of medical reports. Health Inf. Sci. Syst. **8**(1), 1–25 (2020). https://doi.org/10.1007/s13755-020-00108-6

52. Xu, H., Pang, J., Yang, X., et al.: Modeling clinical activities based on multi-perspective declarative process mining with openehr's characteristic. BMC Med. Inform. Decis. Mak. **20**(Suppl 14), 303 (2020)
53. Xu, H., Stenner, S.P., Doan, S., Johnson, K.B., Waitman, L.R., Denny, J.C.: Medex: a medication information extraction system for clinical narratives. J. Am. Med. Inform. Assoc. **17**(1), 19–24 (2010)
54. van Zelst, S.J., Mannhardt, F., de Leoni, M., et al.: Event abstraction in process mining: literature review and taxonomy. Granular Comput. **6**, 719–736 (2021)

# Object-Centric Extraction and Analysis of Scientific Publications


Aaron Küsters[1]([✉]) [iD], Cameron Pitsch[1] [iD], Christian Rennert[1] [iD], Jan Niklas van Detten[2,3], Ali Norouzifar[1] [iD], Viki Peeva[1] [iD], Tian Li[2], and Benedikt Knopp[1] [iD]

[1] Chair of Process and Data Science, RWTH Aachen University, Aachen, Germany
{kuesters,cameron.pitsch,rennert,ali.norouzifar,peeva,
knopp}@pads.rwth-aachen.de
[2] Business Process Management: Foundations and Engineering Group, RWTH Aachen University, Aachen, Germany
{n.vandetten,t.li}@bpm.rwth-aachen.de
[3] Celonis, Munich, Germany



**Abstract.** Object-centric event data is a generalization of case-centric event logs that allows events to be associated with multiple objects of different types. This flexibility allows extracting, modeling, and analyzing real-life processes more accurately by including multiple perspectives. Publicly available datasets are needed to support the development, evaluation, and conceptualization of new object-centric process mining concepts and techniques. In this paper, we present a generic framework to extract public scientific publication data into object-centric event logs. Apart from the publications and their authors, our framework also integrates information on the topics and keywords of works, as well as scientific conferences in the context of which research papers were published or presented. The extraction approach is generic and can extract available works for any given author or keyword, yielding a single object-centric event log as a result. The resulting dataset can then be used in object-centric process mining techniques, as well as for other general analysis, as it contains information on a plurality of different aspects. To demonstrate the feasibility of our approach, as well as the analytical potential of the resulting logs, we present a case study using the publication works of Wil van der Aalst. For example, we showcase how models mined by object-centric process model discovery describe the control-flow of the obtained data and analyze the popularity and development of keywords. The case study's analysis artifacts and the extracted object-centric event log, as well as the extraction framework code, are all publicly available.

**Keywords:** process mining · object-centric · data extraction


## 1 Introduction

*Process mining* is concerned with analyzing processes based on digital track records, called *event logs*. These logs trace the timestamps of performed activities


© The Author(s), under exclusive license to Springer Nature Switzerland AG 2026
J. Mendling et al. (Eds.): Wil van der Aalst Festschrift, LNCS 16480, pp. 662–678, 2026.
https://doi.org/10.1007/978-3-032-17618-9_43

for individual *process executions*. As such, they offer a foundation for a data-based analysis of the underlying process, ideally generating relevant insights.

Traditionally, each process execution referred to the life cycle of an individual *object*. However, real-life processes rarely consist of isolated objects. Instead, they typically contain various objects of different types that interact. *Object-Centric Process Mining (OCPM)* accounts for such interacting objects, allowing a more realistic representation of processes and offering additional analytical opportunities. For the analysis of an *Object-Centric Event Log (OCEL)*, multiple algorithmic techniques have been proposed. They typically involve the construction and verification of an imperative or declarative process model that represents the control flow of all object types. Based on the initial insights gathered on such models, different in-depth analysis techniques for specific aspects can be performed.

However, all of these techniques already assume an OCEL to be given. In practice, though, the availability of OCELs of sufficient quality is a complex challenge. IT systems rarely track process data in a structure that is immediately suitable for representation in OCELs. Instead, they require an *extraction strategy* that combines technical information about the IT systems with domain-specific knowledge to provide a mapping to OCELs.

Existing work on the extraction of OCELs is often limited by the lack of public availability. Software vendors for object-centric process mining techniques provide extensive tooling for data modeling and extraction, but the resulting logs are of a proprietary nature to the respective customers and as such unavailable to the research community. Academic extraction techniques that refer to business processes allow extractions from complex ERP systems such as SAP but, of course, require access to real-life instances of such systems that are rarely available for research purposes. As such, there is a lack of public real-life logs that restricts the development and verification of analysis techniques.

To address this problem, extraction strategies are needed for domains in which the underlying real-life IT systems for process data are generally publicly available. Some existing proposals for this purpose include the extraction of data from public platforms that are in process-driven domains, such as GitHub for open-source software development. However, only a few such approaches exist.

In this work, we address this gap while simultaneously making process data accessible on a very core process of many researchers: publishing papers. We present a general approach to extract data on scientific publications based mainly on publicly available data sources into an object-centric event log, capturing interactions between objects like *authors*, *papers*, *conferences*, and *keywords*. These systems include commonly used platforms for publishing *Call for Papers* of scientific conferences (WikiCFP) and the attribution of metadata to publications (Scopus & OpenAlex). Our approach can be applied to any researcher with published papers that are recorded in the utilized systems, enabling the creation of numerous unique object-centric event logs in a yet unexplored domain.

To showcase the utility of our approach, we perform a case study on the scientific publications of Wil van der Aalst. We use our approach to extract a publicly available object-centric event log evolving around his published papers. Subsequently, we apply a range of recently introduced object-centric techniques to illustrate the analytical potential of the logs exacted with our approach.

## 2   Related Work

We summarize related work on the extraction of object-centric event logs, using the OCEL file format [16]. Approaches for the extraction of object-centric event logs can be categorized into three groups: 1) the general extraction of object-centric event logs from enterprise IT systems, 2) the transformation of alternative formats for object-centric process information into object-centric event logs, and 3) the domain-specific extraction customized for the targeted platform.

Broad approaches for extraction strategies from enterprise systems typically refer to relational databases in general [23] or to specific, but widely used, planning systems such as SAP [5,14]. For research purposes on the resulting logs, those approaches require legitimate access to a real-life instance of those systems. As those are often not available, simulated instances can also be used [25]. The same problem arises for industrial tools for log extraction, which typically include a full tool suite for data modeling. Comparable academic tools of similar generality for this purpose have only recently been proposed in [29].

Approaches that rely on the transformation of data from other sources typically originate from graph-based formalisms. This includes event knowledge graphs [20], which can be constructed with the use of data modeling techniques [28]. Multiple approaches exist to handle the transformation between these graphs and object-centric logs [18,19]. Further transformation techniques attempt to infer object-centric information from traditional event logs [27] or try to preserve as much information as possible from more expressive formats [15].

While the aforementioned approaches attempt to remain domain-agnostic, our work primarily follows approaches that specialize in domain-specific extractions. More specifically, on approaches that focus on underlying publicly available IT systems. Existing work in this direction includes the extraction from publicly available platforms in process-driven domains, such as GitHub for software development [6]. Further domain-specific approaches go even further and consider also more distant areas from the traditional business process setting. Such techniques include the modeling of football games in object-centric event logs [8] or the digital traces left by players in computer games, such as [24]. The corresponding logs challenge many of the existing object-centric analysis techniques with their reflection of large and complex real-life systems.

Further work that should be noted are approaches outside the process mining community that focus on the analysis of scientific publication data. For the underlying systems that we investigate for our extraction, various analyses have been performed already, albeit with very different goals that are not necessarily process-driven. This includes, for example, the analysis of coverage by OpenAlex in comparison to other platforms [9] or the development of a recommendation system for conferences based on WikiCFP [17]. For Scopus, there is an abundance of analytical methods available that range from the improved classification of papers [3] to the detection of problematic journals [1], just to name a few. To the best of our knowledge, our approach is to first enable a process-driven, object-centric analysis on data extracted from these systems.

## 3   Extracting Object-Centric Event Logs

In this section, we discuss the data extraction framework used to extract object-centric event logs for publication data, illustrated in Fig. 1. The framework combines the OpenAlex[1] and Scopus[2] APIs, as well as WikiCFP[3] to extract rich information describing various aspects of the publications. OpenAlex is used as the primary data source to fetch metadata about publications for a keyword or author. Then, Scopus and OpenAlex are further queried to enrich the data, and, finally, WikiCFP is used to extract various timestamps and location data for the conference. Finally, all this information is combined to create the OCEL for the given keyword or author. The extraction pipeline is available on GitHub[4].

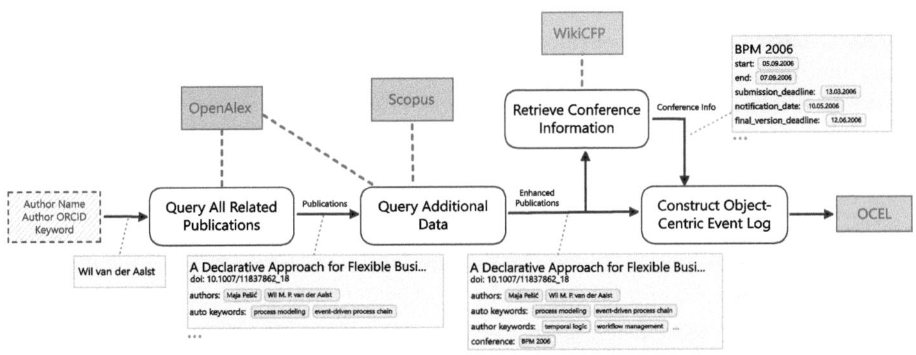


**Fig. 1.** An overview of the extraction approach. Taking an identifier as input, all relevant publications are queried from OpenAlex and then enriched using additional data from OpenAlex and Scopus. Then, conference information is added from WikiCFP.

### 3.1   Data Sources

Before going into detail on the framework itself, we first discuss the reasons that we choose the given data sources and discuss their data quality. OpenAlex [26] is chosen as the primary data source as it is an open-access and extensive library, covering publication data from a wide range of disciplines that further provides

---


[1] https://openalex.org/.

[2] https://www.scopus.com/.

[3] http://www.wikicfp.com/.

[4] https://github.com/cRennert/publication-ocel-extraction.

API access for all relevant publication data. That is, it contains data on over 263 million publications and 2.5 billion references.

Scopus, as a commercial vendor of scientific publication data, includes data on around 97.3 million records and over 2.4 billion references, dating back to 1970 and covering data from more than 7,000 publishers[5]. Therefore, we use Scopus to provide additional data that is not available in OpenAlex, such as the author-provided keywords of a paper or conference names, enriching the data basis that is extracted from OpenAlex. However, since Scopus requires a paid membership, we decide against using it as the main data source but instead use it to enrich the data extracted from OpenAlex. For further information on the suitability of OpenAlex and Scopus as data sources for our framework and regarding data quality, we refer to [2] and [10].

As a data source for conference information, we use WikiCFP since it is one of the only publicly available websites that provides information on conference dates and locations in a structured manner. WikiCFP is a community-driven website that provides information on calls for papers for scientific conferences. In particular, WikiCFP contains important deadlines, conference dates, and locations of selected conferences. As such, for a given conference, WikiCFP is used to extract its location, start and end dates, deadlines for the submission of the abstract, paper, and final version, and the notification date. However, while in many instances, the WikiCFP entry for a call for papers contains correct and complete information, in some instances, entries have missing or incorrect data since they are entered by community members and not validated in any way. Thus, the data extracted from WikiCFP may contain typos in dates or locations or missing data due to the information not being available when the call for papers was entered into WikiCFP. Moreover, the extent of data completeness varies between entries since the minimal entry only contains the submission deadline and start and end dates of the conference. These data quality issues are later addressed in post-processing.

## 3.2   Data Extraction

The extraction framework follows the structure illustrated in Fig. 1. As input, an author's name, ORCID, or a keyword is expected, and related publications are queried from OpenAlex. For each publication, the retrieved data includes its title, DOI, automatically assigned keywords, document type, and number of citations, as well as information on all involved authors. In the next step, for all publications that have a DOI, Scopus is queried to retrieve further information on each document, including the author keywords and the name of the conference it was published at (if any). Scopus and OpenAlex are both used to derive a timestamp of the publication, where the more precise date is used. In addition to this extended publication data, recursive queries are executed to retrieve all works citing the publication from OpenAlex. This information is later used to

---

[5] https://www.elsevier.com/products/scopus/content.

construct `citations` attributes, which include the total number of papers that cited a work at a given timestamp.

Next, all other information on the associated conferences is retrieved from WikiCFP. While we use the official APIs for the querying of OpenAlex and Scopus, data scraping needs to be applied to extract the information from WikiCFP. From this information, `City` and `Country` objects are derived for each conference location, as well as events for the important dates of the conference: `Abstract Deadline`, `Submission Deadline`, `Acceptance Notification`, `Final Version Deadline`, `Start Conference`, and `End Conference`.

Finally, the gathered data is used to construct an OCEL: `Papers`, `Keywords`, `Researchers`, `Conferences`, as well as the `Cities` and `Countries` they are in, are added as objects with respective object types. For events, the publication timestamp is used to add one `Publication` event for each paper, also involving the relevant researcher and keyword objects. Moreover, the information extracted from WikiCFP is used to add relevant conference events, e.g., `Submission Deadline` or `Start Conference` which are also associated with relevant papers or researchers. As further details, for instance on conference participation, are not available, we made some basic assumptions, for example, that the first author of a paper always attends the conference the paper is presented at. To include the temporal dynamics of citation counts, we added a `citations` attribute to `Paper` objects for the total number of citations that changes over time, accounting for the publication dates of the works citing the paper. Similarly, automatically assigned `Keywords` also have a total citation count that changes over time, corresponding to the number of citations of all papers that were assigned to this keyword. Object-to-object relationships are added between relevant object instances, as indicated in Fig. 2. Researchers can be related to other researchers, representing a collaboration between them. The relationship between papers and authors differentiates between first authors and co-authors. Each paper is associated with the conference it was published or presented at, with the conference being associated with the city and country it took place in. To differentiate between automatically generated and manually added author keywords for papers, different relationship qualifiers are used.

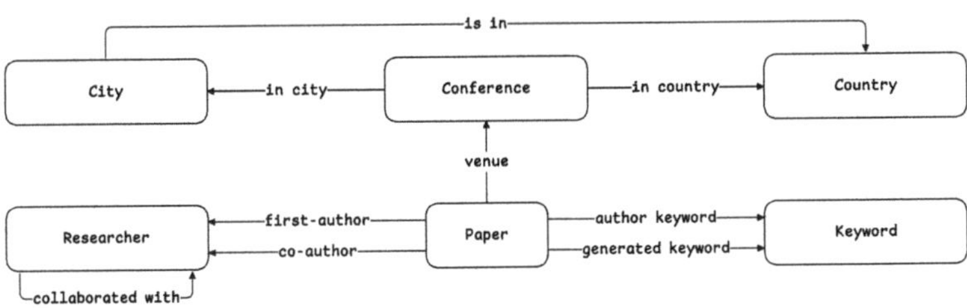


**Fig. 2.** Object-to-object relationships between the included object types and their relationship qualifiers in the scientific publication domain context.

# 4   Case Study: Publications of Wil van der Aalst

In this section, we perform a case study on the scientific publications of Wil van der Aalst. First, we use our approach to extract a corresponding OCEL. We then apply various analysis techniques to showcase the analytical potential of such logs. In particular, we investigate the control flow of the log from an imperative and declarative perspective. Subsequently, we drill down into multiple more detailed aspects, such as the occurrences of keywords, time series analysis, and conference locations. Notably, all of these analyses are based on the extracted OCEL as a single data source. Throughout different parts of the analysis and the preprocessing, we used OCPQ [22] to explore the OCEL and export situation tables. The source code of our case study analysis is available on GitHub[6]. Moreover, the extracted datasets are also available[7].

## 4.1   Object-Centric Event Log Extraction

After extracting the event log using our extraction framework, the data contains a few quality issues. For instance, while OpenAlex features consolidation of multiple spellings of author names, some authors occur in the dataset with different spellings, causing them to be identified as distinct authors. Moreover, this consolidation is not perfect, meaning that certain papers are incorrectly assigned to Wil van der Aalst. Furthermore, the format of the conference information in WikiCFP is not standardized, which means that, also here, formats vary and misspellings occur. To address these issues, we add a post-processing step to the extraction framework, which, given a list of erroneous paper IDs and mappings of incorrect author and location names, repairs the aforementioned issues and typos to create a clean OCEL[8].

The resulting OCEL dataset contains over 2000 events and 5000 objects interconnected by over 30000 event-to-object and 50000 object-to-object relationships. The most frequent event type is `Publication` with over 1500 events. Events based on conferences, such as `Start Conference`, occur less frequently, with the most common ones having just below 100 events each. The objects in the dataset are over 1500 `Paper` and `Keyword` objects, above 900 `Researcher` objects, as well as over 200 `Conference`, 70 `City`, and 30 `Country` objects. Notably, apart from Wil himself, one researcher has participated in over 150 papers of the dataset, 13 researchers have contributed to 50 or more papers, and over 90 researchers have been involved in 10 or more papers.

---

[6] https://github.com/cRennert/publication-ocel-analysis.
[7] https://doi.org/10.5281/zenodo.17769774.
[8] Due to the data completeness and quality issues of the underlying data sources, we do not consider the dataset to be *complete*. Thus, we often focus on analyzing trends and changes, which can also be observed from just a sample.

## 4.2   Object-Centric Control Flow Analysis

**Object-Centric Process Trees.** We utilize object-centric process trees to generate insights into the control flow present in the generated object-centric event log [11]. Conceptually, object-centric process trees summarize the most restrictive control flow across all object types into a joint end-to-end process model. As such, they are used to generate a high-level overview before drilling down into detailed analysis aspects. Additionally, they can be used to identify parts of the process in which the identities of objects are relevant for control flow decisions [13]. We first preprocess the object-centric event log and apply the approach from [11] for the control flow discovery. Then, we proceed with the technique from [13] to detect identity-based relationships between object types.

*Data Preprocessing.* We perform two data preprocessing steps, specific to the subsequent usage of object-centric process trees. This particularly refers to the identification of missing object types and duplicated activity labels.

Missing object types can arise due to flawed data extraction strategies or misinterpreted domain knowledge. As they typically lead to activities without distinct control flow relations, they drastically impede the subsequent discovery of object-centric process trees. As such, they should be ruled out in advance. For this purpose, we use the detection strategy from [12]. Applying it to the generated input logs yields no distinct new object types. As such, we can verify the extraction quality to be sufficient for the use of object-centric process trees.

Activity duplications arise when the same activity label is used in drastically different process contexts. As they are not supported by the formalism of object-centric process trees, we aim to rule them out in advance. To identify such duplications, we perform the following steps on the extracted object-centric event log. We iteratively project the log onto each of the object types and determine the prefixes for each of the activities in the alphabet of the log. Then, we quantify the behavioral differences between the prefixes of the same activity and use this measure as a distance to cluster prefixes. If this step results in multiple clusters, we conclude that the process context for these clusters of events with the same activity is sufficiently different to justify splitting the corresponding label.

Applying this strategy to the generated log yields a single activity with two event clusters that show sufficiently different prefix behavior. The `Publication` activity appears in two extremely different contexts, which seem to correspond to the publication of a paper before and after the review process. We investigated these events and found the first cluster to represent a data quality issue caused by the high granularity of the extracted timestamps. As such, we filtered the respective events.

*Control Flow.* We utilize the approach from [12] to discover the control flow of the mainstream behavior in the input log with the use of object-centric process trees. The approach generates an accumulated directly-follows graph across all object types that excludes behavior induced by resource-like business objects. As such, it reflects the most restrictive control flow across all object types that can

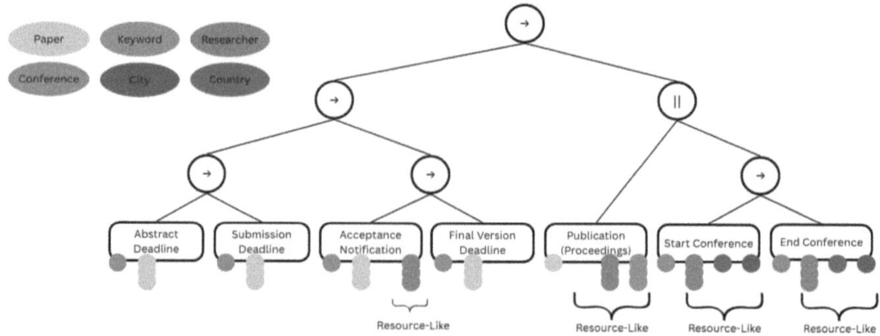



**Fig. 3.** Object-centric process tree for the object-centric event log on academic publications. Note that resource-like object types are not subject to the discovered control flows of sequences (→) and concurrency (||). The involvement of object types in activities is indicated by the respectively colored dot in the leaves. Multiple dots express the option to include multiple objects of that type in the execution of the activity.

be expressed in the utilized representational bias. To focus on the mainstream behavior in the log, we apply a filter to this graph. First, we determine the average edge frequency. Then, we remove all edges with a significantly lower frequency. The resulting object-centric process tree is shown in Fig. 3.

The overall behavior expresses the sequential steps of the review process of a conference. After the review, the final version is submitted and published in the conference proceedings. Concurrently with the publication, the conference is held. Unsurprisingly, the majority of the identified control flow is induced by the object types of papers and conferences. The remaining object types of researches, keywords, countries, and cities mostly exhibit resource-like behavior. This means that over the time span recorded in the input log, researchers wrote multiple papers, visited multiple conferences, and used the same keyword in various papers simultaneously. Note that this type of resource-like behavior is indicated by the respective note in the visualization of the tree.

*Identity Relations.* On top of the discovered object-centric process tree shown in Fig. 3, we apply the approach from [13] to discover parts of the process in which the identities of objects influence their control flow. Applying this technique to the preprocessed object-centric event log exclusively generates results that can be verified in the domain context with superficial knowledge. For example, the discovered restrictions express that across the review, the same paper always implies the same set of researchers. Additionally, the same conference also implies the same country across all activities related to these types.

**OC-DECLARE.** To reveal even more synchronized control flow between objects of different types, we also discover an OC-DECLARE process model using the discovery approach described in [21]. An OC-DECLARE model consists of multiple constraints, visualized as arcs between activity nodes. Figure 4 shows the OC-DECLARE model automatically discovered on the dataset with a noise threshold of $\tau = 0.2$ and without object-to-object relationships, after performing a transitive reduction to remove superfluous constraints. The resulting model consists of 12 individual constraints, with confidence values ranging from 82.22% to 100%. Consider the constraint arc discovered between `Abstract Deadline` and `Submission Deadline` as an example. It encompasses that for each conference in the abstract deadline event, there should be a submission deadline event directly afterwards that also involves all the papers of the first event. Notably, this constraint is not discovered in the preceding direction, i.e., that before each `Submission Deadline` event, there should be an `Abstract Deadline` event. This can be attributed to the fact that not all conferences that have a submission deadline in our dataset also have an abstract deadline, and the preceding constraint would thus not hold with the required confidence. In general, much of the observed synchronization behavior can be attributed to the assumptions made in Sect. 3. For instance, the discovered arc from `Start Conference` to `End Conferences` expresses that all the researchers involved with the start of the conference are also involved in the corresponding end conference event for each city, conference, and country object also involved in the start event. This constraint is violated only in 2.02% of all `Start Conference` events. Manual investigation using OCPQ reveals that for two of the 99 conferences in the dataset, the conference end event has the exact same timestamp as the start event, violating the *eventually-follows* temporal constraint of the corresponding OC-DECLARE arc.

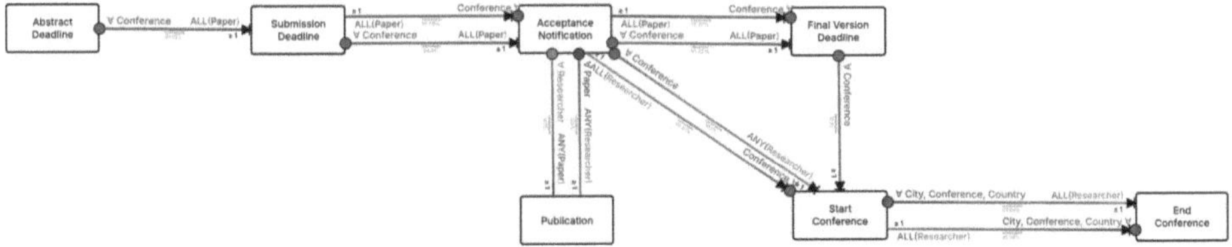

**Fig. 4.** Discovered OC-DECLARE model.

### 4.3  Data Analysis

In this subsection, we use non-process mining techniques to further analyze the data from the OCEL. To this end, we employ visual analytics to show trends in the data, such as in the popularity of keywords and the impact of published papers as measured by citations. Finally, we aggregate conference locations to provide a view on the most visited countries.

*Keyword Analysis.* Trends and developments of research directions can be revealed by examining the frequency and temporal changes of keyword usage in scientific publications. The extracted OCEL dataset contains more than one thousand unique keywords provided by the authors. Since the keywords were

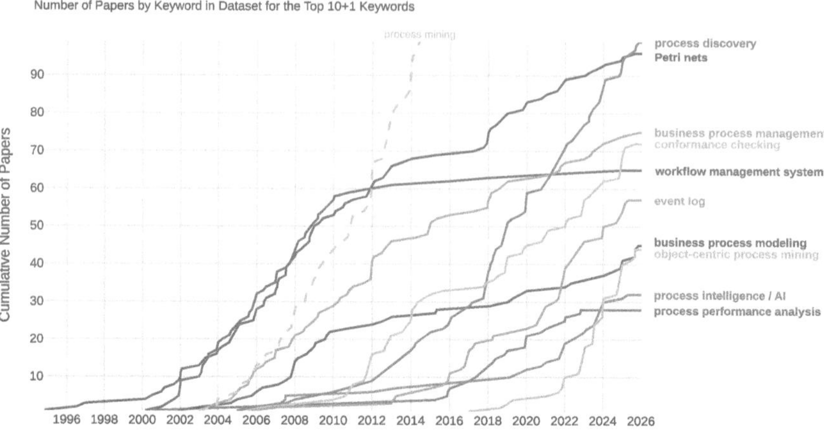



**Fig. 5.** Total number of papers published per keyword over time in the examined dataset for the eleven most frequent keywords. Similar keywords are grouped together and shown for one representative.

freely chosen by the authors, their selection is often inconsistent and does not follow a standardized guideline. This introduces several challenges, such as grammatical variations (e.g., "event log" vs. "event logs"), orthographic differences between British and American English (e.g., "modelling" vs. "modeling"), or the inconsistent use of hyphenation (e.g., "internet of things" vs. "internet-of-things"). A further difficulty arises from the use of different expressions to describe conceptually similar notions, for example, *process improvement* and *process enhancement.*

To address these challenges, we explored embedding models that encode words into a high-dimensional feature space, where each keyword is represented by a numerical vector. In this representation, semantically similar words are located close to each other. We compared embeddings generated by SciBERT [4] and by *text-embedding-3-large*[9], which is an OpenAI model. Based on manual inspection, the embeddings from the OpenAI model aligned more closely with our domain understanding and thus were selected for further analysis. Subsequently, we applied the HDBSCAN clustering algorithm [7] to group semantically related keywords. Finally, each resulting cluster was manually examined and assigned a representative label, ensuring both interpretability and domain relevance.

Figure 5 shows the cumulative number of papers published for the 11 keywords with the most publications in the dataset. The keyword *Petri nets* was among the first terms Wil used in his publications more than 30 years ago. In the early years of his scientific career, *Petri nets* and *workflow management systems* were central research themes. Over time, the figure shows a shift toward *business process management*, reflecting Wil's transition from theoretical foundations to practical applications. After 2010, two new concepts gained prominence, *process*

---

[9] https://platform.openai.com/docs/guides/embeddings.

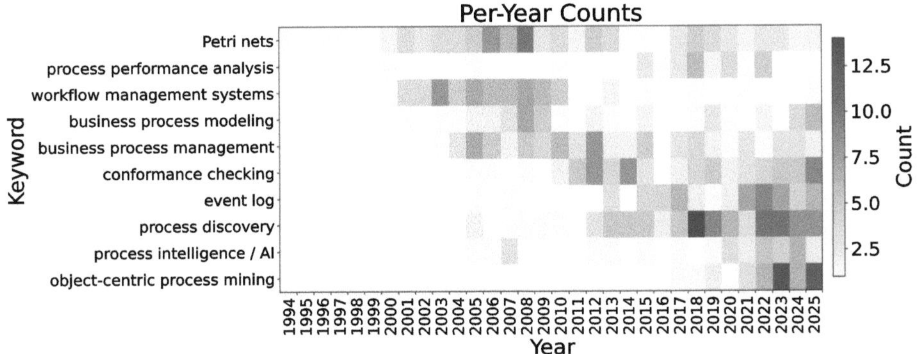


**Fig. 6.** Temporal evolution of keywords in publications (1994–2025).

*discovery* and *conformance checking*, both of which Wil significantly contributed to developing. These areas remain highly relevant after more than a decade of research and today count towards the five keywords with the most published paper in the dataset. The continued focus on the keyword *event log* during this period reflects its essential role, as both process discovery and conformance checking are inherently data-driven. Recently, keywords like *object-centric process mining* and *process intelligence / AI* have attracted growing interest, aligning with broader developments in process mining and data science fields.

The evaluation of research interests is especially observable when considering the number of new papers published for a keyword per year, as shown in Fig. 6. The x-axis denotes the publication year, while the y-axis lists the keywords. The color intensity encodes the yearly frequency of each keyword, with darker shades indicating higher occurrence. For clarity, the figure does not include the dominant keyword *process mining* and only includes keywords with at least 25 papers. Keywords are ordered by their year of first appearance. Notably, there are sometimes *"hot"* and *"cold"* phases of keywords, where more or fewer papers than usual on that keyword are published. For instance, 2014–2016 was a cold phase for the keyword *Petri nets*, while in 2018 there was an exceptionally hot phase for the keyword *process discovery*, with 15 papers published with that keyword in one year.

Recent research interests and emerging developments are not fully visible in Fig. 5 and 6, as low-frequency keywords were excluded, even though such terms may signal new directions in recent years. To highlight these trends, Fig. 7 visualizes the most frequent keywords during the years 1994–2020 and from 2020 to now (2025). In addition to *process mining*, other generic terms such as *event log*, *process discovery*, and *conformance checking* are excluded to emphasize more specific and emerging topics. This figure highlights more recent research themes in Wil's publications, like *object-centric process mining* or *process intelligence / AI*, and also certain terms not frequently used anymore, like *workflow management systems*.

**Fig. 7.** Word clouds of keywords (1994–2020 on the left, 2020–2025 on the right), with word size proportional to the number of papers published in the respective time range.

*Impact of Publications.* In further exploratory data analysis, we visualized trends in the data by means of time series. Our goal is to illustrate the development of the impact of Wil's research on the research community, as reflected in citations of his work. Figure 8 shows the number of new publications each year and the number of citations for these papers per year[10]. Starting in the early 2000s, there is a slow yet stable acceleration of research output, with a significant acceleration from the years 2005 to 2008. After that, there is a stability around the level of 60 publications per year, with a global maximum in the year 2024. Citations increase starting around 2002 and 2003 at a stable pace, peaking in 2012.

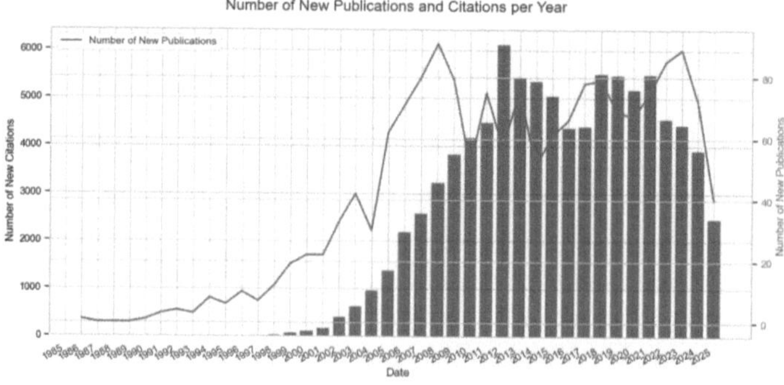



**Fig. 8.** New publications per year (line) and total citations for these publications (bars).

---

[10] Thanks to our master's thesis student Ibrahim Ismail for his work on TSA.

*Conference Locations.* In this study, we analyze the location data found for the conferences in our extracted OCEL for the author *Wil van der Aalst.* In particular, the dataset contains location information for only 99 of the 251 conferences, meaning that a location can be determined for only 174 of the papers. This is because the location data is extracted from a community-driven website, meaning that not every call for papers is recorded.

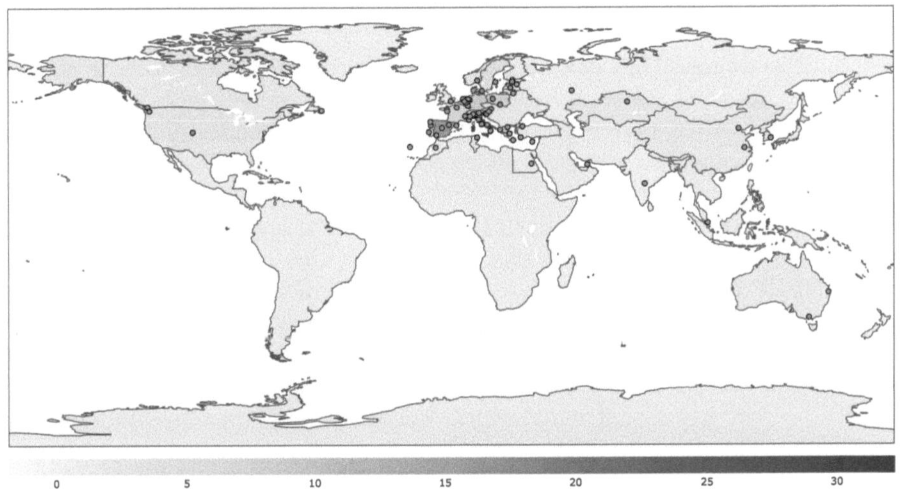

**Fig. 9.** Conference location frequency for papers with *Wil van der Aalst* as co-author. The color of a country indicates its frequency as a conference location, and green points indicate the city in which the conference took place.

Figure 9 shows a map of the locations of the conferences for all papers with *Wil van der Aalst* as a co-author. Countries are colored based on the total number of papers associated with a conference located in that country, and for each paper, the corresponding city is indicated with a green circle. The most common country is Italy, with 32 papers, closely followed by the Netherlands, with 28 papers, and Spain, with 16 papers. Correspondingly, the most common cities were Bolzano, Italy (14); Limassol, Cyprus (13); and Eindhoven, the Netherlands (12). In total, our recorded data covers 33 countries and 5 continents.

## 5   Conclusion

In this paper, we introduced a framework for extracting scientific publication data from public sources, in particular OpenAlex, Scopus, and WikiCFP, and transforming it into an object-centric event log (OCEL), capturing complex interactions between objects of different types, such as papers, researchers, keywords, and conferences. The framework is generic and can be used for generating logs based on any specified author or keyword.

To demonstrate the framework's feasibility and the analytical potential of the resulting OCEL, we conducted a case study on the publication history of Wil van der Aalst. To that end, we included both object-centric and other detailed analyses, for example, on keywords that, while not being inherently object-centric, leverage the interconnected information of multiple objects in the OCEL as a data source. In the object-centric analysis, the employed discovery techniques were able to mine meaningful process models from the events included in the OCEL. The keyword analysis revealed trends and changes of research themes over three decades, and the location analysis showed patterns in conference location attendance. This work serves as both a practical tool for the research community, allowing deep process-based analysis of scientific publications, for instance for literature reviews, as well as a blueprint for enabling the creation of new, diverse datasets to advance object-centric process mining research.

*Future Work.* For future work, our primary goal is to improve the data coverage and quality of the extracted works. To achieve this, additional data sources such as DBLP and arXiv could be integrated. Furthermore, conference-specific information, for example, extracted from EasyChair instances, could be included, which would yield a richer data source for event and timestamp information. As OpenAlex accepts user-provided curation requests, some data quality issues can also be addressed upstream, which would not only benefit our developed approach but also other projects using OpenAlex. Of course, there are also many more opportunities for analyzing the resulting dataset of our case study.

# References


1. Abalkina, A.: Challenges posed by hijacked journals in scopus. J. Assoc. Inf. Sci. Technol. **75**(4), 395–422 (2024)
2. Alperin, J.P., Portenoy, J., Demes, K., Larivière, V., Haustein, S.: An analysis of the suitability of openalex for bibliometric analyses. CoRR abs/2404.17663 (2024)
3. Álvarez-Llorente, J.M., Guerrero-Bote, V.P., de Moya-Anegón, F.: New paper-by-paper classification for scopus based on references reclassified by the origin of the papers citing them. J. Informetrics **19**(2), 101647 (2025)
4. Beltagy, I., Lo, K., Cohan, A.: Scibert: a pretrained language model for scientific text. In: EMNLP/IJCNLP (1), pp. 3613–3618. Association for Computational Linguistics (2019)
5. Berti, A., Park, G., Rafiei, M., van der Aalst, W.M.P.: A generic approach to extract object-centric event data from databases supporting SAP ERP. J. Intell. Inf. Syst. **61**(3), 835–857 (2023)
6. Bosmans, L., Peeperkorn, J., De Smedt, J.: Pystack't: real-life data for object-centric process mining. In: BPM (Demos / Resources Forum). CEUR Workshop Proceedings, vol. 4032, pp. 208–215. CEUR-WS.org (2025)
7. Campello, R.J.G.B., Moulavi, D., Sander, J.: Density-based clustering based on hierarchical density estimates. In: Pei, J., Tseng, V.S., Cao, L., Motoda, H., Xu, G. (eds.) PAKDD 2013. LNCS (LNAI), vol. 7819, pp. 160–172. Springer, Heidelberg (2013). https://doi.org/10.1007/978-3-642-37456-2_14

8. Chan, V., Ebert, L., Hillmann, P.J., Rubensson, C., Mendling, S.A.F.P.J.: Transforming football data into object-centric event logs with spatial context information. In: Business Process Management Workshops (to be published). Lecture Notes in Business Information Processing, Springer (2025)

9. Culbert, J.H., Hobert, A., Jahn, N., Haupka, N., Schmidt, M., Donner, P., Mayr, P.: Reference coverage analysis of openalex compared to web of science and scopus. Scientometrics **130**(4), 2475–2492 (2025)

10. Culbert, J.H., et al.: Reference coverage analysis of openalex compared to web of science and scopus. Scientometrics **130**(4), 2475–2492 (2025)

11. van Detten, J.N., Schumacher, P., Leemans, S.J.J.: Discovering compact, live and identifier-sound object-centric process models. In: ICPM, pp. 113–120. IEEE (2024)

12. van Detten, J.N., Schumacher, P., Leemans, S.J.J.: Object synchronizations and specializations with silent objects in object-centric petri nets. In: BPM. Lecture Notes in Computer Science, vol. 14940, pp. 57–74. Springer (2024)

13. van Detten, J.N., Schumacher, P., Leemans, S.J.J.: Modeling and discovering dynamic identity relations in object-centric process mining. In: ICPM (to be published). IEEE (2025)

14. Fahland, D., Lu, X., Nagelkerke, M., van de Wiel, D.: Discovering interacting artifacts from ERP systems (extended abstract). EMISA Forum **36**(2), 89–92 (2016)

15. Fahland, D., et al.: Towards a simple and extensible standard for object-centric event data (OCED) - core model, design space, and lessons learned. CoRR abs/2410.14495 (2024)

16. Ghahfarokhi, A.F., Park, G., Berti, A., van der Aalst, W.M.P.: OCEL: a standard for object-centric event logs. In: ADBIS (Short Papers). Communications in Computer and Information Science, vol. 1450, pp. 169–175. Springer (2021)

17. Iana, A., Jung, S., Naeser, P., Birukou, A., Hertling, S., Paulheim, H.: Building a conference recommender system based on SciGraph and WikiCFP. In: Acosta, M., Cudré-Mauroux, P., Maleshkova, M., Pellegrini, T., Sack, H., Sure-Vetter, Y. (eds.) SEMANTiCS 2019. LNCS, vol. 11702, pp. 117–123. Springer, Cham (2019). https://doi.org/10.1007/978-3-030-33220-4_9

18. Khayatbashi, S., Hartig, O., Jalali, A.: Transforming event knowledge graph to object-centric event logs: a comparative study for multi-dimensional process analysis. In: ER. Lecture Notes in Computer Science, vol. 14320, pp. 220–238. Springer (2023)

19. Khayatbashi, S., Hartig, O., Jalali, A.: Transforming object-centric event logs to temporal event knowledge graphs (extended version). CoRR abs/2406.07596 (2024)

20. Klijn, E.L., Preuss, D., Imeri, L., Baumann, F., Mannhardt, F., Fahland, D.: Event knowledge graphs for auditing: a case study. In: ICPM Workshops. Lecture Notes in Business Information Processing, vol. 503, pp. 84–97. Springer (2023)

21. Küsters, A., van der Aalst, W.M.P.: OC-DECLARE: discovering object-centric declarative patterns with synchronization. In: BPM. Lecture Notes in Computer Science, vol. 16044, pp. 162–179. Springer (2025)

22. Küsters, A., van der Aalst, W.M.P.: OCPQ: object-centric process querying and constraints. In: RCIS (1). Lecture Notes in Business Information Processing, vol. 547, pp. 383–400. Springer (2025)

23. Li, G., de Murillas, E.G.L., de Carvalho, R.M., van der Aalst, W.M.P.: Extracting object-centric event logs to support process mining on databases. In: Mendling, J., Mouratidis, H. (eds.) CAiSE 2018. LNBIP, vol. 317, pp. 182–199. Springer, Cham (2018). https://doi.org/10.1007/978-3-319-92901-9_16

24. Liss, L., Elbert, N., Flath, C.M., van der Aalst, W.M.P.: Framework for extracting real-world object-centric event logs from game data. In: ICPM Workshops. Lecture Notes in Business Information Processing, vol. 533, pp. 363–375. Springer (2024)
25. Park, G., Leah Tacke, g.U.: Procure-to-payment (p2p) object-centric event log in ocel 2.0 standard (Oct 2023)
26. Priem, J., Piwowar, H.A., Orr, R.: Openalex: a fully-open index of scholarly works, authors, venues, institutions, and concepts. CoRR abs/2205.01833 (2022)
27. Rebmann, A., Rehse, J., van der Aa, H.: Uncovering object-centric data in classical event logs for the automated transformation from XES to OCEL. In: BPM. Lecture Notes in Computer Science, vol. 13420, pp. 379–396. Springer (2022)
28. Swevels, A., Fahland, D., Montali, M.: Implementing object-centric event data models in event knowledge graphs. In: ICPM Workshops. Lecture Notes in Business Information Processing, vol. 503, pp. 431–443. Springer (2023)
29. Wei, J., Ouyang, C., Wang, Y., Huang, L.: Dirigo: a method to extract event logs for object-centric processes. Data Knowl. Eng. **160**, 102485 (2025)

# Hybrid Intelligence and Corporate Governance: Division of Labour or Hybrid Ensembles?

Daniel Hagemeier and Peter Letmathe[(✉)]

School of Business and Economics, RWTH Aachen, Templergraben 64, 52062 Aachen, Germany
{Daniel.Hagemeier,Peter.letmathe}@rwth-aachen.de

**Abstract.** This article explores the corporate governance of Hybrid Intelligence (HI). We distinguish two fundamental modes of HI: *Division of Labour*, where humans and AI each specialise in different tasks, and *Hybrid Ensembles*, where their independent outputs are aggregated. Building on three complementary governance lenses (organisational, human, and societal), we propose a governance framework that synthesises these two modes and examines them across six dimensions: responsibility, transparency, human agency, fairness, risk, and strategic alignment. While HI promises productivity, efficiency, and resilience gains for organisations, it also raises human concerns about fairness, non-discrimination, autonomy, and job security, as well as societal concerns regarding democratic legitimacy. The framework is illustrated through an empirical production dashboard case, showing how HI governance choices shape accountability, autonomy, and legitimacy in practice. We conclude that HI governance is not about choosing one mode over the other but about dynamically balancing them and thus securing value creation and legitimacy across organisational, human, and societal levels. These insights point to future research and practice, highlighting the need to address the temporal dynamics of shifting human–AI roles and to integrate democratic deliberation into corporate governance processes.

**Keywords:** Hybrid Intelligence · Corporate Governance · Human–AI Collaboration · Division of Labour · Hybrid Ensembles

## 1 Introduction

Wil van der Aalst has long argued that the boundary between human and machine work is shifting from task automation to hybrid constellations where people and algorithms collaborate dynamically [1]. Machine learning (ML) may outperform humans in speech or image recognition; yet, human intelligence remains indispensable for contextual knowledge and empathy [1, 2]. Hybrid Intelligence (HI) promises to combine the strengths of both. Still, it also creates new governance challenges: sometimes humans supervise machines ("human-in-the-loop"), sometimes machines supervise humans ("machine-in-the-loop"), and sometimes both are aggregated into a Human-AI ensemble [3] (in the following, we refer to such Human-AI ensembles as Hybrid Ensembles).

© The Author(s), under exclusive license to Springer Nature Switzerland AG 2026
J. Mendling et al. (Eds.): Wil van der Aalst Festschrift, LNCS 16480, pp. 679–714, 2026.
https://doi.org/10.1007/978-3-032-17618-9_44

Systems combining human and machine intelligence are controversially discussed in the literature, specifically with regard to the role of artificial intelligence: what seems like the safer, more risk-averse governance choice may actually lead to greater harm. Should we favour human override even when machines are more accurate? Should we allocate decision-making between humans and algorithms to share accountability, or does this division dilute responsibility to the point where no one is truly accountable? All these points raise a fundamental question: ***how should HI be governed?*** Traditional governance frameworks assume clearly bounded roles: humans decide, machines execute. However, when employing HI, roles are fluid, and collective outcomes can blur accountability. As Dellermann et al. [4, p. 640] define it, HI is "the ability to achieve complex goals by combining human and artificial intelligence, thereby reaching superior results to those each of them could have accomplished separately, and continuously improve by learning from each other." If this is true, governance must move beyond static allocation of authority to frameworks that account for collaboration dynamics, shifting responsibilities, and legitimacy concerns. Grossmann et al. [5] underline this epistemic challenge in their *Science* article: "Just as the prisoners in Plato's Cave Allegory observing shadows on a wall and believing them to represent reality, LLMs rely on 'shadows' of human experiences described in cultural products" [5, p. 1109]. Their metaphor underlines that governance must confront not only questions of responsibility and accountability but also of epistemic legitimacy.

In this article, we address the question presented in our title: "Hybrid Intelligence and Corporate Governance: Division of Labour or Hybrid Ensembles?". We present a governance framework built on six dimensions that encapsulate recurring challenges in both modes of human–AI collaboration: Division of Labour and Hybrid Ensembles. Each dimension is conceptualised as a property range, clarifying the trade-offs that managers and researchers must consider. To demonstrate the framework's analytical use, we apply it to a use case involving Manufacturing Execution Systems (MES) dashboards in a small-scale manufacturing environment. We conclude with a research agenda that links our findings to broader debates on multi-level governance, legitimacy, and the temporal dynamics of HI applications. Figure 1 provides an overview of our analytical approach, connecting the theoretical foundations of HI to the governance framework and its empirical application.

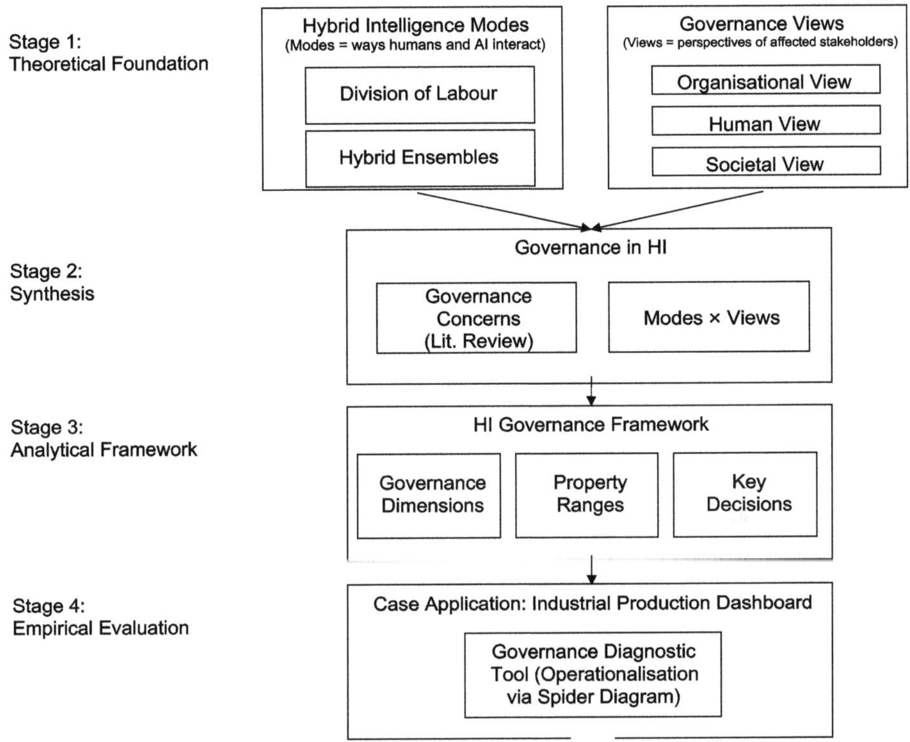


**Fig. 1.** Analytical approach of the study. The figure illustrates the progression from theoretical foundations (HI modes and governance views) to theory synthesis (governance in HI), to the analytical framework (governance dimensions, property ranges, and key decisions), and finally to empirical evaluation through a case application (MES dashboards).

## 2  Theoretical Foundation

### 2.1  HI: Concept, Evolution, and Challenge

The concept of HI refers to the deliberate combination of human and artificial intelligence to achieve outcomes that neither could attain alone. While early research in Artificial Intelligence (AI) emphasised autonomy and automation, the HI perspective highlights complementarity and collaboration between humans and machines [4]. In this sense, HI extends beyond the notion of Augmented Intelligence, where machines merely support human decision-making, by framing humans and AI systems as interdependent human-agent teams with dynamic collaboration [6]. The roots of HI can be traced across several research streams.

- **Human Computer Interaction (HCI):** Early work in HCI emphasised usability and user support, positioning computers as tools that extend human cognitive abilities. Card, Moran, and Newell's [7]. The Psychology of Human-Computer Interaction established this paradigm. The HCI perspective largely retained a human-dominant framing, where technology was viewed as an instrument.

- **Human-in-the-Loop (HITL) approaches:** In machine learning, HITL paradigms introduced iterative interaction, where humans provide feedback to train and correct models. Amershi et al. [8] and Holzinger [9] emphasised the importance of *interactive machine learning*, a process driven by human input to reduce errors. This stream demonstrated that intelligent systems cannot function effectively without continuous human oversight.
- **Augmented Intelligence:** The concept of Augmented Intelligence, popularised by IBM in the early 2010s as part of its Watson and cognitive computing initiatives [10], shifted the focus from automation to supportive AI, emphasising complementarity with human judgment. This reflected a growing recognition in management and computer science that value creation depends on human–machine collaboration. Yet, as Raisch & Krakowski [11] highlight, such augmentation is rarely stable: what begins as support often drifts towards automation, creating an **automation–augmentation paradox** that complicates governance.
- **HI**: Building on these foundations, recent research reframes the relationship as more interdependent: humans and machines are not merely in a tool–user relationship but can form dyadic constellations of intelligence. Akata et al. [6, p. 18] emphasise "collaborative, adaptive, responsible, explainable" as the normative basis for HI. Here, the novelty lies in seeing both sides as capable of co-evolution, where machines learn from humans and humans adapt to algorithmic insights.

Across diverse domains, from corporate decision-making to societal resilience, HI is presented as a pathway to overcome the limitations of either humans or machines in isolation. For example, Steyvers et al. [12] show that ensembles of humans and algorithms ("Hybrid Ensembles") can outperform either agent alone when their errors are weakly correlated. However, it remains an open question as to how humans and machines should be best combined: through a **Division of Labour**, where each specialises in distinct tasks, or through **Hybrid Ensembles**, where outputs are aggregated across agents. Scholars emphasise that this requires managing the paradox between automation and augmentation [11], ensuring error diversity in Hybrid Ensembles [3, 12], and sustaining continuous co-evolution despite differences in human and machine learning dynamics [4].

## 2.2  Collaboration in HI

HI can manifest in two primary modes of collaboration. The first, **Division of Labour,** builds on the principle of specialisation, where humans and AI assume distinct roles. The second, **Hybrid Ensembles**, relies on aggregation, where both agents perform the same task and their outputs are combined to improve accuracy or robustness. These two modes represent distinct logics for combining human and machine intelligence, thereby creating different governance challenges. Table 1 summarises these collaboration modes.

**Table 1.** Modes of HI

|  | **Division of Labour** (Specialisation / Collaboration) | **Hybrid Ensembles** (Aggregation) |
|---|---|---|
| Concept | Humans and AI perform different subtasks according to their comparative strengths | Humans and AI perform the same task, and outputs are aggregated into a collective decision or prediction |
| Mechanism | Complementarity of roles | Error diversity and independence |
| Industrial Examples | **a. Predictive maintenance:** Machine learning predicts possible failures, but engineers decide which maintenance intervention to perform.<br>**b. Financial risk scoring:** Algorithm calculates a credit score; loan officer approves or rejects based on broader context. | **a. Demand forecasting:** Algorithmic forecast of monthly demand is statistically combined with planner adjustments → "forecast consensus" used for production orders.<br>**b. Workforce safety monitoring:** Wearable sensor data suggests fatigue risk; supervisors rate perceived fatigue of their crews. The aggregated index triggers intervention (e.g., extra break, reallocation).<br>**c. Blockchain Decentralized Autonomous Organization (DAO) governance:** Smart contracts + human token holders' aggregate decisions. |
| Strengths | Efficiency gains, leveraging unique capabilities (speed vs. context, scale vs. empathy) | Higher accuracy and quality, robustness as well as efficiency gains. Potential for legitimacy when human input is preserved. |
| Challenges | Dynamic reallocation over time (automation-augmentation paradox), risk of deskilling | Accountability for aggregate outcomes; requires low error correlation |
| Key Sources | Dellermann et al. [4]; Alami & Al-Masaeid [13]; Trunk et al. [14] | Choudhary et al. [3]; Steyvers et al. [12]; Alibašić [15] |

**Division of Labour (Specialisation/Collaboration).** In this mode, humans and AI specialise according to their respective strengths: machines provide speed, scale, and statistical accuracy, while humans contribute contextual and tacit knowledge, creativity, and ethical reasoning [4]. Empirical work illustrates this complementarity in executive settings, where algorithms process large-scale data but strategic judgment remains with human leaders [13]. A recent review further shows how decision-making processes can be decomposed into stages where humans and AI assume distinct roles, ranging from information search to evaluation and implementation [14]. Division of Labour is usually characterised by sequenced task performance, i.e. separate stages where machines execute a task and stages where humans are in charge. Interaction primarily takes place when tasks shift from machines to humans, and vice versa. Yet, Division of Labour is rarely stable. As Raisch & Krakowski [11] note, tasks initially designed as augmentation often drift towards automation and back again, creating an automation–augmentation paradox that makes governance a dynamic rather than a one-off allocation problem.

**Hybrid Ensembles (Aggregation).** In computer science, ensemble methods typically refer to the combination of multiple machine-learning models (e.g., bagging, boosting, random forests) to reduce error through diversity of predictions. In HI, researchers extend this principle to Hybrid Ensembles, where human and AI judgements are aggregated on the same task. The underlying rationale remains the same: when errors are weakly correlated, the combined output outperforms any single contributor [3, 12]. Beyond prediction, ensembles are applied in governance contexts such as blockchains, where algorithmic decisions are combined with expert judgment [15]. In theory, Hybrid Ensembles rely on the aggregation of independent human and AI judgements. In organisational practice, however, co-adoption often occurs: human experts adjust their decisions after seeing algorithmic outputs, and algorithms are retrained on human corrections. This gradual co-adaptation creates a blurred line between independent aggregation and symbiotic co-production. Moreover, both parties of the Hybrid Ensemble (AI and humans) can profit from short- and long-term learning, emphasising the dynamic nature of such ensembles. Although we refrain from considering such learning effects here, this is a highly relevant topic for both theory and practice, as well as a promising avenue for future research. Initial studies already show that such learning can lead to substantial positive performance effects [16]. Overall, Hybrid Ensembles create governance challenges, as responsibility becomes diffuse, raising fundamental questions about who should be held accountable when collective outcomes fail.

## 2.3  Corporate Governance Perspectives on HI

Governance refers to the systems of rules, practices, and processes that determine how decisions are made, who holds authority, and how accountability is ensured. In management research, corporate governance has traditionally been analysed through agency theory, which emphasises the allocation of decision rights and control between principals and agents [17]. Later work has broadened this perspective by linking corporate governance to the creation and reconfiguration of firm capabilities [18]. Comparative governance research further shows that governance is not limited to firms but unfolds at multiple levels, including corporate, national, and supranational, through both internal and external mechanisms [19, 20]. Beyond these, information systems research highlights the importance of governance in inter-organisational infrastructures, such as coordination hubs, where challenges of technology investment, participation, and data require formalised governance arrangements [21].

Recent work on AI, as well as the interplay between human and artificial intelligence, confirms this multi-level governance approach. For instance, Roy and Saha [22] show that regulating AI adoption in workplaces requires reconciling corporate incentives, worker welfare, and democratic legitimacy. Kuziemski and Misuraca [23] discuss AI governance in the public sector as a multi-level game spanning macro (society), meso (organisations), and micro (individuals), and Grossmann et al. [5] highlight how AI reshapes the interplay between individual behaviour, social dynamics, and collective institutions. Building on this multi-level governance literature, we distinguish three complementary governance views that are especially relevant for HI:

- The **organisational view**, concerned with organisational performance, accountability, and risk;
- the **human view**, focused on responsibility, trust, and autonomy at the individual level; and
- the **societal view**, which emphasises legitimacy, fairness, and regulation at the level of public institutions and democratic systems.

These three views provide the analytical lenses through which the corporate governance of HI can be understood. As Table 2 suggests, these three perspectives are not mutually exclusive but represent complementary governance lenses that function at different levels of analysis.

Each perspective offers a unique analytical lens on HI governance. From an **organisational perspective**, HI raises questions of adoption and accountability familiar from AI governance, as well as how firms govern the *teaming* [24] of humans and AI to generate short- and long-term value without losing control. From a **human view**, HI goes beyond algorithmic explainability to address how individuals *calibrate* [25] their reliance on AI partners, preserve autonomy, and avoid deskilling in joint constellations. From a **societal view**, HI highlights the legitimacy of shifting decision-making from clearly identifiable actors towards hybrid human–machine collectives, which challenges established frameworks of regulation and *democratic oversight* [26]. Taken together, the three views underline that HI governance extends beyond traditional AI governance by focusing on the recursive interaction between human and artificial agents.

**Table 2.** Corporate Governance Perspectives and Key Concerns in the HI Field

|  | A. Organisational View | B. Human View | C. Societal View |
|---|---|---|---|
| Unit of analysis | Firm | Individual Human Agent | Society / public institutions |
| Governance Question for HI | How can firms govern HI so that it creates value without losing control? | How can HI governance protect human responsibility, competence, and psychological safety while ensuring trust and explainability in hybrid constellations? | How can HI balance innovation with societal values and democratic legitimacy? |

(continued)

**Table 2.** (*continued*)

| | A. Organisational View | B. Human View | C. Societal View |
|---|---|---|---|
| Key Governance Concerns in the HI area | **(A.1) Technology Adoption & Readiness:** Technology readiness and maturity models (Uren & Edwards [27]); Organizational adoption drivers (Alsheibani et al. [28]); Industry 4.0 readiness (Kovič et al. [29]). **(A.2) Capabilities & Learning:** Dynamic capabilities for digital transformation (Warner & Wäger [30]); AI literacy as organizational capability (Cetindamar et al. [31]); Human-centric AI in corporate learning (Asemota & Owoeye [32]). **(A.3) Human–AI Teaming:** interoperability, trust, dialogue, and organisational governance of human–AI collaboration (Dellermann et al. [4]; Raisch & Krakowski [11]; Simón et al. [24]). **(A.4) Risks:** Automation–augmentation paradox (Raisch & Krakowski [11]); Ethics washing and implementation gaps (de Laat [33]; Bughin [34]); Dark side of AI analytics (Rana et al. [35]). | **(B.1) Trust & Explainability:** How individuals calibrate reliance on AI (Lee & See [25]); need for understandable explanations (Arrieta et al. [36]; Mohseni et al. [37]). **(B.2) Psychological Safety & Emotions:** AI anxiety, fear of replacement, depression, adoption personas (Sarkar [38]; Shen et al. [39]; Kim et al. [40]; Li & Huang [41]). **(B.3) Self-Efficacy & Agency:** How competence perceptions shape adoption; algorithm aversion/appreciation (Park et al. [42]; Hou et al. [43]). **(B.4) Tacit Knowledge & Responsibility Gaps:** Risk of losing tacit expertise (Walker [44]) and assigning accountability to moral crumple zones (Zhang et al. [45]). **(B.5) Trust:** Trustworthy, human-centered AI design (Shneiderman [46]); trust & explainability principles (Chamola et al. [47]); trust linked to legitimacy, morality, robustness (Albahri et al. [48]) | **(C.1) Ethics & Principles:** Normative frameworks (beneficence, autonomy, justice, explicability) (Floridi & Cowls [49]; Floridi et al. [50]). **(C.2) Regulation & Oversight:** Risk-based vs. rights-based models (European Commission [51]; Presno Linera & Meuwese [52]). **(C.3) Democracy & Participation:** AI's role in shaping deliberation, epistemic diversity, elections (Jungherr [53]; Branford et al. [54]; Simons [26]). **(C.4) Public Interest Governance:** Calls for justification, equality, deliberation, transparency (Züger & Asghari [55]) **(C.5) Global Governance:** international legitimacy (Erman & Furendal [56]; Grossmann et al. [5]). |

## 2.4 Interdependencies Between Corporate Governance Perspectives on HI

While the three corporate governance perspectives can be analytically distinguished, they are interdependent in practice. Organisational decisions regarding HI impact individual agency and societal legitimacy. Personal experiences of trust and competence loop back into organisational readiness and societal acceptance. Additionally, societal norms and regulations define the boundaries for what organisations and individuals can do. Recognising these interdependencies highlights that HI governance is not about dealing with siloed views but about managing a dynamic system [5, 23]. How do these interdependencies appear across the different perspectives?

The **organisational view** emphasises how firms adopt and control HI to deliver short- and long-term value while remaining accountable. Corporate decisions regarding adoption and task allocation have a direct impact on human experiences of trust, autonomy, and competence. Over-automation can lead to deskilling and complacency, locking firms into narrow routines and diffusing responsibility [11]. In production settings, case studies demonstrate that HI reconfigures work tasks and intensifies monitoring demands, with risks of psychological stress and a loss of expertise if adoption is not human-centred [57]. At the same time, corporate responsibility is undermined when firms engage in ethics washing, adopting principles without integrating them into their corporate governance practices [33]. Corporate readiness further depends on employees' AI literacy [31] and compliance with external regulations, such as the European Union Artificial Intelligence Act (EU AI Act) [51]. While the literature acknowledges these links, it often treats them separately, leaving little guidance on how firms can simultaneously manage inward (employee) and outward (societal) accountability.

The **human view** mediates between corporate practice and societal acceptance. At the micro level, trust calibration [25] and explainability [36] are critical for individual reliance on AI. However, when organisations fail to support these conditions, the effects do not remain individual. Li and Huang [41] demonstrate how AI anxiety (fear of replacement, privacy violations, and loss of control) spreads widely. Kim et al. [40] found that AI adoption can negatively affect well-being, as it reduces employees' psychological safety ($\beta = -0.324$, $p < 0.001$; a moderate and highly significant effect), thereby causing depression symptoms. However, ethical leadership partially mitigates this effect by strengthening psychological safety in AI adoption situations ($\beta = 0.211$, $p < 0.001$). These experiences demonstrate that when workers feel anxious or unsafe, corporate adoption slows, and societal acceptance is eroded. To address these concerns, frameworks such as **trustworthy AI guidelines** [58] emerge. Yet, as Bughin [34] shows in a survey of 1,615 firms, many companies adopt responsible AI codes that aim to address **societal pressure** but fail to operationalise them. This suggests a governance gap: the human view cannot be treated as an inward-looking HR or ethics issue. Failures of trust, safety, and agency at the organisational level quickly scale into legitimacy crises at the societal level, while societal demands for responsible AI loop back into corporate obligations.

The **societal view** establishes the normative and the legal environment within which corporate and human governance operate. Principles such as beneficence, justice, and explicability [49], as well as regulatory instruments like the EU AI Act [59] and the Council of Europe's Framework Convention [52], define which hybrid constellations are acceptable. For corporate governance, this implies that firms must not only ensure compliance with formal regulation (e.g., risk classifications, transparency obligations, human oversight requirements) but must also build internal structures that translate abstract ethical principles into operational practices. For example, under the EU AI Act, a company deploying an AI recruitment system must document how human oversight is ensured (e.g., documenting algorithmic decisions, monitoring fairness metrics, and reporting to regulators). It turns societal principles of non-discrimination into operational corporate governance obligations. Yet, these frameworks are still subject to debate: some scholars argue that economic considerations overwrite ethical principles [60]. Empirical work also demonstrates how **corporate failures can escalate into societal risks.** Rana et al. [35] demonstrate that failures at the firm or the individual level, such as opacity in analytics, can erode societal legitimacy and prompt stricter oversight. The dependency is recursive: society sets boundaries, but corporate practices and individual experiences constantly reshape those boundaries.

These interdependencies demonstrate that corporate, human, and societal governance must be treated as an interconnected system. The recursive interplays help to explain why the two modes of HI, i.e. Division of Labour and Hybrid Ensembles, generate governance challenges depending on the perspective taken. Section 2.5 synthesises these insights by mapping the concerns of each governance view onto the two HI modes.

### 2.5  Synthesis: HI Modes and Governance Views

The two modes of HI, i.e. **Division of Labour** and **Hybrid Ensembles**, do not raise identical governance concerns. Depending on whether the focus lies on the **organisational**, **human**, or **societal** level, different challenges become evident.

**Division of Labour** emphasises specialisation, where humans and AI take distinct roles. From an **organisational view**, this raises questions of *who* decides *which tasks are automated* and how accountability for outcomes is maintained at the firm level. From a **human view**, the concern lies in deskilling, loss of autonomy, and the danger of humans being reduced to nominal overseers. From a **societal perspective**, legitimacy becomes critical because delegating high-stakes decisions to machines affects fundamental principles of our society (e.g., in domains like justice, healthcare, or education). Unlike human agents, algorithms lack legitimacy under the social contract of modern societies. Therefore, Rahwan [61] advocates for a *"Society in the Loop"* oversight, a governance mechanism that ensures that the values and rights of stakeholders affected by machine decisions are considered in HI systems.

**Hybrid Ensembles**, by contrast, combine human and machine outputs on the same task. At the **organisational level**, this creates challenges of *responsibility diffusion* when aggregated outputs fail, demanding new forms of accountability. At the **human level**, Hybrid Ensembles risk undermining explainability, as joint predictions may become even less transparent than those of single agents. This opacity can also be motivationally induced: individuals may either engage more carefully because their input is aggregated or disengage under the assumption that their contribution is diluted. In this vein, Hybrid Ensembles can draw on characteristics of gamification that can further increase employee motivation [62]. At the **societal level**, the legitimacy of ensemble-based decision-making is a subject of contention. While aggregation may improve accuracy, it also raises questions of fairness and acceptance in collective decision domains such as climate policy or elections.

Table 3 synthesises key governance concerns discussed in this chapter (see Table 2) and contrasts how these concerns manifest differently in the two HI modes.

**Table 3.** Contrasting Governance Concerns in the two HI modes

|  | **Division of Labour** (Task specialisation between humans and AI) | **Hybrid Ensemble** (Aggregation of independent human and AI intelligences) |
|---|---|---|
| Organisational View | Allocation of tasks between humans and AI; maintaining firm-level accountability | Accountability for aggregated outcomes; responsibility diffusion |
| Human View | Risk of deskilling and reduced autonomy; trust in delegated oversight | Transparency of joint predictions; difficulty attributing agency within Hybrid Ensembles; risk of black-box systems |
| Societal View | Legitimacy of automating <u>specific roles in sensitive domains</u> (e.g., justice, healthcare, education); varying public acceptance across contexts | Legitimacy of ensemble-based <u>decisions in collective domains</u> (e.g., climate policy, elections); risk of undermining democratic deliberation |

**Example: The Omission Bias Dilemma in HI Governance.**
A well-known phenomenon in risk perception, *Omission Bias*, illustrates the differences between the two modes of HI. Omission Bias describes the systematic tendency to judge harmful outcomes from action as being worse than equal harms from inaction [63]. Applied to HI adoption, non-use (omission) may feel safer for corporate decision-makers, yet it risks long-term loss of competitiveness, while active use (commission) promises rational benefits but can create human and societal downsides.

- For **Division of Labour**, responsibility for omission (not deploying HI) or commission (activating HI in critical decisions) can be directly attributed to specific managers or engineers.
- In **Hybrid Ensembles**, however, where human and AI judgements are combined, the distinction between omission and commission becomes less clear: was it the human who ignored a signal or was it the ensemble logic that weighted it down? This creates a governance dilemma: how can organisations balance the perceived safety of non-use against the demonstrable advantages of HI use without losing accountability when collective outcomes fail?

Taken together, the synthesis reveals that the governance of HI is not uniform but instead depends on the intersection of mode and view and their specific contexts. Division of Labour highlights issues of allocation and autonomy, while Hybrid Ensembles emphasise aggregation and accountability. These concerns manifest differently across corporate, human, and societal levels, underscoring the need for a multidimensional governance framework. The next chapter builds on this insight by translating these concerns into concrete governance dimensions that together provide a systematic framework for governing HI.

## 3   Governance Framework for HI

### 3.1  Purpose and Approach

Corporate governance of HI remains conceptually fragmented. Existing approaches are either high-level, focusing on general ethical principles and rights, or narrowly domain-specific, such as those in IT and data governance. What is missing is a framework that links the distinctive modes of HI (Division of Labour and Hybrid Ensembles), not only incorporating organisational goals but also integrating the human and societal perspectives into their specific contexts. The purpose of this chapter is to propose such a framework. Our objective is not to prescribe regulatory rules but to develop a **conceptual artefact** that helps academics and managers to analyse, compare, and debate corporate governance challenges in HI.

HI is inherently a matter of collaboration. By definition, it involves the interaction of humans and AI systems, and its governance challenges emerge at the boundaries between individuals, organisations, and societies. Interdependence, uncertainty, and legitimacy concerns are built into the design and use of HI, making it an archetypal case for what Emerson et al. [64] describe as **collaborative governance**. In this vein, Emerson et al.'s Integrative Framework for Collaborative Governance [64] provides a strong conceptual lens for analysing cross-boundary governance challenges. They conceptualise governance not as a static allocation of authority but as evolving regimes shaped by three interrelated areas: system context, collaborative governance regime, and collaboration dynamics. These areas are especially relevant for HI, which is inherently collaborative in nature: it requires coordination between human and artificial agents, as well as between individuals, organisations, and societal institutions.

- **System Context**. The system context describes the background conditions and drivers that create the need for collaboration. In HI, the context is defined by the rise of AI as a general-purpose technology. Uncertainty about how roles and tasks should be distributed between humans and machines, as well as legitimacy concerns in sensitive domains such as healthcare, justice, and public administration, need to be addressed. These contextual conditions generate both the pressures and the constraints under which HI governance must operate.
- **Collaborative Governance Regime**. Emerson et al. define a collaborative governance regime as the institutional arrangements that structure and sustain collaboration over time. In the case of HI, regimes emerge wherever rules and practices determine how humans and AI are combined, for example, through the Division of Labour or Hybrid Ensembles, and how accountability, participation, and decision-making rights are allocated. The notion of regimes draws attention to the fact that HI governance is not a one-time decision but an evolving set of arrangements that must be continuously adjusted as technologies and contexts change.

- **Collaboration Dynamics.** Finally, collaborative governance is sustained through dynamics such as principled engagement, shared motivation, and capacity for joint action. These dynamics highlight that governance is not only about formal structures but also about interactive processes: how stakeholders build trust, commit to shared purposes, and learn and mobilise resources for collective action. For HI, collaboration dynamics manifest in concerns such as transparency, fairness, accountability, and alignment, which condition whether humans, organisations, and societies remain motivated to engage with and accept hybrid constellations.

We utilise these three areas (**system context, collaborative governance regime, and collaboration dynamics**) as **conceptual search spaces** for identifying governance dimensions specific to HI. Within these spaces and guided by the synthesis of HI modes and governance views (Sect. 2.4), we distil six governance dimensions that capture recurring challenges in governing HI in Sect. 3.2. It is essential to recognise that Emerson's framework was developed within the context of **public policy and collective action**. It was not designed with socio-technical systems like HI in mind. As such, their concepts must be **interpreted carefully** when applied to human–AI collaboration. They do not directly specify how to govern machine agents or socio-technical ensembles, but these build a solid search space for dynamics in high-collaborative environments.

Finally, our framework also adopts a design-oriented perspective, making it practical for researchers and decision-makers. Inspired by the latest IT governance approaches, particularly blockchain governance [65] and data governance [66], we present each governance dimension with a **property range** and associated **domain-specific decision questions**. This allows us to move beyond abstract principles and to provide structured categories that clarify the trade-offs involved in governing HI.

### 3.2 Governance Dimensions

Corporate governance challenges of HI can be categorised into six fields defined by the intersection of **modes** (Division of Labour and Hybrid Ensembles) and **governance views** (corporate, human, and societal). Each dimension highlights recurring issues, including accountability, transparency, autonomy, fairness, risk, and alignment. To structure these challenges systematically, we use Emerson et al.'s [64] *Integrative Framework for Collaborative Governance* as a conceptual lens, interpreting each field as pointing to a *dynamic that requires governance.* For example, "system context" highlights legitimacy pressures in sensitive domains, "governance regimes" point to institutional arrangements for allocating decision rights, and "collaboration dynamics" emphasise trust, motivation, and collective capacity.

The six dimensions represent the core areas where HI requires governance attention across organisational, individual, and societal levels. Each dimension is specified along a **property range** (e.g., clear ↔ diffuse accountability; reactive ↔ proactive risk governance) and entails **different domain decisions** depending on whether HI is realised through **Division of Labour** or through **Hybrid Ensembles**. Table 4 provides an overview of these six dimensions, which are then discussed in greater detail.

**Table 4.** HI Governance Framework: Relevant Domain Decisions

| Governance View | Governance Dimension | Property Range | Domain Decision | |
|---|---|---|---|---|
| | | | Division of Labour | Hybrid Ensembles |
| Organisational View | **Responsibility & Accountability** **(1)**: *Who is responsible when outcomes fail?* | Clear ↔ Diffuse responsibility | Who decides which tasks remain human vs. AI, and who carries liability if tasks are misallocated? | Who is accountable for outcomes when human and AI judgements are aggregated? |
| Human View | **Transparency & Explainability** **(2)**: *How understandable are hybrid processes?* | Interpretable ↔ Black-box | How are AI-driven roles explained to humans performing complementary tasks? | How are aggregated predictions and Hybrid Ensemble decisions explained to end-users, managers, and regulators? |
| | **Human Agency & Autonomy** **(3)**: *How do we preserve human competence and decision authority?* | Strong agency ↔ Deskilling | How can role allocation protect human skills and authority? | How can Hybrid Ensemble systems prevent humans from becoming passive overseers? |
| Societal View | **Ethics & Fairness (4)**: *How are biases, justice, and normative principles safeguarded?* | Principle-driven ↔ Outcome-driven | Which tasks should never be delegated to AI (e.g., ethical trade-offs in supply chains, worker safety)? | How can Hybrid Ensemble outcomes be audited for bias and fairness? |

*(continued)*

**Table 4.** (*continued*)

| Governance View | Governance Dimension | Property Range | Domain Decision | |
|---|---|---|---|---|
| | | | Division of Labour | Hybrid Ensembles |
| Societal + Organisational View | **Risk & Resilience (5):** *How are operational and systemic risks managed?* | Reactive incident handling ↔ Systemic resilience | How are risks of automation managed at firm level? | How are systemic risks from Hybrid Ensemble failures (e.g., policy, climate, finance) mitigated? |
| | **Strategic Alignment & Value Generation (6):** *How is HI aligned with organizational goals and societal legitimacy?* | Efficiency-oriented ↔ Legitimacy-oriented | How is task allocation aligned with firm strategy and societal legitimacy? | How do ensemble systems create sustainable value rather than short-term efficiency? |

**Dimension 1: Responsibility & Accountability.** Following Bovens [67], we distinguish between ex ante *responsibility*, which allocates roles and liabilities before an action is taken, and ex post *accountability*, which obliges actors to explain and justify their conduct to a forum that can pass judgement and impose consequences. In HI, this distinction blurs because the "problem of many hands" is amplified: human and AI contributions are entangled, making both ex ante allocations and ex post forums harder to define, specifically in the case of Hybrid Ensembles.

The literature identifies three persistent challenges. First, **responsibility gaps** emerge when no actor can reasonably be held liable for failures. Santoni de Sio and van den Hoven [68] demonstrate that without meaningful human control (defined by *tracking* and *tracing* conditions), accountability bears the risk of collapsing into what they term "an accountability vacuum". Second, **diffuse accountability** arises when algorithmic systems redistribute roles in ways that obscure who can be held accountable. Breidbach and Maglio [69] emphasise that data-driven business models often rely on accountable algorithms, yet in practice they obscure responsibility by embedding decision logic deeply into opaque infrastructures. Third, **unclear liability allocation** persists in human–AI collaboration. Peng et al. [70] demonstrate that perceptions of responsibility differ depending on the collaboration mode: AI supporting a human is judged to be more acceptable than AI supervised by a human.

These challenges justify conceptualising a **range between clear and diffuse responsibility**. At one end, actors are explicitly accountable through defined roles, audit trails, and recourse mechanisms; at the other, accountability disperses across humans and AI with little traceability. The two modes of HI require different responses: Division of Labour magnifies the responsibility gap: when tasks are misallocated between human and AI, liability becomes contested. Governance must therefore answer the question: *who decides which tasks should remain human versus AI, and who bears liability if misallocation leads to harm?* **Hybrid Ensembles** amplify *diffuse accountability*: outcomes emerge from combined human–AI judgements, making attribution complex. Governance must therefore answer the question: *who is accountable for outcomes when human and AI judgements are aggregated?*

**Dimension 2: Transparency & Explainability.** Transparency denotes the degree to which hybrid processes are open to scrutiny, while explainability refers to the provision of intelligible reasons for AI-assisted outcomes. In Emerson et al.'s terms, transparency and explainability sustain principled engagement: only if human and organisational stakeholders understand how outcomes are produced they remain motivated to collaborate within a governance regime.

Three well-documented challenges justify conceptualising a property range between **interpretable** and **black-box processes**. First, **model opacity** is inherent in modern HI applications. Burrell [71] distinguishes between opacity due to secrecy, to technical illiteracy, and to the intrinsic complexity of machine learning, illustrating why even experts often struggle to reconstruct decisions fully. Arrieta et al. [36] similarly stress that the explainability of ML is lacking in an organisational context due to two factors: competence (businesses did not adopt digital transformation skills quickly enough) and the enormous amount of knowledge that ML models can comprise. Second, **instability of explanations** reduces their reliability. Doshi-Velez and Kim [72] highlight that interpretability lacks standardised definitions and evaluation, while Samek et al. [73] discuss how, in complex decision processes, the correct and incorrect decision strategy can refer to the same explanation. Third, the **audience-competence gap** complicates explainability: Mohseni et al. [37] demonstrate that explanations need to differ for different user groups, as mismatches between explanation formats and user competence reduce usability. Chattaraman et al. [74] find empirically that digital assistants are more effective when these consider the target group's experience and competence level.

These challenges are amplified differently in the two modes of HI. In **Division of Labour** settings, explainability must clarify AI-assigned roles and predictions for human collaborators. Caruana et al. [75] demonstrate in a pneumonia risk prediction study that intelligible models (i.e. interpretable by humans) revealed a wrong rule, suggesting that asthma patients had a lower mortality risk than the general population, which reflected biased treatment patterns in the training data. Only transparent rationales allow clinicians to detect such spurious correlations. In **Hybrid Ensembles**, by contrast, accountability depends on clarifying how human and AI judgements are combined. Samek et al. [73] propose faithfulness tests, such as pixel flipping, to ensure that the features identified as important truly drive the outcomes. Without such meta-explanations, regulators cannot audit ensemble decisions for bias or robustness.

From this analysis, two governance questions crystallise. For Division of Labour: *how are AI-driven roles explained to humans performing complementary tasks in ways that are faithful, comprehensible, and adapted to user competence?* As this question is also relevant for Hybrid Ensembles, it must also address the following issue: *how are aggregated predictions and ensemble decisions explained to end-users, managers, and regulators with sufficient fidelity to support audit and accountability?*

**Dimension 3: Human Agency & Autonomy.** Human agency and autonomy refer to the preservation of human competence and decision authority when tasks are distributed between humans and AI. In Emerson et al.'s terms, sustaining agency is part of the dynamics of collaboration: only if humans retain meaningful control and the ability to contest outcomes they remain motivated to engage in HI regimes.

The literature highlights recurring challenges. Raisch and Krakowski [11] describe the ***automation–augmentation paradox***: while AI promises to augment human work, it often reduces discretion and creates cycles of deskilling when humans are removed. Li and Huang [41] conceptualise **AI anxiety** based on eight factors, including fears of learning, job replacement, and loss of control. Sarkar [38] provides qualitative evidence of two primary drivers of human agency: the fear of making mistakes with opaque AI systems and the fear of replacement. Both hinder AI adoption in an organisational context. In addition, empirical studies show that without **psychological safety and trust**, human–AI collaboration often results in passive oversight. Shen et al. [39] find that teachers' continued use of AI tools in classrooms depends critically on psychological safety and trust. Kim et al. [40] confirm this view empirically and outline the conditions under which psychological safety can lead to the adoption of AI.

These challenges justify conceptualising a property range from **strong agency** to **deskilling**. Regarding the Division of Labour, the governance question is how task allocation can protect human skills and authority. In Hybrid Ensembles, the issue is how to prevent humans from becoming passive overseers of aggregated outcomes, a risk reinforced when opacity or fear reduces active participation [38]. From this analysis, two governance questions crystallise. Regarding Division of Labour: *how can role allocation protect human skills and decision authority rather than inducing deskilling?* For Hybrid Ensembles: *how can ensemble systems be designed to prevent humans from becoming passive overseers and to ensure that their agency remains meaningful regarding aggregated outcomes?*

**Dimension 4: Ethics & Fairness.** Ethics and fairness concern how biases, justice, and normative principles are safeguarded when human and AI judgements are combined. In Emerson et al.'s terms, they are part of the *collaboration dynamics*: without shared ethical standards and safeguards, trust and legitimacy in hybrid regimes cannot be sustained. Empirical and review studies on ethics and fairness concerns converge on two problems that we take into account. First, **algorithmic bias: For instance,** in HR and workplace analytics, algorithmic monitoring can shift organisations towards compliance logics that crowd out human sense-making [76]. An HR decision algorithm can create anticipatory conformity. Second, **principles-to-practice gaps:** Floridi and Cowls [49] propose a unified framework of five principles for AI (beneficence, non-maleficence, autonomy, justice, and explicability), placing explicability as a meta-principle that links fairness to transparency and accountability. Yet, Cousineau et al. [77] find that developers struggle to operationalise such principles: fairness definitions are fragmented, regulation is unclear, tools are immature, and auditing standards are inconsistent. This gap helps to explain why companies often adopt ethical codes without embedding them into practice, leading to "ethics washing" [33]. Empirical work confirms these risks in regulated domains. In accounting, Lehner et al. [78] show that AI-based decision systems can institutionalise bias unless systematic auditing practices are adapted to include algorithmic components. This illustrates how aggregation opacity challenges fairness even in contexts with strong governance traditions.

These findings justify conceptualising a property range between **principle-driven and outcome-driven governance**. Principle-driven approaches anchor decisions in normative standards such as justice and dignity, even at the expense of efficiency. Outcome-driven approaches judge fairness primarily by results, for example, equalised error rates across groups, focusing on measurable performance rather than underlying principles. The two HI modes face distinct fairness issues. Regarding the **Division of Labour**, the question is that of which tasks should never be delegated to AI because they require inherently normative judgment. Judicial sentencing and end-of-life medical decisions illustrate contexts where principle-based human reasoning remains indispensable, and AI requires an ethical design [58]. For **Hybrid Ensembles**, fairness risks emerge through aggregation: combining human and AI judgements can conceal discriminatory effects and complicate auditing. From this analysis, two governance questions crystallise. For Division of Labour: *which tasks should never be delegated to AI, and how are such boundaries enforced?* Additionally, for Hybrid Ensembles: *how can aggregated outcomes be audited to ensure they remain fair and aligned with societal values?*

**Dimension 5: Risk & Resilience.** Risk and resilience describe how hybrid systems can withstand failures, disruptions, and external shocks. Unlike other dimensions, this is inherently cross-view: firms must ensure corporate resilience through business continuity, cybersecurity, and supply chain stability, while societies must safeguard democratic institutions, employment, and public trust. In Emerson et al.'s terms, this dimension reflects the *system context* of HI.

The literature highlights different layers of risk. At the **organisational level**, Modgil et al. [79] demonstrate, through interviews with supply chain professionals during the COVID-19 pandemic, that many firms turned to AI to strengthen their resilience by improving transparency, forecasting, and last-mile delivery. They conclude that high AI readiness enhances dealings with shock-induced risks, such as COVID-19. Contingency structures and dynamic capabilities are crucial. At the **societal level**, Roy and Saha [22] demonstrate with a formal model that democracy regulates automation to protect workers, albeit in distortionary ways: it may lead either to full automation accompanied by fiscal populism or to Luddite-style restrictions, where vulnerable groups gain little. Both outcomes highlight distributional risks that can undermine the resilience of democratic systems when facing automation. Jungherr [53] similarly warns that AI can **undermine democratic resilience** through the manipulation of information environments, the erosion of equality, and asymmetries between democracies and autocracies if safeguards are absent.

These challenges justify conceptualising a property range between *reactive* and *proactive* risk governance. At the reactive end, organisations respond only after disruptions occur, while societies struggle with legitimacy crises and political backlash. At the proactive end, firms embed redundancy and monitoring into their operations, and societies invest in safeguards that preserve trust and stability in the face of shocks.

The two modes of HI face different resilience demands. For **Division of Labour**, continuity depends on clear fallback structures when either humans or AI fail, such as ensuring that clinicians can override malfunctioning triage algorithms. In **Hybrid Ensembles**, the problem is correlated failure: if human and AI judgements share the same blind spots, aggregation may amplify rather than mitigate risks. From this analysis, two governance questions crystallise. For Division of Labour: *how can fallback structures ensure continuity when one actor fails?* For Hybrid Ensembles: *how can aggregated systems be stress-tested to prevent correlated failures that endanger both corporate performance and societal resilience?*

**Dimension 6: Strategic Alignment & Value Generation.** Strategic alignment and value generation concern the degree to which HI is embedded in organisational goals. In Emerson et al.'s Terms, this dimension reflects *collaborative governance regimes*: HI only becomes sustainable if it aligns with institutional strategies and generates value that stakeholders recognise as legitimate. Without such alignment, hybrid systems risk being treated as isolated technical pilots rather than integrated socio-technical capabilities. The literature highlights persistent gaps. In their classic study, Henderson and Venkatraman [80] have already demonstrated the challenge of aligning IT with business strategy. This difficulty also extends to AI. Cockburn et al. [81] argue that recent advances in deep learning should be understood not only as productivity enhancers but also as a method of invention for general purposes, which changes the innovation process itself. Yet Raisch and Krakowski [11] caution that many AI deployments get caught in the automation–augmentation paradox, creating efficiency gains without building complementary capabilities that secure long-term value. Finally, Braun et al. [82] argue that trust in AI cannot be established solely through checklists or regulatory principles. Instead, it requires ongoing deliberation and openness, because trust remains fragile and distrust plays a constructive role in democratic negotiation. This highlights that AI alignment must go beyond efficiency and also address the conditions under which stakeholders grant legitimacy to HI. In corporate contexts, this legitimacy is not abstract but specifically links to the recognition of measurable value (disutility) by customers, employees, regulators, and shareholders. Rahwan's [61] "Society in the loop" perspective reminds us that corporate value creation also depends on achieving broader algorithmic stakeholder consensus in HI settings.

These insights justify conceptualising a property range between **efficiency-oriented and legitimacy-oriented alignment**. At one end, HI is used tactically to optimise productivity and reduce costs. At the other, it is embedded in corporate strategy and value generation to ensure legitimacy, stakeholder acceptance, and sustainable growth.

The two HI modes face different challenges. For **Division of Labour**, alignment depends on whether task allocation directly advances strategic achievements, e.g., as for claims that automation contributes to compliance and customer satisfaction. For **Hybrid Ensembles**, aggregated HI outcomes must align with corporate strategy and demonstrate measurable value creation, as acceptance of HI use depends on tangible results: managers demand short-term performance evidence, while stakeholders require proof of long-term value and legitimacy. From this, the following two governance questions arise, for Division of Labour: *how can task allocation ensure contributions to strategic goals*; and for Hybrid Ensembles: how *can aggregated outcomes be aligned with corporate value creation?*

## 3.3   Applying as an Assessment Tool

To make the governance framework actionable, we propose using a **spider diagram** as an analytical instrument to position the specific use case of HI along the six dimensions (see Fig. 2). Each axis represents one corporate governance dimension, marked with its property range (e.g., clear ↔ diffuse accountability; efficiency-oriented ↔ legitimacy-oriented alignment). By plotting a system's current position, managers and researchers can visualise the overall governance profile of a hybrid intelligent system. This enables structured comparisons across cases, tracking of changes over time, and identification of misalignments, such as a system that is transparent and ethically fair but fragile in terms of resilience.

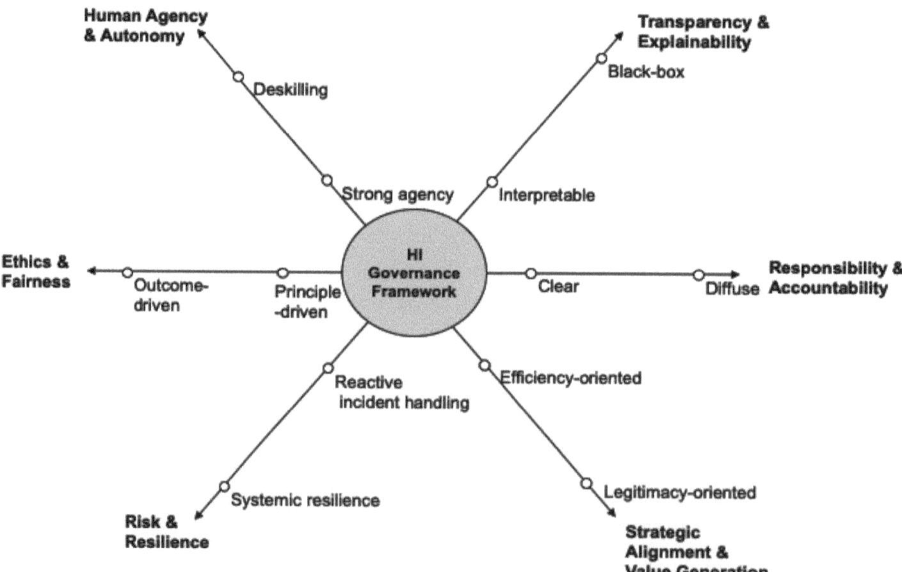


**Fig. 2.** Analytical Instrument for Mapping HI Governance Profiles (to be applied in use case analysis)

The practical value of this instrument lies in surfacing **counterintuitive governance dynamics** that might otherwise remain undetected. Hybrid Ensembles, often expected to reduce individual error through aggregation, may instead create governance problems by diffusing accountability or amplifying correlated risks. Similarly, efficiency-oriented alignment can undermine legitimacy: a system may be technically optimised yet fail if it erodes human autonomy or public trust. By linking abstract dimensions to a concrete mapping tool, the framework provides a structured basis for discussion, reflection, and comparison.

The framework and instrument contribute conceptually and practically: they highlight where governance tensions in HI emerge, show how these can be visualised and compared across cases, and provide a foundation for structured debates, while recognising that specific governance arrangements must still be developed contextually.

## 4  Applying the HI Governance Framework: The Production Dashboard Use Case

The following case study illustrates how our governance framework can be applied in practice. It draws on findings from our ongoing research on MES Dashboards in small-scale manufacturing [83]. Here, we only present a condensed version. The purpose is not to provide full empirical detail but to demonstrate how the six governance dimensions can be used as an analytical lens for characterising a concrete HI application.

### 4.1  Case Context and Intervention

The use case is drawn from a German family-owned company producing electric motors in a make-to-order setting with batch sizes ranging from 10 to 1,000 units. The company operates a three-shift system, where late and night shifts are typically characterised by limited managerial presence. This context created a governance challenge: how to ensure productivity and reliability when direct supervision is absent. In January 2023, the company introduced real-time MES dashboards across 12 assembly lines (see Fig. 3). Each dashboard displayed key performance indicators such as target versus actual output, Overall Equipment Effectiveness (OEE), availability, and interruptions. The intervention was designed to provide shift teams with transparent performance feedback, enabling greater self-regulation and reducing reliance on supervisors.

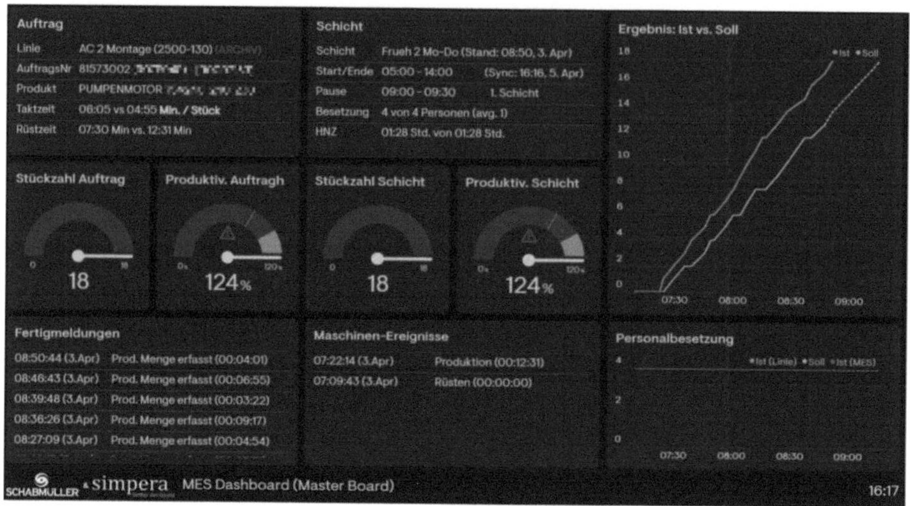


**Fig. 3.** MES Dashboard for Assembly Line Workers (Case Study)

The dashboard provides real-time visibility into production targets, OEE, and avail-ability, making performance transparent to shopfloor teams and reducing dependence on supervisors. A quasi-experimental research design compared performance before and after the rollout and was complemented by a survey of operators. The findings, which are subject to a separate publication, show that the dashboards increased produc-tivity overall and, significantly, indicate behavioural learning effects: workers not only reacted to being monitored but also engaged with the dashboards as valuable tools for self-regulation. *How does it reduce reliance on supervisors?* Before the introduction of the dashboard, supervisors coordinated shift performance by monitoring progress ex-post, highlighting deviations, and motivating teams. Now, dashboards partly assume this role by providing real-time performance transparency to all team members work-ing on an assembly line. This visibility allows workers to collectively self-regulate, distribute tasks, and correct issues without waiting for managerial intervention. Conse-quently, supervision shifts from direct oversight to a more indirect form of governance, **with accountability embedded in human–machine interaction rather than enforced through hierarchical control.**

The dashboard qualifies as a *softer form of HI*. It does not follow the classic Human-in-the-Loop logic, where humans and machines interact through explicit continuous decision cycles. Instead, the interactions are primarily indirect: the system visualises key performance indicators, while operators interpret these signals and adjust their behaviour accordingly. Four criteria justify the dashboard as a kind of HI application. First, **context adaptation:** the dashboard updates in real time to reflect disruptions, absences, or pro-cess variations. Second, **human learning:** workers begin to anticipate the consequences of their actions, while the aggregated data simultaneously support organisational learn-ing. In our working paper, we assume that these learning effects partly substitute the need for human supervision. Third, the **actions proposal:** by highlighting gaps between target and actual output, the dashboard implicitly suggests corrective measures. Finally, the dashboard triggers **ongoing human–machine interaction:** operators continuously engage with the information to regulate their performance. In this sense, the dashboard forms a hybrid collaboration: less direct and interventionist than in common Human-in-the-Loop systems, but constituting a socio-technical form of intelligence that reshapes both worker behaviour and organisational coordination.

## 4.2   Interpreting the MES Dashboard Application Through HI Governance

Having qualified the MES dashboard as a form of HI, the next step is to classify it within our framework. The dashboard does not aggregate human and AI judgements into a joint outcome, as Hybrid Ensembles would. Instead, it provides real-time information that redistributes roles between humans and digital systems: the AI component monitors and visualises performance. In contrast, human operators interpret the information and take action accordingly. This makes the MES dashboard an example of **Division of Labour**, where human and machine responsibilities remain distinct but complementary.

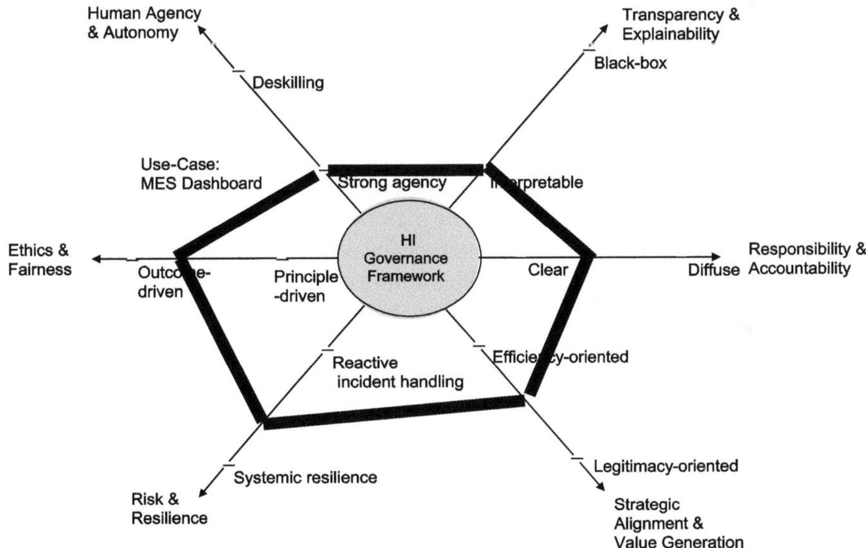


**Fig. 4.** HI Governance profile of the MES dashboard use case across six dimensions.

How does the dashboard organise the collaboration in this industrial use case? To assess the various aspects, we utilise our HI Governance Framework and evaluate the six governance dimensions. The evaluation was validated through an expert interview with the Application Developer, following a semi-structured guideline aligned with the six governance dimensions. The expert provided qualitative assessments for each dimension, which are summarised in the appendix. The spider diagram (Fig. 4) visualises this assessment. Importantly, the ratings are not all positioned at the extreme ends of the spectrums, but in intermediate positions that reflect the nuanced nature of the case and the framework as an assessment tool.

1. **Responsibility & Accountability** are **moderately clear**. During the rollout, the workers' council raised concerns that dashboards could expose individual performance and be misused for surveillance. To address this, the company decided to display only team-level results, ensuring that accountability remained collective. This design choice clarified responsibility without creating undue individual pressure.
2. **Transparency & Explainability** lie **near the interpretable end**. Real-time data allow workers to see immediately how their actions translate into productivity. For instance, when someone steps away from the line, the dashboard instantly shows the effect on efficiency. This transparency increases attentiveness, but it also requires contextual knowledge to interpret whether deviations reflect controllable factors or external events.
3. **Human Agency & Autonomy** is positioned towards **strong agency**. By providing continuous feedback, the dashboard enables teams to self-regulate without managerial oversight. The immediacy of the feedback loop ensures that improvements are visible within minutes, empowering workers to experiment and adjust their performance.
4. **Ethics & Fairness** has an **intermediate position**. On the one hand, fairness is explicitly designed into the system: the "ideal" productivity baseline is adjusted for external conditions such as machine defects or reduced staffing, so that workers are not penalised for factors beyond their control. On the other hand, personal circumstances like illness or fatigue (e.g., a worker suffering from a migraine) are not accounted for, leaving some performance variations to appear outcome-driven and potentially unfair.
5. **Risk & Resilience** is **partly proactive**. The dashboard reduces dependency on supervisors, particularly during night shifts, by making performance self-regulating. At the same time, the system creates a new dependency on technical reliability: if dashboards fail or data are inaccurate, the risk of disruption could be amplified.
6. **Strategic Alignment & Value** shows a balance of **efficiency and legitimacy orientation**. On the one hand, dashboards contribute to productivity improvements; on the other, workers perceive them as helpful tools rather than as intrusive surveillance, which in turn strengthens dashboards' acceptance and legitimacy. This is only possible because governance choices, such as focusing on team rather than individual metrics, address workers' concerns.

Taken together, the MES dashboard case demonstrates that real-world HI systems are rarely positioned at the extremes of governance spectrums. Instead, they often inhabit negotiated middle positions shaped by design choices, social dialogue, and perceptions of fairness.

### 4.3 Reflections and Limits

The MES dashboard case highlights how governance choices often involve counterintuitive trade-offs. Making performance visible at the team level improves fairness and legitimacy, but leaves responsibility less clearly defined at the individual level. Adjusting productivity baselines for external events can increase perceptions of fairness; however, personal factors such as illness or fatigue remain unaccounted for, leaving outcome-driven tensions unresolved. The case also shows that transparency can both empower autonomy and expose new vulnerabilities if data are misinterpreted or systems fail. These insights underline that HI governance is rarely about moving fully to one end of a spectrum; instead, it is about negotiating workable positions positioned in the middle of the spectrum.

At the same time, the case remains limited: it is drawn from a single firm and one-year observation, and its findings cannot be generalised without caution. Its value lies in illustrating how the governance framework can surface hidden tensions and help to structure practical debates about HI in real workplaces.

## 5   Research Agenda for HI Governance

Directions for future research relate to the very distinction that frames this paper: **Division of Labour versus Hybrid Ensembles**. While prior research agendas rarely differentiate between modes of HI, our framework suggests that governance tensions manifest differently depending on how human and AI roles are combined. Our analysis suggests that future research on HI governance should extend beyond familiar concerns, such as explainability, fairness, and trust, to address the **dynamic, systemic, and political** challenges that emerge when human and artificial agents co-evolve. Building on both our framework and the MES dashboard case, we highlight three promising directions:

1. **Governance Drift and Temporal Dynamics:** HI systems are not static: what begins as augmentation often drifts towards automation, shifting the balance of roles and responsibilities. Raisch and Krakowski [11] describe this as the *automation–augmentation paradox*, illustrating how governance arrangements that initially appear stable can erode over time. Our case illustrates this in two ways. First, dashboards initially strengthened worker agency, but novelty effects may fade, and monitoring could gradually shift into compliance. Second, the system also produced **unintended governance uses**: once performance became transparent, managers could identify systemic absence patterns across teams and shifts, insights that were not detectable in the original design, giving the application an almost **emergent character that requires proactive steering.** This demonstrates that governance drifts are not only about automation gradually taking over but also about **emergent uses and re-purposings** of hybrid systems as they evolve. Future research should therefore examine how governance regimes change longitudinally, how responsibilities shift when new affordances become visible, and what mechanisms can recalibrate governance before human agency and accountability are lost.

2. **Embedding Democratic Deliberation:** Jungherr [53] demonstrates that AI is not only a technical artefact but also a force that shapes democratic processes, epistemic diversity, and legitimacy on different levels. Our case provides a micro-level example: the works council's involvement in the rollout was crucial in defining accountability (team-level rather than individual metrics), which increased acceptance and legitimacy. However, the legal situation regarding whether and how to involve workers' councils in HI design was not fully clear, and deliberation only happened because developers proactively sought it out. This highlights a governance gap: democratic elements of HI governance cannot depend on the discretion of system designers and developers but must be systematically built into governance models. Future research

should therefore explore how such requirements can be formalised, for instance, through procedural standards that ensure employee representation and stakeholder deliberation in the design of HI systems.

3. **Reflexive and Multi-Level Governance:** Grossmann et al. [5] emphasise that AI reshapes not just individual behaviour but also social dynamics, creating multi-level governance challenges. Our case illustrates this: the introduction of dashboards required alignment across multiple levels of the socio-technical system, from integrating data sources and ensuring technical reliability, to redesigning shopfloor work routines, supporting employees in learning to interpret the dashboards, and securing managerial acceptance. This highlights that HI governance is not confined to a single organisational level but depends on **coordination across technical, human, and institutional domains**. Future research should therefore investigate how governance mechanisms can be designed to handle such multi-level interdependencies, ensuring that HI systems remain resilient and legitimate as they become embedded in organisational and societal structures.

Taken together, these directions highlight that the future of HI governance lies in understanding change over time, inclusion of democratic voices, and reflexive adaptation across levels of analysis. By addressing these challenges, research can move from abstract principles to governance models that are not only ethical and legitimate but also resilient in the face of technological and societal transformation.

## 6  Conclusion

This article shows that a **Division of Labour** between humans and machines or through **Hybrid Ensembles** that aggregate their judgements are two fundamental modes of HI. Division of Labour raises issues of allocation, autonomy, and deskilling, while Hybrid Ensembles surface challenges of accountability diffusion, fairness, and systemic risk. The proposed governance framework highlights six dimensions that help decision-makers and researchers navigate these trade-offs, and the MES dashboard case illustrates how such tensions can play out in practice.

Yet the more profound lesson is that corporate HI governance cannot be reduced to choosing between labour division and aggregation. Instead, the real challenge lies in **managing the dynamics between the two**: systems drift over time, deliberation and participation shape their legitimacy, and reflexive governance is needed to adapt across organisational and societal levels. These insights point to a broader research agenda that treats HI governance as a **living system**, where the Division of Labour and Hybrid Ensembles are not static categories but evolving configurations that require steering.

Our case also highlights a practical paradox: as technical development accelerates, governance risks are being pushed to the background in organisational debates. Firms often focus on speed of deployment and efficiency gains, while the slower, more complex questions of responsibility, fairness, and legitimacy are sidelined. This makes it even more urgent for research and practice to keep governance at the centre of HI, not as an afterthought, but as an integral part of innovation and system design. Therefore, the proposed six-dimensional governance framework is more than a descriptive tool. It offers a diagnostic instrument that enables decision-makers to identify where governance risks emerge and which trade-offs require attention. By making these tensions visible and comparable, the framework provides a structured basis for both academic analysis and practical implementation of HI initiatives.

In this sense, the question posed in our title remains deliberately open. Governance will not be about selecting one mode over the other but about developing frameworks that can flexibly assess and balance **Division of Labour and Hybrid Ensembles.**

# Appendix

To ensure a transparent and reproducible mapping of Hybrid Intelligence (HI) applications within the six-dimensional governance framework, each dimension was operationalised through three guiding questions. Each question was rated on a three-point ordinal scale, where **1** corresponds to the left-hand side of the property range, **3** to the right-hand side, and **2** represents an intermediate configuration between both poles. The evaluation was conducted together with the developer and operator of the dashboard.

| Dimension | Property Range | Evaluation Questions | MES Dashboard Example Case | |
|---|---|---|---|---|
| | | | Rating 1–3 | Justification |
| Responsibility & Accountability | Clear ↔ Diffuse responsibility | Q1. Is accountability for system outcomes formally assigned to a human role? | 1 | Accountability clearly remains at team level and production manager. |
| | | Q2. Can accountability be traced across the human–AI interface when errors occur? | 2 | All dashboard data derive from existing ERP and machine logs, ensuring traceability to human inputs. Realtime human input data and machine data are visible in the board supporting this tracability. |

(continued)

(*continued*)

| Dimension | Property Range | Evaluation Questions | MES Dashboard Example Case | |
| --- | --- | --- | --- | --- |
| | | | Rating 1–3 | Justification |
| | | Q3. Are escalation processes clearly defined for failures? | 1 | Escalation follows existing operational routines with clear human responsibility. Without MES dashboards, the shift performance of previous day is discussed and analysis in next day stand-up production meeting. These processes are kept same. |
| | | | | → Average: **1.3** (moderately clear responsibility) |
| Transparency & Explainability | Interpretable ↔ black-box | Q1. Can decision rationales and system outputs be explained in understandable terms? | 1 | Workers understand how actions affect displayed efficiency. Interactions (such as sick leave) are directly shown result-wise on the MES dashboard. |
| | | Q2. Are the system's limitations documented and communicated? | 1 | Documentation exists and was communicated during introduction phase. |
| | | Q3. Can humans contest or verify system outputs through tangible evidence? | 1 | Operators can verify values directly against machine data. The connection between human interaction and machine data is immediately apparent as visual feedback. |
| | | | | → Average: **1.0** (high interpretability) |

(*continued*)

*(continued)*

| Dimension | Property Range | Evaluation Questions | MES Dashboard Example Case | |
|---|---|---|---|---|
| | | | Rating 1–3 | Justification |
| Human Agency & Autonomy | Strong agency ↔ Deskilling | Q1. Do humans retain the competence to act independently from system outputs? | 1 | Teams continue to decide and act without managerial intervention. |
| | | Q2. Are training and feedback loops in place to maintain human decision capability? | 1 | Continuous visual feedback reinforces learning and competence. |
| | | Q3. Does system design encourage critical reflection by users? | 1 | Real-time data invite reflection, though engagement varies by user. The daily data transparency allows employees to detect errors in SAP source data, e.g. wrong machine setup times. |
| | | | → Average: **1.0** (strong agency) | |
| Ethics & Fairness | Principle-driven ↔ Outcome-driven | Q1. Are ethical considerations normative principles of the application design? | 3 | While the dynamic baselining mechanism prevents operators from being penalised for machine-related downtime, this remains a technical fairness safeguard rather than a principled ethical requirement. |

*(continued)*

*(continued)*

| Dimension | Property Range | Evaluation Questions | MES Dashboard Example Case | |
|---|---|---|---|---|
| | | | Rating 1–3 | Justification |
| | | Q2. Are fairness or non-discrimination checks applied? | 2 | Fairness is addressed through the dynamic adjustment of productivity baselines depending on available capacity. Baselines were derived from standardized REFA time measurements, which ensure procedural consistency and objective criteria. However, they do not account for individual differences in skills, experience, or training level and therefore provide only a partial fairness safeguard. |
| | | Q3. Are ethical evaluations based on values (principles) or mainly on achieved outcomes (utility)? | 3 | Performance evaluations rely exclusively on achieved outcomes. No principle-oriented ethical criteria or individual-level contextual adjustments are incorporated |
| | | | → Average: **2.6** (mainly outcome-driven) | |
| Risk & Resilience | Reactive incident handling ↔ Systemic resilience | Q1. Are risk controls primarily reactive or proactive? | 2 | The Dashboard prevents issues through continuous visibility and the ability to react to it. |

*(continued)*

*(continued)*

| Dimension | Property Range | Evaluation Questions | MES Dashboard Example Case | |
|---|---|---|---|---|
| | | | Rating 1–3 | Justification |
| | | Q2. Is performance monitoring systematic? | 2 | Teams monitor deviations visually and act promptly. |
| | | Q3. Are contingency plans and redundancies built into the socio-technical system? | 1 | No fallback exists if data transmission or dashboard fails. |
| | | | → Average: **1.6** (balanced systemic / pro-active) | |
| Strategic Alignment & Value Generation | Efficiency-oriented ↔ Legitimacy-oriented | Q1. Is the primary goal performance improvement or also trust? | 2 | Efficiency is primary, but design fosters acceptance through team metrics. |
| | | Q2. Are broader stakeholder interests included in performance evaluation (e.g. societal stakeholders)? | 2 | Workers' concerns were addressed to ensure acceptance. |
| | | Q3. Is value creation measured beyond short-term productivity? | 1 | No |
| | | | → Average: **1.6** (balanced orientation) | |

# References


1. Van Der Aalst, W.M.P.: Hybrid Intelligence: to automate or not to automate, that is the question. Int. J. Inf. Syst. Proj. Manag. **9**(2), 5–20 (2021). https://doi.org/10.12821/ijispm 090201
2. Schuster, D., Benevento, E., Aloini, D., Van Der Aalst, W.M.P.: Analyzing healthcare processes with incremental process discovery: practical insights from a real-world application. J. Healthc. Inform. Res. **8**(3), 523–554 (2024). https://doi.org/10.1007/s41666-024-00165-6
3. Choudhary, V., Marchetti, A., Shrestha, Y.R., Puranam, P.: Human-AI ensembles: when can they work? J. Manag. **51**(2), 536–569 (2025). https://doi.org/10.1177/01492063231194968
4. Dellermann, D., Ebel, P., Söllner, M., Leimeister, J.M.: Hybrid intelligence. Bus. Inf. Syst. Eng. **61**(5), 637–643 (2019). https://doi.org/10.1007/s12599-019-00595-2

5. Grossmann, I., Feinberg, M., Parker, D.C., Christakis, N.A., Tetlock, P.E., Cunningham, W.A.: AI and the transformation of social science research. Science **380**(6650), 1108–1109 (2023). https://doi.org/10.1126/science.adi1778

6. Akata, Z., et al.: A research agenda for hybrid intelligence: augmenting human intellect with collaborative, adaptive, responsible, and explainable artificial intelligence. Computer **53**(8), 18–28 (2020). https://doi.org/10.1109/MC.2020.2996587

7. Card, S.K., Moran, T.P., Newell, A.: The psychology of human-computer interaction. Am. J. Psychol. **97**(4), 625–627 (1984). https://doi.org/10.2307/1422176

8. Amershi, S., Cakmak, M., Knox, W.B., Kulesza, T.: Power to the people: the role of humans in interactive machine learning. AI Mag. **35**, 105–120 (2014). https://doi.org/10.1609/aimag.v35i4.2513

9. Holzinger, A.: Interactive machine learning (iML). Informatik Spektrum **39**(1), 64–68 (2016). https://doi.org/10.1007/s00287-015-0941-6

10. Kelly, J.E.: Computing, cognition, and the future of knowing: how humans and machines are forging a new age of understanding. Comput. Res. News **28**(8). https://cra.org/crn/wp-content/uploads/sites/7/2016/09/CRN_Sept_2016.pdf. Accessed 27 Sept 2025

11. Raisch, S., Krakowski, S.: Artificial intelligence and management: the automation-augmentation paradox. AMR **46**(1), 192–210 (2021). https://doi.org/10.5465/2018.0072

12. Steyvers, M., Tejeda, H., Kerrigan, G., Smyth, P.: Bayesian modeling of human–AI complementarity. Proc. Natl. Acad. Sci. **119**(11), e2111547119 (2022). https://doi.org/10.1073/pnas.2111547119

13. Alami, R., Al-Masaeid, T.: The AI-executive partnership: a new paradigm for decision-making and strategic leadership. J. Inf. Knowl. Manag. 2550065 (2025). https://doi.org/10.1142/S0219649225500650

14. Trunk, A., Birkel, H., Hartmann, E.: On the current state of combining human and artificial intelligence for strategic organizational decision making. Bus. Res. **13**(3), 875–919 (2020). https://doi.org/10.1007/s40685-020-00133-x

15. Alibašić, H.: A multi-paradigm ethical framework for hybrid intelligence in blockchain technology and cryptocurrency systems governance. FinTech **4**(3), 34 (2025). https://doi.org/10.3390/fintech4030034

16. Letmathe, P., Rößler, M.: Should firms use digital work instructions?—Individual learning in an agile manufacturing setting. J. Oper. Manag. **68**(1), 94–109 (2022). https://doi.org/10.1002/joom.1159

17. Eisenhardt, K.M.: Agency theory: an assessment and review. Acad. Manag. Rev. **14**(1), 57–74 (1989). https://doi.org/10.2307/258191

18. Teece, D.J.: Explicating dynamic capabilities: the nature and microfoundations of (sustainable) enterprise performance. Strateg. Manag. J. **28**(13), 1319–1350 (2007). https://doi.org/10.1002/smj.640

19. Aguilera, R.V., Desender, K., Bednar, M.K., Lee, J.H.: Connecting the dots: bringing external corporate governance into the corporate governance puzzle. Acad. Manag. Ann. **9**(1), 483–573 (2015). https://doi.org/10.5465/19416520.2015.1024503

20. Aguilera, R.V., Judge, W.Q., Terjesen, S.A.: Corporate governance deviance. Acad. Manag. Rev. **43**(1), 87–109 (2018)

21. Markus, M.L., Neo Bui, Q.: Going concerns: the governance of interorganizational coordination hubs. J. Manag. Inf. Syst. **28**(4), 163–198 (2012). https://doi.org/10.2753/MIS0742-1222280407

22. Roy, J., Saha, B.: Democratic regulation of AI in the workplace. Games Econ. Behav. **152** (2025). https://doi.org/10.2139/ssrn.4638665

23. Kuziemski, M., Misuraca, G.: AI governance in the public sector: three tales from the frontiers of automated decision-making in democratic settings. Telecommun. Policy **44**(6), 101976 (2020). https://doi.org/10.1016/j.telpol.2020.101976

24. Simón, C., Revilla, E., Jesús Sáenz, M.: Integrating AI in organizations for value creation through human-AI teaming: a dynamic-capabilities approach. J. Bus. Res. **182**, 114783 (2024). https://doi.org/10.1016/j.jbusres.2024.114783
25. Lee, J.D., See, K.A.: Trust in automation: designing for appropriate reliance. Hum. Fact. J. Hum. Fact. Ergon. Soc. **46**(1), 50–80 (2004). https://doi.org/10.1518/hfes.46.1.50_30392
26. Simons, J.: Algorithms for the People: Democracy in the Age of AI. Princeton University Press (2023). https://doi.org/10.2307/j.ctv2vjrj0m
27. Uren, V., Edwards, J.S.: Technology readiness and the organizational journey towards AI adoption: an empirical study. Int. J. Inf. Manag. **68**, 102588 (2023). https://doi.org/10.1016/j.ijinfomgt.2022.102588
28. AlSheibani, S., Cheung, Y., Messom, C.: Artificial intelligence adoption: AI-readiness at firm-level. Presented at the Twenty-Second Pacific Asia Conference on Information Systems. Association for Information Systems, Japan (2018)
29. Kovič, K., Tominc, P., Prester, J., Palčič, I.: Artificial intelligence software adoption in manufacturing companies. Appl. Sci. **14**(16), 6959 (2024). https://doi.org/10.3390/app14166959
30. Warner, K.S.R., Wäger, M.: Building dynamic capabilities for digital transformation: an ongoing process of strategic renewal. Long Range Plan. **52**(3), 326–349 (2019). https://doi.org/10.1016/j.lrp.2018.12.001
31. Cetindamar, D., Kitto, K., Wu, M., Zhang, Y., Abedin, B., Knight, S.: Explicating AI literacy of employees at digital workplaces. IEEE Trans. Eng. Manag. **71**, 810–823 (2024). https://doi.org/10.1109/TEM.2021.3138503
32. Asemota, M.O., Owoeye, G.: Integrating human-centric AI into corporate learning: balancing automation with empathy. Dev. Learn. Organ. Int. J. (2025). https://doi.org/10.1108/DLO-01-2025-0014
33. De Laat, P.B.: Companies committed to responsible AI: from principles towards implementation and regulation? Philos. Technol. **34**(4), 1135–1193 (2021). https://doi.org/10.1007/s13347-021-00474-3
34. Bughin, J.: Doing versus saying: responsible AI among large firms. AI Soc. **40**(4), 2751–2763 (2025). https://doi.org/10.1007/s00146-024-02014-x
35. Rana, N.P., Chatterjee, S., Dwivedi, Y.K., Akter, S.: Understanding dark side of artificial intelligence (AI) integrated business analytics: assessing firm's operational inefficiency and competitiveness. Eur. J. Inf. Syst. **31**(3), 364–387 (2022). https://doi.org/10.1080/0960085X.2021.1955628
36. Arrieta, A.B., et al.: Explainable Artificial Intelligence (XAI): concepts, taxonomies, opportunities and challenges toward responsible AI. Inf. Fusion **58**, 82–115 (2020). https://doi.org/10.1016/j.inffus.2019.12.012
37. Mohseni, S., Zarei, N., Ragan, E.D.: A multidisciplinary survey and framework for design and evaluation of explainable AI systems. ACM Trans. Interact. Intell. Syst. **11**(3–4), Article 24 (2021). https://dl.acm.org/doi/10.1145/3387166
38. Sarkar, A.: From anxiety to advantage: guiding employees to embrace AI at work. Organ. Dyn. 101170 (2025). https://doi.org/10.1016/j.orgdyn.2025.101170
39. Shen, L., Qiu, N., Wang, Z.: Psychological safety and trust as drivers of teachers' continued use of AI tools in classrooms. Sci. Rep. **15**(1), 31426 (2025). https://doi.org/10.1038/s41598-025-13789-4
40. Kim, B.-J., Kim, M.-J., Lee, J.: The dark side of artificial intelligence adoption: linking artificial intelligence adoption to employee depression via psychological safety and ethical leadership. Human. Soc. Sci. Commun. **12**(1), 704 (2025). https://doi.org/10.1057/s41599-025-05040-2

41. Li, J., Huang, J.-S.: Dimensions of artificial intelligence anxiety based on the integrated fear acquisition theory. Technol. Soc. **63**, 101410 (2020). https://doi.org/10.1016/j.techsoc.2020.101410

42. Park, N., Jang, K., Cho, S., Choi, J.: Use of offensive language in human-artificial intelligence chatbot interaction: the effects of ethical ideology, social competence, and perceived humanlikeness. Comput. Hum. Behav. **121**, 106795 (2021). https://doi.org/10.1016/j.chb.2021.106795

43. Hou, T.-Y., Tseng, Y.-C., (Tina) Yuan, C.W.: Is this AI sexist? The effects of a biased AI's anthropomorphic appearance and explainability on users' bias perceptions and trust. Int. J. Inf. Manag. **76**, 102775 (2024). https://doi.org/10.1016/j.ijinfomgt.2024.102775

44. Walker, A.M.: Tacit knowledge. Eur. J. Epidemiol. **32**(4), 261–267 (2017). https://doi.org/10.1007/s10654-017-0256-9

45. Zhang, Z., Chen, Z., Xu, L.: Artificial intelligence and moral dilemmas: perception of ethical decision-making in AI. J. Exp. Soc. Psychol. **101**, 104327 (2022). https://doi.org/10.1016/j.jesp.2022.104327

46. Shneiderman, B.: Human-centered artificial intelligence: reliable, safe & trustworthy. Int. J. Hum.-Comput. Interact. **36**(6), 495–504 (2020). https://doi.org/10.1080/10447318.2020.1741118

47. Chamola, V., Hassija, V., Sulthana, A.R., Ghosh, D., Dhingra, D., Sikdar, B.: A review of trustworthy and Explainable Artificial Intelligence (XAI). IEEE Access **11**, 78994–79015 (2023). https://doi.org/10.1109/ACCESS.2023.3294569

48. Albahri, A.S., et al.: A systematic review of trustworthy and explainable artificial intelligence in healthcare: assessment of quality, bias risk, and data fusion. Inf. Fusion **96**, 156–191 (2023). https://doi.org/10.1016/j.inffus.2023.03.008

49. Floridi, L., Cowls, J.: A unified framework of five principles for AI in society. Harvard Data Sci. Rev. **1**(1) (2019). https://doi.org/10.1162/99608f92.8cd550d1

50. Floridi, L., et al.: AI4People—an ethical framework for a good AI society: opportunities, risks, principles, and recommendations. Mind. Mach. **28**(4), 689–707 (2018). https://doi.org/10.1007/s11023-018-9482-5

51. European Union, Regulation (EU) 2024/1689 of the European Parliament and of the Council of 13 June 2024 laying down harmonised rules on artificial intelligence and amending Regulations (EC) No 300/2008, (EU) No 167/2013, (EU) No 168/2013, (EU) 2018/858, (EU) 2018/1139 and (EU) 2019/2144 and Directives 2014/90/EU, (EU) 2016/797 and (EU) 2020/1828 (Artificial Intelligence Act) (2024). http://data.europa.eu/eli/reg/2024/1689/oj/eng. Accessed 27 Sept 2025

52. Presno Linera, M.Á., Meuwese, A.: Regulating AI from Europe: a joint analysis of the AI act and the framework convention on AI. Theory Pract. Legislat. 1–20 (2025). https://doi.org/10.1080/20508840.2025.2492524

53. Jungherr, A.: Artificial intelligence and democracy: a conceptual framework. Soc. Media + Soc. **9**(3), 20563051231186353 (2023). https://doi.org/10.1177/20563051231186353

54. Branford, J., Soulier, E., Fichtner, L.: Generative AI and democratic culture. Philos. Technol. **38**(3), 123 (2025). https://doi.org/10.1007/s13347-025-00953-x

55. Züger, T., Asghari, H.: AI for the public. How public interest theory shifts the discourse on AI. AI Soc. **38**(2), 815–828 (2023). https://doi.org/10.1007/s00146-022-01480-5

56. Erman, E., Furendal, M.: The global governance of artificial intelligence: some normative concerns. Moral Philos. Polit. **9**(2), 267–291 (2022). https://doi.org/10.1515/mopp-2020-0046

57. Schierhorst, N.J., et al.: Hybrid intelligence in production systems and its effects on human work: insights from four use-cases. Procedia Comput. Sci. **232**, 2901–2910 (2024). https://doi.org/10.1016/j.procs.2024.02.106

58. Winfield, A.F., Michael, K., Pitt, J., Evers, V.: Machine ethics: the design and governance of ethical AI and autonomous systems [scanning the issue]. Proc. IEEE **107**(3), 509–517 (2019). https://doi.org/10.1109/JPROC.2019.2900622

59. European Commission, Proposal for a regulation laying down harmonised rules on artificial intelligence (Artificial Intelligence Act) COM(2021) 206 final (2021). https://eur-lex.europa.eu/legal-content/EN/TXT/?uri=CELEX:52021PC0206. Accessed 26 Sept 2025

60. Hagendorff, T.: The ethics of AI ethics: an evaluation of guidelines. Mind. Mach. **30**(1), 99–120 (2020). https://doi.org/10.1007/s11023-020-09517-8

61. Rahwan, I.: Society-in-the-loop: programming the algorithmic social contract. Ethics Inf. Technol. **20**(1), 5–14 (2018). https://doi.org/10.1007/s10676-017-9430-8

62. Friedrich, J., Becker, M., Kramer, F., Wirth, M., Schneider, M.: Incentive design and gamification for knowledge management. J. Bus. Res. **106**, 341–352 (2020). https://doi.org/10.1016/j.jbusres.2019.02.009

63. Anderson, C.J.: The psychology of doing nothing: forms of decision avoidance result from reason and emotion. Psychol. Bull. **129**(1), 139–167 (2003). https://doi.org/10.1037/0033-2909.129.1.139

64. Emerson, K., Nabatchi, T., Balogh, S.: An integrative framework for collaborative governance. J. Publ. Admin. Res. Theory **22**(1), 1–29 (2012). https://doi.org/10.1093/jopart/mur011

65. Beck, R., Müller-Bloch, C., King, J.L.: Governance in the blockchain economy: a framework and research agenda. J. Assoc. Inf. Syst. **19**(10) (2018). https://doi.org/10.17705/1jais.00518

66. Khatri, V., Brown, C.V.: Designing data governance. Commun. ACM **53**(1), 148–152 (2010). https://doi.org/10.1145/1629175.1629210

67. Bovens, M.: Analysing and assessing accountability: a conceptual framework. Eur. Law J. **13**(4), 447–468 (2007). https://doi.org/10.1111/j.1468-0386.2007.00378.x

68. Santoni De Sio, F., Van Den Hoven, J.: Meaningful human control over autonomous systems: a philosophical account. Front. Robot. AI **5** (2018). https://doi.org/10.3389/frobt.2018.00015

69. Breidbach, C.F., Maglio, P.: Accountable algorithms? The ethical implications of data-driven business models. J. Serv. Manag. **31**(2), 163–185 (2020). https://doi.org/10.1108/JOSM-03-2019-0073

70. Peng, C., Van Doorn, J., Eggers, F., Wieringa, J.E.: The effect of required warmth on consumer acceptance of artificial intelligence in service: the moderating role of AI-human collaboration. Int. J. Inf. Manage. **66**, 102533 (2022). https://doi.org/10.1016/j.ijinfomgt.2022.102533

71. Burrell, J.: How the machine "thinks": understanding opacity in machine learning algorithms. Big Data Soc. **3**(1), 2053951715622512 (2016). https://doi.org/10.1177/2053951715622512

72. Doshi-Velez, F., Kim, B.: Towards a rigorous science of interpretable machine learning. arXiv arXiv:1702.08608 (2017). https://doi.org/10.48550/arXiv.1702.08608

73. Samek, W., Montavon, G., Lapuschkin, S., Anders, C.J., Muller, K.-R.: Explaining deep neural networks and beyond: a review of methods and applications. Proc. IEEE **109**(3), 247–278 (2021). https://doi.org/10.1109/JPROC.2021.3060483

74. Chattaraman, V., Kwon, W.-S., Gilbert, J.E., Ross, K.: Should AI-Based, conversational digital assistants employ social- or task-oriented interaction style? A task-competency and reciprocity perspective for older adults. Comput. Hum. Behav. **90**, 315–330 (2019). https://doi.org/10.1016/j.chb.2018.08.048

75. Caruana, R., Lou, Y., Gehrke, J., Koch, P., Sturm, M., Elhadad, N.: Intelligible models for healthcare: predicting pneumonia risk and hospital 30-day readmission. In: Proceedings of the 21th ACM SIGKDD International Conference on Knowledge Discovery and Data Mining, pp. 1721–1730. ACM (2015). https://doi.org/10.1145/2783258.2788613

76. Leicht-Deobald, U., et al.: The challenges of algorithm-based HR decision-making for personal integrity. J. Bus. Ethics **160**, 377–392 (2019). https://doi.org/10.1007/s10551-019-04204-w

77. Cousineau, C., Dara, R., Chowdhury, A.: Trustworthy AI: AI developers' lens to implementation challenges and opportunities. Data Inf. Manag. **9**(2), 100082 (2025). https://doi.org/10.1016/j.dim.2024.100082

78. Lehner, O.M., Ittonen, K., Silvola, H., Ström, E., Wührleitner, A.: Artificial intelligence based decision-making in accounting and auditing: ethical challenges and normative thinking. Acc. Audit. Acc. J. **35**(9), 109–135 (2022). https://doi.org/10.1108/AAAJ-09-2020-4934

79. Modgil, S., Singh, R.K., Hannibal, C.: Artificial intelligence for supply chain resilience: learning from Covid-19. Int. J. Logist. Manag. **33**(4), 1246–1268 (2022). https://doi.org/10.1108/IJLM-02-2021-0094

80. Henderson, J.C., Venkatraman, H.: Strategic alignment: Leveraging information technology for transforming organizations. IBM Syst. J. **32**(1), 472–484 (1993). https://doi.org/10.1147/sj.382.0472

81. Cockburn, I., Henderson, R., Stern, S.: The Impact of Artificial Intelligence on Innovation. National Bureau of Economic Research, Cambridge, MA, Working Paper 24449 (2018). https://doi.org/10.3386/w24449

82. Braun, M., Bleher, H., Hummel, P.: A leap of faith: is there a formula for "trustworthy" AI? Hastings Cent. Rep. **51**(3), 17–22 (2021). https://doi.org/10.1002/hast.1207

83. Hafner, M., Hagemeier, D., Letmathe, P., Iravanimanesh, S.: Operational MES dashboards in small-scale manufacturing: reducing supervision, enhancing performance. In: Working Paper, RWTH Aachen University (2025)

# Privacy and Confidentiality in Process Mining: An Overview of Challenges, Methods, and Future Research Directions

Majid Rafiei[✉] [iD]

SAP SE, Walldorf, Germany
`majid.rafiei@sap.com`

**Abstract.** This paper focuses on the definitions of privacy and confidentiality in the context of process mining, the specific disclosure risks that arise when applying process mining to sensitive event logs, the general activities involved in privacy-aware process mining, categories of current methods for mitigating privacy risks, and an extensive discussion of future research directions. The objective is to provide a structured overview to capture the breadth of challenges and potential research opportunities in this field.

**Keywords:** Privacy · Confidentiality · Process mining · Event data

## 1 Introduction

Process mining has rapidly developed into one of the most influential approaches for analyzing and improving business processes. Unlike traditional business process management (BPM), which relies primarily on normative models and interviews, process mining extracts knowledge directly from the rich event data recorded in enterprise information systems. These event logs provide unprecedented visibility into how processes actually unfold in practice, enabling organizations to identify bottlenecks, detect compliance deviations, and discover optimization opportunities.

Yet, the same characteristics that make event logs so powerful also introduce serious challenges concerning privacy and confidentiality. Logs often contain detailed information about individuals (patients, customers, employees) as well as business-critical activities (pharmaceutical manufacturing steps, financial transactions, logistics chains). Inappropriate handling of such data can lead to regulatory violations, reputational harm, competitive disadvantage, and ethical breaches.

The rise of regulations such as the General Data Protection Regulation (GDPR) in Europe [21], the Health Insurance Portability and Accountability Act (HIPAA) in the United States [1], and the upcoming EU AI Act underscores the urgency of embedding privacy and confidentiality into process mining. These


J. Mendling et al. (Eds.): Wil van der Aalst Festschrift, LNCS 16480, pp. 715–727, 2026.
https://doi.org/10.1007/978-3-032-17618-9_45

legal frameworks require organizations not only to protect sensitive data but also to demonstrate compliance and accountability.

This paper summarizes and elaborates on the key contributions of the dissertation Privacy and Confidentiality in Process Mining [11]. Key findings from the dissertation are consolidated while expanding the discussion towards new opportunities and challenges. By systematically exploring definitions, risks, methodological categories, and future research directions, it positions privacy and confidentiality as central pillars for the future of responsible process mining.

## 2   Privacy and Confidentiality in Process Mining

Although the terms privacy and confidentiality are often used interchangeably, they represent distinct yet complementary concepts in the realm of process mining, each with its own set of concerns and protective measures [5].

### 2.1   Privacy in Process Mining

Privacy refers to the rights of individuals to control how their personal data is collected, stored, processed, and shared. In the context of process mining, privacy concerns primarily focus on the traces or event logs that capture the activities associated with individual cases. These cases could represent patients in a hospital's Electronic Health Records (EHR) system, customers interacting with an e-commerce platform, or employees participating in organizational processes. The concern is that event logs may contain sensitive information that could potentially be used to identify or infer personal details about individuals, which can lead to privacy violations if not properly protected.

For example, in healthcare, patient data may be captured during a medical procedure, and in e-commerce, customer behavior or purchase history may be recorded. Both types of data, if mishandled or improperly shared, can lead to violations of privacy laws such as GDPR in Europe HIPAA in the United States. A key component of privacy protection in process mining is ensuring that individuals cannot be re-identified from anonymized event logs or that traces cannot be linked back to specific individuals.

### 2.2   Confidentiality in Process Mining

Confidentiality is more closely aligned with the organizational perspective and refers to the protection of sensitive business information from unauthorized access. In process mining, confidentiality concerns are focused on preventing the exposure of proprietary business information that might be embedded in event logs, such as internal workflows, compliance strategies, trade secrets, or competitive strategies. Unlike privacy, which directly impacts individuals, breaches of confidentiality primarily harm organizations, potentially leading to financial losses, reputational damage, or the leakage of critical business insights to competitors [5].

For example, a process execution model of a production line might reveal proprietary insights into the efficiency of a manufacturing process or expose trade secrets regarding resource allocation. The exposure of such information to unauthorized parties could compromise the competitive advantage of a company, even though no personal information about individuals is directly implicated. In these cases, protecting confidentiality could involve securing event log data with encryption, ensuring that only authorized stakeholders have access to the underlying process data or limiting the sharing of process models that reveal sensitive organizational knowledge.

In the context of process mining, confidentiality often requires safeguards around access control, data encryption, and model security. Organizations typically establish clear protocols for who can view, analyze, or share certain aspects of the process data to prevent unintentional leaks. As such, confidentiality measures are crucial for maintaining the integrity and trustworthiness of business operations.

### 2.3   Overlap and Interdependence

In practice, privacy and confidentiality often overlap, and ensuring the responsible application of process mining requires addressing both concerns. For instance, the anonymization of event logs to protect privacy may also serve to safeguard confidentiality by preventing unauthorized individuals from linking sensitive data to specific employees or patients. On the flip side, confidentiality measures such as encryption may also contribute to safeguarding personal information. For instance, Homomorphic Encryption techniques can be utilized to preserve privacy of individuals in inter-organizational settings [22].

## 3   Disclosure Risks in Process Mining

Event logs in process mining are quite unique in structure, which introduces specific disclosure risks that extend beyond the general concerns associated with traditional data analysis. These risks are particularly critical because process mining often relies on granular event data to uncover process insights, which can inadvertently expose sensitive information.

### 3.1   Case Disclosure

Case disclosure refers to the risk of identifying individuals represented as cases within an event log. It quantifies how uniquely the trace owners, i.e., cases, can be re-identified [13]. For instance, in a healthcare setting, linking a treatment sequence in a hospital's event log to a patient's known identity could represent a case disclosure. This is especially concerning when combined with other data sources, as it may allow an adversary to re-identify a patient and deduce private health conditions or treatment details. Note that case disclosure is not limited to healthcare but applies to any domain where individual-specific information is recorded, such as customer interactions in e-commerce or employee activities in business workflows.

## 3.2  Trace Disclosure

Trace disclosure occurs when entire behavioral patterns or sequences of events corresponding to a particular case are exposed, making it possible for attackers to infer future behavior, predict outcomes, or uncover confidential business operations. It quantifies how confidently the trace attribute of cases, as a sensitive attribute, can be specified [13]. Note that trace disclosure could happen without a successful case disclosure. For example, when there are different patients, i.e., cases, with the same sequence of treatment activities in a hospital, where one of those patients is an attacker's target patient, the attacker would be able to know the complete sequence of activities performed for the target patient without the need to know the exact case id.

## 3.3  Additional Disclosure Risks

One could also analyze the disclosure risks from the perspective of different data attributes in event logs. In the following, we provide some examples [14].

**Activity-based disclosure:** This risk arises when infrequent or rare activities recorded in event logs can be linked to specific sensitive attributes or behaviors. For instance, an uncommon medical procedure or a rare business event might be highly indicative of a sensitive condition or process when combined with other data.

**Resource-based disclosure:** This occurs when an individual's or a professional's unique work patterns in the event log can be used to profile them. For example, consistent task sequences or time logs tied to specific employees may expose personal working habits, potentially leading to unintentional disclosure of private details (such as performance reviews or personal characteristics).

**Time-based disclosure:** This type of disclosure involves re-identifying cases by aligning the detailed timestamps of events in the log with external knowledge. For example, a timestamped medical procedure may be linked with public data, such as hospital schedules or insurance records, to identify the patient. Similarly, for business processes, time-based information could help correlate specific events to known organizational timelines, leading to the identification of confidential operations.

**Combined Attacks:** Attackers may exploit correlations between different attributes—such as resource patterns and time stamps—leading to a combined attack that increases the likelihood of re-identification or inference. By cross-referencing event log data with external sources, attackers may expose sensitive organizational or personal information.

## 3.4  The Challenge of Balancing Utility and Protection

The disclosure risks could further be amplified by other aspects of responsible process mining, such as transparency. Moreover, there always exists a trade-off

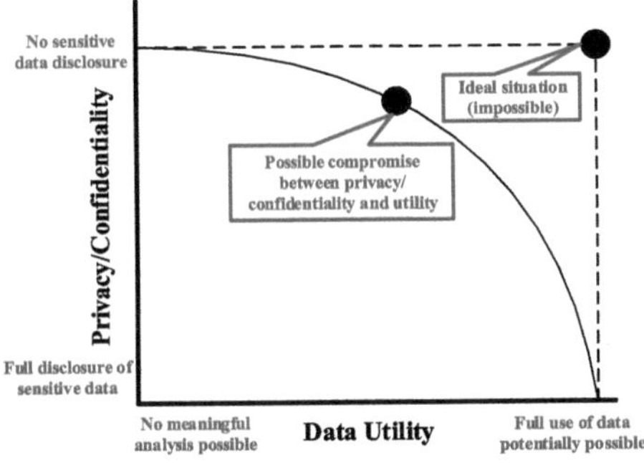


**Fig. 1.** Trade-off between sensitive data protection and data utility preservation [11].

between maximizing data protection, i.e., reducing the disclosure risks, and preserving a good level of data/result utility. As shown in Fig. 1, the ideal situation where there exists no sensitive data disclosure and no data utility degradation is impossible. However, it is possible to compromise between sensitive data protection and data utility preservation [11]. A privacy-preservation technique is of higher performance in comparison with other techniques if it is able to provide higher data utility preservation for the same privacy guarantees. Thus, it is important to have measures for evaluating both privacy protection and utility preservation. This is where one needs to come up with rigorous measures for quantifying the introduced disclosure risks.

## 4    Privacy-Related Activities in Process Mining

Privacy-related activities may be explored from the perspective of two distinct types of scenarios: (i) scenarios involving a single event log and (ii) scenarios involving multiple event logs.

### 4.1    Privacy-Related Activities for Single Event Log Scenarios

Figure 2 presents an overview of privacy-related activities in process mining, with a particular focus on scenarios involving a single event log. In this context, a single event log refers to a case where one data owner is responsible for a single, associated event log. Based on this assumption, the main activities can be categorized as follows: (A1) Privacy and confidentiality preservation techniques, (A2) Disclosure risk analysis of event logs, (A3) Data utility analysis, (A4) Result utility analysis, and (A5) Disclosure risk analysis of results.

The privacy and confidentiality preservation techniques involve applying basic anonymization methods to ensure data protection (A1). These techniques take an original event log as input and produce an anonymized version of it. Disclosure risk analysis can be performed both on the original and anonymized event logs to assess the effectiveness of the protection mechanisms (A2). Additionally,

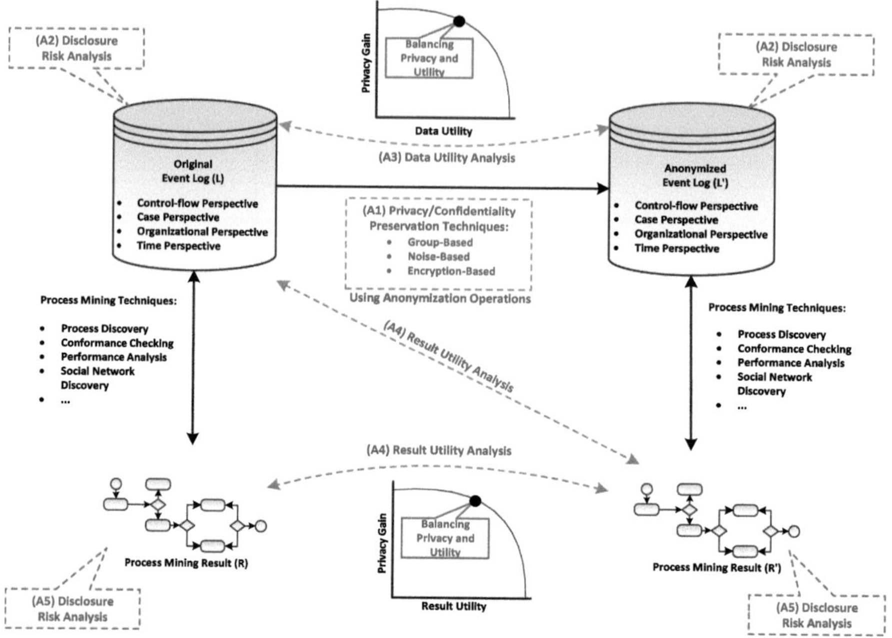



**Fig. 2.** A general overview of privacy-related activities in process mining considering a single event log. A1 to A5 show the main types of activities [11].

comparisons between the original and anonymized event logs can evaluate the extent to which data utility is preserved (A3). The overarching goal is to develop protection techniques that both enhance privacy or confidentiality and maintain the utility of the data.

As with original event logs, process mining techniques can also be applied to anonymized event logs. However, process models—one of the primary outputs of process mining—can still reveal sensitive information. Therefore, disclosure risk analysis must also be conducted on the results produced from anonymized logs (A5). The aim is for the results derived from anonymized event logs to closely resemble those obtained from the original event logs, thereby balancing privacy protection with the preservation of analytical insights.

The results derived from anonymized event logs should closely resemble those obtained from the original event logs. To assess this similarity, result utility analyses are conducted (A4). It is important to distinguish between data utility preservation and result utility preservation. The former is a broader concept: if two event logs are similar, the results they produce should also be similar. However, in some cases, privacy protection techniques may focus on a specific aspect of an event log that directly influences a particular type of result. In such situations, result utility preservation may be sufficient, offering more flexibility for protection techniques while ensuring higher privacy guarantees.

## 4.2  Privacy-Related Activities for Multiple Event Logs Scenarios

As previously mentioned, Fig. 2 primarily focuses on single event logs, where there is only one data owner and a single event log owned by that entity. However, there are common process mining scenarios that involve multiple event logs, such as *distributed settings* and *continuous publishing*.

In a distributed setting, multiple data owners each possess their own event logs. For example, in a supply chain scenario, several organizations collaborate to produce a product, with each organization maintaining its own event log and associated privacy or confidentiality concerns. Despite these individual concerns, all organizations may want to access a joint process model that represents the overall collaboration without compromising their privacy or confidentiality.

Continuous publishing involves a scenario where there is a single data owner but multiple event logs. In this case, business processes are executed continuously, generating new events that must be recorded in real time. To ensure that process mining results remain current, these event logs containing the latest events need to be published on an ongoing basis (e.g., daily, weekly, etc.). We refer to this process as Continuous Event Data Publishing (CEDP).

## 5  Categories of Current Methods

The current privacy and confidentiality protection techniques can be broadly categorized as follows.

### 5.1  Anonymization Operations

Anonymization operations are the primary mechanisms used to modify the original event log in order to meet specific privacy requirements, and they may involve any number of parameters. These operations can be applied at either the case or event level, with their target being a case, an event, or their respective attributes. Common anonymization operations are as follows:

**Suppression:** This involves removing specific identifiers from the log, such as names or ID numbers. For example, in healthcare, patient IDs might be suppressed in event logs to prevent the identification of individuals. In the context of process mining, as examples, in [7,14], the authors employ suppression operations to provide group-based privacy protections.

**Substitution:** Sensitive information is replaced with random or generalized values. For instance, instead of storing the exact time a specific medical procedure took place, the log may store a random time within a given range, making it harder to link events to a specific patient. In [12], a substitution technique is used in order to mine roles from event logs while preserving privacy.

**Condensation:** Condensation begins by grouping cases into clusters with similar sensitive attribute values. Within each cluster, the sensitive values are then replaced with a representative statistical measure of the group, such as the mean, mode, or median. In [2], the authors introduced a condensation-based approach for privacy preservation in process mining.

**Swapping**: In this technique, attributes are exchanged between records in a way that preserves overall statistics but makes it difficult to trace back the information to a specific individual. Individual cases selected for exchanging sensitive attribute values are expected to have similar values for those attributes. Consequently, cases must be grouped into clusters based on the similarity of their sensitive attribute values.

**Generalization**: This operation replaces certain values, determined by the operation's target and possibly specific conditions, with a parent value from the attribute's taxonomy tree. The inverse of generalization is referred to as specialization. For example, replacing "patient age = 45" with "patient age group = 40–50". This ensures the individual's identity is less discernible while still providing useful aggregated data for analysis. In [7], this operation has been used to generalize trace variants.

### 5.2   Encryption-Based Techniques

Encryption techniques are employed to protect the data during analysis, ensuring that sensitive information remains confidential even when the data is shared across different entities. Examples of encryption-based approaches include:

**Secure Multiparty Computation (SMPC)**: SMPC enables multiple parties to collaboratively analyze data without revealing the actual data to each other. For example, in a supply chain, different organizations may wish to collaborate on process mining without sharing their individual logs. SMPC allows them to compute joint insights while keeping their logs private [4].

**Homomorphic Encryption**: This technique allows computations to be performed on encrypted data, so that data remains encrypted during the entire process. For instance, an organization can run process mining algorithms on encrypted event logs, and the final result can still provide useful insights, without decrypting the underlying data at any point [8].

### 5.3   Group-Based Methods

Group-based techniques convert the input data into masked tables by leveraging data similarity. These methods aim to form groups of identical data items, based on assumptions about the background knowledge an adversary might possess. Group-base techniques are more intuitive. However, a key limitation of these techniques is their reliance on assumptions about background knowledge. Examples include:

$k$**-anonymity**: This technique ensures that for every case in the event log, there are at least $k$ other cases that are similar in terms of specific attributes. For example, if an event log contains information about patient treatments, $k$-anonymity might group patients with similar treatment sequences together, ensuring that no single patient can be uniquely identified.

**$l$-diversity**: An extension of $k$-anonymity, $l$-diversity aims to ensure that each group of anonymized cases contains at least $l$ distinct values for sensitive attributes. For instance, in a healthcare setting, if a group of patients has the same treatment sequence, the $l$-diversity technique ensures that there is sufficient variety in other sensitive attributes, such as diagnoses, to prevent attackers from making inferences about any individual.

**$t$-closeness**: This approach ensures that the distribution of sensitive attributes within any group of cases is similar to the distribution of those attributes in the entire dataset. This can be particularly useful in preventing attackers from gaining insight into sensitive conditions or outcomes, such as specific diseases.

Examples of group-based privacy-preservation techniques in process mining are [7,14], and [19]. These group-based methods ensure that, even if an adversary has access to the event logs, they cannot make meaningful inferences about individual cases.

### 5.4   Noise-Based Methods

Noise-based methods introduce controlled randomness into the event logs to protect individual privacy while still preserving the overall structure of the data. These methods are especially important in the context of statistical analysis, where small deviations can significantly reduce the risk of identifying individual data points. These techniques are often on the basis of Differential Privacy [3].

Differential Privacy adds noise to the data or results of analysis in such a way that the presence or absence of any single individual's data has little to no effect on the overall outcome. For example, adding random noise to a count of patients undergoing a particular treatment prevents an attacker from inferring whether a specific patient was part of the dataset. There are several papers in the process mining context using noise-based techniques to provide privacy guarantees, including [9,20,24,25], and [6].

## 6   Future Research Directions

This section aims to highlight potential research directions that have either not yet been explored or have only received limited attention, indicating a need for more comprehensive investigation.

### 6.1   Privacy in Object-Centric Process Mining

Object-centric process mining (OCPM) captures interactions between multiple entities (e.g., orders, customers, products). Traditional privacy-preserving methods often fail here because relationships between entities can themselves reveal sensitive information. Future work could develop graph anonymization techniques or relationship-based k-anonymity to mask interactions while retaining analytical power. For example, in a supply chain setting, anonymization must hide the connection between a supplier and a critical component while still enabling analysis of bottlenecks.

## 6.2 Privacy-Aware Federated Process Mining

Federated process mining enables multiple organizations to collaboratively discover and analyze processes without centralizing sensitive data. For example, a consortium of hospitals could jointly analyze patient treatment pathways across regions without sharing raw patient data, ensuring compliance with GDPR while still learning from broader patterns. This research direction has recently garnered increasing attention within the community, with several papers addressing key activities of process mining in inter-organizational settings—particularly in the areas of process discovery [4,16] and conformance checking [18]. Nevertheless, there is considerable scope for further research and development.

## 6.3 Continuous Event Data Publishing (CEDP)

In some contexts, process mining involves the continuous publishing of event data, where new event logs are generated and published on a regular basis. While this provides the advantage of up-to-date process insights, it also introduces unique privacy risks, such as Temporal Privacy Leakage. When logs are published over time, the accumulation of historical data may allow attackers to infer sensitive information based on changes in patterns or the timing of specific events. For example, a hospital might continuously release data on patient treatments, and over time, an adversary might be able to deduce a patient's condition based on trends in treatment sequences. CEDP creates ongoing challenges for privacy preservation, as each incremental release of event logs increases the risk of revealing sensitive information over time. There are a few papers in process mining targeting these types of challenges [15,17].

## 6.4 Synthetic Event Log Generation

Generative models such as GANs and large language models (LLMs) open new opportunities for synthetic log generation, where data is statistically similar to real logs but free of direct identifiers. However, care must be taken to avoid memorization that inadvertently leaks real cases. Hybrid approaches could combine differentially private training with domain-specific constraints to ensure both realism and privacy. For example, a bank could release synthetic transaction logs for academic research, preserving the utility for fraud detection while ensuring no real customer data is exposed. Recently, this approach has gained some attention in process mining, but there remains significant potential for further research [25].

## 6.5  Privacy-by-Design Algorithms

Rather than applying privacy measures after data collection, algorithms can be designed to be inherently privacy-preserving. For instance, process discovery techniques could work directly with aggregated statistics instead of raw event traces, and conformance checking might employ encrypted pattern matching. This approach aligns with the GDPR's "privacy by design" principle. As an example, a hospital could perform compliance checks against treatment guidelines using encrypted patient traces, ensuring the confidentiality of doctors' actions. To date, only a few studies in process mining have explored this direction [10, 23].

## 6.6  Context-Aware Confidentiality

Not all stakeholders require the same level of detail. Future systems could provide context-aware confidentiality, tailoring protections based on user roles or contractual obligations. This could be implemented with policy-aware process mining frameworks, automatically adjusting data sharing depending on context. For example, regulators may see detailed compliance deviations, while external auditors see only aggregated results.

## 6.7  Fairness and Privacy in Workforce Analytics

Organizational mining often reconstructs social networks of employees. While anonymization protects identities, biases may persist if certain groups are disproportionately represented or excluded. Research could focus on fairness-preserving anonymization, ensuring privacy while preventing discriminatory outcomes. For example, in HR analytics, ensuring that anonymized performance data does not inadvertently reveal or disadvantage specific minority groups.

## 6.8  Interdisciplinary Bridges

Privacy in process mining is not only a technical challenge but also a legal and ethical one. Future research should explore bridges with explainable AI, AI ethics, and accountability frameworks. For example, privacy-aware process models could be paired with explainability modules that clarify how protections were applied and what risks remain. For example, a company presenting anonymized process models to regulators could include an "explainability certificate" documenting the privacy-preservation methods applied.

**Acknowledgments.** Looking back on my PhD journey, I remain deeply grateful for the guidance and inspiration I received from Prof. Wil van der Aalst (Wil). My doctoral years at RWTH Aachen University were marked by an environment that encouraged curiosity, precision, and creativity—values he consistently embodied. His ability to combine rigorous scientific thinking with genuine enthusiasm for discovery shaped not only my research, but also my approach to problem-solving and collaboration. Thanks, Wil!

# References


1. HIPAA privacy rule and its impacts on research (2017). https://www.hhs.gov/hipaa/for-professionals/special-topics/hipaa-privacy-rule-research/index.html
2. Batista, E., Solanas, A.: A uniformization-based approach to preserve individuals' privacy during process mining analyses. Peer-to-Peer Netw. Appl. **14**(3), 1500–1519 (2021). https://doi.org/10.1007/s12083-020-01059-1
3. Dwork, C.: Differential Privacy: A Survey of Results. In: Agrawal, M., Du, D., Duan, Z., Li, A. (eds.) TAMC 2008. LNCS, vol. 4978, pp. 1–19. Springer, Heidelberg (2008). https://doi.org/10.1007/978-3-540-79228-4_1
4. Elkoumy, G., Fahrenkrog-Petersen, S.A., Dumas, M., Laud, P., Pankova, A., Weidlich, M.: Secure Multi-party Computation for Inter-organizational Process Mining. In: Nurcan, S., Reinhartz-Berger, I., Soffer, P., Zdravkovic, J. (eds.) BPMDS/EMMSAD -2020. LNBIP, vol. 387, pp. 166–181. Springer, Cham (2020). https://doi.org/10.1007/978-3-030-49418-6_11
5. Elkoumy, G., et al.: Privacy and confidentiality in process mining: threats and research challenges. ACM Trans. Manag. Inf. Syst. **13**(1), 11:1–11:17 (2022). https://doi.org/10.1145/3468877
6. Elkoumy, G., Pankova, A., Dumas, M.: Differentially private release of event logs for process mining. Inf. Syst. **115**, 102161 (2023)
7. Fahrenkrog-Petersen, S.A., van der Aa, H., Weidlich, M.: PRETSA: event log sanitization for privacy-aware process discovery. In: International Conference on Process Mining, ICPM 2019, Aachen, Germany, June 24-26, 2019, pp. 1–8. IEEE (2019). https://doi.org/10.1109/ICPM.2019.00012
8. Kazemian, M., Helfert, M.: A lightweight encryption method for privacy-preserving in process mining. In: 2023 IEEE Intl Conf on Dependable, Autonomic and Secure Computing, Intl Conf on Pervasive Intelligence and Computing, Intl Conf on Cloud and Big Data Computing, Intl Conf on Cyber Science and Technology Congress (DASC/PiCom/CBDCom/CyberSciTech), pp. 0228–0233 (2023).https://doi.org/10.1109/DASC/PiCom/CBDCom/Cy59711.2023.10361442
9. Mannhardt, F., Koschmider, A., Baracaldo, N., Weidlich, M., Michael, J.: Privacy-preserving process mining - differential privacy for event logs. Bus. Inf. Syst. Eng. **61**(5), 595–614 (2019). https://doi.org/10.1007/s12599-019-00613-3
10. Michael, J., Koschmider, A., Mannhardt, F., Baracaldo, N., Rumpe, B.: User-centered and privacy-driven process mining system design for IOT. In: International Conference On Advanced Information Systems Engineering, pp. 194–206. Springer (2019)
11. Rafiei, M.: Privacy and confidentiality in process mining. Ph.D. thesis, RWTH Aachen University (2023). https://doi.org/10.18154/RWTH-2023-11015, https://publications.rwth-aachen.de/record/973807/files/973807.pdf
12. Rafiei, M., van der Aalst, W.M.P.: Mining roles from event logs while preserving privacy. In: Francescomarino, C.D., Dijkman, R.M., Zdun, U. (eds.) Business Process Management Workshops - BPM 2019 International Workshops, Vienna, Austria, September 1-6, 2019, Revised Selected Papers. Lecture Notes in Business Information Processing, vol. 362, pp. 676–689. Springer (2019). https://doi.org/10.1007/978-3-030-37453-2_54, https://doi.org/10.1007/978-3-030-37453-2_54
13. Rafiei, M., van der Aalst, W.M.P.: Towards quantifying privacy in process mining. In: Leemans, S.J.J., Leopold, H. (eds.) Process Mining Workshops - ICPM 2020 International Workshops, Padua, Italy, October 5-8, 2020, Revised Selected Papers. Lecture Notes in Business Information Processing, vol. 406, pp. 385–397. Springer (2020). https://doi.org/10.1007/978-3-030-72693-5_29

14. Rafiei, M., van der Aalst, W.M.P.: Group-based privacy preservation techniques for process mining. Data Knowl. Eng. **134**, 101908 (2021). https://doi.org/10.1016/j.datak.2021.101908
15. Rafiei, M., van der Aalst, W.M.P.: Privacy-Preserving Continuous Event Data Publishing. In: Polyvyanyy, A., Wynn, M.T., Van Looy, A., Reichert, M. (eds.) BPM 2021. LNBIP, vol. 427, pp. 178–194. Springer, Cham (2021). https://doi.org/10.1007/978-3-030-85440-9_11
16. Rafiei, M., van der Aalst, W.M.P.: An abstraction-based approach for privacy-aware federated process mining. IEEE Access **11**, 33697–33714 (2023). https://doi.org/10.1109/ACCESS.2023.3263673
17. Rafiei, M., Elkoumy, G., van der Aalst, W.M.P.: Quantifying temporal privacy leakage in continuous event data publishing. In: Sellami, M., Ceravolo, P., Reijers, H.A., Gaaloul, W., Panetto, H. (eds.) Cooperative Information Systems - 28th International Conference, CoopIS 2022, Bozen-Bolzano, Italy, October 4-7, 2022, Proceedings. Lecture Notes in Computer Science, vol. 13591, pp. 75–94. Springer (2022https://doi.org/10.1007/978-3-031-17834-4_5, https://doi.org/10.1007/978-3-031-17834-4_5
18. Rafiei, M., Pourbafrani, M., van der Aalst, W.M.P.: Federated conformance checking. Inf. Syst. **131**, 102525 (2025). https://doi.org/10.1016/j.is.2025.102525, https://www.sciencedirect.com/science/article/pii/S0306437925000109
19. Rafiei, M., Wagner, M., van der Aalst, W.M.P.: TLKC-privacy model for process mining. In: Dalpiaz, F., Zdravkovic, J., Loucopoulos, P. (eds.) Research Challenges in Information Science - 14th International Conference, RCIS 2020, Limassol, Cyprus, September 23-25, 2020, Proceedings. Lecture Notes in Business Information Processing, vol. 385, pp. 398–416. Springer (2020).https://doi.org/10.1007/978-3-030-50316-1_24, https://doi.org/10.1007/978-3-030-50316-1_24
20. Rafiei, M., Wangelik, F., van der Aalst, W.M.P.: TraVaS: differentially private trace variant selection for process mining. In: Process Mining Workshops. Lecture Notes in Business Information Processing, Springer (2023)
21. Regulation, E.G.D.P.: Regulation (EU) 2016/679 of the european parliament and of the council of 27 april 2016 on the protection of natural persons with regard to the processing of personal data and on the free movement of such data, and repealing directive 95/46/ec (general data protection regulation) 2016. OJ L **119**(1) (2016)
22. Rennert, C., Albers, J., Leemans, S.J.J., van der Aalst, W.M.P.: Your secret is safe with me: federated directly-follows graph discovery. In: 7th International Conference on Process Mining, ICPM 2025. IEEE (2025)
23. Schulze, M., Zisgen, Y., Kirschte, M., Mohammadi, E., Koschmider, A.: Differentially private inductive miner. In: 2024 6th International Conference on Process Mining (ICPM), pp. 89–96. IEEE (2024)
24. Ueck, H., Andrews, R., Wynn, M.T., Leemans, S.J.J.: Differentially private event logs with case attributes. In: Process Mining Workshops, pp. 240–252. Springer Nature Switzerland, Cham (2025)
25. Wangelik, F., Rafiei, M., Pourbafrani, M., van der Aalst, W.M.P.: Releasing differentially private event logs using generative models. Data Knowl. Eng. **159**, 102450 (2025). https://doi.org/10.1016/j.datak.2025.102450

# How Students and Robots Can Profit from Process Mining

Hayyan Helal, Tarik Viehmann, and Gerhard Lakemeyer(✉)

Knowledge-Based Systems Group, RWTH Aachen University, Ahornstr. 55,
52056 Aachen, Germany
`{helal,viehmann,gerhard}@kbsg.rwth-aachen.de`
`https://www.kbsg.rwth-aachen.de/`

**Abstract.** In this chapter we outline the outcome of our fruitful collaboration with Wil's research group in two very distinct application areas: helping students in designing their individual study plans and analyzing the performance of robots in production logistics scenarios.

The complexity of modern study programs, particularly within large higher education institutions, increasingly challenges both students and curriculum designers. While formal examination regulations and recommended study plans provide a regulatory backbone, they often fail to accommodate the dynamic and heterogeneous nature of individual student progress. The collaboration with Wil's group, as part of the AIStudyBuddy project, introduces a novel, multi-layered research program that addresses this issue. By integrating process mining, rule-based reasoning, and AI planning, this body of work proposes a novel framework for supporting personalized study planning and monitoring based on real-world data.

For many years, our group has been engaged in the RoboCup Logistics League, where teams of robots compete in game-like setting manufacturing product variants with the help of machines. During a game product orders arrive randomly with deadlines attached for delivery. The goal is to fulfill as many of the orders during a game as possible. While a large body of data has been collected over the years from actual games, both real and in simulation, a challenge has been how to make use of that data in order to analyze and ultimately optimize the behavior of the robots. We will show how object-centric process mining can play a key role in addressing this challenge.

## 1  Introduction

Process mining has proven to be a very important discipline and has led to powerful tools for the discovery, analysis and optimization of business processes [1]. In this chapter we outline the outcome of our fruitful collaboration with Wil's research group in two application areas, which are somewhat unusual in the context of process mining: university student study plans and robots in production logistics scenarios.


J. Mendling et al. (Eds.): Wil van der Aalst Festschrift, LNCS 16480, pp. 728–740, 2026.
https://doi.org/10.1007/978-3-032-17618-9_46

Our collaboration regarding study plans came about when we were partners in the project *AIStudyBuddy* funded by the German Federal Ministry of Education and Research (BMBF). The idea was to apply AI techniques to help students choose their individual study plans and curriculum designers in improving their design decisions. While the work in our group focused on formalizing existing curricula and using rule-based reasoning as well as automated planning techniques to devise study plans, Wil's group applied process mining techniques to analyze actual study plans and their outcomes in order to fine tune recommendations for students faced with the task of deciding which courses to take and when.

In robotics our group has been, for many years, engaged in the RoboCup Logistics League, where teams of robots compete in a game-like setting manufacturing product variants with the help of machines. During a game product orders arrive randomly with deadlines attached for delivery. The goal is to fulfill as many of the orders during a game as possible. While a large body of data has been collected over the years from actual games, both real and in simulation, a challenge has been how to make use of that data in order to analyze and ultimately optimize the behavior of the robots. We will show how object-centric process mining can play a key role in addressing this challenge.

The rest of the paper is organized as follows. Section 2 introduces the AIStudyBuddy project and gives a brief overview of three joint papers. In Sect. 3 we introduce the RoboCup Logistics League, show how data collection is enhanced to arrive at object-centric event logs, and give an outlook on how process mining can yield new insights into robot performance during a game. We end with a brief conclusion.

## 2 Data-Driven Study Planning and Monitoring for the Project *AIStudyBuddy*

The *AIStudyBuddy* project was conceived as a response to the growing complexity and personalization needs of academic study planning within higher education institutions. Traditionally, students receive static recommended plans that assume a linear progression through a curriculum. However, student behavior frequently deviates from these templates due to various personal, administrative, or academic factors. These deviations, while common, are often not sufficiently accounted for in current advising or planning systems.

The project addresses this gap by combining methods from process mining, explainable AI, and educational analytics to build a smart, interactive assistant for students and a diagnostic tool for curriculum designers (see Fig. 1 for a visual representation). The system comprises two primary modules:

- StudyBuddy: A rule-aware, data-informed planning tool that allows students to propose and validate personalized study plans. It ensures formal compliance with examination regulations while providing data-driven recommendations based on successful patterns mined from historical student data.

– BuddyAnalytics: A platform for academic advisors and program designers to explore real-world study paths, detect significant deviations from recommended plans, evaluate the effectiveness of curricular sequences, and derive actionable insights from process mining models.

The core idea is to provide individualized, yet regulation-compliant planning guidance, using a combination of the research interests of our group, the *Knowledge Based Systems Group* (KBSG) and Wil's group. *Process and Data Science* (PADS):

– Rule-based AI, KBSG.
– Declarative behavioral models, PADS.
– Statistical pattern mining from event logs, PADS.
– Automated planning with hard and soft constraints, KBSG.

This project was the joint work of three German universities: RWTH Aachen University, University of Wuppertal, and University of Bochum. It covered different subjects such as Computer Science, Economics, and Mechanical Engineering. Anonymized student logs from the Campus Management System (CMS) of each university, and detailed descriptions of the diverse study programs served as the foundation for training, evaluation, and deployment of the AIStudyBuddy components. Through this architecture, the project delivers both personalized support for learners and strategic insights for institutional decision-making.

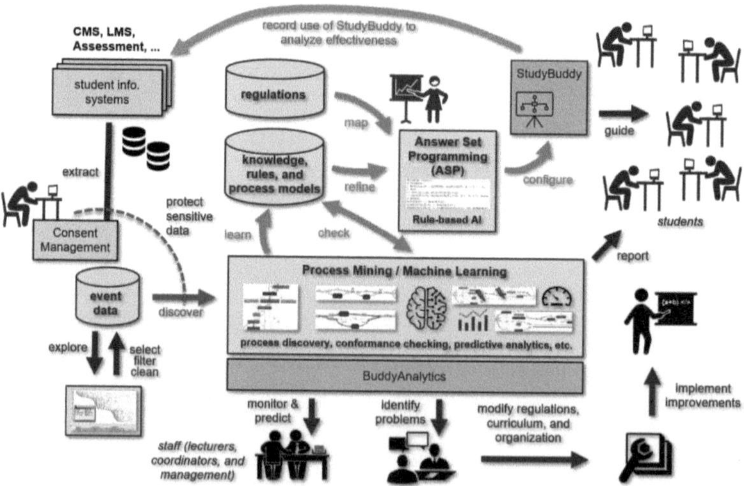


**Fig. 1.** Overview of the project, showing the two parts: StudyBuddy and BuddyAnalytics and their relationships to the different systems and techniques.

The following three publications reflect the layered development of this research agenda, from foundational system architecture, to behavioral pattern extraction, to their integration in intelligent planning systems.

## 2.1 Rule-Based and Process-Aware Study Planning: System Architecture and Foundations

The foundational paper in this research stream, *A Combined Approach of Process Mining and Rule-based AI for Study Planning and Monitoring in Higher Education* [12], presents the conceptual and technical framework of the AIStudyBuddy project. The architecture integrates rule-based reasoning (using Event Calculus and Answer Set Programming) with process mining (PM) techniques applied to event logs extracted from the CMS. To ensure differentiating between correctness and optimality, we distinguish between two types of constraints: hard constraints, which are mandatory (e.g., course prerequisites), and soft constraints, which are statistically derived from past successful student behavior but remain optional.

The paper motivates its approach by emphasizing the limitations of static planning in the face of real-world variability. For example, students' deviations from recommended study plans often stem from employment, family responsibilities, or repeated exam attempts, yet such deviations are poorly captured in traditional systems. We take a deeper look into the data: In Fig. 2, we show the grade distribution of different student groups, some deviating from the recommended plan (red) and some not (green). We can easily see that deviating students usually get lower grades.

We address this by validating students' individualized study plans against both hard and soft constraints. Meanwhile, BuddyAnalytics enables administrators to visualize how actual student paths deviate from expected ones using models such as Petri nets, process trees, and Directly-Follows Graphs (DFG) [12].

We demonstrate the system's implementation using data from the Computer Science and Mechanical Engineering Bachelor's programs at RWTH Aachen University. The event data, comprising course registrations, exam attempts, and grades is transformed into event logs suitable for PM techniques such as inductive mining and conformance checking. By comparing discovered models against normative ones, the system highlights where students are deviating, and why such deviations might be meaningful rather than problematic. This blend of descriptive, predictive, and prescriptive analytics makes the system highly adaptable to the complexity of educational processes.

## 2.2 Mining Behavioral Patterns for AI Planning: Formalizing Soft Constraints

Building upon the system-level architecture of AIStudyBuddy, the second paper, *Incorporating Behavioral Recommendations Mined from Event Logs into AI Planning* [9], introduces a formal method for mining behavioral recommendations from event logs and integrating them into AI planning frameworks.

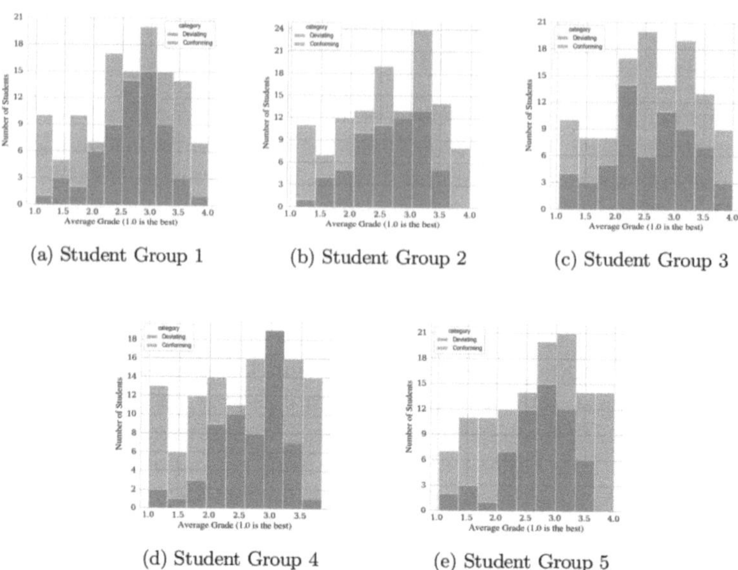

(a) Student Group 1     (b) Student Group 2     (c) Student Group 3

(d) Student Group 4     (e) Student Group 5

**Fig. 2.** Distribution of average grades for 'Conforming' and 'Deviating' students. This histogram represents the count of students within each average grade interval, highlighting differences in grade distributions between the two categories.

Using the Declare framework, we mine behavioral patterns expressed as temporal constraints (e.g., Precedence(Course A, Course B)) and validate them through LTLf (Linear Temporal Logic on Finite Traces, [5]) checks and statistical hypothesis testing (Mann-Whitney U Test, [7]). Only statistically significant patterns are retained as behavioral recommendations. These are then incorporated into a planning framework that uses preference-based AI planning to generate study plans that satisfy all hard constraints while maximizing adherence to beneficial patterns.

For example, suppose a significant number of students who took "Algorithms" before "Advanced Data Structures" achieved higher grade point averages (GPAs). The system would encode this as a weighted preference, encouraging future students to follow the same sequence. The empirical evaluation, conducted again on RWTH Aachen student data, reveals that plans incorporating such recommendations improve academic performance, especially in terms of grades and completion time. This paper makes a critical theoretical contribution by formalizing the integration of mined empirical insights into AI planners. It thus advances the field beyond traditional static curriculum planning to adaptive, explainable, and data-grounded planning.

## 2.3   Extracting Interpretable Rules for Study Path Guidance

The most recent contribution, *Extracting Rules from Event Data for Study Planning* [11], focuses on producing interpretable, data-driven rules from CMS event logs using decision tree models. Unlike the previous two works that emphasize process model discovery and AI planning, this study focuses on classification models that map descriptive features of student behavior (e.g., course order, semester of enrollment, reattempts) to academic outcomes, i.e., the grade corresponding to the exam performance.

The study introduces various atomic and non-atomic features, including course-semester mappings, course-order patterns, and time gaps between course attempts. These features are then used to train decision trees whose leaf nodes generate interpretable rules. For example, "If course A is taken in semester 1 and course B is taken in semester 2, then the expected grade is better than 2.0." (2.0 corresponds to B in the British/American system).

The simplicity and transparency of these rules make them particularly useful for direct student-facing applications, academic counseling, and curriculum reform. Empirical results from RWTH Aachen show that the models are both accurate and insightful. In particular, they reveal that while following the official study plan often correlates with good outcomes, certain deviations also lead to academic success, suggesting that study plans should be both flexible and adaptive. This work contributes a complementary layer of explainability and transparency, vital for stakeholder trust in intelligent educational systems.

## 2.4   The AIStudyBuddy Tool

Besides producing conceptual ideas, the project also involved the development of the AIStudyBuddy tool. In its final version, the study plan is presented in the form of an interactive table, where columns represent academic semesters and rows correspond to distinct knowledge areas defined within the curriculum of a given study program. This structured layout provides an intuitive overview of the student's academic progression, aligning visual clarity with curricular organization. In Fig. 3, we show the user interface of the StudyBuddy tool. When hovering over a course, the prerequisites of it are shown as arrows (solid for hard and dashed for soft). Additionally, on the right side, a list of recommendations is shown. Initially, the tool displays a pre-filled recommended study plan based on the institution's formal regulations and typical course sequences.

Students can actively modify this plan through drag-and-drop interactions, moving individual courses across semesters and knowledge domains. The system provides real-time feedback when a course is placed in a semantically invalid or structurally infeasible position, such as violating prerequisite dependencies or credit constraints, thereby guiding students toward feasible alternatives without requiring detailed prior knowledge of the regulations.

Beyond constraint validation, the tool offers personalized recommendations, which are dynamically generated based on the student's individual academic history, previous performance, and the course choices planned for future semesters.

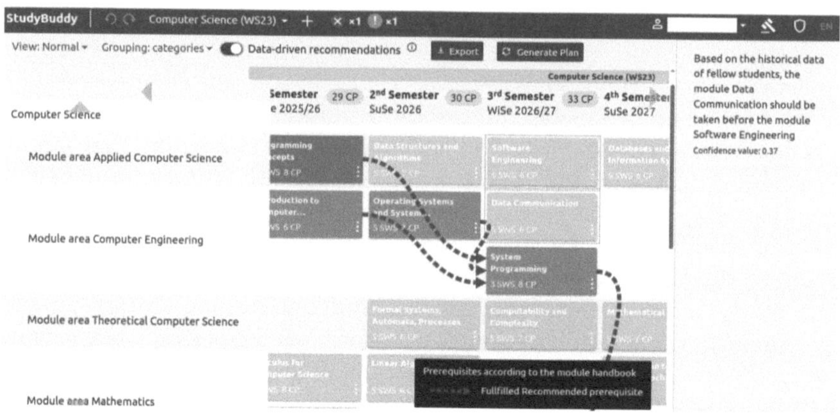

**Fig. 3.** The interactive student interface of the study buddy tool.

Each recommendation is accompanied by a textual explanation that details the underlying reasoning, along with a quantitative weight indicating the relative importance or statistical strength of the suggestion. This approach ensures transparency and interpretability, both of which are crucial for fostering trust in AI-supported decision systems.

After any number of manual adjustments, students may invoke an automated plan refinement function. This feature utilizes a solver-based optimization engine that attempts to complete and correct the current plan by searching for a configuration that satisfies all hard constraints while maximizing the weighted sum of fulfilled recommendations. The result is a study plan that not only adheres to institutional rules but is also aligned with empirically validated patterns of academic success.

Throughout the development and evaluation phases of the project, the tool has been subjected to multiple rounds of user testing. Feedback from students has been overwhelmingly positive, with many reporting that the combination of flexible planning and data-informed recommendations significantly enhanced their confidence and decision-making in course selection and sequencing.

## 3    Process Mining in The RoboCup Logistics League

The *RoboCup Logistics League* (RCLL) [8] is a robotic competition that focuses on research challenges in smart factories and Industry 4.0 scenarios. In contrast to traditional large-scale manufacturing, the RCLL addresses highly flexible production environments where small batches and customized products must be produced autonomously and efficiently.

Each team operates up to three autonomous mobile robots on a shared factory floor. The robots must transport workpieces between a set of static production machines that perform assembly tasks in order to fulfill customer orders.

Each team has exclusive access to its own set of machines. Figure 4 shows images of different stages of robot – machine interaction in the RCLL

**Fig. 4.** Scenes of robot – machine interactions in the RCLL. Left: Robot in the foreground, machine in the background. Middle: Robot approaching a machine. Right: Robot picking up a base from a machine.

The league provides a benchmark for research in several core areas:

- **Autonomous Navigation:** Safe and efficient movement in dynamic factory environments.
- **Perception and Manipulation:** Object recognition, alignment with machines, and precise handling of parts.
- **Task Planning and Scheduling:** Real-time decision-making under uncertainty, including handling failures and machine downtime.
- **Multi-Robot Coordination:** Cooperation and communication to avoid conflicts and optimize throughput.

A semi-autonomous game-controller, the *referee box* (refbox) takes care of creating individual game instances, randomly generating

- a field layout (positions of machines on the field).
- customer requests consisting of color configurations for individual parts (base, up to three additional rings and a cap, examples are shown in Fig. 5) as well as temporal constraints specifying the desired delivery window and time, when the order is placed,
- material costs for the assembly of rings (requiring a randomized amount of additional input material depending on the color),
- and temporary maintenance intervals of machines, which become unavailable for a period of time during production without prior notice.

**Fig. 5.** The product on the left consists of a black base and a grey cap, while the product on the right consists of a yellow base, three rings (blue, yellow, and orange), and a black cap. (Color figure online)

While the RCLL provides a realistic and challenging environment for autonomous decision-making, assessing the *quality* of those decisions is non-trivial. A team's success is typically measured by aggregate production metrics (e.g., the number of completed products or accumulated points), which do not directly reveal how well individual planning, scheduling, or coordination decisions contributed to performance. Due to the dynamic and stochastic nature of the environment,where machine states, order arrivals, and robot interactions constantly change, it is difficult to identify causal relationships between actions and outcomes using traditional evaluation methods.

### 3.1   Object-Centric Process Mining

This complexity motivates the use of *process mining* [3] and related data-driven analysis techniques to extract, visualize, and evaluate operational processes from execution logs. By reconstructing the actual decision and execution flows of autonomous agents, process mining can help to reveal behavioral patterns, detect inefficiencies, and validate whether decision-making strategies align with optimal or expected production workflows. Such analysis enables more systematic validation and improvement of autonomous decision systems.

Due to the complexity of the underlying problem, traditional process mining via event logs fail to capture the RCLL scenario properly, as they are centered around single objects. In contrast, in the RCLL, robots, workpieces and machines all contribute to the individual events. Wil's group developed *Object-Centric Process Mining* (OCPM) [2], where a refined data format centered around *Object-Centric Event Data* (OCED) is presented, which considers processes where multiple object types are considered. In order to leverage techniques in the field, a standardized data format called *Object-Centric Event Logs* (OCEL) was introduced [6] and later refined in version 2 [4].

## 3.2   Providing Data via the Referee Box

To enable process mining in the RCLL context, the refbox must be capable of capturing all events that characterize the production process.

This includes not only high-level task executions such as order creation, machine processing, and product delivery, but also fine-grained events like robot task assignments, navigation goals, and machine state transitions. The refbox uses MongoDB[1] as data backend and stores all information it has on machine events, field layout and customer orders. However, data about robot tasks has to be captured as well, hence a first step was to extend the data exchange such that robots also provide high level descriptions of their atomic tasks (mainly, driving, picking up objects and placing them down). Afterwards the relevant data consists of *agent task history* (robot movements and activities), *machine history* (machine state changes), *machines* (machine positions), *orders* (order details), *robot history* (robot state changes), *shelf slot history* (storage slot contents), *start timestamp* (activity timing), and *workpiece history* (workpiece states). Next, a data pipeline was created in order to extract the data from the database into a suitable format for generating OCELs and traditional event logs. Additionally, over 600 games were simulated to provide data for subsequent analysis.

## 3.3   Object-Centric Event Log Extraction

The work described here was performed in the context of Jord Piciri's Master thesis [10]. To generate an OCEL from the RCLL simulation data, object and event types were first defined to compose several different OCEL representations of different abstraction levels.

Based on the RCLL rule book, four primary object types were derived: *game ID*, *robot*, *machine*, *workpiece*, and *order*. Relationships between the object types are depicted UML-style in Fig. 6.

However, one could further distinguish machines by their roles (there are a set of machines performing production steps and a different set purely for providing or consuming material). Additionally, workpieces could also be split into multiple object types based on the progress, e.g., base pieces, bases with $n$ rings, or bases with $n$ rings and a cap.

Similarly, the primary events are the atomic robot actions *MOVE*, *RETRIEVE*, and *DELIVER* and the machine steps for getting a base, adding rings and caps and providing additional assembly material to a station.

These configurations allow flexible analysis depending on the desired process granularity. Finally, using the process mining framework PM4Py[2], the OCELs can be filtered by object type to obtain traditional event logs when required, thereby maintaining a unified and reusable data representation for both object-centric and conventional process mining analyses.

---

[1] https://www.mongodb.com/.

[2] https://processintelligence.solutions/pm4py.

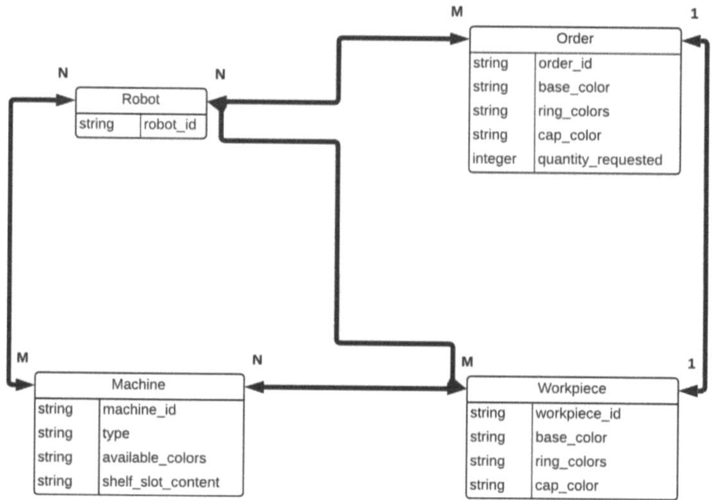

**Fig. 6.** Relationship between the primary object types in the RCLL.

## 3.4    Outlook: Analysis and Prediction

The present work has focused on establishing a reliable data pipeline to position the RCLL as an attractive benchmark environment for OCPM research. By enabling the extraction of OCELs, it becomes possible to reconstruct the underlying RCLL processes in detail, facilitating retrospective analyses that uncover bottlenecks, inefficiencies, and strategic behavioral patterns.

A compact representation of robot utilization throughout a game, generated from OCEL data, is shown in Fig. 7. This visualization highlights how each robot contributes over time, making it easier to identify periods of high activity, idle times, or coordination inefficiencies.

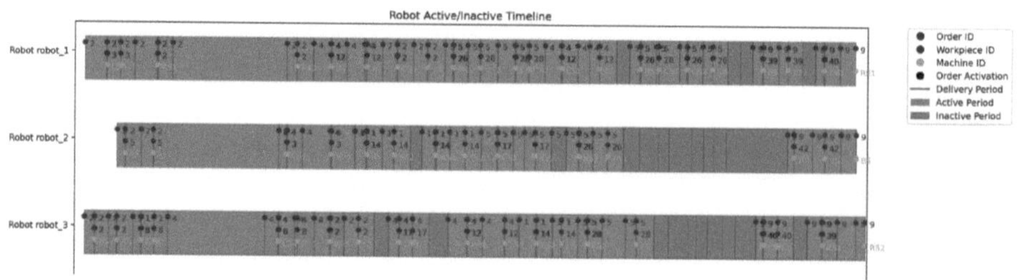

**Fig. 7.** Visualization of robot activity generated from OCEL data.

Looking ahead, the integration of OCPM with *Predictive Process Monitoring* (PPM) offers promising opportunities to further enhance robot coordination, production efficiency, and strategic decision-making within the RCLL. Future research should emphasize the quantification of team and system performance through well-defined *Key Performance Indicators* (KPIs), such as machine utilization, cycle time, or robot idle ratios. These indicators would yield interpretable measures of efficiency and collaboration, enabling teams to systematically compare strategies across matches and competition seasons. Beyond performance evaluation, predictive methods could forecast process outcomes, such as potential production delays or resource conflicts, based on historical OCEL data, ultimately paving the way for proactive and adaptive decision support in dynamic manufacturing scenarios.

## 4  Conclusion

In this chapter we have demonstrated that both students and robots can benefit from process mining. While the AIStudyBuddy project has come to a close with solid results, both conceptually and empirically, the application of process mining to robotics is still ongoing. In particular, we believe that much more can and should be done to refine and analyze the event logs obtained from RCLL games in order to optimize the behavior of our robots. Lastly we would like to thank Wil and his group for their dedication and willingness to share their insights into process mining with us. It has been a fun journey. Thank you, Wil!

**Acknowledgments.** Tarik Viehmann was funded by the Deutsche Forschungsgemeinschaft (DFG, German Research Foundation) under Germany's Excellence Strategy – EXC-2023 Internet of Production – 390621612, the EU ICT-48 2020 project TAILOR (No. 952215) and the Research Training Group 2236 (UnRAVeL).

Hayyan Helal was funded by the German Federal Ministry of Education and Research (BMBF) for the project AIStudyBuddy (No. 16DHBKI016), and the EU ICT-48 2020 project TAILOR (No. 952215).

## References

1. van der Aalst, W.M.P.: Process mining. Commun. ACM **55**(8), 76–83 (2012)
2. van der Aalst, W.M.P.: Object-centric process mining: unraveling the fabric of real processes. Mathematics **11**(12) (2023)
3. van der Aalst, W.M.P., Carmona, J. (eds.): Process Mining Handbook. Lecture notes in business information processing, vol. 448. Springer, Cham, Switzerland (Jul (2022)
4. Berti, A., et al.: Ocel (object-centric event log) 2.0 specification (2024)
5. De Giacomo, G., Vardi, M.Y.: Linear temporal logic and linear dynamic logic on finite traces. In: Proceedings of the Twenty-Third International Joint Conference on Artificial Intelligence, pp. 854–860. IJCAI '13, AAAI Press (2013)
6. Ghahfarokhi, A.F., Park, G., Berti, A., van der Aalst, W.M.P.: Ocel: A standard for object-centric event logs. In: Bellatreche, L., et al., (eds.) New Trends in Database and Information Systems, pp. 169–175. Springer International Publishing, Cham (2021)

7. Mann, H.B., Whitney, D.R.: On a test of whether one of two random variables is stochastically larger than the other. Ann. Math. Stat. 50–60 (1947)
8. Niemueller, T., Lakemeyer, G., Ferrein, A.: The RoboCup Logistics League as a Benchmark for Planning in Robotics. In: 2nd ICAPS Workshop on Planning in Robotics (PlanRob) (2015)
9. Park, G., Rafiei, M., Helal, H., Lakemeyer, G., van der Aalst, W.M.P.: Incorporating behavioral recommendations mined from event logs into AI planning. In: International Conference on Advanced Information Systems Engineering, pp. 20–28. Springer (2024)
10. Piciri, J.: Process Mining in the RoboCup Logistics League. Master's thesis, RWTH Aachen Univserity, Aachen, Germany (2025)
11. Rafiei, M., et al.: Extracting rules from event data for study planning. In: International Conference on Process Mining, pp. 361–374. Springer (2023)
12. Wagner, M., et al.: A combined approach of process mining and rule-based AI for study planning and monitoring in higher education. In: International Conference on Process Mining, pp. 513–525. Springer (2022)

# Process Mining in the Era of Smart Manufacturing: Applications, Limitations, and Opportunities


Minseok Song[1][(✉)] and Jae-Yoon Jung[2]

[1] Department of Industrial and Management Engineering, Pohang University of Science and Technology (POSTECH), Pohang, South Korea
`mssong@postech.ac.kr`
[2] Department of Industrial and Management Systems Engineering, Kyung Hee University, Yongin, South Korea
`jyjung@khu.ac.kr`



**Abstract.** Process mining has emerged as a key enabler of smart manufacturing. It provides techniques for process discovery, conformance checking, and performance analysis to enhance operational transparency and efficiency. With the growing availability of data from enterprise resource planning (ERP) systems, manufacturing execution systems (MES), and industrial Internet of Things (IIoT) platforms, manufacturers are increasingly leveraging process mining to enhance efficiency, quality, and flexibility. This paper presents a structured review of process mining in manufacturing, synthesizing one and a half decades of research. The reviewed studies are organized into core application areas, including discovery, conformance, performance analysis, and predictive or prescriptive analytics, with a particular focus on synergies with digital twins, operations research, simulation, and machine learning. We further identify domain-specific challenges, including heterogeneous data sources, high process variability, scalability, and real-time requirements, and discuss the limitations of existing approaches. Finally, we outline emerging directions—including online process mining, multi-level system integration, sustainability-driven analytics, and human–machine collaboration—highlighting how process mining can accelerate the transition toward smart and resilient manufacturing. This review consolidates prior work, reveals research gaps, and provides a roadmap for advancing process mining in the manufacturing domain.

**Keywords:** Process Mining · Smart Manufacturing · Shop Floor · Production · Industry 4.0


## 1 Introduction

The rapid digitalization of manufacturing has led to an unprecedented growth in data generated across production systems, supply chains, and enterprise platforms. Advanced information systems such as enterprise resource planning (ERP), manufacturing execution systems (MES), and increasingly industrial Internet of Things (IIoT) platforms, continuously record detailed event data that capture the execution of operational processes. Leveraging these data to gain transparency, identify inefficiencies, and support decision-making is a central challenge in the era of Industry 4.0 [5].

Process mining has emerged as a promising discipline for addressing this challenge. Positioned at the intersection of data science and business process management, process mining offers a collection of techniques for discovering process models from event logs, checking conformance between actual and designed processes, and enhancing processes with performance insights. While process mining has been successfully applied in domains such as healthcare, finance, and telecommunications, its adoption in manufacturing is comparatively still in its early stages but rapidly accelerating. The complexity of manufacturing processes, with their intertwined material flows, resource constraints, and human-machine interactions, presents both opportunities and unique challenges for process mining research and practice.

A growing body of studies has investigated the use of process mining in manufacturing, focusing on objectives such as cycle-time reduction, bottleneck detection, workload balancing, lean manufacturing, and integration with digital twins, operational analytics, and simulation. However, the literature remains fragmented across multiple research communities, including industrial engineering, information systems, and computer science. To the best of our knowledge, there is no comprehensive review that systematically synthesizes these contributions, categorizes their approaches, and identifies open research challenges specific to the manufacturing domain.

The objective of this paper is therefore twofold. First, we provide a structured review of existing research on process mining in manufacturing, classifying contributions according to their methodological focus and application context. Second, we analyze the limitations of current work and highlight future directions with particular emphasis on real-time analytics, data integration across heterogeneous systems, and the role of process mining as a core enabler of smart manufacturing. This review covers one and a half decades of published studies, drawing from academic databases and industrial case studies.

The remainder of the paper is organized as follows. Section 2 describes the methodology employed to conduct the literature review. Section 3 presents a detailed overview of process mining applications in manufacturing, while Sect. 4 synthesizes and classifies research themes. Section 5 outlines key challenges and limitations, followed by Sect. 6, which explores emerging trends and future directions. Section 7 concludes the paper with final remarks.

## 2    Methodology of the Review

In this study, we followed a structured process comprising three main steps: a literature search, the application of inclusion and exclusion criteria, and the development of a classification framework.

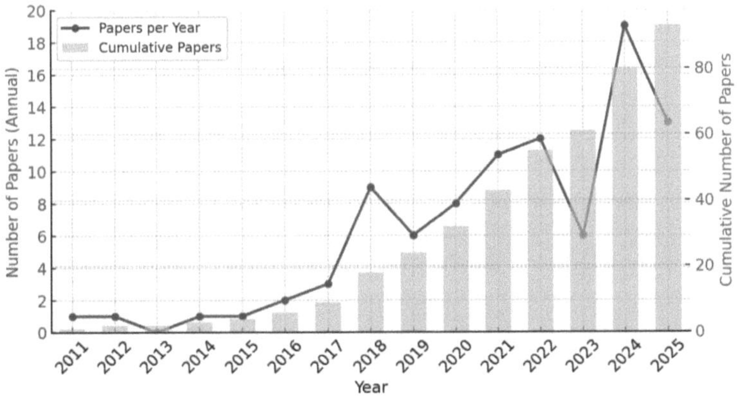


**Fig. 1.** Number of process mining papers published by year.

The literature search was designed to capture the breadth of research on process mining in manufacturing. We conducted the search exclusively in the *Scopus* database, which is one of the largest and most comprehensive sources of peer-reviewed literature, covering journals, conference proceedings, and technical papers. The search covered publications from **2011 to 2025**, reflecting one and a half decades of research since the emergence of process mining as a formal discipline.

Search keywords combined *"process mining"*, with manufacturing-related terms including *"manufacturing," "shop floor," "production,"* and *"Industry 4.0."* A dedicated search in **Scopus** was conducted using the query:

TITLE ("process mining" AND ("manufacturing" OR "shop floor" OR "production" OR "industry 4.0")) AND (LIMIT-TO(DOCTYPE, "cp") OR LIMIT-TO(DOCTYPE, "ar")) AND (LIMIT-TO(LANGUAGE, "English"))

This returned **93 documents** (as of 2025), shown in Fig. 1. The temporal distribution shows a clear increase in publications after 2015, with a peak in 2024 (19 documents), followed by continued high activity in 2025. Regarding the type of document, the majority were **conference papers (69.9%)** while **journal articles accounted for 30.1%**. In terms of subject areas, the most contributions came from **Computer Science (30.7%) and Engineering (27.5%)**, followed by Decision Sciences (11.6%), Mathematics (11.1%), and Business / Management (9.5%). This suggests that research on process mining in manufacturing is inherently interdisciplinary, with a strong orientation toward computer science methods, yet substantial application relevance in engineering and management.

The selected literature was analyzed and categorized using an iteratively developed classification framework. Each paper was coded along three main dimensions:

- **Process mining applications:** Discovery, conformance checking, performance analysis, and predictive and prescriptive applications.

- **Manufacturing research themes:** Operational analytics, simulation and process improvement, bottleneck detection and resource management, lean manufacturing, and quality improvement.
- **Data source and system context:** ERP, MES, IIoT/sensors, machine-level data, material handling data, and hybrid sources.

As summarized in Table 1, simulation and process improvement (20.0%) and bottleneck detection and resource management (18.1%) emerge as the most prominent research themes in the manufacturing domain, followed by quality improvement (10.5%). Within process mining applications, performance analysis (16.2%) and discovery (9.5%) are the most frequently addressed, whereas ERP (14.3%) and machine-level data (10.5%) constitute the predominant data sources across studies.

**Table 1.** Distribution of Themes in Process Mining Literature for Manufacturing

| Category | Theme | Percentage (%) |
|---|---|---|
| Process Mining Applications | Performance analysis | 16.2 |
| | Discovery | 9.5 |
| | Predictive/Prescriptive | 4.8 |
| | Conformance checking | 3.8 |
| Manufacturing Research Themes | Simulation and process improvement | 20.0 |
| | Bottleneck detection and resource management | 18.1 |
| | Quality improvement | 10.5 |
| | Operational analytics | 9.5 |
| | Lean manufacturing | 5.7 |
| Data Source and System Context | ERP | 14.3 |
| | Machine-level data | 10.5 |
| | IIoT/sensors | 3.8 |
| | MES | 2.9 |
| | Material handling data | 1.0 |

This framework enabled a structured synthesis of contributions and facilitated the identification of research trends, common challenges, and emerging opportunities in applying process mining to manufacturing.

## 3   Applications of Process Mining in Manufacturing

The manufacturing sector offers fertile ground for process mining, due to its reliance on well-defined processes, the increasing availability of event data, and the ongoing demand for efficiency, quality, and flexibility. Recent studies demonstrate that process mining has been applied in diverse contexts in manufacturing, ranging from shop floor optimization to digital twins and sustainability analysis. This section reviews applications in five main dimensions: data sources, process discovery, conformance checking, performance analysis, and predictive or prescriptive applications.

### 3.1   Data Sources in Manufacturing

The success of process mining depends critically on the availability and quality of the event data. In manufacturing, event logs can be generated from multiple layers of information systems and physical infrastructure:

- **ERP and MES**: ERP platforms (e.g., SAP, Oracle) record transactions related to order management, procurement, and inventory, and have been used for production planning, cost analysis, and standardization of business processes. MES platforms, in turn, track shop floor activities, including scheduling, routing, and work-in-progress management. Several case studies demonstrate how process mining on MES logs enables the reconstruction of production flows and the identification of bottlenecks [16].
- **IIoT, sensors and machine controllers**: With the proliferation of connected devices, IIoT platforms, sensors, automated material handling systems (AMHS, e.g. OHT, AS/RS, AGV/AMR) and machine controllers (e.g., PLCs, SCADA systems) enable near real-time monitoring of machine conditions, environmental factors, and production parameters. These data sources support predictive maintenance, anomaly detection, and integration with cyber-physical production systems [3, 30].

The integration of these heterogeneous sources poses challenges due to the differing formats, granularity, and semantics; however, collectively, they form the foundation for applying process mining in manufacturing.

### 3.2   Process Discovery in Manufacturing Contexts

Process discovery has been widely used in manufacturing to uncover actual execution flows. Unlike in transactional domains, manufacturing processes often involve concurrency, resource sharing, and rework cycles. Applications include reconstructing production flows to support lean manufacturing and reduce waste [22], and mapping end-to-end order processing in production networks [31]. Discovery techniques such as inductive mining and heuristic mining have been adapted to handle noisy and incomplete shop floor logs [16, 28, 29]. These methods have identified loops in automotive assembly and other discrete manufacturing contexts [8], providing data-driven foundations for continuous improvement and dynamic process mapping.

### 3.3   Conformance Checking for Quality and Compliance

Conformance checking is particularly important in manufacturing, where compliance with standards, regulations, and safety requirements is critical. Studies apply conformance analysis to verify compliance with production plans, quality assurance procedures, and zero-defect manufacturing initiatives [9, 18]. Advanced techniques such as alignment-based conformance checking and token replay have been extended to manufacturing data, enabling systematic detection of deviations and supporting both operational audits and certification requirements.

### 3.4   Performance Analysis and Bottleneck Detection

Performance analysis is among the most prevalent applications of process mining in manufacturing. By enriching process models with time, cost, and resource information, managers can systematically detect bottlenecks and evaluate throughput efficiency. Reported applications include bottleneck detection in discrete assembly systems [10], value-stream-based throughput optimization in production networks [20], and the integration of process mining with simulation to assess rescheduling and resource allocation strategies [23]. Furthermore, process mining has been applied to eliminate non-value-added activities and to optimize process flows under resource constraints [22].

### 3.5   Predictive and Prescriptive Applications

More recent studies extend process mining from retrospective analysis toward predictive and prescriptive analytics, aligning with smart manufacturing and Industry 4.0 goals.

**Predictive process monitoring.** leverages historical event logs to forecast outcomes such as remaining cycle times [6], defect probabilities, and machine failures [12,13]. Machine learning methods are increasingly integrated with process mining for shop-floor decision support [17].

**Prescriptive process analytics.** goes further by recommending actions to optimize outcomes. Applications include dynamic rescheduling in cellular manufacturing systems [21], prescriptive process design and data-processing workflows in production and logistics [14], and proactive decision support enabled by the coupling of process mining with digital twins and simulation [25].

## 4   Research Themes in the Manufacturing Domain

### 4.1   Operational Analytics and Optimization

In modern manufacturing, data-driven analytics has become a cornerstone for process optimization and operational excellence. The integration of machine learning (ML) and deep learning (DL) techniques enables the extraction of actionable insights from large-scale event logs, supporting operational analytics such as predictive maintenance, quality analytics, anomaly detection, and process improvement [24]. For instance, ML models can predict machine failures, allowing preventive interventions that reduce unplanned downtime and improve overall equipment effectiveness [19].

Beyond operational analytics, operations research (OR) methods such as scheduling, resource allocation, and optimization benefit significantly from process mining insights. By leveraging event log data, these approaches can dynamically adapt production schedules, optimize job-shop routing, and balance workloads across machines [1]. Combining ML and OR facilitates real-time decision-making and continuous improvement, as manufacturers can simulate alternative strategies and select optimal process configurations.

Furthermore, process mining supports performance benchmarking by providing empirical evidence of process behavior. Key performance indicators (KPIs), such as throughput times, cycle times, and process variants, offer quantitative measures for evaluating operational efficiency. This enables organizations to identify underperforming units, allocate resources more effectively, and design targeted interventions for process enhancement [4].

## 4.2   Simulation and Process Improvement with Digital Twins

Discrete-event simulation (DES) is essential for enhancing manufacturing process efficiency. Process mining provides event log data that fuels accurate simulation models, enabling manufacturers to conduct "what-if" analyses under varying production scenarios [26]. Such simulations allow for testing production changes virtually, reducing the risk of costly disruptions in live operations.

Digital twins, representing virtual replicas of physical manufacturing systems, further expand the scope of process improvement. Enriched with real-time event logs and predictive models, digital twins allow for monitoring, forecasting, prediction, and optimization of manufacturing operations [32]. They provide a platform for scenario testing, including machine failure simulations, production ramp-ups, and workflow adjustments, facilitating proactive decision-making.

In addition, process mining contributes to quality management by integrating with simulation and digital twin frameworks. Machine-level monitoring, root cause analysis, and defect prediction models derived from event logs enhance product quality and reduce scrap rates [27]. The combination of simulation, digital twins, and process mining thus forms a robust methodology for continuous process improvement, enabling manufacturers to maintain high standards of operational accuracy and product reliability.

## 4.3   Bottleneck Detection and Resource Management

Identifying and managing bottlenecks is crucial for improving production throughput. Process mining techniques enable detailed visualization of resource utilization, task sequences, and process delays, revealing hidden bottlenecks that limit throughput [15]. By analyzing event logs, organizations can detect congested workstations, overloaded resources, or inefficient routing patterns that negatively impact process performance [4].

Resource management, closely tied to bottleneck analysis, leverages process mining to ensure equitable distribution of tasks and optimize workforce or machine deployment. Integrating resource analysis with scheduling and dispatching strategies allows manufacturers to reduce idle time, prevent resource conflicts, and enhance production responsiveness. Dynamic monitoring of workloads also supports predictive adjustments, enabling real-time interventions to mitigate potential disruptions.

Moreover, process improvement initiatives such as the Theory of Constraints and Six Sigma can utilize insights from process mining to systematically reduce inefficiencies. By combining bottleneck identification, workload optimization, and performance analysis, manufacturers can establish a foundation for operational excellence and long-term process automation [1].

## 4.4  Lean Manufacturing and Quality Improvement

Lean Manufacturing principles aim to eliminate waste, enhance efficiency, and maximize value delivery in production systems. Process mining provides a data-driven approach to identify non-value-added activities, redundancies, and process deviations [4]. By visualizing workflows and quantifying cycle times, organizations can implement lean strategies more effectively, targeting specific areas for improvement.

Quality improvement is another key research theme enabled by process mining. Event logs facilitate defect detection, root cause analysis, and predictive quality assurance measures [27]. For example, continuous monitoring of process deviations and machine behaviors allows for early detection of quality issues, minimizing scrap and rework. Integrating quality analytics with Lean initiatives ensures that process improvements do not compromise product standards, fostering both efficiency and reliability.

In combination, Lean Manufacturing and quality improvement strategies, supported by process mining, create a holistic framework for enhancing production performance. By leveraging detailed operational data, manufacturers can achieve sustainable improvements in throughput, quality, and overall operational excellence.

## 5  Challenges and Limitations

While process mining has shown significant potential in manufacturing, its application is not without challenges. The unique characteristics of production systems introduce limitations that affect the reliability, scalability, and interpretability of results. This section synthesizes the main barriers reported in the literature and observed in practice.

## 5.1  Application Highlights and Comparative Insights

Case studies provide evidence that process mining adds value in various manufacturing environments. Comparative insights highlight several dimensions of variation across studies. From an industry-specific perspective, discrete manufacturing often emphasizes variability and rework, whereas continuous manufacturing focuses on consistency and throughput. In terms of data availability, advanced applications are more common in sectors with mature MES and IIoT infrastructures [30], while others remain limited to ERP-level analysis [16]. Methodologically, most studies focus on discovery and conformance check [28,29], while predictive and prescriptive approaches are still emerging and are frequently reported in pilot or experimental settings [6,12,13]. These findings suggest that while adoption is advancing, maturity levels vary considerably across industries and use cases.

## 5.2   Data Quality and Event Log Generation

Generating high-quality event logs presents a persistent challenge. Unlike transactional domains, manufacturing data is diverse and encompasses various sources such as ERP transactions, MES events, and IIoT sensor streams [16,30]. To effectively integrate these sources, extensive preprocessing is required, which includes synchronizing timestamps, constructing case identifiers, and reducing noise. Without systematic data pipelines in place, the results of process mining may be incomplete or misleading.

## 5.3   Complexity and Variability in Manufacturing Processes

Manufacturing processes are inherently complex, involving parallel operations, rework cycles, and dynamic routing. Such variability complicates process discovery and often produces overly detailed models that are difficult to interpret [28,29]. Moreover, the continuous evolution of product designs and scheduling rules demands adaptive mining techniques, which remain an emerging area of research.

## 5.4   Scalability and Real-Time Requirements

The widespread adoption of IIoT devices generates massive event streams that often exceed the capacity of traditional mining techniques. The discovery and conformance checking in large-scale manufacturing logs remains a significant challenge [11]. Real-time requirements further intensify these difficulties, as predictive monitoring and scheduling applications demand immediate feedback [6,17]. Although simulation-based methods offer partial support for scenario testing [23], industrial acceptance of streaming and online mining techniques is still limited.

## 5.5   Interpretability and Human–Machine Collaboration

Interpretability and usability continue to be significant challenges. Highly complex models can impede adoption on the shop floor, where various stakeholders need clear and accessible insights. Recent studies highlight the importance of visualization and decision support integration in building trust and promoting collaboration [14,21,25]. To bridge this gap, we need advances in explainable analytics and the creation of user-centered process mining tools specifically designed for manufacturing environments.

## 6   Emerging Trends and Future Directions

As process mining becomes integral to smart manufacturing, its role is expanding beyond traditional analytics to enable real-time, integrated, and autonomous production environments. This section highlights how process mining is evolving in the context of smart manufacturing, drawing on recent literature and industry trends.

## 6.1  Real-Time and Online Process Mining

Smart manufacturing environments are characterized by high-velocity data streams from IIoT devices, sensors, and automation systems. Real-time and online process mining is emerging as a key enabler for continuous monitoring, anomaly detection, and adaptive control in these settings. Grobis and Ihlenfeldt demonstrate how process mining supports data processing and process design in production and logistics, emphasizing the need for scalable, online mining architectures that can handle large volumes of streaming data [14]. The ability to analyze event data as it is generated allows manufacturers to respond instantly to deviations, bottlenecks, or equipment failures, supporting predictive maintenance and minimizing downtime. However, challenges remain in ensuring low-latency insights and integrating process mining with edge and cloud computing infrastructures [14].

## 6.2  Cross-System and Multi-Level Process Integration

Smart manufacturing systems span multiple layers from ERP to shop-floor automation and machine-level control. Integrating process mining across these layers is essential for end-to-end visibility and optimization. De Oliveira highlights the importance of technology-specific frameworks and maturity models to guide the integration of process mining across different manufacturing systems [7]. Object-centric and hierarchical process mining approaches are being developed to harmonize event logs from diverse sources, enabling holistic analysis of dependencies and interactions across organizational levels [2]. This integration supports advanced use cases such as tracing how MES-level scheduling decisions impact shop-floor bottlenecks or how machine-level variability propagates to overall production performance [14].

## 6.3  Sustainable and Resilient Manufacturing for Industry 5.0

Sustainability and resilience are central to the vision of Industry 5.0, which emphasizes not only efficiency but also adaptability and environmental responsibility. Process mining is increasingly leveraged to identify waste, optimize resource usage, and support green manufacturing initiatives. Khakpour et al. demonstrate how integrating process mining with zero-defect manufacturing can improve sustainability by predicting and preventing defects in production [18]. Recent reviews also show how process mining can uncover inefficiencies in energy consumption, logistics, and supply chains, enabling targeted interventions to reduce carbon footprints and improve circularity [7]. Moreover, process mining supports resilience by enabling rapid detection of disruptions and facilitating adaptive responses to supply chain shocks or equipment failures. Future research will likely focus on integrating process mining with sustainability metrics and resilience modeling, supporting manufacturers in achieving both operational excellence and long-term viability [7].

## 6.4  Autonomous Manufacturing and AI Factory

The convergence of process mining with autonomous systems and AI-driven factories is accelerating the transformation of smart manufacturing. Technologies such as cobots and AGV/AMR generate rich event data that can be mined for optimization and self-adaptation. Jessen et al. discuss how AI and process mining can be combined to provide actionable insights and support autonomous decision-making in manufacturing processes [17]. Software-defined manufacturing (SDF) and generative AI are also emerging as enablers of flexible, intelligent production environments. As these technologies mature, future research should address the challenges of explainability, human–AI collaboration, and the ethical deployment of autonomous manufacturing systems [14].

## 7  Conclusion

This paper has reviewed process mining applications in manufacturing, synthesizing two decades of research at the intersection of data-driven analysis and industrial process management. Process mining provides a powerful framework for analyzing, monitoring, and continuously improving manufacturing systems by bridging the gap between event data and operational decision-making. It thus holds significant potential as a cornerstone of digital transformation in industry. As a future work, it is crucial for future studies to broaden database coverage and keyword scope to capture a wider and more diverse body of research, thereby paving the way for more comprehensive and insightful findings.

## References


1. van der Aalst, W.M.P.: Process mining: data science in action. Springer, 2nd edn. (2016)
2. van der Aalst, W.M.P.: Object-centric process mining: Dealing with divergence and convergence in event data. In: Ölveczky, P.C., Salaün, G. (eds.) Software Engineering and Formal Methods, pp. 3–25. Springer International Publishing, Cham (2019)
3. van der Aalst, W.M.P., et al.: Removing operational friction using process mining: shallenges provided by the internet of production (IOP). Commun. Comput. Inf. Sci. **1446**, 1–31 (2021)
4. Bolt, A., Sepúlveda, M.: Process mining in the manufacturing industry: challenges and opportunities. J. Manuf. Syst. **61**, 1–14 (2021)
5. Brecher, C., et al.: Internet of production: fundamentals, methods and applications. Springer, 1st edn. (2023)
6. Choueiri, A.C., Sato, D.M.V., Scalabrin, E.E., Portela Santos, E.A.: An extended model for remaining time prediction in manufacturing systems using process mining. J. Manuf. Syst. **56**, 188 – 201 (2020)
7. de Oliveira, J.V.G., Portela Santos, E.A., Detro, S.P.: Uncovering the potential and pitfalls of process mining in manufacturing. Procedia CIRP **132**, 19–24 (2025), 12th CIRP Global Web Conference (CIRPe 2024)

8. Dišek, M., Šperka, R., Kolesár, J.: Conversion of real data from production process of automotive company for process mining analysis. Smart Innovation Syst. Tech. **74**, 223–233 (2018)
9. Dogan, O., Areta Hiziroglu, O.: Empowering manufacturing environments with process mining-based statistical process control. Machines **12**(6) (2024)
10. Fang, Z., Yu, C.: Bottleneck mining: a data-driven bottleneck identification method via process mining in manufacturing systems. In: 2024 IEEE 20th International Conference on Automation Science and Engineering (CASE), pp. 1626–1631 (2024)
11. Fischer, M., Pourbafrani, M., Kemmerling, M., Stich, V.: A framework for online detection and reaction to disturbances on the shop floor using process mining and machine learning. In: Proceedings of the Conference on Production Systems and Logistics, pp. 387 – 396 (2020)
12. Friederich, J., Lazarova-Molnar, S.: Process mining for reliability modeling of manufacturing systems with limited data availability. In: 2021 8th International Conference on Internet of Things: Systems, Management and Security (IOTSMS), pp. 1–7 (2021)
13. Friederich, J., Lazarova-Molnar, S.: Data-driven reliability modeling of smart manufacturing systems using process mining. In: 2022 Winter Simulation Conference (WSC), pp. 2534–2545 (2022)
14. Grobis, M., Ihlenfeldt, S.: Process mining for supporting data processing and process design in production and logistics. Procedia CIRP **136**, 468–473 (2025), 35th CIRP Design 2025
15. Heo, G., Lee, J., Jung, J.Y.: Analyzing bottleneck resource pools of operational process using process mining. ICIC Express Lett. Part B: Appl. **9**(5), 437–441 (2018)
16. Hong Tu, T.B., Song, M.: Analysis and prediction cost of manufacturing process based on process mining. In: 2016 International Conference on Industrial Engineering, Management Science and Application (ICIMSA), pp. 1–5 (2016)
17. Jessen, U., Schroth, L., Mühllechner, M.: From data to actionable insights: utilizing ai and process mining in manufacturing processes. Lecture Notes Bus. Inf. Process. **527 LNBIP**, 462 – 471 (2024)
18. Khakpour, R., Ebrahimi, A., Seyed-Hosseini, S.M.: An integrated approach of zero defect manufacturing and process mining to avoid defect occurrence in production and improve sustainability. Int. J. Lean Six Sigma **16**(3), 660–685 (2025)
19. Klinkmüller, C., Fahland, D., Weidlich, M., Weske, M.: Efficient detection and prediction of performance problems based on process mining techniques. Inf. Syst. **90**, 101446 (2020)
20. Kroeger, S., Rafles, A., Jordan, P., Soellner, C., Zaeh, M.F.: Data model to enable multidimensional process mining for data farming based value stream planning in production networks. Prod. Eng. Res. Devel. **19**(2), 307–327 (2025)
21. Kurakado, H., Nishi, T., Liu, Z.: Data-driven scheduling of cellular manufacturing systems using process mining with petri nets. IFIP Adv. Inf. Commun. Techn. **729 IFIP**, 17 – 28 (2024)
22. Laghouag, A.A., Zafrah, F.B., Qureshi, M.R.N., Sahli, A.A.: Eliminating non-value-added activities and optimizing manufacturing processes using process mining: a stock of challenges for family smes. Sustainability (Switzerland) **16**(4) (2024)
23. Langer, A., Ortmeier, C., Martin, N.L., Abraham, T.G.M., Herrmann, C.: Combining process mining and simulation in production planning. In: Proceedings of the Conference on Production Systems and Logistics, pp. 264 – 273 (2021)

24. Leemans, S.J.J., Fahland, D., van der Aalst, W.M.P.: Discovering block-structured process models from event logs containing infrequent behavior. Data Knowl. Eng. **116**, 123–145 (2019)
25. Lugaresi, G.: Process mining as catalyst of digital twins for production systems: challenges and research opportunities. In: Proceedings - Winter Simulation Conference, pp. 3082 – 3093 (2024)
26. Mannhardt, F., de Leoni, M., Reijers, H.A., van der Aalst, W.M.P.: The impact of event log quality on process discovery results. Inf. Syst. **75**, 50–69 (2018)
27. Nguyen, T., Tran, H., Do, N.: Applying process mining for quality assurance in manufacturing: defect detection and prevention. Procedia CIRP **93**, 202–207 (2020)
28. Rudnitckaia, J., Venkatachalam, H.S., Essmann, R., Hruška, T., Colombo, A.W.: Screening process mining and value stream techniques on industrial manufacturing processes: Process modelling and bottleneck analysis. IEEE Access **10**, 24203–24214 (2022)
29. Santos, C., Fialho, J.R.S., Silva, J., Neto, T.: Process mining in a line production. Lecture Notes Netw. Syst. **921 LNNS**, 241 – 257 (2024)
30. Saraeian, S., Shirazi, B.: Process mining-based anomaly detection of additive manufacturing process activities using a game theory modeling approach. Comput. Ind. Eng. **146** (2020)
31. Schuh, G., Gützlaff, A., Schmitz, S., Kuhn, C., Klapper, N.: A methodology to apply process mining in end-to-end order processing of manufacturing companies. Lecture Notes in Mechanical Engineering , pp. 127 – 137 (2022)
32. Tao, F., Qi, Q., Liu, A., Kusiak, A.: Data-driven smart manufacturing. J. Manuf. Syst. **48**, 157–169 (2019)

# Author Index





J. Mendling et al. (Eds.): Wil van der Aalst Festschrift, LNCS 16480, pp. 755–756, 2026.
https://doi.org/10.1007/978-3-032-17618-9